ENCYCLOPEDIA OF WORLD BIOGRAPHY

14

ENCYCLOPEDIA OF WORLD BIOGRAPHY

SECOND EDITION

Schiele
Stuart

14

DETROIT • NEW YORK • TORONTO • LONDON

Staff

Senior Editor: Paula K. Byers
Project Editor: Suzanne M. Bourgoin
Managing Editor: Neil E. Walker

Editorial Staff: Luann Brennan, Frank V. Castronova, Laura S. Hightower, Karen E. Lemerand, Stacy A. McConnell, Jennifer Mossman, Maria L. Munoz, Katherine H. Nemeh, Terrie M. Rooney, Geri Speace

Permissions Manager: Susan M. Tosky
Permissions Specialist: Maria L. Franklin
Permissions Associate: Michele M. Lonoconus
Image Cataloger: Mary K. Grimes

Production Director: Mary Beth Trimper
Production Manager: Evi Seoud
Production Associate: Shanna Heilveil
Product Design Manager: Cynthia Baldwin
Senior Art Director: Mary Claire Krzewinski

Research Manager: Victoria B. Cariappa
Research Specialists: Michele P. LaMeau, Andrew Guy Malonis, Barbara McNeil, Gary J. Oudersluys
Research Associates: Julia C. Daniel, Tamara C. Nott, Norma Sawaya, Cheryl L. Warnock
Research Assistant: Talitha A. Jean

Graphic Services Supervisor: Barbara Yarrow
Image Database Supervisor: Randy Bassett
Imaging Specialist: Mike Lugosz

Manager of Data Entry Services: Eleanor M. Allison
Data Entry Coordinator: Kenneth D. Benson

Manager of Technology Support Services: Theresa A. Rocklin
Programmers/Analysts: Mira Bossowska, Jeffrey Muhr, Christopher Ward

ISBN 0-7876-2221-4 (Set)
ISBN 0-7876-2554-X (Volume 14)

Library of Congress Cataloging-in-Publication Data

Encyclopedia of world biography / [edited by Suzanne Michele Bourgoin and Paula Kay Byers].
p. cm.
Includes bibliographical references and index.
Summary: Presents brief biographical sketches which provide vital statistics as well as information on the importance of the person listed.
ISBN 0-7876-2221-4 (set : alk. paper)
1. Biography—Dictionaries—Juvenile literature. [1. Biography.] I. Bourgoin, Suzanne Michele, 1968- . II. Byers, Paula K. (Paula Kay), 1954- .
CT 103.E56 1997
920'.003—dc21 97-42327
CIP
AC

Printed in the United States of America
10 9 8 7 6 5 4 3 2

ENCYCLOPEDIA OF WORLD BIOGRAPHY

14

S

Egon Schiele

Egon Schiele (1890-1918) was an Austrian Expressionist painter and draftsman, whose reputation increased greatly through the years.

Egon Schiele was born in 1890 in Lower Austria as the third child in his family. His father was a rail-road civil servant who died in 1905. His uncle became his guardian but did not support his artistic career. Nevertheless, Schiele entered the academy in Vienna where he quickly ran into difficulties with his teacher, the then famous Professor Griepenkerl.

In 1907 he met Gustav Klimt, whom he admired, who assisted him in obtaining his first commissions and who influenced his early drawing style. Following Klimt's suggestion, Schiele entered four paintings in the Vienna International Exhibition of 1909, where works by Oskar Kokoschka and Vincent Van Gogh were also shown. In the same year he left the academy and, with other young artists, formed the short-lived artist group "Neukunstgruppe"; however, the first exhibition was not successful. By 1910 he had found his own style with its strong emphasis on the contour line and vibrant colors.

In 1911 he moved to the small town of Krumau, where he painted a number of townscapes. His lifestyle caused problems in the town and he moved with his model Wally Neuziel to Neulengbach where in 1912 he was arrested and charged with immorality and seduction. Some of his drawings were confiscated; one was even burned by the judge in the courtroom. He spent 24 traumatic days in jail and returned to Vienna upon his release.

His first important exhibitions were held in Germany: in 1913 in the famous Galerie Goltz in Munich and in the Folkwangmuseum in Hagen, followed by one-man exhibits in Hamburg, Breslau, Stuttgart, and Berlin, where the Expressionist journal *Die Aktion* published his drawings as well as his poetry. In 1915 he married Edith Harms, and a few days later he was drafted into the army. After having been assigned to guard Russian prisoners of war, the *Die Aktion* journal published a special issue with his drawings and the Berlin Sezession exhibited his works.

In 1917 he was transferred to the Army Museum in Vienna, which provided him with some time to paint again. A portfolio of 12 drawing reproductions was published. He was invited to participate in exhibits in Munich, Dresden, Amsterdam, and Stockholm, but his poverty remained unchanged. The first truly great success came in 1918 with his exhibit at the Vienna Secession (no less than 19 paintings and several drawings). He received a number of commissions, and 25 of his works were exhibited in Zurich. Shortly thereafter, however, his wife—who was expecting a child-died of the Spanish influenza epidemic, and three days later the artist succumbed to the same disease.

Schiele was an extraordinary artist who—together with the young Kokoschka—must be considered the outstanding Austrian Expressionist. His dominating theme was the human body, which he depicts in truly singular forms. The many nudes, female as well as male, are devoid of any then-acceptable concept of beauty and are like psychograms emphasizing tensions and even tragedy. Likewise in his paintings of children he emphasized their awkward bodies and their earnest eyes, and yet, the impact of these works on the viewer is very strong because the depictions are forthright and direct. His eros knows more of unresolved tensions and painful dreamstates than of joy. Even his marvelous townscapes frequently lack perspective dimensions and let the windows of the houses appear like blind eyes; they are expressions of the artist's mood more than topographical depictions; they are images of fall—with isolated, dry trees standing in the cold wind.

Schiele's symbolic works, such as "Death and the Maiden," "The Hermits," or even such seemingly happy themes as "Mother with Two Children," show the same penetrating insight for which his portraits have become famous, giving less a literary likeness than a psychogram of the sitters and subjects. His many self-portraits are proof of his continuous struggle with what he considered the soul of the arts: the depiction of that truth which lies below the surface. While the subject matter seems to be depressing, his works prove otherwise. The extraordinary ability to form the three dimensional body through dominating contour lines, his choice of very strong and forthright colors, the frequently ambiguous spaces, and his extraordinary sensitivity, which transforms even a seemingly quick drawing into a complete work of art, have allowed Schiele's fame to continue to grow. The feverish erotic states which so frequently dominate Schiele's works have by now lost their shock and have been recognized as unique depictions of human life as seen by one of the great artists of the 20th century.

Further Reading

The oeuvre catalogues of Schiele's works (paintings as well as graphics) have been published by Otto Kallir-Nirenstein (1966; 1970). To these can now be added the 1973 volume by Rudolf Leopold. Arthur Roessler published Schiele's letters and prosepoems in 1921, and Christian M. Nebehay in 1979 published a biography together with many newly discovered letters and some of the poems. Special aspects of Schiele's life and works have been treated by contemporaries, such as Heinrich Benesch in *My Way with E.S.* (1965), and Alexandra Comini wrote a monograph on Schiele's portraits and a number of important articles. Of equal importance are the many exhibition catalogues, which not only attest to the artist's growing fame but frequently contain important critical contributions.

Additional Sources

Egon Schiele and his contemporaries: Austrian painting and drawing from 1900 to 1930 from the Leopold collection, Vienna, Munich: Prestel; New York: Distributed in the USA and Canada by te Neues Pub. Co., 1989.

Kallir, Jane, *Egon Schiele, the complete works: including a biography and a catalogue raisonne,* New York: H.N. Abrams, 1990. □

Jacob Henry Schiff

Jacob Henry Schiff (1847-1920) was the outstanding member of the American-German banking group that became important after the Civil War. He played a major role in railroads and in industrial mergers at the turn of the century.

Jacob Schiff was born in Frankfurt am Main, Germany, on Jan. 10, 1847, of a middle-class family and a long line of rabbis and bankers. At the age of fourteen he was apprenticed to a business firm. In 1865 he emigrated to New York and soon set up his own brokerage office. In 1872 Schiff went to Germany to go into banking.

When Schiff returned to New York in 1875, he was invited to join the private banking firm of Kuhn, Loeb and Company. He soon became a leading member of the house and in 1885 its senior partner. Interested in railroad financing, Schiff found his big chance when he and E. H. Harriman (America's greatest railroad man) took over the Union Pacific Railroad in 1897.

Schiff and Harriman set out to acquire the Northern Pacific Railroad from J. P. Morgan and James J. Hill by stock-exchange maneuvers. The result was a financial panic in 1901. The titans settled on a holding company, the Northern Securities Company, which owned the stock of the Northern Pacific, the Great Northern, and the Burlington railroads, with the Schiff-Harriman interests fully recognized. Thanks to Schiff and J. P. Morgan, this was the golden age of American railroading; and Schiff was recognized as Morgan's peer.

Also between 1895 and 1910 Schiff's firm headed banking syndicates (using European money markets for funds and as outlets for the new securities) that formed several important American industrial mergers. From 1897 to 1906 Kuhn, Loeb and Company cooperated with other firms to market over $800 million in securities; during 1907-

1912 it alone underwrote $530 million worth, and with other houses an additional $821 million. Schiff was imaginative enough to see that an American capital market had developed, and he floated dollar bonds to finance Mexican railroads and to raise money for Japan's war against Russia. Unlike Morgan, Schiff was not interested in voting trusts or in sitting on the boards of the companies he organized or reorganized, and he did not seek to become their depositories. His company did not control a group of banks or dominate credit agencies; to this extent, therefore, he did not earn the censure of the Pujo Committee's Money Trust Investigation of 1913.

As a devout Jew, Schiff became a spokesman for those Jews who believed in assimilation into American culture. He helped establish Jewish philanthropic agencies—hospitals, family-and child-care societies, recreation and settlement house centers—to help less fortunate coreligionists adjust to American life. Schiff also helped put the Jewish Theological Seminary on a sound footing, created the Semitic Museum at Harvard, and financed the departments of Semitic literature at the New York Public Library and the Library of Congress. He died in New York on Sept. 25, 1920.

Further Reading

Although *Jacob H. Schiff: His Life and Letters,* edited by Cyrus Adler (2 vols., 1928), is useful, more exciting and informative about Schiff's business life is Stephen Birmingham, *Our Crowd* (1967). Fritz Redlich, *The Molding of American Banking* (1968), is very good on Schiff and is the best discussion of investment banking extant. □

Edward Schillebeeckx

The Belgian Roman Catholic theologian Edward Schillebeeckx (born 1914) was one of the most influential Catholic thinkers of his day.

Edward Schillebeeckx was born November 12, 1914, in Antwerp, Belgium. The sixth of fourteen children of Johanna and Constant Schillebeeckx, he grew up in Flemish-speaking northern Belgium and attended a high school run by the Jesuits. His father was an accountant in the Public Records Office, and an older brother became a Jesuit missionary in India. But Edward found himself more attracted to the Dominicans, whom he joined when he was 19. He has said that the Dominicans seemed to him warmer, and that their stress on the doctrine of God in philosophy and on social questions in theology struck a responsive chord.

Schillebeeckx did his novitiate and philosophical studies in Ghent, Belgium, after which he performed his compulsory military service. The next stage in his formation was theological studies at the Catholic University of Louvain, where he found himself dissatisfied with the neoscholastic approach then in favor. On the advice of a Dominican superior, he began reading the works of Karl Adam, a Catholic theologian teaching at Tubingen, Germany. Adam was trying to restate Catholic faith in non-scholastic terms, by returning to the Bible and the patristic tradition. From the Jesuit theologian Pierre Rouselot, as well as Adam, Schillebeeckx learned to stress experience—both the believer's experiential struggles with faith and the human experience of Jesus. The works of the Dominican Yves Congar and the Jesuit Karl Rahner also helped him escape the impasse of neo-scholasticism.

Schillebeeckx was ordained a priest in 1941. His next period of study took place in France, at the Sorbonne and Le Saulchoir, the French Dominican house of studies. His doctorate in theology came from Le Saulchoir, and the greatest influence on him in those years was M.D. Chenu, a Dominican who was deeply interested in "the signs of the times" that theology had to read if it were to communicate the relevance of faith. Chenu supported the French worker-priest movement (an effort to meet the laboring classes, who were disaffected from the Church, on their own ground), and Schillebeeckx imbibed a deep sympathy for this approach to priestly ministry. Church authorities in Rome condemned Chenu's views, but he carried on peacefully. Years later, when Schillebeeckx himself was suspect in Rome, he kept in mind the fortitude that Chenu had shown.

From his experience in France, Schillebeeckx was convinced that theology ought to reflect on the practice of faith. Unless theologians were in touch with people's actual experience, including their efforts to establish a just social order, they would not be effective. This conviction anticipated the Latin American liberation theologians of the 1970s and

1980s, for whom Schillebeeckx later maintained great sympathy. Working with refugees one summer building houses, Schillebeeckx found that reflecting with students on this experience in the evenings brought a rich yield for theological investigation.

From 1943 Schillebeeckx was teaching theology at the Catholic University of Louvain. He was responsible for the entire curriculum of dogmatic theology (that which exposes the basic tenets of church doctrine), which was spread over a four-year cycle. Thus he was forced to consider the entire corpus of Catholic doctrine and think about the interrelations among the different tracts. His first publications, beginning in the early 1950s, dealt with sacramental theology. Translated into English as *Christ, The Sacrament of Encounter with God* (1962), his first book received a warm reception. Schillebeeckx was rethinking the sacraments in non-scholastic, personalist categories, searching for the presence of Christ in and through the signs of the sacramental ceremonies. His next book, on Mary, treated her in the context of Christology, rather than in the ecclesiastic context usually employed. The result was to humanize Mary, tying her to the humanity and work of Jesus. This focus, more limited than the previous tendency to associate Mary with the entire sweep of the history of salvation, was more congenial to Protestant theologians, who feared idolatrous overtones in Catholic devotion to Mary.

In addition to teaching dogmatic theology at Louvain, Schillebeeckx also gave spiritual direction to numerous students. His tendency in that work was to relax the previously rigid rules and support a training regime both permissive and progressive. This succeeded in reducing tensions between students and faculty, and it put into practice the positive, hopeful, humanistic theology that he was developing from his studies in the history of theology and the Bible. His goal was to be not so much a superior as a friendly, understanding, kindly older brother.

In 1957 Schillebeeckx was appointed to Nimegen University in Holland, where he wrote his most influential books. At first he was depressed by the conditions at Nimegen, which were considerably more constrictive than those at Louvain. But his work as a *peritus* (expert) before and during the Second Vatican Council (1962-1965) put him in contact with the leading bishops and theologians of the world-wide church and caught him up in the euphoria of an unprecedented effort to update the Church by bringing it into dialogue with the modern world. He gave numerous lectures to bishops, explaining recent advances in theology, and he contributed to the chapter on marriage and the family in the key conciliar document *Gaudium et Spes* (The Church in the Modern World). Reflecting years later, he found the achievement of the council to be ambiguous, because it brought some progress but by no means the radical reforms for which he had hoped. Popes Paul VI and John Paul II both put brakes on such reforms and clamped down on theologians who stressed freedom of conscience or democratic processes in the Church. Schillebeeckx found himself most sympathetic to the "critical communities" that arose in Europe after the council. These grass-roots churches sought to criticize church practice in view of its social and experiential impact, as well as its fidelity to tradition.

Schillebeeckx's greatest books, on Christology, appeared in Dutch in 1974 and 1977. Translated as *Jesus* (1979) and *Christ* (1980), they have set the standard for contemporary studies of Jesus. With great erudition, Schillebeeckx sought to retrieve the experience of both the man Jesus and the early Christian community that became convinced he was alive in their midst (through the resurrection). Together, these books were a *tour de force,* joining biblical scholarship with hermeneutical (interpretational) acumen and speculative power in a fresh synthesis. The two books brought Schillebeeckx under a cloud in Rome, because they do not use traditional language and do not make the formulas of the Council of Chalcedon (451), where the divinity and humanity of Jesus were defined classically, the template for all Christological reflection.

Schillebeeckx bore the attacks on his writings patiently, continuing to produce controversial studies in other areas. For example, his book on ministry (1980) argued for the ordination of women and against priestly celibacy. He also continued his leadership in Concilium, an international publishing venture designed to help theologians from all over the globe collaborate on important current issues.

Schillebeeckx retired from Nimegen in 1982, the same year in which he received the Erasmus Prize, one of Europe's most prestigious awards. He continued to study and write, remaining a quiet, soft-spoken advocate of a free, engaged, personalist Christian faith. He lived in a book-lined room at the Albertinum, a Dominican community residence in Nijmegan. The silver-haired theologian was in personality similar to his books; he spoke, sometimes opaquely, only to his peers and never tried to popularize. Dignified, reserved, soft-spoken, and somewhat nervous, he looked like the scholar he was. Schillebeeckx suffered from heart trouble. As for prayer, he said he has "never found it difficult" to "speak to God" as "a man speaks to his friend."

Further Reading

Schillebeeckx's major works are *Christ: The Sacrament of the Encounter with God, Jesus, Christ, Ministry,* and *The Church with a Human Face* (1985), an expanded version of *Ministry.* A good sampling of the major themes of his work are available in *The Schillebeeckx Reader,* edited by Robert Schreiter (1984). Schillebeeckx also published some of his sermons (*God Among Us,* 1986) and a short book *On Christian Faith.* The best introduction to his life and thought is his *God is New Each Moment* (1983), a series of interviews he gave to Dutch journalists. Also useful is John Bowden's *Edward Schillebeeckx* (1983). □

Johann Christoph Friedrich von Schiller

The German dramatist, poet, and historian Johann Christoph Friedrich von Schiller (1759-1805) ranks

as one of the greatest of German literary figures. He was a founder of modern German literature.

Friedrich von Schiller was born at Marbach, Württemberg, on Nov. 10, 1759. His father, Johann Kaspar Schiller, was an army captain in the service of Duke Karl Eugen of Württemberg. His mother, Elisabeth Dorothea, the daughter of a Marbach innkeeper, was a gentle and religious person. Schiller had four sisters, one older and three younger.

As a boy, Schiller, under the influence of Philipp Ulrich Moser, a parson, wanted to become a preacher. He attended the duke's military academy, the Karlsschule, near Stuttgart for two years. After the academy was moved to Stuttgart, Schiller endured five more years of harsh discipline there. He studied medicine because that was the domineering duke's will. In spite of frequent illnesses, fevers, stomach upsets, and headaches, he wrote his final dissertation on the interrelationship between man's spiritual and physical natures. At the same time he was writing his first play, *Die Räuber,* which was published in 1781. It ranks as one of the literary monuments of the German *Sturm und Drang* period.

Early Works

In December 1780 Schiller was appointed medical officer to a regiment stationed in Stuttgart at a pitiably low salary. A loan toward the publication of *Die Räuber* marked the beginning of a succession of agonizing debts that characterized Schiller's early career. In 1782 *Die Räuber* received its first stage performance, in Mannheim. It brought him both public acclaim and the wrath of the duke, who forbade him to write anything except medical treatises. That same year Schiller published the *Laura-Oden* in his *Anthologie auf das Jahr 1782.* The inspiration for these poems was a 30-year-old widow, Dorothea Vischer, who had three children. She had rented a simple ground-floor room to Schiller and another lieutenant.

Meantime, Schiller's conflict with the Duke of Württemberg forced him to flee Stuttgart in September 1782. A period of great deprivation and uncertainty followed until Schiller became dramatist at the Mannheim theater in September 1783. During this time he composed *Die Verschwörung des Fiesko zu Genua* (1783) and *Kabale und Liebe* (1784). He also began work on *Don Carlos, Infant von Spanien,* which appeared in 1785 and in its revised form in 1787.

In 1784 Schiller completed *Die Schaubühne als moralische Anstalt betrachtet,* which appeared in his *Rheinische Thalia,* a literary journal, in 1785. The second issue of *Thalia* contained Schiller's hymn *An die Freude,* which later inspired Ludwig van Beethoven to create his magnificent Ninth Symphony in D Minor. In the third issue of *Thalia* Schiller published part of *Don Carlos.* During this period Christian Gottfried Körner generously offered Schiller financial help and hospitality, becoming his patron and friend.

Don Carlos was important in Schiller's dramatic development not only for its use of a historical setting but also for its employment of blank verse. For the first time, too, Schiller accomplished the presentation of a perfectly drawn and perfectly convincing noblewoman. The character of Queen Elisabeth of Valois was to some extent based on that of Charlotte von Kalb, an intimate friend.

Schiller occupied himself for many years afterward with the themes he employed in this drama. In *Don Carlos* the conflict between love and the demands of the state was exalted into the idea of the dignity and freedom of man. The struggle against love is a struggle for a high goal, and it is not the love of Don Carlos for the Queen or his friendship for the Marquis of Posa that forms the crux of the play but the ideal of spiritual and national freedom.

In all of Schiller's earliest tragedies—*Die Räuber, Die Verschwörung des Fiesko,* and *Kabale und Liebe*—he presents either a great criminal, a great adventurer, or a great enthusiast. All of his characters speak in the grand style. Schiller captures the secret of great passion even in his earliest dramas. The robber chieftain Karl Moor of *Die Räuber* judges himself when he admits that two men like him would destroy the organic structure of the civilized world. Fiesko contemplates the idea that it is great to win a crown but that it is divine to be able to cast it off.

In 1787 Schiller paid a visit to his friend Frau von Kalb in Weimar, the residence of Johann Wolfgang von Goethe, who at that time was traveling in Italy. The two great German poets met the following year in the house of Frau von Lengefeld (later to be Schiller's mother-in-law) in Rudolstadt. They had met once before, in December 1779, when Duke Karl August of Weimar and Goethe had come to the Karlsschule in Stuttgart to award the annual student prizes. Schiller had received three silver medals.

In 1788 Schiller's poems *Die Götter Griechenlands* and *Die Künstler* appeared, and that same year he published *Geschichte des Abfalls der vereinigten Niederlande,* a history of the revolt of the Netherlands against Spain. These works assured Schiller's fame and social position. Together with Goethe's support they gained him a professorship of history at the University of Jena in 1789. He held this position for 10 years. Schiller's inaugural, *Was heisst und zu welchem Ende studiert man Universalgeschichte,* caused a sensation. Afterward more than 500 students paid homage to the poet, but at later lectures the number of students in attendance dwindled considerably. Early in 1790 Schiller married Charlotte von Lengefeld, a gifted writer. In February 1803 he was created a nobleman.

Esthetic Theory

After 1790 Schiller became intensely interested in the philosophy and esthetics of Immanuel Kant. His *Geschichte des Dreissigjährigen Krieges,* a history of the Thirty Years War, appeared in 1791-1792. His studies in esthetics accompanied his historical researches. Schiller strove to capture the essence of "freedom and art." He determined not to read the works of any modern writer for 2 years. In his poem *Die Götter Griechenlands* Schiller had looked upon Greece with the eyes of Johann Joachim Winckelmann, the classical archeologist and historian of ancient art. Under the influence of Winckelmann's conception of the "schöne Antike," Schiller became convinced that only art can ennoble the barbarian and bring him culture. Art became, for Schiller, in the Platonic sense a basis of education. In 1795 he wrote in his *Über die aesthetische Erziehung des Menschen,* "There is no other way to make the sensuous man rational and reasonable than by first making him esthetic." The iron necessity of man's daily existence degraded him, said Schiller, and utility became the idol of the masses. But by means of the esthetic form man can "annihilate" the material aspects of life and triumph over transient matter. Man thus becomes the creator of a pure and permanent world.

In his grandiose philosophic poem *Die Künstler,* Schiller venerated art as the ennobling power that can create a higher culture and disclose a world harmony. In the opening strophe of this work, man, standing on the threshold of a new century, is depicted as the master of nature. He is shown as free, enlightened, strong through laws, great in his gentleness, matured through time, proud, and manly. Art, said Schiller, teaches man how to overcome his desires. Art is the first step away from the bondage of the flesh into a realm where the nobility of the soul reigns. The artist frees form from material in the same manner that waves separate a reflection from its source. In nature the artist discovers the laws of beauty. For example, in a tree he perceives the form of a pillar, and in the crescent moon the artist becomes aware of the mystery of the universe. For Schiller reality was merely illusion; only in the higher, spiritual realm was truth to be found. Just as the stage had changed into a tribunal in his famous poem *Die Kraniche des Ibykus,* so to him true art changes into higher reality.

Schiller wrote his important essay in esthetics, *Über naive und sentimentalische Dichtung,* in 1795-1796. It forms the basis of modern poetry criticism. In it Schiller points out that the "naive" poet has an advantage over other poets in his powerful, sensitive, and inherent clarity, while the "sentimentalische" poet has an advantage in his power of moral enthusiasm. By now Schiller had reached an artistic maturity incompatible with moralizing. In his philosophical poem *Das Ideal und das Leben* (1795) the poet presents no clumsy didactic lesson. No mention of reward or recompense for the sufferer, or of moral striving after inner freedom, is made. The subject of this poem is purely the growth of a powerful personality beyond the confines of the self into a higher world.

Later Dramas

In 1798-1799 Schiller completed his great trilogy on Albrecht von Wallenstein, the condottiere of the Thirty Years War. These three plays—*Wallensteins Lager, Piccolomini,* and *Wallensteins Tod*—represent Schiller's most powerful tragedy. In them he comes nearest to the tragic grandeur of William Shakespeare and Heinrich von Kleist. The *Wallenstein* plays stress Schiller's view of man as a creative force, and they exhibit his concept of historical inevitability. Schiller ennobles Wallenstein as a great creative statesman who bows before inexorable fate. Wallenstein recognizes his guilt and acknowledges the justice of his end because he realizes that every evil deed brings with it its angel of revenge.

The famous literary friendship between Goethe and Schiller began in earnest in 1794. On July 20, 1794, after a meeting in Jena of a nature society of which both were honorary members, Goethe went to Schiller's house to continue a discussion on the interpretation of natural phenomena, the metamorphosis of plants, and the interrelationship or separation between idea and experience. Goethe believed he had "observed with his own eyes" tangible truths of nature that Schiller, however, called "ideas." An important correspondence between the two poets followed. Schiller enjoyed the friendship of Goethe, with whom he began editing the literary journals *Horen* (1795-1797) and *Musenalmanach* (1796-1800). Goethe's residence in Weimar was a main reason for Schiller's move there, from Jena with his family, in 1799. During his Weimar years Schiller created many of his finest plays and poems.

Schiller wrote his most popular play, *Maria Stuart,* in 1800. He employed tragic irony as an artistic means in the memorable scene between the two queens in which Mary speaks daggers to Elizabeth but is hoist with her own petard. Mary remains a noble and tragic character right up to the scaffold. As with Elizabeth, the decisive factor in her fate lies in her personality and not in politics. Mary's death is subject not to "poetic justice" but to the justice of human conscience. By her death she atones for a previous guilt.

Schiller's next play, *Die Jungfrau von Orleans* (1801), is his poetically richest drama. Its theme is again guilt and redemption. Compared to *Maria Stuart,* it is loosely constructed, diffuse, and romantic not only in regard to the material itself but also in regard to the poetic character of the heroine. On the other hand, *Die Braut von Messina* (1803) is compact and stylized. Artistry dominates it at the cost of poetry. This play reflects Schiller's interest in classical antiquity. Its chorus has passages of lyrical and rhetorical magnificence.

In the preface to the first edition of this play, Schiller explained his views on the function of the chorus. The chorus, he wrote, should not be an accompaniment to the drama as in some ancient plays. Rather it should bring out the poetry of the play, thereby converting the modern world into a poetic one. The chorus should express the depth of mankind, and it should be a judging and clarifying witness of the actions in that it reflects them and endows them with spiritual power.

Schiller revealed his technical mastery at its most supreme in *Wilhelm Tell* (1804). Although this play is stylized, its artistry is less obvious than that of *Die Braut von Messina*. Schiller created the character of Wilhelm Tell as a manly hero without making him into a leader. When Gessler, the governor, brutally interferes with life and nature, the Swiss, and with them Wilhelm Tell, fight for family and freedom. In this play Schiller for once placed history and hero in favorable conjunction.

In the fragmentary drama *Demetrius,* Schiller unfolds a mysterious fate, revealing through his analytical dramatic technique a past crime more terrible to contemplate than any dread of the future. Whereas Oedipus in the hands of Sophocles subjects himself to divine command, Schiller's Demetrius defies his fate in order to perish.

Schiller's final tragedies are concerned with man's profoundest experience, the assertion and attainment of free will despite bodily claims or passion. After months of intermittent illness, Schiller died in Weimar on May 9, 1805.

Further Reading

An early biography of Schiller is Thomas Carlyle, *The Life of Friedrich Schiller* (1825; 2d ed. 1845). Of the many critical biographies see William Witte, *Schiller* (1949) and *Schiller and Burns* (1959). Other useful studies include Henry B. Garland's three works, *Schiller* (1949), *Schiller Revisited* (1959), and *Schiller: The Dramatic Writer* (1969); Ernst L. Stahl, *Friedrich Schiller's Drama: Theory and Practice* (1954); William F. Mainland, *Schiller and the Changing Past* (1957); and the essay on Schiller in Thomas Mann, *Last Essays* (trans. 1959). Other useful studies are Stanley S. Kerry, *Schiller's Writings on Aesthetics* (1961); Elizabeth M. Wilkinson and L. A. Willoughby, eds., *Schiller: On the Aesthetic Education of Man, in a Series of Letters* (trans. 1967), which has an extensive introduction about Schiller along with some of his works; and John Martin Ellis, *Schiller's Kalliasbriefe and the Study of His Aesthetic Theory* (1969). For a discussion of *Sturm and Drang* and Weimar classicism see the relevant chapters in Ernst L. Stahl and W. E. Yuill, *Introductions to German Literature,* vol. 3: *German Literature of the 18th and 19th Centuries,* edited by August Closs (1970). □

Solomon Schindler

Solomon Schindler (1842-1915), German-American rabbi and social theorist, contributed to the reform movement in Judaism and to the religious socialism of his era.

Solomon Schindler was born in Neisse, Germany, on April 24, 1842, the son of a rabbi. Although he was prepared for the rabbinate, his liberal religious tendencies caused him to enter the Royal Teachers' Seminary at Büren, from which he graduated in 1870. He had married Henrietta Schutz. His unusual conduct and ideas closed certain opportunities, and his openly antipatriotic stand during the Franco-Prussian War made it desirable for him to leave the country.

Schindler and his family arrived in America without resources. Reluctantly, because of financial need, he accepted a post as rabbi in Hoboken, N. J. In 1874 he became reader, teacher, and preacher of a temple in Boston. He proceeded to transform this temple into the Jewish church of his dreams, dispensing with many orthodox rituals and Americanizing the institution in every way possible. Although this lost him some of his congregation, he gained many more. In 1885 a new temple was dedicated with such liberal Protestant ministers as Phillips Brooks and Edward Everett Hale attending.

Schindler expanded his social concerns in ways that made him popular among Bostonians of various religions. He was a friend of the Catholic editor and poet John Boyle O'Reilly. His sermons collected as *Messianic Expectations and Modern Judaism* (1885)—critical of what he deemed outmoded and unwarranted illusions—were circulated by the *Boston Globe.* His hope for the world was social reform, particularly as expounded by Edward Bellamy in his novel *Looking Backward,* which Schindler translated into German. Schindler also wrote a sequel, *Young West* (1894).

Schindler's approach to religion and social reform brought him local popularity, so that from 1888 to 1894 he was elected to the Boston School Board by all factions. Nevertheless he lost his appeal for his congregation, which sought a native pastor and dismissed Schindler in 1893. He went on to found the pioneer Federation of Jewish Charities of Boston and was its superintendent until 1899. Thereafter until his retirement in 1909, he headed the Leopold Morse Home for Infirm Hebrews at Mattapan, Mass. Schindler in later years offered a sermon, "Mistakes I Have Made," which modified the sweeping nature of his criticism of traditional Judaism. He died on May 5, 1915.

Further Reading

Schindler's reputation has been lost in the uncertain currents of the Christian Socialism of his time. The one treatment of him in modern times, an incomplete analysis, is in Arthur Mann, *Yankee Reformers in the Urban Age* (1954). See also B. O. Flower, *Progressive Men, Women and Movements of the Past Twenty-five Years* (1914), and Arthur E. Morgan, *Edward Bellamy* (1944). David Philipson, *The Reform Movement in*

Judaism (1907; new and rev. ed. 1931), does not include Schindler but develops some of the principles that influenced his thought. □

Karl Friedrich Schinkel

The German architect, painter, and designer Karl Friedrich Schinkel (1781-1841) was one of the most important and influential architects of his time. He was equally at home with the medieval and the classical tradition.

Karl Friedrich Schinkel was born on March 13, 1781, in Neuruppin west of Berlin; the family moved to the Prussian capital in 1794. Inspired by Friedrich Gilly's 1796 project for a monument to Frederick II (Frederick the Great), Schinkel turned to architecture and studied with Gilly (1798-1800). Schinkel traveled in Italy and France (1803-1804). He became a painter of romantic landscapes and panoramas (*Medieval City by the Water,* 1813) and stage sets (*Magic Flute,* 1815). In 1813 he designed the Iron Cross, Germany's highest military award. In 1815 Frederick William III appointed him Prussian state architect.

Although Schinkel designed important buildings for cities other than Berlin, such as the church of St. Nicholas in Potsdam (1826-1837) and the Guard House in Dresden (1833), his major works were erected in the capital. In fact, he reshaped the monumental center of the city, and before its destruction during WWII it was said that he who knew Berlin knew Schinkel. His first building was the Royal Guard House (Neue Wacht-Gebäude) on the Unter den Linden (1816). A stone block with Doric portico, it established Schinkel as a master of Neo-Greek forms.

The reshaping of the Lustgarten (now Marx-Engels-Platz), a square at the eastern end of the Unter den Linden in front of the Royal Palace (now demolished), occupied the architect's attention during the 1820s. He remodeled the Cathedral to the east, but his major work was a new museum (now the Altes Museum) opposite the palace (designed 1822; finished 1830). A low block with a central rotunda for sculpture flanked by courts and surrounded by galleries for paintings, the museum closed the north side of the square with a majestic row of 18 Ionic columns framed by a podium below, entablature above, and pilasters to either side. The museum was Schinkel's masterpiece, one of the principal monuments of European neoclassicism and a continuing source of inspiration for classically oriented architects of the 20th century, such as Ludwig Mies van der Rohe and Philip Johnson.

Schinkel's other notable buildings in Berlin show the variety of his work. The Theater (Schauspielhaus) on the Gendarmenmarkt (1818; gutted 1945) sat on a podium with its Ionic portico contrasting with the low, flat, pilastered wings. The whole was capped by sculpture-enriched pediments. It was meant to form a unit with the porticoed and domed French and German churches that flank it. The monument to Napoleon's defeat that still crowns the Kreuzberg is a cast-iron Gothic pinnacle designed in 1818 (finished 1821; site later altered). For the Friedrich Werder Church near the Lustgarten, Schinkel submitted alternative designs, one classical and one medieval; the existing church (finished 1831) is Neo-Gothic.

The School of Architecture (Bauakademie) on the Spree River near the Lustgarten (1831-1835; destroyed) was characteristic of Schinkel's later work. A simple redbrick block enriched on the exterior by shallow pilasters and restrained decoration, it was a direct statement of structure and enclosure without overt historical details. Schinkel was appointed professor of architecture at the academy in 1820, and through his students his influence continued long after his death. He died in Berlin on Oct. 9, 1841.

Further Reading

The basic works on Schinkel are in German. A brief discussion of Schinkel's buildings in the context of the architecture of the early 19th century is in Henry-Russell Hitchcock, *Architecture: Nineteenth and Twentieth Centuries* (1958). Schinkel as city planner of Berlin is discussed in Hermann G. Pundt, *Schinkel's Berlin: A Study in Environmental Planning* (1972). □

Phyllis Schlafly

Phyllis Schlafly (born 1924) was an American conservative political activist and author, noted for her vocal and well-organized opposition to the Equal Rights Amendment.

Phyllis Stewart was born August 15, 1924, in St. Louis, Missouri. She received a mainly Catholic education but transferred from a Catholic college to Washington University in St. Louis in 1942. While there she had a World War II defense job in an arms plant test-firing ammunition. After her graduation in 1944 she went on to Radcliffe, where she received an M.A. in government in 1945. She worked for a year in Washington, D.C., for the American Enterprise Association (now Institute). In 1946 she returned to St. Louis, where she became a research director for two banks and worked in a campaign to return a conservative congressman to office. In 1949 she married Fred Schlafly, a wealthy lawyer from Alton, Illinois, a devout Catholic, and an ultraconservative anti-Communist. The Schlaflys raised six children, four boys and two girls. Phyllis Schlafly received her law degree in 1978 from Washington University.

Political Action

In 1952, during the Korean War, Schlafly made her first unsuccessful run for Congress from the 24th Illinois District in a right-wing conservative, Cold War, and anti-Communist issues campaign against big government and the conduct of the war. Throughout the 1950s she made statewide speeches as a state officer and national defense chairman of the Daughters of the American Revolution. Schlafly self-published two bibliographical pamphlets, *A Reading List for Americans* (1954) and *Inside the Communist Conspiracy* (1959). She wrote and spoke for the Cardinal Mindszenty Foundation, co-founded by her sister and a missionary priest and, in 1971, co-authored *Mindszenty the Man* with the anti-Communist Hungarian prelate's secretary. She was president of the Illinois Federation of Republican Women from 1956 to 1964. In 1963 she was chosen Woman of Achievement by the St. Louis *Globe-Democrat.* A delegate to Republican national conventions beginning in 1956, she went to the 1964 convention pledged to the conservative Senator Barry Goldwater.

In 1964 Schlafly published *A Choice Not an Echo,* a paperback history of Republican national conventions that told how the "kingmakers"—the party's eastern, internationalist wing—had cheated the "grass roots" of their choices. It championed Goldwater, and its three million copies were in part responsible for his winning the Republican presidential nomination. His landslide loss in the election to incumbent President Lyndon B. Johnson intensified a conservative-moderate power struggle that was developing within Republican ranks. In 1967 Schlafly lost a bitter fight for the presidency of the National Federation of Republican Women; founded the *Phyllis Schlafly Report,* a monthly newsletter for her growing corps of ultraconservative women supporters; and published *Safe—Not Sorry,* with comments on urban Black ghetto riots and other topics.

In 1970, during the unpopular Vietnam War and in a tense climate generated by the riots, she again ran unsuccessfully for Congress in Illinois, waging a militant law-and-order, Cold War issues campaign. She charged that federal bureaucrats had created a permanently impoverished welfare class and that civil rights and New Left groups "saturated by Communists" and federal poverty workers (among others) had organized the riots. She opposed the war as a no-win Soviet trap to divert U.S. resources from a strong defense.

Between 1964 and 1976 she wrote five books on national defense with retired Rear Admiral Chester Ward: *The Gravediggers* (1964); *Strike from Space* (1965); *The Betrayers* (1968); *Kissinger on the Couch* (1975); and *Ambush at Vladivostok* (1976). The books charged that an elite group of men—the "gravediggers"—chief among them Robert S. McNamara, secretary of defense (1961-1968), and Henry A. Kissinger, secretary of state (1973-1976), had undermined American defenses during the 1960s and 1970s by negotiating U.S.-Soviet weapons agreements and détente and by scrapping U.S. weapons systems. The personal attack style of the books and their idiosyncratic conservative content offended liberals, moderates, and some conservatives—even the far-right John Birch Society.

The Equal Rights Amendment

During the 1970s Schlafly almost single-handedly prevented ratification of the Equal Rights Amendment (ERA), a proposed constitutional amendment guaranteeing equality of rights for women. In 1972 the amendment passed Congress, and 30 of the 38 state legislatures needed for ratification passed it. Schlafly opposed it for allegedly striking at traditionalist family and religious values (opening the door to legalization of homosexual marriage, abortion, and conscription of women), for tampering with financial support and protective labor laws for women, and for transferring state power to the federal government.

Throughout the 1970s she barnstormed the country with her supporters, lobbied state legislatures, and debated feminist leaders. Schlafly founded the Eagle Forum, a national organization of volunteers to champion conservative causes, in 1976. *The Positive Woman,* in which she compared a traditional wife and homemaker, pro-family and pro-defense ideal, to feminist ideals and values, was published in 1978. Her style and content again offended readers across the political spectrum, but some commentators acknowledged a strong vein of common sense in her arguments, and the women's movement became less insensitive to her constituency and changed some of its tactics. The ratification period for the amendment expired in June 1982.

After the ERA

Schlafly was awarded seven medals by Freedoms Foundation (1970) and in 1975 received the Brotherhood Award of the National Conference of Christians and Jews. In the 1980s she continued to lobby for ultraconservative and traditionalist causes—e.g., for school prayer and against equal pay for women for comparable work. For three decades she was a populist who spoke effectively to and for the resentments of her constituency and a salient precursor of a 1980s resurgence of conservatism. Her opponents found her to be an incredibly fierce and capable fighter for her views.

By the mid-1990s, the author of 16 wide-ranging books focused her considerable energies on Eagle Forum campaigns, a syndicated column appearing in 100 newspapers, a daily radio show on 270 stations, and a radio talk show on education broadcast weekly on 50 stations. She remained a spokeswoman for conservative causes, speaking around the country and presenting her views on day care, comparable worth, and the Family Medical Leave Act to the U.S. Congress. She weathered attempts to discredit her family-values message, most notably when the news media took great glee reporting in 1992 that her son was a homosexual. She was voted Illinois Mother of the Year that same year.

Further Reading

The only biography as of the mid-1990s of Schlafly was Carol Felsenthal's fair and thought-provoking *The Sweetheart of the Silent Majority* (1981). Other articles appeared in *Rolling Stone* (November 26, 1981); *Ms.* (January and September 1982); *Newsweek* (February 28, 1983 and September 28, 1992); and *National Review* (October 19, 1992). Articles by Schlafly appeared in *The Humanist* (May/June 1986); and *The Congressional Digest* (May and November 1988) as well as in dozens of other publications. An Internet site maintained by the Eagle Forum offers a large selection of Schlafly's writings. □

Friedrich von Schlegel

The critic and author Friedrich von Schlegel (1772-1829) was one of the chief founders of the German romantic movement. He is best known for his writings in literary theory and cultural history.

Friedrich von Schlegel was born in Hanover on March 10, 1772. He studied philosophy and literature at Göttingen University and later at Leipzig. Between 1794 and 1796 he lived in Dresden, later moving to Jena, making acquaintances in the literary circles of both cities. In Jena, Schlegel was especially influenced by the philosophy of Johann Gottlieb Fichte, whose teachings he later applied to literary theory.

In 1797 Schlegel moved to Berlin, where he associated with such romantic writers as Ludwig Tieck. In 1798 Schlegel published two essays, *Vom Studium der griechischen Poesie* (On the Study of Greek Poetry) and *Geschichte der Poesie der Griechen und Römer* (History of the Poetry of the Greeks and Romans), in which he expounded the thesis that the Greeks had achieved perfect harmony in their civilization and art. With other members of the romantic movement he edited the literary quarterly *Athenaeum* (1798-1800). In its pages he developed his literary theories—he considered romantic poetry to be a "progressively universal poetry," expanding its subject matter to include all aspects of life. An example of such "poetry" was Schlegel's experimental novel, *Lucinde* (1799), in which he analyzed the psychological details of his relationship with Dorothea Veit, the daughter of the Jewish intellectual Moses Mendelssohn. Friedrich and Dorothea were married in 1804.

After teaching briefly at the University of Jena, Schlegel moved to Paris in 1802, where he studied Oriental literature and culture. In 1808 he went to Cologne, converted to Roman Catholicism, and published a study of Indian culture, *Über die Sprache und Weisheit der Indier* (On the Language and Wisdom of the Indians).

Although Schlegel had previously taught absolute freedom in thought and action and preached free love in his novel, in later years he tended toward increasing intellectual and political conservatism. He became affiliated with the Austrian government, at that time a reactionary force in European politics. In 1809 he became court secretary in Vienna, although he continued his literary activities. Between 1810 and 1812 he gave lectures in Vienna on medieval poets as forerunners of romanticism, and he perfected his philosophy of history, which viewed national cultures as organic developments. Among his translated lectures are

The Philosophy of History, The Philosophy of Life and the Philosophy of Language, and *The History of Literature.*

In 1815 Schlegel assisted the Austrian delegation at the Congress of Vienna. In his later years he served as editor of the conservative journal *Concordia.* He died in Dresden on Jan. 12, 1829.

Further Reading

The best extensive treatment of Schlegel, especially his theoretical writings, is in Oskar Walzel, *German Romanticism* (1932). Walzel demonstrates Schlegel's central importance as a romantic theorist. More general discussions of Schlegel's life and work are in Walter Silz, *Early German Romanticism* (1929), and Ralph Tymms, *German Romantic Literature* (1955).

Additional Sources

Eichner, Hans, *Friedrich Schlegel,* New York, Twayne Publishers 1970.

Peter, Klaus, *Friedrich Schlegel,* Stuttgart: Metzler, 1978. □

Friedrich Ernst Daniel Schleiermacher

The German theologian and philosopher Friedrich Ernst Daniel Schleiermacher (1768-1834) held that man's consciousness of being springs from the presence of God within him. He believed that all morality is an attempt to unite man's physical nature with his mind.

Born on Nov. 21, 1768, Friedrich Schleiermacher was educated at Moravian Church schools and destined to be a pastor. Doubting religion, he studied at the University of Halle, becoming absorbed first in Kantian philosophy and then in Plato, Baruch Spinoza, and Johann Gottlieb Fichte. He became one of the early Berlin romantics and associated particularly with Friedrich von Schlegel. In 1799 he published his famous *Reden über die Religion,* in which he claimed that religion was separate and apart from morality and knowledge. His *Monologen* (1800) outlined his ethical system. His *Grundlinien einer Kritik der bisherigen Sittenlehre* (1803) was a philosophical work, and his *Die Weihnachtsfeier* (1806) outlined his views on Jesus. He was pastor at Stolp from 1802 to 1804 and then became a professor at Halle until 1809, when he moved to Berlin, where he remained until his death on Feb. 12, 1834.

Schleiermacher was the most influential thinker of 19th-century Protestantism. In philosophy, however, he was overshadowed by G. W. F. Hegel. Schleiermacher was an idealist, holding that human knowledge was at best a mere approximation to reality and that man arrives at this knowledge by a conflict (the *Dialektik*). All German idealism was somehow saddled with the a priori conviction that reality was either very difficult to reach or totally unreachable in

itself. Schleiermacher labored with this a priori in his attempt to establish his religious beliefs on a solid foundation. In this he was a child of the Enlightenment and a victim of the romantic illusion that in the final analysis it was only the ego or the individual who counted. This illusion cohered with his Protestant persuasion that the individual conscience was the ultimate criterion of what was correct in belief and good in morality.

Religion, Schleiermacher held, results from the feeling man has that he is absolutely dependent. He derived the structure of his theology from this basic notion. He considered Christianity to be the highest stage of the monotheistic urge in man. To Christ, Schleiermacher assigned a role of mediator, thereby leaving great doubts as to the divinity of Jesus and his identity with God. He reinterpreted the traditional Christian doctrines of sin, justification, Christology, Last Judgment, hell, and heaven.

Schleiermacher foreshadowed the later religious thought of the 19th and early 20th centuries. His doctrine concerning the rise of natural and supernatural religions is a foretaste of the later evolutionary theories. His attempt to bridge rationalism and supernaturalism invoked the theories and the principles which animated Ethical Culture movements of the 20th century.

Further Reading

Terence N. Tice, *Schleiermacher Bibliography* (1966), is highly recommended as an extensive guide to the literature by and about Schleiermacher. Aspects of his life and thought are discussed in Richard B. Brandt, *Philosophy of Schleiermacher* (1941), and Jerry F. Dawson, *Friedrich Schleiermacher: The Evolution of a Nationalist* (1966).

Additional Sources

Christian, C. W., *Friedrich Schleiermacher,* Peabody, Mass.: Hendrickson Publishers, 1991, 1979.

Clements, K. W. (Keith W.), *Friedrich Schleiermacher: pioneer of modern theology,* London; San Francisco, CA: Collins, 1987. □

Oskar Schlemmer

Oskar Schlemmer (1888-1943) was a German painter, sculptor, and stage designer. His single subject was the human figure, which he reduced to puppet-like, two-dimensional shapes that were expressive of the human body as a perfect system of proportions and functions analogous to the machine age.

Oskar Schlemmer was born on September 4, 1888, in Stuttgart to Carl Leonhard Schlemmer and his wife Mina Neuhaus. The youngest of six children, Schlemmer learned at an early age to provide for himself following the untimely death of both his parents around 1900. As early as 1903 the young Schlemmer was completely independent and supporting himself as an apprentice in an inlay workshop.

In 1906 Schlemmer enrolled at the Stuttgart Academy, where he studied under Landenberger until he left for Berlin to work independently in 1910. While in Berlin Schlemmer painted his first important pictures—some landscapes and two rare self-portraits. These early pictures anticipate Schlemmer's life-long search for the geometric order and structure that characterize his later figurative work. It is also during this period that he first became interested in dance and the theater.

By 1912 Schlemmer was back in Stuttgart, studying under the artist Adolf Hoelzel. He remained there until World War I found him fighting on the western front in 1914. After being wounded twice Schlemmer was appointed to a military cartography unit in Colmar, where he resided until the end of the war. In 1918 he was, once again, back in Stuttgart working under Hoelzel.

The following year Schlemmer turned, for the first time, to the art of sculpture. The relief sculpture entitled *Figure of a Youth in Components* (1919) typifies his approach to the human form, a subject from which he rarely strayed. Schlemmer depicted the profile of a male youth reduced to basic geometric shapes abstracted from nature to reveal the figure's basic structure. Thus he illustrated not a specific figure within a time-defined realm but, instead, a figure that embodies the idea of man and his never changing structure.

The 1920s were Schlemmer's most productive years. After his marriage to Helena Tutein in 1920 he accepted the post of master of form at Walter Gropius' Bauhaus in Weimar. At the Bauhaus Schlemmer was first appointed as a master of the mural painting and sculpture workshops before heading the theater workshop in 1923. Schlemmer's interest in the theater was essentially in the ballet. His *Triadic Ballet,* first performed in Stuttgart in 1922, was a great success at the Bauhaus in 1923. With music composed by Paul Hindemith, Schlemmer used three dancers dressed in puppet-like costumes before various backdrops. The ballet was choreographed to reveal the figures' relationships to each other as well as to the space around them. Schlemmer saw the puppet as an idealization of the human form, a form that was able to move with perfect machine-like grace once it was liberated from the earthbound realm by the puppetmaster. Thus Schlemmer created a human form that was at once timeless in the perfection of its parts and contemporary in its mechanical movement.

Schlemmer's paintings from this period reflect the spatial concerns evident in his theatrical productions. The *Dancer,* painted in 1923, shows a single puppet-like figure frozen in step. Unlike the earlier *Figure of a Youth* Schlemmer set this figure within a vague stage setting where the figure interacts with the surrounding space. In other pictures from this period Schlemmer often included several figures in the same composition.

The conservative political climate of the Weimar Republic in the 1920s forced the Bauhaus to move to Dessau in 1925. Schlemmer accepted the offer to head the experimental theater workshop in Dessau. He remained there until 1929, when he took a teaching post at the Breslau

Academy. While at Breslau, Schlemmer resumed work on the mural commission he received in 1928 for the Fountain Hall of the Folkwang Museum in Essen and designed stage sets for an opera and ballet by Igor Stravinsky.

The 1930s were difficult years for Schlemmer and his family. In 1933 he was dismissed from his teaching position at Breslau by the Nazis, who considered his art degenerate. The Schlemmers then moved to Eichberg near the Swiss border. Unable to show or sell his work, Schlemmer's painting took on a decidedly mystical tone. The former balance that Schlemmer achieved between the rounded conical forms of his figures and their placement on a two-dimensional surface gave way to very flat, almost transparent, figures bathed in a mystical light. In 1937 Schlemmer moved to Sehringen before his pictures were displayed at the National Socialist exhibition of "Degenerate Art."

Schlemmer's last years were spent working at a paint factory owned by Kurt Herbert in Wuppertal. The factory offered Schlemmer the opportunity to paint without the fear of persecution. His last series, the so called "Window Pictures," were very small pictures painted while looking out the window of his house and observing neighbors engaged in their domestic tasks.

During the summer of 1942 Schlemmer fell ill. After clinical treatments at numerous hospitals Oskar Schlemmer died in Baden-Baden in April 1943.

Further Reading

Museum catalogues provide the fundamental information on Schlemmer's art. His letters and diaries are available in English translation edited by his wife: Tut Schlemmer, *The Letters and Diaries of Oskar Schlemmer* (1972). Useful background material may be found in H. H. Arnason, *History of Modern Art* (1968) and in Frank Whitford, *Bauhaus* (1984). ☐

Arthur Meier Schlesinger

The American historian Arthur Meier Schlesinger (1888-1965) was one of the pioneers in the study of the social aspects of American history.

Arthur M. Schlesinger was born in Xenia, Ohio, on Feb. 27, 1888, the son of a first-generation immigrant. Schlesinger graduated in 1910 from Ohio State University. As a graduate student at Columbia, he was influenced by Herbert Levi Osgood, James Harvey Robinson, and Charles A. Beard. His dissertation, finished in 1917, was *The Colonial Merchants and the American Revolution* (1918), which Sir Denis Brogan called "perhaps the most remarkable Ph.D. dissertation in modern American historiography." Schlesinger had used Osgood's methods and Beard's insights.

While finishing his dissertation, Schlesinger taught at Ohio State, beginning in 1912. He became a full professor in 1917, the same year he received his doctorate. During his stay at Ohio State, he married Elizabeth Bancroft. In 1919 he moved to the State University of Iowa as chairman of the history department. In 1922 he inaugurated a course entitled "Social and Cultural History of the United States," the first of its kind in the country. His *New Viewpoints in American History* (1922) presents his ideas on the craft and content of history. He joined Harvard in 1924 as a visiting professor of history and became Francis Lee Higginson professor of history in 1939. He was a charter member of the Social Science Research Council, an organization he later chaired (1930-1933).

The first four volumes of *A History of American Life,* under the joint editorship of Schlesinger and Dixon Ryan Fox, appeared in 1927. Schlesinger's own contribution was volume 10, *The Rise of the City, 1878-1898* (1933), an outstanding pioneer effort in social and urban history. The 13-volume series was completed in 1948 and was an original attempt to portray the everyday life of ordinary people, touching on health, public welfare, and recreation. Schlesinger also wrote college texts during this period. His interest in immigration led him to finish two books by Marcus Lee Hansen: *The Atlantic Migration, 1607-1860* (1940), which won a Pulitzer Prize, and *The Immigrant in American History* (1940). His presidential address to the American Historical Association in 1942, reprinted in his *Paths to the Present* (1949), again called attention to the study of American character.

Schlesinger retired from Harvard in 1953. He died on Oct. 30, 1965. His son, Arthur M. Schlesinger, Jr., became famous as a historian and also as part of President John F. Kennedy's intellectual group.

Further Reading

The best account of Schlesinger's professional life is his autobiography, *In Retrospect: The History of a Historian* (1963). His ideas are set forth in his *New Viewpoints in American History* (1922) and *Paths to the Present* (1949; rev. ed. 1964), as well as in John Higham, Leonard Kreiger, and Felix Gilbert, *History* (1965).

Additional Sources

Depoe, Stephen P., *Arthur M. Schlesinger, Jr., and the ideological history of American liberalism,* Tuscaloosa: University of Alabama Press, 1994. ☐

Arthur Meier Schlesinger Jr.

Arthur Meier Schlesinger, Jr. (born 1917) was an outstanding historian of the United States and an influential activist in the Democratic Party. What was unique was the extent to which he brought his scholarship to bear upon his partisan politics.

Arthur M. Schlesinger, Jr. was born in 1917 with the name Arthur Bancroft Schlesinger, later changed by dropping his mother's maiden name and taking his father's full name. This emulation was one of many in the most famous father-son combination in the history of American historians, for Schlesinger Jr. was raised in the home of one of the leading historians of the 1920s and 1930s. Arthur Schlesinger, Sr. taught one of the first college courses in American social and cultural history (in the early 1920s), pioneered in the scholarship of social history, and, as a professor at Harvard between the two world wars, directed the graduate work of several students who became distinguished social and intellectual historians.

Precocious Arthur Jr. graduated from Harvard College *summa cum laude* at age 20 and published his honor's thesis one year later, *Orestes A. Brownson: A Pilgrim's Progress* (1939). He spent a year studying in England, but did not pursue further formal academic training. Membership in the Society of Fellows at Harvard allowed him to do the research for *The Age of Jackson,* published when he was only 27 in 1945. (After 1942 Schlesinger Jr. had been involved in the World War II effort in Washington, D.C. and overseas.) The Pulitzer Prize was awarded *The Age of Jackson,* and Schlesinger Jr. was appointed to the Harvard history department, where his father was still a professor.

Schlesinger Jr. moved his scholarly focus from the pre-Civil War period to that of the New Deal while he was a Harvard professor. Teaching American intellectual history from the colonies to the present, he concentrated his research upon the *Age of Roosevelt* and published the first three volumes covering the years to 1936: *The Crisis of the Old Order* (1957); *The Coming of the New Deal* (1958); and *The Politics of Upheaval* (1960). In the mid-1980s he resumed work on his multi-volume history of the New Deal.

If Schlesinger Jr. had only published these historical works he would be known to the educated public as well as to historians, for all of his books are well written and widely read. But it was his political involvements and the relation of his writing to these involvements which made Schlesinger a public figure of unusual interest.

He became the Albert Schweitzer Professor of Humanities at the City University of New York in 1966 and president of the American Institute of Arts and Letters in 1981.

Actively Supported Stevenson

Though Schlesinger Sr. (1888-1965) was a liberal, a Democrat throughout the 1920s, and a supporter of the New Deal, his scholarship did not visibly manifest his political views and his partisan political activity was slight. Schlesinger Jr. was more active personally in partisan politics, and his scholarship seemed to cast votes. *The Age of Jackson,* written during FDR's fourth term, argued that the pre-Civil War reform era was one of a series of alternating liberal cycles which followed conservative periods, each of which failed to address the nation's political, economic, and social problems. Schlesinger attempted to demonstrate that Jacksonian democracy was a conscious social movement emanating mainly from "have-nots" in the eastern and southern parts of the country. The alleged class conscious eastern radicalism and the regional alignment suggested, of course, links with the New Deal, and it was said that *The Age of Jackson* "voted" for Roosevelt, as well as Jackson.

In 1949 Schlesinger Jr. published *The Vital Center: The Politics of Freedom,* a history of American social thought organized around the political issues of the post-World War II years. *The Vital Center* voted retrospectively for Truman in the election of 1948, both in terms of domestic New Deal programs and in the formulation of opposition to totalitarianism, whether of fascism on the right or communism on the left. Written for the moment, *The Vital Center* remains a remarkably enduring testament for the mainstream of the Democratic Party almost 40 years after it was published.

An active supporter of Adlai Stevenson in his unsuccessful bids for the presidency in 1952 and 1956, Schlesinger Jr. switched his speech-writing to John Kennedy for the election of 1960. *Kennedy or Nixon: Does it Make Any Difference* (1960) made his case for JFK. After serving in the White House as a special assistant to Kennedy and resigning his Harvard faculty position, Schlesinger wrote *A Thousand Days: John F. Kennedy in the White House* (1965), for which he was again awarded a Pulitzer Prize.

His political visibility obscured the fact that Schlesinger Jr. remained an acute scholarly commentator in book reviews on the monographic works of other historians in American intellectual, political, and social history. In addition, he served as editor of the *History of American Presidential Elections* (4 volumes, 1971) and in 1986 wrote 14 stylish essays describing *The Cycles of American History.*

Old Ideals Recycled

Following Bill Clinton's proclamation of a new covenant in his 1992 presidential acceptance speech, Schlesinger asserted that a new era had begun. He based his assertion on the cycles of American history theory put forth by his father. The elder Schlesinger predicted in 1939 that the New Deal would run out of steam in the mid-1940s. It would give way to a conservative tide, he predicted, which in turn would yield a new liberal epoch starting in 1962. The next conservative phase would begin around 1978.

On the strength of this record, it was logical to predict, as the younger Schlesinger did in 1986, that at some point, shortly before or after the year 1990, there should come a sharp change in the national mood and direction. The reason each phase recurred at roughly 30-year intervals, Schlesinger asserted, was because generational change was the cycle's mainspring. But because each generation kept faith with its youthful dreams, Schlesinger argued, the forward momentum was guaranteed.

During the 1990s, Schlesinger was among an increasing number of writers, analysts and political observers who recognized that all was not well with multiculturalism and politically correct trends.

Further Reading

The best essay on Arthur Schlesinger, Jr. as a historian was by Marcus Cunliffe, "Arthur M. Schlesinger, Jr.," in *Pastmasters: Some Essays on American Historians,* edited by Marcus Cunliffe and Robin Winks (1969). For an interesting analysis by Schlesinger Jr. of perhaps the most influential historian of his own age in his own field of scholarship see Schlesinger Jr., "Richard Hofstadter," in *Pastmasters.* For background on the historical profession in the United States during Schlesinger Jr.'s lifetime, see John Higham, *History* (1965), chapters I-III. Schlesinger has been featured on the A&E Biography television program; a brief biography can be accessed at the Website www.biography.com (July 1997). He has authored more than a dozen books. □

James Rodney Schlesinger

James Rodney Schlesinger (born 1929) was an intelligent and strong-minded conservative whose professorial expertise led to a controversial career in government which included several appointments by President Nixon, one of which was secretary of defense, from which he was fired by President Ford, and his appointment by President Carter as secretary of energy, from which he was forced to resign.

James R. Schlesinger was born and reared in a middle-class Jewish family in New York City. His early years coincided with the Great Depression and World War II. But the most indelible mark left on him was that of the formative years of the Cold War, which he experienced as a student at Harvard where he earned A.B., A.M., and Ph.D. degrees in economics. During these years he toured Europe on a fellowship and emerged with a no compromise attitude towards the Soviet Union. He also converted to the Lutheran Church and married Rachel Mellinger. Together they had eight children (four sons and four daughters).

In 1955 Schlesinger began his professional career as assistant professor of economics at the University of Virginia. His first and only monograph, *The Political Economy of National Security* (1960), received mixed reviews, including one which noted a tendency to speak *ex cathedra.* Despite that early indication of an impolitic style, the conservative content attracted the favorable attention of the RAND Corporation, which Schlesinger joined in 1963. He rose to the position of director of strategic studies and also served as a consultant to the Bureau of the Budget.

With Richard Nixon's presidential victory in 1968 Schlesinger became assistant director of the Office of Management and Budget, where he earned a reputation for winning a six billion dollar cut in the Defense Department budget. This cutback did not stem from a "dovish" perspective. On the contrary, one of the central tenets of Schlesinger's thought was the belief that the Soviet leadership could not be trusted. A corollary was that the United States must maintain military supremacy at all costs. This "hard line" did not, however, lock Schlesinger into any one system or weapon. In 1974, for example, he proposed the development of the MX missile, yet as a member of the Scowcroft Commission in the early 1980s he opposed its further development.

Environmentalists—Friends or Foes?

Another major element in his thinking was concern for the environment. This played a role in his appointment as chairman of the Atomic Energy Commission (A.E.C.) in 1971 and as energy secretary in 1977. In both instances his environmental concern was supposed to balance a known bias for the development of nuclear power. As A.E.C. chairman he did not halt a nuclear bomb test on an Aleutian island. Rather, he attempted to demonstrate its safety by taking his wife and two of his daughters to view it. As secretary of defense he approved the chemical extermination of hundreds of thousands of blackbirds which were causing problems at several military bases despite the pleas of environmentalists, especially bird-watchers, who had counted Schlesinger as one of their own.

Later, as energy secretary, he weighed the case of the snail darter—a rare, tiny fish whose survival since prehistoric times was now endangered by the Clinch River nuclear power project—and found it wanting. His minimizing of the danger at Three Mile Island proved to be the proverbial last straw, evoking a flood of verbal abuse from environmentalists and powerful politicians. Speaking for the environmentalists, Jane Fonda declared, "Putting Energy Secretary James Schlesinger in charge of nuclear power is like putting Dracula in charge of the blood bank." Never timid, Schlesinger replied in kind, dismissing the *ad hominem* analogy as an expression of "the same people who were for Ho Chi Minh." Senator George McGovern's description of Schlesinger's performance as a "disaster" was not so easily contradicted, and congressional opposition ultimately led to Schlesinger's resignation from the center stage of national politics.

Schlesinger's style was a constant problem. After one of his earliest meetings with Nixon, the president reportedly told an aide, "Never bring him in here again," because he was put off by Schlesinger's abrasive challenges to more senior aides. Later, Nixon was offended by Schlesinger's condescending call for the president to use his forensic ability in getting the Soviets to yield in the SALT I talks, describing the comment as an insult to everyone's intelligence, "particularly to mine." Gerald Ford's perception of Schlesinger as patronizing was even stronger, dating back to Ford's days in the House. Moreover, Ford perceived Schlesinger's relations with congressmen as a liability, so when they differed on the defense budget as well as the handling of the Mayaquez incident, Ford fired him. Schlesinger first allied with the Reagan camp. When this bid failed, he joined forces with Carter, forming an especially close personal relationship. This bond preserved his place in Carter's inner circle even after it was clear that Schlesinger's congressional opponents would not be satisfied until he was out of office. Their deep-seated opposition may also account for the fact that Schlesinger remained in academe after his resignation in August 1979, serving as a senior adviser and later as counselor at the Georgetown Center for Strategic and International Studies despite the return of conservative Republicanism to the White House in 1981.

When in 1990, President George Bush proposed arms reductions with Russia, Schlesinger argued that a U.S. presence in Europe of 75,000 to 100,000 would be sufficient to represent America's commitment to Europe and assure stability on the continent.

Aligned with Jesse Helms

In May of 1996 during the heat of the U.S. Presidential campaign, Schlesinger and two former secretaries of defense, Caspar Weginberger and Donald Rumsefeld, along with nuclear scientist Edward Teller and former CIA director James Woolsey, testified in favor of mandating the deployment of a nationwide system of satellites, radars, and missile interceptors by the year 2003. However, independent polls and focus groups showed little public interest, and soon Republican candidates began walking away, convinced that they should not raise the issue in their campaigns.

In April 1997 four former defense secretaries lined up with Senator Jesse Helms against the chemical weapons treaty. One of them was James Schlesinger, who said it would tie U.S. hands in developing defenses against the very weapons America was swearing off. Schlesinger argued that the treaty would ban use of crowd-control chemicals such as tear gas, impair development of defenses against chemical weapons, and open the way for industrial espionage in the chemical industry.

Further Reading

There were no published works or lengthy articles which focused exclusively on Schlesinger, and he has not published an autobiography. Hence, his career and character were best gleaned from the memoirs of Nixon, *RN: The Memoirs of Richard Nixon* (1978); Ford, *A Time To Heal* (1979); Carter, *Keeping Faith* (1982); and those of cabinet members such as Kissinger. Studies of the Department of Defense, such as Douglas Kinnard, *Secretary of Defense* (1981), also include treatment of Schlesinger. ☐

Friedrich Albert Moritz Schlick

The German physicist and philosopher Friedrich Albert Moritz Schlick (1882-1936) revived positivism as a leading force in 20th-century thought and was the founding spirit of the Vienna Circle.

Moritz Schlick was born in Berlin on Feb. 28, 1833, and educated there. His secondary school training was largely focused on mathematics and physics, and he pursued these subjects further in his university studies at Heidelberg, Lausanne, and Berlin. His doctoral thesis at Berlin, written under Max Planck, was *Reflection of Light* (1904).

By 1910 Schlick's interests had shifted from physics proper to epistemology and the philosophy of science. With his inaugural dissertation, "The Nature of Truth in the Light of Modern Physics," he began his teaching career at Rostock. There he continued to follow developments in physics, partly through his friendship with Planck and Albert Einstein; and he wrote the first interpretation of the latter's relativity theory in 1917. Also during this period, Schlick worked out his fundamental ideas on scientific knowing and published them as *The General Theory of Knowledge* (1918). This earned him wide attention and a call to a professorship, first at Kiel in 1921 and a year later at Vienna.

At Vienna, Schlick quickly became the center of a group of men interested in scientific philosophy, logic, and mathematics. The group included among others Otto Neurath, Rudolf Carnap, Herbert Feigl, Friedrich Waismann, and Kurt Gödel and later the English philosophers Alfred Ayer and Susan Stebbing and an American, Charles Morris. There were weekly meetings to discuss fundamental questions in logic and the philosophy of science. Setting very exact (critics would say "narrow") criteria for knowledge, the group rejected metaphysical propositions as meaningless and severely limited the range of significant speech in ethics and esthetics. In 1929, on the occasion of Schlick's return from a guest lectureship at Stanford, Calif., he was presented with a pamphlet describing the history, membership, orientation, and goals of the group. It was called "The Scientific View of the World: The Vienna Circle."

The reading of Ludwig Wittgenstein's *Tractatus* in 1921 fundamentally altered Schlick's conception of the task of philosophy. He now held that philosophy's task was the analysis of the concepts used in science and the language spoken in everyday life. Widely propagated by members of the Vienna Circle, this is the dominant view in English and American philosophy today.

Schlick was shot by a deranged former student while on his way to lecture at the University of Vienna on June 22, 1936. Owing to his death and to the hostility of the Nazi regime after the Anschluss, the members of the Circle were widely dispersed to Scandinavia, England, and the United States.

Further Reading

There is no major work on Schlick. Victor Kraft, *The Vienna Circle: The Origin of Neo-positivism* (1953), gives an account of the history and central doctrines of the group. □

Heinrich Schliemann

Heinrich Schliemann (1822-1890) was a German merchant, world traveler, and archeologist. A man of enormous linguistic ability and personal determination, he combined a romantic enthusiasm and the calculating abilities of a practical realist in his search for the historical sites of Homeric Greece.

Heinrich Schliemann was born on Jan. 6, 1822, at Neubukow in Mecklenburg. The early death of his mother and the financially straitened circumstances of his poor pastor father made it necessary for the family to separate when Schliemann was 9 years old. He was brought up by an uncle, but further family misfortunes forced him to leave high school and to attend a commercial school, from which he graduated in 1836.

Apprenticed to a small grocer, Schliemann labored in unhappiness and desolation for 5 years until a working accident forced him to give up this life. Determined to seek a new situation, he embarked upon a voyage to Venezuela, where he hoped to find more congenial employment. Shipwrecked off the coast of Holland, he found a position with a commercial firm in Amsterdam and engaged in intensive language study during his spare time. He devised his own method and learned English and French in 6 months each, adding Dutch, Spanish, Italian, and Portuguese in even shorter periods of study.

In 1844 Schliemann became corresponding clerk and bookkeeper with B. H. Schröder and Company. This firm's Russian connections induced him to add that language to his linguistic accomplishments, and in 1846 his employers sent him to St. Petersburg as their commercial agent. Although he continued to represent the Dutch firm for 11 years, Schliemann founded a mercantile house of his own in 1847 to which he added a Moscow branch in 1852. His enterprises flourished, aided by the demand for war materials during the Crimean War, and he accumulated a huge fortune.

Travels of Leisure

In 1863 Schliemann gave up his Russian enterprises to devote his time and wealth to the pursuit of his childhood dream, the discovery of historical Troy and Homer's Greece. He set out in 1864 on a world tour which took him to Carthage, India, China, Japan, and America, where he received citizenship, for which he had applied during an earlier visit. He settled in Paris, published his first book, *La Chine et le Japon* (1865; *China and Japan*), and engaged in studies in preparation for his archeological search. In 1868 he proceeded to Greece, where he visited various Homeric sites. From these experiences he published the book *Ithaka, der Peloponnes und Troja* (1869), in which he advanced two theories (later to be tested and borne out) that Hissarlik, not Bunarbashi, was the true site of Troy and that the Atreid graves at Mycenae were situated inside the walls of the citadel. This work earned him a doctorate from the University of Rostock.

Excavation of Troy

In 1870 Schliemann's excavations at Troy began in earnest. He discovered a great treasure of gold jewelry and other objects and published his findings in *Antiquités troyennes* (1874). Largely because of poor illustrations and organizational shortcomings, the book was not well received. In addition, he encountered difficulties from the Turkish government regarding permission to continue his excavations. He went to Mycenae, where he began to dig near the Lion Gate, eventually unearthing the famous Dome Tombs, the burial place of the Mycenaean kings. The finds of gold, silver, bronze, stone, and ivory objects were enormous, perhaps the greatest treasure trove ever discovered, and eventually led to Schliemann's book *Mycenae* (1877).

In 1878 Schliemann returned to Troy to resume the excavations. His finds were published in *Ilios, City and Country of the Trojans* (1880). In 1881 he presented his Homeric treasures to the German people to be housed in specially designated Schliemann Halls in the State Museum of Berlin.

Having meanwhile worked at another Homeric site, Orchomenos, Schliemann returned to Troy in 1882, accompanied by Wilhelm Dörpfeld, whose archeological and architectural knowledge introduced much-needed professional methodology into the excavations. The resulting evaluations were published as *Troja* (1884) and were a much-improved sequel to Schliemann's *Ilios* of 1880.

The last 6 years of Schliemann's life were spent with further excavations at the citadel of Tiryns (1884) and at Orchomenos (1886), with plans for work in Egypt and Crete and with actual excavation starts on Cythera and in Pylos. On Dec. 25, 1890, while Dörpfeld was leading another dig at Troy, Schliemann died in Naples. He had had a life of great accomplishments, rushing impatiently and with insurmountable energy from project to project. Although his findings frequently lacked a correct final interpretation, his drive and enthusiasm subjected the world of Homer and the profession of archeology to a fresh breeze which blew away the cobwebs of established assumptions and ushered in a new era of archeological scholarship.

Further Reading

Schliemann's own account remains important as a basic source: *Mycenae: A Narrative of Researches and Discoveries at Mycenae and Tiryns* (1880; repr. 1967), which includes over 700 engravings and drawings. A sympathetic biography that contains many quotations from Schliemann's writings and letters is Emil Ludwig, *Schliemann of Troy: The Story of a Gold-seeker* (1931). Lynn and Gray Poole, *One Passion, Two Loves* (1966), describes Schliemann's life after 1869 and focuses on his close relationship with his second wife, Sophia. The most scholarly work on his excavations is Karl Schuchhardt, *Schliemann's Excavations: An Archaeological and Historical Study* (trans. 1891), which includes many sketches, pictures, and diagrams of the sites. Pierre S. R. Payne, *The Gold of Troy* (1959), with a chapter on Schliemann scholarship and a select bibliography, is useful for the general reader.

Additional Sources

Brackman, Arnold C., *The dream of Troy,* New York: Van Nostrand Reinhold Co., 1979, 1974.

Burg, Katerina von, *Heinrich Schliemann: for gold or glory?,* Windsor: Windsor Publications, 1987.

Deuel, Leo, *Memoirs of Heinrich Schliemann: a documentary portrait drawn from his autobiographical writings, letters, and excavation reports,* New York: Harper & Row, 1977.

Traill, David A., *Schliemann of Troy: treasure and deceit,* New York: St. Martin's Press, 1996. □

Andreas Schlüter

Andreas Schlüter (ca. 1660-1714), German sculptor and architect, was the greatest exponent of the baroque style in northern Germany. His works are characterized by powerful, dynamic forms and great dignity.

Andreas Schlüter whose exact birth date is uncertain but which must have been in the early 1660s, came from the north of Germany, probably Hamburg or Danzig. Little is known of his early training. He worked in Warsaw as a sculptor (1689-1693). In 1694 he was working in Berlin as a sculptor, apparently called there by the prince-elector of Brandenburg, Frederick III, who later became King Frederick I of Prussia. In 1695 Schlüter was sent on a brief study trip to France and, in 1696, on one to Italy at the expense of the elector. Later that year Schlüter produced statues for the Long Bridge leading to the palace in Berlin, as well as over 100 decorative heads of warriors for the keystones of the arches of the Arsenal in Berlin. These heads were largely produced by his assistants after his models.

Monument to the Great Elector

In 1696 Schlüter began his designs for the bronze equestrian monument to the King's father, the Great Elector, his most famous work in sculpture. This overlife-size statue was executed between 1698 and 1700, and the four enchained warriors, symbolizing the four temperaments, at its base were completed in 1708. The monument was originally on the Long Bridge, but after World War II it was placed in front of the Charlottenburg Palace. Inspired by such monuments as the Marcus Aurelius on the Capitol in Rome and François Girardon's equestrian statue of Louis XIV, the monument of the Great Elector is noteworthy for its great vitality and movement. Yet the dynamism of its large forms is more reminiscent of Gian Lorenzo Bernini than the aforementioned classical or classicizing examples.

Berlin Schloss

In 1699 Schlüter was appointed surveyor general of works for the elector, in charge of all buildings, and began work on a new palace on the island in the Spree, the famous Berlin Schloss. For it he designed not only the massive block of the structure itself but also all decorative details and the interiors. His organizational abilities were as important as his architectural talents in this enterprise, for he held the same sort of position in Berlin during the first decade of the 18th century that Bernini had earlier held in Rome, controlling all aspects of every architectural undertaking.

The construction of the Schloss was under Schlüter's direction until 1707, after which work continued under his successors, such as Eosander von Göthe. Those parts that were after Schlüter's designs were the Great Court, the Great Portal, and the main rooms of the first floor. All revealed Schlüter's basically sculptural approach to architectural problems: his tendency to enliven large areas through the dramatic use of strongly projecting articulating elements. The sculptural decoration of the stairway and the ceiling of the Hall of the Knights (Rittersaal), representing the four continents, were also his. The Schloss, although less damaged during World War II than many other buildings in Berlin, was the victim of political considerations and was demolished by the East German authorities in 1950. Only the sculpture is preserved (Bode Museum, Berlin).

In Berlin, Schlüter also designed and executed such works as the pulpit in St. Mary's Church (1703), the Alte Post (1701-1704; destroyed in the late 19th century), and the Münzturm (1706), a water tower attached to the Mint. The imminent collapse of this tower, and the discovery of structural problems in his other buildings, notably the Arsenal, led to the downfall of the architect. Although he demolished the water tower himself and sought to justify his errors, his enemies at court thoroughly discredited him. He lost one office after another and became seriously ill. By 1710 he was in disgrace at court and was permitted to work only as a sculptor. The sarcophagus of the elector (1713) was his last important work in Berlin.

In 1714 Schlüter left for St. Petersburg, where he had been offered employment. He died there the same year shortly after his arrival.

Further Reading

The standard monographs on Schlüter are in German. In English only Eberhard Hempel, *Baroque Art and Architecture in Central Europe* (1965), deals with the artist to any degree. □

Helmut Schmidt

Social Democrat Helmut Schmidt (born 1918) served as chancellor of the Federal Republic of Germany (West Germany) from 1974 to 1982. He led his nation into a more prominent role in European and Atlantic alliance affairs and strengthened the West German economy.

Helmut Schmidt was born in a working class section of Hamburg on December 23, 1918. His stern father and his brother were teachers, and he married a teacher. Schmidt received a good education, becoming fluent in English and an accomplished musician. He maintained a student's passion to always learn and the schoolmaster's impatience with those who are lazy. He was 14 when Hitler came to power and was 16 or 17 when he was told and then guarded the dangerous family secret: his paternal grandfather was Jewish.

In 1937 Schmidt was drafted, spending eight years in the army, participating in the 1941 invasion of Russia, and earning an Iron Cross as an artillery officer before being captured by the English in April 1945. He became politicized in the prisoner of war camp, formally joining the Social Democratic Party of Germany (SPD) in 1946. He studied economics at the University of Hamburg and entered the administration of his native city. At age 35 in 1953, he was elected Social Democratic deputy, establishing himself in the capital in Bonn as an expert on transportation and as a quick thinker and good speaker, often sharp and sarcastic but rarely boring. In the late 1950s he gained prominence by denouncing the government's bid for West German atomic weapons as nationalist "megalomania" while also participating as a reserve officer in army maneuvers. His book *Defense or Retaliation* (1961) established his expertise in strategic matters.

Entered City Politics

Tiring of his role as deputy in a seemingly perennial opposition, Schmidt turned to city politics and immediately demonstrated his organizational skills in coping with Hamburg's devastating flood of February 16, 1962, which killed more than 300 people. Schmidt returned to the national scene after the election of 1965, helping to steer the Social Democratic Party into the "Great Coalition" with the reigning Christian Democratic Party. As party floor leader between 1966 and 1969, Schmidt established himself as a politicians' politician. In 1969 when Willy Brandt became the first Social Democratic chancellor since 1930, Schmidt became the first Social Democratic defense minister since 1920. His book *Balance of Power* (1969) pointed to a policy of détente.

In the months preceding the 1972 elections Schmidt replaced his one-time teacher Professor Karl Schiller as "superminister"—minister of both finance and economics—when Schiller resigned over economic policy. As Brandt's crisis manager Schmidt restored confidence and

helped secure the election victory for the Social Democratic/Free Democratic coalition. But, unhappy with the increasingly lax leadership style of Brandt, Schmidt contemplated leaving national politics, but stayed on as finance minister. When Brandt resigned in May 1974 amidst a spy scandal, Schmidt was the obvious choice for his replacement. He was the one politician who could revive and redirect the five year ruling coalition, and no one else had his command of economics, defense, and diplomacy.

The transfer of power to Schmidt was orderly and peaceful. This remarkable stability is in great contrast to the Weimar Republic, which during its fourteen years had twenty-one governments. Unlike the visionary—at times messianic—leadership of Brandt, the pragmatic Schmidt was intent on grounding his countrymen and his allies in the "given realities." In a matter-of-fact way he continued Brandt's policy of reconciling West Germany with her eastern neighbors, but he also made the West German presence more strongly felt in the Western alliance. "We are not small enough to keep our mouths shut, but we are too small to do more than talk," he would say. Stalemated Western European unity and the strains in the Atlantic alliance made the international community more receptive to Schmidt, the spokesman of West Germany, the symbol of a divided Europe trying to make peace with itself. A close working relationship with French President Giscard d'Estaing consolidated the ties between the two countries. Schmidt's chancellorship expressed a new national self-assurance within the void created by an America preoccupied with Vietnam and Watergate and by an aging Kremlin leadership.

Prestige Abroad and a Firm Base at Home

Schmidt's astute handling of the West German economy in the aftermath of the oil crisis of 1973/1974 earned him prestige abroad and a firm base at home. Unlike Brandt, whose passionate following within the Social Democratic Party was never reflected in the German public, Schmidt's general popularity translated to only lukewarm support in and for his party. After the 1976 election he was chosen chancellor in Parliament by a one-vote majority. Yet Schmidt's prestige soared as he effectively rode out the wave of terrorism that reached its peak in 1977.

Germans have been the main beneficiaries of détente; they were also the most threatened by the decline of American nuclear superiority in Europe. Schmidt tried to steer the North Atlantic Treaty Organization (NATO) toward a two-track strategic policy: serious negotiations for arms control with the Russians while calling for medium-ranged nuclear weapons in Western Europe, mostly on German soil. Efforts to get superpower agreement on Euro-rockets led to frustration, and détente was undone by the ideological turn in world politics that came with the Soviet invasion of Afghanistan, the Polish crisis, and the election of Ronald Reagan in the United States.

The West German electorate repudiated Schmidt's conservative challenger, Franz Josef Strauss, in the 1980 elections, but Schmidt's party barely held its own. The chancellor found himself caught in the middle: the left-wing of his party was rebellious, while his junior coalition partner—the Free Democrats—moved to open defection and creation of a new conservative government under Helmut Kohl. Impaired by ill health, Schmidt's eight and a half years as chancellor came to an end in 1982.

In retirement Schmidt remained undaunted, as critical in *A Grand Strategy for the West* (1985) of the neutralists of his own party as he was of the American military build-up through deficit spending. In June of 1997, Schmidt called on his successor Helmut Kohl and Finance Minister Theo Waigel to resign over what he said was the government's fiscal mismanagement. Schmidt said he saw no way for Waigel to lead Germany out of its fiscal troubles and that Waigel himself was chiefly to blame. "The only thing left to do is to make room for people with new ideas," said Schmidt. "And that is even more applicable for his government chief."

Further Reading

Jonathan Carr's *Helmut Schmidt, Helmsman of Germany* (London, 1985) employed candid interviews to create a clear picture of Schmidt's childhood and career. Wolfram F. Hanrieder (editor), *Helmut Schmidt, Perspectives on Politics* (1982) provides a selection of speeches and interviews. Alfred Grosser's *Germany in Our Time: A Political History of the Postwar Years* provides a useful synopsis of West German political, economic, and social developments. Also see *People and Politics: The Years 1960-1975* by former chancellor Willy Brandt. A number of review articles discuss significant recent interpretations of the Federal Republic's history and politics: Peter J. Katzenstein's "Problem or Model? West Germany in the 1980s," in *World Politics;* Wilhelm Bleek's "From Cold War to Ostpolitik: Two Germanys in Search of Separate Identities," in *World Politics;* and Klaus Epstein's "The German Problem 1945-50," in *World Politics.* Of more specific relevance: Helmut Schmidt's own *Men and Powers: a Political Retrospective* (1989), translated by Ruth Hein. □

Gustav Friedrich von Schmoller

The German economist Gustav Friedrich von Schmoller (1838-1917) broadened the study of economics by insisting that it be studied dynamically in the context of history and sociology.

Gustav Schmoller was born on June 24, 1838, in Württemberg-Baden. He was from a family of civil servants and continued in that tradition. His studies in civic administration at the University of Tübingen included public finance, statistics, economics, administration, history, and sociology. He served as professor of civic administration at the universities of Halle (1864-1872), Strassburg (1872-1882), and Berlin (1882-1913). He was also a member of academies in Berlin, Munich, St. Petersburg, Copenhagen, Vienna, and Rome.

In the early 1860s Schmoller defended the commercial treaty between France and the German Customs Union, negotiated with Prussian leadership. This defense curtailed his career in Württemberg but gained favor for him with Prussian authorities, and he was appointed official historian of Brandenburg and Prussia in 1887. He became a member of the Prussian state council in 1884 and representative of the University of Berlin in the Prussian upper house in 1889. He died at Bad Harzburg on June 27, 1917.

Schmoller was the founder and leader of the Association of German Academic Economists. He was also editor of several publications series, one of which was later known as *Schmoller's Yearbook* (from 1881). One of the first great organizers of research in the social sciences, he dominated for several decades the development of economics and of related social sciences. During this time hardly a chair of economics in German universities was filled without his approval.

In political activities Schmoller was a royalist, favored strong government, and had high regard for the Prussian civil service. He was a conservative social reformer who wanted to improve working-class conditions by means of better education, government regulations, cooperatives, and other reforms.

Schmoller's contribution to economics was to reject its study in a narrow analytical view and to place it in the context of the other social sciences. Opposing a theoretical approach, he preferred to include in economics relevant aspects of history, statistics, sociology, social psychology, social anthropology, geography, and even ethics and philosophy. He was eclectic in assembling these aspects into a panorama of the social sciences. He was challenged as superficial by theoretical economist Carl Menger of Vienna in an 1883 pamphlet, by historian Georg von Below in 1904, and by others. Modern critics view Schmoller's long dominance of German social scientists as unfortunate because its effect was to retard development of economic theory in Germany. Outside Germany his influence in economics was small, although he did influence American institutional economics.

Further Reading

For evaluations of Schmoller's place in economics and the social sciences see Charles Gide and Charles Rist, *A History of Economic Doctrines from the Time of the Physiocrats to the Present Day* (trans. 1915; 2d ed. 1948); Karl Menger, *Problems of Economics and Sociology,* edited with an introduction by Louis Schneider (1963); and Jurgen Herbst, *The German Historical School in American Scholarship: A Study in the Transfer of Culture* (1965).

Additional Sources

Balabkins, Nicholas, *Not by theory alone: the economics of Gustav von Schmoller and its legacy to America,* Berlin: Duncker & Humblot, 1988. □

Rose Schniederman

Rose Schneiderman (1882-1972) played a leading role in labor organizing and in the improvement of working conditions for women.

Rose Schneiderman was born in a Polish village on April 6, 1882. Her Orthodox Jewish parents both worked to support the family, her father as a tailor, her mother as a seamstress. In 1890 the family immigrated to the United States, settling in the lower East Side of New York City. When her father died two years later, her mother tried to make ends meet by taking in boarders and sewing, but she was forced to place her children in orphanages for more than a year.

At the age of 13 Schneiderman left school, where she had completed the ninth grade, to work as cash girl in a department store. Three years later she moved to a higher paying job manufacturing caps, even though her mother protested that factory work was not "genteel." Schneiderman was introduced to socialism and trade unionism during a visit to Montreal in 1902. When she returned to New York the next year she organized a women's local in her shop for the United Cloth Hat and Cap Makers' Union. She quickly demonstrated her leadership abilities, and in 1904 she was elected to the general executive board of the national union, which sent her to organize women cap makers in New York and New Jersey.

In 1905 Schneiderman joined the National Women's Trade Union League (WTUL), a recently formed coalition of workers and middle- and upper-class reformers whose purpose was to organize women into unions and to promote legislation protecting women in the workplace. She soon became vice-president of the New York league and its paid organizer of Jewish women employed in East Side garment factories. Her impressive contributions to the organizing campaigns and strikes in the women's garment industry from 1909 to 1914 led to her election as an officer in two New York locals and to her employment as national organizer for the International Ladies' Garment Workers Union in 1915 and 1916. Frustrated by the male union leaders' refusal to entrust her with full responsibility, she resigned in 1917.

In 1908 Schneiderman had joined the Equality League of Self-Supporting Women, organized by Harriet Stanton Blatch to mobilize employed women in the woman suffrage campaign. As Schneiderman grew disillusioned with the male-dominated labor movement and with the difficulties of organizing women workers she increasingly saw the ballot as the essential pre-condition to obtaining protective legislation and to unionizing women workers. In 1913 the National American Woman Suffrage Association hired her to organize and speak for the Ohio referendum, and she worked in the New York campaigns in 1915 and 1917.

Schneiderman had begun her political life as a member of the Socialist Party. In 1919 she helped found the Labor Party in New York, and she ran on its ticket for the United States Senate in 1920. But shortly thereafter she became an active Democrat, in part through her growing association with Eleanor and Franklin Roosevelt. Eleanor Roosevelt had joined the WTUL in the early 1920s, and Schneiderman was among the individuals who instructed both Roosevelts about industrial work and labor unions. Their friendship grew, and Schneiderman was a frequent visitor at the Roosevelt homes in New York City and Hyde Park.

Schneiderman had become president of the New York WTUL in 1917 and in 1926 was elected to the national presidency. Throughout the 1920s the league focused its energies on the passage of protective labor legislation, an orientation in conflict with the National Woman's Party (NWP) and other feminists promoting an equal rights amendment to the U.S. Constitution. Because such an amendment would invalidate protective labor laws which applied only to women, Schneiderman and the WTUL vigorously opposed the amendment. At the same time, they found their efforts to pass minimum wage laws for women obstructed by the NWP. In the 1930s, however, Schneiderman enjoyed the fruits of her campaign when New York passed minimum wage and maximum hours laws.

Appointed by President Franklin Roosevelt in 1933 as the only woman on the labor advisory board of the National Recovery Administration (NRA), Schneiderman endeavored to see that workers were treated fairly in the codes written to standardize practices within industries. She described her work in the New Deal as "exhilarating and inspiring," yet she was not able to eliminate the provisions in some of the codes which established lower wages for women doing essentially the same work as men.

When the NRA was declared unconstitutional in 1935, Schneiderman returned to New York and was appointed secretary of that state's Department of Labor. Finding little to challenge her in this administrative job, she resigned in 1943. She remained president of the WTUL until it disbanded in 1950, and she continued to be active in the New York league. Its demise in 1955 marked the end of her public career. During retirement she wrote her autobiography, and she died in 1972 at the age of 90.

Further Reading

The most complete story of Schneiderman's life is her autobiography, *All for One* (1967). Her career as labor activist is discussed in Philip S. Foner, *Women and the American Labor Movement; from the First Trade Unions to the Present* (1982), and in Nancy Schrom Dye, *As Equals and as Sisters: Feminism, the Labor Movement, and the Women's Trade Union League of New York* (1980). □

Arthur Schnitzler

The Austrian dramatist and novelist Arthur Schnitzler (1862-1931) is at his best in one-act plays and novellas that often deal with extreme situations—death, sexual conflicts, and neurotic and even psychotic states.

Born of Jewish parents in Vienna, where he spent almost his entire life as a physician, Arthur Schnitzler looked upon himself primarily as a scientist and never gave up his medical practice. His first creative period (1893-1900) saw the publication of numerous poems and sketches, largely centered on themes of infidelity and jealousy, and two major works, his first novella, *Sterben* (1894; *Dying*), and his first successful play, *Anatol* (1893).

In the mid-1890s Schnitzler was associated for a short time with a literary movement of impressionist writers, including Hugo von Hofmannsthal, who were violently opposed to the naturalism then in vogue in Berlin. But soon he broke away from café society—the Jung-Wien group, which gathered in Vienna's famous Café Griensteidl—and he never again joined any literary circle.

The highlight of Schnitzler's second phase (1900-1912) was his famous play *Reigen* (1900; *La Ronde*), which Eric Bentley has called "a great 'comedy' of sexual promiscuity." Banned, attacked, censored on its first appearance, and later withdrawn by Schnitzler himself, it has gradually won the reputation of a masterpiece of modern drama. *La Ronde,* in 10 brief dialogues between a man and a woman, reveals the attitudes of partners from all social classes before and after the act of love. Modern critics no longer see this play as pornographic but rather as a bitter, witty, and yet tender and melancholy examination of the human condition expressed through the metaphor of man's endless "round dance" of sexuality and desire.

As a writer of fiction, Schnitzler developed early in his career the technique known as stream of consciousness and later made famous by James Joyce. The best examples are two of his stories, *Leutnant Gustl* (1900; *None but the Brave*) and *Fräulein Else* (1925). The former is a long interior monologue describing an unpleasant young lieutenant who, insulted by a baker, broods until he reaches the decision to commit suicide in order to preserve his honor, only to be saved accidentally by the knowledge that the baker has died of a heart attack. In *Fräulein Else* Schnitzler used the stream-of-consciousness technique to reveal a psychotic young girl's motives for disrobing in a hotel lobby.

Schnitzler's third and last period, from 1912 to the time of his death, has often been referred to as "retrospective." To this phase belong such masterpieces as *Frau Beate und ihr Sohn* (1913; *Beatrice*) and *Casanovas Heimfahrt* (1918; *Casanova's Homecoming*) and the novella *Traumgekrönt* (1925; *Rhapsody*). In two important works, his long autobiographical novel, *Der Weg ins Freie* (1908; *The Road to the Open*), and the play *Professor Bernhardi* (1913), Schnitzler deals with racial and religious prejudice, specifically with anti-Semitism, which he sees as a problem of general human concern. He chooses many of his characters from the medical profession and assigns to them the role of the *raisonneur* who expresses his own tolerant views on life and love.

Further Reading

Schnitzler's *My Youth in Vienna,* translated by Catherine Hutter (1970), is his diary of his early years, through the 1870s. The most complete study of him in English is Solomon Liptzin, *Arthur Schnitzler* (1932). A good sampling of critical investigations is the eight papers delivered at the University of Kentucky in 1962: *Studies in Arthur Schnitzler: Centennial Commemorative Volume,* edited by Herbert W. Reichert and Herman Salinger (1963). The most comprehensive and reliable guide to the literature by and about Schnitzler is Richard H. Allen, *An Annotated Arthur Schnitzler Bibliography 1879-1965* (1966).

Additional Sources

Psychoanalysis and old Vienna: Freud, Reik, Schnitzler, Kraus, New York: Human Sciences Press, 1978. □

Arnold Schoenberg

Arnold Schoenberg (1874-1951) was an Austrian composer whose discovery of the "method of composition with twelve tones" radically transformed 20th-century music.

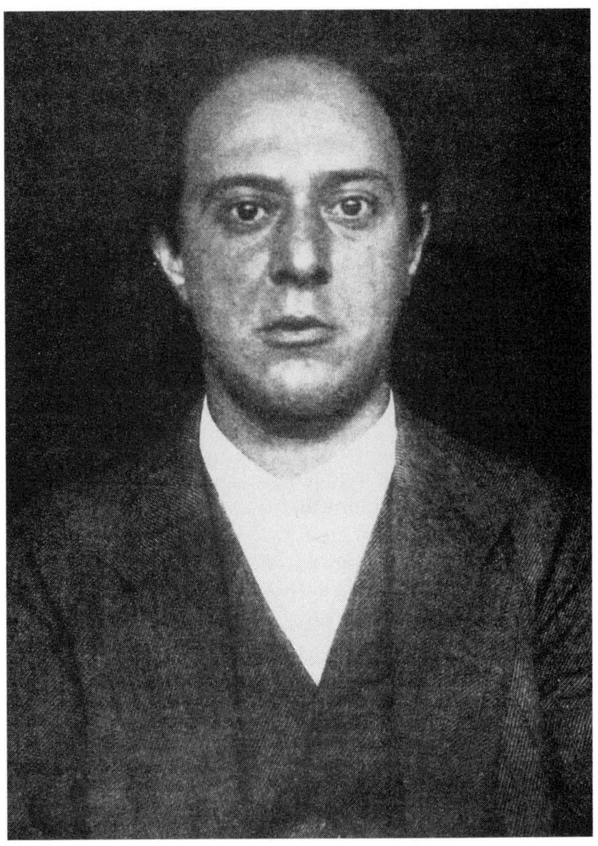

The early music of Arnold Schoenberg represents the culmination of romantic musical ideals. His gigantic cantata *Gurre-Lieder* is, together with Gustav Mahler's Eighth Symphony, one of the last great works in the monumental style. It seemed impossible for music to develop any further in this direction. Thus, Schoenberg became one of the first 20th-century composers to write for small, specialized chamber ensembles. He transcended traditional tonal limitations and began to write "atonal" or "pantonal" music without a key center. This new style offered much freedom, but there was need of a system to control the new harmonic material thus made available.

After a period of experimentation, Schoenberg developed such a system: the method of composition with twelve tones. So far-reaching were the results of this discovery that Schoenberg's theories became, for a time, more famous than his compositions. However, since his death, his music has received more of the recognition that it deserves. Most important musical developments of the second half of the 20th century owe their impetus directly or indirectly to him.

Schoenberg was born in Vienna on Sept. 13, 1874. His interest in music began early. When he was eight years old, he started to learn the violin, and he soon began composing violin duets. His parents were not musicians—his father, Samuel, owned a shoe store—but they enjoyed music and were sympathetic to his musical development.

Early Works

In the amateur orchestra Polyhymnia, Schoenberg met Alexander von Zemlinsky. They became close friends, and Zemlinsky began to give Schoenberg instruction in composition, the only formal teaching of this sort that he ever had. The String Quartet in D Major (1897, published 1966) is a good example of the immediate results. This was Schoenberg's first work to be played publicly in Vienna. As its Brahmsian style was quite accessible to the conservative taste of the audience, it was well received.

Quite different is Schoenberg's *Verklärte Nacht* (Transfigured Night), a string sextet inspired by Richard Dehmel's poem of the same name. While the orchestral tone poem, or symphonic poem (a composition telling a story in music), was common in the 19th century, Schoenberg's work represents the first attempt to transfer this form to chamber music. It was written in the summer of 1899. Zemlinsky tried to have it performed that fall, but its Wagnerian style was rejected by the conservative program committee of the Tonkünstlerverein. It was finally premiered in 1903. At that time it was still considered controversial, and audience reaction was hostile. Since then it has become one of Schoenberg's most popular works, especially in its versions for string orchestra.

From 1901 to 1903 Schoenberg lived in Berlin, where he conducted at the Überbrettl cabaret and later taught composition at the Stern Conservatory. He became friendly with Richard Strauss, who suggested Maurice Maeterlinck's *Pelléas et Mélisande* to him as a good subject for an opera. Without knowing of Claude Debussy's opera based on this play, Schoenberg began to write a symphonic poem on the same subject; he completed it in 1902. It is his only orchestral tone poem in the tradition of Franz Liszt and Richard Strauss.

Development of Atonality

Back in Vienna, Schoenberg began to teach privately. He attracted talented pupils: Alban Berg and Anton Webern came to him at this time. A stylistic change was beginning to occur in Schoenberg's work. Tonality, which had been more and more freely treated in such pieces as his Second String Quartet, was finally abandoned. The date of completion of the piano piece Opus 11, no. 1 (Feb. 19, 1909), is an important one in the history of music, for this is the first composition to dispense completely with traditional tonality. In this new style any chord combination can be freely used, and there is no differentiation in the treatment of consonances and dissonances.

Writing about his new music in connection with a concert on Jan. 14, 1910, at which the piano pieces Opus 11 were premiered, Schoenberg said: "I have succeeded for the first time in approaching an ideal of expression and form that had hovered before me for some years. Hitherto I had not sufficient strength and sureness to realize that ideal. Now, however, that I have definitely started on my journey, I may confess to having broken the bonds of a bygone esthetic; and if I am striving toward a goal that seems to me to be certain, nevertheless I already feel the opposition that I shall have to overcome. I feel also with what heat even those of the feeblest temperament will reject my works, and I suspect that even those who have hitherto believed in me will not be willing to perceive the necessity of this new development."

Twelve-tone System

Schoenberg was right in his fears that he would be misunderstood. Even more misunderstood was his next stylistic change, which was gradually being prepared between 1916 and 1920. During those years he completed no major compositions; instead, he worked toward a solution of the structural problems of nontonal music. One day in July 1921 Schoenberg told his pupil Josef Rufer, "Today I have discovered something which will assure the supremacy of German music for the next hundred years." It was the method of composition with twelve tones. The Prelude of Schoenberg's Piano Suite, Opus 25 (completed July 29, 1921), is probably the first twelve-tone composition.

In the twelve-tone method each composition is based on a row, or series, using all twelve notes of the chromatic scale in an order chosen by the composer. Besides being presented in its original form, the row may be inverted, played backward, played backward in inversion, or transposed to any scale step. All harmonies and melodies in a composition are derived from its special row; thus, unity is assured. While some critics feared that music written in this way might become mechanical and inexpressive, Schoenberg continued to write highly personal and expressive compositions, using the expanded resources made available by the new method. From time to time he would return to traditional tonality in one or more works. However, it really made no difference to him whether his compositions were tonal, atonal, or twelve-tonal. As he said once, "I like them all, because I liked them when I wrote them."

In the 1920s Schoenberg seemed to have reached a peak in his career. His appointment as director of a composition class at the Prussian Academy of Arts, Berlin, took effect in 1926. Four years later he began his great biblical opera, *Moses und Aron.* (He never finished this work, but in its incomplete, two-act form it became, after his death, one of his greatest popular successes.) Under normal circumstances he might well have spent the rest of his life in Berlin. However, when the Nazis assumed power in Germany, Schoenberg's Jewish heritage made him unwelcome. In September 1933 he was dismissed from the academy. The next month he sailed for America.

American Works

Schoenberg's first American teaching post was at the Malkin Conservatory in Boston (1933-1934). His health suffered from the climate, and he decided to move to Los Angeles. There, he taught first at the University of Southern California and then at the University of California, until age forced his retirement in 1944. He wrote some of his finest instrumental music in California: the Fourth String Quartet (1936), the Violin Concerto (1934-1936), the Piano Concerto (1942), and the String Trio (1946).

After his retirement, Schoenberg had hoped to find time to complete *Moses und Aron* and the oratorio *Die Jakobsleiter* (Jacob's Ladder), which he had begun in 1917. However, his poor health and the necessity of earning a living by private teaching made this impossible. During the last year of his life, he wrote a series of texts called *Modern Psalms,* which he described as "conversations with and about God." He was still able to compose part of the first psalm; the last words he set to music are "und trotzdem bete ich" (and yet I pray). On July 13, 1951, he died in Los Angeles.

Further Reading

A representative collection of Schoenberg's correspondence is in *Letters,* edited by Erwin Stein (trans. 1964). Of Schoenberg's other writings, the collection of essays *Style and Idea,* edited by Dika Newlin (trans. 1950), has the greatest general interest. A useful preliminary biography, though not a definitive study, is H. H. Stuckenschmidt, *Arnold Schoenberg* (trans. 1959). Harold C. Schonberg, *The Lives of the Great Composers* (1968), briefly discusses Schoenberg. Dika Newlin, *Bruckner-Mahler-Schoenberg* (1947; rev. ed. in preparation), presents Schoenberg's work as the culmination of a historical development that can be traced back to the 18th-century classical Viennese School. René Leibowitz, *Schoenberg and His School* (trans. 1949), takes a similar viewpoint but carries the line of development to Berg and Webern. A helpful general discussion of twelve-tone music is George Perle, *Serial Composition and Atonality: An Introduction to the Music of Schoenberg, Berg and Webern* (1962; 2d rev. ed. 1968). K. H. Wörner, *Schoenberg's Moses and Aaron* (trans. 1963), offers a detailed musical and textual analysis of what is probably Schoenberg's most important work.

Additional Sources

MacDonald, Malcolm, *Schoenberg,* London: Dent, 1976.

Neighbour, O. W. (Oliver Wray), *The New Grove Second Viennese School: Schoenberg, Webern, Berg,* New York: Norton, 1983.

Newlin, Dika, *Schoenberg remembered: diaries and recollections, (1938-76),* New York: Pendragon Press, 1980.

Reich, Willi, *Schoenberg: a critical biography,* New York: Da Capo Press, 1981.

Rosen, Charles, *Arnold Schoenberg,* Chicago, Ill: University of Chicago Press, 1996.

Schoenberg, Arnold, *Arnold Schoenberg, Wassily Kandinsky: letters, pictures, and documents,* London; Boston: Faber & Faber, 1984.

Small, Christopher, *Schoenberg,* Borough Green, Kent: Novello, 1977.

Stuckenschmidt, Hans Heinz, *Arnold Schoenberg,* Westport, Conn.: Greenwood Press, 1979, 1959. □

Gershom Scholem

The Jewish scholar Gershom Scholem (1897-1982) was a noted authority on Jewish mysticism. He examined the origins and influence of the Cabalist movement.

Born in Berlin, Germany, on December 5, 1897, Gershom Scholem was educated at Berlin, Jena, Bern, and Munich universities. In 1923 he emigrated to Palestine, which became his permanent residence. In 1925 he became professor of Jewish mysticism at the Hebrew University, a post he retained until 1965. He was dean of the university from 1941 to 1943. In 1946 he was assigned the task of salvaging Jewish cultural treasures in the aftermath of World War II. He was a visiting professor and lecturer at many American universities, including Brown University (1956-1957).

Scholem's scholarly achievements were enormous in the field of Jewish mysticism. No other contemporary writer and, indeed, no former student of this field equaled him in breadth of knowledge, depth of perception, and power of synthesis. His publications were numerous, and they included *Das Buch Bahir* (1923); *Bibliografia Kabbalistica* (1927); *Major Trends of Jewish Mysticism* (1946); *The Beginnings of Kabbalism* (1949); *Sabbatai Zvi and the Sabbataian Movement* (2 vols., 1957); *Jewish Gnosticism and Talmudic Tradition* (1960); *Zur Kabbala und ihrer Symbolik* (1960); *Von der mystischen Gestalt der Gottheit* (1962); *Judaica* (1963); *On the Kabbalah and Its Symbolism* (1965); *Walter Benjamin* (1965); *The Messianic Idea in Judaism* (1971); *Kabbalah* (1974); and *On Jews and Judaism in Crisis* (1976).

Before Scholem's time academic study of Jewish mysticism was not well developed. Scholem set out to master the manuscriptal tradition and thus to provide himself with an indispensable and superb instrument for analyzing the origin, the nature, and the history of Jewish mysticism. His work emphasized the Cabalist movement, since this was the only genuine form of mysticism developed by Judaism. Scholem examined the 12th-century rise of Cabalism in Provence, France. He concentrated on the *Book of Bahir,* the oldest Cabalist text known in the 12th century, and the Cabalist works composed in Provence during the 12th century. His analysis of the *Bahir* led him back to the early Jewish Gnosticism of the Middle East. He showed that even in the early Middle Ages and in strictly rabbanate circles, Gnostic doctrines and ideas flourished. This was probably because of the proximity of Syrian Gnostic and Mandaean sects. Sometime around the end of the 11th and the beginning of the 12th century, this Gnostic tradition met with a very vibrant Neoplatonism in southern France. A century later a fresh school of Cabalist mysticism sprang up in Spain around the town of Gerona in Catalonia.

Scholem established relationships between the Kathari movement, the teaching of John Scotus Erigena, and these traditions, besides elucidating the lines and teaching of many renowned Cabalists. He also demonstrated the influence of Cabalism on the Haskalah and Hasidic movements of the 18th and 19th centuries and noted its impact on the Zionist movement. From 1968-1974, Scholem was president of the Israel Academy of Science and Humanities. He died in Jerusalem on February 20, 1982.

Further Reading

Scholem wrote his autobiography, *From Berlin to Jerusalem* in 1978. His work was often cited in Alexander Altmann, *Studies in Religious Philosophy and Mysticism* (1969). □

Martin Schongauer

The German engraver and painter Martin Schongauer (ca. 1435-1491) was the first identifiable maker of fine prints in Germany and the finest master of this medium before Dürer.

Martin Schongauer was the son of Caspar Schongauer, a goldsmith who moved from Augsburg to Colmar, on the upper Rhine, where he became a citizen in 1445. The earliest paintings of Martin have not been identified with certainty, but he apparently worked near Ulm about 1462. He is documented in 1465 as matriculating for a semester at the University of Leipzig, either to study or else to undertake some artistic commission; between that year and his reappearance in the records of Colmar in 1469, art historians have assumed a trip to the Netherlands.

The records show that Schongauer owned a house in Colmar in 1477. After 1488 he was working on the *Last Judgment fresco,* traces of which were uncovered in 1932, in the church at Breisach, where he died in 1491.

His Paintings

Schongauer's one certain extant panel painting is the magnificent *Madonna in the Rose Garden* (1473), a life-sized image commissioned by the church of St. Martin in Colmar. Monumental yet intimate, Mary bends her head in humility as two angels hover above with a golden crown, her attribute as Queen of Heaven. The figure style is based on that of the Dutch painter Dirk Bouts, but the dense and minutely described trellis of rose vines and birds which enclose her betray the hand of an engraver.

Two other paintings, both small, reveal Schongauer's characteristic style and, because of their high quality, are probably by his own hand: a *Nativity* and a *Holy Family.* Both seem to reflect the mature style of his engravings from the late 1470s.

Late Gothic Master

It is as engraver that Schongauer's importance in the development of European art justly lies. Since original prints may exist in many "originals" and are highly mobile, the master's fame quickly spread in his own lifetime. The young Albrecht Dürer journeyed to Colmar to meet him—in vain, as it turned out, for the master had recently died.

Schongauer forms a link between the early engravers, as represented by Master E. S., and the Renaissance ideals first forcibly expressed by Dürer. In both subject matter and style his prints manifest the quintessence of the late Gothic spirit in a special way, as do the sculptures of Tilman Riemenschneider and the paintings of Rogier van der Weyden.

All of Schongauer's 115 engravings bear his monogram, but none is dated, so that time sequence is based on stylistic grounds. There is, however, a distinction between early and late in the rendering of the "M" of the monogram: in the earlier the lines of the "M" are vertical, and in the later they are flared. The first period dates from about 1465 to 1475, the second from about 1475 until his death.

Quite a number of Schongauer's religious compositions were derived from paintings by the Flemish masters Jan van Eyck, Hugo van der Goes, Bouts, and especially Van der Weyden. Schongauer never slavishly copied but recreated their world of concrete forms, based on realistic observation, into a wonderfully spiritualized, late Gothic form world that is abstracted in the pure terms of black and white lines.

His Engravings

The *Virgin and Child with a Parrot,* one of his earliest engravings and dating possibly about 1465, with a half-length Madonna and nude Child in an abstracted architectural setting, is related to a painting by Bouts. Schongauer's progress in the technique of engraving over his predecessor, Master E. S., is evidenced by the use of modeling lines that follow the forms and reveal their shapes and of cast shadows and reflected lights. Whereas the background in this print is merely a filler, Schongauer soon developed this space so that it is filled with exciting and varied passages, as in the early *Nativity,* the figures of which are inspired by Van der Weyden's *Bladelin Triptych.* Schongauer's *Death of the Virgin* presents a dramatic perspective rendering which has a parallel in design and emotion in the painting by Van der Goes, dating about 1480. Finally, a lost painting by Jan van Eyck, the *Road to Calvary,* was the inspiration for Schongauer's largest and most famous print. The composition teems with caricatured figures in a dramatically pictorial landscape setting.

Strictly Schongauer's own invention is the famous *Temptation of St. Anthony* print, in which the resolute man of God is shown airborne, being assaulted by wildly imaginative zoomorphic creatures. Also original and unprecedented is the greatly detailed rendering of the *Censer,* a reminiscence in the artist's later years of his earliest years in his father's goldsmith shop.

Schongauer made series of prints unified in theme and size. In his late style are the 10 exquisite figures of the *Wise* and *Foolish Virgins,* silhouetted against the pure whiteness of the paper sheet. In his own day, and down to the present, the most famous series is the *Passion of Christ,* a set of 12 plates. Innumerable copies of these designs were made throughout Europe, and they achieved almost canonical importance in the art of the time.

Among other prints in Schongauer's mature style is the stunning pair of the *Annunciation,* with Gabriel and Mary on separate sheets. These decoratively abstracted figures possess a refined metallic brilliance and subtle tone expressive of the particular nature of engraving that can only be called classic. Schongauer's art, especially his prints, marks a milestone in the history of draftsmanship.

Further Reading

There is no book-length study of Schongauer in English. The paintings and engravings are most conveniently reproduced in the German edition by Julius Baum, *Martin Schongauer*

(1948). For the engravings alone, and for a fine text in English, see Alan Shestack, *The Complete Engravings of Martin Schongauer* (1969). □

Franz Xaver Schönhuber

Franz Xaver Schönhuber (born 1923) gained wide notoriety as leader of the right-wing political party, the Republicans, in what was then West Germany.

Franz Schönhuber was born on January 19, 1923, in the Bavarian town of Trostberg an der Alz. His father, a Catholic butcher, joined the Nazi Party in 1931. Young Schönhuber attended Catholic boarding school in Bavaria but finished his secondary education in Dresden and Munich, as his family moved to those cities.

In 1942, at age 19, Schönhuber volunteered for service in the elite military wing of the Nazi SS (Schutzstaffel), the Waffen-SS. He was posted to France, Corsica, Italy, and Yugoslavia. In 1943 he was decorated with the Iron Cross, Second Class. After the war he was interned by the British military forces and served the occupation authorities as an interpreter.

Returning to Bavaria, Schönhuber worked for a time as an actor in provincial theaters. He then turned to journalism and became editor of a tabloid newspaper in Munich. He married a woman from Hungary who was of half Jewish parentage, but they were divorced after the birth of a daughter. Later he married again, a lawyer who was for a time a Social Democratic deputy in the Munich city assembly. Between 1972 and 1982 Schönhuber was employed by the Bavarian State Radio, first as a reporter and then as host of a popular television show. He was dismissed following the publication in 1981 of his autobiography, in which he defended his wartime activities.

After he lost his job in television, Schönhuber became aligned with the new party of Republicans. It was founded in late 1983 by two former deputies of the conservative Bavarian Christian Social Union (CSU) in the West German parliament who had resigned from that party. They disapproved of CSU leader Franz Josef Strauss' domination of the party and also of his abandonment of hard-line anticommunism and acceptance of the West German government's policy of recognizing East Germany and extending financial aid to it in hopes of ameliorating the lot of the East German population.

By 1985 Schönhuber, whose television following and fiery oratory soon established him as the most magnetic personality among the Republicans, had become chairman of the Republicans. Under his leadership the new party espoused a conservative, nationalistic program and appealed particularly to West German discontent with the presence in their society of millions of workers from Turkey and other foreign countries who competed with Germans for increasingly scarce jobs while enjoying the full benefits of West Germany's elaborate and expensive welfare state. The Republicans also criticized the policy of conciliation toward East Germany followed by Chancellor Helmut Kohl of the Christian Democratic Union (CDU) and called for a crusade against communism. Despite Schönhuber's vigorous campaigning, his party tallied a mere three percent of the vote in the Bavarian state election of 1986.

During 1987 and 1988 Schönhuber's Republicans carried their organizing efforts into the northern parts of West Germany. In January 1989, to the surprise of political observers, they won 7.5 percent of the votes in West Berlin and captured 11 of the 139 seats in the city parliament. In June 1989 they gained 7.1 percent of West German ballots for the European Parliament by securing the support of over two million voters. Schönhuber and five other Republicans were elected to seats in the Strasbourg Assembly, where they soon aligned themselves with the French National Front of Jean-Marie Le Pen. The two rightist parties had much in common, drawing support from disgruntled elements of society who believed they were being treated unfairly by their governments and resented the presence of large numbers of foreigners in their countries.

The upheaval that brought down the East German regime in the fall of 1989 and set in motion the unification of the two Germanys eclipsed Schönhuber and the Republicans. In the midst of momentous events that were reshaping the German nation, their carping criticisms of the government of Chancellor Helmut Kohl came to sound increasingly petulant and irrelevant—when they were noticed at all. In March 1990 the party was excluded, on the grounds of extremism, from participation in the first free parliamentary election in East Germany. When voters went to the polls in May 1990 in two of West Germany's federal states, Lower Saxony and Rhineland-Westphalia, the Republicans tallied only 1.5 percent and 1.8 percent of the ballots, respectively.

At the end of May 1990 Franz Schönhuber resigned as chairman of the Republicans when the party executive withdrew its confidence from him. With the party's promise of national reunification through militant anticommunism rendered outdated by events, the Republicans displayed every sign of disintegration as the 1990 election of the first all-German postwar parliament approached. Nevertheless, the 67-year-old Schönhuber, reluctant to abandon a political career that had thrust him into national prominence, engaged during the summer and autumn of 1990 in a public struggle for control of what remained of the Republicans' organization against the increasingly strident opposition of younger party members.

Schönhuber was able to revive the Republican Party. In the 1992 and 1993 elections the Republican Party, still under his leadership, was able to muster votes, in a few districts. During this time reports of Nazi terrorism spread across Germany. Nazi activities were principally directed at refugees and at Roma people. As a member of the European Parliament Schönhuber may have legitimized the Nazi movement in the eyes of his true believers. By 1994 the Neo-Nazis were making use of modern technology and establishing electronic communication networks, as well as computer bulletin boards and Internet Web pages.

Further Reading

The greatest source of additional information on Franz Schönhuber was in his own book, *Ich war dabei* (Munich, 1981), which may be translated as "I Was a Witness." For a dissident view of the union of the two Germanys see *Two States—One Nation* (1990) by the noted German writer Gunter Grass. A James Jackson article in *Time* (June 6, 1994), provided a summary of Neo-Nazi activities. □

Henry Rowe Schoolcraft

The American explorer and ethnologist Henry Rowe Schoolcraft (1793-1864) was one of the earliest writers on Native American culture and history.

Henry Schoolcraft was born on March 28, 1793, in Albany County, N.Y. His father was a glassmaker. After attending local schools, Schoolcraft took up glassmaking, which he combined with private study and lectures at Middlebury College.

Between 1810 and 1817 Schoolcraft managed factories in New York, Vermont, and New Hampshire and wrote a treatise on glassmaking. In 1818 he traveled westward to pursue his geological interests. *A View of the Lead Mines of Missouri* (1819) established his scientific reputation and won him a place with an expedition to the copper mines around Lake Superior. He wrote of this adventure in *Narrative Journal of Travels through the Northwestern Regions of the United States . . . to the Mississippi River* (1821).

By 1821 Schoolcraft was a well-known geologist, but he had become acquainted with the Native Americans living in the North, and in 1822 he was appointed Indian agent in Sault Ste. Marie, Mich. In 1823 he married Jane Johnston. He pursued Native American studies, carried on negotiations between the Native Americans and the government, and was promoted to superintendent of Indian affairs for Michigan. As Indian superintendent, he negotiated several important Native American treaties transferring land to the state.

Although as Indian agent Schoolcraft deprived the Native Americans of vast tracts of land, he demonstrated a sympathetic, if somewhat paternalistic, concern for their welfare. His treaty of 1836 provided for a system of annuities to be paid individually to the Native Americans rather than in lump sums to tribal chiefs. He supported government schools and mission schools as well, in the belief that it was necessary to "Christianize" Native Americans in order to educate them. He urged the teaching of agriculture to compensate for the loss of their hunting grounds and took a strong stand against alcohol.

Schoolcraft is best remembered as a scholar of Indian ethnology. Among his numerous volumes containing descriptions of Native American life and culture are *Algic Researches* (2 vols., 1839); *Oneóta* (8 vols., 1844-1845); *Notes on the Iroquois* (1847); *Personal Memories . . . of Thirty Years with the Indian Tribes* (1851); and *Historical and Statistical Information Respecting the History, Condition, and Prospects of the Indian Tribes of the United States* (6 vols., 1851-1857). These accounts of Native American life and folklore contributed greatly to anthropological science. Schoolcraft died on Dec. 10, 1864.

Further Reading

Schoolcraft is a neglected figure, but Chase S. and Stellanova Osborn have a long, appreciative account in *Schoolcraft, Longfellow, Hiawatha* (1942). See also Edmund W. Gilbert, *The Exploration of Western America, 1800-1850* (1933), and Rufus W. Griswold, *Henry Rowe Schoolcraft* (1849).

Additional Sources

Bremer, Richard G., *Indian agent and wilderness scholar: the life of Henry Rowe Schoolcraft,* Mount Pleasant: Clarke Historical Library, Central Michigan University, 1987.

Schoolcraft, Henry Rowe, *Personal memoirs of a residence of thirty years with the Indian tribes on the American frontiers,* New York: AMS Press, 1978. □

Arthur Schopenhauer

The German philosopher Arthur Schopenhauer (1788-1860), whose pessimistic philosophy was widely known in the late 19th century in Europe and the United States, held that ultimate reality was

nothing but senseless striving or will, having no divine origin and no historical end.

Arthur Schopenhauer was born in Danzig on Feb. 22, 1788. His father, a successful Dutch businessman, had a taste for urbane living, travel, and bourgeois culture, while his mother aspired to the more exotic culture of writers and nonconformists. When Schopenhauer was 5, Danzig, formerly a free mercantile city, was annexed by Poland. As a consequence, his family moved to Hamburg, Germany, in search of a more congenial setting for his father's business. In 1797 Schopenhauer was sent to stay with a family in France, returning to Hamburg after 2 years to enter a private school. Later he became interested in literature, earning the disapproval of his father, who nonetheless gave him the choice of pursuing serious literary studies or traveling with the family for 2 years. Schopenhauer chose to travel.

His voyages over, Schopenhauer took a job as a clerk in a Hamburg merchant's office. That year, 1805, his father died, apparently a suicide. The mercantile world held only drudgery for young Schopenhauer, whose ambitions and desires were both unfocused and frustrated. Feeling constrained by a promise to his father, Schopenhauer remained at work until 1807, when he joyfully resigned in order to study Greek and Latin in a school at Gotha. Having enraged an unsympathetic instructor, he transferred to a school in Weimar, where his mother had already established herself as mistress of a literary salon frequented by Goethe and other notables. But Schopenhauer had earlier quarreled with his mother, whom he thought too free with her ideas and her favors. He therefore resided with his mentor, the philologist Franz Passow, who paid his tuition. Schopenhauer's studies went well, and in 1809, on acquiring a handsome legacy, he enrolled at the University of Göttingen. He studied mostly the sciences and medicine but eventually turned to philosophy.

Philosophical Studies

Schopenhauer's new passion for philosophy led him to the University of Berlin, where he hoped to cull the wisdom of Johann Gottlieb Fichte, then the foremost philosopher in Germany. He was disappointed in Fichte but remained at the university until 1813, when Prussia mobilized to expel the French after Napoleon's defeat. Seeing the dangers of staying in Berlin and having no heart for nationalistic fervor, Schopenhauer sought refuge in Rudolstadt. There he completed his doctoral dissertation, which he submitted successfully to the University of Jena. He published the dissertation at his own expense and then returned to Weimar. He met Goethe, who seemed sympathetic to his thinking. One fruit of their conversations was Schopenhauer's brief study *Über das Sehn und die Farben* (1816; *On Vision and Colors*).

The World as Will and Idea

Schopenhauer's unhappy relations with his mother finally terminated in open hostility, and he moved to Dresden. By this time the central and simple idea of his philosophy had taken hold in his mind. The principal source of this idea was his own experience and moods, but the expression of it owed much to the philosophies of Plato and Immanuel Kant and the mystical literature of India. He foresaw that his reflections would eventually lift him above the absurd stresses and conflicts of his life, and he thought that ultimately his writings would usher in a new era not only in philosophy but also in human history. Whereas former philosophies had been parceled into schools and special problems, his own, as he envisaged it, would be a single, simple fabric. The simplest expression of this potent idea is probably the very title of the book he wrote at Dresden, *Die Welt als Wille und Vorstellung* (*The World as Will and Idea*). The world is necessarily present to a subject that perceives it; thus the world is "idea" or "representation." Yet the world is not created or constructed by the subject or the mind; its own nature is will, or blind striving. "My body and my will are one," and in the final analysis one person's will is indistinguishable from every other form of willing.

The book was printed by a reluctant publisher in 1818 and failed to gain a public. Nevertheless, with two books to his credit, Schopenhauer was given a lectureship in philosophy at the University of Berlin. At that time G. W. F. Hegel was the center of attention, and Schopenhauer decided to compete with him by lecturing at the same hour. But he addressed an empty room, and shortly his academic career was over.

Other Writings

In 1831 cholera was epidemic in Berlin, and Schopenhauer fled to Frankfurt, where he stayed for the rest of his life. In 1836 he published a study of contemporary science, *Über den Willen in der Natur* (*On the Will in Nature*), showing that his philosophy was consistent with the sciences. In 1839 he won a prize from the Norwegian Scientific Society for an essay on freedom of the will. To this essay he added another, publishing them in 1841 as *Die Beiden Grundprobleme der Ethik* (*The Two Fundamental Problems of Ethics*). During these years he revised and augmented the text of *The World as Will and Idea,* which was republished in 1844 with 50 new chapters. In 1847 he republished his dissertation, *Über die vierfache Wurzel des Satzes vom zureichenden Grunde* (*On the Fourfold Root of the Principle of Sufficient Reason*). By now he was attracting some notice, but the fame he had predicted for himself was still only a dream.

Schopenhauer's style of life in his Frankfurt years has always both fascinated and puzzled his admirers. Though he wrote about the ultimate value of negating the will, he displayed unusual willfulness; though he extolled tranquility, he was always energetic; though he wrote savage diatribes against women, he could not forgo female company.

Parerga und Paralipomena

At last, in 1851, Schopenhauer published the book that brought him fame and followers. Titled *Parerga und*

Paralipomena, it was a collection of highly polished, insightful essays and aphorisms. Its style was probably the chief reason for the book's immediate success. Yet the ideas were important too, particularly the notion that will was primary over intellect. The pessimism that follows from such a notion was already in vogue, and Schopenhauer became its voice. Another reason for his fame was surely his appeal to the inner experience of moods and feelings, in contrast to the more traditional appeals to history, reason, authority, and objective evidence. His philosophy takes its source in "the selfsame unchangeable being which is before us." Life is all suffering, he said, but it can be reflected upon, and then it will be seen to be "nothing." Schopenhauer died on Sept. 21, 1860. By then he had countless followers, and he was idolized as a kind of savior.

Further Reading

Schopenhauer's own writings are readily available in translation. Particularly noteworthy is a selection of the essays and aphorisms from *Parerga and Paralipomena,* edited and translated by R. J. Hollingdale (1970), which includes an introduction containing biographical information. Patrick Gardiner, *Schopenhauer* (1963), is a study of the philosopher's life and works. Schopenhauer's life is presented in detail in Helen Zimmern, *Arthur Schopenhauer: His Life and Philosophy* (1876), and in William Wallace, *Life of Schopenhauer* (1890). A more critical assessment of Schopenhauer's work is in Frederick Copleston, *Arthur Schopenhauer: Philosopher of Pessimism* (1946).

Additional Sources

Safranski, Reudiger, *Schopenhauer and the wild years of philosophy,* Cambridge, Mass.: Harvard University Press, 1990.

Janaway, Christopher, *Schopenhauer,* Oxford; New York: Oxford University Press, 1994.

Simmel, Georg, *Schopenhauer and Nietzsche,* Urbana: University of Illinois Press, 1991. □

William Cornelius Schouten

William Cornelius Schouten (ca. 1580-1625) was a Dutch explorer and navigator. In 1616 he discovered a new route to the Pacific via Cape Horn.

The exact birth date of William Schouten is unknown, but the year was probably 1580 and the place Hoorn in what is now Holland. He became a seafarer and made three trips to the East Indies between 1601 and 1603. His reputation as a navigator and interest in exploring distant parts attracted the attention of Isaac Le Maire, a wealthy Amsterdam merchant who in 1615 appointed him to command the *Eendracht* on a voyage to the Pacific.

One object was to search for the great south land about whose existence and riches rumors abounded. Another was to find a route into the Pacific other than those then known to exist via the Strait of Magellan and the Cape of Good Hope. The Dutch East India Company alone was permitted to use these routes; thus it had a monopoly over trade in the Pacific. Le Maire, who had formed a rival trading company, believed that another entrance lay south of the Strait of Magellan. If it could be found, the trade of the Pacific would be open to his company.

The *Eendracht,* accompanied by the *Hoorn,* later destroyed by fire in Patagonia, sailed for South America on June 14, 1615. Schouten's official position was that of master mariner, and Le Maire's son Jacob accompanied the voyage as merchant and president. In January 1616 their first goal was attained when a new entrance to the Pacific around Cape Horn was discovered and named after their hometown.

From there they sailed across the Pacific, passing through some of the islands of the Tuamoto and Tonga groups. They moved on to New Ireland and to other islands of the Bismarck Archipelago and later spent some time examining the northern coastline of New Guinea. From there they sailed among more of the Pacific islands, arriving at Ternate on Sept. 17, 1616, where they encountered a large Dutch fleet under Adm. van Spilbergen.

Their efforts were favorably received, but at Batavia, their last port of call, the Dutch governor general, Jan Pietersz Coen, refused to believe that they had discovered a third route into the Pacific. Viewing them as trespassers who had broken the East India Company's charter, he confiscated their ship and sent them back to Holland under arrest. Eventually Le Maire succeeded in clearing their name and securing recompense for their treatment.

Following his release Schouten published a narrative of the voyage under his own name, thereby precipitating a clash with Jacob Le Maire, who objected to being given no credit. A later edition of the same work was issued by Le Maire, and some historians believe that he was justified in claiming most of the credit. Schouten in September 1619 captained a vessel of the Dutch East India Company and made several voyages to the East Indies. In 1625 bad weather forced him into Antongil Bay, on the east coast of Madagascar, where he died.

Further Reading

Biographical details about Schouten are scarce and mainly found scattered in Dutch sources. Accounts of Schouten's voyage are in Alexander Dalrymple, *Historical Collection of the Several Voyages and Discoveries in the South Pacific Ocean* (1770-1771; repr. 1967), and John C. Beaglehole, *The Exploration of the Pacific* (1934; 3d ed. 1966). See also Peter H. Buck, *Explorers of the Pacific* (1953). □

Erwin Schrödinger

The Austrian physicist Erwin Schrödinger (1887-1961) was the founder of wave mechanics and described the quantum behavior of electrons.

For nearly 5 decades, Erwin Schrödinger, one of the most creative theoretical physicists of the 20th century, contributed papers to the scientific literature. Yet, from the start, his intellectual life was broadly based. He illustrated the breadth of his interests when he described how he intended to fulfill the duties of a professorship he expected to receive in 1918 at Czernowitz, Austria: "I was prepared to do a good job lecturing on theoretical physics . . . but for the rest, to devote myself to philosophy, being deeply imbued at the time with the writings of Spinoza, Schopenhauer, Mach, Richard Semon and Richard Avenarius." This professorship did not materialize. Nevertheless, throughout his life his philosophical concerns came to the surface, principally because he recognized that physics alone cannot provide an answer to Plotinus's ancient question, "And we, who are we, anyway?" Schrödinger's life was unified by his search for an answer to that simple but profound question.

Schrödinger was born on Aug. 12, 1887, in Vienna, the son of a successful and cultured businessman. In 1906 he entered the University of Vienna, where he was most stimulated by the experimental physicist Franz Exner and the theoretical physicist Fritz Hasenöhrl. After Schrödinger completed his doctoral degree in 1910, he remained as an assistant to Exner. In that capacity he explored various problems, many in solid-state physics.

In 1914 Schrödinger became privatdozent at Vienna but almost immediately found himself serving as an artillery officer in Italy. Shortly after he married Annamaria Bertel in 1920, he went to the University of Jena as an assistant to Max Wien. Within the next year he was called, first as associate professor to the Technische Hochschule in Stuttgart, then as full professor to the University of Breslau, and finally as full professor to the University of Zurich. His years at Zurich (1921-1927) were, scientifically speaking, the most productive in his career.

Discovery of Wave Mechanics

In the immediate post-World War I years, Schrödinger worked on a variety of problems in different areas of physics: general relativity, statistical mechanics, radiation theory, the theory of colors, solid-state physics, and atomic spectroscopy. Some of his results are of great historical interest but have been superseded by new insights; others have remained of permanent interest. All of this work was but a prelude to those famous 2 months in 1925/1926, when, in an outburst of genius, he discovered wave mechanics.

When Schrödinger learned of Louis de Broglie's "matter-wave" hypothesis, he immediately tried to use it to explain the bright line spectrum emitted by the hydrogen atom; that is, he tried to apply it to the case of a single electron electrically "bound" to a proton. The results of his investigations—the wave equation he postulated and to which he applied the appropriate "boundary conditions"—were not in agreement with experiment. Discouraged, he put the work aside for some months—until one day in late 1925 the thought struck him that perhaps he should go against his instincts and not take account of the relativistic mass increase of the electron. The results were in striking agreement with experiment! Interestingly, it is now known that even Schrödinger's first, relativistic treatment of the problem is essentially correct—earlier, he had simply not taken account of the "spin" of the electron, a concept unknown to him at the time.

The nonrelativistic wave equation that Schrödinger assumed to govern the behavior of the electron in the hydrogen atom was of course the equation now universally known as the Schrödinger wave equation, the fundamental equation of wave mechanics. In less than 2 months he discovered his equation and began applying his elegant and beautiful theory to enough physical situations to carry complete conviction of its correctness. The capstone of his achievements was his proof of the logical equivalence of wave mechanics and "matrix mechanics," the latter discovered almost simultaneously by Werner Heisenberg in 1926.

Later Scientific Work

In 1927 Schrödinger became Max Planck's successor at the University of Berlin, where he remained until the political events of 1933 and the accompanying anti-Semitic attacks on many of his colleagues forced him, as a matter of conscience, to resign his position. That year he received the Nobel Prize in physics, sharing it with Paul Dirac.

Schrödinger was a fellow at Oxford University from 1933 to 1936, when he accepted a professorship at the University of Graz. After Hitler annexed Austria in 1938, Schrödinger's outspoken anti-Nazism forced him to flee to Italy. As a member of the Pontifical Academy in Rome, he was reasonably safe and began to explore an idea communicated to him earlier by Eamon De Valera, a mathematician who at the time was also president of the Irish Republic, to establish a research institute in Dublin modeled after the Institute for Advanced Study in Princeton. Schrödinger went to Dublin in 1939 as director of the institute's School of Theoretical Physics. By the time he left Dublin in 1956 for Vienna (where a special chair in theoretical physics was created for him), his health was badly damaged and his productive life in physics was over.

During the preceding 3 decades, however, Schrödinger had continued to contribute to the development of quantum theory. He explored the theory of the Compton effect and potential barrier-penetration problems, and he developed the elegant factorization ("ladder operator") technique for generating solutions to the Schrödinger equation for some particular problems. In 1930 he demonstrated that a Dirac electron traveling in free space has superimposed on its motion a very small oscillatory motion, or *Zitterbewegung,* an insight which was subsequently of considerable theoretical importance for certain studies. Schrödinger carried out studies on relativity, cosmology, the unified field theory, meson physics, counter (detector) statistics, and statistical mechanics. He rarely worked with a colleague or student. Like Albert Einstein, he was a "horse for single harness" whose influence was disseminated and perpetuated not by a band of devoted followers but, rather, by his extensive writings.

Humanistic Concerns

Schrödinger was always deeply concerned with philosophical questions—not only those that pertain to scientific issues but also those that pertain to essentially humanistic issues. The fundamental reason for his concern with these issues was his full recognition of the limitations of science. He was convinced, for example, that Heisenberg's uncertainty principle has nothing whatsoever to do with the age-old question of human free will. He believed that to illuminate questions such as these—to obtain a complete world picture—one requires the union of all knowledge, the insights achieved in all disciplines.

Schrödinger's quest to understand the nature of science and self led him to the study of history, particularly ancient history. He regarded Thales of Miletus as the first scientist because of Thales's profound insight that nature is understandable or comprehensible and not characterized by a capricious interplay of superstitions and uncontrollable forces. A century later Heraclitus concluded that this comprehensibility is possible only if the world is so constructed as to appear the same to all sane, waking, persons—only if there exists a "world in common."

According to Schrödinger, this world in common is discovered through observation in combination with insights of a metaphysical nature—hunches, spontaneous creative thought, and the like—that guide the interpretation of the observations. He believed that this world in common, to be comprehensible, had to be to a large degree a deterministic, causal world. Chance elements could enter only through the "intersection of causal chains"; these chance elements are precisely the sort of events that scientists prefer not to talk about, but that theologians and philosophers are profoundly interested in. Thus, once again, Schrödinger was led to conclude that the only way to achieve a complete world picture is to take account of nonscientific as well as scientific knowledge. He felt this to be particularly true when discussing questions like the origin and nature of life, as well as the profoundly interesting role that chance played in Darwinian evolution.

Schrödinger died in Vienna on Jan. 4, 1961.

Further Reading

Schrödinger discussed his work in his Nobel lecture, reprinted in *Nobel Lectures in Physics,* vol. 2 (1965). A collection of letters exchanged by Schrödinger, Einstein, Planck, and Hendrik Lorentz is *Letters on Wave Mechanics,* edited by K. Przibram and translated by M. J. Klein (1967). The most complete source of information on Schrödinger and his work is William T. Scott, *Erwin Schrödinger: An Introduction to His Writings* (1967), which includes a bibliography. An obituary by Walter Heitler is in the *Biographical Memoirs of Fellows of the Royal Society of London,* vol. 7 (1961). For the historical significance of Schrödinger's work see Max Jammer, *The Conceptual Development of Quantum Mechanics* (1966).

Additional Sources

Mehra, Jagdish, *Erwin Schrödinger and the rise of wave mechanics,* New York: Springer-Verlag, 1987.

Moore, Walter John, *A life of Erwin Schrödinger,* Cambridge; New York: Cambridge University Press, 1994.

Moore, Walter John, *Schrödinger, life and thought,* Cambridge; New York: Cambridge University Press, 1989.

Schrödinger, Erwin, *What is life?: the physical aspect of the living cell; with, Mind and matter; & Autobiographical sketches,* Cambridge; New York: Cambridge University Press, 1992. □

Patricia Scott Schroeder

Patricia Scott Schroeder (born 1940) served as the first U.S. congresswoman from Colorado beginning in 1973. She was outspoken about what she considered wasteful spending by the Defense Department and championed women's and children's issues. When she retired from Congress in January 1997, she was the longest-serving woman in Congress.

Patricia Scott Schroeder, daughter of Lee and Bernice Scott, was born July 30, 1940, in Portland, Oregon. She received her Bachelor's degree in 1961 *magna cum laude* from the University of Minnesota where she was a member of Phi Betta Kappa. While studying law at Harvard she met James Schroeder, whom she married in 1962.

After receiving her law degree in 1964 the Schroeders moved to Denver, Colorado. Patricia worked as a field attorney for the National Labor Relations Board until 1966. In 1968, she became Democratic precinct committeewoman and in 1969 she worked as a lecturer and law instructor in Colorado. She served as a hearing officer for the Colorado Department of Personnel and as legal counsel to Planned Parenthood of Colorado from 1970-1972.

In 1972, Schroeder ran for Congress at the urging of her husband. Running on a liberal, anti-war platform, she was elected representative to the 1st District of Colorado. Schroeder had chosen not to assume a safe middle-of-the-road position. She was outspoken against the Vietnam War and asked for a reordering of national priorities with emphasis on health services, environmental protection, education, and health care. Although a virtually unknown candidate, she was able to capture the Democratic primary and upset the Republican incumbent with 51.6 percent of the vote. Schroeder would remain in office for 25 years.

As the first woman ever elected to the U.S. House of Representatives from Colorado in its 79-year history, she quickly became aware of entrenched attitudes against females in Congress. When a colleague asked her how she, a mother of two small children, could be a legislator at the same time, she responded, "I have a brain and a uterus and I use them both."

Schroeder surprised those who thought she would prefer a House committee dealing with quality of life or women's issues by negotiating a seat on the powerful Arms Services Committee, headed by F. Edward Hébert. There she tried to expose what she viewed as the waste and folly of defense policies and to channel "saved" funds into social welfare programs.

Soon she appeared to threaten the long standing, good relationship between the committee and the Pentagon. She denounced their Military Procurement Authorization Bill as "frivolous," "a boon-doggle," and a "colossal waste of money." She chided those who thought that "killing an enemy fifteen times over makes us more secure than if we can kill him only five times over," and condemned her committee as "the Pentagon's lobby on the Hill." She accused the committee of being frightened of open debate on defense issues and challenged their logic in arguing either that "the Russians are doing it and therefore we must do it in order to avoid falling behind" or "the Russians are NOT doing it and therefore we must do it in order to stay ahead."

Her comments put her at odds with Hébert, who disliked having dissenting views aired in public, and he became openly critical of Schroeder. He once refused to approve her as a member of the U.S. delegation to a Strategic Arms Limitation Treaty (SALT) disarmament conference, telling her, "I wouldn't send you to represent this committee at a dog fight," but she went after the rule requiring the chairman's approval and the rule was later dropped. Eventually Hébert was deposed and Schroeder claimed it as her greatest victory.

Schroeder was also active in women's and children's issues, attempting to eliminate gender inequities, introducing legislation providing funds for child-abuse centers, cosponsoring legislation to expand Head Start programs, and supporting year-round use of recreational facilities for poor children. As chairman of the National Task Force on Equal Rights for Women she called for federal payments for abortions. In March, 1985, she was a regular on news programs denouncing the violent tactics of anti-abortionists.

Although Schroeder believed some improvement had been made in women-related legislation, such as gains in the military and certain areas of credit, she felt that one of the most important issues of the 1980s was to solve problems such as pension and job inequities, Social Security, and other inequalities based on sex. She also believed it urgent that women become more politically active, although she was not optimistic that they would become office-holders in large numbers. Other crucial issues of the 1980s, she believed, were the continuing problems of environment, military expenditures, and the need to convince other countries to share more of their defense costs. In 1988 Schroeder was appointed chair of the Defense Burden Sharing Panel, a component of the House Armed Services Committee. Schroeder enthusiastically undertook a challenging cause: that of women and their participation in the military. In 1989, following the U.S. invasion of Panama, she introduced legislation which would afford women a greater chance of participation in all areas of the military

Other legislation introduced by Schroeder would also have a profound effect on the lives of American women and children. In 1993, the Breast and Cervical Cancer Mortality Prevention Act provided breast and cervical cancer screening to poor women and the National Child Protection Act provided for child care providers access to a national database of information on child abusers for the purpose of background checks. The Violence Against Women Act of

1994 was enacted to assist law enforcement professionals and victims rights organizations to fight rape and other forms of violent crime against women.

As a congresswoman Schroeder avoided the Washington social scene, preferring to be with her husband and children. She frequently returned to Colorado to report to her constituents. In 1987, however, she became more of a national figure as she travelled the country to see if she should become a candidate for president the following year. After five months of "testing" she decided not to enter the race.

The decision to retire from the House of Representatives came only after the 1994 Republican "House cleaning" that removed much of the power of the Democratic party within the House. She announced in 1995 that she would not seek another term, and she spent much of 1996 campaigning on behalf of President Bill Clinton and then turned to teaching and writing.

Further Reading

See Schroeder, Pat; Camp, Andrea; and Lipner, Robyn. *Champion of the Great American Family* (Random House, 1989). Biographical data for Patricia Schroeder can be found in Esther Stineman's *American Political Women.* Additional materials concerning Schroeder's life and political activities are in Ilene Barth's "Congresswoman Pat Schroeder: She Calls Herself a Troublemaker," *Ms.* (June 1976); Norma L. Friedman's "Patricia Schroeder: Wife, Mother, Congresswoman—She Shows Us How," *Vogue* (November 1978); and Karen Elliott House's "That's No Pretty Young Thing . . . That's Congresswoman Pat Schroeder," *Family Circle* (July 1975). □

Franz Peter Schubert

Franz Peter Schubert (1797-1828), an early romantic Austrian composer, is best known for his lieder, German art songs for voice and piano.

The lieder of Franz Schubert assumed great importance during the 19th century as a result of several concomitant cultural and sociological developments in Germany, which included the new profusion of lyric poetry, particularly in the works of Goethe, and the evolution of the piano into a highly complex mechanism. As a composer, Schubert possessed an astonishing lyric gift and at times turned out several songs in a day.

In musical history Schubert stands with others at the beginning of the romantic movement, anticipating the subjective approach to composition of later composers but lacking Beethoven's forcefulness and inventive treatment of instrumental music. Despite his more conservative tendencies, however, Schubert's contributions include the introduction of cyclical form in his *Wanderer Fantasy* for piano, the use of long-line melodies—instead of motto-type themes—in his piano sonatas and chamber music, and the increased emphasis on the role of the piano accompaniments in his lieder. Many of his large-scale instrumental pieces were unknown until after the middle of the 19th century. (The *Unfinished* Symphony, for example, did not receive its first public performance until 1865, 43 years after it was written!) Furthermore, unlike many of the other romantic composers, such as Carl Maria von Weber, Hector Berlioz, Franz Liszt, and Richard Wagner, Schubert did not engage in a literary career; nor was he a conductor or virtuoso performer. Consequently he did not achieve considerable public recognition during his lifetime.

Childhood and Training

Schubert was born in Vienna on Jan. 31, 1797, the fourth son of Franz Theodor Schubert, a schoolmaster, and Elizabeth Vietz, in domestic service in Vienna. Franz received instruction in the violin from his father, his older brother Ignaz, and Michael Holzer, the organist at the Liechtenthal parish church. In 1808, through a competitive examination, Franz was accepted into the choir of the Imperial Court Chapel as well as the Stadtkonvikt (Royal Seminary), where he received a fine education and his talents were encouraged by the principal. A 20-year-old law student, Joseph Spaun, who founded an orchestra among these students, formed a lifelong friendship with Schubert.

In 1814 the genius of Schubert was first manifest in *Gretchen am Spinnrade,* inspired by his reading of Goethe's *Faust.* His first Mass, which included solos for a young woman friend, Therese Grob, and his first symphony appeared about this time and showed the influence of Franz Joseph Haydn. Schubert modeled his earliest songs, particularly the ballads, for example, *Hage's Klage* (1811), after

those by Johann Rudolf Zumsteeg. Besides *Gretchen,* Schubert wrote five other Goethe songs that year. Before he died, he had set approximately 57 poems by the poet, at times exceeding in his music the high attainment of Goethe in the poetry.

Early Period, 1814-1820

By the end of 1814 Schubert was an assistant in his father's school and had begun to make the acquaintance of numerous poets, lawyers, singers, and actors, who soon would be the principal performers of his works at private concerts in their homes or in those of their more affluent friends. Spaun, now a student at the University of Vienna, introduced Schubert to his colleagues at the school, Johann Mayrhofer and Franz von Schober, the latter a dilettante in law, acting, writing, and publishing, who in turn introduced Schubert to the renowned singer Michael Vogl.

In 1816 Spaun sent a volume of Schubert's songs to Goethe for his consideration. All the songs were to texts by Goethe, and some, *Gretchen, Wandrers Nachtlied, Heidenröslein,* and *Erlkönig,* are among Schubert's most celebrated songs. Eventually Goethe returned the album, but he was unimpressed. Other 18th-century lyric poets whose works Schubert set include J. G. von Herder, the collector and translator of folk songs, and F. G. Klopstock. Friedrich von Schiller's poems account for 31 settings. None can compare, however, with the remarkable Goethe lieder. Even the uninitiated must respond to the excitement of the *Erlkönig,* where by means of changing accompaniment figures, sharp dissonance, and effective modulations Schubert differentiates the four characters of the ballad—narrator, father, son, and Erlking—and creates one of the masterpieces of romantic music.

The significance of Schubert's lieder tends to eclipse his equally fine choral writing in his six Masses. Unfortunately we cannot say the same of his approximately 11 completed works for the stage. Schubert's lyrical gift did not extend to large-scale dramatic works; his talents showed themselves most effectively in the more precise miniatures.

While still a schoolmaster, Schubert composed Symphonies No. 2 through No. 5, the outer two works being in the key of B-flat, a tonality he seems to have favored. At this time he also wrote many of the delightful dances, waltzes, and *Ländler* for which he was known during his lifetime. By 1817 Schubert was installed in the home of his friend Schober, where the presence of an excellent instrument may have inspired him to write several piano sonatas. In his father's house there had been no piano. Examination of the sonatas will prove Schubert to have been rather daring in his juxtaposition of keys, particularly in development sections.

In addition to instrumental compositions of 1817, lieder still flowed from Schubert's pen (50 that year). Among the best are Schiller's *Gruppe aus dem Tartarus;* the delightful *Die Forelle,* which later provided the theme for the variation movement of the so-called *Trout* Quintet; *An die Musik,* Schubert's hymn to music which was inspired by Schober's poem; and *Der Tod und das Mädchen* to words by the minor poet Claudius. This last song appears again as the theme of the variations in the second movement of the String Quartet *Death and the Maiden.* In July 1817 Schubert was appointed to the ménage of Count Esterhazy, who, with his wife and children, spent winters in an estate slightly north of Schönbrunn and summers at Zseliz in Hungary. There Schubert composed many of his four-hand works.

Middle Period, 1820-1825

Between 1820 and 1823 Schubert achieved his musical maturity. Two of his operettas and several of his songs were performed in public; amateurs and professional quartets sang his part-songs for male voices; and some of his works began to be published. Private concerts at the Sonnleithners and other middle-class residences soon brought Schubert a degree of renown.

In September 1821 Schubert and Schober left Vienna for the country with the intention of writing *Alfonso und Estrella,* his only grand opera. Shortly after his return to the city, he met Edward Bauernfeld, who introduced him to Shakespeare's works. In the fall of 1822, having completed his Mass in A-flat, Schubert began work on the Symphony in B Minor, which became known as the *Unfinished.* Three movements were sketched; two were completed. The reasons for the work being left incomplete are open to conjecture.

Schubert's health deteriorated, and in May he spent time in the Vienna General Hospital. Soon afterward, while working on the third act of another opera, *Fierabras,* he began his remarkable song cycle *Die schöne Müllerin* to the poetry of Wilhelm Müller. *Rosamunde,* a play for which Schubert had written incidental music—only the overture and ballet music are heard today—failed in 1823 and brought to a close his extended efforts to achieve a successful opera.

Schubert now turned to chamber music. At the Sonnleithners he had met Ferdinand Bogner, a flutist, and Count Troyer, a clarinetist. The latter commissioned Schubert's Octet for woodwinds and strings, which in style and number of movements closely resembles Beethoven's Septet, Opus 20. The A Minor and D Minor (*Death and the Maiden*) Quartets stem from 1824, the G Major from 1826. In 1825 Schubert moved again, this time next door to the artist Moritz Schwind. There, with Bauernfeld and Spaun, they formed the mainstay of the Schubertiads, evenings at which Vogl and others sang Schubert's songs. Schwind's illustrations of these evening musicales are among the best contemporary descriptions left to us.

Final Years, 1826-1828

In 1826 and 1827, despite a recurrence of his illness, Schubert wrote four masterpieces, each of which has remained a staple in the repertory: the String Quartet in G, the Piano Sonata in G, the Piano Trio in B-flat (all 1826), and the second Piano Trio in E-flat (1827). In his final years his style changed considerably. On March 26, 1827, Beethoven died, and Schubert, who, with the Hüttenbrenners, had supposedly visited the dying man on March 18, was one of the torchbearers at the funeral. Toward the end of that year Schubert completed his two series of piano pieces that he himself entitled *Impromptus,* thus enabling us to disregard

Robert Schumann's suggestion that D. 935 (Opus 142) was conceived as a sonata.

In 1828, the last year of his life, Schubert composed several first-rate works: the magnificent F-Minor Fantasy for piano duet dedicated to Esterhazy, the C-Major Symphony, the E-flat Mass, and nine songs to Ludwig Rellstab's poems, which Schubert may have intended as a cycle. Seven of these songs, six Heinrich Heine songs, and one setting of a poem by J. G. Seidl appeared as *Schwanengesang* (Swansong), a title given them by the publisher. On March 26, 1828, Schubert participated in the only full-scale public concert devoted solely to his own works.

On November 11, suffering from nausea and headache, he took to his bed in the house of his brother Ferdinand. Five days later the doctors diagnosed typhoid fever. One of the two doctors was a specialist in venereal disease; thus the suspicion that Schubert had syphilis is well founded. He was correcting the proofs of the second set of his song cycle *Die Winterreise* when he became delirious and died 2 days later on Nov. 19, 1828. Schubert's meager estate and all his manuscripts were left by default to his brother Ferdinand, who, fortunately for posterity, worked ceaselessly to enlist the aid of publishers, editors, and conductors in having them published.

In 1830 a subscription fund helped to raise money for a memorial stone over Schubert's grave. The dramatist Franz Grillparzer wrote this much-criticized epitaph: "The Art of Music here entombed a rich possession but even far fairer hopes." Schubert's closest friends were unaware of his achievement. A wealth of scholarly material has been devoted to the composer in recent years. Nobody, however, has done as much to correct the record as the great scholar O. E. Deutsch, whose initial is now inextricably linked to each Schubert work in his catalog.

Further Reading

On Schubert's life, the two works edited by Otto E. Deutsch are definitive, *The Schubert Reader: A Life of Franz Schubert in Letters and Documents* (trans. 1947), with commentary designed to bring the documents into sharper focus, and *Schubert: Memoirs by His Friends* (1958). Two books by Maurice J. E. Brown, *Essays on Schubert* (1954) and *Schubert: A Critical Biography* (1958), are reliable. Marcel Brion, *Daily Life in the Vienna of Mozart and Schubert* (trans. 1962), describes the milieu in which Schubert lived and worked.

Alfred E. Einstein, *Schubert: A Musical Portrait* (1951), and Gerald Abraham, ed., *The Music of Schubert* (1947), offer valuable insights into the man and his music. Martin Chusid, ed., *Schubert's Unfinished Symphony* (1968), a critical edition of the score, treats a particular piece to a stylistic analysis, offering a historical essay, analytical notes, and a section on contemporary views and comments. Richard Capell, *Schubert's Songs* (2d ed. rev. 1957), is worth consulting. Ernest Porter, *Schubert's Song Technique* (1960), is easy to read. Particularly important is Otto E. Deutsch, *Schubert Thematic Catalogue* (1950), a list of all the works in chronological order. □

Gunther Schuller

The versatility of the American musician Gunther Schuller (born 1925) was recognized when he received the Alice M. Ditson Award from Columbia University in 1970: "You have already achieved distinction in six careers, as conductor, as composer, as horn virtuoso and orchestral musician, and as author and educator."

Gunther Schuller was born in New York City on November 22, 1925, the son of a New York Philharmonic Orchestra violinist. He sang as a boy soprano in the St. Thomas Church choir, studied flute and French horn privately, and studied music theory at the Manhattan School of Music. Before he was 20, he was a professional hornist, playing in the Ballet Theater Orchestra and later with the Cincinnati Symphony. From 1945 to 1959 he played with the Metropolitan Opera Orchestra.

Schuller's first published compositions date from 1950, but it was his *Seven Studies on Themes of Paul Klee* (1959) that brought him wide attention through performances by many orchestras and through recordings. In this piece Schuller revealed himself as a masterful orchestrator in complete control of a serialism inspired by Anton Webern. The piece had wit and charm, unusual components of serial compositions. In some of the Studies Schuller matched the color of the pictures with orchestral color, and in others, such as "The Twittering Machine," and the "Arab Village," he reflected the mood and atmosphere of the pictures in the music.

There was a strong jazz influence in all of Schuller's compositions. The composer called the combination of jazz elements with serial practices "third stream" music, a term which has been generally adopted to describe this typically American musical development. During the 1960s Schuller received a number of grants that allowed him to devote himself entirely to composition.

In 1965, as composer-in-residence in Berlin, Schuller completed his opera *The Visitation,* first produced in Hamburg in 1966. For his libretto the composer adapted Franz Kafka's story *The Trial,* changing the setting to the American South and the characters to African-Americans. Thus altered, it became a powerful and timely statement of the plight of black Americans. The music was in Schuller's "third stream" manner with much jazz. *The Visitation,* a sensational success in its first European productions, was less successful when produced in the United States. He subsequently wrote two more operas, *The Fisherman and His Wife* (1970) and *A Question of Taste* (1989).

In 1968 Schuller published the first volume of his monumental history of jazz, proving himself to be the outstanding authority in this field. After teaching at Yale, he became president of the New England Conservatory in 1966, and a few years later, director of the Berkshire Music Center in Tanglewood as well (1970-1985). He was unrivaled among American musicians of his generation for the versatility and quality of his accomplishments. In 1993, Schuller received *Down Beat* magazine's prestigious Hall of Fame and Lifetime Achievement awards.

During the 1990s, Schuller broadened his conducting repertoire and also published *The Compleat Conductor* (1997), a detailed analysis of eight symphonic works in which he compared the composer's written intentions with the actual recorded performances of those pieces over the last 50 years.

Further Reading

David Ewen, *The World of Twentieth-century Music* (1968), provides biographical information and a discussion of Schuller's works. A short biography of him was in Gilbert Chase, ed., *The American Composer Speaks* (1966). He was profiled in *Down Beat* (September 1993). □

Charles M. Schulz

Cartoonist and creator of "Peanuts," Charles M. Schulz (born 1922) was the winner of two Reuben, two Peabody, and five Emmy awards and a member of the Cartoonist Hall of Fame.

Charles Schulz was born in Minneapolis, Minnesota, on November 26, 1922, the son of Carl (a barber) and Dena (Halverson) Schulz. At school in St. Paul he was bright and rapidly promoted, which made him often the smallest in his class, a fact that may have been of psychological significance in his later development. Noting his aptitude for drawing, his mother encouraged him to take a correspondence course from the Federal School in Minneapolis.

In World War II Schulz was drafted and sent to Europe, mustering out after the war as a sergeant. He returned to Minnesota as a young man strongly imbued with Christian beliefs. For a while he free-lanced for a Catholic magazine and taught in the correspondence school, which had been renamed the Art Instruction Institute. Some of his work appeared in the *Saturday Evening Post,* and eventually he created a cartoon entitled "Li'l Folks" for the *St. Paul Pioneer Press,* signing it "Sparky," a nickname conferred on him by an uncle.

In 1950 the United Feature Syndicate of New York proposed publication of a new comic strip, which Schulz wished to call "Li'l Folks" but which was named "Peanuts" by the company. In 1950 the cartoon made its debut in seven newspapers with the characters Charlie Brown, Shermy, Patty, and Snoopy. Within a year the strip appeared in thirty-five papers, and by 1956 in over a hundred. Characters were added slowly, and psychological subtleties were much developed. Lucy, Linus, and Schroeder appeared; then Sally, Charlie Brown's sister; Rerun, Lucy's brother; Peppermint Patty; Marcie; Franklin; Jose Peterson;

Pigpen; Snoopy's brother, Spike; and the bird, Woodstock. In 1955, and again in 1964, Schulz received the Reuben award from the National Cartoonists Society.

By this time Schulz' popularity was enormous and had become world-wide. "Peanuts" appeared in over 2,300 newspapers. The cartoon branched out into television, and in 1965 the classic "A Charlie Brown Christmas," produced by Bill Melendez and Lee Mendelson, won a Peabody and an Emmy award. Many more television "specials" and Emmys were to follow. An off-Broadway production, "You're a good man, Charlie Brown," staged in 1967, ran four years. In 1969, National Aeronautics and Space Administration astronauts named their command module "Charlie Brown" and their lunar lander "Snoopy." Many volumes of Schulz' work were published in at least 19 languages, and the success of "Peanuts" inspired many licensed products in textiles, stationery, toys, games, etc. Schulz also authored a book, "Why, Charlie Brown, Why?" (which became a CBS television special) to make the dreaded subject of cancer understandable to children (his mother had died of cancer during World War II).

Besides the previously mentioned awards, Schulz received the Yale Humor Award, 1956; School Bell Award, National Education Association, 1960; and honorary degrees from Anderson College, 1963, and St. Mary's College of California, 1969. A "Charles M. Schulz Award" honoring aspiring comic artists was created by the United Feature Syndicate in 1980. The year 1990 marked the 40th anniversary of "Peanuts." An exhibit at the Louvre, in Paris, called "Snoopy in Fashion," featured 300 Snoopy and BELLE plush dolls dressed in fashions created by more than 15 world-famous designers. It later traveled to the United States. Also in 1990, the Smithsonian Institution featured an exhibit titled, "This Is Your Childhood, Charlie Brown . . . Children in American Culture, 1945-1970."

The "Peanuts" cartoons were centered on the classically simple and touching figures of a boy and his dog, Charlie Brown and Snoopy, surrounded by family and school friends. Adults were present only by implication, and the action involved ordinary, everyday happenings, transformed by childhood fantasy.

Charlie Brown was the quintessence of ordinariness, as his name and his visible form suggest. His round head had minimal features, half-circles for ears and nose, dots for eyes, a line for a mouth, the rest of the body compressed to pint size. He was a combination of ineptness and puzzlement in the face of problems that life and his peers dealt out to him: the crabby superiority of Lucy; the unanswerable questions of Linus, a small intellectual with a security blanket; the self-absorption of Schroeder the musician; the teasing of his school mates; and the behavior of Snoopy, the flop-eared beagle with the wild imagination and the doghouse equipped with a Van Gogh, who sees himself as a World War I Flying Ace trying to shoot down the Red Baron when he is not running a "Beagle Scout" troop consisting of the bird Woodstock and his friends.

Charlie Brown's inability to cope with the constant, predictable disappointments in life, the failure and renewal of trust (typified by Lucy's tricking him every time he tries to kick the football), his touching efforts to accept what happens as deserved, all were traits shared in a lesser degree by his companions. Even crabby Lucy cannot interest Schroeder or understand baseball; Linus puzzled over life's mysteries and the refusal of the "Great Pumpkin" to show up on Halloween. The quirks and defects of humanity in general were reflected by Schulz' gentle humor, which constituted the appeal of the cartoon to the public, as it pinpointed our own adult weaknesses in a diminished and entertaining form, with a dash of pathos.

Part of the pleasure of "Peanuts" was the readers' expectation fulfilled, as the build-up to the penultimate frame reached the let-down of the final. "I realize . . . I am not alone . . . I have friends!" says Charlie Brown, momentarily reassured by "psychiatrist" Lucy. "Name one!" retorts Lucy, returning to her usual role.

Some writers find a moral and religious gospel to be drawn from Charlie Brown's dilemmas. Schulz maintained that he was more preoccupied by getting the strip on the drawing board. However, even to the casual reader "Peanuts" offered lessons to be learned. Schulz employed everyday humor, even slapstick, to make a point, but usually it was the intellectual comment that carries the charge, even if it was only "Good Grief!" Grief was the human condition, but it was good when it taught us something about ourselves and was lightened by laughter.

Schulz was twice married, to Joyce Halverson in 1949 (divorced 1972) and to Jean Clyde in 1973. He had five children by his first marriage: Meredith, Charles Monroe, Craig, Amy, and Jill. He was an avid hockey player, had a passion for golf, and enjoyed tennis.

Charles Schulz and the "Peanuts" characters remained a mainstay in the late 1990s. Schulz's work was beloved by the masses. He has had two retrospectives dedicated to his work within the past 15 years. The first was in 1985 at the Oakland Museum in Oakland, California and the second occurred in 1990 at the Louvre's Museum of Decorative Art in Paris. As of the late 1990s the syndicated cartoon strip of the "Peanuts" ran in over 2000 newspapers throughout the world on a daily basis.

Further Reading

The most complete biography was Rheta Grimsley Johnson, *Good Grief: the Story of Charles M. Schulz* (1989). *The Funnies, An American Idiom,* edited by David Manning White and Robert H. Abel (Part V, 1963), contained interesting comment placing Schulz in the context of American cartoonists. *The Gospel According to Peanuts* (1964) by Robert L. Short pointed out the similarity between "Peanuts" and many passages of the Bible. *Charlie Brown & Charlie Schulz* (1970) by Lee Mendelson with Charles M. Schulz presented useful comments but is somewhat dated. *America's Great Comic-Strip Artists* (Part 16, 1989), edited by Richard Marschall, provided up-to-date commentary on Schulz and other cartoonists and some comparison.

Among Schulz' best-known works were: *Happiness Is a Warm Puppy* (1962); *Good Grief, Charlie Brown* (1963); *A Charlie Brown Christmas* (1965); *Charlie Brown's Yearbook* (1969); and *You're A Good Sport, Charlie Brown* (1976). Additional information may be obtained at http://www.united-media.com (July 1997). □

Kurt Schumacher

Kurt Schumacher (1895-1952) was the leading German socialist statesman during the period of recovery and reconstruction following World War II. Although his views on the future organization of Germany were not accepted, he continued to exercise an important influence on the political ideas of his countrymen decades after his death.

Born into a West Prussian merchant family of liberal political views, Schumacher shared the exhilaration followed by disillusionment which so many young men of his generation experienced during World War I. He volunteered for military service, but after being seriously wounded he returned to the study of law. He felt increasingly drawn to politics, however, and in 1918 he joined the Social Democratic Party. Active at first as a journalist and politician in the state of Württemberg, Schumacher was elected to the Reichstag in 1930. His vigorous opposition to National Socialism led not only to his banishment from public life in 1933, but to imprisonment in a succession of concentration camps and to brutal hardship which permanently impaired his health. Learning in the last weeks of the war that his name was on a Nazi execution list, he went underground until the collapse of the Third Reich in the spring of 1945.

Welcomed as one of the "good Germans" who had resisted the Hitler tyranny, he immediately plunged into the work of rebuilding the Social Democratic Party. Fearing that a union with the Communist Party, which the Soviets were encouraging in their zone of occupation, would lead to domination by the Communists, he concentrated on the creation of a vigorous independent socialist movement in the parts of Germany occupied by the Western allies. At the first postwar convention of the Social Democratic Party in May 1946, he rejected the theory of class conflict, emphasizing the importance of political freedom and economic justice for all groups in society. He hoped thereby to broaden the social base of his party and to attract democratic forces within the bourgeois camp. He defined his brand of socialism as the "economic liberation of the moral and political personality." Regarding the future organization of the German state, he favored a democratic federal union with a central government strong enough to maintain economic unity, financial independence, and social welfare. The administrative system, he insisted, should be "as centralistic as necessary, but as federalistic as possible."

His views soon brought him into conflict with the occupying powers. He charged, not without justice, that the Allied authorities (France, Great Britain, United States) opposed his socialist policies and that they therefore favored "candidates of the bourgeois parties" for key positions in politics, economics, and administration. Their disapproval was sharpened by his convictions regarding what the international position of the new Germany should be. Hoping to avoid the permanent division of his country into two hostile states, he advocated neutrality in the incipient Cold War between the United States and the Soviet Union. A believer in a united Europe, he nevertheless continued to cling to the concept of a strong German national state, embracing all four occupation zones (the Allies plus the Soviet Union), which could play an important role in the political affairs of the continent. Above all, he opposed the military alignment of his country with either East or West, maintaining that reunification could be achieved only by a policy of strict neutrality. His goal was a united, democratic, socialistic, and peaceful Germany acting as a diplomatic buffer between the two superpowers.

In the political battles of the early postwar years Schumacher was defeated by his opponent Konrad Adenauer, leader of the middle-of-the-road Christian Democratic Union. This was partly a result of the indirect support which the latter received from the Allied occupation authorities; partly it was due to Schumacher's own brusqueness and irritability, aggravated by his declining health. But the main reason was that most Germans, eager for American aid in the recovery of their ravaged economy and convinced that entry into the North Atlantic Treaty Organization (NATO) would hasten the political rehabilitation of their country, favored close ties to the West.

The German Federal Republic, as it developed in the period after its founding in 1949, did not follow the policies urged by Schumacher. While material prosperity and political respectability have been amply achieved, chances for the reunification of Germany seem as remote today as ever. Yet Schumacher's vision continues to appeal to many of his countrymen. The concept of a socialist Germany in which the rights of property are subordinated to society's collective welfare is still central to the program of the Social Democratic Party, and the longing for the union of all Germans—those in the German Democratic Republic in the East with those in the German Federal Republic—remains undiminished. The ideals Schumacher advocated have survived the political disappointments and defeats he suffered during his lifetime.

Further Reading

Although Schumacher's speeches and writings have been published in several editions, none, unfortunately, has been translated into English. There is, however, a first-rate study of his public career: Lewis J. Edinger, *Kurt Schumacher: A Study in Personality and Political Behavior* (1965). In addition, any book dealing with the recovery of Germany after World War II is bound to contain information about him. See, for example, Richard Hiseacks, *Democracy in Western Germany* (1957) or Harold Zink, *The United States in Germany, 1944-1956* (1957). Finally, there are several contemporary articles by well-known journalists and scholars, among them Flora Lewis, "The Hard-Bitten Herr Schumacher," *New York Times Magazine* (July 31, 1949); Theodore H. White, "Kurt Schumacher: The Will to Power," *The Reporter* (December 11, 1951); and Felix Hirsch, "Adenauer or Schumacher?" *Current History* (February 1952).

Additional Sources

Kurt Schumacher, Dusseldorf; New York: ECON, 1988. □

Robert Schuman

The French statesman Robert Schuman (1886-1963) was the public author of the plan that pooled the French and German coal and steel industries into the European Coal and Steel Community.

Born in Luxembourg on June 29, 1886, into a prosperous family from Lorraine, Robert Schuman was educated in Germany as a lawyer. Of military age during World War I, he did not serve in the German army, although later his political opponents often made that accusation. After the Treaty of Versailles restored Lorraine to France in 1919, Schuman was elected to the French Parliament, a deputy of the Catholic Popular Democratic party.

Exerting a generally conservative influence, Schuman was a member of the parliamentary finance commission for 17 years and its president in 1940. Undersecretary of state for refugees in the Paul Reynaud government after March 1940, he was arrested by the Gestapo in September and confined at Neustadt. Schuman escaped in 1942 and immediately joined the resistance movement. During this time he played an important role in the creation of the Popular Republican Movement (MRP), which after 1945 replaced his former party as the major organ of French Christian democracy.

Elected to the Constituent Assembly in 1945, Schuman was appointed its finance chairman. Minister of finance under Georges Bidault and Paul Ramadier during 1946-1947, Schuman favored a program of austerity. Becoming prime minister in late 1947 amid widespread Communist-inspired strikes and disorders, Schuman and his interior minister, Jules Moch, stood firm, facing down the Communist challenge and enabling the Fourth Republic to survive its first great crisis. Forced to resign after only 7 months in office, Schuman held the post again for a few days in September 1948.

Schuman earned his greatest fame as foreign minister in 10 successive governments from July 1948 to December 1952. He stood as the foremost advocate of Franco-German reconciliation and European unity. He was the enthusiastic sponsor in 1950 of Jean Monnet's plan for combining French and German coal and steel production, which was later realized with the formation of the European Coal and Steel Community in June 1952. In 1950 Schuman also launched a plan for an integrated European army, but that project was defeated in the French Chamber in 1954.

In 1958 Schuman was elected first president of the European Parliamentary Assembly, the consultative body of the Common Market, a position in which he served for 2 years. For his efforts in the cause of European unity he was awarded the Charlemagne Prize by the city of Aachen in 1958 and the Erasmus Prize by the European Cultural Foundation in 1959. Schuman died near Metz on Sept. 4, 1963, after a long illness.

Further Reading

There is no biography of Schuman in English. His role in the Fourth Republic is extensively discussed in Alexander Werth, *France, 1940-1955* (1956). Useful works for historical background are Herbert Luethy, *France against Herself* (trans. 1955); John T. Marcus, *Neutralism and Nationalism in France* (1958); and Frederick F. Ritsch, *The French Left and the European Idea, 1947-1949* (1966). □

Robert Alexander Schumann

The music of the German composer and critic Robert Alexander Schumann (1810-1856) made a significant impact on the burgeoning romantic movement in its rhythmic novelty and harmonic and lyrical expressiveness.

Robert Schumann created no intrinsically new forms, but he infused them with a personal subjectivity and emotional intensity that transformed an inherited classical tradition into the quintessence of romantic experience. Much of his music is characterized by literary allusions and autobiographical references, which are "nothing more than delicate directions for performance and understanding" added to the music to indicate the composer's poetic intent. Yet he was not averse to experimenting with the contrapuntal devices of a J. S. Bach or the symphonic structures of a Beethoven. He thus stands midway between the conservatives and ultraprogressives of the 19th century.

Schumann was born at Zwickau on June 8, 1810, the youngest of the five children of Friedrich Schumann, a bookseller and publisher, and Johanna Schumann. Robert spent hours in his father's bookshop and developed a lifelong interest in German literature, especially the works of Jean Paul (Richter), Heinrich Heine, and Joseph von Eichendorff. At 7 Robert went to a private school and studied piano with the local church organist, who introduced him to the works of C. P. E. Bach, Franz Joseph Haydn, and Wolfgang Amadeus Mozart. By the time Robert was 9, he had begun his first efforts at composition.

During his years in secondary school (1820-1828) Schumann continued to practice the piano, often participating in concerts at the school and in the salons of eminent patrons. By 1825 he had made such progress in improvisation and composition that his father tried to interest Carl Maria von Weber in becoming Robert's teacher, but Weber was on his way to England and nothing came of the attempt. The following year Schumann's sister, Emilie, committed suicide as the result of a mental disorder, and his father, also suffering from a nervous illness, died a few months later.

In 1828 Schumann began to study law at his mother's request at the University of Leipzig. After a short visit to Munich, where he met Heine, Schumann returned to his law studies in earnest. He continued his musical studies with Friedrich Wieck, an eminent piano teacher. At his teacher's home Schumann met Wieck's daughter Clara, already a remarkable pianist at the age of 9. In 1829 Schumann moved to Heidelberg, ostensibly to continue his law studies but essentially to study composition and piano. He frequented the home of the law professor Anton Thibaut, a musical amateur who was instrumental in reviving an interest in the choral music of the Renaissance and the baroque. That summer Schumann went on holiday to Switzerland and Italy and wrote the first part of his *Papillons* for piano.

A concert by Niccolo Paganini in 1830 in Frankfurt was the decisive factor that turned Schumann permanently to music. After some stormy correspondence with his mother, she finally agreed to let him continue his studies with Wieck. He took up residence in the Wieck home and concentrated on developing into a virtuoso pianist. In his anxiety to make rapid progress he experimented with a sling device to strengthen his fingers; by irrevocably straining his right hand he ruined all chance of becoming a virtuoso. He therefore decided to concentrate on his composition studies and worked with Heinrich Dorn, choirmaster at the Leipzig opera, under whom Schumann completed the second part of the *Papillons* and an Allegro for piano. He also embarked on an intensive study of the music of J. S. Bach.

In 1834 the first issue of the *Neue Zeitschrift für Musik* (New Journal for Music) appeared. It was the organ of the Davidsbündler, a group of musicians, named for the Old Testament King David, who concentrated their struggle against the musical Philistines of their own day. Schumann edited this reforming journal until 1844, and it became a model for music criticism. In order to observe music from all points of view, Schumann invented three artistic characters: the stormy, impetuous Florestan; the gentle, lyrical Eusebius; and the arbiter between the two, Master Raro. In later years Schumann signed many of his own compositions with these appellations.

Schumann's *Twelve Symphonic Études* appeared in 1834, and the next year saw the completion of *Carnaval* and the Piano Sonata, Opus 11. His mother died in 1836. He stayed on in Leipzig with the Wiecks, fell in love with Clara, and, over the strong objections of her father, became engaged to her in 1837. Through the success of his journal, Schumann became an eminent voice in cultural matters and an artistic critic of European rank, more famous for his writings than for his compositions, which most musicians found too difficult to play. Nevertheless, he kept on composing and produced such pianistic masterpieces as the *Études symphoniques,* the *Scenes from Childhood,* the *Kreisleriana,* and the *Fantasy.* On a visit to Vienna in 1838 to further the aims and influence of his journal, he made the sensational discovery of Franz Schubert's C-Major Symphony, which Mendelssohn eventually performed.

In February 1840 Schumann was honored by a doctorate from the University of Jena. A month later he met Franz Liszt, who played part of Schumann's *Carnaval* at a recital in Leipzig. Schumann married Clara, against her father's will, in September. Seven children were born of this union.

The ensuing years were a high point in Schumann's compositional activity. During 1840 he wrote a veritable outpouring of songs, including the cycles *Myrthen* (Myrtles), *Frauenliebe und Leben* (Women's Love and Life), and *Dichterliebe* (Poet's Love). The next year he composed his Symphony No. 1, the *Spring* Symphony and in 1842 he wrote many of his finest pieces of chamber music, including three String Quartets dedicated to Mendelssohn and the Quintet in E-flat for piano and strings. The Piano Concerto in A Minor and the Symphony No. 2 were also well under way.

A crisis of mental exhaustion followed on these productive years. A visit from Hector Berlioz in 1843, however, inspired Schumann to new activity, and he began his *Paradise and the Peri* for solo voices, chorus, and orchestra. That same year Mendelssohn called him to teach composition at the newly founded Leipzig Conservatory. In 1844, after a reconciliation with Wieck, the Schumanns embarked on a successful concert tour of Russia. On their return to Leipzig, Schumann suffered a serious nervous breakdown which caused him to resign as editor of the *Neue Zeitschrift.* The Schumanns moved to Dresden in December 1844, where they became acquainted with Richard Wagner, whose stage technique Schumann admired more than his music. In Leipzig, Schumann founded the Society for Choral Singing and taught privately for a living. Here he finished his Piano Concerto in A Minor, which was premiered by Clara in 1846, and the Symphony No. 2. He completed his opera *Genoveva* early in 1848.

In 1849 Schumann's health improved dramatically, and he composed more than 20 works that year, including the *Album for the Young,* the incidental music to Lord Byron's *Manfred,* and a group of short works for various instruments.

In 1850 Schumann became civic music director in Düsseldorf. The Düsseldorf years were not happy ones. Times of great inspiration in composition alternated with profound periods of melancholy and despondency, often lasting weeks or even months. His overall creativity began to lag so that one critic dared to write of him, "Schumann has worked his way down from genius to talent." Nonetheless these years witnessed the completion of the *Scenes from Goethe's "Faust,"* the *Waldscenen* (Woodland Scenes) for piano, innumerable songs, and Symphony No. 3, the *Rhenish.*

Wagner had once remarked on Schumann's "strange lack of skill in conducting," and this unsuitability for the conductor's post led to constant bickering with the authorities in Düsseldorf. His choir also began to grow more and more recalcitrant. Eventually Schumann was left to conduct his own works only, and all the other conducting was entrusted to the concertmaster.

In 1853 Schumann's Symphony No. 4 was performed successfully at the Lower Rhine Festival, but his mental condition continued to deteriorate. The only bright spot in his life that year was a visit from Johannes Brahms, whom Schumann greatly admired and in whose behalf he wrote a laudatory article, "New Paths," for the *Neue Zeitschrift.* There was also a brief concert tour of Holland with his wife and a visit to Hanover, where Joseph Joachim conducted Schumann's Symphony No. 4 and played the *Fantasy* for violin and orchestra.

Schumann went completely berserk on Feb. 27, 1854, when he threw himself into the Rhine in a suicide attempt. He was rescued by some passing fishermen, and at his own request he was taken to an asylum in Endenich. Clara, aided by their loyal friend Brahms, did all that was possible to bolster Schumann's spirits but to no avail. He died on July 29, 1856.

Further Reading

There is unfortunately no really good work on Schumann in English. Even the monumental German study, *Robert Schumann* by Wolfgang Boetticher (1941), is marred by Nazi overtones. Very useful are Joan Chissell, *Schumann* (1948), and Gerald Abraham, ed., *Schumann: A Symposium* (1952). Percy M. Young, *Tragic Muse: The Life and Works of Robert Schumann* (1957), is also worth examining. For general historical background Donald Jay Grout, *A History of Western Music* (1960), is recommended. □

Joseph Alois Schumpeter

Joseph Alois Schumpeter (1883-1950) was an Austrian economist who advocated the view that business cycles are an integral part of the process of economic development in a capitalist economy.

Joseph Schumpeter was born in Triesch in Moravia (now Czechoslovakia) on Feb. 8, 1883, the only son of Alois Schumpeter, a clothing manufacturer who died when Joseph was 4 years old. Because of his mother's remarriage 7 years later to the commanding general of all Austrian troops in Vienna, Schumpeter was raised in the manner traditional to the Austrian aristocracy. In 1901 he graduated with high honors from the Theresianum, a school distinguished for its classical education.

From 1901 to 1906 he studied law and economics at the University of Vienna, where he attended the seminars of Eugen Philippović, Friedrich von Wieser, and Eugen Böhm-Bawerk. He received the degree of doctor of law in 1906 and spent a brief period visiting England and practicing law in Egypt. In 1909 he returned to Austria, where he accepted a professorship in economics at the University of Chernovtsy. In 1911 he joined the faculty at the University of Graz, where, except for the academic year 1913/1914, he remained until 1918. During this period he had written his first major article and three important books and had established his preeminence in economic theory.

During World War I Schumpeter took part in the intrigues to negotiate a separate peace for Austria and in putting forward proposals for economic reconstruction. In 1919 he became finance minister in the coalition government of the Austrian Republic but was forced to resign before even presenting his financial proposals to Parliament.

Next, Schumpeter became president of a private bank in Vienna which, because of economic conditions and the dishonesty of some of his associates, failed in 1924. He returned to academic life, accepting a professorship at the University of Bonn in 1925. He visited Harvard in the following year and again in 1930 and, in 1932, moved there permanently. During his years at Harvard he produced several more major books, the last of which was in rough manuscript at his death and was edited and published by his wife, Elizabeth Boody Schumpeter. Schumpeter died in his sleep, of a cerebral hemorrhage, on Jan. 8, 1950.

Schumpeter's work, published in 15 books and pamphlets, over 200 articles, book reviews, and review articles, defies classification by school of thought or by methodology. Although his *Theory of Economic Development* (1912) is a classic in the abstract-deductive tradition of Léon Walras and Böhm-Bawerk, many of his articles and his *Business Cycles* (1939) demonstrate his interest in and capacity for statistical and econometric research. Finally, his writings on socialism, *Imperialism and Social Classes* (1951) and *Capitalism, Socialism and Democracy* (1942), and on the history of economic theory, *Economic Doctrine and Method* (1914) and *History of Economic Analysis* (1954), reveal an insight into the broad sweep of sociological and historical forces on economic ideas and events that can be compared only to that of Marx.

Further Reading

Seymour E. Harris, ed., *Schumpeter, Social Scientist* (1951), contains a number of excellent essays about Schumpeter's life and work. Richard V. Clemence and Francis S. Doddy, *The Schumpeterian System* (1950), is a study of his system of economic analysis. His career is discussed briefly in Joseph Dorfman, *The Economic Mind in American Civilization* (5 vols., 1946-1959), and Ben B. Seligman, *Main Currents in Modern Economics: Economic Thought since 1870* (1962).

Additional Sources

Allen, Robert Loring, *Opening doors: the life and work of Joseph Schumpeter,* New Brunswick, N.J.: Transaction Publishers, 1991.

Mearz, Eduard, *Joseph Schumpeter: scholar, teacher, and politician,* New Haven: Yale University Press, 1991.

Schneider, Erich, *Joseph A. Schumpeter: life and work of a great social scientist,* Lincoln: Bureau of Business Research, University of Nebraska-Lincoln, 1975.

Stolper, Wolfgang F., *Joseph Alois Schumpeter: the public life of a private man,* Princeton, N.J.: Princeton University Press, 1994.

Swedberg, Richard, *Joseph A. Schumpeter: his life and work,* Cambridge, UK: Polity Press, 1991.

Swedberg, Richard, *Schumpeter: a biography,* Princeton, N.J.: Princeton University Press, 1991. □

Carl Schurz

The most prominent foreign-born American in 19th-century public life, Carl Schurz (1829-1906) was soldier, statesman, and journalist. He was at the center of many political reform movements.

Carl Schurz was the foremost of a remarkable group of emigrés who went to the United States after the failure of the 1848-1849 revolution in Germany. In his adopted land Schurz crusaded against slavery, campaigned for his friend Abraham Lincoln, fought for the North in the Civil War, helped shape a Reconstruction policy that enfranchised the freed slaves, championed civil service reform, founded the Liberal Republican movement, was a leader of the "Mugwump" exodus from the Republican party, and denounced American imperialism in the Spanish-American War.

Carl Schurz was born on March 2, 1829, in Liblar near Cologne, Germany. He graduated from the gymnasium at Cologne and entered the University of Bonn in 1847 as a candidate for the doctorate in history. At the age of 19 he was a leader of the student movement that became the spearhead of democratic revolutionary ferment in many parts of Germany. In 1849 Schurz was commissioned a lieutenant in the revolutionary army, which was finally defeated by the Prussians. Knowing he would be shot if captured, he fled the country. He later returned under a false passport to rescue a professor from Spandau prison and spirit him out of Germany in the most daring exploit of the entire revolution.

American Civil War Record

After short residences in France and England, in 1852 Schurz went to the United States. He joined the antislavery movement and helped build the Republican party in Wisconsin, where he settled in 1856. An excellent orator, Schurz made speeches for John C. Frémont in the 1856 presidential election and for Lincoln against Stephen Douglas in the 1858 Illinois senatorial campaign. He was chairman of the Wisconsin delegation to the 1860 Republican convention. He campaigned tirelessly in the 1860 election and was gratified by a letter from Lincoln declaring that "to the extent of our limited acquaintance, no man stands nearer my heart than yourself." Rewarded by appointment as minister to Spain, Schurz resigned that post in 1862 and returned to the United States to work for Union victory and emancipation.

Schurz's military experience was limited to a few weeks of fighting in Germany 13 years earlier, but he worked hard at mastering military strategy and was finally promoted to major general of volunteers in 1863. He was popular with his troops, but his battle record was mixed. After limited success as a division commander at Chancellorsville and a corps commander at Gettysburg, he was given charge of an instruction corps at Nashville. This was not to his liking, and in 1864 he obtained release from command to campaign for Lincoln's reelection. Schurz finished out the war as a chief of staff in William T. Sherman's army.

Postwar Political Career

In the summer of 1865 Schurz began investigating Southern conditions for President Andrew Johnson and a Boston newspaper. He found that many Southerners were defiant and recalcitrant, determined to keep Negroes subordinate. Schurz's long report contradicted the premises of Johnson's Reconstruction policy, and the President did not acknowledge the report. But congressional Republicans secured its publication and wide distribution. This document was of great influence in molding a radical Reconstruction policy based on Negro suffrage.

Schurz was Washington correspondent of the *New York Tribune,* then editor of the *Detroit Post,* and in 1867 he became part owner and editor of the German-language *St. Louis Westliche Post.* Schurz made the keynote address at the Republican national convention in 1868 and the next year was elected to the U.S. Senate from Missouri. His views on Reconstruction had become less radical; he advocated the removal of all political disabilities from former Confederates and was increasingly critical of Federal intervention in behalf of what he considered corrupt and oppressive Republican regimes in Southern states.

A proponent of civil service reform, Schurz was also repelled by the corrupt political atmosphere of Ulysses S. Grant's administration. In 1872 he led reformers out of the regular Republican party and organized the Liberal Republican party, which nominated Horace Greeley to run against Grant. Schurz's actions split the Republican party in Missouri and allowed the Democrats to capture the legislature, so he was not reelected to the U.S. Senate in 1875. In 1876 he returned to the regular Republican party and supported the presidential reform candidacy of Rutherford B. Hayes. Schurz was rewarded with appointment as secretary of the interior, and he made considerable progress in reform of Indian affairs and introduction of the merit system into the department.

Journalism and Reform

In 1881 Schurz returned to journalism, serving for 2 years as an editor of the *New York Evening Post* and of the *Nation.* For several years thereafter he free-lanced, and from 1892 to 1898 he was chief editorial writer for *Harper's Weekly.* In 1884 he joined the revolt of the "Mugwumps" (reform Republicans) against the party's presidential nominee, James G. Blaine, and supported Grover Cleveland. Schurz was president of the National Civil Service Reform League (1892-1900) and of the Civil Service Reform Association of New York (1893-1906). Opposing the Spanish-American War in 1898, he became a leading anti-imperialist, urging independence for the Philippines rather than American colonialism there. Schurz died in New York City on May 14, 1906. His wife had died some years before; he was survived by three of his five children.

Further Reading

The basic source for Schurz's life is *The Reminiscences of Carl Schurz* (3 vols., 1907-1908). Also of value are Frederic Bancroft, ed., *Speeches, Correspondence and Political Papers of Carl Schurz* (6 vols., 1913), and Joseph Schafer, ed., *Intimate Letters of Carl Schurz, 1841-1869* (1928). There is no biography of Schurz incorporating modern scholarship. The best account is Claude M. Fuess, *Carl Schurz, Reformer* (1932). □

Kurt von Schuschnigg

The Austrian statesman Kurt von Schuschnigg (1897-1977) served as chancellor of Austria from 1934 to 1938. He succeeded in preventing German absorption of Austria until he lost the support of Mussolini in 1937.

Kurt von Schuschnigg was born on December 14, 1897, at Riva on Lake Garda (now a part of Italy). He was the son of an Austrian army officer. Educated in a Jesuit gymnasium at Feldkirch, Schuschnigg served in the Austro-Hungarian army on the Italian front in World War I. He was decorated for bravery and was a prisoner of war during 1918-1919. In 1922 he received a doctorate in law from the University of Innsbruck.

After practicing law in Innsbruck, Schuschnigg became a candidate of the Christian Socialist party for Parliament and, through the backing of the influential Christian Socialist leader Ignaz Seipel, was elected to Parliament in 1927. In 1932 Schuschnigg was named Austrian minister of justice, and in 1933 he assumed the portfolio of the Ministry of Education in addition to his earlier post. After the assassination of the Christian Socialist chancellor Engelbert Dollfuss during the abortive Nazi putsch of July 25, 1934, Schuschnigg became Austrian chancellor, pledged to defend Austria's independence from Nazi Germany.

Schuschnigg's political views were characteristic of Austrian clerical conservatism. He was a zealous Catholic, staunch antileftist, vehement anti-Nazi, and fervent legitimist. He would have preferred to solve Austria's political problems through the restoration of the Hapsburg dynasty. Schuschnigg had no recourse but to follow Dollfuss's reliance on Italian premier Benito Mussolini's protection against Nazi Germany's desire for Anschluss. The imposition by the League of Nations of sanctions against Italy for its aggression against Ethiopia in 1935 drove Italy into the arms of Germany and rendered Mussolini unable further to defend Austrian independence from German encroachment.

On February 12, 1938, Adolf Hitler summoned Schuschnigg to Berchtesgaden, where he demanded that Schuschnigg order the amnesty of jailed Austrian Nazis and that he include Nazis in his Cabinet, particularly Artur Seyss-Inquart. Schuschnigg agreed to Hitler's demands, but on his return to Vienna he restated his vow to preserve Austria's independence. Hitler then ordered the Austrian Nazis to foment disorder throughout the country. When Schuschnigg ordered a plebiscite to ascertain the country's opinion of his determination to maintain Austria's independence, Hitler demanded the plebiscite's delay and he ordered troops to Austria's border on Schuschnigg's refusal. Schuschnigg then resigned, and he was succeeded by Seyss-Inquart, who called German troops into the country in March 1938.

After the German Anschluss, Schuschnigg was imprisoned by the Germans until 1945, when he was liberated by American troops. He then emigrated to the United States and became professor of political science at St. Louis University, Missouri, until 1967 when he returned to Austria and retired. He died in 1977.

Further Reading

There were few sources available in English for a study of Schuschnigg. His own works, such as *Farewell Austria* (1937; trans. 1938) and *Austrian Requiem* (1946), contained valuable information but must be used cautiously. Perhaps the best discussion of Schuschnigg's career as Austrian chancellor was in John A. Lukacs, *The Great Powers and Eastern Europe* (1953). See also Dieter Wagner and Gerhard Tompowitz, *Anschluss: The Week That Hitler Siezed Vienna* trans. 1972). □

Elisabeth Schüssler Fiorenza

Feminist biblical scholar and theologian Elisabeth Schüssler Fiorenza (born 1938) provided models, methods, and metaphors for biblical interpretations and a reconstruction of early Christianity in which women shared the center and were restored to human subjectivity.

One of the foundational maxims of the feminist movement—the personal is political—provided a significant lens through which to view the life of Elisabeth Schüssler Fiorenza. Born in Romania in 1938 and fleeing to what would become West Germany with her family during World War II, she desired, as a young German woman, to become a professional theologian in the Roman Catholic Church, which defined her role and mission as a "lay" woman within the world rather than within the church. Her 1963 licentiate thesis from the University of Würzburg, where she was the first woman to enroll in the theological course required of students for priesthood, was therefore her first public and political articulation of her work toward a redefinition of the Catholic Church so that it included women in their full personhood, able to exercise their gifts and power. This thesis was published in 1964 as her first book, *The Forgotten Partner: Foundations, Facts and Possibilities of the Professional Ministry of Women in the Church.*

As a professional theologian Schüssler Fiorenza's specialty, demonstrated in her doctoral thesis, "Priest for God: A Study of the Motif of the Kingdom and Priesthood in the Apocalypse," for the Catholic Theological Faculty, Wilhelms-Universität, Münster, was biblical studies and the history of early Christianity. Through the publication of significant books, articles, and coedited projects as well as participation in numerous conferences and workshops both in the United States and internationally, she contributed to the feminist redefinition of theological and biblical interpretation both within the academy and the churches. Her academic career took her from Germany to the United States, where she held positions at the University of Notre Dame, Indiana; the Episcopal Divinity School, Cambridge; and as Krister Stendahl Professor of Divinity at the Harvard Divinity School.

A collection of essays, *Discipleship of Equals: A Critical Feminist Ekklesia-logy of Liberation* (1993), provided a brief glimpse of her wide contribution to women in the churches as well as to a theoretical articulation of critical feminist theology of liberation. A reading of the summary that precedes each article highlighted Schüssler Fiorenza's courage within the struggle against patriarchal structures in both church and academy. This characterized her life and her writing, as did the mutual support, encouragement, and shared creative path-finding that came from the community or *ekklesia* of women similarly committed.

The publication of *In Memory of Her: A Feminist Reconstruction of Christian Origins* in English in 1983, and subsequently in a number of other languages, brought Schüssler Fiorenza's feminist framework for biblical interpretation and historical/theological reconstruction to international attention. She provided the first comprehensive articulation of a feminist critical model of historical-theological interpretation. It incorporated a hermeneutics (an interpretation) of suspicion that questioned the way in which women had been represented in the androcentric (male centered) documents of early Christianity. A hermeneutics of remembrance enabled a new reconstruction of the history of early Christianity so that it included the hints, the traces of women's agency within that history. In the following year the collection of essays *Bread Not Stone: The Challenge of Feminist Interpretation* further developed her hermeneutical framework, incorporating a focus on rhetorics and providing a comprehensive model of biblical interpretation.

As a teacher, Schüssler Fiorenza involved her students and workshop participants in the theological interpretive process. In this she not only taught but demonstrated the necessity of what she called "liberative vision and imagination" in order to retell the biblical stories in a variety of media and in a variety of settings so that women's suffering, struggles, agency, and dreams take their place at the center of the retold biblical story. One can experience this creativity in her 1992 book *But She Said: Feminist Practices of Biblical Interpretation.* She opened each chapter with a poem capturing an aspect of women's experience or vision as it shapes the interpretive process of that chapter. Most chapters closed with a creative re-telling or re-contextualizing of the story under consideration written by her students as they explored the gospel stories of women.

The personal and the political intersect in the pathfinding or path-creating dimensions of Schüssler Fiorenza's life and work. She was actively involved in a number of women's organizations that found their voice in the closing decades of the 20th century. With Judith Plaskow she founded and coedited the *Journal of Feminist Studies in Religion,* a forum for feminist inter-religious studies that more traditional journals failed to offer. She was likewise founding co-director of the section of Feminist Theology in *Concilium,* an international theological review within the Roman Catholic tradition. She was the editor of a three-volume work, *Searching the Scriptures,* the first volume of which was published November 1993. It entailed collaborative work with a wide range of authors and resulted in a collection that represented the multidimensional nature of feminist biblical interpretation. Being the first woman scholar to be elected president of the Society of Biblical Literature, she forged another path along which women could walk.

Schüssler Fiorenza's dream to become a professional biblical scholar and theologian would seem to have been realized far beyond even her own creative imagining. She stood within a host of feminist theologians and biblical scholars as co-worker, envisioning and enacting new possibilities for women in the academy, in church, and in society. She was model and mentor for those who followed in her footsteps or who opened up new paths in feminist biblical interpretation and in the redefinition of church and world. For her, however, the theological task would not be complete until all women were free, free from all patriarchal oppression. Her creative work helped shape her own life as well as that of many other women and men in the academies and in the churches.

In *Jesus: Miriam's Child, Sophia's Prophet: Critical Issues in Feminist Christology* (1994), Schüssler Fiorenza deconstructed Christian doctrine to allow new interpretations likely to prove more fruitful for women and all oppressed groups. She saw these doctrines not as truths but as rhetorical strategies that retarded liberation. She viewed her approach as more radically inclusive than Marxism on questions of gender, sexual orientation, and race, and as more positively disposed toward the roles of religion and ideology. While strongly supportive of a diversity of feminist groups with different experiences and voices, she warned against the balkanization of the movement and its fragmentation into racial, religious, sexual orientation, and age-determined special interest groups. Her work was regularly cited for its creativity and forcefulness of analysis. She was, however, criticized by some for being pedantic, jargonistic, and accessible only to a closed circle of theologians and academicians.

She was married to Francis Schüssler Fiorenza, a theologian who shared with his wife a professorship at the Harvard Divinity School. They had a daughter, Kristina.

Further Reading

Elisabeth Schüssler Fiorenza's best known work was *In Memory of Her: A Feminist Reconstruction of Christian Origins* (1983). *Bread Not Stone: The Challenge of Feminist Interpretation* (1984) supplemented this earlier volume and her hermeneutical model. She published numerous articles in both German and English for scholarly journals and for more generally accessible publications. She coedited five volumes of *Concilium* on feminist theology, one volume of *Semeia* on interpretation for liberation, and other collections of essays. *Revelation: Vision of a Just World* (1991) continued her work on the Book of Revelation begun in her doctoral studies. A later book, *But She Said: Feminist Practices of Biblical Interpretation* (1992), supplemented her hermeneutical model with rhetorical reading strategies, while Discipleship of Equals: A Critical Feminist Ekklesia-logy of *Liberation* (1993) provided a "cartography of struggle" of this feminist theologian. As mentioned in the text, she edited *Searching The Scriptures—Volume 1: Feminist Introduction* (1993), and *Volume 2: A Feminist Commentary* (1995). Her *Jesus: Miriam's Child, Sophia's Prophet: Critical Issues in Feminist Christology* (1994), provides social and political contexts for the Christological issues in the light her position as a "biblical scholar working within the discourses of feminist liberation theology." □

Heinrich Schütz

The German composer Heinrich Schütz (1585-1672) is credited with an important role in bringing the Italian baroque style to Germany.

Born in Köstritz, Saxony, to prosperous, middle-class parents, Heinrich Schütz learned the rudiments of music in the chapel choir of Moritz, Landgrave of Hesse-Cassel. In 1608 Schütz entered the University of Marburg to study law, but when the landgrave, who recognized his extraordinary musical gift, offered to support him, Schütz was able to leave for Venice in 1609 to study with Giovanni Gabrieli. Schütz returned in 1613 after his teacher's death.

While in Italy, Schütz published his first collection, *Il primo libro de madrigali* (1611), dedicated to Landgrave Moritz. These 19 chromatic madrigals reveal the close attention Schütz was always to give both the syntax and content of his texts. Even more Italianate are the *Psalmen Davids* (1619), published after the composer became kapellmeister to Johann Georg, Elector of Saxony, in Dresden. In these 26 works, composed for multiple groups of vocal and instrumental soloists, reinforced by two or more choruses, Schütz brought to northern Europe the colorful, polychoral methods of his beloved master, Gabrieli. The music, of overwhelming grandeur, was written for the enhancement of the Protestant liturgy and the edification of the court.

Schütz's *Historia der Auferstehung Jesu Christi* (1623), the Easter Story, was his first oratorio in the Italian style. While the Evangelist performs solos to the accompaniment of four viols, the roles of Jesus and Mary Magdalene are sung as duets over the basso continuo. In his next important work, the *Cantiones sacrae* (1625), Schütz seemed to return to the older polyphonic style. But their chromaticism, "madrigalisms" illustrating the text, and intensely subjective qualities relate these sacred songs more closely to the madrigals of 1611.

To fulfill his task of transforming church music through the southern concerted style, Schütz made a second pilgrimage to Italy in 1628. Now he studied the techniques of Claudio Monteverdi as he observed them in the vocal and instrumental writing of the great Italian. The first fruits of the visit appeared the following year as part 1 of Schütz's *Symphoniae sacrae*. Solo singing with obbligato instruments over the continuo—such was the new style exemplified by the masterpiece of this first collection, *Fili mi, Absalon*.

A short while after Schütz returned to Germany, he found musical activity severely curtailed because of the religious wars raging throughout Saxony. During the 1630s and early 1640s he stayed only intermittently at Dresden, obtaining permission from the elector to work in Copenhagen, Wolfenbüttel, Hanover, and Weimar. Because of limited resources, the master now wrote shorter compositions for one to five parts with continuo. Two such collections were issued in 1636 and 1639 with the title *Kleine Geistliche Konzerte*.

By 1647 conditions at the Saxon court had improved somewhat, and Schütz released part 2 of his *Symphoniae sacrae*. Unlike part 1, which had Latin settings for voices and various obbligato instruments, part 2 was set to German words and used only the strings and continuo. In part 3 of the *Symphoniae sacrae* (1650) Schütz joined the polychoral writing of his early *Psalmen Davids* with the soloistic style he learned from Monteverdi. The masterpiece *Saul, Saul, was verfolgst du mich?* is scored for a six-voice ensemble, two four-voice choruses, and two obbligato instrumental parts. In few of his later pieces did he go beyond the resources of these compositions, which are truly cantatas.

Although Schütz was the foremost German protagonist of the new baroque style, he did not foresee that his apparent deemphasis of counterpoint would persuade younger compatriots to abandon it. By 1648 this danger had become so manifest that Schütz was persuaded to publish his *Geistliche Chormusik,* a collection of 29 motets in the older style, to show young composers "before they proceed to concertizing music to crack this hard nut (wherein the true kernel and the right foundation of good counterpoint is to be sought) and to pass their first tests in this category." Schütz obviously viewed his artistic mission as a union of counterpoint and *stile recitativo, a cappella* and *concertato,* rather than as a rejection of the older Flemish style.

In 1665 Schütz completed three Passions according to Luke, John, and Matthew. What first impresses us in these works is their external austerity. Gone are the instrumentally accompanied recitative of the Easter Story and the polychoral writing with instruments in part 3 of the *Symphoniae sacrae.* Here the Bible narrative is sung *a cappella* with solo portions chanted in a "Germanized" plainsong.

Even though these works seem archaic, it would be incorrect to believe that Schütz rejected his entire mission of a concerted, soloistic church music. Only a year or two before, he had composed the *Historia der Freuden-und Gnaden-reichen Geburt Gottes und Marien Sohnes Jesu Christi,* the Christmas Story, in the richly concerted style he had espoused for over 50 years. In the Passions he abandoned the luxuriant apparatus for pure chant and polyphony, in part as an object lesson to younger composers and in part to demonstrate that his own era could still use the *a cappella* style of the past.

Schütz passed the last of his 55 years of service to the elector of Saxony in Weissenfels and in Dresden, where he died. Through his efforts German church music took on features we easily recognize as baroque. In the way he put polyphony on an equal footing with the new concerted style, Schütz resembles Monteverdi, who also brought the past into the present and subjected it to a new esthetic.

Further Reading

Hans J. Moser, *Heinrich Schütz: His Life and Work* (1936; trans. 1959), is the most complete study of the master. The music of Schütz in relation to his contemporaries is treated in Manfred E. Bukofzer, *Music in the Baroque Era: From Monteverdi to Bach* (1947), and in Claude V. Palisca, *Baroque Music* (1968).

Additional Sources

Geier, Martin, *Music in the service of the church: the funeral sermon for Heinrich Schütz (1585-1672),* St. Louis, MO: Concordia Pub. House, 1984.

Horton, John, *Schütz: October 1585-6 November 1672,* London: Novello, 1986. □

Philip John Schuyler

The American Revolutionary War general Philip John Schuyler (1733-1804) was a leader in the political and commercial life of his state and nation.

Philip Schuyler was born in Albany, N. Y., on Nov. 11, 1733, into an old, aristocratic Dutch family, one of the colony's largest landholders. He received an excellent education. After commanding a company of New York militia in the French and Indian War, he managed the large estate left him by his father in the Mohawk and Hudson River valleys.

At the same time, Schuyler was active in supporting the colonial cause in the controversy with Great Britain. He argued the colonial position in the provincial Assembly in 1768 and went to the Second Continental Congress in May 1775 as delegate from New York. There he served with George Washington on a committee to make rules and regulations for the army. In June 1775, shortly after the Revolution began, Congress appointed him a major general, one of four to serve under Washington.

Schuyler's assignment was to command the Northern Department (consisting of New York) and to prepare an attack on Canada. After raising and supplying an army and strengthening Ticonderoga and Crown Point on the route north, he was forced by ill health to turn over command of the troops to Gen. Richard Montgomery. The attack failed, and Schuyler was given much of the blame. He had, actually, delayed too long in ordering the army to get under way and had been too slow and deliberate in executing his plan, but the true cause of the defeat lay in factors beyond his control. He also made some bad decisions during the course of the campaign of British general John Burgoyne in northern New York in 1777; one of these contributed to the loss of Ft. Ticonderoga, an American stronghold. Ac-

cusations of incompetence were leveled against him, along with a rumor of intrigue with the enemy. In 1778 Schuyler demanded a court-martial to air the charges. He was acquitted that October but felt it best to resign his commission.

After leaving the army, Schuyler was active in politics, holding office continually until 1798, when illness forced his permanent retirement. He served as state senator for 13 years and for 3 years as U.S. senator from New York under the new Federal Constitution, in whose creation he had played a leading role with his son-in-law, Alexander Hamilton. Schuyler died in Albany on Nov. 18, 1804.

Further Reading

The best biography of Schuyler is Benson J. Lossing, *The Life and Times of Philip Schuyler* (2 vols., 1872-1873). Bayard Tuckerman, *Life of General Philip Schuyler* (1903), is good for Schuyler's military phase. For special aspects of Schuyler's life see George W. Schuyler, *Colonial New York: Philip Schuyler and His Family* (2 vols., 1885), and Don R. Gerlach, *Philip Schuyler and the American Revolution in New York, 1733-1777* (1964).

Additional Sources

Taormina, Francis R., *Philip Schuyler: who he was, what he did,* Schenectady, N.Y.: F.R. Taormina, 1992. □

Charles Michael Schwab

Charles Michael Schwab (1862-1939), American industrialist, became a multimillionaire in the steel industry but died bankrupt.

Charles M. Schwab was born on Feb. 18, 1862, in Williamsburg, Pa. He graduated from high school in 1880 and 2 years later joined the steel enterprise of Andrew Carnegie as an unskilled manual laborer. In 6 months he was an assistant manager. He was appointed superintendent of Carnegie's Homestead Works in 1887. No wonder Carnegie declared about Schwab, "I have never met his equal."

The steel industry at the turn of the 20th century was in the throes of a competitive struggle in which Carnegie was the ruthless competitor and other firms attempted to achieve stability. Schwab served as the intermediary between Carnegie and banker J. P. Morgan, and the sale of Carnegie's company became the main step in organizing the U.S. Steel Corporation in 1901. Morgan chose Schwab as president of the new giant corporation. In 1903 Schwab left because of internal disagreements with his associates.

Schwab acquired control of the Bethlehem Steel Company in 1901. When the concern was merged into the United States Shipbuilding Company, Schwab's stock was exchanged for bonds. When this company failed owing to an improper financial policy, Schwab as the prime creditor became the owner. Bethlehem Steel Corporation, organized in 1904, was his own creation, and he made it a major steel producer and a worthy competitor of U.S. Steel. During World War I Bethlehem Steel became an important producer of materiel for the Allied war effort. He also spurred the American shipbuilding program to new heights after he was appointed director of the Emergency Fleet Corporation in April 1918.

After the war Schwab entered into semiretirement. He continued as the chairman of the board of directors of Bethlehem Steel until his death but delegated the responsibility to the president. During the 1930s Bethlehem was accused of having earned extortionate profits during the war, but the courts upheld the company's actions. Schwab died in London, England, on Sept. 18, 1939.

Further Reading

There is no biography of Schwab. Information on various phases of his career must be pieced together from works which have another emphasis: James H. Bridge, *The Inside History of the Carnegie Steel Company* (1903); Ida M. Tarbell, *The Life of Elbert H. Gary* (1925); Arundel Cotter, *The Story of Bethlehem Steel* (1916) and *United States Steel: A Corporation with a Soul* (1921); Burton J. Hendrick, *The Life of Andrew Carnegie* (2 vols., 1932; new introduction, 1969); Stewart H. Holbrook, *Age of the Moguls* (1953); Joseph Frazier Wall, *Andrew Carnegie* (1970); and Louis M. Hacker, *The World of Andrew Carnegie* (1968). Both Arthur S. Dewing, *Corporate Promotion and Reorganizations* (1914), and Henry R. Seager and Charles A. Gulick, Jr., *Trust and Corporation* (1929), contain a chapter on the U.S. Shipbuilding Company.

Additional Sources

Hessen, Robert, *Steel titan: the life of Charles M. Schwab,* Pittsburgh, Pa.: University of Pittsburgh Press, 1990. □

Theodor Schwann

The German biologist Theodor Schwann (1810-1882) is considered a founder of the cell theory. He also discovered pepsin, the first digestive enzyme prepared from animal tissue, and experimented to disprove spontaneous generation.

Theodor Schwann was born at Neuss near Düsseldorf on Dec. 7, 1810. At the University of Bonn, which he entered in 1829, he met Johannes Müller, the physiologist, whom he assisted in his experiments. Schwann continued his medical studies at the University of Würzburg and later at the University of Berlin, from which he graduated in 1834. His doctoral dissertation dealt with the respiration of the chick embryo.

Contributions to Physiology and Anatomy

At the University of Berlin, Schwann again came into contact with Müller, who convinced him that he should follow a scientific career. Very soon after he began to work under Müller, he had his first success. From extracts which he made of stomach lining, Schwann demonstrated that a factor other than hydrochloric acid was operating in digestion. Two years later, in 1836, he succeeded in isolating the active principle, which he named pepsin.

Between 1834 and 1838 Schwann undertook a series of experiments designed to settle the question of the truth or falsity of the concept of spontaneous generation. His method was to expose sterilized (boiled) broth only to heated air in a glass tube, the result being that no microorganisms were detectable and no chemical change (putrefaction) occurred in the broth. He was convinced that the idea of spontaneous generation was false. His sugar fermentation studies of 1836 also led to his discovery that yeast originated the chemical process of fermentation.

At Müller's suggestion, Schwann also began research on muscle contraction and discovered striated muscles in the upper portion of the esophagus. He also identified the delicate sheath of cells surrounding peripheral nerve fibers, which is now named the sheath of Schwann.

Cell Theory

In 1838 Schwann became familiar with Matthias Schleiden's microscopic research on plants. Schleiden described plant cells and proposed a cell theory which he was certain was the key to plant anatomy and growth. Pursuing this line of research on animal tissues, Schwann not only verified the existence of cells, but he traced the development of many adult tissues from early embryo stages. This research and the cell theory which followed were summarized in *Mikroskopische Untersuchungen ueber die Uebereinstimmung in der Struktur und dem Wachstum der Thiere und Pflanzen* (1839; *Microscopical Researches on the Similarity in the Structure and the Growth of Animals and Plants,* 1847). This work, which in Schwann's own words demonstrated that "the great barrier between the animal and vegetable kingdoms, viz. the diversity of ultimate structure, thus vanishes," established the cell theory to the satisfaction of his contemporaries.

Schwann proposed three generalizations concerning the nature of cells: First, animals and plants consist of cells plus the secretions of cells. Second, these cells have independent lives, which, third, are subject to the organism's life. Furthermore, he realized that the phenomena of individual cells can be placed into two classes: "those which relate to the combination of the molecules to form a cell. These may be called plastic phenomena," and "those which result from chemical changes either in the component particles of the cell itself, or in the surrounding cytoblastema [the modern cytoplasm]. These may be called metabolic phenomena." Thus Schwann coined the term "metabolism," which became generally adopted for the sum total of chemical processes by which energy changes occur in living things.

Contributions to Histology

Schwann also contributed to the understanding and classification of adult animal tissues. He classified tissues into five groups: separate independent cells, such as blood; compacted independent cells, such as skin; cells whose walls have coalesced, such as cartilage, bones, and teeth; elongated cells which have formed fibers, such as tendons and ligaments; and finally, cells formed by the fusion of walls and cavities, such as muscles and tendons. His conclusions were also basic to the modern concept of embryology, for he described embryonic development as a succession of cell divisions.

This generalization of the essential structural kinship of all living things had been denied for centuries by the old Aristotelian doctrine of vegetable and animal souls. Perhaps Schwann's findings were more disturbing than he liked to admit, since he realized that they supported an ultimate physical rather than a theological explanation. Schwann saw the implications of his discovery, and the idea of the world of life being nothing more than a machine appalled him. He found refuge in the Roman Catholic faith, choosing, as he said, a God "more sensitive to the heart than to reason."

In 1839 Schwann was appointed professor of anatomy at the University of Louvain, Belgium, where he remained until 1848, when he accepted a professorship at the University of Liège. He remained there until his retirement in 1880. After leaving the influence of Müller, Schwann's productivity practically ceased; in Belgium he published only one paper, on the use of bile. He was an excellent, conscientious teacher, loved and appreciated by his students.

Schwann's work was ultimately recognized by scientists in other countries, and in 1879 he was made a member of the Royal Society and also of the French Academy of Science. In 1845 he had received the Copley Medal. Death came to Schwann on Jan. 11, 1882, 2 years after his retirement, in Cologne.

Further Reading

Excerpts in English translation from *Mikroskopische Untersuchungen* are found in the following works: Forest Ray Moulton and Justus J. Schifferes, eds., *The Autobiography of Science* (1945; rev. ed. 1960); Augusto Pi Suñer, *Classics of Biology* (1955); Friedrich S. Bodenheimer, *The History of Biology: An Introduction* (1958); and George Schwartz and Philip W. Bishop, eds., *Moments of Discovery* (2 vols., 1958). There is no biography of Schwann. Gilbert Causey in *The Cell of Schwann* (1960) devotes the first chapter to a sparse recital of the essential details of Schwann's life. Erik Nordenskiöld, *The History of Biology* (1928; new ed. 1935), gives a brief biographic account, as does Gordon R. Taylor, *The Science of Life* (1963). A good treatment of the cell theory and Schwann's part in it is in William A. Locy, *Biology and Its Makers* (1908; rev. ed. 1915). □

Norman Schwarzkopf

General Norman Schwarzkopf (born 1934) earned the moniker Stormin' Norman during the Persian Gulf War, when he became famous for planning a strategic military strike that almost immediately crippled Iraqi forces.

"As a commander you have to walk that difficult balance between accomplishing your mission and taking care of the men and women whose lives have been entrusted to you," *People* magazine quoted General Norman Schwarzkopf as saying. The four-star army general who led allied forces to victory in the Persian Gulf became the first bona fide U.S. military hero since the era of General and President Dwight D. Eisenhower." I don't consider myself dovish and I certainly don't consider myself hawkish," General Schwarzkopf told Eric Schmitt of the *New York Times.* "Maybe I would describe myself as owlish—that is, wise enough to understand that you want to do everything possible to avoid war then be ferocious enough to do whatever is necessary to get it over with as quickly as possible in victory." At 6'3" and 240 pounds, the general is a grizzly bear of a man with a teddy bear side, a rare blend, as *People* magazine put it, of "martial mastery and human sensitivity."

Commanded Over 500,000 Troops

As he commanded an allied force of over 500,000 troops in a quick mop-up of Iraqi forces, the commander emerged as a TV-ready hero perfect for the nightly news—a smooth composite of traditional and contemporary concepts of masculinity and leadership. "Norman Schwarzkopf is America's hero," trumpeted *20/20,* ABC-TV's news magazine show. Described in appearance as a "fatherly meatpacker" by *Newsweek,* a "230 pound pussy cat" by one supermarket tabloid, and "Stormin' Norman" by innumerable headline writers, the General seemed to spend

most of his time in the aftermath of the Persian Gulf war explaining himself to America. "I've been scared in every war I've ever been in," he told Barbara Walters, who interviewed him on *20/20.* "Any man who doesn't cry scares me a little." A second-generation general, he told *Insight* magazine's Richard Mackenzie that his first priority in the war was protecting the well-being of his troops: "I have loved soldiers since my first platoon, the first I ever commanded."

Although Iraqi resistance crumbled faster than expected, the general did not claim tactical genius in orchestrating the victory. Although he was able to keep the enemy in the dark about allied troop position, he attributed victory largely to the poor quality of Iraqi military leadership, training, and morale. The enemy's forces, he said to *Newsweek*'s Tom Mathers, simply were inadequate. "This was a lousy outfit. Lousy." His famous one-word answer when asked his opinion of Iraqi dictator Saddam Hussein? "Hah."

After the war ended Schwarzkopf had a more elaborate description. Ticking off Saddam's deficiencies on the fingers of one hand, the general declared the Iraqi commander was "neither a strategist, nor is he schooled in the operational art, nor is he a tactician, nor is he a general, nor is he a soldier." Having run out of fingers, he added sarcastically, "Other than that he is a great military man." Schwarzkopf also blamed Saddam's penchant for shooting his own soldiers. "I gotta tell you," he remarked to *Newsweek,* "a soldier doesn't fight very hard for a leader who is going to shoot him on a whim."

In the years following the war, other issues arose for Schwarzkoph, namely evasive illnesses suffered by many Persian Gulf War veterans from the U.S. The medical problems suffered by U.S. forces are believed to be caused by biological and chemical weapons. Some officials claim that the disorders could have been caused by a chemical warfare antidote administered to soldiers by the U.S. military without approval. On January 29, 1997, Schwarzkopf told senators he knew nothing of the war's most notorious nerve gas release or that an antidote given to half a million soldiers lacked government approval. Government investigations, including examinations of Schwarzkoph's war log, have not uncovered an answer and medical disorders associated with the Persian Gulf remain a mystery.

Earlier in the war, especially at moments when the United States' victory seemed less than certain, the general displayed the four-star temper he tried to keep under wraps. Reporters who wrote stories he thought were less than favorable suddenly found their access to sources had dried up as fast as rainfall in the desert sand. One reporter who questioned Schwarzkopf's battlefield tactics got his answer fired back in the form of a question; "You ever been in a minefield?" Despite his thin skin for bad press, and little taste for what he saw as an argumentative and ill-informed media disdainful of security issues, he displayed a sure touch when he did see a use for the media. Dramatically dropping to his knees when he arrived to liberate Kuwait and bottling Kuwaiti sand to take home to his family, Schwarzkopf set a new definition of photo opportunity. On network primetime TV he told Barbara Walters he would not rule out running for President: "Never say never."

Grew up an Army Brat

Born in Trenton, New Jersey, in 1934, the future war hero grew up an army brat, the only son of World War I general Herbert Norman Schwarzkopf (his father decided against passing on the name Herbert). The elder Schwarzkopf was between army stints when his son was born, serving as the founding commander of the New Jersey state police. In this capacity he had tracked down and arrested Bruno Richard Hauptmann, convicted of murder in the celebrated Charles Lindbergh baby kidnapping case, and the notoriety had brought him a weekly spot as narrator of a popular radio program, *Gangbusters.* One of his son's earliest memories is staying up late to listen to the broadcasts.

When world war broke out again, his father rejoined the Army. The remaining Schwarzkopf household was predominantly female, a fact the future general recalls as bearing no small impact on his developing personality. "I wasn't your normal, tough, macho young boy," he told *Insight.* "Maybe it was the influence of my mother and my sisters, the fact that I had this responsibility on my shoulders. I can remember being pushed around a lot. I can't really say why. I learned to hate the bully. I learned to hate the playground group that went around pushing other people around. I never ran with that bunch as a young boy." Later on he boarded at the Bordentown Military Institute near his hometown.

After the war ended his father was shipped out to Iran to establish a police force for the Shah, a strong ally. Young Norman went over to join his father in Teheran, and stayed several months before the rest of the family came over. He recalls being impressed by the admiration his father received from his subordinates. He himself admired his father as a war hero, much like General Eisenhower. "My father was a very honorable man," he told *Insight.* "He epitomized the best [West] Point graduate of his day that's totally committed to a sense of duty, totally committed to a sense of honor, totally dedicated to his country, and a selfless servant."

He did have another role model: Alexander the Great. He told Charlayne Hunter-Gault of public television's *MacNeil/Lehrer NewsHour,* "When I was a young man, everything was shades of black and white, and Alexander the Great was one of my heroes, because he conquered all the known world by the time he was twenty-eight." (His more enduring role models are two later generals, Ulysses S. Grant and Creighton Abrams, the latter his Vietnam commander, "because they didn't worry about who got the credit. They just got the job done.")

Schwarzkopf followed his father on other assignments. The military was helping to rebuild Europe under the Marshall Plan, and the general was shuttled from country to country for the next five years; first Italy, then Germany, then Switzerland. His classmates included Iranians, displaced Jews, Germans, Italians, Yugoslavians, and various other ethnic groups and nationalities. The experience permanently broadened his mind, he recalled years later to *Insight.* "I came to understand that you judge a person as an individual. I also learned that the American way is great, but it's not the only way. There are a lot of other ways things are done that are just as good, and some of them are better."

Began Military Career

He eventually returned to the United States and entered West Point, as his father had done before him. He graduated 42nd out of 485 in the class of l956. Upon graduation he joined the army as a second lieutenant in the infantry, attending the Infantry Officer Basic course and Airborne School at the Army's Infantry School at Fort Benning, Georgia. In March l957 he was sent to Fort Campbell, Kentucky, where he served as a platoon leader and later as an executive officer in the 2nd Airborne Battle Group, the 187th. That assignment lasted about two years.

In July 1959 Schwarzkopf was sent to Germany for a year to serve as a platoon leader in the 6th Infantry. The following year he was named aide-de-camp to the commanding general of the Berlin Command. In September 1961 he shipped back to Fort Benning to continue advanced infantry officer training, then enrolled at the University of Southern California in Los Angeles and pursued a master's program in guided missile engineering, graduating in June 1964. He returned to West Point and taught in the department of Mechanics for a year.

Then came the Vietnam War. In June 1965 he was sent over with an airborne brigade and served his 300 days' duty in what the army calls an "advisory capacity." He returned to a staff job in Washington, then returned to West Point to resume teaching there. He was back in the classroom as a student the next year, this time at General Staff College at Fort Leavenworth, Kansas. He returned to army headquarters for another staff job supporting efforts in Vietnam, then in December 1969 shipped over there for a second tour of duty as commander of the 1st Battalion, 6th Infantry, 198th Infantry Brigade of the 23rd Infantry Division. During this stint he was awarded two Purple Hearts and three Silver Stars.

Reputation Tarnished by Casualties

His reputation, however, was tarnished by casualties, including eight deaths, that occurred as a result of "friendly fire" from U.S. artillery. The callous way the army handled the incidents gave rise to a public sense that the army had lost control over the situation. Form letters that went out under the name of Lt. Colonel Schwarzkopf implicated him in the debacle. The incidents were recounted in the book *Friendly Fire,* published in 1976, and fictionalized by Hollywood in a feature film that appeared soon thereafter.

Schwarzkopf returned home from Vietnam livid over the way Washington had handled its part of the entire war effort. The war, he felt, had been lost by the politicians on the battlegrounds of the media. He told *Insight'* s Richard Mackenzie, "The United States military did not lose the war in Vietnam period. In the two years I was in Vietnam I was in many battles. I was never in a defeat—came pretty close a couple of times, but we were never defeated. The outcome of the Vietnam War was a political defeat, but it was not a military defeat."

Back in Washington, the soldier alternated administrative work and advanced military and technical training for several years. In October 1974 the lieutenant colonel was made deputy commander of the 172nd Infantry Brigade in Fort Richardson, Alaska, was appointed a full colonel in 1975, and made commander of the First Brigade, 9th Infantry Division, in Fort Lewis, Washington. He retained that post nearly two years.

Became General

In July 1978 he was sent to Hawaii to serve two years at the Pacific Command post at Camp H. M. Smith; when he returned to Washington he was made a general. In August 1980 he shipped out to Europe for two years, as assistant division commander of the 8th Infantry Division. Back in Washington he handled administrative work for a year, then was assigned to Fort Stewart, Georgia, as deputy commanding general of the 24th Infantry Division. From this post he served as deputy commander of the U.S. invasion of Grenada.

Schwarzkopf's high-visibility performance in Grenada did not escape attention from the Pentagon. After another year of staff work he was assigned to I Corps at Fort Lewis, as commanding general. Then, in August 1987, he returned to the capitol as senior army member of the Military Staff Committee of the United Nations. In November 1988 he was appointed full general and moved to the top of the U.S. Central Command. In this capacity he began planning U.S. military strategies in the event of a Persian Gulf showdown.

Much of the general's popularity rests on his family-man image. The general is married to the former Brenda Holsinger, whom he met at a West Point football game in 1967, when she was a 26-year-old TWA flight attendant. The couple married in 1968; they have three children plus a sizable household menagerie: a black Labrador retriever, a cat, a gerbil, and two parakeets. According to an account in *People,* the General's hobbies include hunting and fishing; dining on a thick cut of steak, rare, followed by Breyer's mint-chocolate chip ice cream. He likes to watch TV, tuning in *Jeopardy!* and *Cheers* as well as Clint Eastwood westerns and Charles Bronson flicks. To this list, he says, you can add opera. (During his senior year at West Point he conducted the academy choir.) The difference between conducting music and troops, he quipped to a *People* reporter, is that in war "the orchestra starts playing, and some son of a bitch climbs out of the orchestra pit with a bayonet and starts chasing you around the stage."

Further Reading

Insight, March 18, 1991.
New York Times, January 28, 1991.
People, March 11, 1991.
USA Today, January 30, 1997. □

Albert Schweitzer

Albert Schweitzer (1875-1965) was an Alsatian-German religious philosopher, musicologist, and medical missionary in Africa. He was known especially for founding the Schweitzer Hospital, which provided unprecedented medical care for the natives of Lambaréné in Gabon.

Albert Schweitzer, the son of an Evangelical Lutheran minister, was born on Jan. 14, 1875, in Kaysersberg, Alsace, which was then under German rule. Albert's early life was both comfortable and happy. One Sunday morning, when he was about 8, he had an experience that helped to shape his life. At the strong urging of another lad, he reluctantly aimed his slingshot at several birds which, as he later wrote, "sang sweetly into the morning sunshine." Moved, he "made a silent vow to miss. At that moment, the sound of church bells began to mingle with the sunshine and the singing of the birds. . . . For me, it was a voice from heaven. I threw aside my slingshot, shooed the birds away to protect them from my friend's slingshot, and fled home."

When Albert was 10 years old, he went to live with his granduncle and grandaunt in Mulhouse so that he could attend the excellent local school. He graduated from secondary school at the age of 18. During these 8 years he learned directly from his elderly relatives the demanding ethical code and rigorous scholarly outlook of their early-1800s generation.

In 1893 Schweitzer enrolled at the University of Strasbourg, where, until 1913, he enjoyed a brilliant career as student, teacher, and administrator. His main field was theology and philosophy, and in 1899 he won a doctorate in philosophy with a thesis on Immanuel Kant.

Schweitzer also made a profound study of Nietzsche and Tolstoy, recoiling from Nietzsche's adulation of the all-conquering "superman" and being greatly attracted to Tolstoy's doctrine of love and compassion. The definitive influence, however, on Schweitzer was the life of Jesus, to whose message and messiahship he devoted years of research and reflection. His classic work *The Quest of the Historical Jesus* (1906) deals with major scholarly writings on Jesus from the 17th century onward; the volume was well received and quickly became a standard source book.

Renunciation and Dedication

Meanwhile, Schweitzer's biography of J. S. Bach, written in 1905, had also proved an immediate success. At 30 years of age Schweitzer was tall, broad-shouldered, darkly handsome, and a witty, charismatic writer, preacher, and lecturer: clearly, a bright future lay before him. However, one spring morning in 1905, he experienced a stunning religious revelation: it came to him that at some point in the years just ahead he must renounce facile success and devote himself unsparingly to the betterment of mankind's condition.

Accordingly, several years later, Schweitzer threw over his several careers as author, lecturer, and organ recitalist and plunged into the study of medicine—his aim being to go to Africa as a medical missionary. He won his medical degree in 1912. The year before, he had married Helene Bresslau, a professor's daughter who had studied nursing in order to work at his side in Africa; in 1919 the couple had a daughter, Rhena.

Establishment in Africa

In 1913 the Schweitzers journeyed to what was then French Equatorial Africa. There, after various setbacks, they founded the Albert Schweitzer Hospital at Lambaréné, on the Ogooué River, "at the edge of the primeval forest." This area now lies within the independent West African republic of Gabon. Funds were scarce and equipment primitive, but native Africans thronged to the site, and in the decades that followed, many thousands were treated.

Reverence for Life

One hot afternoon in 1915, as he sat on the deck of an ancient steamboat chugging its way up the Ogooué, Schweitzer noticed on a sandbank nearby four hippopotamuses with their young. Instantly, "the phrase Reverence for Life struck me like a flash." He had anticipated this phrase more than 3 decades earlier in his refusal to shoot his slingshot at the sweetly singing birds; now, it became the coping stone of his philosophical system and of his everyday life at the hospital.

Somewhat to Schweitzer's chagrin, the news of his lonely, heroic witness at Lambaréné spread abroad, and he became a world-famous exemplary figure. An American named Larimer Mellon, a member of the wealthy Mellon family, was one of the many whose lives were affected by Schweitzer. Inspired by Schweitzer's example, Mellon, then in his late 30s, returned to college, obtained his medical degree, and with his wife, Gwen, set up the Albert Schweitzer Hospital deep in a primitive rural area of Haiti. Many hundreds of lives were similarly changed by Schweitzer's charismatic witness.

Despite his demanding schedule at Lambaréné, Schweitzer found time to lecture in the United States in 1949, received the Nobel Peace Prize in 1952, and published in 1957 and 1958 notable appeals to the superpowers in the name of humanity, urging them to renounce nuclear-weapons testing. He died at Lambaréné on Sept. 4, 1965; at the time, he was still working vigorously on the third volume of his monumental *Philosophy of Civilization.* On his death his medical associates and his daughter, Mrs. Rhena Eckert-Schweitzer, took over direction of the hospital with the aim of carrying out Schweitzer's wish that its facilities be drastically modernized.

Further Reading

The best introduction to Schweitzer's thought and personality is through his own engagingly written autobiographical works: *At the Edge of the Primeval Forest* (1922), *Memoirs of Childhood and Youth* (1925), and *Out of My Life and Thought* (1933). One of the best studies of Schweitzer is George Seaver, *Albert Schweitzer: The Man and His Mind* (1947). Also valuable are Norman Cousins, *Dr. Schweitzer of Lambaréné* (1960), and Henry Clark, *The Philosophy of Albert Schweitzer* (1964).

Lively personal and pictorial introductions to Schweitzer are Erica Anderson, *Albert Schweitzer's Gift of Friendship* (1964) and *The Schweitzer Album: A Portrait in Words and Pictures* (1965). Two general, readable studies of Schweitzer are Dr. Joseph F. Montague, *The Why of Albert Schweitzer* (1965), which includes a bibliography of Schweitzer's writings, and Magnus Ratter, *Schweitzer—Ninety Years Wise* (1964). Also consult Hermann Hagedorn, *The Prophet in the Wilderness* (1947; rev. ed. 1962); Erica Anderson, *The World of Albert Schweitzer* (1955); Robert Payne, *The Three Worlds of Albert Schweitzer* (1957); and Werner Picht, *The Life and Thought of Albert Schweitzer* (trans. 1964). □

Kasper von Schwenckfeld

The Silesian nobleman and theologian Kaspar von Schwenckfeld (1489/1490-1561) formulated doctrines concerning the nature of Christ and the Eucharist that caused him to break with Luther and spend much of his life in exile as a religious outlaw.

Kaspar von Schwenckfeld was born in the town of Ossig in Silesia. After university training he became sympathetic to the principles of the early Lutheran Reformation, and his influence at the court of the Duke of Liegnitz was instrumental in bringing the Reformation to Silesia. Schwenckfeld, however, did not agree with Martin Luther on all points, and he disagreed particularly on the questions of "real presence" (that is, whether or not Christ is present in the Eucharist) and on the nature of Christ.

In 1525 Schwenckfeld went to Wittenberg to discuss his differences with Luther, but the two failed to agree. Another opponent of Luther, Ulrich Zwingli, then published a treatise by Schwenckfeld, and the ensuing difficulties in Silesia forced Schwenckfeld to leave his home in 1529, the first of many such journeys. From 1529 to 1533 Schwenckfeld lived in Strasbourg, the home of many Reformation exiles. In 1533, however, Schwenckfeld's doctrines came under heavy criticism from Martin Bucer, and their condemnation at the Synod of Strasbourg in 1533 caused Schwenckfeld to leave that city. From 1533 to 1538 Schwenckfeld lived in Ulm, but eventually another controversy arose over his Christological doctrines, and he left Ulm in 1538. Schwenckfeld's doctrines were again formally condemned at Schmalkalden in 1540.

At this time Schwenckfeld wrote his most important treatises on theology: *Vom Fleische Christi* (1540; *On the Body of Christ*) and *Grosse Confession* (1541; *The Great Confession*). From 1540 until his death, Schwenckfeld produced many letters and treatises, so many that Philip Melancthon referred to Schwenckfeld as a "hundred-

hander''—a man who wrote so much that he must have had a hundred hands. Schwenckfeld's chief influence lay in his Christological doctrines. He was particularly concerned with the process of human salvation and saw this process as an indwelling of Christ in the saved man. Besides this concern, however, there lay also his opposition to religious persecution and his persistent defense of freedom of conscience and religious liberty.

Schwenckfeld's place in the Reformation has long been obscured because of the many condemnations heaped upon him and his followers in their own time both by Protestants and by Catholics. Schwenckfeld's harried later years drew more opposition down upon him, and when he died, he was buried under the house of friends in Ulm so that his body could not be exhumed and burned as that of a heretic. After his death his followers published his works and lived in Silesia until the arrival of the Jesuits in 1719. They then emigrated to Saxony, to England, and finally to North America, where they settled in eastern Pennsylvania in 1734.

Further Reading

The best biography of Schwenckfeld in English is Selina Gerhard Schultz, *Caspar Schwenckfeld von Ossig* (1946). Schwenckfeld's place in the Reformation is examined in George H. Williams, *The Radical Reformation* (1962). His theology is discussed in the good study by Paul L. Maier, *Caspar Schwenckfeld on the Person and Work of Christ* (1959), which also contains further bibliographical references to Schwenckfeld's life and thought.

Additional Sources

McLaughlin, R. Emmet, *Caspar Schwenckfeld, reluctant radical: his life to 1540,* New Haven: Yale University Press, 1986.

McLaughlin, R. Emmet, *The freedom of spirit, social privilege, and religious dissent: Caspar Schwenckfeld and the Schwenckfelders,* Baden-Baden: V. Koerner, 1996. □

Rosika Schwimmer

Rosika Schwimmer (1877–1948) was a Hungarian feminist and international peace activist during the First World War.

A spirited speechmaker and polemicist, Rosika Schwimmer was one of the first international feminists. First in her native Hungary, then throughout Europe, Britain, and the United States, she argued for women's rights and the dignity of working women. The outbreak of World War I diverted her energy into the cause of peace, but two years of intense work yielded few results. The war dragged on, her health and her spirit broke, and she lived a long, disappointing later life as an exile in America.

Born to a wealthy Jewish family in Budapest, Schwimmer was the daughter of an agricultural scientist. But when her father's efforts to develop grain hybrids were unsuccessful, the family fell on hard times. To help support them she went to work as a bookkeeper at the age of 18, and after two years, in 1897, volunteered to work with a trade union, the National Association of Women Office Workers. Before long she was its crusading president. In 1903, she founded the Hungarian Association of Working Women, then traveled to Germany as its delegate in the following year to attend the first meeting of the International Woman Suffrage Alliance (IWSA). Forming yet another association for Hungarian feminists on her return, this time helped by Budapest friend and teacher, Vilma Glucklich, Schwimmer inaugurated a campaign for women's votes which ultimately gained its objective in 1920 at the end of the First World War.

These early experiences led her to favor expanded job opportunities for women, dress reform, and improved legal rights. She shared with her American contemporary Charlotte Perkins Gilman the conviction that housework should be done by efficient women's collectives rather than separately in every household, freeing women for more interesting and rewarding pursuits. She translated into Hungarian Gilman's book *Women and Economics* in which these ideas were advanced and justified. In 1908 and then again in 1912 and 1913, she toured Eastern Europe with the American women's rights champion Carrie Chapman Catt, the two of them making brilliant speeches in support of women's suffrage and law reform. All who met Schwimmer were impressed by her dynamism and energy. Historian Caroline Moorehead writes:

> She was eloquent, tough, and indefatigable, producing opinions and pamphlets on everything from state

> child care to home economics and marriage in both Hungarian and German, writing short stories and a novel and delivering innumerable lectures. She wore brightly colored, loose fitting dresses and no corset, as was only proper for a follower of the dress-reform movement, and a pince nez. . . . [S]he referred to herself as a "very, very radical feminist."

The climax of Schwimmer's early work for women's rights came in 1913 when she hosted the IWSA annual conference in Budapest, with its record number of 3,000 participants. At the end of the conference, Catt, who was then president of IWSA, wrote her a warm letter of thanks, adding a memento of their first meeting:

> When I remember the young girl who could understand no English and who knew so little about the movement for the enfranchisement of women only nine years ago, and then see the wonders of your own development and growth, and the great work you have accomplished in Hungary, I am filled with amazement, gratitude, and pride.

In 1914, the year the First World War began, Schwimmer was at work in London as the press secretary to the IWSA and as a well-paid journalist for several European newspapers. This was a crucial moment in the history of the British women's suffrage campaign. Many prominent suffragists, led by Emmeline and Christabel Pankhurst, had undertaken the tactic of direct action in the last few years, smashing windows, sabotaging the mail, and defacing public monuments to publicize their cause. One feminist, Emily Davison, had dramatically rushed onto the Derby race course, snatched the bridle of the King's horse, and been trampled to death, becoming a martyr to the cause of suffrage. But as soon as the war began, many British feminists put the issue to one side and became fervent supporters of war against Germany and Austria. Others, with Schwimmer's support, believed that rights for women and world peace were inseparable issues and pledged themselves to advance their work despite the war.

By this time, Schwimmer had mastered nine languages, which was the ideal preparation for her international peace work in the following years. She was well-informed about Eastern European affairs from her extensive travels and had a huge circle of friends and acquaintances from her work in the IWSA. In 1909, she had been the first foreign woman to address the House of Commons Foreign Affairs Committee and was by now a familiar figure in Parliament. (She even had breakfast with Chancellor of the Exchequer David Lloyd George and pointed out that the assassination of the Austrian Archduke augured a world war. He admitted after the fighting began that she alone among his friends and advisors had had the prescience to grasp the consequences of the killing.)

Pacifism ran deep in Schwimmer's family. One of her uncles, Leopold Katscher, had founded the Hungarian Peace Society, while another uncle, Edler von Lederer, even though an army officer, also spoke out against militarism. When a family friend, Baroness Bertha von Suttner, had tried to organize a pan-European peace movement, Schwimmer appealed to the U.S. government to use its influence to prevent bloodshed. Just after the war began, she sailed for America to promote this scheme, believing that President Woodrow Wilson could convene a conference of neutral powers to preside over negotiations. Her repute was sufficient to win her an audience with Secretary of State William Jennings Bryan, himself very eager to keep out of the war, then with the President, who at this stage was also ardently opposed to intervention but made no promises. But when she spoke to the press afterwards, she angered Wilson by misrepresenting his remarks, and he refused to see any peace workers for several months. Undeterred, Schwimmer toured the country, making speeches against war to women's groups, again being helped by her friend from the IWSA, Carrie Catt. The two women were slightly at odds. With her country already at war, peace had become the overriding issue to Schwimmer, whereas women's suffrage remained uppermost in Catt's mind and she wanted to direct Schwimmer's marvelous oratory in support of it. During the tour, Schwimmer met Jane Addams, founder of the Hull House social settlement, in Chicago. A British feminist and peace worker, Emmeline Pethick-Lawrence, was also touring America on behalf of a negotiated peace, and the two women joined forces.

Although they were technically enemies with their countries at war, Schwimmer and Pethick-Lawrence, speaking dramatically side by side, were the first to suggest a specifically women's peace movement. But given their situation they needed the help of renowned indigenous American women, such as Addams, who had already written *Newer Ideals of Peace* (1907) and who had a national reputation. The stirring lectures given by the two Europeans led to the creation of emergency peace committees in several cities, including Boston, Nashville, St. Paul, and Chicago. Addams agreed to call a peace meeting in Washington, D.C., in January 1915, with a view to forming a Women's Peace Party (WPP), but Schwimmer, afraid that the meeting had been hijacked by divisively militant suffragists, at first declined to take part except as a journalist. Reassured by the irenic ("conciliatory") tone of the meeting, Schwimmer changed her mind and spoke in praise of the American women's action. She added that peacemaking and women's votes went hand in hand because at present the women in her audience were "voiceless to prevent some incident" that might "bring for your children what has happened to our children."

Three months later, Schwimmer sailed back to Europe and spoke at the International Congress of Women, convened by the talented Dutch feminist Dr. Aletta Jacobs. Although the Congress was to have met in Berlin, the German faction—realizing that women from enemy nations would be excluded—settled for The Hague instead. As it was, most of the British women who had hoped to attend were denied passports by the British government, which also declared Schwimmer an enemy alien, so that she could not return. The conference participants passed resolutions urging an end to the fighting, immediate peace talks, the right of all peoples to self-government, and equal rights for women—some of which would show up again in 1918 among Woodrow Wilson's "Fourteen Points." Schwimmer wanted members of the conference to take the resolution personally to heads of government in the belligerent and neutral nations, and made a passionate floor speech to promote the idea of personal missions: "When our sons are killed by millions, let us, mothers, only try to do good by going to the kings and emperors, without any other danger than a refusal!" Though many had misgivings about the value of these excursions, the delegates voted in favor, and Schwimmer was asked to lead a group of representatives to Denmark, Norway, Sweden, Russia, and the Netherlands. The government officials they met were polite but noncommittal, and the women's actions generated a disappointingly small amount of discussion and publicity.

Back in America in mid-1915, Schwimmer, always eager for prompt and dramatic action, learned that the automobile magnate, Henry Ford, was devoting himself to peacemaking. An American woman named Rebecca Shelly, who was convinced that God was directing her to make peace, arranged a massive antiwar demonstration in Detroit to draw Ford's attention when he refused to meet her in person. Schwimmer spoke to the meeting and won an audience with Ford on November 18, explaining to him her plan for a mediated peace. Louis Lochner, head of the National Peace Federation, joined them the next day, and together they persuaded Ford of the plan's viability. Ford in turn approached President Wilson and asked him to establish an official neutral commission which he, Ford, would finance. Wilson politely declined.

The Women's Peace Party tried to increase the pressure on Wilson by holding a large demonstration in Washington, D.C., on November 26 with Schwimmer as keynote speaker. Unfortunately, when Henry Ford followed her to the podium after another of her rousing speeches, he claimed that he would find a way to "get the boys out of the trenches by Christmas," then only a month away. This assertion was bound to be refuted by the facts and helped undermine rather than strengthen the movement. Ford also financed a ship, the *Oscar II,* to take peace delegates to a second European conference the following week. Schwimmer, now marked by the press as Ford's "expert assistant," was making a poor impression on many of the leading American pacifists, who considered her hotheaded and thoughtless. Her calls for immediate peace negotiations seemed not to be backed by consideration of the political complexities of the issue, and some WPP women, concluding that she was hurting rather than helping their cause, declined to join the peace ship.

The voyage of the *Oscar II* received much adverse publicity, and many of the journalists traveling on it (there were almost as many newspapermen as delegates) treated the whole venture as a joke. Fear of being torpedoed by a German submarine, overcrowding, and a rough winter sea led to constant animosities among the passengers. Schwimmer, whose behavior historian Barbara Steinson describes as "secretive and authoritarian," asserted that she had a bagful of documents proving that the warring powers were ready to negotiate, but when she showed them to eager passengers they turned out to be no more than the vague promises her earlier mission had elicited. She declared that Ford had promised the International Committee $200,000, but no money was forthcoming.

Tiring of the venture in Christiana, Sweden, when it yielded no quick results, Ford soon slipped away, while Schwimmer and Lochner carried on with the project, setting up a Neutral Conference for Continuous Mediation in Stockholm. Finally the two of them fell out and Schwimmer resigned in protest from the Conference, pursued by malicious rumors that she was actually an agent being paid by the Central Powers (for which Hungary was fighting) to bring the peace process into disrepute. Almost at once she collapsed with a serious heart condition and had to take an unaccustomed three-month break from work. She spent the rest of the war in Stockholm, depressed at the mounting casualties and the seeming futility of all the peace efforts to date, but returned to Hungary in November 1918.

At the end of the war the Austro-Hungarian Empire collapsed. Count Michael Károlyi, one of Schwimmer's friends, overthrew Emperor Charles I in a bloodless coup and invited Schwimmer to become a member of his National Council of Fifteen. The liberal-minded Károlyi then invited Schwimmer to become ambassador to Switzerland, making her the first woman ambassador in Hungarian history. While there, she worked on another women's peace conference but had hardly started her official duties when she was recalled to Budapest, partly because she had equipped herself as ambassador by using state funds for a fur coat, an expensive apartment in Berne, and a chauffeured limousine. At a time when people all over Europe, including Hungary, were starving to death, these seemed like outrageously provocative purchases, even if they were designed to bolster her dignity as ambassador. The next month, Károlyi was overthrown by the Communist coup d'état of Béla Kun. Denied a passport, Schwimmer was unable to attend the fourth Women's International Congress at Zurich. Delegates sent her letters of encouragement (though some were secretly relieved by her absence), and then constituted themselves as the Women's International League for Peace and Freedom (WILPF).

The Communists treated Schwimmer as a bourgeois ("middle class") enemy for her work in the Károly regime and denied her the right to work, but worse was to follow. The fascist regime of Admiral Nicolas Horthy, which soon overthrew the Hungarian Communists, began to purge the Jews and singled out Schwimmer for extermination. Loyal friends, Quakers, and American peace workers managed to smuggle her out of Hungary on a Danube steamer and into Vienna in 1920, and from there she was able to make her way to the United States. But America was then undergoing a "Red scare" of its own, a panicky reaction to the Russian Revolution abroad and labor militancy at home. In the worst violation of civil rights since slavery, the Attorney General, A. Mitchell Palmer, was summarily deporting, without trial, hundreds of foreign-born citizens suspected of radical sympathies. Not surprisingly in this atmosphere, the old accusation that Schwimmer was a spy came up again, along with the allegation that her peace work between 1914 and 1917 had been aimed at neutralizing America for the benefit of the Central Powers. Other critics suggested, ludicrously enough, that she might be the source of Henry Ford's growing anti-Semitism.

Her sister Franciska, a New York pianist, and her friend Lola Maverick Lloyd, a wealthy woman whom she had first met in 1914, supported Schwimmer when she was at first denied the right to work. By now she was suffering from a severe case of diabetes and found it more difficult than previously to lead an active life. Hoping nevertheless to resume her work as a journalist and lecturer, Schwimmer applied for citizenship, but the oath taken by new citizens required candidates to swear that they would bear arms in defense of America if necessary. As a pacifist she refused to take the oath, but sued for citizenship nevertheless, declaring that as a point of conscience she would be unable to take up arms for any country or any cause. The case went all the way to the Supreme Court which ruled, in 1929, that she should not be granted citizenship. Justices Oliver Wendell Holmes and Louis Brandeis dissented from the majority opinion, claiming that her case should be considered as a First Amendment freedom of thought issue. Holmes wrote: "The applicant seems to be a woman of superior character and intelligence, obviously more than ordinarily desirable as a citizen of the United States." Superior character and intelligence did not make her likable, however, and even her supporters were finding her dogmatic and high-handed ways hard to endure.

Permitted to stay in America as a stateless person, she remained intensely devoted to the peace cause. In 1925, she attended the first Conference on the Cause and Cure of War, in Washington, D.C., but found it too halfhearted in its approach. The second conference, the following year, seemed even worse to her, especially as all 30 of the lecturers were men, and Schwimmer rebuked the organizer—her old friend Carrie Catt—for this gender imbalance. Catt was not the only one she annoyed. Gradually, as she aged, she became increasingly abrasive, launching a succession of libel suits against journalists who had handled the peace ship scheme roughly; she also began a prolonged correspondence with Henry Ford and his associates, who she believed had wronged her and damaged her reputation.

Despite her deteriorating health, Schwimmer kept busy in America. She and Lola Maverick Lloyd founded the Campaign for World Government in 1937, in the years when another world war seemed imminent and the hopeless failure of the League of Nations was apparent to all. At first the organization was a small antiwar group dedicated to world government, but its ranks swelled during the Second World War, especially after the Hiroshima and Nagasaki nuclear bombings of 1945. She started, but never finished, an autobiography and began to work at creating a world center for women's archives, but once again her personal tactlessness alienated many of the people whose help and cooperation she needed. Schwimmer died in 1948 of bronchial pneumonia after living largely on her sister's and Lloyd's charity for 27 years. It was a disappointing end for the woman who had seemed incandescent to her associates before, and in the early days of, the First World War.

Further Reading

Hershey, Burnet. *The Odyssey of Henry Ford and the Great Peace Ship.* Taplinger. 1967.

Kraft, Barbara S. *The Peace Ship: Henry Ford's Pacifist Adventure in the First World War.* Macmillan, 1978.

Moorehead, Caroline. *Troublesome People: Enemies of War, 1916-1986.* London: Hamish Hamilton, 1987.

Steinson, Barbara J. *American Women's Activism in World War I.* Garland, 1982.

Wiltsher, Anne. *Most Dangerous Women: Feminist Peace Campaigners of the Great War.* London: Pandora, 1985. □

Kurt Schwitters

The painter, collagist, typographer, and poet Kurt Schwitters (1887-1948) was the creator of MERZ-art, which is two and three dimensional collage-like works using paper and discarded objects of everyday use.

Kurt Schwitters was born in 1887 in Hannover, Germany. His parents were reasonably well-to-do retailers who made possible his studies at the Arts and Crafts school in Hannover and four years at the Art Academy in Dresden (1909-1914). He then settled in Hannover, married Helma Fischer, served for a short time in the army, and turned away from figurative painting and began to write his first poems. In 1918 he created his first "MERZ" picture. The name derived from a piece of paper with the word "Kommerz"—the letter-head of a bank—which formed part of the collage. He had his first exhibition of these new works in 1919 at the famous Der Sturm Gallery in Berlin, directed by Herwarth Walden, who was also the editor of the *Sturm* journal. Schwitters' only son Ernst was born while Schwitters studied two more semesters in Hannover. In 1919 he published several articles and poems in the *Sturm* journal, including his famous "Anna Blume" poem, and established friendships with several avant-garde artists in Germany. His apolitical stance caused Richard Huelsenbeck, one of the leaders of the Berlin Dada group, to exclude him from their activities, but the friendship with another member of this group—Raoul Hausmann—lasted through Schwitters' lifetime. In 1920 the Societe Anonyme of Katharine Dreyer in New York showed some of Schwitters' works for the first time in the United States.

At the Dada congress in Weimar in 1922 he met the Dutch artist Theo van Doesburg and thus established connections with the De Stijl movement. In 1923 he began to publish (in irregular intervals) the MERZ magazine and saw the first of his works bought by a museum (Dresden). In 1924 a record was cut of his recitation of the "Ursonate," a sound-poem in the Dada tradition, originally inspired by Raoul Hausmann.

At this time Schwitters began to work on his MERZ column (which he called "Cathedral of Erotic Misery" [Kathedrale des erotischen Elends]), a stalactite-like three-dimensional construction of many different materials which filled not only his studio but grew so high that the removal of the ceiling became necessary for its further expansion. The witty title referred in part to the many small "caves" (later covered) in which he imbedded small objects which were tokens of memory to various friends as well as objects which he found here and there. He considered this sculpture the most important part of his life's work; it was destroyed by bombs during World War II. He started a second one during his exile in Norway (which was destroyed by fire) and a third one in England. From 1930 on he spent considerable time every year in Norway, emigrating there in 1937 after the Nazis had confiscated 13 of his works from various museums and exhibited four of them in the infamous "Degenerate Art Exhibit" in Munich in 1937. When the Germans invaded Norway in 1940 he escaped to England, where he was for 17 months, after which he lived with his son in London. After suffering a stroke in 1944 he moved to the Lake District. In 1945 his wife died in Hannover. The Museum of Modern Art in New York, which had exhibited his works since 1936, provided him a grant to recreate the MERZ column. After prolonged illnesses, Schwitters died on January 8, 1948, in Kendal near Ambleside, England.

Schwitters' fame rests on his MERZ pictures, his collages and assemblies, the MERZ column (preserved only photographically), and his poetry, as well as on his inventiveness as a typographer and advertising designer. He freed the various materials from their original intent and fused them into singular works of art. A stylistic development can be recognized moving from the early expressionistic collages and drawings to the incorporation of constructivist and De Stijl (The Style) elements. His humor and wit (sometimes expanded to the titles of his works) can also be seen in his charming children books (in collaboration with Kate Steinitz). It is revealing that from 1918 on Schwitters incorporated in his works the discarded trash of the everyday, thus creating something like an analogue to the old Germany's collapse after World War I. He always believed that art represented liberation and should provide enjoyment at the same time. That the general public was shocked by his works as well as by recitations of his poetry (often taking on the forms of an "event"), he accepted, since art was to him "a spiritual function of man with the task to liberate him from the chaos and the tragedy of life. . . ."

Further Reading

The most comprehensive monograph on the artist is by Werner Schmalenbach (Cologne, 1967), which includes many illustrations and an extensive bibliography by Hans Bolliger. Since the comprehensive retrospective of Schwitters' works in 1956 which traveled from Hannover to Berne, Amsterdam, and Brussels his fame has grown, and the catalogues of later exhibitions have become important contributions to the understanding of the artist. The 1920 defense of the artist by his publisher Christof Spengemann, "Die Wahrheit ueber Anna Blume" ("The Truth concerning A.B.") provides a good sketch of the spirit of the times. Kate Steinitz published her memories of the artist (1918-1930) in 1963 in Zurich, which in an enlarged form (translated by R. B. Haas) was published by the University of California Press in 1968. John Elderfield's catalogue for the 1985 retrospective of New York's Museum of Modern Art is lucid and thorough.

Additional Sources

Dietrich, Dorothea, *The collages of Kurt Schwitters: tradition and innovation,* Cambridge; New York: Cambridge University Press, 1993. □

Publius Cornelius Scipio Africanus Major

Publius Cornelius Scipio Africanus Major (236-184 B.C.) was a Roman official during the Second Punic War. He defeated Hannibal in the Battle of Zama and was a champion of both Roman imperialism and the enlightened pro-Hellenic spirit of a new age.

Scipio was married to Aemilia, sister of Lucius Aemilius Paullus (victor of Pydna in 168 B.C.), and became the father of Cornelia, mother of the Gracchus brothers.

As a youth of about 18, Scipio was credited with having saved his father's life at the Battle of the Ticinus (Ticino) in 218, and as military tribune in 216, he rallied the survivors after the disastrous defeat of Cannae. The young Scipio held the office of curule aedile in 213. When, in 211, Lucius and Gnaeus Scipio, his father and uncle, fell in Spain, he was appointed by vote of the Roman people to their proconsular command, the first *privatus* (private citizen) in Roman history to obtain this privilege.

Punic Wars

In Spain, Scipio seized New Carthage, the enemy's headquarters, but won great sympathy by his humane treatment of his Spanish captives. In 208 he defeated Hasdrubal Barca at Baecula but was unable to prevent the enemy's escape and march across the Pyrenees. After defeating two other enemy armies at Ilipa, he captured Gades (Cadiz), the last stronghold of the Carthaginians in Spain. In 206 he left for Rome to stand for the consulship.

As consul in 205, Scipio was assigned the province of Sicily and, after strong senatorial opposition, also the province of Africa. In 204 he crossed to Africa with 35,000 men. He besieged Utica for 40 days until the beginning of winter forced him to encamp on a nearby headland. Early in the following year he defeated the Carthaginians at Campi Magni, overran their territory, and captured Tunis. Scipio granted the enemy an armistice to seek peace terms in Rome, but late in 203 Hannibal returned to Africa to renew the war. Landing his troops at Leptis, Scipio headed for Zama, a 5 days' march west of Carthage. Here the decisive battle took place, ending in a complete victory for Scipio and King Masinissa, his Numidian ally. Scipio concluded the peace and returned to Rome, where he celebrated his triumph. Henceforth he carried the honorary cognomen Africanus.

Elected censor in 199, Scipio became *princeps senatus* (leader of the Senate) till the end of his life. Consul for the second time in 194, he was thwarted by the Senate in his desire to obtain the province of Macedonia, where he hoped to pursue his pro-Hellenic policy against the threat of the Syrian king Antiochus III. In the following year he was sent to Africa to arbitrate in a border conflict between Carthage and King Masinissa. In 190 Scipio was instrumental in obtaining for his brother Lucius, consul of the year, the command against Antiochus by offering to accompany him as legate on his campaign.

Seriously ill in Asia Minor, Scipio Africanus took no part in the decisive victory of Magnesia in 189 but was active again during the peace negotiations at Sardis. When the two brothers returned to Rome, they were immediately attacked by the party of Cato the Elder, a vigorous opponent of the pro-Hellenic policy of the Scipios.

Lucius was accused of embezzling the money paid by Antiochus as a war indemnity to the Roman people. Asked to produce the account books, Scipio Africanus tore them up before the eyes of the senators. When, according to one tradition, he was himself accused of accepting bribery from Antiochus, he invited the people to follow him up to the Capitol in order to give thanks to Jupiter for the victory of Zama. His power broken, Scipio left Rome as a private citizen, disillusioned and ill, to retire on his estate at Liternum in Campania.

Further Reading

The definitive biography is Howard Hayes Scullard, *Scipio Africanus: Soldier and Politician* (1970). Extremely valuable are Scullard's *Scipio Africanus in the Second Punic War* (1930) and Richard M. Haywood, *Studies on Scipio Africanus* (1933). Designed for the general reader are Basil Henry Liddell Hart, *A "Greater than Napoleon": Scipio Africanus* (1926), and the fictional account by Friedrich Donauer, *Swords against Carthage,* translated by F. T. Cooper (1932). Recommended for general historical background are J. B. Bury and others, eds., *The Cambridge Ancient History,* vol. 8 (1930), and Howard H. Scullard, *A History of the Roman World from 753-146 B.C.* (1935; rev. ed. 1951) and *Roman Politics 220-150 B.C.* (1951). □

Publius Cornelius Aemilianus Scipio Africanus Minor

Publius Cornelius Aemilianus Scipio Africanus Minor (c. 185-129 B.C.) was a Roman official and general in Africa and Spain. He was also the brilliant leader of the so-called Scipionic Circle, a group of pro-Hellenic philosophers, poets, and politicians.

The second son of Lucius Aemilius Paullus, Scipio was adopted by Publius Cornelius Scipio, son of Scipio Africanus Major, and married Sempronia, sister of the Gracchus brothers. As a youth of 18 years, Scipio accompanied his father to Greece in 168 B.C., fought in the Battle of Pydna, and participated in his father's triumph. Among the Achaean hostages was the historian Polybios, who remained in the house of Paullus and won the friendship of young Scipio. In 151, although assigned to the province of Macedonia, Scipio volunteered to serve as military tribune with Lucullus in Spain. Scipio distinguished himself in single combat with a Spanish horseman, won the mural crown, and negotiated the surrender of the city of Intercatia.

War against Carthage

Sent by Lucullus to Africa to procure elephants for the Celtiberian War, Scipio mediated peace between the Carthaginians and the Numidian king, Masinissa. Back in Rome he aided in the release of Polybios and the other Achaean hostages. In 149 Scipio served as military tribune under Manilius in Africa, where he won the crown of siege by saving a beleaguered force against the attack of Hasdrubal.

After the death of King Masinissa in 148, Scipio settled the succession to the Numidian kingdom by dividing it among the King's sons. Returning to Rome to stand for the aedileship, Scipio was elected consul instead. The vote of the people exempted him from the laws on legal age and granted him the command against Carthage without the lot.

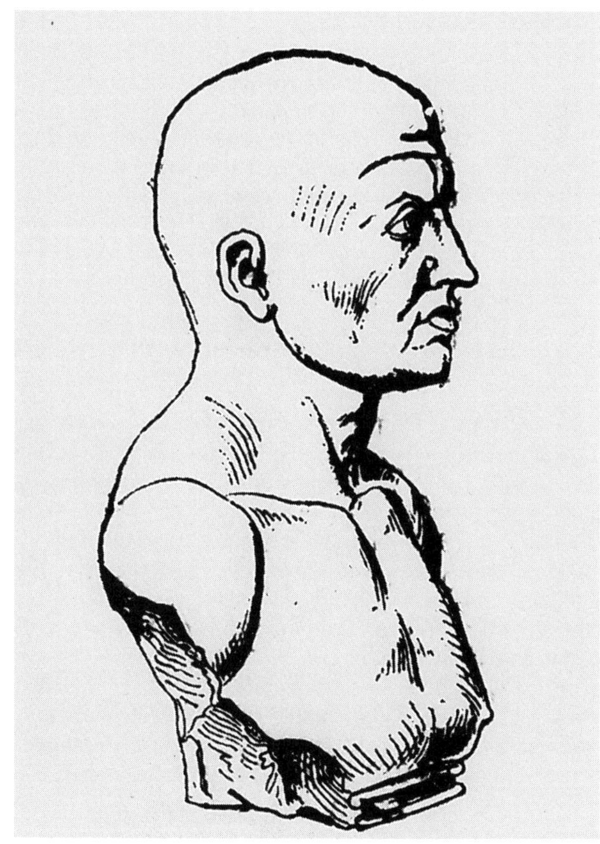

Crossing over to Utica, Scipio blockaded Carthage and in 146 captured and destroyed the city. Tradition reports that Scipio, while gazing at the city in flames and meditating on the uncertainties of human events, feared for his own city and wept. At any rate, he cursed the site, sold the remaining population into slavery, organized the new province of Africa, and returned to Rome to celebrate a brilliant triumph, accepting his inherited cognomen, Africanus, for his own merits.

During his censorship in 142, which gained him a reputation for severity, Scipio completed the building of the Aemilian Bridge. As head of an embassy to the East in 140, he observed and settled Roman relations with the Eastern allies. In 134 a special dispensation exempted him from the law on reelection to the consulship, and, again, he was granted a military command by popular vote, this time in Hither Spain (Tarraconensis). After restoring discipline in the army, he blockaded and destroyed the Spanish stronghold of Numantia in 133.

Civil War in Rome

While still in Spain, Scipio received the news of the stormy tribunate and death of Tiberius Sempronius Gracchus and expressed his undisguised hostility to Gracchus's agrarian program and unconstitutionality. After celebrating his second triumph Scipio continued to oppose the pro-Gracchan party by rejecting the proposal of the tribune Carbo to legalize repetition of the tribunate and by sponsoring a measure which deprived the Gracchan land commission of its judicial function.

Tension rose to a climax during the Latin Festival of 129, when Scipio faced the populace in a public address which ended in hostile altercations. Escorted home by an impressive throng, he withdrew to his bedroom to compose another speech for the next day. In the morning he was found dead. Carbo, Gaius Gracchus, Scipio's wife Sempronia, and his mother-in-law Cornelia were all suspected of responsibility for his death. However, the eulogy written by his friend Gaius Laelius made no mention of a violent death.

Scipio, though liberal in culture and a great admirer of Greek literature and learning, was basically a political conservative who vigorously supported senatorial control of the constitution and Roman dominion in the provinces. Emerging as the ideal statesman during the century of revolution, Cicero chose Scipio as the central figure for his dialogue *On the Commonwealth* and celebrated Scipio's lifelong friendship with Laelius in his essay *On Friendship.*

Further Reading

Ancient sources on Scipio's life are Livy, Polybios, and Cicero. The definitive modern biography is A. E. Astin, *Scipio Aemilianus* (1967). For an understanding of Scipio and his friends see Ruth M. Brown, *A Study of the Scipionic Circle* (1934). Recommended for general historical background are Tenney Frank, *Roman Imperialism* (1914); J. B. Bury and others, eds., *The Cambridge Ancient History,* vol. 8 (1930); and Howard H. Scullard, *Roman Politics 220-150 B.C.* (1951). □

Martin Scorsese

Martin Scorsese (born 1942) is a director and writer of highly personal films about intense loners who struggle against their own inner demons and the violence of their urban environments. While many of his works reflect his experience as an Italian-American growing up in New York City, he has also made highly regarded movies of great works of literature and other stories.

Film director Martin Scorsese was born on November 17, 1942, in Flushing, New York to Charles, a clothes presser, and Catherine, a seamstress. They raised their son in the Little Italy neighborhood of New York City. Plagued by severe asthma as a child, Scorsese was fascinated with movies. He watched films on television and attended local theaters frequently while his healthier peers engaged in sports and more social activities. After initially pursuing a career in the priesthood, Scorsese dropped out of the seminary after a year and entered the prestigious Film School at New York University. Scorsese's *It's Not Just You Murray!* won the Producer's Guild Award for best student film in 1964, and he also received awards for other film shorts that he made as an undergraduate.

Drew from Own Urban Experience

After graduating, Scorsese remained at New York University as an instructor in basic film technique and criticism while at the same time beginning his career as a director. His 1968 short film, *The Big Shave,* won Le Prix de L'Age d'Or at Ledoux's Festival of Experimental Cinema. Scorsese's first feature film, *Who's That Knocking at My Door,* was first screened in 1969. It was produced by Haig Moonigan, one of Scorsese's teachers at New York University. This strongly autobiographical film about an Italian-American youth also introduced the actor Harvey Keitel, who became a frequent participant in Scorsese's works. The director also frequently casts his mother, Catherine, in his films, and Scorsese himself has acted in some of his own films and those made by others.

Outraged by the killing of four Kent State Student protesters and the Vietnam War in general, Scorsese and some of his students formed the New York Cinetracts Collective in 1969 as a means to film student protests against the conflict. The result was *Street Scenes,* screened at the 1970 New York Film Festival, which called for a withdrawal of U.S. troops from Vietnam as well as an end to military ROTC activities on all U.S. college campuses.

Scorsese worked as a film editor before his directing career was established, most notably as a co-supervising editor of the documentary *Woodstock* in 1970. (Many years later his interest in music would lead him to direct a music video for pop legend Michael Jackson's "Bad.") He also had a brief stint with the CBS television unit covering Hubert Humphrey during the 1972 presidential election. In the early 1970s he moved to Hollywood and met the producer/director Roger Corman, who asked him to direct a sequel to his *Bloody Mama.* Instead, Scorsese directed Corman's *Boxcar Bertha,* a 1972 gangster film somewhat resembling *Bonnie and Clyde.* According to Ephraim Katz in *The Film Encyclopedia, Boxcar Bertha* "gave the young director [Scorsese] the opportunity to work within the Hollywood system and paved the way to his phenomenal rise in the coming years."

Began Successful Collaboration with De Niro

Next on the filmmaker's career path was a return to familiar turf in *Mean Streets,* a 1973 release about a young Italian-American trying to get by in a low-life environment. Emphasizing character development over plot, *Mean Streets* featured a jumpy cinematic style of quick cuts that foreshadowed Scorsese's later work *Taxi Driver.* It also marked the director's first creative pairing with the actor Robert De Niro, whom Scorsese had grown up with in Little Italy. Their partnership evolved into one of the most successful director/actor collaborations in modern film. Years later in 1981, *Taxi Driver* gained some notoriety when John Hinckley, Jr. claimed that Jodie Foster's role in the film was his inspiration for trying to assassinate President Ronald Reagan.

Scorsese also began directing documentaries in the 1970s. These included *Italianamerican,* a profile of his parents released in 1974, and *American Boy,* a 1978 account of a friend who had immersed himself in the drug culture of the 1960s. He veered away from his usual movie themes with *Alice Doesn't Live Here Anymore* in 1975, a film about a recently widowed mother trying to find herself. According to Leslie Halliwell in *Halliwell's Film Guide,* the *New Yorker* claimed the movie was "full of funny malice and breakneck vitality." Scorsese followed with his major hit, *Taxi Driver,* in which he returned to his usual urban setting. Halliwell called it an "unlovely but brilliant made film" that "haunts the mind and paints a most vivid picture of a hell on earth." *Taxi Driver* was awarded the International Grand Prize at the Cannes Film Festival.

The director's nostalgic look at his city after World War II called *New York, New York* proved a critical failure in 1977, despite having the star power of Robert De Niro and Liza Minnelli. Halliwell said that it was "hampered by gross overlength, unattractive characters and a pessimistic plot." Scorsese became depressed as well as physically ill and required hospitalization following the making of this film. A failed marriage and drug problems further debilitated him. He returned to documentaries in the late 1970s by directing a film of The Band's final concert entitled *The Last Waltz.* Then he got back on track in feature films after De Niro convinced him to direct *Raging Bull,* a saga of the boxer Jake LaMotta. The movie earned Scorsese the National Society of Film Critics Award for Best Director, as well as his first Academy Award nomination. *Raging Bull* was later named the best film of the decade in a movie critics' poll.

King of Comedy, a 1983 film about a failed comic who kidnaps a famous talk-show host, was one of Scorsese's less successful efforts. In *Partisan Review,* Morris Dickstein called it "a pointless and irritating film with a few brilliant touches." Accolades came his way again, though, for his direction of *After Hours,* an unusual black comedy about a mild-mannered New York City resident who gets involved in a series of late-night mishaps. "A film so original, so particular, that one is uncertain from moment to moment exactly how to respond to it," said film critic Roger Ebert about the 1985 release, according to *Halliwell's Film Guide.* Scorsese was honored with the Best Director Award at the Cannes Film Festival for this effort.

Box-office success greeted Scorsese's *The Color of Money* in 1986, a sequel to *The Hustler* starring Paul Newman. It represented one of Scorsese's few big-budget productions up to that time. Certain religious groups were outraged by his next release, 1988's *The Last Temptation of Christ,* which dealt with an alternative interpretation of Jesus' acceptance of his role on earth. Although *Variety* as cited by Halliwell called *Last Temptation* "a film of challenging ideas," its pre-release notoriety and long running time hampered its success at the box office. Scorsese returned to more comfortable cinematic ground in 1990 with *Goodfellas,* a violent tale of Mafia hoodlums in New York City that earned him Best Director Awards from the National Society of Film Critics, New York Film Critics, and Los Angeles Film Critics.

Showed Versatility with Period Piece

After the 1991 release of his remake of *Cape Fear,* Scorsese surprised the film community by his filming of *Age of Innocence,* the Edith Wharton novel set in nineteenth-century New York City. "I had the script in my mind for two years and wrote it in two and half weeks, with Jay Cocks," Scorsese told *Interview* about the film in 1993. Lavishly produced and slowly paced, it resembled nothing in Scorsese's directorial past. It proved not to be a trend, however, as Scorsese jumped back to modern times with a tale of greed and deception in Las Vegas with his 1995 release, *Casino.*

Scorsese showed his support of film history in 1990 by becoming president of the Film Foundation, an organization dedicated to film preservation. He has also been very active in promoting independent film makers, and in 1994 became a member of the advisory board for the Independent Film Channel on cable television. On October 9, 1996, the American Film Institute announced that Scorsese would be awarded its 1997 Life Achievement Award, which he accepted on February 21, 1997. In addition, he received the prestigious Wexner Prize in March 1997, for originality in the arts. His next film, *Kundun,* the story of Tibet's exiled spiritual leader, the Dalai Lama, was released in September 1997. A director of 20 feature films and documentaries, he has also written a number of screenplays since his first film was released in 1968. His steady output as a filmmaker is expected to continue into the twenty-first century.

Further Reading

Katz, Ephraim, *The Film Encyclopedia,* Harper & Row, 1979, p. 1028.

Halliwell, Leslie, *Halliwell's Film Guide,* 7th ed., Harper & Row, 1989, pp. 22, 135, 560, 584, 665, 723, 994-995.

Interview, October 1993, pp. 62-63, 135.

Los Angeles Times, February 22, 1997, p. F1.

New York Times, March 8, 1997, p. A13.

Partisan Review, 1994, pp. 658-664.

"http://www.msstate.edu/Movies/search.html," in *Internet Movie Database,* 1996. □

Dred Scott

Dred Scott (1795-1858), in an effort to gain his freedom, waged one of the most important legal battles in the history of the United States.

Dred Scott was born a slave in Southampton County, Va. in 1795. Industrious and intelligent, he was employed as a farmhand, stevedore, craftsman, and general handyman. In 1819 his original owner moved to Huntsville, Ala., and later to St. Louis, Mo. In 1832 he died, and Scott was sold for $500 to a surgeon in the U.S. Army who took Scott to the free state of Illinois in 1834 and on to Wisconsin Territory. Later the doctor returned with Scott to Missouri.

When the surgeon died, Scott passed to John Sanford. During these years he had married and had two daughters. Scott had tried unsuccessfully to escape from slavery and later to buy his freedom. In 1846 he filed suit in the Missouri state courts for his freedom on the grounds that residence in a free territory had liberated him.

Scott's suit finally came before the U.S. Supreme Court. On March 6, 1857, in *Dred Scott v. John Sanford,* after much debate the Supreme Court ruled against Scott 7 to 2, with Chief Justice Roger B. Taney giving the majority opinion. According to Taney, Scott could not sue Sanford because he was not a U.S. citizen. The justice argued that Scott was not a citizen because he was both a black man and a slave. Taney's remarks that black men "had no rights which the white man was bound to respect" came as a severe blow to abolitionists.

This crucial decision electrified the country, for Taney had ruled that African Americans were not citizens of the United States and that an act of Congress (the Missouri Compromise of 1820) was unconstitutional. He also had redefined the relationship between the states and the Federal government, making possible the expansion of slavery into the territories. Southerners rejoiced at the verdict; abolitionists denounced it and even went as far as discrediting the legitimacy of the Court itself.

A few months after the decision, on May 26, 1857, Scott's owner freed him. Scott continued to live in St. Louis until his death on Sept. 17, 1858. Although African Americans would not become citizens of the United States until the ratification of the 14th Amendment (1868), Scott's bid for freedom remained the most momentous judicial event of the century.

Further Reading

The best account of Scott and his case is Vincent C. Hopkin, *Dred Scott's Case* (1951). Alfred H. Kelly and Winfred A. Harbison, *The American Constitution: Its Origins and Development* (4th ed. 1970), is a useful text in examining the constitutional questions. Stanley I. Kutler, *The Dred Scott Decision: Law or Politics?* (1967), provides a critical assessment of the controversial issues and implications surrounding the case. Another invaluable aid in understanding the case and its ramifications is Loren Miller, *The Petitioners: The Story of the Supreme Court of the United States and the Negro* (1966). An excellent background study is John Hope Franklin, *From Slavery to Freedom: A History of American Negroes* (1947). □

Francis Reginald Scott

The poet, political activist, and constitutional theorist Francis Reginald Scott (1899-1985) was a catalyst in the struggle for Canadian political, legal, and literary independence; for human rights and fundamental freedoms in Canada; and for Quebec nationalism.

Francis Reginald Scott was born in Quebec City in 1899, the son of a well known poet and Anglican clergyman, Canon F. G. Scott. The young Scott inherited his father's social concerns and his poetic interest in the Canadian northland. A Rhodes scholar at Oxford University, he received a B.A. in 1922 and a B. Litt. in 1923. He then returned to Canada, where he graduated from McGill University with a B.C.L. in 1926. As a young man who came of age in the 1920s—a strongly nationalist period in Canadian history—Scott became a catalyst in the struggle for Canadian political, legal, and literary independence.

A shaping component in F. R. Scott's nationalism was the land itself. After his three years abroad he found Canadian culture superficial. Canada had nothing in the way of an historical past to match that of Europe—nothing, that is, except the vast, open stretches of the pre-Cambrian shield. He recalled that "the Laurentian country was wonderful, open, empty, vast, and speaking a kind of eternal language in its mountains, rivers, and lakes. I knew that these were the oldest mountains in the world. . . . Geologic time made ancient civilization seem but yesterday's picnic." For Scott, the great age of the land seems to have been transmuted into a substitution for an historical past. Yet because of its association with the new Canadian nationalism ("the true north strong and free"), and because it was unpeopled, the land was a clean canvas for the artist's impression. He soon realized that it was on this natural landscape that Canada's new literature must be built:

> Who would read old myths
> By this lake
> Where the wild duck paddle forth
> At daybreak?

With the poet-critic A. J. M. Smith, Scott helped found the avant-garde *McGill Fortnightly Review* (1925-1926), a little magazine now synonymous with modernism in Canadian poetry. He was also co-editor of its short-lived successor, *The Canadian Mercury* (1928-1929). In 1936 he helped edit the first anthology of modern Canadian poetry, *New Provinces: Poems of Seven Authors.* In 1942 he was one of the organizers of *Preview,* the dominant literary magazine of the decade. In March 1944 he received the Guarantor's Prize from *Poetry: A Magazine of Verse* for a group of war poems.

Scott's first collection of poems, delayed by the Depression, was *Overture* (1945), followed by *Events and Signals* (1954); a collection of satires, *The Eye of the Needle* (1957); *Signature* (1964); *Selected Poems* (1966); *Trouvailles* (1967); and *The Dance Is One* (1973). His poetry developed in four successive stages. In the late 1920s he wrote a northern landscape poetry influenced by the Imagists, by T. S. Eliot's fertility myth, and by Henri Bergson's *élan vital.* In the 1930s, in response to the Depression, he wrote a basically socialist, often satiric, program poetry: some of these poems—notably "Social Notes"—are blunt satires on social evils. In the 1940s his preoccupation with landscape and political reform was fused into a larger humanist structure. In the 1950s and 1960s, in response to an emerging Quebec nationalism, Scott became a pioneer translator of Quebeçois poetry.

His poetic subject is most often man (in the generic sense) silhouetted against a natural horizon. His characteristic metaphors develop from the exploration of man's relationship to nature and society: they involve time and infinity, world and universe, love and spirit—terms that emerge as 20th-century humanist substitutes for the Christian vocabulary. A typical Scott poem moves from the natural landscape, as in "Laurentian Shield" ("Hidden in wonder and snow, or sudden with summer, / This land stares at the sun in a huge silence"), or from a specific image—the great Asian moth of "A Grain of Rice," for example—to a consideration of the significance of the image in the larger pattern of human life.

The frame of our human house rests on motion
Of earth and of moon, the rise of continents,
Invasion of deserts, erosion of hills
The capping of ice.
Today, while Europe tilted, drying the Baltic,
I read of a battle between brothers in anguish.
A flag moved a mile.

Distressed by the social misery of the Depression, Scott became active in left-wing political movements such as the Fabian-inspired League for Social Reconstruction (1932), which published *Social Planning for Canada* in 1935. He was national chairman of the Co-operative Commonwealth Federation (now the National Democratic Party) from 1942 to 1950 and co-author of *Make This Your Canada: A Review of CCF History and Policy* (1930). He wrote *Canada and the United States* (1941) after a year spent at Harvard on a Guggenheim fellowship. He also contributed to the important symposium *Evolving Canadian Federalism* (1958) and was a co-editor of *Quebec States Her Case* (1964), a series of essays on the new Quebec nationalism. Scott, an authority on constitutional law and civil rights, was described by the legal historian Walter Tarnopolsky as an "architect of modern Canadian thought on human rights and fundamental freedoms." He argued several major civil rights cases before the Supreme Court of Canada, including *Switzman* v. *Elbing* (1957), *Roncarelli* v. *Duplessis* (1958), and *Brodie* v. *The Queen* (1961), better known as the *Lady Chatterly* case.

In 1952 Scott was briefly a technical-aid representative for the United Nations in Burma; from 1961 to 1964 he was dean of law at McGill; and from 1963 to 1971 he was a member of the Royal Commission on Bilingualism and Biculturalism. Scott—who contributed equally to Canadian law, literature, and politics in both official languages—was elected to the Royal Society of Canada in 1947, awarded the Lorne Pierce Medal for distinguished service to Canadian literature in 1962, and received a Molson Prize for outstanding achievements in the arts, the humanities, and the social sciences in 1967. His career as an interpreter of Quebec poetry culminated with a Canada Council Translation Prize for *Poems of French Canada* (1977); his work as a social philosopher culminated with a Governor General's award for *Essays on the Constitution: Aspects of Canadian Law and Politics* (1977); and his poetry was crowned with a Governor General's award for *The Collected Poems of F. R. Scott* (1981).

Further Reading

One of the first studies of F. R. Scott's poetry was W. E. Collin's *The White Savannahs* (1936), which connects Scott's landscape poems with T. S. Eliot's *The Waste Land* and notes their connection with the loss of Eden and the desire for an ideal. Desmond Pacey in *Ten Canadian Poets* (1958) recognizes Scott's excellence in the three fields of law, literature, and politics but concludes that he "will be remembered as a poet primarily for his social satire," a view shared by K. L. Goodwin writing in *The Journal of Commonwealth Literature* in 1967. Stephen Scobie, in *Queen's Quarterly* of 1972, emphasizes the punning ambivalence of some of Scott's best poems. Other excellent essays include Elizabeth Brewster's "The I of the Observer" and Germaine Warkentein's "Scott's 'Lakeshore' and Its Tradition" in *Canadian Literature* in 1978 and 1980, respectively. Peter Stevens' *The McGill Movement: A. J. M. Smith, F. R. Scott and Leo Kennedy* (1969) places Scott in the context of the 1920s. Special issues of *Canadian Literature* in 1967 and *Canadian Poetry* in 1977 feature Scott. For a larger study of Scott as poet, political activist, and constitutional theorist see *On F. R. Scott: Essays on His Contributions to Law, Literature and Politics,* edited by Sandra Djwa and R. St. J. Macdonald (1983). □

Robert Falcon Scott

The English naval officer and polar explorer Robert Falcon Scott (1868-1912) made monumental scientific findings in Antarctica, and his geographical discoveries were extensive. He failed in his attempt to be the first to reach the South Pole.

Robert F. Scott was born on June 6, 1868, at Devonport. In 1880 he entered the naval college, H.M.S. *Britannia,* and 2 years later became a midshipman. He was promoted to first lieutenant in 1897. As early as 1887 Scott had come to the attention of Sir Clements Markham, the principal promoter of British exploration in the late 19th century. In 1899, after Markham had won partial government backing for the intended dash to the pole, Scott was chosen to head the National Antarctic Expedition.

Leaving England in August 1901, the *Discovery,* with Scott as commander, sailed south and reached the Ross Sea in January 1902. For 2 years the ship remained off Hut Point, Ross Island, in McMurdo Sound, and it was from here that many sledge journeys, including two led by Scott himself, began. On Dec. 30, 1902, Scott and two of his associates reached latitude 82°16′33″S over the Antarctic Plateau; this was then the southern record. A year later Scott reached latitude 77°59′S, longitude 146°33′E. A general reconnaissance of the area around South Victoria Land and the Ross Sea and Ross Shelf Ice was undertaken, and the findings added much to man's knowledge of Antarctica. The expedition ended when the *Discovery,* with the relief ships *Morning* and *Terra Nova,* reached New Zealand in April 1904. Promoted to captain on his return to England in 1904, Scott commanded, in turn, three warships and in 1909 became a

naval assistant at the Admiralty. Scott recorded his impressions of his first expedition in *The Voyage of the "Discovery"* (1905).

Enthusiasm for Antarctic explorations had waned after 1904, but in 1909 Scott announced plans to reach the South Pole. British and Dominion governments gave financial support, and the *Terra Nova* sailed in June 1910. While at sea, Scott learned that Roald Amundsen and his Norwegian party were also attempting to reach the pole. The race was on. From winter headquarters at Cape Evans (latitude 77°38′24″S), Scott began his sledge journey on Nov. 1, 1911. He had placed much faith, too much as events were to prove, on motor sledges and ponies. The former broke down; the latter either died in crevasses or were shot for food. Consequently, the strength of Scott and his men was taxed even before they left the last supporting party at latitude 86°32′S on Jan. 4, 1912, for the attempt on the pole. On January 18 the party, composed of Scott and four others, reached the South Pole and found there the Norwegian flag, a tent, and a note left for Scott by Amundsen, who with his excellent knowledge and use of dogs, had reached the goal on December 14, 1911.

Heartbroken and weary, the party now turned for base camp. But weakened by the strain and lack of warm food, which brought on frostbite, the men became involved in a "race against time to reach one depot after another" before their strength gave out. At latitude 79°40′S, 11 miles from One Ton Depot, the remaining three members of the party made camp for the last time. On March 29 Scott made his last journal entry. Eight months later a relief expedition found the tent, bodies, journals, and records. In 1964 an account of this expedition was published as *Scott's Last Expedition: From the Personal Journals of Captain R. F. Scott.*

When news of the tragic and heroic end reached London and Europe, admiration was forthcoming from many quarters. A lasting action was the opening of a fund to commemorate the explorers which enabled publication of their scientific results and the opening of the great Scott Polar Research Institute in Cambridge, England.

Further Reading

Biographies of Scott are Stephen Gwynn, *Captain Scott* (1930); Martin Lindsay, *The Epic of Captain Scott* (1934); George Seaver, *Scott of the Antarctic: A Study in Character* (1940); and Maude Carter, *Captain Scott: Explorer and Scientist* (1950). Illuminating works on his second expedition are Leonard Huxley, *Scott's Last Expedition* (1913), and Edward Ratcliffe Garth Russell Evans, *South with Scott* (1921). The scientific findings of this voyage were published in *British Antarctic Expedition ("Terra Nova"), 1910-13: Scientific Results* (1914).

Additional Sources

Huntford, Roland, *The last place on earth,* New York: Atheneum, 1985.

Huntford, Roland, *Scott and Amundsen,* New York: Atheneum, 1984, 1983.

Huxley, Elspeth Joscelin Grant, *Scott of the Antarctic,* Lincoln: University of Nebraska Press, 1990, 1977.

Johnson, Anthony M., *Scott of the Antarctic and Cardiff,* Cardiff, U.K.: University College Cardiff Press, 1984.

Sanderson, Marie, *Griffith Taylor: Antarctic scientist and pioneer geographer,* Ottawa: Carleton University Press, 1988. ☐

Sir Walter Scott

The Scottish novelist and poet Sir Walter Scott (1771-1832) is the acknowledged master of the historical novel. He was one of the most influential authors of modern times.

Walter Scott was born in Edinburgh on Aug. 15, 1771, the son of a lawyer with a long family tradition in law. By birth Scott was connected with both the rising middle class of Britain and the aristocratic Scottish heritage then passing into history. He was educated at Edinburgh University and prepared for a career in law, but his avocations were history and literature. He read widely in English and Continental literatures, particularly medieval and Renaissance chivalric romances, German romantic poetry and fiction, and the narrative folk poems known as ballads.

Translations and Poetry

From these intense interests Scott's earliest publications derived: a translation of J. W. von Goethe's play *Götz von Berlichingen* (1799) and other translations from German;

Minstrelsy of the Scottish Border (1802-1803), a collection of ballads that generated great interest in folk poetry; and a succession of narrative poems, mainly of chivalric or historical action. These poems—including *The Lay of the Last Minstrel* (1805), *Marmion* (1808), and *The Lady of the Lake* (1810)—became best sellers, and Scott established his first literary reputation as a poet of the romantic school.

During these years Scott also pursued a legal career, rising to the official position of clerk of the Court of Session. His enormous energies allowed him to engage in scholarly and journalistic activities. His edition and biography of John Dryden, the English poet and dramatist, published in 1808, remains of value. His politically motivated founding of the *Quarterly Review,* a literary journal, helped make Edinburgh the most influential center of British intellectual life outside London. In these years Scott also began to create an estate, Abbotsford, to reflect his antiquarian interests. He modeled its furnishings and architecture on the traditions of the medieval era.

Waverley Novels

When sales of his verse narrative *Rokeby* (1813) declined and a new poet, Lord Byron, appeared on the literary scene, Scott began to develop another of his many capacities. Picking up the fragment of a novel he had begun in 1805, he tried his hand at fiction, and his most fully characteristic novel, *Waverley* (1814), resulted. As its subtitle, *'Tis Sixty Years Since,* established, *Waverley* was a historical novel about the 1745 rebellion to restore the Stuart line to the British throne. By leading a young and naive Englishman through a wide range of Scottish classes, political factions, and cultural modes, Scott built up a substantial picture of an entire nation's life at a dramatic historical juncture.

The success of *Waverley* established Scott in the career of a novelist, but it did not establish his name in that role. Unwilling to stake too much on his venture into fiction, he had published *Waverley* anonymously. Finding that the mask of anonymity had stimulated public interest, Scott signed his subsequent novels "by the Author of Waverley." This signature became his trademark, the novels bearing it being called the "Waverley" novels. The Waverley novels exercised enormous fascination not only for Scots and Englishmen but also throughout the Continent. These novels provided the characters and plots for innumerable stories, plays, and operas, the most famous of which is Gaetano Donizetti's opera *Lucia di Lammermoor.*

Scott's achievement as a novelist can best be summarized by grouping his novels according to their themes and settings. His first successes were largely in the realm of Scottish history. In the order of their chronological setting, the Scottish novels are *Castle Dangerous* (1832) and *The Fair Maid of Perth* (1828), both set in the 14th century; *The Monastery* and *The Abbot* (both 1820), its sequel, set during the 16th century's religious upheavals; *A Legend of Montrose* (1819) and *Old Mortality* (1816), which deal with the campaigns of the 17th-century civil wars; and a series of novels of the Jacobite (Stuart) rebellions of the 18th century—*Rob Roy* (1817), *Waverley,* and *Redgauntlet* (1824). Other Scottish novels indirectly related to historical themes are *The Black Dwarf* (1816), *The Heart of Midlothian* (1818), *The Bride of Lammermoor* (1819), and *The Pirate* (1822). Scott also wrote a group of novels set in nearly contemporary times: *Guy Mannering* (1815), *The Antiquary* (1816), and *St. Ronan's Well* (1824).

English Novels

At a critical point of his career, Scott turned to English history for his subject matter. Critics are generally agreed that the English (and Continental) novels, mainly set in medieval times, are inferior in social and psychological realism, but they include Scott's most enduringly popular works. He began with *Ivanhoe* (1820) and then wrote three other novels set in the period of the Crusades: *The Talisman* (1825), *The Betrothed* (1825), and *Count Robert of Paris* (1832). *Quentin Durward* (1823) and *Anne of Geierstein* (1829) deal with the later Middle Ages, and the Renaissance is represented by *Kenilworth* (1821) and *The Fortunes of Nigel* (1822). The English phases of the civil-war and Restoration periods were rendered in *Woodstock* (1826) and *Peveril of the Peak* (1822), respectively.

So massive a literary corpus cannot be reduced to broad generalizations. Most critics and readers seem to prefer Scott's early novels. On the whole, Scott's work is flawed by sentimentality and rhetoric, but his novels command the power to put modern readers in touch with men of the past.

Scott's later years were clouded by illness, throughout which he continued to write. He spent the energies of his last years trying to write enough to recover honorably from the bankruptcy of a publishing firm in which he had invested heavily. He died at Abbotsford on Sept. 21, 1832.

Further Reading

The authorized biography by Scott's son-in-law, John Gibson Lockhart, *Memoirs of the Life of Sir Walter Scott* (3 vols., 1837-1838), has been supplemented by the definitive, scholarly work of Edgar Johnson, *Sir Walter Scott: The Great Unknown* (2 vols., 1970), which combines biography and criticism. The most thorough critical examination of the novels is Francis R. Hart, *Scott's Novels: The Plotting of Historical Survival* (1966). Another approach is presented in Alexander Welsh, *The Hero of the Waverley Novels* (1963). The most influential recent interpretation is that of George Lukács, *The Historical Novel* (1962). □

Winfield Scott

The American Winfield Scott (1786-1866) was the leading general of the Mexican War and a superb tactician. He was the Whig nominee for president in 1852.

Winfield Scott became a soldier at a time when the U.S. Army was very ineffective. By study and hard work, he made himself the best military man in the country, wrote the standard manuals on tactics and infantry, and upgraded the Army into an effective unit. Moreover, he was a negotiator who avoided war on several occasions. Yet the presidency, which he coveted, eluded him.

Scott was born near Petersburg, Va., on June 13, 1786. Failing to inherit the family wealth through legal technicalities, he attended William and Mary College but quit because he disapproved the irreligious attitude of the students. After reading law, he was admitted to the Virginia bar in 1806 and practiced until appointed a captain in the military in 1808. Sent to New Orleans, he was soon in trouble. He declared that the commanding general of the department, James Wilkinson, was as great a traitor as Aaron Burr; Scott was court-martialed and suspended from the Army for a year (1810).

War of 1812

A lieutenant colonel at the outbreak of war, Scott distinguished himself in a number of battles. Several times wounded, the 6-foot 5-inch, 230-pound officer showed such judgment and courage that he was promoted to brigadier general, was breveted a major general, and was voted the thanks of Congress and a gold medal. He declined the offered position of secretary of war in James Madison's administration.

Scott went to Europe in 1815 and in 1829 to study foreign military tactics, and he wrote military manuals for the Army that remained standard for half a century. He married Maria D. Mayo of Richmond, Va., in 1817. He also conducted military institutes for the officers of his command, the Eastern Division, which was headquartered in New York City.

In 1828 Scott participated in the Black Hawk War. Four years later President Andrew Jackson sent him to South Carolina during the nullification controversy, and his tact prevented civil war at that time. In 1835 Jackson sent him to fight the Seminole and Creeks in Florida, but he was deprived of materials and moved slowly. Jackson removed him from command to face a board of inquiry. The board promptly exonerated him with praise for his "energy, steadiness and ability."

Following the abortive Canadian revolt of 1837, President Martin Van Buren sent Scott to bring peace to the troubled Niagara region. Later in 1838 Scott convinced 16,000 outraged Cherokee that they should move peacefully from Tennessee and South Carolina to the Indian Territory; he also persuaded them to be vaccinated. His tact and skill as a negotiator in 1839 brought peace in the "Lumberjack War" over the boundary between Maine and New Brunswick. In reward for these activities, he was named general in chief of the Army in 1841, a position he held for 20 years.

Mexican War

Scott's name had been mentioned prominently for the Whig nomination for president in 1840 and 1844; thus, at the outbreak of the Mexican War, President James K. Polk did not want Scott to achieve the prominence that would earn him the presidential nomination. When Zachary Taylor's campaign in northern Mexico failed to achieve victory, however, Polk had to turn to Scott. Scott's strategy proved effective: landing at Veracruz in March 1847, he was in Mexico City within 6 months after brilliant victories at Cerro Gordo, Molino del Rey, and Chapultepec. His force then became an army of occupation, restoring order so effectively that a delegation of Mexicans asked him to become dictator of the nation. Polk wanted to court-martial Scott and thereby discredit him as a rival, but Congress voted Scott a second gold medal and thanks for his conduct of the war. Polk's charges were withdrawn.

Presidential Nominee

In 1848 the Whig party elected Zachary Taylor to the White House. In 1852 the Whig presidential nomination went to Scott, but he was defeated easily in a pompous and lackluster campaign. Congress 3 years later recognized his accomplishments by naming him a lieutenant general, the first American to hold that rank since George Washington.

In 1857 Scott argued against the "Mormon War" in favor of negotiation. Though President James Buchanan sent him to negotiate a dispute with England over the San Juan Islands in the Pacific Northwest in 1859, he refused Scott's advice to strengthen Southern forts and posts to avoid their capture should civil war break out.

In 1861, at the beginning of the Civil War, Scott stayed in the Union Army despite his Virginia heritage. He recommended the policy of dividing and containing the South to President Abraham Lincoln, a policy later followed successfully. On Nov. 1, 1861, Scott retired at his own request. Lincoln summarized the nation's sentiment when he said, "We are . . . his debtors." Scott died on May 29, 1866, at West Point, N.Y., and was buried in Arlington National Cemetery.

Scott's insistence on maintaining strict standards of dress and discipline in the Army caused the troops to refer to him as "Old Fuss and Feathers." Opposed to the use of strong alcoholic beverages, he once ordered that any soldier found intoxicated had to dig a grave for his own size and then contemplate it, for soon he would fill it if he persisted in drinking. His arguments against alcoholic beverages led to the founding of the first temperance societies in the United States.

Further Reading

Memoirs of Lieut.-General Scott, LL.D., Written by Himself (2 vols., 1864), filled with rhetorical flourishes, contains Scott's own version of his life and times. Two standard biographies are Charles W. Elliott, *Winfield Scott: The Soldier and the Man* (1937), and Arthur D. H. Smith, *Old Fuss and Feathers: The Life and Exploits of Lt.-General Winfield Scott* (1937). Justin H. Smith, *The War with Mexico* (2 vols., 1919), traces Scott's activities in that conflict.

Additional Sources

Keyes, Erasmus D. (Erasmus Darwin), *Fighting Indians in Washington Territory,* Fairfield, Wash.: Ye Galleon Press, 1988. □

Alexander Nikolayevich Scriabin

The composer and pianist Alexander Nikolayevich Scriabin (1871-1915) was a striking representative of the early modern school of Russian music. The romantic symbolism of his late work often obscures his genuine innovations.

Alexander Scriabin was born in Moscow on Dec. 25, 1871. His musical talent was discerned at an early age. He studied piano and, at the age of 14, took theory and composition instruction from Alexander Taneev. Scriabin entered the Moscow Conservatory in 1888; one of his classmates was Sergei Rachmaninov. Scriabin graduated with the Gold Medal in 1892. His accomplishment as a pianist outweighed the value of his early, Chopin-like compositions for piano, and it was as a performer that he began appearing abroad. Except for a 6-year term (1897-1903) as a piano teacher at the Moscow Conservatory, he spent most of his mature years in the West, years in which his zest for living brought him almost as much attention as his art.

From about the turn of the century Scriabin began to cast away both his tonal and formal moorings: he is often lauded for the former and criticized for the latter, but the phenomena are inseparable. The steady progression is seen in his numerous short piano pieces—nocturnes, mazurkas, études, and preludes—and becomes focused in the last sonatas (Nos. 6-10, 1912-1913) and the remarkable orchestral works: the Third Symphony (*Divine Poem;* 1905), the Fourth Symphony (*Poem of Ecstasy;* 1907), and the Fifth Symphony (*Poem of Fire or Prometheus;* 1910).

In pushing away from tonality Scriabin developed chords from superimposed fourths, including the "mystic chord." He handled form in erratic time segments; some of his études are only seconds long. Overlaying this technical and expressive development was a highly personal, egocentric, verbose, quasi-devout mysticism which has led some biographers to judge Scriabin insane. Indeed, sketches for a final, unfinished work, *Mystery,* seem musically senseless; it was to be performed as a "multimedia" event on a Tibetan mountain by thousands of supplicants and, in Scriabin's imagination, was to bring the world to a close.

On April 14, 1915, Scriabin died in Moscow. His family, whom he legitimized at the end, was left with little money, and Rachmaninov, among others, came to their aid. Scriabin's son, Julian, seemed a prodigious copy of the father; he, too, died early and tragically in 1919.

Scriabin stands somewhat aside from the mainstream of musical development and seems unclassifiable in either Russian or Western terms. His contribution may best be seen in his small piano pieces. He wrote no chamber music, no opera, and very little vocal music, so his influence is uniquely limited. The innovative sophistication and mysticism of his later works were not appreciated by the ideologists of the young Soviet Union, and this, too, was a

limiting factor. Like many of his generation, he moves in and out of vogue. But his legacy, though limited, is of lasting value.

Further Reading

Biographers either fight shy of or linger dotingly on some of the extramusical sensations in Scriabin's life. The soberer accounts are those of Arthur E. Hull (1916) and Alfred Swan (1923). The works by Leonid Sabaneev (1923) and Faubion Bowers (2 vols., 1969) are less restrained; the Bowers book is unusually entertaining though not altogether accurate. Chapters on Scriabin appear in M. Montagu-Nathan, *Contemporary Russian Composers* (1917); M. D. Calvocoressi and Gerald Abraham, *Masters of Russian Music* (1936); David Brook, *Six Great Russian Composers* (1946); and William Austin, *Music in the Twentieth Century* (1966).

Additional Sources

Bowers, Faubion, *Scriabin, a biography,* New York: Dover, 1995.

Schloezer, Boris de, *Scriabin: artist and mystic,* Berkeley: University of California Press, 1987. □

Edward Wyllis Scripps

The confidence of Edward Wyllis Scripps (1854-1926) in free enterprise and democracy enabled him to create the first newspaper chain in the United States and to contribute significantly to the new journalism of his era.

Born in Rushville, Ill., on June 18, 1854, E. W. Scripps came from a publishing family. His grandfather had issued the *London Literary Gazette,* and relatives in America were associated with newspapers. Scripps was raised on the family farm in Winchester, Ohio. At 18 he became an office boy on the *Detroit Advertiser and Tribune,* managed and owned by his half brother James Scripps. Later he served in business and editorial capacities for James. Borrowing money from relatives, notably his half sister Ellen, who would be his close associate for 40 years, Scripps founded the *Cleveland Penny Press* in 1877.

Scripps was a philosopher of journalism as well as a businessman. He believed that the psychology of people had to be studied if they were to be satisfied. He reached controversial conclusions over the years, as when he held that "one mature white American is a better prospect [as a newspaper purchaser] than two or three Negroes or comparatively recent immigrants. . . ." On the other hand, he thought that the differences between people were the products of accident and environment. He fought boldly and under stress for the right to print news independently, and he was conspicuous in battles against municipal corruption.

In 1880 Scripps again joined relatives to take on the *St. Louis Evening Chronicle* and then the paper that became the *Cincinnati Post.* With the Detroit and Cleveland papers,

they constituted the first newspaper chain in the country. Disagreements in policy, particularly Scripps's liberal, prolabor views, caused Scripps to leave the group with only the *Cincinnati Post.* He began a drive which multiplied his newspaper holdings in the Midwest and South, retaining 51 percent of stock in all papers. In 1889 he and Milton A. McRae founded the Scripps-McRae League of Newspapers. Dissatisfied with telegraphic news from the Associated Press and opposing its monopolistic features, in 1897 Scripps organized the Scripps-McRae Press Association, later the United Press Association. Scripps later developed a feature service, the Newspaper Enterprise Association.

Although Scripps maintained rigid control of his properties, he sought to spread responsibility for them among associates, and by the time of his death on March 12, 1926, he owned only 40 percent of the stock. Scripps's interest in science expressed itself in his organization (1920) of the journalistic Science Service. With his sister he also endowed what became the Scripps Institution of Oceanography at La Jolla, Calif.

Further Reading

Scripps speaks for himself in two books: one arranged by his family and edited by Charles R. McCabe, *Damned Old Crank* (1951), the other edited by Oliver Knight, *I Protest* (1966), a volume of "selected disquisitions." Biographical accounts written by associates are Gilson Gardner, *Lusty Scripps: The Life of E. W. Scripps* (1932), and Negley O. Cochran, *E. W. Scripps* (1933). Scripps figures also in Milton A. McRae, *Forty Years in Newspaperdom* (1924).

Additional Sources

A Celebration of the legacies of E.W. Scripps: his life, works and heritage: symposium: Ohio University, Athens, Ohio, March 2-3, 1990, Athens, Ohio: Ohio University, 1990.

Preece, Charles, *Edward Willis and Ellen Browning Scripps: an unmatched pair: a biography,* Chelsea, MI: Bookcrafters, 1990.

Trimble, Vance H., *The astonishing Mr. Scripps: the turbulent life of America's penny press lord,* Ames: Iowa State University Press, 1992. □

James Henry Scullin

James Henry Scullin (1876-1953) was an Australian politician and the first native-born Labour prime minister of Australia.

James Scullin was born the son of a railway worker near Ballarat, Victoria. He was brought up a Roman Catholic and formally educated only at primary school, but he later attended evening classes. He became a small grocer and editor of a newspaper in Ballarat before turning his attention to politics.

Scullin joined the Labour party in 1903 and was organizer for the Australian Workers Union for 4 years until, in 1910, he was elected to the federal Parliament. He lost his seat in 1913 and became editor of the *Ballarat Echo,* an evening daily. He returned to Parliament in 1923 and became deputy leader of the Labour party in 1927 and leader the following year. In the election of October 1929 he decisively defeated the governing Liberal and Country parties, and the Labour party gained its largest parliamentary majority since the federation in 1901.

Scullin lacked ministerial experience when he became prime minister, and though he was a man of moderate views and was respected on all sides for his integrity, his modesty and gentleness ill matched the heavy burdens that were to fall on his shoulders. As the effects of the worldwide economic depression spread to Australia, his ministry was torn by internal dissension. His task was made more difficult by a hostile upper house, where, in contrast to its large majority in the lower house, the Labour party held only 7 of the 36 seats and was thus powerless to put several of its proposals into effect.

Because of the economic crisis, Scullin's government was obliged to repudiate election pledges and to assume responsibility for deflation, retrenchment, reduction in wages and the standard of living, and, at the end of 1931, a devaluation of the Australian pound in terms of sterling. Throughout his tenure of office Scullin was harassed by political difficulties arising out of his government's management of the economic crisis.

In August 1930 Scullin left to attend the imperial conference in London, where one of his duties was to advise the King that, in accordance with Labour party views in Australia, the next governor general should be an Australian. In his absence, his parliamentary following split on economic policy, and when he returned, there was outright defection. Five members from New South Wales left the federal Labour party and formed themselves into a group attached to the policies of John Thomas Lang, the controversial Labour premier in their state; and Joseph Lyons, the postmaster general, resigned from the ministry and joined the opposition. In the election of December 1931 the opposition was led by Lyons and supported by some other erstwhile members of the Labour party.

The crippled Labour government was swept from office, and Scullin was replaced as prime minister by his former lieutenant. He continued as leader of the Labour party until 1935, when he resigned on account of ill health. He remained in Parliament until 1949 and died on Jan. 28, 1953.

Further Reading

W. E. Denning, *Caucus Crisis* (1937), is an account of the rise and fall of Scullin's government. Edward R. Walker, *Australia in the World Depression* (1933), and D. B. Copland, *Australia in the World Crisis, 1929-1933* (1934), cover the economic problems of the period. See also William R. McLaurin, *Economic Planning in Australia, 1929-36* (1937).

Additional Sources

Robertson, John, *J. H. Scullin: a political biography,* Nedlands: University of Western Australia Press, 1974. □

Glenn Theodore Seaborg

The American chemist Glenn Theodore Seaborg (born 1912) won the Nobel Prize for the discovery of transuranium elements and served as chairman of the Atomic Energy Commission.

Glenn T. Seaborg was born on April 19, 1912, in the iron-mining town of Ishpeming, Michigan to Swedish immigrants Herman Theodore Seaborg, a machinist, and Selma O. (Erickson). At his mother's urging, the family moved to the Los Angeles, California, area when he was ten, in an effort to locate better educational opportunities for the children. In 1929 he entered the University of California at Los Angeles, majored in chemistry, and then went on as a graduate student at University of California at Berkeley (1934-1937).

Berkeley was exciting for a budding scientist of the time. The chemistry department was led by a figure of world renown, Gilbert N. Lewis, while the physics department boasted the young Ernest O. Lawrence, who had invented the cyclotron. Seaborg received his Ph.D. in chemistry, although he did his research on a problem in nuclear physics. In this way he obtained knowledge of both fields, a valuable background for what became his major life work.

Research for Nuclear Weapons

Without a job after graduation in 1937, Seaborg was surprised and delighted when Lewis asked him to be his personal assistant. Shortly thereafter, Seaborg met Lawrence's secretary, Helen L.Griggs, whom he married in 1942. Seaborg was able to continue working in his own specialty area: the discovery and chemical characterization of the radioactive isotopes of various elements, including iodine-131, iron-59, and cobalt-60. At this time Enrico Fermi in Rome seemed to be producing an assortment of so-called transuranium elements (because they were beyond uranium, element 92, in the periodic table) when he bombarded uranium with neutrons. The German radiochemists Otto Hahn and Fritz Strassmann, however, found clear evidence of elements from the middle of the periodic table, and by early 1939 it was recognized that uranium was splitting, or fissioning, in these experiments, rather than capturing a neutron to evolve into an element with a higher atomic number.

This discovery, coming on the eve of World War II, generated much thought about the possibility of nuclear weapons. It also stimulated much basic nuclear research. In particular, it seemed possible that transuranium elements could really be produced, and Berkeley physicists Edwin McMillan and Philip Abelson, using the new 60-inch cyclotron, did indeed create element 93, neptunium, in 1940. McMillan then began the search for element 94, but turned the task over to Seaborg when he was called away on war research. Seaborg, by now an instructor in the Chemistry Department (1939-1941), produced and chemically identified plutonium in February 1941 by bombarding neptunium with deuterons, the nuclei of the hydrogen isotope deuterium. A month later he and Emilio Segre showed that the isotope plutonium-239 fissioned with slow neutrons, opening the possibility of using it as fuel for a nuclear reactor or the explosive heart of a nuclear weapon.

Seaborg was made an assistant professor in 1941. Early the next year John Gofman, a student working with him, created and chemically identified a new isotope of uranium, U-233, which would be of great commercial importance if thorium, readily abundant, ever became a common reactor fuel. With America's entry into the war and the organization of scientific activity for military purposes, Seaborg took leave from the University of California and joined the nuclear research group, *The Manhattan Project,* at the University of Chicago. There he was in charge of the investigation of transuranium elements, especially the task of learning plutonium's chemical properties so the element could be extracted from uranium.

Visible amounts of plutonium were extracted by the summer of 1942. The microgram quantities produced were used to devise chemical separation techniques tested in a pilot plant at Oak Ridge, Tennessee, and scaled up to industrial size for the plutonium-producing reactors built at Hanford, Washington. The plutonium separated there was transported to Los Alamos, New Mexico, where it was fashioned into components for the bomb tested at Alamogordo in July 1945 and for the weapon dropped on Nagasaki in August.

Scientific and Administrative Tasks

Seaborg returned to Berkeley in the spring of 1946 as a full professor. While still in Chicago, he and his colleagues synthesized and separated elements 95 and 96, americium and curium, respectively, and Seaborg fashioned the concept of the actinide group to place the heavy elements in the periodic table. This idea enabled him to predict the chemical properties of still-higher numbered transuranium elements. At Berkeley between 1946 and 1958 he and his group (sometimes collaborating with other laboratories) discovered six more elements: berkelium (97), californium (98), einsteinium (99), fermium (100), mendelevium (101), and nobelium (102). Element 106 was found some years later.

With scientific distinction came additional responsibilities. Seaborg was director of Berkeley's Nuclear Chemistry Division (1946-1958 and 1972-1975) and an associate director of the campus' Radiation Laboratory (1954-1961 and after 1972), founded by Ernest Lawrence. He also served on the national scene. President Truman appointed him a member of the Atomic Energy Commission's first General Advisory Committee (1947-1950), which was chaired by Robert Oppenheimer.

These positions did not pull Seaborg away from laboratory work, but a request from a most unexpected direction began that process. Berkeley's chancellor, Clark Kerr, asked Seaborg, a sports fan, to be the faculty representative to the Pacific Coast Intercollegiate Athletic Conference. He accepted and served (1953-1958) during a time of scandals that forced the conference's dissolution and the creation of a successor organization. Indeed, he was a leading figure who displayed administrative skills in navigating through that troubled period. When Kerr was elevated to the presidency of the multi-campus University of California in 1958, he asked Seaborg to be the next chancellor at Berkeley.

Seaborg served in this position during a period of great activity: various departments, colleges, and institutes were created, while others were restructured. Increased federal funding offered greater opportunities for graduate education, numerous buildings were constructed or planned, programs to improve the quality of teaching were initiated, and teams in several sports were remarkably successful. Seaborg responded to invitations at the national level as well and was appointed by President Eisenhower to the President's Science Advisory Committee (1959-1961) and to the National Science Foundation's National Science Board (1960-1961).

Nuclear Power for War and Peace

In early 1961 newly inaugurated President Kennedy appointed Seaborg chairman of the Atomic Energy Commission (AEC). He held this post for ten years—longer than any other chairman—under Presidents Kennedy, Johnson and Nixon. As it was a full-time job requiring residence in Washington D.C., Seaborg took an extended leave of absence from the University of California. The AEC's mission was two-fold: to design and build nuclear weapons and to encourage peaceful uses of nuclear energy. The commission's history during this period has not yet received enough attention, so Seaborg's leadership cannot be fully evaluated. New weapons—such as the Minuteman intercontinental ballistic missile—were deployed, while other weapons—such as missiles with multiple warheads—were developed. The nation's stockpile of arms reached a point where the production of fissionable material was reduced. Seaborg also was involved in the government's successful effort to negotiate the Limited Nuclear Test Ban Treaty (1963) and the Non-Proliferation Treaty (1970).

As the discoverer of plutonium Seaborg preferred to encourage its use for peaceful purposes rather than as the prime ingredient in atomic bombs or the trigger in hydrogen bombs. His years at the AEC were ones in which the peaceful atom seemed likely to succeed. Radioactive materials were used in medical diagnosis and treatment, industrial product testing, the dating of archeological artifacts, power packs for instruments that must be left unattended, and other applications that are noncontroversial. But the major uses, once so promising, were dead or moribund by 1985. The AEC's Plowshare program, in which nuclear explosives would carve out harbors and canals and pulverize rock for easier mineral extraction, proved to be neither economically nor politically viable. The same is true of the nuclear-powered spacecraft (which never got off the drawing board) and nuclear-powered merchant ships (which were built). During the early 1960s electrical utilities could not sign up fast enough for construction of nuclear reactors. By the end of the decade and through the 1970s they cancelled contracts faster than they sought new ones. Unanticipated time delays, enormous cost overruns, smaller demand for electricity, construction quality problems, safety uncertainties, public opposition, and other factors turned nuclear power into an industry with a great future behind it. But if this has been a failed generation of reactors, a number of them nevertheless were built and more will come on line in the future. Support for the next generation—breeder reactors—which would produce more fissionable material than they consume and which would utilize the presently "wasted" uranium-238 or thorium-232 (the latter yields U-233, discovered by Gofman and Seaborg) had been withdrawn by the federal government.

Seaborg returned to Berkeley in 1971 as a University Professor of Chemistry. During his years in Washington D.C. and after he served on numerous other governmental committees and played an active role in professional societies. He was president of the American Association for the Advancement of Science in 1972 and of the American Chemical Society in 1976. Nearly 50 colleges and universities awarded him honorary degrees; he was an honorary member of many foreign scientific societies and the recipient of numerous medals and prizes, the most notable being the Nobel Prize for Chemistry, which he shared in 1951 with McMillan.

He was one of the founders of, and in 1981, the president of the International Organization for Chemical Sciences in Development (IOCD), an organization that tried to solve Third World problems through scientific collaboration. In the 1980s, he published two books, the first being *Kennedy, Krushchev and the Test Ban* (1981). In 1987 *Stem-*

ming the Tide: Arms Control in the Johnson Years was published. Outside the political and scientific arenas, Seaborg was a devoted family man and outdoor enthusiast.

Further Reading

Factual information about his life may be found in a directory like *American Men and Women of Science* (1982). For an interesting analysis of his career from an unusual perspective, see Rae Goodell, *The Visible Scientists* (1977). Seaborg's leadership of the AEC was reviewed critically in H. Peter Metzger's *The Atomic Establishment* (1972). Most useful was an autobiographical entry Seaborg wrote for the volume edited by Irving Stone, *There was Light. Autobiography of a University. Berkeley: 1868-1968* (1970). □

Samuel Seabury

The American theologian Samuel Seabury (1729-1796) was an important figure in the establishment of the Episcopal Church in the United States.

Samuel Seabury was born in Groton, Conn., on Nov. 30, 1729, a son of Samuel Seabury, a minister of the Congregational Church who became a convert to the Church of England and was ordained in its ministry in 1730. Young Seabury graduated from Yale College in 1748, went to England in 1751, studied medicine in Edinburgh, and was ordained in 1753. A year later he returned to America under the auspices of the Society for the Propagation of the Gospel and became rector of Christ Church, New Brunswick, N.J. Later he served churches in Jamaica and Westchester, N.Y.

Conflict characterized Seabury's life. He was a High Churchman and a royalist. He believed that the establishment of a strong episcopate in America should take precedence over the organization of a national church. An early controversy left a mark on him. Dissenters, who were in the majority in the Jamaica vestry, opposed the governor's action in making Seabury, rather than the man they had chosen, the town minister. Later, in Westchester, using a pseudonym, he wrote pamphlets in defense of the Church of England and of British rule in America. In November 1775 he was arrested but was permitted to return to Westchester 2 months later. He sought refuge behind the British lines in September 1776 and in 1778 was appointed chaplain to a British regiment. After the war he received a pension from the British government.

In 1783 Seabury was chosen by the Connecticut clergy to obtain consecration as a bishop. The lack of bishops in America had been an obstacle to the growth of the Church, for ordination could be effected only in England. But the English authorities would not agree to Seabury's candidacy, and he was consecrated in the Episcopal Church of Scotland in November 1784. The following year he returned to America as rector of St. James Church, New London, Conn., and bishop of Connecticut, the first bishop of the Episcopal Church in the country.

Samuel Seabury (holding cane)

Efforts to establish a national Episcopal Church had begun during Seabury's absence. His position as bishop caused some opposition to unification; some clergymen condemned him because of his actions in support of the British; others doubted the validity of his consecration. He was strongly supported by most of the New England clergy, however, and Church unity was achieved at the General Convention of 1789 in Philadelphia. Seabury died on Feb. 25, 1796, in New London.

Further Reading

James Thayer Addison, *The Episcopal Church in the United States, 1789-1931* (1951), gives an account of Seabury's activities. Raymond W. Albright, *A History of the Protestant Episcopal Church* (1964), contains more detail and documentation. The classic biographical sketch of Seabury is in *The Episcopate in America* by William Stevens Perry (1895).

Additional Sources

Mitgang, Herbert, *The man who rode the tiger: the life of Judge Samuel Seabury and the story of the greatest investigation of city corruption in this century,* New York: Norton, 1979, 1963.

Seabury, Samuel, *Moneygripe's apprentice: the personal narrative of Samuel Seabury III,* New Haven: Yale University Press, 1989. □

Robert George Seale

Robert George Seale (born 1936) was a militant activist who, with Huey P. Newton and Bobby Hutton, founded the Black Panther Party for Self Defense in 1966.

Born to a poor African American carpenter and his wife in Dallas, Texas, on October 22, 1936, Robert George (Bobby) Seale and his family moved to Port Arthur, Texas, and then to San Antonio, Texas, before finally settling in Oakland, California, during World War II. Attributing his failure to make the basketball and football teams to racial prejudice, Seale quit Oakland High School and joined the U.S. Air Force. After three years in the Air Force, Seale was court-martialed and given a bad conduct discharge for disobeying a colonel at Ellsworth Air Force Base in South Dakota.

Seale returned to Oakland and, while working as a sheet metal mechanic in various aerospace plants, earned his high school diploma through night school. In 1962 he began attending Oakland City College (Merritt College). Seale became aware of the African American struggle for civil rights when he joined the Afro-American Association (AAA), a campus organization that stressed black separatism and self-improvement. Through the AAA he met activist Huey P. Newton in September 1962. Seale and Newton soon became disenchanted with the AAA, however, believing that the organization offered little more than ineffectual cultural nationalism. In their view, this cultural nationalism would not help lessen the economic and political oppression felt in the African American community, especially in the Ghetto. Both greatly admired Malcolm X and were particularly impressed with his teachings. They were especially drawn to the idea that Black people had to defend themselves against white brutality and inaccurate education. The assassination of Malcolm X in 1965 pushed them to adopt Malcolm's slogan, "Freedom by any means necessary," and they founded the Black Panther Party for Self-Defense in October 1966.

The Black Panther Party for Self-Defense

Beginning as an armed patrol dedicated to the defense of Oakland Blacks against the brutality of the city police, the Black Panthers gained local notoriety for their fearlessness and militant demand for Black rights. In 1967 the Black Panther Party (BPP) garnered national attention when it sent an armed contingent to the state capitol in Sacramento to protest a proposed gun-control law and to assert the constitutional right of Blacks to bear arms against their white oppressors. Coupling food programs for needy families and "liberation schools" for political education with defiant calls for Black control of community institutions and for "power to the people," the BPP opened recruitment centers across the nation in 1968. According to J. Edgar Hoover, the head of the Federal Bureau of Investigation (FBI), the BPP had become "the No. 1 threat to the internal security of the nation." Fearful of the growing popularity of the BPP and their insistence that Black Power grows out of the barrel of a gun, Hoover ordered the FBI to employ "hard-hitting counterintelligence measures to cripple the Black Panthers" in November 1968

For their participation in the demonstrations at the Democratic National Convention in Chicago in 1968, Seale was brought to trial with seven white radicals, including Youth International Party founders Jerry Rubin and Abbie Hoffman, and the founders of Students for a Democratic Society, Tom Hayden and Rennie Davis, on September 24, 1969. The eight were indicted in a federal court in Chicago under the new anti-riot provision of the 1968 Civil Rights Act, which made it illegal to cross state lines to incite a riot or instruct in the use of riot weapons. Because his attorney, Charles Garry, had just undergone surgery and could not be present, Seale asked for a delay two weeks before his trial. Judge Julius Hoffman refused. Seale then retained William Kunstler, who was representing the other seven defendants. Upon Garry's advice, fired Kunstler and asked to represent himself, which would have given him the opportunity to cross-examine witnesses and present evidence during the trial. However, Judge Hoffman insisted that Kunstler was sufficient representation and proceeded with the trial.

When Seale continued to protest, with repeated outbursts and by refusing to follow courtroom procedure and decorum, Hoffman had him bound and gagged during the trial. On November 5, 1969, the judge sentenced Seale to four years in jail for 16 counts of contempt of court, each of which contributed three months to his sentence. During his prison term Seale was also indicted for ordering the torture and execution of Alex Rackley, former Black Panther suspected of being a government informer. On May 25, 1971, the conspiracy trial ended in a hung jury and the judge ordered all charges dropped against Seale and the other defendants. The following year the federal government suspended the contempt charges and released Seale from prison.

Return to Politics

Seale returned to Oakland to find the BPP decimated by police infiltration, killings, and arrests. At least two dozen Black Panthers had died in gun fights with the police and dozens more had been imprisoned. The BPP had also been rendered impotent by internal disputes in which Black nationalist advocates warred against the program of revolutionary socialism called for by Newton and Seale. In 1973 Seale ran for mayor of Oakland, finishing second out of nine candidates with 43,710 votes to the incumbent's 77,476.

Claiming combat weariness, Seale left Oakland and the Panthers in 1974. In 1978 he published his autobiography, *A Lonely Rage,* which described the emotional and psychological changes he had undergone as a black activist. His 1970 book, *Seize the Time,* portrayed the story of the Black Panthers and the political views of Huey Newton. In retrospect, Seale found consolation in Newton's belief that, to move a single grain of sand is to change a world. "We moved a grain of sand and several hills beside," Seale affirmed. "I swear I'm surprised we lived through it."

Throughout the 1980s Seale continued to develop and support organizations dedicated to combating social and political injustices. He still lectures about his past and current experiences struggling for civil rights for African Americans. In 1987 he published *Barbeque'n with Bobby,* the proceeds from which go to various non-profit social organizations.

Further Reading

The career and beliefs of Bobby Seale are dramatically described in *A Lonely Rage: The Autobiography of Bobby Seale* (1978); and in his *Seize the Time: The Story of the Black Panther Party and Huey P. Newton* (1970). Also see his contributions to G. Louis Heath, editor, *The Black Panther Leaders Speak* (1976) and Philip S. Fonder, editor, *The Black Panthers Speak* (1970). Further background on Seale's life and activities as a leader of the Black Panther Party appear in Gene Marine's history *The Black Panthers* (1969), Don A. Schanche's analysis *The Panther Paradox: A Liberal's Dilemma* (1970), and Reginald Major's study of the party's roots and development, *A Panther Is a Black Cat* (1971). His murder trial is studied by Gail Sheehy, *Panthermania: The Clash of Black Against Black in One American City* (1971). □

Elizabeth Cochrane Seaman

Journalist and reformer Elizabeth Cochrane Seaman, better known as Nellie Bly (1864-1922), gained fame at the end of the nineteenth century for her investigative reports of abusive conditions in the cities of Pittsburgh and New York. Her writing style was marked by first-hand tales of the lives of the underclass, which she obtained by venturing into their world in a series of undercover adventures. She riveted the attention of the nation with a more lighthearted assignment in the winter of 1889-90 when she successfully imitated Jules Verne's fictional journey *Around the World in Eighty Days* in only 72 days.

Elizabeth Cochrane Seaman, who wrote under the pen name Nellie Bly, was a journalist who gained nationwide fame for her investigative reports on abuses in various companies and public institutions. Her stories were not only reform-minded, but filled with first-hand adventure; she undertook such stunts as having herself admitted to an insane asylum, working in a factory sweatshop, and getting herself arrested in order to get a glimpse of the experiences of some of the most downtrodden of urban America. In her greatest escapade, Bly set out to imitate Jules Verne's imaginary trip around the world in less than 75 days while Americans anxiously awaited tales of her travel. Bly distinguished herself as a reporter at a time when the field was dominated by men, and her accomplishments won a greater measure of acceptance for other women journalists.

Bly was born Elizabeth Cochran on May 5, 1864, in Cochran Mills, Pennsylvania. She was the youngest of three children of Michael and Mary Jane Cochran. The Cochrans had both been married previously. Mary Jane, who came from a wealthy Pittsburgh family, was a widow with no children from her first marriage. Michael Cochran was a self-made industrialist who had begun his career as a laborer and eventually became a mill owner, property owner, and associate judge. He had seven children from his earlier marriage, including five boys. As a child, Bly was determined to keep up with her older brothers. She would join in even the roughest activities, including races and climbing trees, to prove herself their equal.

Bly was educated at home by her father in her early years, but he died in 1870 when she was only six years old. Her mother married a third time, but it was an unhappy relationship that ended in divorce. She and her mother lived for a while on the money her father had saved and Bly was sent to school near their home to prepare for a teaching career. While her performance at school was not impressive, she proved to be a creative and talented writer. At the age of 16, the family funds were depleted and Bly and her mother moved to stay near relatives in Pittsburgh. Around this time, she added the e' to her last name, feeling that "Cochrane" had a more elegant air.

Became Reporter in Pittsburgh

Once in Pittsburgh, Bly looked for a way to make a living so her relatives would not have to support her. At that time, a single woman had few professional options. Basically, she could become a teacher or a companion for a wealthy woman. Bly, however, wanted to become a writer. While the odds were not with her, Bly was able to make a profession out of writing due to her extraordinary personality and determination. She got her break in 1885, after a letter she had written to the *Pittsburgh Dispatch* caught the eye of the paper's editor, George A. Madden. In response to an editorial maintaining that women should remain at home rather than entering the professional or political sphere, Bly had written a spirited letter that argued women were perfectly capable of independent thought and meaningful careers. Impressed with the words of the piece, which was signed only "Lonely Orphan Girl," Madden published an ad requesting to speak with the writer of the letter. Bly responded, and at a meeting between the two, Madden asked what kind of stories she might write if she could be a journalist. She indicated that she wanted to tell the stories of ordinary people, and so Madden gave Bly her first journalistic assignment—a piece on the lives of women. Upon receiving her submission, Madden was pleased with the results and published it under the "Lonely Orphan Girl" pseudonym.

For her next article, Bly suggested the topic of divorce. Her editor was unsure that a single young woman could write a convincing article on the subject, but Bly produced a well-researched piece that included some of her father's legal notes on divorce as well as interviews with women who lived near her. Madden agreed to publish the article, but insisted that she find a different pen name—it would seem inappropriate for a story on divorce to be signed by "Little Orphan Girl." The story appeared under the name Nellie Bly—inspired, according to some stories, by the popular Stephen Foster song "Nelly Bly"—and this became the moniker that she would work under for the rest of her career.

Uncovered Factory Hazards and Abuses

Bly was hired as a full-time reporter for the *Dispatch,* earning a salary of five dollars a week. Her initial stories concerned the welfare of Pittsburgh's working class and poor, and the depressed and dangerous conditions she uncovered led to a number of reforms. She developed a reputation for bringing her readers a first-hand look at these topics. To investigate an unsafe factory, she took a job there herself and reported how the establishment was a firetrap that paid low wages to women who were required to work long and difficult shifts. She also traveled to the slums of the city to present a picture of children forced to work all day in order to provide for their families. While Bly's stories raised the indignation of Pittsburgh's citizens and inspired changes, the institutions she attacked were displeased and threatened to remove their advertisements from the newspaper. To appease their customers, the editors of the *Dispatch* changed the focus of Bly's writing, giving her cultural and social events to cover. While the caliber of her writing remained high, Bly yearned to continue her investigative work. She decided to go to Mexico and write about the conditions of the poor there. For several months, she contributed stories about disparities in Mexican society to the *Dispatch.* She then returned to Pittsburgh in 1886.

Reported on Asylum Conditions

Seeking a job as a serious journalist, not just a society columnist, Bly moved to New York City in 1887. There she sold some of her stories about Mexico to newspapers, but found that no one wanted to hire a female as a reporter. Resourceful as ever, Bly managed to turn this experience itself into a story that she sold to her former employers in Pittsburgh. Finally, she managed to arrange an interview with the managing editor of the *New York World,* John Cockerill. Cockerill and the paper's owner, Joseph Pulitzer, liked Bly's stories, but were seeking something more dramatic and attention-getting. Bly was ready for the challenge. With Cockerill, she devised the idea of getting herself admitted to New York's insane asylum for the poor, Blackwell's Island, in order to discover the truth behind reports of abuses there. After being placed in the institution, Bly dropped her act of insanity, but found that doctors and nurses refused to listen to her when she stated she was rational. Other disturbing practices there included feeding the patients vermin-infested food, physical and mental abuse by the staff, and the admission of people who were not psychologically disturbed but simply physically ill or maliciously placed there by family members—as in the case of one woman who was declared insane by her husband after he caught her being unfaithful. After ten days in the asylum, Bly was removed by a lawyer from the newspaper, as had been previously arranged. The resulting stories by Bly caused a sensation across the country, effected reforms at Blackwell's Island, and earned her a permanent post at the *World.*

New York was ripe with possibilities for Bly's style of reporting, and she gained a national reputation for her daredevil methods of getting a story. To get an inside view of the justice system, she pretended to commit a robbery and found that women prisoners were searched by male officers because no women were employed by the jail. She also exposed a fraudulent employment agency that was taking money from unsuspecting immigrants, a health clinic where unqualified doctors experimented on patients, and a lobbyist who had successfully bribed a number of state politicians. Her work also included interviews with some of the most famous figures of the day, including Buffalo Bill and the wives of presidents Ulysses S. Grant, James Garfield, and James K. Polk.

Raced around the World

Bly's most notorious stunt, however, was her trek across the globe in the spirit of the 1873 book *Around the World in Eighty Days* by French author Jules Verne. Bly's plan was to accomplish the feat in only 75 days. Traveling alone, Bly began her journey on November 14, 1889, on an ocean liner heading from New Jersey to London. As she made her way from Europe to the Middle East, Ceylon, Singapore, Hong Kong, and Japan, Americans kept up on her progress through her stories sent in by cable. The *World* made the most of the adventure, turning Bly into a celebrity who inspired songs, fashion, and even a game. She returned to New York in triumph on January 25, 1890, after only 72 days. The town welcomed her arrival with a huge celebration and parade.

Bly was married in 1895 to Robert Livingston Seaman, a millionaire who owned the Iron Clad Manufacturing Company and the American Steel Barrel Company. She retired from writing to assist her husband in his businesses and became president of his companies after Seaman's death in 1904. Her business instincts were poor, however, and in 1911 she declared bankruptcy and returned to journalism. During this period of her career she covered World War I from the Eastern Front and then took a job with the New York *Evening Journal.* But her days as a household name were long past. Upon her death from pneumonia on January 27, 1922, in New York, few people remarked on her passing. Only the *Evening Journal* published a piece on her significance, calling her the country's best reporter. Despite her relative obscurity at the end of her life, Bly's impact was a lasting one. Her unique and energetic approach to reporting launched new trends in journalism, and her insistence on covering difficult topics—despite her gender—set a precedent for journalistic careers for women.

Further Reading

For more information see Belford, Barbara, *Brilliant Bylines: A Biographical Anthology of Notable Newspaperwomen in America,* Columbia University Press, 1986; Kroeger, Brooke, *Nellie Bly: Daredevil, Reporter, Feminist,* Times Books, 1994; and Rittenhouse, Mignon, *The Amazing Nellie Bly,* E. P. Dutton, 1956. □

Seattle

Seattle (1788-1866) is regarded as the last great leader of the native bands that lived in the Pacific Northwest.

Generally regarded as the last great leader of the native bands that lived in the Pacific Northwest, Seattle was responsible for continued good relations between Native Americans and the new white settlers. He was born around 1788 to Schweabe, his Suquamish father, and Scholitza, his Duwamish mother, in the area of central Puget Sound, Oregon Region (now Washington State). As a member of a patrilineal society, Seattle learned and spoke the Suquamish dialect of his father.

When Seattle was four years old, whites arrived in the Puget Sound area, and the process of cultural assimilation began. By the 1830s, when he was in his mid-forties, Seattle had converted to the Catholicism of the French missionaries and was baptized as "Noah." With his new-found faith, he instituted morning and evening church services among Native Americans that were continued even after his death.

The City

The California Gold Rush of 1849 deluged the Pacific Northwest with white settlers intent on exploring the natural wealth of the area. Seattle, then principal chief of the united Suquamish and Duwamish nations—both Coast Salishan bands—counseled friendship, open trade, and accommodation of white settlers.

In respect for their friend and ally, the whites at Puget Sound took Seattle's name for their own settlement in 1852. Among the Salishan Indians of the Pacific Northwest, however, it was believed that the frequent mention of a dead person's name would disturb that person's eternal rest. In order to use his name—Seattle—as the name of their city, white settlers agreed to prepay the chief for the trouble that his spirit would later experience when his name was mentioned; Seattle was compensated with moneys from a small tax imposed on the settlers prior to his death.

The Land

As white settlers continued to pour into the area, the U.S. Government pressed the issue of land purchase from the Indians. In December of 1854, Seattle met with Washington territorial governor Isaac Stevens to discuss the sale of native lands in exchange for smaller reservations and government annuities. His speech at this meeting was translated into English and transcribed by Henry A. Smith, a poet. Seattle agreed to accommodate the whites and the U.S. Government by moving the Puget Sound bands to a reservation. In 1855, at the age of 67, Seattle became the first signer of the Port Elliott Treaty between the Puget Sound Indians and the United States. But soon after the treaty was made, the terms were broken by whites, leading to a series of Native American uprisings from 1855 to 1858, including the Yakima War of 1855-1856 east of the Cascade Moun-

tains, and the unsuccessful 1856 attack on Seattle's village by Nisqually warriors from west of the Cascade Mountains.

In accordance with the treaty stipulations, Seattle and his people moved to the Port Madison reservation, located west-northwest across the Puget Sound from the current city of Seattle, on the east shore of Bainbridge Island. There he lived in the Old Man House—a large community building.

The Speech

Seattle's 1854 address to the Washington territorial governor regarding the status of his people and their future was said to be eloquent and moving, but today there are at least four variations of the text, which raises the question of cultural authenticity. Seattle spoke in either Suquamish or Duwamish, which was then translated immediately into Chinook, and then into English for the U.S. Government representatives. The only surviving transcript of Seattle's oration was derived from the notes in English that were purportedly taken by Dr. Smith as Seattle spoke. On October 29, 1887, the *Seattle Sunday Star* published what Dr. Smith claimed was a representative transcription of Chief Seattle's spoken words, although he noted his text "contained none of the grace and elegance of the original." The text begins: "Yonder sky that has wept tears of compassion upon my people for centuries untold, and which to us appears changeless and eternal, may change. Today it is fair. Tomorrow it may be overcast with clouds. My words are like the stars that never set. Whatever Seattle says, the great chief at Washington can rely upon with as much certainty as he can upon the return of the sun or the seasons."

Two years later, in 1889, Washington became a state. A year after that, the city of Seattle erected a monument to its ancestral namesake, chief of the Suquamish and Duwamish peoples. Both of these Native American tribal bands are now extinct, but Seattle's speech has continued to fascinate scholars throughout the twentieth century. In the 1960s poet William Arrowsmith revised the speech into modern-day English. Arrowsmith's version begins: "Brothers: That sky above us has pitied our fathers for many hundreds of years. To us it looks unchanging, but it may change. Today it is fair. Tomorrow it may be covered with clouds." Perry's letter, featured in an ecology movie titled *Home,* is based loosely on Dr. Smith's transcription of Seattle's 1854 oration: "The Great Chief in Washington sends word that [he] wishes to buy our land. The Great Chief also sends us words of friendship and goodwill. This is kind of him, since we know he has little need of our friendship in return. But we will consider your offer. For we know that if we do not sell, the white man may come with guns and take our land. How can you buy or sell the sky, the warmth of the land? The idea is strange to us."

Seattle was married twice and had six children, four of whom died in childhood. He passed away on June 7, 1866, at the age of 78, on a Washington reservation. His famous speech and its current interpretations and use continue to challenge academics, but according to Native American history expert Herman Viola, as quoted in *Newsweek,* Seattle's discourse—whether accurate or embellished—undoubtedly "conveys the feeling a lot of Indians had."

Further Reading

Kaiser, Rudolf, "Chief Seattle's Speech(es): American Origins and European Reception," in *Recovering the Word: Essays on Native American Literature,* University of California Press, 1987.

Leitch, Barbara A., *A Concise Dictionary of Indian Tribes of North America,* Algonac, Michigan, Reference Publications, 1979.

Native North American Almanac, edited by Duane Champagne, Detroit, Gale Research, 1994; 1157.

Waldman, Carl, *Who Was Who in Native American History,* New York, Facts On File, 1990; 318.

Watt, Roberta Frye, *Four Wagons West,* Portland, Binsford & Mort, 1934.

Buerge, David, "Seattle's King Arthur: How Chief Seattle Continues to Inspire His Many Admirers to Put Words in His Mouth," *Seattle Weekly,* July 17, 1991.

"Chief Seattle's Treaty Oration—1854," *Seattle Sunday Star,* October 29, 1887.

Jones, Malcolm, Jr., and Ray Sawhill, "Just Too Good to Be True: Another Reason to Beware of False Eco-prophets," *Newsweek,* May 4, 1992; 68.

Information from Nancy Zussy, State Librarian, Washington State Library, Olympia, Washington. □

Richard John Seddon

Richard John Seddon (1845-1906) was a New Zealand political leader and Liberal prime minister who instituted liberal reforms and advocated imperial solidarity and expansion.

Richard John Seddon was born at St. Helens, Lancashire, England, on June 22, 1845, the son of a schoolmaster. He left school at the age of 12 and at 18 emigrated to Australia, where he worked on the goldfields in Victoria. He moved on to New Zealand in 1866 and established himself as a hotelkeeper. He entered local politics in 1869 and 10 years later transferred to the House of Representatives as a Liberal.

Seddon soon showed himself to be an astute party manager, a hard worker, and a loud, forceful, and verbose speaker who had little time for experts and possessed a strong faith in the virtues of the common man. In 1891 he became minister of public works, defense, and mines in the Liberal government, and in 1892, when John Ballance, the prime minister, became ill, Seddon acted as leader of the House. When Ballance died in 1893, Seddon was invited to form a government.

Seddon was prime minister for 13 years, and his administration pursued an energetic social program. Graduated land and income taxes were introduced, large holdings were broken up by means of taxes on unimproved property and estates with absentee owners, and attempts were made to encourage the small farmers. In 1894 industrial concilia-

tion and arbitration boards were set up for what was the first compulsory system of state arbitration in the world. An 8-hour working day was established by law in 1897, old-age pensions were introduced in 1898, the free place system in secondary schools was established in 1903, and, somewhat by chance, female suffrage was adopted in 1893.

In external affairs Seddon was the most prominent colonial advocate of imperial preference. He favored a policy of imperial solidarity and expansion: the Cook Islands were annexed to New Zealand in 1900, and a contingent of New Zealand troops was dispatched to support the British Empire in the Boer War.

The social reforms were not necessarily Seddon's own handiwork, of course, but his support was always an essential factor in getting legislation passed. Personally, he was gross, vulgar, domineering, and probably dishonest, but he was well liked and gained a firm hold on the affections of the general public. He centralized the administration too much, and he held too many ministerial portfolios himself, but his personal style became the model for later leaders in New Zealand politics. He died in office on June 10, 1906.

Further Reading

The best biography is Randal M. Burdon, *King Dick: A Biography of Richard John Seddon* (1955). An earlier but still useful work is James Drummond, *The Life and Work of Richard John Seddon* (1907). □

Adam Sedgwick

The English geologist Adam Sedgwick (1785-1873) was the founder of the Cambrian system, the first period of the Paleozoic geologic era.

Adam Sedgwick was born on March 22, 1785, at Dent in his ancestral region of the Yorkshire Dales. In 1804 he entered Trinity College, Cambridge, which became his chief home for the rest of his life. After being made a fellow in 1810, he was ordained; he later became a canon of Norwich. In 1818 he was elected to the professorship of geology, not because he knew anything about geology but on his general merits. However, he began enthusiastically to study the subject, giving lectures and making geological tours, but he constantly allowed himself to be diverted by business irrelevant to his geological work.

During 1821-1824 Sedgwick carried out researches in the north of England—on the Magnesian Limestone and New Red Sandstone and in the Lake District—but he delayed in the announcement and publication of his findings. Nevertheless, his standing in the world of science at that time and his general popularity were recognized by his being elected president of the Geological Society of London in 1829 and president of the British Association for the Advancement of Science in 1833.

In 1831 Sedgwick began the work which will always be associated with his name: the establishing of a rock-succession, the revealing of a grand structure among the mountains of North Wales, and the consequent founding of the Cambrian system. He did not put his researches into writing, and this was the chief cause of the regrettable controversy which eventually developed with Roderick Murchison over priorities of discovery and nomenclature among these Lower Paleozoic rocks (as they soon came to be called). However, Sedgwick did compose a few important treatises on the structure of rock-masses. In 1839 he and Murchison reported the results of their joint work which founded the Devonian system.

Thereafter Sedgwick's duties at his college and university caused his geological work, other than his lectures and the augmentation of his collections, to be almost entirely laid aside. Sedgwick never married. He died at Cambridge on Jan. 27, 1873. His lasting memorial is the Sedgwick Museum at Cambridge, opened in 1904, one of the most famous geological schools.

Sedgwick's reputation as a geologist and as a man rests almost entirely on his personality, which was conspicuous for its integrity, vigor, and charm, though he could be bitter in controversy. The influence of his presence and the power of his spoken word are not to be gathered from contemporary written records.

Further Reading

Sedgwick's *A Discourse on the Studies of the University* was recently reprinted with an introduction by Eric Ashby and Mary Anderson (1969), which focuses on Sedgwick's person-

ality, his career as a teacher, and his efforts at educational reform. The standard biography is John Willis Clark and Thomas McKenny Hughes, *The Life and Letters of the Reverend Adam Sedgwick* (2 vols., 1890). Additional light is thrown on Sedgwick and his work in Sir Archibald Geikie, *The Founders of Geology* (1897; 2d ed. 1905), and Horace B. Woodward, *The History of the Geological Society of London* (1907). A good profile of Sedgwick is in Carroll Lane Fenton and Mildred Adams Fenton, *Giants of Geology* (1945; rev. ed. 1952).

Additional Sources

Speakman, Colin, *Adam Sedgwick, geologist and dalesman, 1785-1873: a biography in twelve themes,* Broad Oak, Heathfield, East Sussex: Broad Oak Press, 1982. □

Pete Seeger

The American folksinger and activist Pete Seeger (born 1919) was associated with the Communist and Progressive parties in the 1940s and 1950s, but later focused on environmental issues. He was especially admired for his fight against the blacklisting of entertainers in the 1950s because of left wing political beliefs.

American folksinger, composer, song collector and five-string banjo virtuoso Pete Seeger was born in New York City in 1919 into a family of Juilliard music professors. He spent his early years in private schools and studied sociology at Harvard College. It was in 1938, when he dropped out of Harvard after two years to ride the rails and hitchhike all over the United States, that he immersed himself in folk music. He traveled all around the country collecting songs, meeting the greats of American folk music: Leadbelly, Woody Guthrie and Earl Robinson. Two years later he briefly served as an assistant in the Archive of Folk Song at the Library of Congress. He then helped organize the Almanac Singers in 1941. The group campaigned against American entry into World War II, until Germany invaded Russia. The Almanacs then sang on behalf of the Allies. Following the war Seeger worked for better relations between the United States and international Communism, most notably by campaigning for Henry Wallace for president in 1948. During these early years Seeger was closely associated with the legendary folk singer and composer Woody Guthrie. He was also the national director of People's Songs, Inc., an effort to institutionalize left-wing music.

"Goodnight Irene" Number One Hit

In 1948 Seeger organized another singing group, the Weavers, with whom he achieved his greatest popular success. They appeared on national radio and television and recorded a song, "Goodnight Irene," that was the number one hit in 1950. But with the rise of anti-Communist feeling

in the nation, the Weavers were blacklisted, along with hundreds of other leftist or formerly leftist entertainers. With the mass media closed to them, the Weavers disbanded. Seeger, who composed as well as performed and had a personal following, survived the blacklist by making recordings and giving concerts. In 1964-1965 he made a world tour with his family, performing in 24 countries. In 1967, with the blacklist easing, he appeared on the Smothers Brothers television show. But Seeger had missed the folksong vogue which flourished briefly in the late 1950s and early 1960s and never recovered his earlier popularity.

Seeger was especially active in the civil rights movement of the 1960s, appearing at rallies and fund-raising concerts. The simplicity and directness of this cause were well suited to his musical talents. He customarily appeared in shirtsleeves rolled to the elbow, accompanying himself on a banjo. Seeger did more than anyone else to revive interest in this American instrument.

Without entirely abandoning his other causes, Seeger became an effective environmentalist, water pollution being his particular object of concern. Using the Hudson River sloop *Clearwater* as a dramatic prop, he was a leader in the struggle to reclaim that river. He also sang on behalf of similarly endangered bodies of water.

Active as an Organizer and Promoter

Though best known as a folksinger, Seeger was equally active as an organizer and promoter, not only of sociopolitical causes but also of purely musical events. Among these were the Newport (Rhode Island) Folk Festivals and appearances of the reconstituted Weavers. He took particular pride in having been one of the first white Northerners to recognize the value of Southern folk music, which he ardently encouraged for close to 50 years. Dubbed "America's tuning fork" by Carl Sandburg, Seeger has written more than 100 songs in addition to manuals on playing the 5-string banjo and 12-string guitars.

The autumn of his life turned into an awards season for Seeger, as he received honors from places where he was once denounced. In 1955, after refusing to answer questions from the House Committee on Un-American Activities, Seeger was branded unpatriotic and blacklisted from television and major concert halls for 17 years; but in 1994 he returned to Washington to accept the National Medal of the Arts from President Clinton. In 1965, Seeger was accused of threatening to stop Bob Dylan's electrified rock performance at the Newport Folk Festival; in 1996, he was inducted into the Rock and Roll Hall of Fame. In the late 1930s, Seeger had dropped out of Harvard after losing a partial scholarship; just before his 77th birthday, he was honored as a distinguished alumnus at that university's Arts First festival.

Further Reading

Seeger can be seen in a film of the last concert of the Weavers that is often aired on public television. A fine biography is David King Dunaway's *How Can I Keep from Singing* (1981). Seeger is a walking history book of American music. Songs he wrote and popularized like "If I Had a Hammer," "Kisses Sweeter Than Wine," and "Where Have All the Flowers Gone?" have become standards, and many of them are available on CDs and other sound recordings, such as *The Almanac Singers: Their Complete Recordings.* Seeger (along with Blood Seeger) authored *Where Have All the Flowers Gone: A Singer's Stories, Sings, Seeds, Robberies* in 1993. Seeger has been featured on the Arts & Entertainment (A&E) television program *Biography* (www.biography.com). □

George Seferis

The Greek poet and statesman George Seferis (1900-1971) combined a diplomatic career with the creation of a body of poetic works unique for their synthesis of modern man's anguished estrangement and the redemptive promise of an ancient artistic heritage.

The son of a law professor who was a poet in his own right, George Seferis or Georgios Seferiadis, spent the first 14 years of his life at his birthplace, Smyrna (Izmir), Turkey. The Seferiadis family fled Asia Minor with the outbreak of World War I, taking up residence first in Athens, where George completed secondary school, then in 1918 moving to Paris, where his father pursued a law practice. Richly endowed from childhood with the poetic experience of a living, oral literature and encouraged by the example of his father, Seferis found himself very early divided between the exigencies of a practical and a literary career. While studying law in Paris, he began writing poetry, and his first titled composition (1924, published later), "Fog," dates from a stay in London, where Seferis had gone to perfect his English prior to taking the Greek Foreign Service examination. Seferis returned to Athens and to the Foreign Ministry in 1925, continuing to write verse and to produce translations and literary criticism until, in 1931, his first collection of poems, *Strophe* (*Turning Point*), appeared.

Diplomacy summoned Seferis to London, where he served as vice-consul until 1934, all the while continuing to publish works (notably "The Cistern," 1932) in magazines and reviews. His next major collection—*Mythistorema* (*Mythical Story,* 1935)—represented an evolution away from the rigidly "pure," stylistically self-conscious early works toward the sober, almost denuded manner that marked the best of his mature poetry, keeping it attuned to real patterns of speech.

Modern desolation for Seferis expressed itself amid particular ruins—the broken statues and columns of an immensely rich Greek heritage. The enduring materiality of these past creations weighed heavily on Seferis, living on for the poet as proof of human continuity, of a glorious but evolving Hellenism.

In *Kichle* ("The Thrush," written during World War II), Seferis faced the ravaged modern world defiantly: "the fragments/ Are not the statues./ You are yourself the remains." But new ruins were being made of Greece. The poet-diplomat continued his dual service, fleeing with the Free Greek government during the Nazi occupation. His published works swelled by five volumes during the war: *Himerologion katastromatos* (*Log Book*) *I, II,* and *III; Tetradio gymnasmaton* (*Exercise Book*); and *Poiïmata* (*Poems*). Married in 1941, Seferis had journeyed with his wife Maria in official exile from Ankara to South Africa, to Cairo, and to Italy; he wrote all the while—including a group of *Dokimes* (*Essays*) in 1944—becoming more and more a recognized poet of his unsettled times. In 1947 Seferis received the Palamas Prize from the Athens Academy, and during the postwar years he held diplomatic assignments of ever-increasing responsibility. By the time he returned to Great Britain as Greek ambassador in 1957, his official stature in public service and in letters was already internationally recognized. Seferis retired from the Foreign Service in 1962. He won the Nobel Prize for literature in 1963. Seferis died in Athens on Sept. 20, 1971.

Further Reading

Recent translations of Seferis's works include those of Rex Warner, *Poems* (1960) and *On the Greek Style* (*Dokimes*) (1966), and Edmund Keeley and Philip Sherrard, *George Seferis: Collected Poems, 1924-1955* (1967), annotated with bibliography. No complete translation or definitive critical presentation has been undertaken to date. Background may be found in Edmund Keeley and Philip Sherrard, trans. and eds., *Six Poets of Modern Greece* (1961), and Philip Sherrard, *The Marble Threshing Floor: Studies in Modern Greek Poetry* (1970). A brief biography and Nobel Prize presentation and acceptance speech appear in Horst Frenz, ed., *Nobel Lectures: Literature, 1901-1967* (1969).

Additional Sources

Seferis, George, *Days of 1945-1951; a poet's journal,* Cambridge, Mass., Belknap Press of Harvard University Press, 1974.

My brother George Seferis, St. Paul, Minn.: North Central Pub. Co., 1982. □

George Segal

American sculptor George Segal (born 1924) placed cast human figures in settings and furnishings drawn from the environment of his home in southern New Jersey.

George Segal was born on November 26, 1924, in New York City. He attended Stuyvesant High School in Manhattan. In 1940 his family moved to South Brunswick, New Jersey, where his father, who had previously worked as a butcher, operated a chicken farm. Segal attended art classes at Cooper Union in New York in 1941-1942. From 1942 to 1946 he studied literature, psychology, history, and philosophy in evening classes at Rutgers University in New Jersey. Before receiving his B.S. degree in art education from New York University in 1949, he took classes at the Pratt Institute of Design in New York. While attending New York University, Segal studied collage with the sculptor Tony Smith and also took classes with the painter William Baziotes.

The 1950s were difficult years for Segal financially, but he continued painting and developed important friendships with other artists who were in the New York area. He operated a chicken farm across the road from his parents' from 1949 to 1958, but, faced with bankruptcy, he began teaching in various public schools in New Jersey from 1957 to 1964. In 1961 he entered the Master of Fine Arts program at Rutgers University and received his degree in 1963.

Segal's earliest exhibited works were paintings. Unlike the work of most artists in New York in the late 1940s and 1950s, Segal's paintings were representational and frequently included human figures in an interior environment. By the time of his third one-man exhibition at the Hansa Gallery in New York in 1958, Segal's paintings were life-size in scale, intensely colored, and mainly represented figures painted with heavy, expressive brush strokes. The problem of resolving the conflict between the two-dimensional, formal space of abstract painting and his interest in depicting three-dimensional figures led Segal, in 1959, to exhibit plaster figures placed in front of his paintings. These three-dimensional sculptures could exist in real space, while the flat canvases served to form an environmental setting created by flat areas of color. These tentative sculptures were made of wood and plaster, materials familiar to Segal from his construction activities on his farm.

His Future is Cast

In the summer of 1961 a student in an art class Segal was teaching brought him some bandages used to set broken bones. When these plaster-impregnated strips are wet and molded in place they harden into a cast. He began experimenting by making plaster casts of his body and assembled the parts into a sculpture of a seated figure. The full sculpture, *Man Sitting at a Table,* included a real chair and a table to which a window had been nailed. The mullions of the window form a grid through which the viewer looks, as if into an illusionary painted canvas. The incorporation of an environmental setting for the figure grew partly from his combining of painted settings with his first sculptures two years earlier, but the idea is also related to parallel artistic concepts that were then being developed by a number of Segal's contemporaries.

Allan Kaprow, whom Segal met in 1953, organized Happenings—partially improvised, non-narrative dramatic performances. His first Happening was held on Segal's farm. Kaprow was one of a number of artists exploring the integration of multi-sensory experience within an environment that often depended on random or improvisational techniques. The composer John Cage was a major influence on the artists who participated in this avant-garde circle that included Robert Rauschenburg, Red Grooms, Kaprow, and some of the performers who formed the Fluxus Group. In encompassing human figures, and on at least one occasion sound, and an environmental milieu, Segal's sculpture has some affinity to approaches being explored by these artists. Segal's work is distinguished by his emphasis upon formal values, his use of familiar settings and objects, and his use of such traditional themes as figures at a table, female nudes, and even on a few occasions religious subjects.

Segal generally made his sculptures by molding cloth strips dipped in hydrostone, an industrial plaster, over the person serving as his model. The surfaces of the sculpture were manipulated freely by the artist as he worked with the strips of plaster-soaked cloth. Sometimes he used these casts of the figure as a negative mold into which he poured plaster in order to produce a positive cast, but he generally preferred the greater artistic activity involved in working with the exterior surface of the initial cast. On rare occasions these sculptures were then cast in bronze and painted with a white finish. Segal at times painted the surface of his sculptures, first in *The Costume Party* (1965), and more frequently in the mid-1970s—*Couple on Black Bed* (1976), *Red Girl in Blanket* (1975), and *Magenta Girl on Green Door* (1977), for example—but most of his sculptures are white. The whiteness separates their reality as expressive of the artist's intuition and feelings from that of the colored environment in which Segal places them, while their naturalism provides a bridge between the real world and the artist's personal vision. For Segal, the primary colors that he sometimes used are meant to communicate psychological states and thus can be used arbitrarily with no immediate reference to the actual appearance of the subject.

Segal's sculptures of the 1960s were often mundane in subject, such as *Woman Painting Her Fingernails* (1962), and were cast from personal friends and neighbors. A large number of sculptures, beginning with his first cast work discussed earlier, incorporate windows. Windows remind one of the definition of illusionistic painting as a mirror or a window through which one has a view of the visible world. In many of Segal's works the presence of an actual window (with a real three-dimensional space) clarifies the nature of the space as concrete, not an illusion.

An Art Movement

A considerable number of Segal's sculptures of the 1960s and 1970s have the theme of transit—for example, *Man on a Bicycle* (1962, Moderna Museet, Stockholm), *The Bus Driver* (1962, Museum of Modern Art, New York), *The Bus Riders* (1962, Hirshhorn Museum and Sculpture Garden, Washington, D.C.), *The Gas Station* (1963-1964, The National Gallery of Canada, Ottawa), *The Truck* (1966, Art Institute of Chicago), and *To All Gates* (1971, Des Moines Art Center, Iowa). These and a number of other works of figures in a doorway, such as *Woman in a Doorway I* (1964, Whitney Museum of American Art, New York) or other sculptures where the theme is even more obvious, an example being *Bas-Relief: Girl with Clock* (1972), all relate to the theme of passage or the transitory nature of temporal existence.

Segal's concern with the timeless and universal within the context of modern life includes sculptures showing figures involved in their work, making love, eating, or located in settings characteristic of contemporary American culture. His accomplishment is in having found a compelling way to synthesize modern sensibility and artistic approaches with these enduring philosophical and artistic issues.

Segal is best known for his sculptures, but in 1994 he returned to painting, often exploring depth and space in these works. Works of this period are drawn with charcoal on house paint, in shades of gray, black and white. He also applies stucco layers for texture.

In 1995 Segal wrapped Israeli statesman Abba Eban's body in plaster-impregnated bandages in the first step in the making of the cast that was to become *Portrait of Abba Eban.* The sculpture shows a seated, life-size Eban (covered in the dark acrylic paint) in front of a black, wooden wall with a map of Israel silkscreened on it. Eban asked Segal to make the sculpture for the Abba Eban Center for the Diplomacy of Israel, a part of Hebrew University in Jerusalem.

Segal was commissioned to produce three bronzes for the Franklin Delano Roosevelt Memorial, dedicated in 1997: *The Fireside Chat, The Rural Couple,* and *The Breadline.* Encompassing over seven acres, the FDR Memorial is situated between the Lincoln and Jefferson memorials, and creates a park-like sequence of four outdoor galleries, each depicting a term in office.

Segal has long pursued a personal interest in interpreting the Bible through his work. Five tableaux—all drawn from the Book of Genesis—were seen together for the first time in early 1997 in a museum setting at the Skirball Cultural Center and Museum. The institution emphasizes art related to the Jewish experience.

Further Reading

For a major comprehensive study of Segal's work see *George Segal* by Jan Van der Marck (revised edition, 1979), which has many illustrations, a list of exhibitions, and a useful bibliography. For a briefer treatment that includes commentaries by Segal see *George Segal: Sculptures,* by Martin Friedman and Graham W. J. Beal, catalogue of an exhibition held at the Walker Art Center, Minneapolis, Minnesota; San Francisco; and New York in 1978-1979. The photographs of Segal's working method are especially useful. Also see the *Modern Masters Series* (v.5, p. 123-125) (1983). For more recent work see articles in *Art News* magazine or use one of the many search engines, such as AltaVista, to find listing on the WWW of galleries, dealers and museums currently exhibiting the artist's works. Segal was also featured on the Arts & Entertainment television network's program *Biography,* and additional information is available from their web page (www.biography.com). □

Andrés Segovia

Andrés Segovia (1893-1987) was one of the most important musicians of the twentieth century. Perhaps the greatest testament to what he accomplished for the guitar was the renaissance in music composed for it by important composers,

He established the guitar as an important concert instrument, made prolific recordings, and inspired generations of guitarists. Many composers began using the instrument in their works, including Manuel de Falla, Heitor Villa-Lobos, Manuel Ponce, Mario Castelnuovo-Tedesco, Joaquín Turina, and Joaquín Rodrigo. This astounding enrichment of the guitar's repertoire stands in stark contrast to the eighteenth and nineteenth centuries, when practically none of the major composers—like Mozart, Hayden, and Beethoven—wrote music for the guitar.

Renaissance of the Guitar

In the first part of the nineteenth century, the guitar, which for centuries had been considered an accompanying instrument for singing and dancing, staked out its own territory as an appropriate instrument for music in the classical style. The Spaniard Fernando Sor and the Italian Mauro Giuliani were the two most important figures for the renaissance of this instrument, both of whom were virtuoso performers and prolific composers.

But by 1840 both Sor and Giuliani were dead, and the guitar seemed to be languishing along with them. In Segovia's own words, "the guitar was caught in kind of vicious circle: there were few guitarists because no music was being written for it, and no music was being written for it because there were so few guitarists."

Yet the tradition survived, thanks to at least one major figure in the succeeding generations who kept the spirit of Sor and Giuliani alive. In the 1840s and 1850s the Frenchman Napoleon Coste performed and composed for the guitar, and toward the end of the century the Spaniard Francisco Tárrega composed important works of a more national character for the instrument, in addition to transcribing the music of Bach, Mendelsohn, and Albéniz for the guitar.

In the first part of the twentieth century, though there were guitarists of renown, like Tárrega's disciple Miguel Llobet and the Paraguayan Augustín Barrios, Segovia was by far the predominant figure in the renaissance classical guitar enjoyed. Segovia added to the repertoire with important transcriptions—Bach's "Chaconne" being perhaps the most famous—and discoveries of forgotten composers—like the seventeenth-century lutenist Robert de Visée. In addition, he achieved a status for the guitar that it never was able to attain in the nineteenth century: that of an appropriate and even majestic concert instrument.

"Don Quijote de la Guitarra"

Segovia's rise to success was remarkable considering the obstacles he was forced to overcome. Born into a very humble family in Linares in the South of Spain in 1893, he was brought up by his Uncle Eduardo and Aunt María, and spent most of his youth in Granada. His family opposed his interest in music, and as Segovia explained, "Since I had to fight against the stubborn opposition of my family, I had to forego teachers, conservatories, or any other accepted method of instruction." Segovia taught himself not only the rudiments of his instrument, but the ability to read music as well. "From that time I would be my own master and disciple," he commented.

He gave his first concert at the "Círculo Artístico" of Granada in 1910, at the age of 16. Concerts followed in Seville, and then the young Segovia departed for Madrid. In his autobiographical writings Segovia neglected to assign dates to many key events, but he must have been 17 or 18 years old when he made this trip to the Spanish capital. While on the train, Segovia told of a conversation he had with his traveling companions, during which he put forth an eloquent defense of the guitar. "First, no string instrument offers such complete harmonic potential; second, it is light and can be transported effortlessly from one place to another; and thirdly, its sound is naturally melancholic and beautiful." As they left the train, one of the passengers said, "So long, Don Quijote of the Guitar, may the world restore your sanity."

Concerts in Spain and Abroad

After some difficulty in Madrid, Segovia enjoyed his first great stroke of luck: not the concert which had been arranged at the *ateneo* of Madrid, but rather his encounter with the guitar maker Manuel Ramírez. In what became a famous anecdote, Segovia offered to rent a guitar from Ramírez for his concert, much in the same way a piano would be rented locally for touring musicians. Yet when Ramírez heard the young Segovia play one of his guitars, he said, "Take it; its yours."

The concert took place in 1913, and though it received mixed reviews, it attracted considerable attention to Segovia and his instrument. Concerts followed in Valencia, where one reviewer praised Segovia for "bypassing the guitar's hackneyed repertoire and playing instead works by Debussy, Tchaikovsky, and other 'strangers' to the instrument." Perhaps more significant than these concerts, Segovia met and befriended Miguel Llobet, the most important disciple of the great Francisco Tárrega. Llobet invited Segovia to follow him to his native Barcelona, where he helped arrange recitals for the 25-year-old Segovia, the most important being in Barcelona's famous *Palau* or "Palace." The large hall was filled to capacity. "In a night abounding in emotions," Segovia recalled, "the one that moved me most was the realization that I had broadened the scope of the guitar and proved it *could* be heard from any stage."

Until 1920, Segovia continued giving concerts all over Spain, played for the Queen, and met the impresario Quesada, who was to act as his agent until 1956. Quesada organized Segovia's first venture abroad, a South American tour which began in 1920. Yet before his departure, he had secured an important landmark for his instrument. "For the first time, a composer who was not a guitarist wrote a piece for the guitar. It was Federico Moreno-Torroba [who] in a few weeks came up with the truly beautiful *Dance in E Major*. . . . That success prompted Manuel de Falla to compose his very beautiful *Homage,* and Joaquín Turina his splendid *Sevillana.*" Even before Segovia left Spain, these compositions had elevated the rank of the guitar to a level that it had not reached in a century.

Segovia's successful pattern of playing concerts while continually broadening his instrument's horizons continued in Latin America. Once again he showed the guitar to be an immensely appealing concert instrument, while inspiring composers who heard him to direct their efforts to the guitar. In Mexico he made the acquaintance of Manuel Ponce, who would go on to become one of the guitar's greatest composers. Segovia said of Ponce's *Folías de España* that "it is the most important work that has been written for the solo guitar."

But perhaps the event that sealed Segovia's success was his Paris debut. It took place on April 7, 1924, in the concert hall of the Conservatoire and was attended by a capacity audience. One of the pieces on the program was a newly composed virtuoso piece called "Segovia" by Roussel. Rarely had a performer enjoyed such a prestigious public. Present at the recital were Paul Dukas, Manuel de Falla, Albert Roussel, Joaquín Nin, and even the philosopher Miguel de Unamuno, who heard the recital from Madame Debussy's box. This recital came to be considered one of the most important musical events of the century, perhaps after Igor Stravinsky's debut of *The Rite of Spring* in the same city ten years earlier. After a European tour that led him through England, Italy, Germany, Hungary, and the Soviet Union, Segovia's next great success was in the New York Town Hall on January 8, 1928. This was followed by concert tours of Japan, the Philippines, China, and Indonesia.

The Spanish Civil War, and then World War II, interrupted Segovia's residence in Barcelona, and he spent those years in the Americas, especially in Mexico, Uruguay, and New York. He resumed world touring afterwards, and began pursuing intensely a routine of university teaching, especially at the Academia Chigiana in Sienna, Italy. He also gave classes at the University of California at Berkeley, and held annual master classes at Santiago de Compostela in Spain. Thousands of guitarists received instruction from him, and the greatest of the following generation, including John Williams, Julian Bream, Alirio Diaz, Oscar Gighlia, and Christopher Parkening, were largely indebted to him for their stature.

Segovia continued playing, teaching, and recording—almost 30 records with Decca and several more with RCA—up the to end of his life in 1987. He received numerous awards and honors during his lifetime, including an honorary Doctor of Music degree from Oxford University in 1974, being made Marquis of Salobrena by a royal Spanish decree in 1981, and the Gold Medal of the Royal Philharmonic Society of London in 1985.

Further Reading

Clinton, George, *Andrés Segovia,* London, 1978.

Grunfeld, Frederic, *The Art and Times of the Guitar,* London, 1969.

Segovia, Andrés, *Andrés Segovia: An Autobiography of the Years 1893-1920.*

Guitar Review ("La guitarra y yo"—a series of autobiographical articles by Segovia), Nos. 4 (1947), 6 (1948), 7 (1948), 10 (1949), 13 (1952). ☐

Florence B. Seibert

A biochemist who received her Ph.D. from Yale University in 1923, Florence B. Seibert (1897-1991) is best known for her research in the biochemistry of tuberculosis. She developed the protein substance used for the tuberculosis skin test.

The protein substance used for the tuberculosis skin test was developed by Florence B. Seibert and was adopted as the standard in 1941 by the United States and a year later by the World Health Organization. In addition, in the early 1920s, Seibert discovered that the sudden fevers that sometimes occurred during intravenous injections were caused by bacteria in the distilled water that was used to make the protein solutions. She invented a distillation apparatus that prevented contamination. This research had great practical significance later when intravenous blood transfusions became widely used in surgery. Seibert authored or coauthored more than a hundred scientific papers. Her later research involved the study of bacteria associated with certain cancers. Her many honors include five honorary degrees, induction into the National Women's Hall of Fame in Seneca Falls, New York (1990), the Garvan Gold Medal of the American Chemical Society (1942), and the John Elliot Memorial Award of the American Association of Blood Banks (1962).

Florence Barbara Seibert was born on October 6, 1897, in Easton, Pennsylvania, the second of three children. She was the daughter of George Peter Seibert, a rug manufacturer and merchant, and Barbara (Memmert) Seibert. At the age of three she contracted polio. Despite her resultant handicaps, she completed high school, with the help of her highly supportive parents, and entered Goucher College in Baltimore, where she studied chemistry and zoology. She graduated in 1918, then worked under the direction of one of her chemistry teachers, Jessie E. Minor, at the Chemistry Laboratory of the Hammersley Paper Mill in Garfield, New Jersey. She and her professor, having responded to the call for women to fill positions vacated by men fighting in World War I, coauthored scientific papers on the chemistry of cellulose and wood pulps.

Although Seibert initially wanted to pursue a career in medicine, she was advised against it as it was "too rigorous" in view of her physical disabilities. She decided on biochemistry instead and began graduate studies at Yale University under Lafayette B. Mendel, one of the discoverers of Vitamin A. Her Ph.D. research involved an inquiry into the causes of "protein fevers"—fevers that developed in patients after they had been injected with protein solutions that contained distilled water. Seibert's assignment was to discover which proteins caused the fevers and why. What she discovered, however, was that the distilled water itself was contaminated—with bacteria. Consequently, Seibert invented a distilling apparatus that prevented the bacterial contamination.

Seibert earned her Ph.D. in 1923, then moved to Chicago to work as a post-graduate fellow under H. Gideon Wells at the University of Chicago. She continued her research on pyrogenic (fever causing) distilled water, and her work in this area acquired practical significance when intravenous blood transfusions became a standard part of many surgical procedures.

After her fellowship ended, she was employed part-time at the Otho S. A. Sprague Memorial Institute in Chicago, where Wells was the director. At the same time, she worked with Esmond R. Long, whom she had met through Wells's seminars at the University of Chicago. Supported by a grant from the National Tuberculosis Association, Long and Seibert would eventually spend thirty-one years collaborating on tuberculosis research. Another of Seibert's long-time associates was her younger sister, Mabel Seibert, who moved to Chicago to be with her in 1927. For the rest of their lives, with the exception of a year in Sweden, the sisters resided together, with Mabel providing assistance both in the research institutes (where she found employment as secretary and later research assistant) and at home. In 1932, when Long moved to the Henry Phipps Institute—a tuberculosis clinic and research facility associated with the University of Pennsylvania in Philadelphia—Seibert (and her sister) transferred as well. There, Seibert rose from assistant professor (1932–1937), to associate professor (1937–1955) to full professor of biochemistry (1955–1959). In 1959 she retired with emeritus status. Between 1937 and 1938 she was a Guggenheim fellow in the laboratory of Theodor Svedberg at the University of Upsala in Sweden. In

1926 Svedberg had received the Nobel prize for his protein research.

Seibert's tuberculosis research involved questions that had emerged from the late-nineteenth-century work of German bacteriologist Robert Koch. In 1882 Koch had discovered that the tubercle bacillus was the primary cause of tuberculosis. He also discovered that if the liquid on which the bacilli grew was injected under the skin, a small bite-like reaction would occur in people who had been infected with the disease. (Calling the liquid "old tuberculin," Kock produced it by cooking a culture and draining off the dead bacilli.) Although he had believed the active substance in the liquid was protein, it had not been proven.

Using precipitation and other methods of separation and testing, Seibert discovered that the active ingredient of the liquid was indeed protein. The next task was to isolate it, so that it could be used in pure form as a diagnostic tool for tuberculosis. Because proteins are highly complex organic molecules that are difficult to purify, this was a daunting task. Seibert finally succeeded by means of crystallization. The tiny amounts of crystal that she obtained, however, made them impractical for use in widespread skin tests. Thus, she changed the direction of her research and began working on larger amounts of active, but less pure protein. Her methods included precipitation through ultrafiltration (a method of filtering molecules). The result, after further purification procedures, was a dry powder called TPT (Tuberculin Protein Trichloracetic acid precipitated). This was the first substance that was able to be produced in sufficient quantities for widespread use as a tuberculosis skin test. For her work, Seibert received the 1938 Trudeau Medal from the National Tuberculosis Association.

At the Henry Phipps Institute in Philadelphia, Seibert continued her study of tuberculin protein molecules and their use in the diagnosis of tuberculosis. Seibert began working on the "old tuberculin" that had been created by Koch and used by doctors for skin testing. As Seibert described it in her autobiography *Pebbles on the Hill of a Scientist,* old tuberculin "was really like a soup made by cooking up the live tubercle bacilli and extracting the protein substance from their bodies while they were being killed." Further purification of the substance led to the creation of PPD (Purified Protein Derivative). Soon large quantities of this substance were being made for tuberculosis testing. Seibert continued to study ways of further purifying and understanding the nature of the protein. Her study in Sweden with Svedberg aided this research. There she learned new techniques for the separation and identification of proteins in solution.

Upon her return from Sweden, Seibert brought the new techniques with her. She began work on the creation of a large batch of PPD to serve as the basis for a standard dosage. The creation of such a standard was critical for measuring the degree of sensitivity of individuals to the skin test. Degree of sensitivity constituted significant diagnostic information if it was based upon individual reaction, rather than upon differences in the testing substance itself. A large amount of substance was necessary to develop a standard that ideally would be used world-wide, so that the tuberculosis test would be comparable wherever it was given. Developing new methods of purification as she proceeded, Seibert and her colleagues created 107 grams of material, known as PPD-S (the S signifying "standard"). A portion was used in 1941 as the government standard for purified tuberculins. Eventually it was used as the standard all over the world.

In 1958 the Phipps Institute was moved to a new building at the University of Pennsylvania. In her memoirs, Seibert wrote that she did not believe that the conditions necessary for her continued work would be available. Consequently, she and Mabel, her long-time assistant and companion, retired to St. Petersburg, Florida. Florence Seibert continued her research, however, using for a time a small laboratory in the nearby Mound Park Hospital and another in her own home. In her retirement years she devoted herself to the study of bacteria that were associated with certain types of cancers. Her declining health in her last two years was attributed to complications from childhood polio. She died in St. Petersburg on August 23, 1991.

In 1968 Seibert published her memoirs, which reveal her many friendships, especially among others engaged in scientific research. She particularly enjoyed international travel as well as driving her car, which was especially equipped to compensate for her handicaps. She loved music and played the violin (privately, she was careful to note).

Further Reading

New York Times, August 31, 1991. □

Sejo

The Korean king Sejo (1417-1468) was an effective yet cruel ruler. In his attempt to maintain royal prerogative against the pressures of the Confucianist gentry-officials, his ruthlessness nurtured a reaction which in time led to a net loss of power for his successors.

Sejo, formally named Yi Yu, and known as Prince Suyang before taking the throne, was born Nov. 7, 1417, the second son of the great king Sejong. Among eight royal heirs Sejo was perhaps the most capable, but since the designation as crown prince had gone to his elder brother (Yi Hyang, who reigned as Munjong, 1450-1452), Sejo was from the beginning cut off from the succession. Throughout Sejong's reign the royal brothers worked well together, directed by an even-handed father who kept them busy. Sejo was well informed on military affairs, having observed frontier operations against the Jürchen and participated in the development of munitions and ordnance during the early 1440s. He made a major contribution as director of his father's land-survey commission; the formulas developed by his body for measuring crop yields and assessing taxes became a fundamental part of Yi-dynasty fiscal structure. Sejo as a prince also wrote in the vernacular an account of the Buddha's life, which provided the inspiration for his father's Buddhist poetry.

Sejo's brother Munjong succeeded Sejong in 1450 and was competent enough as king; but his health was poor, and he quickly became a target for bureaucrats and officials. Sejo and his younger brother, Prince Anp'yong (1418-1453), helped their weaker brother by seeing that the throne's interests were asserted. But when on the King's premature death, in 1452, Munjong's 10-year-old son, Tanjong (Yi Hongwi, also known as Prince Nosan), succeeded, a rift grew between the two brothers over the exercise of power during Tanjong's minority.

Finally, in November 1453, Sejo, charging Prince Anp'yong and his followers with plotting to overthrow the young king, banished his brother to an island, where he was forced to commit suicide, and murdered the principal men of his faction. With Sejo now in complete control, Tanjong grew increasingly edgy. Convinced that Sejo's coups were not yet over, he abdicated on July 25, 1455. Sejo took the throne the same day, while Tanjong moved to a lonely exile in remote Kangwon Province.

Sejo justified his usurpation on the grounds that unless a strong king sat on the throne the royal power would steadily be eroded. But many men of his day felt he had gone too far, and inevitably a movement grew to restore Tanjong. A group of loyalists planned a coup for July 1456 but were betrayed by an informer. Sejo personally carried out their interrogation, subjecting the six plotters to unspeakable torture and mutilation. The historical accounts of this confrontation show the six men composing defiant poetry and lecturing Sejo to silence before finally breathing their last. Soon afterward Sejo ordered Tanjong's suicide.

These murders echoed through the centuries that followed, with the overwhelming opinion falling on the side of the boy king and the "Six Dead Ministers," as they came to be called. (Six sympathetic officials who went into lifetime retirement to protest Sejo's action are called the "Six Live Ministers.") Tanjong and all loyalists were posthumously rehabilitated during the 17th century, but long before that the reverberations of the affair had precipitated factional struggles and purges (notably in 1498, when defense of the loyalists was adjudged *lèse-majesté*).

From 1456 on, Sejo's power was not again questioned. He had his way in virtually everything, and it can be said in his favor that, once established, he was a remarkably effective king. Among his achievements were lavish support of Buddhist writings and their publication, effective frontier defense, suppression of a major rebellion, and institution of the "secret censor" system, by which royal spies circulated covertly through the provinces ferreting out and summarily punishing corruption. In time these posts became themselves major focuses of graft, but the original idea of incorruptible censors had a long life in popular fiction.

Sejo abdicated in favor of his son Yejong on Sept. 22, 1468, and died the next day of an incurable disease.

Further Reading

There is no biography of Sejo in English. Some details of his reign appear in such standard survey histories as Takashi Hatada, *A History of Korea,* translated and edited by Warren W. Smith, Jr., and Benjamin H. Hazard (1969); and Woo-keun Han, *The History of Korea,* edited by Grafton Mintz (trans. 1970). □

Sejong

Sejong (1397-1450) was a Korean king and inventor of the Korean alphabet. His long reign, 1418-1450, is generally acknowledged to have been the most brilliant period of the Yi dynasty.

Sejong, formally named Yi To, and known as Prince Ch'ungnyong before taking the throne, was born on May 7, 1397. Since his eldest brother, Prince Yangnyong, had been designated crown prince in 1404, Sejong in early life did not anticipate the throne. But Yangnyong's erratic behavior led to his deposition and Sejong's elevation in July 1418. (An unofficial tradition holds that Prince Yangnyong feigned instability so that Sejong might rule.) Sejong became king, following his father's abdication, on Sept. 7, 1418.

During his reign Sejong introduced improved administrative procedures, new census laws, penal reforms, and some civil rights for slaves and outcast groups. He maintained proper relations with China and a firm stance with Japan. His devastating attack on the island of Tsushima in 1419, in retaliation for the coastal raids of Japanese pirates, eliminated the immediate peril and ultimately led to a treaty (1443) which established a long-lasting, peaceful relationship with Japan. To the north he incorporated new territory south of the Yalu and Tumen rivers, which until then had been occupied or threatened by the Jürchen barbarians. Korea's modern borders are thus one of his legacies.

In the cultural field, Sejong ordered the compilation of outstanding historical works, and his system of branch depositories for historical records ensured the survival of many valuable books through the destructive Japanese invasions of 1592-1598. He reformed the court music. Voluminous encyclopedias of agriculture, medicine, military science, and public administration were compiled. He sponsored the compilation of gazeteers, instituted standardized weights and measures, and installed rain gauges throughout the country, all of which contributed to his rationalization of tax-assessing procedures. His researchers designed clepsydras, armillary spheres, and other scientific instruments.

Sejong's greatest achievement was the alphabet. It was first announced late in 1443 and formally proclaimed in 1446. Sejong was not merely the patron of this alphabet but its actual theoretician and inventor. It reflects in its structure and graphic symbolism a very sophisticated understanding of linguistics. Although the script was coolly received by his officials and did not for many years completely replace the classical Chinese in which they wrote, it was a long-run success and is today the writing system of all Koreans.

Sejong was quick to promote those who showed promise; especially intelligent young men received his "reading vacations," paid leaves for untrammeled study. The most promising scholars were appointed to the famous "College of Assembled Worthies" (organized 1420), where the research for his cultural and technical projects was done. Many of their publications survive today and reveal a uniformly high standard of scholarship. Sejong's friendship with his scholars was legendary. In political life too he got on well with his highest officers.

But beginning in the late 1430s, Sejong's relations with his officials became strained over two issues. The first was his attempt to delegate certain royal duties to the crown prince in order to conserve his own health. From about 1437, Sejong suffered from rheumatism and diabetes, and about 1442 his eyesight also began to fail. He repeatedly asked his ministers' assent to his plans for the crown prince; just as regularly this assent was withheld. (Korean kings, while theoretically all-powerful, were by tradition and practice required to obtain a consensus of support for their actions.) The debate was resolved only in 1445, when the crown prince finally took over limited duties, but the ill feeling remained.

A second issue was Sejong's belief in Buddhism. The Yi dynasty had come to power partly as a reaction against the previous dynasty's excessive patronage of Buddhism, and from the beginning it had enforced strict limitations on the numbers of monks and monasteries and on tenable church property. As king, Sejong enforced these public policies, but personally he was a devout believer, especially after the death of his wife, Queen Sohon, in 1446. For this he suffered constant abuse from his Confucianist officials. Some of the opposition to his alphabet was doubtless a result of this antagonistic atmosphere.

Because of these struggles and his increasingly poor health, Sejong after 1446 began to turn from his official duties to his private pursuits. In addition to the assistance of the crown prince (later reigned as Munjong, 1450-1452), Sejong was helped by two other capable sons, Princes Anp'yong and Suyang (Sejo). Sejong spent his last years writing Buddhist devotional poetry, much of which still survives. Early in 1450, he left the palace and retired to the Seoul residence of his youngest son, where he died of a massive stroke on March 30, 1450.

Further Reading

Sejong's reign is discussed in Takashi Hatada, *A History of Korea,* translated and edited by Warren W. Smith, Jr., and Benjamin H. Hazard (1969); and Woo-keun Han, *The History of Korea,* edited by Grafton Mintz (trans. 1970).

Additional Sources

King Sejong the Great: the light of fifteenth century Korea, Washington, D.C.: International Circle of Korean Linguistics, 1992. □

Seleucus I

Seleucus I (ca. 358-281 B.C.), a Macedonian general, was a Companion of Alexander the Great, king of Babylonia and Syria, and founder of the Seleucid empire and dynasty.

The son of a Macedonian nobleman, Seleucus was born between 358 and 354 B.C. in Macedonia, then ruled by Philip II. He grew up with the king's son, Alexander, and became Alexander's close associate during his expedition through Persia. Seleucus was present with Alexander at Susa in 324, and according to Alexander's bidding, Seleucus married the Bactrian princess Apama. Unlike many of the Macedonians, Seleucus never repudiated this political marriage.

Scramble for the Throne

When Alexander died in 323, Seleucus ranked well below the leading "successors." The kingship went jointly to Alexander's epileptic and half-witted half brother, Philip Arrhidaeios, and the unborn child carried by Alexander's Bactrian wife, Rhoxana. Perdikkas, the leading general and Macedonian nobleman in Babylon, became their regent. Of the other prominent generals, Ptolemy sought the satrapy of Egypt; Antipater remained in Greece as governor and, allied with Craterus, crushed the Athenian rebellion; Lysimachus obtained Thrace; and Antigonus "the One-eyed" gained the powerful satrapy of Phrygia.

Opposition arose to Perdikkas, and in 321 war erupted. Caught between the northern powers and Ptolemy to the south, Perdikkas divided his forces. Seleucus, who had received no lands or personal power other than a generalship under Perdikkas, supported the regent. Perdikkas and Seleucus marched against Ptolemy and three times failed to cross the Nile Delta.

Seleucus, wishing to overthrow his perpetual subordination, turned on Perdikkas and joined in his assassination. Consequently, Seleucus gained the satrapy of Babylonia and the power he sought. Although the satrapy of Babylonia remained the heart of Alexander's empire, Seleucus found the borders difficult to maintain. In Asia Minor, Antigonus rapidly gained more power, and leaders in Media and Susiana also sought to overthrow Seleucus.

When Antipater, the new royal regent, died in 319, Antigonus sought greater power and larger realms. In 321 Antipater had appointed Antigonus commander of the royal armies in Asia, and Antigonus desired to reunite Alexander's empire. When royalist uprisings in Asia threatened Seleucus's insecure power, out of necessity he summoned Antigonus's assistance. Once in Babylonia, Antigonus assumed supreme command and reduced the royalists, and in 316 Seleucus fled to Egypt and Ptolemy's protection. Together, Ptolemy, Cassander (the son of Antipater), and Lysimachus opposed Antigonus and demanded that Seleucus be restored to Babylonia. By 311, with Antigonus back in Asia Minor, Seleucus and Ptolemy entered Pales-

son by Apama, Antiochus (I), ruled as viceroy of the dominions east of the Euphrates. Seleucus's love for Antiochus was such that he divorced his second wife, Stratonice, in 293 to allow his son to marry her.

In 293 Seleucus occupied Cilicia in eastern Asia Minor and began to plot against Demetrius (his former father-in-law), who had seized the Macedonian throne. Seleucus once again allied himself with Ptolemy and Lysimachus. Lysimachus, however, took Macedonia for himself, and Seleucus turned against him. In the spring of 281 Seleucus set out to conquer Asia Minor and to defeat Lysimachus. With him was the eldest son of Ptolemy I, Ptolemy Keraunos, who continually intrigued against his father and against Seleucus. The aged Ptolemy I failed to aid Lysimachus, who fell to a traitor's spear. But when Seleucus advanced on Macedonia that summer, Ptolemy Keraunos stabbed him to death in a vain attempt to claim the Macedonian throne.

Further Reading

Edwyn Bevan, *The House of Seleucus* (2 vols., 1902), remains the major study of Seleucus and the Seleucid dynasty. General studies of the Hellenistic era are W. W. Tarn and G. T. Griffith, *Hellenistic Civilization* (1927; 3d rev. ed. 1952), and Pierre Grimal and others, *Hellenism and the Rise of Rome* (1968). □

tine. The victorious Seleucus headed for Babylon, gaining the support of the people, the armies, and minor officials. From 311 on, Seleucus retained Babylonia. Pushing eastward Seleucus rapidly conquered the once rebellious Media and Susiana. Antigonus, however, remained a threat and regained Palestine.

Securing a Power Base

In 311 Seleucus founded Seleucia on the Tigris as his new capital. It replaced ancient Babylon and became an eastern outpost of Greek civilization—a major entrepôt blending Greeks, Babylonians, and Jews. With the Chaldean Magi, Seleucus also founded the eastern city of Ctesiphon across the Tigris from Seleucia.

During the next 9 years Seleucus strengthened his eastern borders and crossed the Indus River and invaded India. In the west Antigonus still dominated and in 305 assumed the royal title. In Babylonia, Seleucus ruled a tight, efficient government modeled upon the earlier Persian absolutism. He developed his army and the bureaucracy and built new cities during a humane and able kingship.

In 302 Seleucus marched against Antigonus and entered Phrygia. In the following spring he allied once again with the "separatist generals" Ptolemy, Cassander, and Lysimachus, and at Ipsus in a heated battle he defeated and killed Antigonus. As booty, Seleucus obtained Syria. Seleucus thus gained the chief military and political position among the kings, which caused an estrangement with them. In Syria he built Antioch-on-the-Orontes in 300. Seleucus's

Edwin Robert Anderson Seligman

The American economist and editor Edwin Robert Anderson Seligman (1861-1939) was known as editor in chief of the *Encyclopaedia of the Social Sciences* and for editing the *Columbia University Studies in History, Economics, and Public Law.*

On April 25, 1861, Edwin R. A. Seligman was born in New York City, where his father was a banker of some prominence in both national and international financial circles. For his early education (until the age of 11) he was tutored at home. He then entered the innovative Columbia Grammar School, and at the age of 14 he entered Columbia College, where he received his bachelor's degree in 1879. He then went abroad to study at universities in Berlin, Paris, and Heidelberg.

In 1882 Seligman returned to Columbia to pursue simultaneously graduate studies in economics and in law; he received his master's in economics and was admitted to the New York State bar in 1884. In the same year, he received an appointment as lecturer in economics in the faculty of political science at Columbia. This discipline had been newly established under the aegis of John W. Burgess and was a truly pioneering development in the history of American education. In 1888 Seligman was promoted to adjunct professor of political economy and in 1891 received the rank of professor of political economy and finance, which he retained until his death.

Seligman's efforts through his life were dispersed over a wide range of activities. Not only was he energetically engaged in academic, professional, and editorial areas, but he worked in governmental and civic spheres, especially with groups concerned with promoting various social reforms. He was a cofounder of the American Economic Association and served as its president (1902-1904). He was president of the National Tax Association (1913-1915) and was one of the moving forces behind the founding of the American Association of University Professors in 1915, serving as its president (1919-1920). He was also a frequent adviser to New York State and New York City tax commissions, this being the area of his special competency. In the same capacity he acted as consultant to the League of Nations (1922-1923) and the reform-minded government of Cuba in 1931.

At Columbia, Seligman taught mainly in the field of political economy and the history of economic doctrines, originally a subfield of political philosophy, which attained an independent status in the 20th century. Recent thought on this matter, however, has reverted to the ancient view that economics cannot be really considered or understood apart from political philosophy, which sets the goals for economic activities. Seligman was one of a small group of scholars who worked actively to establish economics as an independent discipline. His own works on the history of economic doctrines and on economic terminology exercised an important influence in the United States and Europe; several of them were translated and are still cited today in professional works. His works on taxation were quite influential when written, but unlike his treatments of the development of economic doctrine, they are less frequently cited today. Many of the tax reforms that he advocated were adopted, such as the progressive income tax.

Perhaps Seligman's chief contribution to modern education, however, was his editorship (1927-1935) of the influential and highly esteemed *Encyclopaedia of the Social Sciences,* the most important and comprehensive reference work in the social sciences. In the original edition, Seligman himself wrote several articles reflecting his own wide interests, including an introductory essay, "What Are the Social Sciences?"

Further Reading

There is no definitive biography of Seligman. Some information on his life is in *Edwin R. A. Seligman, 1861-1959: Addresses Delivered at the Memorial Meeting Held on December the Thirteenth, 1939* (1942), and his career is discussed in Joseph Dorfman, *The Economic Mind in American Civilization* (5 vols., 1946-1959), and Ralph G. Hoxie and others, *A History of the Faculty of Political Science, Columbia University* (1955). His position in the history of economic thought is assessed in Ben B. Seligman, *Main Currents in Modern Economics: Economic Thought since 1870* (1962). A list of Seligman's works is included in Columbia University, Faculty of Political Science, *A Bibliography . . . 1880-1930* (1931). □

Selim I

Selim I (ca. 1470-1520), the ninth Ottoman sultan, was the instigator of large-scale conquest and administrative consolidation in Asia that left the Ottomans dominant in the Middle East.

The son of Bayezid II (Bajazet), Selim gained administrative experience as governor of Trebizond and Semendra. In contention for the succession with his older brothers, Selim won with the support of the Janissaries, who forced Bayezid to abdicate on April 25, 1512.

For a year the new sultan was preoccupied with eliminating his brothers and nephews. Then he turned to consolidating Ottoman power in Anatolia, which was threatened by religious attractions from Persia. In the fall of 1513 lists were prepared of Shiite heretics. Some 40,000 died, and others were imprisoned or deported in the persecution that followed.

Selim's declaration of war on Iran the following spring initiated a famous correspondence between himself and Shah Ismael. The Sultan, later remembered as a poet, wrote in an elegant style—the message, however, proving provocative and insulting. On Aug. 23, 1514, Turkish artillery routed the Persians at Chaldiran.

To quiet Janissary opposition to the war, Selim executed several leaders, a procedure for which his reign is noted. He later appointed men from his own household as generals in order to increase control over the Janissary group. Selim is called "Yavuz" ("the Grim"), connoting both respect and fear. Essentially a stern ruler, he nevertheless survives in Ottoman history as a hero.

Selim campaigned in eastern Anatolia again in 1515 and resumed the attack on Persia the following year. In August, however, the Turks encountered the Mamluk ruler of Egypt, a supporter of Ismael, and defeated him in a brief battle north of Aleppo. Egyptian forces were unpaid, undisciplined, and dissentious, the state weakened by the recent loss of Eastern trade to the Portuguese.

The Levantine cities surrendered peacefully, and Ottoman administrators took over but with remarkably few changes. When the new Egyptian sultan executed Selim's ambassadors, who were bearing offers of peace in exchange for acceptance of Turkish sovereignty, the Ottomans moved on Cairo, which fell in January 1517. En route to Egypt, Selim made a pilgrimage to Jerusalem.

During his months in Cairo, Selim accepted the voluntary submission of the sharif of Mecca, thus bringing the holy places under Ottoman control. Tradition has it that one consequence of this campaign was the official surrendering to the Ottomans of the paraphernalia of the Caliph (the Prophet's standard, mantle, and sword) by the last "Abbasid" caliph, al-Mutawwakil, captured from the Egyptians at Aleppo. This alleged transference of authority was the later legal justification for Osmanli use of the title, although Selim had earlier referred to himself as caliph.

Selim returned to Istanbul in July 1518. As skilled at administration as in military affairs, he subsequently devoted himself to government. On Sept. 20, 1520, he suddenly died, apparently of cancer.

Further Reading

General works on Selim's period include G. W. F. Stripling, *The Ottoman Turks and the Arabs, 1511-1574* (1942), and A. D. Alderson, *Structure of the Ottoman Dynasty* (1956). □

Selim III

Selim III (1761-1808), the twenty-eighth Ottoman sultan, was a late-18th-century reformer who sought to end the stagnation and decay weakening the empire.

Born on Dec. 24, 1761, Selim was the son of Mustafa III and successor to his uncle Abdul Hamid I, who died April 7, 1789. As a youth, the new sultan had benefited from a moderately free existence in contrast to the century-old custom of caging Osmanli princes. He was better educated then most of his recent predecessors.

Selim initially devoted himself to prosecuting the 2-year-old Austro-Russian War, an outgrowth of the first detailed plan to divide the Ottoman Empire, drawn up by Austria and Russia in 1782. The Peace of Sistova, in August 1791, involved no territorial changes with Austria, but the Peace of Jassy (Iaşi), in January 1792, advanced the Russian border to the Dniester.

Internal Reforms

Profiting from unrest in Europe which preoccupied his enemies, Selim introduced domestic reforms to strengthen his government. He solicited suggestions throughout the governing institutions. As a basis for change, he created a new treasury, filled, in large part, from confiscatory punishment leveled at fief holders who had ceased to respect their military obligations.

Among the changes was an attempt to curtail the grand vizier's power by enlargement of the Divan and insistence that important issues be brought before it. Schools were opened, attention was given to printing and to the circulation of Western translations, and young Turks were sent to Europe for further study. The most significant reforms, however, involved the military. The navy was strengthened, and a navigation school was opened. The army commissariat was changed, officer training was improved, the Bosporus forts were strengthened, the artillery was revitalized, and the new engineering school was reorganized. Foreign advisers, largely French, assisted.

The major innovation was the founding of a new body of regular troops known as *nizam-i-jedid* (new regulation), a term also applied to the reforms as a whole. The first of these new units, uniformed, well disciplined and drilled, was formed in 1792 by a former Turkish lieutenant in the Russian army. Other units followed, involving, in some instances, extensive barracks building with related town facilities, such as the mosques and baths of Scutari. Such buildings constitute Selim's major architectural legacy.

Foreign Relations

On the international scene all remained peaceful until 1798, although foreign affairs received considerable attention. New resident embassies were established in Britain, France, Prussia, and Austria. Selim, a cultured poet and musician, carried on an extended correspondence with Louis XVI. Although distressed by the establishment of the republic in France, the Porte (Ottoman government) was soothed by French representatives in Istanbul who maintained the goodwill of various influential personages, including the later Swedish minister, Mouradgea d'Ohsson, whose *Tableau de l'Empire Othoman* (1820) provides a good overview of this period.

On July 1, 1798, however, French forces landed in Egypt, and Selim declared war on France on September 4. In alliance with Russia and Britain, the Turks were in periodic conflict with the French on both land and sea until March 1801. Peace came in June 1802.

The following year brought trouble in the Balkans. For decades a sultan's word had had no power in outlying provinces, prompting Selim's reforms of the military in order to reimpose central control. This desire was not fulfilled. One rebellious leader was Austrian-backed Osman Pasvanoglu, whose invasion of Wallachia in 1801 inspired

Russian intervention, resulting in greater autonomy for the Dunubian provinces.

Serbian conditions also deteriorated. They took a fateful turn with the return, in 1799, of the hated Janissaries, ousted 8 years before. These forces murdered Selim's enlightened governor, ending the best rule this province had had in the last 100 years. Their defiant, outrageous actions prompted the anti-Janissary revolt of 1804. Neither arms nor diplomacy could restore Ottoman authority.

French influence with the Porte did not revive until 1806, but it then led the Sultan into defying both St. Petersburg and London, and Turkey joined Napoleon's Continental System. War was declared on Russia on December 27 and on Britain in March 1807. Meanwhile, reform efforts had continued, but in March 1805 a general levy for new troops had led the Janissaries to revolt. These events culminated in the murder of reform leaders and, on May 29, 1807, the deposition of Selim. He was charged with childlessness and the use of military innovations to incite revolt.

Incarcerated in the *saray,* or palace, by his cousin, the new sultan Mustafa IV, Selim occupied himself instructing Mustafa's brother Mahmud in the art of government. On July 28, 1808, he was executed, as supporters, demanding his reinstatement, broke down the palace gates. Mustafa gained nothing, however; he was replaced by Mahmud II.

Further Reading

For general biographical information on Selim III see A. D. Alderson, *Structure of the Ottoman Dynasty* (1956). V. J. Puryear, *Napoleon and the Dardanelles* (1951), considers diplomacy. □

5th Earl of Selkirk

Thomas Douglas, 5th Earl of Selkirk (1771-1820), was a Scottish colonizer in Canada. Concerned about the depressed state of the Highlands of Scotland and Ireland, he devoted much of his fortune, and his health, to establishing new communities in North America.

Thomas Douglas was born in Kirkcudbrightshire on June 20, 1771, the seventh son of the 4th Earl of Selkirk. With little prospect of family support, he went to the University of Edinburgh to study law and there developed an interest in social and political affairs. In 1792, a tour of the Highlands convinced him that the lot of its people could never be improved and their only hope lay in emigration.

The breakdown of the clan system and the conversion of large areas of the Highlands into sheep walks had reduced the crofters to a life of marginal existence. Douglas was even more shocked by the condition of the Irish peasantry. His concern led to the passion of his life, the colonization of these people in North America, where their economic prospects would be improved and the British Empire strengthened. He was able to do something about it when the last of his brothers died in 1797, and he succeeded to the family estate 2 years later.

Selkirk besieged the Colonial Office with his emigration schemes and was finally granted permission in 1803 to undertake his first ventures. Lands in Prince Edward Island and in Upper Canada were granted, and his first two colonies were planted. Selkirk spent most of 1803 and 1804 in British North America supervising his experiments. The former colony prospered, but the second, at Baldoon, was less successful and collapsed.

Settlement of the Red River

Selkirk returned to England in 1804 and then devoted several years to politics as a Whig. He was married in 1807 to Jean Wedderburn-Colville, whose family was involved in the Hudson's Bay Company. The following year Selkirk began to acquire stock in the company. His old interest in colonization rekindled. His attention shifted westward to the Red River valley, and he began to plan the migration for which he is best remembered. In 1811 he received from the company a grant of 116,000 square miles in what is now Manitoba, Minnesota, and North Dakota. In July the first of a stream of Selkirk settlers set out for their new home.

They had to contend not only with natural hazards but also with the hostility of the North West Company, which felt settlement threatened the fur trade, a business that Selkirk "hated from the bottom of his heart." In 1815, and again the following year, the colony was attacked by the traders, with considerable loss of life on the second occasion. Selkirk arrived at Red River in 1817 and began the task of reconstruction, establishing a school and a church. His arrest of some of the traders resulted in a drawn-out trial which eventually exonerated the Nor'westers.

Selkirk returned home in 1818. He died at Pau, France, on April 8, 1820. His humanitarian impulse had broken his health and consumed his fortune, but it left a warm and cherished memory in the Canadian west.

Further Reading

The best and probably definitive study of Selkirk is John M. Gray, *Lord Selkirk of Red River* (1963). Older but still useful are George Bryce, *Mackenzie, Selkirk, Simpson* (1905) and *The Life of Lord Selkirk: Coloniser of Western Canada* (1912), and Chester Martin, *Lord Selkirk's Work in Canada* (1916).

Additional Sources

MacEwan, Grant, *Cornerstone colony: Selkirk's contribution to the Canadian West,* Saskatoon, Sask.: Western Producer Prairie Books, 1977. □

Wilfred Sellars

The influential American philosopher Wilfred Sellars (1912-1989) developed a unified and novel philosophical system that had wide influence on Ameri-

can philosophy. Sellars was a president of the American Philosophical Association and the author of many books and articles, most notably *Science, Perception and Reality* and *Science and Metaphysics.*

Wilfred Sellars was born on May 20, 1912, in Ann Arbor, Michigan. He was the son of the American philosopher Roy Wood Sellars, who was an influential participant in the critical realist movement within the United States. He was educated at various universities in the United States and Great Britain and began his teaching career as an assistant professor at the University of Iowa in 1938. In 1947 he accepted a position at the University of Minnesota as professor of philosophy and remained there until 1958, at which time he accepted a position at Yale University. In 1963 he accepted the position of professor of philosophy at the University of Pittsburgh.

The characteristic mark of American philosophy during the middle half of the 20th century was an unwillingness to construct unified systems of thought that responded to most, if not all, the perennial questions of philosophy. American philosophers during this period fell under the influence of empiricist and linguistic assaults on traditional metaphysics and became skeptical of the very enterprise of building philosophical systems. Wilfred Sellars rejected this skeptical loss of nerve and constructed a system of ideas that originated from his solution to what he considered the primary philosophical problem of our epoch—the problem of connecting scientific with ordinary accounts of the world. He refers to these accounts as the "scientific and manifest images."

The manifest image or the common sense account of the world is, at first glance, inconsistent with the scientific account of the world since ordinary men never see neutrons or use electron microscopes. However, the manifest image is, according to Sellars, never completely abandoned by science because scientific proof requires that evidence be available to anyone and hence scientific evidence ultimately must end up appealing to the manifest image. Furthermore, the objects of science are, for Sellars, modeled on ordinary objects. These two domains are separate, irreducible domains but they are interconnected. Both domains are dialectically dependent on one another in the sense that we need the scientific image to validate the hypotheses of science and we need the scientific image to provide the ontology of the manifest image while the manifest image provides the epistemological foundation of the scientific image. What unites these two realms is that both are intrinsically realistic in that both domains posit the existence of realities that exist independently of our cognitive processes.

Science then must never abandon ordinary objects if it is to retain its universal status. This is because ordinary common sense postulates the existence of chairs and tables but these objects do not "explain" our sensations. This is the empiricist trap. Rather, these ordinary objects are "directly perceived" and these directly perceived objects are models for forming abstract pictures of sensations. The world of perception is a construct based on the contents of the manifest or common sense picture of the world. Furthermore, believing in ordinary objects, such as chairs and tables, is, for Sellars, not a synthetic or casual belief. It is an analytic belief in the sense that the meaning of our most basic scientific terms, such as sensation or perception, assume these ordinary objects as models for explaining what a sensation or perception is. The scientific image is also realistic. It postulates not ordinary objects but theoretical objects to account for our complex scientific experience. These theoretical objects are, according to Sellars, parasitic on ordinary objects in the sense that the scientist will always require ordinary objects to explain what he means by theoretical objects.

This view of science plays a crucial role within Sellars' conception of the human mind. The central theme of his picture of the mind is that the mind in both its actions (remembering, seeing, feeling, etc.) and its contents (memories, sensations, sentiments, etc.) can be interpreted neutrally without assuming that minds are either material objects or immaterial objects. He therefore rejects claims such as "the mind is the brain" as well as claims such as "the mind is a spirit." For Sellars, they might be either, but the philosophy of the human mind by itself cannot lead to either conclusion. The reason or basis for this neutralist view of the mental is that, according to Sellars, all mental events are functional. A functional event is what is minimally needed to predict the occurrence of the second event, given the occurrence of the first within the appropriate circumstances. Thus, if one takes an aspirin when one has a headache, the belief that aspirin reduces pain is functional in the sense that it connects taking aspirin with having a headache. For Sellars, functional mental events are minimal events and, since they are minimal, they must be neutral with respect to being either material or immaterial.

Sellars' ethical writings concern themselves with fitting ethical discourse within this functional, scientific realism. The heart of his moral concern is to establish that moral acts are free in the sense that they are caused by a certain type of mental event called a volition and the absence of volition to do an act X makes act X determined or accidental rather than free. Volitions are thus the functional element within morality. But while volition or freedom is at the core of the moral evaluation of persons, it is not, for Sellars, at the core of the moral evaluation of actions. Actions, he claimed, must be viewed from the viewpoint of general consequences for relevant communities. It is the general welfare of the relevant community that constitutes the realistic basis for justifying which actions ought to be freely committed. In short, Sellars' ethics is systematically unified with both his philosophy of mind and his theory of knowledge.

Further Reading

Reading the works of Wilfred Sellars will require time and patience. It is recommended that he be read with help. Perhaps the best available help for young readers interested in his work is *The Synoptic Vision* (1977) edited by Delaney, Loux, Gutting, and Solomon. Also, Richard Bernstein's *Praxis and Action* (1971) contains some very helpful comments on Sellars' philosophical system. Finally, Bruce Aune's *Knowledge,*

Mind and Nature (1967) is an excellent source of information on Sellars.

Additional Sources

Evans, Joseph Claude, *The metaphysics of transcendental subjectivity: Descartes, Kant, and W. Sellars,* Amsterdam: B.R. Gruner, 1984. □

Peter Richard Henry Sellers

Peter Richard Henry Sellers (1925-1980) was a British comedy genius of theater, radio, television, and movies.

Peter Sellers was born in Southsea, Hampshire, in southern England, where by chance his parents were performing in a local vaudeville show, on September 8, 1925. His father was William Sellers, a pianist and musical director, and his mother was Agnes Marks, a character actress. Sellers was ethnically half-Jewish from his mother's side, but was not religious. He was educated in a Catholic school (St. Aloysius College, Highgate, London) and his funeral service in 1980 was Anglican.

Sellers loved his mother and the show business family around him, which included his eight uncles (stage producers) and his maternal grandmother (renowned for bringing swimmers in a glass tank to the music hall stage, among other things). Peter made his stage debut at the age of five in his grandmother's review, *Splash Me!* His early life was filled with music hall goings-on, backstage gossip, his parents' search for "digs" (provincial lodgings suitable for entertainers), and theatrical odd jobs for himself—"head sweeperouter" in the auditorium, for instance.

Peter, a weak student at St. Aloysius, decided to become a drummer, and he secured a job with a dance band. World War II found him, at the age of 18 in 1943, with the Royal Air Force (RAF). He joined ENSA (the forces entertainment company) and served in Burma, India, and the Middle East in camp comedy shows, later touring with the RAF "Gang Show." Sellers enjoyed his time with ENSA entertaining troops. In 1946 he was demobilized; he said it was "like coming out of the sunshine into the shade."

The two "demob" years (1946-1948) were, in fact, doldrums for Sellers. He went the exhausting round of visits to dispirited theatrical agent, he got the seasonal job of entertainment director of a holiday camp, and he played the ukelele in comic skits at clubs. Finally, with an audition at the famous Windmill Theatre in London in 1948, his career made a turn, albeit his act was scheduled between nude performances. He began to make a name for himself in variety shows, appearing at the London Palladium. Sellers telephoned a BBC producer, effectively mimicking two radio stars, Richard Murdoch and Kenneth Horne, as if they were recommending him for a job. The producer gave Sellers his first radio spot. Radio was a successful field for him, with his uncanny mimicry of voices.

In January 1952 Sellars, Spike Milligan, and Harry Secombe launched the *Goon Show* on BBC radio, an irreverent, impious show where the Goons jested in dozens of voices of imaginary characters—which Goon was which voice, no one cared. The *Goon Show* took the British nation by storm; it was a hit for nine years. Tapes of episodes of the *Goon Show* were still being sold worldwide almost 40 years later. On British television Spike Milligan and Peter Sellers later produced their satires: *A Show Called Fred, Son of Fred* and *Yes, It's the Cathode Ray Tube Show.*

The motion picture debut for Peter Sellers (after a number of small films, like *Down Among the Z Men*) was a small part in *The Ladykillers* (1956), starring Alec Guiness. More films came in 1957 to 1959 including *Carlton-Browne of the F.O.* starring Terry-Thomas (1959, titled in America *Man in a Cocked Hat*). This was the first movie Sellers made with the production and direction team of John and Ray Boulting. Sellers signed a five-year contract with the Boultings, but with two films in 1959, *The Mouse That Roared* and *I'm All Right, Jack,* he established his movie career. In the former he played the multiple parts of a prime minister, a duchess, and a constable in a mythical, debt-ridden European nation that decides to declare war on the United States, to be later rehabilitated (like Germany and Japan) by the Americans. In the latter film he played a self-important shop steward in a British postwar factory, pitting his cunning against management. Both movies were instant hits.

The World of Henry Orient (1964) was the first "American" movie that Sellers made and was the official U.S. entry in the Cannes Film Festival. He played a vain and lecherous pianist being chased by two teenagers. But his visit to Hollywood was cut short: he had divorced his first wife, Anne Howe, and married 19-year old Britt Ekland, a rising Swedish film star, in February 1964; and he had the first of his heart attacks in April at the age of 38.

In England the first of his *Pink Panther* films was opening to enthused crowds while he recuperated. As inspector Clouseau, Peter Sellers gained his biggest audience. He played the Inspector as an imperturbable Gallic blunderer, a detective who could detect without knowing what he had done. The sequel, *A Shot in the Dark,* was released in the same year. Subsequent *Pink Panther* films were *Return of the Pink Panther* (1975) and two movies which exceeded $100 million each in revenues, *The Pink Panther Strikes Again* (1976) and the *Revenge of the Pink Panther* (1978).

In contrast, also released in 1964 was the satiric film *Dr. Strangelove, or How I Learned to Stop Worrying and Love the Bomb,* in which Sellers played three parts: the mad scientist, Dr. Strangelove; the U.S. President Muffley; and RAF Group-Captain Mandrake. The 1960's were a busy time for Sellers. During this time he also made *What's New, Pussy Cat?* He played Fritz Fassbender, a psychiatrist with psychotic problems; it was a pure farce.

During his life, Sellers was featured in 52 movies: some were mediocre and some were a financial failure. *Being There* (1979) was the finest film he ever made, and he knew it. The movie, based on the novel and script by Jerzy Kosinski, concerned a strange case of mistaken identity in which a passive, harmless, and not-so-simple-minded gardener ("Chance" or Chauncey Gardiner) hooked on television was believed by the people around him to be an economic genius and oracle. Sellers (as Chance) becomes an adviser to the U.S. President, and in line for the presidency himself. Wry, understated humor marked Seller's performance in this film, in contrast with the farcical *Pink Panther* movies and the zany *Goon Show.* Without eccentric accents, multiple characters (he plays only Chance), and buffoonery, Sellers masterfully portrayed a man made illustrious by what other people detected in him, whether it was true or not.

In *The Fiendish Plot of Dr. Fu Manchu* (1980) he was co-author and director of the movie and played Dr. Fu Manchu. He gave himself, as Dr. Fu Manchu, a significant line:

> -"I suppose you think I'm too old for a young, ravishing creature like yourself?"
> -"How old are you?"
> -"One hundred and sixty eight."
> -"You know, I don't think age matters, really."

Peter Sellers was married four times: to Anne Howe (1951-1964), an English actress with whom he had two children, Michael and Sarah; to Britt Ekland (1964-1969), a Swedish actress with whom he had a daughter, Victoria; to Miranda Quarry (1970-1974), a stepdaughter of an English peer; and to Lynne Frederick, an actress whom he married in 1977 (She turned 26 the day after Sellers died). He fell in and out of love with unexpected impetus: he surprised even himself. Sellers himself said: I seem to marry young people. I never grew up, you see—I'm still the same idiot I was at 18 or 20." This frankness about himself was there in 1960 when he painted himself as being a man of a thousand voices: "As far as I am aware I have no personality of my own whatsoever." He was very superstitious about everything, especially about his acting: "I have the feeling that the film character enters my body as if I were a kind of medium. It's a little frightening." For all the hype of an interview with a film star, he may have been telling the truth.

Apparently by temperament and personality he was a fit subject, predisposed to heart problems; he was demanding in the theater (he hated "hamming" and amateurism). He was given to temper tantrums and was restless and quixotic by nature, and he could not stand pettyminded bureaucrats, officers, landladies, and people of that sort. He had disputes with his colleagues, for instance Blake Edwards, who had directed the *Pink Panther* films.

Sellers had a script for a revival, called *The Romance of the Pink Panther,* in his possession at the Dorchester Hotel on the day of his death. His weak heart, which gave him trouble in 1964, 1977, and again in 1979, finally caused his death in 1980.

Further Reading

Peter Sellers co-authored two books, *Seller's Market* (1966) with Joe Hyams, and *The Book of the Goons* (1974) with Spike Milligan. Other books on Sellers include Peter Evans, *Peter Sellers: The Man Behind the Mask* (1968, rev. ed. 1981); A. Walker, *Peter Sellers: The Authorized Biography* (1981); Michael Sellers with Sarah and Victoria Sellers, *P.S.: I Love You, Peter Sellers, 1951-1980* (1981); and D. Sylvester, *Peter Sellers: An Illustrated Biography* (1981).

Additional Sources

Evans, Peter, *Peter Sellers, the mask behind the mask,* New York, N.Y.: New American Library, 1980.

Lewis, Roger, *The life and death of Peter Sellers,* London: Century, 1994.

Sellers, Michael, *P.S. I love you: an intimate portrait of Peter Sellers,* New York: E.P. Dutton, 1982.

Walker, Alexander, *Peter Sellers, the authorized biography,* New York: Macmillan, 1981. ☐

Ousmane Sembène

The Senegalese writer and filmmaker Ousmane Sembène (born 1923) is one of Africa's great contemporary novelists and the father of African cinema. His work is characterized by a concern with ordinary decent people who are victimized by repressive governments and bureaucracies. Several of his films have been censored in Senegal because of their political criticism.

Ousmane Sembène was born on Jan. 8, 1923, at Ziguinchor in the southern region of Casamance in colonial French West Africa, now Senegal. Among Francophone African writers, he was unique because of his working-class background and limited primary school education. Originally a fisherman in Casamance, he worked in Dakar as a plumber, bricklayer, and mechanic. In 1939 he was drafted into the colonial army and fought with the French in Italy and Germany and then participated in the liberation of France. He settled in Marseilles, where he worked on the piers and became the leader of the longshoremen's union. His first novel, *Le Docker noir* (1956; translated into English in 1981 as *The Black Docker*), is about his experiences during this period.

Sembène soon turned to writing full-time. He returned to Senegal a few years before it gained independence in 1960. He became an astute observer of the political scene and wrote a number of volumes on the developing national consciousness. In *Oh pays, mon beau peuple!*, he depicts the plight of a developing country under colonialism. *God's Bits of Wood* (1960) recounts the developing sense of self and group consciousness among railway workers in French West Africa during a strike. *L'Harmattan* (1964) focuses upon the difficulty of creating a popular government and the corruption of unresponsive politicians who postpone the arrival of independence.

Father of African Cinema

In the early 1960s, Sembène studied film in Moscow at the Gorki Studios. He turned to film to reach the 90 percent of the population of his country that could not read. Sembène soon gained an international reputation by directing films based on his movies. His 20-minute long short feature film, *Borom Sarat,* a simple story about a day in the miserable life of a Dakar cart-driver, was the first film made by an African on a fictional subject to be widely distributed outside Africa. It is remarkable for the cleavages Sembène revealed in contemporary African society between the masses of the poor and the new African governing class who stepped into the positions of dominance left by the French.

His breakthrough film was *Black Girl,* the first sub-Saharan film ever shown at the prestigious Cannes Film Festival. It tells the story of a Senegalese woman who is lured from her homeland by the promise of wealth and becomes lost in a morass of loneliness and inconsiderateness. Sembène's prize-winning work *Mandabi (The Money Order)* (1968) shows what happens to an unemployed illiterate when he tries to cash a large money order from his Parisian nephew; he is crushed by an oppressive bureaucracy and unsympathetic officials. Michael Atkinson, in *Film Comment,* called it "a virtual comic flowchart of the traditional tribal world lost in modern-day red tape." It was the first of Sembène's films to be produced in the native Wolof language and targeted at a broader Senegalese audience. Sembène was the first director to have his characters speak an African language.

Many of Sembène's films, including *Xala* (1974) and *Ceddo* (*The Outsiders;* 1976), were censored or temporarily banned by Senegal's government because of their powerful social and political messages. His 1971 film *Emitai* centered on a wartime French force's seige of a desert tribe, the Diola. *Xala* is a comic, satiric dissection of the greed of the post-independence Senegalese upper class. *Ceddo* is set in the 17th century and depicts the conflicts in a village between adherents to the ancient tribal religion and Muslims who are trying to stamp out paganism.

Filming on the Fly

Even after 30 years of writing, directing and producing films, Sembène still was making his movies dirt-cheap, finding actors and settings as he moved across his poor country. Sembène's 1987 film *The Camp at Thiarove* depicted a 1944 colonial massacre in Africa. It was the first African feature film produced completely without European technical aid or financing. In 1992, Sembène produced *Guelwaar,* a story about the tangled politics, religious squabbles and bureaucracy surrounding a man's burial. Desmond Ryan of Knight-Ridder/Tribune News Service noted the case of the missing body was for Sembène "a means of raising larger issue that Sembène believes are leading Senegal to fratricidal destruction. . . . His sardonic view of his country as it struggles for national identity and solvency resounds with laughter tinged with deep bitterness." Atkinson called it a "lean and eloquent masterwork."

Writing in *Film Comment,* Atkinson noted Sembène's reliance on straightforward storytelling: "The best of his work possesses a natural-born faith in the naked austerity of events, expressed via amateurish yet relaxed performances . . . Camera movement is rare, closeups even rarer, and many of the images have the fading, overexposed tint of aging home movies. . . . Sembène's modern folk art has all the power and glory of Old Testament myths, while casting an ice-cold contemporary eye at the socioeconomic tarpit of African nations wrangling with their newfound independence and the crippling reverb of colonial control."

In a 1990 interview published in *Africa Report,* Sembène recounted how he organized "traveling picture shows"—going to a village to show a movie and then moderating a discussion about it. "In colonial times, the cinema was a form of entertainment for foreigners," he said. "Now, however, African filmmakers are raising real issues. . . . People are thus slowly starting to identify with their history and the cinema is becoming something real." Over the years, Sembène's films have questioned colonialists, fundamentalists, peasants, and the new bourgeoisie. "It's not me, it's my people that evolve," Sembène said. "I live among them; I'm like the thermometer."

Further Reading

Michael Atkinson's "Ousmane Sembène" *Film Comment* is one of the best sources on Sembène's films. Claude Wauthier's descriptive summary of a host of black writers, including Sembène, appeared in English as *The Literature and Thought of Modern Africa* (1964; trans. 1966). A chapter on Sembène is in A.C. Brench, *The Novelists' Inheritance in French Africa: Writers from Senegal to Cameroon* (1967). An interview with Sembène by Daphne Topouzis appears in *Africa Report* (November-December 1990). ☐

Nikolai Nikolaevich Semenov

The Russian physicist and physical chemist Nikolai Nikolaevich Semenov (1896-1986) is famous for his experiments explaining chemical reactions by means of the mechanism of chain reactions.

Nikolai Semenov was born on April 15, 1896, in Saratov. He displayed a keen interest in the physical sciences by the time he was 16 and in 1913 entered the physics and mathematics department of the University of St. Petersburg (later Petrograd and now Leningrad). At the age of 20 he published his first paper on the collision of molecules and electrons. In 1917 he ended his studies at the University of Petrograd, obtained a position as physicist in the Siberian University of Tomsk and later, in 1920, returned to work for the next 11 years at the Petrograd (in 1924 Leningrad) Institute of Physics and Technology.

In 1928 Semenov became a professor at the Leningrad Polytechnical Institute and organized its physics and mathematics department. Three years later he was appointed scientific chief of the Institute of Physical Chemistry of the Soviet Academy of Sciences. In 1932 he was elected to full membership in the academy, and from 1957 to 1963 he was the academy's secretary of the division of the chemical sciences. In 1944 he was assigned to the University of Moscow, heading the department of chemical kinematics. He also was instrumental in launching scientific journals and organizing Soviet conferences on physical chemistry.

Semenov's scientific investigations dealt primarily with molecular physics and electronic phenomena, the mechanism of chemical transformations, and the propagation of explosive waves. He published in "The Oxidation of Phosphorus Vapor at Low Pressures" (1927) his discovery of branching reaction chains in chemical transformations having the character of an explosion. Semenov intensively continued his researches in chemical reactions involving the chain theory and published his results in *Chemical Kinetics and Chain Reactions* (1935) and in the exhaustive two-volume study *Some Problems in Chemical Kinetics and Reactivity* (1958-1959). For his contributions to reaction kinetics, Semenov was awarded the Nobel Prize in 1956, the first resident Soviet citizen to achieve this distinction.

Semenov also played an active role in his country's affairs. He first joined the Communist party of the Soviet Union in 1947, served as a deputy in the Supreme Soviet in 1958, 1962, and 1966, and in 1961 was elected an alternate member of the party's Central Committee. In the Soviet Union he fought for the liberty of experimentation for the scientist, freedom of expression for the artist, and "chain reactions of success" for humanity as a consequence of international scientific exchanges. In 1971, Semenov, along with thirteen other Soviet scientists, signed a cablegram letter to President Richard Nixon, expressing concern that the Federal murder trial of African American militant and philosophy teacher Angela Davis be conducted such that

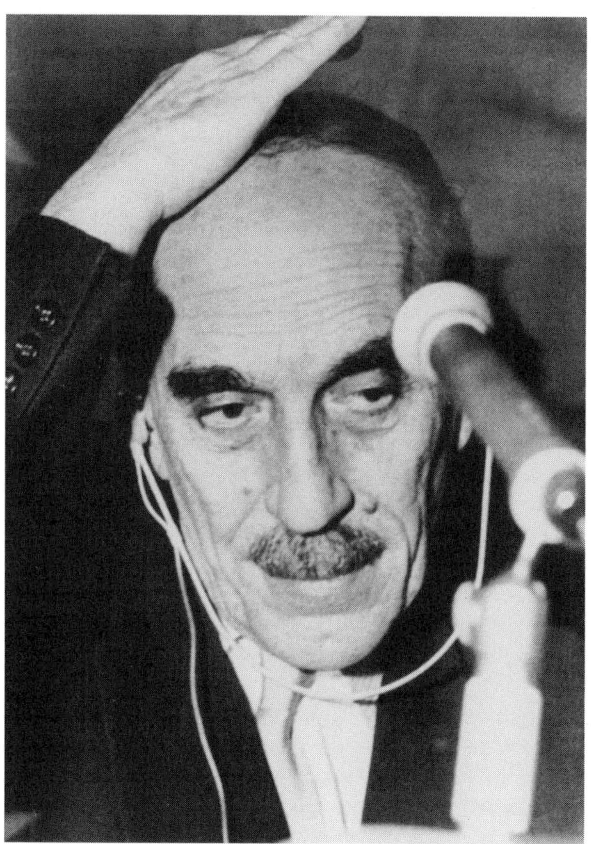

her life would be spared (she was a member of the Communist party). Nixon responded by inviting all the scientists to attend her trial. Semenov died in 1986.

Further Reading

Only scattered articles on Semenov have thus far appeared in English and Russian newspapers and journals. A brief biographical sketch of Semenov by Albert Parry is in George W. Simmonds, ed., *Soviet Leaders* (1967). Semenov's scientific contributions receive mention in the comprehensive work of V. N. Kondratev, *Chemical Kinetics of Gas Reactions,* translated by J. M. Crabtree and S. N. Carruthers (1964), and in Keith J. Laidler, *Reaction Kinetics* (1966). □

Ignaz Philipp Semmelweis

The Hungarian physician Ignaz Philipp Semmelweis (1818-1865) was a pioneer of antisepsis in obstetrics and demonstrated that many cases of puerperal fever could be prevented.

Ignaz Philipp Semmelweis, the son of a prosperous shopkeeper, was born on July 1, 1818, at Buda, a city united with Pest in 1873 to form Budapest. After 2 years at the University of Pest, 19-year-old Ignaz matriculated at the University of Vienna as a law student. Unhappy, he returned to the University of Pest and studied medicine (1838-1840). After completing further studies at the University of Vienna, he received a medical degree in April 1844. Following 4 months of special instruction in midwifery, Semmelweis became a provisionary assistant at the First Obstetric Clinic in the large Vienna Lying-In Hospital. Two years later he became a regular assistant to the director of this clinic.

Semmelweis was especially distressed by the horrors of puerperal fever. Within a few hours after delivery, numerous mothers would be afflicted with high fever, rapid pulse, distended abdomen, and excruciating pain. One out of 10 would die as a result of this infection. One observation haunted Semmelweis. The hospital was divided into two clinics: the first for the instruction of medical students, the second for the training of midwives. The mortality due to puerperal fever was significantly greater in the first clinic. Traditional ideas ascribed puerperal fever to epidemic influences; if this were true, both clinics should be equally affected. Overcrowding was suggested; yet the second clinic was ordinarily more crowded than the first. Semmelweis incessantly searched for a better understanding of his puzzling observations.

In 1847 Semmelweis's colleague J. Kolletschka unexpectedly died of an overwhelming infection following a wound he sustained while performing an autopsy. Semmelweis realized that the course of the disease in his friend was remarkably similar to the sequence of events in puerperal fever. Here was an explanation of the difference in mortality between the two clinics: the medical students and teachers dissected corpses, whereas the midwives did no autopsies. The teachers and pupils could thus carry infectious particles from the cadavers to the natural wounds of a woman in childbirth. Accordingly, teachers and students who had been dissecting were requested to wash their hands with a solution of chlorinated lime before examining the laboring patients. As a result, during 1848 the mortality of the first clinic was less than that of the second clinic.

Surprisingly, opposition to Semmelweis's observations was intense, for the paradox of being healer and murderer was intolerable for most. When confronted with Semmelweis's explanations, conscientious obstetricians pleaded "not guilty." Semmelweis could not understand these reactions. A few outstanding doctors supported him; nevertheless, the tide of controversy grew to such an extent that Semmelweis was "retired" from his position as assistant at the first clinic. In 1850 he left Vienna and returned to Budapest.

At the St. Rochus Hospital in Budapest, Semmelweis was allowed to introduce disinfection in the obstetrical division. In 1855 he became professor of theoretical and practical midwifery at the University of Pest. In 1857 he married. But the deaths of two children during the next few years added personal grief to professional suffering, a suffering that intensified as opposition to his ideas spread throughout Europe.

With much reluctance Semmelweis organized his observations and published his great work on puerperal fever, *The Etiology, Concept, and Prophylaxis of Childbed Fever* (1861). Even this did not silence his opponents, and Semmelweis, unable to accept this resistance, was committed to an insane asylum in 1865, where he died of blood poisoning. Not until 1883 did the Boston Lying-In Hospital introduce methods of antisepsis, methods similar to those used several decades earlier by Semmelweis.

Further Reading

The most readable biography of Semmelweis is Frank G. Slaughter, *Immortal Magyar: Semmelweis, Conqueror of Childbed Fever* (1950). For greater detail, especially about the opposition to Semmelweis's views, see Sir William J. Sinclair, *Semmelweis: His Life and His Doctrine* (1909).

Additional Sources

Childbed fever: a scientific biography of Ignaz Semmelweis, Westport, Conn.: Greenwood Press, 1994.

Slaughter, Frank G. (Frank Gill), *Immortal Magyar: Semmelweis, conqueror of childbed fever,* New York, Schuman, 1950. □

Raphael Semmes

Raphael Semmes (1809-1877), American naval officer of the Confederacy, commanded the *Sumter* and *Alabama* in their daring raids on Northern shipping during the Civil War.

Raphael Semmes was born in Charles County, Md. Appointed a midshipman in the U.S. Navy at 16, in 1837 he was promoted to lieutenant. During the long periods of inactivity that characterized naval service in those days, Semmes had the opportunity to study and then to practice law.

During the Mexican War, Semmes commanded the brig *Somers* and then served with distinction in the campaign against Mexico City. He recounted these experiences in *Service Afloat and Ashore during the Mexican War* (1851).

Soon after Alabama seceded from the Union, Semmes resigned his commission and accepted an appointment as commander in the Confederate Navy. In April 1861 he was assigned to command the C.S.S. *Sumter* at New Orleans. The *Sumter* ran the Federal blockade in June and, during a long voyage that culminated at Gibraltar, took 18 prizes. Semmes left the worn-out *Sumter* at Gibraltar and started back to the Confederate States. At Nassau he was intercepted by orders to take command of the English-built steam bark *Enrica,* which he armed and on Aug. 24, 1862, commissioned off the Azores islands as the C.S.S. *Alabama.*

During almost 2 years on the high seas commanding the *Alabama,* Semmes burned, sank, or captured and sold 55 Union vessels. But on June 19, 1864, the *Alabama's* career abruptly ended at Cherbourg, France, where the U.S.S. *Kearsarge* had blockaded it. In an ill-advised burst of chivalric resolve, Semmes had challenged the better-equipped *Kearsarge* to combat. Superficially the antagonists were evenly matched; in reality the odds heavily favored the *Kearsarge.* After an engagement of about half an hour, the *Alabama* struck its colors and then sank. Semmes was rescued by an English yacht, one of many that had come to witness the engagement.

Returning to the Confederacy, Semmes was promoted to rear admiral and assigned to command the James River squadron. When Richmond fell, he destroyed his gunboats and retreated south with his sailors. He and his men were included in the surrender of Gen. Joseph E. Johnston's army on April 26, 1865.

After the war Semmes (like many Confederates) spent several months in Federal prison. Afterward he was occupied variously as a teacher, editor, and lawyer. He also wrote his famous *Memoirs of Service Afloat* (1869), a vivid account of the voyages of the *Sumter* and the *Alabama* in which he took literary revenge on the enemy. In 1877 he died at his home in Mobile after a brief illness.

Further Reading

Semmes's *Memoirs of Service Afloat, during the War between the States* (1869) is available in an abridged version, *The Confederate Raider Alabama,* edited with an introduction by Philip Van Doren Stern (1962). Biographies of Semmes include Colyer Meriwether, *Raphael Semmes* (1913); Walter Adolphe Roberts, *Semmes of the Alabama* (1938); and Edward Carrington Boykin, *Ghost Ship of the Confederacy: The Story of the Alabama and Her Captain* (1957).

Additional Sources

Semmes, Raphael, *Memoirs of service afloat during the War Between the States,* Baton Rouge: Louisiana State University Press, 1996.

Taylor, John M., *Confederate raider: Raphael Semmes of the Alabama,* Washington: Brassey's, 1994.

Tucker, Spencer, *Raphael Semmes and the Alabama,* Fort Worth, TX: Ryan Place Publishers, 1996. □

Lucius Annaeus Seneca the Younger

Lucius Annaeus Seneca the Younger (ca. 4 B.C.-65 A.D.) was a Roman philosopher important in his own day as tutor and "prime minister" of the emperor Nero.

The philosophical works of Seneca although not especially original, show such nobility of sentiment that Christian writers on morality and ethical conduct have drawn on him over the centuries; he seems to have invented a highly rhetorical type of tragedy, the influence of which was especially widespread in the Renaissance; and his literary style, terse, epigrammatic, and full of intermittent brilliance, provided a respectable rhetorical alternative to the long, periodic sentences of Cicero and had some influence on the development of the normal literary prose style of English, French, and other languages.

Seneca was born in Cordova, Spain, about 5 or 4 B.C., the son of the famous writer on rhetoric known as Seneca Rhetor. Seneca's elder brother was proconsul of Achaea in A.D. 51-52 and was the "Gallio" before whose tribunal Paul was brought. His younger brother was the father of the poet Lucan. His mother was Helvia, a cultivated woman deeply interested in philosophy, and one of her sisters was the wife of a man who was later prefect of Egypt. This sister brought Seneca to Rome as a small child.

Seneca's schooling had a great influence on his later life. He disliked his studies under teachers who insisted on verbal criticism and on detailed learning, but his rhetorical studies, under the leading men of his day, including his own father, left a deep impression on his style. He was, however, most deeply involved in the study of philosophy. His teachers, disciples of the eclectic but basically Stoic Roman philosopher Quintus Sextius, filled him with an enthusiasm for philosophy which he never lost and never wholly lived up to, and the rigorous asceticism into which he plunged so weakened his already poor constitution that his health began to decline. He thought of suicide, but was stopped by his regard for his father, who also pointed out that he might be mistaken for a devotee of certain foreign superstitions which the emperor Tiberius was attempting to stamp out. Instead, Seneca was sent to visit his aunt in Egypt.

After his return from Egypt, Seneca secured election (ca. A.D. 31) to the quaestorship as a result of his aunt's

influence and began his legal career. His oratory (all of it lost) rapidly gained him renown, which became dangerous after the accession in 37 of Emperor Caligula, who wanted no rivals in this field. Seneca would probably have been murdered if Caligula had not been informed that Seneca was very sick and could not live long. Seneca then betook himself to other literary fields, to alternating periods of retreat and meditation with his public work, and to building his private fortune.

Trial and Exile

After the accession of Claudius as emperor in 41, Seneca was for a while prominent in the court as a member of the party of Agrippina and Julia Livilla, Claudius's nieces. The empress Messalina, however, whose influence over Claudius was all-powerful, saw the two princesses as dangerous rivals and secured the banishment of Julia Livilla in 41 on charges of immorality. Seneca was accused of being her lover and condemned to death by the Senate, but his punishment was changed to banishment to Corsica by the Emperor.

Seneca spent the next 8 years in exile on Corsica. He was miserable. He was a literary man, without access to learned men; a man who loved human society, removed from his friends; a man of acquisitive instincts, deprived of his property; and a man who enjoyed power and influence, reduced to impotence and apparent friendlessness. Cringing flattery of the Emperor and of the Emperor's powerful freedman Polybius proved useless, but in 49 he was recalled at the behest of Agrippina, who had survived Messalina and married her uncle Claudius. Seneca was to be tutor to Nero, her son and the adopted son of Claudius, and he was appointed praetor for the year 50.

Life under Nero

Claudius was murdered by Agrippina in 54, and Nero acceded to the throne. The next 5 years, while Nero was under the influence of Seneca and Sextus Afranius Burrus, became famous for their good government and general happiness. The court was also aware of crimes and intrigues, most notably the murder of Britannicus, Claudius's son, and thus Nero's most dangerous rival, in 55. In 55 or 56 Seneca was appointed to a suffect consulship.

In 59 Agrippina, who had been Seneca's patroness, was murdered by her son—quite possibly, as Nero explained to the Senate in a statement written by Seneca, as the result of the discovery of plots on her part against the throne. In 62 Burrus died, and one of his successors, Ofonius Tigellinus, soon came to exercise an evil influence over his master. Realizing that his major support was gone and that Tigellinus was working for his removal, Seneca, who must have been sick of being compromised by the necessities of state, asked to be allowed to retire and offered to put at Nero's disposal the vast fortune he had acquired in his service; Nero permitted his retirement but refused the proferred wealth.

Seneca devoted the next 3 years of his retirement to his studies and writings, but in 65 he was implicated (along with, among others, his nephew Lucan) in Piso's conspiracy, and his death became inevitable. He was ordered to commit suicide by Nero, according to Tacitus.

Much of the shabbiness of Seneca's life was made up for by the manner of his death, calm and philosophical, which showed true Stoic nobility. Tacitus related that Seneca's body had become so thin from fasting that he had difficulty in getting the blood to flow from his opened veins. His second wife, Pompeia Paulina, wanted to commit suicide with him but was prevented from doing so.

Philosophical Works

Seneca's philosophical works are marked by neither originality of thought nor depth of speculation, but rather by enthusiasm of presentation and an understanding of the practical limitations of life and the weaknesses of human nature. The chronological arrangement of these works is uncertain, but it is generally agreed that very few of them predate his exile.

Ten works, in 12 books, have been handed down to us under the name *Dialogues,* although only one of them could be considered an actual dialogue. Three of these are *consolationes,* treatises, partly philosophical, partly rhetorical, attempting to cure grief. In addition, there are three books composing *On Anger. On the Happy Life* develops the standard Stoic view that happiness is to live in accordance with nature and to practice virtue, and it contains an interesting defense of the wise man's possession and good use of wealth. There are three works addressed to Annaeus Serenus, *On the Constancy of a Wise Man, On Tranquility of Mind,* and the fragmentary On Leisure.

Some other philosophical works of Seneca are seven books called *Natural Questions,* written in 62-63, a loosely arranged compilation of information on natural science, which formed the standard work on cosmology for the Middle Ages until the rediscovery of Aristotle. The 124 *Epistles* to Lucilius contain innumerable digressions which give a fascinating picture of Roman life.

His Tragedies

Ten plays are ascribed to Seneca. One of these, the *Octavia,* the only extant Roman historical drama, is almost universally rejected as being written by Seneca. The *Hercules Oetaeus* has also been generally rejected, but the consensus of scholarship favors Senecan authorship for the *Hercules Furens, Troades, Medea, Phaedra, Phoenissae, Oedipus, Agamemnon,* and the *Thyestes,* the only play whose Greek model has not been preserved. Nothing is known about the time of composition of these plays.

Seneca's major inspiration was Euripides, the source of half of his dramas. He took from Euripides an interest in psychological analysis, especially of abnormal types, in philosophical speculation, and in rhetorical effect and developed each of these to what often seems an excessive degree. The Stoic doctrine which proclaimed that a good man is totally good and a bad man totally evil makes his characters less humanly alive than the Greek characters. In these plays Seneca's rhetoric is almost unrestrained: overelaboration of realistic detail until it becomes ludicrous, mythological pedantry, and unending verbal cleverness and epigrammatic morality are but part of an overall exaggeration and declamatory urgency which soon wearies the reader.

Seneca's tragedies were not written for actual performance but for dramatic reading. Some actions, such as the murder of Medea's children, could hardly have been presented on an ancient stage, and many speeches and choruses, while too long to be tolerable in the theater, would have been especially pleasing as readings to literary circles trained to appreciate ingenious rhetoric and description. Seneca wrote a very cruel and witty satire on the deification of Claudius, the *Apocolocyntosis* ("Pumpkinification"). The Emperor's habits, such as his fondness for acting as a judge and playing dice, speech mannerisms, and physical infirmities are mercilessly parodied. The work is, in form, a Menippean satire, composed of mingled prose and verse, and is amusing for its use of legal language and parodies of Claudius's and Augustus's prose styles.

Further Reading

The best biography of Seneca in English is Francis C. Holland, *Seneca* (1920); the best brief account appears in J. Wight Duff, *A Literary History of Rome in the Silver Age from Tiberius to Hadrian* (1927; 3d ed., edited by A. M. Duff, 1964). Seneca's philosophical works are discussed in E. Vernon Arnold, *Roman Stoicism* (1911); Richard Mott Gummere, *Seneca the Philosopher and His Modern Message* (1922); and T. P. Hardeman, *The Philosophy of Lucius Annaeus Seneca* (1956). The best account of Seneca's *Apocolocyntosis* is in Allen Perley Ball, *The Satire of Seneca on the Apotheosis of Claudius* (1902), but see also J. Wight Duff, *Roman Satire: Its Outlook on Social Life* (1936).

Almost all of the numerous studies of Seneca's tragedies concentrate either on the use he made of his Greek models or on his influence on later tragedy. Among these studies are John William Cunliffe, *The Influence of Seneca on Elizabethan Tragedy* (1893; repr. 1925); Frank Laurence Lucas, *Seneca and Elizabethan Tragedy* (1922); Howard Vernon Canter, *Rhetorical Elements in the Tragedy of Seneca* (1925); Norman T. Pratt, *Dramatic Suspense in Seneca and in His Greek Precursors* (1939); and Charles W. Mendell, *Our Seneca* (1941).

Additional Sources

Sussman, Lewis A., *The elder Seneca,* Leiden: Brill, 1978.

Srensen, Villy, *Seneca, the humanist at the court of Nero,* Chicago: University of Chicago Press, 1984. □

Ludwig Senfl

Ludwig Senfl (ca. 1486-1543) was a German composer of Swiss birth. His Masses, motets, and vernacular lieder mark the adoption by 16th-century German masters of Franco-Flemish imitative polyphony emanating from the Low Countries.

Ludwig Senfl was born in Basel. As a young boy, he sang first at Augsburg and later at Vienna in the imperial choir of Maximilian I of Austria. During this period he studied with Heinrich Isaac, official court composer of the Hapsburgs, and subsequently succeeded to the same post. In later years Senfl offered homage to Isaac by completing the older master's unfinished cycle of Mass Propers, printed in 1550 as the *Choralis Constantinus,* and by apotheosizing him in an original poem set to music.

After the death of Emperor Maximilian in 1519 and the dissolution of the imperial chapel choir the following year, Senfl traveled to Augsburg to supervise the publication of a motet collection, *Liber selectarum cantionum,* as a memorial to the late monarch. By 1523 he found a new position with William IV of Bavaria, at whose court in Munich he remained for the rest of his life.

Like many artists and musicians of the time, Senfl was drawn into the vortex of religious strife attending the Reformation. Although he served only Catholic rulers and never formally abandoned the older faith, he corresponded with and occasionally sent compositions to Martin Luther, with whom he seems to have been on friendly terms. For the most part, however, Senfl's service music was composed for Catholic worship. A self-effacing, lovable, and versatile composer, he was widely respected by his contemporaries and honored by his employer.

Senfl's extant works number 7 Masses, 240 motets, 262 lieder, and a few pieces for instruments. His beautifully chiseled imitative polyphony discloses the unmistakable influence of his two great predecessors, Josquin des Prez and Isaac. Two of the Masses are "parodies," or reworkings,

of earlier polyphonic pieces. This new technique stamps him as the first German master to abandon the older *cantus firmus* Mass. Among the motets are many Mass Propers composed for divine services at the Bavarian court. Although Senfl generally wrote for four voice parts, some ceremonial pieces were for as many as eight. Throughout his works is a profound understanding of both the declamation and meaning of the text.

In Senfl's lifetime more of his lieder were published than either the Masses or motets. Like earlier masters, he set the old "court" tunes in polyphonic garb, but he devoted far more attention to arranging "folk" and "popular" songs. His melodic inventiveness, smooth linear writing, and polished counterpoint made them universal favorites.

Further Reading

Some of Senfl's works are analyzed in Gustave Reese, *Music in the Renaissance* (1959). For background on the music of the period see Paul Henry Lang, *Music in Western Civilization* (1941). □

Léopold Sédar Senghor

Léopold Sédar Senghor (born 1906) was an African poet, philosopher, and president of Senegal. He was one of the originators of "Negritude," a "black is beautiful" doctrine begun in Paris during the 1930s.

The map of Africa as it exists today owes something to the efforts of Léopold Senghor who took a leading role in the negotiations that led to independence of France's sub-Saharan colonies. He established relations with the former mother country that endure to this day. While asserting the uniqueness and greatness of black culture, the equal in every respect to that of the Greeks and the French, he held out the promise of an eventual synthesis of diverse peoples' contributions to a coming great "civilization of the universal."

Senghor was born on October 9, 1906, at Joal, the son of a wealthy Catholic trader who descended from a Serer royal family. Raised as a Catholic among an overwhelmingly Moslem population, Senghor attended the school of the Fathers of the Holy Ghost at N'Gazobil in 1914 and went on to pursue his studies in Dakar until 1928, when he left for France. In Paris he was the first African to be awarded an *agregation* certificate, in 1935, qualifying him to teach at a lycee, which he did from 1936 to the outbreak of the war, first in Tours and then in Paris. Captured while fighting against the Germans in 1940, he organized a resistance among his fellow prisoners.

Political Career

After the war, Africa's representation in the French National Assembly was greatly increased, and opportunities for indigenous political activity were expanded. In 1945 Senghor joined with Lamine Gueye in cofounding a new political party affiliated with the French Socialist party, the Bloc Africain, which appealed to newly enfranchised peo-

ple in the rural areas. In the same year, and again in 1946, the people of Senegal elected Senghor as deputy to the French National Assembly. In 1946 he was also selected the official grammarian for the new constitution of the Fourth Republic.

Senghor's alliance with Lamine Gueye soon grew thin, as Senghor turned to cultivate his rural following and as he rejected Gueye's assimilation politics. In 1948 Senghor formed his own political party and rejected affiliation with all metropolitan organizations. In 1951 his organization won both seats to the National Assembly. Senghor's proposal in 1953 that the French government divide French West Africa into two federations, one with its capital at Dakar in Senegal and the other at Abidjan in the Ivory Coast, was defeated. This defeat, as Senghor predicted, meant the "Balkanization" of West Africa, the creation of many small, not really economically viable, political units.

Senghor served as a minister in the Edgar Faure government in 1955; the following year Senghor's group, for the final time, won the elections to the National Assembly and then won 47 out of 60 seats in the newly established territorial council of Senegal. A division occurred among African leaders over the value of these councils, for some saw them as a positive step toward self-government, but others (Senghor foremost among them) argued that what counted was the unity of the region as a whole and that "territorialization" would only make this task more difficult.

Unlike the modernizing Africans in the British colonies, Senghor also argued that "mere political independence" could be a sham and therefore was not necessarily the highest goal African peoples should seek. Economic and technological realities in his day meant that even the "super powers" could not go it alone; what chance then for Senegal by itself? Not surprisingly, in 1958, when the new DeGaulle government offered the territories of West Africa the chance to "opt for independence" in a referendum—on the understanding that all financial and technical aid would be immediately withdrawn—Senghor, in spite of much domestic opposition, campaigned against this type of "self-government." Senegal joined the Sudanese Republic in 1959 to form the short-lived Mali Federation. Finally, on Aug. 20, 1960, Senegal became independent but remained part of a reconstituted "French community."

Thereafter Senghor survived several attempted coups d'etat, the most serious occurring in 1962, at least one assassination effort (1967), and widespread riots and demonstrations against rising prices and government financial policies (1968 and 1969). Nevertheless, throughout all these developments, he maintained his position as president of the republic and head of the governing political party while absorbing the major organized opposition groups and appeasing the central elements of his own coalition.

Negritude and Socialism

The evolution of Senghor's doctrine occurred in three distinct periods—the era preceding World War II, the period of achieving independence, and the epoch following independence. Senghor argued that the work of the black has distinction not in substance or subject matter but, rather, in a special approach, method, and style. In the pre-World War II period, Senghor particularly argued that one must look for the black person's uniqueness in the person himself. "Negritude" arises first, then, from the singular racial characteristics of the black. Later, after the war, Senghor became caught up in the problem of reorganizing societies—in Europe after fascism, in Africa after colonialism.

Revolted by Nazism, he placed increasing emphasis in his theory of Negritude on the historical context of the black evolution as an explanation for the rise of unique civilizations. Socialism he viewed as a way toward a renewed humanism through the ending of exploitation. Revolutionary change in France and the West as well as in the developing areas would allow a new type of community to be created. After independence in 1960, Senghor turned increasingly to the day-to-day problems of building a viable economy.

Significantly, Senghor used the term Senegalese socialism for the first time early in 1962. His ideas and ideology became increasingly pragmatic and technocratic as he attempted to maximize the effectiveness of modern agricultural methods, capital, industry, and social engineering.

Senghor resigned in 1981 after 20 years of being president. He devoted much of time afterwards to developing and publishing his philosophical contributions to the realization of a single, planetary civilization.

His Writings

The year 1945 marked not only Senghor's entry into political life but also the publication of his first collection of poems, *Chants d'ombre.* In 1948 he published another volume of poetry, *Hosties noires,* and edited an anthology of new Negro and Malagasy poetry. Later poetic offerings were *Chants pour Naëtt* (1949), *Éthiopiques* (1956), and *Nocturnes* (1961).

Senghor's major prose works were *Nation et voie africaine du socialisme* (1961), *Pierre Teilhard de Chardin et la politique africaine* (1962), *Liberté I: Négritude et humanisme* (1964), *Les Fondements de l'Africanité ou Négritude et Arabité* (1967), and *Politique, nation et developpement moderne* (1968).

Further Reading

A substantial collection of Senghor's poetry is in *Selected Poems,* translated and introduced by John Reed and Clive Wake (1964). Several of Senghor's major political writings were translated by Mercer Cook in *On African Socialism* (1964). Irving Leonard Markovitz, *Léopold Sédar Senghor and the Politics of Negritude* (1969), which has an exhaustive bibliography, traces the development of Senghor's ideas from 1931 and views them within the changing social, political, and historical scene of French colonialism and African development. See also Michael Crowder, *Senegal: A Study in French Assimilation Policy* (1962), for a good general treatment of the historical background. □

Sennacherib

Sennacherib (reigned 705-681 B.C.), a king of Assyria, was one of the four great kings of the late Assyrian Empire. He rebuilt Nineveh and destroyed Babylon.

Sennacherib is the biblical form of the name Sin-akhe-eriba. Though a younger son, he was chosen as heir by his father, Sargon II. As crown prince, he gained experience fighting on the northern frontier. On hearing of Sargon's death, he hastened back to Nineveh, but rebellion broke out. In Babylonia, a Chaldean, Merodach-Baladan, seized the throne, supported by the Elamites, but he was put to flight and the Chaldean tribes surrendered. The city-states and kingdoms of Syria and Palestine, encouraged by Egypt, refused tribute. In 701 B.C. Sennacherib marched to the coast and occupied Ascalon and Sidon; Judah was next invaded, Lachish captured by assault, and Jerusalem invested. Hezekiah, King of Judah, defied the Assyrians and was forced to pay a heavy indemnity. Sennacherib then attempted to invade Egypt, but disaster, perhaps plague, struck his army and he was forced to turn back.

A second rebellion in Babylonia was foiled, and Sennacherib made his son, Assur-nadin-shum, king of Babylon. Merodach-Baladan took refuge in the marshes of southern Elam. Seven years later, after repeated provocation, Sennacherib decided to seek him out; building a fleet at Nineveh, he sailed the ships downriver to Opis, then dragged them overland to the Euphrates, and thence to the Persian Gulf. After a sea battle, Elamite coastal towns were destroyed. Meanwhile, Assur-nadin-shum was murdered and replaced by an Elamite nominee. In 689 Sennacherib avenged his son. Marching to Babylon, he took the city by storm and mercilessly destroyed it, deporting the inhabitants and flooding the ruins. This sacrilege to a holy city shocked the ancient world but effectively discouraged further rebellion.

The war annals of Sennacherib depict him as a ruthless destroyer, "the flame that consumes those who will not submit." In his building inscriptions, however, he appears as "he who cares for the welfare of Assyria." His greatest achievement was the rebuilding of Nineveh, the ancient capital. He strengthened the walls, cut new streets, and replanned the water system. Water was brought from the hills 50 miles away and carried over a valley on a stone aqueduct—one of the engineering feats of antiquity. His palace, built on an artificial platform, covered 8 acres and was surrounded by parks and orchards stocked with exotic plants and animals. In January 681, while at prayer, Sennacherib was murdered by his own sons.

Further Reading

The events of Sennacherib's reign are recounted in volume 3 of the *Cambridge Ancient History* (1925), as well as in A. T. Olmstead, *History of Assyria* (1923), and H. Saggs, *The Greatness That Was Babylon* (1962). Daniel D. Luckenbill collected the inscriptions in *Ancient Records of Assyria and Babylonia,* vol. 2 (1927). For Sennacherib's rebuilding of Nineveh see R. Campbell Thompson, *A Century of Exploration at Nineveh* (1929). On the reliefs from his palace, most of which are in the British Museum, consult C. J. Gadd, *The Stones of Assyria* (1936) and *Assyrian Sculptures in the British Museum, from Shalmaneser III to Sennacherib* (1938). See also T. Jacobsen and S. Lloyd, *Sennacherib's Aqueduct at Jerwan* (1935). □

Mack Sennett

The American silent-screen producer and director Mack Sennett (1884-1960) is frequently considered the originator of film comedy. He perfected the art of silent-screen slapstick in his "Keystone" series.

Mack Sennett was born Michael Sinnott on Jan. 17, 1884, in Quebec, Canada. He emigrated to New York at the beginning of the 20th century to act in films by D. W. Griffith. Not very successful, Sennett turned to movie direction, and his first two efforts, *Comrade* (1911) and *One-round O'Brien* (1912), were so popular that sequels were immediately demanded. Assured of financial backing, he formed his own organization, the Keystone Company, and moved to Hollywood, Calif.

During the first year Sennett produced 140 "Keystone Comedies," the most famous of which were *Uncle Tom without the Cabin* and *Salome vs. Shenandoah.* Unable to direct every comedy personally, Sennett supplied himself with a talented crew of gag writers, comedians, cameramen, and stunt men. At the completion of each film, he would attend the final screening and perfect the structure and timing through careful editing. All of these films were made so that, in projection, the action was faster than life.

Sennett's comic philosophy is perhaps best expressed in his comments on the Italian folk form commedia dell'arte: "The round, fat girls in nothing much doing their bumps and grinds, the German-dialect comedians, and especially the cops and tramps with their bed-slats and ladders appealed to me as being funny people. Their approach to life was earthy and understandable. They made fun of themselves and of the human race. They reduced convention, dogma, stuffed shirts . . . to nonsense, and then blossomed into pandemonium. . . . I especially enjoyed the reduction of authority to absurdity, the notion that sex could be funny, and the bold insults that were hurled at pretension."

The Sennett films defied logic and gravity in their epic chases and wild pie-throwing contests. In a Sennett comedy it was not unusual for a bandit to rob a bank with a vacuum cleaner or for a flood to carry a man out of his house in a bathtub. The Sennett Bathing Beauties, which featured such curvaceous creatures as Louise Fazenda and Gloria Swanson, added a touch of sexual delight to the then puritanical American film. Sennett's comedies, when they are at their best, are a combination of impudent satire, vulgar burlesque, and exhilarated madness.

The tragedy of Sennett's career was the arrival of sound in movies in the late 1920s; he was unable and unwilling to adjust to its demands. In 1928 Sennett permanently closed his studio. That same year the Academy of Motion Picture Arts and Sciences awarded the classic innovator a special award, "for his lasting contribution to the comedy technique of the screen." He died on Nov. 6, 1960, in Woodland Hills, Calif.

Further Reading

The standard biography of Sennett is Cameron Shipp, *King of Comedy* (1954). Excellent critical studies of the film maker's work are in Gilbert Seldes, *The Seven Lively Arts* (1924); James Agee, *Agee on Film* (1958); Edward C. Wagenknecht, *The Movies in the Age of Innocence* (1962); and Kenneth McGowan, *Behind the Screen* (1965).

Additional Sources

Sennett, Mack, *King of comedy,* San Francisco: Mercury House; St. Paul, Minn.: Distributed to the trade by Consortium Book Sales & Distribution, 1990. □

Lucius Septimius Severus

Lucius Septimius Severus (146-211) was a Roman emperor. His reign is notable for the militarization of the government, growing Oriental influences in society, and high development of civil law.

Severus was an African from Leptis Magna. He rose through the regular course of Roman offices, was consul in 190, and was serving as governor of Upper Pannonia in 193, when Emperor Pertinax was murdered by the praetorian guard. Severus's command of 12 legions and proximity to Rome made him a favored contender for the throne. He appeared in Rome as the dead emperor's avenger and won the senators' approval by promising them respectful treatment, by disbanding the praetorian guard, which he replaced with elite from the legions, and by naming his Western rival, Albinus, his caesar (successor-designate).

After defeating his more formidable rival, Pescennius Niger, in 194, Severus started a successful campaign against the Parthians. But fear of the activities of Albinus in the West led Severus to break off his campaign and hurry back to Gaul to meet and defeat his rival at Lyons in early 197.

Now firmly established, Septimius began to show more candidly his sentiments toward Roman traditions. He had 29 senators executed on suspicion of favoring Albinus, and their property was confiscated. Famous cities, such as Byzantium, Antioch, and Lyons, were humiliated or destroyed. And his elder son, Bassianus (Caracalla), was renamed Marcus Aurelius Antoninus, in pretense that Septimius had been adopted into the prestigious Antonine family of emperors.

A Parthian attack in 197 brought the Emperor back to the East. He captured the Parthian capital at Ctesiphon and reestablished a province of Mesopotamia. From 199 to 202 the Emperor visited various Eastern provinces, where he

established frontier outposts and improved the living conditions of the soldiers.

For the next 6 years Septimius remained chiefly in Rome. His administrative activities included pay raises for the troops, whom he also allowed for the first time to marry while in service. Veterans were given rapid advancement in the civil service, and the bureaucracy became militarized. Italy's formerly preferred status in the empire was lessened, while favored status was given to many places in his native Africa and his wife's homeland in Syria. Severus appointed prominent jurists to high administrative posts; and the appearance of a number of Rome's greatest legal names on the Emperor's council brought a humane approach and increased protection for the humble in the legislation of the Emperor.

From 208 to his death at York in 211 Septimius was in Britain fighting the Caledonians. Whether or not he really advised his sons on his deathbed to enrich the soldiers and disregard all others, the anecdote is a just estimate of the direction he gave the Roman world.

Further Reading

An ancient life of Severus in *Scriptores historiae Augustae* was translated by David Magie for the Loeb Classical Library (3 vols., 1921-1932). The standard life is Maurice Platnauer, *The Life and Reign of the Emperor Lucius Septimius Severus* (1918). A more recent work is Gerard J. Murphy, *The Reign of the Emperor L. Septimius Severus* (1945).

Additional Sources

Birley, Anthony Richard, *Septimius Severus: the African emperor,* New Haven: Yale University Press, 1989, 1988.

Rubin, Z., *Civil-war propaganda and historiography,* Bruxelles: Latomus, 1980. □

Sequoyah

Sequoyah (ca. 1770-1843), Cherokee scholar, is the only known Native American to have formulated an alphabet for his tribe. This advance enabled thousands of Cherokee to become literate.

Sequoyah was born at the Cherokee village of Taskigi in Tennessee. His father probably was Nathaniel Gist, a trader. His mother was part Cherokee and was abandoned by her husband before the birth of Sequoyah. He used his Cherokee name until he approached manhood, when he assumed the name George Guess (as he understood his father's last name to be).

Crippled for life in a hunting accident, Sequoyah became an excellent silversmith. As an adult, he had contacts with whites which piqued his curiosity about "talking leaves," as he called books. In 1809 he determined to master this secret and to apply it to his own people. After a dozen years of ridicule and insults, he invented a Cherokee alphabet of 85 or 86 characters that allowed every sound in Cherokee to be written.

In 1821 Sequoyah demonstrated his invention before the Cherokee council, which approved his work. Within 2 years thousands of Cherokee had mastered the syllabary, an advance which stimulated the printing of books in the Cherokee language as well as some newspapers printed partly in Cherokee.

In 1823 Sequoyah went to Arkansas to teach his syllabary to the Cherokee who already had migrated westward, and he moved with them to Oklahoma in 1828. He became somewhat active in tribal politics and was a Cherokee delegate to Washington, D.C., in 1828. With his syllabary a success, Sequoyah devoted much of his time to studying other tribal languages in a search for common elements. His tribe recognized the importance of his contribution when, in 1841, it voted him an allowance, which became an annuity of $300.

Early in 1843 Sequoyah became interested in a tribal tradition that said that part of the Cherokee nation had migrated west of the Mississippi River prior to the American Revolution. He set out to find this group, a trek that led him westward and southward, and he died in August 1843, possibly in the state of Tamaulipas in Mexico.

Sequoyah is commemorated by the state of Oklahoma, which placed a statue of him in the nation's capital. Also, a redwood tree, the Sequoia, was named in his honor, as was the Sequoia National Park.

Further Reading

The standard biography of this great Native American is Grant Foreman, *Sequoyah* (1938). Brief but useful is Kate Dickinson Sweetser, *Book of Indian Braves* (1913). Grace S. Woodward, *The Cherokees* (1963), assesses the impact of Sequoyah's syllabary. □

Junípero Serra

A Franciscan missionary and founder of the Spanish missions of California, Junípero Serra (1713-1784) was one of the most respected and best-known figures in California history.

Junípero Serra whose sobriquets "Apostle of California" and "Father of the Missions" typify the love and esteem with which he is still regarded, was born Miguel José Serra at Petra on the island of Majorca just off the eastern coast of Spain. Educated by the Franciscan fathers at Palma, Serra joined the order in 1730 and took the name Junípero in memory of a companion of St. Francis of Assisi. For several years following his ordination, Serra remained at Palma as both student and teacher. He received a doctorate in theology in 1742 and served as professor of theology at the Franciscan university in Palma from 1744 to 1749.

Then, at the age of 36, Serra joined a group of missionaries setting out for Mexico. In company with his pupil and friend Fray Francisco Palóu, Serra arrived in Mexico City in December 1749. Shortly thereafter he volunteered to go to the mission field of Sierra Gorda in northeastern Mexico, where for 8 years he served as preacher and teacher. He learned the Otomí language of the natives, built several churches which are still in use today, and established a successful and thriving mission system.

In 1758 Serra prepared for a new assignment at Mission San Sabá on the Texas frontier, but before he could go north, hostile Comanches attacked and burned the mission. The Church then ordered Serra to the Franciscan college of San Fernando in Mexico City, and from 1758 to 1767 he served as home missionary, preached throughout Mexico, and served as a commissioner of the Holy Office, or Inquisition.

California Missions

In 1767, when the Spaniards expelled the Jesuit order from New Spain, Serra became president of the former Jesuit missions in Baja California. He arrived at Loreto in April 1768 and immediately set about the task of improving and enlarging the mission establishments. In 1769 he volunteered to go to Alta California to establish the first missions there. During the march north Serra suffered from painful bleeding ulcers on his legs and feet, but he refused to turn back. He arrived at San Diego in late June 1769 and immediately began construction of the first mission plant.

During the next 15 years Serra devoted his time and energy to the Franciscan establishment in California. When others despaired, Serra persevered. By 1782 the indefatigable priest had founded nine missions: San Diego, San Carlos Borromeo de Monterey (Carmel), San Antonio, San Gabriel, San Luis Obispo, San Francisco, San Juan Capistrano, Santa Clara, and San Buenaventura. Slowly he overcame the fear and hostility of the natives and converted them to the Christian religion. Serra was as concerned with the Native Americans' physical well-being as with their spiritual life. He introduced domestic animals and new agricultural methods and trades to the neophytes at his missions and did everything possible to help the natives adjust to a different way of life. Under his care the California missions became the most successful and prosperous in all of New Spain.

Not only did Serra have responsibility for the missions, but after the founding of the pueblos of San José and Los Angeles he also administered the churches there as well as those at the presidios of San Diego, Monterey, San Francisco, and Santa Barbara. His devotion and constancy were in large part responsible for the growth and development of Spanish California.

Serra died in August 1784 at Mission San Carlos Borromeo and was buried in the mission church (at present-day Carmel), which has become a shrine to his memory. Monuments to Serra dot the map from Majorca to San Francisco, and several societies, including Serra International, have been established in his honor.

Further Reading

Although adulatory, the work by Serra's friend and companion Francisco Palóu, *Life of Fray Junípero Serra* (1787; trans.

1955), is the best known of the Serra biographies, available in several editions and translations. The best of the modern works is Maynard J. Geiger, *The Life and Times of Fray Junípero Serra* (2 vols., 1959). The study by Katherine and Edward Maddin Ainsworth, *In the Shade of the Juniper Tree: A Life of Fray Junípero Serra* (1970), is thoroughly researched, but the wealth of factual material tends to obscure Serra's personal qualities. Most histories of California devote at least part of a chapter to Serra's career. Particularly recommended is the discussion in Charles E. Chapman, *A History of California: The Spanish Period* (1928).

Additional Sources

Habig, Marion Alphonse, *Junípero Serra,* Chicago, Ill.: Franciscan Herald Press, 1987.

Morgado, Martin J., *Junípero Serra's legacy,* Pacific Grove, Calif.: Mount Carmel, 1987.

Pirus, Betty L., *Before I sleep,* New York: Vantage Press, 1977.

Sullivan, Marion F., *Westward the bells: a biography of Junípero Serra,* Boston, MA: St. Paul Books & Media, 1988.

Weber, Francis J., *A bicentennial compendium of Maynard J. Geiger's The life and times of Fr. Junípero Serra,* S.l.: s.n., 1988, Santa Barbara, CA: Kimberly Press.

Weber, Francis J., *Some "fugitive" glimpses at Fray Junípero Serra,* S.l.: s.n., 1984. □

Jorge Antonio Serrano Elías

Jorge Antonio Serrano Elías (born 1945) was president of Guatemala from 1991 to 1993, the first active Protestant to be elected president of a Latin American nation. He continued civilian rule of the country amid growing economic and political problems until the military removed him from office on June 1, 1993.

Jorge Antonio Serrano Elías was born in Guatemala City in 1945. He graduated from the University of San Carlos of Guatemala in industrial engineering and then earned a graduate degree in economic development at Stanford University.

A prosperous Guatemalan businessman, Serrano Elías was an active Roman Catholic until 1975, when he became a "reborn" evangelical Baptist. He joined the U.S.-based Full Gospel Business Men's Fellowship and later the Pentecostal Church of the Word, headed in Guatemala by retired general Efraín Ríos Montt. Ríos Montt had seized power in Guatemala in March 1982 and ruled until another coup ousted him in August 1983.

Through a family tie with an elder in the church, Serrano Elías became an advisor to President Ríos Montt and served as president of his Council of State. He differed with the general on some issues, however, and Serrano Elías's own presidential ambition strained relations between the two. Thus, Serrano Elías joined the Pentecostal Elim Church, where he held the title of "Prophet." That church's preference for General Ríos Montt as a presidential candidate led Serrano Elías to join El Shaddai, an upper-class Protestant congregation formed by a U.S. missionary following the 1976 earthquake. Linked to a California sect by satellite television transmissions, the central feature of Shaddai was its obsession with demons it associated with Guatemala's pre-Columbian Mayan heritage.

When the army decided in 1984 to allow free elections, Serrano Elías formed the Solidary Action Movement (MAS). He was MAS' candidate in the 1985 presidential campaign, in which he placed third among eight candidates. He again was a candidate in a large field in the 1989 election, but most of the evangelical churches favored the candidacy of Ríos Montt. Ríos Montt led the polls during this campaign. Six weeks before the election Serrano Elías had only 2 percent of the vote. The 1985 constitution forbade anyone from holding public office who had led a military revolt, however, and two weeks before the November 11 election the Court of Constitutionality disqualified Ríos Montt.

Serrano Elías's support immediately soared. His anti-politician rhetoric gained Catholic as well as Protestant support. Although some Catholics campaigned against him on religious grounds, calling him the Antichrist, religion was not the deciding element. Continued political turmoil, economic decline, and charges of corruption against the Christian Democratic (PDC) government of Mario Vinicio Cerezo had brought the authoritarian Ríos Montt considerable support, which Serrano Elías now inherited. Serrano Elías took 24.1 percent of the votes, a close second to Jorge Carpio Nicolle of the National Centrist Union (UCN), who garnered only 25.7 percent. In the runoff on January 6, 1991, Serrano Elías won 68 percent of the vote and became the first active Protestant to win election as president of a Latin American nation. His inauguration on January 14, 1991 was the first transfer of power from one elected civilian president to another in Guatemalan history. Abstention of the electorate was alarmingly high, however, as Guatemalans were losing faith in the democratic process. Only 44 percent of registered voters participated in the November 1990 elections and only 30 percent voted in the January 1991 runoff. Serrano Elías thus won with only about 20 percent of eligible voters. He also came to power with little support in Congress, his MAS party holding only 18 of the 116 seats in Congress.

In his inaugural address Serrano Elías called for a Social Pact" among business, labor, and popular organizations, but he did not mention Guatemala's Mayan majority. His government was neoliberal and private-sector oriented. He sought to downsize government, increase exports of non-traditional products, promote *maquiladora* assembly production, and privatize government-owned enterprises. He was strongly influenced by the Guatemalan Research and Social Studies Association (ASIES) and the United States Agency for International Development (AID), which encouraged ending the import substitution approach of the 1960s and 1970s in order to create economies friendlier to U.S. imports and investment. As elsewhere in Central America, there was much talk of structural adjustments. Serrano Elías skillfully formed an alliance in Congress between his own MAS, the PDC, and the UCN, and during his first year in office he made some progress in stabilizing the economy.

Serrano Elías joined other Central American leaders in attempting to revitalize Central American economic integration. Agreements of April 23 and May 14, 1993 (the Guatemala Protocol), reduced tariffs and modified the 1960 Central American Economic Integration Treaty (SIECA), moving the Central American Common Market away from import substitution toward an open economy in which labor, capital, and goods could move freely throughout the isthmus. Serrano Elías also worked toward settling the historic Guatemalan-Belize dispute. His recognition of Belizean sovereignty in September 1991, ratified by Congress in November 1992, was unpopular, however, among Guatemalan nationalists, who challenged it in the courts.

Flagrant abuse of human rights under Serrano continued, related to the continuing civil war against leftist guerrillas. Many labor leaders, intellectuals, journalists, and human rights activists remained in exile. Before taking office, as leader of the National Reconciliation Commission Serrano Elías had initiated talks with the guerrillas. Extended talks between his government and the guerrillas' Guatemalan National Revolutionary Union (URNG), however, failed to reach a lasting agreement. Serrano Elías defended the military and absolutely refused to agree to investigation of past human rights abuses as a condition for an agreement.

Charges of corruption and maladministration of justice added to Serrano Elías's difficulties. In September 1992 his support of a plan, in league with Panamanian interests, to establish a casino and race track at the old hippodrome was especially damaging. Serrano Elías's ownership of thoroughbred race horses and polo ponies and links of the casino deal to drug trafficking interests, which had also grown rapidly in Guatemala during his administration, discredited Serrano Elías and undermined his ability to govern.

In May 1993, rising unrest characterized by student riots, public employee strikes, guerrilla activity, and ordinary crime precipitated a political crisis. Although Serrano Elías's MAS party had made small gains in Congress and in controlling of municipal governments, public confidence in his administration had declined and he had lost significant business support because of the secretive and unclear way he had handled privatization. On May 25, 1993, Serrano Elías suspended constitutional guarantees and dissolved the Congress and the Supreme Court. Although the military supported this action, other elements of the country protested. The human rights ombudsman, Ramiro de León Carpio, ceased his activities and the Court of Constitutionality declared Serrano Elías's act unconstitutional. A private National Consensus Forum and a group headed by Nobel Peace Prize winner Rigoberto Menchú petitioned for restoration of constitutional order. Small but noisy street demonstrations erupted. The URNG suspended the peace negotiations. An international protest joined the domestic opposition. The United States froze all economic aid and threatened to remove trade privileges it had extended to Guatemala. The European Community also suspended aid. Then the military reversed its position and forced Serrano Elías to resign on June 1, 1993. He fled to El Salvador, subsequently settling in Panama. On June 5, 1993 the Guatemalan Congress, now reconvened, elected Ramiro de León Carpio as the new president.

Serrano Elías remained in Panama. On July 16, a Guatemalan judge ruled that the government had no legal standing to extradite Serrano Elías. de León subsequently withdrew the Guatemalan ambassador in Panama, Juan Delpree, in an effort to force the extradition of Serrano Elías.

Serrano Elías's election in 1991 raised predictions the demise of the Catholic Church as a force in Guatemalan politics and throughout Latin America. His ouster revived misgivings about the role of evengelicals in high elected office.

Further Reading

For a detailed overview of recent Guatemalan political history, see James Dunkerley, *Power in the Isthmus, A Political History of Modern Central America* (London, 1988). Some detail on Serrano Elías's presidential administration may be found in Howard H. Lentner, *State Formation in Central America: The Struggle for Autonomy, Development, and Democracy* (1993). For current development in Guatemala, see *Inforpress Centroamericana* (Guatemala), or its condensed English-language weekly, *Central America Report* (Guatemala). For an excellent summary and analysis of Serrano Elías's religious background see David Stoll, "Guatemala Elects a Born-Again President," *Christian Century* (February 20, 1991). For a perceptive description of Guatemala prior to and during the administration of Serrano Elías see Víctor Perrera, *Unfinished Conquest: The Guatemalan Tragedy* (1993). For an assessment of the impact of Serrano Elías's demise on the role of evangelicals in Guatemalan government, see Stephen Sywulka, "Evangelical president ousted in power struggle," *Christianity Today* (July 19, 1993). □

Jean-Jacques Servan-Schreiber

Jean-Jacques Servan-Schreiber (born 1924) excelled as a journalist and writer on public affairs. His efforts to revive the Radical-Socialist Party in France succeeded temporarily, but he discovered that one cannot breathe life into moribund entities.

Jean-Jacques Servan-Schreiber was born on February 13, 1924. His parents, Emile Servan-Schreiber and Denise, née Bresard, lived in the fashionable 16th arrondissement of Paris. His father, in partnership with his uncle, had founded *Les Echos,* the first financial newspaper of France, and it might be said that Jean-Jacques was born to become a journalist. He carried out his secondary studies at the Lycée Janson-de-Sailly in Paris and graduated from the Lycée de Grenoble. He then returned to Paris, where he entered the Ecole Polytechnique, one of the grandes écoles that were the cradles of France's intellectual elite. In 1947 he graduated and also married Madeleine Chapsal on September 18. That marriage ended in divorce several years later, and on

August 11, 1960, he married Sabine Becq de Fouquières. He fathered four sons: David, Emile, Franklin, and Edouard.

His career as a journalist began immediately after his graduation in 1947 when he joined the newspaper *Le Monde* as a reporter. In 1953 he became its diplomatic editor. Like many French newspaper reporters, he held a second job, first as a European correspondent for the American journal *The Reporter* (1949) and then as foreign affairs writer for *Paris-Presse* (1951-1952). He was also a freelance contributor to *TIME* and *The New York Herald Tribune.* In 1953 he followed the example of his father and established a periodical, a weekly called *L'Express,* in partnership with Françoise Giroud. He served as director and writer, with a weekly column—*Bloc notes*—covering mainly but not exclusively political topics. He served in this capacity until 1970, and from 1968 to 1970 was president-general director, then president of the oversight council (1970-1971) of the Express Group. The Express Group was an incorporated fusion of the Société d'Etudes et de Presse and of the Société Express-Union and published the weekly *L'Express.* By the mid-1960s he had made the periodical a moderately left-wing journal with a format modeled on *TIME* and *Newsweek.* Some of his critics accused him of having abandoned his socialist beliefs. A fairer evaluation has been offered by David Caute, "Servan-Schreiber does indeed embody all the self-conscious modern-mindedness of the Kennedy generation in America." His political convictions bring together the "traditional attachment of the left to social justice and social mobility with an admirable grasp of modern economics and technological realities."

At the turn of the decade Servan-Schreiber decided to enter politics actively. In October 1969 he was chosen secretary general of the Radical and Radical-Socialist Party, the oldest political party in French politics, having been founded in 1901-1902. It had been blamed for France's lack of preparation for World War II in 1939—a false accusation, but nonetheless it had not recovered its prewar status. J.-J. S.-S. (as he was known) set out to revive it and to make it a party with the mission to reform France. This meant both the "Americanization" of the economy and extensive social reforms. He was largely responsible for the party's platform calling for an end to the right of private inheritance and to the "grandes ecoles" which created an intellectual and bureaucratic oligarchy and for the creation of a system of civilian economic and social service to replace compulsory military service. This became the manifesto of the party when it was approved by the party's congress of February 14-15, 1970. The next year he was elected president of the party, a post he held until 1979.

Before this occurred he decided to run in a by-election in the district Meurthe-et-Moselle (Nancy) in June 1970 for the National Assembly. A wealthy man by now, he decided to use the tactics that had proved successful in American elections: extensive publicity through the use of television and the press and through travel. He was already well known for his books and his column in *L'Express.* Reporters began to see him as the "French Kennedy," as the "media man." As though bent upon living up to this he flew 40 reporters from Paris to Nancy and lodged them in a disaffected abbey. He gave numerous press conferences, winning national and international attention. This rather noisy campaigning did not mean that J.-J S.-S. was merely posing. He ran on a platform intended to raise the issue of decentralization in France, where Paris controlled the destinies of all citizens, and he relentlessly blamed the planners in Paris for the economic problems of the Lorraine region. Once endowed with autonomy, he argued, local people would solve their own problems. His candidacy was successful in the first circumscription of Nancy, and he won again in March 1973 and March 1978. However, the Constitutional Council invalidated this last election in June.

This was not his first electoral set-back. Shortly after his initial success in Nancy he decided to challenge the new premier, Jacques Chaban-Delmas, in another by-election in Bordeaux, the second circumscription of Gironde. Once more he resorted to electioneering "ä l'Américaine," with a one hour and 40 minutes appearance on the program "A armes égales" of the French Radio Television Office and numerous two minute appearances. His critics accused him of running in numerous elections as a form of plebiscite and of aiming at the presidency. If this was his ambition, he failed badly; Chaban-Delmas, mayor of Bordeaux, won 63.5 percent of the vote, an unusual victory. J.-J. S.-S. never fully recovered from this defeat of his national and international ambitions.

It was his reputation as a writer that kept his name before a broad audience. *Lieutenant in Algeria* (1957) is a monumental attack on French government policy in Algeria during the 1950s. J.-J. S.-S. was not a novice in military matters; he had escaped to England during World War II, served in the Free French Air Force, and in 1943 received the military cross for bravery, as well as the Médaille des Evadés and the Médaille des Engagés Volontaires. Drafted into the French army in Algeria, perhaps because of his political stance, he served from 1956 to 1957 and became a lieutenant. After demobilization he founded the National Federation of Algerian Veterans and was its president from 1958 to 1965. For many, his book was a betrayal of France's mission in North Africa; the book, however, clearly indicates that, in his opinion, France had no mission. The government and its politically appointed officers were certainly not interested in a *mission civilisatrice* that would have won the loyalty of most natives. Rather, the brutalities carried out against *fellagha* rebels prompted the natives to take sides against the French government. The minister of defense accused him of weakening the morale of the army. He was acquitted of this charge, and his book was one of the many published works that convinced the French that they could not hold Algeria by force of arms.

France's retreat from Algeria released enormous energy in the country; her economy began to take off. But J.-J. S.-S. feared that France was still too ineffective, so he wrote *The American Challenge* to demonstrate how France and Europe could revitalize themselves. Arthur Schlesinger, Jr. caught his meaning. Unlike General de Gaulle, who wished to seal France off from American economic penetration, J.-J. S.-S. advocated a process of "discriminating Americanization." American dynamism lay not in capital investment abroad, not in inventions or technology, but in skilled management, individual initiative, the flexibility of business structure, and decentralized business decisions.

The benefits of decentralization were also the basis of two later books: *The Spirit of May* (1968) about the student revolt of 1968 and *The Radical Alternative* (1970), a challenge to the traditional system of centralizing all power of decision in Paris. In 1974 President Giscard d'Estaing named him minister of reform. However, when he spoke out against the resumption of nuclear tests in the South Pacific he was removed, his ministry having lasted only 12 days.

In recompense he became president of the Regional Council of Lorraine (1976-1978). After that he was active in informational services, serving as president for the Centre Mondial pour l'Informatique et les Resources Humaines beginning in 1982.

Nearly 30 years after the publication of *The American Challenge*, journalists, politicians and historians reference it as they try to explain how and why a new-world capitalism is spreading all over the world. As noted in *The Economist* newspaper of July 13, 1996: Conglomerates are being broken up; shareholders are clamoring for their rights; the old stable links between managers, owners and bankers are being burst apart. As before, many Europeans fear that this spells the end of Europe's business civilization. They foresee an American maelstrom of atomistic competition, job insecurity and social division. Books such as Servan-Schreiber's have engraved on European minds the sense that American capitalism is a threat. Despite recession and unemployment, many Europeans remain proud of a brand of capitalism that for decades seemed to offer both prosperity and social justice.

Further Reading

Additional information on J.-J. S.-S. can be found in Raymond Barrillon, *Servan-Schreiber, pour quoi faire?* (1971). Other sources include the *Times Literary Supplement* (November 23, 1967, and July 25, 1968), the *New York Review of Books* (June 20, 1968), the *New York Times Book Review* (July 28, 1968, and March 16, 1969), *LIFE* (May 17, 1968), *Newsweek* (July 22, 1968, and June 24, 1974), and *The Economist* (July 13, 1996). □

Michael Servetus

The Spanish religious philosopher Michael Servetus (ca. 1511-1553), often called the first Unitarian, denied the divinity of Christ and the doctrine of the Trinity. His views made him abhorrent to both Catholics and Protestants.

Michael Servetus was born at Villanueva. The son of a notary, he became a law student in Toulouse, where he developed an avid interest in the Bible. A Franciscan named Juan de Quintana befriended him in 1525. Quintana became confessor to Emperor Charles V in 1530, and that year Servetus accompanied Quintana to Bologna for Charles's coronation. There the pomp surrounding the Pope repelled him and tended to alienate him from the Roman Catholic Church. This journey was decisive in shaping Servetus's thought, for he also visited Augsburg, where he came into immediate contact with Protestantism, which impressed him favorably. He soon became acquainted with the leading spirit of Rhenish Protestantism, Martin Bucer.

Servetus then published a book that separated him philosophically not only from Catholicism but also from all the current reforming movements: *De Trinitatis erroribus* (1531; On the Errors of the Trinity). Its erudition was astonishing in light of the fact that its author was so young. But its thesis horrified Servetus's contemporaries, making him in their eyes a heretic. Servetus viewed Jesus as a man upon whom God had bestowed divine wisdom. Jesus came forth as a prophet bearing God's precious gift, but he did not partake of God's immortality.

If Servetus denied Jesus' equality to the godhead, he yielded to none in his praise of Jesus, calling him the Light of the World. Servetus insisted that those who believed in the Trinity were tritheists who could not escape the logic that they denied the One True God.

Because of these views Servetus was forced to take flight, moving in 1532 from Switzerland to France. There he lived for a time unmolested, traveling in 1536 to Paris to study medicine. He met John Calvin briefly, but Servetus concentrated for a time on medicine rather than on religious

reform. He became assistant to the physician Johann Günther and continued to study avidly, taking up theology and Hebrew as well as medicine.

In 1546 Servetus wrote to Calvin, sending him elaborate manuscripts on his theological views. Calvin answered without warmth, letting Servetus know he would not be welcome in Geneva. The reformer very probably, through correspondence, was partially responsible for Servetus's arrest by the inquisitor general of Lyons on April 4, 1553. On April 7 Servetus escaped, turning up 4 months later in Geneva. He was seized, tried, and on Oct. 27, 1553, burned alive with the acquiescence of Calvin.

Further Reading

A scholarly biography of Servetus is Roland H. Bainton, *Hunted Heretic: The Life and Death of Michael Servetus* (1953; new foreword, 1960). Also useful is John F. Fulton, *Michael Servetus: Humanist and Martyr* (1953). A good account of Servetus's theology is in Louis Israel Newman, *Jewish Influence on Christian Reform Movements* (1925).

Additional Sources

Friedman, Jerome, *Michael Servetus: a case study in total heresy,* Geneve: Droz, 1978. □

Toya Sesshu

The Japanese painter and Zen priest Toyo Sesshu (1420-1506) is generally regarded as Japan's greatest painter. His Zen-inspired paintings are credited with establishing a truly Japanese style of ink painting which had a great influence on all later Japanese painting.

The Muromachi, or Ashikaga, period during which Sesshu lived was profoundly influenced by Zen Buddhism, which had been introduced from China during the Kamakura period. Under its impact the Chinese-style ink paintings of the great masters of the Southern Sung period, especially the landscape painters Ma Yüan and Hsia Kuei and the Ch'an painters Mu Ch'i and Yu-chien, served as models for the Japanese painters. Not only did these artists derive their style from China, but the landscape they represented was also that of South China in spite of the fact that many of them had never been there.

Sesshu was born in Bitchu Province in western Honshu. As a youth, he became a Buddhist novice at the Shokoku-ji, a well-known Zen temple in Kyoto which was not only a famous Buddhist sanctuary but a celebrated cultural center as well. At the monastery young Sesshu came under the influence of the famous painter Shubun, who was a fellow monk, and the Zen master Shunrin Suto, who became his spiritual adviser.

Little is known about Sesshu's early artistic work prior to his journey to China (1467-1469), during which he visited Buddhist monasteries and traveled as far as Peking. Although the artist was well received and also much impressed by the grandiose landscape, he was disappointed with the state of painting in Ming China, which to his way of thinking compared unfavorably to the painting of the Sung period some 2 centuries earlier.

Returning to Japan in 1469, Sesshu moved from place to place in northern Kyushu to avoid the civil war which was raging in Kyoto and finally settled in Oita, where he enjoyed the patronage of the Otomo family. His friend, the monk Bofu Ryushin, in commenting upon Sesshu's position at this time, reported that everyone from the nobility to the common people of Oita admired his painting and asked for examples of his work. Between 1481 and 1484 the artist made a long journey through Japan, visiting many parts of the country and making numerous sketches of the landscape.

After Sesshu returned to western Japan, he settled at Yamaguchi in Suho Province, where he set up the Tenkaitoga-ro studio and enjoyed the patronage of the Mori family. He spent the remainder of his life at Yamaguchi, enjoying ever-growing fame as Japan's leading artist.

Landscape Paintings

Of all the various subjects treated by Sesshu, landscapes form by far the largest and most important category. The earliest of these is a set of hanging scrolls depicting the four seasons (National Museum, Tokyo). Painted either in China or shortly after his return, they reflect the rather dry and academic style of the Chinese Che school of the time. His mature style is best seen in a pair of landscape scrolls depicting fall and winter, which originally belonged to the Manju-in in Kyoto (now in the National Museum, Tokyo). Painted in ink on paper in a vigorous and expressive manner, they show the artist at his very best. The style and the subject are derived from Chinese models, but Sesshu's paintings show far greater contrasts between solid blacks and lighter tones, more emphasis on heavy lines, and a flatter space than would be found in Chinese Sung painting.

While these pictures are in the form of hanging scrolls, called kakemono, other landscapes by Sesshu are in the form of horizontal hand scrolls known as makimono. The most famous of these, and perhaps Sesshu's most outstanding work, is the long scroll landscape (collection of the Mori family, Yamaguchi). Measuring more than 50 feet in length and painted in 1486, when the artist was at the peak of his power, it represents suiboku ink painting at its best, combining magnificent brushwork with a profound interpretation of the moods and aspects of nature. Starting with a spring landscape, it ends with winter scenes depicting mountains, gnarled pines, picturesque rocks, tiny figures, fishing boats, village huts, and town houses.

Two other celebrated Sesshu landscapes are the *haboku sansui scroll* (National Museum, Tokyo) of 1495 and the *Ama-no-hashidate,* or Bridge of Heaven scroll (National Museum, Kyoto), a work from the very end of Sesshu's life, about 1502 to 1506. The *haboku sansui* is painted in the so-called spilled-ink style, a free and very spontaneous manner derived from the Zen tradition. The *Ama-no-hashidate,* which is a kind of topographical painting of a celebrated beauty spot located on the Japanese sea coast, is executed in a very meticulous style. Several other landscapes can with more or less certainty be attributed to Sesshu, but none of them is equal in quality to these masterpieces. Among the landscapes in American collections which are attributed to Sesshu, the spilled-ink-style picture in the Cleveland Museum is the most authentic as well as the finest esthetically.

Zen Subjects

Although Sesshu remained a Buddhist monk all his life and his landscape painting was religious in inspiration, several of his other works are Zen paintings in a more specific sense. Among these is a large scroll painted in 1496 (collection of the Sainen-ji, Aichi prefecture). It depicts Hui-ko cutting off his arm to demonstrate his will power to the founder of Zen, Bodhidarma, or Daruma, as he is called in Japan. Both the bold, inspired brushwork of the picture and the choice of the subject matter are typical of Zen Buddhist thought. The portrait of Daruma, with bushy eyebrows and a fierce expression, reveals his spiritual power in a masterful way.

Bird and Flower Paintings

The third main category of Sesshu's work consists of decorative screen paintings depicting birds and flowers as well as monkeys and all sorts of trees and plants. This type of painting, which was particularly popular in Ming China, is very different from Sesshu's other work owing to its greater attention to realistic detail and emphasis on decorative design rather than religious feeling. The format too tends to differ from most of his other works, for these paintings tend to be folding screens instead of scroll paintings. Among the screens of this type, the finest is a pair showing birds and flowers rendered in a very decorative and detailed manner (Kosaka Collection, Tokyo).

The best such painting in America is the monkey screen (Museum of Fine Arts, Boston), which, although signed and dated 1491, is no longer believed to be by Sesshu. However, since he had many followers working in his style, the question of which works are actually by the master and which are by his workshop or his followers is very difficult to determine.

Further Reading

The most complete work on Sesshu in English is still Jon Carter Covell, *Under the Seal of Sesshu* (1941). A more recent work is Tanio Nakamura, *Sesshu Toyo, 1420-1506,* with an English text by Elise Grilli (1957). There is a brief introduction to Sesshu's life and work in the Tokyo National Museum's edition of *The Masterpieces of Sesshu* (1956). □

Roger Huntington Sessions

The works of the American composer Roger Huntington Sessions (1896-1985) are characterized by a dense chromaticism of an expressive and individual character. He was also an influential teacher.

Roger Sessions was born December 28, 1896, in Brooklyn, New York. He entered Harvard at the age of 14. Later he studied music under Horatio Parker at Yale and Ernest Bloch at the Cleveland Institute of Music (1919-1922) and then stayed on at the institute as Bloch's assistant. Sessions' first major orchestral work, *The Black Maskers* (1923), is usually heard today in its form as a suite. It remains the best introduction to his music by virtue of its accessibility: the warmth and color of the orchestral writing and the rhythmic ingenuity create an immediacy of excitement not characteristic of his later style; at the same time, he is in command of every compositional detail.

In following Sessions' development, one realizes that his music, though unmistakably "progressive" in style, was independent of the current trend at any given moment. Thus his *First Piano Sonata* (1930) opens in an atmosphere reminiscent of César Franck or Gabriel Fauré; and Sessions' music of the 1930s, in general, bears only the most superficial imprint of neoclassicism. The pandiatonicism of the *Violin Concerto* (1935) is perhaps the closest he ever approached to Aaron Copland's manner, while the four piano pieces known as *From My Diary* (1937-1940) far surpass in harmonic and gestural complexity anything to be found in American neoclassic works of the period.

The 1930s were a time of compositional struggle for Sessions and of readjustment to America after 8 years spent in Europe. Returning in 1933, he immediately began teaching at Princeton, moving to Berkeley in 1945, then back to Princeton in 1953. After he retired from Princeton in 1964, he taught at the Juilliard School in New York until his death in 1985.

The later years brought noticeable changes in Sessions' music. While the pieces of the 1930s and 1940s were produced slowly and sporadically, the works of the 1950s and 1960s came in fair profusion. Six Symphonies, two Piano Concertos, and a Mass were written between 1957 and 1968. The harmonic complexity of the middle years proceeds quite inevitably through the "diatonic atonality" of the Second String Quartet (1951) to a chromaticism reminiscent of Arnold Schoenberg, beginning with the *Idyll of Theocritus* (1956). He also wrote a *String Quartet* (1958), *Psalm 140 for Soprano and Orchestra* (1963), a total of ten symphonies, the *Concerto for Chamber Orchestra* (1970), and *Five Pieces for Piano* (1974). The affinity with Schoenberg is seen especially in the later orchestral works, with their motivic elaboration, contrapuntal density, long-breathed lines, and kaleidoscopic play of instrumental color.

Sessions' music has been called difficult, but for those familiar with the more advanced 20th-century works it poses no problems. It is consistently serious in tone; even the most gently lyrical moments are internally too complex to be considered "light" or "charming." But the complexity has expressive force and is entirely appropriate to the scope and grandeur of design typical of his large-scale works.

Sessions was held in high regard by his contemporaries and students. He received countless honors and many commissions. Of his several books and articles *Harmonic Practice* (1951) and three collections of lecture-essays, of which *The Musical Experience of Composer, Performer, Listener* (1950), *Questions about Music* (1970), and *Roger Sessions on Music* are the most significant. He won a Pulitzer Prize for one of his concertos in 1981.

Further Reading

Posthumously, *The Correspondence of Roger Sessions* by Roger Sessions (edited by Andrea Olmstead) was released in 1992. There is no full biography of Sessions, but considerable information is in several background works: Gerald Abraham, *A Hundred Years of Music* (1938; 3d ed. 1964); David Ewen, *World of 20th Century Music* (1968); and H. H. Stuckenschmidt, *Twentieth Century Music* (1969). □

Elizabeth Ann Bayley Seton

Elizabeth Ann Bayley Seton (1774-1821), the first American woman to be beatified, founded the first American order of nuns, initiated the parochial school system, and established the first Catholic orphanage in the United States.

Elizabeth Bayley was born in New York City on Aug. 28, 1774, a daughter of Richard Bayley, health officer for the port of New York and professor of anatomy at King's College. The Bayley family were members of the Episcopal Church. Elizabeth grew up in fashionable New York society. In 1794 she married William Magee Seton, a prosperous New York banker and merchant. They had five children. Seton was so active in her aid to the sick, the poor, and the unfortunate that she became known as the "Protestant Sister of Charity."

In the fall of 1803 the Setons went to Italy to visit friends, the Filicchi family, who were prominent bankers and shippers. Mr. Seton, already ill, was seriously affected by the voyage and died in December. The Filicchis introduced Mrs. Seton to Catholicism, and Antonio Filicchi accompanied her when she returned to America in 1804. Despite the opposition of her close friend, the Episcopal minister John Henry Hobart, she joined the Catholic Church in March 1805.

For her conversion Seton was ostracized by New York society. She had difficulty in supporting her family, although Antonio Filicchi was generous in giving her aid. She considered going into a convent but followed the advice of Bishop John Carroll of Baltimore and did not do so. Father William Dubourg of Baltimore told her that he wanted to establish a school in that city, and in September 1808 she opened a boarding school for girls. She and her small group of assistants adopted the name Sisters of Charity of St. Joseph. The rules of the order were similar to those of a French order, the Daughters of Charity of St. Vincent de Paul. In 1809 the

sisters moved to Emmitsburg, Md., to property which had been given the Church for use in the education of the poor.

The first winter in the new location was harsh. The house was incomplete and the food inadequate, but within a few months the school was thriving. Members of the group took over an orphanage in Philadelphia in 1814 and established orphanages and schools in New York and Philadelphia.

Mother Seton died on Jan. 4, 1821. She was declared venerable on Dec. 18, 1959, and was beatified on March 17, 1963.

Further Reading

Joseph I. Dirvin, *Mrs. Seton: Foundress of the American Sisters of Charity* (1962), is a detailed, scholarly biography, based on an impressive bibliography, including many primary materials. Leonard Feeney, *Mother Seton: An American Woman* (1947), is written in a somewhat popular style, but it contains excerpts from some of Seton's letters. □

Ernest Thompson Seton

Ernest Thompson Seton (1860-1946) was best known as the author of *Wild Animals I Have Known* and as co-founder of the Boy Scouts of America.

Seton was born on August 14, 1860, in South Shields, England, the eighth of the ten sons of Alice Snowdon Thompson and Joseph Logan Thompson. At the age of 21 he took the surname Seton in the belief that his father was the true heir to the lands and titles of Lord Seton, Earl of Winton. After an appeal from his mother in 1887, he resumed the Thompson surname and began using the *nom de plume* Ernest Seton-Thompson on his published works; in 1901 he changed his name legally to Ernest Thompson Seton. These changes have caused confusion in identifying his earlier work.

Joseph Thompson owned a small fleet of merchant sailing ships, but when forced out of business by competition from steam-powered ships in 1866, he emigrated to Canada with his family to become a farmer. On the farm near Lindsay, Ontario, Seton developed the interest in animal life that became the basis of his career as both artist and naturalist. The Thompsons, however, were unsuccessful as farmers, and after four years they moved to Toronto; here Seton discovered the wildlife of Toronto Island and the Don River valley. His adventures in the valley may be found in *Two Little Savages* (1903).

In 1876 he was apprenticed to the Toronto portrait painter John Colin Forbes and began night classes at the Ontario School of Art and Design. Although he won a seven year scholarship to London's Royal Academy of Arts in January 1881, he abandoned his studies after only seven months and returned to Canada, this time to settle on his brother Arthur's Manitoba homestead. His wildlife research on the prairie resulted in the publication of his first scientific

article in 1883 and provided material for many of his later books, among them *The Trail of the Sandhill Stag* (1899).

Seton completed his art training between 1890 and 1896 at the Académie Julian in Paris. It was in France that he met the writer Grace Gallatin, the daughter of a San Francisco financier. They were married in New York in June 1896 and settled near Greenwich, Connecticut. Their only child was Anya Seton, the novelist. The marriage ended in divorce in 1935.

In 1898 Seton published his first book of animal stories, *Wild Animals I Have Known,* telling the stories of Lobo, King of Currumpaw; Silverspot, the crow; and Raggylug, the cottontail rabbit, from the animals' points of view. Lavishly illustrated with Seton's unique drawings and paintings, the book was an instant success, and Seton went on tour telling his stories and showing slides of his illustrations. For the next ten years he turned out at least one book of stories annually, including *The Biography of a Grizzly; Lives of the Hunted; Monarch, the Big Bear of Tallac; Woodmyth and Fable;* and *Animal Heroes.*

The popularity of his stories was temporarily halted in 1903 when the naturalist/philosopher John Burroughs accused him in an article in the *Atlantic Monthly* of "faking" his animal tales. Seton responded to this attack by investing the next five years in the research and writing of the two-volume *Life Histories of Northern Animals* which earned him the Camp Fire Gold Medal for 1909 and the renewed popularity of his books. Later he enlarged the *Life Histories* and published them in four volumes between 1925 and 1928 as *Lives of Game Animals,* this time earning the John Burroughs Memorial Society's Bronze Medal.

In 1902 Seton organized the Woodcraft Indians for boys in order to encourage outdoor activities, and in 1904 he presented a copy of his *Birchbark Roll of the Woodcraft Indians* to Sir Robert Baden-Powell, the hero of the seige of Mafeking, South Africa, asking him to help popularize Woodcraft summer camps in England. Instead, Baden-Powell introduced his own organization—the Boy Scouts—into England in 1908, incorporating most of the games and activities Seton had included in the *Birchbark Roll.* When it appeared that Baden-Powell intended to move the Boy Scout organization into the United States, Seton joined forces with other youth leaders to form the Boy Scouts of America in 1910, and he became the first Chief Scout. However, five years later he was forced out of the Boy Scouts because he was a pacifist.

In 1930 Seton settled on a 2,300-acre tract of land near Santa Fe, New Mexico. Here he married his second wife, Julia Moss Buttree, and with her he founded the Seton College of Indian Wisdom (later the Seton Institute of Indian Lore). Here for the next ten years they conducted summer courses in arts and crafts, outdoor activities, and leadership skills. He published his autobiography in 1940 and his last animal story book, *Santana, the Hero Dog of France,* in 1945. He continued to write and lecture until two months before his death on October 23, 1946.

Further Reading

A complete biography of Seton is *Black Wolf: The Life of Ernest Thompson Seton* by Betty Keller (1984). His autobiography, *Trail of an Artist-Naturalist* (1940), and Julia M. Seton's *By a Thousand Fires: Nature Notes and Extracts from the Life and Unpublished Journals of Ernest Thompson Seton* (1967) reveal Seton's story-telling ability, but the facts contained in them are somewhat suspect. His early development as a naturalist is documented in *Ernest Thompson Seton in Manitoba 1882-1892* (The Manitoba Naturalists Society, 1980), while John Wadland's *Ernest Thompson Seton: Man in Nature and the Progressive Era: 1880-1915* (1978) provides an appraisal of his scientific contributions and his part in the founding of the Boy Scouts of America. Grace Gallatin Seton-Thompson's *A Woman Tenderfoot in the Rockies* (1900) and *Nimrod's Wife* (1907) describe Seton's research expeditions. More information on the early stages of the scouting movement may be found in *Mafeking: A Victorian Legend* by Brian Gardner (1966) and Daniel Carter Beard's autobiography *Hardly a Man Is Now Alive* (1939).

Additional Sources

Anderson, H. Allen (Hugh Allen), *The chief: Ernest Thompson Seton and the changing West,* College Station: Texas A&M University Press, 1986.

Keller, Betty, *Black Wolf: the life of Ernest Thompson Seton,* Vancouver: Douglas & McIntyre, 1984.

Redekop, Magdalene, *Ernest Thompson Seton,* Don Mills, Ont.: Fitzhenry & Whiteside, 1979.

Seton, Ernest Thompson, *Trail of an artist-naturalist: the autobiography of Ernest Thompson Seton,* New York: Arno Press, 1978, 1940.

Seton, Ernest Thompson, *The worlds of Ernest Thompson Seton,* New York: Knopf: distributed by Random House, 1976.

Wadland, John Henry, *Ernest Thompson Seton: man in nature and the Progressive Era, 1880-1915,* New York: Arno Press, 1978. □

Georges Pierre Seurat

The French painter Georges Pierre Seurat (1859-1891) was the leading figure in the neoimpressionist movement of the 1880s and in the development of the technique of pointillism.

The impressionist style, which marked a radical shift in the course of Western painting, blossomed for the most part in the 1870s. During the next 2 decades a number of young painters sought to work out the tenets of impressionism in terms of their personal styles. These artists are generally separated into two groups: the postimpressionists, which included Vincent Van Gogh, Paul Gauguin, and Paul Cézanne, and the neoimpressionists, which included Georges Seurat and Paul Signac. In particular, Seurat wished to carry the theories of impressionism to their logical conclusions and to establish an art with a truly scientific base.

Seurat was born in Paris on Dec. 2, 1859. As a student, he worked in the school of the sculptor Justin Lequien, and, for less than a year during 1878-1879, he studied at the École des Beaux-Arts. During these years Seurat developed a deep respect for antique sculpture and Renaissance painting. In terms of his own century, he particularly admired the painting of J. A. D. Ingres, and he made a careful study of the new landscape tradition that had begun with the Barbizon school and culminated in impressionism.

Development of Pointillism

But Seurat was interested in science as well as art, especially in scientific color theory. During the late 1870s and the early 1880s he read numerous treatises on this subject, including those by M. E. Chevreul, H. von Helmholtz, and O. N. Rood; he also studied Eugène Delacroix's writings on color.

Essentially, Seurat's aim was to separate each color into its component parts (this process is known as divisionism) and to apply each of the component colors individually on the canvas surface. In order to have the colors blend optically, each one had to be applied in the form of a small dot of pigment. The phenomenon whereby colors were allowed to blend optically instead of being mixed on the palette had been the discovery of the impressionists, but Seurat carried the process further. He analyzed it scientifically and developed a theory to explain it. The term "pointillism" refers to the actual application of these theories to painting.

His Paintings

Seurat's first major demonstration of pointillism was *A Sunday Afternoon on the Island of La Grande Jatte* (1884-1886). This is also his most celebrated painting. A large work, it is extremely complicated, consisting of numerous figures scattered both across and into pictorial space. The scene itself is typically impressionist in presenting an outdoor world. Yet the work departs radically from impressionism: it was painted entirely in the studio with each of its many elements being carefully calculated in terms of color, light, and composition. *La Grande Jatte* is thus a tour de force in revealing Seurat's painstaking method: like his academic predecessors, he made careful studies for each figure. As a result, each seems frozen in its position, but each scintillates because it is composed of a myriad of individual color spots. As a whole, the painting is at once both classical and modern.

Seurat, Signac, and Odilon Redon were instrumental in organizing the Société des Artistes Indépendants, which had its first exhibition in 1884. Like the impressionists before them, these artists originated their own shows because their radical art had been rejected by the juries of the official Salon. And although these shows contained a wide variety of individual styles, Seurat's ambitious demonstrations of pointillism clearly established him as the major figure of neoimpressionism. Between 1886 and 1890 his influence thus spread to numerous other painters, including Gauguin, Camille Pissarro, Van Gogh, and Henri de Toulouse-Lautrec, all of whom went through pointillist periods in their own work.

After completing *La Grande Jatte,* Seurat consciously sought to expand the expressive range of his work. He became interested in motion and in the emotional quality of linear rhythms. Seurat's friend, the esthetician Charles Henry, encouraged and shared these interests, which are reflected in *La Parade* (1887-1888), *La Chahut* (1889-1890), and the *Circus* (unfinished). In contrast to the formality of *La Grande Jatte,* these works contain moving figures, sparkling lights, and a generally lyric atmosphere. In spite of this expanded content, however, Seurat did not relinquish his methodical, scientific technique. He continued to work slowly, carefully developing his theories and producing numerous drawings and oil studies for each painting.

His Drawings

Because of his painstaking working process, Seurat completed relatively few major paintings. Throughout his life, however, he was a tireless and consummate draftsman. As a student, he made drawings of classical sculpture, architectural motifs, and the human figure. Many of these are reminiscent of the touch and style of Ingres. But by the early 1880s Seurat began to evolve a more personal style, generally employing Conté crayon and an unusually high-grain paper. The range of feeling in these drawings is extraordinary—and occasionally surprising in comparison to the rather cool tenor of his paintings. The master delicately used his materials to suggest figures, spaces, and atmosphere; frequently he allowed the grain of the paper to show through the Conté crayon and achieved a sense of quiet intimacy that has few parallels in the history of the medium.

Early in 1891 Seurat contracted infectious angina. He died on March 29 at the height of his artistic powers.

Further Reading

The most authoritative treatment of Seurat's techniques and color theories is William Innes Homer, *Seurat and the Science of Painting* (1964). Monographs on the artist include Daniel Catton Rich, ed., *Seurat: Paintings and Drawings* (1958), and John Russell, *Seurat* (1965). For Seurat's drawings see Robert L. Herbert, *Seurat's Drawings* (1962). For a general survey see John Rewald, *Post-Impressionism, from Van Gogh to Gauguin* (1956; 2d ed. 1962). □

Gino Severini

Gino Severini (1883-1966) was one of the leading painters of the Italian futurist movement, which proposed a radical renovation of artistic activity in keeping with the dynamism of modern mechanized life.

Gino Severini was born on April 7, 1883, in Cortona. In Rome in 1901 he met Umberto Boccioni, and the following year he became acquainted with Giacomo Balla, who had studied in Paris. Severini and Boccioni became Balla's pupils. Thus Severini was acquainted with the theories of divisionism when he himself arrived in Paris in 1906. There it was Georges Seurat, above all, who impressed Severini.

In his studio at the Impass Guelma, Severini created his most famous futurist pictures, such as *Le Boulevard* (1909) and *Danse du Pan Pan au Monico* (1911). He was particularly attracted by subject matter connected with cabarets and night clubs, and his paintings represent hectic rhythms with dissected and multiplied forms, as in the *Dynamic Hieroglyphic of the Bal Tabarin* (1912). He was one of the five artists who signed the Futurist Manifesto in 1910, and he took part in the historic exhibitions of the futurist group in Paris, London, and Berlin.

Severini's pictures, painted in Seurat's clear colors, influenced the cubists to lighten their palette, and his personal contribution was to combine the futurist program with the analytical and geometrical spirit of cubism.

In 1915 Severini joined the artists of the Effort Moderne. The experimental work produced in the style of the Section d'Or group led Severini into a transitional period, which he described in his book *Du Cubisme au classicisme* (1921). In the 1920s he was drawn more to murals than to easel painting, creating a series of harlequins and frescoes, based on the commedia dell'arte, at the Castle of Montefugoni near Florence (1922). He also executed frescoes in Switzerland for churches at Semsales and La Roche (1926-1927), the Capuchin church at Sion, and Notre Dame du Valentin in Lausanne (1935). Severini designed mosaics for the University of Fribourg, Switzerland (ca. 1925), and for the Palace of Art (1933) and the Palace of Justice (1939) in Milan.

Severini's development from a cubist to a neoclassicist style occurred under the influence of Pablo Picasso and the Valori Plastici group. About 1930, however, Severini returned to a sort of decorative cubism. His late work showed a tendency toward concrete art.

In 1950 Severini won a prize at the Venice Biennale. He died in Paris on Feb. 26, 1966.

Further Reading

Severini is discussed in Alfred H. Barr, Jr., *Cubism and Abstract Art* (1936). Raffaele Carrieri, *Avant-garde Painting and Sculpture in Italy, 1890-1955* (1955), gives a panorama of the development of modern Italian art with detailed studies of the leading artists. See also James Thrall Soby and Alfred H. Barr, Jr., *Twentieth Century Italian Art* (1949), and Guido Ballo, *Modern Italian Painting from Futurism to the Present Day* (1958).

Additional Sources

Severini, Gino, *The life of a painter: the autobiography of Gino Severini,* Princeton, N.J.: Princeton University Press, 1995. □

John Sevier

John Sevier (1745-1815), American frontiersman, soldier, and politician, was a leading figure during the frontier period in the Old Southwest and became the first governor of Tennessee.

John Sevier was born on Sept. 23, 1745, in the Shenandoah Valley of Virginia. The eldest of seven children, he worked for his father, who had a farm, kept a tavern, traded for furs, and speculated in real estate. At the age of sixteen John married Sarah Hawkins and began a similar career.

By his late twenties Sevier had decided to go west, and in 1771 he purchased land on the Holston River in eastern Tennessee. Two years later he moved his wife and seven children there. Sevier gained his new neighbors' respect, and soon they elected him to positions of leadership which included membership on the local Committee of Public Safety and one term in the North Carolina Provincial Congress. Although a lieutenant colonel in the militia, he took little part in the War for Independence until 1780, when he led several hundred frontiersmen east to help defeat the British at Kings Mountain. Shortly after this, he led a punitive expedition against the Cherokee in Tennessee, the first of many such campaigns.

In 1784 North Carolina ceded its western lands to the Confederation Congress to reduce the state war debt and tax burden. This cession stimulated a movement for statehood among the frontiersmen living beyond the Appalachians. In August 1784 they held a convention and decided to petition

Congress for statehood, but before they acted, North Carolina rescinded its land cession. The settlers met again in spite of this, adopted the North Carolina statutes temporarily, and elected John Sevier as governor of the state of Franklin. Opposition from the United States, North Carolina, the Native Americans, and some settlers defeated the statehood movement by 1788.

The next year Sevier began a single term in the U.S. House of Representatives, and in 1791 he became a brigadier general in the territorial militia. Three years later he was elected as the first governor of the new state of Tennessee, an office he held for the constitutional limit of three consecutive terms. Then, after he had been out of office for 2 years, the voters chose him for still another three terms. Following that, Sevier served in the Tennessee Senate and in 1811 was elected to the U.S. House of Representatives, where he served until his death in 1815.

Further Reading

The best study of Sevier is Carl S. Driver, *John Sevier: Pioneer of the Old Southwest* (1932), which gives an accurate discussion of his activities as land speculator, militiaman, and politician, although it fails to present much personal material. Samuel C. Williams, *History of the Lost State of Franklin* (1924; rev. ed. 1933), offers the most complete account of Sevier's role in the movement for statehood.

Additional Sources

Gilmore, James R. (James Roberts), *John Sevier as a commonwealth-builder; a sequel to The rearguard of the revolution,* Spartanburg, S.C.: Reprint Co., 1974 c1887. □

Samuel Sewall

The voluminous diary of Samuel Sewall (1652-1730), American jurist, provides a vivid picture of the Boston of his day as well as of himself.

Samuel Sewall was born on March 28, 1652, in North Baddesley, Hampshire, England. His father was an occasional minister and cattle raiser who had spent from 1634 to 1646 in Massachusetts, where he had met his wife. After study at a grammar school, Samuel went to Newbury, Mass., where his father had returned two years earlier. Samuel's education continued under the local minister. In 1667 he entered Harvard; he graduated in 1671 and became master of arts in 1674. Unlike most of his classmates, he did not become a minister.

In 1676 Sewall married the daughter of a prosperous merchant. The story that his wife's dowry was her weight in the pine-tree shillings her father minted may not be apocryphal. Sewall went to work for his father-in-law. He became a constable in 1679, and in 1681 he was appointed to the Massachusetts General Court. His wife's inheritance after her father's death in 1683 was substantial, and it permitted Sewall to shift from business to civic service.

Sewall's diary records his daily life, with few opinions and no introspection. He was mainly conservative, conventionally religious, worldly but charitable, a Puritan and a Yankee. His diary indirectly reveals contemporary attitudes. It covers a business trip he made to England in 1688-1689. It is less detailed than one might wish on the Salem witch trials of 1692, when he served as one of seven judges. Eventually he saw the evil of which he had been guilty by his condemnation of "witches," and in 1697 he publicly acknowledged his error.

Following the witch trials, Sewall was appointed a judge of the Superior Court of Massachusetts, a post he held for twenty-five years. Then for eleven years he was chief justice. He was devoted to the cause of Christianizing Native Americans and freeing slaves. To the latter cause he devoted a pamphlet, *The Selling of Joseph* (1700). Another pamphlet, *Phaenomena quadem Apocalyptica ad aspectum Novi Orbis configurata* (1687), argued that New England was a suitable site for the new Jerusalem.

Sewall's wife died in 1717. Of their fourteen children, only five survived her. Sewall married two more times. One failed courtship attempt is described in one of the diary's most attractive episodes. Sewall died in Boston on Jan. 1, 1730.

Further Reading

Sewall's diary was published by the Massachusetts Historical Society in three volumes (1878-1882); abridged versions were edited by Mark Van Doren (1963) and Harvey Wish (1967). An attractive biography is Ola E. Winslow, *Samuel Sewall of Boston* (1964). The Salem witchcraft trials are treated in Chadwick Hansen, *Witchcraft at Salem* (1969). □

William Henry Seward

William Henry Seward (1801-1872), American statesman, is noted for his staunch opposition to the spread of slavery and for his handling of foreign affairs as a member of Abraham Lincoln's Cabinet during the Civil War.

William H. Seward was born on May 16, 1801, in Florida, N.Y. He attended school there and at the age of fifteen entered Union College. In 1818, after a disagreement with his father over money matters, Seward ran away to Georgia, where he taught school and learned something of the South and slavery. He returned and in 1820 graduated from Union.

Seward then studied law and was admitted to the bar in 1822. He began practice as a junior partner of Judge Elijah Miller in "the bustling village of Auburn." He married the judge's capable daughter, Frances, and success came at once. The rise of the Anti-Masonic party lured him into politics, where he came into contact with master politician Thurlow Weed, who became his political mentor and shrewd guide into public office. Seward was elected state senator in the fall of 1830 as the advocate of internal improvements, sound banking, and social reforms. Following defeat in 1833, he cast his lot with the Whigs.

New York Governor

With Weed's help, Seward became the Whig candidate for governor of New York, and in 1837, when the poor economic situation made those in office look bad, he was elected. As governor for two terms, he attracted wide attention for his battle with Southern governors over the return of fugitive slaves and his efforts to secure equal opportunity for the education of Catholic children in New York. In 1842 he returned home to resume his law practice and to restore his depleted finances.

Seward was not, however, out of the public eye. His position against slavery had given him a leading place in the formation of the new Liberty party. His own idea was to take a firm but moderate course. "Let the world have assurance that we neither risk nor sympathize with convulsive, revolutionary or sanguine measures." He was for compensation to the slaveholder with "regard for his feelings" and for equal compassion "to the slave."

In 1846 two African Americans, both clearly mentally ill, were brought to trial in Auburn on the charge of murder.

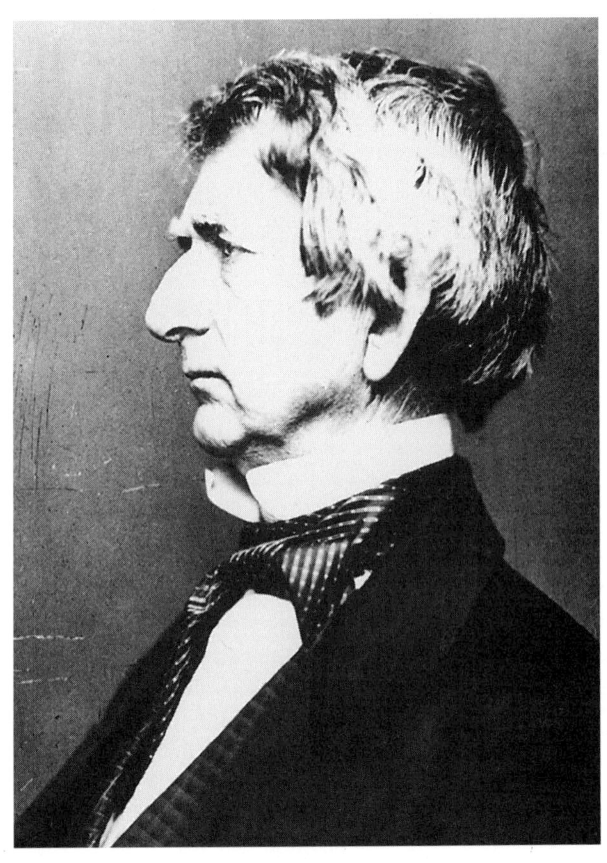

Seward's eloquent defense of these two "spread his fame far and wide and his *Argument in Defense of William Freeman* . . . went into four editions the same year." William Gladstone called his summation "the finest forensic effort in the English language."

Seward was elected to the U.S. Senate in 1849. Sectional feelings had meantime become intense, and the Mexican War had raised again the issue of slavery in the territories. Seward supported a proviso barring slavery from any territory acquired from Mexico but sharply opposed Henry Clay's compromise bill, which left the slavery issue unsettled. Seward was reelected in 1854, the year Stephen A. Douglas introduced his Kansas-Nebraska Bill and the Republican party was created. He spoke against Douglas's bill but only gradually shifted to the new party.

In Lincoln's Cabinet

With the Republican victory in November 1860, Lincoln quickly chose Seward as secretary of state. Seward accepted with the assumption that responsibility for conducting the administration rested on his shoulders. He would assume the role of "prime minister" for a president who was inferior in experience and abilities to himself. Though he soon learned better, only the modesty and wisdom of a Lincoln would have endured Seward's unsolicited advice and his independent course in dealing with Southern matters. When he finally discovered that a conciliatory attitude and a willingness to leave slavery to each state was not enough to preserve the Union, Seward became one of Lincoln's most loyal defenders and, in the end, one of the nation's greatest secretaries of state.

Although Seward's conduct during the period that the Southern states began seceding from the Union is open to serious criticism, his handling of foreign affairs deserves the highest praise. While the North rejoiced at the seizure of two Confederate agents on board the British ship *Trent,* Seward wisely accepted England's protest and returned the men. He handled the matter of English and French recognition of the Confederacy with such dignity and firmness that neither took official action. His pressure, coupled with a veiled threat of dangerous consequences, caused British officials to "take due precautions" in outfitting Confederate privateers.

Seward urged Lincoln to run again in 1864. Seward was connected so closely with all that Lincoln represented that an attempt was made on his life the same night the President was assassinated. Seward remained in the Cabinet after Lincoln's death and supported President Andrew Johnson's efforts to bring the Southern states back into the Union. He remained loyal even when impeachment proceedings were brought against the President.

Seward rounded out his diplomatic career by crowding France and Maximilian out of Mexico, settling the Alabama Claims, and purchasing Alaska from Russia. He spent his last days traveling, ending with a trip around the world. He died at his home in Auburn, N.Y., on Oct. 10, 1872.

Further Reading

Seward's writings and speeches are gathered in *The Works of William H. Seward,* edited by George E. Baker (5 vols., 1884-1889). An indispensable biography is Glyndon G. Van Deusen, *William Henry Seward* (1967). The older, once standard life by Frederic Bancroft, *The Life of William H. Seward* (2 vols., 1900; repr. 1967), which devotes less space to Seward's personal life, remains useful for reference. Other biographies are T. K. Lothrop, *William Henry Seward* (1896), and Edward E. Hale, Jr., *William H. Seward* (1910). Seward figures prominently in James G. Randall, *Lincoln the President* (4 vols., 1946-1965).

Additional Sources

Taylor, John M., *William Henry Seward: Lincoln's right hand,* New York, NY: HarperCollins, 1991. □

Anne Sexton

A contemporary American poet, Anne Sexton (1928-1974) was best known for the relentlessly autobiographical nature of her poetry and for her personal "confessional" voice, which led some fans to believe, mistakenly, that everything she wrote had actually happened to her.

Anne Sexton was born Anne Gray Harvey on November 9, 1928, in Newton, Massachusetts. The youngest of three daughters born to prosperous parents, Sexton began writing poetry as a result of an emotional breakdown that led to serious depression. Her first of several suicide attempts was an overdose of Nembutal. Despite a lasting relationship with her psychiatrist, Martin Orne, Sexton lived a troubled life. As part of her therapy, Orne suggested Sexton write poetry, and she did. She eloped with and married Alfred Muller "Kayo" Sexton, II, on August 16, 1948.

Sexton began writing seriously in 1957, publishing *To Bedlam and Part Way Back* in 1960, a collection that won her significant praise for a first book. Though she received little formal training in poetics, claiming to learn meter by watching I. A. Richards on television, her poetry has notable formal sophistication. She is best known for the intensely personal quality of her work that early mentors, including John Holmes, tried to discourage in her. Sexton wrote about subjects that were previously unexplored in poetry, such as abortion, menstruation, and the allure of suicide for her. At a time when the most critically acclaimed poetry was considered "representative" of the human condition, Sexton wrote unabashedly about herself, writing on topics that some found "embarrassing" and others didn't even consider appropriate for poetry. Also noteworthy was the fascination with death that her poetry reveals, a fascination she shared with friend and fellow poet Sylvia Plath, whom she met while taking a writing seminar with Robert Lowell at Boston University. Previously, in a Holmes workshop, Sexton had met and struck up an important and lasting friendship with

the poet Maxine Kumin. Kumin was the one with whom Sexton shared her ideas and early drafts of poems. In 1967 Sexton received the Pulitzer Prize for *Live or Die* (1966) as well as the Shelley Memorial Prize. Other significant awards included a 1969 Guggenheim Foundation grant to work on her play *Mercy Street* and the American Academy of Arts and Letters travel grant in 1963.

Though there is much scholarly disagreement about which poets should be included in what M. L. Rosenthal labeled the "confessional" school of poetry—so named because of the confessional quality in the work—no one seems to argue with Sexton's placement therein. Others sometimes grouped with her as confessional poets include Robert Lowell, Sylvia Plath, John Berryman, Allen Ginsberg, and Theodore Roethke. While this label is used disparagingly at times to describe Sexton's work, it is certainly an appropriate label, though Rosenthal actually fashioned it for Lowell rather than Sexton.

Despite frequent stays in a mental hospital and continual psychiatric therapy, Sexton published seven poetry collections in her lifetime with three more published posthumously. Her best work is probably found in *All My Pretty Ones* (1962), which bears an epigraph from Shakespeare's *Macbeth.* In that collection, too, Sexton professes her commitment to personal, confessional poetry in "With Mercy For The Greedy," writing:

> I was born
> doing reference work in sin, and born
> confessing it. This is what poems are

Among her best-known poems are "Her Kind," after which Sexton named the band with which she later performed; "The Abortion"; "Letter Written on a Ferry While Crossing Long Island Sound"; "In Celebration of My Uterus"; and "The Ambition Bird."

Notable in her work is the collection published in 1971 titled *Transformations.* In these poems Sexton retells some well-known Grimm's fairy tales from the perspective of "a middle-aged witch, me," creating some comic moments and leading to some surprising conclusions that are not part of the original tales.

Sexton was an enormously popular reader on the poetry reading circuit. So popular was she, in fact, that she was able to command reading fees far in excess of those most poets received at the time. She was a glamorous woman—her early career before writing poetry included a brief stint as a model—and she had many fans, both inside and outside academia. Many thought of her as a celebrity first and a poet second.

Sexton made her final—this time successful—suicide attempt on October 4, 1974.

Further Reading

Sexton's works include: *To Bedlam and Part Way Back* (1960), *All My Pretty Ones* (1962), *Live or Die* (1966), *Love Poems* (1969), *Transformations* (1971), *The Book of Folly* (1972), *The Death Notebooks* (1974), *The Awful Rowing Toward God* (1975), *45 Mercy Street* (1976), and *Words for Dr. Y.: Uncollected Poems* (1978). Her poems have also been collected in *The Complete Poems* (1981). Also of interest is Sexton's *No Evil Star: Selected Essays, Interviews, and Prose* (1992), edited by Steven E. Colburn.

Further information about her life and work can be found in Diane Wood Middlebrook's *Anne Sexton: A Biography* (1991). Reviews of her work and critical essays can be found in Diane Hume George's *Sexton: Selected Criticism* (1988); Linda Wagner-Martin's *Critical Essays on Anne Sexton* (1989); and Steven E. Colburn's *Anne Sexton: Telling the Tale* (1988). Sexton's *The Complete Poems* also contains a useful introduction to the poet by her friend and fellow poet Maxine Kumin. □

Horatio Seymour

Horatio Seymour (1810-1886), a governor of New York, was a leading figure in the Democratic party. He owed his influence to his absolute integrity and his ability to bring conflicting factions together.

Horatio Seymour was born of a well-to-do family (his father was a banker) in the frontier village of Pompey Hill, N.Y., on May 31, 1810. He was admitted to the bar but practiced only briefly. From 1833 to 1839 he served as military secretary to New York governor William M. Marcy, his lifelong friend.

In 1841 Seymour entered the lower house of the New York Legislature. Although the conflict between two party factions endured for nearly 2 decades, Seymour was one of the few leaders capable of reconciling them even temporarily. Since he never sought to create a personal following through the use of patronage and generally followed a moderate course, he was able to command wide respect. He served as Speaker from 1845 to 1847 and in 1850 was elected governor, serving for two terms.

In national politics Seymour used his influence to preserve Democratic party harmony by supporting candidates, such as James Buchanan, who took the position that the Federal government lacked the power to regulate slavery. At the outbreak of the Civil War, he supported the Union cause but only in the expectation that a peaceful settlement would be arranged.

In 1862 Seymour was again elected governor, defeating a Radical Republican. Although he criticized Abraham Lincoln's excessive use of executive power and condemned the Emancipation Proclamation (which he ascribed to abolitionist influence), he worked diligently to fill New York's troop quotas for fighting the Civil War. Erroneous reports (propagated by Radical Republicans) that he had failed to take strong measures to repress the draft riots of 1863 in New York City because he wished to aid the Southern cause led to his defeat when he sought reelection in 1864.

In 1868 Seymour was nominated as the Democratic candidate to run against Ulysses S. Grant in the presidential election. A compromise candidate, he repudiated the party's written platform during his campaign. In spite of this action, he lost the election by a margin of only 300,000 votes. Refusing further offices, he continued to be a major influence in party politics. He aided Samuel J. Tilden in breaking the Tweed ring and backed efforts to reform Tammany Hall. He died in Albany on Feb. 12, 1886.

Further Reading

Stewart Mitchell, *Horatio Seymour of New York* (1938), is an excellent biography. See also De Alva S. Alexander, *A Political History of the State of New York* (4 vols., 1906-1923), and New York State Historical Association, *History of the State of New York,* edited by Alexander C. Flick (10 vols., 1933-1937; new ed., 5 vols., 1962). □

Lodovico Sforza

The Duke of Milan Lodovico Sforza (1452-1508) was a notable patron of the arts, presiding over the final and most productive stage of the Milanese Renaissance.

Lodovico Sforza, born on July 27, 1452, was the fourth son of Francesco I Sforza and, as such, was not expected to become ruler of Milan. Nevertheless his mother, Bianca, prudently saw to it that his education was not restricted to the classical languages. Under the tutelage of the humanist Francesco Filelfo, Lodovico received instruction in the beauties of painting, sculpture, and letters, but he was also taught the methods of government and warfare. Lodovico was called "the Moor" because of his dark complexion.

When Francesco I Sforza died in 1466, he was succeeded by the dissolute Galeazzo Maria, elder brother of Lodovico. Galeazzo Maria ruled until his assassination in 1476, leaving his throne to his 7-year-old son, Gian Galeazzo, Lodovico's nephew. A bitter struggle for the regency with the boy's mother, Bona of Savoy, followed, from which Lodovico emerged the victor in 1481. For the next 13 years he controlled Milan as regent.

Lodovico contented himself with the realities rather than the appearance of power. He poured money into agriculture, horse and cattle breeding, and the metal industry. Some 20,000 workers were employed in the silk industry. Artists and craftsmen labored to make the court of Milan the most splendid in Italy. Lodovico continued work on the Cathedral of Milan and had the streets of his capital widened and adorned with gardens. The universities of Pavia and Milan flourished under his generous hand. There was some grumbling at the heavy taxation necessary to support these ventures, and a few riots resulted.

In 1491 Lodovico married Beatrice d'Este of the ruling house of Ferrara. The 14-year-old princess brought to Milan an artless gaiety that quickly transmitted itself to all around her. Her joy in life, her laughter, and even her extravagance charmed the court. With her guidance the Sforza castle became the center of sumptuous festivals and balls where she entertained philosophers, poets, diplomats, and soldiers. Beatrice had good taste, and under her prompting her husband's patronage of artists became more selective. Leonardo da Vinci and Donato Bramante were employed at the court.

In 1493 Beatrice bore a son whose future was insecure because Lodovico was only regent. Lodovico then secretly asked Maximilian, soon to become Holy Roman emperor, for the title of Duke of Milan. Maximilian agreed, in exchange for the hand of Bianca, Lodovico's niece.

In 1494 the new king of Naples, Alfonso, allied himself with Pope Alexander VI and threatened Milan. Lodovico, feeling himself isolated, fell into a panic and made the fatal mistake of offering the king of France, Alfonso's rival, free passage through Milan so that he might attack Naples. But French ambitions did not end with Naples, and Lodovico later bitterly regretted his decision when France claimed Milan.

Gian Galeazzo died in 1495, and Lodovico hastened to assume the ducal title. But his fortunes continued to descend rapidly. In 1497, as the result of a difficult child-birth, Beatrice died. Lodovico was inconsolable, and the entire court was shrouded in gloom. Then Louis of Orléans became king of France, and in 1498 he descended upon Milan. None of the other Italian states would help the ruler who had invited the French into Italy 4 years earlier. Lodovico managed to escape the French armies and, in 1499, sought help from Maximilian. Meanwhile the French had entered Milan.

Lodovico returned with an army of mercenaries and reentered Milan in February 1500. Two months later he was betrayed by his soldiers and given over to the French, who took him as a prisoner to France. Deprived of all the amenities of life, he spent his last years in the underground dungeon at Loches, where he died on May 17, 1508.

Further Reading

Cecilia Ady, *A History of Milan under the Sforza* (1907), is both delightful and scholarly. Julia Cartwright, *Beatrice D'Este: Duchess of Milan, 1475-1497* (1899; 8th ed. 1920), is of great value in its treatment of the court of Milan under Lodovico. □

Shaaban Robert

Shaaban Robert (1909-1962) is considered by many to be the greatest author to have written in the Swahili language.

Shaaban bin ("son of") Robert was born January 1, 1909, in the tiny village of Vibamba south of the town of Tanga in northeastern Tanzania (then Tanganyika) in East Africa. Not much is known of his parents or of the actual details of his early life. It has been asserted that his parents came from a clan of Yao witchdoctors, but this has been disputed. The surname Robert is most likely a name his father was given when he went to primary school. Shaaban himself for a time wrote it Roberts rather than Robert. Whatever his parental origin, Shaaban Robert never referred to himself as Yao and was one of the earliest to call himself a Swahili person.

From 1922 to 1926 he was educated in Dar es Salaam (the capital of Tanzania), coming in second in a class of 11 to receive the School Leaving Certificate under the then British colonial educational system in Tanganyika. He married three times and was widowed twice. His first wife, Amina, died as a young woman and is the subject of one of his best known poems, which he named for her. He had ten children; five were still living at the time of his death.

After receiving the school certificate Shaaban worked at various posts as a colonial government civil servant. From 1926 to 1944 he was a customs official at different locations throughout the territory. From 1944 to 1946 he worked for the Game Department. From 1946 to 1952 he worked in the Tanga District Office, and from 1952 to 1960 he was in the Survey Office there. Many of his civil service experiences are woven into his writings. Shaaban Robert died on June 22, 1962, and is buried in the town of Machui near his birthplace. During his lifetime he received the Margaret Wrong Memorial Prize for writing and was honored by the British government as a Member of the British Empire (M.B.E.).

Shaaban Robert has been called both the "poet laureate of Swahili" and the "Father of Swahili" for his work as a literary figure and champion of the Swahili language. Much of what we know of his life comes from a two-part autobiographical work published in Swahili in 1958: *Maisha Yangu na Baada ya Miaka Hamsini* (*My Life* and *After Fifty Years*). Part One, *My Life,* is the work for which he received the Margaret Wrong Memorial Prize. He also wrote about his childhood, but this was a handwritten piece in one copy which he mailed in to a writing competition and never saw again!

In his autobiographical writing Shaaban Robert incorporated a number of poems written as reflections upon particular times of his life. Among the best known are *Amina, Utenzi wa Hati* ("Poem for Hati"), *Utenzi wa Adili* ("Poem for Adili"), and *Ujane* ("Widowhood"). His literary talents extended from poetry and autobiography to biography, fiction, and essay writing. He is known for having written the biography of the noted Zanzibari popular singer Siti binti Saad (Siti daughter of Saad), who was famous throughout East Africa and as far away as India. A striking feature of Shaaban's biography of Siti is his sensitivity to the singer's struggle as a woman in a nontraditional role in a male-dominated Islamic society. Shaaban extols Siti's virtue, successes, and determination as a model for women to follow in countries such as his own emerging from a colonial past and developing self-reliance.

Shaaban himself gained a wide reputation for his literary endeavors. His background as a civil servant, his education, and his tendency to philosophize combined to give his works a broader base than other East African Muslim writers before him. He was the first Swahili writer to try his hand at popular biography and fantasy. His approach to literature was modern and humane; his words appeal to those interested in new ways of thinking and seeing the world.

His short fictional allegory *Adili na Nduguze* ("Adili 'the Just' and His Brothers") is set in a make-believe land peopled by characters representing and named for distinct human qualities. The tale is told in the person of Adili in the process of recounting events before the king and in the presence of two baboons Adili has been accused of abusing. We are taken back in time to when Adili's brothers, Hasidi ("spite") and Mwivu ("envy"), coveted his beloved Mwelekevu ("instructress"). The rulers of the spirit world punished the brothers by turning them into baboons and ordering Adili to beat them nightly. Thus, Adili tells the king, he is not really abusing baboons but doing the will of the spirit world. The king (Rai, "Prudence") then takes justice into his own hands and restores the brothers to their human forms. In the end Adili is reunited with Mwelekevu and each brother (having been suitably punished) finds a suitable lover of his own.

Shaaban is best known for his poetry and for its versatility. He wrote *tendi* (or *tenzi:* sq. *utenzi*) which are poems in verses of four lines, the first three rhyming together internally and the fourth forming an end rhyme throughout. These are written in a narrative didactic style and may be as long as 3,000 lines in length. Shaaban was an innovator in writing Swahili poetry using the roman alphabet rather than the traditional Arabic script. Thirty-five of his poems are published in a collection entitled *Pambo la Lugha* ((*The Adornment of Language*). In addition to *tendi,* Shaaban was a master of writing *guni* (known by some as "defective" rhyme) in which final verse lines do not rhyme as they do in the non-defective *tendi.* Shaaban also employed the poetic form *takhmis,* a modern form in six lines (12 half lines or *vipande*).

Using the essay as his medium of expression, Shaaban Robert wrote of poetry as a universal phenomenon occurring in nature as well as in culture. One distinction between Swahili and Western poetry is that Swahili poems are composed to be sung. As writing alters this poetic essence, rhyme (as an evocation of tune) is all important. In his essays Robert emerged as the first person to write about Swahili literature as a genre. His *Kielezo cha Insha* ("A Comment on the Essay") is an essay on essay-writing for people wanting to learn to write well using Swahili.

Though most of Shaaban Robert's writing is in Swahili, he did translate at least one of his poems into English with the assistance of the African literature scholar Gerald Moore. This poem appears in English as "Our Frame" and has to do with the implications of human bodily impermanence:

> . . . at the time of death when life fails
> A grave keeps us
> To cover rottenness—our bad smells
> It is not human custom
> To dwell in purity—whatever one's internal state
> may be.

Shaaban wrote this when he was turned down for an insurance policy because of the frailty of his own health.

Shaaban's life spanned the time of German rule in East Africa through independence from British colonial rule in Tanganyika. His works reveal the process of developing both individual and national self-reliance in an ever-changing cultural context. Perhaps what he himself considered to be his *magnum opus* was a work published posthumously—his *Utenzi wa Vita ya Uhuru* ("Epic on the War of Freedom"). This consisted of 3,000 rhyming stanzas dealing with World War II and the effects Shaaban perceived it to have on Africa.

One feature of Shaaban Robert's Swahili writing is that it seems to translate well into English without losing its charm and metaphor (maybe because he was at home in an English speaking world to a great extent).

Shaaban Robert was a Swahili writer writing for Swahili people. Unfortunately the audience for whom he intended his works is limited so far by the fact that only a small number of people are yet literate in Swahili in the Roman script. In this vein, Shaaban is also remembered for his work to standardize the Swahili language and for his service on the Language Board of Tanzania, on the East African Swahili Committee, and with the East African Literature Bureau. These endeavors contributed greatly to Swahili having been chosen as the national language of Tanzania and as a national and official language in Kenya. Today the language is being taught and used as a medium of instruction in both countries. As a member of the Tanga Town Council in Tanzania, Shaaban was also committed to the idea of nation-building and to the role of Swahili in that process. For his work with the language as well as for his literary output in it, Shaaban Robert is revered as "Mr. Swahili."

His lasting influence on East Africa may be seen in the fact of a population rapidly becoming literate in the language and in an emerging regional literature. Authors in East Africa seem to have opted for Swahili (and other vernacular languages) instead of English as their literary means of expression, in contrast to authors in West Africa, who have largely chosen French.

Further Reading

There is little written about Shaaban Robert in English. Another Swahili author, Salim Kombo, is said to have a biography in progress. What we now know of his life comes mostly from his own autobiographical writing and from the notes to the Nelson editions of his works written in Swahili by the late Swahili scholar J.W.T. Allen. Readers interested in Swahili literature in general and in achieving a sense of Shaaban Robert's place in its growth and development might read Lyndon Harries' *Swahili Poetry* (Oxford, 1962) or Jan Knappert's *Traditional Swahili Poetry* (Mouton, The Hague, 1968). Edgar C. Polome (in *Swahili Language Handbook,* 1967) and Wilfred H. Whiteley (in *Swahili: The Rise of a National Language,* 1969) both mention Shaaban Robert's role in the growth of Swahili language use and literary output in East Africa. The journal *Research in African Literatures,* which publishes scholarly articles about literature throughout Africa, from time to time publishes articles of interest to people who wish to know more about the history of Swahili literature and language and the role of Shaaban Robert. □

Shabaka

Shabaka (reigned ca. 712-ca. 696 B.C.) was a Nubian king who established the Twenty-fifth Dynasty in Lower Egypt and thus became the first of the "Ethiopian" pharaohs.

Shabaka succeeded his brother Piankhi as ruler of the Nubian kingdom of Kush in what is now northern Sudan. At this time the people of the Mediterranean world called all black people south of Egypt "Ethiopian," so this name became associated with the Egyptian dynasty of Nubian kings. Shabaka and his successors, however, had nothing to do with the modern country called Ethiopia.

Piankhi had subdued Lower Egypt 10 years before Shabaka came to power but had failed to leave a permanent administration there. Thus Shabaka had to undertake the task of reconquering Lower Egypt completely anew. Despite the fact that Shabaka, unlike Piankhi, established an effective administration over all of Egypt, Piankhi received more attention in the histories because he left much more detailed written descriptions of his activities.

During Shabaka's reign Egypt experienced the prelude to the Assyrian conquest. Shabaka appreciated the serious danger of the growing power of the Assyrians to the northeast of Egypt, and he tried to get Syria and Palestine to revolt in order to create buffer states. This attempt failed when the Assyrians put down the revolts, and Assyria and Egypt approached a major confrontation. It is, however, unclear whether any battle actually took place at this time. Shabaka is often identified with the "So" of the Old Testament who fought the Assyrians, but this identification is highly tenuous.

The remainder of Shabaka's reign seems to have been peaceful. He established his capital at Thebes in Middle Egypt and fostered the priesthood and religious architecture. He restored the ancient temple at Thebes and completed much repair work on temples throughout Upper and Lower Egypt. According to Herodotus, he abolished capital punishment in Egypt.

About 696 he was succeeded by his nephew Shabataka (Shebitku). The threat of Assyrian attack still hung over the kingdom, so Shabataka also placed his younger brother Taharqa on the throne as coregent, as had been commonly done throughout Egyptian history in order to assure the development of strong leadership.

After Shabataka died 5 years later, Taharqa became the sole ruler, but he was eventually driven out of Lower Egypt by the Assyrians and the Twenty-fifth Dynasty came to an end. Shabaka's descendants did, however, continue to rule in Kush for another thousand years, while Egypt continued in its decline under a succession of foreign conquerors.

Further Reading

Relatively little is known about the life of Shabaka. Some contemporary records pertaining to him and the other Nubian pharaohs can be found in English translation with commentary in Ernest A. W. Budge, *Egyptian Literature,* vol. 2 (1912). Several general histories are also useful: James Henry Breasted, *A History of Egypt* (1905; 2d rev. ed. 1909); A. J. Arkell, *A History of the Sudan* (1955; 2d rev. ed. 1961); and Cyril Aldred, *The Egyptians* (1961). References to "So" can be found in 2 Kings of the Old Testament. □

Betty Shabazz

After the assassination of her husband, civil rights leader Malcolm X, Betty Shabazz (1936-1997) persevered to raise her six children, receive her doctorate, and continue a career, all the while staying true to her values as a member of the Nation of Islam religion. She chose mainly to operate outside of the spotlight, but made occasional appearances to promote civil rights and to relate her husband's message to the public.

When Betty Shabazz married the dynamic civil rights leader Malcolm X, she could not anticipate the extent of her husband's fame or the course that their lives would take. Shabazz was catapulted into the American consciousness and the media spotlight following her husband's assassination in 1965 by three members of the Nation of Islam. Formerly an esteemed leader of the Nation, Malcolm broke with the black nationalist organization in 1963 after revising his separatist ideals and embracing a new philosophy of global unity. His young widow, pregnant with twin daughters at the time of his murder, was left to raise them—and their four sisters—by herself. In the ensuing years, Shabazz avoided publicity when she could, opting instead to provide a quiet, normal home life and full education for her children.

Shabazz was born on May 28, 1936, in Detroit, Michigan. As an adopted child who grew up in a fairly sheltered, middle-class household in Detroit, her early social life consisted of the local Methodist church with her parents on Sundays, parties on some Saturday nights with church friends, and movies on Fridays. While attending Northern High School, she joined the Del Sprites, a sorority affiliate. After high school graduation, she attended Tuskegee Institute in Alabama and encountered her first racial hostilities, which she didn't understand, and her parents refused to acknowledge. "They thought [the problems] were my fault," she later wrote in an autobiographical portrait printed in *Essence* magazine. After two years in Alabama, she moved to New York City to attend nursing school at Brooklyn State Hospital.

While at school in New York, a friend invited her to hear Malcolm X speak at an Islamic temple. When this friend said she'd arrange for them to be introduced after his speech, Betty's initial reaction was "big deal," she related in *Essence* in 1992. "But then," she continued, "I looked over and saw this man on the extreme right aisle sort of galloping to the podium. He was tall, he was thin, and the way he was

Betty Shabbaz (right)

galloping it looked as though he was going someplace much more important than the podium. . . . Well, he got to the podium—and I sat up straight. I was impressed with him." They were introduced later, and she became even more impressed. They talked about the racism she encountered in Alabama, and she began to understand its causes, pervasiveness, and effects. Soon Betty was attending all of Malcolm's lectures. By the time she graduated from nursing school in 1958, she was a member of the Nation of Islam.

Betty Shabazz explained in *Essence,* "I never 'dated' Malcolm as we think of it because at the time single men and women in the Muslims did not 'fraternize' as they called it. Men and women always went out in groups." In addition, Malcolm was busy with a relentless schedule of speaking engagements for the Nation of Islam. Nevertheless, their connection grew strong. Soon after she finished nursing school, Malcolm, who was traveling the country at the time, called her from Detroit and proposed. Before the week was out, they were married.

They were not together as long as either had hoped. On February 21, 1965, while speaking at the Audubon Ballroom in Harlem, Malcolm X was gunned down. Shabazz had brought their four daughters to hear him speak that day. As the first of the gunshots rang out, she threw her children down and covered them with her own body. After the shooting ended, she tried to help her husband, but someone held her back. When she finally did reach him, he was dead, and she wondered if she would survive herself.

For three weeks, Shabazz did not sleep. She kept seeing her husband's body fall. "I really don't know where I'd be today if I had not gone to Mecca to make Hajj [a spiritual pilgrimage] shortly after Malcolm was assassinated," she confided in *Essence.* "Two young doctors—one from Harvard and the other from Dartmouth—invited me to go to Mecca in my husband's stead. And that is what helped put me back on track. I remembered Malcolm saying, 'Don't look back and don't cry. Remember, Lot's wife turned into a pillar of salt.' I began to understand the meaning of that statement." She also had six daughters to raise. (The twin daughters were born seven months after their father's death; Attallah, Malcolm and Betty's eldest daughter, was only six at the time of the assassination.)

After returning from Mecca, Shabazz did not allow herself to grieve further—at least not visibly; her children needed her strength. "The girls knew only that something terrible had happened," she told *Look* magazine a few years after his death. "After the shock, as I became aware again, I tried to soothe them. I couldn't let them see hysteria on my part. Later, I learned that I had to adopt a personality of positiveness and high humor. For, if I laughed, they laughed. . . . I learned that I couldn't even express sadness around them. I didn't want them to worry." She threw herself into their care and education. They studied French and Arabic, as well as ballet. Attallah even took classes in medicine offered to children by Columbia University.

The Shabazz children also studied black history. "Malcolm was a firm believer in the value and importance of our heritage. He believed that we have valuable and distinct cultural traditions which need to be institutionalized so that they can be passed on to our heirs." Shabazz further explained her educational perspective to *Ebony* in 1969: "I . . . want them to travel so they can know more about Africa, the West Indies and the Middle East. I want them to go to some of the places that their father visited. In this way I feel they will broaden their scope and become of maximum use to themselves, their families, and their people."

Although raising and educating her daughters took up most of her time, Shabazz still managed to further her education. Between 1970 and 1975, she completed a master's degree in public health administration and received a doctorate in education from the University of Massachusetts at Amherst. In 1976, she joined the faculty of Medgar Evers College in Brooklyn as associate professor of health administration. Shortly thereafter, she became director of the school's Department of Communications and Public Relations.

Although Shabazz made occasional appearances on behalf of civil rights, she remained a private person, preferring the intimacy of her family and close friends to any suggestion of public life. She was, however, "committed to the broadest possible distribution [of Malcolm's message]" as she told *Publishers Weekly* in 1991. She also wanted to protect his image from base commercialization. She served as a consultant on the Spike Lee film *Malcolm X,* which opened in 1992, and also hired a licensing firm to help maintain some control over the use of his name. In the following years, she entered into several legal battles over copyright infringements of his writings, name, and the symbol *X*. As she told the *Washington Post,* the marketing of his image had "gotten out of hand."

In 1994, nearly 30 years after the assassination of Malcolm X, Shabazz spoke out in a television interview for the first time against the Nation of Islam and linked Nation leader Louis Farrakhan to his death. It was known for years, however, that she had suspected Farrakhan of some involvement in the killing. Farrakhan denied the allegations, claiming only that the turbulent, racially hostile atmosphere of the 1960s was responsible for Malcolm's end. Then in January of 1995, Shabazz's daughter, Qubilah, was accused of hiring a hit man to murder Farrakhan, whom she said was planning to kill her mother. Charges were later dropped when Qubilah signed a plea agreement maintaining her innocence but admitting some responsibility in the plot against Farrakhan. In May of 1995, Betty Shabazz and Farrakhan shook hands at a fundraiser at the Apollo Theater in Harlem, thus ending decades of hostile feelings. *Jet* reported that Shabazz said to Farrakhan at the event, "May the god of our forefathers forever guide you on your journey."

In many respects Betty Shabazz's adult life was defined by her relatively brief marriage to Malcolm X; she did, however, built her own life and success, and found contentment. "My life today is very peaceful," she told *Essence.* "I'm a Sunni [orthodox] Muslim and as observant as I can be. . . . I've made pilgrimage. I acknowledge the oneness of God. I pray. I contribute to charity. I fast. And I work hard."

Shabazz, who saw her husband assasinated and sought to preserve his memory and teachings in life that became a symbol of perseverance to African Americans, died on June 23, 1997, at a Bronx hospital, three weeks after suffering extensive burns in a fire apparently set by her troubled 12-year-old grandson. Her death was met with an outpouring of grief and solemn statements by her family, political and civil rights leaders, colleagues and friends, and hundreds of ordinary people whose lives she had touched.

Further Reading

Ebony, June 1969, p. 172; February 1984, p. 127; November 1995, pp. 62, 64.

Essence, May 1979, p. 88; February 1985, p. 12; February 1992, pp. 50+.

Jet, October 5, 1992, p. 36; April 5, 1993, p. 46; May 22, 1995, pp. 12-13.

Look, March 4, 1969, p. 74.

New York Times, June 24, 1997.

Publishers Weekly, August 9, 1991, p. 13; October 18, 1991, p. 14.

Rolling Stone, November 30, 1989, p. 76

Variety, November 23, 1992, p. 62.

Washington Post, November 18, 1992, p. C1.

Associated Press wire report, April 3, 1994. □

Sir Ernest Henry Shackleton

The British explorer Sir Ernest Henry Shackleton (1874-1922) is known for his ambitious examination of sections of Antarctica.

In the early 20th century, certain nations, especially Great Britain, Norway, and the United States, participated in attempts to reach the highest latitudes north and south. The motives for these expeditions were scientific attainment and national prestige. Sir Ernest Shackleton was to play an important role in the British expeditions to Antarctica.

Shackleton was born at Kilkee, County Kildare, Ireland, on Feb. 15, 1874. It has been noted that his "descent from north of England Quaker stock on his father's side and his Irish ancestry on his mother's may have accounted for the mingling of caution, perseverance, reckless courage, and strong idealism which were his leading characteristics." He joined the merchant service in 1890 and became a qualified master (1898) and a sublieutenant in the Royal Naval Reserve (1901). Desirous of adventure and fame, he applied for a position in Robert F. Scott's *Discovery* expedition to the Antarctic in 1901. With Scott and one other, he sledged to 82°16′33″S latitude over the Ross Shelf Ice.

Returning home due to illness, in 1903, Shackleton undertook numerous engagements: secretary of the Royal Scottish Geographical Society (1904-1905) and employee of an engineering company in Glasgow. But his determined ambition lay in Antarctic conquest, and in 1907 he made his plans public. His principal object was to reach the South Pole; other aims were to explore the Ross Shelf Ice and King Edward VII Land and to reach the south magnetic pole. The expedition was largely financed by guarantees which would be redeemed by proceeds from lectures and publications following the voyage.

The *Nimrod,* a small whaler, reached the Ross Shelf Ice in January 1908. Shackleton discovered the Beardmore Glacier, attained 88°23′S on the Antarctic Plateau on Jan. 9, 1909, and sent expeditions which reached the south magnetic pole and the summit of Mt. Erebus. On his return to England he became a popular hero, was knighted, and received numerous awards from geographical societies. The British government granted £20,000 toward the cost of the expedition. Shackleton made a lengthy lecturing tour and complied his account of the expedition, *The Heart of the Antarctic* (1909).

Shackleton now proposed to determine the extent of the Weddell Sea and adjacent lands and to complete a trans-Antarctic expedition. The *Endurance* and *Aurora* under government auspices sailed in 1914 for South Georgia. When the *Endurance* was crushed in the ice, Shackleton led heroic sledge and boat parties first to Elephant Island (reached April 15, 1916) and then to South Georgia (August 30), a total of some thousand miles. He completed the rescue operation in the Ross Sea, where the transpolar party was waiting, and returned home to write his account, *South* (1919).

Then followed numerous tasks, including a mission to South America on behalf of the British government to explain Allied war aims, and an expedition to northern Russia to organize winter equipment. But after World War I Shackleton returned to polar exploration and led an expedition financed by John Quiller Rowett to explore Enderby Land. Shackleton, however, died suddenly of angina pectoris on Jan. 5, 1922, and was buried on South Georgia Island.

Further Reading

Shackleton's accounts of his explorations are in his *The Heart of the Antarctic* (2 vols., 1909) and *South* (1919). Two biographies are Hugh Robert Mill, *The Life of Sir Ernest Shackleton* (1923), and Margery and James Fisher, *Shackleton* (1957). Books dealing with his polar exploits include Frank Wild, *Shackleton's Last Voyage* (1923), and Frank Hurley, *Shackleton's Argonauts* (1948). Useful background information on Shackleton and his expeditions is given in L. P. Kirwan, *A History of Polar Exploration* (1960). See also Robert F. Scott, *Voyage of the "Discovery"* (2 vols., 1905), and Frank Arthur Worsley, *Endurance: An Epic of Polar Adventure* (1931). □

Peter Levin Shaffer

Peter Levin Shaffer (born 1926) became one of England's most popular and respected playwrights; his work was equally successful in the United States, where he chose to live.

Born May 15, 1926, Peter Shaffer worked as a conscript in the coal mines in England from 1944 to 1947; that is, during the last year of World War II and the immediate postwar period. He graduated from Trinity College of Cambridge University in 1950.

The following year he joined with his fraternal twin, Anthony, to publish the first of three mystery novels, *Woman in the Wardrobe,* under the joint pseudonym of Peter Anthony. He and Anthony, later best known as the author of the play *Sleuth,* repeated their success with *How Doth the Little Crocodile* in 1952 and *Withered Murder* in 1955.

In 1951 his first radio play, *The Prodigal Father,* was presented on the BBC and his initial venture into television drama, *The Salt Land,* appeared on ITV. It was followed in 1957 by *Balance of Terror* on BBC-TV. (Many years later, in 1989, he returned to radio with the dramatic monologue *Whom Do I Have the Honour of Addressing?* on BBC.) During these years Shaffer worked at the New York Public Library (1951-1954) and for the music publisher Bosey and Hawkes (1954-1955) and served as a literary critic for *Truth* (1956-1957).

In 1958 Shaffer had his first great theatrical success with *Five Finger Exercise,* which opened in London, enjoyed a two-year run, and won the *Evening Standard* Drama

Award. It was produced in New York the following year and received the New York Drama Critics Circle Award in 1960. A conventional realistic drama about what has come to be called a dysfunctional family, it surely contains autobiographical elements in the character of the 19-year-old Clive, torn between his unimaginative businessman father and his doting, overindulgent mother. Critic Charles Lyons believed it "manifests the playwright's skill in providing arresting theatrical images. . . ." Ironically, it is in part Shaffer's later plays that make this early work seem dated.

There followed a number of short plays of varying success: the double bill of *The Private Ear* and *The Public Eye* opened in London in 1962 and in New York a year later; *The Merry Roosters Panto* (1963); *Black Comedy,* written to accompany *Miss Julie* with Maggie Smith and Albert Finney, premiered at Chichester in 1965. It was produced in New York in 1966, accompanied by a companion piece written especially for the American production, titled *White Lies.* While *Black Comedy* was received with wild enthusiasm, *White Lies* was not, prompting Shaffer to rework it twice; the subsequent effort was titled *The White Liars* and *White Liars.* The revisions, however, were no better received than the original; when the double bill was revived by off-Broadway's Roundabout Theater in 1993, the consensus of critics and viewers was that *White Liars* had to be endured in order to get to *Black Comedy.*

Shaffer had begun writing screenplays in 1963, collaborating with Peter Brook on *Lord of the Flies,* and added *The Pad (and How to Use It*), based on *The Private Ear,* in 1966; *Follow Me!* in 1971; and *The Public Eye* in 1972.

His next great stage success occurred with *The Royal Hunt of the Sun,* which opened at Chichester in 1964, was moved to London later that year, and appeared in New York in 1965. Obviously indebted to French theorist Antonin Artaud (who had himself toyed with the idea of a play titled *The Conquest of Mexico*), the tragedy is as much a spectacle as a drama. Shaffer was delighted with the work, writing, "I do not think that I ever enjoyed doing anything so much . . . ," and generally the critics were equally pleased. One of the commentators who had a mixed reaction was Robert Brustein: "While lauding the spectacular theatricality," he felt that the story of Pizarro's conquest of Peru and the death of Incan Emperor Atahuallpa displayed a very conventional set of liberal notions about the noble savage, the ignoble Catholic."

In 1970 Shaffer's most American play, *The Battle of Shrivings,* opened in London. The designation was his and he explained that he associated it most strongly with sojourns in New York City in 1968 and 1969" when he became obsessed by the fever of that time." But the story of a community of pacifists, protesters, and vegetarians led by Sir Gideon Petrie, a combination of Gandhi, Martin Luther King, Daniel Berrigan, and Abbie Hoffman, had no success with either the critics or the public, and plans to take it to New York were dropped. Shaffer rewrote it and retitled it *Shrivings,* but it was kept alive in the printed version only.

Shaffer had a resounding hit with *Equus* in 1974, which ran for over 1,000 performances in London. But if the British liked it, the Americans were ecstatic over the story of a young man who is put into the hands of a psychiatrist after blinding six horses. In his splendid introduction to his collected plays (1982), the playwright tells of the true story that prompted the work and shows how he adapted it to achieve greater universality. In Manhattan in 1975 it won the Antoinette Perry Award (the Tony), the New York Drama Critics Circle Award, and the Outer Critics Circle Award, but the critical reception was enormously varied. Brendan Gill in the *New Yorker* called it "a melodrama continuously thrilling on its own terms" and John Russell Taylor labeled it "at once a spectacular drama and a thinkpiece"; John Simon in *New York* magazine, on the other hand, opined that "it falls into that category of wornout whimsy wherein we are told that insanity is more desirable, admirable, or just saner than sanity." It was made into a film for which Shaffer wrote the script in 1977.

Even more successful was the 1979 drama *Amadeus,* about the relationship between the genius Mozart and the near-great Salieri, who, according to one not widely credited tradition, had murdered his young rival, driven by jealousy. Like *Equus* this work ran for over 1,000 performances in London; it won the *Evening Standard* Drama Award for 1979 and the Antoinette Perry Award in New York. Made into a film, with Shaffer doing the screenplay, it won an Oscar award for best film in 1984. Generally, it was well received: Frank Rich in *The New York Times* hailed the triumphant production," while Steve Grant in the *Observer* called it marvelously engrossing and moving . . . a feast for the eye and ear." Among the few dissenters was Jascha Kessler of KUSC-TV, who dismissed it as an example of cultural pretentiousness at its intellectual best today."

In 1985 came *Yonadab,* based on a story of incest in the Old Testament book of *Samuel* but prompted by Dan Jacobson's novel *The Rape of Tomar,* which had attracted Shaffer since its publication. It remained in the repertory of the National Theater in London, where it won great praise from Irving Wordle in the *Times,* who acclaimed it as a spectacle of the utmost virtuosity," and Jack Kroll of *Newsweek,* who thought it Shaffer's most daring, most personal, most honest play." Despite these reviews, it was never taken to New York.

Lettice and Lovage, written as a gift for Maggie Smith, opened in 1987 and ran for three years in London, with a shorter run in New York. A frankly commercial comedy, it was labeled "original" by both the *Times* and the *Daily Telegraph* in London; while on this side of the Atlantic Henry Popkin in *Theater Week* judged it "surely the most effective laugh-machine that Broadway has seen in many years."

In *The Gift of the Gorgon* (1992), Shaffer considers the quest for identity, creativity, and the boundary between justice and revenge in a flashy vehicle drawn from Greek mythology. As usual, critics were divided and audience response was far more uniformly enthusiastic. Aleks Sierz wrote of the production that "as theater it is flamboyant, exciting, brilliant: on cooler reflection, the ideas seem facile, the conflicts simplified, the gore too gruesome."

Taken as a whole, Shaffer's work, as he recognized, was concerned with the dichotomy laid down by Friedrich

Nietzsche between the Apollonian (the intellectual, the rational) and the Dionysiac (the emotional, the irrational), with the playwright often coming down on the side of the latter. His oeuvre is important in the history of 20th-century British theater. Benedict Nightingale probably best summed it up in *The New York Times:* "His plays traverse the centuries and the globe, raising questions that have perplexed minds from Job to Samuel Beckett."

Shaffer received the William Inge Award for Distinguished Achievement in the American Theater in 1992. He was appointed Cameron Mackintosh Visiting Professor of Contemporary Theatre at Oxford University in 1994.

Further Reading

Shaffer's introduction to the 1982 volume *The Collected Plays of Peter Shaffer* is most helpful to an understanding of his work. Published during the height of Shaffer's popularity, critical volumes worth attention are *Peter Shaffer* by C. J. Gianakaris; *Peter Shaffer: A Casebook,* edited by Gianakaris; *Peter Shaffer* by Dennis A. Klein; and *Peter Shaffer: Roles, Rites, and Rituals in the Theater* by Gene A. Plunka. □

1st Earl of Shaftesbury

Anthony Ashley Cooper, 1st Baron Ashley and 1st Earl of Shaftesbury (1621-1683), was one of the most controversial and powerful English politicians of the Restoration period.

Anthony Ashley Cooper was born to wealth and comfort. In his early political career he had considerable difficulty in obtaining his seat in Parliament, and although he aligned himself with the King at the beginning of the civil war, he had similar difficulties in obtaining the powers of the posts he was appointed to in the royal forces. He was unforgiving of this lack of trust.

By 1644 Cooper had become frustrated in the royal cause, and he shifted to the parliamentary forces. Although he performed admirably in his military capacity, Parliament refused to seat him. At this juncture he withdrew from national affairs only to resurface in the Cromwellian Parliaments. He was finally admitted to Cromwell's Council of State in 1653.

By 1656 Cooper had joined the parliamentary opposition to Cromwell, and in the last years of the interregnum he moved violently from one position to another until he finally was placed on the commission to recall Prince Charles in 1660. In the spring of 1660 he received a pardon from King Charles II for his part in Cromwellian affairs. As a companion of the King and as a rising official, he was created 1st Baron Ashley in 1661, but his rise was checked by his opposition to the Earl of Clarendon and the Cavalier-Anglican party.

After the fall of Clarendon, Ashley became a member of the coalition ministry of the Cabal and worked closely with the 2d Duke of Buckingham. By 1670 Ashley had become

formally estranged from the Duke of York, and he began his career as an exclusionist with attempts to legitimatize the Duke of Monmouth to deprive York of the succession. The alienation of York also led Ashley into the camp of the fervent anti-Catholics.

Ashley's progression from liberal tolerationist in the 1660s to rabid anti-Catholic in the 1670s brought him into a position of opposition to the court. Thus, although he was a member of the Cabal ministry, he was not informed of the secret Treaty of Dover of 1670. Further, though he sponsored the Dutch War, he opposed the raising of funds to support that was as his position had changed from ministership to opposition during the progress of the war. In the same vein he supported Charles's Declaration of Indulgence in Council, but he opposed it in Parliament because it offered toleration for Catholics as well as for Protestant nonconformists. Created 1st Earl of Shaftesbury, he became lord chancellor in 1672. He was dismissed from office in 1673.

During the Earl of Danby's ministry Shaftesbury's position hardened, and he shared with Buckingham the leadership in attacking the ministry. In 1677 he was imprisoned in the Tower for the violence of his statements, and he was released only upon his submission in 1678.

With the outbreak of the Popish Plot hysteria in 1678, Shaftesbury not only fanned the flames of fanaticism but also actively colluded with Titus Oakes and other informers to direct their testimony toward a more meaningful political end—the exclusion of the Duke of York from the succession. His personal role in the parliamentary leadership of the lower house and the Green Ribbon Club cannot be substantiated in any final form because his heirs destroyed much of his correspondence. All contemporary evidence, however, points toward Shaftesbury's as being the final voice in Whig circles.

By 1681 the Popish Plot had blown itself out, and reaction had set in against the Whigs over the extremity of their demands. Shaftesbury was isolated and, although the Whig sheriff of London by empaneling a Whig jury was able to save him from a trial on the charge of treason, he was forced to flee to the Continent.

Shaftesbury was an infinitely complex personality who was at one and the same time motivated by high-minded principles and base ambitions. He could show, upon occasion, selfless sacrifice and then turn to the most duplicitous and cynical actions. His principal weaknesses were his belief that what was expedient for him was moral for the nation and his necessity to destroy what he could not dominate.

Further Reading

The best and most complete biography is W.D. Christie, *Life of Anthony Ashley Cooper, First Earl of Shaftesbury* (2 vols., 1871). K. H. D. Haley, *The First Earl of Shaftesbury* (1968), provides new insights into both the man and the period. See also Louise Fargo Brown, *The First Earl of Shaftesbury* (1933). Shaftesbury's career is given considerable attention in John Pollock, *The Popish Plot: A Study in the History of the Reign of Charles II* (1903; new ed. 1944), and in David Ogg, *England in the Reign of Charles II* (2 vols., 1934; 2d ed. 1956).

Additional Sources

Battiscombe, Georgina, *Shaftesbury: the great reformer, 1801-1885,* Boston: Houghton Mifflin, 1975, 1974.

Catherwood, H. F. R. (Henry Frederick Ross), Sir, *The difference between a reformer and a progressive,* London: Shaftesbury Society, 1977.

Chapman, Hester W., *Four fine gentlemen,* London: Constable, 1977; Lincoln: University of Nebraska Press, 1977.

Finlayson, Geoffrey B. A. M., *The seventh Earl of Shaftesbury, 1801-1885,* London: Eyre Methuen, 1981.

Voitle, Robert, *The third Earl of Shaftesbury, 1671-1713,* Baton Rouge: Louisiana State University Press, 1984.

Pollock, John Charles, *Shaftesbury: the poor man's earl,* London: Hodder and Stoughton, 1985. □

3d Earl of Shaftesbury

The moral philosopher Anthony Ashley Cooper, 3d Earl of Shaftesbury (1671-1713), made his chief contributions in the fields of moral philosophy and esthetics.

On Feb. 26, 1671, Anthony Ashley Cooper was born in London. His grandfather gave the responsibility for the boy's education to John Locke. Locke hired a tutor, Mrs. Elizabeth Birch, for young Anthony, and her efforts met with such success that before his twelfth birthday he could easily read both Latin and Greek. Following the death of his grandfather in 1683, his parents enrolled him in Winchester College. Here, however, he was insulted and abused, perhaps because of his grandfather's activities as a Whig. After 3 years at Winchester, he persuaded his father to allow him to travel abroad. Together with two friends and tutors he spent 3 years on the Continent (1686-1689) before returning to England.

Cooper's health was poor, and the climate of London served to aggravate his asthma. In 1689 he was offered a seat in Parliament, but he did not accept at this time because of his desire to devote himself exclusively to his studies. In 1695 he was elected to Parliament as a Whig. As a member, he argued relentlessly for liberty and for the legal rights of the accused. His poor health forced him to resign his seat in 1698, and he then spent several months in Holland. After the death of his father in 1699, he assumed the title and the responsibilities of the 3d Earl of Shaftesbury. King William II offered him the post of secretary of state, but Shaftesbury declined the offer because of his health. The only official position he held was that of vice admiral of Dorsetshire.

Shaftesbury married Jane Ewer, whom he hardly knew, in 1709. They had one son, who became the 4th Earl of Shaftesbury.

Shaftesbury devoted his life almost exclusively to his studies and to his writing after Queen Anne assumed the throne in 1702. Although his health was poor, Shaftesbury was diligent about his studies. Shaftesbury's writings were, for the most part, occasional pieces rather than systematic

treatises. His essays include "An Inquiry concerning Virtue or Merit" (1699), "A Letter concerning Enthusiasm" (1708), "Sensus Communis, an Essay on the Freedom of Wit and Humour" (1709), "The Moralists, a Philosophical Rhapsody" (1709), and "Soliloquy, or Advice to an Author" (1710). These essays were republished in a three-volume collection as *Characteristics of Men, Manners, Opinions, Times* (1711). For this collection Shaftesbury wrote an introduction entitled "Miscellaneous Reflections on the Preceding Treatises." Seeking a more congenial climate, Shaftesbury left England in 1711. He finally settled in Naples, Italy, where he died on Feb. 4, 1713.

In his moral philosophy Shaftesbury asserted that men by nature are not inherently selfish and can, even without the aid of religion, lead virtuous lives. He found true morality in a balance between egoism and altruism. This balance becomes possible because a harmony exists between society and the individual that makes the general welfare identical with individual well-being. Man is innately equipped with spontaneous instincts to develop and promote this harmony.

Further Reading

A collection of Shaftesbury's essays, *Characteristics of Men, Manners, Opinions, Times* (3 vols., 1711), was later edited by John M. Robertson (2 vols., 1900; repr. 1963). *The Life, Unpublished Letters, and Philosophical Regimen of Anthony, Earl of Shaftesbury,* edited by Benjamin Rand (1900), contains some additional notes and letters and a brief account of Shaftesbury's life written by his son. Studies of Shaftesbury include Charles Elson, *Wieland and Shaftesbury* (1913); Florence M. G. E. Higham, *Lord Shaftesbury: A Portrait* (1945); R. L. Brett, *The Third Earl of Shaftesbury: A Study in Eighteenth-century Literary Theory* (1951); and Dorothy B. Schlegel, *Shaftesbury and the French Deists* (1956). □

7th Earl of Shaftesbury

The English social reformer and philanthropist Anthony Ashley Cooper, 7th Earl of Shaftesbury (1801-1885), was a leading exponent in Victorian England of reform of a multitude of social evils.

Anthony Ashley Cooper was born on April 28, 1801, and was known as Lord Ashley until he succeeded his father as Earl of Shaftesbury in 1851. His childhood was not happy, his father's relationship with him being both distant and harsh. For reasons not completely known, though partly through the influence of a family servant, Lord Ashley early became an Evangelical and always remained, as he put it, "an Evangelical of the Evangelicals." This creed meant a fervent belief in Protestant Anglicanism; the orientation of his life and work by religion; hostility to modernism and secularism on the one hand and to Rome and Roman Catholic tendencies in his Church on the other; and, finally, infinite compassion for the poor, the helpless, and the unfortunate. "God had called me," he wrote, "to labour among the poor."

After Lord Ashley's election in 1826 as a Conservative member of Parliament, his first important speech urged the improvement of laws governing the treatment of the insane. He became chairman of the Lunacy Commissioners, established in that year, and he continued in that office until his death. In 1845 he wrote parliamentary acts to strengthen the controls against unjust institutionalization, to protect patients, to extend facilities, and to professionalize public supervision. He conducted a similar campaign against the employment—often under horrifying conditions—of small boys as chimney sweeps, and he became chairman of the Climbing Boys' Society, a typical Victorian reform society. After repeated efforts he finally secured passage of an effective statute in 1875 that introduced public licensing of the trade.

In the 1840s Lord Ashley adopted the Ragged School movement as another cause. This movement involved the provision of rudimentary education and housing for thousands of homeless children in London. His Lodging House Act (1851) provided for public licenses and inspection of lodgings, and during the Crimean War he instituted the Sanitary Commission. These achievements arose from his conversion to the cause of public health and from his service, from 1848 to 1854, as a commissioner of the new Board of Health.

Lord Ashley's most important and most famous work was conducted as a member of Parliament between 1832 and 1850. He was the leader of the struggle for statutory intervention in the hours and working conditions of children in English textile mills and also of women and children

employed in mines. He later recorded that he took up the first cause quite unexpectedly and became suddenly convinced of his duty by "meditation and prayer." Over nearly 2 decades of deep social unrest he steadily fought for the limitation of the work of women and children to 10 hours a day, and he represented in Parliament a massive popular movement by the workers of Lancashire and Yorkshire. The victory in this cause was substantially won, after piecemeal acts in 1833 and 1844, by the famous Ten Hours Act of 1847. He had briefly withdrawn from Commons in 1846 and therefore could not lead the final effort. Earlier, in 1842, he had won a much quicker and more personal success with his Mines Act, which prohibited work underground by small boys and females.

Curiously, Lord Ashley's dedication was accompanied by a keen sense of the wearisome, thankless, and often inconclusive character of these reform efforts. Moreover, as a reformer, he was limited and even anachronistic in his outlook for his generation. He was antagonistic to political democracy and to trade unionism, to socialism and to public agitation arising from the lower classes, to secular education and to advances in scientific inquiry. His self-appointed career kept him aloof from politics, especially after 1846. When Lord Shaftesbury died, on Oct. 1, 1885, he had been much honored for his work, but he had also been bypassed by the political and social changes of the later Victorian era.

Further Reading

The best-known and most accessible biography of Shaftesbury is J. L. and Barbara Hammond, *Lord Shaftesbury* (1923; 4th ed. 1936). The standard Victorian study is Edwin Hodder, *Life and Work of the Seventh Earl of Shaftesbury* (3 vols., 1886-1887), which is valuable particularly for the extensive quotations from Shaftesbury's diaries. For a general discussion of Victorian social reform see David Roberts, *Victorian Origins of the British Welfare State* (1960). Cecil Driver, *Tory Radical: The Life of Richard Oastler* (1946), contains a rich and lively account of the movement for the Ten Hours Act. □

Shah Jahan

Shah Jahan (1592-1666) was the fifth Mogul emperor of India. During his reign, from 1628 to 1658, the Mogul Empire reached its zenith in prosperity and luxury. He is remembered as the builder of the Taj Mahal.

The third son of Emperor Jahangir, Shah Jahan was born at Lahore on Jan. 5, 1592, and was given the name of Khurram. During his father's reign he distinguished himself in many military campaigns, especially in Mewar (1615), the Deccan (1617 and 1621), and Kangra (1618). During Jahangir's closing years, Shah Jahan came into open conflict with Empress Nur Jahan, but his rebellion against his father, in 1622, was unsuccessful. On the death of Jahangir on Oct. 29, 1627, disputes for the succession broke out, and Shah Jahan emerged successful. He was proclaimed emperor at Agra on Feb. 4, 1628.

Despite his Hindu mother, Shah Jahan did not follow the liberal religious policy instituted by his grandfather, Emperor Akbar. In 1632 he ordered all Hindu temples recently erected or in the process of erection to be torn down. Christian churches at Agra and Lahore were also demolished. In the same year the Portuguese settlement at Hooghly near Calcutta was also attacked. The Portuguese were accused of piracy and of kidnaping Mogul subjects, infecting them with Christian doctrines, and shipping them as slaves to Europe. The settlement was reduced, and several thousand Christians were killed.

Between 1630 and 1636 Shah Jahan reduced the independent kingdoms of the Deccan. Ahmadnagar was taken in 1632, Golkonda in 1635, and Bijapur in 1636. In the northwest, however, imperial armies were unsuccessful. The attempt in 1647 to annex Balkh and Badakshan, ancestral possessions of Babur, the founder of the Mogul Empire, failed.

Patron of the Arts

Shah Jahan had three wives. His second wife, Mumtaz Mahal, whom he had married in 1612, died in 1631. She had been the mother of 14 of his 16 children. It was to her memory that the Taj Mahal was built. In this most beautiful

Shah Jahan (center)

of the world's tombs, the minutest detail has been carefully thought out and executed with tireless precision. In inscribing texts from the Koran round the tall doorways, the artists have shown themselves such masters of perspective that the letters 30 feet or more above the line of the eye appear to be exactly of the same size as those a foot above the floor level. Onyx, jasper, cornelian, carbuncle, malachite, lapis lazuli, and other precious stones are studded in the mosaic. It has been described as "A Dream in Marble."

The Jama Mosque of Delhi and the Pearl Mosque of Agra are two other masterpieces. Near the city of Old Delhi, Shah Jahan built a new capital, Shahjahanabad, with its magnificent Red Fort. Within the fort is the Hall of Public Audience, and here Shah Jahan sat on the Peacock Throne, which consisted entirely of jewels and precious metals and stones. Four legs of gold supported the seat; 12 pillars of emeralds held up the emerald canopy; each pillar bore two peacocks encrusted with gems; and between each pair of peacocks rose a tree covered with diamonds, emeralds, rubies, and pearls.

Under Shah Jahan's patronage jewelry reached a high degree of perfection, and jewelers from both Asia and Europe visited the Mogul court to sell their craft and gems. Yet in spite of all these lavish expenditures, the imperial treasury was never in debt; in fact, Shah Jahan ended his reign with more money in the treasury than he had at the beginning of his reign.

Patron of Letters

Hindi language was coming into vogue, and Shah Jahan himself spoke Hindi and patronized Hindi poets like Sundar Das and Chintamani and Hindi musicians like Jagan Nath, Sukh Sen, and Lal Khan. His reign also saw the rendering into Persian of several Sanskrit classics; some of these translations were patronized by his son Dara Shikoh.

Shah Jahan had begun his reign by killing his brothers and all male members of their families. His sons likewise recognized no kinship in their pursuit of kingship. In 1657, when the Emperor's health appeared to be failing, his four sons, Dara Shikoh, Shuja, Murad Baksh, and Aurangzeb, began to take steps to secure the succession. Eventually the contest resolved itself between Dara Shikoh and Aurangzeb, and the latter proved successful. On June 8, 1658, Aurangzeb entered Agra, made a captive of his father, and assumed the throne. For 8 years Shah Jahan remained a prisoner in the Agra Fort, attended by his faithful daughter Jahanara and gazing, it is reported, most of the time upon the Taj Mahal, where he was to be laid to rest beside his favorite consort.

In some respects Shah Jahan is a paradox. He employed many non-Moslems at his court but nevertheless showed considerable intolerance to Hinduism and Christianity. His son Aurangzeb continued this illiberal policy to its worst extent. Shah Jahan's court was enormously rich, and he spent a vast sum on splendid buildings. His was an age of luxury. Yet he did nothing to arrest the decline in Mogul economy. The policy of reducing the Deccan and conquering the northwest, also continued by his successor, proved disastrous and shook public confidence in the Mogul imperium. Though he was a just man, he was also at times quite vengeful, and he set into motion wars of succession from which the Mogul polity never recovered. But as the builder of the Taj Mahal, he ensured himself a place in world history.

Further Reading

The best biography of Shah Jahan is Banarsi Prasad Saksena, *History of Shahjahan of Dihli* (1932). For a contemporary account of his reign see François Bernier, *Travels in the Mogul Empire, A.D. 1656-1668,* translated by A. Constable and edited by V. A. Smith (1914). Shah Jahan's architecture is dealt with in Percy Brown, *Indian Architecture: The Islamic Period* (1942; 3d ed., 2 vols., 1959-1960). □

Ben Shahn

Ben Shahn (1898-1969), American painter, graphic artist, and photographer, was devoted to the figurative tradition. He was one of the most significant social critics among painters of the 20th century.

Born in Kaunas, Lithuania, Ben Shahn emigrated with his family to the United States in 1906. From the age of 15 to 18, Shahn was apprenticed to a New York lithographer. In 1919 he enrolled at New York University, completing his studies at the City College of New York in 1924. After 2 years studying at the National Academy of Design, Shahn traveled in Europe and North Africa. Returning to America, he had his first one-man show in 1929.

Shahn's mature style and his emphasis on specific social themes date from the 1930s. His art was influenced by photographer Walker Evans, with whom he shared quarters. In 1931-1932 Shahn painted 23 gouaches and 2 mural panels based on the Sacco and Vanzetti case. The best known is the *Passion of Sacco and Vanzetti;* executed in tempera, with elongated bodies and slight caricature of the faces, the work is a masterpiece of understatement. This style remains consistent throughout his work. Fifteen gouache studies (1932-1933) dealing with labor leader Tom Mooney aroused the interest of Mexican mural painter Diego Rivera. Shahn became Rivera's assistant on the murals for the RCA Building in Rockefeller Center, New York City.

Shahn used techniques learned from Rivera in murals and panel paintings commissioned by numerous Federal agencies. The eight paintings on the theme of prohibition for the Public Works Arts Project are good; the one titled *W.C.T.U. Parade* (1933-1934) is best known. His mural for the Community Center of the Federal Housing Development in Roosevelt, N.J. (1937-1938), is the most typical. Shahn's themes were a variety of topical problems—from anti—semitism to unfair labor conditions; he framed them into a continuous wall plane that is subdivided by architectural devices. Though he borrowed the organizing motifs from Rivera, Shahn's murals are generally more readable and less crowded. Less well known are his photographs for

the Farm Security Administration; typical is the one titled *Arkansas Share Cropper's Family.*

During the 1940s Shahn executed graphics for the Office of War Information and, later, for the Congress of Industrial Organizations (CIO). *Register, Vote,* a 1944 employment poster for the CIO, shows his concern with social equality and his ability to integrate language and visual form in a coherent design. He had a retrospective exhibition at the Museum of Modern Art in New York in 1947.

After the 1940s Shahn moved from what he called "social realism" to a "personal realism." He also increasingly turned to tempera painting and graphics. Yet his iconography was never "personal" or autobiographical. Rather, he reached a universal expression through the devices of symbolism and allegory, the stylized line, and the colorful palette, which are hallmarks of his style. Whether his subject was music or a theme after the Spanish artist Francisco Goya, he could evoke worlds with a single pen stroke or color overlay. *Blind Botanist,* a drawing for a painting (1954), demonstrates Shahn's ability to express the poignant, often tragic, state of mankind.

Shahn's *Lucky Dragon* series (1960-1962) visualizes the tragedy of the Japanese fishing vessel that sailed into an atomic testing area in 1954. Perhaps his greatest honor was his appointment as Charles Eliot Norton professor of poetry at Harvard University (1956-1957). Shahn then continued to work prolifically and with social responsibility. He taught and lectured at a variety of educational institutions.

Further Reading

Essential reading includes Shahn's Harvard lectures entitled *The Shape of Content* (1957). The best illustrations and general introduction to Shahn's work are in James Thrall Soby, *Ben Shahn: His Graphic Art* (1957) and *Paintings* (1963). The best critical study of Shahn is Seldon Rodman, *Portrait of the Artist as an American: Ben Shahn, a Biography with Pictures* (1951). □

Shahpur II

Shahpur II (310-379) was a Persian king during whose reign the Sassanian dynasty reached a new height in military power and territorial expansion.

Posthumous son of Hormozd II, Shahpur was elected king before his birth, or possibly as an infant. During his minority reign Persia had a weak government of regents and suffered raids from its neighbors, particularly the Arabs who invaded southern Persia. Rome, however, which had gained some of the western Persian cities in Mesopotamia during the reign of Narse, Shahpur's grandfather, left Persia in peace.

Once grown up, Shahpur proved a formidable soldier and a capable ruler. After subduing the Arabs and conquering Bahrain on the southern littoral of the Persian Gulf, he turned his attention to his western frontiers with a view to restoring the Persian provinces lost earlier to Rome and establishing Persian power over Armenia and Iberia. Perso-Roman relations had latterly become further complicated by the conversion to Christianity of the Armenian king Terdat and by Emperor Constantine's proclaiming himself a protector of the Christians.

In the military operations which ensued, Shahpur had achieved a measure of success when, about 350, raids by the Huns drew his attention to the eastern frontiers. His successful campaign against the Huns (350-357) resulted in the expansion of the eastern boundaries and the inclusion of Hunnish contingents in the Persian army. Relieved of the problems of the East, Shahpur now turned his whole attention to Rome, demanding in a letter to Constantine the restoration of the lost Persian provinces. This led again to a series of wars which began in 359 and continued into 363, when Julian, the Roman emperor, despite the initial successes which took his armies to the gates of Ctesiphon, was forced to retreat and died of battle wounds on the way.

The peace treaty signed in 363 with Julian's successor, Jovian, rewarded Shahpur's skill and tenacity of purpose and was a severe blow to the Roman influence in the East. The five provinces beyond the Tigris, as well as the fortified city of Nisibi, the center of Rome's operations on its eastern frontiers, were returned to Persia, and Armenia was placed outside the sphere of Roman influence. Rome also agreed to cooperate with Persia in the upkeep of fortifications in the Caucasus in order to ward off Barbarian invasions.

During Shahpur's reign the Christians of Iran, who had been drawn into the Perso-Roman conflict, became the subject of renewed persecutions, which seem to have been motivated more by political consideration than by religious prejudice. On the other hand, Shahpur is reported to have been kind to the Jews.

Shahpur is considered one of the mightiest of the Sassanian kings. Of an imperious nature, he was tall in stature and strongly built. His title, *Dhu'l-Aktaf* (Lord of the Shoulders), may refer to his being broad-chested. His long reign of about 70 years coincided with the reign of 10 Roman emperors, beginning with Galerius and ending with Valentinian II.

Further Reading

George Rawlinson discusses the reign of Shahpur II, mainly on the basis of classical sources, in his *The Seventh Great Oriental Monarchy* (1876), as does Percy Sykes in *A History of Persia* (2 vols., 1915; rev. ed. 1930). □

Shaka

Shaka (ca. 1787-1828) was an African warrior leader and creator of the Zulu military monarchy. His career was a transforming influence in the history of southern and central Africa.

Shaka was the son of the Zulu chieftain Senzangakona, but doubt surrounds his legitimacy, and it seems that his mother, Nandi, was soon expelled with her child from Senzangakona's household. Thus Shaka grew up an exile in the territories of neighboring chiefs. The distortions in his adult personality, his indifference to suffering, his fierce devotion to his mother, and his urge to dominate may, in some measure, be attributable to the experiences of those years.

The latter phase of this period of exile was spent in the territory of the Mthethwa chief Dingiswayo. Here Shaka found himself at the center of military activity and political change, for Dingiswayo was engaged in subjugating his weaker neighbors and establishing a confederacy of chieftainships under Mthethwa overlordship.

Upon reaching adulthood, Shaka was drafted into the Mthethwa army and rapidly distinguished himself. By 1816 he had been promoted to a position of command and had won Dingiswayo's patronage. With this backing Shaka plotted successfully for the assassination of his own half brother Sigujana, who had succeeded Senzangakona, and then seized the Zulu chieftainship for himself.

Leader of the Zulu

As chief of the Zulu people, Shaka stood in a client relationship to Dingiswayo, but after the Mthethwa chief's death (ca. 1818) Shaka launched an independent career of conquest. A master of strategy and battle tactics, he injected a new ferocity into warfare by subjecting his men to iron discipline and training them in novel methods of close combat. Shields were exploited as weapons for disarming the enemy, and short-handled stabbing spears were introduced in place of the traditional throwing assegais.

Shaka also built as he conquered. His regiments were not enrolled territorially; instead, as he expanded his domains, he drafted the men of the conquered chiefdoms into age regiments under a system of centralized command. Thus traditional local loyalties were deprived of any means of military expression, and the men of fighting age were made wholly dependent on the will of their new ruler. Even marriage was prohibited except to men of regiments that had earned this privilege by service in arms.

Shaka's most decisive victory (ca. 1818/1819) was probably that against the Ndwandwe chief, Zwide, who had been Dingiswayo's most dangerous rival. After that, there was no serious obstacle to the expansion of Shaka's power, and by 1824 his rule extended over the country east of the Drakensberg from the southern frontiers of present-day Swaziland to the lands of Natal beyond the Tugela River. Dingiswayo had established a Mthethwa overlordship; Shaka created a centralized monarchy in which the chiefdoms of the past were obliterated except in certain privileged enclaves and on the marches of his kingdom, where some chiefly lines seem to have retained a measure of local authority under a client relationship.

Repercussions of Shakan Militarism

Shaka's influence was not confined to the region of his own conquests. In several instances chiefs who were the victims of his attacks, or who feared his wrath, fled with their followers and began careers of plunder that contributed to disruption far beyond the area in which the Zulu armies were operating. This upheaval (the *Difaqane*) affected the patterns of population distribution over a large part of southern and central Africa.

In Natal and in the central plateau region the devastation was such that the Afrikaners (South Africans of European descent) and Boers (South Africans of Dutch or Huguenot descent) found apparently empty lands awaiting them when they spread out from the Cape in 1836-1838. Elsewhere, either in imitation of Shaka's military state or in response to the critical conditions resulting from the *Difaqane,* new polities were constructed by the Bantu-speaking peoples which profoundly influenced the history of southern and central Africa.

By sending refugees spilling southward, Shaka's campaigns increased the pressures on the already-troubled Cape eastern frontier. And by permitting white traders and hunters to establish themselves at Port Natal in 1824, he nurtured the seeds of a new British colony that would ultimately annex Zululand and carry it into a white-controlled Union of South Africa.

Shaka lived long enough to have only a limited awareness of the changes wrought by his career. In 1827, after the death of his mother, he imposed extravagant mourning ceremonies that left loyalty strained, and in 1828 he was assassinated by two of his half brothers, Dingane and Mhlangana, acting in conspiracy with his personal attendant, Mbopa. However, the Zulu kingdom remained an important factor in South African politics until its defeat by Britain in 1879, and a sense of Zulu nationhood survives to this day.

Further Reading

E. A. Ritter's popular biography *Shaka Zulu: The Rise of the Zulu Empire* (1955) is enriched by oral tradition but marred by a tendency to romanticize. It should be read with Alfred T. Bryant, *Olden Times in Zululand and Natal* (1929); Donald R. Morris, *The Washing of the Spears* (1965); and John D. Omer-Cooper, *The Zulu Aftermath* (1966). Also helpful is Monica Wilson and Leonard Thompson, eds., *The Oxford History of South Africa* (1969). □

William Shakespeare

The English playwright, poet, and actor William Shakespeare (1564-1616) is generally acknowledged to be the greatest of English writers and one of the most extraordinary creators in human history.

The most crucial fact about William Shakespeare's career is that he was a popular dramatist. Born 6 years after Queen Elizabeth I had ascended the throne, contemporary with the high period of the English Renaissance, Shakespeare had the good luck to find in the theater of London a medium just coming into its own and an audience, drawn from a wide range of social classes, eager to reward talents of the sort he possessed. His entire life was committed to the public theater, and he seems to have written nondramatic poetry only when enforced closings of the theater made writing plays impractical. It is equally remarkable that his days in the theater were almost exactly contemporary with the theater's other outstanding achievements—the work, for example, of Christopher Marlowe, Ben Jonson, and John Webster.

Shakespeare was born on or just before April 23, 1564, in the small but then important Warwickshire town of Stratford. His mother, born Mary Arden, was the daughter of a landowner from a neighboring village. His father, John, son of a farmer, was a glove maker and trader in farm produce; he had achieved a position of some eminence in the prosperous market town by the time of his son's birth, holding a number of responsible positions in Stratford's government and serving as mayor in 1569. By 1576, however, John Shakespeare had begun to encounter the financial difficulties which were to plague him until his death in 1601.

Though no personal documents survive from Shakespeare's school years, his literary work shows the mark of the excellent if grueling education offered at the Stratford grammar school (some reminiscences of Stratford school days may have lent amusing touches to scenes in *The Merry Wives of Windsor*). Like other Elizabethan schoolboys, Shakespeare studied Latin grammar during the early years, then progressed to the study of logic, rhetoric, composition,

oration, versification, and the monuments of Roman literature. The work was conducted in Latin and relied heavily on rote memorization and the master's rod. A plausible tradition holds that William had to discontinue his education when about 13 in order to help his father. At 18 he married Ann Hathaway, a Stratford girl. They had three children (Susanna, 1583-1649; Hamnet, 1585-1596; and his twin, Judith, 1585-1662) and who was to survive him by 7 years. Shakespeare remained actively involved in Stratford affairs throughout his life, even when living in London, and retired there at the end of his career.

The years between 1585 and 1592, having left no evidence as to Shakespeare's activities, have been the focus of considerable speculation; among other things, conjecture would have him a traveling actor or a country schoolmaster. The earliest surviving notice of his career in London is a jealous attack on the "upstart crow" by Robert Greene, a playwright, professional man of letters, and profligate whose career was at an end in 1592 though he was only 6 years older than Shakespeare. Greene's outcry testifies, both in its passion and in the work it implies Shakespeare had been doing for some time, that the young poet had already established himself in the capital. So does the quality of Shakespeare's first plays: it is hard to believe that even Shakespeare could have shown such mastery without several years of apprenticeship.

Early Career

Shakespeare's first extant play is probably *The Comedy of Errors* (1590; like most dates for the plays, this is conjectural and may be a year or two off), a brilliant and intricate farce involving two sets of identical twins and based on two already-complicated comedies by the Roman Plautus. Though less fully achieved, his next comedy, *The Two Gentlemen of Verona* (1591), is more prophetic of Shakespeare's later comedy, for its plot depends on such devices as a faithful girl who educates her fickle lover, romantic woods, a girl dressed as a boy, sudden reformations, music, and happy marriages at the end. The last of the first comedies, *Love's Labour's Lost* (1593), is romantic again, dealing with the attempt of three young men to withdraw from the world and women for 3 years to study in their king's "little Academe," and their quick surrender to a group of young ladies who come to lodge nearby. If the first of the comedies is most notable for its plotting and the second for its romantic elements, the third is distinguished by its dazzling language and its gallery of comic types. Already Shakespeare had learned to fuse conventional characters with convincing representations of the human life he knew.

Though little read and performed now, Shakespeare's first plays in the popular "chronicle," or history, genre are equally ambitious and impressive. Dealing with the tumultuous events of English history between the death of Henry V in 1422 and the accession of Henry VII in 1485 (which began the period of Tudor stability maintained by Shakespeare's own queen), the three "parts" of *Henry VI* (1592) and *Richard III* (1594) are no tentative experiments in the form: rather they constitute a gigantic tetralogy, in which each part is a superb play individually and an integral part of an epic sequence. Nothing so ambitious had ever been attempted in England in a form hitherto marked by slapdash formlessness.

Shakespeare's first tragedy, *Titus Andronicus* (1593), reveals similar ambition. Though its chamber of horrors—including mutilations and ingenious murders—strikes the modern reader as belonging to a theatrical tradition no longer viable, the play is in fact a brilliant and successful attempt to outdo the efforts of Shakespeare's predecessors in the lurid tradition of the revenge play.

When the theaters were closed because of plague during much of 1593-1594, Shakespeare looked to nondramatic poetry for his support and wrote two narrative masterpieces, the seriocomic *Venus and Adonis* and the tragic *Rape of Lucrece,* for a wealthy patron, the Earl of Southampton. Both poems carry the sophisticated techniques of Elizabethan narrative verse to their highest point, drawing on the resources of Renaissance mythological and symbolic traditions.

Shakespeare's most famous poems, probably composed in this period but not published until 1609, and then not by the author, are the 154 sonnets, the supreme English examples of the form. Writing at the end of a brief, frenzied vogue for sequences of sonnets, Shakespeare found in the conventional 14-line lyric with its fixed rhyme scheme a vehicle for inexhaustible technical innovations—for Shakespeare even more than for other poets, the restrictive nature of the sonnet generates a paradoxical freedom of invention that is the life of the form—and for the expression of emotions and ideas ranging from the frivolous to the tragic. Though often suggestive of autobiographical revelation, the sonnets cannot be proved to be any the less fictions than the plays. The identity of their dedicatee, "Mr. W. H.," remains a mystery, as does the question of whether there were real-life counterparts to the famous "dark lady" and the unfaithful friend who are the subject of a number of the poems. But the chief value of these poems is intrinsic: the sonnets alone would have established Shakespeare's preeminence among English poets.

Lord Chamberlain's Men

By 1594 Shakespeare was fully engaged in his career. In that year he became principal writer for the successful Lord Chamberlain's Men—one of the two leading companies of actors; a regular actor in the company; and a "sharer," or partner, in the group of artist-managers who ran the entire operation and were in 1599 to have the Globe Theater built on the south bank of the Thames. The company performed regularly in unroofed but elaborate theaters. Required by law to be set outside the city limits, these theaters were the pride of London, among the first places shown to visiting foreigners, and seated up to 3,000 people. The actors played on a huge platform stage equipped with additional playing levels and surrounded on three sides by the audience; the absence of scenery made possible a flow of scenes comparable to that of the movies, and music, costumes, and ingenious stage machinery created successful illusions under the afternoon sun.

For this company Shakespeare produced a steady outpouring of plays. The comedies include *The Taming of the Shrew* (1594), fascinating in light of the first comedies since it combines with an Italian-style plot, in which all the action occurs in one day, a more characteristically English and Shakespearean plot, the taming of Kate, in which much more time passes; *A Midsummer Night's Dream* (1595), in which "rude mechanicals," artisans without imagination, become entangled with fairies and magic potions in the moonlit woods to which young lovers have fled from a tyrannical adult society; *The Merchant of Venice* (1596), which contributed Shylock and Portia to the English literary tradition; *Much Ado about Nothing* (1598), with a melodramatic main plot whose heroine is maligned and almost driven to death by a conniving villain and a comic subplot whose Beatrice and Benedick remain the archetypical sparring lovers; *The Merry Wives of Windsor* (1599), held by tradition to have been written in response to the Queen's request that Shakespeare write another play about Falstaff (who had appeared in *Henry IV*), this time in love; and in 1600 the pastoral *As You Like It,* a mature return to the woods and conventions of *The Two Gentlemen of Verona* and *A Midsummer Night's Dream,* and *Twelfth Night,* perhaps the most perfect of the comedies, a romance of identical twins separated at sea, young love, and the antics of Malvolio and Sir Toby Belch.

Shakespeare's only tragedies of the period are among his most familiar plays: *Romeo and Juliet* (1596), *Julius Caesar* (1599), and *Hamlet* (1601). Different from one another as they are, these three plays share some notable features: the setting of intense personal tragedy in a large world vividly populated by what seems like the whole range of humanity; a refusal, shared by most of Shakespeare's contemporaries in the theater, to separate comic situations and techniques from tragic; the constant presence of politics; and—a personal rather than a conventional phenomenon—a tragic structure in which what is best in the protagonist is what does him in when he finds himself in conflict with the world.

Continuing his interest in the chronicle, Shakespeare wrote *King John* (1596), despite its one strong character a relatively weak play; and the second and greater tetralogy, ranging from *Richard II* (1595), in which the forceful Bolingbroke, with an ambiguous justice on his side, deposes the weak but poetic king, through the two parts of *Henry IV* (1597), in which the wonderfully amoral, fat knight Falstaff accompanies Prince Hal, Bolingbroke's son, to *Henry V* (1599), in which Hal, become king, leads a newly unified England, its civil wars temporarily at an end but sadly deprived of Falstaff and the dissident lowlife who provided so much joy in the earlier plays, to triumph over France. More impressively than the first tetralogy, the second turns history into art. Spanning the poles of comedy and tragedy, alive with a magnificent variety of unforgettable characters, linked to one another as one great play while each is a complete and independent success in its own right—the four plays pose disturbing and unanswerable questions about politics, making one ponder the frequent difference between the man capable of ruling and the man worthy of doing so, the meaning of legitimacy in office, the value of order and stability as against the value of revolutionary change, and the relation of private to public life. The plays are exuberant works of art, but they are not optimistic about man as a political animal, and their unblinkered recognition of the dynamics of history has made them increasingly popular and relevant in our own tormented era.

Three plays of the end of Elizabeth's reign are often grouped as Shakespeare's "problem plays," though no definition of that term is able successfully to differentiate them as an exclusive group. *All's Well That Ends Well* (1602) is a romantic comedy with qualities that seem bitter to many critics; like other plays of the period, by Shakespeare and by his contemporaries, it presents sexual relations between men and women in a harsh light. *Troilus and Cressida* (1602), hardest of the plays to classify generically, is a brilliant, sardonic, and disillusioned piece on the Trojan War, unusually philosophical in its language and reminiscent in some ways of *Hamlet.* The tragicomic *Measure for Measure* (1604) focuses more on sexual problems than any other play in the canon; Angelo, the puritanical and repressed man of ice who succumbs to violent sexual urges the moment he is put in temporary authority over Vienna during the duke's absence, and Isabella, the victim of his lust, are two of the most interesting characters in Shakespeare, and the bawdy city in which the action occurs suggests a London on which a new mood of modern urban hopelessness is settling.

King's Men

Promptly upon his accession in 1603, King James I, more ardently attracted to theatrical art than his predecessor, bestowed his patronage upon the Lord Chamberlain's Men, so that the flag of the King's Men now flew over the Globe. During his last decade in the theater Shakespeare was to write fewer but perhaps even finer plays. Almost all the greatest tragedies belong to this period. Though they share the qualities of the earlier tragedies, taken as a group they manifest new tendencies. The heroes are dominated by passions that make their moral status increasingly ambiguous, their freedom increasingly circumscribed; similarly the society, even the cosmos, against which they strive suggests less than ever that all can ever be right in the world. As before, what destroys the hero is what is best about him, yet the best in Macbeth or Othello cannot so simply be commended as Romeo's impetuous ardor or Brutus's political idealism (fatuous though it is). The late tragedies are each in its own way dramas of alienation, and their focus, like that of the histories, continues to be felt as intensely relevant to the concerns of modern men.

Othello (1604) is concerned, like other plays of the period, with sexual impurity, with the difference that that impurity is the fantasy of the protagonist about his faithful wife. Iago, the villain who drives Othello to doubt and murder, is the culmination of two distinct traditions, the "Machiavellian" conniver who uses deceit in order to subvert the order of the polity, and the Vice, a schizophrenically tragicomic devil figure from the morality plays going out of fashion as Shakespeare grew up. *King Lear* (1605), to many Shakespeare's masterpiece, is an agonizing tragic version of a comic play (itself based on mythical early English history), in which an aged king who foolishly deprives his only loving daughter of her heritage in order to leave all to her hypocritical and vicious sisters is hounded to death by a malevolent alliance which at times seems to include nature itself. Transformed from its fairy-tale-like origins, the play involves its characters and audience alike in metaphysical questions that are felt rather than thought.

Macbeth (1606), similarly based on English chronicle material, concentrates on the problems of evil and freedom, convincingly mingles the supernatural with a representation of history, and makes a paradoxically sympathetic hero of a murderer who sins against family and state—a man in some respects worse than the villain of *Hamlet.*

Dramatizing stories from Plutarch's *Parallel Lives, Antony and Cleopatra* and *Coriolanus* (both written in 1607-1608) embody Shakespeare's bitterest images of political life, the former by setting against the call to Roman duty the temptation to liberating sexual passion, the latter by pitting a protagonist who cannot live with hypocrisy against a society built on it. Both of these tragedies present ancient history with a vividness that makes it seem contemporary, though the sensuousness of *Antony and Cleopatra,* the richness of its detail, the ebullience of its language, and the seductive character of its heroine have made it far more popular than the harsh and austere *Coriolanus.* One more tragedy, *Timon of Athens,* similarly based on Plutarch, was written during this period, though its date is obscure. Despite its abundant brilliance, few find it a fully satisfactory play, and some critics have speculated that what we have may be an incomplete draft. The handful of tragedies that Shakespeare wrote between 1604 and 1608 comprises an astonishing series of worlds different from one another, created of language that exceeds anything Shakespeare had done before, some of the most complex and vivid characters in all the plays, and a variety of new structural techniques.

A final group of plays takes a turn in a new direction. Commonly called the "romances," *Pericles* (1607), *Cymbeline* (1609), *The Winter's Tale* (1611), and *The Tempest* (1611) share their conventions with the tragicomedy that had been growing popular since the early years of the century. Particularly they resemble in some respects plays written by Beaumont and Fletcher for the private theatrical company whose operation the King's Men took over in 1608. While such work in the hands of others, however, tended to reflect the socially and intellectually narrow interests of an elite audience, Shakespeare turned the fashionable mode into a new kind of personal art form. Though less searing than the great tragedies, these plays have a unique power to move and are in the realm of the highest art. *Pericles* and *Cymbeline* seem somewhat tentative and experimental, though both are superb plays. *The Winter's Tale,* however, is one of Shakespeare's best plays. Like a rewriting of *Othello* in its first acts, it turns miraculously into pastoral comedy in its last. *The Tempest* is the most popular and perhaps the finest of the group. Prospero, shipwrecked on an island and dominating it with magic which he renounces at the end, may well be intended as an image of Shakespeare himself; in any event, the play is like a retrospective glance over the plays of the 2 previous decades.

After the composition of *The Tempest,* which many regard as an explicit farewell to art, Shakespeare retired to Stratford, returning to London to compose *Henry VIII* and *The Two Noble Kinsmen* in 1613; neither of these plays seems to have fired his imagination. In 1616, at the age of 52, he was dead. His reputation grew quickly, and his work has continued to seem to each generation like its own most precious discovery. His value to his own age is suggested by the fact that two fellow actors performed the virtually unprecedented act in 1623 of gathering his plays together and publishing them in the Folio edition. Without their efforts, since Shakespeare was apparently not interested in publication, many of the plays would not have survived.

Further Reading

Alfred Harbage, ed., *The Complete Pelican Shakespeare* (1969), is a sound one-volume text with useful introductions and bibliographies. For editions of individual plays the New Arden Shakespeare, in progress, is the best series. The authoritative source for biographical information is Sir Edmund K. Chambers, *William Shakespeare: A Study of Facts and Problems* (2 vols., 1930). Reliable briefer accounts are Marchette G. Chute's highly readable *Shakespeare of London* (1949) and Gerald E. Bentley, *Shakespeare: A Biographical Handbook* (1961).

The body of Shakespeare criticism is so large that selection must be arbitrary. Augustus Ralli, *A History of Shakespeare Criticism* (2 vols., 1932), is a guide through the thickets of the past. Ronald Berman, *A Reader's Guide to Shakespeare's Plays* (1965), provides helpfully annotated bibliographies. *Samuel Taylor Coleridge's Writings on Shakespeare,* edited by Terence Hawkes (1959), offers invaluable and influential criticism by a great romantic poet, and A. C. Bradley, *Shakespearean Tragedy: Lectures on Hamlet, Othello, King Lear, Macbeth* (1904), remains one of the indispensable books. Twentieth-century criticism can be sampled in Leonard F. Dean, *Shakespeare: Modern Essays in Criticism* (1957; rev. ed. 1967), and Norman Rabkin, *Approaches to Shakespeare* (1964). Other noteworthy studies include G. Wilson Knight, *The Wheel of Fire: Interpretations of Shakespeare's Tragedy* (1930; 5th rev. ed. 1957); Derek A. Traversi, *An Approach to Shakespeare* (1938; rev. ed., 2 vols., 1968); Mark Van Doren, *Shakespeare* (1939); Harley Granville-Barker, *Prefaces to Shakespeare* (1946-1947), edited by M. St. Clare Byrne (4 vols., 1954); John Russell Brown, *Shakespeare and His Comedies* (1957; 2d ed. 1962); C. L. Barber, *Shakespeare's Festive Comedy: A Study of Dramatic Form and Its Relation to Social Custom* (1959); L.C. Knights, *Some Shakespearean Themes* (1959); Norman Rabkin, *Shakespeare and the Common Understanding* (1967); and Stephen Booth, *An Essay on Shakespeare's Sonnets* (1969).

Studies of the theaters are in C. Walter Hodges, *The Globe Restored: A Study of the Elizabethan Theatre* (1953), and A. M. Nagler, *Shakespeare's Stage* (1958); and of the staging, in Bernard Beckerman, *Shakespeare at the Globe, 1599-1609* (1962). The standard account of the audience is Alfred Harbage, *Shakespeare's Audience* (1941). The best account of early Renaissance drama is in Frank P. Wilson and Bonamy Dobrée, eds., *Oxford History of English Literature,* vol. 4 (1969). Oscar J. Campbell and Edward G. Quinn, eds., *The Reader's Encyclopedia of Shakespeare* (1966), is a compendious handbook. □

John Malchase David Shalikashvili

U.S. General John Malchase David Shalikashvili (born 1936) was appointed chairman of the Joint Chiefs of Staff in August 1993, culminating a military career that began in 1958.

John Shalikashvili was born in Warsaw, Poland, on June 27, 1936, one of three children of Dimitri Shalikashvili and Maria Ruediger, daughter of a czarist general. Dimitri Shalikashvili, who had gone into exile from his native Georgia following communist victory in the Russian Civil War, was serving as a contract (foreign national) officer in the Polish army when World War II began. Demobilized after Poland's surrender to Germany, Dimitri Shalikashvili joined the Georgian Legion in 1942, a military unit composed of Georgian expatriates who believed they could free their homeland from communist oppression by aligning themselves with Germany. The Georgian Legion was later placed under the direct command of the Waffen SS, an elite branch of the German armed forces that included Germans as well as foreign troops hostile to Soviet communism.

Until 1944 the Shalikashvili family lived in relative comfort given Poland's status as a defeated and occupied nation. During the uprising of Warsaw underground forces, however, fighting raged around the apartment building where the family was living, and for weeks Maria

Shalikashvili and her children took refuge in the basement. Once the resistance was suppressed, the Shalikashvilis were among many civilians evacuated to transit camps along the border between Poland and Germany. To evade the advancing Red Army, the family settled in Pappenheim, a village in Bavaria where Maria Shalikashvili had wealthy relatives who provided them with a residence and a livelihood. In 1952 the Shalikashvilis emigrated to Peoria, Illinois, where a distant relative resided.

John Shalikashvili, who was fluent in Polish, German, and Russian, enrolled as a junior in Central High School in Peoria. He improved his English, the story goes, by watching John Wayne films. In 1958 he graduated from Bradley University with a degree in mechanical engineering. Drafted into the army, Shalikashvili was accepted in Officer Candidate School (OCS) at Fort Sill, Oklahoma, after completing his training. He was commissioned a second lieutenant in 1959 and assigned to a mortar battery in Alaska. Deciding to make a career in the army, Shalikashvili served as an instructor (1961-1963) and staff officer (1963-1964) at the Army Air Defense School and Center in Fort Bliss, Texas, and then joined the 32nd Army Air Defense Command in Germany (1965-1967). He had been promoted to captain in 1963 and became a major in 1967. In 1966 he married Joan E. Zimpelman; the couple had one son.

Service at Home and Abroad

In January 1968 he began an 18-month assignment as senior advisor in the Trieu Phong district, Advisory Team 19, with the United States Military Assistance Command in Vietnam. Shalikashvili's responsibilities included training local militia and accompanying Vietnamese militia units into combat as well as working with officials on rice production and other civilian economic and political tasks. In the decade following his service in Vietnam, Shalikashvili studied at both the Naval War College (1969-1970) and the Army War College (1977-1978) as well as at George Washington University, which awarded him a Master's degree in international relations (1970). He had staff assignments overseas in South Korea (1971-1972) and Italy (1978-1979) and twice served at Fort Lewis, Washington, the second time as commander of the 1st Battalion, 84th Field Artillery (1975-1977). He was promoted to lieutenant colonel in 1974 and to colonel five years later.

Between 1979 and 1981 Shalikashvili was in Germany with the 1st Armored Division. He was then transferred to Washington, D.C., where he served as chief of the politico-military division and then as deputy director of the Strategy, Plans and Policy Directorate. In 1983 he was promoted to brigadier general and to major general in 1986. By this time Shalikashvili, who was regarded as both a soldier's general and a skilled planner, was established as a so-called "fast-burner," someone who was on a career path that could well lead to high command. From 1984 to 1986 he again served in Germany as assistant commander of the 1st Armored Division, after which he had duty in the Pentagon as the army's director of strategy, plans, and policy (1986-1987). Shalikashvili next commanded the 9th Infantry Division before returning to Germany in 1989 as deputy commander-in-chief, United States Army, Europe.

Shalikashvili was in Germany when the Persian Gulf War began. He did not participate in the war. In its aftermath, however, Iraqi forces had driven the substantial Kurdish minority within Iraq from their home area in the north into harsh mountainous terrain along the borders between Iraq, Iran, and Turkey. President George Bush gained approval to organize an international relief expedition to serve in what was identified as Operation Provide Comfort. Military contingents as well as medical personnel from the United States and a dozen other countries began entering the area in April 1991. Shalikashvili, a lieutenant general since 1989, was named commander. The operation, which had as its stated goals the provision of humanitarian aid and the establishment of a safe haven for the Kurds in northern Iraq, lasted until July and was perceived as a success. Soon it was being analyzed by defense intellectuals as a model for the type of quasi-military scenario that appeared likely to occur in any of several troubled areas. That is, at a time when the possibility of a land confrontation between North Atlantic Treaty Organization (NATO) forces and the former Soviet army had receded, military operations were apt to be modest in scale and unconventional in nature, combining both peacemaking and peacekeeping missions as well as the distribution of humanitarian aid. The successful commander would need diplomatic skills as well as the intellectual flexibility to judge when, where, and how much force to apply.

From Europe to the Pentagon

With the conclusion of his service in the Middle East, Shalikashvili completed his assignment in Europe, and in August 1991, reported to the Pentagon as assistant to General Colin Powell, chairman of the Joint Chiefs of Staff (JCS). The following June he became Supreme Allied Commander, Europe (SACEUR). As head of NATO forces, Shalikashvili, now a full (four-star) general, had to provide leadership in evaluating the alliance's mission as well as prepare it for possible operations in such places as Bosnia, where problems existed that were even more daunting than those seen in northern Iraq.

In August 1993 Shalikashvili, known to many as General Shali, was chosen to become chairman of the JCS by President Bill Clinton. Although it was unusual for one army general to replace another in this position that would normally have been rotated to a navy or air force officer, the unassuming Shalikashvili, seemed to have unsurpassed qualifications to deal with post-Cold War problems in places like Somalia and Bosnia.

"If Clinton is going to send Americans in harm's way, he needs a chairman who is seen as offering independent operational judgments. He chose the right man," observed a Brookings Institution analyst at the time of Shalikashvili's nomination. Secretary of Defense Les Aspin, who was believed to have been General Shali's foremost advocate in the Clinton administration, was impressed not only by the general's service record but by his tact and astuteness in dealing with leaders of many nationalities. He had already developed expertise in arms control issues during an earlier tour at the Pentagon. Taking office at a time of realignment in international affairs and budget cutbacks at home, Shalikashvili faced formidable challenges. Not least was the task of succeeding Colin Powell, arguably the nation's most popular military leader since Dwight Eisenhower nearly half a century earlier.

As Chairman of the Joint Chiefs, Shalikashvili oversaw the risky invasion of Haiti which reinstated the elected President Jean-Bertrand Aristide and then transferred peacekeeping duties to a U.N. force. Confronted with the war in Bosnia, he argued for military representatives during the Dayton Peace Accords, for clear mission goals, objectives, and prohibitions for the U.S. force sent to Bosnia, and for a straightforward chain of command, robust rules of engagement, and sufficient force to get the job done. He continued the simultaneous downsizing and technological upgrading of U.S. military forces. Since 1989, active all-volunteer forces were reduced by 700,000 persons, nearly 1/3 of active forces.

He stood as a strong advocate for technological upgrading of the armed forces; for maintaining strong alliances throughout the world and enlargement of NATO; for engagement with great powers, particularly with China; for maintaining military strength commensurate with U.S. worldwide interests and obligations well into the future. He developed Joint Vision 2010, a unified conceptual template whereby all the services would plan development, training, and re-equipment, and strategic planning jointly.

In late January, 1997, Shalikashvili announced his plans to retire from his position in keeping with the tradition of Chairmen of the Joint Chiefs serving two two-year terms.

Further Reading

No biography of General Shalikashvili has yet been published. Information about the general and his background is sparse and must be gleaned from many sources. His father, Dimitri, prepared an account (in Russian) of the family's adventures in the turmoil of Europe. It is available at the Hoover Institution in Stanford, California. Lieutenant Colonel John P. Cavanaugh, *Operation Provide Comfort: A Model for Future NATO Operations* (School of Advanced Military Studies, United States Army Command and General Staff College, Fort Leavenworth, Kansas, 1992) provides a valuable assessment of the assignment that brought Shalikashvili to prominence.

Much of the information that has appeared on General Shalikashvili in newspapers is based on standard Pentagon press releases. But conspicuous for their thoroughness and analysis are articles by William Drodziak in the *New York Times,* March 28, 1993; Melissa Healy in the *Los Angeles Times,* May 28, 1993; Barton Gellman in *The Washington Post,* August 12, 1993; Michael R. Gordon and also by Tim Weiner in the *New York Times,* August 12, 1993; and John Lancaster in *The Washington Post,* September 21, 1993. Bruce B. Auster, "Western Leader from the East," *U.S. News & World Report* (November 9, 1992), is of interest. Also relevant are Fred Barnes, "Shali, Shan't He," *New Republic* (September 13, 1993) and two articles in *Congressional Quarterly Weekly Report:* Pat Towell with Matthew Phillips, "Shalikashvili Wins Praise as Joint Chiefs Nominee" (August 14, 1993), and Gregory J. Bowens, "Senators Question Shalikashvili, Seek Assurance on NATO Post" (September 25, 1993). His November 7, 1996 speech to the Council of Foreign Relations, "The United States Armed Forces: A Prospectus," *Vital Speeches* (January 1, 1997), outlines his own assessment of many of his undertakings and states his goals and principles. □

Yitzchak Shamir

Yitzak Shamir (born 1914) was prime minister of Israel (1983-84, 1987-88), leader of the Likud Party and vice premier and minister of foreign affairs in the National Unity government (1984-86).

Yitzak Shamir (Yizernitsky) was born in 1914 in eastern Poland. While a student at the Hebrew "gymnasium" in Bialystok he was also involved with the Revisionist Zionist movement known as Brit Trumpeldor, or Betar. In 1935 instead of pursuing law studies in Warsaw he immigrated to Palestine, where he worked as a construction worker and accountant in addition to studying at the Hebrew University. During the next decade Shamir was involved with the Jewish underground movement as a member of the more militant and nationalist groups pledged to resisting the British mandate authorities as well as retaliating against acts of Arab violence directed at the Jewish community.

Unlike most of the Jewish underground, which chose to fight alongside of the British during World War II, Shamir remained firmly opposed to Britain's presence in Palestine. In 1940 he left the Irgun organization and helped to form the Lehi (Lohamei Eretz Yisrael), or Fighters for the Freedom of Israel, also known as the "Stern Gang" because of its commander, Avraham Stern. When Stern was captured and killed by the British, Shamir was a member of the triumvirate which took charge of Lehi in 1942, until Menachem Begin assumed command in 1943.

As Lehi chief of operations, Shamir was involved in a number of underground attacks and daring exploits. After the famous bombing incident at the King David Hotel, the British command center in Jerusalem, he was captured and deported to a prison camp in Eritrea in 1946, but escaped in 1947 to Djibouti, where he was detained by the French authorities. Only at the end of May 1948 was Shamir able to make his way back to what by then had become the independent state of Israel.

The next 20 years are almost a blank in the biography of Yitzak Shamir. The record suggests that for much of the period he operated inconspicuously deep within the structure of the Israeli secret intelligence service, the Mossad. Toward the end of the 1960s he left this service to manage several businesses in the private sector and to campaign on behalf of Soviet Jewry.

Shamir's career entered a new, more public phase in 1970, when he joined the opposition Herut Party headed by his former commander, Begin. In the 1973 elections he became a member of the Knesset, Israel's parliament. Then, following the Herut-led Likud bloc's dramatic 1977 electoral victory, Shamir was elected speaker of the Knesset. In this position he chaired the historic session on November 20, 1977, when Egypt's president launched his peace initiative by coming to address the Knesset. However, at a crucial moment in the peace process Shamir chose to abstain on the key vote which endorsed the 1978 Camp David accords. Feeling that Prime Minister Begin had made excessive concessions to Egypt by returning all of the Sinai Peninsula, Shamir showed consistency when he also abstained from approving the final Israel-Egypt Treaty in March 1979. Still, in later years he pledged to uphold the agreement, while giving it a hard-line interpretation.

In October 1979, following the resignation of Moshe Dayan as minister of foreign affairs, Begin turned to Shamir in seeking a successor. Despite his lack of experience in international diplomacy, Shamir applied himself to the post and with time impressed outside observers and foreign statesmen as hard-working, receptive, and devoted. In the early 1980s he was active in pursuing closer ties with France, in exploring a dialogue with the Soviets and their Eastern European allies, in renewing relations with African states, and in developing economic trade in Latin America. However, whether due to his loyalty to Begin or to other reasons, Shamir came in for indirect criticism by the Kahan Commission set up to inquire into aspects of the 1982 Lebanese intervention; while cleared of complicity in the specific Sabra and Shatilla camp massacres, he was faulted in the final report with having ignored early rumors.

On August 28, 1983, Premier Begin made a surprise announcement that, due to personal reasons, he was resigning, having led the Herut in opposition and in power for over 35 years. In an effort at filling this void, a hastily-convened Herut Party on September 2 selected Shamir as its leader. In the coming five weeks of arduous inter-party negotiations Shamir finally succeeded in putting together a viable coalition with 64 Knesset votes, giving it a four vote majority. The coalition, however, lasted less than a year. In the 1984 national elections Shamir headed the Likud campaign. When the results were tabulated, Likud gained 41 Knesset seats as against 44 for the Labour/Alignment, giving neither of the two main parties a clear majority. The political stalemate was resolved only through a unique arrangement based on the principle of rotation. By the terms of the agreement, Labour's head, Shimon Peres, served as prime minister for the initial two years, with Shamir as vice premier and minister of foreign affairs, after which the two men switched positions.

Despite skepticism on the part of the experts, this arrangement held together; while not exactly a cordial relationship, Peres and Shamir were sufficiently motivated by a sense of national responsibility to preserve good working relations. Under the National Unity government, and while waiting for the rotation to take place, Yitzak Shamir in the years 1984-86 was fully preoccupied with two principal tasks: maintaining leadership of his fractious Herut-Likud political movement in the post-Begin era, and improving

Israel's international diplomatic position in the post-Lebanon period.

Shamir took a hard line against the Palestinian uprisings that began on the West Bank and in Gaza in late 1987. He remained prime minister, as head of a Likud-Labor coalition, following the elections of November 1988.

After the government lost a vote of confidence in March 1990, Shamir put together a coalition of Likud and several right-wing and religious parties. He agreed to participate in the comprehensive Middle East peace talks that began in 1991, but his ardent support for new Jewish settlements on the West Bank hampered negotiations with the Palestinians and strained relations with the United States. When Likud lost the parliamentary elections of June 1992, Yitzhak Rabin succeeded Shamir as prime minister. In March 1993 Benjamin Netanyahu succeeded him as head of Likud.

On July 12, 1992, Shamir bid farewell as Prime Minister. In a televised speech he gave to his Cabinet, he claimed advances in employment, in securing Israel against foreign attacks and in opening relations with a host of foreign countries during his last two years in power. Shamir concluded: "I seriously doubt if any past government in Israel has had such achievements."

The uncompromising comments from Shamir appeared to be aimed at easing the shock of the election defeat. Citizens reduced Likud's share of the vote to less than 30 percent. Voters apparently did not agree with Shamir that a government which had left the country in a recession, had been reluctant to offer a long-term solution to the Palestinian conflict, had quarreled with Washington, and had botched the chore of welcoming tens of thousands of Russian immigrants could be ranked among Israel's greatest.

Further Reading

There is no published biography of Shamir to date. Background information can be found in Robert Freedman, editor, *Israel in the Begin Era* (1982) and in Bernard Reich, *Israel: Land of Tradition and Conflict* (1985). Updated information gathered from the Los Angeles Times "Shamir Says Farewell," July 13, 1992; Britannica Online, *The Cambridge Biographical Encyclopedia*. □

Shammai

Shammai (active 1st century B.C.), called Hazaken, or Elder, was a Jewish sage. He founded the Bet Shammai, the "School of Shammai," which was the persistent opponent of the rival Bet Hillel, the "School of Hillel."

Shammai was probably a little older than Hillel (ca. 60 B.C.-ca. A.D. 10). The two sages formed the last of the five Zuggot, or Pairs, who transmitted the Unwritten or Oral Tradition (as distinguished from the Written or Scriptural) to successive generations over a period of about 2 centuries (ca. 175 B.C.-A.D. 10). Shammai was the *Av Bet Din,* the "Father," or Senior Judge, of the Court of the Great Sanhedrin, and Hillel was its *Nasi,* or President. Shammai, a conservative, belonged to the upper classes and followed strictly the older, rigid, Oral Tradition. Hillel, a liberal, attempted to broaden the tradition by means of interpretation of the biblical text. In order to give the law greater flexibility he sought out its intent.

Shammai's rigorous adherence to literal rather than liberal truth is illustrated by the opinion of his school that even a bride is to be lauded only on what she actually is, in accordance with the biblical principle "Keep thyself far from falsehood" (Exodus 23:7). But the Hillelites took a far more generous attitude and held that "every bride may be described as comely and graceful." The Shammaites also supported the view that a husband may divorce his wife only for infidelity, while Hillel maintained that a husband could do so for any reason.

The rivalry of the schools of Shammai and Hillel, which began in the first pre-Christian century, continued through the period of Roman rule and the stormy Judean revolt. At that time, it was natural that non-Jews would be suspect and the loyalty of proselytes would be questioned. Shammai insisted on a stringent policy toward proselytes, to discourage their admission to the Jewish fold. He rebuffed a prospective convert who was ready to accept Judaism provided he could abide only by the Written (Scriptural) Law, but Hillel patiently explained to him the importance of the Oral Law. Shammai also harshly rebuked a proselyte who undertook to become a Jew if he would be made a priest, but Hillel had the proselyte understand that the priesthood was limited only to the descendants of Aaron. Pagan proselytes consequently declared "that the irritability of Shammai could drive one from the world, while the tolerance of Hillel brought them under the wings of the *Shechinah* ("Divine Presence"). Despite Shammai's reputation for severity, his favorite maxim was: "Make the study of Torah thy chief occupation; say little and do much, and receive all men with a cheerful countenance" (Abot 1:15).

The Shammaites evidently prevailed in their viewpoint until the fall of the Jewish state in A.D. 70, but their school hardly survived the disaster. Their debates with the Hillelites added vital content to Judaism.

Further Reading

A good study of Shammai and his school is in Solomon Zeitlin, *The Rise and Fall of the Judaean State,* vol. 2 (1967). Nahum N. Glatzer, *Hillel the Elder* (1956), and Louis Finkelstein, *The Pharisees* (2 vols., 1938; 3d ed., 1962), make frequent reference to Shammai and the Shammaites. Judah Goldin's "The Period of the Talmud" in Louis Finkelstein, ed., *The Jews* (2 vols., 1949; 3d ed. 1960), sketches the development of the Halakah (Jewish law). □

Shang Yang

Shang Yang (ca. 390-338 B.C.) was a Chinese statesman and political philosopher. He was one of the

founders of Chinese Legalism and organized the rise to power of the Ch'in dynasty.

The real name of Shang Yang was Kung-sun Yang; he was also known as Wei Yang. He was born in Wei, a state in north-central China. His mother was a concubine of a member of the Wei royal family. In his youth he specialized in criminal law and served as tutor to the Wei princes. He was a favorite of the Wei prime minister, who recommended to the Wei ruler that Shang Yang succeed to the ministry upon his death. This request was denied, and Shang Yang, feeling that he was not appreciated in Wei, journeyed to the western state of Ch'in, which had been seeking men who could offer practical advice on state affairs.

Becoming the confidant of Duke Hsiao, who was just then embarking on a program of military expansion and revitalization of the state, Shang Yang presented him with a comprehensive plan for the accomplishment of these ends. He proposed a complete reform of the political, social, and economic structure of the state. He advocated strengthening the judicial system and the imposition of severe punishments for crimes of all kinds.

There was to be a group sharing of guilt and punishment, and people were required to inform on lawbreakers. Those who failed to denounce a criminal were cut in two. Rank and position would be given only to those who distinguished themselves in military affairs. Membership in the Ch'in royal clan was denied to nobles who achieved no military success.

Central to Shang Yang's economic theory was an overwhelming emphasis on agriculture and a rejection of "nonessential" activities such as commerce and manufacturing. He proposed that anyone engaging in secondary professions be sold as slaves. His most famous economic reform was the abolition of the idealized system of landholding known as the "well-field system," in which a section of land was divided into nine portions, tilled by eight families in common, with the produce from the ninth portion reserved for the overlord.

Shang Yang reportedly substituted for this system individual ownership of property and had new land brought under cultivation. He also introduced a poll tax and a produce tax. Actually, the well-field system may well have been abolished already, and Shang Yang may not have had anything to do with originating this reform.

Given a high military post, Shang Yang led an expedition against his home state of Wei, which he conquered in 350 B.C. He supervised the building of a new capital at Hsien-Yang. He applied his laws so strictly and impartially that even the crown prince was punished on several occasions, even having his nose sliced off. In 341 Shang Yang led another expedition against Wei and forced it to cede to Ch'in all of the land west of the Yellow River. For his services, Shang Yang was rewarded with a fief of 15 cities in Shang (modern Shensi), from which his names Lord Shang and Shang Yang are derived.

Duke Hsiao died in 338, and his successor was the crown prince whom Shang Yang had punished earlier. Shang Yang was then charged with plotting rebellion and forced to flee. One account states that he tried to take refuge in an inn but was refused entrance because the law of Lord Shang prohibited the lodging of fugitives! He tried to return to Wei, but he was sent back to Ch'in. Shang Yang was finally killed making a stand at his fief in Shang. His body was pulled apart by chariots and his whole family executed.

Shang Yang is credited with the authorship of the *Book of Lord Shang* (*Shang-Chün shu*), a collection of economic, legal, and political treatises, many of which are elaborations of the program he developed in Ch'in. It is doubtful that this book actually comes from his hand, nor is it the work of a single author. Because of its emphasis on law, this work is considered one of the major ancient Chinese works on Legalist philosophy.

Further Reading

The best work on Shang Yang is J.J.L. Duyvendak, *The Book of Lord Shang* (1928). Some information on Shang Yang appears in Cho-yun Hsu, *Ancient China in Transition: An Analysis of Social Mobility, 722-222 B.C.* (1965), and Joseph R. Levenson and Franz Schurman, *China: An Interpretative History—From the Beginnings to the Fall of Han* (1969). For general background see Edwin O. Reischauer and John K. Fairbank, *A History of East Asian Civilization,* vol. 1: *East Asia: The Great Tradition* (1958). □

Shankara

Shankara (ca. 788-820) was an Indian philosopher and reformer. He founded the advaita, or nondual, school of vedanta philosophy.

Shankara, also called Shankaracharya, "Master Shankara," was born of Brahman parentage in southern India. His intellectual powers were soon evident, and he mastered a wide range of religious and philosophical materials. His major goal was to synthesize the immensely diverse spectrum of Hindu philosophical and theistic symbolism into a single coherent system. He was quite orthodox in his commitment to the *Veda*—the most ancient body of Hindu religious literature; but he tried to harmonize its many paradoxical and often contradictory teachings by centering on the last Vedic section, the *Upanishads* ("esoteric" teachings, also called the *Vedanta,*" end of the *Veda*").

Shankara ascribed the founding of the Vedanta school to the sage Badarayana (ca. 400 B.C.), whose writings formed the basis for some of shankara's most important treatises. But despite his claim that he was only expounding the *Vedanta,* Shankara was unquestionably one of the most creative intellects in Indian history. he travelled widely, founding numerous monastic centers and elaborating his philosophy. Though his life was short, he was an untiring worker and a brilliant dialectician whose lasting prestige was fully established by the time of his death. The doctrine which he espoused became the most influential of all Hindu philosophies, providing the basis for theological innovations, cultic integration, and reform.

The basic elements of Shankara's philosophy are derived from selected aspects of the *Upanishads.* Though the texts are very diverse, they are—in shankara's view—dominated by a teaching which asserts that the true self (*atman,* "soul") of every individual has a qualitative and essential relationship to an overarching universal Soul (*Atman*) which in its ultimate sacred form is called Brahman: "Brahman exists eternal, pure, enlightened, free, omniscient, and all powerful." It is the source and end of all phenomena.

This metaphysic has two particularly important aspects: since only Brahman is ultimately real and eternal, all particular worldly entities are regarded as illusory and transient; but since these transient forms are also manifestations of Brahman, "illusion" itself has a positive ontological status. The technical term for illusion is *maya;* but it also signifies the *power* of illusion. Shankara's doctrine is therefore called *advaita*—nonduality—because it strives to ascribe all reality to a single dynamic, unitary source.

Through the sensual perceptions of the everyday world, man apprehends only the illusory and deceptive appearances of the ultimate reality. This conditioned and finite knowledge is, in the ultimate sense, ignorance (*avidya,* "nonknowledge"), because it is not attuned to that which transcends and yet incorporates all space-time phenomena. And this ignorance is exacerbated by the confusion of the transcendental spirit with empirical forms—an error which is the "source of all evil."

However, within the lower and provisional framework of existence, certain essential forms have a permanent sanctity: the sacred scriptures, the cults and forms of traditional worship, the law of karmic retribution, and the caste system itself. These are essential "qualities" (*gunas*) of the order of the universe. Therefore, while it is true that Brahman as absolute existence and ultimate truth transcends these forms and is "without qualities" (*nirguna*), in its diverse manifestations it also possesses the secondary qualities of a personalized god, Hindu institutions, law, and ethics: Brahman is the source of "scripture and all knowledge, and is responsible for the distinctions into gods, animals, humans, classes, the stages of life."

Adherence to these secondary forms through worship, self-discipline, and appropriate demeanor prepares the religiously perceptive individual for the higher knowledge of the transcendent Brahman. In this purified form, knowledge is the source of a final and transforming intuition of the absolute unity of the individual soul with Brahman—an experience of liberation and release from the snares of worldly delusion and transmigration "the *Upanishads* aim to eliminate delusion by the attainment of the knowledge of the unity of the self [with Brahman]." This mystical philosophy would seem to undercut all other forms of traditional Hinduism, since worldly distinctions are illusory; but they are also regarded as aspects of the divine self-manifestation. So Shankara rigorously upholds the integrity of Hindu social institutions and the *Veda,* interpreted through the ultimate revelation contained in the *Upanishads.*

There is much in Shankara's mystical teaching which suggests the influence of Buddhist philosophy, and he was accused of being a crypto-Buddhist during his own lifetime. But his successful philosophical synthesis was a factor in precipitating the final decline of Buddhism in India. In this way Shankara did much to assure the triumph of Hinduism and its institutions. In addition to his philosophical innovations, he was also an ardent exponent of the devotional poems and prayers which reflect the immense range of his religious sensibilities.

Further Reading

Background on Shankara is in Surendra Dasgupta, *A History of Indian Philosophy,* 5 vols. (1922-1955), and Sarvepalli Radhakrishnan and Charles Moore, eds., *A Sourcebook in Indian Philosophy* (1957). Indian sources include V. Raghavan, trans., *Prayers, Praises and Psalms* (Madras, 1938); Nalinimohan Mukherji, *A Study of Shankara* (Calcutta, 1942); and Ram P. Singh, *The Vedanta of Sankara: The Metaphysics of Value* (Jaipur, 1949). For general background consult A. L. Bashman, *The Wonder That Was India* (1937; rev. ed. 1963). □

Albert Shanker

Over four decades, Albert Shanker (born 1928) rose from public school mathematics teacher to national educational statesman. Shanker's militant leadership of New York's United Federation of Teachers in the 1960s brought him personal notoriety and won for teachers substantial improvements in compensation, working conditions, and bargaining power. President of the 700,000-member American Federation of Teachers from 1974 into the 1990s, Shanker was an effective advocate of sweeping national educational reform.

Born September 24, 1928, Albert Shanker grew up in a working-class Jewish family in the borough of Queens in New York City. His parents, Mamie and Morris Shanker, were emigrants from Poland. Both were union members; his father a union newspaper deliveryman, and his mother a sewing machine operator and member of the Amalgamated Clothing Workers Union. The Shanker family's deeply held political views were staunchly pro-union, following the socialism of Norman Thomas and including ardent support of Franklin Roosevelt and the New Deal.

Early on, Shanker exhibited the voracious thirst for information, the love of philosophy, and the dedication to human rights causes that characterized his life's work. As a boy he read several newspapers daily, and by the time he was a teen, he was avidly reading the humanitarian philoso-

phy of Thomas Hook. He idolized Franklin D. Roosevelt, Clarence Darrow, and Bayard Rustin, the civil rights leader.

Shanker's social and political activism began during his undergraduate years at the University of Illinois in Urbana-Champagne. Shanker picketed segregated movie theaters and restaurants and was a member of the Young People's Socialist League and chair of the Socialist Study Club. Shanker majored in philosophy and graduated with honors. Shanker then took graduate courses in philosophy and mathematics at Columbia University, receiving an M.A. degree and completing the coursework, but not the dissertation, required for a Ph.D. in philosophy.

Classroom Work to Union Organizer

Shanker's graduate work ended in 1952, when he took a one-year leave of absence from his graduate program and accepted a temporary position teaching mathematics at an East Harlem School. He taught mathematics in New York City public schools from 1952 to 1959, making $42 a week in take-home pay and experiencing firsthand the poor treatment of teachers, the ineffectiveness of traditional teaching methods, and the conflict and frustration that dominated inner-city classrooms. During this time he joined the New York Teachers Guild and devoted increasing time and energy to union work.

Shanker became a full-time union organizer for New York City's United Federation of Teachers (Local No. 2 of the American Federation of Teachers) in 1959. His ascent within the union was swift. By 1964 he was president, a position he held until 1985. During the 1960s, Shanker received national attention and considerable criticism for his aggressive union leadership and skillful negotiation of pay increases for New York City teachers. In 1967, and again in 1968, he served jail sentences for leading illegal teachers' strikes. The 1968 strike closed down almost all New York City schools for 36 days. The stimulus for the strike was teacher transfers out of ghetto schools during school decentralization experiments. The strike exacerbated racial tensions in ghetto schools, although the real issue was protecting teachers' rights from excessive local control.

During the 1960s Shanker was also active in the civil rights movement. He was a charter member of the Congress of Racial Equality (CORE). He participated in several major civil rights marches and the sit-ins in Selma and Montgomery. He led a delegation of teachers to protest Martin Luther King's murder. All of this notwithstanding, Shanker's positions on minority hiring quotas and busing in the early 1970s were criticized by some Black leaders. Shanker promoted the development of magnet schools rather than busing to achieve racial balance. He opposed quota hiring of minority teachers, believing such quotas to be essentially discriminatory, and instead supported educational programs within his union to qualify Blacks and other minorities for teaching positions.

As a result of his controversial views and his militant union leadership, Shanker was considered something of a loose cannon through the 1960s and early 1970s. This image was captured by Woody Allen's 1973 movie *Sleeper,* in which the main character wakes up in the year 2173 and is told that the United States had been destroyed because one hundred years ago a man called Albert Shanker got hold of a nuclear warhead."

Union President and Reformer

Beginning in the early 1970s and with his 1974 election as president of the American Federation of Teachers (AFT), Shanker's image mellowed, and he became a nationally respected proponent of educational reform. This change was attributed in part to Shanker's paid weekly column in the *New York Times,* Where We Stand." This AFT-sponsored commentary on educational issues ran in the *New York Times* and 60 other papers nationwide beginning in 1970. In this column, Shanker anticipated, analyzed, and advocated major changes in education. Through this forum and his role as national president of the American Federation of Teachers, Shanker's focus broadened from improving teachers' working conditions to improving the performance of the educational system as a whole through sweeping restructuring and reform. In Shanker's view, essential elements of such reform are increased teacher competence, responsibility, and accountability: elements that are a significant departure from traditional union views.

Foremost among the changes Shanker promoted and facilitated in the 1980s were the creation of a national examination for beginning teachers, the utilization of a team approach to school organization and management, and pedagogy that emphasized cooperative learning and highly participative instruction rather than classrooms dominated by teacher talk. Shanker was a strong advocate of increased use of computer technology, not only to provide individualized instruction for students, but also to create a national database and communication network for the dissemination of the best available instructional materials and techniques.

Shanker's educational reform efforts largely paralleled the changes occurring in American industry as a result of quality and productivity problems. Shanker frequently cited the relatively poor academic performance of American students as evidence of the necessity for change in our educational system. At the heart of Shanker's reform recommendations was the exploration of organizational structures and management systems that empower teachers to generate improvements and controls, as well as the provision of a broad range of incentives to motivate teachers, schools, and school systems to make the needed improvements.

Shanker's influence towards these ends was considerable and extended far beyond the 700,000-member American Federation of Teachers. His leadership of the American Federation of Teachers and his successful influence on national opinion regarding educational issues were credited with pushing the two million-member National Education Association (NEA) from resistance to active support of school reform in the 1980s, just as his success with collective bargaining in the 1960s is thought to have stimulated NEA affiliates to negotiate contracts and call strikes. In 1985 Shanker's initiative sparked the formation of the National Board for Professional Teaching Standards, which in the early 1990s was working toward the implementation of a national examination system for beginning teachers.

Shanker's influence extended to corporate and government leadership as well. Beginning in the mid-1980s he was a member of the prestigious Committee for Economic Development, an alliance of national corporate leaders that was working to improve schools. He served on national committees such as, the Carnegie Forum on Education and the Economy and on President Bush's Educational Policy Advisory Committee. Shanker's long held views and ideas on national standards were the foundation for educational reforms outlined by President William Clinton during the State of the Union Address in 1997. After the address, Clinton called Shanker and said to him we should have listened to your sooner.'' Sara Mosle described Shanker as the most important American educator in half a century.''

Further Reading

The best source on Shanker's views and work in education is his Sunday *New York Times* column, Where We Stand,'' starting in 1970. Sara Mosle, *The New Republic* (March 17, 1997), provides information on his life, contributions to education and union activity. □

Claude Elwood Shannon

The American mathematician Claude Elwood Shannon (born 1916) was the first to apply symbolic logic to the design of switching circuits, and his work on the mathematics of communication is central to modern information theory.

Claude Shannon was born on April 30, 1916, in Gaylord, Michigan. After graduating from the University of Michigan in 1936, he went to the Massachusetts Institute of Technology. There he made a mathematical discovery of considerable potential in the field of technology, and one which pointed the direction of his subsequent career. While studying the design of switching circuits, he saw how to apply symbolic logic to establish an economy of design. By employing the language of logic in plotting the alternative flow paths of the electric current through a switching series, redundant controls could be discovered and eliminated.

On completion of his doctorate in 1940, Shannon joined Bell Telephone Laboratories. He was interested in the problem of ascertaining the efficiency of various electrical devices for the transmission of information, with a view to the selection of the most efficient one—and the increase of its efficiency. Involved in this problem is that of communication in general, and in applying mathematics to this problem, Shannon, following H. Nyquist and R. V. L. Hartley, laid the foundations of information theory.

In a communication system, a source information selects a message which is transformed into a signal by a transmitter, which in turn directs the signal along a channel to a receiver. The receiver converts the signal back into a message which is then available at its destination. In any system, and especially a mechanized one, there is a tendency for distortions, errors, and redundant signals to affect the accuracy of the signal, and these may all be classed as noise.'' The problems associated with the system may be concerned with the amount of information; the capacity of transmitter, channel, and receiver; the encoding process; and noise. Information'' in this sense is a measure of the freedom of choice available when selecting a message, and the theory of probability involved in estimating the freedom of choice. The capacity of the transmitter and of the channel may be related in a theorem by means of which the maximum transmission rate possible may be calculated. And, further, by introducing the noise factor it is possible to calculate under what conditions transmissions low in error may be achieved.

Shannon's work on information systems not only had important implications in the whole theory of communications but was of considerable value in the development of computers. His demonstration of the central importance of a knowledge of symbolic logic as basic to understanding of circuit design has ensured a level of efficiency essential to the increasingly complex computer systems. He remained as a consultant with Bell Laboratories until 1972. Shannon was also a Donner Professor of Science from 1958-78, becoming Professor Emeritus in 1978 (he was also a visiting fellow at All Souls College in Oxford, England that year). Shannon was awarded the Kyoto Prize in 1985.

Further Reading

Some information on Shannon appears in *Mathematics in the Modern World: Readings from Scientific American,* with an introduction by Morris Kline (1968). The importance of his work in the computer age is also highlighted in *On the Shoulders of Giants: From Boole to Shannon to Taube* (June, 1993) in *Information Technology and Library.* □

Ralph Shapey

Beginning in the early 1950s, the American composer, conductor, and teacher Ralph Shapey (born 1921) devoted himself to the cause of new music. His own powerful and complex compositions reflect a personal vision uncompromised by rapidly changing trends.

Ralph Shapey was born on March 12, 1921, Philadelphia, Pennsylvania. At age seven he began studying the violin, which he continued later under Emmanuel Zeitlin. He rose through the ranks of the Philadelphia National Youth Symphony Orchestra, first as a playing member, then as youth conductor, and finally as assistant conductor (1938-47). The later years also included study with his principal composition teacher, Stefan Wolpe.

After three years in the army he moved to New York City in 1951. Here, through the early 1960s, Shapey established himself by composing, conducting, and teaching both privately and at the Third Street Music Settlement. His conducting abilities, especially in new and difficult works, led to other assignments with orchestras and chamber groups in Buffalo, New York; London, Ontario, Canada; New York City; and Philadelphia. From 1963 to 1964 he taught at the University of Pennsylvania, and in 1964 he accepted a post at the University of Chicago, where he founded the Contemporary Chamber Players. Maintaining this post, later as professor of music, Shapey achieved considerable success both with his own compositions and with the ensemble, whose performances have become the major impetus for new music in the Midwest.

"The Concept of It Is, Rather than the Traditional It Becomes"

Rugged independence and raw emotional power—perhaps reminiscent of the American composer Carl Ruggles—characterize his music. It acquires its boldness and immediacy through the initial presentation of ideas in their completely developed form, which Shapey calls the concept of 'it is', rather than the traditional 'it becomes'." While his works are atonal, not all of them adhere strictly to 12-tone principles, and none is as minutely controlled as the compositions of Milton Babbitt and other contemporaries. Shapey achieves order through diminutions of the musical image, and form often results from the initial image exploding into its own various states of being, juxtaposed against itself in ever new focuses." To aid the definition of these juxtaposed images or mosaics, Shapey very often divides his ensemble, both in terms of timbre and in actual placement on the stage. Larger ensembles may be broken into as many as seven distinct groups, as in *Ontogeny* for orchestra (1958).

In other respects Shapey's music closely follows the Schoenberg tradition. Except for a few compositions, such as *Songs of Ecstasy* for soprano, piano, percussion and electronic tape (1967), he uses traditional instruments sounded in their normal manner. Notation, too, is for the most part traditional. He has been called an Abstract Expressionist, no doubt after the painters with whom he associated in New York, but this label is misleading in that music is inherently an abstract art and Shapey's is certainly no more so than other Expressionists such as Schoenberg. Aleatoricism plays only a small part in Shapey's compositions, usually in the form of improvisation between worked out sections, as in the second movement of *Rituals* for orchestra (1959), or in one group playing material similar to another's, but at a different or unfixed tempo, as in *Dimensions* for soprano and 23 instruments (1960).

"A Protest Against All the Rottenness in the Musical World"

In addition to his teaching duties at the University of Chicago, Shapey was active as an educator in composing didactic pieces. In the late 1960s he contributed music to the University of Illinois String Research Project in an effort to fill the gap in contemporary music that is suitable for the early stages of string instruction.

In 1969 Shapey requested a moratorium on the performance of his works as a protest against all the rottenness in the musical world and in the world in general." A performance of his oratorio, *Praise,* for bass-baritone, double chorus, and ensemble (1971) in 1976, marked his return before an ever-increasing public.

Other important compositions by Ralph Shapey include the *Violin Concerto* (1959); *Evocation* for violin with piano and percussion (1959); *Incantations* for soprano and ten instruments (1961); *Discourse* for four instruments (1961); *String Quartet Number 7* (1971-1972); *Fromm Variations* for piano (1973); *Songs of Eros* for soprano and orchestra (1975); *Oh Jerusalem* for soprano and flute (1975); *Passacaglia* for piano (1982); *Double Concerto* for violin and cello (1982); and the *Mann Duo* for violin and viola (1983).

Recognition for his work has come in the form of numerous awards, grants, and commissions including the following: Alma Morgenthau Commission (1953) for *String Quartet Number 4;* Dimitri Mitropoulos Commission (1953) for *Challenge—The Family of Man;* representative for the United States (1958) at the I.S.C.M. Festival in Strasbourg, France; Stern Foundation Award (1959) for *Rituals;* Fromm Foundation Commission (1960) for *Dimensions* and (1967) for *Songs of Ecstasy;* Brandeis Creative Arts Award (1962); Rockefeller Foundation Grant (1964); Naumburg Recording Award (1966) for *Rituals;* National Institute of Arts and Letters Award (1966); Koussevitzky Foundation Commission (1967) for the *Partita-Fantasy;* Fromm Music Foundation Commission (1972) for *String Quartet Number 7;* and Elizabeth Sprague Coolidge Foundation Commission (1979) for *Song of Songs.* Shapey's music is published by Theodore Presser and is recorded mostly on the CRI label.

In honor of his 75th birthday, a concert featuring the strikingly dissimilar works of Shapey and Brahms was conducted at Columbia University's Miller theater. As if to confirm his curmudgeonly reputation Shapey, despite his relative obscurity away from the University of Chicago, refused to provide biographical information or program notes in the timeless belief that the music be allowed to speak for itself."

Further Reading

Little has been written on Shapey, but in the past, he has refused to provide biographical information or program notes in the belief that the music be allowed to speak for itself." Wilfrid Mellers' *Music in a New Found Land* and Eric Salzman's *Twentieth Century Music: An Introduction* both contain good but short descriptions placing Shapey in historical context. Good biographical coverage appears in David Lewin's *American Composers: A Biographical Dictionary.* To get beyond surface detail and into the music itself one must take recourse to periodicals, newspaper articles, and record jackets. Of these, Donal J. Henahan's articles in *The Musical Quarterly,* LII (1966) and LIII (1967), and in the *New York Times* (January 26, 1984); John Rockwell's article in the *New York Times* (January 13, 1984); and the liner notes for the recording of *Evocation* (CRI-141) are especially informative. □

Harlow Shapley

The American astronomer Harlow Shapley (1885-1972) proved that our solar system is only a peripheral member of our galaxy. He is credited with bringing Harvard Observatory into a position of preeminence in the world of astronomy.

Harlow Shapley was born on Nov. 2, 1885, in Nashville, Missouri, where his father was a successful hay producer and dealer. Harlow received his early education in a one-room country schoolhouse. About age 15, he went to a kind of business school in Pittsburg, Kansas, and within a year, became a newspaper reporter. He saved his money and resolved to get educated." He was accepted by the Carthage Collegiate Institute, from which he graduated in 1907 as valedictorian of his class.

Shapley then entered the University of Missouri, intending to study journalism, but, finding no degree program available, took up astronomy—and never put it down. In 1910 he received his bachelor's degree; the following year he completed his master's degree. He received the valuable Thaw fellowship of Princeton University and began studying under H. N. Russell. In 1913 Shapley received his doctoral degree.

Shapley's thesis, a lasting contribution to astronomy, dealt with methods for determining the physical properties—for example, the period of revolution, the orbital inclination, and the mean density—of eclipsing binary (double) stars from their light curves" (their intensity as a function of time). From the outset of his work, however, he had a pressing desire to determine the distances to these stars, and, after a trip of several months to Europe, Shapley went in 1914 to Mt. Wilson Observatory to study stellar distances. He made a giant step forward in his research program when, within a year, he realized that the variable Cepheid stars are not eclipsing binaries but single pulsating stars. Their distances, therefore, could be determined by measuring their *apparent* magnitudes, using Henrietta S. Leavitt's 1912 period-luminosity relationship to obtain their *absolute* magnitudes, and employing the inverse-square law. Furthermore, since pulsating Cepheid stars frequently occur in the so-called globular clusters, Shapley could employ the former to determine distances to the latter.

Using Mt. Wilson's 60-inch reflecting telescope, Shapley took numerous photographs from 1916 to 1917. Analyzing them, he discovered that although the globular clusters are symmetrically distributed about the plane of the

Milky Way, most appear to be concentrated in the direction of the constellation Sagittarius. From these observations, Shapley drew the revolutionary conclusion that our solar system is not at the center of our galaxy but is actually far (roughly 50,000 light-years) off-center. Thus Shapley in 1917 displaced the sun from the center of our galaxy. Moreover, Shapley concluded that our galaxy, lens-shaped, is of immense dimensions: 300,000 light-years in diameter and 30,000 light-years thick. (These estimates had to be revised later to take account both of interstellar absorption and W. Baade's work.)

This revolutionary discovery stimulated protracted debate and was undoubtedly Shapley's greatest single achievement. But his contributions to astronomy by no means stopped in 1917. Four years later he became director of Harvard Observatory and for more than three decades thereafter, simultaneously carried out creative research and fulfilled his administrative duties. He became known as Mr. Magellanic Clouds" for his many studies on this pair of relatively close-by, irregularly shaped galaxies; he discovered in 1938 the first of the dwarf sculptor-type galaxies; he directed immense surveys of stellar spectra and galactic populations—all this, and much more, while bringing the overall research and instructional programs of Harvard Observatory to a position of preeminence in the world.

In addition to being elected to the National Academy of Sciences in 1924, Shapley received numerous honorary degrees, medals, and other high honors. In 1952 he became director emeritus and Paine Professor of Astronomy at Harvard, and in 1956 professor emeritus. He died in 1972.

Further Reading

A selected bibliography is included in Shapley's delightfully written reminiscences, *Through Rugged Ways to the Stars* (1969). A chapter on his life and work is in Navin Sullivan, *Pioneers in Astronomy* (1964). For more general background see Sir William C. Dampier, *A History of Science* (1943); Bernard Jaffe, *Men of Science in America* (1944); and Willy Ley, *Watchers of the Skies* (1963). □

Ali Shariati

Ali Shariati (1933-1977) has been called the "Ideologue of the Iranian Revolution." His reinterpretation of Islam in modern sociological categories prepared the way for the Islamic revival that shook Iran in 1979, attracting many young Muslims who had been alienated both from the traditional clergy and from Western culture.

Shariati was born in Mazinan, Khurasan, a small village in Eastern Iran, in 1933 and was educated by his father, Aqa Muhammad Taqi Shariati. His youth was spent in Meshad where his father established the Center for the Propagation of Islamic Teachings. After high school he entered Teachers' Training College and became an active member of his father's center. He entered the University of Meshad in 1956, graduating in 1960. From 1960 to 1964 a state scholarship enabled him to study at the University of Paris, where he gained sociological insight and pursued Islamic studies with the renowned French scholar Louis Massignon. In France he was influenced by the radical Marxism of Jean-Paul Sartre, Albert Camus, and Franz Fanon. Despite this influence he criticized these thinkers for their rejection of traditional religion and suggested that the only way the deprived nations could counterbalance Western imperialism was through the cultural identity preserved by religious traditions.

While in France Shariati had joined with such other Iranian expatriates as Mehdi Bazargan and Bani Sadr who supported resistance to the shah of Iran. Not unexpectedly, he was imprisoned for a time on his return to Iran in 1964. Although turned down for a teaching position at the University of Teheran, he taught at a variety of high schools until a position became available at the University of Meshad. There he became a popular teacher, using an innovative method which expounded Islamic doctrine using a sociological approach. While some Muslim clergy criticized his lack of Islamic expertise, others sympathized with his attempt at modernization and helped him revise the content of his writings. His classes, however, threatened the government establishment, which had them suspended.

In 1965 he established a center of Muslim religious teaching, the Husaniya-yi Irshad in Teheran, and he moved there in 1967. The choice of an institution dedicated to the martyrdom of Husayn in the struggles against the Ummayyads (660-750 A.D.) emphasized his commitment to the struggle against the tyranny of the shah's regime in Iran. His political influence was so great that the regime had him arrested again in 1973 and closed down the Husaniya, banning his works. Although released in 1975, his freedom was restricted. In June 1977 he travelled to England, where he died under circumstances that his supporters insisted suggested the involvement of SAVAK, the Iranian secret police.

Tawhid: Unity in Shariati's Thought

The guiding principle of Shariati's thought, like that of Islam generally, is *tawhid* or unity. On one level this refers to the excellence of the human being. God creates humanity out of clay and spirit, thus enabling a unity of all elements in creation. The human being is thereby made the vice-regent (*kalifa*) for God, bringing perfection to the created world. On another level the principle of unity must be applied to the social world. Every corruption and injustice in the world comes from a lack of unity. The Muslim proclamation that God alone is to be worshipped, made five times daily, conquers greed, envy, and fear by liberating the individual from selfishness.

The implications of this view are radical. If the central significance of the Muslim creed is individual liberation, then any form of dependency is wrong. The Muslim clergy have embraced the principle of imitation (*taqlid*) rather than creative innovation (*ijtihad*) as the basis for deciding Islamic behavior. Shariati opposed blind traditionalism, citing the Koranic statement that "God does not change what is in a people until they change what is in themselves" (Sura 13, Aya 11). The test of a Muslim society lies less in its traditionalism than in its ability to utilize traditional thought to meet the challenge of creating a just society. The ideal of unity requires individuals who can lead a society to the virtues it represents and the social justice which it demands.

Shariati's View of the Religious Leader

Attaining *tawhid* requires the help of religious leaders, but they must be leaders of the right type. The ideal of Mohammad stands as the model of a leader who can use religious insight and knowledge of social norms to transform society. The true religious leader is one who takes up the social responsibility that Mohammad displayed and gains the confidence of the people, thereby educating the society, transmitting religious teachings, and improving the condition of human society. He found the radical emphasis on change and the role of leadership echoed in classical Muslim sources. The Koran proclaims that Allah (God) and the people (*al nas*) are often identical. In order to know God's will it is important, then, to look to what the people are saying, thinking, and doing. Since the time of Muhammad and his early successors (and Shariati aroused dissent by accepting much of the Sunnite evaluation of those leaders despite his own commitment to Shi'ite Islam) religious leadership has waned. He declared that in the modern period it was necessary to return to the primal responsibilities of social consciousness and creativity.

In practical terms he took this to mean that the intellectuals rather than the clergy would bring about the return to the original meaning of Islam. He looked forward to a new type of religious leader. The qualifications were not only knowing the Koran, but knowing its social message and its vision of a new social world, not only being an expert in the biography of the Prophet, but recognizing the place of the Prophet in a Koran-oriented society; not only knowing Islamic history but having the ability to use that knowledge as a model of just social behavior; and, finally, being acquainted with Islamic culture as the basis for Muslim identity.

The problem with the traditional clergy, he explained, was that they were content to look at Islam as a set of general universal principles. Instead, they should apply Islamic ideals to the particulars of Muslim society, the particular problems with which both individuals and the community as a whole must struggle. Such views irritated many of the clergy, and in 1968 Ayatollah Motahari, a disciple of Ayatollah Ruhollah Musavi Khomeini, resigned from the Teheran Husaniya in protest against Shariati's anticlericalism, anticipating the anti-intellectualism that followed the 1979 revolution. Shariati himself responded to such critics by vigorously attacking the established clergy. Despite the victory of the clerical leaders in the Iranian revolution, however, his ideas continued to be influential among younger Iranian Muslims.

Further Reading

There is no single biography available for Ali Shariati. A useful article, "Ali Shariati: Ideologue of the Iranian Revolution," by Abulaziz Sachedina, can be found in *Voices of Resurgent Islam,* edited by John L. Esposito (1983). Books concerned with modern Islam in general or with Iran often included sections on Shariati; see in particular Michael Fischer, *Iran From Religious Dispute to Revolution* (1980) and Malaise Ruthven, *Islam in the World* (1984). Many of Shariati's pamphlets and essays have been translated into English. See especially his *Marxism and Other Western Fallacies* (1980) and *On the Sociology of Islam* (1979). □

Ariel Sharon

Following a distinguished, if controversial, military career, General Ariel Sharon (born 1928) entered Israeli politics in 1973. He then became a prominent public figure, serving as defense minister during the 1982 Israeli invasion of Lebanon.

Ariel ("Arik") Sharon, one of Israel's most controversial military and political figures, was born in 1928 at Kfar Mallah, an early Jewish farming settlement in the central Sharon valley of what was then British-mandated Palestine. His parents were Shmuel and Dvora Scheinerman, ardent Zionists who had emigrated from Russia following World War I. Growing up at a time when the Arab-Jewish struggle over Palestine intensified, young

Sharon combined a high school education with membership in the underground Jewish military organization, the Haganah.

In 1945 Sharon began a military career which continued until 1973 and which saw him participate in each of the major campaigns waged by the Israel Defense Force (IDF). Prior to Israel's establishment as a nation in 1948 he completed an officer's training course and served as an instructor for Jewish police units. During the War of Independence he fought as a platoon commander in the battle of Latrun, where he was seriously wounded. Afterwards Sharon became a military intelligence officer, and in 1952 he obtained a leave of absence to study Middle Eastern affairs at the Hebrew University.

The following year Sharon was chosen to form and lead a small elite commando force trained for special operations behind enemy lines. Both Sharon and Unit 101'' were to become famous for their carrying out of a series of daring raids across Israel's vulnerable borders, thus enforcing a defense doctrine of retaliation for Arab violations of the 1949 armistice agreements and attacks against Israeli civilian targets.

Sharon Continued to Rise through the Ranks of the IDF

In the 1956 Sinai campaign against Egypt, Sharon commanded a paratroop brigade, which came under heavy fire and suffered many casualties in the Mitla pass. By then he already had the reputation of a tough, unconventional fighter whose undisciplined, independent action in battle bordered in the view of his superiors on insubordination. Still, Sharon continued to rise through the ranks of the IDF. After a year's interlude at the Staff College in Camberley, England, where he studied military science, Sharon, promoted in 1958 to colonel, spent the next three years as senior administrative officer in the training division of the General Staff, heading the Infantry School. Successive assignments were: brigade commander of the armored corps, 1962; chief of staff at Northern Command headquarters, 1964; and head of training division of the General Staff, 1966. During that period he received a law degree, and he was promoted to major-general in early 1967.

The next Arab-Israeli conflict, the Six Day War in June 1967, saw Sharon commanding a brigade on the southern front, where he again distinguished himself in battling against Egyptian forces in the Sinai desert. After two years as brigadier-general at the Southern Command during the 1968-70 war of attrition'' along the Suez Canal, Sharon in 1970 was entrusted with the difficult task of suppressing Palestinian terrorist activity in the Gaza Strip. He succeeded in restoring internal security there despite charges of ruthlessness. He generated additional controversy inside the IDF by challenging the prevailing notion of a static defense line at the Suez Canal. Nevertheless, he was appointed head of the Southern Command in 1970.

Sharon, denied his ambition to become the next chief of staff, resigned from the army and entered politics in July 1973. Identifying with the right-of-center Gahal alignment, he helped to negotiate the formation of a Likud (unity) front headed by opposition leader Menachem Begin in September. In October, however, the Yom Kippur war intervened and Sharon once more saw battle when urgently summoned to lead a reserve army division in containing the Egyptian advance. It was then that Sharon registered his greatest military success. Smashing through the enemy lines, he personally led the Israeli forces in establishing a bridgehead at Ismailia and in crossing to the western side of the canal, thereby regaining the initiative.

Returning to politics after the war, Sharon was elected to the Knesset (Israel's parliament) on the Likud ticket in December 1973. However, he resigned a year later; shortly thereafter, in 1975, Premier Yitzhak Rabin appointed him to the post of special advisor on security affairs, which he relinquished in 1976 in order to form the independent Shlomtzion (peace of Zion) Party pledged to retaining the territories occupied in the 1967 war. When he only succeeded in gaining two seats in the May 1977 elections, Sharon opted to merge with the victorious Likud block. Appointed to the cabinet post of minister of agriculture by Prime Minister Menachem Begin, Sharon actively promoted Jewish settlement in the territories, especially in Judea and Samaria on the West Bank of the Jordan River.

Advocated a Forceful Approach

During the second Begin government Sharon served as minister of defense from 1981 to 1983. In this capacity he advocated a forceful approach to the increased military presence and activity of the Palestine Liberation Organization in Beirut and in southern Lebanon. He is widely regarded as having been the principal architect of operation peace for Galilee launched into Lebanon in June 1982, from which Israel did not disengage until June 1985. Sharply criticized for the conduct of the war and the siege of Beirut, Sharon remained in the public eye, successfully defending himself in a libel suit against *Time* magazine in 1984. He even resumed his political career as minister of industry and trade in the National Unity Government, formed in September 1984 under Premier Shimon Peres.

Further Reading

Ariel Sharon's military exploits are described in Ze'ev Schiff, *A History of the Israeli Army* (1974); and he is a central figure in the account of operation peace for Galilee" by Schiff and Ehud Yaari, *Israel's Lebanon War* (1984). The libel suit against *Time* is covered in Renata Adler's *Reckless Disregard: Westmoreland v. CBS et al; Sharon v.Time* (1986). Information on Ariel Sharon can also be found through online resources, such as Magazine Index Plus, ProQuest's Newspaper Abstract, both available in many public libraries, or using one's PC to access NewsWorks (www.newsworks.com), a consortium owned by nine major media companies. The Electric Library (www.elibrary.com/) (a subscription service) is an excellent source for information from a variety of media, ranging from radio scripts to books (such as *Countries of the World,* which list Sharon in at least two chapters. ☐

Al Sharpton

To critics, he is known as "Al Charlatan" or "Rev. Soundbite," a rabble-rousing racial ambulance chaser who never met a video camera he didn't like. To others Al Sharpton (born 1955) is a voice for the disenfranchised, an intelligent, articulate activist who knows how to play the media and speak for the underclass.

The Reverend Al Sharpton has emerged as a voice that people listen to—even if they don't like what they hear. Sharpton, a Pentecostal minister without a parish, uses his theatrical style and inflammatory rhetoric to make himself as familiar a front-page figure as New York City residents Donald Trump and Leona Helmsley. The self-declared civil rights leader injected himself into many of the city's stickiest issues—the Tawana Brawley case, the Bensonhurst racial murder trial, the Bernhard Goetz shooting—often making himself part of the controversy.

Even Sharpton's harshest critics admit he touches a nerve by tapping into a vein of black discontent with white society. Revelations that would devastate other leaders, such as the news that Sharpton secretly worked as an FBI informant and tape-recorded conversations with blacks, rarely stick to Sharpton because they merely confirm the view of his supporters that the white media and the white criminal justice system are out to get him.

Creature of Media

Sharpton is "a creature of the New York media," Wilbert Tatum, publisher of New York's black newspaper, the *Amsterdam News,* told *Newsday.* "When they saw Al Sharpton, who was articulate, fat and wore jogging suits, with a medallion around his neck and processed hair, they thought that he would be the kind of caricature of black leadership they could use effectively to editorialize without editorializing at all. . . . While white media were using Al as a caricature, he was organizing the troops to do what respected black leadership could not do: speak to the issues without fear or favor, and use media in the process. Media thought they were using Al, and Al was using media."

On January 12, 1991 Sharpton was stabbed in the chest minutes before he was to lead a protest march through a predominantly white Brooklyn neighborhood where a black teenager was slain by a mob of white youths two years earlier. In stable condition at the hospital the next day, he did something typical—he called a press conference. As *Esquire*'s Mike Sager wrote, "Sharpton has been defined by his sound bites, nine or 10 seconds of the most explosive rhetoric the reporter or TV producer can find. Of course, Sharpton comes from a tradition of hyperbole; he started preaching in the Pentecostal church at age four."

Born in the Brownsville section of Brooklyn where he still lives, Sharpton was drawn to the spotlight at a young age. He says that he decided early on to become a preacher, and began delivering sermons before entering kindergarten. By 13, he had become an ordained Pentecostal minister and was known as "the boy wonder," preaching gospel in local churches and accompanying entertainers such as Mahalia Jackson on national religious tours.

Sharpton graduated from Brooklyn's Tilden High School, a classmate and friend of longtime major league baseball player Willie Randolph. He briefly attended Brooklyn College before dropping out. Sharpton's father was a well-off contractor who bought a new car each year. But when Al was ten, he told the *Los Angeles Times,* his father deserted the family, forcing his mother to work as a cleaning woman and go on welfare. After his father left, Sharpton attached himself to a series of father figures, from U.S. Congressman Adam Clayton Powell to Jesse Jackson to singer James Brown.

Became Youth Director

In 1969 Jackson, then a young Chicago minister, named the 14-year-old Sharpton as youth director of his group, Operation Breadbasket. Around the same time, Sharpton grew close to Brown, whose son, a friend of Sharpton's, had been killed in a car accident. "He sort of adopted me," Sharpton told the *Washington Post.* "He lost a son, didn't have a father, so he made me his godson." Brown hired the stout teenager as a bodyguard, and introduced him to his business agents. Before he even finished high school, Sharpton was working in the concert promotion business.

Brown introduced Sharpton to two other people who would figure prominently in his life. One was backup singer Kathy Jordan, whom Sharpton met in 1972 and married in l983. (Together they have two daughters, and Jordan now works for the U.S. Army.) The other was boxing promoter Don King, whom Sharpton met in 1974 while promoting a Brown concert that coincided with the Muhammad Ali-George Foreman heavyweight title fight. Soon, Sharpton was seen at the ringside of major prize fights. Years later, Sharpton and King would team up to win a $500,000 contract to promote Michael Jackson after threatening to organize a boycott of Jackson's concert tour because of lack of minority involvement.

In the early 1970s Sharpton founded the National Youth Movement, an organization with the stated purpose of fighting drugs and raising money for ghetto youth. As the l6-year-old director of the organization, Sharpton made his first newspaper headlines in 1971 by urging black children in Harlem to participate in the African celebration of Kwanza instead of traditional Christmas events. The organization was later renamed the United African Movement, which Sharpton touted as a charitable anti-drug group with 30,000 members in 16 cities. But Victor Genecin, a New York state prosecutor, told the *Washington Post* that the group was "never anything more than a one-room office in Brooklyn with a telephone and an ever-changing handful of staffers who took Al Sharpton's messages and ran his errands."

Began Protesting

In 1974 Sharpton again made headlines when he led a group of older black leaders into a meeting with New York City's deputy mayor to protest the police shooting and death of a 14-year-old black youth. The meeting was prompted by a Sharpton-led demonstration of 500 people at City Hall. Later in the decade Sharpton began experimenting with protest tactics of disorderly conduct. He was arrested for the first time in 1970 after a sit-in at New York City Hall to demand more summer jobs for teenagers. Later, he was ejected from a Board of Education meeting after sitting in front of the board president during a protest. Another time, he led a group along Wall Street, painting red X marks on office buildings he claimed were fronts for drug dealing. Sharpton told the *Washington Post* he borrowed such tactics from Martin Luther King, Jr. "How did King establish his leadership? By marching, by putting people in the streets. Tell me when in the history of the civil rights movement the goal wasn't to stir things up."

By and large, however, Sharpton was not known beyond his Brooklyn neighborhood. That changed in 1984, when he led the demands for a murder indictment for white subway gunman Bernhard Goetz, who shot four unarmed black teenagers he said were trying to rob him. Goetz was indicted on a murder charge but acquitted on all but minor gun charges. As Goetz's trial unfolded, Sharpton led daily protests on the courthouse steps, often finding his way onto the nightly news.

Sharpton gained national prominence with his tactics in the 1986 Howard Beach racial killing. In that case, three black men leaving a pizza parlor in the community were assaulted by a group of bat-wielding white youths. One black man died when he was chased into traffic and run over by a car. Sharpton led a "Days of Outrage" protest that shut down traffic on the Brooklyn Bridge and halted subway service in Brooklyn and Manhattan. A year later, he became closely involved with the case of 15-year-old Tawana Brawley, an upstate New York girl who claimed she was raped by five or six white men, one of whom had a police officer's badge. Sharpton, as one of Brawley's three "advisers," publicly accused several officers of the crime and persuaded Brawley not to cooperate with the state investigation. Eventually, several inquiries strongly indicated that Brawley had fabricated the entire incident.

Sharpton "seemed utterly out of control, likening the state attorney general to Adolf Hitler and demanding the arrest of Duchess County officials without a shred of proof," wrote the *Philadelphia Inquirer*'s Claude Lewis. "Both Brawley and Sharpton proved to be among the saddest of figures, using their talents at deceit to fool the public. They thought that by merely being mysterious they could bamboozle us. They refused to speak specifics about the case and employed mysticism to enhance charges of racism to put the authorities in a defensive position. Both proved to be virtuosos at distorting reality. They are brazen people with no scruples." Sharpton remains unrepentant about his role in the Brawley case. "We don't let nothing slip through the cracks, and that case is still unresolved," he told the *Los Angeles Times.* "We've only won when we hit the streets and stay out in the streets and keep this town in disruption."

To the amazement of many, Sharpton survived his curious role in the Brawley affair, as well as revelations in

1988 that he was an informant for the FBI. Sharpton confirmed that for five years he secretly supplied federal law enforcement agencies with information on Don King, reputed organized crime figures, black leaders, and elected officials.

Sharpton a Survivor

In 1989 and 1990 Sharpton again beat the odds, prompting *Newsday* columnist Murray Kempton to compare him to "a cat who has nine lives. He just keeps surviving." First, Sharpton beat a tax evasion rap, which he called a government vendetta. Then, in 1990, he was acquitted on charges that he pocketed more than half of the $250,000 he raised through the National Youth Movement. At the beginning of the case, Sharpton wrote to the grand jury: "Since I was a young child, I was a minister. I know no other life than serving others and allowing God to take care of me. I never owned a car, house, jewelry, etc. My intent is my causes, not wealth."

Sharpton's most recent cause was Yusef Hawkins, a black 16-year-old who was killed by a bat-wielding mob in Bensonhurst in August 1989. The murder stunned New York, which was already beset by spiraling racial tensions. To many New Yorkers it symbolized a breakdown in racial civility that had no quick explanation or readily available cure. Hawkins's father, Moses Stewart, called Sharpton for help the day after the murder. "I wanted someone who was going to take my plight and scream for justice," Stewart told the *Washington Post*. "I didn't want anyone to come to me with a compromise. I wanted the world to know that my son was murdered because he was black. This is what Sharpton does. He brings it to the forefront."

Sharpton led protest marches through Bensonhurst and led a group standing a noisy vigil outside the courtroom where two white teens were being tried for Hawkins's murder. Not-guilty verdicts, Sharpton told *Time* magazine, would be "telling us to burn down the city." Eventually, one of the teens was convicted for the murder.

Recovers from Stabbing

On January 12, 1991, while preparing to lead a march in that same Bensonhurst neighborhood to protest the light sentence given to Hawkins's killer, Sharpton was attacked by a man who stabbed him in the chest. The attack occurred in front of more than 15 supporters and 100 police officers. Sharpton was hospitalized, but officials said his wound was not serious. Michael Riccardi, 27, of Bensonhurst, was immediately arrested and charged with the stabbing.

Shortly following this incident, Sharpton visited London in the Spring of 1991 in an attempt to call attention to the killing of Rolan Adams, a black London teenager who had been allegedly stabbed to death by a gang of whites. However, Sharpton was less then credible with his facts—he did not know Adam's correct name or age and showed marked confusion over police attempts to bring the perpetrators to justice. Sharpton quickly returned to New York where citizens and the media were more amenable to his often outrageous charges and accusations than their English counterparts.

In early 1992 Michael Riccardi was found guilty of stabbing Sharpton and was sentenced to a 5-15 year jail term. Sharpton, always aware of the media spotlight, pleaded on his assailants behalf and asked Judge Francis X. Egitto for leniency when sentencing Riccardi. In a show of Christian forgiveness Sharpton told the court that with the proper help Riccardi could be rehabilitated.

In April 1993 Sharpton was recognized as a ". . . dedicated leader who remains steadfast in the fight for equality" when he was presented with the National Action Network Award. At the awards ceremony New York City Councilman Adam Clayton Powell IV and New York mayor David Dinkins had nothing but accolades for Sharpton. Now that he was being praised by politicians why not become one? In late 1992 Sharpton had entered the New York U.S. Senate primary and ran a lively if futile campaign against Geraldine Ferraro and garnered a surprisingly high 166,000 votes. In 1993 talk of a senate seat for Sharpton was revived and there was much talk in his camp mounting a similar campaign against Senator Daniel Patrick Moynihan. It was hoped by some, and undoubtedly feared by others, that Sharpton's name on the ballot would empower many otherwise disenfranchised-enfranchised black voters. Sharpton subsequently mounted an aggressive primary challenge to Moynihan but the *New York Times* dubbed it as a campaign more ". . . pragmatically aimed at feeding his own outsider's ascendancy in black politics." He did not win the primary but he did win a place as a power-broker on the New York political scene.

Changes Demeanor

With the Tawana Brawley fiasco all but forgotten and with Sharpton now being courted by various politicos his demeanor was rapidly changing. In 1995 *New York* said Sharpton was no longer the "Winnie Mandela of African-American politics," but was rather adopting a more conciliatory style reminiscent of the late Dr. Martin Luther King Jr. With Sharpton's entry into mainstream politics a kinder and gentler Al was calling for racial harmony and a Christian attack on the politics of meanness. Leading a 1995 March from New York City to Albany in protest of Governor George Pataki's budget cuts Sharpton told his fellow marchers:

> There is a mean-spiritedness in the land. If the poor can be scapegoated today, who can be tomorrow? It's as though it's somehow criminal to be unfortunate. Over 60 percent of the children who are classified as poor in this country are the children of people who work every day. This is a battle for the soul of this country. A battle between the Christian right and the right Christians. The Christian right says cut the poor. The right Christians say feed the poor.

In a December 1995 article *Newsday* wrote that to his admirers Sharpton is an authentic leader, a courageous standard-bearer, and a champion of causes where others fear to tread. To his detractors however Sharpton is an inflammatory race-baiting agitator and a ". . . self-aggrandizing, publicity-seeking manipulator of the media."

Sharpton took it all in stride, he's heard it all before, and announced a possible challenge to Rudolph Giuliani's mayoralty. On June 21, 1997, he formally announced his candidacy for New York City's Democratic mayoral nomination.

In 1996 Sharpton published his autobiography *Go and tell Pharaoh: the autobiography of Reverend Al Sharpton.*

Further Reading

Estell, Kenneth, ed., *The African-American Almanac,* Gale Research, 1994.

Sharpton, Al, *Go and tell Pharaoh: the autobiography of Reverend Al Sharpton,* Doubleday, 1996.

Albany Times-Union, April 11, 1990.

Atlanta Constitution, May 12, 1989.

Buffalo News, August 26, 1990; October 15, 1990.

Esquire, January 1990.

Gentleman's Quarterly, December 1993.

Jet, April 6, 1992; April 26, 1993.

Los Angeles Times, September 27, 1989; January 13, 1991.

Miami Herald, July 14, 1989. *Newark Star-Ledger,* August 26, 1990.

New Republic, September 19-26, 1994.

Newsday (Long Island), January 20, 1988; January 22, 1988; June 22, 1988; January 6, 1989; April 27, 1989; June 30, 1989; May 21, 1990; August 12, 1990; January 13, 1991; January 18, 1991; December 14, 1995.

Newsweek, May 13, 1991.

New York, April 3, 1995.

New York Times, January 21, 1997.

Orlando Sentinel, May 25, 1990.

Philadelphia Inquirer, May 24, 1990.

Time, May 28, 1990.

Washington Post, July 14, 1988; September 5, 1990. □

Anna Howard Shaw

Anna Howard Shaw (1847-1919), American suffragist leader, reformer, and feminist, was the fourth president of the National American Woman Suffrage Association.

Anna Howard Shaw was born in Newcastle-upon-Tyne, England, on Feb. 14, 1847, but was raised near Big Rapids, Michigan. She studied at Alma College in Michigan and at Boston University's theological school, from which she graduated in 1878. Pastoral work grew tiresome, and at the age of 35 she entered Boston University's medical school, receiving her medical degree in 1886. The practice of medicine proved equally unsatisfying, and she abandoned it for lecturing and temperance activities. She rose to head the suffrage department of the Women's Christian Temperance Union before leaving for the National American Woman Suffrage Association (NAWSA).

Susan B. Anthony, then president of NAWSA, valued Dr. Shaw's oratorical talents highly and put them to frequent use. But when Anthony resigned in 1900, she chose Carrie Chapman Catt to succeed her. Four years later Catt resigned, and Dr. Shaw's loyalty was rewarded. Although she was president of NAWSA for 11 years, her tenure was not a success. NAWSA had become a large national organization that demanded diplomatic, political, and administrative talents that Dr. Shaw lacked. Moreover, she was a hot-tempered, pugnacious woman and offended both friends and enemies of woman's suffrage. An associate said that she was very witty, but always terribly down on men, and sometimes one really almost winced when she attacked them so vigorously that they got red in the face and looked ready to do murder."

By 1915 it was apparent that while support for women's suffrage was growing, Dr. Shaw was incapable of translating this into votes for women. Accordingly, she was replaced by Carrie Chapman Catt, who led NAWSA to victory in less than five years. Dr. Shaw accepted this demotion with good grace and distinguished herself as chairman of the Woman's Committee of the Council of National Defense, when the United States entered World War I. Though the Woman's Committee was only a symbol of the government's appreciation of women's eagerness to serve, it amounted to more than that, thanks largely to Dr. Shaw, whose stubborn energy compelled the government to give women more responsibility. She died in Moylan, Pennsylvania, on July 2, 1919, only 16 months before she would have exercised the right to vote; the right for which she gave half her life to win.

Further Reading

Anna Howard Shaw's autobiography, *The Story of a Pioneer* (1915), is revealing. Much useful material on her is in *History*

of Woman Suffrage vol. 4, edited by Susan B. Anthony and Ida Husted Harper (1902), and vols. 5 and 6, edited by Ida Husted Harper (1922). William L. O'Neill, *Everyone Was Brave: The Rise and Fall of Feminism in America* (1969), discusses her work on the Woman's Committee. □

George Bernard Shaw

The British playwright, critic, and pamphleteer George Bernard Shaw (1856-1950) produced more than 52 plays and playlets, three volumes of music and drama criticism, and one major volume of socialist commentary.

George Bernard Shaw's theater extended to his personal life. He considered himself a cultural miracle, and a partisan conflict among his readers and playgoers provoked a massive body of literature for and against him and his work. Much recent criticism concludes that he ranks as the greatest English dramatist since William Shakespeare.

Shaw was born in Dublin, Ireland, on July 16, 1856. At an early age he was tutored in classics by an uncle, and when he was 10 years old, he entered the Wesleyan Connexional School in Dublin. There his academic performance was largely a failure. Shaw later described his own education: "I cannot learn anything that does not interest me. My memory is not indiscriminate, it rejects and selects; and its selections are not academic." Part of his nonacademic training was handled by his mother, a music teacher and a mezzo-soprano; Shaw studied music and art at the same time. He became a Dublin office boy in 1871 at a monthly salary equivalent to $4.50. Success in business threatened him: "I made good," he wrote, "in spite of myself and found, to my dismay, that Business, instead of expelling me as the worthless imposter I was, was fastening upon me with no intention of letting me go. . . . In March, 1876, I broke loose." Resigning a cashier's position, Shaw joined his mother and two sisters in London, where they conducted a music school. Shaw had started writing, at the age of 16, criticism and reviews for Irish newspapers and magazines; in 4 years only one piece was accepted. Shaw lived in London for the 9 years after 1876 supported by his parents and continued to write criticism. He also entertained in London society as a singer.

Shaw as a Novelist

Between 1876 and 1885 Shaw wrote five novels. *Immaturity,* the first, remained unpublished, and the other four, after a series of rejections from London publishers, appeared in radical periodicals. *To-Day* published *An Unsocial Socialist* in 1884; it was designed as part of a massive projected work that would cover the entire social reform movement in England. *Cashel Byron's Profession* (1882) also appeared in *To-Day;* juvenile, nonsensical, at times hilarious, it was produced in 1901 as the drama *The Admirable Bashville; or, Constancy Unrewarded. The Irrational Knot,* a portrayal of modern marriage that Shaw asserted anticipated Henrik Ibsen's *A Doll's House,* appeared in another radical periodical, *Our Corner,* as did *Love among the Artists* (1887-1888).

Political Activities and Writings

At the age of 23 Shaw had joined a socialist discussion group, of which Sydney Webb was a member, and he joined the Fabian Society in 1884. *Fabian Essays* (1887), edited by Shaw, emphasized the importance of economics and class structure; for him, economics was "the basis of society." In 1882 Shaw's conversion to socialism began when he heard Henry George, the American author of *Progress and Poverty,* address a London meeting. George's message "changed the whole current of my life." His reading of Karl Marx's *Das Kapital* in the same year "made a man of me." For 27 years Shaw served on the Fabian Society's executive committee. In his role as an active polemicist he later published *Common Sense about the War* on Nov. 14, 1914, a criticism of the British government and its policies. *The Intelligent Woman's Guide to Capitalism and Socialism* (1928) supplied a complete summary of his political position. It remains a major volume of socialist commentary. For 6 years Shaw held office on a municipal level in a London suburb.

Shaw's other careers continued. Between 1888 and 1894 he wrote for newspapers and periodicals as a highly successful music critic. At the end of this period, he began writing on a regular basis for Frank Harris's *Saturday Review;* as a critic, he introduced Ibsen and the "new" drama to the British public. Shaw's *Quintessence of Ibsenism* appeared in 1890, *The Sanity of Art* in 1895, and *The Perfect Wagnerite* in 1898. All of them indicate the formation of his esthetics. He married Charlotte Payne-Townshend, an Irish heiress and fellow socialist, in 1898. She died in 1943.

The Plays

Shaw wrote drama between 1892 and 1947, when he completed *Buoyant Billions* at the age of 91. *Widowers' Houses,* his first play, was produced in 1892 at London's Royalty Theater. He identified this and the other early plays as "unpleasant." *Widowers' Houses* was about slum landlordship. Preoccupied by the "new" woman, Shaw wrote *The Philanderers* in 1893. Also written in the same year but not produced until 1902 because of British censorship, *Mrs. Warren's Profession* revealed, he wrote, "the economic basis of modern commercial prostitution." Shaw's first stage successes, *Arms and the Man* and *Candida,* both of them "pleasant" plays, were produced in 1894. *You Never Can Tell,* first produced in 1896 and not often revived, is Shaw's most underrated comedy. The Vedrenne-Barker productions at the Royal Court Theater in London of Shaw, Shakespeare, and Euripides between 1904 and 1907 established Shaw's permanent reputation; 11 of his plays received 701 performances.

Shaw began as a dramatist writing against the mechanical habits of domestic comedy and against the Victorian romanticizing of Shakespeare and drama in general. He wrote that "melodramatic stage illusion is not an illusion of real life, but an illusion of the embodiment of our romantic imaginings."

Shaw's miraculous period began with *Man and Superman* (1901-1903). It was miraculous even for him; in a late play, *Too True to Be Good* (1932), one of the characters speaks for him: "My gift is divine: it is not limited by my petty personal convictions. Lucidity is one of the most precious of gifts: the gift of the teacher: the gift of explanation. I can explain anything to anybody; and I love doing it."

Major Barbara (1905) is a drama of ideas, largely about poverty and capitalism; like most of Shaw's drama, *Major Barbara* poses questions and finally contains messages or arguments. *Androcles and the Lion* (1911) discusses religion. *John Bull's Other Island* (1904), which is the least known of his major plays, concerns political relations between England and Ireland. *Heartbreak House* analyzes the domestic effects of World War I; written between 1913 and 1916, it was first produced in 1920. Most of the plays after *Arms and the Man* carry long prefaces that are often not directly related to the drama itself. Shaw systematically explored such topics as marriage, parenthood, education, and poverty in the prefaces.

Shaw's popular success was coupled with a growing critical success. *Heartbreak House, Back to Methuselah* (1921; he called it his "metabiological pentateuch"), *Androcles and the Lion,* and *Saint Joan* (1923) are considered his best plays. They were all written between the ages of 57 and 67.

Shaw Explaining Shaw

The plays of Shaw express, as did his life, a complex range of impulses, ambitions, and beliefs. Reflecting on his life and his work, he explained at 70: "If I am to be entirely communicative on this subject, I must add that the mere rawness which soon rubs off was complicated by a deeper strangeness which has made me all my life a sojourner on this planet rather than a native of it. Whether it be that I was born mad or a little too sane, my kingdom was not of this world: I was at home only in the realm of my imagination, and at ease only with the mighty dead. Therefore I had to become an actor, and create for myself a fantastic personality fit and apt for dealing with men, and adaptable to the various parts I had to play as an author, journalist, orator, politician, committee man, man of the world, and so forth. In all this I succeeded later on only too well."

Shaw was awarded the 1925 Nobel Prize for literature. At the patriarchal age of 94, he died in his home at Ayot St. Lawrence, England, on Nov. 2, 1950.

Further Reading

The literature on Shaw is extensive. Shaw wrote numerous letters, some of which are in *Bernard Shaw: Collected Letters, 1874-1897,* edited and with an introduction by Dan H. Laurence (1965), the first of a projected multivolume collection of his correspondence. Not particularly revealing of Shaw's private life is the *Autobiography,* edited by Stanley Weintraub (2 vols., 1969-1970), an assemblage of Shaw's personal writings on a host of topics over a half century.

The standard biography of Shaw is Archibald Henderson, *Bernard Shaw: Playboy and Prophet* (1932). William Irvine, *The Universe of G.B.S.* (1949), is one of many attempts at a definitive critical biography. Stanley Weintraub, *Journey to Heartbreak: The Crucible Years of Bernard Shaw, 1914-1918* (1971), is a fascinating biographical study of Shaw during World War I. Two good introductions to Shaw and his work are G. K. Chesterton, *George Bernard Shaw* (1909), and Eric Bentley, *Bernard Shaw* (1947; 2d ed., 1967). Recently there has been a critical reassessment of Shaw. The most important works are Richard M. Ohmann, *Shaw: The Style and the Man* (1962), and Martin Meisel, *Shaw and the Nineteenth-century Theater* (1963). □

Lemuel Shaw

Lemuel Shaw (1781-1861) was one of America's leading judges during the time the common law was being developed.

Lemuel Shaw was born on Jan. 9, 1781, in Barnstable, Mass. Educated mostly at home by his father, he entered Harvard and graduated in 1800. After 3 years of legal study he was admitted to the New Hampshire bar in 1804. After his fiancée died, Shaw did not marry until 1818, when he wed Elizabeth Knapp. She died in 1822, leaving a son and daughter. In 1827 Shaw married Hope Savage; they had two sons.

Returning to Boston, Shaw was admitted to the bar in 1804 and began his slow but certain climb to the top of the profession in Massachusetts. Shaw's legal training was supplemented by political activities. In politics he consistently followed Daniel Webster and was first a Federalist and then a Whig. Shaw served in the General Court as a representative (1811-1814, 1820) and as a senator (1821-1822). He was a delegate to the state constitutional convention (1822) and drew up Boston's first city charter in 1822. Much of Shaw's law practice was commercial. When the governor appointed him chief justice of the Supreme Judicial Court in 1830, he accepted, even though his judicial salary of $3,500 was approximately one-fifth his income as a lawyer.

Shaw's fame rests on his judicial career. In 30 years on the bench he delivered approximately 2,200 opinions. Because Massachusetts was the center of burgeoning commerce, Shaw's opinions on commercial matters were later cited throughout the country, as other areas evolved from agrarian to industrial economies. His sold reasoning helped adjust the venerable common law to the changing economy.

Shaw was an adherent of judicial restraint, and his court voided only 10 laws in 30 years, leaving the legislature uninhibited in providing for society's needs. Shaw believed in the commonwealth idea, individualism, human rights, law and order, in business as the source of progress, and in the need to preserve the Union. Implicit in his judicial opinions, these values were at times in conflict. He believed that business should be supported by the state but he subject to regulation for the common good. Though convinced that slavery was wrong, he could not override his belief in judicial restraint or the deeper conviction that application of the Constitution's fugitive-slave clause was necessary to preserve the Union; and so he refused to invalidate the Fugitive Slave Act of 1850, despite considerable antislavery agitation.

His adherence to individualism overrode Shaw's concern for business in his ruling that employees had the right to organize to gain their ends, including establishing a closed shop. He was also responsible for the entry of the "separate but equal" doctrine into American law in the school segregation case of *Roberts v. Boston* (1849).

Shaw resigned from the bench in 1860. He died on March 30, 1861. Oliver Wendell Holmes, Jr., said of Shaw: "The strength of that great judge lay in an accurate appreciation of the community. . . . Few have lived who were his equals in their understanding of the grounds of public policy to which all laws must ultimately be referred."

Further Reading

Shaw is eulogized in Frederic Hathaway Chase, *Lemuel Shaw* (1918). Leonard W. Levy, *The Law of the Commonwealth and Chief Justice Shaw* (1957), relates Shaw's work to his environment. Judge Elijah Adlow, *The Genius of Lemuel Shaw* (1962), analyzes Shaw's opinions. Oscar and Mary Flug Handlin, *Commonwealth: A Study of the Role of Government in the American Economy, Massachusetts, 1774-1861* (rev. ed. 1969), is indispensable for understanding the economic background.

Additional Sources

Levy, Leonard Williams, *The law of the commonwealth and Chief Justice Shaw,* New York: Oxford University Press, 1957.

□

Mary Shaw

Mary Shaw (born 1943), a professor of computer science and Dean for Professional Programs at Carnegie-Mellon University in Pittsburgh, has made major contribution to the field of computer science. She also has been involved in the development of computer science education.

Professor of computer science and dean of professional programs at Carnegie-Mellon University in Pittsburgh, Pennsylvania, Mary Shaw has made major contributions to the analysis of computer algorithms, as well as to abstraction techniques for advanced programming methodologies, programming-language architecture, evaluation methods for software performance and reliability, and software engineering. She has also been involved in the development of computer-science education. She was elected to the Institute of Electrical and Electronic Engineers in 1990 and the American Association for the Advancement of Science in 1992; she received the Warnier Prize in 1993.

Mary M. Shaw was born in Washington, D.C., on September 30, 1943, to Eldon and Mary Holman Shaw. Her father was a civil engineer and an economist for the Department of Agriculture, and Shaw attended high school in Bethesda, Maryland, at the height of the Sputnik—the first artificial satellite—era, when the country was making a concerted effort to bolster science and mathematics education. Her father encouraged her interest in science with books and simple electronic kits when she was in the seventh and eighth grades, and her high-school years provided opportunities to delve more deeply into both computers and mathematics.

An International Business Machines (IBM) employee named George Heller from the Washington area participated in an after-school program which taught students about computers; he arranged for the students to visit an IBM facility and run a program on an IBM 709 computer. This was Shaw's introduction to computers. For two summers during high school, as well as during the summer after she graduated, she worked at the Research Analysis Corporation at the Johns Hopkins University Operation Research Office. This was part of a program begun by a woman named Jean Taylor to give advanced students a chance to explore fields outside the normal high school curriculum. "They would give us a system analysis problem and ask us to investigate," Shaw told contributor Rowan Dordick. Among the problems she worked on was a study of the feasibility of using irradiated foods to supply army units.

Shaw entered Rice University with the idea of becoming a topologist, having become enamored with Moebius strips and Klein bottles while in high school. She quickly changed her mind, however, after looking through a textbook on topology. Though there were no courses at that time in computer science, there was something called the Rice Computer Project, a group which had built a computer—the Rice I—under the leadership of an electrical engineering professor named Martin Graham. Shaw wandered into the project area one day and asked a question about the computer. By way of an answer, she was given a machine reference manual and was told to read it first and then come back. She surprised the project members by doing just that. It was a small group, consisting mostly of faculty and graduate students, and Shaw ended up working with the project part-time during her last three years, under the mentorship of Jane Jodeit, the head programmer. Shaw gained valuable experience on the Rice I; she worked on a programming language, wrote subroutines, and helped figure out ways to make the operating system run faster.

After her junior year, Shaw attended summer school at the University of Michigan, where she met Alan Perlis, a professor at Carnegie Mellon University. After receiving her B.A. *cum laude* in mathematics from Rice in 1965, she entered Carnegie Mellon, where Perlis became one of her advisors. She received her Ph.D. in 1971 in computer science, with a thesis on compilers—programs that translate language a human can easily understand into language that the computer understands. Shaw was invited to join the faculty after receiving her degree. One of her first notable accomplishments, in collaboration with Joseph Traub, was the development of what is known as the Shaw-Traub algorithm, an improved method for evaluating a polynomial which allows computers to compute faster. This effort was part of a general interest Shaw had in finding ways to formalize computations in order to make them more efficient.

Shaw's focus on improved software design led her to pursue an approach to the organization of computer programs called abstract-data types. This approach is one of the foundations of object-oriented programming. Large programs are difficult to read or modify unless there is some intrinsic structure, and this is the problem abstract-data-type programming was designed to address. Abstract-data types is a method of organizing the data and computations used by a program so that related information is grouped together. For example, information about electronic details of a telephone-switching network would be grouped in one part of the program, whereas information about people and their telephone numbers would be grouped in another part.

Shaw's work in this area came to fruition in two ways. The first was in the creation of a programming language called Alphard that implemented abstract-data types; she developed this language with William A. Wulf and Ralph L. London between 1974 and 1978. The second, more theoretical result, was the clarification of abstractions in programming. Shaw made it easier to design programs that are more abstract—the word "abstract" in this context means that elements of the program are further removed from the details of how the computer works and closer to the language of the problem that a user is trying to solve. This work can be viewed as a continuation of the trend in programming languages, begun with FORTRAN, to write programs in a higher-order language that reflects the nature of the problem, as opposed to programming in the binary machine language—ones and zeros—that the computer understands.

Shaw's concerns with abstraction proved a natural bridge to a more general issue, which she posed to herself as a question: What other ways are there of organizing programs? The answer emerged as Shaw came to realize that what she was really looking for was the organization of software engineering. In "Prospects for an Engineering Discipline of Software," she wrote: "The term 'software engineering' was coined in 1968 as a statement of aspiration—a sort of rallying cry." The problem, as she and others realized, was that the term was not so much the name of a discipline as a reminder that one did not yet exist.

Through historical study of the evolution of civil and chemical engineering, Shaw has developed a three-stage model for the maturation of a field into a complete engineering discipline. She has shown that an engineering discipline begins with a craft stage, characterized by the use of intuition and casually learned techniques by talented amateurs; it then proceeds through a commercial stage, in which large-scale manufacturing relies on skilled craftsmen using established techniques that are refined over time. Finally, as a scientific basis for the discipline emerges, the third stage evolves, in which educated professionals using analysis and theory create new applications and specialties and embody the knowledge of the discipline in treatises and handbooks.

Shaw has concluded that contemporary software engineering lies somewhere between the craft and commercial stages, and this conclusion has led to an effort on her part first to promote an understanding of where software engineering should be headed and second to develop the scientific understanding needed to move the discipline into the third stage.

The transformation of a discipline proceeds through its practitioners, so it is natural that Shaw has devoted much of her career to improving computer-science education. She was a coauthor of the first undergraduate text to incorporate the concept of abstract-data structures, and she led a group that redesigned the undergraduate computer-science curriculum. She was also involved in the execution of an innovative Ph.D. program that has been widely adopted.

Shaw's accomplishments are not limited to computer science. She was the National Women's Canoe Poling Champion from 1975 to 1978, and she placed in the Whitewater Open Canoe National Championships in 1991. Her marriage to Roy R. Weil—a civil engineer, software engineer, and commercial balloon pilot—spurred an interest in aviation. She has become an instrument-rated pilot, a single-engine commercial glider pilot, and a Federal Aviation Administration (FAA) certified ground instructor. □

Richard Norman Shaw

The British architect Richard Norman Shaw (1831-1912) is noted for his domestic work, in which he was one of the most gifted designers in the Queen Anne, or "Shavian," style.

Richard Norman Shaw was born in Edinburgh on May 7, 1831. His architectural training began at 15 in the London office of William Burn, a domestic architect of some distinction. In 1854 Shaw won the Gold Medal of the Royal Academy, and its traveling scholarship permitted a journey that resulted in the publication of his *Architectural Sketches from the Continent* (1858), a folio of 100 lithographed vignettes of medieval ecclesiastical and domestic architecture in France, Italy, Germany, and Belgium.

In 1858 Shaw succeeded Philip Webb as chief assistant to George Edmund Street, the leading Victorian Gothic church architect. In 1862 Shaw set up his own practice in London in loose partnership (until 1868) with William Eden Nesfield, to whom his early work owes much.

Shaw began as a builder of Gothic revival churches, such as that at Bingley in Yorkshire (1864), but he is now remembered for his Queen Anne country houses, for example, Leys Wood in Sussex (1868; demolished), which was early and influential, and Adcote in Shropshire (1879). These houses, vaguely based upon older vernacular architecture, exhibited richly textured and parti-colored materials such as brick, tiles, and half-timbering arranged into irregular, many-gabled piles; the rambling plans were composed of loosely grouped rooms, variously sized and shaped. The influence of these "Shavian" houses reached across the Atlantic via magazine illustrations to affect the domestic work of Henry Hobson Richardson and others.

The style could be urbanized, as in Shaw's New Zealand Chambers in London (1872-1874; destroyed) and his own house in Hampstead (1875), or it could be adopted for a total environment. At Bedford Park in London, Shaw laid out (1876-1880) the first garden city, with small gabled houses, a gabled inn and stores, and a church. He thus initiated the planned suburban living that carried over into the 20th century in the work of Charles F. A. Voysey and the partnership of Richard Barry Parker and Sir Raymond Unwin.

The Queen Anne style gave way in Shaw's work of the 1880s and 1890s to a more formal, if no less influential, Neo-Georgian manner, as at Bryanston in Dorset (1889-1890). His late work, such as the Picadilly Hotel in London (1905-1908), is of less interest today, and his alteration of John Nash's Regent Street in London has been lamented by later critics.

The most distinguished scholar-architects of the next generation, including William R. Lethaby, Thomas G. Jackson, and Sir Reginald Blomfield, his biographer, were all trained in Shaw's office. Shaw died in London on Nov. 17, 1912.

Further Reading

The uncritical biography of R. T. Blomfield, *Richard Norman Shaw* (1940), should be supplemented by a chapter on Shaw in Nikolaus Pevsner, *Victorian Architecture,* edited by Peter Ferriday (1963). For Shaw and the architecture of his time see Henry-Russell Hitchcock, *Architecture: Nineteenth and Twentieth Centuries* (1958).

Additional Sources

Saint, Andrew, *Richard Norman Shaw,* New Haven: Published for the Paul Mellon Centre for Studies in British Art (London) by Yale University Press, 1976. □

Daniel Shays

Daniel Shays (ca. 1747-1825), American Revolutionary War captain, is best known for leading a rebellion of western Massachusetts farmers in 1786-1787 seeking relief from oppressive economic conditions.

Daniel Shays was born in Middlesex County, Mass. His father had emigrated from Ireland as an indentured servant. Barely educated, Daniel began work as a farm laborer. At the start of the Revolution he joined the local militia. He rose to captain in the 5th Massachusetts Regiment of the Continental Army. Those who served with Shays recalled him as a brave soldier and a good officer.

In 1780 Shays returned to western Massachusetts, a region suffering economic dislocation from the war. The farmers were particularly hurt by the scarcity of money created by the decline of the state's shipping, fishing, whaling, and distilling industries and by the heavy taxes imposed to prosecute the Revolution. Shays suffered with his neighbors. Elected to local office, he was soon representing them in county conventions (between 1782 and 1786), at which petitions were drawn reciting the farmers' distress and demanding relief for debtors in the form of paper money, reduction in government expenditures, restraints on court and attorney fees, and suspension of debt executions. Though Shays managed to keep his farm, other farmers saw mortgage foreclosures take everything but the clothes off their backs. Debtors were imprisoned and even sold to work off their debts.

In 1786 farmers in western Massachusetts organized, took up arms, and forced the courts to suspend sessions. Though Shays headed one of these "regiments," he later denied being the "generalissimo" of the rebellion. Other leaders took no orders from him, but Shays did head the largest band of insurgents, some 1,200, which sought to seize the Federal arsenal at Springfield in January 1787. They were repulsed and scattered by militia. The remainder, pursued by an army of state troops, were surprised on Feb. 4, 1787, and captured in great numbers. Some, like Shays, fled the state. The rebellion was over by the end of February, although intermittent fighting occurred until the summer. Finally pardoned, as were all of the rebels, Shays lived in New York until his death on Sept. 29, 1825.

Perhaps the most significant impact of Shays' Rebellion was the impetus it gave the movement to replace the Articles of Confederation by a new constitution, creating a stronger national government.

Further Reading

There are no biographies of Shays. The fullest analysis of the rebellion is in Robert J. Taylor, *Western Massachusetts in the Revolution* (1954). Marion L. Starkey, *A Little Rebellion* (1955), is a human-interest reconstruction of the episode without much depth. Richard B. Morris provides an excellent capsule treatment of the insurrection in Daniel Aaron, *America in Crisis: Fourteen Crucial Episodes in American History* (1952). A brief account written for school children is Monroe Stearns, *Shays' Rebellion, 1786-1787* (1968), which supplies more details about Shays himself than do many scholarly works. Edward Bellamy's novel *The Duke of Stockbridge: A Romance of Shays' Rebellion* (1879; republished 1962, Joseph Schiffman, ed.) re-creates the country of the Shaysites. □

Anatoly Borisovich Shcharansky

For nine years (1977-86), Anatoly Shcharansky (born 1948) personified the desperate plight of many Soviet Jews. Caught in the vice of great power politics,

Shcharansky suffered a prolonged and difficult imprisonment because of his wish to emigrate to Israel and his prominence in the Helsinki Watch Group. After his release he was welcomed in Israel as a conquering hero.

Anatoly Borisovich Shcharansky, now known as Natan Sharansky, was born on January 20, 1948, in Donetsk, Ukraine, where his father was a journalist for a Communist Party newspaper. A good student, he was admitted to the Moscow Physical Technical Institute, where he studied mathematics and computer science. Upon graduation in 1972 he took a position as a computer scientist at the Oil and Gas Research Institute. Shortly afterwards he and his future wife Natalia Stieglitz (Avital) decided to emigrate to Israel and requested exit visas.

Avital's request was approved, but Shcharansky was denied permission to leave because of his professional training and position, and possibly because of his activism in support of the right of Jews to emigrate. Like other refuseniks'' (those refused permission to leave), Shcharansky was a frequent participant in demonstrations around the Moscow synagogue in 1973 and early 1974. But, unlike many others, including Avital's brother Misha (who was granted permission to leave in late 1973), Shcharansky was frequently detained. Avital was granted permission to leave and the couple anticipated that his exit permit would soon follow. The couple married on July 3, 1974, just before Avital was scheduled to leave Moscow.

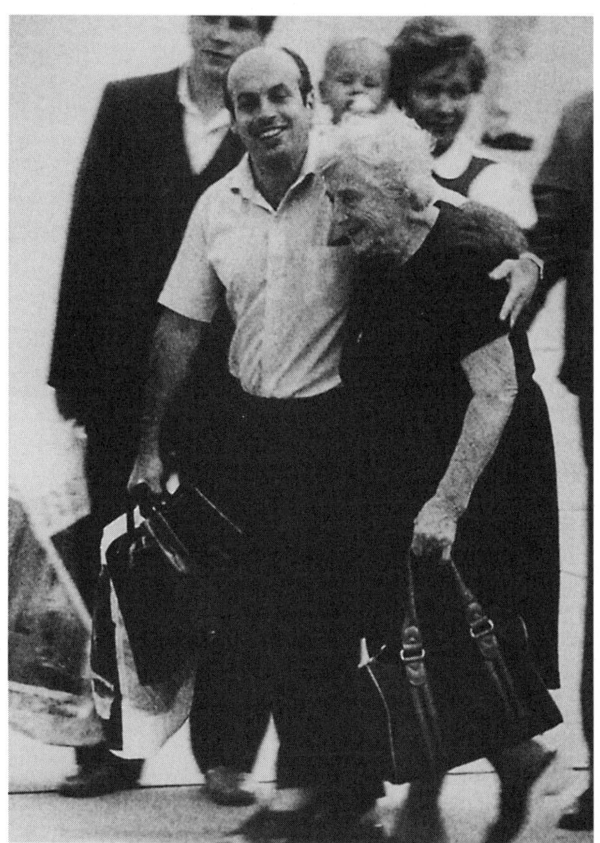

Anatoly Shcharansky (arm around woman)

Helped Organize Helsinki Watch Group in Moscow

His anticipated exit permit never came, and Shcharansky soon became a leading member of the Moscow refusenik'' community. After the Helsinki declaration was signed in 1975 guaranteeing'' human rights, he helped organize the Helsinki Watch Group in Moscow, which was designed to monitor Soviet violations of the accord. Fluent in English, he soon emerged as the group's leading spokesman. Western reporters frequented his apartment. His name, and the story of his separation from Avital, became well known to Western readers.

Soon after his election, President Jimmy Carter made the issue of abuse of human rights a priority matter in his relations with the Soviet Union. Soviet authorities were angered by this approach and felt they had to send a clear signal of their displeasure. Shcharansky soon fell victim to a classic entrapment. His roommate, secretly working for the KGB, made contact with U.S. Central Intelligence Agency agents in Moscow and apparently began passing information on the Helsinki Watch Group. American suspicions soon caused the ties to be broken, but the damage was done. On March 15, 1977, surrounded by a crowd of Western reporters who Shcharansky had invited to walk with him to see what it's like to be constantly shadowed,'' he was arrested. In July 1977 the 30-year-old dissident went on trial for high treason, accused of passing information to an unnamed Western intelligence agency.

The four day trial captured the attention of the Western press for both personal and political reasons. Shcharansky refused to accept his KGB-appointed lawyer and, even though he risked the death penalty, defended himself. He was refused the right to call witnesses or to cross-examine his accusers. At the same time, the desperate unhappiness of his mother, Ida Milgrom, who kept a lonely vigil outside the closed Moscow courtroom, raised the sympathies of millions of Americans. So, in the end, did the shock of Shcharansky's 13-year sentence, although it was a moderate sentence considering the alternative possibilities. Also important were the implications of this show trial'' for Soviet-American relations and President Carter's human rights policies. From this point onwards, it was clear that Carter's terms for improving detente were not acceptable to Soviet rulers.

Shcharansky was never far from Western political consciousness during the long years of his imprisonment. As his physical condition deteriorated, and as reports reached the West of his courageous resistance during his trial and afterwards, his moral stature increased. He soon came to symbolize the plight of persecuted Jews everywhere, and particularly in the U.S.S.R. There was little hope, however, of his early release.

Soviets Agree to His Release as Part of an Exchange of Agents

In late 1985, however, after the historic first meeting between Chairman Mikhail Gorbachev and President Ronald Reagan in Geneva, the new Soviet leader decided to make a gesture in the direction of improved relations. Still officially insisting that Shcharansky was a spy, the Soviets agreed to his release as part of an exchange of convicted espionage agents on both sides. He was released early on the morning of February 11, 1986, at the border separating East and West Berlin. Shcharansky was allowed to go alone to his freedom before the others, as if those releasing him were acknowledging his special status. His important role as a symbol of repression was thus evident at the end of his long ordeal, as it had been at the beginning. Perhaps to end the Shcharansky symbolism,'' the U.S.S.R. permitted five of his relatives to follow him to Israel in July 1986.

There, in response to the perceived failure of the government to meet the demands of the people, he formed the Israel on the Rise'' movement, comprising emigrants from the former Soviet Union. Nearly 20 percent of the country's population are emigrants from the former Soviet Union.

In 1989 he was nominated as Israeli ambassador to the U.N. In January of 1997, as the Israeli Cabinet minister of industry and trade, Shcharansky, who changed the spelling of his surname to Sharansky, returned to Moscow to sign an economic cooperation agreement with Moscow Mayor Yuri Luzhkov to boost trade between Israel and the city. According to Sharansky, the ceremony took place in a sparkling hall, next door to the building where he was arrested 20 years earlier; the last time he saw anything of Moscow other than Lefortovo Prison. It was very funny,'' Sharansky said. Here I was arrested, and 20 years later I'm received with state honors in the next building.''

Further Reading

Shcharansky's ordeal and life are discussed in Martin Gilbert's *Shcharansky: Hero of Our Time* (1986) and in *Anatoly and Avital Shcharansky: The Journey Home* by the *Jerusalem Post* (1986). Shcharansky also has been profiled on the Arts & Entertainment Television Network's *Biography* (www.biography.com). With Ilana Ben-Josef, he authored *Next Year in Jerusalem.* In addition, he has authored or co-authored books with his wife Avital, including: *Anatoly and Avital Shcharansky: The Journey Home* (1986); and *Fear No Evil* (1988). □

Charles Sheeler

The work of American painter Charles Sheeler (1883-1965) is, in its pragmatic association with the American scene and its consistently lucid technique, central to the precisionist style. His techniques varied from photographic realism to modified abstraction.

Born in Philadelphia, Charles Sheeler attended the School of Industrial Art (1900-1903) and the Pennsylvania Academy of the Fine Arts (1903-1906), studying with the William Merritt Chase. With a fellow student, Morton Schamberg, Sheeler set up a studio in Philadelphia in 1908. In Europe the next year, he and Schamberg were impressed by the elegant formalism of the Italian Renaissance painters. In Paris they experienced some of the ferment of modernism and saw the radical manifestations of Pablo Picasso's and Georges Braque's analytical cubism and the Fauve expressionism of Henri Matisse's painting. After this trip Sheeler devoted himself to working in essentially analytical styles.

In 1910 Sheeler and Schamberg rented a farmhouse in Bucks County, Pa., where they sketched on weekends. Sheeler worked as a commercial photographer and did commissions for local architects. Although he always regarded photography as subordinate to his painting, it became an important means of research for his paintings. He is regarded as one of the pioneers of innovative American camera work.

Sheeler exhibited in the 1913 Armory Show, which dramatically introduced the spectrum of European modernism to America. The exhibition's French section led Sheeler into stronger abstraction; in *Landscape* (1915) he applied the standard cubist devices of flattened, overlapping, and quasi-transparent planes to build an analytical composition.

The cubist clarity never left Sheeler's painting, although by the mid-1920s he had divested himself of its stylistic mannerisms. (He returned to these in later works.) *Church Street El* (1920), a dramatic cityscape, brilliantly applies cubist formalism to the American urban scene. In *Bucks County Barn* (1923) he applied the cubist doctrine to an American countryside subject. Sheeler equated the austere functionalism of anonymous rural American architecture with the complex technical efficiency of present-day industry and alternated between these themes, representing each with objectivity.

Sheeler sought inherently abstract subjects, which he further simplified. *Upper Deck* (1929), a portrayal of shipboard architecture, is a study of geometric metal shapes. It illustrates the relationship between Sheeler's photographic studies and paintings so pronounced throughout his mid-1920s and 1930s work, evident in the series of photographs and paintings of stairway themes. Sheeler's black-and-white Conté drawings, selectively based on his photography, are particularly strong. Although he used color sensitively, his paintings remain essentially value studies in dark and light. His Bucks County Conté-crayon drawings, such as *Interior with Stove* (1932), are among his most authoritative. *View of New York* (1931), an eloquently simple study, consists of shapes floated on a vertical-horizontal grid; a photographer's table, chair, and lamp, seen against a window, are treated as pure abstract elements.

A 1927 photographic assignment from the Ford Motor Company led to such literal works as *City Interior* (1936), a one-point perspectival view of an industrial street spanned by complex heavy pipes and trusses; tiny figures of workers are isolated in this overwhelming environment. (This is one of the few works in which human figures appear.)

In Sheeler's art all components of the industrial environment were regarded with the same dispassion; he gave as much attention to a wraith of factory smoke as to a gigantic turbine. During the 1940s he moved toward modified abstraction, his paintings more and more rigorously controlled. Devices derived from photography, such as double exposure, provided new sources of abstract forms. These are the basis of such works as *Continuity* (1957), a factory scene. In his midwestern barn paintings of this period, realistically detailed elements of landscape and rural architecture are prismatically juxtaposed and fused with anonymous shapes derived from surrounding trees, buildings, and clouds. Some compositions of the 1950s combine elements of several sites.

A strongly moralistic attitude characterized Sheeler's choice of subjects; in his paintings, American functionalism merged with technological perfection. He painted a universe whose elements relate in perfect harmony. No storm clouds appear in his blue skies; no sign of deterioration is permitted; old barns avoid picturesque sentimentalism; every field is green. The time is the idealized present. Yet for all his seemingly detached concern with the abstract purity of American rural architecture and the industrial environment, Sheeler remained a highly introspective, lyrical painter.

Further Reading

The most comprehensive work on Sheeler is the National Collection of Fine Arts catalog, *Charles Sheeler* (1969), which includes essays by Martin Friedman, Bartlett Hayes, and Charles Millard and a complete chronological table of Sheeler's life and paintings. Sheeler's relevance to precisionism is illustrated by Martin Friedman in the Walker Art Center catalog, *The Precisionist View in American Art* (1960). See also Constance M. Rourke, *Charles Sheeler* (1938), and William Carlos Williams's introduction to the Museum of Modern Art catalog, *Charles Sheeler* (1939).

Additional Sources

Sheeler, Charles, *Charles Sheeler,* New York: Watson-Guptill Publications, 1975. □

Fulton J. Sheen

During the 1950s, Catholic clergyman Fulton Sheen (1895-1979) hosted *Life is Worth Living,* a popular television show for which he earned an Emmy Award, and on which he presented his views on religious topics, everyday life, and politics.

One of the unlikeliest successful television personalities of the "Golden Age" in the 1950s was a Catholic clergyman named Fulton Sheen. He was on a small network with few affiliates as a throwaway program slotted against the hugely popular Milton Berle, but caught on and became one of the most popular figures in the country, even drawing admirers from among those who dislike Catholicism. While never really becoming a major figure in the hierarchy of the Catholic church, Sheen was one of its most visible members and an excellent ambassador for the church to the secular world.

Early Years

Peter John Sheen was born May 8, 1895 in El Paso, Illinois, the first of four sons born to Newton Morris Sheen and the former Delta Fulton. The child suffered from tuberculosis at an early age, and was often cared for by his mother's family. They enrolled him in school as "a Fulton," and that maiden name became his first name. It was a farming family, but Fulton knew early on he wanted a career in the priesthood. He attended parochial schools in Peoria, Illinois, and at St. Viator's College in Kankakee, Illinois, then at St. Paul's Seminary in Minnesota before becoming ordained in Peoria in 1919.

Education

Being a good student, Sheen was sent to the Catholic University of America in Washington, D.C., then to the University of Louvain in Belgium. He obtained his doctorate there in 1923, and received a degree in philosophie with highest honors in 1925 while studying in Paris and Rome. He was teaching theology at St. Edmund's College in Ware, England, when he was called home to Peoria to take over his first parish.

Eight months later he was transferred to a teacher of philosophy job at Catholic University. He drew attention to himself there through his total dedication to his work, neither smoking nor drinking, taking no holidays, enjoying no luxuries and giving away almost all his earnings. He rose quickly to the rank of full professor, and also was promoted to papal chamberlain, then domestic prelate and Bishop.

Broadcast Career Begins

In 1930 Sheen began his broadcast career, hosting the Sunday evening *Catholic Hour* program on NBC Radio. In the 1940s he performed some religious services on television, and in 1948 he was guest speaker on the television program *Television Chapel* on WPIX in New York. Director Edward Stasheff remembered for *Television Quarterly,* "His whole technique was the magnetic effect of the way he looked into the camera. I hate to use a cliché, but the word is 'telegenic.' He was made for the medium."

In 1952 Milton Berle owned Tuesday night television with his 8 p.m. show, *Texaco Star Theatre.* The small DuMont network decided to put Sheen on the air opposite Berle as something of a sacrificial lamb, thinking a program with no potential may as well be on in a time slot with no chance. *Life is Worth Living* premiered on February 12, 1952, with the Bishop Fulton Sheen appearing in a long cassock, a gold cross and chain on his chest, a long purple cape and a skull cap, speaking from a set designed to look like a rectory study before an audience at the Adelphi Theatre in midtown Manhattan. The half-hour program consisted of a one-minute commercial for Admiral, followed by a 28-minute talk delivered without notes or teleprompter by the bishop, ended with a two-minute peroration and the sign-off "God love you," followed by another one-minute commercial for Admiral. This formula proved to be a success.

Sheen's talks were never straight appeals for loyalty to the Catholic church, but universal in nature, designed to appeal to people of any faith. "Starting with something that was common to the audience and me, I would gradually proceed from the known to the unknown or to the moral and Christian philosophy," he is quoted as saying in his posthumously published biography, *Treasure in Clay.* "When I began television nationally and on a commercial basis, I was no longer talking in the name of the church."

Popularity Increases

Initially, *Life is Worth Living* aired on only three stations nationwide. The show proved popular with audiences, however, and immediately began cutting into the ratings of Berle and Frank Sinatra, who had a Tuesday night show on CBS. Within two months Sheen's show was seen on 15 stations, and the bishop was overwhelmed with fan mail and requests to sit in the studio audience. NBC even tried to lure him away from DuMont at one point, but loyalty bid the bishop decline. At the 1952 Emmy Awards, Sheen defeated Edward R. Murrow, Lucille Ball and Arthur Godfrey for the title of Most Outstanding Television Personality. Upon accepting his award, he said, "I wish to thank my four writers, Matthew, Mark, Luke and John."

Eventually Sheen's program was seen by 20 million viewers on 123 stations. His fame grew along with his audience, and one of the things he became known for was performing conversions to Catholicism of well-known people, including Fritz Kreisler, Heywood Broun, Clare Boothe Luce, Henry Ford II and Louis Budenz. He also attracted attention for his political views, and at various times drew heat from both conservatives and liberals. He supported the anti-communist Franco in the Spanish Civil War, while conceding the dictator's fascism; he also defended corporal punishment in schools and spoke out against Freudian psychology. Following the reforms of Vatican II—which Sheen advised on mission problems—he spoke out against poverty and nuclear war, and alternately opposed and supported U.S. involvement in the Vietnam War. Throughout the '50s and most of the '60s, he also served as national director of the Society for the Propagation of the Faith, raising funds for missions around the world.

Sheen Named Archbishop

In 1966 Sheen was named archbishop of Rochester, New York, amid speculation as to whether the church was trying to promote him or neutralize him. He continued the church's reforms in that area, and was considered progressive in his policies. Questions were raised about his administrative practices, however, and he opted for early retirement in 1969, at the age of 74. He was named titular archbishop and moved to a small apartment in New York City. He underwent open heart surgery in July 1977, and was largely confined to his home until his death from heart disease in 1979. □

Charles M. Sheldon

Charles M. Sheldon (1857-1946) was an American social reformer who was best known for his authorship of the best selling inspirational novel *In His Steps* (1897). A longtime pastor in Topeka, Kansas, he was an early advocate of civil rights and social services for African Americans and a firm believer in putting one's religion into practice in daily life.

Charles M. Sheldon was born on February 26, 1857, at Wellsville, New York. His father was a minister, and the family moved frequently until, in 1869, they homesteaded a frontier tract and lived in a log cabin in the Dakota Territory for several years. Sheldon went to school at Phillips Academy, Brown University, and Andover Theological Seminary, completing his theological degree in 1886. He then accepted a pastorate in the Congregational Church at Waterbury, Vermont, but stayed only two years, since he desired a new church he could help direct from the beginning. He got his wish when he was called to the pastorate of the newly founded Central Congregational Church in Topeka, Kansas, where he took up duties in 1889.

Sheldon quickly exhibited a flair for unusual projects. Shortly after his arrival in Topeka, in the middle of an economic depression, he wanted to understand how the unemployed felt, so he donned old clothes and applied for work at nearly every store in town, only to be turned down every time. He also noted that a colony of impoverished former slaves had become established very near his church, and he spurred Topekans to undertake relief projects for these unfortunate souls. Thus was founded the first kindergarten for African American children west of the Mississippi River. The Village Improvement Society helped residents to improve their homes, and jobs were located for many who had been unemployed. Sheldon's vision of race relations and justice for minorities was far ahead of its time.

After a year or so in Topeka, Sheldon became displeased that the audiences at his Sunday evening services were not nearly as large as those at the morning services. Looking for ways to get more people out, he hit upon the idea of reading "sermon stories"—serial stories in which each installment ended at a tense moment in the narrative. (In one early story, for example, the hero was at the bottom of a mine shaft with water pouring in as the first episode ended.) People wanted to come back to find out what happened next, and within three weeks Sheldon's church was overflowing on Sunday evenings.

In the fall of 1896 the sermon story was entitled "In His Steps." It was a tale of a group of committed Christians who resolved to ask themselves whenever they had hard decisions to make, "What would Jesus do?" Their dedication led them to avoid the easy choices, instead opting for difficult but spiritually rewarding projects in service of others. The story was a big hit when it was first read in Topeka, and it quickly gained a national audience through its publication as a serial story in a religious magazine that winter. In 1897 it was issued in book form, and sales were large from the beginning. Two years later other publishers learned that the book had a defective copyright, and that anyone could publish the popular novel without payment of royalties. Thus unauthorized editions sprang up by the dozens. Eventually over 70 American, British, and Canadian publishers issued the book, and it was translated into over two dozen foreign languages. Sheldon, however, received only minimal royalties from what some regard as the best selling novel of all time. Estimates of the number of copies published range as high as 30 million or more in book form and tens of millions more in other forms, such as newspaper supplements.

One episode in *In His Steps* involved a Christian newspaper editor who decided to edit his paper according to the "What would Jesus do?" standard and thus changed his guidelines for news coverage and began to reject advertising he found unwholesome. The publisher of one of Topeka's daily newspapers decided to try the idea in real life, offering Sheldon the editorship for a week. Sheldon accepted the offer, and for a week in March 1900 the Topeka *Daily Capital* was a very unusual paper indeed. Gone were stories of boxing matches and violent crimes; in their place Sheldon ran inspiring stories about social reform, the progress of Christian missions, and crises needing attention from good people. In the latter category was a famine in India; Sheldon ran stories about it every day, and by the end of the week huge sums of money had been raised for relief. Farmers also donated a boatload of grain which was shipped to the starving nation. Meanwhile, advertising also was changed at the Sheldon *Capital;* out went ads for products of which Sheldon disapproved, such as corsets, patent medicines, alcohol, and tobacco. Sheldon even changed ads for unoffensive products so that their claims would not be exaggerated. The newspaper was heavily promoted and was a huge success; over 300,000 persons around the world subscribed for the week, and many more bought the paper on newsstands.

Sheldon pursued many reform projects for the rest of his life. Among them were prison reform, the upgrading of police departments, the improvement of schools, and providing people with what he considered moral entertainment. Two projects stand out above the others, however. The first was prohibition. Sheldon from childhood had opposed the use of alcohol, and for decades he worked tirelessly for national prohibition, taking great joy in its enactment in 1918. He did not confine his efforts to the United States, but toured the world, applying his great fame as an author to the cause of enacting prohibition elsewhere. The second great cause he espoused was world peace; even during World War II he wore the unpopular label of pacifist cheerfully. Again he took to the road, speaking out for the cause of peace, and at one point erected highway billboards urging the nation to disarm.

Sheldon's most important contribution to his causes was not theory, but popularization. He had a knack for easy-to-read writing, and in his time he was one of the world's most widely read authors. Nearly a century later *In His Steps* still sells thousands of copies a year, evidence that Sheldon's influence is still alive.

Further Reading

Sheldon's most famous book, by far, was *In His Steps* (1897). Among the more popular of his approximately 50 other books were *The Crucifixion of Philip Strong* (1898), *Robert Hardy's Seven Days* (1893), *The Reformer* (1901), and *His Brother's Keeper* (1896). He also published hundreds of magazine articles, most frequently in *The Christian Herald.* He published an autobiography, *His Life Story* (1925). No major biography of Sheldon has been published, although one is in progress. A pamphlet of some value is Glenn Clark, *The Man Who Walked In His Steps* (1946). Several master's theses have been written on Sheldon; probably the best is David G. Johnson, *A Study of the Ideas of Charles M. Sheldon* (University of Kansas, 1965). Many histories of the social gospel period in American religious history make brief references to Sheldon.

Additional Sources

Miller, Timothy, *Following in his steps: a biography of Charles M. Sheldon,* Knoxville: University of Tennessee Press, 1987. □

Mary Wollstonecraft Shelley

Mary Wollstonecraft Shelley (1797-1851) is best known for her novel *Frankenstein; or, The Modern Prometheus* (1818), which has transcended the Gothic and horror genres and is now recognized as a work of philosophical and psychological resonance. In addition to *Frankenstein,* Shelley's literary works include several novels that were mildly successful in their time but are little known today and an edition of poetry by her husband, the Romantic poet Percy Bysshe Shelley, which she issued with notes that are now regarded as indispensable. Her reputation rests, however, on what she once called her "hideous progeny," *Frankenstein.*

Shelley's personal life has sometimes overshadowed her literary work. She was the daughter of Mary Wollstonecraft, the early feminist and author of *A Vindication of the Rights of Woman,* and William Godwin, the political philosopher and novelist. Her parents' wedding, which occurred when Wollstonecraft was five months pregnant with Mary, was the marriage of two of the day's most noted freethinkers. While they both objected to the institution of matrimony, they agreed to marry to ensure their child's legitimacy. Ten days after Mary's birth, Wollstonecraft died from complications, leaving Godwin, an undemonstrative and self-absorbed intellectual, to care for both Mary and Fanny Imlay, Wollstonecraft's daughter from an earlier liaison. Mary's home life improved little with the arrival four years later of a stepmother and her two children. The new Mrs. Godwin, whom contemporaries described as petty and disagreeable, favored her own offspring over the daughters of the celebrated Wollstonecraft, and Mary was often solitary and unhappy. She was not formally educated, but absorbed the intellectual atmosphere created by her father and such visitors as Samuel Taylor Coleridge. She read a wide variety of books, notably those of her mother, whom she idolized. Young Mary's favorite retreat was Wollstonecraft's grave in the St. Pancras churchyard, where she went to read and write and eventually to meet her lover, Percy Shelley.

An admirer of Godwin, Percy Shelley visited the author's home and briefly met Mary when she was fourteen, but their attraction did not take hold until a subsequent meeting two years later. Shelley, twenty-two, was married, and his wife was expecting their second child, but he and Mary, like Godwin and Wollstonecraft, believed that ties of the heart superseded legal ones. In July 1814, one month before her seventeenth birthday, Mary eloped with Percy to the Continent, where, apart from two interludes in England, they spent the next few years traveling in Switzerland, Germany, and Italy. These years were characterized by financial difficulty and personal tragedy. Percy's father, Sir Timothy Shelley, a wealthy baronet, cut off his son's substantial allowance after his elopement. In 1816, Mary's half-sister Fanny committed suicide; just weeks later, Percy's wife, Harriet, drowned herself. Mary and Percy were married in London, in part because they hoped to gain custody of his two children by Harriet, but custody was denied. Three of their own children died in infancy, and Mary fell into a deep depression that was barely dispelled by the birth in 1819 of Percy Florence, her only surviving child. The Shelleys' marriage suffered, too, in the wake of their children's deaths, and Percy formed romantic attachments to other women. Despite these trying circumstances, both Mary and Percy maintained a schedule of rigorous study—including classical and European literature, Greek, Latin, and Italian language, music and art—and ambitious writing; during this period Mary completed *Frankenstein* and another novel, *Valperga* (1823). The two also enjoyed a coterie of stimulating friends, notably Lord Byron and Leigh Hunt. The Shelleys were settled near Lenci, Italy, on the Gulf of Spezzia in 1822 when Percy drowned during a storm while sailing to meet Leigh and Marianne Hunt. After one mournful year in Italy, Mary returned permanently to England with her son.

Shelley's life after Percy's death was marked by melancholy and hardship as she struggled to support herself and her child. Sir Timothy Shelley offered her a meager stipend, but ordered that she keep the Shelley name out of print; thus, all her works were published anonymously. In addition to producing four novels in the years after Percy's death, Mary contributed a series of biographical and critical sketches to *Chamber's Cabinet Cyclopedia,* as well as occasional short stories, which she considered potboilers, to the literary annuals of the day. The Shelleys' financial situation improved when Sir Timothy increased Percy Florence's allowance with his coming of age in 1840, which enabled mother and son to travel in Italy and Germany; their journeys are recounted in *Rambles in Germany and Italy in 1840, 1842, and 1843* (1844). Too ill in her last few years to complete her most cherished project, a biography of her husband, Shelley died at age fifty-four.

Although *Frankenstein* has consistently dominated critical discussions of Shelley's oeuvre, she also composed several other novels in addition to critical and biographical writings. Her five later novels attracted little notice, and critics generally agree that they share the faults of verbosity and awkward plotting. After *Frankenstein, The Last Man* (1826) is her best-known work. This novel, in which Shelley describes the destruction of the human race in the twenty-first century, is noted as an inventive depiction of the future and an early prototype of science fiction. *Valperga* and *The Fortunes of Perkin Warbeck* (1830) are historical novels that have received scant attention from literary critics, while *Lodore* (1835) and *Falkner* (1837), thought by many to be autobiographical, are often examined for clues to the lives of the Shelleys and their circle. Shelley's stories were collected and published posthumously, as was *Mathilda,* a novella that appeared for the first time in the 1950s. The story of a father and daughter's incestuous attraction, it has been viewed as a fictional treatment—or distortion—of Shelley's relationship with Godwin. The posthumously published verse dramas, *Proserpine* and *Midas* (1922), were written to complement one of Percy Shelley's works and have garnered mild praise for their poetry. Critics also admire Shelley's non-fiction: the readable, though now dated, travel volumes, the essays for *Chamber's Cabinet Cyclopedia,* which are considered vigorous and erudite, and her illuminating notes on her husband's poetry.

Since Shelley's death, critics have devoted nearly all of their attention to *Frankenstein.* Early critics, generally with some dismay, usually relegated the novel to the Gothic genre then practiced by such popular authors as Ann Radcliffe and Matthew Gregory "Monk" Lewis. While most early Victorian reviewers reviled what they considered the sensationalist and gruesome elements in *Frankenstein,* many praised the anonymous author's imagination and powers of description. In the later nineteenth century and throughout *Frankenstein* criticism, commentators have focused on Prometheanism in the novel, an aspect that Shelley herself highlighted in the book's subtitle. This line of inquiry, which continues to engage critics, likens Dr. Frankenstein to the Greek mythic figure who wreaks his own destruction through abuse of power. Percy Shelley treated the same mythic-philosophic theme in his poetry, most notably in *Prometheus Unbound,* and critics have searched for his influence on *Frankenstein,* particularly in the expression of Romantic ideals and attitudes. Scholars have also debated the value of the additional narratives that he encouraged her to write. While some have praised the novel's resulting three-part structure, others have argued that these additions detract from and merely pad the story, although most have valued the other-worldly Arctic scenes. Commentators have also frequently noted the influence of Shelley's father, tracing strains of Godwin's humanitarian social views; in addition, some critics have found direct thematic links to his fiction, particularly to his novel, *Caleb Williams.* Other literary allusions often noted in *Frankenstein* include those to John Milton's *Paradise Lost,* the source of the book's epigraph, as well as Johann Wolfgang von Goethe's *Faust* and Coleridge's "The Rime of the Ancient Mariner."

Frankenstein criticism has proliferated since the 1950s, encompassing a wide variety of themes and approaches. The monster, who is often the focus of commentary, has been interpreted as representing issues ranging from the alienation of modern humanity to the repression of women. Many commentators have viewed the monster as Dr. Frankenstein's double, an example of the doppelganger archetype. In a similar vein, critics have discussed Dr. Frankenstein and the monster as embodying Sigmund Freud's theory of id and ego. Students of the Gothic, supernatural horror, and science fiction novel have adopted *Frankenstein* as a venerable forebear and have approached it from a historical slant. Alternately, Shelley's life has served as a starting point for those who perceive in the novel expressions of the author's feelings toward her parents, husband, children, and friends. Recent feminist critics, in particular, have found Shelley and *Frankenstein* a rich source for study, describing it, for example, as a manifestation of the author's ambivalent feelings toward motherhood.

Leigh Hunt once characterized Shelley as "four-famed—for her parents, her lord / And the poor lone impossible monster abhorr'd." Today, she has emerged from the shadow of her parents and husband as an artist in her own right. The volume and variety of *Frankenstein* criticism attests to the endurance of her vision.

Further Reading

Bloom, Harold, editor, *Mary Shelley: Modern Critical Views,* Chelsea House, 1985.

Church, Richard, *Mary Shelley,* Gerald Howe, 1928.

Dunn, Jane, *Moon in Eclipse: A Life of Mary Shelley,* St. Martin's, 1978.

Gerson, Noel B., *Daughter of Earth and Water: A Biography of Mary Wollstonecraft Shelley,* Morrow, 1973.

Gilbert, Sandra, and Susan Gubar, *The Madwoman in the Attic,* Yale University Press, 1979.

Grylls, Glynn R., *Mary Shelley: A Biography,* Oxford University Press, 1938.

Harris, Janet, *The Woman Who Created Frankenstein: A Portrait of Mary Shelley,* Harper, 1979. □

Percy Bysshe Shelley

The English romantic poet Percy Bysshe Shelley (1792-1822) ranks as one of the greatest lyric poets in the history of English literature.

Percy Bysshe Shelley was born at Field Place near Horsham, Sussex, on Aug. 4, 1792. He was the first son of a wealthy country squire. Shelley as a boy felt persecuted by his hardheaded and practical-minded father, and this abuse may have first sparked the flame of protest which, during his Eton years (1804-1810), earned him the name of "Mad Shelley." In the course of his first and only year at Oxford (1810-1811), Shelley and his friend Thomas Jefferson Hogg issued a pamphlet provocatively entitled *The Necessity of Atheism.* Their "atheism" was little more than a hieroglyph connoting their general revulsion against establishment authoritarianism. However, both students were expelled from the university.

This event—soon combined with the influence of *Political Justice* by anarchist reformer William Godwin—merely intensified Shelley's rebelliousness against accepted notions of law and order, both in his private life and in the body politic. In the summer of 1811 Shelley met and married Harriet Westbrook, and he tried to set up, with her and Hogg, one of those triangular relationships that were to become characteristic of his love life, presumably because he saw in them a way to materialize his noble ideal of freedom in love and togetherness in human relationships. In the early months of 1812 Shelley evinced more than theoretical interest in the Irish cause, another manifestation of his desire for political reform.

Shelley's First Poems

Shelley attempted to convey his views on these and sundry other topics in *Queen Mab* (1813), a juvenile allegorical romance that, nevertheless, contained the germ of his mature philosophy: the ontological notion that throughout the cosmos there is "widely diffused/A spirit of activity and life," an omnipresent nonpersonal energy that, unless perverted by man's lust for power, can lead mankind to utopia.

By the summer of 1814 Shelley had become closely involved with Godwin, his debts, and his daughter Mary. For a brief while, the poet contemplated settling down with both Mary (as his "sister") and Harriet (as his wife); but the latter did not agree, and in late July Shelley eloped to the Continent with Mary, taking along her half sister, Claire Clairmont.

Shelley's *Alastor*

Back in England, Shelley was increasingly driven to the realization that utopia was not just around the corner, and this may have prompted the writing of *Alastor, or the Spirit of Solitude* in December 1815. This ambiguous poem is a dialectical analysis of the tragic irony in the poet's fate as he is caught between the allurements of extreme idealism and his awareness that the very nature of man and the world precludes the achievement of his highest purpose. *Alastor* represents a transient but necessary phase in Shelley's evolution. He was hence-forth to return with unrelenting determination to his dual poetic task of defining the romantic ideal of universal harmony and of striving to bring about the reign of love and freedom in human society.

The first fruits of this ripening were the *Hymn to Intellectual Beauty* and *Mont Blanc,* which were planned in 1816, during a stay in Geneva. Both poems constitute an impressive statement of Shelley's fundamental belief in an everlasting, benevolent "Spirit," the hidden source of splendor and harmony in nature and of moral activity in man.

The Revolt of Islam

The winter of 1816/1817 was a period of great emotional disturbance for Shelley. Harriet died, presumably by suicide, in December, and the courts refused to grant Shelley the custody of the two children she had borne him. In addition, he was beginning to worry about his health. However, there were encouragements as well. Partly thanks to Leigh Hunt (to whom he gave financial help with his customary generosity), Shelley was gaining some recognition as an original and powerful poet.

During the spring and summer of 1817, Shelley composed his most ambitious poem to date, *The Revolt of Islam.* In this work the crude allegorical didacticism of Queen Mab gave way to genuine, although at times still turgid, symbolism. The theme of love between man and woman was adroitly woven into the wider pattern of mankind's love-inspired struggle for brotherhood. Like the French Revolution, the failure of which had preoccupied Shelley for a long time, *The Revolt of Islam* ends in disaster. But the poet had now come to a mature insight, absent from *Alastor,* into the complex interplay of good and evil. Man's recognition of his boundaries is the first step to wisdom and inner liberty; martyrdom does not put an end to hope, for it is a victory of the spirit and a vital source of inspiration. *The Revolt of Islam* illustrates a discovery that often signaled the romantic poet's accession to wisdom and that John Keats described, in April 1819, as the recognition of "how necessary a World of Pains and troubles is to school an Intelligence and make it a Soul."

Exile and *Prometheus Unbound*

In March 1818 the Shelleys (still accompanied by Claire Clairmont) left England, never to return. The bulk of the poet's output was produced in Italy in the course of the last 4 years of his short life. Though life in Italy had its obvious rewards, this period was by no means one of undiluted happiness for Shelley. He was increasingly anxious about his health; he was beginning to resent the social ostracism that had made him an exile; exile itself was at times hard to bear, even though the political and social situation in England was most unattractive; and his son William died in June 1819.

However, although a note of despondency can be perceived in some of his minor poems, such as the *Stanzas Written in Dejection near Naples,* the major ventures of Shelley's later years testify to the relentless energy of an imaginative mind steadily concerned with fundamentals and ever eager to diversify its modes of expression. In *Prometheus Unbound* (1818-1819), Shelley turned to mythical drama to convey, in a more sensitive and complex way, the basic truth that had been expressed through the narrative technique of *The Revolt of Islam.* Moreover, the same dialectical reconciliation of the puzzling dualities of life received more purely lyrical shape in the *Ode to the West Wind* of October 1819.

Dramas and Social Tracts

Like the other romantic poets, Shelley was aware of the limitations of lyrical poetry as a medium of mass communication. He, too, endeavored to convey his message to a larger audience, and he experimented with stage drama in *The Cenci* (1819), a lurid but carefully constructed tragedy which illustrates the havoc wrought by man's Jupiterian lust for power, both physical and mental, in the sphere of domestic life.

Shelley's interest, however, lay in wider issues, which he now began to tackle in unexpectedly robust satires and with scathing polemical aggressiveness, venting his social indignation in the stirring oratory of *The Masque of Anarchy* (1819); in *Peter Bell the Third* (1819), a parody of William Wordsworth and an ironic comment on the elder poet's political and artistic disintegration; in *Oedipus Tyrannus, or Swell-foot the Tyrant* (1820), a mock tragedy on the royal family; and in *Hellas* (1821). The last of his major political poems, *Hellas* celebrates the Greek war of liberation, in which Lord Byron was involved in more active ways; it crowns a large series of minor poems in which Shelley, throughout his writing career, had hailed the resurgent spirit of liberty, not only among the oppressed classes of England but also among the oppressed nations of the world.

Final Poems and Prose Works

Shelley's concern with promoting the cause of freedom was genuine, but his personality found a more congenial outlet in his "visionary rhymes," in which the peculiar, dematerialized, yet highly sensuous quality of his imagery embodied his almost mystical concepts of oneness and love, of poetry and brotherhood, without destroying their ethereal ideality. Such themes remained the fountainhead of his inspiration to the last, but—as he was nearing 30—with a more urgent, yet less strident sense of the unbridgeable gap between the ideal and the real. He conveyed this sense with poignantly subdued elegiac tones in *The Sensitive Plant* (1820) and in the poem that he composed on the death of John Keats, *Adonais* (1821).

Samuel Taylor Coleridge and Wordsworth had been about the same age, some 20 years earlier, when they had expressed, in *Dejection* and the *Immortality Ode,* their disenchanted consciousness and stoical acceptance of the decay that life and experience had brought to their visionary powers. Shelley too, it seems, came to be affected with a similar dismaying sense of fading imagination; his response, however, was significantly different from theirs. Far from submitting to the desiccating consequences of growth, he wrote the *Defence of Poetry* (1821), one of the most eloquent prose assessments of the poet's unique relation to the eternal. And, in 1822, he focused on the poet's relation to earthly experience in *The Triumph of Life,* which T. S. Eliot considered his "greatest though unfinished poem." This work contains an impassioned denunciation of the corruption wrought by worldly life, whose "icy-cold stare" irresistibly obliterates the "living flame" of imagination.

Shelley's death by drowning in the Gulf of Spezia near Lerici, Italy, on July 8, 1822, spared him—perhaps mercifully—the hardening of the spirit that, in his view, had destroyed Wordsworth.

Further Reading

Newman Ivey White, *Shelley* (2 vols., 1940), is still the standard biography. Other biographical studies include Edward Dowden, *The Life of Percy Bysshe Shelley* (1909); Edmund Charles Blunden, *Shelley: A Life Story* (1947); A. B. C. Whipple, *The Fatal Gift of Beauty: The Final Years of Byron and Shelley* (1964); Jean Overton Fuller, *Shelley: A Biography* (1968); and George Bornstein, *Yeats and Shelley* (1970). A convenient introduction for the general reader is Desmond King-Hele, *Shelley: His Thought and Work* (1960).

For general critical studies of the poetry see Carlos H. Baker, *Shelley's Major Poetry: The Fabric of a Vision* (1948); Peter Butter, *Shelley's Idols of the Cave* (1954); Neville Rogers, *Shelley at Work: A Critical Inquiry* (1956; 2d ed. 1967); Milton T. Wilson, *Shelley's Later Poetry: A Study of His Prophetic Imagination* (1957); Harold Bloom, *Shelley's Mythmaking* (1959); Ross Greig Woodman, *The Apocalyptic Vision in the Poetry of Shelley* (1964); and George M. Ridenour, ed., *Shelley: A Collection of Critical Essays* (1965).

Other aspects of Shelley's thought are studied in Ellsworth Barnard, *Shelley's Religion* (1936); Kenneth Neill Cameron, *The Young Shelley: Genesis of a Radical* (1950); Earl J. Schulze, *Shelley's Theory of Poetry: A Reappraisal* (1966); and John Pollard Guinn, *Shelley's Political Thought* (1969). More specifically concerned with Shelley's philosophy are A. M. D. Hughes, *The Nascent Mind of Shelley* (1947); J. A. Notopoulos, *The Platonism of Shelley* (1951); and C. E. Pulos, *The Deep Truth: A Study of Shelley's Scepticism* (1954).

Since Harold Leroy Hoffman wrote *An Odyssey of the Soul: Shelley's "Alastor"* (1933), several studies have been devoted to single works: Bennett Weaver, *Prometheus Unbound* (1957); Donald H. Reiman, *Shelley's "The Triumph of Life"* (1965); and Earl R. Wasserman, *Shelley's "Prometheus Unbound": A Critical Reading* (1965). For assessments of Shelley's influence and reputation see Sylva Norman, *Flight of the Skylark: The Development of Shelley's Reputation* (1954), and Roland A. Duerksen, *Shelleyan Ideas in Victorian Literature* (1966). □

Alan Shepard

The first American in space, Alan Shepard's (born 1923) 1961 flight was immortalized in the book and movie, *The Right Stuff.*

Alan Shepard was born on November 18, 1923, in East Derry, New Hampshire, a small village a few miles south of Manchester. He was the son of an army colonel. As a small child, Shepard attended school in a one-room schoolhouse, where he was a good student, particularly in mathematics. He graduated from the Pinkerton Academy in Derry, New Hampshire, and entered the U.S. Naval Academy in Annapolis, Maryland, in 1941.

During World War II, Shepard served as an ensign aboard the destroyer Cogswell in the Pacific. Following the war, he began flight training and qualified as a pilot in 1947. As a Naval pilot, Shepard served in Norfolk, Virginia, Jacksonville, Florida, and aboard several aircraft carriers in the Mediterranean. In 1950, he became a test pilot, and over the next eight years he tested a variety of aircraft and worked as a flight instructor. He was also assigned to duty aboard a carrier in the Pacific and eventually earned an appointment to the staff of the Atlantic fleet's commander in chief.

One of the First Astronauts

In 1958, Shepard was one of 110 test pilots chosen by NASA as prospective astronauts. NASA planned to judge the applicants based on physical and mental criteria, looking, as NASA administrator T. Keith Glennan stated, for "men of vision . . . with a practical, hardheaded approach to the difficult job ahead." After a battery of physical and psychological tests, seven men were selected as the nation's first astronauts: John Glenn, M. Scott Carpenter, Virgil Grissom, Donald Slayton, Leroy Cooper, Walter Schirra, and Alan Shepard. Following the announcement Shepard said, "My feelings about being in this program are really quite simple. . . . I'm here because it's a chance to serve the country. I'm here, too, because it's a great personal challenge: I know [space travel] can be done, that it's important for it to be done, and I want to do it."

Shepard began intensive training for space flight. Courses in biology, geography, astrophysics, astronomy, and meteorology supplemented his physical training, which included exposure to conditions much more severe than were anticipated during space travel. Shepard also spent long hours performing weightlessness tests, preparing for

the weaker gravitational pull outside the earth's atmosphere.

First American in Space

Early in 1961, NASA chose Shepard over Glenn and Grissom, the two other finalists, to be the first American in space. The astronauts themselves had attempted to downplay the importance of the selection of the first astronaut. John Glenn said, "We have tried to do away with a lot of this talk about who is going to be first on this, because we feel very strongly that this is so much bigger than whose name happens to be on the first ticket." Preparations for America's first manned space flight therefore commenced in a spirit of cooperation. Glenn acted as Shepard's back-up, ready if Shepard became unable to fly, and Slayton served as Shepard's radio contact at the Mercury Control Center. The other astronauts also had responsibilities during Shepard's flight.

On May 5, 1961, Freedom 7 lifted off from Cape Canaveral, Florida. Shepard piloted the Mercury capsule 115 miles above the earth's surface and 302 miles across the Atlantic Ocean. After landing safely in the Atlantic, Shepard was picked up from the water by helicopter pilot; his first words were, "Man, what a ride!" Although the trip lasted for only about fifteen minutes, Shepard's journey was almost technically perfect, and it paved the way for many more flights by U.S. astronauts. Shepard returned to ticker-tape parades, and he received a medal from President John F. Kennedy.

After his historic flight Shepard looked forward to future missions. In 1963, however, he was diagnosed as having Meniere's syndrome, a disease of the inner ear that produces nausea, vertigo, and hearing impairment. NASA removed Shepard from active flight duty and reassigned him to NASA's Houston, Texas, facility, where he became chief of the Astronaut Office. Although he became quite wealthy as a result of real estate and banking investments during the next few years, he yearned for space flight. In 1968, he underwent a successful operation in which a small drain tube was implanted in his inner ear. Shepard applied for readmission to active duty, and in 1969 his patience and determination were rewarded when NASA chose him to command the Apollo 14 flight to the moon. "I think if a person wants something badly enough," Shepard once said, "he's just got to hang in there and keep at it."

Went to the Moon

Apollo 14 became an important mission for the U.S. space program. Apollo 13 had been a disappointment; technical difficulties had prevented it from landing on the moon as planned and placed the astronauts in danger, and the space program was losing public support. The Apollo 14 astronauts were scheduled to test new equipment on the moon's surface and to spend longer periods outside the space capsule. Shepard and Edwin Mitchell were assigned to land on the moon while Stuart Roosa orbited the moon in the command module, the Kitty Hawk.

On January 31, 1971, Apollo 14 blasted off from Cape Kennedy, nearly ten years after Shepard's first space flight. Five days later Shepard and Mitchell landed on the moon's surface, the third group of astronauts to do so. From their lunar module, the two astronauts stepped out into the Fra Mauro Highlands, as the world watched on television. Shepard said, "Wow, it's really wild up here. . . . It certainly is a stark place." The astronauts had brought a lunar cart with them, and during two trips outside the lunar module, each lasting more than four and a half hours, they conducted experiments and gathered rock specimens. On one excursion Shepard hit a golf ball across the moon's surface. In addition, the astronauts left behind a multi-million dollar mini-scientific station that would continue to send messages to scientists on earth. Thirty-three and a half hours after they landed, the two astronauts completed a successful docking with Kitty Hawk. The 240,000-mile journey back to earth ended with a splash-down near Samoa in the South Pacific on February 9. By all accounts, the voyage was a big success.

Immortalized in *The Right Stuff*

The story of the 1961 flight was immortalized in a book by Tom Wolfe and 1983 movie, both titled *The Right Stuff.* Both the movie and the book found a sizable audience, but Shepard wasn't that impressed, as he told *Publisher's Weekly.* "Wolfe never talked to any of us original seven guys. His book was based on hearsay, on what he got from second generation astronauts. The story line was good, but the characterizations left a little to be desired."

Shepard and Deke Slayton, another former astronaut, sought to set the story straight when they contracted to write their own account of the Mercury, Gemini and Apollo programs, tentatively titled *Giant Steps: The Inside Story of the American Space Program.* "The other books written about the space program have been maybe more like stories by engineers than by reporters," Shepard told *Publisher's Weekly.* "Ours has a little more drama." Asked why he had waited until the mid-1990s to tell his story, he told *Publisher's Weekly,* "It's been in the back of my mind, but I've been busy with other things until now, until these guys came to me."

Shepard retired from NASA in 1974. Always a successful entrepreneur, he developed a wholesale beer distributorship and a real estate firm in the Houston area. Shrewd investments in horses, banks, oil, and real estate have made him a multimillionaire. He has been married for over 40 years and has two daughters, lives in Houston and chairs the board of the Mercury 7 Foundation, the original astronauts' educational organization. Although no longer active in the space program, Alan Shepard will be remembered both as the first American in space and as one of a handful of men to walk on the moon.

Further Reading

Caiden, Martin, *The Astronauts: The Story of Project Mercury,* Dutton, 1961.

Carpenter, M.C., and others, *We Seven, By the Astronauts Themselves,* Simon & Schuster, 1962.

MacMillan, Norman, *Great Flights and Air Adventures,* St. Martin's, 1965, pp. 202-203.

Silverberg, Robert, *First American Into Space,* Monarch Books, 1961.
AdAstra, July/August 1991.
Life, May 12, 1961, pp. 18-27.
Publisher's Weekly, March 15, 1993.
Time, February 1, 1971, p. 46; October 3, 1980, pp. 40, 58.
U. S. News and World Report, May 15, 1961, pp. 53-59; May 10, 1976, p. 49; February 15, 1971, pp. 29-31. □

Sam Shepard

Sam Shepard (Samuel Shepard Rogers VII; born 1943) began his career as a playwright in the lively off-off-Broadway scene of the 1960s and became one of the United States' most prolific and acclaimed dramatists. He was also a rock music performer and a film actor.

Samuel Shepard Rogers VII was born on November 5, 1943, at Fort Sheridan, Illinois, the son of a career Army man whose assignments took him to many locations, including Guam, while his son was growing up. After his father retired from the service, the family settled on a ranch in Duarte, California, where they grew avocados and raised sheep.

Shepard (there is some debate as to when he dropped the Rogers from his name) worked as a stable hand at the Conley Arabian Horse Ranch in Chino, California, from 1958 to 1960. Upon graduation from high school he attended Mount Antonio Junior College for a year, majoring in agriculture with some thought of becoming a veterinarian.

When he left college, he joined the Bishop's Company Repertory Players, a touring theater group with which he spent 1962 and 1963. He went to New York in 1963, where he got a job as a busboy at the Village Gate in Greenwich Village, hung out with the son of the famous jazz musician Charles Mingus, and, encouraged by Ralph Cook, the founder of Theater Genesis, began to write plays.

In the 1960s the New York theater scene consisted of three levels. There was Broadway, the center of commercial theater; off-Broadway, which presented some new works as well as revivals of classics not economically viable on Broadway, such as those by Ibsen and Strindberg; and off-off-Broadway (OOB), devoted to experimental works and often housed in bars or lofts in Greenwich Village and on Manhattan's Lower East Side, with little or no admission charged. The most celebrated OOB groups, in addition to Theater Genesis, were the Caffe Cino, La Mama Experimental Theater Company, the Open Theater, and the Judson Poets' Theater.

Shepard debuted at Theater Genesis on October 16, 1964, with the double bill *Cowboys* and *Rock Garden.* In 1965 he presented *Up to Thursday* and *4-H Club* at Theater 65, *Dog* and *Rocking Chair* at La Mama, *Chicago* at Genesis, and *Icarus's Mother* at the Cino.

In 1966 he received the first of several grants, this one from the University of Minnesota, and presented *Fourteen Hundred Thousand* at the Firehouse Theater in Minneapolis; that same year *Red Cross* was given at the Judson.

The *Village Voice* was the chief organ of the counterculture in the 1960s and specialized in covering both off-Broadway and off-off-Broadway. From the start of Shepard's career, *Voice* critic Michael Smith had been an enthusiastic fan, writing that there was something so free and direct about those plays. They seemed to catch the actual movement of the minds of people I know. It was something I had never seen before." The *Voice* annually presented awards called Obies for work in the theater and Shepard was given an unprecedented trio of them in 1966 for *Chicago, Icarus's Mother,* and *Red Cross.*

The *Voice*'s support was vital to the young playwright's career, because the mainstream critics, those from the major newspapers, ranged from lukewarm to hostile. Jerry Tallmer, the *New York Post*'s eye on OB and OOB, could summon no enthusiasm, while Clive Barnes of the *New York Times* (later a supporter) called Shepard's early plays disposable . . . like Kleenex." Indeed, years later, in his introduction to *The Unseen Hand and Other Plays* (1986), Shepard himself wrote, Basically, without apologizing, I can see that I was learning to write," and confessed, some of that work is slightly embarrassing to me now."

In 1967 Shepard wrote *La Turista,* his first full-length play, which won a 1967 Obie; *Melodrama Play,* an Obie winner the following year; *Cowboys #2,* which premiered in Los Angeles; and *Forensic and the Navigators,* which also won a 1968 Obie. He also received two more grants, one from the Rockefeller Foundation in 1967 and one from the Guggenheim Foundation in 1968.

In 1968 Shepard began a three-year stint with the Holy Modal Rounders, a rock group, playing drums and guitar. Interestingly, in an interview conducted in 1971, he stated that he would rather be a rock star than a playwright, yet he did not abandon writing while he was playing, completing *Holy Ghostly* and *The Unseen Hand* in 1969, *Operation Sidewinder* and *Shaved Splits* in 1970, and *Mad Dog Blues* and *Back Bog Beast Bait* in 1971. He was awarded a second Guggenheim in 1971.

Leaving the Holy Modal Rounders, Shepard went to England, and his next five plays were premiered there: *Cowboy Mouth* (written with Patti Smith), *The Tooth of Crime, Blue Bitch* (presented on BBC television), *Geography of a Horse Dreamer,* and *Little Ocean.* When *The Tooth of Crime,* widely acclaimed in England, was presented in the United States, it won an Obie in 1973. That same year saw the publication of his first book of essays and poems, *Hawk Moon.* Two other similar collections followed in 1977 and 1982.

Back in the United States, Shepard became the playwright in residence at the Magic Theater in San Francisco, a position he held from 1974 to 1984. His plays *Killer's Head* and *Action* opened in New York in 1975, the latter winning an Obie that year. The year 1976 saw *Suicide in Band Angel City;* 1977, *Inacoma,* and 1978, *The Sad Lament of Pecos Bill on the Eve of Killing His Wife* and *The Curse of the Starving Class,* a critical success.

It was also in 1978 that Shepard began his career as a film actor, appearing in *Renaldo and Clara* and *Days of Heaven.* He also started his collaboration with Joseph Chaikin on the theater piece *Tongues;* this was a stage work, with music, heavily dependent on the theories of Antonin Artaud. Shepard and Chaikin collaborated on two more pieces, *Savage/Love* in 1979 and *War in Heaven,* presented on WBAI radio in 1985.

In 1979 Shepard achieved his warmest critical reception with *Buried Child,* which won both an Obie and the Pulitzer Prize for drama. Writing in the *Washington Post,* critic David Richards said, Shepard delivers a requiem for America, land of the surreal and home of the crazed . . . the amber waves of grain mask a dark secret. The fruited plain is rotting and the purple mountain's majesty is like a bad bruise on the landscape."

Shepard continued to write plays, including *Seduced* in 1979; *True West,* which had a run of over 600 performances in New York in 1980-81; *Fool for Love,* which won him his 11th Obie in 1984; and *A Lie of the Mind,* which garnered the New York Drama Critics Circle Award in 1986. In 1987 the one-act *True Dylan,* was published in *Esquire* magazine.

At the same time, however, he was expanding his work in film, not only writing screenplays but taking on more acting roles. He appeared in *Resurrection* in 1980, *Raggedy Man* in 1981, *Frances* in 1982, *The Right Stuff in* 1983, *Country* in 1984, and *Fool for Love* in 1985. He was nominated for an Academy Award for his portrayal of jet pilot Chuck Yeager in *The Right Stuff.* He had worked on several screenplays, including *Me and My Brother* and *Zabriskie Point,* but achieved his greatest success in this genre with *Paris, Texas,* which was given a Golden Palm Award at the Cannes Film Festival in 1984. He also wrote the script for *Fool for Love* in 1985.

Shepard continued to demonstrate his rich multi-dimensional talents during the 1990s. *States of Shock* was produced in 1991 and *Curse of the Starving Class* in 1997. The Signature Theater, in New York City devoted a whole season (1996-97) to plays by Shepard. He was awarded the American Academy of Arts and Letters Gold Medal for Drama in 1992.

Writing in the *New Republic,* Robert Brustein called Shepard one of our most celebrated writers," adding that his plays have overturned theatrical conventions and created a new kind of drama." And, in his introduction to *Sam Shepard: Seven Plays,* Richard Gilman writes, Not many critics would dispute the proposition that Sam Shepard is our most interesting and exciting playwright."

Further Reading

Books on Shepard abound, although many of them have a shrill, cheerleading tone. Probably the best is Ellen Oumano's *Sam Shepard: The Life and Work of an American Dreamer* (1986). Also worthwhile are Kimball King's *Sam Shepard: A Casebook* (1988) and Ron Mottram's *Inner Landscapes: The Theatre of Sam Shepard* (1984). Newer works on Shepard include: Leonard Shewey, editor, *Rereading Shepard: Contemporary Critical Essays on the Plays of Sam Shepard,* (1993); Don Shewey, *Sam Shepard* (1997); and Leslie Wade, *Sam Shepard and the American Theater* (1997). In addition, John Blackburn wrote a Master's Thesis *Portrait of the Artist: Sam Shepard and the Anxiety of Identity* (University of Virginia, 1996). □

Thomas Sheraton

The English furniture designer Thomas Sheraton (1751-1806) brought about the transition from the late-18th-century Adam and Hepplewhite style to that of the Regency period.

Born at Stockton-on-Tees, County Durham, Thomas Sheraton had little education and worked at first as a journeyman cabinetmaker. He went to London about 1790 and is said to have "supported himself, a wife, and two children by his exertions as an author." From then on he probably lived chiefly from the sale of his furniture designs, but it is extremely unlikely that he made any furniture after his early years.

In 1799 Sheraton left London to become a Baptist minister at Stockton and Darlington, Yorkshire, and continued in this work until 1802. He passed his last years in London, where he died on Oct. 22, 1806. The Edinburgh publisher Adam Black wrote of Sheraton's abject poverty and spoke of his gifts as a scholar, designer, and teacher.

Sheraton's first and most important publication, *The Cabinet-maker and Upholsterer's Drawing Book,* was issued in 49 separate parts between 1791 and 1794. His designs were intended "to exhibit the present taste of furniture" and "at the same time to give the workman some assistance." They represent an advance upon the neoclassic designs of Robert Adam and George Hepplewhite in the direction of even greater elegance and refinement and in the preference for chair backs and mirror frames of square shape instead of the oval forms favored by these two predecessors. Sheraton's early designs, usually intended to be carried out in satinwood, are often highly ornamental and strongly express the influence of Louis XVI furniture, especially in the shaping of tabletops with serpentine or bowed breakfronts and quadrant ends, in the delicate scrolling of flower and leaf patterns, inlaid or painted, with ribbon decoration, and especially in his use of slender turned colonnettes and feet of "spinning-top" design. Some elements of his designs, such as "reeding" and splayed "claw legs" for tables, persisted as late as 1820.

Of greater significance for the Regency period, however, was Sheraton's *The Cabinet Dictionary* (1803), in which he emphasized the new severer and more archeologically correct aspect of the classical spirit, which he had derived from French Directoire designs and from the work of Giovanni Battista Piranesi, Henry Holland, Charles Heathcote Tatham, and Thomas Hope. Sheraton now included animal motifs such as lion masks and lion monopodia, or lion-shaped supports for chairs and tables. He also showed the curved-saber, or scimitar, leg of the typical Regency chair and made use of dolphins and other marine motifs such as anchors, masts, cordage, oars, and sails in furniture designs associated with Nelson's nautical victories.

Thirty of the projected 150 parts of Sheraton's third work, *The Cabinet-maker, Upholsterer and General Artists' Encyclopaedia,* were issued from 1804 to 1806. Increasingly in his later years his designs showed signs of eccentricity, but a selection of the best designs from his three works, published as *Designs for Household Furniture* (1812), did much to establish his influence in early 19th-century furniture design and production.

Further Reading

Ralph Fastnedge, *Sheraton Furniture* (1962), is an admirable comprehensive and well-illustrated account of the designer's life and work. A selection of his work is in *Sheraton's Furniture Designs,* with a preface by Ralph Edwards (1949). Recommended for general background are Ralph Fastnedge, *English Furniture Styles from 1500 to 1830* (1955); Peter Ward-Jackson, *English Furniture Designs of the Eighteenth Century* (1958); and Clifford Musgrave, *Regency Furniture, 1800-1830* (1971) and *Adam and Hepplewhite and Other Neo-classical Furniture* (1966).

Additional Sources

Fastnedge, Ralph, *Sheraton furniture,* Woodbridge, Suffolk, England: Antique Collectors' Club, 1983. ☐

Philip Henry Sheridan

Philip Henry Sheridan (1831-1888), American soldier, was noted for his part in the 1864-1865 Virginia campaigns of the Civil War.

Philip H. Sheridan was born in Albany, N.Y., on March 6, 1831, the son of Irish immigrant parents who soon moved to Somerset, Ohio. At the age of 14 he went to work as a store clerk. Inspired by the Mexican War, he secured an appointment to the U.S. Military Academy at West Point in 1848. A year's disciplinary suspension delayed his graduation until 1853. Tours of duty in California and Oregon made him into a military jack-of-all-trades and doubtless helped him develop self-reliance and resourcefulness.

Following the outbreak of the Civil War, Sheridan received a captaincy in the 13th Infantry, and after several irksome administrative assignments he was made colonel of the 2d Michigan Volunteer Cavalry. After duty in northern Mississippi he was promoted on July 1, 1862, to brigadier general. Shifted soon afterward to the infantry, he competently commanded a division during the western campaigns.

In March 1864 Sheridan was ordered to Virginia to command the cavalry corps. Following an undistinguished performance at the Battle of the Wilderness, he led a long raid against Gen. Robert E. Lee's communications, which devastated Confederate supply depots and railroads.

On August 1 Gen. Ulysses S. Grant ordered Sheridan to take command in the Shenandoah Valley and dispose of Gen. Jubal Early's force, which had nearly taken Washington in July and still lingered threateningly in the lower valley. With 40,000 infantry and cavalry Sheridan defeated Early's vastly outnumbered force three times in September and October 1864 and finally dispersed the remnant at Waynesboro in March 1865. Meanwhile he had systematically devastated the valley. Sheridan then marched unopposed through central Virginia, reaching Grant in time to participate in the final campaign against Lee.

When the war ended, Sheridan was sent to police the Texas-Mexican border. In 1867, following passage of the Reconstruction Acts, he was assigned to command the Fifth Military District, comprising Louisiana and Texas. President Andrew Johnson, believing Sheridan too heavy-handed in civil affairs, transferred him to the Department of the Missouri to direct operations against the Plains Indians. He was promoted to lieutenant general in 1869, and after succeeding Gen. William T. Sherman as general in chief, he became a full general in 1888. Sheridan completed his memoirs shortly before his death on Aug. 5, 1888, in Nonquitt, Mass.

Further Reading

For Sheridan's own account of his life see his *Memoirs* (1888). An excessively laudatory study is Richard O'Conner, *Sheridan, the Inevitable* (1953). Other studies are W.H. Van Orden,

General Philip H. Sheridan (1896); John McElroy, *General Philip Henry Sheridan* (1896); and Joseph Hergesheimer, *Sheridan: A Military Narrative* (1931). For background information consult Edward J. Stackpole, *Sheridan in the Shenandoah* (1961).

Additional Sources

Hutton, Paul Andrew, *Phil Sheridan and his army,* Lincoln: University of Nebraska Press, 1985.

Morris, Roy, *Sheridan: the life and wars of General Phil Sheridan,* New York: Vintage Books, 1993.

Sheridan, Philip Henry, *Indian fighting in the fifties in Oregon and Washington Territories,* Fairfield, Wash.: Ye Galleon Press, 1987.

Sheridan, Philip Henry, *Personal memoirs of P.H. Sheridan, General United States Army,* New York: Da Capo Press, 1992.

□

Richard Brinsley Sheridan

The British playwright and orator Richard Brinsley Sheridan (1751-1816) wrote two comic masterpieces for the stage, *The Rivals* and *The School for Scandal.* In his own time, Sheridan was equally celebrated as a great Whig orator.

Richard Brinsley Sheridan was born in Dublin, Ireland, on Oct. 30, 1751. His father, Thomas, was an actor and theater manager; his mother, Frances, was the author of novels and plays. The family moved to London in 1758, and Sheridan was educated at Harrow (1762-1768). His first publication, a joint effort with a school friend, N.B. Halhead, was a metrical translation of Aristaenatus (1771). With this friend Sheridan also wrote his first play, a farce called *Jupiter,* which was rejected by both David Garrick and Samuel Foote.

Courtship and Marriage

In 1770 the Sheridans moved to Bath. There Richard, his brother Charles, and his friend Halhead were among the many who fell in love with a beautiful young singer, Elizabeth Linley. The most importunate of her admirers was a Capt. or Maj. Mathews. Terrified by his persecutions, she decided to seek shelter in a French convent, and Sheridan offered to protect her on her journey. In March 1772 they fled to France and were secretly married there. Leaving her at the convent, Sheridan returned to England and fought two duels with Mathews. Elizabeth was brought back to Bath by her father, and Sheridan was sent to London by his, but on April 13, 1773, they were allowed to marry openly.

Though at first the young couple had nothing to live on except a small dowry, in January 1775 Sheridan solved the problem of their support with the production of *The Rivals* at Convent Garden. A comedy of manners that blended brilliant wit with 18th-century sensibility, it became and remained a great successes. One measure of its popularity

was that it gave a new word to the English language, "malapropism," based on Mrs. Malaprop's mistakes.

The year 1775 was a productive one for Sheridan. In May his farce, *St. Patrick's Day, or the Scheming Lieutenant,* was performed, and in November Sheridan's comic opera, *The Duenna,* was produced with the help of his wife's father at Covent Garden. A son, Thomas, was also born to the Sheridans in 1775.

Drury Lane

In June 1776 Sheridan purchased Garrick's share of the Drury Lane Theater and became its manager. No fault can be found with his theatrical sense, but misfortunes and financial carelessness plagued him in this career. At first, however, Sheridan prospered, and 2 years after purchasing Garrick's interest he was able (with his partners) to buy the other half of the theater.

On May 8, 1777, Sheridan presented his new play, *The School for Scandal.* It was immediately, and throughout Sheridan's management, the most successful piece in the repertory of the Drury Lane. This comedy is an ingenious blending of two plots, one concerning the young, country-bred wife of a middle-aged husband who is taught town manners by a "school" of scandalmongers, the other concerning the amorous and financial adventures of the Surface brothers, whose contrasting reputations also contrast with their true characters.

In October 1779 Sheridan produced the last play of his own authorship, *The Critic,* in which he deftly mocked the follies of everyone, from playwright to spectator, connected with the theater. Though he continued as manager of Drury Lane, and though, in 1799, he had a hand in translations of two German plays, *Pizarro* and *The Stranger* at the age of 28 Sheridan had virtually completed the first of his careers.

Parliamentary Career

Sheridan had long been sympathetic to the position of Charles James Fox and his fellow Whigs; his first service to that party was his extensive contributions to their periodical, the *Englishman* (March 13-June 2, 1779). In October 1780 Sheridan entered Parliament as the member for Stafford.

It soon became apparent that the Whigs had another great orator to add to Edmund Burke and Fox. In 1782 and 1783 Fox's friends briefly held office, and Sheridan was respectively undersecretary for foreign affairs and a secretary of the Treasury. His greatest orations, however, were delivered in the 7-year impeachment proceedings against Warren Hastings, the first governor general of British India.

On Feb. 7, 1787, Sheridan spoke for 5 hours on the crimes of Hastings against the begums (princesses) of Oudh. A typical response to this speech was that of a Mr. Logan, who, before he heard it, had written a spirited defense of Hastings. After the first hour Logan remarked, "All this is declamatory assertion without proof"; after the second, "This is a most wonderful oration"; after the third, "Mr. Hastings has acted very unjustifiably"; after the fourth, "Mr. Hastings is a most atrocious criminal"; and at the end, "Of all monsters of iniquity the most enormous is Warren Hastings!" Many of Sheridan's other parliamentary addresses were also greatly admired, but few of them were preserved.

A friend of the Prince of Wales (later George IV), an ally of Fox, an independent after Fox's death, Sheridan was treasurer of the navy in the Whig administration of 1806. In 1804 the prince had appointed him receiver of the duchy of Cornwall, and in 1808 Sheridan at last began to benefit from this office. But his fortunes were on the decline, and in 1812 he lost his seat in Parliament.

Sheridan's first wife died in 1792, and in 1795 he married Esther Jane Ogle. In 1792-1794 Sheridan had to rebuild Drury Lane Theatre, incurring great debts. In 1809 it burned. The theater was again rebuilt, by subscription, but Sheridan did not receive enough for his share to prevent his being harassed by creditors before his death on July 7, 1816. He was buried in Westminster Abbey.

Further Reading

The most complete modern edition of Sheridan's works is *The Plays and Poems of Richard Brinsley Sheridan,* edited by Raymond C. Rhodes (3 vols., 1928). *The Letters of Richard Brinsley Sheridan* (3 vols., 1966) were well edited by Cecil Price.

The earliest relatively impartial biography was by Irish poet Thomas Moore, *Memoirs of the Life of the Right Honourable Richard Brinsley Sheridan* (2 vols., 1825), which omits some of the information made available by Sheridan's family. Early accounts by John Watkins, *Memoirs of the Public and Private Life of . . . Richard Brinsley Sheridan* (2 vols., 1817), and by William Smyth, *Memoir of Mr. Sheridan* (1840), started many false and scandalous stories. Sheridan's sister, Alicia Lefanu, replied to Watkins in her biography of her mother, *Memoirs of the Life and Writings of Mrs. Frances Sheridan, Mother of . . . Richard Brinsley Sheridan* (1824). Of the later accounts, recommended are those of William F. Rae, *Sheridan: A Biography* (2 vols., 1896), and Walter S. Sichel, *Sheridan, from New and Original Material* (2 vols., 1909). Raymond Rhodes wrote the most substantial critical study, *Harlequin Sheridan: The Man and the Legends* (1933). A good brief study is William A. Darlington, *Sheridan* (1933). □

John Sherman

John Sherman (1823-1900), American politician, was the most significant congressional figure in the development of American fiscal policy during the "gilded age."

John Sherman was born in Lancaster, Ohio, on May 10, 1823. He participated in the frantic development of his native state, working on canal improvements at the age of 14 and becoming a supervisor of canal construction at 16. He soon turned to the study of law and in 1844 was admitted to the Ohio bar. In 1854, at the age of 31, he was elected to Congress and, until 1898, served without interruption in Federal office.

Sherman maintained a moderate stance in the tense congresses of the 1850s. Although he criticized the Radical

Republicans during the Civil War, in the end he voted with them. He served in the Senate after 1861. His knowledge of the complexities of currency and finance helped to make him head of the Senate Finance Committee, where in 1874 he engineered several bills concerned with the retirement of the wartime paper money. A man with presidential ambitions, Sherman found it useful to work with conservative eastern financiers, such as August Belmont, who insisted on a solidly based stable dollar, while still serving moderate financial interests in his home state.

Sherman managed Rutherford B. Hayes's difficult nomination and election to the presidency in 1876. He was instrumental in securing Louisiana's disputed electoral votes for Hayes and fully supported the President's program to establish a conservative, white-dominated Republican party in the South. The program failed, but Sherman became Hayes's secretary of the Treasury and a leading candidate for the Republican nomination in 1880.

In 1880 Sherman's candidacy was passed over in a deadlocked convention, and his own campaign manager, James A. Garfield, was nominated. Sherman's failure to secure the nomination stemmed not from his political philosophy but from his inability to inspire excitement in either prominent politicians or the voters. A small dour man, he was an adequate orator and one of the most accomplished governmental technicians of his day. But in his long career he had made many enemies who also blocked his nomination in succeeding conventions.

In the Senate again (1881-1897), Sherman was best known for his sponsorship of the Sherman Silver Purchase Act and the Sherman Antitrust Act. The latter was not really Sherman's work at all; his name was attached to lend it prestige.

In 1897 William McKinley named Sherman secretary of state as a final honor and in order to create a Senate vacancy for Mark Hanna. Sherman was ill-fitted for the position and soon found himself at odds with McKinley's imperialist policies. Sherman resigned a year later. He died in Washington on Oct. 22, 1900.

Further Reading

Until the biography currently being prepared by Jeannette Nichols is completed, the reader must refer to old and outdated works: Theodore E. Burton, *John Sherman* (1906), and Winfield S. Kerr, *John Sherman* (1908). H. Wayne Morgan, *From Hayes to McKinley* (1969), deals with the era of Sherman's prominence. □

Roger Sherman

Roger Sherman (1721-1793), American patriot, was a signer of the Declaration of Independence and a formidable voice at the Constitutional Convention.

Roger Sherman was born of humble origins. As a youth, he worked as a cordwainer and cobbler on the family farm in Stoughton, Mass. In 1743 he moved to New Milford, Conn., where he was variously employed as a surveyor, storekeeper, almanac compiler, and lawyer. He also began his long career as a public official, serving as juryman, deacon, town clerk, school committeeman, justice of the peace, assemblyman, and commissary officer for the Connecticut militia. In 1761 he moved permanently to New Haven, where he continued his mercantile enterprises until 1772, when he retired to devote full time to public affairs. He served long terms as a member of the upper house of the Connecticut Legislature (1766-1785) and as a judge of the superior court (1766-1789), while also acting as treasurer of Yale College, from which he received an honorary master's degree in 1768.

As the Revolution approached, Sherman opposed the Stamp Act, supported the Sons of Liberty, enforced nonimportation agreements, and headed the New Haven Committee of Correspondence. He served in the Continental Congress from 1774 to 1781 and again in 1783-1784. He often counseled caution and moderation but without compromising American self-determination. He signed the Articles of Association of 1774, the Declaration of Independence (serving on its drafting committee as well), and the Articles of Confederation. After the war he returned to New Haven, where he was faced with severe financial reverses stemming from his support of the Revolution, the collapse of some of his businesses, and the demands of a large family (seven children by his first wife and eight by his second).

Though Sherman had consistently sought to strengthen the powers of Congress, he went to the Constitutional Convention of 1787 convinced that it would suffice to "patch up" the Articles of Confederation. He added constructively to debates, often leading the small-state opposition to the Pennsylvania-Virginia insistence on representation according to population. He also fought to uphold the supremacy of state legislatures. In the end, he helped devise the "Great Compromise," approved the Constitution, and defended it in the ratification debates. As an elder statesman, he served for 2 years in the first Federal House of Representatives and then for 2 years in the Senate.

Further Reading

Sherman's letters are in E.C. Burnett, ed., *The Letters of the Members of the Continental Congress* (8 vols., 1921-1938). His speeches are in *The Annals of Congress* (16 vols., 1857-1861), and in Max Farrand, ed., *The Records of the Federal Convention* (4 vols., 1937). The standard biography is Roger S. Boardman, *Roger Sherman: Signer and Statesman* (1938). See also Lewis H. Boutell, *The Life of Roger Sherman* (1896). Clinton Rossiter, 1787: *The Grand Convention* (1966), gives a lively, sympathetic account of Sherman's role.

Additional Sources

Rommel, John G., *Connecticut's Yankee patriot, Roger Sherman,* Hartford, Conn.: American Revolution Bicentennial Commission of Connecticut, 1979, 1980. □

William Tecumseh Sherman

William Tecumseh Sherman (1820-1891), American soldier, was a Union general during the Civil War. He captured Atlanta and Savannah and wrought great destruction in marches through Georgia and the Carolinas.

William T. Sherman was born in Lancaster, Ohio, on Feb. 8, 1820. After his father died, "Cump," as he was known, was raised by the Thomas Ewings. Sherman attended the U.S. Military Academy at West Point, graduating in 1840. He served in the Second Seminole War (1840-1842). Stationed in California during the Mexican War, he had little chance for combat honor, although he was awarded one brevet. He resigned from the Army on Sept. 6, 1853, and entered civilian life, working in banks in California and New York City. He also practiced law unsuccessfully in Kansas and was superintendent of a military academy at Alexandria, La. (now Louisiana State University), when the Civil War came.

Early Civil War Service

Returning to the Army in May 1861, Sherman commanded a brigade at First Bull Run on July 21, 1861. From August to November he was with the Department of the Cumberland in Kentucky, eventually taking command of that department. Nervous, overly alarmed at Confederate capabilities, and racked with hostility toward newspapermen, he suffered an emotional breakdown and was transferred to Missouri for a time. Returning to Tennessee, he supported Gen. Ulysses S. Grant in victorious campaigns against Ft. Henry and Ft. Donelson in February 1862.

Sherman formed a close friendship with Grant and, as a division commander, accompanied Grant's army as it moved southward to Pittsburg Landing. When the Union force was surprised by the massive attack of Confederate general Albert Sidney Johnston at Shiloh on April 6, Sherman reacted vigorously in helping stem the tide of Union defeat; he had four horses shot out from under him. The next day, reinforced by troops from Gen. Don Carlos Buell's force, the Federals drove the enemy from the field. In late 1862 Sherman occupied Memphis but, in his movement against Vicksburg, was repulsed at Chickasaw Bluffs at the end of December. Now a major general of volunteers, and in command of the XV Corps, he served with Grant's Army of the Tennessee in the eventually successful operations against Vicksburg in the first half of 1863.

Later Civil War Service

When Grant was ordered to relieve the Union army at Chattanooga in late 1863, Sherman went along and participated in the Battle of Chattanooga. His attacks at Tunnel Hill on November 24 were repelled, but other Federal assaults succeeded in driving out the Confederate force. Sherman then moved to relieve Knoxville in December. In February 1864, he captured the enemy base at Meridian, Miss.

When Grant became general in chief of all the Union armies, Sherman succeeded him in command in the West. Battle strategy determined that simultaneous advances would be made in May 1864 against Gen. Robert E. Lee, defending Richmond, and Gen. Joseph E. Johnston, defending Atlanta. Sherman began his campaign for Atlanta with 100,000 men as against Johnston's 60,000. In a series of flanking maneuvers, Sherman steadily worked his way to the vicinity of Atlanta. He was unwittingly aided when the rash Gen. John B. Hood superseded Johnston.

Sherman captured the important city on September 2. Then, sending Gen. George H. Thomas back to check Hood's countersortie into Tennessee, Sherman embarked with 62,000 men on his famed "March to the Sea." He captured Savannah on Dec. 21, 1864. This was followed by a swing northward through the Carolinas, against minor opposition, and culminated in the capitulation of Johnston's army at Durham Station on April 17.

Postwar Duty

When Grant became U.S. president in 1869, Sherman replaced him as general in chief, a post he held with distinction until he retired from the army in 1883 as a four-star general. He was still tall and erect, with graying reddish hair and furrowed face. Residing in St. Louis and then New York City, Sherman continued to be active as a speaker and writer. He died in New York on Feb. 14, 1891. Never an outstanding battle captain, he nevertheless won high honors by his talent for devising sweeping campaign plans and by his ability in carrying out great marches with sure logistic support.

Further Reading

The primary personal account is *Memoirs of General William T. Sherman* (2 vols., 1875), an uneven but provocative and intelligent reminiscence. An informed though hostile critique of the memoirs is Henry V. Boynton, *Sherman's Historical Raid* (1875). Of value are Rachel S. Thorndike, ed., *The Sherman Letters: Correspondence between General and Senator Sherman from 1837-1891* (1894), and Mark A. DeWolfe Howe, ed., *Home Letters of General Sherman* (1909).

The ablest, most thoroughly researched biographies are Basil H. Liddell Hart, *Sherman: Soldier, Realist, American* (1929); Lloyd D. Lewis, *Sherman, Fighting Prophet* (1932), brilliantly written and containing much information on Ulysses S. Grant; and James M. Merrill, *William Tecumseh Sherman* (1971), a reassessment of Sherman based on letters discovered by the author and never before used by historians. Useful for Sherman's campaigns are George W. Nichols, *The Story of the Great March* (1865); Jacob D. Cox, *Atlanta* (1882); and John G. Barrett, *Sherman's March through the Carolinas* (1956). □

Sir Charles Scott Sherrington

The English physiologist Sir Charles Scott Sherrington (1857-1952) described the fundamental mechanisms of the working of the mammalian nervous system. He formulated the principle of the reciprocal innervation of effectors and discovered the functional significance of muscle receptors.

Charles Scott Sherrington was born on Nov. 27, 1857, in Islington. He began his medical studies at the Royal College of England and ended them in 1879 at St. Thomas Hospital in London as a fellow of the Royal College of Surgeons. Then he went to Cambridge, where he soon became a fellow of Caius College.

Neurophysiology soon attracted Sherrington, and his first two publications, which he authored in collaboration with J. W. Langley, were devoted to the study of secondary degenerations of the spinal cord of a dog which had undergone an experimental excision of the cerebral cortex. These papers revealed Sherrington's mastery over histological techniques which were such an important asset in his later research.

In 1892 Sherrington married Ethel Wright. In 1895, after a short period devoted to travel during which he was attracted by anatomopathology and bacteriology, he was appointed to the chair of physiology at Liverpool, which allowed him to develop his experimental activity in a well-equipped laboratory.

At the end of the 19th century neurophysiology had just accomplished a decisive step. The spinal cord was no longer a bundle of conducting fibers with no other function

than connecting the brain with the somatic receptors and the muscles, for the demonstration had been made once and for all of its reflexive function. It was also demonstrated that the column of gray matter, interposed between the dorsal and ventral roots, played an important role in nerve cord performance and that this gray matter was composed of myriads of nerve cells linked to one another without protoplasmic confluence. The notion of a relation between the irreciprocity of central nervous conduction and the existence of this structural and trophic discontinuity of the central neuronal nets had become apparent. On the other hand, the study of the neural reactions in invertebrates had revealed the interplay of elementary processes very similar to those whose participation in the functioning of the neuraxis of vertebrates was only beginning to appear.

No coherent doctrine had emerged from these fragmentary observations until 1906, when Sherrington's *Integrative Action of the Nervous System* was published. This book, which contained the Silliman Lectures he delivered at Yale University in 1904, was a milestone in its field.

Integrative Action

The chain of processes, making the spinal cord isolated from the brain a mechanism of high precision and a perfect functional unity, was set forth in a series of logically ordered chapters. Locomotion in mammals was shown to be the result of the orderly cooperation of a group of reflexes admirably adapted to their ends, successively calling each other in a strict temporal and causal seriation through the action of dynamic factors. The study of certain rhythmical reflexes led to the fundamental distinction of the respective functional roles of interneurons and motor neurons. The organization of central autochthonal rhythms was the prerogative of the former, whereas the emission of efferent impulses, both reflex and voluntary ones, was the function of the latter, constituting a "final commonpath."

Sherrington described another more complex neural machinery: the decerebrated preparation with its peculiar characteristic of the permanent contraction of muscles which antagonize gravitation. He definitively characterized as genuine reflexes such brief contractile responses as are aroused by tendinous percussion acting through the sudden elongation of the neuromuscular spindles. The cerebral cortex, which is the warden of associative memory, informed by the telereceptors which greatly enlarge the perceptual space, crowns the neural construction of mammals. It confers unto the creature the power of adaptation to the incessant variations of the environment within which it must defend its ephemeral integrity to ensure the survival of the species. Such was, in its majestic order, this henceforth classical monument of neurophysiology.

Other Discoveries

World War I, in which Sherrington served for the National Defence, interrupted his physiological research at Liverpool. Then came his work at Oxford. This stage of his career permitted him, assisted by enthusiastic young researchers, to add to the edifice of his work the precision and the enriching which electronic progress now made possible. He introduced the notions of central excitatory and central inhibitory states, neutralizing each other algebraically and interpreted as the manifestations of opposite changes in the nervous cells' membrane polarization. The nice intracellular oscillographic recordings, realized by one of his assistants, which Sherrington did not live to see, confirmed the soundness of his foresight through the materialization of postsynaptic potentials of excitation and inhibition. From the same period dates the analysis—a model of quantitative precision—with E. G. T. Liddell, of the myotatic reflex, base of the muscular tonus. Sherrington also discovered the functional role of the thin motor fibers which innervate the neuromuscular spindles.

Sherrington's scientific accomplishment was astounding by its wideness and diversity. For example, he collaborated on a set of excellent studies on primate cerebral cortex between 1901 and 1917. These studies confirmed the explanatory value of the dynamic factors of the central nervous apparatus deduced from the analysis of the spinal mechanisms.

In 1932 Sherrington shared the Nobel Prize in physiology or medicine with E. D. (later, Lord) Adrian. In honoring their work the Nobel Prize Committee acknowledged that biological research inspired solely by philosophical curiosity and free from any concern with immediate medical application would some day help those whose work was aimed directly toward the improvement of the human lot.

In *Man on His Nature* (1942), which is Sherrington's philosophical testament, and in the preface which he wrote in 1947 for the sixth edition of *Integrative Action,* he explained what he meant by the word "integration." He underlined the distinction necessary between the purely motor integration of the decerebrate animal and the complete conscious one of the sensing being. An excerpt from the preface sheds more light on his position concerning the mind-brain problem and explains why Ivan Pavlov once harshly accused him of dualism and of animism. With regard to psychophysiological parallelism, Sherrington mentions the two complementary syntheses which occur simultaneously in the intact nervous system: the physicochemical, which makes an aggregate of interdependent organs into a goal-seeking machine, and the psychological, which integrates an array of perceptual processes into an individual conscience, with its emotions, its aspirations, its volitions, and its memory. He wonders whether these two parallel integrations are commensurable. His position was definitely not the expression of a religious belief. It simply translated the anxiety of the philosopher and the poet of *Man on His Nature* faced with the mystery of human destiny.

Further Reading

The most complete biography of Sherrington is by E. G. T. Liddell in the Royal Society of London, *Obituary Notices of Fellows of the Royal Society,* vol. 8 (1952-1953). Liddell wrote of "Sherrington and His Times" in his *The Discovery of Reflexes* (1960). Ragnar Granit, *Charles Scott Sherrington: An Appraisal* (1967), is an authoritative analysis of Sherrington's work. □

Robert Emmet Sherwood

Robert Emmet Sherwood (1896-1955) was an American playwright whose penetrating dramas often showed an idealistic hero confronted with war.

Robert E. Sherwood was born in New Rochelle, N.Y., on April 4, 1896. He graduated from Milton Academy (1914) and from Harvard (1917). Rejected for service in World War I, he enlisted in the Canadian Black Watch; he was wounded and gassed. He worked for *Vanity Fair* magazine in 1919 and a year later joined the staff of *Life* magazine, becoming its film editor. In 1922 he married Mary Brandon, an actress. Their daughter was born in 1923. He edited *The Best Moving Pictures of 1922-23* and in 1924 became editor of *Life.* The first of his many film credits was *Oh, What a Nurse!* (1926). Sherwood made his stage debut with *The Road to Rome* (1927), a humorous, sophisticated treatment of Hannibal. *Reunion in Vienna* (1931) charmed audiences with its urbane comedy about an old love newly ignited. While publishing a novel, *The Virtuous Knight* (1931), he worked in Hollywood as a dialogue writer and scenarist on his own plays. *Acropolis* (1933), dealing with the problems of Athens and Sparta, was a quick failure. From this time, however, his works became serious.

In 1934 Sherwood was divorced; he married Madeline Hurlock Connelly in 1935. During the next few years, he reached his peak as a dramatist. *The Petrified Forest* (1935), a pertinent assessment of romanticism and reality in American culture, was followed by *Idiot's Delight* (1936). This uncanny prediction of World War II won a Pulitzer Prize. An adaptation, *Tovarich* (1936), preceded the brilliant *Abe Lincoln in Illinois* (1938), another Pulitzer Prize play and the first production of the Play-wrights Company, which Sherwood helped organize. *There Shall Be No Night* (1940), a compelling depiction of the Finish involvement in the war, won Sherwood his third Pulitzer Prize. *Abe Lincoln in Illinois* led to an association with Eleanor Roosevelt.

At the outbreak of World War II Sherwood entered public service as special assistant to the secretary of war (1940), director of the overseas branch of the Office of War Information (1942), and special assistant to the secretary of the Navy (1945). His film play *The Best Years of Our Lives* (1946) won many Academy Awards, and his historical work *Roosevelt and Hopkins* (1948) earned him several awards. He died in New York City on Nov. 14, 1955.

Further Reading

The major works on Sherwood are R. Baird Shuman, *Robert E. Sherwood* (1964), which contains biographical information and a good critical discussion of the plays, and John Mason Brown, *The Worlds of Robert E. Sherwood: Mirror to His Times, 1896-1939* (1965), an excellent biography of Sherwood's life up to the time of his public service in 1940. Recommended for background reading are John Howard Lawson, *Theory and Technique of Playwriting* (1936; rev. ed. 1949); Winifred L. Dusenbury, *The Theme of Loneliness in*

Modern American Drama (1960); and Casper H. Nannes, *Politics in the American Drama* (1960).

Additional Sources

Brown, John Mason, *The worlds of Robert E. Sherwood: mirror to his times, 1896-1939,* Westport, Conn.: Greenwood Press, 1979, 1965. □

Lev Shestov

Russian Jewish thinker and literary critic Lev Shestov (Lev Isaakovich Schwarzmann; 1866-1938) was obsessed with what he considered to be the inevitable struggle between religious faith and reason. An irrationalist and fideist, this Nietzschelike figure was fascinated with religious faith, though it was perhaps the independent Promethean man that appealed to him more than the God of the Hebrews.

Lev Shestov (pseudonym of Lev Isaakovich Schwarzmann) was born in Kiev on January 31/February 13, 1866. His father, Isaak, was a Jewish merchant and committed Zionist who attended the synagogue, but was reputed to be a "freethinker."

As a youth Shestov was attracted to radical ideas, and it was involvement in political activities in his Kiev gymnasium which forced him to continue his studies at a Moscow school, from which he graduated in 1884. At Moscow University he first studied mathematics, but then transferred to law. His political views forced his transfer to Kiev University. He graduated in 1889, but his dissertation on worker laws was not approved for publication by the censors. Though Shestov was probably interested in Marxism for a time, his anarchistic tendencies and his distaste for determinism probably inclined his sympathies toward the Russian populists.

After a brief stint in the military, and a short time as an assistant to a lawyer in Moscow, his father's failing business compelled him to return to Kiev in the early 1890s. By this time his focus of attention had shifted from economics and politics to literature and philosophy.

In 1895 Shestov suffered a complete physical and mental breakdown. It is likely that the crisis was primarily caused by the tremendous tension caused by being caught between a strong-willed, authoritarian father and his romantic involvements with Russian Orthodox women, marriage to whom his father would never approve.

Attempting to regain his health, Shestov traveled to Europe in the spring of 1896. Early the next year, he met a bright, young Russian medical student in Rome, Anna Berezovskaia, who helped nurse him back to health and who eventually became his wife. They had two children, Tatiana (1897) and Nathalie (1900).

Since Shestov never did tell his father about his marriage to Anna, he mainly lived in Russia until mid-1910, while his family remained elsewhere in Europe. One of the happiest and most productive periods for Shestov was when he lived in Coppet, Switzerland, with his family (1910-1914). From September 1914 until July 1918, the Shestovs lived in Moscow. They then moved to Kiev, which was immersed at the time in the violent struggles between Germans, Bolsheviks, and Ukrainian nationalists. Despite Shestov's criticism of the Bolsheviks, he survived and was able to emigrate with his family to Paris early in 1920.

In his first book, *Shakespeare and his Critic Brandes* (published in Russian in 1898), Shestov desperately attempted to find meaning and purpose in all human tragedies. In *The Good in the Teaching of Tolstoy and Nietzsche* (1900), he no longer found it possible to argue that every tragedy is a secret manifestation of the good. Reality now included unexplained tragedy and unanswered questions. In *Dostoevsky and Nietzsche: The Philosophy of Tragedy* (1902), Shestov proposed that it is not just the outside world with its abstract laws of nature and morality which threatens man, but also the pervasive reality of ever-present egoism.

Nowhere in his 13 published volumes does Shestov seem closer to nihilism than in *The Apotheosis of Groundlessness* (1905). His carefully-fashioned pensees are like thought-grenades which Shestov hurled at the cornerstones of the West's most cherished ideals. "Everything we see is mysterious and incomprehensible," Shestov declared. Though bordering on philosophical anarchism, the work revealed its author to be a master of the aphorism genre.

In *Beginnings and Endings* (1908) and *Great Vigils* (1911), though somewhat less caustic, Shestov continued to develop the themes of his previous work. He concluded *Beginnings* with the assertion that "everyone has long been sick of universally binding truths. . . . . It is necessary to find a way to break free from the power of every sort of truth." According to one of Shestov's most perceptive contemporary critics, Simon Frank, when you finish reading Shestov "your soul is left with a suffocating feeling of melancholy— the sort of melancholy which arises during moments of spiritual vacuum."

During the second decade of the 20th century Shestov was for more interested in discussing the attempts of great thinkers to provide solutions to the human predicament. His work of these years on Greek and medieval philosophy and on Martin Luther (*Sola Fide,* 1916) and *Potestas Clavium* (1923) exhibits a real longing for a transcendent God. In *Sola Fide* he contends that "reality is irrational, absolutely unknowable, and our science is only an idealistic ignorance of life."

From 1922 until his death Shestov taught a course in philosophy at the Institut d'Etudes Slaves in Paris. He became quite well-known in French intellectual circles, particularly after one of his articles on Dostoevsky was published in *Nouvelle Revue Francaise* (1922).

Shestov lectured in Germany, Holland, Poland, and, near the end of his life, in Palestine (1936). In the mid 1920s Shestov was selected for membership in the Kant and Nietzsche societies. During the 1920s and 1930s Shestov had contacts with some of the most influential literary figures of the time: Andre Gide, Thomas Mann, Charles Du

Bos, Martin Buber, Edmund Husserl, Martin Heidegger, as well as many other Russian and French luminaries. It was Husserl who in 1928 suggested that Shestov read Soren Kierkegaard—a writer destined to become one of Shestov's favorites and the subject of one of his most important books: *Kierkegaard and Existential Philosophy* (1936, in French). Through this work and other writings Shestov had an impact on other contemporary existentialists, such as Albert Camus, who discussed Shestov in his *Myth of Sisyphus.*

In addition to publishing articles in Russian emigre journals, Shestov's works were translated into French, German, and other languages. His fifth book appeared in English (under the title of *Penultimate Words and Other Essays*) as early as 1916, followed four years later by his fourth book (under the title of *All Things Are Possible*). In addition to his book on Kierkegaard, the fruit of Shestov's emigre writings include two of his most significant works: *In Job's Balances* (1929) and *Athens and Jerusalem* (1938).

Shestov died on November 22, 1938, in Paris. Posthumous works that have appeared thus far: *Speculation and Revelation: The Religious Philosophy of Vladimir Solovev and Other Essays* (1963, in German) and *Turgenev* (1982, in Russian), an unfinished manuscript begun in 1903.

Convinced that scientism, reason, and objective knowledge were but impotent idols of the modern age, Shestov steadfastly insisted that meaning could only be found in that which was subjective and beyond the boundaries of traditional reason and morality.

Shestov has often been presented to readers by Western commentators as a man of profound religious faith. But though he often used biblical vocabulary, the Judaeo-Christian conception of a god who acts in history in ways which are at least partially intelligible to man and who reveals truths which men can communicate with others is foreign to Shestov. For Shestov, original sin was not disobedience to God, but the acquisition of rational knowledge.

In retrospect, this gifted, enigmatic Russian thinker often seemed far more concerned with achieving a god-like freedom for the individual than with discovering a god who might make demands on his human creations. Thus, though Shestov continually criticized the modern age, he seems in many ways to be a modern man par excellence.

Further Reading

All of Shestov's works were written in Russian. Unless otherwise indicated, dates in the text after publications indicate the year the work first appeared in print. If no language is indicated, text reference is to a Russian edition.

Eight of Shestov's thirteen published books are available in English translation in six volumes published by Ohio University Press: *Dostoevsky, Tolstoy and Nietzsche* (1969; Shestov's second and third books); *All Things Are Possible* and *Penultimate Words and Other Essays* (1977; his fourth and fifth books); *Potestas Clavium* (1968); *In Job's Balances* (1975); *Kierkegaard and the Existential Philosophy* (1969); and *Athens and Jerusalem* (1966). In addition, Ohio University Press has published *A Shestov Anthology* (1970), which includes an article on Martin Buber from a book which is not available in English translation. The anthology is a good introduction to Shestov's thought.

For published surveys of Shestov's life and thought in English, the reader is referred to the introductions by Bernard Martin which are in all of the Ohio University Press volumes. The most detailed analysis is to be found in *Athens and Jerusalem.* The best, most complete compilation of biographical materials on Shestov is a two-volume Russian work by his daughter, Nathalie Baranoff: *Zhizn' L'va Shestova* ("The Life of Lev Shestov"; Paris: La Press Libre, 1983). The work quotes liberally from unpublished correspondence and secondary sources not readily available.

Those who have understood Shestov best have tended to be his contemporaries, such as Nicolai Berdiaev and Simon Frank, and their analyses are generally not available in English. One of the most detailed descriptions of Shestov's thought by one of the few people Shestov considered to have understood him is that of the poet and philosopher Benjamin Fondane: *Rencontres Avec Leon Chestov* (Paris: Plasma, 1982). Fondane was a Romanian Jew who emigrated to France in 1923 and died in the gas chambers of Auschwitz in 1944. He was greatly influenced by Shestov.

The most detailed bibliographies on Shestov have been published by the Institut d'Etudes Slaves (Paris): *Bibliographie des Oeuvres de Leon Chestov* (1975) and *Bibliographie des Etudes sur Leon Chestov* (1978). Both works were compiled by Nathalie Baranoff, and she is also responsible for a catalogue (1977) of Shestov manuscripts (including an unpublished work on Plotinus), which is now located at the Sorbonne Library in Paris. The Shestov Archive is also at the Sorbonne and includes Shestov's correspondence, his library, and secondary works on him.

Additional Sources

Valevicius, Andrius, *Lev Shestov and his times: encounters with Brandes, Tolstoy, Dostoevsky, Chekhov, Ibsen, Nietzsche, and Husserl,* New York: P. Lang, 1993. □

Eduard Amvrosevich Shevardnadze

Eduard Amvrosevich Shevardnadze (born 1928) rose to prominence as the foreign minister of the U.S.S.R. under Mikhail Gorbachev. After the breakup of the Soviet Union he was elected President of his native Georgia.

At the end of the September 1990 mini-summit conference in Helsinki, while Presidents Bush and Gorbachev were giving their television press conference, the cameras also focused on the front row of VIPs—Barbara Bush, Raisa Gorbachev, James Baker (the American secretary of state), and Eduard Shevardnadze (the Soviet foreign minister). As with each of the annual summits between the United States and the Soviet Union after 1985, somewhere in every picture, standing near Gorbachev, was Eduard Shevardnadze. Thus, it was a shock not only to the Soviet president but throughout the U.S.S.R. and abroad when Shevardnadze suddenly resigned December 20, 1990. He left with an ambiguous warning of an impending dictatorship.

In his post of foreign minister, Shevardnadze had become one of the most easily recognized Soviet leaders abroad. While Gorbachev was the chief architect of the Soviet foreign policy called *novoe myshlenie* (new thinking), his chief disciple was Shevardnadze. He was always present at international gatherings, having prepared the way, yet appropriately retreating to the background and surrendering center stage to Mikhail Gorbachev when high-level meetings actually took place.

There could hardly be a greater difference in style between the smiling, urbane Shevardnadze and his more somber predecessor, Andrei Gromyko. Self-assured and charming, Shevardnadze was a sunny contrast to the gloomy Gromyko, who was identified with the Soviet "*nyet*" in the United Nations. Shevardnadze displayed an ease in dealing with Western and Third World diplomats that won him respect and admiration. Gromyko was respected, even feared, but rarely admired. When Gorbachev came to power, Gromyko was among the first of the "old guard" to be shifted to another position and given an honorary title. Shevardnadze, at first glance, was an unlikely candidate for minister of foreign affairs. Most of his career prior to 1985 had been dedicated to the Komsomol (Communist Youth League), and police work. He was a "law and order" man from the unruly Republic of Georgia.

A Georgian by nationality, he was born in a small town, Mamati, near the Black Sea on January 25, 1928. At 18 he was a Komsomol instructor and at 20 joined the Communist Party of the Soviet Union (CPSU). His formal education included the Higher Party School of the Communist Party of Georgia, from which he graduated in 1951, and a teaching degree, by correspondence, from the Kutaisi State Pedagogical Institute (1960). He married a journalist and was believed to have children.

In the 1950s he principally worked for the Komsomol, rising to the position of first secretary of the Komsomol of Georgia (1957-1961). He was also a member of the Central Committee of the All-Union (national) Komsomol. From 1958 to 1964 Shevardnadze was a member of the Central Committee of the Communist Party of Georgia. In the 1960s he worked within the Communist Party of Georgia for several years at the *raikom* (district) level and then for the Georgian Ministry of Internal Affairs (MVD), the civilian police, where he served for seven years as minister of internal affairs (1965-1972). In 1972 Shevardnadze was appointed first secretary of the Communist Party of Georgia. In this position he built up a reputation as the man who cleaned up, at least temporarily, corruption in the Georgian Republic. It is believed that his life was threatened on several occasions because of his efforts to eliminate corruption.

His work as first secretary of the Communist Party of the Georgian Republic for 13 years attracted the attention of the national party. In 1976 he was elected to the Central Committee of the CPSU and in 1978 was made a candidate member of the Politburo. This was the same year that Gorbachev was brought to Moscow to serve as Central Committee secretary for agriculture, and one can assume that their close association began at least by 1978.

In 1985 Gorbachev appointed Shevardnadze to be his foreign minister, replacing the long-term (28 years) foreign minister, Gromyko. Shevardnadze also became a full member of the Politburo, the first Georgian since Stalin to serve on the highest organ of the party. In the next five years Shevardnadze made his mark in foreign policy, and virtually everyone forgot that he had little prior experience in external affairs. He soon gained respect and admiration for his keen intelligence and ability to deal rationally with international problems. Shevardnadze was constantly on the road after his appointment, visiting the United States numerous times, Great Britain, China, France, Japan, Germany, and many other countries. In superpower politics, foreign minister was probably the most exhausting position apart from the presidency. Shevardnadze built up a good rapport with his American counterparts, Secretaries of State George Shultz (1985-1988) and James Baker (1989-1990).

At the 28th Congress of the Communist Party in July 1990, Shevardnadze, a party member since he was 20 years old, stated his intention not to run again for the Politburo. He expressed the view, as did other officials, that it was appropriate for government ministers to separate themselves from serving on the Politburo. Several other Politburo members did not stand for reelection or were retired while the first secretaries of the republic were admitted. Hence, the turnover in the composition of the Politburo was substantial after the 28th congress. No longer serving on the Politburo were the members of Gorbachev's Presidential Council—Nikolai Ryzhkov, Alexander Primakov, Vladimir Kryuchkov, Alexander Yakovlev, Vadim Medvedev, and

Shevardnadze. (Kryuchkov, the chief of the dreaded secret police, the KGB, was later arrested as one of the Gang of Eight in the failed coup of 1991.)

Shevardnadze had spoken out strongly at the 28th party congress against the conservative criticism of Gorbachev's administration, which was led by Yegor Ligachev. Unlike some occasions when he did little but report on foreign policy, Shevardnadze actively responded to the charges against new thinking and Soviet foreign policy. But he was a troubled man. Six months later he suddenly resigned as foreign secretary, December 20. A little more than six months after that he quit the Communist Party. Meanwhile he became head of the new Movement for Democratic Reform, built around such liberals as former Presidential Council member Alexander Yakovlev, sometimes called the father of *perestroika;* industrial specialist Arkady Volsky; legislator Ivan Laptyev; mayor of Moscow Gavril Popov; and St. Petersburg (Leningrad) mayor Anatoli Sobchak.

To replace Shevardnadze, Gorbachev appointed career diplomats Alexander Bessmertmykh and then Boris Pankin. Gorbachev wanted to bolster his flagging prestige and persuaded Shevardnadze to return to his old foreign ministry post on November 19, 1991. However, the breakup of the Soviet Union the next month brought an end to the Cold War. The U.S. recognized the independence of Georgia on December 25, 1991 and provided aid for food, fuel and medicine. The popularly elected Georgia president, Zviad Gamsakhurdia, was overthrown by opponents of his increasingly dictatorial regime and replaced with a military council. In March 1992 Shevardnadze returned to Georgia to head a four-person State Council, which replaced the military council.

On October 11, 1992 voters elected a new parliament, with Shevardnadze as chairman. By September 14, 1993 the political and economic situation in Georgia had so deteriorated that Shevardnadze resigned to protest the parliament's blocking of his ministerial appointees. At the request of the parliament, he returned to office two days later. Turmoil and conflict continued in Georgia with minorities and separatists fighting for control of power and resources. Shevardnadze continued to guide the country, challenging Western nations "to rise above national interests and establish a post-Cold War order." During a visit to the U.S. in 1994, President Bill Clinton described Shevardnadze as "a statesman whose vision and diplomacy have played an immeasurably important role in bringing a peaceful end to the Cold War." In 1995 Shevardnadze survived an assassination attempt and the same year was elected Georgia President in a popular election. He continued to guide the Georgia state through the uncertainty of the post-Cold War period.

Further Reading

The best source of information on Shevardnadze is his political memoir, *The Future Belongs to Freedom* (1991). There has been relatively little written about Shevardnadze. Some sources which shed insight on his career and role in the Gorbachev administration since 1985 include Donald R. Kelley's *Soviet Politics from Brezhnev to Gorbachev;* and Baruch A. Hazan's *From Brezhnev to Gorbachev: Infighting in the Kremlin.* Several works chronicle his service as foreign minister, including Richard Staar's *USSR Foreign Policies after Detente;* and Raymond F. Smith's *Negotiating with the Soviets.* For a general overview of the evolution of Soviet foreign policy, Nogee and Donaldson's *Soviet Foreign Policy Since World War II;* and Alvin Z. Rubinstein's *Soviet Foreign Policy Since World War II: Imperial and Global* are recommended; Misha Glenny, in a personal interview, described him as the "Bear in the Caucasus" (*Harper's Magazine,* March 1994). Information on Georgia and Shevardnadze can be found in articles and fact sheets published in the *US Department of State Dispatch.* ☐

Fu'ad Shihab

Fu'ad Shihab (1903-1973) was the Father of the Lebanese Army, which he organized after World War II and headed until his election as president of Lebanon in 1958. Although he worked hard to forge a sense of national unity among Christian and Muslim Lebanese, this legacy was lost in the period following his retirement and death.

Fu'ad Shihab (also spelled Chehab) was a scion of the princely family which had ruled Lebanon from 1711 to 1842. Fu'ad Shihab was born in 1903 in the town of Ghazir in Kisrwan and was the fourth generation descendant of Prince Hasan, the brother of Prince Bashir II (the Great) who was the ruler (Hakim) of Lebanon intermittently during the period 1788-1840.

Father of the Lebanese Army

Shihab studied at the School of Freres Maristes in Junya and after finishing his secondary school enrolled in the military academy in Damascus, from which he graduated as a lieutenant in 1923. He continued his military studies in France at L'Ecole d'Application de L'Infanterie à Saint Maixent and at L'Ecole Supérieure d'Etat-Major de Versailles. In 1930 he was appointed commander of the Rashaya (Southern Biqa') garrison, a position he held until 1937. In 1938 he was sent to Paris to study at L'Ecole Supérieure de Guerre.

During World War II he was in charge of organizing the forces called Troupes Spéciales du Levant which participated in fighting on the side of the Allies in North Africa, Italy, and France. On August 1, 1945, he was promoted to the rank of general and became commander-in-chief of the Troupes Spéciales du Levant which rallied under the Lebanese flag to become the Lebanese army. The Lebanese army was built under Shihab on a non-sectarian basis, creating an institution which instilled in its members the spirit of loyalty to Lebanon rather than to their religious sects.

Whenever Lebanon was engulfed in a crisis the assistance of General Shihab was invariably sought. For instance, in the political crisis which centered around the demand for the resignation of President Bishara al-Khuri (1943-1952) in September 1952, General Shihab was appointed prime minister for a brief transitional period until a new president was elected. In the civil war of May to October 1958 President Camille Chamoun (1952-1958) was challenged by an armed opposition whose leaders were mostly Muslim and Druze politicians. General Shihab as the commander of the Lebanese army neither allowed the opposition to overthrow Chamoun nor agreed to put down the rebellion by force. He kept his army united and acted as the indispensible arbiter, furnishing the basis for his election as president on July 31, 1958.

Shihab's Presidency, 1958-1964

Coming to power in the wake of the 1958 crisis, President Shihab (a Maronite Christian) tried to inculcate a sense of national unity among the Lebanese. He pursued a foreign policy which reaffirmed the unwritten pact of 1943 by coming to terms with the rising tide of Arab nationalism, led by Gamal Abdel Nasser of Egypt, without infringing upon Lebanese sovereignty. The amicable understanding between Shihab and Nasser stabilized Lebanon and consolidated Shihab's popularity among Lebanese Muslims.

Domestically, Shihab sought to introduce reforms in the civil service by establishing a Civil Service Council and a Central Inspection Board to reduce corruption and to base civil service recruitment more on merit rather than on patronage. He also initiated the policy of equal division of administrative posts between Christians and Muslims.

Politically, Shihab expanded the Lebanese Parliament to 99 members, rendering it more representative in order to lessen the chances for the use of violent non-democratic means to achieve political objectives. This was particularly significant in light of the abortive coup d'etat attempted by a few army officers and the Syrian Social Nationalist Party on December 31, 1961. Their major grievance was Shihab's foreign policy, which was favorable to Nasser. The heavy-handedness of Shihab's security apparatus in dealing with the leaders of the coup d'etat tarnished the image of his presidency, but it was to his credit that none of the political prisoners was executed and that within a decade they were all freed.

President Shihab realized that no national unity could last unless the underprivileged population in the less developed regions of Lebanon were drawn into the political process. With this objective in mind Shihab asked Louis Joseph Lebret of the Institut de Recherches et de Formation en vue de Développement (IRFED) to undertake a thorough social and economic study of Lebanon. This resulted in a report which has ever since been regarded as a landmark in determining the development needs of Lebanon as a whole.

Shihab's Legacy

Shihab's influence continued throughout the 1960s. However, he declined, in 1970, to run again for the presidency, and his handpicked candidate was defeated in the elections. Consequently, Shihabism came under attack and Shihabist officers were purged from the army. Fu'ad Shihab died on April 25, 1973, and his political legacy appears, in the light of the later civil wars and foreign interventions, to have been all but forgotten.

Further Reading

Additional information on Shihab and on Lebanon during the period of his rule can be found in Marius Deeb, *The Lebanese Civil War* (1980); Michael C. Hudson, *The Precarious Republic: Political Modernization in Lebanon* (1968); and Kamal S. Salibi, *Crossroads to Civil War 1958-1976* (1976). □

Shih Ko-fa

The Chinese scholar-soldier Shih Ko-fa (died 1644), also named Hsien-tze and Tao-lin, is a national hero for his defense of Yangchow against the Manchus.

Born in Hsiang-fu, Chihli (Hopei), of a poor family, Shih Ko-fa lived in a period of war and invasion. From an early age he had a profound love for his country and felt an irreconcilable hatred toward the enemy. He regarded the patriot Wen T'ien-hsiang as his greatest inspiration.

Shih had remarkable records in the preliminary examination held in his native town, qualifying him to take the prefectural examination, with the degree of *hsiu-t'sai* (flowering talent—that is, licentiate or bachelor). Tso Kuang-tou, superintendent of examinations, arranged for him to be educated in a *shu-yüan* (private academy), with free maintenance and tuition. In 1624/1625 Shih passed the provincial examination with the degree of *chü-jen* (recommended man). At that time Tso became involved in a political intrigue; he was imprisoned and tortured to death. At the risk of his life, Shih visited the prison and gave proper burial to his patron's body.

In 1628 Shih passed the state examination at Peking, the capital, with the highest degree of *chin-shih* (presented scholar). He became a member of the Han-lin-yüan (Board of Academicians) and later was appointed governor general of Honan and Anhwei. He was very successful in his military campaign against the rebels. By 1643 he had risen to be minister of the Board of War at Nanking, taking command of the armies south of the Yangtze.

In 1644, when the capital fell to the Manchus, a young prince, Fu Wang, was enthroned to continue the imperial line. Shih was then promoted to *ta-hsüeh-shih* (grand secretary) in charge of the defense of Yangchow (Kiang-tu). The feeble Ming government, however, exhibited little fervor to defend itself against the onslaughts of the Manchus. As a result, Shih's defense plan was thwarted, and the approaching Manchu troops quickly encircled Yangchow. Shih, refusing to acknowledge the inevitable, led his gallant army and people in a determined resistance. As one story has it, he might have saved the city had he been willing to open the canals and drown the enemy. But he said, "Our people will die in greater number than the Manchu troops!" So the city was taken and sacked, a bloody massacre continuing for many days. Shih was captured and slain.

Years later a shrine at Mei-hua-lin (Plum-flower Hill), Yangchow, where Shih's costume and symbolic articles were buried, was built in his honor. In the reign of Ch'ien-lung (1735-1796) he was given the posthumous designation Ch'ung Ch'eng (Man of Loyalty and Integrity). His writings are preserved in *Shih Ch'ung Ch'eng Chi* (Collected Writings of Shih Ko-fa).

Further Reading

This period of Chinese history is well treated in Kenneth Scott Latourette, *The Chinese: Their History and Culture* (4th ed. 1964). □

Shih Le

Shih Le (274-333) was the founder of the Latter Chao empire and is an example of a man of the humblest social origins who, during troubled times, rose to the highest position of ruler of almost all of North China.

Shih Le was a Chieh, a Hsiung-nu tribe which seems to have spoken a Turkic language. He came from southeastern Shansi, and although his biography says he was descended from small-tribe chief-tains, his early life shows him to have been very poor indeed. In 285 he went to Lo-yang, the capital, accompanying a merchant from his native place. Shih reached the lowest point in his fortunes when he was sold into slavery to a Chinese in Shantung. He then joined, and eventually became the leader of, a group of bandits. At this time he took the Chinese name of Shih Le.

After some striking victories, in 307 Shih threw in with the self-styled king of the barbarian "Han" dynasty, Liu Yüan, and remained, ostensibly at least, in the service of that "dynasty" until he founded his own kingdom in 319. In the intervening years he piled up victory upon victory, invading the Pei-ho Basin down to the Yellow River in 308, ambushing and killing Wang Yen, close to 50 members of the imperial Chin family, and 100,000 troops in eastern Honan in 311, the year Lo-yang was burned and sacked by Liu Yüan's successor, Liu Ts'ung.

By killing two of his allies and annexing their armies that same year, Shih became an independent force; and when he, counseled by his wise Chinese adviser, Chang Pin, took Peking by ruse from the rebel Chin general, Wang Chün, in 314, he became the de facto ruler of eastern China. When Liu Ts'ung died in 318, Shih Le became vice-regent of the "Han" empire with Liu Yao; but a palace revolution which occurred that year forced him to break with Liu Yao, and the two barbarian leaders set up rival capitals: Liu Yao in Ch'ang-an, and Shih Le in Hsiang-kuo, southern Hopei.

Since both took the name Chao for their kingdoms, historians have called Liu Yao's dynasty "Former Chao" and Shih Le's "Latter Chao." In 328, after 5 years of intermittent warfare, Liu Yao occupied Lo-yang (about midway between the two capitals). The next year Shih Le personally led his troops against his rival, taking the ancient capital and capturing Liu Yao (who was dead drunk at the time). Thus in 329 Shih Le was the ruler of almost all of North China, and in March-April 330 he assumed the imperial throne of the Latter Chao, although, with modesty that was unique among his barbarian peers, he refused the title of emperor, contenting himself with "Heavenly Prince of the Great Chao."

Illiterate, having received no schooling whatsoever in his indigent youth, Shih Le was by no means lacking in intellectual curiosity. He was an admirer of Chinese culture and of Buddhism, the patron of the great monk Fot'u-teng, and the builder of splendid monasteries in his capitals. It is true that the histories seem only to remember his interest in the magical aspects of Buddhism, his belief in and fear of Fo-t'u-teng's power to see the future and to work miracles, but they also tell us that late in life "he liked to listen to scholars read to him and when, from time to time, he was wont to discourse on the faults and virtues of men of ancient and modern times, all those who heard him assented with delight." His imperial status was short-lived, for he fell seriously ill in 333 and died on August 17.

Shih Le was an astute and, according to the standards of the age, a humane leader. He strove to Sinicize and bring racial harmony to his realm, but he was unable to achieve real prosperity. The incessant warfare that characterizes his entire reign was, of course, the main reason, but his complete reliance on the semifeudal regional Chinese Great Families made it impossible for him to institute centralized civil administration with power to protect the peasants and keep the bitter racial animosities between the Chinese and barbarians in check. The result was that 2 years after the death of his nephew and successor, Shih Hu, in 349 (a ruler as ruthless as his uncle had been benign), the empire, torn by internal strife, simply collapsed.

Further Reading

There is no work on Shih Le in English. A background study which discusses him is William Montgomery McGovern, *The Early Empires of Central Asia: A Study of the Scythians and the Huns and the Part They Played in World History* (1939). □

Edward Albert Shils

Edward Albert Shils (1911-1995), American sociologist, studied the sociology of culture, with special attention to the role of ideology in culture and the part played by intellectuals in the formation and shaping of ideology. He also studied the sociology of science, of higher education, and of literature, plus the sociology of sociology itself.

For whatever reason, Edward Albert Shils chose to keep most of the facts of his life closed to public view. We do know, however, that he was born in 1911 and received a Bachelor's degree in foreign languages from the University of Pennsylvania some 20 years later. He worked as a social worker for several years, including one year in New York.

On September 22, 1932, this young man [as he described himself in one of his articles] without social airs and without social ambitions, poor, rather ignorant, serious, and intellectual, launched on a quest without knowing what he was looking for'' and went to the University of Chicago. There he found an atmosphere that permitted him to grope, along with professors who were themselves groping, trying to find answers to questions about human social life. Shils was particularly influenced by the economist Frank H. Knight, the economic historian John U. Nef, and the sociologist Robert E. Park. Each of them opened aspects of behavior to Shils that he had never thought related to one another and that he increasingly felt could only be answered through a sociological framework.

Shils became a research assistant in sociology (and took a decrease in his monthly salary from the $125 he had earned as a social worker to $86.11) but, he says, he never took a course for credit at the university because the requirements were not up to my standards.'' Consequently, this distinguished sociologist completed not a single course in the field, nor did he receive a Ph.D. Such was the latitude for individual growth and discovery provided at that time by the University of Chicago (from which he retired as a distinguished professor in 1985).

Work at Home and Abroad

His linguistic ability brought him into contact with the writings of the German sociologists Georg Simmel, Max Weber, and Karl Mannheim and the French sociologist Emile Durkheim. During his Chicago years, these writers helped to shape Shils' thinking about the relation between social groups, the shaping of ways of thinking through group membership, and the role played by scholars and scholarship in human affairs. These ideas led him to collaborate in the launching of the *Bulletin of the Atomic Scientists* with scientists who had worked in the top-secret Manhattan Project to produce the first atomic bombs during World War II and who, emerging from secrecy after the war, attempted to alert governments to the risks of nuclear weaponry.

Shils joined the staff of the London School of Economics in 1946 and taught sociology. While there, as he watched the British Empire begin to divest itself of its colonies, including the vast subcontinent of India, he raised questions about intellectuals in the new states.'' In 1947 he delivered a series of lectures in London on primary groups in the social structure, focusing especially on some earlier research he had done (with Morris Janowitz) on the dissolution of the German army during the war. Meanwhile, he continued his close connection with the atomic scientists' movement.

In 1949 the sociologist Talcott Parsons invited Shils to Harvard University to join him in writing what was to become a major sociological document of the mid-20th century—*Toward a General Theory of Action* (1951)—and in developing what they called action theory.'' Shils' acceptance renewed a friendship that had begun in 1936, when they first met at the University of Chicago. Together Parsons and Shils attempted to construct an all-inclusive sociological theory that would provide a unified understanding of society, that would find an interconnectedness of all things social. Shils described Parsons as a saint of sociology,'' and their collaboration persisted until Parsons' death in 1979.

Return to the University of Chicago

From 1952 to 1953 Shils lectured at the University of Manchester, and in late 1953 he returned to the University of Chicago with a joint appointment to its Committee on Social Thought, an interdisciplinary program in the social sciences, and to the Department of Sociology. Here he remained until his retirement in 1985.

New interests now engaged him: the plight of the intellectual in a time of conservative reaction to thought deemed to be radical or unpopular; academic freedom; mass culture; and the proper organization of intellectual institutions which would enable them to meet their intellectual and social obligations.'' He visited India for an extended period in 1955 and 1956, and returned every year but one until 1967. In 1962 he created the quarterly journal *Minerva* to deal with matters of science policy and higher education. He was invited by the University of Kent in Canterbury to deliver the T.S. Eliot Memorial Lectures in 1974; his subject was the part played by tradition in modern life. In 1983 he received the International Balzan Prize, awarded by an Italian foundation for fields without Nobel Prizes. In presenting Shils the prize, the foundation cited him for combining the empiricism of American sociology with the theoretical thinking of European sociologists, thus contributing toward a truly universal general sociology.'' He was the first sociologist, and the second social and moral'' scientist after Jean Piaget, to be given that honor.

Although Shils investigated a wide variety of social phenomena, the central concern of his work was his attempt to answer the age-old question: how is society possible? His answer was a sociological one, rooted both in the classic sociological tradition of Georg Simmel, Max Weber, and Emile Durkheim and in the American writings of Robert E. Park, W. I. Thomas, and Charles Cooley. He argued that societies exist through the varieties of ties people form to one another—in small groups, large collectivities, or even social classes or nations—the ideologies or systems of beliefs that make some ties more permanent than others, more important than others. One can understand a particular society or societies in general by looking not at a single moment in time but at a series of connected moments—developing what Park called a natural history'' and noting the consistencies or changes from moment to moment.

However, the strength or location of social ties does not yet tell the whole story. Ideology, religion, science, and media culture are all essential to persistence and change in society, and, unless they are understood in all their richness and variety, one cannot possibly understand the social order. It was Shils' sensitivity to the interplay between ideas and action that was at the core of his sociological work and which linked him to the larger tradition of social thought. Perhaps Shils best characterized his efforts (on the opening page of the first issue of *Minerva*) as the improvement of understanding.''

Shils taught every year for 56 years—teaching his last class at the age of eighty-four. In the last fifteen years of his life he concentrated his attention on clarifying the nature of what he called collective self-consciousness. By the term collective self-consciousness, he meant the self-consciousness of a collectivity, in particular a society. He thought that society was a real entity.

Among his good friends were to be found many scientists: the Hungarian physicist Leo Szilard, the German physicist Heinz Maier-Leibniz, and the American physicist Alvin Weinberg. He knew much about governmental policy toward the natural sciences; one of the areas covered by *Minerva*) was the influence of government on scientific research.

In 1979, he was selected by the National Council on the Humanities to give the Jefferson Lecture, the highest national honor given in the field of the humanities.

Further Reading

One can best learn of Shils as person and sociologist by reading his own work. Collections of his papers include: *Selected Essays* (1970), whose contents cover the breadth of his concerns and include what has become a sociological classic: "The Calling of Sociology." In addition, there are *The Intellectuals and the Powers and Other Essays* (1972) and *Center and Periphery: Essays in Macrosociology* (1975). He is the author of *The Present State of American Sociology* (1948); *Political Development in the New States* (1962); *The Torment of Secrecy* (1974 reprint with new introduction); *Tradition* (1981); *Cambridge Women: Twelve Portraits* (1996); and *Portraits: A Gallery of Intellectuals* (1997). He edited with Talcott Parsons *Toward a General Theory of Action* (1951); and, with Parsons, Kaspar D. Naegele, and Jesse R. Pitts, *Theories of Society* (1961). He also was the editor of a selection of articles from *Minerva, Criteria for Scientific Development: Public Policy and National Goals* (1968). The titles indicate the subjects of the books. A set of essays in honor of Edward Shils," *Culture and Its Creators,* assembled by two of his students, Joseph Ben-David and Terry Nichols Clark, appeared in 1977; it contains an all-too-brief assessment of the character and contributions of Shils. His obituary appeared in the January 29, 1995, *Chicago Tribune* and *New York Times.* □

Shinran

The Japanese Buddhist monk Shinran (1173-1262) was the founder of the True Pure Land sect, or jodo shin shu. He was the most famous disciple of Honen and was active in developing and transforming Amidist beliefs in Japan.

The son of a court noble, Shinran entered the Tendai monastery on Mt. Hiei in 1182. But he found Tendai teachings inadequate. He is said to have turned to belief in Amida as the result of a dream in which he was so instructed by the bodhisattva Kwannon.

In 1207 Shinran was exiled to Echigo in the north at the same time as his master Honen, returning to the capital with him in 1211. The reason for Shinran's banishment was that he had taken a wife, thus defying the vow of celibacy. The woman was alleged to be a daughter of the Fujiwara regent Kanezane, and Honen was said to have commanded the marriage.

Although there is some doubt about the identity of Shinran's wife, there is none at all that he wished to show by this act that monastic discipline was not necessary for salvation if one put oneself completely at the mercy of the Buddha Amida as Honen required. He further wished to demonstrate that the family should be the center of religious life. Shinran felt that he was merely carrying to its logical conclusion Honen's idea that if salvation meant consigning oneself completely to Amida's grace other religious practices were superfluous.

It was Shinran's belief that he should exert himself to the utmost to propagate belief in Amida among the simple people. He was himself obliged to live among the people, in a sense a social outcast. And he thought of himself as a lost soul. He even went so far as to claim that the wicked had more chance for salvation than the good, for the former relied more on Amida's grace than the latter, who counted too much on their good works. "If even good people can be reborn in the Pure Land, how much more the wicked man!"

Certain more conservative followers of Honen claimed that the continual calling of the Buddha's name, the *nembutsu,* was a most desirable religious act. Honen himself is said to have recommended multiple invocation. Shinran, however, believed that quantity had little to do with the Buddha's grace and that a single repetition of his name was all that was necessary. Multiple repetition seemed to him to be, in fact, a practice through which one strove to attain salvation other than by complete reliance on Amida's mercy.

Shinran's innovation in Japanese Amidism was the abolishment of monasticism and the authorization of a married priesthood. He himself was a *shami,* a person who leads a religious life but does not follow the monastic discipline.

Further Reading

An account of Shinran's life and excerpts from his writings are in Ryusaku Tsunoda and others, eds., *Sources of the Japanese Tradition* (1958), and a detailed discussion of Shinran's beliefs is in Alfred Bloom, *Shinran's Gospel of Pure Grace* (1965). □

Edward Shippen

Edward Shippen (1728-1806), American jurist, was a Tory during the Revolution but later rose to the post of chief justice of the Supreme Court of Pennsylvania.

Edward Shippen was the scion of a patrician Pennsylvania family. He was born on Feb. 16, 1728, received his first schooling in Philadelphia, and studied law at the Middle Temple in London. By virtue of his own ability and his family's eminence, he became a successful lawyer in Philadelphia almost from the date of his admission to the bar in 1750.

Shippen's reverence for European education and intellect made it difficult for him to move with the times during the period of estrangement from England prior to the Revolution. That Shippen would remain a Tory was never in doubt. Although appalled at English coercion, he could never bring himself to do more than protest mildly; he remained conservative, aligned with those Pennsylvanians who ultimately opposed any break with England.

Shippen's legal and public careers were stalled only temporarily by the Revolution. Though his son-in-law was Benedict Arnold (married to his daughter Margaret, known as "Peggy the Tory Belle") and his sympathies had been well publicized, he was never expelled from Pennsylvania, nor was his property confiscated. He was merely interned at his country estate, where it was virtually impossible for him to actively aid the English cause. Moreover, like many Tories, he had taken an oath of neutrality that later stood him in good stead.

With the return of peace, Shippen resumed his legal career and within a short time received a series of judicial appointments. In 1784 he was named president of the Court of Common Pleas of Philadelphia; soon afterward he rose to the High Court of Errors and Appeals. In 1791 he was named an associate justice of the Supreme Court of Pennsylvania, and in 1799 chief justice.

With the changing values after the turn of the century, however, Shippen's conservatism threatened his career once more. As in the days of the Revolution, when loyalism was punishable, so it was that Federalism—and Shippen was a Federalist—became a cause for political retribution in post-1800 Pennsylvania. In 1804 he and two colleagues were impeached on clearly political grounds. Although acquitted in 1805, Shippen resigned from the bench less than a year later because of failing health. He died on April 15, 1806.

Further Reading

Surprisingly little has been written about Shippen. For brief but cogent insights into his life see Carl and Jessica Bridenbaugh, *Rebels and Gentlemen: Philadelphia in the Age of Franklin* (1942), and Elisha P. Douglass, *Rebels and Democrats: The Struggle for Equal Political Rights and Majority Rule during the American Revolution* (1955). □

William L. Shirer

An eyewitness to many of the critical events in Europe in the 1930s, William L. Shirer (1904-1993) reported the key developments leading to World War II and wrote widely on the history of Nazi Germany.

Born in Chicago, Illinois, on February 23, 1904, William Lawrence Shirer was the son of Seward Smith, a lawyer, and Josephine (Tanner) Shirer. After graduating from Coe College in 1925, Shirer left his home in Cedar Rapids, Iowa, to set out for Paris on one last youthful fling before settling down to work in the United States. Crossing the Atlantic via a cattle boat, Shirer dreamed of becoming a poet and novelist. Hundreds of other American men and women with similar dreams were then coming to Paris, however, and Shirer could not find work with the major American newspapers with Paris editions.

On the morning of his last day in France, resigned to returning to what he called the land of "Prohibition, fundamentalism, puritanism, Coolidgeism, [and] Babbitry," the editor of the Paris edition of the *Chicago Tribune* offered Shirer a job. The next day he was sitting at the *Tribune* copy desk next to a fellow expatriate-turned-copywriter, James Thurber.

For the next two years Shirer wrote sports and human interest stories for the *Paris Tribune* and studied European history at the College de France. Increasingly, he turned away from fiction and poetry toward "what was going on in the world. "History now seemed more interesting to me, especially contemporary history. . . ." Vaguely the idea began to take root that there might be a great deal of history to write about from here for a daily newspaper back home."

Shirer's *Tribune* editors agreed, and from 1927 to 1932 he served as a foreign correspondent for the home newspaper, roaming from one European capital to another.

Working subsequently for the Paris edition of the *New York Herald,* the Universal News Service, and the Columbia Broadcasting System (CBS), Shirer spent much of his time in Berlin, Prague, and Vienna, reporting on the rise to power of Hitler and the Nazis and on the coming of World War II. Shirer's dramatic radio reports won him the Headliners Club Award in 1938 and 1941. His observations of the tumultuous events in Europe in the 1930s formed the basis of his best known books: *Berlin Diary: The Journal of a Foreign Correspondent, 1934-1941* (1941); *The Rise and Fall of the Third Reich: A History of Nazi Germany* (1960); and *The Nightmare Years, 1930-1940* (1984), each one a blend of journalism and history.

Shirer returned to the United States in December 1940, continuing to work as a radio commentator for CBS until 1947 when he joined the Mutual Broadcasting System. His support for the Hollywood Ten during the postwar "Red Scare" caused him to be blacklisted from broadcasting, and in 1950 he turned to lecturing and writing to support his family during the McCarthy era. Shirer spent much of the next decade utilizing his own reports on the events of the 1930s, transcripts of the Nuremberg Trials, and captured German documents to write his panoramic *The Rise and Fall of the Third Reich,* which won the 1961 National Book Award and Sidney Hillman Foundation Award.

His major works after 1960 include a memoir of Gandhi, an analysis of the fall of the third French Republic in 1940, a book on Leo Tolstoy (the great Russian writer), and a memoir of his exciting life and times. Married in 1931 to Theresa Stiberitz and divorced in 1970, Shirer had two daughters, Eileen Inga and Linda Elizabeth. He lived in Lenox, Massachusetts and died in Boston in 1993, a few months prior to his 90th birthday.

Further Reading

Shirer's major writings include *Berlin Diary: The Journal of a Foreign Correspondent, 1934-1941* (1941); *Midcentury Journey: The Western World Through Its Years of Conflict* (1952); *The Rise and Fall of the Third Reich: A History of Nazi Germany* (1960); *The Collapse of the Third Republic: An Inquiry into the Fall of France in 1940* (1969); *Twentieth-Century Journey: A Memoir of a Life and the Times,* Vol. I: *The Start, 1904-1930* (1976), and Vol. II: *The Nightmare Years, 1930-1940* (1984); *A Native's Return* (1990); *Gandhi: A Memoir* (1980); and his last major work, *Love and Hatred: the Troubled Marriage of Leo and Sonya Tolstoy* (1994). For biographical and critical information on his life and writings see *Dictionary of Literary Biography: American Writers in Paris, 1920-1939* (1980) and articles in the *New Republic* (November 14, 1960, and February 12, 1977); *Atlantic* (December 1960 and December 1969); *Saturday Review* (August 21, 1976, and January 19, 1980); and *New York Times Book Review* (October 10, 1976, and July 24, 1977). □

Shivaji

The Indian military leader Shivaji (1627-1680) fought the Mogul Empire to establish a Maratha kingdom free from Mogul domination.

Shivaji was the son of Shahji Bonsale, a kingmaker in the Moslem kingdoms of Ahmagnagar and Bijapur in the Deccan. He was born on April 10, 1627 (March 19, 1630, according to some sources), in the Shivneri fort north of Poona in the state of Maharashtra, India. He was brought up by his mother, Jijabai, and tutor, Dadaji Kondadeva, who instilled in him a love for independence and Hinduism and basic skills in military and administrative leadership.

Shivaji began his career by gathering round him bands of the hardy peasantry called the Mavales and waging guerrilla wars against the kingdom of Bijapur. Between 1646 and 1658 he captured a number of Bijapuri strong-holds and in 1659 killed Afzal Khan, a renowned Bijapur general sent against him with a strong army. In the course of his wars against Bijapur, Shivaji also attacked Mogul territories in the Deccan, and this brought him into direct conflict with Aurangzeb, last of the great Moguls.

In 1664 Shivaji sacked the preeminent port city of Surat on the western coast, which brought retaliation from Aurangzeb in the form of a vast army led by the Rajput general Jai Singh. Shivaji could not withstand this offensive and signed the Treaty of Purandar in 1665, by which he surrendered 23 forts and agreed to enroll in the Mogul imperial service as a faithful retainer. In 1666 he visited Aurangzeb's court in Agra, where he was virtually kept in confinement, but escaped through a clever stratagem.

During 1667-1669 Shivaji kept his peace but renewed his wars with a second sack of Surat, in 1670. During the next 4 years he expanded his power in the western coastal lands and the south and on June 6, 1674, climaxed his career with his formal coronation in the fort of Raigarh, heralding the birth of the new and sovereign state of the Marathas. The last years of his life were spent in extending the territories under the control of his new state. Shivaji died on April 4, 1680.

Shivaji was no mere warrior or "freebooter," as his adversaries described him. He was a man with a grand vision for the liberation of the Hindus from Mogul rule and the creation of a government inspired by principles of unity, independence, and justice. His charisma united the caste-ridden people of Maharashtra, and in his administrative arrangements he displayed an uncommon wisdom. He also appreciated the growing importance of naval power in the politics of 17th-century India and began to create a navy of his own, one of the few rulers of India to do so. In his personal appearance he was of medium stature but well built, quick and piercing of eye, ready to smile and chivalrous in his dealings with all, including his erstwhile foes. Shivaji's significance in Indian history lies in the hammerblows he struck against the Mogul Empire and the dynamism he imparted to the Marathas, which helped them go on to stake imperial claims during 1720-1760.

Further Reading

The best and most authoritative single work on Shivaji is Jadunath Sarkar, *Shivaji and His Times* (1919; 5th ed. rev. 1952). G. S. Sardesai, *New History of the Marathas,* vol. 1 (1946), contains a comprehensive account of Shivaji's career based on original Marathi documents. Mahadev Govind Ranade, *Rise of Maratha Power* (Delhi, 1961), offers perceptive views of the background to the Maratha revolution. For general background consult W. H. Moreland and Atul Chandra Chatterjee, *A Short History of India* (1936; 3d ed. 1953).

Additional Sources

Daud, Tafazzul, *The real Sevaji,* Karachi: Indus Publications, 1980.

Kincaid, Dennis, *Shivaji, the founder of Maratha empire: The grand rebel,* Delhi: Discovery Pub. House; New Delhi: Distributors, Uppal Pub. House, 1984.

Lajpat Rai, Lala, *Shivaji, the great patriot,* New Delhi: Metropolitan, 1980.

Pagdi, Setumadhava Rao, *Shivaji,* New Delhi: National Book Trust, India, 1983.

Studies in Shivaji and his times, Kolhapur: Shivaji University, 1982.

Takakhav, N. S. (Nilkant Sadashiv), *Life of Shivaji, founder of the Maratha Empire,* Delhi, India: Sunita Publications, 1985.

Verma, Virendra, *Shivaji, a captain of war with a mission,* Poona: Youth Education Publications: distributors, Youth Book Agencies, 1976. □

William Shockley

Physicist William Shockley (1910-1989) shared the 1956 Nobel Prize in physics for inventing the transistor. He was also involved in the controversial topic of the genetic basis of intelligence.

William Shockley was a physicist whose work in the development of the transistor led to a Nobel Prize. By the late 1950s, his company, the Shockley Transistor Corporation, was part of a rapidly growing industry created as a direct result of his contributions to the field. Shockley shared the 1956 Nobel Prize in physics with John Bardeen and Walter Brattain, both of whom collaborated with him on developing the point contact transistor. Later, Shockley became involved in a controversial topic for which he had no special training, but in which he became avidly interested: the genetic basis of intelligence. During the 1960s, he argued, in a series of articles and speeches, that people of African descent have a genetically inferior mental capacity when compared to those with Caucasian ancestry. This hypothesis became the subject of intense and acrimonious debate.

William Bradford Shockley was born in London, England, on February 13, 1910, to William Hillman Shockley, an American mining engineer, and May (Bradford) Shockley, a mineral surveyor. The Shockleys, living in London on a business assignment when William was born, returned to California in 1913. Shockley did not enter elementary

school at the usual age, however, because, as he told *Men of Space* author Shirley Thomas, "My parents had the idea that the general educational process was not as good as would be done at home." As a result, he was not enrolled in public schools until he had reached the age of eight.

Shockley's interest in physics developed early, inspired in part by a neighbor who taught the subject at Stanford and by his own parents' coaching and encouragement. By the time he had completed his secondary education at Palo Alto Military Academy and Hollywood High School at the age of seventeen, Shockley had made his commitment to a career in physics. Shockley and his parents agreed that he should spend a year at the University of California at Los Angeles (UCLA) before attending the California Institute of Technology (Caltech), where he earned a bachelor's degree in physics in 1932. Offered a teaching fellowship at the Massachusetts Institute of Technology (MIT), Shockley taught while working on his doctoral dissertation, "Calculations of Wave Functions for Electrons in Sodium Chloride Crystals," for which he was awarded his Ph.D. in 1936. Shockley later told Thomas that this research in solid-state physics "led into my subsequent activities in the transistor field."

Upon graduation from MIT, Shockley accepted an offer to work at the Bell Telephone Laboratories in Murray Hill, New Jersey. An important factor in that decision was the opportunity it gave him to work with Clinton Davisson, who was to win the 1937 Nobel Prize in physics for proving Louis Victor de Broglie's theory that electrons assumed the characteristics of waves. Shockley's first assignment at Bell was the development of a new type of vacuum tube that would serve as an amplifier. But, almost as soon as he had arrived at Bell, he began to think of a radically new approach to the transmission of electrical signals using solid-state components rather than conventional vacuum tubes. At that time, vacuum tubes constituted the core of communication devices such as the radio because they have the ability to rectify (create a unidirectional current) and multiply electronic signals. They have a number of serious practical disadvantages, however, as they are relatively fragile and expensive, and have relatively short life-spans.

As early as the mid–1930s, Bell scientists had begun to think about alternatives to vacuum tubes in communication systems, and by 1939, Shockley was experimenting with semiconducting materials to achieve that transition. Semiconductors are materials such as silicon and germanium that conduct an electrical current much less efficiently than do conductors like silver and copper, but more effectively than do insulators like glass and most kinds of plastic. Shockley knew that one semiconductor, galena, had been used as a rectifier in early radio sets, and his experience in solid-state physics led him to believe that such materials might have even wider application in new kinds of communication devices.

The limited research Shockley was able to complete on this concept of alternative conductors was unsuccessful, largely because the materials available to him at the time were not pure enough. In 1940, war was imminent, and Shockley soon became involved in military research. His first job involved the development of radar equipment at a Bell field station in Whippany, New Jersey. In 1942, he became research director of the U.S. Navy's Anti-Submarine Warfare Operations Research Group at Columbia University, and served as a consultant to the Secretary of War from 1944 to 1945.

In 1945, Shockley returned to Bell Labs as director of its research program on solid-state physics. Together with John Bardeen, a theoretical physicist, and Walter Brattain, an experimental physicist, Shockley returned to his study of semiconductors as a means of amplification. After more than a year of failed trials, Bardeen suggested that the movement of electric current was being hampered by electrons trapped within a semiconductor's surface layer. That suggestion caused Shockley's team to suspend temporarily its efforts to build an amplification device and to concentrate instead on improving their understanding of the nature of semiconductors.

By 1947, Bardeen and Brattain had learned enough about semiconductors to make another attempt at building Shockley's device. This time they were successful. Their device consisted of a piece of germanium with two gold contacts on one side and a tungsten contact on the opposite side. When an electrical current was fed into one of the gold contacts, it appeared in a greatly amplified form on the other side. The device was given the name transistor (for *trans* fer re *sistor*). More specifically, it was referred to as a point contact transistor because of the three metal contacts used in it.

The first announcement of the transistor appeared in a short article in the July 1, 1948 edition of the *New York*

Times. Few readers had the vaguest notion of the impact the fingernail-sized device would have on the world. A few months later, Shockley proposed a modification of the point contact transistor. He suggested using a thin layer of P-type semiconductor (in which the charge is carried by holes) sandwiched between two layers of N-type semiconductor (where the charge is carried by electrons). When Brattain built this device, now called the junction transistor, he found that it worked much better than did its point contact predecessor. In 1956, the Nobel Prize for physics was awarded jointly to Shockley, Bardeen, and Brattain for their development of the transistor.

Shockley left Bell Labs in 1954 (some sources say 1955). In the decade that followed, he served as director of research for the Weapons Systems Evaluation Group of the Department of Defense, and as visiting professor at Caltech in 1954–55. He then founded the Shockley Transistor Corporation to turn his work on the development of the transistor to commercial advantage. Shockley Transistor was later incorporated into Beckman Instruments, Inc., and then into Clevite Transistor in 1960. The company went out of business in 1968.

In 1963, Shockley embarked on a new career, accepting an appointment at Stanford University as its first Alexander M. Poniatoff Professor of Engineering and Applied Science. Here he became interested in genetics and the origins of human intelligence, in particular, the relationship between race and the Intelligence Quotient (IQ). Although he had no background in psychology, genetics, or any related field, Shockley began to read on these topics and formulate his own hypotheses. Using data taken primarily from U.S. Army pre-induction IQ tests, Shockley came to the conclusion that the genetic component of a person's intelligence was based on racial heritage. He proposed that people of African ancestry were inherently less intelligent than those of Caucasian lineage. He also surmised that the more "white genes" a person of African descent carried, the more closely her or his intelligence corresponded to that of the general white population. He ignited further controversy with his suggestion that inferior individuals (those whose IQ numbered below 100) be paid to undergo voluntary sterilization.

The social implications of Shockley's theories were, and still are profound. Many scholars regarded Shockley's whole analysis as flawed, and they rejected his conclusions. Others were outraged that such views were even expressed publicly. Educators pointed out the significance of these theories for their field, a point pursued by Shockley himself when he argued that compensatory programs for blacks were doomed because of their inherent genetic inferiority. For a number of years, Shockley could count on the fact that his speeches would be interrupted by boos and catcalls, provided that they were allowed to go forward at all.

During his life, Shockley was awarded many honors, including the U.S. Medal of Merit in 1946, the Morris E. Liebmann Award of the Institute of Radio Engineers in 1951, the Comstock Prize of the National Academy of Sciences in 1954, and the Institute of Electrical and Electronics Gold Medal in 1972 and its Medal of Honor in 1980. He was named to the National Inventor's Hall of Fame in 1974. Shockley remained at Stanford until retirement in 1975, when he was appointed Emeritus Professor of Electrical Engineering. In 1933, Shockley had married Jean Alberta Bailey, with whom he had three children, Alison, William, and Richard. After their 1955 divorce, Shockley married Emily I. Lanning. He died in San Francisco on August 11, 1989, of prostate cancer.

Further Reading

McGraw-Hill Modern Scientists and Engineers, Volume 3, McGraw-Hill, 1980, pp. 111–12.

National Geographic Society, Special Publications Division, *Those Inventive Americans,* National Geographic Society, 1971, pp. 209–16.

Thomas, Shirley, *Men of Space,* Volume 4, Chilton Books, 1962, pp. 170–205.

Nobel Prize Winners, H. W. Wilson, 1987, pp. 962–64. □

Sholem Aleichem

The Jewish author Sholem Aleichem (1859-1916) wrote with great humor of Jewish life in eastern Europe and America.

Sholem Aleichem was born Sholem Rabinowitz on March 3, 1859, in Freislav, Poltava district, in the Ukraine. He received a traditional Jewish education but also attended a state school. His mother died when he was 13, and he suffered considerable hardship at the hands of his stepmother. At 17 he made his first literary attempts. The following year he was employed by a Jewish landowner in Kiev as a tutor. He remained at the estate for 3 years but was forced to leave at the discovery of his secret romance with the young lady he tutored. In 1880 he began to serve as a rabbi in a Jewish town. At this time he began to publish his writings in both the Hebrew and Russian press. In 1883 his first Yiddish works were published. In that year he married his former pupil and left his position to return to her father's estate. After the death of his father-in-law he became executor of the inheritance and from 1887 resided in Kiev, where he was involved in various business enterprises.

Sholem Aleichem continued his literary work, publishing several stories as well as the series of *Die Yiddische Volksbibliothek* (The Yiddish Folk Library). In 1890 he suffered great financial losses and went to Paris, and then to Vienna and Czernowitz (Chernovtsy). Between 1893 and 1899 he lived in Kiev and wrote works in both Yiddish and Russian. During this period he began his renowned works *Tevya the Dairyman* and *Menachem Mendel.*

Following the 1905 Kiev pogrom he decided to emigrate to America, and in October 1905 he reached New York. In 1908 he embarked on a lecture tour in Russia during which he fell seriously ill with a lung ailment. His impaired health, however, did not affect his literary output, and during those years he published many works, among them *Motel Ben Pasey the Chazan, The Flood,* and *The*

Correspondence of Menachem Mendel and His Wife Shayndel Shaynda.

At the outbreak of World War I Sholem Aleichem and his family were displaced to Copenhagen, where he began writing his tragicomedy *It's Hard to Be a Jew.* Later in 1914, he returned to New York, and there he published his autobiography, *From the Market-place,* as well as stories about the war. In 1915 he wrote his well-known play *The Great Prize.* He died in New York on May 13, 1916. His funeral was attended by 300,000 mourners, and he was eulogized in the U.S. Congress.

Sholem Aleichem depicted Jewish life in the Diaspora with great affection and heartfelt humor. His portrayals are sharply drawn and highly incisive characterizations of simple folk plagued by the problems of earning their daily bread, merchants, rabbis, teachers, and cantors—all animated by a humor born of oppression. Sholem Aleichem wrote little in Hebrew, preferring what was then the language of the masses, Yiddish. He frequently used the monologue as a vehicle of expression, allowing characters to speak for themselves in their own idiom. His fidelity to the speech of the people being depicted contributes much to the realism of his characterizations. The bittersweet humor of Sholem Aleichem pervades his portrayal of the lot of his people as that of the Wandering Jew.

Further Reading

There are scholarly studies of Sholem Aleichem in Hebrew. In English see Maurice Samuel, *The World of Sholom Aleichem* (1943); Melech W. Grafstein, ed., *Sholom Aleichem Panorama* (1949); Marie Waife-Goldberg, *My Father, Sholom Aleichem* (1968); and Louis Falstein, *The Man Who Loved Laughter: The Story of Sholom Aleichem* (1968). General works include Sol Liptzin, *The Flowering of Yiddish Literature* (1964), and Charles A. Madison, *Yiddish Literature: Its Scope and Major Writers* (1968).

Additional Sources

Butwin, Joseph, *Sholom Aleichem,* Boston: Twayne Publishers, 1977.

Samuel, Maurice, *The world of Sholom Aleichem,* New York: Atheneum, 1986, 1970. □

Mikhail Aleksandrovich Sholokhov

The Soviet novelist Mikhail Aleksandrovich Sholokhov (1905-1984) won an international reputation for an epic novel, "The Silent Don," dealing with his native Don Cossack land. Sholokhov won the Nobel Prize for literature in 1965.

Mikhail Sholokhov was born on May 24, 1905, in a village in the Don Cossack region of Russia. His mother was a peasant, and his father came from the middle classes. Sholokhov's education was interrupted by the civil war, in which he served as a member of a Red grain-requisitioning detachment. He then went to Moscow, where he joined a group of young proletarian writers, supporting himself as a manual laborer. However, he soon returned to his native region, where he lived the rest of his life.

Sholokhov's first works were sketches and stories of the civil war, collected in 1925 as *Tales of the Don.* Thereafter he continued to write short stories. In 1928 the first installments of his epic novel, *The Silent Don,* appeared, and this work established his reputation. Its final installment appeared in 1940.

The Silent Don is a panoramic novel based on the life of the Don Cossacks before, during, and after the Revolution. Its hero, Grigory Melekhov, a Cossack peasant, is a natural leader with a fiery spirit of independence and a strong sense of decency and justice. In World War I he fights valiantly against the Germans. Confused by the events and issues of the Revolution and civil war, he fights at first on the White side, then with the Reds, and finally joins a band of Cossack nationalist guerrillas fighting the Reds. After 7 years of conflict, Grigory is morally exhausted. His plight, similar to that of millions of Russians during those years, is shown so poignantly that he has become the most popular tragic hero of Soviet literature. A passionate and violent tale that profoundly depicts the connection between man and his physical surroundings, *The Silent Don* ranks as the greatest epic novel of Soviet literature.

Sholokhov interrupted his work on *The Silent Don* to begin another large novel, *Virgin Soil Upturned,* the first volume of which appeared in 1932. Also set in the Don Cossack region, it deals with the violent social upheavals caused by the forced collectivization of agriculture in the 1930s. The second volume of this novel was published in 1960.

Sholokhov's third important novel concerns World War II. Entitled *They Fought for Their Country,* it has been published only in chapters and remains unfinished. Sholokhov also published one excellent story about World War II, "The Fate of a Man" (1957).

Sholokhov received the Nobel Prize for literature in 1965. A longtime Communist, he was a member of the Supreme Soviet for many years and received countless official honors.

Further Reading

The Silent Don was published in English in two volumes: *And Quiet Flows the Don* (1935) and *The Don Flows Home to the Sea* (1941). *Virgin Soil Upturned* (1957) also appears in two volumes: *Seeds of Tomorrow* (1935) and *Harvest on the Don* (1960). Studies of Sholokhov in English include: Lev Grigorevich Iakimenko, *Sholokhov: A Critical Appreciation* (1973), C. G. Bearne, *Sholokhov* (1969) and D. H. Stewart, *Mikhail Sholokhov: A Critical Introduction* (1967). Extensive studies of Sholokhov are also in the following works: Gleb Struve, *Soviet Russian Literature, 1917-1950* (1951); Ernest J. Simmons, *Russian Fiction and Soviet Ideology* (1958); Helen Muchnic, *From Gorky to Pasternak* (1961); and Edward J. Brown, *Russian Literature since the Revolution* (1969). □

Dmitri Dmitrievich Shostakovich

Dmitri Dmitrievich Shostakovich (1906-1975) was a Soviet composer who, after Prokofiev's death in 1953, stood quite alone at the summit of Soviet Russian music.

Widely imitated, Dmitri Shostakovich was perhaps the first great composer purposely and consciously to develop a political awareness as an integral part of his art and to accept, even seek, creative guidance from ideological, extramusical sources. His career was troubled and tense at times, yet he was honored more than any other composer of his time, possibly excepting Igor Stravinsky. A natural bent for the stage seemed thwarted by early criticism, and it is chiefly for his 14 symphonies that he is best known.

Shostakovich was born in St. Petersburg and grew up in that city through its war and revolutionary (Petrograd; later Leningrad) periods. He was only 11 at the time of the Revolution, and his family was affested by political troubles: His mother's family was of the petty bourgeois that Lenin abhorred. Dmitri attended the Glasser school; in 1919 he entered the Petrograd Conservatory under the protective wing of the composer Alexander Glazunov. Shostakovich studied both piano and composition, the latter with Maximilian Steinberg. The training was rigorous. Shostakovich's diploma work, the First Symphony (1924-1925), was received with unusual enthusiasm by Western audiences eager for the musical fruits of the Bolshevik experiment, and it is still frequently programmed in the West.

Early Works

Socially and politically aware, Shostakovich worked with the Leningrad workers' schools (*rabfak*) and began to aim his talents toward the stage. At the same time he concertized and did musical "odd jobs." An opera, *The Nose* (1928), and a ballet, *The Golden Age* (1929), both satirical, were successful, although his Second and Third Symphonies were not. He began the opera *Lady Macbeth of Mzensk* (later *Katerina Izmailova*) in 1930; it was to be the first of a trilogy on the fate of women in past periods. It contains some of Shostakovich's most effective music both in lyric, solo vocal pieces and in grotesque orchestral interludes. It was staged successfully throughout the world.

Relations with the Party

In 1936 the opera was officially condemned and the composer taken to task in the Communist party press. Stalin was personally and directly involved (he attended a performance), and the overt issues were those of "formalism," crude eroticism, and musical inaccessibility. The incident served as a platform for the party's ideological guidance of the art; the vocabulary of political control of music was begun, and Shostakovich abandoned the stage for years. He withdrew his Fourth Symphony (it was already in rehearsal) and wrote the Fifth Symphony as an apology and expression of gratitude for the instruction he had received. This work, too, became popular in the West.

With other Soviet artists, Shostakovich benefited from the relaxation of controls which the party deemed necessary during the war years. During this relatively free period he wrote his Sixth through Ninth Symphonies. The Seventh, called the *Leningrad* Symphony, was begun in that besieged city and finished in an evacuation center. It was received with intense emotion throughout the world. But after the war, and until Stalin's death in 1953, life was a nightmare for intellectuals and artists, a fact now conceded in the Soviet Union. Shostakovich was vigorously attacked not only for a number of his works but also for matters of attitude, origin, and taste. In company with other criticized composers, he apologized in the pattern established in the political trials of the mid-1930s and thanked the party for its concern.

After Stalin died, a thaw began, which remained a peripatetic, unpredictable feature of Soviet intellectual life for several decades following. Shostakovich's Tenth Symphony was first heard late in 1953. Although it has remained a controversial item, it is still occasionally played. The Eleventh (1957) and Twelfth (1961) Symphonies, both programmatic and based on revolutionary-political themes, were ideologically proper but not musically long-lived.

Late Works

In 1963 Shostakovich rewrote *Lady Macbeth of Mzensk* as *Katerina Izmailova,* and the opera was quite successful. A comparison of the two versions reveals curiously little change. In the later version Shostakovich was a more painstaking craftsman and editor. He removed certain blatantly erotic portions. In general, he abandoned the complexities of characterization; Katerina, in particular, is no longer the complicated creature that Lady Macbeth was. Also in 1963 Shostakovich resumed teaching—he had lost his teaching posts in 1948.

Shostakovich's works not only grace the symphonic repertoire, but those of chamber and piano music as well. He wrote 12 String Quartets, and his sets of Preludes and Fugues for piano are contemporary classics. His two Concertos for violin and orchestra and his Concerto for cello and orchestra have proved hardy. The Cello Concerto is an outstanding work on which the composer sought the collaboration of Mstislav Rostropovich, the cellist for whom it was written. Shostakovich's Thirteenth Symphony was a symphonic setting of Yevgeny Yevtushenko's poetry, including his protest against Soviet anti-Semitism, *Babi Yar.* The work was, in effect, banned. The Fourteenth Symphony is also a setting of poetic texts— poems of death by various authors, Russian and Western. It is an unusual expression in a milieu which values optimism.

In 1968 at the Fourth Congress of Soviet Composers, Shostakovich reaffirmed his belief that "Soviet music is a weapon in the international ideological battle. . . . Soviet artists cannot remain indifferent observers in the struggle." It was statements like this which led most to regard Shostakovich as an orthodox Communist, content to toe the party line. Not until after his death when his memoirs were published in the West, did the general public realize how perilous Shostakovich's situation was for most of his career. He was the embodiment of the enlightened Russian intellectual in his work and way of life: rational, disciplined, and self-critical. His constitution was not strong and he often was force to spend time in sanatoriums. Although he was diagnosed with an incurable myelitis in 1959, his death in 1975 came as the result of his third heart attack. Shostakovich's music unites powerful emotional expression with formal mastery, tragedy and humour, pugnacious vitality and resignation. A wide range of stylistic influences, from Bach to revolutionary song, from Russian folk music to 20th-century atonality, combine and merge in a synthesis forged by his genius.

Further Reading

Dmitri Shostakovich: About Himself and His Times (1981), compiled by L. Grigoriyov and I. Platek, discusses his life and music in his own words. Shostakovich is the subject of biographies by Seroff (1943), Martynov (1947), and Rabinovich (1959). Seroff is out of date, and Martynov and Rabinovich emphasize a Soviet view not altogether useful to the Western reader. Any book on contemporary music will devote considerable space to Shostakovich, as does William Austin, *Music in the Twentieth Century* (1966). Chapters on Shostakovich are found in Gerald Abraham, *Eight Soviet Composers* (1943), and Stanley D. Krebs, *Soviet Music and Musicians* (1970). □

Shotoku Taishi

Shotoku Taishi (573-621), the Prince of Holy Virtue, was a Japanese regent, statesman, and scholar. He prepared the Seventeen-article Constitution in 604 and contributed significantly to the political-cultural development that led to the Taika Reform of 645-649.

Prince Shotoku was the second son of Emperor Yomei (Prince Oe) and his consort, Anahobe Hashihito. According to legend, his mother bore him unexpectedly and with no labor pains while on her routine inspection of the imperial stable. While an infant, the prince already began to show evidence of exceptional intellect, and he began reading extensively in his early childhood. He is said to have listened once to eight persons simultaneously pleading to him and to have understood every word. Emperor Yomei's love for his prodigious son was so great that he had the prince live in a specially reserved part of the palace known as the Jogu, or Upper Palace. The three different personal names of the prince were derived from these episodes: Umayado no Miko (Prince of the Stable Door), Yatsumimi no Miko (Prince of Eight Ears), and Kamitsumiya no Miko or Jogu Taishi (Prince of the Upper Palace).

Power Struggles

When Shotoku was 13 years old, Emperor Bidatsu (reigned 572-585) died, and a bloody struggle for royal succession took place involving the heads of two powerful noble families, the Sogas and the Mononobes. The Sogas favored Oeno Oji (Prince Oe, father of Shotoku) as the new sovereign, and the Mononobes preferred Anahobe no Miko. The violent feud ended in victory for Prince Oe, who ascended the throne in September 585, to be known as Emperor Yomei. Because of his poor health, however, the reign of Yomei was short-lived.

When the Emperor became seriously ill, the prince, who was by now a devout Buddhist, sat by his father's bedside day and night praying fervently for his recovery. It was probably because of this princely devotion that the Emperor announced his intention to become a Buddhist believer.

The demise of Emperor Yomei in 587 set off another and more serious strife between the Sogas and the Mononobes, and this struggle ended when troops of the Sogas killed Prince Anahobe and Mononobe no Moriya. Shotoku, then 15, participated in the campaign and prayed to Shi-Tenno (Four Heavenly Guardians of Buddhism) for victory. Subsequently, he had the Shitennoji erected. Prince Hasebe, a son of one of Soga no Umako's younger sisters, was enthroned as Emperor Sushun. A strong animosity soon developed, however, between the Emperor and his overbearing uncle, Umako, and the outcome was that Emperor Sushun (reigned 588-592) was assassinated by one of Umako's men.

When Princess Sukiya-hime ascended the throne as Empress Suiko, Umako nominated as heir apparent and regent not one of her sons but Prince Shotoku. It is not quite clear why Umako selected the prince, but it is believed that Umako recognized Shotoku's great qualities and thought it prudent to keep him on the Soga side. From then until his death, Shotoku figured as the actual ruler of Japan.

Protector of Buddhism

Shotoku moved the Shitennoji from its original site at Tamatsukuri to its present location in Osaka in his very first year as the prince regent. He issued a rescript in the following year calling for worship of the three treasures—Buddha, Buddhist teachings, and priesthood. Two Korean high priests arrived in Japan in 595—Eji from the kingdom of Koryo (Koma) and Eso from the kingdom of Paekche (Kudara). The prince almost immediately became a disciple of Eji and from him formally received the Buddhist commandments.

Shotoku studied them carefully and wrote commentaries on three Buddhist sutras, *Hokke, Yuima,* and *Shoman.* A number of temples, including the Horyuji, were built under the personal supervision of the prince. The massive importation of Buddhism into Japan now signaled not only an introduction of a religion that was far more sophisticated than the current native cults of Japan but also a conscious attempt at the adoption of the more advanced continental culture, including literature, art, sciences, and political systems.

The cultural importation process had begun as early as 552, when the king of Paekche presented Emperor Kimmei with several copies of Buddhist sutras and Confucian classics. Under the sponsorship of Prince Shotoku, many sculptors, temple builders, artists, tilers, and other artisans were invited from Korea. Among the Confucian scholars who were invited to Japan was Kakuga (or Doctor Kak-ka), under whom the prince acquired profound knowledge of Confucian classics.

Both Buddhist and Confucian teachings appeared to flower simultaneously in Japan at the time, and Japan enjoyed a splendid cultural advancement. The famed Horyuji, containing beautiful murals and other fine artistic works, was completed in 607. Because the capital in those days was located in the Asuka district, this first flowering of the continental culture and fine arts in Japanese history is referred to as the Asuka period.

Cap Ranks and the Constitution

The Chinese practice of distinguishing official ranks by the form and materials of the official cap was adopted by the Japanese court, and Shotoku in 604 promulgated the system of 12 cap ranks. The introduction of this system can be said to be the beginning of the formal differentiation of governmental roles in Japan. The 12 grades were: *Dai-toku* (greater virtue), *Sho-toku* (lesser virtue), *Dai-nin* (greater humility), *Sho-nin* (lesser humility), *Dai-rei* (greater decorum), *Sho-rei* (lesser decorum), *Dai-shin* (greater faith), *Sho-shin* (lesser faith), *Dai-gi* (greater righteousness), *Sho-gi* (lesser righteousness), *Dai-chi* (greater knowledge), and *Sho-chi* (lesser knowledge). Shotoku also adopted the continental calendar system taught by a Korean priest, Kanroku, which resulted in the official adoption of the first lunar calendar in Japan.

In 604 Shotoku distributed to his officials the famous Seventeen-article Constitution, which is known as the first written law of Japan. In reality, it was a collection of moral maxims rather than legal norms. Many of the moral commandments were obviously derived from the Analects of Confucius and other Confucian writings of ethical and political doctrines. Buddhism, however, was specifically named as the supreme object of faith.

An abiding concern of Shotoku was evidenced, however, by the first article, which declared that the virtue of wa, or concord or harmony, should be valued. The constitution also emphasized the supremacy of the imperial throne, defined the duties of ministers, forbade provincial authorities to levy exactions, and admonished them to use forced labor only "at seasonable times."

Foreign Affairs

Official relations between Japan and China opened in 607, when Shotoku sent Ono no Imoko as an envoy of the Japanese emperor to Emperor Yang of the Sung dynasty with a message which read, "The Emperor of the country where the sun rises greets the Emperor of the country where the sun sets." Subsequently, Japanese scholars were sent to China to study the continental culture and Chinese political system.

One of Shotoku's most significant accomplishments was the compilation of the first history of Japan in 620, a year before his death. The history book was later burned when the residence of the Soga family was destroyed by fire following the assassination of Soga no Iruka, which marked the inauguration of the Taika Reform (645). Shotoku died on Feb. 2, 621.

Further Reading

A study of Shotoku is Masaharu Anesaki, *Prince Shotoku, the Sage Statesman* (1948). There are nine entries on Shotoku in *Nihongi: Chronicles of Japan from the Earliest Times to A.D. 697,* translated by William G. Aston (1896; repr. 1956). Many entries on the prince in the *Nihongi* are quoted in Ryusaku Tsunoda and others, *Sources of Japanese Tradition* (1958). George Sansom, in *A History of Japan to 1334* (3 vols., 1958), doubts that Shotoku could have accomplished all the things which are attributed to him during his relatively short life and regency. □

Henry Miller Shreve

Henry Miller Shreve (1785-1851), American steamboat designer and builder, improved water transportation and navigation on the western rivers. He helped make possible the great era of steamboat traffic prior to the Civil War.

Henry Shreve was born on Oct. 21, 1785, in Burlington County, N.J. When he was 3 years old, the family moved to western Pennsylvania. He grew up on the Youghiogheny River, watching the steady movement of men and goods bound westward for the nation's interior. At about the age of 15 he began working on the keelboats, barges, and pirogues which plied the Monongahela and Ohio rivers. He spent the rest of his life on the western rivers.

Shreve owned and operated keelboats and barges in the years when Robert Fulton was developing the first steamboat. In 1813 Shreve himself entered the business of building and operating steamboats. One of his boats, the *Enterprise,* made the first complete upriver trip from New Orleans to Pittsburgh. In 1816 he designed and built a new kind of steamboat which became the prototype for the great Mississippi steamers. This boat, the *Washington,* had a shallow-keeled hull, a main deck housing engines, and an upper cabin deck topped by the pilot house. All the great steamboats of the ensuing era were built from the design conceived by Shreve.

Shreve successfully fought to break the monopoly on steam navigation enjoyed by Fulton and Robert R. Livingston. These two had obtained a 14-year monopoly from officials of the Orleans Territory, and they tried to prevent Shreve's vessels from operating in the lower Mississippi. In 1818 the courts dismissed a suit against Shreve for navigating restricted waters, thus opening the river to all potential entrepreneurs. Full development of the commercial opportunities in the interior followed.

In 1827 the Federal government appointed Shreve superintendent of western river improvements, a post within the War Department. He began a vigorous program of removing obstacles to the safe passage of river traffic. He designed new boats to dislodge and remove snags from the rivers, a constant source of danger to steamboats. By 1834 boats ran at night through many channels formerly unsafe even in daylight. Shreve's work made travel much safer on the western rivers. He retired in 1841 to a residence outside St. Louis and died there on March 6, 1851.

Further Reading

Information on the life of Shreve is available in Herbert Quick, *Mississippi Steamboatin'* (1926); Stewart H. Holbrook, *Lost Men of American History* (1946); and Walter Havighurst, *Voices on the River* (1964). A good analysis of the river trade is Louis C. Hunter, *Steamboats on the Western Rivers* (1949).

Additional Sources

McCall, Edith S., *Conquering the rivers: Henry Miller Shreve and the navigation of America's inland waterways,* Baton Rouge: Louisiana State University Press, 1984. □

Shubert Brothers

The Shubert brothers were theatrical managers and producers of the largest theater empire in the 20th

century. They were Lee Shubert (1873?-1953), Samuel S. (1875?-1905), and Jacob J. (1879?-1963).

Samuel S., Jacob J., and Lee Shubert were born in Eastern Europe on uncertain dates in the latter part of the 19th century. Their parents, David and Catherine, brought the family to Syracuse, New York, in 1882. David Shubert, an alcoholic, could not support his family in their new home, and the boys were forced to go to work. At the age of ten Lee Shubert began selling newspapers in front of a local theater. He was soon joined by his brother, Sam, who found his way inside of the theater when he was cast in a small part in a play directed by David Belasco, a prominent theater director. Sam quickly fell in love with the glamour of the theater and adopted many of Belasco's mannerisms. He went from actor to program boy at the Bastable Theatre, to assistant treasurer of the Grand Opera House, to treasurer of the Wieting, Syracuse's most distinguished theater.

As Sam Shubert was ascending the ladder of theatrical management, a pattern was established among the brothers of backing each other's work. This pattern would remain with them throughout their careers. When Sam Shubert was named manager of the Bastable Theatre (1897), Jacob, the youngest brother, was working at the Wieting, and Lee was the bookkeeper for both theaters. By keeping their hands in as many theaters as possible the Shubert brothers began building what was to become the largest theatrical empire in the United States.

Jacob Shubert

Lee Shubert

Their first business venture in the theater was to attain the New England touring rights to Hoyt's *A Texas Steer.* Shortly after this success the brothers formed their own theater, the Baker, in Rochester. While Jacob Shubert turned the Baker into a successful stock company (with shows running in repertory), Sam and Lee acquired the Grand Opera House in Syracuse. By 1900 the brothers managed five theaters in New York state. They had also defined their individual roles in the business—Sam was the creative leader, Lee developed the business, and Jacob dealt with out-of-town productions.

The brothers had raised themselves swiftly out of poverty and had become respected theater managers. But this was not enough. They wanted to produce their own plays, and their intense ambitiousness drove them to New York City. In 1900, with borrowed money, the brothers moved to New York City and acquired the Herald Square Theatre. Although they didn't produce their own plays, they turned the Herald Square into one of the most successful theaters in New York with smash hits such as *Arizona,* the first Western, by Augustus Thomas and featuring Lionel Barrymore, and *The Belle of New York,* an English import. By 1904, after ten years in the business, they had acquired ten theaters, including the Casino and the Princess in New York City; the Hyperion in New Haven, Connecticut; the Dearborn in Chicago; and the Colonial in Boston. Around 1901 the brothers had also begun to produce plays of their own, with successful productions including *The Chinese Honeymoon* and *Emerald Isle* (1902).

On May 12, 1905, at the age of 30, Sam Shubert died of injuries sustained in a train wreck near Harrisburg, Pennsylvania. At the time of his death he had 13 theaters that included one in London, a string of producing credits, and a play (*Fantasia*) to his credit. He was also involved in a theatrical war. The rapid growth of the Shubert Company was a threat to the Syndicate, a group of producers and theater owners who literally controlled American theater in the early 20th century. The Syndicate, led by Abe Erlanger and several other producers, owned three quarters of the theaters in the country; therefore, if someone wanted to work in the theater they were practically forced to work for the Syndicate.

After Sam's death Lee Shubert was ready to sell out to the Syndicate, until Erlanger made the mistake of insulting Sam's memory. From then on the Shuberts fought the Syndicate fiercely, until they won the battle and eventually turned into the same kind of controlling force they had once publicly decried. If they knew anything it was how to publicize. The brothers claimed to be on the side of the theater workers by breaking the Syndicate's control. The newspapers and theater people loved them for it. They produced a farewell tour for the idolized actress Sarah Bernhardt, and when the Syndicate closed them out of a city they produced the show in tents. The press sympathized with their plight. (In actuality, a tent held more seats than a theater, so they were making more money.)

This was only the beginning. In 1924 the Shuberts had 86 theaters in the United States alone; they were making $1 million a week in ticket sales; and they controlled 60 percent of the legitimate theater in the United States. In addition, they owned their own ticket brokerage, a dancing and singing school, and an enormous amount of real estate. They were also producing one quarter of the plays in America, and Lee Shubert was on the board of MGM.

While the brothers had essentially formed their own trust and were in constant litigation, the Shuberts did introduce to the stage many of the finest actors of the time, including the Marx Brothers, Will Rogers, Jack Benny, Al Jolson, Eddie Cantor, Bert Lahr, the Barrymores, Spencer Tracy, and dozens more. They also add to their credit the U.S. premiere of the innovative director Max Reinhardt's production of *Sumurun* (1911); the premiere of the well-known *Children's Hour* (1934) by Lilian Hellman; the production *Hellzapoppin* (1938), one of the longest running plays in history; and the development of the "spectacle," with the creation of a 40-foot-deep water tank at the Hippodrome.

Yet despite the fact that Lee had written a play and Jacob directed frequently, their contribution to the theater was not artistic—it was strictly business. Ironically, it was Lee who was named head of the Little Theatre, America's first attempt at creating a national theater based on artistic rather than commercial aims.

At the time of Lee Shubert's death in 1953 at the age of 80, the brothers had produced 600 shows under the credit of "Mssrs. Shubert presents." They had also booked 1,000 shows into their numerous theaters. They had essentially stopped producing their own shows and were primarily backing other productions and booking companies around the country. In 1956 they were faced with an anti-trust suit and were forced to stop their booking business, yet their vast acquisitions of theater real estate continued to make the Shubert Corporation one of the largest theater operations in the country. Still controlled by the Shubert family in the mid-1980s, the company continued to lease theaters and manage real estate.

The Shubert brothers developed new theater districts all over the United States. They employed thousands of theater people over the years. They were partially responsible for the formation of Actor's Equity (the actors needed a union in order to face their power). They had also turned theater into a large scale, commercial business which concerned itself with popular taste rather than art.

Jacob Shubert died in 1963 at the age of 85.

Further Reading

The Brothers Shubert (1968) by Jerry Stagg provides an in-depth look at the history of the Shubert brothers. *Theatre in America—The Impact of Economic Forces, 1870-1967* (1968) by Jack Poggi puts in excellent perspective the effects of the Shuberts on American theater. In addition, *Matinee Tomorrow* (1949) by Ward Morehouse refers to the Shuberts in terms of their relationship to actors and play production. The Shubert brothers are listed in *Who's Who in Theatre* (1939), edited by John Parker. □

George Pratt Shultz

George Pratt Shultz (born 1920), a labor and economics specialist, educator, author, businessman, and international negotiator, served under three U.S. presidents. He was the first director of the Office of Manpower and Budget and served as secretary of the Department of Labor, of the Department of the Treasury, and of the Department of State.

George P. Shultz was born in New York City on December 13, 1920, the only child of Birl E. and Margaret Lennox (Pratt) Shultz. He spent his childhood in Englewood, New Jersey, and attended private school in Windsor, Connecticut. He majored in economics at Princeton University, where he received a B.A. degree in 1942. During World War II he joined the United States Marine Corps, served in the Pacific arena, and advanced to the rank of captain. While in Hawaii he met Helena Maria O'Brien, an Army nurse. They were married on February 16, 1946, and had three daughters and two sons.

Shultz resumed his academic career by enrolling at the Massachusetts Institute of Technology in 1945. He earned his Ph.D. degree in 1949 within the program of industrial economics, specializing in the problems of labor relations, employment, and unemployment. Shultz stayed on at the university until 1957 to teach industrial relations. During this time period he began to serve on arbitration panels for labor-management conflicts, a role he was to enact many times over the next decade. He also served at the first of his many national government posts when he was appointed senior staff economist to President Dwight Eisenhower's Council of Economic Advisors.

In 1957 Shultz joined the University of Chicago Graduate School of Business, where he also taught industrial relations. He became dean of the school in 1962. Presidents John Kennedy and Lyndon Johnson appointed him to serve on several government task forces and committees related to labor-management and employment policies.

President Richard Nixon named Shultz to the post of secretary of labor on December 11, 1968. Although he advocated that the government not intervene in labor bargaining or strikes, circumstances thrust the secretary into many such disputes. One major crisis that forced his attention was the 1970 postal workers strike, which required sending the National Guard into New York City to sort the mail. During his term in office Shultz defended the Nixon administration's reluctance to pursue affirmative action programs aggressively and the administration's active campaign on union reform. He worked hard to keep wages from rising in both the private and public sectors.

After 18 months at the Labor Department, he accepted President Nixon's appointment to become the first director of the Office of Management and Budget (which replaced the Bureau of the Budget in a major administrative reorganization). In this position he continued to face problems of wage control and price freezes, as well as major private industry strikes.

In May 1972 Shultz again changed posts in the Nixon administration. He was appointed secretary of the treasury, where he became a key adviser to the president on matters of the federal debt and both domestic and international economic policies. On the domestic front, Shultz was involved in efforts to defeat the rising inflation of the early 1970s. On the international side, he travelled abroad many times to negotiate a multi-national "floating" currency system with exchange rates set by the marketplace and several trade agreements with the former Soviet Union (now the Russian Federation, comprised of 21 autonomous republics, 49 oblasts, and 6 krays). When the Organization of Petroleum Exporting Countries (OPEC) drastically increased oil prices after October 1973, causing rapid inflation, Shultz's call for an international rollback of prices went unheeded and he worked hard to stop the recession in the American economy.

Shultz resigned from government service in March 1974 and entered the business community. He became an executive vice president of the Bechtel Corporation, an international construction and engineering firm based in San Francisco. He later became president and a director of the Bechtel Group, Inc.

Nominated as the 60th secretary of state by President Ronald Reagan, Shultz was sworn in on July 16, 1982. As the nation's major adviser and negotiator of international affairs, Shultz was intimately involved with the important problems of the world. He sought plans to end conflicts in the Middle East and in Central America and to deal with international terrorism. As a member of the president's team, he supported a strong American defense program, including a space-based anti-missile defense system (the Strategic Defense Initiative, or Star Wars). He guided U.S. arms limitation talks with the Soviet Union. A constant international traveller, he attended President Reagan's meetings with Soviet leaders. His academic and labor arbitration background molded his approach to his work as secretary of state. He proved to be a thoughtful and careful operator and a firm believer in quiet diplomacy. He served as Secretary of State from 1982 to 1989, at which time he returned to the private sector as an educator (Stanford University's Hoover Institute and Graduate School of Business) and writer. His entire cabinet service spanned over twelve years and covered four separate cabinet posts (Secretary of State, Secretary of Labor, Secretary of Treasury, and Director of OMB.) He maintained a residence in Stanford, California.

Further Reading

Shultz authored a semi-autobiographical novel, *Turmoil and Triumph: My Years as Secretary of State* (1993), which was well reviewed. Accounts of his career during President Nixon's administration are in Dan Rather and Gary Paul Gates, *The*

Palace Guard (1974) and in William Safire, *Before the Fall* (1975). His early days in the Reagan administration are discussed in Laurence I. Barrett, *Gambling With History: Reagan in the White House* (1983). Shultz has written several works on economic policy and labor relations. One book that contains his insights and thoughts on economic policy issues and the government's role is George Shultz and Kenneth W. Dam, *Economic Policy Beyond the Headlines* (1978). □

Jean Julius Christian Sibelius

Jean, Julius Christian Sibelius (1865-1957) was one of the leading postromantic composers and Finland's greatest musician. His music is both nationalistic and universal and is most effective in conveying mood or atmosphere.

Jean Sibelius—he adopted the French form of his first name as a student—was born on Dec. 8, 1865, in the garrison town of Hämeenlinna, where his father was a military doctor. The family was a musical one, and Sibelius learned the rudiments very early. Destined for the law, he found the attractions of music so strong that he overcame family opposition and began formal conservatory training by 1886. His goal was to become a violin virtuoso—a dream which later found possible sublimation in the only concerto he composed, that for violin (1903), plus some shorter solo pieces.

As the star pupil of the conservatory's founder, Sibelius found his path directed increasingly toward composition. He studied in Berlin, Leipzig, and Vienna (1889-1891). He won his first public triumph in 1892 with his symphonic poem *Kullervo,* for voices and orchestra, based on parts of the *Kalevala,* the Finnish national epic which inspired so many of his works. That year he married Aino Järnefelt.

Sibelius became an active member of a circle of artists and writers in Helsinki fired by nationalistic spirit. This spirit was reflected in some evocative scores he composed to accompany a series of patriotic and historical stage tableaux in 1899, among them the famous *Finlandia*. Other important works of this period were his first great symphonic poem, *En Saga* (1893); the *Four Legends of Lemminkäïnen* (finished 1895), one of which is *The Swan of Tuonela;* and his only opera, *The Maiden in the Tower* (1896).

In 1897 Sibelius won a state pension, which made it possible for him to devote the balance of his career to unhindered composition. He composed the flamboyantly romantic First Symphony (1898-1899) and the richly scored Second Symphony (1901-1902). In 1904 he built a villa in the forest near the town of Järvenpää which he named Ainola after his wife and where he lived for the rest of his life.

Sibelius's mature years became a regular alternation of steady composition and international travel. He composed another *Kalevala* -inspired symphonic poem, *Pohjola's Daughter* (1906), his only published string quartet, entitled *Voces intimae* (1909); and three more Symphonies—the transitional Third (1904-1907), the austere and enigmatic Fourth (1910-1911), and the confidently triumphant Fifth (1914-1915). His tours brought him particular attention and success in Germany, England, and the United States. In 1922-1924 he wrote the serene and pastoral Sixth Symphony and the Seventh Symphony, a terse, economically developed one-movement fantasia. *Tapiola* (1926) is his spare evocation of the Finnish forests.

This proved to be Sibelius's last major work, and only a few trifles followed in what came to be called "the silence from Järvenpää." He was internationally famous, especially in the English-speaking countries, where many regarded him as the savior of the symphonic form and the champion of the faction which rejected the radical doctrines of atonalism. Why he withdrew from active composition has been much debated. One explanation is that he became increasingly fearful that he might not be able to go on living up to his own reputation. A living legend and a national monument in his own land, he persevered in his strict retirement for the remaining 32 years of his life. He died on Sept. 20, 1957.

Sibelius's output was extensive, including a large number of piano pieces, mainly short, and nearly 100 solo songs, most of them to texts in Swedish, Finland's old literary language. Like most northern composers, he wrote many incidental scores for stage plays, the most noteworthy being those to Adolf Paul's *King Christian II* (1898), to Arvid Järnefelt's *Kuolema* (1903: source of the *Valse triste*), to Maurice Maeterlinck's *Pelléas et Mélisande* (1905), to

Hjalmar Procopé's *Belshazzar's Feast* (1906), and, perhaps the finest of all, to Shakespeare's *The Tempest* (1926).

Further Reading

There are numerous studies on Sibelius, many reflecting the adulation heaped on him in his late years and the mythology about him, which Sibelius himself often encouraged. Good examples of this are the quasi-official biography by Karl Ekman, *Jean Sibelius: The Life and Personality of an Artist* (trans. 1935); Cecil Grey's more concise *Sibelius* (1931); and Nils-Eric Ringbom, *Jean Sibelius: A Master and His Work* (1948; trans. 1954). Sections in Constant Lambert, *Music Ho!* (1934), illustrate the assessments of Sibelius as herald of the true "music of the future." A critical attempt to penetrate the myths and deflate the adulation is Harold E. Johnson, *Jean Sibelius* (1959). Robert Layton, *Sibelius* (1966), offers a balanced, if still admiring, perspective at greater distance.

Additional Sources

Goss, Glenda Dawn, *Jean Sibelius and Olin Downes: music, friendship, criticism,* Boston: Northeastern University Press, 1995.

Gray, Cecil, *Sibelius,* Westport, Conn.: Hyperion Press, 1979.

James, Burnett, *Sibelius,* London; New York: Omnibus Press; New York, NY, USA: Exclusive distributors, Music Sales Corp., 1989.

Johnson, Harold Edgar, *Jean Sibelius,* Westport, Conn.: Greenwood Press, 1978, 1959.

Ringbom, Nils-Eric, *Jean Sibelius: a master and his work,* Westport, Conn.: Greenwood Press, 1977.

Tawaststjerna, Erik, *Sibelius,* Berkeley: University of California Press, 1976-1986. □

Walter Richard Sickert

Walter Richard Sickert (1860-1942) was one of England's greatest impressionist painters. His cityscapes and music hall scenes were frequently based, compositionally, on Degas's paintings.

Walter Sickert was born in Munich to a Danish father, Oswald Sickert, a painter and journalistic draftsman, and an English mother. Oswald emigrated with his family to England in 1868 to keep his sons from being conscripted into the German army. In 1875 Walter enrolled at King's College in London. In 1881 he entered the Slade School in London, but he soon left to help James McNeill Whistler print his etchings. In 1883 Sickert, by then Whistler's apprentice, took a painting by Whistler to Paris, where he met Edgar Degas, whose devoted follower he became from then on. Sickert had come to feel that Whistler painted with too much surface facility.

In 1885 Sickert and his wife honeymooned in Dieppe. His scenes of Dieppe date from 1885, but especially after 1899 street scenes of Dieppe were a recurring subject. Sickert, especially from about 1895, was a prolific writer, and he also taught extensively. He visited Venice in 1895, in the winter of 1900/1901, and in 1903-1904, when he did views of St. Mark's Square. From 1900 to 1905 he lived mainly in France.

The years 1907-1914 were Sickert's Camden Town period, in which he showed forlorn people in dreary rooms with cheap Victorian furniture. In these works he used a thick and broken impasto, as in *Girl Reading* (1907) and *Ennui* (1913). In 1911 he founded an association of painters called the Camden Town group, most of whose members did not share his impressionistic leanings. From 1919 to 1922 Sickert lived in Dieppe and then settled permanently in London. He died in Bath.

Outside of Sickert and Sir William Orpen, England did not produce any first-rate painters who followed the lead of the French impressionists. Sickert, though often influenced by Degas not only in the choice of subject matter but also in the methods of cutting figures and in the choice of unusual viewpoints, nonetheless had his own flavor. In his many music hall scenes executed between 1887 and 1899, Sickert showed a greater interest in the audience than did Degas, and he had a preference for earthy, low-life, somewhat ribald types, such as the theatergoers in the *Old Bedford, a Corner of the Gallery* (ca. 1897). He was fascinated with the mundane, seamy side of English life, and he emphasized the dreary mood of his subject matter by low-keyed tones, in contrast to most of the work of the French impressionists.

Further Reading

The biographical study of Lillian Browse, *Sickert* (1960), shows Sickert as only peripherally dependent upon the French impressionists.

Additional Sources

Emmons, Robert, *The life and opinions of Walter Richard Sickert,* London: Lund Humphries, 1992, 1941.

Sutton, Denys, *Walter Sickert: a biography,* London: Joseph, 1976.

Woolf, Virginia, *Walter Sickert: a conversation,* Norwood, Pa.: Norwood Editions, 1978. ☐

Henry Sidgwick

The English philosopher and moralist Henry Sidgwick (1838-1900) was the author of *The Methods of Ethics,* which has been described as the "best treatise on moral theory that has ever been written."

Henry Sidgwick was born in Yorkshire and attended Rugby before entering Trinity College, Cambridge. After a distinguished undergraduate career, he was elected a fellow in 1859. Because he could not in conscience subscribe to the Thirty-nine Articles as a condition for holding a fellowship, Sidgwick resigned but remained at Cambridge as a lecturer. He became Knightbridge professor of moral thought in 1883. Together with his wife, Eleanor, a sister of Arthur Balfour, the British prime minister, he helped to establish Newnham, the Cambridge University college for women. Sidgwick was also one of the founders and the first president of the influential Society for Psychical Research. In addition to the classic *The Methods of Ethics* (1874), Sidgwick's writings include *Principles of Political Economy* (1883), *Outlines of the History of Ethics for English Readers* (1886), *The Elements of Politics* (1891), *Practical Ethics* (1898), *Philosophy: Its Scope and Relations* (1902), and *Lectures on the Philosophy of Kant and Other Philosophical Lectures and Essays* (1905). During his long association with Cambridge, Sidgwick taught and influenced several important future thinkers, including John McTaggart, G. E. Moore, and Bertrand Russell.

Ethical methodology concerns the ways in which men make decisions about how they should act. Sidgwick, as an ethical historian, saw that ethical decisions resulted from a particular conception of the end or purpose of life. Philosophers have been divided into two groups on this subject: those who think that happiness is the chief purpose of existence, and a minority group that acknowledges that there are ends other than happiness, such as self-realization or perfection, that are also intrinsically desirable.

The methods of non-Eudamonistic ethics rest on some type of intuition into the nature of moral principles that extend beyond happiness. The philosophic difficulty of intuitionalism is its inability to establish the universal validity of such insights as transcendent values. Sidgwick described happiness ethics as utilitarian and distinguished between systems that aim at the happiness of individuals (egoistic hedonism) and those that aim at happiness for all. In these systems, methodology consists of designating actions as right or wrong in terms of the amount of happiness produced for the self or for others. Sidgwick admitted that he distrusted intuitional systems because of their subjectivity, and he considered himself to be a utilitarian until he came to perceive "the profound discrepancy between the natural end of action, private happiness, and the end of duty, general happiness."

Thus the central problem of ethics for Sidgwick was located in the conflict between personal inclination and duty toward others. Eventually Sidgwick admitted that without some sort of religious sanction, the attempt rationally to demonstrate the ethical necessity of extending self-love to love for others was a failure.

Further Reading

A biography by A. and E. M. Sidgwick, *Henry Sidgwick: A Memoir* (1906), contains useful sources and a complete bibliography. The best secondary references are C. D. Broad's *Five Types of Ethical Theory* (1930) and *Ethics and the History of Philosophy* (1952).

Additional Sources

Schneewind, J. B. (Jerome B.), *Sidgwick's ethics and Victorian moral philosophy,* Oxford; New York: Clarendon Press, 1977. ☐

Sir Philip Sidney

The English poet, courtier, diplomat, and soldier Sir Philip Sidney (1554-1586) realized more dramatically than any other figure of the English Renaissance the ideal of the perfect courtier and the universal gentleman.

The son of a noble and well-connected family, Philip Sidney was born at Penshurst, his father's estate in Kent. His formal education began with his entrance into the Shrewsbury School in 1564. In 1568 he moved on to Christ Church, Oxford. Sidney's correspondence and school records indicate that as a youth he already showed clear signs of brilliance but that he was of sober temperament and uncertain health. Leaving Oxford without a degree, as was not uncommon for noblemen, Sidney completed his education with a 3-year tour of the Continent (1572-1575), visiting France, Germany, Austria, Poland, and Italy.

Life at Court

On his return to England, Sidney entered quickly into the life of the aristocracy, dividing his time between the London house of his uncle, the powerful Earl of Leicester, and the country home of his sister, the Countess of Pembroke. Late in 1576 he paid a visit to his father, then Lord Deputy of Ireland, and observed political and social conditions in Ireland firsthand. Upon returning to England he addressed to the Queen a *Discourse on Irish Affairs,* defending his father's administration from the many criticisms leveled against it. In 1577 Sidney was sent on a diplomatic mission to Germany, during which he enthusiastically but unsuccessfully attempted to reconcile the quarreling Protestant factions and to organize a unified resistance against the Catholic nations.

Sidney's interests and relationships, however, were not restricted to the worlds of the court and diplomacy. He enjoyed frequent contacts with a variety of literary men, notably Thomas Drant, Fulke Greville, Edward Dyer, and Edmund Spenser. In his attempt to share in their efforts to create a new English poetry, Sidney wrote a number of experimental poems in nonrhyming quantitative meters. Other works probably written during this period include his *Lady of May,* an elaborate entertainment performed in honor of Queen Elizabeth I (1578), a large part of his sonnet sequence *Astrophel and Stella,* and the first draft of his prose romance, the *Arcadia.* His *Apology for Poetry* was probably composed shortly after the publication of Stephen Gosson's *School of Abuse* (1579), an attack on the theater that had been dedicated to Sidney without his knowledge or approval.

Marriage and Death

Meanwhile, Sidney's situation at court was not entirely satisfactory. He had for some years been regarded as a young man of promise and importance; but he was still without any steady and remunerative position. Other disappointments may have added to his discouragement: he had for some time known and admired Penelope Devereux, the daughter of the Earl of Essex, who clearly inspired the "Stella" of his sonnet sequence. But she married Lord Rich in 1581. Two years later Sidney married the daughter of Sir Francis Walsingham. He was knighted the same year.

Sidney had been a leader of the strong Puritan faction promoting English involvement in the wars of the Protestant Dutch against their Spanish rulers. In 1585, after Elizabeth I finally acceded to this faction's demands and sent an army to the Netherlands, Sidney was named governor of Flushing, one of the towns that the Dutch had ceded to the Queen in return for her support. For several months he fought and commanded troops at the side of his uncle, the Earl of Leicester, in Flanders. At the battle of Zutphen on Sept. 22, 1586, he was fatally wounded. A biography written by his friend Greville tells how Sidney was vulnerable because he had generously lent a part of his protective armor to a fellow knight.

Major Works

During his lifetime Sidney's works circulated only in manuscript. His *Arcadia* was the first to be printed, in 1590. Combining elements drawn from the pastoral tradition, the heroic epic, and the romances of chivalry, this long mixture of prose and verse summed up the heroic ideals that inspired Sidney's life. The *Arcadia* is noted for its complex plot, for its earnest digressions on such topics as justice, atheism, virtue, honor, and friendship, and for its involved and elaborate style. The published version of 1590 was a revision, much amplified and elaborated by comparison with the first draft.

In *Astrophel and Stella,* first printed in 1591, Sidney expressed varying moods and intensities of passionate love, in imitation of Italian and French sonneteers of the Petrarchan tradition. Sidney's simple yet delicate verse is markedly superior to that of his contemporaries. His *Apology for Poetry* (first published in 1595) was the first major critical essay in Renaissance England. Drawing on such foreign critics as Julius Caesar Scaliger and Lodovico Castelvetro, Sidney condensed the classical defense of "poetry" (by which he meant all forms of creative writing), and he insisted on the ethical value of art, which aims to lure men to "see the form of goodness, which seen they cannot but love ere themselves be aware, as if they took a medicine of cherries." This critical essay, perhaps more than any other work, has assured Sidney's position in the history of literature. All three of his major works, however, hold an important place in one of the most brilliant eras of English literary creativity.

Further Reading

Sidney's *Complete Works* were edited by Albert Feuillerat (4 vols., 1912-1926). An excellent edition of the *Poems* was prepared by William A. Ringler, Jr. (1962). Full biographies of Sidney include Malcolm W. Wallace, *The Life of Sir Philip Sidney* (1915); Mona Wilson, *Sir Philip Sidney* (1931); and Kenneth Muir, *Sir Philip Sidney* (1960). Other helpful studies include Kenneth Orne Myrick, *Sir Philip Sidney as a Literary Craftsman* (1935; 2d ed. 1965); John Buxton, *Sir Philip Sidney and the English Renaissance* (1954; 2d ed. 1964); and Frederick Samuel Boas, *Sidney: His Life and Writings* (1955). Recent critical assessments are available in Robert L. Montgomery, Jr., *Symmetry and Sense* (1961); David Kalstone, *Sidney's Poetry: Contexts and Interpretations* (1965); and Neil L. Rudenstine, *Sidney's Poetic Development* (1967). For general literary background see Douglas Bush, *The Renaissance and English Humanism* (1939); S. T. Bindoff, *Tudor England* (1951); Hallett Darius Smith, *Elizabethan Poetry* (1952); and C. S. Lewis, *English Literature in the Sixteenth Century, Excluding Drama* (1954).

Additional Sources

Duncan-Jones, Katherine, *Sir Philip Sidney, courtier poet,* New Haven: Yale University Press, 1991.

Greville, Fulke, Baron Brooke, *The life of the renowned Sr Philip Sidney (1652),* Delmar, N.Y.: Scholars' Facsimiles & Reprints, 1984.

Greville, Fulke, Baron Brooke, *Sir Fulke Greville's Life of Sir Philip Sidney,* Norwood, Pa.: Norwood Editions, 1978.

Hamilton, A. C. (Albert Charles), *Sir Philip Sidney: a study of his life and works,* Cambridge Eng.; New York: Cambridge University Press, 1977.

Lloyd, Julius, *The life of Sir Philip Sidney,* Folcroft, Pa. Folcroft Library Editions, 1974.

Sidney in retrospect: selections from English literary renaissance, Amherst: University of Massachusetts Press, 1988.

Wilson, Mona, *Sir Philip Sidney,* Norwood, Pa.: Norwood Editions, 1978. □

Benjamin Siegel

Bugsy Siegel (1906–1947) was a gangster and gambler who felt class was everything. He is considered responsible for putting Las Vegas, Nevada on the map.

Bugsy Siegel believed that in order to get ahead, you had to have class. As a gangster who ran gambling rackets, he was something of a visionary. As part of an expansion of gambling activities in the West, he is credited with putting the small Nevada town of Las Vegas on the map as the king of the world gambling capitals.

Fiery Youth

Benjamin Siegel was born on 28 February 1906 in Brooklyn, New York. In a manner similar to fellow gangster Louis Lepke, Siegel began his criminal career by preying upon pushcart vendors with a sidekick named Morris Sedway. Unlike Lepke, Siegel did not usually beat the vendors he was trying to convince to buy protection from him. Rather he would simply have Sedway pour kerosene over the vendors' merchandise and then light it on fire. It usually only took a vendor one lesson to decide to pay the "insurance."

Gambling Rackets

During the 1920s and 1930s Siegel continued his climb up the underworld ladder until he became involved in a killing in the early part of the 1930s. As a result of this murder, several attempts were made on his life. With the heat turned up, he reportedly approached syndicate leaders regarding a plan to consolidate criminal undertakings in California with Jack Dragna, who at the time controlled the underworld in that state. Siegel contacted an old friend with whom he had grown up in New York, the film actor George Raft, who reportedly liked Siegel and was happy to introduce him to various Hollywood actors and studio directors. With the help of Dragna, Siegel operated various gambling establishments, including a floating casino. Siegel was reportedly involved in the murder of a gangster named Harry Greenberg after it was rumored that Greenberg had become a police informant. He was later acquitted of the murder and turned more of his attention to increasing gambling revenue for the syndicate.

The Flamingo

In 1945 Siegel decided to establish a gambling hotel in a small town called Las Vegas, Nevada. According to reports, he borrowed $3 million from the syndicate and eventually spent $6 million total in building the Flamingo Hotel. As the first legalized gambling casino in the United States, the Flamingo became famous nationwide, and Bugsy drew enormous profits from it. At some point in 1946 or 1947, he apparently had a disagreement with the syndicate regarding its claim to the $3 million it had put up to help finance the hotel.

A Bad Roll of the Dice

On behalf of the syndicate, Lucky Luciano contacted Bugsy and instructed him to meet with syndicate members in Havana, Cuba, which was then one of the gambling centers of the world, often frequented by American gangsters. Siegel apparently refused to return the $3 million, perhaps thinking that as a gambling crime czar he had little to fear from the syndicate. He was wrong. On 20 June 1947, as Siegel sat in the living room of his girlfriend, syndicate prostitute Virginia Hill, he was shot three times in the head and killed instantly. At about the same time, his longtime friend and companion Moey Sedway, accompanied by several syndicate members, appeared at the Flamingo Hotel and informed the manager that they were taking over.

Further Reading

Biographies that may be of interst include George Carpozi, Jr., *Bugsy: The Bloodthirsty, Lusty Life of Benjamin "Bugsy" Siegel* (1992); Dean Jennings, *We Only Kill Each Other* (1992); and David Hanna, *The Man Who Invented Murder, Inc.* (1974). The 1991 Film *Bugsy,* focused on Siegel's dream to build the Flamingo Hotel in Las Vegas. The television show A&E Biography profiled Siegel in the December 1996 bio *Bugsy Siegel: Gambling in the Mob.* □

Henryk Sienkiewicz

The Polish novelist and short-story writer Henryk Sienkiewicz (1846-1916) wrote historical novels on an epic scale. His evocations of the Middle Ages and the 17th century, as well as the early Christian era, are vivid, stirring, and often beautiful.

Born on May 4, 1846, in Wola Okrzejska in Russian-occupied Poland, Henryk Sienkiewicz enjoyed a peaceful childhood in the country, encountering the conflicts of his divided land only when his family moved to Warsaw and the boy began secondary school. An average student, Sienkiewicz graduated to a post as tutor in a wealthy family before returning to Warsaw University; there he hesitated between medicine and law, finally transferring to the faculty of history and literature. He left the university in 1871 without taking his examinations. During the next 5 years Sienkiewicz painfully established himself as a free-lance writer and journalist. He distinguished himself as a chronicle writer, a popular reporting genre that took him to Vienna, Ostend, and Paris; his regular *feuilletons* contained charming, entertaining episodes of daily life as well as serious treatments of pressing social issues. In 1876 the successful journalist was sent to the United States, and Sienkiewicz sent back from America a collection of short stories (*Charcoal Sketches*) and material for his *American Letters.*

Returning to Europe in 1878, Sienkiewicz lived for a time in Paris and Italy, writing short stories ("Orso," "Yanko the Musician," "From the Memoirs of a Poznan Tutor," and "After Bread") and lecturing on his American experiences. His marriage to Maria Szetkiewicz in 1881 marked the beginning of the most contented and richly productive period of his life. Appointed editor of a new Warsaw daily, he continued writing chronicles and short stories. Concerned with the oppressed peasantry, he wrote tragic narratives of a divided people that were occasionally censured, and even such American tales as "Sachem" and "The Lighthouse Keeper" revealed his deep national feeling.

These years witnessed as well the most important transformation in Sienkiewicz's artistic career: his turning away from journalism and the short narrative to embark upon the creation of epic tableaux from Poland's national past. From 1882 to 1887 his trilogy appeared, first as a serial, then with even greater success in book form. Recreating the 17th-century struggle for existence of the Polish-Lithuanian commonwealth, *With Fire and the Sword, The Deluge,* and *Pan Michael* traced a people's heroic resistance to invasion by the Cossacks and the Swedes. Sienkiewicz's purpose was to revive national sentiment with a vision of ancestral vigor. He gained overwhelming public approval for his encouraging evocation of a glorious past.

Sienkiewicz next turned to a contemporary setting, offering a lengthy diagnosis of the Polish upper-class finde-siècle malaise in *Without Dogma* (1890); its somewhat morbid hero was sharply contrasted with the progressive and robust characters of *Children of the Soil* (1894). In 1893 Sienkiewicz began work on his best-known historical novel, *Quo Vadis?* Its story of early Christian persecution paralleled the political upheavals Sienkiewicz had traced for

Poland in his trilogy. This novel is considered a stylistic masterpiece, and it remained for many years the most successful fictional publication in history. Sienkiewicz gained international celebrity with *Quo Vadis?*, but his patriotic sense of a distinct national past led him to turn next to Poland's dark ages, with *The Teutonic Knights* (1900), tales of rapacious foreigners and of long-suffering Poles.

Sienkiewicz enjoyed a jubilee celebration in his honor in 1900, and he was at the height of personal fame when he received the Nobel Prize for literature in 1905. His remaining work showed a decline in conceptual strength. *On the Field of Glory* (1905) returned to the era of the trilogy, but with less success. *In Desert and Wilderness* (1911) was a children's story reminiscent of Rudyard Kipling and Daniel Defoe, rich in a positivistic didacticism then out of date. Sienkiewicz's last important work, *Whirlpools* (1910), reflected alarm at the outbreaks of revolutionary activity in Russia, that "storm from the East" threatening to "cover our tradition, civilization, culture—the whole Poland and turn it into a desert."

World War I drove Sienkiewicz into exile in Switzerland, where he directed Polish relief work and where he died on Nov. 14, 1916.

Further Reading

Critical treatments of Sienkiewicz include Monica Gardner, *The Patriot Novelist of Poland, Henryk Sienkiewicz* (1926); Waclaw Lednicki, *Henryk Sienkiewicz: A Retrospective Synthesis* (1960); and Mieczyslaw Giergielewicz, *Henryk Sienkiewicz* (1968). A brief biography is contained in Horst Frenz, ed., *Nobel Lectures: Literature, 1901-1967* (1969). For a study of Sienkiewicz's place in Polish literature see Czeslaw Milosz, *The History of Polish Literature* (1969). □

Justo Sierra

Justo Sierra (1848-1912) was a Mexican educator, writer, and historian. As one of Mexico's leading liberal historians and as minister of education, he was responsible for considerable educational reform and expansion during the first decade of the 20th century.

Justo Sierra was born in Campeche, Yucatán, on Jan. 26, 1848. His father, Justo Sierra O'Rielly, was one of Yucatán's foremost intellectuals. Young Sierra studied in Campeche and Mexico City, receiving a law degree at the age of 23. Elected to the Mexican Congress in 1872, he quickly gained a reputation as a formidable debater. He served 2 years on the Supreme Court prior to his designation as subsecretary of justice and public education in 1902. In 1905 he was appointed minister of public education and fine arts, a post which he held until the fall of the regime of Gen. Porfirio Díaz in 1911.

Sierra insisted that educational progress parallel economic growth, both to train the populace in the requisite skills and to preserve the national identity in the face of an influx of foreign capital and methodology. Consequently, he stressed science and Mexican history in his curriculum. In 1910 he sponsored the First National Congress of Primary Education and revived the National University of Mexico, which had splintered into separate colleges.

One of the foremost propagandists of his day, Sierra edited and wrote regular columns for several newspapers. Though a member of the Díaz Cabinet, he did not hesitate to criticize the regime and never fully accepted the positivism that constituted the official ideology. Maintaining an independent intellectual stance, he considered himself primarily a humanist.

Sierra is best known for his voluminous historical works. Although he attempted to synthesize the broad sweep of human development for the general reader in his *Historia general* (1896), most of his volumes focused on Mexican history. His interpretation was liberal, and he contended that Mexico had experienced only two revolutions worthy of the name: the Independence movement and the War of the Reform (1854-1867). In *México: su evolución social* (1902), Sierra argued that the Díaz era was the culmination of Mexican development. He defended Benito Juárez in *Juárez: su obra y su tiempo* (1905), contending that his era of liberal government constituted the pivotal period of Mexican history.

Sierra's most famous work is *La evolución política del pueblo mexicano* (1900-1902; *The Political Evolution of the Mexican Nation,* 1946), intended as a "popular synthesis." In this volume he applied the prevailing evolutionary theories to Mexican history, emphasizing the importance of the liberal revolution of the mid-19th century. He condemned the Mexican leaders of the early portion of that century as petty individuals seeking only self-aggrandizement.

After the collapse of the Díaz regime in 1911, Sierra was appointed ambassador to Spain. He died in Madrid on Sept. 13, 1912.

Further Reading

The best source available in English on Sierra is the introduction to his *The Political Evolution of the Mexican Nation,* translated by Charles Ramsdell, with notes and introduction by Edmundo O'Gorman (1969). William Rex Crawford, *A Century of Latin-American Thought* (1944; rev. ed. 1961), discusses Sierra's ideas. Carlos González Peña, *History of Mexican Literature* (trans. 1943; 3d ed. 1968), examines Sierra's life and career. □

Comte Emmanuel Joseph Sieyès

The French statesman and political writer Comte Emmanuel Joseph Sieyès (1748-1836) known as the Abbé Sieyès, upheld the interests of the Third Estate. His effort to consolidate a moderate republican gov-

ernment established Napoleon Bonaparte as the head of state.

Born at Fréjus on May 3, 1748, Emmanuel Joseph Sieyès got his primary education from the Jesuits in his hometown and continued into advanced study in theology. Appointment as a canon in the cathedral chapter of Tréguier (1775) brought him the appellation of Abbé (used in France not only for abbots but also for churchmen without a parish), and by the eve of the French Revolution he had been promoted to vicar general of the bishop of Chartres. But his interests in these years of intensive political debate turned from theology and Church administration to public affairs, and when the government called for proposals on ways to hold the elections to the Estates General, one of his three pamphlets on the issue was of critical importance in rallying the Third Estate as a force independent of, and even hostile to, clergy and nobility. This was the famous *Qu'est-ce que le tiers état?* (1789; *What Is the Third Estate?*), which proclaimed in phrases of ringing clarity that the commoners had been nothing and should be all, as the essential component of the French nation.

Sieyès was elected a deputy of the Third Estate and not of his own Estate, and he played a key role in the events of the first months of the Revolution. He proposed the name National Assembly for the combined single chamber established unilaterally by the Third Estate, with some support from liberal clergy and nobles, on June 17; drew up the "Tennis Court Oath," by which the deputies pledged themselves to the defense of the National Assembly as the embodiment of the sovereignty of the people, on June 20; and took the initiative in the decision of the Constituent Assembly (as the National Assembly was called in its self-assumed task of writing a constitution) to continue its work despite the King's order to disband on June 23. He was also active in the formulation of the Declaration of the Rights of Man.

Further events showed Sieyès to be a moderate within the Revolutionary movement. He favored the widest personal rights of citizens as against arbitrary government power, limitation of the right to vote to property holders (because the votes of the poor, he argued, would be easily bought by the rich), and extreme economic individualism, without restriction upon the right of persons to amass wealth. He was not elected to the Legislative Assembly but was chosen a deputy to the Convention. As the Revolution swung into its radical phase, he chose the path of caution and avoided a prominent role during the Reign of Terror. Asked afterward what he had done during that perilous period, he answered tersely, "J'ai vécu" (I stayed alive). To do so, he had voted for the death penalty against Louis XVI; but after Maximilien de Robespierre's fall, he resumed political activity.

As a member of the Thermidorean Committee of Public Safety and then of the Council of Five Hundred, Sieyès favored an annexationist foreign policy and internal consolidation. After serving as ambassador to Berlin in 1798-1799, he returned to Paris to become a member of the Directory, the executive branch of government. When it became clear that the Directory was supported by only a minority in the nation, with both radical republicans and royalists in active opposition, he and a fellow Director sought the support of the army in the person of Gen. Bonaparte in the coup d'etat of 18 Brumaire (Nov. 9, 1799). However, in the new government of three consuls conceived by Sieyès, it was Napoleon Bonaparte who took the post of first consul for himself, and Sieyès was sent into innocuous but prestigious posts, especially after Bonaparte became Emperor Napoleon. He was named to the Senate and became its president, was named a count of the empire, and was elected to the French Academy.

However, when the Bourbon monarchy was finally restored in 1815, Sieyès was banned as a regicide and fled to Brussels, where he lived as an exile until the Revolution of 1830. Returning home, he died in Paris on June 20, 1836, remembered in history chiefly for his inflammatory pamphlet of 1789 and his dupe's part in the overthrow of the Directory.

Further Reading

Sieyès's *What is the Third Estate?*, edited with historical notes by S. E. Finer (trans. 1964), has a detailed biographical introduction by Peter Campbell. John Harold Clapham, *The Abbe Sieyès: An Essay on the Politics of the French Revolution* (1912), is by a distinguished economic historian. Glyndon G. Van Deusen, *Sieyès: His Life and His Nationalism* (1932), is a good general account. ☐

Clifford Sifton

Clifford Sifton (1861-1929) was a politician who did more than anyone else to turn the Canadian West into a premiere agricultural area.

Clifford Sifton's father, John Wright Sifton, was a farmer, oil man, and banker and a devout Methodist. Of Irish origin, he moved his family to England and then to Canada, where Clifford was born in a farmhouse near Arva, Canada West (Ontario), on March 10, 1861. Clifford's older brother, Arthur Lewis Sifton (born October 26, 1858), was also destined to play an important role in the early political life of western Canada.

In 1874 John moved the Sifton family again, this time to Selkirk, Manitoba. Clifford and his brother attended two Methodist institutions, Wesley College in Winnipeg and Victoria College in Cobourg, Ontario. Clifford graduated in 1880 as the gold medalist. The two brothers articled (were apprentices) in Winnipeg and set up law practice in the town of Brandon, Manitoba. Clifford's father broke ground for his sons in politics, running for office six times, although with only moderate success.

Clifford won his first provincial election in Brandon North as a Liberal in 1888, eloquently denouncing the monopolistic privileges of the powerful Canadian Pacific Railway (CPR). As attorney general of Manitoba, 1891-1895, he inherited the volatile, complex school issue that turned on the rights guaranteed to French and Catholic Manitobans to support their own schools. His passionate opposition to religious instruction in the schools brought him to national prominence. The issue was tearing Manitoba apart and presenting an intractable thorn in the side of the French and Catholic prime minister, Wilfrid Laurier. In 1896 Sifton worked out a "compromise" that effectively curtailed the separate schools but managed to save face for the prime minister.

Laurier was impressed and brought Sifton into the federal cabinet as minister of the interior and superintendent general of Indian affairs. Despite a deafness that afflicted him all his life, Sifton's high energy, mastery of political organization, and incisive analytical mind set him apart, even in Laurier's talented cabinet. He negotiated the important Crow's Nest Pass Agreement with the CPR. He was responsible for the administration of the Yukon during the turmoil of the Klondike Gold Rush, and he was the agent in charge of presenting Canada's case to the Alaska Boundary Tribunal in 1903.

Despite his successes, Sifton found it necessary to silence some of his critics in the highly partisan world of the press. He purchased the *Manitoba Free Press* newspaper in 1897 and hired as his editor John W. Dafoe, one of the ablest journalists in Canadian history (and a future biographer).

Sifton's greatest accomplishment was the organization of a massive immigration into the Canadian West. From 1880 to 1891 over one million Canadians and immigrants had left Canada for the United States. Sifton had an unbounded confidence in the future prosperity of the Canadian West, and he determined to ensure that Canadian (that is, British), not American, institutions be established on the northern prairie. A born organizer, he eliminated the bureaucratic fumbling that frustrated settlers trying to buy land, simplified procedures, centralized decisions, and orchestrated a massive publicity campaign in Europe and North America. He dispatched lecturers to fall fairs in the United States and distributed pamphlets and ads in thousands of American newspapers. Six hundred U.S. editors (in an early version of the modern "media tour") were given free trips to Canada, as were British members of Parliament (MPs). Agents scoured Britain, Germany, and other European countries to publicize the "golden fields" of the West and to lure the "peasants in sheepskin coats" of present-day Ukraine and Romania to the Canadian West. Despite repeated attacks by nativists, Sifton's "stalwart peasants" turned some of the most difficult areas of the West into productive farms. Sifton's campaign stands as the greatest and most successful public relations campaign in Canadian history, bringing more than two million newcomers to Canada between 1896 and 1911.

Sifton resigned from the federal cabinet on February 27, 1905, following a dispute with Laurier over school policy for the new provinces of Alberta and Saskatchewan. In 1911 he broke with the Liberal Party on its policy of "reciprocity" (free trade) with the United States, supporting the protectionist Conservatives. Though he did not run for Parliament again, he remained an influential presence in public life. He was chairman of the Canadian Commission of Conservation from 1909 to 1918, promoting conservation measures far ahead of their time. He was knighted by King George V on January 1, 1915.

Sifton died on April 17, 1929, in New York, where he had gone to consult a specialist in heart disease. Despite the suspicion of many contemporaries that he was fabulously wealthy, he left an estate officially valued at $3.2 million, though the government valued it at much more. He was highly secretive about his business affairs, and his biographers have still not discovered how, in the words of one critic, he came to Ottawa a poor man and left it a rich man. Many considered him ruthless and unprincipled, but Sifton was a man of exceptional achievement. He had a deep and persistent faith in Canada's future, and he left an imposing monument in the settlement and development of one of the world's greatest agricultural areas, the Canadian West.

Further Reading

J.W. Dafoe's *Clifford Sifton in Relation to His Times* (1931) is a personal and sympathetic memoir. David J. Hall, *Clifford Sifton,* 2 vols. (1981, 1985), is a thorough, scholarly, and readable biography and contains a detailed bibliography. The best general history of Canada in Sifton's time is Robert Craig Brown and Ramsay Cook, *Canada 1896-1921: A Nation Transformed* (1974).

Additional Sources

Hall, D. J. (David John), *Clifford Sifton,* Vancouver: University of British Columbia Press, 1981-1985. □

Sigismund

Sigismund (1368-1437) was king of Hungary from 1385 to 1437, Holy Roman emperor from 1411 to 1437, and king of Bohemia from 1420 to 1437.

Born on Feb. 15, 1368, Sigismund was the second son of the emperor Charles IV and the brother of the emperor Wenceslaus. His reign as king of Hungary and Holy Roman emperor witnessed three of the most crucial events in later medieval history: the Turkish invasion of Hungary and the defeat of the ill-fated Crusade of Nicopolis in 1396; the burning of John Hus as a heretic and the subsequent revolution of the Hussites in Bohemia; and the important Council of Constance (1415-1417), over which Sigismund presided and which ended the Great Schism in the Roman Catholic Church (1378-1415) but which alienated Sigismund from the Czechs and deprived him of the Bohemian resources of the imperial house of Luxemburg, of which he was the last member.

King of Hungary

Sigismund's debut in the political life of eastern Europe occurred at the age of 17, when the death of Louis the Great of Hungary left the crown of Hungary to Louis's daughter Mary (reigned 1382-1395) and to Sigismund, her fiancé. After invading Hungary, Sigismund was recognized as king in 1387 but at the cost of losing Poland to the Jagiellon dynasty of Lithuania and, after 1389, of losing large portions of southern and eastern Hungarian territory to the Ottoman Turks, who established their footing in continental Europe with a shattering victory over Sigismund's crusading army at Nicopolis in 1396.

After Sigismund became king of Hungary, his lavish scale of living—as well as his military expenses and the cost of his later candidacy for the imperial crown—rapidly depleted the resources of the Hungarian royal treasury. Sigismund's fiscal policies crushed the Hungarian peasantry with unbearable burdens of taxation and alienated the restive Hungarian aristocracy. Although Sigismund's prestige in Hungary was somewhat enhanced by his position as Holy Roman emperor after 1411 and by his nominal kingship of Bohemia after 1420, neither of these titles aided Hungary, and Sigismund's reign was a failure.

Holy Roman Emperor

Having spent much of his youth in Hungary, Sigismund was unknown in the West when he was elected emperor in 1411. He was a brave fighter, as his conduct at Nicopolis and elsewhere testified. Sigismund was reasonably well educated, he was a good Latinist, and he remained a patron of learning. In addition to these attributes, however, Sigismund had less attractive ones. He had many amorous adventures; he was subject to fits of extreme cruelty; and his limitless ambition to make his imperial title a reality in the western parts of the empire ill suited his limited financial resources.

The political conditions of the German part of the empire had steadily deteriorated under Sigismund's two immediate predecessors, Wenceslaus (reigned 1376-1400) and Rupert of the Palatinate (reigned 1400-1410). The lack of a uniform law code; the rivalry among electors, lesser nobles, and the city-leagues; and the empire's diversified territories in Germany, Italy, Bohemia, and Hungary—all required the hand of a great ruler with infinite financial and administrative resources. In addition, Sigismund's diplomatic connections distracted his attention far to the east and north, where he established the Hohenzollern house in Brandenburg and negotiated with the Teutonic Knights in their struggle with newly Christianized Lithuania.

Council of Constance

Sigismund's greatest imperial project was the calling of the Council of Constance in 1415. Since 1378 two popes had claimed legitimacy, and since 1409 three had simultaneously claimed St. Peter's chair. Christendom was politically and ecclesiastically fragmented along the lines of loyalty to one or the other of the three popes, and Sigismund saw an opportunity to fulfill his duties as protector of the Church and to enhance his own status. The council settled the papal schism, but it also violated the safe-conduct that the Emperor had issued to the Bohemian reformer John Hus. The council ordered Hus burned at the stake as a heretic. His death aroused great indignation among the Czechs and inaugurated a bloody social war that lasted for 2 decades.

Sigismund's prestige in Bohemia was greatly diminished. Sigismund's other imperial reform activities during the period 1415-1417 met equally disastrous results.

Last Years

Sigismund's last years were spent in diplomatic activities on the borders of his wide territories. Problems in Poland, the Bohemian revolt, the Turks in Hungary, and political factionalism in Germany wore the Emperor down. His own limited resources and resistance on the part of his subjects and rivals in the kingdoms over which he ruled made all his attempts at reform fruitless. The settlement that he had greatly helped the Church to achieve was threatened at the Council of Basel, which lasted from 1431 until after Sigismund's death. Only the compromise in Bohemia, which brought the Hussite wars to an end in 1436, brightened the Emperor's last years. He was finally crowned emperor by the Pope in 1433, and the pacification of Bohemia was his last effective act. At his death on Dec. 9, 1437, Sigismund was once again planning to intervene between Pope and council.

Further Reading

The Cambridge Medieval History, edited by J. B. Bury (8 vols., 1913-1936), gives a good account of Sigismund's reign. William Stubbs, *Germany in the Later Middle Ages, 1200-1500,* edited by Arthur Hassall (1908), contains a chapter on Sigismund, and its conclusions can be checked with those of Geoffrey Barraclough, *The Origins of Modern Germany* (1946; 2d rev. ed. 1957). Standard histories of the Hussite movement, such as Frederick G. Heymann, *John Zizka and the Hussite Revolution* (1955), and of the Council of Constance also contain detailed information on Sigismund. □

Luca Signorelli

The Italian painter Luca Signorelli (ca. 1445-1523) anticipated the style of the High Renaissance. His masterpiece is the fresco cycle in Orvieto Cathedral.

Luca Signorelli was born in Cortona. According to Giorgio Vasari, who claimed a kinship with him that has since been disproved, Signorelli was born in 1441, but scholars now doubt Vasari, and a birth date in the late 1440s is most commonly accepted.

The earliest mention of Signorelli is in 1470, and after that his life is well documented. For instance, he served in a variety of official municipal offices in Cortona, was on a committee to judge projects for the facade of the Cathedral in Florence, and once borrowed money from Michelangelo, who complained that Signorelli was slow in repaying the loan. According to Vasari, Signorelli was widely admired throughout Italy. He reported that Signorelli lived more like a gentleman than an artist, dressing in fine clothes and displaying fine manners and conversation. He died in Cortona in 1523 probably on October 16.

Signorelli trained under Piero della Francesca, and his earliest work reflects his debt to Piero, especially in the use of broad planes to model forms. But Signorelli rejected Piero's static figures and was most concerned with depicting the human body in action, an interest he may have acquired from the Florentine painter and sculptor Antonio Pollaiuolo. Among Signorelli's most important early works are the frescoes (late 1470s) in the Sacristy of the Basilica of the Holy House, Loreto; the *Flagellation* (1480-1481) in the Brera, Milan; the *Testament and Death of Moses* (ca. 1482) in the Sistine Chapel in the Vatican, Rome; the S. Onofrio altarpiece (1484) in the Cathedral Museum, Perugia; and the frescoes (mid-1490s) in the cloister of the Abbey of Monte Oliveto Maggiore near Siena.

The frescoes depicting the Last Judgment in the S. Brizio Chapel of the Cathedral in Orvieto are Signorelli's masterpiece. Called to Orvieto in 1499 to complete the vault decorations begun by Fra Angelico and Benozzo Gozzoli, Signorelli worked until 1504 painting the walls with a vivid narrative, including the *Preaching of the Antichrist,* the *End of the World,* the *Resurrection of the Dead,* and the *Damned and the Elect.* He suppressed details of environment to concentrate attention on the numerous nude figures that dominate the compositions. These frescoes, which Vasari claimed Michelangelo admired, were the most compelling depiction of the Last Judgment before Michelangelo's great fresco in the Sistine Chapel.

Signorelli never equaled the expressive power of these works in the paintings of his last 20 years. His late works were mainly formal altarpieces in which the hands of assis-

tants may be seen. In them Signorelli made use of the simple bilateral symmetry so frequently seen in Perugino's altarpieces.

Further Reading

Maud Cruttwell, *Luca Signorelli* (1899), is a full-length biography. Information on the artist can be found in J. A. Crowe and G. B. Cavalcaselle, *A History of Painting in Italy* (2 vols., 1871; 2d ed., 3 vols., 1912), and Bernhard Berenson, *The Drawings of Florentine Painters* (2 vols., 1903; rev. ed., 3 vols., 1938) and *Italian Painters of the Renaissance* (1930).

Additional Sources

Kury, Gloria, *The early work of Luca Signorelli, 1465-1490,* New York: Garland Pub., 1978. □

Prince Norodom Sihanouk

A Cambodian nationalist and political leader, Prince Norodom Sihanouk (born 1922) secured Cambodia's independence from French colonial rule and sought to protect his country from the repercussions of Great Power rivalries.

The first of the four children of Prince Norodom Suramarit and Princess Monivong Kossamak, Prince Norodom Sihanouk was born in the Cambodian capital of Phnom Penh on Oct. 31, 1922. He was a direct descendant of the great 19th-century King Norodom, who was succeeded upon his death in 1904 by a half brother rather than a son. The colonial French encouraged Sihanouk's selection as king in 1941 because they feared the outspokenly nationalist heir apparent of the line of King Norodom's half brother. Sihanouk, who already enjoyed a reputation as a playboy, was picked because the French perceived him as pliable.

Sihanouk was raised in a quite modest environment by his musically talented parents, in whose footsteps he partly followed as an accomplished saxophonist. Educated in French at an ordinary day school in Phnom Penh, Sihanouk was subsequently sent to a secondary school in Saigon in Vietnam, which, like Cambodia, was then part of French Indochina. He did not complete his secondary schooling, however—let alone continue on to a university—because of his recall to Phnom Penh in 1941, at the age of 18, to be enthroned as king.

Sihanouk's coronation took place 10 months after the fall of France, whose Indochinese empire fell under the practical direction of the expanding Japanese—who controlled neighboring Vietnam and Laos. During the first years of his reign as king, Sihanouk was a prisoner in his own palace. Although he subsequently proclaimed Cambodian independence from France in March 1945, encouraged by the retreating Japanese, he came fairly quickly to terms with the returning French after the war. He also opposed demands by the national legislatures elected in 1947 and 1951 for a redeclaration of independence from France.

Emergent Nationalist

Somewhat surprisingly, in light of his dissolution of a legislature that demanded immediate independence, Sihanouk proceeded to France to advance this very demand. Rebuffed by the French, he went into exile in Thailand in 1953, successfully embarrassing France into acquiescence to his country's independence. This independence was in effect completed in 1954 with the Geneva Agreements, which terminated the 8-year Franco-Indochinese War. This war was fought largely in adjacent Vietnam, but there were a few Vietnamese Communist partisans in Cambodia and a handful of Cambodian sympathizers. Sihanouk held up final approval of the Geneva Agreements until his demand for the complete withdrawal of the Vietnamese Communists from his country was met.

Sihanouk accepted American military and economic assistance after the end of the First Vietnamese War (1945-1954) and even initially sought to join the Southeast Asian Treaty Organization (SEATO). He terminated United States aid in 1963, however—and broke off diplomatic relations in 1965 (resumed in 1969)—because of the spillover into Cambodia of American war activity in adjacent South Vietnam and American diplomatic support of (and military aid to) another neighbor and historical foe, Thailand.

Monarchy without a King

Although he was still king when independence came, Sihanouk stepped down as monarch in 1955 in order to play a more active day-to-day role in Cambodian politics. He was succeeded on the throne by his father. The mercurial Sihanouk served a half dozen times as premier in the years 1955-1960, frequently resigning from the post for one reason or another, and became "chief of state" in 1960—shortly after the death of his father, the king. Although Cambodia continued to call itself a monarchy and was led by a former king—Sihanouk—it was the only monarchy in the world without a ruling sovereign.

Sihanouk formed the Popular Socialist Community party after his abdication as a means of preserving his political preeminence. This party won all the seats in the National Assembly vote of 1955 and subsequent elections throughout the 1960s, making Cambodia a one-party state in terms of representation in its government, and Sihanouk the political, if not reigning, king. The outbreak of North Vietnamese-encouraged Communist rebellion on Cambodian soil in 1967, however, indicated that there was at least this kind of opposition to Sihanouk's continued control of Cambodian political life.

For the first decade and a half of Cambodia's resumed independence, Sihanouk symbolized his nation to both his countrymen and the world beyond Cambodia. A devout Buddhist, he also sought to modernize his country's traditional agricultural economy, accepting aid from all quarters (until his termination of United States assistance in 1963). Assuming the posture of an outspoken neutralist in the second half of the 1950s, he tried both to restrict the role of the Great Powers in his country and to block the extension of the Vietnam War to Cambodia—with a surprising degree of success. He visited Peking, and he even recognized the Communist "Provisional Revolutionary Government" (Vietcong) in South Vietnam in 1969.

On March 18, 1970, while Sihanouk was returning from a health cure in France via Moscow, he and his government were overthrown by Lt. Gen. Lon Nol and Prince Sisowath Sirik Matak. This pro-Western coup resulted in Sihanouk's forming a government-in-exile in Peking and in the declaration of Cambodia as a republic. At that time he also announced his support of the Cambodian Communist Khmer Rouge under General Pol Pot in their efforts to overthrow Lon Nol.

In 1975 Lon Nol's government was overthrown by the Khmer Rouge and Sihanouk was returned to his position as head of state. In 1976, however, he was placed under house arrest by Pol Pot who assumed control of the government as the country's prime minister. In 1979, the Khmer Rouge government fell when the North Vietnamese invaded and occupied the country. Pol Pot and his allies fled to southwestern Cambodia and engaged in guerilla warfare against the new Vietnamese-backed government, while Sihanouk fled once again into exile in China, where he remained for 12 years. There he formed a coalition government-in-exile composed of royalists, rightists, and the Khmer Rouge. His government-in-exile in China succeeded in gaining a seat at the United Nations as the legitimate government of Cambodia.

In 1989, the Vietnamese withdrew and left behind a pro-Vietnamese government under Prime Minister Hun Sen. Sihanouk and Hun Sen began negotiations for his return. In 1991, Sihanouk returned to Cambodia and became president. He repudiated the Khmer Rouge at that point, denounced them as criminals, and called for the arrest and trial of their leaders. The Khmer Rouge returned to its position of armed opposition. In a U.N.-sponsored election in 1993, Sihanouk's royalist party was elected to power and approved a new constitution that reestabished the monarchy. In September 1993 Sihanouk was again crowned king of Cambodia. He governed with two co-prime ministers, his son Norodom Ranariddh and Hun Sen.

In 1996 the Khmer Rouge splintered apart. The moderate faction defected to Sihanouk and hard-liners under Pol Pot continued guerilla warfare from the mountain jungles. In June 1997, following a disintegration of leadership in the Khmer Rouge, fighting broke out between forces loyal to the two co-prime ministers. In early July, Norodom Ranariddh was deposed by Hun Sen.

Further Reading

The personality and views of Prince Sihanouk emerge strongly in John P. Armstrong, *Sihanouk Speaks* (1964), a book which quotes Sihanouk at considerable length on a wide range of subjects. In 1995 Sihanouk himself published *Charisma and Leadership* in which he describes his personal encounters with some of the great leaders of the twentieth century. *Politics and Power in Cambodia: The Sihanouk Years* (1973) and *Sihanouk: Prince of Light, Prince of Darkness* (1994) both by Milton E. Osborne offer useful information and insights. *Cambodia: The Search for Security* (1967), by British scholar Michael Leiffer, is a perceptive study of Cambodian foreign policy, highlighting Sihanouk's dominant role in its formation and execution. An earlier and still very useful book on the same subject, which gives an illuminating portrait of Sihanouk in action, is Roger Morton Smith, *Cambodia's Foreign Policy* (1965). Martin Florian Herz, *A Short History of Cambodia* (1958), is a good, if very brief, introduction to Cambodian history. □

Igor Sikorsky

The Russian-American aeronautical engineer, aircraft manufacturer, and inventor Igor Sikorsky (1889-1972) designed such famous aircraft as the flying clipper and was the major developer of the helicopter.

Igor Sikorsky was born in Kiev, Russia, where his father was a professor of psychology at St. Vladimir University. Following his graduation from the Naval Academy at St. Petersburg, he studied in Paris and at the Polytechnic Institute in Kiev. While in Germany in 1908, he heard of the dirigible flights of Count Zeppelin and returned to Paris to study aviation. At the age of 20 he built his first helicopter.

He then turned to more conventional planes, and in 1910 his S-2 achieved some success. In 1913 he built the world's first four-engine plane, the *Grand,* which was adopted by the Russian army and used during World War I.

Sikorsky was not sympathetic with the Bolshevik Revolution of 1917 and in 1918 left for Paris, where he lost money attempting to build his aircraft. In 1919 he came to the United States, hoping to find a broader opportunity to exercise his engineering talents. His initial experience was discouraging, and he was forced to take a teaching position in a school for Russian immigrants. Then, in 1923, he joined with other Russian refugees to form the Sikorsky Aero Engineering Company. The composer and concert pianist Sergei Rachmaninov was a large investor and became vice president of the new firm.

Within a few years the firm became a part of the giant United Aircraft and Transport Company. Sikorsky and his fellow Russians were excellent engineers but poor businessmen. In 1928 they began work on large flying boats for Pan American Airways and lost $1 million on the contracts. In 1929 Sikorsky sold 56 "aerial yachts" to wealthy subscribers, most of whom were deeply involved in the stock market. When the market crashed in October 1929, they defaulted and left Sikorsky in a difficult financial situation.

United took closer charge of Sikorsky's business but continued to support his work on flying boats, which culminated with the building of the S-42 Clipper Ship for Pan American. These were magnificent engineering achievements but still lost money for the firm. Their construction was abandoned in 1938. United, however, fortunately chose to support Sikorsky in a return to his early work on helicopters.

The helicopter had long been realized to be theoretically workable, and a number of people during the 1920s and 1930s, both in the United States and abroad, experimented with its design. In 1939 Sikorsky tested his VS-300, the first truly practical helicopter. His success lay partly in his use of propeller blades the pitch of which could be controlled so as to change the direction of flight. During World War II helicopters were not used until 1944, and their real contributions to both war and peace came only in the 1950s, when Sikorsky was one of the leading manufacturers in the field.

Further Reading

Sikorsky's autobiography is entitled *The Story of the Winged S* (1939). A full-length account of Sikorsky is Frank J. Delear, *Igor Sikorsky: His Three Careers in Aviation* (1969). A biographical chapter on him is in Robert M. Bartlett, *They Work for Tomorrow* (1943). His work is placed in context by John B. Rae in *Climb to Greatness: The American Aircraft Industry, 1920-1960* (1968). Charles Lester Morris, *Pioneering the Helicopter* (1945), is an account by Sikorsky's test pilot. ☐

John Silber

Philosopher, educator and controversial President of Boston University, John Silber (born 1926) was an internationally recognized authority on ethics, education and the philosophy of Immanuel Kant.

John Silber was born August 15, 1926, in San Antonio, Texas, the second son of Paul G. Silber, a German-American architect, and Jewell Joslin Silber, an elementary school teacher. His family was economically comfortable until, like most all middle-class American families, the Great Depression of the 1930s depleted their earning sources. The Silbers were a proud family and the father refused to relinquish the practice of architecture despite the absence of demand brought upon by the depression. This under-employment made it necessary for the mother to teach grammar school in order to keep the family fed and clothed.

The atmosphere of the Silber household was one of gentility and culture. There were constant reminders not to allow their financial status to interfere with the diligent pursuit of learning. Bible verses were memorized, chores completed, books read, concerts attended, and school assignments mastered.

John was born with a right arm which ended in a stump right below his elbow. He first discovered a difference between himself and other children when he was four. The ridiculing attitude of his fellow students was a problem to him and led to constant fighting. Named "One-Armed Pete," young Silber discovered he could apply the stump squarely to the face of an opponent and be at an advantage.

He fought continuously until the fifth grade. Nora Ephron, in a 1977 *Esquire* magazine article, suggested that "In some sense, John Silber never stopped fighting on the playground."

John Silber received his undergraduate education at Trinity College (Texas), graduating *summa cum laude* in 1947 with majors in fine arts and philosophy. Following his undergraduate work he married Kathryn Underwood, a fellow student. Through his interest in philosophy and theology he considered the ministry as a career and attended Yale Divinity School for a year. An attraction to law led him to the University of Texas Law School, but also for only a year. He finally decided on the discipline of philosophy, the work of Immanuel Kant, in particular, and graduated from Yale with an M.A. degree in 1952 and a Ph.D. degree in 1956. The following year he returned to Texas where he was appointed assistant professor of philosophy at the University of Texas in Austin.

At the University of Texas (U.T.) Silber quickly developed a reputation as a demanding teacher with liberal social views. Students reported his teaching style as Socratic as well as abrasive, consisting of relentless questions and uncomfortable confrontations. They found his expectations of them high with good grades difficult to obtain. Silber was, however, nominated by students for three outstanding-teacher awards. His reputation for liberal social views came from his service as chair of the Texas Society to Abolish Capital Punishment and his outspoken views in favor of racial integration. He was promoted to professor and named chairperson in 1962 and became dean of the College of Arts and Sciences in 1967. By 1970 Silber had crossed swords with the University of Texas' biggest booster and chair of the board of regents, Frank C. Irwin, Jr. Ostensibly the conflict was over a proposal to split the college into two smaller schools, but *TIME* magazine reported Silber became "a target because of his liberalism, aggressiveness, and potential candidacy for the U.T. presidency." The university dismissed him from his position as dean.

Meanwhile, a new academic opportunity was developing in Massachusetts. Boston University is located directly across the Charles River from and overshadowed by Harvard and M.I.T. It had been under pressure from emerging institutions such as the University of Massachusetts and Northeastern which could undercut the cost of private education. A Methodist institution, B.U.'s most famous graduate was Martin Luther King, Jr., from the school of theology. Early in 1970 Arland Christ-Janer resigned as president of the school. Boston University needed credible leadership to advance its strength and reputation. A 21-member search committee, following several months of deliberation and nonconclusive actions, asked Silber to come to Boston for an interview. Silber's manner was blunt, arrogant, and cold in the interview process; he called the B.U. campus "the ugliest damned place he'd ever seen." Yet, he mesmerized the committee with his vision for the university, especially for the improvement of undergraduate education. He set conditions related to faculty hiring and personal manipulation of the endowment, to which there was agreement. Silber was hired.

In January 1971 John Silber began his first year as president of Boston University. The trustees gave him money to begin recruiting outstanding faculty from throughout the country. He dove into public life, making speeches and attending public events. An article in *Esquire* described his speaking style as similar to that of a Southern evangelist. The Texas liberal began to sound like a Massachusetts conservative.

Among his early conflicts as president was the row with his faculty over the hiring of new faculty. The new faculty members he was authorized to recruit were brought in with minimal consultation of the departmental chairpersons. There was a general feeling among other faculty that Silber was simply an autocrat. Silber fared even worse with students. In early 1972 he called in the police to break up a demonstration opposing the restoration of armed forces recruitment on campus. Later that year his residence was destroyed by fire, and Silber's family lost all their personal belongings.

Among Silber's recruits to the Boston University faculty were the author Saul Bellow and Elie Wiesel, writer and concentration camp survivor. Silber possessed special sensitivity toward Jewish people, which was heightened while he was a Fulbright scholar at the University of Bonn, West Germany. It was there he learned his father's side of the family was Jewish and that his aunt had been killed at Auschwitz. His father had never said anything about it.

The 1970s marked a period of constant tension at Boston University. The president accused the faculty of mediocrity and the students of fostering anarchy, and they, in turn, accused him of tyrannical rule. Essentially, in response to the Silber administration, the faculty organized a union in 1974 and the following year voted to affiliate with the American Association of University Professors. The administration would not negotiate with the union, and in 1976 the refusal was challenged in a lawsuit. Two-thirds of the faculty and deans demanded the board of trustees fire Silber. The board refused. In 1978 the courts decided in favor of the AAUP position and Boston University was forced to negotiate. The faculty conducted a brief strike in 1979 which was followed by a clerical workers' walkout in which several faculty members refused to cross the picket line. Silber charged five of these faculty members with negligence and moved to have them disciplined. At that point faculty members throughout Boston signed a petition to have Silber removed. In 1984 the courts ruled that the local AAUP chapter could not engage in collective bargaining.

Silber's popularity and support rose during the 1980s. Boston University had improved its campus, vastly increased its endowment, and attracted a blue-chip faculty. His support among alumni and friends of the university was high, as evidenced by financial and other support given to B.U. Silber was a welcomed guest at the White House during both the Reagan and Bush administrations and they, in turn, were commencement speakers and recipients of Boston University honors.

John Silber made a foray into politics by exploring the possibility of candidacy for governor of Massachusetts. He took a leave of absence from the university and formed a political organization. This followed on the heels of Boston University's successful assumption of the responsibility for the operation of the Chelsea, Massachusetts, school system. Polls showed Silber popular among Massachusetts voters, especially in light of the unpopularity of Governor Michael Dukakis.

Silber swept to victory in the 1990 Democratic primary but lost the election by about 77,000 votes (out of more than 2.2 million cast) to William Weld, a 46-year-old Republican lawyer. Silber resigned his post as president of Boston University in 1995 to be appointed as the school's first Chancellor. As Chancellor, Silber served in an advisory capacity and focused on venture capital operations. Even though Weld had defeated Silber in 1990, the Democratic governor appointed Silber to head the state's Board of Education in 1996.

Silber authored scholarly works on Kant including: *The Ethical Significance of Kant's Religion, Procedural Formalism in Kant's Ethics* and *The Natural Good and the Moral Good in Kant's Ethics.* In 1989 Harper published Silber's *Straight Shooting: What's Wrong with American and How to Fit It.* A German edition of *Straight Shooting* was published in 1992, and a Japanese edition was published in 1993.

Further Reading

Except for the popular press there is little published material on John Silber. One of the best personality profiles of Silber is Helen Epstein, "Crusader on the Charles," in the *New York Times Magazine* (April 23, 1989). □

Leslie Silko

Leslie Silko (born 1948) is one of the foremost authors to emerge from the Native American literary renaissance of the 1970s. She blends western literary forms with the oral traditions of her Laguna Pueblo heritage to communicate Native American concepts concerning time, nature, and spirituality and their relevance in the contemporary world.

Silko, of Laguna Pueblo, Plains Indian, Mexican, and Anglo-American descent, was born in Albuquerque and raised on the Laguna Pueblo Reservation in northern New Mexico. As a child she attended schools administered by the Bureau of Indian Affairs and also learned about Laguna legends and traditions from her great-grandmother and other members of her extended family. She graduated magna cum laude from the University of New Mexico in 1969 and briefly attended law school before deciding to pursue a writing career. While working on her fiction, Silko has taught at several universities and colleges throughout the southwest. She is also the single parent of two sons.

Silko's first novel, *Ceremony* (1977), is a nonchronological work that interweaves free verse poetry and narrative prose. The story is set primarily in the years following World War II and revolves around Tayo, a veteran of mixed white and Laguna heritage who returns to the reservation shattered by his war experiences. He ultimately finds healing, however, with the help of Betonie, an elderly man who, like Tayo, is an outcast from Laguna society due to his white heritage, and T'seh Montano, a medicine woman who embodies the feminine, life-giving aspects of the earth. Through them, Tayo learns that his community's ancient ceremonies are not merely rituals, but a means of achieving one's proper place within the universe. To underscore this concept, Silko incorporates Laguna myths and historical incidents, reflecting the Pueblo's abiding connection to the natural world which counteracts the despair and alienation engendered by white society. Critics applauded *Ceremony,* echoing Frank McShane's estimation that the novel "is one of the most realized works of fiction devoted to Indian life that has been written in this country, and it is a splendid achievement."

Silko's next work, *Storyteller* (1981), is comprised of poems from her earlier collection *Laguna Woman* (1974) as well as short stories, anecdotes, folktales, historical and autobiographical notes, and photographs. According to Bernard A. Hirsch, "this multigeneric work lovingly maps the fertile storytelling ground from which [Silko's] art evolves and to which it is here returned—an offering to the oral tradition which nurtured it." Several of the pieces from this work have been accorded significant attention. One such story, "Yellow Woman," is based on traditional abduction tales in which a kachina, or mountain spirit, kidnaps and seduces a young woman on her way to draw water. In Silko's version, a contemporary Pueblo woman realizes that

her liaison with a cattle rustler is in fact a reenactment of the "yellow woman" legend. The boundary between her experience and the myth slowly dissolves as she becomes aware of her active role in the traditions of her community. Upon returning to her family, she hopes that the story of her affair will be passed on as a new episode in the visionary drama kept alive by the oral tradition.

In *Almanac of the Dead* (1991) Silko presents an apocalyptic vision of North America in which Native Americans reclaim their ancestral lands after whites, lacking the spiritual and moral force of the Indian world, succumb to crime, perversion, drug addiction, and environmental degradation. Some critics have objected to what they perceived as Silko's exaggeration of corruption in Anglo-American society. Malcolm Jones, Jr., observed that "in [Silko's] cosmology, there are good people and there are white people." However, most have praised her vivid characterizations and inventive plotting, contending that while *The Almanac of the Dead* may perturb some white readers, it is a compelling portrait of a society founded upon the eradication of Native Americans and their cultures.

Further Reading

Allen, Paula Gunn, editor, *Studies in American Indian Literature: Critical Essays and Course Designs,* Modern Language Association of America, 1983, pp. 127-33.

Authors and Artists for Young Adults, Volume 14, Gale, 1995.

Contemporary Literary Criticism, Gale, Volume 23, 1983, Volume 74, 1993.

Dictionary of Literary Biography, Volume 143: *American Novelists since World War II, Third Series,* Gale, 1994.

Native North American Literature, Gale, 1994.

Patraka, Vivian, and Louise A. Tilly, editors, *Feminist Re-Visions: What Has Been and Might Be,* University of Michigan Press, 1983, pp. 26-42.

Scholer, Bo, editor, *Coyote Was Here: Essays on Contemporary Native American Literary and Political Mobilization,* Seklos, 1984, pp. 116-23. □

Karen Silkwood

Karen Silkwood (1946-1974), a nuclear plant laborer who died while investigating safety violations made by her employer, is viewed as a martyr by anti-nuclear activists. Her story was made into a film, *Silkwood,* in 1983.

On the night of November 13, 1974, Karen Silkwood, a technician at the Kerr-McGee Cimarron River nuclear facility in Crescent, Oklahoma, was driving her white Honda to Oklahoma City. There she was to deliver a manila folder full of alleged health and safety violations at the plant to a friend, Drew Stephens, a *New York Times* reporter and national union representative. Seven miles out of Crescent, however, her car went off the road, skidded for a hundred yards, hit a guardrail, and plunged off the embankment. Silkwood was killed in the crash, and the manila folder was not found at the scene when Stephens arrived a few hours later. Nor has it come to light since. Although Kerr-McGee was a prominent Oklahoma employer whose integrity had never been challenged, as a part of the nuclear power industry it had many adversaries. The controversy ignited by Silkwood's death regarding the regulation of the nuclear industry was intense, with critics finally finding an example around which to focus their argument. The legacy of the Silkwood case continues to this day in the on-going debate over the safety of nuclear technology.

Early Life

Silkwood seemed an unlikely candidate to have had such a dramatic impact on American society. One biographer commented that "most of her life was distinguished by how ordinary it was, as ordinary as her death was extraordinary." Silkwood grew up in Nederland, in the heart of the Texas oil and gas fields. The oldest of three daughters of Bill and Merle Silkwood, Silkwood led a normal life. In high school she played on the volleyball team and flute in the band, and was an "A" student and a member of the National Honor Society. She excelled in chemistry and, upon graduation, went to Lamar College in Beaumont to become a medical technician.

After her first year of college, Silkwood eloped with Bill Meadows. They moved around Texas, where Meadows worked in the oil industry and Silkwood took care of their three children. After years of financial struggle (they finally

declared bankruptcy), Silkwood left him in 1972 when she discovered Meadows was having an affair with her friend. Giving Bill custody of the children, she moved to Oklahoma City. There she found a job at Kerr-McGee's Cimarron River plant in Crescent, thirty miles north of Oklahoma City, soon joined the Oil, Chemical and Atomic Workers Union, and walked the picket line during their largely unsuccessful nine week strike in 1972.

Concerned about Safety

The Cimarron facility manufactured fuel rods that were used in nuclear fission reactors. Contained within these fuel rods were particles of plutonium, an element created from uranium atoms, and the most toxic substance then known. Even pollen-sized grains of plutonium can cause cancer, as had been shown in animal experiments, but the workers at the plant were not alerted to any danger. Nonetheless Silkwood became increasingly concerned about health and safety violations that went uncorrected by management, and as 1974 drew on, got involved with the bargaining committee for the union. The Cimarron plant was experiencing sixty percent employee turnover a year, was using second-hand equipment, and was behind on production.

Desperate to avoid another strike, which was looming, Kerr-McGee organized a union de-certification vote which, though ultimately failing, galvanized the union into bringing the safety violations to the attention of federal officials. Silkwood and two other local union officials went to Washington, D.C., to confer with national union leaders and the Atomic Energy Commission. Chief among their allegations were the lack of training given employees, failure to minimize contaminations, and poor monitoring, including the finding of uranium dust in the lunchroom. At this meeting Silkwood secretly agreed to obtain before and after photomicrographs of faulty fuel rods showing where they were being ground down to disguise faults.

Contaminated by Radioactivity

After this meeting Silkwood began carrying around notebooks to document a variety of safety violations at the plant. Her assertion was that people were being contaminated by plutonium all the time, and indeed there were at least seventeen acknowledged incidents of exposure involving seventy-seven employees in the recent past. Silkwood's concern was obsessive. As her friend Stephens remarked: "She just lived it, couldn't let it go and relax, particularly in the last month she was alive." On November 4 and 5, 1974, for two consecutive days, Silkwood was contaminated by radioactivity, detected by plant electronic monitors when leaving work. By November 7, her urine showed very high levels of radioactivity. When tested, her apartment also showed high levels, especially in the refrigerator. At this time Silkwood was convinced she was going to die of plutonium poisoning. She and her roommate and Stephens were sent to Los Alamos, New Mexico, to be more thoroughly tested. The exposure level was deemed not serious.

Car Went off the Road

On November 13, Silkwood attended a local union meeting then got into her car to drive to Oklahoma City to deliver the manila folder of evidence, the results of her seven week vigil, to *New York Times* reporter David Burnham. Ten minutes later her car went off the road and Silkwood died. The state patrol ruled it an accident, saying "it's pretty clear she fell asleep at the wheel. She never woke up." While blood tests showed a small amount of alcohol and methaqualone (a prescription sedative) in her system, it is doubtful the amount was sufficient to induce sleep in ten minutes. A subsequent investigation by a private detective concluded that she had likely been forced off the road by another car; a dent in the rear bumper showed metal and rubber fragments, as if another car had rammed her from behind. The manila folder was not recovered from the site of the crash, though other personal effects were.

A subsequent Justice Department investigation also ruled it an accident. Congressional hearings, along with a lawsuit on behalf of Silkwood's children, however, have revealed an intriguing and bizarre story to discredit critics, involving the FBI, newspaper reporters, and the nuclear industry, a story largely left untold. It is possible Silkwood's phone had been tapped and that she had been under surveillance for awhile. Union official Jack Tice has said that Silkwood had been alarmed prior to her death: "She was starting to think someone was out to get her."

The truth of what happened the night of November 13, 1974, may never be known. What is clear is that the death of Silkwood has become a rallying point for anti-nuclear activists and put the nuclear industry on the defensive. The Atomic Energy Commission confirmed three violations at the Cimarron plant, which eventually shut down. And a major questioning of the nuclear industry has occurred as a result of the revelations which have come to light. In a suit filed by Bill Silkwood on behalf of his grandchildren, a jury in May, 1979, awarded the Silkwood estate over ten million dollars in punitive damages and cleared Silkwood of the allegation that she had stolen plutonium from the plant. It also found that Kerr-McGee had been negligent and that someone had planted plutonium in her apartment. Though an appeals court overturned the decision, the Supreme Court eventually agreed with the lower court, reinstating the victory for the Silkwood Family and saying that punitive damages could be awarded in cases involving the nuclear industry, effectively allowing state and jury regulation. Though many mysteries remain surrounding the death of Silkwood, the public has gained much awareness about nuclear issues and has pressured the industry to become more responsible to health and safety concerns. As former Congresswoman Bella Abzug has commented, the issues stemming from the Silkwood case are "a matter of concern both in regard to public safety and the rights of individuals."

Silkwood's story was unveiled to a much greater audience in the 1983 film directed by Mike Nichols. Meryl Streep starred as Karen Silkwood with Kurt Russell and Cher in supporting roles. *Silkwood* garnered numerous Academy Award and Golden Globe nominations for acting, directing, and screenplay writing. Cher won a Golden Globe for Best Supporting Actress.

Further Reading

Kohn, Howard, *Who Killed Karen Silkwood?,* Summit Books, 1981.

Rashke, Richard, *The Killing of Karen Silkwood,* Houghton, 1981.

Ms., April, 1975, pp. 59-76.

Newsweek, September 9, 1978, p. 26.

Rolling Stone, June 11, 1992, pp. 92.

Science News, February 4, 1984, pp. 74. □

Benjamin Silliman

The most prominent and influential man of science in America during the early 19th century, Benjamin Silliman (1779-1864) was a chemist, naturalist, and editor.

Benjamin Silliman was born on Aug. 8, 1779, in what is now Trumbull, Conn., and brought up in nearby Fairfield. He entered Yale in 1792 at the age of 13, graduating in 1796. He spent 2 years partly at home and partly teaching in a private school in Connecticut, then returned to Yale to begin studying law and to tutor. He was admitted to the bar in 1802.

That same year, with no background for the position, Silliman was appointed to the newly established professorship of chemistry and natural history at Yale, with permission to qualify himself for the job before beginning his duties. His preparation included attending lectures at the Philadelphia Medical School; work with the chemist Robert Hare; occasional visits to John Maclean, professor of chemistry at Princeton; and 2 years at Edinburgh, Scotland. In 1808 he assumed full professorial duties at Yale, lecturing in chemistry, geology, and mineralogy.

Although Silliman was a competent researcher, he was not an original scientist. However, he was without a peer in his contributions to the institutional development of science. During nearly 50 years as a professor, he was instrumental in establishing the sciences at Yale, arranging for the college to receive the finest mineral collection in America, aiding in establishing the Yale Medical School in 1813, and persuading the Yale Corporation to establish the "department of philosophy and the arts," where science could be studied intensively. Within a few years the department had grown into the Yale Scientific School, which subsequently became the Sheffield Scientific School, Yale's most distinctive contribution to American education in the 19th century.

In July 1818 Silliman issued the first number of the *American Journal of Science and Arts,* of which he was founder, proprietor, and sole editor for almost 20 years. Devoted to the publication of original papers, notices, and reviews in the broad field of the natural and physical sciences, it won international acclaim. Even more important, he, and later his junior editors, used the journal to introduce the latest in European science to American readers. In its pages Americans first learned of such advances as the natural system of classification, the classification of rocks in

terms of the fossils they contained, the chemical approach to mineralogy, and Darwin's theory of evolution.

A brilliant lecturer, Silliman was much in demand by popular audiences for lectures on chemistry, geology, and the bearing of science on religion throughout the 1830s and 1840s. He spent his last years compiling memoirs and conducting his voluminous correspondence. He died on Nov. 24, 1864.

Further Reading

A biography of Silliman is John F. Fulton and Elizabeth H. Thompson, *Benjamin Silliman* (1947). George P. Fisher, *Life of Benjamin Silliman* (2 vols., 1866), is useful primarily for its verbatim quotations from reminiscences, diaries, and correspondence. For Silliman's part in establishing the teaching of science at Yale see Russell H. Chittenden, *History of the Sheffield Scientific School of Yale University, 1846-1922* (2 vols., 1928).

Additional Sources

Benjamin Silliman and his circle: studies on the influence of Benjamin Silliman on science in America: prepared in honor of Elizabeth H. Thomson, New York: Science History Publications, 1979.

Brown, Chandos Michael, *Benjamin Silliman: a life in the young republic,* Princeton, N.J.: Princeton University Press, 1989. □

Beverly Sills

Beverly Sills (born 1929) was a child performer, coloratura soprano, and operatic superstar who retired from her performance career in 1980 to become general director of the New York City Opera Company and a prominent public figure.

Beverly Sills was born Belle Miriam Silverman in Brooklyn, May 25, 1929, during the era of Shirley Temple and other child stars. Her father, son of a Romanian immigrant, was an insurance salesman who wanted his daughter to become a teacher. Her mother, however, had different plans for her daughter, nicknamed "Bubbles." Sills was on the radio by age three singing "The Wedding of Jack and Jill" and winning a Brooklyn contest for "the most beautiful baby of 1932." At the age of four she was a regular on a children's Saturday morning radio program; at seven she sang in a movie and had already memorized 22 arias from Galli-Curci recordings. By 1938 she was a weekly performer on "Major Bowes' Capitol Family Hour," and by the age of ten she was one of the principal actors on the radio program "Our Gal Sunday." She performed in an ad for Rinso White soap and appeared on an early, prophetic television program called "Stars of the Future." She left radio work at age 12, wanting to pursue her love of the Opera.

When she graduated from Public School 91 in Brooklyn, Beverly Sills was voted "Prettiest Girl," "Fashion Plate," "One with the Most Personality," and the "One Most Likely to Succeed." She graduated from the Professional Children's School in New York City and had learned 20 operatic roles by the time she was 15 and 50 to 60 operas by the age of 19. She studied voice privately with her lifelong associate Estelle Liebling and eventually achieved professional competence on the piano as well, studying with Paolo Gallico.

Billed as "the youngest prima donna in captivity," Sills joined a Gilbert and Sullivan touring company in 1945. Two years later she sang her first operatic role, Frasquita in *Carmen,* with the Philadelphia Opera Company. In 1948 she toured college towns with a choir known as the Estelle Liebling Singers. In 1951 and 1952 she toured with the Charles L. Wagner Opera Company in the roles of Violetta in *La Traviata* and Micaela in *Carmen.* In 1953 Sills performed the title role in *Manon* with the Baltimore Opera and, with the San Francisco Opera, performed Elena in Boïto's *Mefistofele,* Donna Elvira in *Don Giovanni,* and Gerhilde in *Die Walküre.*

Sills made her debut with the New York City Opera on October 29, 1955, singing Rosalinde in *Die Fledermaus.* The critics loved her and predicted great success for her career. Later in the season she sang Oxana in Tchaikovsky's *The Golden Slippers.* Eventually she would command a vast repertoire of 100 roles, actively performing 60 of them in 100 opera or concert appearances each year at the peak of her career. Sills' great memory allowed her not only to master her own enormous repertoire of roles but to grasp the other principal roles in the operas she knew as well. This accounts, in part, for her equal reputation as an actress as well as a specialist in the *bel canto* style of singing associated with both Sills and her Australian-born contemporary Joan Sutherland.

In 1956 Sills married Peter Bulkeley Greenough, associate editor of the Cleveland *Plain Dealer,* a newspaper his family partially owned. She and her husband had two children but, unfortunately, one was born hearing impaired and the other developmentally disabled. Her disabled daughter required great care, and her developmentally disabled son had to be institutionalized when he was six. Beverly Sills carried two watches, one set to her son's schedule in the time zone where he lived, so that she could always know what he was doing. These tragedies would lead Sills into philanthropic work later in her career.

In addition to the *bel canto* repertoire, Sills performed modern American operas, including *The Ballad of Baby Doe* by Douglas Moore. She performed avant garde works such as Hugo Weisgall's opera, *Six Characters in Search of an Author,* in 1959 and, in 1965, the American premiere of *Intolleranza 1960,* by Luigi Nono. In 1963 she managed to perform all three roles in Puccini's trilogy of one act operas, *Il Trittico.* On July 8, 1966, she sang Donna Anna in *Don Giovanni* with the Metropolitan Opera, although her formal debut with the Metropolitan Opera did not actually occur until 1975, a fact which led to the growth and popularity of a number of small opera companies in America.

Another historic departure associated with Sills was her delayed appearance in the European opera capitals. Sills was able to rise to the top of her profession before touring Europe. She finally did so in 1967, a guest of the Vienna State Opera, and sang in Buenos Aires that year as well. In 1969 she sang Pamira in Rossini's *Le Siège de Corinth* and the title role in *Lucia di Lammermoor* at La Scala in Milan. She repeated her Lucia at Covent Garden, London, late that same year and went on to sing Violetta in Naples and at the Deutsche Opera in Berlin in January of 1970 and Constanza in *The Abduction from the Seraglio* in Israel in 1971, in addition to a recital in Paris that same year.

Sills became an operatic superstar in the fall of 1966 with the overwhelming success of her performance of Cleopatra in Handel's *Julius Caesar* at the Lincoln Center in New York City. The recording of this role, released in 1967, is among her many highly valued records. Sills' own favorite role was Elizabeth I in Donizetti's *Roberto Devereux,* which resulted in her being the subject of a *TIME* magazine cover story in 1971.

On October 27, 1980, Sills gave her last performance, one which the opera critics said was overdue as her voice had been deteriorating for some time. The very next day she assumed the general directorship of the New York City Opera. She displayed great administrative skill and public relations talent, appearing on popular television programs and in other ways representing opera to a wide, general audience and helping to pull the Opera out of both financial and public crisis. She is the author of three autobiographies which have enjoyed a large readership. She received honorary doctoral degrees from Harvard, New York University, Temple University, the New England Conservatory, and the California Institute of the Arts. In 1973 she was given the Handel Medallion, New York City's highest cultural award. Sills added philanthropy to her list of careers, and, in 1972, she was the national chairman of the Mothers' March on Birth Defects. She continued to be a highly visible, greatly active public figure in promoting opera and philanthropic causes well into the 1980s.

In 1989, Sills formally retired and remained in quiet seclusion with her husband for about five years. In 1994, she returned to public life as the chairwoman of the Lincoln Center for the Performing Arts. At this point in her life, Sills says "I've done everything I set out to do . . . sung in every opera house I wanted to . . . to go on past the point where I should, I think would break my heart. I think my voice has served me very well."

Further Reading

For additional information, see Beverly Sills' three autobiographies: *Beverly, an Autobiography* (1987), written with Lawrence Linderman; *Bubbles: A Self Portrait* (1976); *Bubbles: an Encore* (1981). Articles on Beverly Sills appear in *The New Grove Dictionary of Music and Musicians* (London, 1980) and in *Baker's Biographical Dictionary* (1978). She is also dealt with in W. Sargent *Divas* (1973), J. B. Steane *The Grand Tradition* (1974), and J. Hine *Great Singers on Great Singing* (1982). As a performer and a public figure, Beverly Sills is extensively treated in the periodical literature. Of particular interest is the *TIME* cover story of November 22, 1971. A selective list of other articles follows: *Opera News* (February 11, 1967); *New York Times Magazine* (September 17, 1967); *Newsweek* (April 8, 1968, and April 21, 1969); *Opera News* (September 19, 1970); J. Barthel: "Bel canto Beverly: at 46, a Superstar Makes Her Debut at the Met," *New York Times Magazine* (April 6, 1975); *TIME* (April 7, 1975); and D. Henahan: "A Tough New Role for Beverly," *New York Times Magazine* (September 23, 1979). □

Ignazio Silone

The Italian novelist and essayist Ignazio Silone (1900-1978) was one of the founding members of the Italian Communist Party. He directed international attention to Italian political and social realities and at the same time presented an unconventional picture of the Italian South.

Ignazio Silone was born Secondino Tranquilli on May 1, 1900, at Pescina dei Marsi in the Abruzzi. His father was a small landowner. In 1915 Silone lost both parents and five brothers as a result of an earthquake. He received part of his education at the local seminary and continued his studies in Reggio Calabria but interrupted them at the end of World War I, when he became interested in politics. The circumstances forced him, as he once said, to endure first-hand three essential experiences: poverty, religion, and communism. Thus he took part in the founding of the Italian Communist party (PCI) in 1921 as a representative of the Socialist Youth movement. Subsequently, he became a member of the directorate of the PCI, which he represented at several international conferences. He also was editor of various Communist papers.

After the Fascist takeover Silone went into hiding and worked against the regime. After disagreements over the issue of following central party directives, however, he broke with the Communist party, left the country, and settled in 1930 in Switzerland. There he began to write his first book. After his return to Italy in the fall of 1944, he was for a time a member of the Socialist party and editor of *Avanti!*, its daily. After the split in the party, however, he retired from active politics.

Silone was one of the few contemporary Italian novelists who were actively involved in the political issues of their time, an involvement which for Silone became the very theme of his fiction. The particular subject of almost all his novels is the poor, ignorant peasant world of the South and the millenary injustice meted out to it by whatever oppressive superstructure has been in power. It was Silone who introduced the *cafoni* of his native countryside into literature in works of an extreme stylistic simplicity which are meant to accuse and yet at times read like a eulogy of a world constant, simple, and uncontaminated.

Fontamara (1933), written in a Swiss sanatorium and subsequently translated into over 2 dozen languages, was Silone's first book. The novel does not present theoretical and polemic arguments, as might be expected. It is the simple story of village peasants being condemned to wretchedness and unemployment by a ubiquitous big landowner who thwarts their attempts to use the water of a brook to irrigate their plots. The following two novels, *Pane e vino* (1937; *Bread and Wine*) and *Il seme sotto la neve* (1940; *The Seed Beneath the Snow*), deal with the problematic relationship between party ideology and the exigencies of the *cafoni's* life.

Una manciata di more (1952) takes up again the failure of political parties to right the wrongs of poverty and injustice in the social structure of society. And again, the discrepancies are seen not in terms of specific political parties but as an oppression of the poor by the rich, with whom any political party will come to terms. Thus, changes on the political scene mean next to nothing if the socially oppressive structure is not changed. In *Il segreto di Luca* (1956; *The Secret of Luca*) outward sociopolitical aspects seem to be less obtrusive, but even here, where the right to a personal life clashes with the demands of the state, political overtones are determinant after all. *La volpe e le camelie* (1960; *The Fox and the Camellias*) is the first novel of Silone's that is not placed in the Italian South, but it, too, takes up political aspects and their moral and social consequences under Fascist rule. *L'avventura d'un povero cristiano* (1968), which was awarded the Campiello Prize, depicts the historical clash between popes Celestine V and Boniface VIII and the conflict of individual spirituality with institutionalized religion.

Silone wrote little in the last decades of his life. At a symposium with Arthur Koestler in 1968, Silone called himself "a socialist without a party, a Christian without a church." His last novel, *Severina,* was finished and largely written by his wife. It was his only work to feature a female protagonist. He died in Geneva, Switzerland, in 1978.

Further Reading

Most analysis of Silone's literary works is in Italian. English profiles: Hanne, Michael, *The Power of the Story: Fiction and Political Change,* Berghahn Books, 1994; *Rebels and Reactionaries: An Anthology of Great Political Stories,* Dell, 1992; Woodcock, George, *Writers and Politics,* Black Rose, 1990; Origo, Iris, *A Need to Testify: Portraits of Lauro de Bosis, Ruth Draper, Gaetano Salvemini, Ignazio Silone, and an Essay on Biography,* John Murray, 1984. Also see "Socialism and Sensibility" in *The New Republic* October 26, 1987, and "The Last Hours of Ignazio Silone" in *Partisan Review,* 1984. A biographical sketch and discussion of Silone's work is in Donald W. Heiney, *America in Modern Italian Literature* (1965). His career is also analyzed in Nathan Alexander Scott, *Rehearsals of Discomposure: Alienation and Reconciliation in Modern Literature* (1952), and Richard W.B. Lewis, *The Picaresque Saint: Representative Figures in Contemporary Fiction* (1959). For general historical background see Sergio Pacifici, *A Guide to Contemporary Italian Literature: From Futurism to Neorealism* (1962). □

Abba Hillel Silver

Abba Hillel Silver (1893-1963), rabbi and Zionist leader, was considered among the most prominent leaders of American Judaism.

Abba H. Silver, the son of Moses and Diana Silver, was born in Neinstadt, Lithuania, on Jan. 28, 1893. He was the fifth rabbi in his family. He emigrated with his parents to New York City in 1902. In 1915 he graduated from the University of Cincinnati and in the same year received his rabbinical degree from the Hebrew Union College there. After serving for 2 years as rabbi in Wheeling, W.Va., in 1917 he joined the Temple of Cleveland, Ohio, the largest Reform congregation in the United States. He remained its spiritual leader until his death.

During World War I Silver served with the American forces in France and was decorated for his performance by the French government as *Officier de l'Instruction Publique.* In addition to his activities as president of the Central Conference of American Rabbis (1945-1947), he was a founder of the Cleveland Bureau of Jewish Education and its first president (1924-1932). He was president of the United Palestine Appeal (1938-1943) and co-chairman of the United Jewish Appeal (1938-1944). Silver was president of the Zionist Organization of America (1945-1946), chairman of the American Zionist Emergency Council (1933-1934 and 1945-1949), and chairman of the Jewish Agency for Palestine—American Section (1946-1948).

After World War I Silver was among the supporters of Louis Brandeis in the Zionist controversy, but later he supported Chaim Weizmann and Louis Marshall on the issue of enlarging the Jewish Agency for Palestine, a proposal approved in 1929. He was against the 1937 recommendation of the British Peel Commission to partition Palestine into Jewish and Arab states and a British area comprising strategic sites. Silver claimed that the British mandatory administration in Palestine violated the mandate. He participated as a representative of the Jewish Agency at the United Nations General Assembly sessions in 1947-1948, at which the Nov. 29, 1947, Partition Resolution was adopted. This resolution was one of the international legal bases for the proclamation of the independence of the state of Israel on May 14, 1948.

As a rabbi, Silver was known for his sermons, which were unusual in style, oratory, and content, which was strongly Zionist. His *Messianic Speculations in Ancient Israel* (1927) earned him a high place in rabbinical scholarship. His *World Crisis and Jewish Survival* (1941) dealt with the crisis of Jewry in World War II. Silver died on Nov. 29, 1963.

Further Reading

Biographical information on Silver is in Daniel Jeremy Silver, ed., *In the Time of Harvest* (1963), and Herbert Weiner, ed., *Therefore Choose Life* (1967).

Additional Sources

Raphael, Marc Lee, *Abba Hillel Silver: a profile in American Judaism,* New York: Holmes & Meier, 1989. □

Georges Simenon

The Belgian novelist Georges Simenon (1903-1989), who wrote in French, was one of the most productive and popular writers of the twentieth century. Author of more than 500 novels, translated into dozens of languages, he was most famous for his detective novels featuring Inspector Maigret.

Georges Simenon was born in Liège on Feb. 13, 1903. An able pupil, he was determined to become a writer at the age of 11 and left school 4 years later. In 1919 he began working as a reporter for a Liège newspaper and after military service published his first novel under the pen name of Georges Sim. Between 1921 and 1934 he wrote nearly 200 novels, which he published under more than a dozen pseudonyms. Simenon moved to Paris in 1924, and in 1930 he began the famous Maigret series of detective novels, which he published under his own name. Through the dozens of novels in which he appears, as well as through many films and television adaptations of them, Inspector Maigret, of police headquarters in Paris, has become as well known as Arthur Conan Doyle's Sherlock Holmes. Maigret, a sensible and tolerant but not brilliant man with simple tastes, puzzles his way to the solution of his cases by patient thought and insight—all the while peacefully puffing his pipe. The added psychological dimension enriches the reader's normal interest in learning the solution to the mystery.

For many critics, however, Simenon's best novels are those that lie outside the Maigret series. In the 1930s he

wrote many other thrillers, a notable example being *L'Homme qui regardait passer les trains* (1938; *The Man Who Watched the Trains Go By*). *Pedigree,* written during the war years and published in 1948, is a largely autobiographical novel that presents a powerful and convincing picture of the life of a boy and his parents in Liège from 1903 to 1918. Subsequently Simenon wrote novels in which the psychological analysis of the leading character, exceptional in some way, forms the center of interest. Examples include *Les Volets verts* (1950; *The Heart of a Man*), which portrays the closing stages in the life of a great actor, and *Le Petit saint* (1965; *The Little Saint*), which treats the formative years in the life of a great artist.

Simenon is above all a storyteller; his readers are immediately gripped by their desire to know "what happens next" and by the compelling atmosphere. An astonishing range of characters move through Simenon's world; he said, "Some people collect stamps; I collect human beings." He excludes politics, religion, history, and metaphysics from his books, concentrating on psychology and on the minor details, often extraordinary, of human existence. Simenon's style is deliberately simple, "since I do not write for a single language." He aims at a kind of "universal vocabulary," building up action and atmosphere through careful brief touches.

Simenon retired from writing fiction in 1974 after producing a range of novels, short stories, diaries, and other works. His last long novel was *Intimate Memoirs* (1984), written as an attempt to explore the causes of his daughter's suicide in 1978. Although he described himself as a craftsman, his popular Maigret novels as well as his more serious works came to be admired by distinguished French critics. Nobel laureate André Gide called him "perhaps the greatest and most genuine novelist of today's French literature." He died in Lausanne, Switzerland, in 1989.

Further Reading

Many studies of Simenon's life and work have been published in recent years: Assouline, Pierre, *Simenon: A Biography,* Knopf, 1997; Bertrand, Alain, *Maigret,* Labor (Bruxelles, Belgium), 1994; Bertrand, Alain, *Georges Simenon,* La Manufacture, 1988; Marnham, Patrick, *The Man Who Wasn't Maigret,* Harcourt Brace & Co., 1994; Eskin, Stanley, *Simenon: A Critical Biography,* McFarland & Co., 1987; Bresler, Fenton, *The Mystery of Georges Simenon: A Biography,* Beaufort Books, 1983; Young, Trudee, *Georges Simenon: A Checklist of His "Maigret" & Other Mystery Novels & Short Stories in French & in English Translations,* Scarecrow Press, 1976; Foord, Peter, *Georges Simenon: A Bibliography of the British First Editions in Hardback and Paperback and/or the Principal French and American Editions, with a Guide to Their Value,* Dragonby, 1988; Raymond, John, *Simenon in Court* (1968), a penetrating critique that contains much valuable information. □

Georg Simmel

The German sociologist and philosopher Georg Simmel (1858-1918) wrote important studies of urban sociology, social conflict theory, and small-group relationships.

Georg Simmel was born on March 1, 1858, in Berlin, the youngest of seven children. His father was a prosperous Jewish businessman who became a Roman Catholic. His mother, also of Jewish forebears, was a Lutheran. Georg was baptized a Lutheran but later withdrew from that Church, although he always retained a philosophical interest in religion.

His father died when Georg was very young. A family friend and music publisher became his guardian and left him an inheritance when he died which enabled Simmel to pursue a scholarly career for many years without a salaried position. He studied history and philosophy at the University of Berlin, earning a doctoral degree in 1881. He was a lecturer at the University of Berlin from 1885 to 1900 and professor extraordinary until 1914. He then accepted his only salaried professorship at the provincial University of Strassburg. There he died on Sept. 26, 1918.

Simmel's wide interests in philosophy, sociology, art, and religion contrasted sharply with those of his more narrowly disciplined colleagues. Eschewing pure philosophy, he preferred to apply it functionally as the philosophy of culture, of money, of the sexes, of religion, and of art. Similarly in sociology, the field of his lasting renown, he favored isolating multiple factors. In 1910 he helped found the German Sociological Association. His sociological writings were on alienation and on urban stresses and strains;

his philosophical writings foreshadowed modern existentialism.

Although a popular and even brilliant lecturer, academic advancement eluded Simmel. The reasons for this include prewar Germany's latent anti-Semitism, the unorthodox variety of subjects he pursued rather than following a more acceptable narrow discipline, and perhaps jealousy at his sparkling originality. Ortega y Gasset compared him to a philosophical squirrel, gracefully acrobatic in leaping from one branch of knowledge to another. Unable or unwilling to develop consistent sociological or philosophical systems, Simmel founded no school and left few disciples. "I know that I shall die without intellectual heirs," he wrote in his diary. "My legacy will be, as it were in cash, distributed to many heirs, each transforming his part into use conformed to *his* nature. . . ." This diffusion occurred, and his ideas have since pervaded sociological thought. His insightful writings still stimulate while more systematic contemporaries are less read. Robert K. Merton called Simmel a "man of innumerable seminal ideas."

Further Reading

The best biographies and analyses of Simmel's writings are by Kurt H. Wolff, ed., *Georg Simmel, 1858-1918* (1959), and Lewis A. Coser, ed., *Georg Simmel* (1965).

Additional Sources

Formal sociology: the sociology of Georg Simmel, Aldershot, Hants, England; Brookfield, Vt., USA: E. Elgar, 1991.

Frisby, David, *Georg Simmel,* Chichester: E. Horwood; London; New York: Tavistock Publications, 1984.

Georg Simmel and contemporary sociology, Dordrecht; Boston: Kluwer Academic Publishers, 1990.

Jaworski, Gary D., *Georg Simmel and the American prospect,* Albany: State University of New York Press, 1997. ☐

William Gilmore Simms

American author William Gilmore Simms (1806-1870), the dominant literary personality of the antebellum South, is chiefly remembered for his novels on subjects derived from American history.

William Gilmore Simms was born in Charleston, S.C. His father, "unfortunate in business," moved west; his mother died when he was an infant. He was raised by his maternal grandmother. His education was poor, but he read widely, then studied law. He visited his father in Mississippi, absorbing local color he used later in his books.

Returning to Charleston, in 1826 Simms married and was admitted to the bar a year later. A successful lawyer, by 1830 he had published five books of verse and assisted in editing several literary magazines. By 1832, after his wife's death, he was fully committed to a literary career.

Simms went north, establishing contacts with publishers and making important literary friends. His annual visit north (until the Civil War) to see his books through the press, his prodigious output, and his personality made him one of the most influential figures in American letters. Before sectional controversy eroded his popularity in the North, Simms was second only to James Fenimore Cooper as a popular novelist.

Simms began his literary career an ardent nationalist and Unionist, but he became an advocate of Southern causes in the 1840s and eventually a secessionist, and his writing increasingly turned to Southern material. His achievement was his historical romances. *Guy Rivers* (1834) is set in northern Georgia, then a frontier. *The Yemassee* (1835), his most popular colonial novel, deals with an Indian uprising in 1715. *The Partisan* (1835) was the first of a sequence of seven Revolutionary War novels which ends with *Eutaw* (1856). This series includes *Woodcraft* (1852), his best book, notable for Captain Porgy, an earthy character who contrasts with the aristocratic heroes of the series.

In 1836 Simms married Chevillette Roach, daughter of a wealthy landowner, and thereafter was master of a South Carolina plantation. During the Civil War, Simm's plantation with its extensive library was burned by Union soldiers, leaving him impoverished. He wrote doggedly but with little success and died much honored in his native state but little regarded elsewhere.

Further Reading

A primary source is the *Letters of William Gilmore Simms,* edited by Mary C. Simms Oliphant, Alfred T. Odell, and T.C. Duncan Eaves (5 vols., 1952-1956). Two biographies of Simms, neither entirely satisfactory, are Joseph V. Ridgely, *William Gilmore Simms* (1962), and William P. Trent, *William Gilmore Simms* (1895), the latter more complete. The best brief criticism of Simms is in Jay B. Hubbell, *The South in American Literature, 1607-1900* (1954), which includes a bibliography. Vernon L. Parrington's chapter on Simms in his *Main Currents in American Thought* (1927) seriously argues that Simms's artistic growth was stunted by patrician Charleston. A chapter in William R. Taylor, *Cavalier and Yankee: The Old South and American National Character* (1961), places Simms in the context of Southern literary culture and society. See also *A Bibliographical Guide to the Study of Southern Literature,* edited by Louis D. Rubin, Jr. (1969).

Additional Sources

Guilds, John Caldwell, *Simms: a literary life,* Fayetteville: University of Arkansas Press, 1992.

Trent, William Peterfield, *William Gilmore Simms,* Boston, New York, Houghton, Mifflin and company, 1892. □

Herbert Alexander Simon

The study of decision-making behavior, especially in large organizations, led Herbert Simon (born 1916) to develop new theories in economics, psychology, business administration, and other fields. He was awarded the Nobel Prize in economics in 1978. He was also the first social scientist elected to the National Academy of Sciences.

Herbert Alexander Simon was born in Milwaukee, Wisconsin, on June 15, 1916. He received an A.B. from the University of Chicago in 1936 and a Ph.D. in 1943. He stayed on at Chicago for two years as a research assistant before becoming a staff member of the International City Managers Association and assistant editor of the Public Management and Municipal Year Book (1938-1939). The following year he joined the University of California as director of administrative measurement studies. After a teaching post at the Illinois Institute of Technology (1942-1949), Simon joined the teaching staff of the Carnegie-Mellon University, first as professor of administration and psychology (1949-1955) and later as professor of computer science and psychology (1956 to the mid-1980s).

In his work Simon brought greater realism to neoclassical economic models, which he found to be lacking because of their idealized vision of the "rational" consumer, businessperson, or worker. Instead of maximizing their welfare, profits, or wages on the marketplace, Simon believed that lack of information about alternatives and the impossibility of foreseeing the future makes all of these participants "satisficers." Their rational behavior is "bounded" by the cost of obtaining information and uncertainty; hence Simon proposed the concept of "bounded rationality." That is, economic agents try to do as well as possible given the constraints, but these constraints keep them from ever achieving what neo-classical economists would call a "maximum" (of profits, for example). Simon argues that individuals would be acting rationally by "satisficing," given real world circumstances.

The notion of "bounded rationality" is explained by analogy to the search for a needle in the haystack. The neoclassical approach would be to search for the needle in the stack (a maximization process). Simon's approach is to find the needle which is sharp enough to handle the contemplated sewing tasks (a "satisficing" process).

In another example, consider a chess game: every move involves potentially millions of calculations about alternative actions. Since it is impossible for players to examine all the possibilities, they learn to follow promising lines of play and to utilize "rules of thumb" in decision-making. Over time these rules of thumb change as outcomes are evaluated.

Simon's views on rationality have been expounded in numerous books and articles, including *Models of Man* (1956), *Human Problem Solving* (with Allen Newell, 1972), *The Sciences of the Artificial* (1969), *Models of Discovery* (1977), and *Models of Bounded Rationality and Other Topics in Economic Theory* (1982).

Simon also disputes whether economic models centered on "equilibrium" solutions are useful or accurate. The idea of equilibrium derives from the science of mechanics and was adapted to economic problems by neo-classical economists of the late 19th century. Most modern American economists until the mid-1970s also utilized this methodology. Simon, in his Richard T. Ely Lecture to the American Economic Association in 1978, argued that: "when the system is complex and its environment continually changing (that is, in the conditions under which biological and social evolution actually takes place), there is no assurance that the system's momentary position will lie anywhere near a point of equilibrium."

Simon made other significant contributions to economic analysis. The Hawkins-Simon theorem (1949) contains a powerful test for the sustainability of an economy as measured by input-output tables. In the area of production scheduling Simon co-authored the "Certainty Equivalent" theorem (1956, 1960), which provided practical help to businesses concerned with the needs for labor and inventory when demand fluctuates.

In spite of his own mathematical prowess, Simon sought to break economic methodology out of the rigorous mathematical modeling which requires strong assumptions and quantifiable data into a broader arena of qualitative analysis using interdisciplinary theories. Indeed, he believed economists have much to learn from other social sciences and in his own career he drew widely from them. Much of his writing dealt with issues in psychology as applied to organizations, or what Simon called "micro-micro-economics." To promote these views Simon, along with colleagues at Carnegie-Mellon, founded *The Journal of Organizational Behavior.* Simon's textbook *Administrative Be-*

havior was first published in 1947 and became a classic in the field, going through several editions.

Simon was a consultant to the International City Managers Association (1942-1949), the U.S. Bureau of the Budget (1946-1949), the U.S. Census Bureau (1947), and the Cowles Commission for Research in Economics (1947-1960); chairman of the board of directors of the Social Science Research Council (1961-1965); member of the President's Scientific Advisory Committee (1969-1971); chairman of the Committee on Air Quality Control of the National Academy of Sciences (1974); chairman of the Committee on Behavioral Sciences of the National Science Foundation; winner of the Award for Distinguished Scientific Contributions of the American Psychological Association (1969), and Distinguished Fellow of the American Economic Association (1976). He lectured extensively around the world and received nine honorary degrees.

For his many and diverse contributions Herbert Simon was awarded the Alfred Nobel Memorial Prize in Economics in 1978. Yet the label "economist" is far too narrow for this extraordinary social scientist and philosopher. While not a household name, Simon is still widely-read and has had a profound influence on the underpinnings of nearly every social science. Often referenced in both the abstract as well as the specific, some of Simon's views were discussed in 1996 by Herbert Kaufman in his acceptance of the Dwight Waldo Award of the American Society for Public Administration (ASPA), of which Simon is a previous recipient.

Further Reading

Further information on Herbert Simon can be found in articles by two leading economists in H. W. Spiegel and W. J. Samuels (editors), *Contemporary Economists in Perspective* (1984), and Mark Blaug, *Great Economists Since Keynes* (1985). Simon's own autobiographical work, *Models of My Life* (1991), received generally favorable reviews. ☐

Jules François Simon

The French philosopher, writer, and statesman Jules François Simon (1814-1896) was a leader of the moderate republican faction in the early years of the Third Republic.

Jules Simon was born François Jules Simon Suisse at Lorient on Dec. 27, 1814, but he later dropped the family name. Graduating from the École Normale, he taught philosophy at Caen in 1836 and at Versailles in 1837. Victor Cousin employed him to make translations of Plato and Aristotle, for which Cousin took credit, and Simon soon became Cousin's deputy in the chair of philosophy at the Sorbonne. He also lectured at the École Normale and began his literary career—editing the works of Nicolas Malbranche, René Descartes, Jacques Bossuet, and Antoine Arnauld; writing the *Histoire de l'école d'Alexandrie* (2 vols., 1844-1845); contributing to the *Revue des deux mondes;* and helping to found the journal *Liberté de penser* in 1847.

In 1848 Simon was elected to the Constituent Assembly from the Côtes-du-Nord, and in April 1849 he became a member of the Council of State. However, he was not reelected to the council or elected to the Legislative Assembly. After the coup d'etat of Dec. 2, 1851, he condemned the new regime and was dismissed from the Sorbonne and the École Normale. He then spent his time in writing and produced *Le Devoir* in 1854, which achieved great popularity. This was followed by *La Religion naturelle* (1856), *La Liberté* (1857), and a number of other works.

In 1863 Simon was elected deputy from the eighth district of Paris and won fame as a member of the republican opposition. He opposed the Franco-Prussian War in the legislature and became minister of instruction in the provisional government of 1870. After the fall of Paris, Simon was sent to Bordeaux to oblige Léon Gambetta to accept the government's electoral provisions. Eventually Gambetta resigned, but his enmity for Simon endured.

Simon was elected to the National Assembly from the Marne, and Adolphe Thiers entrusted him with the Ministry of Instruction until 1873. In 1875 he was elected permanent senator and member of the French Academy. Simon became premier and minister of interior under President MacMahon on Dec. 13, 1876. He retained these positions until, after the Chamber adopted a motion urging the Cabinet to repress clerical agitation, MacMahon demanded Simon's resignation in the "Sixteenth of May" incident of 1877. This

began a series of crises which eventually gave the republicans control of the whole government and discouraged later presidents from using their full constitutional powers.

Simon was largely responsible for rejection of Article 7 of Jules Ferry's Education Act, which would have forbidden members of nonauthorized congregations to teach. In his later years Simon exercised influence chiefly through his writings. He died in Paris on June 8, 1896.

Further Reading

There are no biographies of Simon in English. His career is recounted in Denis W. Brogan, *The Development of Modern France, 1870-1939* (1 vol., 1947; rev. ed., 2 vols., 1966), and Guy Chapman, *The Third Republic of France: The First Phase, 1871-1894* (1962). □

Paul Simon

Paul Simon (born 1928) was a newspaper publisher, state legislator, lieutenant governor, and U.S. representative and senator, serving a total of 22 years in Congress. He was a "self-made" man who rose from being a "boy-wonder" in journalism and politics to a candidate for president of the United States.

Paul Simon was born November 29, 1928, in Eugene, Oregon. His parents, the Rev. Martin Paul and Ruth (Troemel) Simon, had only recently returned to the United States from Lutheran missionary work in China so that their child could be born in America.

Simon grew up in Eugene and entered the University of Oregon at age 16 to study journalism. In 1946 he transferred to Dana College in Blair, Nebraska, after his parents moved to Illinois to publish a religious periodical.

At age 19, Simon became the youngest editor-publisher in America. In 1948 he dropped out of college to purchase the *Troy Tribune,* a defunct weekly newspaper in a small southern Illinois town. He resurrected the paper and before long he made his reputation as a crusading journalist by exposing vice and syndicate gambling connections with local government officials. Simon eventually built a chain of 14 weekly newspapers. He sold them in 1966 to devote full time to public service, teaching, and writing.

Simon served a two year hitch as an enlisted soldier in the U.S. Army between 1951 and 1953. He was assigned to the Counter Intelligence Corps and spent most of his tour of duty along the former "Iron Curtain" in Europe. (The term, "Iron Curtain" referred to the political and ideological barrier between Western Europe and the Soviet Bloc nations, which continued from the end of World War II in 1945, until 1990).

Returning from service in the armed forces, Simon, a Democrat, was elected to the Illinois House of Representatives in 1954 at the young age of 25. He was reelected in 1956, 1958, and 1960.

On April 21, 1960, he married Jeanne Hurley, an attorney and state legislator. They became the first husband and wife team to serve in the Illinois General Assembly. He and his wife wrote a book, *Protestant-Catholic Marriages Can Succeed* (1967), to discuss interfaith marriages such as theirs. They had two children, Sheila and Martin.

Simon ran successfully for the Illinois Senate in 1962 and was reelected in 1966. He was respected as a reformer and hard worker, as seen by the record number of awards he garnered. The Independent Voters of Illinois, for example, granted him the "Best Legislator" award during each session he served.

The next stage of public service was reached in 1968. Simon became the lieutenant governor of Illinois. He was the first—and only—lieutenant governor to be elected with a governor of another political party. After his election, the Illinois constitution was changed to provide for the joint election of governor and lieutenant governor, thus assuring that the two office-holders would be members of the same party.

Simon entered the Democratic primary for governor in 1972. He lost by a narrow margin. It was his only loss at the polls. Out of public office, Simon turned to teaching. He taught history and government at Sangamon State University in Springfield, Illinois, and lectured at Harvard University's John F. Kennedy Institute of Politics.

Urged to return to public service, he focused on the national level. Simon ran for the U.S. House of Representatives from a large southern Illinois district. He was first elected in 1974 and then re-elected four times. Serving on the House Education and Labor Committee, he became one of the leading advocates of teacher and educational quality. He was a strong supporter of arms control talks and civil rights.

In 1984 Simon upset three-term Republican incumbent Charles Percy to win a seat in the U.S. Senate. As a senator, he worked on legislation to achieve arms control, to support health care for the elderly, and to promote human rights and a balanced budget. He strove to combat adult illiteracy and wrote about that in one of his many books, *The Tongue-Tied American* (1980). His legislative priority was a public works program that would guarantee a job to anyone who wanted to work. His eleventh book, *Let's Put America Back To Work* (1986), outlined his ideas for the locally run, project-oriented public programs.

On May 18, 1987, Simon announced that he would seek the nomination for president in the 1988 elections. At 58, he was the oldest announced candidate in the Democratic Party race and the one with the most electoral experience. Simon was distinguishable from the other announced contenders in both his appearance and issue stands. Dressed in the bow tie and horned-rimmed glasses that are his trademark, Simon sought to get across his image as a modern day Harry S. Truman and standard-bearer for traditional Democratic Party liberal ideas.

On the day he announced his candidacy, Simon declared his unwillingness to bend to any prevailing political winds. He stated: "I stand here as a Democrat, not as a neo-anything, as one who is not running away from the Democratic tradition of caring and daring and dreaming." He emphasized willingness to use the tools of government in programs for employment, education, farmers, housing, and long-term care for senior citizens. But Simon did not fare well in the Democratic caucuses and primaries, winning only his home state of Illinois.

For the next decade, Simon maintained keen interest in the politics of elections and their financing. In 1995, along with former governor William Stratton, a Republican, Simon led the newly-created Illinois Campaign Finance Task Force. Simon retired in early 1997 after serving 22 years in Congress. He intended to return to teaching at Southern Illinois University in Carbondale, Illinois, and to head a public policy institute there.

Further Reading

No biography has been written about Paul Simon. However, he has authored many works which give an understanding of his interests and positions. Simon was a newspaper columnist for 40 years and the author of 11 books, including: *Lincoln's Preparation for Greatness* (1965), with which he acquired a reputation as a Lincoln scholar and admirer; *The Politics of World Hunger* (1973), written with his brother, Arthur Simon, a Lutheran minister, to highlight the problem and press for public aid programs; *The Once and Future Democrats: Strategies for Change* (1981); and *The Glass House: Politics and Morality in the Nation's Capital* (1984), in which he explained the institutional and moral problems facing members of Congress. He also wrote: *Lovejoy: Martyr to Freedom* (1984), a book about Elijah Lovejoy, an abolitionist; *A Hungry World* (1966); *You Want To Change the World? So Change It* (1971); and *Advice and Consent: Clarence Thomas, Robert Bork, and the Intriguing History of the Supreme Court's Nomination Battles* (1992). □

Konstantin Mikhailovich Simonov

The Russian poet and novelist Konstantin Mikhailovich Simonov (1915-1979) is best known for his patriotic verse dealing with World War II and for his vivid prose descriptions of Soviet troops in action during the war.

Konstantin Simonov was born on Nov. 28, 1915, in St. Petersburg. His father took an active part in the revolution and served throughout the civil war as a commander in the Red Army. Simonov traveled with his father's division and received his secondary education at various provincial schools, chiefly in Ryazan and Saratov. He finished school in 1930. Between 1930 and 1934 Simonov attended university part-time while working as a lathe operator in Saratov and Moscow. In 1934 he entered the Gorky Institute of Literature, studying there until 1939. He received his degree in literature and completed a year of graduate study at the institute.

Simonov's first verses were published in 1934. He continued to write poetry throughout the 1930s, and his first book, *Verses, 1939,* was published in 1940. Much of its contents was inspired by a trip that Simonov made to Mongolia in 1939 as a war correspondent. In 1939 Simonov became a member of the Communist party, and in June 1941 he was called to military duty as a correspondent for the journal *Red Star.* His wartime dispatches were read by a wide audience, and he was awarded several medals for his work, including the Stalin Prize. After World War II Simonov traveled extensively as a member of various literary and journalistic delegations, visiting Japan, China, the United States, and Western Europe. A member of the editorial boards of various Soviet journals and publishing houses, Simonov twice served as a deputy to the Supreme Soviet of the U.S.S.R.

Simonov's literary output was large and varied. He is primarily known for his poetry about the suffering that war causes both to men at war and to their families. Although not innovative, his poetry communicates a personal compassion for its subjects. Its style often draws on colloquial speech and conversational rhythms. Simonov's prose is also noteworthy. His most widely read novel is *Days and Nights* (1944), which deals with the courage of Soviet forces during the siege of Stalingrad. Simonov does not limit himself to the depiction of heroic acts alone but also portrays the deep emotions of men under stress. His prose exhibits an economy of style and a sense of dramatic action unusual in war novels of the cold-war era, which generally glorified the Soviet government and were expected to function as propa-

Konstantin Simonov (foreground)

ganda for the Soviet system. Simonov's postwar novels deal largely with the conflict between the Soviet Union and the United States. In *Smoke of the Fatherland* (1947), he blames the United States for the cold war but asserts the need for common understanding.

Simonov was a proponent of conventional values in officially acceptable Soviet literature, the only literary expression possible for a writer after modernism and the expression of individual vision or creativity were suppressed in the 1920s and 1930s. In the less repressive Khrushchev era after 1953, he was able to create more independent characters who revealed more of the true circumstances of Soviet life. While he was editor of the distinguished journal *Novy Mir* (1954-57), he published an essay criticizing Soviet Realism, the doctrine that all literature must further the goals of the Soviet political system and present only a positive view of Soviet life. In 1957 he was removed as editor for publishing controversial works.

In 1968 he and other high-ranking members of the Union of Soviet Writers refused to sign a statement of official support for the government's invasion of Czechoslovakia; yet he remained an esteemed member of the Soviet literary establishment. Throughout the 1970s he served as secretary of the Union of Writers. He died in Moscow in 1979.

Further Reading

Discussions of his writing are in *Biographical Dictionary of the Former Soviet Union,* Bowker-Saur, 1992; *Encyclopedia of World Literature in the 20th Century,* Continuum Publishing, 1993; Gleb Struve, *Soviet Russian Literature, 1917-1950* (1951); and Vera Alexandrova, *History of Soviet Literature* (1963). □

George Gaylord Simpson

George Gaylord Simpson (1902-1984), an American paleontologist, moved frequently from New York's American Museum of Natural History, where he was curator, to lecture halls and remote fossil fields. His mastery of the fossil record led to significant advances in theoretical evolution and taxonomy.

Paleontology gives rise to the greatest source of empirical knowledge about the history of life. Yet paleontology, which grew and flourished as a descriptive science throughout the 19th and into the early 20th century, contributed little to the theoretical understanding of biology before 1940. George Gaylord Simpson entered this profession in the mid-1920s and demonstrated in the following years that quantitative and deductive methods could lead to accurate and not otherwise accessible conclusions about the history of life.

Education in Colorado and at Yale

George Gaylord Simpson was born in Chicago on June 16, 1902. While he was still very young, his parents, Julia Kinney and Joseph Alexander Simpson, moved to Denver, Colorado, where his father first worked as a railroad claim adjuster and later speculated in irrigation, land development, and mining. George frequently accompanied his father on travels through the mountains, and this led to a lasting fondness for outdoor life and exploration.

Simpson slid easily through grade school, Latin school (ninth grade), and high school in East Denver. Though missing much school for illness, he learned well on his own and graduated in 1918. The following autumn he entered the University of Colorado, where he acquired a particular interest in historical geology, an interest that was sparked and fanned by Arthur Jerrold Tieje. Tieje left Colorado in 1922 and encouraged Simpson to transfer to Yale, which was strong in both geology and zoology. Simpson's senior year was spent at Yale. After graduation in 1923 he immediately entered graduate school and studied with Richard Swan Lull, a leading American paleontologist.

Simpson as Professional Paleontologist

Simpson had begun his professional career even before finishing graduate school. In the summer of 1924 he accompanied William Diller Matthew, paleontologist at the American Museum of Natural History, on a collecting expedition to Texas and New Mexico. Returning to Yale, Simpson con-

tinued his study of Mesozoic mammals—the oldest fossilized mammals, of which there was a rare collection in the Peabody Museum at Yale. These mammals became the subject of Simpson's dissertation and led in the year following his graduation to a study of the European Mesozoic mammals at the British Museum. From this work came his first published monograph (1928), although since 1925 he had written somewhat over 30 articles (at his death he had over 700 publications, nearly 50 of which were books).

While in England Simpson received job offers from Yale and from the American Museum of Natural History in New York City. He chose a position with the latter and remained there as curator of vertebrate paleontology until 1959. He served as chairman of the Department of Geology and Paleontology from 1944 to 1958 and held a joint appointment with Columbia University, where he taught vertebrate paleontology from 1945 to 1959. As curator at the museum Simpson received many opportunities to carry out fossil collecting expeditions.

Simpson's early expeditions included travels to Florida, Montana, New Mexico, Argentina (specifically Patagonia), and Venezuela. The Scarritt Expeditions (funded by Horace Scarritt, a wealthy banker) occupied much of the 1930s. Under these Simpson went twice to Patagonia (1930-1931 and 1933-1934). First studying the country's fossil collections in museums at Buenos Aires and La Plata, he later tracked down in Patagonia a field rich with fossil mammals from the early Cenozoic period (the Age of Mammals). At that time little was known of early mammalian history, and the lack of information about South American mammals represented an unusually large gap.

The description and interpretation of Simpson's findings in Patagonia were set forth in his classic work *The Beginning of the Age of Mammals in South America* (Vol. I, 1948; Vol. II, 1967). Here Simpson told of finding only three groups of mammals in the lower strata (ungulates, edentates, and marsupials). He surmised that South America had been isolated from animal immigration shortly after the origin of mammals in the late Mesozoic (Age of Reptiles) and had remained that way during most of mammalian history (the Cenozoic began approximately 60 million years ago). During this time of isolation, however, South America had received one installment of mammals from another continent. A group of primates and rodents, in a manner which Simpson was unable to explain, colonized South America and flourished toward the middle of the Age of Mammals. Then, in recent time (geologically speaking, in the last few million years) with the origin of a land bridge between North and South America, the southern continent received a flood of invaders from the north and experienced a great increase in mammalian diversity.

Contributions to Evolutionary Thought

Simpson's life changed in two major ways late in the 1930s. First, his marriage failed. It had been a tumultuous one nearly from its beginning in 1923. In 1938 Simpson remarried, and his second wife, a childhood friend, Anne Roe, an academic psychologist, collaborated with him on a textbook, *Quantitative Zoology* (1939). This book was an outpouring of their mutual belief that most zoologists were inadequately trained in statistics, and it served to give impetus to a shift in zoological methodology. A second change is related. Simpson's expertise in statistics prepared him to take on theoretical problems in biology.

Simpson's first major contribution to theoretical biology was in the area of evolution. Since Darwin, paleontologists had almost exclusively been evolutionists, but, again with little exception, they failed to accept Darwin's mechanism for evolution—natural selection. They commonly believed, as epitomized by H. F. Osborn (a colleague of Simpson at the American Museum during Simpson's early years) that long-term phenomena of evolution (macro evolution), such as speciation or major changes in a line of descent (for example, the shift from three-toed to one-toed horses), required explanations that could only be reached through studies of the fossil record.

Simpson was not a typical paleontologist, however. He had always been adept at mathematics, and Anne Roe had introduced him to the powerful statistical techniques used regularly in her field. Consequently, Simpson was able to recognize the efficacy with which a small group of genetic statisticians were solving problems in evolution. In the 1920s and 1930s R. A. Fisher, J. B. S. Haldane, and Sewall Wright had independently worked out statistical principles by which an advantageous variation could be carried through a population in time and subsequently change the adapted nature of that population. That is, they demonstrated that natural selection could theoretically work.

Simpson reconciled these advances in genetics with the fossil record.

Tempo and Mode in Evolution (1942) advanced paleontology in a number of ways. It proposed many means by which evolution might work and demonstrated that hypothesis does have a role in paleontology. It answered the question of whether the fossil record could be reconciled with the new statistical approach that geneticists had applied to natural selection and laid the groundwork for a union of micro and macro evolution in a single principle. It also showed that the fossil record can be described and interpreted quantitatively. Broadly, it formed part of the greater synthesis which united all the various biological subdisciplines in a common understanding of evolution.

Simpson also became an expert on the classification of mammals. Shortly after being hired by the American Museum, he began compiling a catalogue to facilitate storage and retrieval of the museum's extensive collection of mammals. He collected all the contemporary studies in mammalian taxonomy and produced a systematic classification of the mammals organized down to the level of family. This was published in 1931. By 1942 Simpson had written a greatly expanded version. This book, published in 1945, was praised as the first attempt to organize and set forth explicitly the principles of an evolutionary taxonomy.

The Halcyon Period

Simpson called the period 1944 to 1956 the halcyon period of his life. He continued studies in evolution, participated in the founding of the Society for the Study of Evolution, and wrote two books on this subject. *The Meaning of Evolution* (1949) was written for a wide audience and became Simpson's most popular book. *Major Features of Evolution* (1953) was an extensively revised version of *Tempo and Mode in Evolution*. During this period Simpson also wrote a general book on paleontology, *Life of the Past* (1953), and continued his research on fossil mammals.

Research in 1954 took him to Brazil under invitation from the Brazilian National Research Council. There he lectured, consulted Brazilian scientists, and studied mastodons in museums and in the field.

A second expedition to Brazil, in 1955, ended with a severe accident, which forced Simpson to be immediately transported back to New York City and left him crippled for two years. During his recuperation he published a textbook on general biology, *Life* (1957), with C. S. Pittendrigh and L. H. Tiffany. The text was used extensively and employed a novel approach to biology, presenting evolution as the central principle while ignoring the traditional dichotomy between plants and animals.

As a consequence of his lingering disability, Simpson was removed from the chairmanship of the Department of Geology and Paleontology at the American Museum. Subsequent developments led to his resignation as curator of vertebrate paleontology at the museum and as professor at Columbia University in 1959. Shortly thereafter Simpson became the Alexander Agassiz Professor at the Museum of Comparative Zoology (aligned with Harvard University).

Simpson carried on his research from Cambridge for the following eight years. During this time he published his favorite book, *This View of Life* (1964), which was a collection of previous, shorter works (Simpson preferred to lecture from a written text rather than from notes). Simpson also travelled extensively during this period. The height of these travels was perhaps an African expedition with Louis and Mary Leakey when they made their famous discovery of a 14 million year old human ancestor at the Olduvai Gorge in Kenya.

The Later Years

In 1967 the failing health of both Simpson and his wife forced them to move to Tucson, Arizona. Simpson remained employed half-time by the Museum of Comparative Zoology and continued his research under its auspices until 1970. In addition, he served as part-time professor at the University of Arizona, where he remained until full retirement in 1982.

During the late 1960s and early 1970s Simpson and Anne Roe continued to travel extensively, despite failing health. In Patagonia in 1933 Simpson had made an extensive collection of fossil penguins. He worked on this collection only sporadically, but after his partial retirement in 1970 he found great pleasure in studying them. This study took him and Anne to museums in London and Stockholm; on field expeditions to South Africa, Australia, and New Zealand; and on three cruises to Antarctica. The result was the book *Penguins: Past and Present, Here and There* (1976).

Throughout his life, Simpson worked tirelessly and with great enthusiasm. Complete retirement in 1982, when he left his professorship at the University of Arizona, was merely a nominal change-two books published after retirement—*Fossils and the History of Life* (1983) and *Discoverers of the Lost World* (1984)—attest to his tenacious desire to work, ending only with his death late in 1984.

Further Reading

There is not much secondary literature on Simpson's life and work. Further details can be found in his autobiography, *Concession to the Improbable* (1978). Stephen Jay Gould has written a short article on Simpson's role in the union of paleontology and theoretical evolution in *The Evolutionary Synthesis,* edited by Ernst Mayr and William B. Provine (1980). In the same work Mayr has written a short biography of Simpson that focusses on his scientific achievements.

On the other hand, a wealth of primary works is readily available, and one can find a comprehensive list of Simpson's publications up to 1971 in Hecht, et. al., "George Gaylord Simpson: His Life and Works to the Present," *Evolutionary Biology* 6 (1972). Simpson's book *Attending Marvels* (1934) is a charming account of his travels in Patagonia. □

Louis Aston Marantz Simpson

American poet, critic, and educator Louis Aston Marantz Simpson (born 1923) was widely recognized for the elegance of his verse.

Louis Simpson was born on March 27, 1923, in Kingston, Jamaica, in the British West Indies, the son of Aston and Rosalind (Marantz) Simpson. In 1949 he married Jeanne Rogers, but was divorced in 1953. He married for the second time to Dorothy Roochvarg in 1955, but was divorced in 1979. The son of his first marriage is Matthew Simpson; the children of his second marriage are Anne Simpson and Anthony Simpson.

He came to the United States in 1940 and in World War II served in the U.S. Army from 1943 to 1946. He was promoted to sergeant; was awarded the Bronze Star with Oak Leaf Cluster; was twice awarded the Purple Star; and, as a member of his unit, received a Presidential Citation. Educated after the war at Columbia University, New York City, he earned his B.S. degree in 1948, M.A. in 1950, and Ph.D. in 1959.

Upon completion of the M.A. degree in 1950. He served as editor with the Bobbs-Merrill Publishing Company in New York City until 1955. He served as instructor in English at Columbia University from 1955 to 1959; assistant and full professor at the University of California, Berkeley, from 1959-1967; and as professor of English and comparative literature at the State University of New York at Stony Brook from 1967 to the 1990s.

In 1957 he received a fellowship in literature (Prix de Rome) at the American Academy in Rome; the Hudson Review fellowship in 1957; the Columbia University distinguished alumni award in 1960; the Columbia University medal of excellence in 1965; the Edna St. Vincent Millay Award in 1960; a Guggenheim fellowship in both 1962 and 1970; an American Council of Learned Societies grant in 1963; the Pulitzer Prize for poetry in 1964; the American Academy of Arts and Letters award in literature in 1976; and the D.H.L. from Eastern Michigan University in 1977.

His publications include *The Arrivistes: Poems, 1940-1949* (1949); *Good News of Death and Other Poems* (1955); editor, with Donald Halland Robert Pack, of *New Poets of England and America* (1957); a book of poems, *A Dream of Governors* (1959); the novel *Riverside Drive* (1962); *James Hogg: A Critical Study* (1962, 1977); another volume of poems, *At the End of the Open Road* (1963); *Selected Poems* (1965); *Adventures of the Letter I* (poems; 1972); *North of Jamaica* (autobiography; 1972, published in England as *Air with Armed Men,* 1972); *Three on the Tower: The Lives and Works of Ezra Pound, T. S. Eliot and William Carlos Williams* (1975); *Searching for the Ox* (poems; 1976); and *A Revolution in Taste: Studies of Dylan Thomas, Allen Ginsberg, Sylvia Plath and Robert Lowell* (1978). He also contributed poems, plays, and articles to literary periodicals, including *American Poetry Review, Listener, Hudson Review, Paris Review,* and *Critical Quarterly,* and poems to Thom Gunn and Ted Hughes, editors, *Five American Poets* (1963).

Drawing subject matter from modern life and time, Simpson was a traditionalist in verse. Turning to modern suburban life in *The Best Hour of the Night,* he recognized the realities of modern living without embarrassment but with poetic transcendence. His *Collected Poems* draw from as wide and varied a human experience as his lifetime attests; the range and scope provide a panorama of the century.

Throughout the 1980s and 1990s Simpson continued major contributions to poetry and literature with: *An Introduction to Poetry* (1986); *The Character of the Poet* (1986); and *In the Room We Share* (1990). Two of his best works *Ships Going into the Blue* (1994) and *The King My Father's Wreck* (1995) were collections of autobiographical essays and memoirs. *Ships Going into the Blue* provides an account of the Poetry Center at Stoney Brook University that he founded and directed.

Further Reading

Additional information on Louis Simpson and his work can be found in C. B. Cox, "The Poetry of Louis Simpson," *Critical Quarterly 8* (Spring 1966); John Brennin and Bill Read, *Twentieth Century Poetry: American and British (1900-1970),* (1970), and Ronald Moran, "Walt Whitman at Bear Mountain and the American Illusion," *CP,* 2 (Spring 1969). Hank Lazer provides an informative review of Simpson's life and works in

On Louis Simpson: Depths Beyond Happiness, University of Michigan Press, 1988. □

Further Reading

An excellent biography of Sims is Elting E. Morison, *Admiral Sims and the Modern American Navy* (1942). □

William Sowden Sims

William Sowden Sims (1858-1936), American admiral, commanded United States naval forces in European waters during World War I.

William Sims was born in Port Hope, Ontario, on Oct. 15, 1858. After graduating from the U.S. Naval Academy in 1880, he served in the Atlantic (1880-1888) and the Pacific (1889-1897). He was American naval attaché in Paris during the Spanish-American War. After additional service as attaché in St. Petersburg, Russia, and further duty at sea, he became inspector of target practice for the U.S. Asiatic fleet. He first came to public notice when he argued vigorously that gunnery was ineffective and in need of modernization. President Theodore Roosevelt made him his naval aide (1907-1909).

In 1909 Sims assumed command of the battleship *Minnesota.* His next assignment was as a student at the Naval War College in Newport, R.I. (1911-1913), to which he returned as president in 1917, after commanding the destroyer flotilla in the Atlantic.

In 1917, after Germany resumed unrestricted submarine warfare against noncombatant vessels, Rear Adm. Sims was dispatched to Europe to establish contact with the naval staffs of the Allies. On April 28 he assumed command of American naval forces in European waters, rising to vice admiral a month later. Sims urged the Navy Department to send all available antisubmarine craft to European waters to participate in convoys and offensive operations against German submarines. At the same time he struggled to build his organization in London. Rapidly gaining the confidence of the British Admiralty, he just as quickly created suspicion in Washington that he was unduly pro-British.

Various controversies with the Navy Department deeply angered Sims, but he remained at his post. Throughout 1917-1918 Sims tried to make the American fleet an effective adjunct of the British fleet, especially in the submarine war, and to provide naval support for the American Army in France. An advocate of close inter-Allied cooperation, he became a leading spirit in the Allied Naval Council, set up in 1917 to coordinate the naval operations of the Western coalition. His contribution to the victory at sea earned him the lasting praise and admiration of his European associates and promotion to full admiral.

After the war Sims resumed the presidency of the Naval War College (1919-1922). In 1920 he presented an angry report to Congress criticizing the wartime conduct of the Navy Department for its failure to react promptly against Germany's submarine warfare. He received a Pulitzer Prize for an account of his wartime service, *The Victory at Sea* (1920). He died in Boston on Sept. 28, 1936.

Jaime L. Sin

Jaime L. Sin (born 1928) was a cardinal of the Roman Catholic Church who served in the Philippines. He was instrumental in the defeat of the Marcos regime and in the installation of Corazon Aquino as president in 1986.

Jaime L. Sin, cardinal of the Roman Catholic Church, was born in the town of New Washington, Aklan, in the Visayan Islands of the Philippines on August 21, 1928. He was the seventh of nine children of Juan Sin and Maxima Lachica.

Cardinal Sin began his missionary career in Jaro, Iloilo, where he attended the Jaro Archdiocesan Seminary of St. Vincent Ferrer. He was ordained a priest on April 3, 1954. He served as priest of the Diocese of Capiz from 1954 to 1957 and became rector of St. Pius X Seminary in Roxas City from 1957 to 1967. While serving in the church he obtained a bachelor's degree in education from the Immaculate Concepcion College in 1959. In 1960 Pope John XXIII named him as domestic prelate.

He assumed several positions in archdioceses in the Visayan Islands—from titular bishop of Obla, auxiliary bishop of Jaro, to apostolic administrator of Seda Plana, archdiocese of Jaro, to titular archbishop of Massa Lubrense and co-adjutor archbishop of Jaro. He subsequently became metropolitan archbishop of Jaro in 1972 and metropolitan archbishop of Manila, the capital of the Philippines, in 1974.

Sin was named cardinal by Pope Paul VI on May 26, 1976. He was elected permanent member of the Synod of Bishops in Rome.

Cardinal Sin was known for his good sense of humor. He jokingly called his residence "the House of Sin" and smiled at the ironic combination of his name and title.

But in a largely Catholic country plagued by a dictatorship from 1972 to 1986, Cardinal Sin often suppressed his smiles. He increasingly criticized the Marcos regime for its indifference to the plight of the poor. While advocating an independent church, he supported intervention in "the morality of politics." Thus he caught the ire of President Marcos and the First Lady many times over his criticisms of the government's human rights violations and over Imelda's extravagant expenditures.

The cardinal became very vocal about the violence and cheating which characterized Philippine elections in the 1970s and 1980s. In the 1978 elections for delegates to the National Assembly, he issued an open letter "calling on church members to report any instances of fraud."

His involvement became more active in 1986 when President Marcos called for snap elections for president and vice-president. Marcos needed a new mandate to convince the world of the legitimacy of his regime.

The opposition saw the opportunity to field candidates against the president. One candidate put up was Corazon Aquino, widow of the senator who was jailed by Marcos, went to self-exile in the United States, and was murdered upon his return to the Philippines in 1983. Cardinal Sin played an important role in unifying several factions and candidates of the opposition. He convinced ex-Senator Salvador Laurel to run for vice-president, with Corazon Aquino as president. Aquino agreed, in turn, to run under Laurel's banner, the UNIDO Party.

The opposition rallied behind the Aquino-Laurel ticket. However, conflicting counts were reported by the government's Commission on Elections (COMELEC) and the volunteer group National Movement for Free Elections (NAMFREL). The Marcos-leaning legislature proclaimed the Marcos ticket victory on the basis of COMELEC tallies. The people protested.

In the military some 300 officers rebelled against the president and Chief of Staff Fabian Ver. The minister of national defense, Juan Ponce Enrile, and deputy chief of staff Fidel Ramos led the rebellion, asking Cardinal Sin to protect the army against the president's reprisal by mobilizing civilian support. The cardinal made an appeal by radio, and the people, Catholic and non-Catholic alike, heeded his call. They went by the millions to stand guard against the gates and fences of the military camp where the rebels stayed. When government tanks and weapons were sent to crush the rebellion, the people's prayers, smiles, and protests prevented the government troops from firing. The president, in desperation, fled the country. The rebel government installed Corazon Aquino as president.

In the 1990s, Cardinal Sin continued to maintain a high profile in the political life of the Philippines. During the 1992 election campaign, Cardinal Sin issued a pastoral letter in which he identified what he considered to be undesirable traits or behaviors in presidential candidates. In 1995, he publicly criticized the Christian Democratic coalition government of Protestant President Fidel Ramos, whom he referred to as a "Marcos clone." He also led massive rallies protesting various governmental policies, including Ramos's one for population control (1995) and for the issuance of national identification (ID) cards (1997). Thus the cardinal who would not intervene played a crucial role in Philippine politics. This was consistent with his reading of the role of the church in a democracy.

He maintained his residence in a suburb of Manila, where he continued to entertain both humble and mighty guests, welcoming all into the "House of Sin" with a modest smile.

Further Reading

Cardinal Sin's bio-data is included in *The Philippines Who's Who* by D. H. Soriano and Isidro L. Retizos (Manila, 1981). Many articles have been written about Cardinal Sin's fight with the Marcoses. Among them are Rodney Tasker's pieces in the *Far Eastern Economics Review:* "Cardinal Sin Speaks Out" (July 21, 1978) and "Archbishop Sin Fights a Boardroom Battle" (August 4, 1978). In the Philippines, several articles have been written about him. These include: C. F. Makabenta's "A Night in the House of Sin," *Expressweek* (November 15, 1979) and Dexter H. Irisar's "Conversation with Archbishop Sin," *Expressweek* (October 10, 1974). The Catholic paper *Veritas* also carried numerous articles about him. □

Kodja Mimar Sinan

Kodja Mimar Sinan (1489-1578) was one of the greatest of the Ottoman architects. His many buildings include some of the most famous landmarks of the Turkish Empire.

Sinan was born in Kaisariya, Anatolia, the son of Greek Christians, on April 15, 1489. His father's name is unknown, but over his non-Turkish origin no doubt has arisen. Caught up in one of the periodic Ottoman levies aimed at drawing off healthy young minority males, who might become revolutionaries, and turning their energies instead into state service, the youthful Sinan was converted to Islam and became a Janissary. He distinguished himself in this famed military service.

Following the 1521-1522 campaigns against Belgrade and Rhodes, Sinan became chief firework operator. During the war with Persia (1534) he contrived an ingenious ferry operation for the successful transporting of troops across Lake Van. Repeatedly promoted, he was a police magistrate at the time of a Turkish invasion of the Danube Valley, during which he constructed a bridge across the river and gained considerable fame. This turned him to full-time architectural activity.

From the end of the 1530s until he died on July 15, 1578, Sinan labored throughout the Ottoman Empire, from Budapest to Mecca, erecting about 340 public structures. The four great mosques for which he is most famous are the Roxelana (1539), the Princes' (1548), which Sinan described as the work of an apprentice, and the Suleimaniye (1550-1556), the work of a journeyman, all three in Stambul (Istanbul); and the Selim II (1551-1574), the work of a master, in Edirne.

Style and Accomplishments

Light but vast domes highlight Sinan's work. Mounted on four-, six-, or eight-sided walls in a style peculiarly Turkish, they encrown extensive interior ceremonial halls. Buttresses bracing the walls were hidden by porches, and conscious attention to exterior appearances led to the development of slim, pencil like, balconied minarets that gave the 16th-century Stambul skyline its magnificent silhouette, which is apparent even today. Interiors were colorfully tiled or paneled in tinted and veined marble with frescoes of flowers or calligraphy decorating the ceilings.

Persian and Byzantine influences, particularly that of Hagia Sophia, can be seen in these structures, as can a trace of Italian Renaissance architecture, but in the work of this Ottoman genius appeared the Turkish style which gave to the reign of Suleiman I (the Magnificent) its cultural distinction. It was in the great central Byzantine dome that Turkish architecture differed from the Persian, which featured open-air central assembly areas flanked by small-domed side halls and massive minarets.

According to a contemporary biographer, the poet Mustafa Sai, Sinan was responsible, in all, for 81 mosques, including domes for the Kaaba, the holy sanctuary at Mecca; 50 chapels or small mosques; 55 madrasahs (schools); 7 Koran schools; 19 tombs; 3 hospitals; 7 aqueducts, including those of Stambul; 8 bridges; 17 poor kitchens; 3 warehouses; 18 caravansaries (fortified rest houses for travelers); 33 palaces, such as those at Scutari; and 33 baths, all commissioned by Suleiman, his daughter Mihrimah, his successors, or noblemen of the empire. Sinan is sometimes credited also with the mosque of Selim I, erected in Stambul in 1521-1522 by the Sultan's son Suleiman I, but this is in doubt: his building period seems to have begun in the late 1530s, when he was about 50 years old. He inspired many followers, including a younger Sinan with whom he is sometimes confused, hence the designation "Kodja" (the Elder). The master's favorite pupil was Yusuf, who is alleged to have built the Mogul palaces at Agra, Delhi, and Lahore.

Further Reading

An article on Sinan appears in volume 13 of McGraw-Hill's *Encyclopedia of World Art* (1965). For background on Sinan see Ulya Vogt-Göknil, *Living Architecture: Ottoman* (1966). Also consult Behçet Ünsal, *Turkish Islamic Architecture* (1959); Ernst Kühnel, *Islamic Art and Architecture* (1962; trans. 1966); and Ekrem Akurgal, Cyril Mango, and Richard Ettinghausen, *Treasures of Turkey* (1966).

Additional Sources

Stratton, Arthur, *Sina,* New York, Scribner 1971, 1972. □

Francis Albert Sinatra

Francis Albert Sinatra (born 1915) may have been the most popular singer in American history, in a career that spanned from the 1930s into the 1990s.

Francis Albert Sinatra was born in Hoboken, New Jersey, on December 12, 1915. He was the only child of Martin and Natalie "Dolly" Sinatra. He lived in a predominantly Italian-American working class neighborhood. As a student at Demarest High School, he became popular by exhibiting the traits he would carry with him throughout his lifetime—those of a generous but pugnacious individual.

Early in his life Sinatra knew he wanted to become a singer. His influences were Rudy Vallee and his idol, Bing Crosby. After dropping out of high school he began to sing at obscure clubs. He got his first big break with Major Bowes and his "Amateur Hour" in 1935, singing in a group called the Hoboken Four. Sinatra, by preference, continued to sing in various New Jersey nightclubs, hoping to attract the attention of the bandleaders who led America into the "Swing Era" on the many hundreds of radio stations that were popping up all over the country.

From the Rustic Cabin Club in Alpine, New Jersey, Sinatra got his first radio play in 1939 on station WNEW in New York City. He then signed with his first bandleader, Harry James, for $75 per week. That same year he married his longtime sweetheart, Nancy Barbato. They would eventually have three children.

After seven months with Harry James, Sinatra joined Tommy Dorsey and his orchestra, causing his career to skyrocket. Dorsey's orchestra was one of the most popular in the land and remained so with Sinatra singing, from 1940 through 1942. During that time he performed with the band in his first two movies—*Las Vegas Nights* (1941) and *Ship Ahoy* (1942). He began his solo career at the end of 1942 and continued his meteoric rise.

As the leading American singer through the war era, he epitomized the evolution of American music with its blends of music that included jazz and the classics. The idiom would come to be known simply as American popular, or pop music. The Swing Era lasted from 1935 through the end of World War II, and Sinatra was by far its best known

vocalist. His musical roots and education were that of the Tin Pan Alley tradition, but he was a diligent student of Italian opera as well. Most important to him throughout his career would be his insistence on his own style and arrangements for whatever music he sang. His unique phrasing of lyrics and his jazzy syncopation of melody lines were delivered in a voice best described as light baritone with a sharp New York accent, resonating deep into his nasal cavities to produce the classic crooning effect.

His wide-shouldered suits and his bow ties were imitated by many men, but his most ardent followers were the teenaged girls, nicknamed the "bobby-soxers," who swooned or screamed for "Frankie" when he sang. For the "Croon Prince of Swing," his widespread appeal was further fueled by America's explosive mass media growth in newspapers, magazines, films, record players, and radio stations. Sinatra was the first to attract the kind of near hysteria that would later accompany live appearances by Elvis Presley and the Beatles. This type of excitement reached its peak in the famed Columbus Day Riot of October 12, 1944, when thousands of his fans (mostly female), denied entry into the already-packed Paramount Theater in New York City, stormed the streets and vented their frustration by smashing nearby shop windows.

Though Sinatra was exempted from military service in World War II because of a perforated eardrum, he helped the war effort with his appearances in movies and benefits for soldiers. He was an outspoken supporter of Franklin D. Roosevelt and liberal viewpoints, including racial and religious tolerance. His charitable appearances were consistent and numerous.

Sinatra's first and only major downfall in the public eye came in 1951 and lasted for almost three years. His extramarital affairs led to his divorce, and his subsequent well-publicized, tempestuous marriage to actress Ava Gardner also ended in divorce in 1957. Rumors of Mafia connections spread, mostly from his socializing with alleged Mafia kingpins, and these rumors persisted, along with publicity about his noted barroom brawls. Musical tastes were changing as well, as "belters" like Eddie Fisher and Frankie Laine were replacing the crooners in popularity. All of these events, in addition to his failure to serve in the military, combined to alienate him from an adoring but fickle public, and especially from the press. The allegations of underworld activity were never proven, and no indictments were ever made. His comeback was secured with his appearance as the feisty Italian-American soldier, Angelo Maggio, in the critically acclaimed film *From Here to Eternity* (1954). The role won him an Academy Award for best supporting actor, and he was back on the record charts as well with "Young at Heart."

Nelson Riddle, his arranger in the 1950s, helped Sinatra stay on the competitive record charts throughout the rest of the decade. In fact, Sinatra stayed on the charts steadily through 1967, despite the sudden and overwhelming pre-eminence of Rock 'n' Roll music. This durability was due in part to the advent of the long-playing album, the LP, upon which Sinatra could surround a central theme with a large collection of songs or ballads. From 1957 through 1966 he had 27 top ten albums without producing one top ten single. These albums were led by *Only the Lonely* (1958), *Come Fly With Me* (1958), and *Come Dance With Me* (1959). The bobby-soxers were now adults, but Sinatra had shifted smoothly to the role of the aging romantic bachelor. This was signified by the image of him leaning alone against a lamppost, raincoat in hand. His movie appearances multiplied during this period, with nine in the span of just two years, including *Guys and Dolls* (1955), *Young At Heart* (1955), *The Tender Trap* (1955), *The Man With the Golden Arm* (1955), and *High Society* (1956).

His music came to be known as "middle of the road," but his ever-present style put him in a class by himself because of his ability to convey the heartfelt romantic message. Additional hits of the 1960s included "It Was a Very Good Year," from his Grammy Award winning album *September of My Years* (1965), and "Strangers in the Night" (1966). He did reach the top of the singles charts in a duet with his daughter Nancy, "Somethin' Stupid," in 1967. A brief marriage to 20-year-old actress Mia Farrow ended in divorce in 1968. He continued his movie roles, including *Tony Rome* (1967) and *Robin and the Seven Hoods* (1964), but they had declined in artistic merit. Critics saw these movies as vehicles for reinforcement of his tough-guy image, as well as his and his friends' answer to the great youth movement that was taking place around them. These friends included entertainers Dean Martin, Sammy Davis, Jr., Joey Bishop, and Peter Lawford, a clique that came to be known as the "Rat Pack."

After his famous recording of "My Way" (1969), Sinatra made an ill-fated attempt to sing some of the lighter tunes of modern rock composers. This led to a brief retirement from entertainment (1971 through 1973), a time that was accompanied by a shift in his politics from liberal to conservative. He had become a close friend of Ronald Reagan's and helped Reagan in his later successsful presidential campaigns.

By this time Sinatra's financial empire produced millions of dollars in earnings from investments in films, records, gambling casinos, real estate, missile parts, and general aviation. He came out of his retirement in 1974 with a renewed interest in the middle of the road genre and older tunes. He was married for the fourth time, in 1976, to Barbara Blakely. His return to the limelight was highlighted by his famous recording of "New York, New York" (1980) as he entered his sixth decade of entertaining.

In 1988, Sinatra joined with Sammie Davis, Jr. and Dean Martin and embarked on a cross-country tour. The tour lasted only one week. Sinatra later organized another reunion tour with Shirley MacLaine in 1992 and it was a resounding success. By 1994, Sinatra was experiencing memory lapses but that did not keep him from performing publicly. He merely added the use of a teleprompter to remind him of the lyrics. After celebrating his 80th birthday at a public tribute and roast at the Los Angeles Shrine Auditorium, new collector's packages of recordings were released and became instant best-sellers.

The legions who grew up with him and his music were complemented by adoration from younger generations, all of whom have made "Old Blue Eyes" the pre-eminent popular singer of the 20th century.

Further Reading

Sinatra had his detractors, as well a controversial man may, but most of his biographers are reverent of him. Two who are generally not reverent are Earl Wilson in *Sinatra: An Unauthorized Biography* (1976), an in-depth study of the man and the allegations that dogged him, and Kitty Kelly in her unsparing portrait, *His Way: The Unauthorized Biography of Frank Sinatra* (1986). Also recommended, though openly admiring of the man, are *Sinatra: An American Classic* (1984), with its fine pictorial display, by John Rockwell; Norm Goldstein's *Frank Sinatra: Ol'Blue Eyes* (1982); and *Frank Sinatra—My Father* (1985) by his daughter Nancy. Gene Ringgold and Clifford McCarty provide an excellent pictorial account of his life in films in *The Films of Frank Sinatra* (1971).

Additional Sources

Ewen, David. *All the Years of American Popular Music* (Prentice-Hall, 1977).

Kelley, Kitty. *His Way: The Unauthorized Biography of Frank Sinatra* (Bantam, 1986).

Simon, George T. *The Big Bands* (Schirmer Books, 1967). □

Upton Beale Sinclair Jr.

Upton Beale Sinclair, Jr. (1878-1968), American novelist and political writer, was one of the most influential muckraking writers of the 1900s. He continued to write and speak for reform for many years.

Upton Sinclair was born in Baltimore, Md., on Sept. 20, 1878. His father, struggling against poverty and liquor, moved the family to New York City when Upton was 10. At 14 Upton entered the College of the City of New York. He graduated in 1897 and went to Columbia University to study law. Through these years he supported himself by writing for adventure-story magazines.

Sinclair moved to Quebec in 1900. His first novel, *Springtime and Harvest* (1901), was a modest success. Three more novels in the next 4 years failed to provide even a bare living. In 1906, however, *The Jungle,* exposing unfair labor practices and unsanitary conditions in the packing houses of Chicago, scored a huge success. The novel's protest about the lot of laborers and the socialist solutions it proposed did not have much immediate effect, but its exposé caused a public outcry. President Theodore Roosevelt invited Sinclair to discuss packing-house conditions, and a congressional investigation led to passage of the Pure Food and Drug Law.

Sinclair divorced his first wife in 1912. The autobiographical novel *Love's Pilgrimage* (1911) treats his marriage

and the birth of his child with a frankness which shocked some reviewers. He married Mary Craig in 1913. *Sylvia* and *Sylvia's Marriage,* a massive two-part story, called for sexual enlightenment. *King Coal* (1917), based on a coal strike of 1914-1915, returned to labor protest and socialistic polemic. *Oil!* (1927) dealt with dishonesty in Warren G. Harding's administration. *Boston* (1928), a novel about the Sacco-Vanzetti case, unearthed much new material and demonstrated the constructive research that always lay beneath Sinclair's protest writings.

Sinclair became a member of the Socialist party in 1902 and was Socialist candidate for Congress from New Jersey in 1906. In 1917 he left the party to support President Woodrow Wilson. He returned to the Socialist camp when Wilson supported Allied intervention in the Soviet Union. In California he stood for Congress on the Socialist ticket (1920), for the Senate (1922), and for governor (1926 and 1930). In 1933, persuaded to campaign seriously for governor, he called his program "End Poverty in California." His cogent presentation of Socialist ideas won him the Democratic nomination, but millions of dollars and a campaign based on falsehood and fear defeated him in the election.

World's End (1940) launched Sinclair's 11-volume novel series attempting to give an insider's view of American government between 1913 and 1949. One of the novels, *Dragon's Teeth* (1942), a study of the rise of Nazism, won the Pulitzer Prize. Before his death on Nov. 25, 1968, Sinclair had produced more than 90 books which netted at least $1 million, most of it contributed to socialist and reform causes.

Further Reading

Sinclair's *My Lifetime in Letters* (1960) and *The Autobiography of Upton Sinclair* (1962) are revealing, if not entirely reliable. Sinclair's work is discussed appreciatively in Alfred Kazin, *On Native Grounds: An Interpretation of Modern American Prose Literature* (1942). A brief essay and a rare reprint of the "End Poverty in California" program are in Arthur M. Weinberg, *Passport to Utopia: Great Panaceas in American History* (1968). □

Isaac Bashevis Singer

Isaac Bashevis Singer (1904-1991), Polish-American author, was admired for his re-creation of the forgotten world of provincial 19th-century Poland and his depiction of a timeless Jewish ghetto existence.

Isaac Bashevis Singer was born on July 14, 1904, in Radzymin, Poland. In his family's rabbinic tradition, he was groomed for Hasidism, attending a Warsaw seminary. However, he decided on a writing career. After completing his seminary studies, he worked as a journalist for the Yiddish press in various parts of Poland. Emigrating to the United States in 1935, Singer became a reporter for the *Daily Forward* in New York City, America's largest Yiddish newspaper. Although he personally adapted to his new habitat, his early literary efforts display nostalgia for the "old country"; the subjects seem part of a distant past remembered from vivid tales of Polish storytellers.

Singer's first novel, *The Family Moskat* (1950), was likened by critics to the narratives of Ivan Turgenev and Honoré de Balzac. Based on Singer's own family, the novel succeeds in translating the almost metaphysical existence of an orthodox Jewish home into a universal reality. Two short stories, "Satan in Goray" and "The Dybbuk and the Golem" (1955), treat the provincialism, superstition, and naiveté of eastern European peasants. A collection of short narratives, *Gimpel, the Fool, and Other Stories* (1957), reworked earlier themes but skillfully avoided repetition. Beneath the grotesque and folk elements, Singer includes in "Gimpel" a psychological-theological moral conflict in which an uncomplicated man finds his idyllic existence threatened by black magic and sorcery.

Modern man is the subject of Singer's novel *The Magician of Lublin* (1960), which portrays a protagonist who dares to violate the sanctity of tradition. The novel lacks the superb intricacy of *The Family Moskat* and the haunting suspense of "Gimpel." Still grappling with the modern experience, Singer sets the 11 short pieces of *The Spinoza of Market Street* (1961) in a post-World War II Polish ghetto. Having departed from his quaintly provincial world into contemporary urban madness, Singer revealed the stylistic limitations of his simple, flowing prose range. "I've always stayed in my same nook, my same corner," Singer reflected

in retrospect. "If a writer ventures out of his corner he is nothing."

The Slave (1962), an epic of 17th-century Poland, recounts the brutal world of Russian Cossacks through the eyes of an enslaved, sensitive, pious Jew; yet somehow the work appeals to modern sensibilities. Once again Singer's flawless prose recaptures a timeless folk element. When a collection of vignettes filled with memories of Singer's childhood in the Warsaw ghetto, *A Day of Pleasure: Stories of a Boy Growing Up in Warsaw* (1969), won the National Book Award for children's literature, Singer remarked that he wrote for young people because "they still believe in God, the family, angels, devils, witches, goblins, and other such obsolete stuff." *A Friend of Kafka,* a collection of short fiction, appeared in 1970.

Recipient of numerous other literary awards, Singer remained an active journalist and critic for the *Daily Forward* throughout. He always wrote in Yiddish and then worked closely with his English translators because of the difficulty in finding equivalents for his subtle verbal nuances. His "simple" and "unchanging" fictions paradoxically have gained in popularity with a new generation possessing a taste for an obscure and sometimes grotesque past which seems more tangible than a nebulous future, for his stories capture the essence of the human condition.

Singer received numerous awards thoughout the latter portion of his life. Some of the more noted include Nobel Prize in literature (1978) and the Gold Medal for Fiction (1989). Singer continued to publish new material until his death in 1991.

Further Reading

Full-length studies of Singer include Irving H. Buchen, *Isaac Bashevis Singer and the Eternal Past* (1968), a critical appraisal of the various themes in Singer's work, and Ben Siegel, *Isaac Bashevis Singer* (1969). Marcia Allentuck, *The Achievement of Isaac Bashevis Singer* (1969), contains appraisals by 12 scholars, and Irving Malin, ed., *Critical Views of Isaac Bashevis Singer* (1969), is particularly useful for explications of obscure elements in Singer's fiction. □

Isaac M. Singer

Isaac M. Singer (1811–1875) was an inventor with many patents who invented the first home sewing machine.

Isaac Singer developed the first practical home sewing machine and brought it into general use. Born in Pittstown, New York, to German-Jewish immigrants, Singer left home at age twelve and roamed the Northeast for many years, working variously in carnivals, as an actor, and a mechanic. In 1839 he patented an excavator, and in the 1840s, a metal and wood-carving machine.

In 1850 Singer was working in a Boston, Massachusetts, machine shop when he was asked to analyze a Blodgett & Lerow sewing machine that had been brought in for repair. Singer developed a new design based on that machine, patented it in 1851, and cofounded (with Edward Clark) the I. M. Singer Company to market it. Although Singer's machine was a great improvement over existing models, partly because of its continuous-feed feature, he was successfully sued three years later for patent infringement by Elias Howe, who had registered his own sewing machine design in 1846. However, the advent of patent pooling and licensing agreements in 1856 allowed the manufacture of Singer machines to continue with constant improvements. By 1860 the Singer Manufacturing Company had become the world's largest maker of sewing machines, and by 1863 Singer had received twenty patents for the machines.

Singer earned millions of dollars from his company and lived flamboyantly, enjoying rides through New York City's Central Park in his yellow coach with his mistresses—not a proper image for a company trying to sell sewing machines to middle-class housewives. Singer retired from the business in 1863, traveling throughout Europe before settling in Torquay, England, where he built a mansion and encouraged his twenty-four children (legitimate and illegitimate) to visit. Upon his death Singer left behind an estate of $13 million.

Further Reading

Brandon, Ruth, *Singer and the Sewing Machine: A Capitalist Romance,* 1996. □

Maxine Singer

Maxine Singer (born 1931) is an advocate of the controversial use of DNA to alter genetic characteristics. She also researches cures for diseases related to genetics.

Maxine Singer, a leading scientist in the field of human genetics, is also a staunch advocate of responsible use of biochemical genetics research. During the height of the controversy over the use of recombinant deoxyribonucleic acid (DNA) techniques to alter genetic characteristics, she advocated a cautious approach. She helped develop guidelines to balance calls for unfettered genetics research as a means of making medically valuable discoveries with demands for restrictions on research to protect the public from possible harm. After the DNA controversy waned, Singer continued to contribute to the field of genetics, researching cures for cancer, hemophilia, and other diseases related to genetics.

Singer was born on February 15, 1931, in New York City, to Hyman Frank, an attorney, and Henrietta (Perlowitz) Frank, a hospital admissions officer, children's camp director, and model. Singer received her B.A. from Swarthmore College in Pennsylvania in 1952, and earned her Ph.D. in biochemistry from Yale in 1957. From 1956 to 1958 she worked as a U.S. Public Health Service postdoctoral fellow at National Institute for Arthritis, Metabolism and Digestive Diseases (NIAMD), National Institutes of Health (NIH), in Bethesda, Maryland. She then became a research chemist on the staff of the section on enzymes and cellular biochemistry from 1958 to 1974. There she conducted DNA research on tumor-causing viruses as well as on ribonucleic acid (RNA). In the early 1970s, Singer also served as a visiting scientist with the Department of Genetics of the Weizman Institute of Science in Rehovot, Israel.

While Singer was working at NIH, scientists learned how to take DNA fragments from one organism and insert them into the living cells of another. This "recombinant DNA" could direct the production of proteins in the foreign organism as if the DNA was still in its original home. This technique had the potential of creating completely new types of organisms. On one hand, the new research brought unprecedented opportunities to discover cures for serious diseases, to develop new crops, and otherwise to benefit humanity. Yet the prospect of creating as-yet-unknown life forms, some possibly hazardous, was frightening to many.

In 1972, one of Singer's colleagues and personal friends Paul Berg of Stanford University was the first to create recombinant DNA molecules. He later voluntarily stopped conducting related experiments involving DNA manipulation in the genes of tumor-causing viruses because of some scientists' fears that a virus of unknown properties might escape from the laboratory and spread into the general population.

Although Berg's self-restraint was significant, the catalyst for the debate over gene-splicing was the 1973 Gordon Conference, an annual high-level research meeting. Singer, who was co-chair of the event, was approached by several nucleic acid scientists with the suggestion that the conference include consideration of safety issues. Singer agreed. She opened the discussion with an acknowledgment that DNA manipulation could assist in combatting health problems, yet such experimentation brought to bear a number of moral and ethical concerns.

The scientists present decided, by ballot, to send a public letter about the safety risks of recombinant DNA research to the president of the National Academy of Sciences, and asked *Science* magazine to publish it. Singer and her co-chair, Dieter Söll of Yale University, wrote the letter warning that organisms of an unpredictable nature could result from the new technique, and suggested that the National Academy of Sciences study the problem and recommend guidelines. Concern generated by this letter led to another meeting at the Asilomer Conference Center in Pacific Grove, California, where a debate ensued. Such proceedings—to consider the ethical issues arising from the new DNA research—were unprecedented in the scientific community. Immediately after the Asilomer Conference concluded, a NIH committee began formulating guidelines for recombinant DNA research.

In helping develop the guidelines, Singer advocated a careful analytic approach. In 1976, she presented four principles to the committee to be used in drafting the guidelines. She advised that certain experiments posed such serious hazards that they should be banned altogether; that experiments with lesser or no potential hazards should be permitted if their benefits are unobtainable through conventional methods and if they are properly safeguarded; that the more risk in an experiment, the stricter the safeguards should be; and that the guidelines should be reviewed annually.

Singer provided a calm voice of reason throughout the public debate over gene-splicing that followed. Committees of lay people, such as the Coalition for Responsible Genetic Research, held demonstrations calling for a complete ban on recombinant DNA research. Some members of the media made analogies to the nightmarish vision contained in Aldous Huxley's book *Brave New World,* which described a genetically altered society. When sent to address a public forum on the issue in 1977, for example, Singer responded to accusations that scientists ignore public concerns. As Clifford Grobstein recounted in his book, *A Double Image of the Double Helix: The Recombinant-DNA Debate,* Singer maintained that "scientists recognize their responsibility to the public . . . (but) dispute over the best way to exercise responsibility must not be confused with the negation of it." According to Grobstein, Singer explained that "while freedom of inquiry is a democratic right, it is clearly unacceptable to cause harm in the name of research. But [Singer] warned that levels of anxiety are not necessarily directly related to levels of real risk."

During her career, Singer has also served on the editorial Board of *Science* magazine and has contributed numerous articles. In her writing for that publication about recombinant DNA research, she stressed the benefits to humanity that recombinant DNA techniques could bring, especially in increasing the understanding of serious and incurable disease. After the NIH guidelines were implemented, she told *Science* readers that "under the Guidelines work has proceeded safely and research accomplishments have been spectacular." By 1980, when public near-hysteria had waned, Singer called for a "celebration" of the progress in molecular genetics. In *Science* she wrote: "The manufacture of important biological agents like insulin and interferon by recombinant DNA procedures," as well as the failure of any "novel hazards" to emerge, was evidence of the value of the cautious continuation of DNA research.

In 1974, Singer accepted a new position at NIH as chief of the Section of Nucleic Acid Enzymology, Division of Cancer Biology and Diagnosis (DCBD) at the National Cancer Institute in Bethesda, Maryland. In 1980 she became chief of the DCBD's Laboratory of Biochemistry. She held this post until 1988, when she became president of the Carnegie Institution, a highly regarded research organization in Washington, D.C. Singer remains affiliated with the National Cancer Institute, however, as scientist emeritus, where she continues her research in human genetics.

In addition to her laboratory research, Singer has devoted considerable time and energy to other scientific and professional pursuits. In 1981, she taught in the biochemistry department at the University of California at Berkeley. A skilled and prolific writer, she has issued more than one hundred books, articles, and papers. Most are highly technical, including numerous articles published in scientific journals. Singer also compiled a graduate-level textbook with Paul Berg on molecular genetics called *Genes and Genomes: A Changing Perspective.* Reviewers gave the work high praise for its clear presentation of difficult concepts. Marcelo Bento Soares in *Bioscience* also commented that the book was "superbly written" and "magnificently captures the sense of discovery, understanding, and anticipation that has followed the so-called recombinant DNA breakthrough."

Singer has also written extensively on less technical aspects of science. She and Berg authored a book for laypeople on genetic engineering, and she continued to promote the benefits of recombinant DNA techniques and battle public suspicion and fear long after the controversy peaked in the 1970s. In the early 1990s, for example, Singer issued an article encouraging the public to try the first genetically engineered food to reach American supermarket shelves. In describing the harmlessness of the "Flavr Savr" tomato, she decried public objections that eating it was dangerous, unnatural, or immoral to readers of the *Asbury Park Press.* Pointing out that "almost all the foods we eat are the product of previous genetic engineering by cross-breeding," Singer said that the small amount of extra DNA in the tomato would be destroyed in the digestive tract, and that people already consume the DNA present in the other foods in their diets. Moreover, she said the decision to eat a genetically altered tomato did not reduce her admiration for nature's creations.

In addition to her writing and lecturing, Singer has served on numerous advisory boards in the United States and abroad, including science institutes in Naples, Italy, Bangkok, Thailand, and Rehovot, Israel. She also has served on an advisory board to the Pope and as a consultant to the Committee on Human Values of the National Conference of Catholic Bishops. She worked on a Yale committee that investigated the university's South African investments, and serves on Johnson and Johnson's Board of Directors. Concerned about the quality of science education in the United States, she started First Light, a science program for inner-city children.

Singer travels extensively and maintains long work weeks to accommodate all her activities. She married Daniel Singer in 1952; the couple have four children: Amy Elizabeth, Ellen Ruth, David Byrd, and Stephanie Frank. Singer is the recipient of more than forty honors and awards, including some ten honorary doctor of science degrees and numerous commendations from NIH.

Further Reading

Grobstein, Clifford, *A Double Image of the Double Helix: The Recombinant-DNA Debate,* W. H. Freeman and Company, 1979, pp. 18–19, 72–73.

Krimsky, Sheldon, *Genetic Alchemy: The Social History of the Recombinant DNA Controversy,* MIT Press, 1982, pp. 181–183.

Lappé, Marc, *Broken Code: The Exploitation of DNA,* Sierra Club Books, 1984, pp. 19–25.

Soares, Marcelo Bento, *Bioscience,* March, 1992, p. 211.

Singer, Maxine F., Curriculum Vitae, current as of August, 1993. *Interview with Donna Olshansky,* conducted August 19, 1993. □

Peter Albert David Singer

The internationally renowned Australian philosopher Peter Albert David Singer (born 1946) is best known for his book *Animal Liberation*. However, he also made important contributions in theoretical ethics and in other areas of applied ethics.

Peter Albert David Singer was born on July 6, 1946, in Melbourne, Australia. His parents, Cora and Ernest Singer, had arrived in Australia eight years earlier, fleeing from their native Vienna to escape the persecution of Jews shortly after the *Anschluss,* the political union of Austria and Germany. By the time Peter was born, his father had become a successful importer of tea and coffee and his mother, already a qualified medical practitioner in Vienna, had cleared all the restrictive barriers then placed in the path of overseas doctors and was once again able to practice her chosen profession.

Keen to integrate their children into Australian society, Cora and Ernest Singer—neither of them religious believers—had decided to send Peter and his sister Joan to prestigious Protestant schools and spoke to them in English only. (It was not until Peter went to high school and university that he finally learned German.) Peter's childhood was comfortable and fairly conventional. He attended Boy Scouts, followed the local football team, went on annual skiing holidays with his family, and did well at school. He went on to study law, history, and philosophy at Melbourne University. It was the study of philosophy that would eventually turn this bright but as yet unremarkable young man into one of the leading and most controversial thinkers of his time.

The story of the radical thinker Singer begins in England in 1970. By that time Singer—now married to Renata, a fellow student from his Melbourne University days—was a graduate student in moral and political philosophy at Oxford University. There he met with other graduate students who abstained from eating meat for purely ethical reasons. Discussions with these vegetarians convinced Singer that it was morally wrong to eat meat; eating animals was, he came to believe, a systematic form of oppression of one species by another. He and Renata became vegetarians themselves.

Five years later, in 1975, Singer published *Animal Liberation,* the book that challenged traditional thinking about the moral status of nonhuman animals and was to provide the intellectual foundation for the worldwide animal liberation movement. The mistreatment of animals in factory farms and as tools for research, Singer argued, is based on an indefensible prejudice in favor of our own species. In these and other practices, the interests of animals are cruelly disregarded to satisfy our own often trivial interests. This is "speciesism," a prejudice akin to that displayed by the racist who discriminates between people on the basis of such morally irrelevant characteristics as the color of their skin.

Animal Liberation sold more than 400,000 copies, was translated into eight languages, and also led to some important practical changes. It has been described as "the bible" of the animals liberation movement—quite an irony, because Singer himself does not subscribe to any religious views and believes that ethics must be based on reason rather than on religion.

While Singer was best known for his book *Animal Liberation,* his standing as a first-rate philosopher and critical thinker does not rest on this book alone. His other books include *Democracy and Disobedience, The Expanding Circle, The Reproduction Revolution* (with Deane Wells), *Should the Baby Live* (with Helga Kuhse), and *How Are We To Live?* There are also two brief introductions to Marx and Hegel, as well as numerous anthologies and collections. In a later collection, *The Great Ape Project,* Singer and his coeditor, Paola Cavalleri, provide evidence that the great apes possess all the morally relevant attributes characteristic of persons and should hence be granted basic human rights.

The best introduction to Singer's work is *Practical Ethics,* first published in 1979 and revised in 1993. In this book Singer defended a consequentialist and utilitarian approach to ethics. The moral nature of actions, he argued, does not depend on adherence to simple moral rules, such as "Do not lie," but rather on the consequences of those actions. While lying is ordinarily wrong, it is not wrong where the telling of truth would result in great harm.

Singer taught and held appointments at various Australian and overseas universities. Beginning in 1977 he was professor of philosophy at Monash University in Melbourne, Australia, and after 1983, director or deputy director of the Monash University Centre for Human Bioethics.

Singer was not only a philosopher; he was also an activist. If there was something seriously wrong with the world, he wanted to change it. He lobbied governments and interest groups and participated in many demonstrations and protests that highlighted wrongful practices. To demonstrate the plight of battery hens, he sat in oversized cages on city squares, led peaceful marches, and held vigil in front of factory farms and fur shops. He got himself arrested for trespassing when he and some fellow animal liberationists tried to take photos of cruelly confined sows on a piggery partly owned by the prime minister of Australia.

A 1989 *Time Australia* profile on Singer bore the headline "Saintly or Satanic?" If Singer's fight for animal rights earned him the adjective "saintly," it was his writings in the field of bioethics that led some to think of him as "satanic." Because he believed that species is not a morally relevant boundary and that the like interests of all beings deserve equal moral consideration, Singer consistently condemned cruel treatment of animals while supporting destructive experimentation on early human *in vitro* embryos. The morally relevant difference, Singer argued, is that animals have interests because they can suffer; early human embryos, on the other hand, are nonsentient beings, cannot suffer, and hence have no interests.

These conclusions sent shock-waves through the Australian and international bioethical community, as did Singer's rejection of the traditional distinction between killing and letting die in the practice of medicine. It is widely believed that it is acceptable to allow a terminally ill patient to die or to refrain from resuscitating a seriously disabled newborn infant. But what, asked Singer, is the moral difference between deliberately allowing a patient to die and helping a patient to die? Is it not sometimes better to take active steps to end a patient's life, particularly if this prevents much unnecessary suffering during the dying process? "Taking active steps" means killing or euthanasia—a practice advocated by Singer under some clearly defined circumstances. Some people find his conclusions so abhorrent that they wish to describe Singer as "satanic." There were even attempts to prevent him from speaking and lecturing in Germany—a country still living in the shadows of the so-called "euthanasia" programs perpetrated under Hitler's Nazi regime.

In his *Rethinking Life and Death* (1994), Singer provoked more controversy when he elaborated on and amplified many of these these conclusions, arguing that, for example, people who no longer have brain function but are not legally dead may have vital organs removed. He argued the ethical propriety af numerous controversial positions on utilitarian grounds and characterized commonly held moral objections to his views as "speciesism." He proposed a radically new ethics based on the quality of life rather than on its sanctity.

Those who knew him well, who were his friends, his colleagues, or his fellow fighters for the rights of animals or the terminally ill, saw Singer as neither saintly nor satanic. They would describe him as a generous and warm-hearted social critic and reformer—and, of course, as one of the outstanding practical philosophers of our time.

Further Reading

The full text of the *Time Australia* profile of Peter Singer is in the issue of November 20, 1989. Books by Peter Singer include *Democracy and Disobedience* (1973); *Animal Liberation: A New Ethics for Our Treatment of Animals* (1975; second edition 1990); *Animal Rights and Human Obligations: An Anthology* (co-editor with Thomas Regan, 1976); *Practical Ethics* (1979; second edition 1993); *Marx* (1980); *Animal Factories* (co-author with James Mason, 1980); *The Expanding Circle: Ethics and Sociobiology* (1981); *Hegel* (1982); *Test-Tube Babies: A Guide to Moral Questions, Present Techniques, and Future Possibilities* (co-edited with William Walters, 1982); *The Reproduction Revolution: New Ways of Making Babies* (co-author with Deane Wells, 1984); *Should the Baby Live? The Problem of Handicapped Infants* (co-author with Helga Kuhse, 1985); *In Defence of Animals* (ed., 1985); *Ethical and Legal Issues in Guardianship Options for Intellectually Disadvantaged People* (co-author with Terry Carney, 1986); *Applied Ethics* (ed., 1986); *Animal Liberation: A Graphic Guide* (co-author with Lori Gruen, 1987); *Embryo Experimentation* (co-editor with Helga Kuhse, Stephen Buckle, Karen Dawson, and Pascal Kasimba, 1990); *A Companion to Ethics* (ed., 1991); *Save the Animals!* (Australian edition, co-author with Barbara Dover and Ingrid Newkirk, 1991); *The Great Ape Project: Equality Beyond Humanity* (co-editor with Paola Cavalieri, 1993); *How Are We To Live? Ethics in an Age of Self-Interest* (1993); and *Rethinking Life and Death* (1994). □

Vishwanath Pratap Singh

Vishwanath Pratap Singh (born 1931) became India's eighth prime minister on December 2, 1989, heading a minority National Front coalition government that ended a decade of continuous Congress Party rule. However, he was ousted less than a year later.

Born in the north Indian city of Allahabad on June 25, 1931, Vishwanath Pratap Singh was adopted by the *raja* (ruler) of Manda principality in the state of Uttar Pradesh. In 1955 he married the former Sita Kumari, who was a close confidante. They had two sons. Educated at the Universities of Allahabad and Poona, Singh held two bachelor's and one law degree. He became involved in politics as vice-president of the student union at Allahabad University, joined the Congress Party, and in 1969 was elected to the Uttar Pradesh legislative assembly.

Two years later Singh became the parliamentary representative from Phulpur constituency in the Uttar Pradesh. In 1974 the then prime minister, Indira Gandhi, named him Union deputy minister of commerce. Within two years he became the minister of commerce. After the Congress Party's defeat in 1977, Singh returned to Parliament as an opposition member until 1980, when the Congress Party once again won a majority. In 1980 he was named chief minister of Uttar Pradesh, where he earned a reputation for honesty in a state known to be difficult to administer with integrity. He resigned in 1982 after failing as promised to curb an upsurge of robberies and killings by gangs of thugs, among whose victims was his brother. Called back to the center, he returned as commerce minister and head of the Department of Supplies in 1983.

After Indira Gandhi's assassination in 1984, her son and successor, Rajiv Gandhi, named Singh as finance minister. In this capacity Singh gained a national and international reputation. Suspicious of the bookkeeping habits of India's major industrial companies, Singh ordered tax raids into the offices of some of the largest and even searched the homes of several chief executive officers, some of whom were close to the Congress Party. Not surprisingly, elements within the Congress and the business community opposed what they termed "heavy handed" tactics. However, Singh gained widespread approval for relaxing industrial controls, rules, and license requirements, thus liberalizing the business climate for Indian and foreign firms alike. He also took an active role internationally at negotiations on aid and trade policies, pressing for special concessions for less-developed countries.

The growth of Singh's personal popular support was viewed with trepidation among Rajiv Gandhi's supporters. Hence, in January 1987 Singh was transferred to the less conspicuous Defense portfolio, a post he held only a few months. Accusations surfaced regarding kickbacks paid to Indian agents for the acquisition of German submarines. Singh immediately ordered an investigation, which was crit-

icized by the prime minister, who said he had not been consulted. Singh resigned from the government, accusing the administration of a cover-up. Shortly thereafter he was expelled from the Congress Party.

In October 1987 Singh formed the Jan Morcha (People's Movement), which he hoped would become a rallying point for opposition parties, which initially paid it little attention. The next year he forged the National Front coalition, including in it the Janata Dal and several smaller parties. However, it was not until almost six months before the November 1989 elections that leaders from other major opposition parties decided that Singh himself was the best bet to defeat the Congress. A loose electoral alliance was formed between the National Front; the right wing Hindu fundamentalist Bharatiya Janata Party (BJP), although Singh refused to support its platform; several regional parties; the Socialists; and the Communists.

Singh campaigned actively on three platform planks. The first was a promise to invest more resources to combat rural poverty, a problem he accused the Gandhi administration of ignoring. Countering allegations that he himself was an aristocrat with vast land holdings without sympathy for the poor, he stressed his participation in the Bhoodan movement during the 1950s. That movement distributed donated land to the landless. In fact, he himself donated a large, well-endowed farm to the movement in 1957. The second plank was to clean up the scandals of the Gandhi administration. Further press disclosures had accused the administration of complicity in another arms pay-off scheme involving the Swedish firm Bofors. Singh promised to use the judicial process to prosecute the guilty, but without vindictiveness, and to create an independent ombudsman's office to handle public complaints. His supporters called him "Mr. Cleaner," juxtaposed against Gandhi's "Mr. Clean" label. The third plank was to make the state-owned radio and television service, which many felt had become a mouthpiece for the Congress, autonomous. Singh proved to be an effective campaigner, drawing larger crowds than any other candidate, especially in the north.

Final election results showed the Congress Party had lost its majority, winning only 192 seats (out of 525). Gandhi resigned after futile attempts to build a coalition. The National Front, which had won only 145 seats—with the Janata Dal making up 141 of those—was then asked to form the government. The electoral coalition needed to be transformed into a governing one: a formidable task since the parties involved ranged from the rightist BJP, with 88 seats, to the socialists and Communists (51 seats), and the National Front in the middle. Despite the qualms felt by the National Front and leftists about Hindu fundamentalism, they decided the BJP had to be included in the coalition in order to have a majority. After delicate negotiations spearheaded by Singh, the coalition was forged.

Singh's leadership was then challenged by two members of the Janata Dal: Devi Lal, chief minister of Haryana, and Chandra Shekhar, a Dal founder and long-standing Congress opponent, who were both interested in the prime ministership. After considerable back-stage maneuvering, Singh nominated Lal as prime minister, which, surprisingly, he declined and in turn nominated Singh, who won the vote. Lal was offered a newly created deputy prime ministership, which he accepted.

To hold this unwieldy coalition together proved to be a formidable task. Additionally, Singh faced secessionist movements in the states of Punjab and Kashmir. The latter threatened to erupt into armed conflict with Pakistan in early 1990 and exacerbated Hindu-Muslim conflict in the country. Known as a consensus builder, skilled negotiator, and a person of strong will, Singh's talents were considerable, but were stretched to their utmost and ultimately failed. Singh held the post as Prime Minister less than a year due to pressures from political rivals and an electorate increasingly polarized along caste and religious lines.

With frequent changes in the India government, Singh joined a growing group of ex-prime ministers. The number of ex-prime ministers had become so large by 1995 that concern for the cost of providing the security services of the Special Protection Group (SPG) became a major political issue. Singh, always putting the plight of the poor before his own, requested that the SPG, in order to save money, no longer provide security for him and his family. In a letter to, then Prime Minister H.D. Deve Gowda, Singh stated, "It will not be possible to accept an alternative cover if it puts the same burden on the treasury and the poor man as the SPG does." In January 1997 Singh announced he was taking a sabbatical from active politics.

Further Reading

There is little published material on Vishwanath Pratap Singh except for news and comment magazines. For example, Edward Desmond, "A brash new middle class is stirring up social revolution" in *TIME* (November 13, 1989), sets the stage for Singh's election victory, while Lisa Berger, "The Fall of the House of Nehru," *TIME* (December 11, 1989), reports the victory of Singh's party. Scattered information on Singh can be found in India newspapers such as *India Today* and *The Hindu*. □

David Alfaro Siqueiros

David Alfaro Siqueiros (1896-1974), one of the great Mexican mural painters, introduced technical innovations in his murals and easel paintings.

David Alfaro Siqueiros was born in Chihuahua. He was educated at the National School of Fine Arts, Mexico City, and did further study in Spain, Italy, and France. He served as an officer in Venustiano Carranza's army (1910-1916) and as military attaché in Paris (1917).

As one of the artists who collaborated in painting the murals for the staircase at the National Preparatory School, Mexico City (1922), Siqueiros became one of the founders of the mural movement in Mexico. He served as secretary general of the Painter's Syndicate and became one of the editors of its publication, *El machete*. With Amado de la Cueva he organized the Alliance of Painters in Guadalajara in 1925, and there he worked with De la Cueva and Carlos Orozco on decorations for the University of Guadalajara. Siqueiros served as a representative of various workers' organizations to Russia in 1928 and as a delegate to workers' meetings in South America in 1929. In 1931 he was exiled to Taxco for political reasons.

Siqueiros was a professor at the Chouinard School of Art, Los Angeles (1932-1933), where he developed new technical processes for outdoor murals, including the use of airbrushes to apply paint. Beginning in 1934 he devoted himself more and more to easel painting and carried out various experiments with Duco paint, for example, *Echo of a Scream* (1937).

Siqueiros was a delegate from the Congress of Mexican Artists to the Congress of Revolutionary Artists in New York City in 1936, and there he established a school in which he set forth his revolutionary artistic ideas. In 1937 he joined the Spanish Republican Army. From 1939 to 1944 he resided in Cuba and Chile.

The principal works by Siqueiros in Mexico City are the *Trial of Fascism* in the Electrical Workers Union building (1939), *Cuauhtémoc against the Myth* in Sonora No. 9 (1944), *New Democracy* in the Palace of Fine Arts (1945), *Patricians and Patricides* in the former Customs House (1945), *Ascent of Culture* in the National University of Mexico (1952-1956), and *Future Victory of Medical Science Against Cancer* in the Medical Center (1958). His best-known mural outside Mexico City, *Death to the Invader,* is in Chillán, Chile (1941-1942).

From 1960 to 1964 Siqueiros was imprisoned by the Mexican government for the crime of "social dissolution," but later he completed a mural commissioned by the Mexican government at Chapultepec Castle. In 1969 he spoke at the First National Painting Contest, in which some 7,000 artists from all parts of Mexico participated.

His next major work was *The March of Humanity* on the Congress Hall of Mexico City, one of the first buildings ever built specifically to house a mural. Incorporating different materials and methods, it united architecture, sculpture, and painting in what was called "a baroque and futuristic extrapolation of realism." In 1968 he became president of the Academy of Arts in Mexico City. A retrospective of his work was shown at the Center for Inter-American Relations, and a three-dimensional mural was permanently installed in the Siqueiros Center in Mexico City.

Further Reading

For more information on Siqueiros, see Shifra Goldman, *Contemporary Mexican Painting in Time of Change,* Austin, (1981). Jean Charlot, *The Mexican Mural Renaissance, 1920-1925* (1963), is an excellent source for Siqueiros's early career. Material on Siqueiros is also in Bernard S. Myers, *Mexican Painting in Our Time* (1956); Alma M. Reed, *The Mexican Muralists* (1960); and Justino Fernández, *A Guide to Mexican Art: From Its Beginnings to the Present* (2d ed. 1961; trans. 1969). □

John Joseph Sirica

U.S. District Court Judge John Joseph Sirica (1904-1992) came to national prominence when he presided over the Watergate affair trials and confronted President Richard Nixon's claim of executive privilege used to protect private presidential tapes.

John Joseph Sirica was born on March 19, 1904, in Waterbury, Connecticut. He was one of the two sons born to Ferdinand ("Fred") and Rose (Zinno) Sirica. His father was an Italian immigrant; his mother was born in New Haven. Sirica's early childhood was spent moving around the South, as his father sought a warm climate for health reasons and employment. Limited finances forced Sirica to work as a boy to help support his family.

Sirica's family settled in Washington, D.C., when he was around 14 years old. He enrolled in the George Washington Law School at the age of 17, never having attended college. Finding his studies too difficult, he left school after one month. Sirica learned to box at the Young Men's Christian Association (YMCA) and supported himself by working as a physical education and boxing instructor for the Knights of Columbus and fighting in occasional boxing matches. Determined to embark on a professional career, Sirica returned to the study of law and earned an LL.B. degree in 1926 from Georgetown University Law School. Later in his distinguished career he was to be awarded ten honorary degrees. He was admitted to the District of Columbia bar shortly after graduation.

Sirica's long legal career began with private practice in 1927. He was appointed an assistant U.S. attorney for the District of Columbia on August 1, 1930, and resigned that post to return to private practice on January 15, 1934. While building his career as a trial lawyer, he became active in Republican Party politics. He worked in five presidential campaigns, beginning in 1936.

President Dwight Eisenhower appointed Sirica to the U.S. District Court for the District of Columbia. He was sworn in on April 2, 1957. Sirica presided over a wide range of complicated and controversial civil and criminal cases and earned a reputation as a tough, law and order, and hardworking judge of high integrity. He was nicknamed "Maximum John" to reflect his inclination to give the longest sentences permitted by the laws.

Sirica became chief judge of the U.S. District Court through seniority on April 2, 1971. The new post gave him administrative responsibilities, including the right to assign special cases to particular judges and to oversee the work of the federal grand juries. In this capacity he assigned to himself the task of presiding over the Watergate cases.

The Watergate affair began on June 17, 1972, with a break-in and electronic wiretapping attempt at the Democratic National Committee headquarters located in a Washington, D.C., residential and office complex called the Watergate. Seven people were arrested. Investigation

showed that there were ties between the burglars and President Richard Nixon's reelection committee.

The trials began on January 10, 1973. Sirica used his power to question witnesses to draw out more information, rather than sit passively watching the attorneys do all the questioning. He also carefully used his power of sentencing to stimulate the convicted men to assist investigators probing the range of illegal activities. These tactics contributed to the gradual uncovering of evidence in the complex political scandal.

The action of most historic value was Sirica's confrontation with President Nixon. This battle began on July 16, 1973, when Alexander Butterfield, a former White House staff member, disclosed that Nixon had been secretly taping conversations in the president's offices. Archibald Cox, appointed as special prosecutor to head the Watergate Special Prosecution Force, went to Sirica's court to seek a subpoena for eight tapes that contained specific White House conversations about the Watergate affair. Although a subpoena had rarely been served on a president, Sirica agreed to issue one. On July 26 the judge received a letter from Nixon in response. In the letter Nixon invoked the doctrine of executive privilege, claiming that the president was not subject to judicial orders to compel action by subpoena.

Sirica was concerned about stepping off into new legal territory and about the effects on Nixon if the tapes were disclosed. Yet, relying on very old precedent, he reached a decision about the next step in this confrontation. On August 29, 1973, he ordered the president to give him the tapes for his own private hearing. In this way Sirica tried to recognize the privilege to protect presidential privacy but also to uphold a principle that the courts could decide what was privileged. Sirica proposed to listen and select which parts of the tapes should be given to the grand jury. The White House appealed the decision. Sirica's opinion was upheld by the circuit Court of Appeals on October 12, 1973. On October 22, Sirica was told by the president's lawyer that the tapes would be submitted.

The confrontation over presidential privilege continued, however. On April 16, 1974, Leon Jaworski, who succeeded Cox as special prosecutor, asked Sirica to subpoena an additional 64 tapes. The judge, thinking the subpoena questions resolved, agreed. The White House refused to honor that subpoena. Jaworski made a dramatic decision, and on May 24 he asked the U.S. Supreme Court for a direct review and immediate consideration of the case, thereby bypassing the appeals process and saving time. The Supreme Court justices, in an unusual July session, upheld the order and issued their milestone ruling interpreting executive privilege on July 24. The public disclosure of the taped conversations was a factor in forcing Nixon to resign from office on August 9, 1974.

Sirica continued to preside over other Watergate trials and sentencing in the succeeding months. When he finally finished the last of that legal business, in the fall of 1977, he had devoted five years to the Watergate affair.

Sirica's treatment of the Watergate trials brought him national recognition. He was chosen "1973 Man of the Year" by *Time* Magazine. A grassroots effort was made to seek a presidential nomination for Sirica in 1976, but he declined to run for that office.

As required by federal law, Sirica stepped down as chief judge of the court on March 18, 1974, having reached his 70th birthday, but he remained a full-time member of the bench. He became senior judge of the court, entering a period of semi-retirement, on November 1, 1977. He chose full retirement October 1, 1986. Sirica lived with his wife, Lucile M. (Camalier), whom he married on February 26, 1952. They raised two daughters and one son. In 1992, at the age of 88, Sirica died of cardiac arrest in Washington, DC.

Further Reading

The judge's perspectives on his life and judicial motives are found in his autobiography, John J. Sirica, *To Set the Record Straight* (1979). This can be supplemented by reading "Standing Firm for the Primacy of Law," *Time* (January 7, 1974). Elaboration on the Watergate court cases and subpoenas can be found in James Doyle, *Not Above the Law* (1977) and in Leon Jaworski, *The Right and the Power* (1976). A nice final tribute to Sirica, *John Sirica: A Man for His Season,* was written by Larry Martz for *Newsweek* (August 24, 1992). ☐

Jean Charles Léonard Simonde de Sismondi

Jean Charles Léonard Simonde de Sismondi (1773-1842) was a Swiss-born historian and political economist. In his histories of France and Italy he placed particular emphasis on the development of constitutional government.

Born on May 9, 1773, Simonde de Sismondi spent a happy childhood on the Swiss country estate of his wealthy aristocratic family. He was educated by his family and by tutors to an ideal of noble service for his fellowman. The family's money had been invested in French public bonds, however, and the collapse of these funds before and during the French Revolution brought about the family's financial ruin. Sismondi worked as a clerk in a countinghouse in Lyons and proved to be a highly competent economist until the fervor of the Revolution drove the family back to Geneva in 1792. Briefly imprisoned there as aristocrats, although they had strong republican sympathies, the Sismondi family fled to England.

During these years of intense financial and political turmoil, Sismondi was constantly at work compiling a vast amount of material collected in notebooks under the title "Researches on the Constitutions of Free Peoples." While in England, he was an industrious student of English constitutional and economic practice and, for a brief time, an advocate of Adam Smith's laissez-faire policies.

Forced back to the warmer climate of the Continent by the illness of his mother, Sismondi settled his family on a farm in Italy, and from 1795 to 1800 he worked by day as a farmer and by night continued his scholarly research. Cognizant now of the periodic unemployment and urban misery brought about by the first and second generations of the industrial revolution in England, Sismondi focused his attention on how free governments, preferably constitutional monarchies, could maintain political and economic freedom.

These years of difficult and strenuous labor resulted in a remarkable series of works. Sismondi published numerous studies of "The Italian Republic" (1807-1820), *The Literature of the South of Europe* (1813), *New Principles of Political Economy* (1819), and the first volume of *History of the French* (1821). In his *Political Economy,* for which he is most famous, he tried to confront the problems created by the industrial revolution. He did not blame technology for the evils of industrialism, nor did he think that socialist proposals were realistic. He recommended that governments, preferably constitutional monarchies, assist the economically weak and poor by legalizing trade unions, establishing standards and wages, abolishing child labor, and requiring factories to provide pensions.

Sismondi spent the last years of his life in Geneva preparing new editions of his writings, finishing his study of the French, and serving as a member of the Geneva Assembly, always a spokesman for freedom with order. He died of stomach cancer on June 25, 1842.

Further Reading

A study of Sismondi's work is Mao-Lan Tuan, *Simonde de Sismondi as an Economist* (1927). A discussion of his life and work is in George P. Gooch, *History and Historians in the Nineteenth Century* (1913; rev. ed. 1952; new preface 1959). □

Nontsikelelo Albertina Sisulu

Nontsikelelo Albertina Sisulu (born 1918) was one of the most important women leaders of the anti-apartheid resistance in South Africa. She was a leader of the African National Congress Women's League and the Federation of South African Women in the 1950s. With the imprisonment of her husband, Walter Sisulu, in 1964, she carried on the resistance, becoming in the 1980s a founder and co-president of the United Democratic Front, contributing to the eventual release of the ANC prisoners.

Albertina Sisulu was born in 1918 among the Xhosa people in the Tsomo district of the Transkei, South Africa. Orphaned in youth, her ambition to be a teacher was frustrated by the need to support her younger siblings. She later finished grade school and trained as a nurse at the Johannesburg Non-European Hospital. In later life she attributed to this youthful self-denial and discipline her manifest strength, steadfastness, and courage through a lifetime of political struggle, supporting her seven children while her husband served a life sentence with his colleague Nelson Mandela and other leaders of the African National Congress of South Africa (ANC).

She met her future husband, Walter Sisulu, in Johannesburg in the early 1940s. Through their courtship she became politically active herself, attending with him the founding discussions of the Youth League, which would transform the moderate ANC into a militant nationalist resistance movement. In July 1944 they were married and settled in the little cinder block house at Orlando Township, Soweto, that would be their home for 45 years. They formed a political union as well. In 1949, as the movement geared up for the anti-apartheid resistance campaigns, Walter Sisulu became the ANC's first full-time general secretary. For this he had given up his income-earning job, and Albertina Sisulu assumed the task of chief family bread-winner.

Over the next 15 years her husband was imprisoned eight times, banned, placed under house-arrest, tried twice for treason, and finally incarcerated for life with Nelson Mandela and six other ANC leaders in 1964. Through these harrowing years Albertina Sisulu had five children and adopted her deceased sister-in-law's two children, supporting her family on her earnings as a nurse. But more, she also became a major political figure in her own right, herself arrested, banned, and imprisoned. Already prominent in the ANC Women's League since 1948, she helped found the non-racial, non-party Federation of South African Women (FSAW) in 1954, later becoming its president. In this capacity she led huge demonstrations against the extension of the hated pass laws to women and against the introduction of the infamous Bantu education system. Her opposition to women's passes brought her first jail sentence in 1958 with Winnie Mandela and others, including Mandela's new baby, which nearly died before they were released.

By the 1960s the women's movement, like the ANC, was being crushed by shootings, arrests, trials, and bans. In 1963, with Walter Sisulu underground in the sabotage campaign of Umkhonto we Sizwe ("Spear of the Nation," the ANC's organization for armed struggle), Albertina Sisulu was also held for three months in solitary confinement under the new 90-day detention law designed to crush opponents without the need for trials. During Walter Sisulu's subsequent treason trial and conviction in 1964, she led the crowds in singing the ANC anthem and saluting the convicted men as the police van carried them off to life imprisonment. Going later with Winnie Mandela on their first semi-annual half-hour visit to their husbands, Albertina Sisulu was reported to have exclaimed, "Oh, our men are shrinking here! . . . But their spirit is strong." And so was

Albertina Sisulu's as she and her children carried on their family commitment to keep resistance alive.

Seventeen years of continuous bans followed—longer than anyone else's in South Africa—including ten years of dusk-to-dawn house arrest. Her livelihood was saved by the intercession of the Johannesburg Nursing Association and financial assistance from the International Defence and Aid Fund for Southern Africa (IDAF). (The IDAF had secretly provided financial help to the family while Walter Sisulu was imprisoned). By the early 1980s, after the 1976 Soweto uprisings, the women's movement, like the ANC, began to re-emerge as the government grappled with massive unrest and attempted cautious reforms.

Albertina Sisulu was arrested again in 1983 and sentenced to four years' imprisonment for leading ANC songs, distributing literature, and displaying its black, green, and gold flag at the funeral of FSAW stalwart Rose Mbele. She managed to get freedom pending appeal and suspension of half the sentence. Meanwhile, in 1983 Albertina Sisulu had helped found the United Democratic Front (UDF), incorporating hundreds of anti-apartheid groups, and was elected one of its three co-presidents from her jail cell. The UDF's purpose was to oppose a new government-inspired constitution that claimed to provide for non-white power sharing (by co-opting the minority Coloureds and Indians) but was immediately recognized as a sham, for it excluded the Black Africans from any participation and kept white supremacy intact.

The formation of the UDF came at an historic turning point. Seemingly triumphant with this cosmetically reformed but re-entrenched apartheid, President P. W. Botha's government now faced a deepening crisis of popular resistance and disorder from 1984 onwards. The government, declaring emergency powers, answered with violent police and military force amid a storm of outrage. Shootings, whippings, thousands of arrests, mass evictions, and mob rule in Black townships by leaderless Blacks attacking police, local officials, and each other produced a profound change of mood within the country and internationally.

Following the horrific destruction by government order of the Crossroads squatter township near Cape Town in 1985, Albertina Sisulu and other UDF leaders were arrested and charged, ironically, with fomenting violent revolution. The case was dismissed for lack of credible evidence. Yet another mass banning came in February 1988, when the UDF, 16 other organizations, and 18 persons, including Albertina Sisulu, now aged 70, were again restricted. With two of her grown children in exile, one detained in the country for over a year, two grandchildren imprisoned, and Walter Sisulu, of course, still under life sentence, the Sisulu family had surely kept faith with its commitment at a fearful price. But the new round of repressions merely signaled the final bankruptcy of government policy. As conditions within the country and in its international position deteriorated with intensified economic sanctions and mounting alarm in business, political, church, and university circles, the call went up more insistently than ever before: seek genuine negotiations or face catastrophe.

Signs multiplied in 1989 that Botha's term of power was nearing its end with his replacement as party leader by the more flexible Frederik W. de Klerk, who became president in September. A clear signal of the impending recognition of Albertina Sisulu's own prominence as a leader and her symbolic importance as Walter Sisulu's wife: the United States and British Governments invited her to visit President Bush and Prime Minister Thatcher "as the patroness of the principal black opposition group in South Africa." Despite her banning order she was granted her first passport by a South African Government anxious to improve its image in the eyes of the world. Before this time no United States president had ever met with an authentic South African Black nationalist leader. But clearly the United States, seeking to restore its credibility among Blacks at home and abroad, now recognized the UDF and by implication the ANC as the essential partners in the negotiated settlement judged necessary to save the future of South Africa. Now also the incarcerated ANC leaders loomed larger than ever as the authentic negotiators, enhanced by their principled refusal to accept Botha's earlier offer of release on condition they accept political immobility. Their essential commitment to moderation and non-racialism was also their great strength: Mary Benson once called them "the African Patriots"—patriots of a common society for all South Africans. Albertina Sisulu and her delegation stood four-square on this proposition. Their message to the American president was that peace could only come with the release of prisoners, the end of repressions, and a national constitutional convention, and to that end he must stick to sanctions and pressure the South African Government to talk on this basis.

On October 14, 1989, came the great turn-about. President de Klerk lifted all restrictions on Albertina Sisulu, and the next day her husband and seven others were released after 26 years of confinement. Nelson Mandela would not come out until the next February, but the die was cast. Consistent with her long struggle, constant and indomitable, she expressed her personal happiness, but it would not be enough. Her husband's freedom would "not minimize the spirit and actions of defiance among our people . . . until we bring the government to a genuine negotiated settlement . . . for a full democratic, participatory non-racial South Africa for all."

This was the hallmark of Albertina Sisulu's principled, selfless, and courageous life: unwavering commitment to the non-racial philosophy of human equality and dignity for all in a common society. She held, miraculously, no bitterness toward the whites of her country as people, distinguishing carefully between the apartheid regime and the people. As she stated in 1987, "The Nationalist Government . . . are the enemies . . . not the White people. White people are just like you and me . . . We are all here to stay. All we want is power-sharing . . . to elect our own government," for a non-racial, democratic united South Africa.

In 1992 as the ANC Women's League Deputy President, Albertina Sisulu proposed that South African women should participate in shaping a Woman's Charter that would be included in an ANC's proposal on gender rights for the new constitution. Later that year, she discussed her belief that education must play a vital role in forming the future of South Africa. She believed that apartheid could only be abolished if women worked together.

In 1994 Albertina Sisulu joined her husband when he returned to Robben Island where he had been imprisoned for 20 years, where he was starring in a film on the International Defence and Aid Fund for Southern Africa (IDAF). Later that year, when Nelson Mandela was elected the first black president of South Africa, she was elected to the South African Parliament. In April 1996 she was honored at the annual dinner of MESAB (Medical Education for South African Blacks, Inc.) in Washington D.C. In 1997 she joined the ANC in the celebration of her husband's 85th birthday. Both she and her husband will be remembered as being dedicated veterans of South Africa's anti-apartheid struggles.

Further Reading

A substantial interview with Albertina Sisulu by Ameen Akhalwaya was published in *Africa Report* (September-October 1987); another by Diana Russell, *Lives of Courage: Women for a New South Africa* (1989); and two brief ones in *Ms.* magazine (April 1986 and October 1988). See also a short reference article in Sheila Gastrow, *Who's Who in South African Politics No. 2* (Johannesburg: 1987). Useful references in the context of the anti-apartheid movement were found in Helen Joseph, *Side by Side: The Autobiography of Helen Joseph* (1986); Mary Benson, *Nelson Mandela: The Man and the Movement* (1986); and Benson's autobiography, *A Far Cry* (London: 1989).

For events in the 1980s see the Institute of Race Relations annual *Race Relations Survey,* especially for 1984, 1987/1988, and 1988/1989. Interesting press reports on Albertina Sisulu's 1989 delegation to Washington and the release of her husband appeared in *The New York Times* (June 17, 1989); *The Los Angeles Times* (June 29 and October 20, 1989); *Atlanta Journal* (July 8, 1989); *Washington Post* (June 30 and July 25, 1989); and *Boston Globe* (October 14, 1989). See also *Ms.* magazine (July-August 1992); *The Times* (October 2, 1992); *The Guardian* (January 25, 1994); and *Maclean's* (May 2, 1994). Information can also be accessed on the internet by doing a search for "Albertina Sisulu" (August 20, 1997). □

Walter Max Ulyate Sisulu

Walter Max Ulyate Sisulu (born 1912) was one of the most important leaders of the African National Congress (ANC) of South Africa. In the 1940s he was a founder of the Congress Youth League, which led the ANC into militant resistance to apartheid. He became general secretary of the ANC and a chief strategist and organizer of the Defiance Campaign in the 1950s. Although a political prisoner for many years, he remained influential and instrumental in the ultimate end to apartheid.

Walter Sisulu was born in 1912 in the South African "native reserve" territory of the Transkei (granted independence in 1976, but reincorporated into the Republic of South Africa in 1994), among the Xhosa-speaking section of the Southern Nguni people. His family were African peasants and members of the Anglican Church. He himself was of racially mixed ancestry. He attended school up to standard IV (the equivalent of American grade 5 or 6), but later in life advanced his education through self-study and correspondence. Unlike most prominent Black leaders of his day, he had neither formal higher education nor professional training, but his intelligence and drive carried him to the foremost rank of African nationalist leadership in the 1940s and 1950s in company with Nelson Mandela and Oliver Tambo.

Sisulu began his working life in 1929 when he migrated to Johannesburg, like so many Africans before and since. He worked in a dairy, in the gold mines, in a kitchen, and as a factory hand during the 1930s. He brought to these experiences a resentment of white paternalism and a political militancy which found expression in labor activism and strike organizing. In 1940 he joined the African National Congress (ANC), then being rejuvenated by the well-known leader A. B. Xuma.

Dissatisfied with the cautious middle class respectability and conservatism of the ANC leadership, he collaborated with other young militants in organizing the Congress Youth League and helped formulate its "Programme of Action" calling for non-violent civil disobedience, strikes, and boycotts to resist South Africa's traditional segregation as well

as new apartheid laws imposed by the post-war Afrikaner Nationalist government.

With the replacement of Xuma with a successor picked by the Youth League—James Moroka—in 1949, Sisulu became the ANC's first full-time secretary-general, conducting the day-to-day operations of the ANC. He served also in this capacity under Moroka's successor, Albert Luthuli, and was responsible for organizing and directing the Defiance Campaign of civil disobedience in the early 1950s during which he was repeatedly arrested, jailed, and put under ban or house arrest.

Sisulu's initial Black nationalist exclusivism softened in these years as he worked with the South African Indian Congress and the small left-wing white Congress of Democrats in a multi-racial umbrella organization called the Congress Alliance. In 1953 he accepted an invitation arranged by Communist members of the Congress of Democrats to visit Europe, Russia, and China with other African leaders. These experiences reinforced a growing interest in socialist ideas, although he was never a Communist himself.

By the mid-1950s Sisulu, in company with other leaders, was subjected to ever-stricter police control and banning orders which reduced his active participation in the resistance movement and weakened its organization, but he continued his leadership behind the scenes. Then in 1956 he was arrested and tried for treason with 156 others. The treason trial lasted until 1961 when, after acquittal, he resumed "illicit" political activity. By this time the ANC resistance movement had come to harrowing days of ideological division with the splitting away of the Pan Africanist Congress under Robert Sobukwe, followed by violent police repression culminating in the Sharpeville massacre of June 1960. Defying house arrest, Sisulu joined Mandela and others in an underground organization called Umkonto we Sizwe (Spear of the Nation) committed to carrying on the resistance in a sabotage campaign. In 1963 he was captured, convicted of sabotage and revolutionary activity, sentenced to life imprisonment, and incarcerated in the political prison on Robben Island in Table Bay. In 1984 he, Mandela, and others still in captivity were moved to the Pollsmoor Prison in Cape Town.

Sisulu's wife Albertina and son Zwelakhe were also harassed by South African authorities for their activism in support of political and economic freedom.

Despite his militancy and radical tendencies, Sisulu was a political pragmatist and essentially a moderate. His early outlook was formed in his Transkei youth under the influence of Xhosa historical traditions and the millenarian movement of Wellington Buthelezi, who was partly inspired by the West Indian Pan Africanist Marcus Garvey. But Sisulu abandoned his early Africanist racial exclusiveness when experience, reflection, and his pragmatic nature led him to a racially inclusive vision of South Africa's future, rooted in the political morality of the Western democratic tradition. Sticking to the Congress Alliance and its multi-racial ideal, he opposed the Pan Africanist split under Robert Sobukwe. With other leaders of the ANC he believed that their non-violent resistance would eventually undermine the hard-line Afrikaner Nationalist apartheid government and persuade disillusioned whites to cooperate in a common South African society with equal rights for all. Tragically, the power, conviction, and ruthless determination of the apartheid regime remained virtually unshaken for yet another generation. But the challenge raised by Sisulu and his colleagues remained the unanswered question of the future, and the issues and alternatives they then courageously and steadfastly defined ultimately prevailed.

Sisulu was released from prison at the end of 1989 by Frederik W. de Klerk, P. W. Botha's successor. In 1991, he was elected ANC deputy president and was a leading figure in the negotiations with de Klerk's government for a transition to a non-racial South Africa. In January 1992, Sisulu, along with colleagues Oliver Tambo and Nelson Mandela, received Isitwalandwe Medals on the 80th anniversary of the ANC Bloemfontein.

In 1994 Sisulu returned to Robben Island where he had been imprisoned for over 20 years, to star in a film on the International Defence and Aid Fund for Southern Africa (IDAF). He officially retired later in 1994, after seeing his friend, Nelson R. Mandela, inaugurated as president. In May 1997, Sisulu was honored at an 85th birthday celebration.

Further Reading

Sisulu figured prominently in political histories of South Africa and its African National Congress, such as Peter Walshe, *The Rise of African Nationalism in South Africa: The African National Congress, 1912-1952* (1971); Mary Benson, *The African Patriots: The Story of the African National Congress of South Africa* (London, 1963); Tom Lodge, *Black Politics in South Africa Since 1945* (Johannesburg, 1983); and the documentary history of African politics by Thomas Karis and Gwendolen Carter, *From Protest to Challenge . . .*, Vols. 2, 3, and 4 (1973 and 1977). Sisulu's biography appeared in Norbert Brockman's, *An African Biographical Dictionary* (ABC-CLIO, Inc., 1994). See also *The Guardian,* January 25, 1995. □

Ndabaningi Sithole

Ndabaningi Sithole (born 1920) is a teacher, clergyman, and politician who played a critical role in the early nationalist movement in Zimbabwe (formerly Southern Rhodesia). A leading African intellectual, he epitomized the plight of Africans during the period of the former Southern Rhodesia's system of racial discrimination.

Ndabaningi Sithole was born on July 21, 1920, in the rural area of Nyamanandhlovu. He was brought up in a pagan household and spent his early years in a typically tribal environment in an isolated part of the country. He was seven years old before he first saw a white person. The family moved to Shabani in 1930, and in 1932 Sithole started attending a school run by British Methodist missionaries. His father, however, opposed the idea, and Sithole left the school at the end of 1932 and became a servant in a white home. But the urge to become educated remained, and in 1935 he defied his father's wishes and ran away to enter the Dadaya Mission school, which was controlled by the Reverend Garfield Todd, who was subsequently to become prime minister of Southern Rhodesia.

Despite his poverty and backwardness in many subjects, Sithole applied himself determinedly and ultimately succeeded. Becoming a Christian, he acquired the National Junior Certificate (Standard Eight), which was then a considerable achievement for an African. He then returned to the Dadaya Mission as a teacher and managed, by private study, to prepare for a Matriculation Exemption Certificate. Also by private study he managed to acquire a bachelor of arts degree through the University of South Africa.

By 1950 Sithole was torn between the vocation of teaching and the Christian ministry. Even as a teacher he had become a Methodist lay preacher, but for over eight years he had been unable to bring himself to enter the Church fully. Finally, in 1953, he did commit himself and applied to the Mission Council of the American Board Mission of Southern Rhodesia, which accepted his application. Under their aegis he spent more than three years in the United States, studying, lecturing, and preaching in many parts of the country. On his return to Southern Rhodesia he became principal of the Chikore Central Primary School and an ordained minister.

Work as a Nationalist

Sithole's attention had become increasingly focused upon politics. In 1957 he completed a short book called *African Nationalism* (published in 1959), which was a very moderate, humane, and balanced account of African grievances in the white supremacist system of Southern Rhodesia. He made it clear that he believed firmly in interracial cooperation. In August 1959 he was elected president of the African Teachers' Association, and from this post he entered politics. Early in 1960 he joined the African nationalist movement, the National Democratic party (NDP), led by Joshua Nkomo, and rapidly rose to the position of treasurer and membership in its executive. By this time he had been forced to resign from his teaching post and was a full-time politician. In December 1960 he was sent to London as an NDP delegate to the Federal Review Conference.

In the 1960s Sithole's career was profoundly affected by the growing authoritarianism of the Southern Rhodesian regime and by the serious split in the nationalist movement. On Dec. 9, 1962, the government proscribed the NDP, but ten days afterward a new nationalist organization, the Zimbabwe African Peoples Union (ZAPU), was founded. Sithole automatically became a leading member, and he represented it abroad. Dissatisfaction with Nkomo's leadership mounted, and Sithole emerged as the leader of a rival faction. Nkomo was accused of indecisiveness and of reluctance to force a confrontation with the government. The split occurred on July 6, 1963, and, despite attempts at reconciliation, it proved to be unbreachable. Sithole was out of the country at the time, but shortly after his return he and his followers founded a new political movement, the Zimbabwe African National Union (ZANU).

In December 1963 Sithole was sentenced to 12 months' imprisonment for distributing an allegedly subversive letter calling upon Africans physically to resist an illegal declaration of independence by the Southern Rhodesian government; but he appealed successfully against the conviction. In February 1964 Sithole, along with hundreds of others, was restricted by the government and placed in a remote detention camp; and in August both ZANU and ZAPU were banned.

Sithole remained in detention for five years. On Feb. 12, 1969, he was sentenced to six years of imprisonment for involvement in a plot to assassinate Ian Smith, prime minister of the illegal Rhodesian regime, and two of his ministers. The conviction rested largely on the authorship of a letter planning the assassinations. A police forensic scientist testified that it had been written by Sithole. Sithole denied this and declared that he had been framed. After sentence had been passed, he said, "I wish publicly to dissociate my name in thought, word and deed from any subversive activities, from any terrorist activities, and from any form of violence."

After his release from prison in 1974, Sithole lived in exile in Zambia with a section of the African National Council, but later withdrew his faction of ZANU from it. In 1976 he attended the Rhodesian Constitutional Conference and served as a member of the Transitional Executive Council in preparation for the long-sought transfer of power to the black majority in Zimbabwe-Rhodesia in 1978-79. After serving that year as a member of Parliament, he ceased to play a substantial role after his long-time rival Robert Mugabe became prime minister in 1980 and established the first free African government in Zimbabwe.

In 1987 he sought refuge in the United States, fearing that Mugabe was trying to kill him. The two had competed for the presidency of ZANU-PF during its early days, and their rivalry intensified when Mugabe took over the party during the guerrilla war against white-ruled Rhodesia. Sithole returned to Zimbabwe in 1991, when he occupied one of two opposition seats in a parliament overwhelmingly controlled by the ZANU-PF party. In 1994 he organized a faction to contest the one-party presidential elections, which Mugabe had again easily won. The following year he was arrested in connection with an alleged plot to assassinate Mugabe, and his weak opposition party was accused of supporting rebels based in nearby Mozambique. Sithole withdrew as an opposition candidate in the 1996 elections, when Mugabe was again elected unopposed.

Sithole continues to be an active member of the opposition Zimbabwe African National Union Ndonga party. In 1997 he publicly reasserted his belief in coups as a legitimate instrument of change in Africa when constitutional means fail. He condemned the Organization of African Unity and its chairman, President Mugabe, as having "no relevance for an independent Africa, which is faced by . . . problems which include continental insecurity and control of the economy by former colonial masters."

Further Reading

Sketch: Sithole's *Hammer & Sickle: Africa's Great Problem* (1991) and *Roots of a Revolution* (1977) are out of print. Sithole's *African Nationalism* (1959; 2d ed. 1968) discusses his own career as well as larger issues. Collected speeches: *In Defence of a Birthright,* Norman Bethune Institute, 1975. His role in the early days of African nationalism is described in "Nbadaningi Sithole, Garfield Todd and the Dadaya School Strike of 1947" in *Journal of Southern African Studies,* June 1992. Profiles: *An African Biographical Dctionary,* ABC-CLIO, 1994; Glickman, Harvey, *Political Leaders of Contemporary Africa South of the Sahara,* Greenwood, 1992; Lipschutz, Mark, *Dictionary of African Historical Biography,* Univ. of California, 1987. His career is discussed in Nathan M. Shamuyarira, *Crisis in Rhodesia* (1965); James Barber, *Rhodesia: The Road to Rebellion* (1967); and B. Vulindlela Mtshali, *Rhodesia: Background to Conflict* (1967). □

Sitting Bull

The American Indian Sitting Bull (ca. 1834-1890), a Hunkpapa Sioux medicine man and chief, was the political leader of his tribe at the time of the Custer massacre and during the Sioux War of 1875-1876.

Sitting Bull was born on the Grand River in South Dakota. He gained some fame as a warrior while in his 20s, but he chose to become a medicine man and a political leader rather than a war chief. He hated the white men and their encroachment on Indian lands. Therefore he stayed off the reservation as much as possible. By the mid-1870s his influence had been extended through several Sioux subtribes and to the Cheyenne and Arapaho Indians. He headed the combined war council of these nations although he was not a war chief.

After miners encroached on Sioux territory during the Black Hills gold rush in 1875, Sitting Bull led his people from the reservation and chose to fight. Warned by Gen. Alfred Terry to return to the reservation, Sitting Bull replied, "You won't need any guides; you can find me easily; I won't run away."

Gen. George Custer and the 7th Cavalry found Sitting Bull and several thousand warriors at the Little Bighorn River on June 25, 1876. Sitting Bull did not take part in the fighting that day but made medicine while Gall and Crazy Horse annihilated Custer and 264 men. Custer's death, however, changed nothing. Gen. Terry and Gen. George Crook pressured the Sioux, and Sitting Bull was forced to lead his people to Canada. Conditions there were no better, and Sitting Bull's following dwindled, especially after 1879, when the U.S. government offered amnesty to those Indians who would surrender. In July 1881 Sitting Bull, with 187 followers, arrived at Ft. Buford to accept the government's offer.

Placed on the Standing Rock Reservation in the Dakota Territory, Sitting Bull found himself famous. During his residence in Canada, stories had circulated in the United States that the Sioux leader was white, a graduate of the U.S. Military Academy at West Point, and a Catholic. In 1878 a book, *The Works of Sitting Bull,* was published ascribing Latin and French poems to his authorship.

When the "ghost dance craze" swept the Indian reservations in 1890, Sitting Bull took no part in it. But soldiers arrested him that December for fear he would lead the Sioux on the warpath. In the fight that followed, Sitting Bull was fatally shot, possibly by accident, possibly by design. He was buried at Ft. Yates, N.Dak., but in 1953 his body was reinterred near Mobridge, S. Dak.

Further Reading

Stanley Vestal, *Sitting Bull: Champion of the Sioux: A Biography* (1932), draws upon both Indian and white sources to present a very sympathetic picture of the chief. Robert M. Utley, *The Last Days of the Sioux Nation* (1963), contains a scholarly assessment, and James McLaughlin, *My Friend the Indian* (1910), provides a contemporary assessment. □

Dame Edith Sitwell

The English poet and critic Dame Edith Sitwell (1887-1964) was one of England's dominating literary figures for half a century and its most eminent woman poet.

Edith Sitwell was born in Scarborough on Sept. 7, 1887, into a family of landed gentry. Her brothers, Osbert and Sacheverell, both younger, also became celebrated writers. She was privately educated on the family estate at Renishaw until she entered the literary circles of London shortly before the beginning of World War I. Her first volume, *The Mother and Other Poems,* was published in 1915, and the following year she began to edit an annual anthology, *Wheels,* which set out to repudiate the comfortable, familiar, English sentimentalities of the Georgian poets. Its bizarre, satirical, self-conscious verse anticipated that judgment of the contemporary scene that was to be perfectly articulated shortly thereafter by T.S. Eliot in *The Wasteland.* Edith Sitwell was thus in the vanguard of the movement that radically changed English poetry at the end of World War I.

Edith Sitwell's early poems, which intermingle startling images of the demonic, the mechanical, and the natural world and employ as their favorite figure the clown or the metaphor of the harlequinade, present an elaborately distorted, nonnaturalistic picture of a world gone mad. Yet they also show evidence of the richness of color and sensuality to which the poet had responded as a rather solitary child and that influenced her poetry throughout her life. They also exhibit an extraordinary sense of rhythm which, with other experiments in sound, proved to be Edith Sitwell's most marked and controversial gift to contemporary poetry.

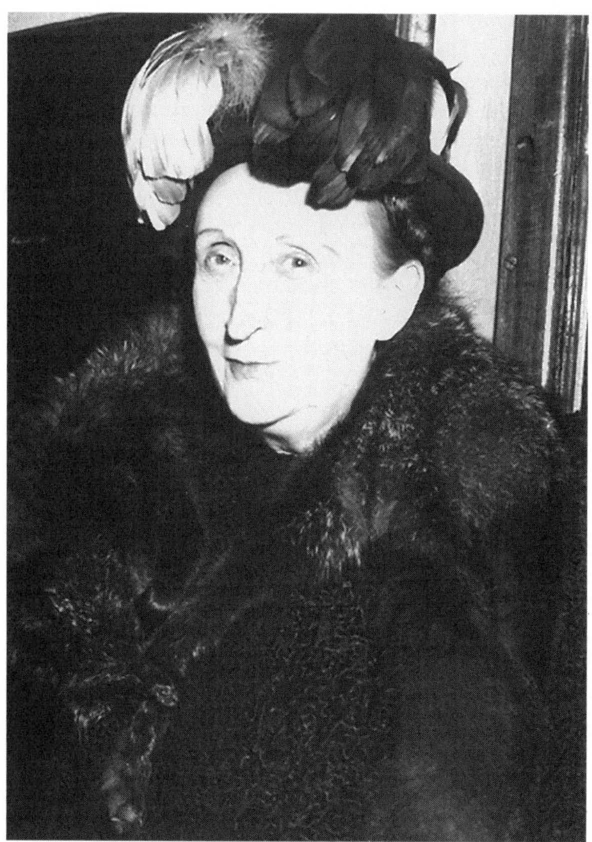

The manner in which Edith Sitwell chose to present her despair at the emptiness and hypocrisy of a world without spirit was so genuinely avant-garde that the audience at the first public theatrical presentation of the lyrics collected under the title *Façade,* in 1923, thought itself the victim of hypocrisy and her poetry the empty hoax.

The apparently cynical, amoral grotesquerie of her early poems may have been less than entirely satisfactory to the maturing Edith Sitwell herself. By the time she published *Gold Coast Customs* in 1929, the pervasive sense of horror—the stifling awareness of the death of the living—was not created within the confined imagery of the artificial commedia dell'arte but spread through a broad anthropological landscape. There are images of vast distance, of journeys, of the sea, and of the visions and barbarities of ancient cultures.

Edith Sitwell wrote little poetry in the 1930s. She exercised herself in the preparation of a number of anthologies and in prose. A critical biography, *Alexander Pope,* was published in 1930. In 1937 she published her only novel, *I Live under a Black Sun;* in 1943, *A Poet's Notebook.* By the time of World War II she had become not merely a literary celebrity but a doyenne of letters whose sponsorship was eagerly sought by younger poets. As a leader in the literary haut monde, she published *Street Songs* in 1942 and *The Canticle of the Rose: Poems 1917-1949* in 1949.

Although her poetic vision remained as much pagan as Christian, Edith Sitwell became a Roman Catholic in 1955. She also became "respectable" and respected. In 1933 she had received the poetry medal of the Royal Society of Literature, and in 1953 she was made a dame commander of the Order of the British Empire. In the 1950s she traveled widely, reading and lecturing to admiring audiences both in England and in the United States. She continued to write and to edit; she left ready for publication after her death, in London on Dec. 9, 1964, an autobiography, *Taken Care Of.* As a poet, Edith Sitwell never achieved the fashionable following she secured as a person. In a sense her own technical brilliance and artistry precluded this.

Further Reading

Edith Sitwell wrote her memoirs in *Taken Care Of: The Autobiography of Edith Sitwell* (1965). So consistently did she associate herself with her brothers, Osbert and Sacheverell, in championing the aristocratic literati that it is difficult to explore her life and thoughts without reference to the family as a whole. Rodolphe L. Megroz, *The Three Sitwells: A Biographical and Critical Study* (1927), is an early example of such a family study. John Lehmann, a friend, publisher, and admirer, wrote *A Nest of Tigers: The Sitwells in Their Times* (1968). The autobiographical works of Osbert Sitwell, comprising *Left Hand, Right Hand!* (1944), *The Scarlet Tree* (1946), *Great Morning* (1948), *Laughter in the Next Room* (1948), and *Noble Essences: A Book of Characters* (1950), are invaluable. John Lehmann, *Edith Sitwell* (1952), is a sympathetic study of her life. Cecil M. Bowra, *Edith Sitwell* (1947), represents the judgment of another close friend. Geoffrey Singleton, *Edith Sitwell: The Hymn to Life* (1960), is recommended.

Additional Sources

Elborn, Geoffrey, *Edith Sitwell, a biography,* Garden City, N.Y.: Doubleday, 1981.

Glendinning, Victoria, *Edith Sitwell, a unicorn among lions,* New York: Knopf, 1981.

Pearson, John, *The Sitwells: a family's biography,* New York: Harcourt Brace Jovanovich, 1979, 1978.

Salter, Elizabeth, *Edith Sitwell,* London: Oresko Books, 1979. □

Śivajī

Indian warrior Śivajī (1627-1680) was the leader of a seventeenth-century independent Hindu nation in the region of Mahārāshtra. By successfully repelling the forces of the invading Mughal empire, often through the use of guerilla warfare, he insured the civil and religious freedom of the Marāthā people.

The warrior Śivajī was the leader of an independent Hindu nation in western India in the 1600s. Although that part of India was primarily controlled by Muslim Mughal forces at the time, Śivajī and his Marāthā people were able to successfully resist the invaders and maintain control of much of the area known as Mahārāshtra, the homeland of the Marāthā people. While his armies could not compare in size with those of the Mughal emperor, Śivajī was able to win many victories by relying more on cunning tactics than strength; he was one of the first military figures to make use of the strategies of guerilla warfare. In his legendary struggle to secure independence and religious freedom for his people, Śivajī became not only a symbol of Hindu strength and pride but also served as an inspiration for the Indian nationalism movement that developed in the twentieth century.

Although he came to be known just by his given name of Śivajī, the future soldier and leader was born Śivajī Bhonsle on April 6, 1627, in Poona, India. Both his mother, Jija Bai, and his father, Shanji Bhonsle, were from prominent families of the Marāthā people, a race originating in the hill region of Mahārāshtra in west central India, but which had spread to neighboring regions in the Deccan plateau of central India as well. The Marāthā had a long tradition of resistance to invaders, and Śivajī was encouraged to develop a strong and aggressive spirit by his mother, who passed on a pride of her family's position in the Hindu warrior caste. The young man's father abandoned his family soon after the birth of his son, so Śivajī was primarily influenced by his mother and a guardian, Dadaji Kondadev. From his mother, he gained not only a warrior's attitude, but also a great love of the Hindu religion. His education was based on great Hindu writings such as the *Rāmāyana* and the *Mahābhārata* and he also developed an appreciation for the devotional music of his faith. Dadaji, who had been an official for the Mughal government of the nearby state of Bijapur, helped to instill in his charge a hatred of the Muslim rulers and a love of the common people of Mahārāshtra. He was also a skilled politician and strategist who demonstrated a strong sense of justice as well as discipline; all of these traits were absorbed by Śivajī and later helped make him an effective and respected leader.

Secured Marāthā Nation

For the first few years of his life Śivajī and his mother moved from place to place in an attempt to avoid capture by Mughal armies. When he was nine, they settled in Poona for ten years before moving to the mountain fort of Rajgarh, a newly-built structure that would become the central post for Śivajī's campaigns and later served as his capital. In his youth in Poona, he spent a great deal of time wandering the territory west of town, becoming familiar with the land and the peasants who lived there. He taught himself how to survive in the wilderness with few provisions and developed the skills of guerilla warfare. Before he had even reached the age of twenty, he began to gain control of a number of districts in the area and had started forming an army of his own. In the districts he ruled, he undertook a number of improvements to strengthen his defenses, rebuilding old forts and organizing local administration. He quickly became a popular leader known for his fairness and intelligence.

After learning of Śivajī's defeat of Afzal Khan, the Mughal emperor, Aurangzeb, grew alarmed. He decided to put an end to the defiant Marāthā, sending a huge force under Shaista Khan to attack Śivajī in January of 1660. The army captured Poona and for the next three years Śivajī was forced to hide in the hills and use guerilla tactics to defend his position and resist capture. He and his army survived by waiting for Mughal forces to enter the hills and then attacking them in a quick, hit-and-run fashion, making the most of their superior knowledge of the local terrain. Śivajī's troops would then return to their forts in the mountains with supplies and weapons plundered from the enemy. The Marāthā resistance efforts switched from a defensive to an offensive tactic in April of 1663, when Śivajī led a daring sneak attack on the personal quarters of Shaista Khan in the Mughal command center, wounding the general and killing dozens of his people. With the khan's forces in confusion after the assault on their leader, Śivajī made use of their immobility and attacked the wealthy port city of Surat, one of the great sources of pride of the Mughal empire. Cursing the "mountain rats" who had the nerve to attack his empire, Aurangzeb redoubled his efforts, sending a new army under Rajput Jai Singh to subdue the Marāthā and their warrior leader.

Forced to Surrender to Mughals

Unaware of the approach of the Mughal army, Śivajī had turned his attention to campaigns in the south of his domain. Jai Singh took control of Poona in March of 1665, and upon hearing the news, Śivajī rushed back to his fortress, Rajgarh. When he arrived, however, the Mughals had already gained a strong foothold in the north, forcing Śivajī to admit he could not defeat their superior power. On June 12, 1665, the Marāthā leader signed a treaty with Jai Singh in which Śivajī agreed to hand over his major strongholds, keeping only a dozen smaller forts for himself. While independence for the Marāthā was beyond hope, Śivajī assumed that he would become a valuable ally of the Mughal emperor, now that they were at peace. In the spring of 1666 he paid his respects to Aurangzeb on the occasion of his formal assumption of the Mughal throne. But rather than reward Śivajī's new loyalty with a top military post, the emperor presented him with only a third-class officer position. Śivajī was infuriated with Aurangzeb's actions and went into a tirade at the imperial court, eventually collapsing from his emotional outburst. Placed under house arrest, Śivajī quickly reevaluated his situation. No longer harboring any hopes for a position of power with the Mughals, he devised a plot to avenge the insult and regain the authority and lands he had lost.

While the Mughal emperor no longer presented a threat to the Marāthā nation, the neighboring Muslim states of Bijapur and Golconda continued to challenge Śivajī's control in the area. For this reason, not all the Marāthā in the Deccan were brought into Śivajī's empire. But his nation, while relatively small, remained stable. After his death of a fever on April 3, 1680, at Rajgarh, Śivajī's sons and subjects carried on his fight. His legacy of resistance insured that the Mughals never gained full control of the Deccan; in fact, even the later invasion by British colonial forces was repelled by the Marāthā. In the centuries since Śivajī's death, the colorful hero who fought for the freedom of the Marāthā people has come to stand as a symbol of Hindu strength and pride. His life is also considered to have been a source of inspiration for the twentieth-century Indian people as they fought their own battles for independence.

Further Reading

Majumdar, R. C., *An Advanced History of India,* 2nd ed., Macmillan, 1961.

Sardesai, G. S., "Shivaji," in *The Mughal Empire,* edited by R. C. Majumdar, Bharatiya Vidya Bhavan (Bombay, India), 1974.

Wolpert, Stanley, *A New History of India,* Oxford University Press, 1982. □

Sixtus V

Sixtus V (1520-1590) was pope from 1585 to 1590. A keenly intelligent man of driving energy and determination, he left his clear impress on the internal organization of the Church and on the physical character of Rome.

Felice Perreti, who became Sixtus V, was born on Dec. 13, 1520, in the village of Grottammare in the Mark of Ancona. His parents were poor, and as a boy he did the hard physical work of a peasant. At the age of 14 he entered the Conventual Franciscans. In his studies, which he pursued in various cities of northern Italy, he manifested a clear and forceful intelligence. In 1547 he was ordained a priest at Siena and the following year received his doctorate in theology from the University of Fermo. His abilities as a preacher and his deep concern for reform in the Church brought him to the attention of prominent churchmen in Rome, including two who subsequently became popes, Pius IV and Pius V. Twice appointed inquisitor in Venice, in 1557 and 1560, Perreti was forced to withdraw from the post because his sternness aroused much antagonism.

Pope Pius V advanced Perreti in several ways, in 1566 by making him bishop of Sant' Agata de' Goti and vicar general of the Conventual Franciscans, in 1570 by appointing him a cardinal, and in 1571 by assigning him to the See of Fermo. On April 24, 1585, Perreti was elected pope and took the name Sixtus V.

Sixtus's short reign of 5 years was filled with enormous achievements. He reorganized the curial system at the Vatican, unifying and amplifying the system of congregations and thereby centralizing the Church's business in Rome. He established 70 as the maximum number for the College of Cardinals, a rule changed in 1958 by Pope John XXIII. With his practical sense he insisted that bishops visit the Holy See periodically to render an account of their dioceses. Impatiently setting aside the scholarship of experts, he took upon himself the enormous task of preparing a revised edition of St. Jerome's translation of the Bible. So marred with mistakes was his work that it had to be corrected under Pope Clement VIII. A master of urban planning, Sixtus changed the face of Rome. By a series of roads which cut through all obstacles, he linked the outlying areas of the city with the

central metropolis. He raised obelisks, brought fresh water by tunnel and aqueduct 14 miles from Palestrina, built the Lateran Palace, and finished the dome of St. Peter's Basilica.

Sixtus pursued foreign policy with equal vigor. Against the potential bloc of massive Spanish influence he worked to preserve France as a strong nation. Only with misgiving did he support the Armada of Philip II against England (1588). There is probably no other pope about whom so many anecdotes are told. Sixtus died on Aug. 27, 1590.

Further Reading

Although research calls for some modification, the best modern comprehensive study of Sixtus V is Ludwig Pastor, *History of the Popes,* vols. 21-22 (trans. 1932). Sixtus V's career is also examined in Henry Daniel-Rops, *The Catholic Reformation* (1955; trans. 1962), and Arthur Geoffrey Dickens, *The Counter Reformation* (1969). □

John Skelton

The English poet and humanist John Skelton (ca. 1460-1529) is chiefly remembered for his satires on the court and the clergy.

Little is known of John Skelton's youth except that he may have come from Yorkshire and that he attended Cambridge. His earliest works, which included a translation of Cicero's *Familiar Letters* and another of Deguileville's *Pèlerinage de la vie humaine,* do not survive. Skelton was declared poet laureate by Oxford in 1488, by Louvain shortly thereafter, and by Cambridge in 1493. These degrees, partly honorary, were also given in recognition of his achievement in grammar. Skelton's earliest poetry is occasional, including, for example, the poem *The Dolorous Death and Most Lamentable Chance of the Most Honorable Earl of Northumberland* (1489). About 1495 Skelton became tutor to Prince Henry (later Henry VIII), a position he held for about 7 years. He was ordained a priest in 1498.

Skelton's first satire, *The Bowge of Court* (1499), was a dream vision attacking the vices of courtiers. In 1501 Skelton wrote *Speculum principis,* an adaption of a Latin version of the *Historical Library* of Diodorus Siculus. The book emphasizes the necessity for virtue and learning among princes.

In 1504 Skelton became rector of Diss, Norfolk. There he wrote some satirical poems on local personages and his famous mock dirge, *Philip Sparrow.* A young nun Skelton knew had lost her pet bird to a voracious cat. Skelton's poem, the first part of which is structured around the Mass for the Dead, represents the nun's lament for her bird. The lament is followed by Skelton's praise of the nun. The tone is pleasant and jocular.

In 1512 Skelton gave up his benefice at Diss and settled at Westminster, where he remained for the rest of his life. He was designated court poet, and he wrote a number of political poems. He also probably wrote a number of plays, but only one of these, *Magnificence* (1516), survives. During this period Skelton also wrote several songs for the court of Henry VIII, such as *Mannerly Margery Milk and Ale.* One of his most important poems, *The Tunnyng of Eleanor Rummyng,* has as its protagonist an amusing variant of an evil old woman.

Between 1521 and 1523 Skelton wrote several satirical attacks on Cardinal Wolsey: *Colin Clout; Speak, Parrot;* and *Why Come Ye Not to Court?* To escape the cardinal's wrath he took refuge with the Countess of Surrey. There he sought to appease Wolsey and to justify himself in *The Garland of Laurel* (1523). His last important work was an attack on heresy, *A Replication against Certain Young Scholars.* His favorite verse forms, consisting of short rhymed *clausulae* of irregular length, are called Skeltonics. Skelton died at Westminster on June 21, 1529.

Further Reading

The Poetical Works of John Skelton was published by the Reverend Alexander Dyce (1843). A modernized version of the poems, *The Complete Poems of John Skelton,* was edited by Philip Henderson (1931; 2d rev. ed. 1948). A good introduction to Skelton is William Nelson, *John Skelton, Laureate* (1939). More recent studies are Ian A. Gordon, *John Skelton, Poet Laureate* (1943), and H. L. R. Edwards, *Skelton: The Life and Times of an Early Tudor Poet* (1949).

Additional Sources

Lloyd, Leslie John, *John Skelton: a sketch of his life and writings,* Philadelphia: R. West, 1978. □

Burrhus Frederic Skinner

The American experimental psychologist Burrhus Frederic Skinner (1904-1990) became the chief exponent of that form of behaviorism known as operationism, or operant behaviorism.

Born in Susquehanna, Ohio, B. F. Skinner attended Hamilton College. He then went to Harvard, where he received a master's degree in 1930 and a doctorate in experimental psychology in 1931. In 1936 he began teaching at the University of Minnesota, the same year he married Yvonne Blue; they had two daughters.

In Skinner's first book, *Behavior of Organisms* (1938), he "clung doggedly to the term *reflex,* thus allowing his immediate psychological roots in classical or early behaviorism." A Guggenheim fellowship enabled him to begin writing *Verbal Behavior* in 1941. He continued on the fellowship through 1945, finishing most of the manuscript. In 1947 he gave a course at Columbia University and the William James Lecture at Harvard, both based on *Verbal Behavior,* which, however, he put off publishing for 20 years. *Walden Two* (1948) described his notions on a feasible design for (utopian) community living.

In 1954 Skinner became chairman of the Department of Psychology at Indiana University and published "Are Theories of Learning Necessary?" Conferences begun at Indiana culminated in 1958 in a new journal, *Journal of the Experimental Analysis of Behavior.*

Air Crib and Skinner Box

Toward the end of World War II, with the birth of his second child, Skinner built an air crib for baby care in which the infant, instead of staying in a tight crib wrapped in layers of cloth, can lie with only a diaper on in an enclosed space which is temperature-controlled and plastic-sheeted, thus allowing the child greater freedom of movement. Many babies are now raised in this way.

During the 1950s, stimulated by an interest in psychopharmacology, Skinner studied operant behavior of psychotics at the Metropolitan State Hospital in Waltham, Mass. For his systematic experiments on this type of behavior, Skinner designed his famous Skinner box, a compartment in which a rat, by pressing a bar, learns to repeat the act because each time he does so a pellet of food is received as a reward. Skinner demonstrated that when these reinforcements accompany or follow certain specific behavior, learning occurs in the experimental animal. Such a response, reinforced by food or other means, is called operant behavior and is distinguished from respondent behavior, which is elicited by a stimulus. Skinner's main concern in

studying operant behavior and its parameters was neither "with the causal continuity between stimulus and response, nor with the intervening variables, but simply with the correlation between stimulus (S) and response (R)."

Two Important Books

Skinner's books *Verbal Behavior* (1957), while omitting the citation of experimental evidence for its assertions, gives a highly objective functional account of language, with the basic unit of analysis being the verbal operant. He explains how differential social reinforcement from other members of the speech community forms, strengthens, or weakens dependency relations between stimulus variables and verbal responses. Included also are discussions of how listener "belief" is fortified by reinforced responses to a speaker's words; how the metaphorical expressions of a speaker reflect the kinds of stimuli which control his behavior; how and why it is that we cease verbalizing; suggestions regarding the nature of aphasia; and logical and scientific verbal behavior.

In *Schedules of Reinforcement* (1957) Skinner and his coauthors reported on a research program that was "designed to evaluate the extent to which an organism's own behavior enters into the determination of its subsequent behavior." They demonstrated that response rates, temporal patterns of rates, and patterning of rate in the temporal vicinity of the reinforcer are dependent upon the schedule of reinforcement. No detailed quantitative laws emerge, however, from their 70,000 hours of data gathering. *Schedules* is suggestive regarding the power of the operant as a tool to investigate psychopharmacological and neurophysiological problems.

Skinner acknowledged Roger Bacon as an influence on his thinking and formulating. Skinner said that he emulated him because Bacon rejected verbal authority; studied and asked questions of phenomena rather than of those who had studied the phenomena; classified in order to reveal properties; recognized that experimentation included all contingencies, whereas mere observation overstresses stimuli; and realized that if nature can be commanded, it must also be obeyed.

Critics of operationism maintained that it disregarded problems such as motives, personality, thought, and purpose or greatly diminished their relevance or importance. Although Skinner dealt with complex psychological problems, his mode of treatment of these problems was criticized as having been seriously limited. His basic behaviorist viewpoint itself has been questioned recently, in part because it rejects consciousness. The concept of consciousness cannot be omitted from psychology without a serious loss in explaining much that man does—since the viewpoint is completely indifferent to introspection.

On August 18, 1990 Skinner died and was buried at the Mt. Auburn Cemetary in Massachussetts. He left behind many distinctive awards and achievements. In 1968 he was awarded the National Medal of Science, in 1971 he was honored with the Joseph P. Kennedy, Jr. Foundation Award, and in 1985 was given the Albert Einstein School of Medecine award for excellence in psychiatry. Skinner continued to write throughout his later years, authoring such works as *Enjoy Old Age* (1983), *Upon Further Reflection* (1986), and *Recent Issues in the Analysis of Behavior.*

Further Reading

Skinner's autobiographical account is in *A History of Psychology in Autobiography,* vol. 5 (1967), edited by E. G. Boring. William S. Sahakian, ed., *History of Psychology: A Source Book in Systematic Psychology* (1968), has representative selections from Skinner's writings. Richard Isadore Evans, *B. F. Skinner: The Man and His Ideas* (1968), is a useful full-length study. Skinner's importance in the history of psychology is analyzed in the excellent study of Henryk Misiak and Virginia Staudt Sexton, *History of Psychology: An Overview* (1966). □

Rudolf Salzmann Slánský

Rudolf Salzmann Slánský (1901-1952) was one of the founding members of the Czechoslovak Communist Party and played a leading role in the Communist takeover of Czechoslovakia in 1948. In the purges of "national Communists" ordered by Joseph Stalin, he was hanged, charged with treason and other crimes in 1952.

Slánský was born on July 31, 1901, in Nezvěstice near Pilsen, in Bohemia, then part of the Austro-Hungarian Empire. He came from a Czech-Jewish middle class background; his father was a small village trader. Slánský himself was educated at the Commercial Academy in Pilsen. After World War I he moved to Prague, capital of the new state of Czechoslovakia, associating with other leftist intellectuals in the so-called "Marxist Club" and joining the Czechoslovak Communist Party when it was established in 1921.

Thereafter, he rose rapidly in the party hierarchy, concentrating his efforts in youth activities and journalism. He became editor of the party's newspaper, *Rudé Právo* (Red Right), and in 1924 he was appointed party secretary in the heavily industrialized northern region of Moravská Ostrava. In 1929 he was elected to the central and executive committees of the party. In the same year, at the Fifth Congress of the Czechoslovak Communist Party, he was raised to membership in the party's presidium and politburo. At the congress he sided with the party faction led by Klement Gottwald, helping the latter retain his post of secretary general.

For several years Slánský, charged by the Czech government with high treason for his illegal underground activities, was forced to live in hiding in interwar Czechoslovakia. Elected a deputy to the National Assembly in 1935, he received parliamentary immunity from arrest. He served in the assembly until 1937. After the infamous Munich Agreement engineered by Adolf Hitler in 1938, Slánský, considered an indispensable Communist leader, was flown to Moscow, where he spent the World War II years from 1939 to 1944. In the Soviet Union he directed the Czech broadcasts of Radio Moscow, helped organize Czechoslovak military units on Russian soil, and trained partisan groups for action in the Czech and Slovak lands. With Gottwald and others, he planned the restructuring of the postwar Czechoslovak government with the Czechoslovak president-in-exile, Eduard Beneš, when the latter visited Moscow in 1943. In 1944 he became the Czechoslovak representative to Partisan General Headquarters in Kiev, then was sent to assist the short-lived Slovak national uprising against the clerico-fascist government of the Slovak Republic, the puppet state set up by Nazi Germany. When the uprising was crushed, Slánský stayed on to lead the remaining partisans in the rugged Tatra Mountains through the forbidding winter of 1944-1945.

After the war Slánský became one of the two top leaders of the Czechoslovak Communist Party, second in status only to his long-time comrade, Gottwald. At the Eighth Party Congress in March 1946 he himself became the party's secretary general, administering its complex internal affairs. Gottwald assumed the newly-created rank of party chairman, retaining general supervision of the party's policy but concentrating on the party's growing role in the government of Czechoslovakia. Slánský also reentered the Czechoslovak parliament in 1945, becoming chairman of the National Assembly's defense committee. In September 1947 he was a delegate to the conference at Wilczagora in Lower Silesia that set up the Cominform, the new Communist international organization.

In February 1948 Slánský, together with Gottwald, led the Communists in their seizure of power in Czechoslovakia through a bloodless coup d'état. Honors flowed to him. On his 50th birthday in July 1951 the regime announced that Slánský's "collected works" were to be published. Four months later, in November, after the post of party secretary general had been abolished and its functions assumed by Party Chairman Gottwald, Slánský was promoted to the rank of vice-premier in the government.

Shortly afterward, on November 27, 1951, it was announced that Slánský had been arrested. He was charged with having organized a "Titoist" conspiratorial center, of being the ringleader of a "Jewish" plot to assassinate Gottwald and overthrow the new Communist regime with American and British assistance. Once the Communists had securely established their rule in Czechoslovakia, intra-party rivalries and hatreds reappeared and coalesced as Soviet dictator Joseph Stalin ordered purges of "bourgeois nationalists," "Titoists," "Trotskyists," and "Zionists" and "dual loyalists" (Jews) throughout the Soviet bloc. Within the Czechoslovak Communist Party two major factions contended, one led by Gottwald, the other by Slánský. Slánský's middle-class, Jewish background made him a likely target, as did his systematic machinations to infiltrate crucial offices within the party and governmental apparatus with his own trusted henchmen. Gottwald, on the other hand, came from Czech (Moravian) peasant stock, had widespread popular support, and, as a devoted supporter of Stalin's policies in the Comintern since 1928, had the Soviet dictator's favor as well. The Soviets, who directed the purge process in all of their satellites, backed Gottwald and abandoned Slánský.

After prolonged police interrogation and the calculated application of physical and psychological pressure, the entire technique supervised by Soviet "advisers," Slánský and 13 other co-defendants (11 of the 14 were Jews) were prosecuted publicly in the notorious "Slánský Trial" held before a "people's court" in Prague from November 20 to 27, 1952. After duly reciting their carefully memorized confessions of high treason, espionage, and sabotage, all were found guilty. On December 2, 1952, Slánský and ten other prominent Czech and Slovak Communists (notably Vladimír Clementis, the eminent Slovak Communist and one-time Czechoslovak foreign minister) were sentenced to death, the three others to life imprisonment at hard labor, including work in Czechoslovakia's uranium mines.

Slánský was hanged the next day, cremated, and his ashes unceremoniously sprinkled on an icy winter road. Slánský's wife, Josefa, was also briefly imprisoned until April 1953. His brother, Richard, was arrested in 1951 while serving as deputy ambassador to Poland, convicted, and sentenced to 25 years in prison. He was released in 1958 and "rehabilitated" in 1963.

After Stalin's death in 1953 and the resulting "thaw" in political conditions throughout the Soviet Union and the entire Soviet bloc, public demands were made in Czechoslovakia, as in the other satellites, for the reinvestigation of the fabricated charges and convictions of the early 1950s. In 1963 Slánský and all of his co-defendants were officially "rehabilitated" legally and as citizens. In May 1968 they were fully rehabilitated and exonerated of their alleged crimes, though none of them were reinstated as members of the Czechoslovak Communist Party.

Further Reading

Victor S. Mamatey and Radomír Luža, editors, *A History of the Czechoslovak Republic, 1918-1948* (1973) is a detailed survey of the country's history from its founding to the Communist coup. There are also two authoritative studies of the rise and triumph of Communism in Czechoslovakia: Josef Korbel, *The Communist Subversion of Czechoslovakia, 1938-1948: The Failure of Coexistence* (1959), and Paul E. Zinner, *Communist Strategy and Tactics in Czechoslovakia, 1918-1948* (1963).

There is no English-language biography of Rudolf Slánský, and biographical material on him is generally scarce. Josefa Slánský's *Report on My Husband* (1969), written by Slánský's wife during the liberal "Prague Spring" period in 1968, includes some intimate personal detail. The documents and accompanying text are especially revealing of the harsh treatment of Slánský's family at the time of his trial and after his execution. Two of the three co-defendants of Slánský who were sentenced to life imprisonment and later released and "rehabilitated" have written their own accounts of their arrest, interrogation, trial, and incarceration: Artur London, *The Confession* (1970), and Eugen Loebl, *Stalinism in Prague: The Loebl Story* (1969). They provide gripping and illuminating, if painful, reading. Jiří Pelikán, editor, *The Czechoslovak Political Trials, 1950-1954* (1971), is the full report (later suppressed) of the official inquiry into the Stalinist purges in Czechoslovakia launched by the ephemeral reform government of Alexander Dubček in 1968. □

Samuel Slater

The English-born American manufacturer Samuel Slater (1768-1835) built the first successful cotton mill in the United States, in 1790.

Samuel Slater was born near Belper in Derbyshire on June 9, 1768, the son of a prosperous yeoman farmer. As a youth, Samuel demonstrated considerable skill as a mechanic, and in school he excelled in arithmetic.

Apprenticeship in the Textile Trade

The Slater farm was located near the river Derwent; the first spinning mill driven by water power was built in Cromford on the Derwent in 1771 by Jedediah Strutt and Richard Arkwright, the inventor of the water-frame spinner. In 1776 they dissolved their partnership, and Strutt took over his own mill in Belper, where Slater began his apprenticeship at the age of 14.

Although the terms of the indenture were harsh and Slater had to work hard, Strutt treated him kindly. Slater learned to operate all the machinery involved in converting raw cotton into yarn. When the machinery broke down—a frequent occurrence since the spinning industry was still in its infancy—he made the necessary repairs.

At the end of his apprenticeship Slater concluded that the best opportunities for advancement in the textile industry were in the United States. Handicraft methods still prevailed there, since no American had yet been successful in constructing a spinning machine, and British law prohibited the export of such machines. In 1789 Slater made his way to London, where he negotiated his passage to America. He told neither his family nor his friends of his plans. According to legend, he sailed from London disguised as a farm laborer, since British law also prohibited the emigration of skilled mechanics.

New Skill to the New World

Within a few days of his arrival in New York City, Slater found a position with the New York Manufacturing Company. He was disappointed, however, because the mill was poorly equipped and lacked access to enough water to provide the necessary power for operating spinning machines. He learned that the firm of Almy and Brown operated a machine spinning mill in Pawtucket, R.I., and wrote to Moses Brown, who had provided most of the capital for building the mill, requesting a job. Slater was hired immediately.

Slater soon became a partner in the firm. His principal responsibility was to design and construct duplicate models of the equipment used in British milling establishments. Brown again supplied the capital. With the aid of a local woodworker, an iron manufacturer, and a general helper, Slater constructed the first practical copies of Arkwright's carders, water-frame spinners, and looms in the United States. The new mill went into operation in December 1790. Slater hired children from the town and surrounding

area and trained them to operate the machinery. This was a common practice in both the United States and England. The raw cotton was sent out to local women for cleaning before it came to the mill for carding.

Soon after the mill went into operation, Slater married Hannah Wilkinson. It is said that she was the first woman in the United States to suggest making sewing thread out of cotton. After her death, he married Esther Parkinson, a wealthy Philadelphia widow.

Building the Textile Industry

The mill did not run smoothly at first. There were problems in securing good-quality raw cotton, and often the equipment broke down. More importantly, the shop was unable to produce cotton yarn in sufficient quantities to meet the demand. In 1793 the firm of Almy, Brown, and Slater decided to expand. Picking a site on the Blackstone River, they constructed a new dam to provide the power and built a large mill. They installed three carders and two spinning frames containing 72 spindles. The mill, called the Old Slater Mill, went into operation in July 1793.

Dissension within the partnership over management of the mill convinced Slater to build his own mill. Still maintaining his interests in Almy, Brown, and Slater, he organized a new firm, Samuel Slater and Company, in 1798. His mill, completed in 1801, was the first in Massachusetts to use the Arkwright system. Slater played an active part in establishing other cotton mills in Rhode Island, Connecticut, Massachusetts, and New Hampshire. By 1828 he had been involved in 13 different partnerships concerned with processing cotton. Because of his contributions to the cotton industry in the United States, he is often referred to as the father of American manufactures.

Further Reading

The most readable, though somewhat subjective, biography of Slater is Edward H. Cameron, *Samuel Slater; The Father of American Manufactures* (1960). George S. White, *Memoir of Samuel Slater: The Father of American Manufactures* (1836; repr. 1967), is a sympathetic contemporary account of Slater's life; it contains numerous primary documents related to early American manufacturing. See also William R. Bagnall, *Samuel Slater and Early Development of Cotton* (1890), and, for broad background, Perry Walton, *The Story of Textiles* (1912). □

John Slidell

John Slidell (1793-1871), American politician, represented the Confederacy in France during the American Civil War.

John Slidell was born in New York City. After graduating from Columbia College in 1810, he entered into business but was ruined by the War of 1812. He then studied law and was admitted to the bar in New York. In 1819 he moved to New Orleans and for the next 42 years was closely identified with Democratic politics in Louisiana.

Slidell ran several times for the U.S. House of Representatives and for the Senate between 1828 and 1843 but was successful only once, in 1843 taking a seat in the House. In 1845 President James K. Polk, wishing to settle various problems with Mexico arising out of the annexation of Texas by the United States, chose Slidell to conduct the negotiations. He arrived in Mexico City in December, but the Mexican government refused to receive him, and he returned home.

Finally Slidell gained a Senate seat by appointment in 1853. During his senatorial years he was one of the most influential members of the Democratic party. He was instrumental in getting James Buchanan nominated and elected in 1856 and wielded great power during his administration. Slidell left the Senate in February 1861, when Louisiana seceded from the Union.

Slidell served the Confederacy as a diplomat. In September 1861 he was appointed commissioner to France, charged with getting the French emperor to recognize the independence of the Confederacy, to break the blockade by the Union Navy of the Southern ports, to permit ships to be built in French yards for the Confederacy, and to provide money. Early in November, Slidell boarded the British steamer *Trent* in Havana for the passage to Europe. On November 8, the second day at sea, a U.S. warship overtook the *Trent* and removed Slidell and James M. Mason, the Confederate commissioner to England. They were taken to Boston as prisoners but were later released when Great Britain protested the action as a violation of international law.

Slidell finally reached France in February 1862 and was received cordially by Napoleon III. But that warm feeling was not translated into policies favorable to the South. The Emperor did not recognize the Confederacy's independence, nor would he use his navy to break the blockade. Slidell did succeed in contracting for six vessels to be built in French yards, but after their completion Napoleon refused to permit Slidell to take possession of them. Slidell convinced a French banker to float $15 million of Confederate bonds, but most of the sum went to commissions. After the war, Slidell remained in France. In 1870 he moved to England, where he died on July 29, 1871.

Further Reading

Louis Martin Sears, *John Slidell* (1925), is a good biography of Slidell. Beckles Willson, *John Slidell and the Confederates in Paris, 1862-65* (1932), is not scholarly, but it is interesting.

Additional Sources

Diket, A. L., *Senator John Slidell and the community he represented in Washington, 1853-1861,* Washington, D.C.: University Press of America, 1982. □

Alfred Pritchard Sloan Jr.

The American automobile executive Alfred Pritchard Sloan, Jr. (1875-1966), pioneered in automotive innovation and built General Motors into one of the world's largest companies.

Alfred P. Sloan, Jr., was born on May 23, 1875, in New Haven, Conn., the son of a prosperous businessman. In New York City he attended the Brooklyn public schools and the Polytechnic Institute, where he passed the exams to enter the Massachusetts Institute of Technology, but he was refused admission because he was too young. At the age of 17 he did matriculate there and received a bachelor's degree in electrical engineering in 1895.

Sloan obtained a position as draftsman in the Hyatt Rolling Bearing Company at Harrison, N.J. By this time he had married Irene Jackson of Boston. At the age of 26 he became president and general manager of the rapidly failing firm when his father and one other man bought control. Sloan quickly resuscitated the firm by moving into the manufacture of steel roller bearings for the mushrooming automobile industry.

While Olds Motor Company was Sloan's first customer, Ford Motor Company became the largest. Hyatt profits ran as high as $4 million annually, but Sloan grew concerned with rumors that General Motors (GM) might produce its own bearings. Instead, William C. Durant, the energetic builder of GM, bought Sloan's firm for $13,500,000 and merged it as part of the United Motors Corporation, with Sloan as president. In 1918 he became a vice president and member of the GM executive committee.

Durant lost control of GM in 1920 to the Du Ponts, but Pierre Samuel du Pont, the new president, knew nothing about automobiles and made Sloan vice president in charge of operations. Three years later Sloan became president of GM and a director of the Du Pont Company. In 1920 GM held a 12 percent share of the market; by 1956, when Sloan retired, the market share stood at 52 percent. He accomplished this not only by innovations such as four-wheel drive, crankcase ventilation, and knee-action brakes but, more importantly, by adopting the staff principle of management. He centralized administration and decentralized production and put each product in its own division and eliminated intracompany competition.

Sloan made a great philanthropic contribution in 1937, when he endowed the Alfred P. Sloan Foundation with $10 million; to 1966, his gifts totaled over $305 million. Major recipients were the Sloan-Kettering Institute for Cancer Research and the Massachusetts Institute of Technology. He died Feb. 17, 1966, in New York City.

Further Reading

The only full-length works on Sloan are autobiographical. An early account of himself, written with Boyden Sparkes, is *Adventures of a White-collar Man* (1941). Sloan's *My Years with General Motors* (1963) is an illuminating book on business history and his role in it. Paul Franklin Douglass, *Six upon the World: Toward an American Culture for an Industrial Age* (1954), includes an essay on Sloan and his significance.

Additional Sources

Sloan, Alfred P. (Alfred Pritchard), *My years with General Motors,* New York: Doubleday/Currency, 1990, 1963.

Weaver, Warren, *Alfred P. Sloan, Jr., philanthropist,* New York: Alfred P. Sloan Foundation, 1975. □

John Sloan

American painter John Sloan (1871-1951) was a pioneer realist. He specialized in city street scenes, New Mexican subjects, and the nude.

Born in Lock Haven, Pa., on Aug. 2, 1871, John Sloan was taken to Philadelphia as a child. After he finished high school, he worked for booksellers and dry-goods dealers. He studied briefly under Thomas Anshutz at the Pennsylvania Academy of Fine Arts and in 1892 was employed by the *Philadelphia Inquirer* as a newspaper artist. Robert Henri encouraged him as a painter, and he was influenced by Japanese prints. In 1895 he moved to the *Philadelphia Press,* for which he drew full-page color pictures until 1902. His early paintings were street scenes, somber in color, vivid and direct in execution. These were first exhibited in 1900 in Chicago and Pittsburgh, and he was included in a New York group show in 1901.

Sloan married in 1901 and in 1904 moved to New York. For many years he supported himself as a magazine illustrator and, after 1906, as a teacher. A series of 10 etchings of city life in 1905-1906, rich in content, often with undercurrents of humor or irony, found no purchasers. Though his work was seen in these years in the Carnegie International Exhibition and the National Academy of Design, more often than not his pungent and unidealized urban scenes were rejected by academic critics. It was in part his rejection by the academy in 1907 that caused Henri to withdraw from that organization. Sloan was one of the group of painters called "The Eight," whose exhibition at the Macbeth Gallery in 1908 called attention to the radical subject matter and vigorous execution of five of the painters—Henri, Sloan, William Glackens, George Luks, and Everett Shinn.

Sloan and his wife joined the Socialist party in 1910, and he became art editor of its magazine, *The Masses,* to which he contributed some of his most compelling drawings. In 1910 and again in 1913 he was an unsuccessful candidate for the New York State Assembly. He withdrew from the party in 1914 but remained on the staff of *The Masses* for 2 more years. He sold his first painting in 1913 to Dr. Albert C. Barnes. He was well represented that same year in the celebrated Armory Show but was too completely a representational artist to have much sympathy for the new European movements exhibited there.

Sloan was an active teacher at the Art Students League and served as its president in 1931. He was president of the Society of Independent Artists from 1918 until his death; this organization staged large, no-jury, no-prize shows from 1917 until 1944.

From 1914 to 1918 Sloan spent the summers in Gloucester, Mass., where he painted landscapes as well as people. He traveled to the Southwest for the first time in 1919, and for the rest of his life spent long periods in Santa Fe, N. Mex., where he built a house in 1940. The life of the Indians, the ceremonial activities of the Spanish inhabitants, and the dramatic desert landscape provided powerful new subjects. In 1931 he was active in organizing a large exhibition of Indian tribal arts.

After about 1930 Sloan painted no more city scenes but became increasingly concerned with studies of the nude. The late paintings are monumental and technically innovative. In contrast to the direct execution of his earlier work, these are carefully constructed with monochrome underpainting, upon which an elaborate surface of bold crosshatchings in color gives startling relief.

The power of Sloan's personality is well conveyed in *Gist of Art* (1939), a compilation of statements made to his students which were recorded by Helen Farr, who became his second wife, in 1944. Sloan died on Sept. 7, 1951, in Hanover, N.H.

Further Reading

Sloan's *Gist of Art* (1939) is an eloquent statement of his attitudes and methods, with interesting comments on his own works. Sloan's *New York Scene: From Diaries, Notes and Correspondence, 1906-1913,* edited by Bruce St. John and introduced by Helen Farr Sloan (1965), describes Sloan and his world. Lloyd Goodrich, *John Sloan* (1952), published in connection with an exhibition at the Whitney Museum, is the best critical study. Van Wyck Brooks, *John Sloan: A Painter's Life,* is a sympathetic personal account. Guy Pène du Bois, *John Sloan* (no date), is a brief but useful picture book. There are interesting personal sidelights in Bennard B. Perlman, *The Immortal Eight* (1962).

Additional Sources

Loughery, John, *John Sloan: painter and rebel,* New York: H. Holt, 1995.

Scott, David W., *John Sloan,* New York: Watson-Guptill, 1975.

□

Claus Sluter

The Dutch-Burgundian sculptor Claus Sluter (ca. 1350-1405/1406) was the most important northern European sculptor of his age. He restored figural sculpture to its former monumental scale. He is considered a pioneer of "northern realism."

Claus Sluter was born in Haarlem. Records indicate that by 1380 he was active in the stonecutters' guild in Brussels. The present state of our knowledge does not afford a satisfactory answer to the question of his training and the formative influences on his style. It is conjectured that in this early period he worked on a set of seated prophets for the Brussels Town Hall.

Sluter's first certain activity occurred in 1385, when Philip the Bold called him to the court at Dijon to assist Jean de Marville in the design and preparation of statues for the facade of the chapel at the Chartreuse de Champmol, a nearby Carthusian monastery founded as a place of interment for the ducal succession. Whatever the nature of Sluter's apprenticeship, he apparently arrived at Dijon a complete master of his craft. At Marville's death in 1389, Sluter succeeded him and is generally credited with the execution of most of the surviving portal sculpture. Life-size portraits of Philip and his duchess, Margaret of Flanders, flank a freestanding group of the Madonna and Child. Not only is this work characterized by an unprecedented degree of sculptural realism, but the artist's feeling for organic form and the expression of human emotions are greatly advanced for the period.

In 1392 Sluter visited Paris to purchase alabaster, and in 1395 he made a trip to the Low Countries to buy marble. His next major commission was a Calvary group intended for the cloister of the Chartreuse de Champmol. Executed between 1395 and 1405, the *Well of Moses,* as it is usually called, is the only extant work entirely by Sluter. Of the original group, six large statues of prophets and an equal number of mourning angels are all that remain. These figures are especially noteworthy for the strong sense of tragedy which they evoke and the highly individualized treatment of character. Sluter's great feeling for sculptural form, combined with rich surface texture, is most fully revealed by the figures of Moses and Isaiah, which rank among the greatest masterpieces of medieval sculpture. His nephew and successor, Claus de Werve, assisted him, and Jean Malouel was responsible for gilding and polychroming the statues. Several of the figures still retain vestiges of the original paint.

When Philip the Bold died in 1404, Sluter was given the task of designing a tomb (now in the Musée des Beaux-Arts, Dijon) for his great patron and benefactor. Though Sluter did not live to see the finished work—it was completed by Claus de Werve in 1410—it is thought that a major part of the carving is by his own hand. Much damaged during the French Revolution, the tomb was heavily restored in 1824. Sluter's chief contribution to the work is the figures of the mourners (*pleurants*), which are located in individual architectural niches below the recumbent form (*gisant*) of the duke. Intensely realistic, yet profoundly emotive, these mourners represent the highest achievement of his art. Too advanced for his age, Sluter had little impact on the subsequent development of late Gothic sculpture.

Further Reading

The most important work on Sluter is in German. A brief but excellent account in English of Sluter's style is in Erwin Panofsky, *Early Netherlandish Painting* (2 vols., 1953). □

Maud Slye

Maud Slye (1879-1954), a pathologist, researched the inheritability of cancer in mice.

Maud Slye devoted her life to cancer research by investigating the inheritability of the disease in mice. Performing extensive breeding studies on the hereditary transmission of cancer, she kept meticulous pedigree records and autopsied thousands of mice during her lifetime. Her work was controversial, however; advocating the archiving of complete medical records for individuals, she believed that human beings could eradicate cancer by choosing mates with the appropriate genotype. Sometimes referred to as "America's Curie," Slye received wide publicity for her work and was honored by many organizations.

Slye was born in Minneapolis, Minnesota, on February 8, 1879, the daughter of James Alvin and Florence Alden Wheeler Slye. Her family, though poor, traced their ancestry back to John Alden of the Plymouth colony. At age seventeen, Slye entered the University of Chicago with savings of forty dollars and the desire to become a scientist. Attending the university for three years, she supported herself by working as a secretary for university president William Harper. After a nervous breakdown, Slye convalesced in Woods Hole, Massachusetts, then completed her B.A. degree at Brown University in 1899. Hired as a teacher at the Rhode Island State Normal School, she stayed at the institution until 1905.

In 1908 Slye received a grant to do postgraduate work at the University of Chicago. Interested in the hereditary basis of disease, she began her work with six Japanese "waltzing" mice which were afflicted with a hereditary neurological disorder. Slye became intrigued by the inheritability of cancer when she heard of several heads of cattle at the Chicago stock yards—all with cancer of the eye—that had come from the same ranch. Inspired by this and other data, Slye went forward with her studies, breeding cancerous mice with one another as well as healthy mice with other healthy mice.

In 1911, Slye became a member of the university's newly created Sprague Memorial Institute, and in 1913 she presented her first paper on cancer before the American Society for Cancer Research. Becoming director of the Cancer Laboratory at the University of Chicago in 1919, she was promoted to assistant professor in 1922, then to associate professor in 1926. In 1936, Slye left her mice in the care of an assistant and took her first vacation in twenty-six years (earlier, when she had visited her ailing mother in California, she rented a boxcar and took her mice with her).

Although Slye discredited a prevailing theory that stated cancer was contagious, it became clear as her work proceeded that the appearance of cancer in an individual was not as simple as the presence of one gene. In later years, Slye posited that two conditions were necessary to produce cancer: inherited susceptibility, and prolonged irritation of the cancer-susceptible tissues. Nonetheless, further studies by other scientists have confirmed that while heredity can be a factor in certain types of cancer, it is much more complex than Slye had perceived.

Slye's work was recognized with several awards and honors, including the gold medal of the American Medical Association in 1914, and the Ricketts Prize in 1915. She also received the gold medal of the American Radiological Society in 1922. A member of the Association for Cancer Research, the American Medical Association, and the American Association for the Advancement of Scence, Slye was the author of forty-two brochures on cancer and two volumes of poetry, *Songs and Solaces* and *I in the Wind.* At the time of her retirement in 1945 Slye was made professor emeritus of pathology, and she spent her retirement years analyzing data accumulated during her years of research. Slye never married. She died September 17, 1954, and was buried in Chicago's Oak Woods Cemetery.

Further Reading

Kass-Simon, G., and Patricia Farnes, editors, *Women of Science: Righting the Record,* Indiana University Press, 1990, pp. 278–279.

O'Neill, Lois Decker, editor, *The Women's Book of World Records and Achievements,* Doubleday, 1979, p. 217.

Reader's Digest, March 1936, pp. 77–80.

Newsweek, April 10, 1937, pp. 26–28.

New York Times, September 18, 1954, p. 15. □

Albion Woodbury Small

The American sociologist and educator Albion Woodbury Small (1854-1926) was instrumental in founding and developing the profession of sociology in the United States.

Albion Small was born in Buckfield, Maine, on May 11, 1854. Though trained as a minister at the Newton Theological Institution (1876-1879), he pursued wider interests at the universities of Leipzig and Berlin (1879-1881), particularly in political economy. Thereafter, till 1889 he taught at Colby College in Maine and embarked on advanced studies in economics and history at Johns Hopkins University. After selection as president of Colby College, he was chosen in 1892 to found a department of sociology at the new University of Chicago. During his tenure at Chicago, Small built the leading department of sociology in the United States, helped in founding the American Sociological Society (of which he was president in 1912 and 1913), and was the first editor of the *American Journal of Sociology.*

Small's teaching and writings were animated by the desire to demonstrate the distinctive nature of the young discipline of sociology, as well as to indicate the interrelations among various social sciences. His first major book, *General Sociology* (1905), viewed the subject matter of sociology as the processes by which various group interests clash and become resolved through accommodations and social innovation. In this work, he summarized and creatively interpreted the writings of Ludwig Gumplowicz and Gustave Ratzenhofer for the first time in English. Further interpretations of European thinkers were included in *Adam Smith and Modern Sociology* (1907), where Small tried to demonstrate the moral and philosophical undergirding of Smith's famous *Wealth of Nations; The Cameralists* (1909), an extremely detailed review of the social theory underlying the public economic policies of Germany from the 16th through the 19th century; and *Origins of Sociology* (1924), a highly erudite reconstruction of German academic controversies that seemed to Small to provide the foundation of modern methodology in social science.

The best summary of Small's overall thinking is contained in *The Meaning of Social Science* (1910), where the thrust of his *General Sociology* is clarified in surprisingly modern terms. Essentially, social science—including sociology—studies continuing processes through which men form, implement, and change valuations of their experiences. Human behavior derives meaning from these valuations, and both values and behavior are simultaneously patterned in the individual (as personality) and in society (through groups and organizations).

Small retired from the university in 1924. He died in Chicago on March 24, 1926. Although his ideas were largely derivative, his contribution to American sociology is incontestable.

Further Reading

Two detailed summaries of Small's works are Edward C. Hayes's "Albion W. Small" in Howard W. Odum and others, eds., *American Masters of Social Science* (1927), and a chapter in Harry Elmer Barnes, ed., *An Introduction to the History of Sociology* (1948). For general background see Harry Elmer Barnes and Howard Becker, *Social Thought from Lore to Science* (2 vols., 1938; 2d ed., 3 vols., 1961), and Bernhard J. Stern, *Historical Sociology* (1960).

Additional Sources

Christakes, George, *Albion W. Small,* Boston: Twayne Publishers, 1978.

Dibble, Vernon K., *The legacy of Albion Small,* Chicago: University of Chicago Press, 1975. □

Robert Smalls

Robert Smalls (1839-1916) was a black American statesman who was born a slave and made a daring escape at the beginning of the Civil War. After the

war he served five terms in Congress as the representative from South Carolina.

Robert Smalls was born a slave, to Robert and Lydia Smalls at Beaufort, S.C., on April 5, 1839. He was taken to Charleston as a youth and worked there at a variety of jobs. He soon mastered the seafaring art and became the de facto pilot of a Confederate transport steamer, the *Planter*. Smalls never accepted his enslaved condition and was determined to free himself. He taught himself to read and write, mastered the tricky currents and channels of Charleston Harbor, and bided his time. Sooner or later his chance would come: he would be free. He *had* to be free.

The Civil War brought his chance. On the morning of May 13, 1862, long before the sun was up and while the ship's white officers still slept in Charleston, Smalls smuggled his wife and three children aboard the *Planter* and took command. With his crew of 12 slaves, Smalls hoisted the Confederate flag and with great daring sailed the *Planter* past the other Confederate ships and out to sea. Once beyond the range of the Confederate guns, he hoisted a flag of truce and delivered the *Planter* to the commanding officer of the Union fleet. Smalls explained that he intended the *Planter* as a contribution by black Americans to the cause of freedom. The ship was received as contraband, and Smalls and his black crew were welcomed as heroes. Later, President Lincoln received Smalls in Washington and rewarded him and his crew for their valor. He was given official command of the *Planter* and made a captain in the U.S. Navy; in this position he served throughout the war.

After the war Smalls returned to South Carolina to enter politics. He served in the Carolina Senate from 1868 to 1870. In 1875 he was elected to the U.S. Congress for the first of five terms. His record as a congressman was progressive. He fought for equal travel accommodations for black Americans and for the civil and legal protection of children of mixed parentage. He was one of the six black members of the South Carolina constitutional convention of 1895.

After leaving Congress, Smalls was duty collector for the port of Beaufort. He retained his interest in the military and was a major general in the South Carolina militia. He died on Feb. 22, 1916.

Further Reading

A fine biography of Smalls is Okon Edet Uya, *From Slavery to Public Service: Robert Smalls, 1839-1915* (1971). Dorothy Sterling, *Captain of the Planter: The Story of Robert Smalls* (1958), written for young people, has an extensive bibliography. A good account of Smalls is in William J. Simmons, *Men of Mark* (1968). Francis B. Simkins and Robert H. Woody, *South Carolina during Reconstruction* (1932), discusses his political career.

Additional Sources

Miller, Edward A., *Gullah statesman: Robert Smalls from slavery to Congress, 1839-1915,* Columbia, S.C.: University of South Carolina Press, 1995. □

Eleanor Smeal

Eleanor Smeal (born 1939), one of the leading feminists in the United States in the last quarter of the 20th century, served as president of the National Organization for Women from 1977 to 1982 and again from 1985 to 1987. She was also president of the Feminist Majority Foundation and continued to organize, publicize and promote feminist issues well into the 1990s.

Eleanor Marie Cutri was born on July 30, 1939, in Ashtabula, Ohio, the daughter of Italian-American parents, Josephine E. Agresti and Peter Anthony Cutri. Eleanor—or Ellie, as she was nicknamed—was the first daughter and fourth child. Her father was born in Calabria, Italy. After immigrating to the United States, he worked as an insurance agent. Eventually the family settled in Erie, Pennsylvania, where Eleanor grew up. Raised as a Roman Catholic, she nevertheless attended Erie public schools, graduating from high school with a record of scholastic excellence.

She continued her academic success at Duke University, from which she graduated Phi Beta Kappa in 1961. As a student she served as president of her dormitory and supported the cause of racial integration. After receiving her

B.A., Eleanor considered pursuing a law degree, but chose not to when she learned of the discrimination against women lawyers (few at that time were accepted into law firms or allowed to practice at court). Instead, she decided to continue her studies in political science and public administration. She received a master's degree in these subjects from the University of Florida in 1963. (She was granted an honorary LL.D. from Duke University in 1991).

At the university she met Charles R. Smeal, a student in metallurgical engineering, whom she married on April 27, 1963. They had two children. After her marriage Eleanor continued work on her doctoral thesis, which concerned attitudes women voters have toward women candidates for office. However, a persistent back illness, which required a year's confinement to bed rest, forced her to abandon the study. Meanwhile, she moved with her family to the Pittsburgh area.

During the late 1960s Smeal became increasingly aware of feminist issues, particularly those affecting homemakers. She had already been confronted with the lack of day care facilities when she tried to work on her thesis with a small child. During her illness she realized that there was no disability insurance for wives and mothers. An awareness of these injustices prompted Smeal to begin research into feminism, and thus, like many other women of the period, she began reading about past women's movements, such as the suffrage campaign, as well as contemporary feminist theory.

In 1968 she began a four-year term on the board of the local League of Women Voters. Two years later she and her husband joined the newly formed—and more militant—National Organization for Women (NOW). Smeal also served in 1971 and 1972 as secretary/treasurer of the Allegheny County Council.

During the 1970s Smeal rose through the ranks of NOW, extending her growing feminist commitment from such local projects as developing nursery schools to assuming in 1977 the presidency of the national organization. From 1971 to 1973 she served as organizer and president of the NOW chapter in South Hills, Pennsylvania. In 1972 she was elected president of the Pennsylvania state NOW, a position she held until 1975. In that capacity she made equal physical education for girls a priority and was successful in having the state's equal rights statute applied in this area.

In 1975 Smeal became chairperson of the board of directors of NOW, having been elected to that board in 1973. She was also active in the NOW legal defense and education fund, particularly in the area of enforcement of Title IX of the 1972 Education Amendments.

On April 23, 1977, Smeal was elected president of the national NOW, by this time an organization of 55,000 persons, the largest feminist association in the world. Smeal's philosophy was that NOW should remain a locally-centered, grass-roots organization that included women from all walks of life, not just educated professionals. To this end she had worked for the establishment of the presidency as a salaried position, so that women who were not independently wealthy or supported by their husbands could serve in the post. Smeal's success as an administrator became clear when she was able to erase a substantial national debt within a year and to double the national membership within two years. She was re-elected president in 1979.

By the late 1970s Smeal had decided that ratification of the Equal Rights Amendment to the Constitution should be a NOW priority. The amendment had passed the Congress in 1972 and had been ratified by 35 states; however, three more states were needed before the amendment would become part of the Constitution. Beginning in February 1977 Smeal (and NOW) organized a boycott of states that had not ratified by organizations that would ordinarily have held conventions in those states. Under Smeal's guidance NOW also worked for the extension of the ratification deadline from 1979 to June 30, 1982. As part of this campaign NOW organized and led a pro-ERA march on Washington on July 9, 1979. It attracted 100,000 demonstrators. After the deadline was extended, Smeal led NOW in heavy lobbying efforts directed against key legislators in key states. But these efforts were not successful, and the deadline passed without ratification.

In 1982, barred by NOW by-laws from seeking a third term as president, Smeal turned her efforts toward writing *Why and How Women Will Elect the Next President* (1984). This "election handbook" focused on the "gender gap," the discrepancy in female and male voting patterns, particularly on issues of social welfare and peace. Smeal stated that if women voted as a bloc, it would be a decisive factor in the

1984 presidential election and in the long run it would be a powerful force for social change. She also urged that the vice presidential candidate of the Democratic Party in 1984 be a woman—an idea that was realized when Walter Mondale selected Representative Geraldine Ferraro as his running mate as a result of NOW lobbying.

In 1985 Smeal successfully sought reelection to the national presidency of NOW, urging that the organization become more militant and activist in its fights for the numerous feminist issues remaining on the agenda, especially abortion rights, the reintroduced ERA, and economic justice for women. She remained president for another two years (until 1987) and promised to take the organization "back to the streets."

In 1987 she became president of Fund for Feminist Majority, based in Arlington, Virginia. In these roles, Smeal continued to bring forward and publicize those feminist issues which she believed were crucial to the future of feminists.

Further Reading

In addition to *Why and How Women Will Elect the Next President* (1984), Smeal was the coauthor (with Audrey Siess Wells) of "Women's Attitudes Toward Women in Politics: A Survey of Urban Registered Voters and Party Committee Women," in Jane Jaquette, editor, *Women in Politics* (1974). See also *People* (August 8, 1977) and *Ms. Magazine* (February 1978). Two discussions of Smeal's views appear in *Ms. Magazine* (May/June 1995) and *The Progressive* (November 1995). Smeal is also listed in the *Marquis Who's Who in America* (1996). □

John Smeaton

The English civil engineer John Smeaton (1724-1792) transformed the handicraft of engineering into a profession by applying experimental science to architectural and mechanical problems.

John Smeaton was born on June 8, 1724, at Austhorpe in Yorkshire. His father was an attorney. As a boy, Smeaton made his own hand tools, casting and forging them himself, and made a small lathe for turning wood. He also made a steam engine, which had the dubious success of pumping dry his father's fish pond.

At 16 Smeaton joined his father's office, where he began legal studies. Two years later he journeyed to London to formally enter the legal profession. However, he was more interested in the mechanical crafts and finally obtained his father's consent to become an instrument maker, a profession which roughly corresponded in terms of mechanical skill to that of a toolmaker of today but which also implied some knowledge of science. In 1750 he opened his own instrument shop.

Smeaton's scientific training came from reading and from attending the meetings of the Royal Society of London. He became a fellow of the Society in 1753 and began contributing articles to the *Philosophical Transactions.* In 1759 he received the Copley Gold Medal for an experimental investigation into windmills and water mills in which he showed how maximum efficiency of waterwheels could be obtained. Later he designed and constructed many waterwheels; his work represented the culmination of the development of this traditional source of water power. Not until the waterwheel was replaced by the turbine was Smeaton's work superseded.

About 1756 Smeaton began his first and most famous engineering project: the reconstruction of the Eddystone Lighthouse in the English Channel. Great Britain was becoming a major naval power, and navigational aids along and in its coastal waters were of vital importance. Eddystone was one of the most important sites. It was a half, and sometimes wholly, submerged reef which was the location of many storms and a frequent cause of shipwrecks. Two previous lighthouses there had been destroyed.

Smeaton decided to make the new lighthouse entirely of stone, a radical departure. He built a scale model of the structure, the rigidity of which was enhanced by dovetailing the courses into one another and into the reef itself. He also developed a cement that solidified and held under seawater. The lighthouse was built between 1757 and 1759. It was replaced in 1877 because that portion of the reef on which it stood had been undermined by the seas of the intervening century.

Smeaton also investigated that machine so essential to the industrial revolution—the steam engine. He was the first engineer to analyze the operation of a steam engine experimentally and to try to increase its efficiency. By about 1770 he doubled the engine's original efficiency, and he later almost tripled it. The efficiency was still very low; nevertheless, by his attention to design he created the best steam engine until James Watt placed his own on the market.

A great many technical innovations were due to Smeaton such as the extensive use of cast-iron parts in moving machinery and the introduction of the use of a diving bell for the construction of bridges and harbor works. He sought to transform what had been the handicraft tradition of engineering, which was based upon practices handed down from master to apprentice, into a profession which applied experimental science to a craft. He was one of the first to call himself a civil engineer. In 1771 he helped establish the first engineering society in the world—the Society of Civil Engineers, also called the Smeatonian Society, which in 1818 became the Institution of Civil Engineers. He died at Austhorpe on Oct. 28, 1792.

Further Reading

John Smeaton's Diary of His Journey to the Low Countries, 1755 was published in 1950. There is no biography of Smeaton, but a sometimes unreliable account is in Samuel Smiles, *Lives of the Engineers,* vol. 2 (1891). Many references to Smeaton's work can be found in H. W. Dickinson, *A Short History of the Steam Engine* (1939), and throughout Charles Singer and others, eds., *A History of Technology* (5 vols., 1958).

Additional Sources

John Smeaton, FRS, London: T. Telford, 1981. □

Bedřich Smetana

The Czech composer Bedřich Smetana (1824-1884), founder of Bohemian national music, is most known for his symphonic poems and operas. His music combines a strong symphonic technique with melodic and rhythmic ideas derived from Bohemian folk traditions.

Born into a large family in the small town of Leitomischel, Bedřich Smetana showed exceptional musical talent as a child, performing on the violin and piano at the age of 5 and writing his first compositions at 8. Despite his father's opposition to his musical training, he quickly gained a reputation as a pianist through his performances of the works of Franz Liszt. After moving to Prague in 1844, Smetana became music teacher to the family of the wealthy Count Thun but left after 4 years. With the help of Liszt, Smetana founded his own piano school.

In 1856 Smetana accepted a position as conductor of the Philharmonic Society of Göteborg, Sweden. While there he wrote his first important symphonic poems, including *Wallenstein's Camp* (1859) after Friedrich von Schiller's great dramatic trilogy. During this time, events were changing in Bohemia. Austria, weakened from futile attempts to maintain control over Italy, granted Bohemia political autonomy in 1860, which elicited strong national feelings from the Bohemians. The following year Smetana returned to Prague to become a leader in the new movement, the first substantial result of which was the establishment in 1862 of a theater where opera and drama could be presented in the Czech language.

Smetana's first major operatic success, *The Bartered Bride* (1866), instantly raised him to the status of Bohemia's leading composer and won for him international success as well as the position as first conductor of the Prague theater. The opera, a humorous tale of peasant life, is full of dance sequences based on Bohemian folk rhythms. The overture, polka, and furiant are often heard in concert. His next opera, *Dalibor* (1868), was more serious, with the hero conceived as a symbol of the Czech soul. Smetana's symphonic orchestration upset some critics, who accused him of imitating Richard Wagner, and throughout his life his serious operas were attacked by many who preferred his lighter works. Today *Dalibor* is considered one of the greatest Czech operas, although it is virtually unknown outside its own country.

Eventually Smetana developed a nervous disorder, continually hearing noises in his head and at times suffering memory lapses. In 1874 he was forced to resign from his conducting position, and at the end of that year he became permanently deaf. From 1874 to 1879 he occupied himself

with the composition of a cycle of six symphonic poems titled *My Country,* of which the best-known are *The Moldau* (1874) and *From Bohemia's Meadows and Forests* (1875). In 1876 he completed his most important chamber work, the string quartet *From My Life.* This composition is unique in the repertoire because of its autobiographical subject matter, reflected in the harrowing screech in the high violin that interupts the dance in the last movement, representing Smetana's own physical disability. In the spring of 1884 he was committed to a mental institution, where he died a few months later.

Further Reading

Two important biographies of Smetana are Liam Nolan and Joseph Bernard Hutton, *The Life of Smetana: The Pain and the Glory* (1968), and Brian Large, *Smetana* (1970), the last of which contains musical analysis as well as biographical material. For general background see Donald Jay Grout, *A History of Western Music* (1960), and Kenneth B. Klaus, *The Romantic Period in Music* (1970).

Additional Sources

Large, Brian, *Smetana,* New York: Da Capo Press, 1985.
Maly, Miloslav, *Bedřich Smetana,* Prague: Orbis, 1976. □

John Smibert

John Smibert (1688-1751), Scottish-born American artist, was a most celebrated painter in the Colonies.

John Smibert was born in Edinburgh, where he was trained as an artisan. Hoping to attain success as a painter, he went to London, working as a coach painter and a copyist. At the age of 28 he became a student at James Thornhill's Great Queen Street Academy. Smibert traveled in Italy from 1717 to 1720, for the grand tour was expected of an aspiring painter, and then reestablished himself in London, where he was regarded as no more than a competent painter.

In 1729 Smibert sailed for America with Dean (later Bishop) George Berkeley, who had organized a movement to establish a college in Bermuda "for converting the Indians to Christianity." Smibert had hoped that in America, where there were no European-trained painters, he would be successful. Berkeley's party landed at Newport, R.I.; as the plan for the college did not materialize, Smibert went to Boston, where he expected to find patrons.

Smibert's *Dean George Berkeley with His Family and Friends* (1729) was the most elaborate and complex painting done in New England to that time. New England portraits usually contained one, two, or at most three sitters, who were shown with few if any accessories. In Smibert's painting, eight sitters, disposed in front of a landscape, are arranged about a table covered with a Turkey-work cloth on which books are placed. Here he introduced a new sophistication and an almost baroque complexity into American art. The gestures of the figures are awkward, and at times the drawing is uncertain, but the faces are rendered honestly, rather than with the facile flattery then characteristic of most English painting.

The homespun, direct quality that Smibert quickly adopted was well received by Bostonians. Some of his portraits, such as that of Nathaniel Byfield (1730), have qualities approaching caricature; others reveal sympathetic psychological penetration. Smibert may also have painted landscapes, for he wrote of working "with somethings in a landskip way." But except for the backgrounds in some of the portraits, including the Berkeley group and the portrait of Jane Clark (ca. 1740), no landscapes survive.

Smibert was one of the first painters in the Colonies to enjoy a status beyond that of an artisan. As such, he set the tone for later painters. He married well; he held civil offices; and he was able to support himself as a settled citizen rather than as an itinerant artist, as was then common. He also submitted some of the first designs for Faneuil Hall in Boston. His son Nathaniel (1734-1756) was also a painter.

Further Reading

The best and most complete study of Smibert is Henry Wilder Foote, *John Smibert, Painter* (1950), which contains a descriptive catalog of the portraits.

Additional Sources

Saunders, Richard H., *John Smibert: colonial America's first portrait painter,* New Haven: Yale University Press, 1995. □

Adam Smith

The Scotch economist and moral philosopher Adam Smith (1723-1790) believed that in a laissez-faire economy the impulse of self-interest would work toward the public welfare.

Adam Smith was born on June 5, 1723, at Kirkcaldy. His father had died 2 months before his birth, and a strong and lifelong attachment developed between him and his mother. As an infant, Smith was kidnaped, but he was soon rescued. At the age of 14 he enrolled in the University of Glasgow, where he remained for 3 years. The lectures of Francis Hutcheson exerted a strong influence on him. In 1740 he transferred to Balliol College, Oxford, where he remained for almost 7 years, receiving the bachelor of arts degree in 1744. Returning then to Kirkcaldy, he devoted himself to his studies and gave a series of lectures on English literature. In 1748 he moved to Edinburgh, where he became a friend of David Hume, whose skepticism he did not share.

Theory of Moral Sentiments

In 1751 Smith became professor of logic at the University of Glasgow and the following year professor of moral philosophy. Eight years later he published his *Theory of Moral Sentiments.* Smith's central notion in this work is that moral principles have social feeling or sympathy as their basis. Sympathy is a common or analogous feeling that an individual may have with the affections or feelings of another person. The source of this fellow feeling is not so much one's observation of the expressed emotion of another person as one's thought of the situation that the other person confronts. Sympathy usually requires knowledge of the cause of the emotion to be shared. If one approves of another's passions as suitable to their objects, he thereby sympathizes with that person.

Sympathy is the basis for one's judging of the appropriateness and merit of the feelings and actions issuing from these feelings. If the affections of the person involved in a situation are analogous to the emotions of the spectator, then those affections are appropriate. The merit of a feeling or an action flowing from a feeling is its worthiness of reward. If a feeling or an action is worthy of reward, it has moral merit. One's awareness of merit derives from one's sympathy with the gratitude of the person benefited by the action. One's sense of merit, then, is a derivative of the feeling of gratitude which is manifested in the situation by the person who has been helped.

Smith warns that each person must exercise impartiality of judgment in relation to his own feelings and behavior. Well aware of the human tendency to overlook one's own moral failings and the self-deceit in which individuals often engage, Smith argues that each person must scrutinize his own feelings and behavior with the same strictness he employs when considering those of others. Such an impartial appraisal is possible because a person's conscience enables him to compare his own feelings with those of others. Conscience and sympathy, then, working together provide moral guidance for man so that the individual can control his own feelings and have a sensibility for the affections of others.

The Wealth of Nations

In 1764 Smith resigned his professorship to take up duties as a traveling tutor for the young Duke of Buccleuch and his brother. Carrying out this responsibility, he spent 2 years on the Continent. In Toulouse he began writing his best-known work, *An Inquiry into the Nature and Causes of the Wealth of Nations.* While in Paris he met Denis Diderot, Claude Adrien Helvétius, Baron Paul d'Holbach, François Quesnay, A.R.J. Turgot, and Jacques Necker. These thinkers doubtless had some influence on him. His life abroad came to an abrupt end when one of his charges was killed.

Smith then settled in Kirkcaldy with his mother. He continued to work on *The Wealth of Nations,* which was finally published in 1776. His mother died at the age of 90, and Smith was grief-stricken. In 1778 he was made customs commissioner, and in 1784 he became a fellow of the Royal Society of Edinburgh. Smith apparently spent some time in London, where he became a friend of Benjamin Franklin. On his deathbed he demanded that most of his manuscript writings be destroyed. He died on July 17, 1790.

The Wealth of Nations, easily the best known of Smith's writings, is a mixture of descriptions, historical accounts, and recommendations. The wealth of a nation, Smith insists, is to be gauged by the number and variety of consumable goods it can command. Free trade is essential for the maximum development of wealth for any nation because through such trade a variety of goods becomes possible.

Smith assumes that if each person pursues his own interest the general welfare of all will be fostered. He objects to governmental control, although he acknowledges that some restrictions are required. The capitalist invariably produces and sells consumable goods in order to meet the greatest needs of the people. In so fulfilling his own interest, the capitalist automatically promotes the general welfare. In the economic sphere, says Smith, the individual acts in terms of his own interest rather than in terms of sympathy. Thus, Smith made no attempt to bring into harmony his economic and moral theories.

Further Reading

John Rae, *Life of Adam Smith* (1895), is still useful and was reprinted (1965) with an introductory essay by Jacob Viner which details the recent scholarship on Smith. William R. Scott, *Adam Smith as Student and Professor* (1937), focuses on Smith's personality. Other biographies include Eli Ginzberg, *The House of Adam Smith* (1934); Sir Alexander Gray, *Adam Smith* (1948); and the not entirely successful work of E.G. West, *Adam Smith* (1969). Robert L. Heilbroner, *The Worldly Philosophers: The Lives, Times, and Ideas of the Great Economic Thinkers* (1953; 3d ed. 1967), has a vivid profile of Smith and his times. Smith's place in the history of economics is assessed in Charles Gide and Charles Rist, *A History of Economic Doctrines from the Time of the Physiocrats to the Present Day* (trans., 2d ed. 1948), and Joseph Schumpeter, *History of Economic Analysis* (1954). □

Alfred Emmanuel Smith

Alfred Emmanuel Smith (1873-1944), American politician, was governor of New York. His race as presidential candidate in 1928 was important as a test of urban influence in American politics.

Alfred E. Smith was born on Dec. 30, 1873, in a tenement on New York City's Lower East Side. He attended St. James's Parochial School until, at the age of 15, he began supporting his widowed mother and sister by working in a fish market. Like other ambitious Irish-Catholic youths of the day, Smith gravitated toward the Tammany Hall political organization, working initially as a subpoena server. As a reward for faithful service, he was picked to run for the New York State Assembly in 1903.

Legislative Career and Governorship

Smith's career in the Assembly represented the politics of the ghetto, combining pragmatic reform with service to the machine. In 1911 he was appointed chairman of the important Ways and Means Committee as well as vice-chairman of the Factory Investigating Commission. This gave him the opportunity to familiarize himself with industrial conditions. He introduced several reform measures representative of the kind of bread-and-butter progressivism that immigrants in New York's ghettos needed. In 1912 he became House floor leader, and the next year the Democrats acknowledged his influence by electing him Speaker.

At the constitutional convention in 1915 Smith demonstrated that he was the best-informed man on the business of the state of New York, and Tammany leaders immediately designated him sheriff of New York County. In 1917 Smith became president of the Board of Aldermen. The following year, upstate delegates to the Democratic convention successfully backed his candidacy for the governorship. To the surprise of many political observers, Smith defeated the Republican incumbent.

Governor Smith, the spokesman for the new urban masses, instituted a number of important social reforms, including an amended workmen's compensation law, higher teachers' salaries, and appropriations for the sick and mentally ill. He also urged the legislature to extend labor laws to protect women in industry and to enact health insurance legislation. His growing popularity was shown in 1920, when a spontaneous parade erupted after his name was placed before the Democratic National Convention for the presidency. His bid for reelection as governor was defeated, however, in the Republican landslide of 1920, but 2 years later he was again elected. In the spring of 1924 he declared his presidential candidacy.

Presidential Ambitions

Smith's candidacy was backed by the urban wing of the Democratic party. The rural wing supported William Gibbs McAdoo. The two-thirds requirement for nomination canceled out Smith and McAdoo, and after a bitter clash the delegates chose John W. Davis on the 103d ballot.

At Davis's behest, Smith again ran for the governorship, defeating Lt. Col. Theodore Roosevelt by 108,000 votes. During his third term Smith continued the fight for Progressive legislation, campaigning for government developed waterpower sites and for administrative reorganization. He won an unprecedented fourth term in 1926.

Smith's presidential nomination in 1928 on the first ballot illustrated the growing power of urban Democrats, but he had little chance of winning against Republican prosperity. He compounded his difficulties by making no effort to unite the factions of his party. His unwillingness or inability to establish a Progressive position that differed sharply from that of his opponent, Herbert Hoover, permitted the campaign to focus on prohibition, personalities, and particularly on Smith's Catholicism. Although soundly defeated, Smith had brought so many foreign-born Americans to the polls that the Democratic party, for the first time, carried the big cities.

In the aftermath of defeat, Smith became increasingly a spokesman and defender of the business community. Beginning in 1933, he condemned the social philosophy and domestic policies of President Franklin Roosevelt. He became in 1934 a charter member of the American Liberty League, an organization of wealthy, conservative industrialists and politicians opposed to the New Deal. Eventually Smith broke with the Democratic party.

Despite an apparent ideological turnabout, Smith's actions were consistent. He was fundamentally conservative, possessing an exaggerated reverence for the institutions and traditions of American society. He had never questioned the assumptions of capitalism and found the notion of a planned society repugnant. If he seemed to have changed in the 1930s, it was only because the times themselves had changed but he had not. He died in New York City on Oct. 4, 1944.

Further Reading

Smith's own account is *Up to Now: An Autobiography* (1929). A recent and probably definitive biography, which makes use of papers of Frances Perkins that have not been accessible to other biographers, is Matthew and Hannah Josephson, *Al Smith: Hero of the Cities* (1969). Also recent and well documented is the lively account by Richard O'Connor, *The First Hurrah: A Biography of Alfred E. Smith* (1970). Oscar Handlin, *Al Smith and His America* (1958), places Smith in the context of his time.

Additional Sources

Eldot, Paula, *Governor Alfred E. Smith: the politician as reformer,* New York: Garland, 1983.

Handlin, Oscar, *Al Smith and his America,* Boston: Northeastern University Press, 1987, 1958. □

Bessie Smith

Bessie Smith (ca. 1894-1937) was called "The Empress of the Blues." Her magnificent voice, sense of the dramatic, clarity of diction (you never missed a word of what she sang) and incomparable time and phrasing set her apart from the competition and made her appeal as much to jazz lovers as to lovers of the blues.

Born into poverty in Chattanooga, Tennessee, Bessie Smith began singing for money on street corners and eventually rose to become the largest-selling recording artist of her day. So mesmerizing was her vocal style—reinforced by her underrated acting and comedic skills—that near-riots frequently errupted when she appeared. Those outside the theaters clamored to get in; those inside refused to leave without hearing more of Smith. Twice she was instrumental in helping save Columbia Records from bankruptcy.

One of the numerous myths about Smith is that she was tutored (some versions claim kidnapped) by Ma Rainey, the prototype blues singer, and forced to tour with Rainey's show. In fact, Rainey didn't have her own show until after 1916, long after Smith had achieved independent success in a variety of minstrel and tent shows. Rainey and Smith did work together, however, and had established a friendship as early as 1912. No doubt Smith absorbed vocal ideas during her early association with the "Mother of the Blues."

Originally hired as a dancer, Smith rapidly polished her skills as a singer and often combined the two, weaving in a natural flair for comedy. From the beginning, communication with her audience was the hallmark of the young singer. Her voice was remarkable, filling the largest hall without amplification and reaching out to each listener in beautiful, earthy tones. In *Jazz People,* Dan Morgenstern quoted guitarist Danny Barker as saying: "Bessie Smith was a fabulous deal to watch. She was a large, pretty woman and she dominated the stage. You didn't turn your head when she went on. You just watched Bessie. If you had any church background like people who came from the [U.S.] South as I did, you would recognize a similarity between what she was doing and what those preachers and evangelists from there did, and how they moved people. She could bring about mass hypnotism."

When Mamie Smith (no relation to Bessie Smith) recorded the first vocal blues in 1920 and sold 100,000 copies in the first month, record executives discovered a new market and the "race record" was born. Shipped only to the South and selected areas of the North where blacks congregated, these recordings of black performers found an eager audience, a surprising segment of which was made up of white Southerners to whose ears the sounds of the blues were quite natural. Smith's first effective recording date, February 16, 1923, produced "Down-Hearted Blues" and "Gulf Coast Blues" and featured piano accompaniment by

Clarence Williams. The public bought an astounding 780,000 copies within six months.

Recorded With the Jazz Elite

Smith's contract paid her $125 per viable recording, with no provision for royalties. Frank Walker, who supervised all of Smith's recordings with Columbia through 1931, quickly negotiated new contracts calling first for 12 new recordings at $150 each, then 12 more at $200, and Smiths's fabulous recording career of 160 titles was successfully launched. On the brink of receivership in 1923, Columbia recovered largely through the sale of recordings by Eddie Cantor, Ted Lewis, Bert Williams, and its hottest selling artist, Bessie Smith. With her earnings, Smith was able to purchase a custom-designed railroad car for herself and her troupe in 1925. This luxury allowed her to circumvent some of the dispiriting effects of the racism found in both northern and southern states as she traveled with her own tent show or with the Theater Owners' Booking Association (TOBA) shows, commanding a weekly salary that peaked at $2,000.

Smith recorded with a variety of accompanists during her ten-year recording career, including some of the most famous names in jazz as well as some of the most obscure. Among the elite were pianists Fred Longshaw, Porter Grainger, and Fletcher Henderson; saxophonists Coleman Hawkins and Sidney Bechet; trombonist Charlie Green; clarinetists Buster Bailey and Don Redman; and cornetist Joe Smith. Perhaps her most empathetic backing came from Green and Smith, examples of which may be found on such songs as "The Yellow Dog Blues," "Empty Bed Blues," "Trombone Cholly," "Lost Your Head Blues," and "Young Woman's Blues." Smith and Louis Armstrong's first collaborations—1925's brilliant "St. Louis Blues" and "Cold in Hand Blues"—marked the end of the acoustic recording era, with Smith's first electrically recorded sides occuring on May 6, 1925. Other standouts with Armstrong include "Careless Love Blues," "Nashville Woman's Blues," and "I Ain't Gonna Play No Second Fiddle." Piano giant James P. Johnson's accompaniment sparkled on 1927's "Preachin' the Blues" and "Back Water Blues" as well as on 1929's "He's Got Me Goin'," "Worn Out Papa Blues," and "You Don't Understand."

Zealous Fans Created Mob Scenes

Feeding on the popularity of her records, Smith's tour date schedule escalated. As she traveled from her home base of Philadelphia, Pennsylvania, to Detroit, Chicago, Washington, D.C., Atlanta, Georgia, and New York City, adoring crowds greeted her at each stop. Extra police became the norm for controling crowd enthusiasm. What was the attraction? Critic and promoter John Hammond wrote in 1937: "Bessie Smith was the greatest artist American jazz ever produced; in fact, I'm not sure that her art did not reach beyond the limits of the term 'jazz.' She was one of those rare beings, a completely integrated artist capable of projecting her whole personality into music. She was blessed not only with great emotion but with a tremendous voice that could penetrate the inner recesses of the listener."

In *Early Jazz,* Gunther Schuller listed the components of Smith's vocal style: "a remarkable ear for and control of intonation in all its subtlest functions; a perfectly centered, naturally produced voice (in her prime); an extreme sensitivity to word meaning and the sensory, almost physical, feeling of a word; and, related to this, superb diction and what singers call projection. She was certainly the first singer on jazz records to value diction, not for itself, but as a vehicle for conveying emotional states. . . . Perhaps even more remarkable was her pitch control. She handled this with such ease and naturalness that one is apt to take it for granted. Bessie's fine microtonal shadings . . . are all part of a personal, masterful technique of great subtlety, despite the frequently boisterous mood or language." Schuller further heralded Smith as "the first complete jazz singer" whose influence on Billie Holiday and a whole generation of jazz singers cannot be overestimated.

Lived and Sang the Blues

In spite of her commercial success, Smith's personal life never strayed far from the blues theme. Her marriage to Jack Gee was stormy, punctuated by frequent fights and breakups despite their adoption of a son, Jack Gee, Jr., in 1926. Their nuptials ended in a bitter separation in 1929; Gee then attempted to keep the boy from Smith for years by moving him from one boarding home to another. Smith also battled liquor. Though able to abstain from drinking for considerable periods, Smith often indulged in binges that were infamous among her troupe and family. Equally well known to her intimates was Smith's bisexual promiscuity.

Smith's popularity as a recording artist crested around 1929, when the three-pronged fork of radio, talking pictures, and the Great Depression pitched the entire recording industry onto the critical list. Though her personal appearances continued at a brisk pace, the price she could demand dipped; she was forced to sell her beloved railroad car, and the smaller towns she played housed theaters in which general quality and facilities were a burden. Even so she starred in a 1929 two-reel film, *St. Louis Blues,* a semi-autobiographical effort that received some exposure through 1932.

Smith's only appearance on New York's famed 52nd Street came on a cold Sunday afternoon in February of 1936 at the Famous Door, where she was backed by Bunny Berigan, Joe Bushkin, and other regulars of the house band. The impact of her singing that day has remained with those present for more than half a century. Much was made of the fact that Mildred Bailey wisely refused to follow Smith's performance. Furthermore, that single afternoon's performance gave rise to other possible Smith appearances with popular swing performers: John Hammond claimed a 1937 recording date teaming Smith and members of the Count Basie band was in the works, Lionel Hampton recalled Goodman's eagerness to record with Smith, and another film was planned. Smith's lean years were ending as the summer of 1937 approached. The recording industry's revival soared on the craziness of the early Swing Era, spearheaded by the success of Benny Goodman's band. Smith had proven adaptable in her repertoire and could certainly swing with the best of them; moreover, blues singing was experiencing a revival in popular taste. Even Smith's personal life was on the upswing with the steady and loving influence of her companion, Richard Morgan.

On the morning of September 26, 1937, Smith and Morgan were driving from a Memphis performance to Darling, Mississippi, for the next day's show. Near Clarksdale, Mississippi, their car was involved in an accident fatal to Smith. A persistent rumor later developed that Smith bled to death because a white hospital refused to admit her. The myth originated in a 1937 *Down Beat* story written by John Hammond and was perpetuated by Edward Albee's 1960 play, *The Death of Bessie Smith.* Thirty-five years after Smith's death, author Chris Albertson finally dispelled the rumor. Albertson won a Grammy award for his booklet that accompanied the 1970 Columbia reissue of Smith's complete works—Columbia's second major reissue project. His deeper investigations resulted in the acclaimed 1972 biography, *Bessie.*

Albertson described Smith's funeral: "On Monday, October 4, 1937, Philadelphia witnessed one of the most spectacular funerals in its history. Bessie Smith, a black superstar of the previous decade—a 'has been,' fatally injured on a dark Mississippi road eight days earlier—was given a send-off befitting the star she had never really ceased to be. . . . When word of her death reached the black community, the body had to be moved [to another location] which more readily accommodated the estimated ten thousand admirers who filed past her bier on Sunday, October 3. . . . The crowd outside was now seven thousand strong, and policemen were having a hard time holding it back. To those who had known Bessie in her better days, the sight was familiar."

Further Reading

Albertson, Chris, *Bessie,* Stein and Day, 1972.

Brooks, Edward, *The Bessie Smith Companion,* Da Capo, 1983.

Donaldson, Norman, and Betty Donaldson, *How Did They Die?,* St. Martin's Press, 1980.

Kinkle, Roger D., *The Complete Encyclopedia of Popular Music and Jazz 1900-1950, Volume 3,* Arlington House, 1974.

Morgenstern, Dan, *Jazz People,* Harry N. Abrams, 1976.

Rust, Brian, *Jazz Records 1891-1942, Volume 2,* 5th revised and enlarged edition, Storyville Publications, 1982.

Schuller, Gunther, *Early Jazz,* Oxford University Press, 1968.

Schuller, Gunther, *The Swing Era,* Oxford University Press, 1989.

Shapiro, Nat, and Nat Hentoff, editors, *The Jazz Makers* (Bessie Smith chapter by George Hoefer), Rinehart and Co., 1957.

Terkel, Studs, and Millie Hawk Daniel, *Giants of Jazz,* revised edition, Thomas Y. Crowell Company, 1975.

Esquire, June 1969.

High Fidelity, October 1970; May 1975.

National Review, July 1, 1961.

Newsweek, February 1, 1971; January 22, 1973.

Saturday Review, December 29, 1951; February 26, 1972. □

David Smith

David Smith (1906-1965), American sculptor and painter, pioneered in exploiting welded, openwork metal sculpture. His art was very influential, and he was one of the most significant American artists during the 1950s.

David Smith was born in Decatur, Ind. The family moved to Paulding, Ohio, in 1921. In 1923 Smith studied art through a correspondence school, and the following year he matriculated for a year at Ohio University. During the summers he worked as a welder and riveter at the Studebaker plant in South Bend, Ind. He also took courses at Notre Dame University and at George Washington University. He entered the Art Students League in New York City in 1927 to study painting with John Sloan; that year he married Dorothy Dehner. The next year he studied privately with the Czech painter Jan Matulka, who introduced him to modern painting and sculpture. To support himself, Smith worked part time as a taxi driver, seaman, carpenter, and salesman. In 1929 he bought an old farm in Bolton Landing, N.Y., and set up the studio he used for the rest of his life.

Early Sculpture

Smith became acquainted with many artists who worked abstractly, and they encouraged him to work in that style. In 1932 he made his first sculptures by attaching stray objects to paintings. On a trip to the Virgin Islands he used coral in his constructions. It was after seeing photographs of Pablo Picasso's metal constructions, however, that he turned wholeheartedly to sculpture. From 1934 to 1940 Smith rented studio space at the Terminal Iron Works in Brooklyn. He would frequently include pieces of "junk" metal in his sculptures. He welded slender lengths of metal strip to circumscribe space in a calligraphic fashion. It was as if Smith were recasting in metal a synthetic cubist painting. A characteristic sculpture of this period is *Aerial Construction* (1936).

Between 1937 and 1940 Smith struck bronze medals, which he called *Medals of Dishonor,* to attack war propaganda, munition makers, bacterial warfare, prostitution, and other social ills. The all-important imagery was borrowed from newspapers, magazines, textbooks on medicine, as well as from Old Masters Francisco Goya, Hieronymus Bosch, Pieter Brueghel, and others. In 1938 Smith had his first one-man show. The next year he executed *Structure of Arches,* a large abstract piece constructed mostly of steel, in which he used arc welding for the first time. In 1940 he made Bolton Landing his permanent residence and supported himself by working part time for the American Locomotive Company in Schenectady, N.Y. After 1944, however, he concentrated on sculpture except for several short-term appointments as a teacher at Sarah Lawrence College, the University of Arkansas, Indiana University, and the University of Mississippi. In 1950 he received a fellowship from the Guggenheim Foundation.

Evolving a Style

In the late 1940s and early 1950s Smith was still evolving a personal style, still searching for and absorbing influences. *Reliquary House* (1945) is reminiscent of Alberto Giacometti's surrealist sculptures. *Royal Bird* (1948) was inspired by a skeleton of a prehistoric bird Smith had seen in the Museum of Natural History in New York; he may have known the influential *Spectre of Kitty Hawk,* a brazed, welded, hammered steel sculpture by Theodore Roszak executed in 1946. *The Letter* (1950), *Twenty-four Y's* (1950), and *Hudson River Landscape* (1951) are highly original works whose imagery is based on the American scene. They are linear and calligraphic in conception. Slender metal strips form an elegant tangle and appear animated as they gesture in turns, bends, thrusts, and counterthrusts. Within the framework of the tangle, relatively self-contained units appear as if suspended. Not infrequently, they suggest arcane hieroglyphs or quasi-semantical designs. He used color in some works which may have been influenced by his friendship with painters such as Robert Motherwell and Kenneth Noland.

Smith's sculpture became better known in the late 1950s. The Museum of Modern Art gave him a one-man show in 1957. He had two other important one-man shows in New York City—at French and Company in 1959 and at the Otto Gerson Gallery in 1961. In 1962 he was commissioned to make 26 sculptures for the Festival of Two Worlds at Spoleto, and went to went to Italy to execute them. During the 1960s he favored larger forms at the expense of the linear. He made works in series such as *Tank Totem, Agricola, Cubi, Menand,* and *Zig.* In *Cubi XXVII* (1965), one of three monumental polished stainless steel "gates," Smith retained the openness and shifting rhythms of his earlier linear sculptures but composed the work by welding together cubic shapes and a cylinder. These have gleaming surfaces buffed to form shifting patterns reminiscent of frost on a windowpane. This work exemplifies Smith's openness to fresh ideas and the constant evolution of his art and his inventiveness.

In 1952 Smith had divorced his first wife, and the following year he married Jean Treas, with whom he had two daughters. The second marriage was dissolved in 1961. On April 23, 1965, Smith died in Albany, N.Y., from injuries sustained in an automobile accident. There have been several exhibitions since his death; the most extensive was in 1969 at the Solomon R. Guggenheim Museum in New York City.

Further Reading

Useful information on Smith is in *David Smith,* text and photos by David Smith, edited by Cleve Gray (1968), and Edward F. Fry, *David Smith* (1969). Jane Harrison Cone, *David Smith, 1906-1965: A Retrospective Exhibition* (1967), is more complete than other works on him, is well researched, and contains 104 monochrome plates. Also recommended is the catalog of Smith's 1969 exhibition at the Guggenheim Museum, which includes excellent plates and an extensive bibliography. Rosalind E. Krauss, *Terminal Iron Works: The Sculpture of David Smith* (1971), is a fine study of the sculptor's imagery.

Additional Sources

Marcus, Stanley E., *David Smith, the sculptor and his work,* Ithaca, N.Y.: Cornell University Press, 1983.

Wilkin, Karen, *David Smith,* New York: Abbeville Press, 1984. □

Donald Alexander Smith

Donald Alexander Smith, 1st Baron Strathcona and Mount Royal (1820-1914), was a Canadian politician, diplomat, philanthropist, and business leader with extensive interests in the fur trade, railroads, and banking.

Donald A. Smith was born on Aug. 6, 1820, at Forres, Morayshire, Scotland. His father was a modestly successful merchant. Donald was educated at the Anderson Institution, Forres. In 1853 he married Isabella Hardisty, daughter of a Hudson's Bay Company official. Their only child was Margaret Charlotte, the heir to Smith's fortune and barony.

John Stuart, a Hudson's Bay Company trader and Smith's uncle, secured Smith's appointment to a company clerkship in 1838. After serving at Lachine and Tadoussac he was transferred in 1847 to Labrador, where he remained 13 years and became a financier. Business associates loaned him their savings, which he used to purchase Bank of Montreal shares. Smith rose through the ranks of the Company and became a chief trader, a chief factor, a company troubleshooter, and finally, in 1869, head of the Montreal Department. He became wealthy and invested heavily in Hudson's Bay Company shares and was a company leader when Canada purchased the company's territories in 1869. He was elected a director in 1883 and served as governor (1889-1914).

The first Riel rebellion (1869-1870) made Smith famous. Sir John Alexander Macdonald's Conservative government feared that the rising might invite American military intervention. Because of Hudson's Bay Company influence, Smith was sent to Red River to negotiate with Louis Riel, leader of the resistance. His impact, although considerable, was not decisive. Smith's confidential report on the rising remains a standard source for students.

Smith capitalized on his notoriety. In 1870 he secured appointment to the Executive Council of the Northwest Territories and was elected to Manitoba's Assembly. Until he resigned his provincial seat in 1874, he was a leader of the lieutenant governor's party. He was federal member of Parliament for Selkirk, Manitoba (1871-1879), until he was unseated for electoral malpractice. He later sat for Montreal West (1887-1896). Smith deserted Macdonald's first confederation government over the Pacific Railway scandal in 1873. Macdonald revived the issue during a debate in 1878. In a famous scene Macdonald declared, "That fellow Smith is the biggest liar I ever met." The Conservative leader then lunged at Smith screaming, "I can lick you quicker than Hell can scorch a feather." Actual blows were prevented, but for years Smith's 1873 desertion rankled Macdonald.

Although a member of Parliament for 17 years, Smith was most interested in business. During the 1870s he became a leading railroader. With several partners, including George Stephen, president of the Bank of Montreal, he purchased the St. Paul-Minneapolis and Manitoba Railway Company and became the firm's vice president. The line gained Smith experience and great wealth. In 1880 he and Stephen dominated the syndicate organized to construct the Canadian Pacific Railway. A major financier as well, Smith was president of the Bank of Montreal (1887-1905). He served as a director of the Patton Manufacturing Company, the New Brunswick Railway, the Canadian Pacific Railway Company, and the Dominion Coal Company.

Prime Minister Sir Charles Tupper appointed Smith Canadian high commissioner to London in 1896. He retained the post until his death in London on Jan. 21, 1914. Tough, proud, unscrupulous, and autocratic, Smith amassed a huge fortune. He was a liberal benefactor who contributed vast sums to such institutions as hospitals and universities—in Canada, Great Britain, and the United States. During the Boer War he equipped, as his personal contribution, a famous mounted regiment, the "Strathcona Horse." Honors were showered upon him, and he was appointed to the Canadian Privy Council in 1896 and to the Imperial Privy Council in 1904. In 1897 he joined the British peerage as Baron Strathcona and Mount Royal.

Further Reading

Beckles Wilson's eulogistic *The Life of Lord Strathcona and Mount Royal* (1915) is the fullest account of Smith's life. John MacNaughton, *Lord Strathcona* (1926), is useful, but W.T.R. Preston, *The Life and Times of Lord Strathcona* (1914), is a shabby polemic. Excellent material on Smith is included in Donald Grant Creighton, *John A. Macdonald: The Old Chieftain* (1956); Heather Gilbert, *Awakening Continent: The Life of Lord Mount Stephen,* vol. 1 (1965); Merrill Denison, *Canada's First Bank* (2 vols., 1966-1967); and Pierre Benton, *The National Dream* (1970) and *The Last Spike* (1971). Recommended for general historical background are Douglas MacKay, *The Honourable Company: A History of the Hudson's Bay Company* (1936; rev. ed. 1966), and G. P. de T. Glazebrook, *A History of Transportation in Canada* (1938; 2d ed., 2 vols., 1964). □

Dora Smith

The American educator Dora Smith (1893-1985) researched, lectured, and wrote extensively about language arts and English curricula in elementary and secondary schools. Dubbed "The First Lady of the United States in the Teaching of English," Smith was also internationally acclaimed as a scholar and consultant.

Dora V. Smith was born on February 14, 1893, to Scottish immigrant parents in Minneapolis. She received her B.A. from the University of Minnesota in 1916 and began her professional career as a high school English teacher in the rural community of Long Prairie, Minnesota. Smith received her M.A. from the University of Minnesota in 1919 and her Ph.D. from the same institution in 1928, working in the interim primarily as an English teacher and supervisor of student teachers at University High School in Minneapolis.

Upon receiving her doctorate, Smith joined the faculty of the University of Minnesota, teaching courses in children's and adolescent literature as well as English and language arts methods. In the early years of her academic career, Smith spent a year in residence at St. George's College at the University of London (1920-1921) and another at Teachers College at Columbia University (1928-1929). In later years she taught summer sessions at Columbia, the University of California, and the University of Hawaii, among others.

Smith's thesis on the effects of class size on high school English teaching methods and outcomes, published by the University of Minnesota Press in 1931, anticipated many of the later controversies over instructional techniques and grouping practices. After comparing freshman English students in two "small" classes of 20 with matched groups of 20 students in two classes of 51, Smith concluded that students in the larger classes performed better in reading literature than their counterparts in smaller classes. She found that successful teachers of larger groups used discussions and projects rather than recitations and worksheets and divided their classes into smaller groups for such tasks as correcting homework, investigating topics, and presenting reports. Long before Robert Slavin's work on cooperative learning and Benjamin Bloom's on mastery learning, Smith advocated having students coach and instruct each other in mixed-ability groups while the teacher provides more intensive individualized instruction to students who need this help.

Smith was interested not only in instructional technique, but also in curriculum content. From 1936 to 1937 she served as a consultant to the New York Regents, investigating that state's response to the challenge of educating college-bound and non-college-bound students from a variety of social classes and settings. Again anticipating contemporary debate, she expressed concern about allowing tests such as the Regents' Examination to drive curriculum decisions.

Smith pursued her interest in curriculum through the National Council of Teachers of English (NCTE). She served as NCTE's president in 1936-1937, then undertook, in 1945, the enormous task of directing and editing the National Council's five-volume series on English curricula from kindergarten to graduate school. The outcomes of the English curricula she proposed were consistent with the tenets of progressive education: to encourage students at all levels to develop solid personal values, understand themselves and others, establish personal reading habits, and learn to think critically, an especially important skill for citizens in a democracy. Throughout the series, she emphasized the importance of beginning where students are and keeping their individual and age-related characteristics in mind.

Smith was no extremist when it came to the educational controversies of her day; instead she consistently advocated flexibility in approach in order to best serve the needs of the individual child. In response to Rudolf Flesch's scathing *Why Johnny Can't Read* (1955), for example, she rebutted the notion that phonics alone could improve reading ability, yet she did not believe that sight word recognition or, as it was popularly known, the "look-say" method of reading instruction could stand alone either. She believed there was a place for basal textbooks in the classroom, but also wanted children to experience the "fun, fact, and fantasy" of real books. As she noted sensibly, "No one method of approaching words will ever suffice. . . . The business of teaching children to read is too important for us to put all our eggs in one basket."

Smith was similarly flexible in addressing the question of whether students should read "classics" or contemporary children's and adolescent literature. She stated that "no single book is so important as to warrant reading at the expense of the development of a voluntary habit of good reading"; yet she urged teachers to guide students to select higher quality mystery stories than the then-popular Nancy Drew and Hardy Boys series. She suggested that teachers tailor their book recommendations to match the interests and tastes of individual students, noting that the "recommendation of a single book which fills a real need in the life of a child will do more to foster mutual relations of interest and good will than all the prescribed reading lists ever printed."

Smith herself was never far from the real needs in the lives of children: throughout her career she served as a consultant for several major U.S. school districts, including Oakland, California; Los Angeles County; Battle Creek, Michigan; Bronxville, New York; Salt Lake City; Austin; and Denver. During a sabbatical leave in the mid 1950s, Smith embarked on a year of international travel to Japan, the Philippines, Indonesia, Thailand, India, Pakistan, Lebanon, Turkey, Greece, and Egypt. Her mission was to find modern books about the customs and cultures of these countries, many of which were just emerging from a period of colonial rule, for American school children. In a newspaper interview prior to the trip, Smith said, "We know the fairy tales and beast fables of many countries, but we have few stories of how children in other countries live, feel, and think today. We do not want our boys and girls to have the notion that the children of India, for example, help to kill giants and go out on errands of magic in company with the genie."

After more than 40 years of scholarship and service in the areas of curriculum development, reading habits, and children's literature, Smith retired from the University of Minnesota as a full professor of general education in 1958. That year she received the highest honor of the National Council of Teachers of English—the W. Wilbur Hatfield Award—for her "long and distinguished service to the teaching of English in the United States." She remained highly productive in her retirement years: her book *Fifty Years of Children's Books, 1910-1960* was published in 1963 and a compilation of her thought entitled *Selected Essays* came out in 1964. Smith died on January 28, 1985, at the age of 92.

Further Reading

Robert C. Pooley provides biographical information in his foreword to *Selected Essays* (1964); that book also serves as a good introduction to Smith's work in language arts and English education. The University of Minnesota Archives has additional biographical material on file, including newspaper clippings and a record of Smith's activity within the university community.

Smith's *Communication, The Miracle of Shared Living* (1955) is intended for general audiences. It emphasizes that communication skills are critical for full and meaningful participation in a democratic society. *Fifty Years of Children's Books* (1963) still reads relevantly, though it, of course, does not take into account later trends in children's literature. Numerous shorter pieces by Smith may be found in education journals such as *English Journal, Elementary English Review, School Review,* and *Review of Educational Research.* □

Gerrit Smith

Gerrit Smith (1797-1874), American philanthropist and reformer, was a founder of the radical-abolitionist Liberty party.

Gerrit Smith was born on March 6, 1797. His father, a partner of merchant John Jacob Astor, was one of the biggest landowners in the nation. Smith graduated in 1818 from Hamilton College. He inherited not only the estate but also his father's intense concern for religious truth. He settled with his first wife, Ann Backus, daughter of Hamilton College's president, in the family home in Peterboro, N.Y.

Smith's concern for religious salvation took him into the Presbyterian Church, where he was associated with such reform causes as tract distribution and Sabbath observance. His developing views, however, caused him to build his own "Church of Peterboro" on more liberal principles, and he himself often preached in the church's chapel. His benefactions ranged from individual gifts to distributions of funds for the relief of old maids and widows and the support of temperance and antitobacco movements.

Smith believed that true religion must express itself in true politics. In 1825 he joined the American Colonization Society, but a decade of experience with the ACS persuaded him that the society's purpose was not to free slaves but to rid the country of free Negroes. He then turned to the American Antislavery Society. One of his most notable acts took place in 1846, when he appointed a committee of land reformers and abolitionists to parcel out a land grant of some 150,000 acres to poor white settlers and blacks. Although much of the land was inferior (and thus failed to demonstrate capacities at land ownership), the grant won wide publicity for the free-soil cause.

In 1840 Smith joined in initiating the Liberty party. He was the party's presidential candidate in 1848, receiving 2,733 votes. In 1853 he was elected as an independent to the Congress, where he mixed defiance of the Fugitive Slave Law at home with a belief that United States annexation of Cuba would be advantageous to its slaves. He resigned his House seat the next year.

Smith's combination of radicalism and conservatism showed itself during the secession crisis. He supported John Brown's assault on Harpers Ferry, Va., but when Smith's position was exposed, he protested his innocence and was sufficiently overwrought to become temporarily insane. When he recovered, he supported the Union, but after the Civil War he held that slavery had been the responsibility of both North and South. Accordingly, he joined with Horace Greeley and Cornelius Vanderbilt to provide bail bond to free Jefferson Davis, holding that his captivity without trial was an injustice to the country. He died in New York City on Dec. 28, 1874.

Further Reading

Octavius Brooks Frothingham, *Gerrit Smith: A Biography* (1878; 3d ed. 1909), though often imprecise, is written by a distinguished transcendentalist. It was deepened and corrected by the scholarly Ralph Volney Harlow and published as *Gerrit Smith: Philanthropist and Reformer* (1939).

Additional Sources

Harlow, Ralph Volney, *Gerrit Smith, philanthropist and reformer,* New York, Russell & Russell 1972. □

Ian Douglas Smith

Ian Douglas Smith (born 1919) was the last white prime minister of Rhodesia before it became the independent nation of Zimbabwe. In an effort to resist African majority rule, he led his extremist white government in a unilateral break with Great Britain and declared Rhodesia a republic, the first such anti-British revolt since the American colonies declared their independence in 1776.

Ian Smith was born on April 8, 1919, in Selukwe, Southern Rhodesia. He attended Selukwe High School; an average student, he was outstanding in sports. His studies at Rhodes University in Grahamstown, South Africa, were interrupted by World War II. He joined the Royal Air Force in 1941, and when his plane crashed in North Africa, Smith received severe injuries in his leg and face. Plastic surgeons literally remade the right side of his face, leaving him with a dour expression which observers later said was an asset in political negotiations. He soon flew again with the 237th (Rhodesia) Squadron. His plane was hit by flak in northern Italy in June 1944. He bailed out and fought for some months with a partisan force against the Germans. Smith crossed the Alps to the Allied lines and joined the

130th Royal Air Force Squadron for the remainder of the war.

Entering Politics

Smith returned to Rhodes University, where he earned the bachelor of commerce degree. He returned to his Selukwe farm and married Janet Watt (they had two sons and a daughter). Deciding to enter politics, he served in the Legislative Assembly as a Rhodesian party member (1948-1953). When the Federation of Rhodesia and Nyasaland was formed in 1953, Smith was elected to the federal Parliament as a member of the ruling United Federal party. After Sir Roy Welensky succeeded to the federal prime ministership, Smith was named chief government whip in 1958.

Observers recall Smith as not particularly notable as a parliamentarian or a popular speaker. He first gained public attention in 1961, when at a party meeting he opposed a constitutional change accepted by the party to give Africans representation in the Southern Rhodesia Legislative Assembly. Smith resigned from the United Federal party that year and was a founding member and vice president of the rightist Rhodesian Front party, which became the ruling party in Southern Rhodesia. Under Prime Minister Winston Field, Smith served as deputy prime minister and minister of the Treasury (1962-1964). When Field was ousted by rightists in his party on April 13, 1964, Smith became prime minister. He also served as minister of defense (1964-1965) and as minister of external affairs (1964).

Crisis and Break with Britain

Smith's rise to leadership fitted Southern Rhodesia's political history. White settler occupancy of the territory had begun in 1890. The settlers received self-governing status in 1923; Britain retained only veto power over legislation discriminatory to Africans. Continuation of minority white rule, critics believed, lay behind the formation of the ill-fated Federation of Rhodesia and Nyasaland (1953-1963). Smith rose to power because of his firm white supremacist stand at a time when African countries to the north were gaining independence under black rule and when Britain was pressing for constitutional changes enabling unimpeded progress toward African majority rule. Smith represented 240,000 whites determined to control a country in which 4.5 million Africans also lived.

On black-white relations, Smith quoted his father as saying, "We are entitled to our half of the country and they are entitled to theirs." Friendly Rhodesians referred to Smith as "Iron Man Ian" or "Good Old Smithy." Critics called him the world's foremost white supremacist. His wife said of him, "No one can influence my husband once he has made up his mind."

Smith's goal was to negotiate independence for Rhodesia under the 1961 Constitution (the name was shortened after Northern Rhodesia became independent as Zambia on Nov. 24, 1964). British prime minister Harold Wilson would not agree without guarantees of unimpeded African progress toward majority rule. Frequent talks in London and Salisbury did not resolve the impasse. Smith was under pressure from whites who were even more extreme than his own government.

On Nov. 11, 1965, Smith issued a declaration of independence reminiscent of the American colonial revolt in 1776. Britain retaliated by cutting off Rhodesia from the sterling trade area, dismissing the Smith government, invalidating Rhodesian passports, and banning purchases of Rhodesia's cash crop of tobacco. Wilson declared that he would not use force to bring Rhodesia to heel. On Dec. 16, 1967, the United Nations Security Council joined Britain's earlier move in imposing economic sanctions against Rhodesia. Despite discomfort from the shortages of some luxuries, Rhodesia received petroleum products and other vital items from the Republic of South Africa, Portuguese Mozambique, and other sources.

Declaration of a Republic

Fruitless talks took place between Smith and Wilson on British ships off Gibraltar in 1966 and 1968. In a constitutional referendum on June 20, 1969, Smith's government received a 72 percent vote approval for a new constitution aimed at legislative parity between whites and Africans when income tax parity was reached (that is, very slowly). He also received an 82 percent vote approval for republican status. On March 1, 1970, Smith declared Rhodesia a republic, severing all ties with Britain.

Urged by Britain, the UN voted to impose economic sanctions against Rhodesia, and African nationalist factions began mobilizing increasingly powerful guerrilla forces in nearby Zambia against the illegal government. In 1973, Smith closed the border with Zambia, causing significant damage to the Rhodesian Railways, which depended on Zambian copper ore.

The civil and guerrilla war escalated in 1975 after the independence of Mozambique opened another base for guerrilla operations. Whites began to flee the border regions as the war continued, adding to the economic hardships imposed by sanctions and the worldwide oil crisis. In the face of diminishing support and supplies from South Africa and increasing international pressure, Smith announced in 1977 that he would enact majority rule in Rhodesia within two years. Later that year he publicly accepted the principle of universal suffrage.

In March, 1978, Smith reached an agreement with African nationalist leaders to set up an executive council while retaining his power in a first step toward majority rule. In 1979 he accepted a shared government with Abel Muzorewa, whose party won the first universal suffrage election in Rhodesian history. Rhodesia was renamed "Zimbabwe Rhodesia," and Muzorewa replaced Smith as prime minister in June 1979. In 1980, Zimbabwe achieved independence from Great Britain under a consitution that guaranteed Europeans 20 out of 100 seats in the national assembly. Robert Mugabe, who had waged a guerrilla campaign, easily won the 1980 elections and established the first free African government in Zimbabwe.

Smith continued to serve in the Parliament as leader of the Republican Front until 1987, when he was suspended. His influence diminished as other RF party members sought to support the Mugabe regime, but he continued to criticize the government and rallied opposition to Mugabe in the 1995 elections.

In his memoirs, *The Great Betrayal,* Smith continued to assert that the black majority should be "gradually" raised to the "standards of Western civilization" and discussed black "terrorists" while downplaying the cruelties of Rhodesia's armed forces during the civil war. He asserted that Britain hypocritically imposed sanctions on Rhodesia even though many of its other states had one-party governments. His own account also emphasized the dictatorial nature of the Mugabe regime and its resistance to democratic reforms. Since leaving politics, Smith has lived on his farm in Zimbabwe

Further Reading

Ian Douglas Smith, *The Great Betrayal: The Memoirs of Ian Douglas Smith,* Blake Publishing, 1997 [reviewed in *Publishers Weekly,* May 26, 1997, and *The Economist,* April 19, 1997]; Peter Joyce, *Anatomy of a Rebel: Smith of Rhodesia,* Graham Publishing, 1974; Philippa Berlyn, *The Quiet Man: A Biography of the Hon. Ian Douglas Smith, I.D., Prime Minister of Rhodesia,* M.O. Collins, 1978; Matthew White, *Smith of Rhodesia,* Printpak, 1978. Sketches: *Political Leaders of Contemporary Africa South of the Sahara: A Biographical Dictionary,* Greenwood, 1992; *An African Biographical Dictionary,* ABC-CLIO, 1994; *Dictionary of African Historical Biography,* U. of Cal. Press, 1986. Useful background works include Franklin Parker, *African Development and Education in Southern Rhodesia* (1960); Lewis H. Gann and Peter Duignan, *White Settlers in Tropical Africa* (1962); and P. E. N. Tindall, *A History of Central Africa* (1968). □

James McCune Smith

James McCune Smith (1813-1865) was the first African American to practice medicine in the United States. He is remembered for his successful work as a physician and for his scholarly writings against slavery.

James McCune Smith was born in New York City on April 18, 1813, the son of a slave and a self-emancipated woman, some sources say that his parents were of mixed race. He attended the African Free School in New York City. According to the *Dictionary of American Biography,* one day the famed Revolutionary War hero, Lafayette, spoke with the students and Smith, then aged 11, was chosen to speak on behalf of the class.

Schooled in Scotland

Smith continued his education at the University of Glasgow in Scotland, where he received his B.A. in 1835, his master's degree in 1836 and his medical degree in 1837. Smith was stocky in build, with a full face and attractive eyes. He was considered an eloquent speaker, according to Carter Woodson's *Negro Makers of History.* He was married and had five children.

Smith worked briefly as a doctor in clinics in Paris, France, but returned to New York City where he opened a pharmacy on West Broadway, the first ever to be operated by an African American. He worked as a physician and surgeon from 1838 until two years before his death in 1865. For 20 years, he served on the medical staff at the Free Negro Orphan Asylum in New York City.

In 1846, a man from Peterboro, New York, donated 120,000 acres in the state to be divided and given to African Americans living in New York City, as reported the *Dictionary of American Biography.* Smith and two members of the African American clergy were given the task of selecting the nearly 2,000 people to receive the land.

Worked Against Sending Blacks Back to Africa

While many people of the day supported the idea that blacks should be returned to Africa, Smith did not. He met with blacks in favor of the move in Albany, New York, in 1852 and persuaded them to adopt a statement urging the New York State Legislature to reject efforts to send black Americans back to Africa. Smith went as far as to challenge a member of Congress from South Carolina, John C. Calhoun, after Calhoun pronounced that African Americans were prone to insanity. Smith's response, showing the information to be false, was called, "The Influence of Climate upon Longevity."

Dedicated to doing all he could to support black emancipation and equality, Smith worked as a supporter of the Underground Railroad, a movement to help slaves escape to freedom. He contributed articles to a publication called *Emancipator* and edited another called *Colored American.*

Wrote Scholarly Articles on Slavery

Regarded as the most scholarly African American of his time, Smith's writings suggest his wide-ranging interests. His articles include "Abolition of Slavery and the Slave Trade in the French and British Colonies," 1838; "On the Haitian Revolutions, with a Sketch of the Character of Toussaint L'Overture," 1841; "Freedom and Slavery for Africans," 1844; "The Influence of Climate upon Longevity: With Special Reference to Life Insurance," 1846; "Civilization: Its Dependence on Physical Circumstances," 1859; "The German Invasion" (which dealt with immigration and how it affected life in America), 1859; "Citizenship" (a report on the Dred Scott decision), 1859; and "On the Fourteenth Query of Thomas Jefferson's Notes on Virginia" (which compared the anatomy of whites and blacks), 1859.

Smith was appointed to teach anthropology at Ohio's Wilberforce University in 1863, but his poor health kept him from taking the position. He died of heart disease at his Long Island, New York, home on November 17, 1865.

Further Reading

Kaufman, Martin, and Todd L. Savitt, editors, *Dictionary of American Medical Biography,* Greenwood Press, 1984, p. 693.

Woodson, Carter G., and Charles H. Wesley, *Negro Makers of History,* Associated Publishers, 6th ed., 1968, pp. 167-168.

Malone, Dumas, editor, *Dictionary of American Biography,* 1935, pp. 288-289.

Blight, David W., *In Search of Learning, Liberty, and Self Definition: James McCune Smith and the Ordeal of the Antebellum Black Intellectual,* Afro-Americans in New York Life and History, Vol. 9(2), 1985, pp. 7-25.

Bulletin of the History of Medicine, Vol. 54(2), 1980, pp. 258-272. □

Jedediah S. Smith

Jedediah S. Smith (1799-1831), trapper, fur trader, and explorer in the American West, was one of the most skillful of the mountain men, although most of his accomplishments were recognized only recently.

Jedediah Smith's activities in the West occurred between 1822 and 1831, a period of rapid American penetration into the Rocky Mountain area and of phenomenal growth in American fur trading and trapping. He was the first reported American to travel overland to California, the first to cross the Sierra Nevada from the west, the first to travel across the Great Basin, north and south as well as east and west, the first to travel north up the California coast to Oregon, and the first to provide a usable description of South Pass.

The fourth of 12 children, Smith was born on Jan. 6, 1799. As a child, he roamed the wooded hills in southwestern New York, and when he was 12, the family moved into Erie County, Pa. From there they moved to the Western Reserve in northern Ohio. Jedediah's activities between 1816 and 1821 are unknown to historians. One author suggests that he got a reasonably good education and then became a clerk on a Lake Erie freighter, learning some business methods and perhaps even meeting Canadian trappers and fur traders. But this is mere conjecture.

By 1821 Smith had arrived in Illinois, still a frontier state. He spent that winter along the Mississippi River. Hearing about Gen. William Ashley's proposed expedition to the Rocky Mountains, he traveled to St. Louis to volunteer. When the keelboat *Enterprise* left St. Louis in May 1822, Smith went along as a hunter. The party reached the mouth of the Yellowstone River in eastern Montana in October. They built a log-surrounded camp called Ft. Henry, which served as their base of supply for the following trapping season. It was here that Smith began his decade of travel in the West.

Trapper and Fur Trader

The winter of 1822/1823 provided a rugged apprenticeship for Ashley's men. After building Ft. Henry, they traveled farther up the Missouri River to trap along its tributary streams. The difficulties of travel through the mountains convinced Maj. Henry that his party needed horses as pack animals, and in spring of 1823 he sent Smith back down the Missouri to tell Ashley. When or where Smith met his employer is not known, but when Ashley's party reached the Arikara Indian villages in late May, Smith was in their company.

Ashley's effort to buy horses from the Arikara led to one of the worst disasters in fur trade history. Because the trappers considered these Indians to be treacherous, Ashley kept part of his 90-man force aboard two keel-boats in the middle of the river. In the afternoon of June 1, one of the chiefs invited the traders to his lodge and there warned Ashley that the braves intended to attack his party. Ashley tried to get his men and horses aboard the keelboats but was unable to do so that evening, and at dawn the following morning the Indians attacked and killed or wounded nearly a third of the party. The remainder retreated downstream.

In September 1823, while Smith was leading a small band of trappers west overland from the Missouri River toward the mountains, a grizzly bear nearly killed him. The beast broke several of his ribs, tore away one eyebrow, gashed his scalp in numerous places, and practically destroyed one of his ears. Smith's companions hurriedly attended to his wounds, but because deep scars remained, Smith wore shoulder-length hair for the rest of his life. After he recovered enough for travel, the party continued west.

The following year Smith and his men traveled with the large Hudson's Bay Company trapping party led by Peter Ogden into the Snake River Valley. Ogden and his superiors wanted to turn the area into a vast fur desert by trapping all of the beaver, thereby discouraging American interest. Smith, however, got ahead of the Canadian trappers and not only gathered large numbers of furs himself but also induced more than 20 of Ogden's party to desert and join the Americans.

During the winter of 1824/1825 Ashley brought trade goods to the mountains, and the next summer Smith accompanied his employer down the Missouri with the fur bundles. That year Ashley decided that he needed a partner who would remain in the mountains and chose Smith. Smith led another party of trappers to the area around the Great Salt Lake. Late in 1826 Ashley sold his interest in the fur trade to Smith, David Jackson, and William Sublette, and these three men dominated American trapping and trading efforts in the northern Rockies until 1830.

In 1830 Smith and his partners sold their holdings to a group of traders called the Rocky Mountain Fur Company. Smith realized that most of the West had been denuded of fur-bearing animals and that increasing competition from rival fur brigades and the need to trap in the Blackfoot Indian country reduced profits and increased the danger. He headed back to St. Louis, where he bought a home and appeared ready to settle down. Instead he soon rejoined Jackson and Sublette and prepared to enter the Santa Fe trade. It was on his first trip west to Santa Fe that a hunting party of Comanche braves surprised Smith alone at a water hole. The Indians ignored his signs of peace, surrounded him, and killed him on May 27, 1831.

Accomplishments as an Explorer

Smith's explorations and his fur trade efforts were interrelated. In 1824 he crossed South Pass, the most important single gap through the Rocky Mountains. Although he was not the first discoverer of this route, his report that wagons could cross there was of major significance because earlier knowledge of the pass had not survived. In 1826, leading a party of trappers south and west across the Great Basin from the Great Salt Lake to the Colorado River and then west to southern California, Smith became the first recorded American to enter California overland from the east. Official suspicion and harassment made his stay unpleasant, so in early 1827 he traveled east across the Sierras, leaving some of his men and all of the furs in California.

Later that same year Smith made a second trip to California. This time he suffered two of the worst defeats in fur trade history. In August 1827 the Mohave Indians attacked his party, killing and capturing most of his men. The remainder struggled on to southern California, where they encountered renewed suspicion and hostility from the Mexican authorities and only with great difficulty finally got permission to leave. They traveled north to Oregon, and in May 1828, while Smith was absent from camp, the Indians killed all but three of his men. Fleeing from this disaster, Smith completed his journey to the Oregon Country. In spite of these defeats, his journeys proved valuable because he provided descriptions of his routes and thus paved the way for later, more extensive travel and exploration in the West.

The Man

Smith was a slender man, perhaps 6 feet tall, with brown hair, blue eyes, and noticeable scars from his encounter with the grizzly. A practicing Methodist, he not only carried a Bible into the mountains but, unlike many of his companions, abstained from liquor and tobacco. His associates liked and respected him for his skill and his courage under fire.

Further Reading

The definitive work on Smith is Dale L. Morgan, *Jedediah Smith, and the Opening of the West* (1953), which also examines his career in the context of the fur trade and international rivalry for the wealth of the Far West. A good recent study, Alson J. Smith, *Men against the Mountains: Jedediah Smith and the Southwest Expedition of 1826-1829* (1964), concentrates mainly on that expedition. Smith is discussed in Gerald Rawling's popularly written *The Pathfinders: The History of America's First Westerners* (1964).

Works including documents on the fur trade and explorations of the period are Harrison C. Dale, *The Ashley-Smith Explorations and the Discovery of a Central Route to the Pacific, 1822-1829* (1918); Maurice S. Sullivan, *The Travels of Jedediah Smith* (1934); and Dale L. Morgan, *The West of William H. Ashley: The International Struggle for the Fur Trade of the Missouri, the Rocky Mts. and the Columbia* (1954). □

John Smith

John Smith (ca. 1580-1631), English colonist in America, was president of the governing council of Jamestown, Va. His writings about Virginia and New England have considerable historical and literary merit.

John Smith's life is known mainly from autobiographical passages in his writing, many details of which have been verified by modern scholarship. He was baptized on Jan. 8, 1579/1580; his birth presumably took place at Willoughby, Lincolnshire, a few days earlier. He was the eldest son of a freeman farmer. He attended school at nearby Louth and was briefly apprenticed to a merchant. In 1596 his father died and Smith inherited the land.

Adventures in Europe

But Smith was eager for adventure: he served for several years in the English army that had been fighting in the Netherlands. Either before or after this term of soldiering, he visited France as a servant to the son of Lord Willoughby, Smith's liege lord. A return to Lincolnshire via Scotland (and shipwreck there) gave him time for thought and reading books on warfare and the responsibilities of leadership. Another educational experience was provided by contact with the learning and horsemanship of the Earl of Lincoln's riding master.

Smith's major Continental adventure began in 1600, when he returned to the Netherlands, where he decided to try his fortune against the Turks. His passage to the Balkans was via France, Italy (which he toured as a sight-seer), the Mediterranean (which he explored as far as Egypt), and

Austria. In Vienna he joined the imperial army. Smith accounted his abilities as a soldier very great. He became captain of 250 cavalrymen and then major. (He preferred the lesser title.) Perhaps his most glamorous undertaking was the killing of three Turks in single combat. This exploit won him a pension, the right to decorate his shield with three Turk heads, and the title of English gentleman. But soon his fortune took a turn for the worse; he was wounded, captured by the Turks, and sold as a slave.

Smith was shipped to Constantinople to be a servant to a young woman. She treated him kindly, but not wishing to have such a man for a slave, she sent Smith to her brother, who made him a farm slave. He was so mistreated that he killed his master. First he fled northward to Muscovy, then to Poland, and finally back to the Holy Roman Empire. Before returning to England, Smith completed this phase of his adventures with a tour of Germany, France, Spain, and Morocco; he also took part in a sea fight off the African coast. Smith returned to England in 1605.

Role in the Colony of Virginia

Somehow, Smith soon met Capt. Bartholomew Gosnold, who had been to America and now was identified with a group planning a colony under the auspices of the London Virginia Company. Perhaps because of his military experience, Smith was selected as one of the seven-man council that was to rule the colony of 100 once it had been established.

The group departed in December 1606 and landed in Chesapeake Bay in April 1607. They named their settlement Jamestown. For some reason Smith was not allowed to serve as an official at first, but soon he began leading explorations of the area, which was occupied by several groups of Indians. Smith began making notes on what was happening. With no leadership being demonstrated by Edward Wingfield, the president of the governing council, the colonists did little. Several men were killed by Indians; others died of disease; and soon the colony was all but incapacitated. In September, Wingfield was replaced by a man named Ratcliffe, and Smith became supply officer.

Smith worked hard to obtain food and bartered with the Indians. On one trip he was captured by Indians and taken to their leader, Powhatan. He was finally released, perhaps at the prompting of Pocahontas, Powhatan's daughter. Smith himself did not include the "Pocahontas episode" in the first of his two accounts of his capture, *A True Relation . . . of Virginia* (1608). The familiar story appears in *The Generall Historie of Virginia, New England, and the Summer Isles* (1624), where it looms less large than people suppose.

In spring 1608 Smith sent to England a letter on the colony's adventures, *A True Relation,* which found its way into print. It is generally recognized as the first American book, though only 44 pages. He continued to play an important role in the colony, and in September 1608 he was elected president of the governing council (not governor, as he called himself later). For a time, real progress in establishing the colony was achieved, but then came the discovery that their grain was rotting and had been eaten by rats. Smith also had difficulty with rebellious colonists. By force of character he led the colonists through a bad winter, but the situation continued to be very difficult. He was badly hurt in a gun-powder explosion and was forced to return to England in October 1609. The colonists barely survived the winter, and they would have given up the project had not reinforcements arrived at the last moment.

Return to England

In England, Smith prepared a report on Virginia, its geography, plants, animals, and Indians, "A Description of Virginia," part of *A Map of Virginia* (1612). In 1614 he visited the coast of Maine and Massachusetts, a trip he described in a propaganda pamphlet, *A Description of New England* (1616). Smith's inclusion of a map of the area resulted in giving many places their present names; Cape Ann, Charles River, and the name New England itself are notable examples.

Smith now enjoyed the support of Sir Ferdinando Gorges of the Plymouth Company. But to his bitter frustration, two efforts to return to America in 1615 and one in 1617 were unsuccessful. All that Smith gained was a title: admiral of New England, Gorges called him.

Smith was still eager to return to America, but now he could not find sponsors. He turned to writing, first with brief pamphlets on efforts to explore and settle New England, *New England's Trials* (1620), and then with a massive compilation, *The Generall Historie of Virginia* (1624), the work which gained him a place in literary history. He poured his early descriptions of Virginia and New England into the work, added to a published account of his Virginia years, and pieced together other men's writings, mostly published ones. He editorialized a good deal and used every occasion to restate his interest in returning to America.

As Smith became more aware of his accomplishments, he tended to exaggerate. He wrote an account of his early years on the Continent, *The True Travels* (1630), and a thoughtful, almost mellow pamphlet on colonization, *Advertisements for the Unexperienced Planters of New England, or Anywhere* (1631). He wrote a little poetry, too. In June 1631 he died in London.

Smith's chief accomplishments were that he saved the first permanent English settlement in America when it was experiencing evil days, and he focused attention on New England so that it attracted settlers. His writings belong with those of the great Elizabethan voyagers collected by Richard Hakluyt. His books, disorganized and often carelessly written, are full of insight and vivid scenes.

Further Reading

Selections from *Travels and Works of Captain John Smith,* edited by Edward Arber (1910), are available in the much shorter *Captain John Smith's America: Selections from His Writings,* edited by John Lankford (1967), which contains an up-to-date review of the literature on Smith. The best and most complete biographical study is Philip L. Barbour's scholarly *The Three Worlds of Captain John Smith* (1964). A study of Smith's work as a writer is Everett H. Emerson, *Captain John Smith* (1971). □

Joseph Smith

Joseph Smith (1805-1844), American religious leader, was the founder of a unique American sect, the Mormons, or the Church of Jesus Christ of Latter Day Saints.

On Dec. 23, 1805, Joseph Smith was born in Vermont; in 1816 his family migrated to western New York. Among the more prominent features of the terrain were the Indian mounds containing the skeletons of long-dead warriors. Shortly after his marriage in 1827, Smith began to talk of some golden plates he had discovered in these mounds under an angel's guidance, as well as magic spectacles that enabled him to decipher the tablets' hieroglyphics. Moving to Pennsylvania, he worked on the translation, which turned out, he said, to be a history by Mormon, an American prophet and historian of the 4th century, telling of two Jewish peoples who had migrated to North America and whom Jesus visited after his ascension. In 1830 the *Book of Mormon* appeared for sale and quickly became important in spreading the Mormon faith.

Smith soon announced the founding of a restored Christian church and proclaimed himself a "seer, a Translator, a Prophet, an Apostle of Jesus Christ and Elder of the Church." Eventually, his claim to special revelations stirred hostility among the residents of New York and Pennsylvania, and in 1831 he summoned his ever-increasing flock to an exodus. Settling in Kirtland, Ohio, the Mormon community evolved into a utopian communal experiment in which the church held all property and each family received sustenance from a common storehouse. When dissension inspired some to move to Independence, Mo., Smith joined them briefly to consecrate ground for a new temple.

In 1833 Smith published the "Word of Wisdom," which encouraged members of the church to abstain from tobacco, alcohol, and hot drinks and to eat meat only in winter. In 1836 Mormon temperance advocates forced a vote for total abstinence. Increasing criticism over his inept management of Kirtland's financial affairs caused Smith to rejoin his Missouri followers. That colony, too, attracted hostility, and Smith had to flee under sentence of death, leading a migration to Nauvoo, Ill.

In the 1840s Smith published a work which elaborated upon the "Hamitic curse" in such a way as to exclude blacks from the Mormon priesthood. At the same time he undertook a history of the Mormon Church. He had also arrived at a doctrinal position which permitted polygamy. He kept this potentially dangerous practice a secret, revealing it only to a privileged few. By 1844 Smith had come to regard Nauvoo as an enclave independent of the United States, and the leaders of his church crowned him king of this new kingdom of God on earth. That same year Smith offered himself for president of the United States, advo-

cating the establishment of a "theodemocracy" and the abolition of slavery.

In 1844 an apostate published an exposé of Mormon polygamy. Smith ill-advisedly permitted his followers to destroy the defector's press, which gave the surrounding "Gentiles" an excuse to retaliate against the Mormons. The Illinois governor sent the militia to arrest Smith for riot, but the militiamen exceeded their orders and brutally murdered Smith on June 27, 1844.

Further Reading

Until recently the literature on Mormonism has been polemical, and the biographies of Smith have reflected either the uncritical views of his followers or the diatribes of disaffected converts. John Henry Evans, *Joseph Smith: An American Prophet* (1933), is a sympathetic account marred by important omissions. The most comprehensive treatment is Fawn Brodie, *No Man Knows My History: The Life of Joseph Smith, the Mormon Prophet* (1945; 2d ed. 1971), which implicitly discounts Smith's claims of special gifts of revelation and prophecy but arrives at a favorable view of his accomplishments. Robert Bruce Flanders, *Nauvoo: Kingdom on the Mississippi* (1965), adds information on Smith's years in Illinois. □

Lillian Eugenia Smith

The Southern writer Lillian Eugenia Smith (1897-1966) was recognized as a passionate critic of white supremacy and segregation. Her main concern was that the traditional pattern of race relations, which she knew intimately from her own experience growing up in Florida and Georgia, was harmful to the humanity of both whites and African Americans.

Born December 12, 1897, in the small, racially-divided north Florida town of Jasper, Lillian Smith was the seventh of nine children. Her father, Calvin Warren Smith, was a successful local businessman and civic leader, while her mother, Anne Hester Simpson, was a descendant of wealthy rice planters. Her parents introduced her to music and literature, but she also was exposed to the accepted views of white supremacy. She later rebelled against the prejudices of her culture, era, and region, and as a writer became recognized as one of the most outspoken opponents of segregation in the South.

Smith graduated from high school in 1915 and spent several years studying, running a hotel her father operated, joining the Student Nursing Corps, and teaching at a rural high school in Georgia. In 1919 she resumed her piano studies at the Peabody Conservatory in Baltimore. Beginning in 1922, Smith spent three crucial years as the music director of an American Methodist school for Chinese girls in Huchow, China. The experience introduced her to Chinese philosophy and the impact of Western imperialism. It also revealed a new perspective on social relations in the South.

Smith, who never married, returned in 1925 to take care of her ailing parents and to help run the Lauren Falls Camp for Girls in Clayton, Georgia. Purchased as a summer home in 1912, the family had moved there permanently in 1915 when the father's business had failed. Under her direction, the camp, which she operated until 1949, became nationally acclaimed for its creative and educational approach.

When the camp was not in session she returned to writing. After producing several manuscripts about her family and her experience in China that went unpublished, in 1935 she and her friend Paula Snelling launched a magazine devoted to Southern politics and culture. It first appeared in the spring of 1936 as *Pseudopedia* (later renamed *The North Georgia Review* and then *The South Today*) with 200 subscribers, and reached a circulation of 10,000 by the time it ceased publication in 1945.

The magazine, which printed the work of African Americans and women, was also a forum for Smith, who criticized racism by appealing to the self-interest of middle- and upper-class whites. She had spent winters in 1927 and 1928 studying psychology at Columbia Teachers College, and her interest in Freud and such other writers as Karl Menninger was evident in her writing. She was interested primarily in the psychological harm of segregation on whites.

Her ideas found wider expression in the controversial and best-selling novel *Strange Fruit,* published in 1944, which was a story about an ill-fated love affair between a young white man from a respected family and a college-educated African American woman working as a housekeeper. It was set in a small town based on her native Jasper. Banned in Boston as obscene, it eventually sold over three million copies and was translated into 16 languages.

The success of the novel gave her financial independence and established her reputation as a critic of segregation. She lectured, wrote for national magazines, and contributed a column for the Black newspaper *The Defender* (Chicago).

Her second major book, *Killers of the Dream* (1949), was nonfiction, blending autobiography and psychology to analyze her upbringing and the pathology of a Southern culture based on white supremacy and segregation. In her view the sickness of the Southern way of life transcended race relations and symbolized the human experience.

Shortly after being treated for breast cancer for the first time, she wrote *The Journey* (1954), which was based on her travels and interviews in the South and investigated the idea of human dignity. The book focused on suffering and pain in the lives of many individuals in the South and expressed her discovery of a religious outlook that replaced the early evangelical Christianity she had rejected in her youth.

After the 1954 historic Supreme Court ruling in *Brown v. Board of Education* (which outlawed segregation in schools), Smith wrote *Now Is the Time* (1955), which urged the South to accept the decision. She published another novel, *One Hour* (1959), which focused on the hysteria of the McCarthy era.

In the changing climate of the early 1960s, Smith gained a wider audience, publishing a revised version of *Killers of the Dream* as well as writing for such mass circulation magazines as *Life, McCalls,* and *Redbook,* and such major newspapers as the *New York Times* and *Atlanta Constitution.* Her final book was a pictorial essay on the civil rights efforts, *Our Faces, Our Words* (1964).

Throughout her career Smith was one of the most outspoken white Southerners on race issues, and she criticized the timidity of moderates and liberals. She had always preferred appeals to white self-interest and personal change, but beginning in the mid-1950s she supported the nonviolent civil rights movement and the leadership of Martin Luther King, Jr. Although she had been an early member of such African American organizations as the National Association for the Advancement of Colored People (NAACP), the Congress of Racial Equality (CORE), and the Student Non-violent Coordinating Committee (SNCC), by the mid-1960s she became critical of the increasingly militant tone of some African American groups.

As a writer Smith never felt appreciated as a creative artist. She was bitter that critics judged her work in terms of social problems rather than viewing it as a metaphor for the alienation of the human condition. Yet from the mid-1930s until her death on September 28, 1966, she was a respected, uncompromising, and influential advocate of desegregation in the South.

Further Reading

Smith's major writing includes the novel *Strange Fruit* (1944) and the nonfiction works *Killers of the Dream* (1949) and *The Journey* (1954). An anthology of her writing from her magazine *The South Today* can be found in *From the Mountain,* Helen White and Redding Sugg, Jr., eds. (1972). Another collection of her writing is *The Winner Names the Age,* edited by Michelle Cliff (1978). A good biography of Smith is *Lillian Smith: A Southerner Confronting the South* by Anne C. Loveland (1986). *How Am I To Be Heard: Letters of Lillian Smith,* edited by Margaret Rose Gladney, was published in 1993.

Additional Sources

Smith, Lillian Eugenia, *Memory of a large Christmas,* Athens: University of Georgia Press, 1996. □

Margaret Chase Smith

Margaret Chase Smith (1897-1995) was one of the most politically powerful women in American history. She served over eight years in the U.S. House of Representatives and was the sole woman senator during her 24 years in the Senate. She was the first woman to have been elected to both houses of Congress and in 1964 became the first woman to have been nominated for the presidency of the United States by a major political party.

Margaret Chase Smith was born in Skowhegan, Maine, on December 14, 1897, the eldest of six children born to Carrie and George Chase. Her career began with typical small-town jobs: clerk, telephone operator, various office jobs. She held high offices in business and professional clubs and in Maine's Republican State Committee. She married Clyde Smith, a businessman and politician who won all the 48 offices he sought.

Margaret Smith's election victories are notable. Following the death of her husband, she waged four successful campaigns in seven months to win his Congressional seat in 1940. In 1948 she scored the greatest total vote majority in Maine's history (over 70 percent), defeating three male opponents without party endorsement because leaders feared she could not be elected to the Senate. In 1960 she received the highest percentage total of all Republican senatorial candidates. Campaigning that year for the presidency, Richard Nixon noted that while some might ride into office on "presidential coattails," in Maine he was trying to "hang onto Margaret's skirts." All her campaigns were low-cost and brief since she thought it important to stay on the job until Congress adjourned.

Margaret Chase Smith became known for her highly independent positions. For example, in her first congressional session she supported President Franklin Roosevelt's peacetime Selective Service Act, the arming of U.S. merchant ships, and the Lend-Lease Act. During World War II

she sometimes supported liberal legislation and voted with Democrats against the Smith-Connally Anti-Strike Act (but supported the post-war Taft-Hartley Act that limited labor activities). As the only House Republican to oppose cuts in Truman's 1947 budget, the *Chicago Tribune* editorialized that she should be "read out of the party." While some thought her a "closet Democrat" she insisted she was a moderate Republican who mainly voted with her party except for a few "dramatic" issues.

A careful examiner of committee witnesses, Smith voted to reject nominees of both Republican and Democratic presidents. She voted against Dwight Eisenhower's nominee Lewis L. Strauss for secretary of commerce; Richard Nixon's Supreme Court nominee, G. Harrold Carswell; and John Kennedy's choice for director of the Central Intelligence Agency, John A. McCone. Drawing upon her expertise in military affairs, Smith rejected promotion for popular actor Jimmy Stewart to Air Force (Reserve) brigadier general until certain additional requirements were met.

She was called a "woman of courage" and a "voice of reason," which seems appropriate. Margaret Chase Smith was the first elected official to speak out against Joseph McCarthy's abuse of Senate privilege in fanning cold-war hysteria in her 1950 "Declaration of Conscience" speech four years before the Senate censured McCarthy. She also warned colleagues that chronic absenteeism in Congress was eroding public confidence in them. (In 1972 she held the all-time consecutive roll-call voting record, rarely missing a vote.) She then introduced a constitutional amendment that would expel any senator who missed more than 60 percent of the yes-no votes. Previously she had proposed another constitutional amendment to abolish the Electoral College and to provide for direct nomination and election of presidents and vice-presidents. Neither proposal passed.

While never concentrating on legislation for women, her career demonstrated concern for them as well as for men. She was affectionately called "Mother of the WAVES" for introducing legislation to create Women Accepted for Voluntary Emergency Service in World War II. When males objected to non-combat overseas assignments for them on the grounds that women should not have to endure such hardships, she declared: "Then we'd better bring all the nurses home." The measure passed. To those who said that the women's place was in the home, Smith replied that women's place was "everywhere." She never considered herself a feminist, but admitted that she hated to leave the Senate (1972) when there was little indication that a qualified woman was coming in.

Smith also gained an international reputation when, as a member of the Armed Forces Committee, she toured several continents to gain information on the state of America's military forces. She frequently met with high foreign officials and was the first woman to address Iran's legislature (1947).

She made several "patriotic" speeches during the turbulent 1960s and drew verbal fire from Nikita and Nina Khrushchev for challenging President Kennedy to match action with his rhetoric over Soviet interference in Cuba. Smith was easily America's "woman legislator of the century." As a powerful force in the Republican Party for many years, she earned the respect of both Republicans and Democrats for her hard work and level-headed approach to congressional affairs during the administrations of five different presidents. In 1964 she was nominated for president at the Republican convention that eventually chose Barry Goldwater as the GOP candidate.

Campaigning in her usual manner, Smith lost her fifth senatorial race in 1972. Analysts believed her age (74) and Maine's economic problems were primarily responsible. The distinguished senator, holder of 85 honorary degrees and noted for the fresh red rose always worn in her lapel, had served her state and her nation for over 32 years. After congressional retirement she was a Woodrow Wilson visiting professor at various major universities from 1973 to 1976 and served on several important boards of directors.

Smith spent the remaining 19 years of her life in semi-retirement, serving on various boards of directors and giving guest lectures and advice to young people.

Further Reading

Autobiographical information and discussion of various career decisions by Margaret Chase Smith are in her *Declaration of Conscience* (with William C. Lewis, 1972). Considerable biographical data is in *Margaret Chase Smith, Woman of Courage* (1964) by Frank Graham, Jr., which concentrates on her while describing the activities of a U.S. senator. For the younger reader Alice Fleming's *The Senator from Maine: Margaret Chase Smith* (1969) is helpful, as is Fleming's *Senator from Maine: Margaret Chase Smith* (1976). Also see MacCampbell, James C., *Margaret Chase Smith: A Biographical Sketch,* (Margaret Chase Smith Library Center, 1982). □

William Smith

William Smith (1727-1803) was a Scottish-born American educator and churchman whose innovative educational ideas and leadership of the Philadelphia Academy during its formative years significantly influenced American education.

William Smith was born in Aberdeen on Sept. 7, 1727. He was educated in the local parish schools and attended the University of Aberdeen (1743-1747). In 1751 he sailed to New York to be a tutor to the sons of a rich Long Island family. In 1753 Smith published a pamphlet entitled *A General Idea of the College of Mirania . . .* , which outlined his utopian ideas for an educational institution appropriate to the new country. There were to be two branches: a Latin school for the "learned professions"; and an English school for the "mechanic professions" with a "useful" curriculum containing no ancient languages. The curriculum for both was essentially secular and included such practical studies as writing, bookkeeping, and French. Such educational ideas were not new in America; they reflected Benjamin Franklin's academy proposals, as well as innovations current in Scotland, but they were broad in conception compared to existing colonial institutions. Smith sent a copy to Franklin and in 1754 went to head the newly formed Philadelphia Academy and College. Over the next 25 years he guided the institution generally along the lines stated in *Mirania*.

Smith became an Anglican priest in 1753 and throughout his life was a strong influence in Church affairs. In 1758 he married Rebecca Moore. He became active in conservative politics during these years, and with the onset of the Revolution he held a loyalist position in fierce opposition to Franklin and the liberals. When the General Assembly revoked the charter of the academy in 1779 on grounds of subversion and issued another charter for a new university of the state of Pennsylvania, Smith left Philadelphia. For 10 years he lived in Maryland, where he organized a new institution, Washington College, and became its first president. During this time Smith, along with other Church leaders, managed to reinstitute the Anglican Church in America as the Protestant Episcopal Church, a name he is supposed to have suggested.

In 1789, when the political winds changed and the original charter of the academy was restored, Smith returned to Philadelphia. Two years later the General Assembly chartered the present University of Pennsylvania, uniting it with the existing university. Smith, however, was not named head. He retired to his country estate near Philadelphia, where he died on May 14, 1803.

Further Reading

Albert Frank Gegenheimer, *William Smith: Educator and Churchman* (1943), is a full biography of Smith; though somewhat uncritical in viewing Smith's inspirational influence on his students, it thoroughly explores his literary and clerical associations. Studies of the educational ideas of the day are

Benjamin Franklin on Education, edited by John Hardin Best (1962), and Frederick Rudolph, ed., *Essays on Education in the Early Republic* (1965). Smith's leadership in educational organizing is examined in Edward Potts Cheyney, *History of the University of Pennsylvania* (1940).

Additional Sources

Jones, Thomas Firth, *A pair of lawn sleeves; a biography of William Smith (1727-1803),* Philadelphia, Chilton Book Co. 1972. □

Robert Smithson

The sculptor, essayist, and filmmaker Robert Smithson (1938-1973) is most known for his sitespecific environmental earth works.

The sculptor Robert Smithson began his career as a painter. Born in Passaic, New Jersey, on January 2, 1938, Smithson was educated in New Jersey public schools. While at Clifton High School he won a scholarship to attend evening classes at the Art Students League. In 1956 he studied at the Brooklyn Museum School. After high school graduation and a brief stint in the Army Reserves, Smithson moved to New York City in 1957. There he painted his first canvasses in an Abstract Expressionist style and developed friendships with poets Allan Brillant and Richard Baker. Smithson's life-long concern for "oppositions" surfaced in these early works where, with a decorative and gestural brushstroke, he painted antithetical religious themes of the celestial and the demonic, the earthly and the spiritual, the sacred and the profane.

Since his childhood Smithson had been interested in natural history. At his family home in New Jersey he built and maintained a museum of reptiles, fossils, and artifacts. In high school he frequented the New York Museum of Natural History, where he was particularly fascinated by the dinosaurs. The artist Nancy Holt, whom he remet in 1959 (they had previously met as youngsters in New Jersey), had a strong concern in her work for biology, and she encouraged Smithson to develop this interest in natural history into sculpture. He soon began to collect specimens—for example, sponges or chemical samples—which he then displayed in an art format to demonstrate that art, like biology, is an inert substance based in nature that can be organized and structured into meaningful relationships.

Creating "Oppositions" Sculptures

In 1964-1965 Smithson created his first large scale sculptures. Many of these works, with their emphasis on geometry, industrial fabrication, and rational appearance, utilized the minimalist vocabulary of artists such as Sol LeWitt, Robert Morris, or Carl Andre. Yet Smithson's intent was to undercut logic and to invert systems by merging his observations of nature with art. *Enantiomorphic Chambers* (1965) combines the artist's interest in crystallography and perception. "Enantiomorphic" refers to crystalline compounds whose molecular structures have a mirrored relationship to each other. Smithson made literal this biological form with a steel structure that holds mirrors at an oblique angle. Vision becomes dispersed as the viewer sees not himself but reflections of reflections, an illusion without an illusion. Thus the crystalline structure acts as a metaphor for art—through a static object it simultaneously refers to both how one sees and to nature. Yet at the same time, this work mirrors no external reality, only itself. Forms based on nature thus point out the ineptness of rational systems and logic.

During this period Smithson often employed mirrors or glass to demonstrate his ideas. This organic material formed into an inorganic shape was either inset, as in *Enantiomorphic Chambers,* or layered, as in *Mirror Strata.* In these mirror and glass works Smithson set up an intriguing dialogue between shape and illusion. If one sees *Mirror Strata* (a large piece formed by overlaid strips of glass) as sculpture, for example, it is necessary to negate the reflective aspect of its material while, on the other hand, if one concentrates on its surface, then its solidity as an object disappears. Appearance and reality play off against one another, allowing the observer to constantly form new definitions and understandings of both the object and the artist's intent. Smithson showed many of these works at his first one-man show at the Dwan Gallery in December-January 1966-1967.

In 1966 Smithson began making excursions to urban, industrial, and quarry sites in New Jersey. At the same time, he published articles on these trips in leading art magazines. These essays both documented his activities and elucidated his artistic theories. One of these articles, "The Monuments of Passaic," a photo essay of his home town, announced Smithson's concern for reclamation of industrial sites and his interest in entropy. Drawing upon the tradition of 18th-century travel books, Smithson here presented "anti-monuments," tributes to suburban sprawl and urban growth that exemplified the decay and deterioration of all things: "One's mind and the earth are in a constant state of erosion, mental rivers wear away abstract banks, brain waves undermine cliffs of thought, ideas decompose into stones of unknowing, and conceptual crystallizations break apart into deposits of gritty reason." Smithson often documented these trips with map-drawings that explored space as both subject matter and formal element. Nancy Holt, whom Smithson married in 1963, often accompanied him on these trips.

Smithson continued to explore entropy and chaos in his dialectical series entitled *Site/NonSite.* In these sculptures Smithson expanded the cartographic aspect of his field trips to disrupt the premises of traditional sculpture. The *Non-Site,* consisting of bins filled with material collected from specific locations, refers back to the *Site* from which it was gathered. The bins are displayed in geometric structures and matched with maps and photographs, thus forming a continuous dialogue between the artist's activity, the object that signifies that activity, and the site in nature from which the object was formed. These *Site/NonSite* works undermined the museum/gallery location even as they made the transformational actions of the artist on raw matter in its original unbounded state even more explicit.

Smithson continued these ideas on a more conceptual level in his *Mirror Displacements.* In this series, which was documented as a published article in *ArtForum* magazine in 1969, Smithson placed nine square mirrors in different surroundings. These mirrors displaced, broke-up, and distorted the world around them. They become both solid and void, object and reflection, positive and negative shape. The artist stressed here the mimetic and illusory aspects of art even as he denied the importance of art objects (the mirrors were immediately dismantled after he photographed them at each site and were stored somewhere in New York). Moreover, the published essay itself became the final artifact of the artist's activity, another mirror that adds one more displacement to our understanding of reality.

Work on a Large Scale

In 1970 Smithson began construction of the large site-specific earth works for which he is most known. *Spiral Jetty,* made of mud, salt crystals, rocks, and water, was built on an abandoned oil rig site on Rozelle Point off of the Great Salt Lake in Utah. The jetty celebrates both technology and nature: although it was built with dump trucks and caterpillar tractors spreading earth and rock from the surrounding desert, it forms a spiral, an elemental form in nature. The spiral can be seen as a schematic image of evolution, a symbol for growth or destruction, or a classical form for the orbit of the moon; it is both an expanding force (as a nebula) and a contracting one (like a whirlpool); it is fairly complex and yet is an essential motif of all ornamental art. At the center, there is nothing but the sun—the beginning and the end of the universe. This large work involving more than 6,650 tons of material is now totally submerged in the lake and exists mainly in its documentary (non-site) form as photographs, a 35-minute 16mm film, and an essay.

For the last two years of his life Smithson sought to use his art as a resource that would mediate between ecology and industry. He contacted many land mining corporations, offering his services as an artist-consultant for land reclamation. He wished to make art out of the decay of discarded land at such sites, thereby restoring art to an everyday function within society. *Broken Circle/Spiral Hill* (1971) was built in Emmen, Holland, on a reclaimed quarry. *Broken Circle* is formed by two semi-circles which are mirrored or doubled—half on land, half on water, half jetty, half canal. In the center is an ancient boulder which could not be moved and formed an "accidental" center, disrupting the dialectic that Smithson had established between the broken circle and the hill. Yet despite this interruption, the two forms constantly refer and relate back to one another: one structure is surrounded by water, the other by land; while the *Broken Circle* is flat, the *Spiral Hill* is three-dimensional, its counterclockwise spiral (white sand on black topsoil) again a symbol for destruction. This work, originally commissioned as a temporary outdoor installation, proved so popular with the people of Emmen that they voted to preserve it as a park.

Smithson continued to explore other sites for his land reclamation earth projects. In 1973 he accepted a private commission to build the *Amarillo Ramp* in Texas. While photographing the site, Smithson died in an airplane crash on July 20, 1973. The work was completed posthumously by Nancy Holt, Richard Serra, and Tony Shafrazi.

Further Reading

Smithson's writings have been gathered together in a book edited by Nancy Holt, *The Writings of Robert Smithson* (1979). The exhibition catalogue for the Smithson retrospective at Cornell, *Robert Smithson: Sculpture* by Robert Hobbs (1982), gives a thorough discussion and illustration of Smithson's sculptural activity. See also Susan Ginsburg, *Robert Smithson: Drawings* (1974).

Additional Sources

Hobbs, Robert Carleton, *Robert Smithson—sculpture,* Ithaca: Cornell University Press, 1981. □

Smohalla

Smohalla (ca. 1815-1895) was a Native American warrior, medicine man, and spiritual leader who is best known for introducing a revitalized Washani religion amongst his people, the Wanapums (Wanapams) of America's Pacific Northwest.

Native American leader Smohalla is closely associated with the Dreamer religion, as the new Washani faith came to be called. It emerged in part as a reaction to the intrusions of a white settlers, the U.S. Army, and the subsequent Indian policies of the U. S. government. The Dreamer faith, which spread rapidly in the mid and late nineteenth century, called for a return to Native American traditions and lifestyles, and a rejection of white cultural influences. Because Smohalla's religious doctrines were so deeply ingrained in the traditional religious beliefs of the Wanapum people, they continued to be a part of the spiritual life of the Native American cultures of the Pacific Northwest well into the twentieth century.

Smohalla was born to the Wanapum or Sokulk tribe around 1815. The tribe belongs to the Shahaptian division of the Shapwailutan linguistic stock. The Wanapums lived along the Columbia River above the mouth of the Snake River and are mentioned by Lewis and Clark in the reports of their western explorations. The chief village of the Wanapums, which was founded by Smohalla in the late 1850s, was on the west bank of the Columbia River at the foot of Priest Rapids in the present day state of Washington. The tribe was always small in number with an estimated population of 1,800 in 1780 but by 1960 it had dropped even further to between 150 and 200.

Smohalla (foreground)

Went by Many Names

Smohalla's birth name was Wak-wei or Kuk-kia, which means "Arising from the Dust of the Earth Mother," but at various times during his life he was called Yuyunipitqana, the "Shouting Mountain," and Waipshwa, the "Rock Carrier." He did not take the name Smohalla, which is Shahaptian for "dreamer," until later in life when he had become a spiritual leader of his people.

Although there is little record of Smohalla's early life, he is known to have been a hunchback at birth and physically unremarkable throughout life. Whites who had met him described Smohalla as being "peculiar" and "not prepossessing at first sight." He did, however, develop oratorical skills and reportedly could hold his followers spellbound with his "magic manner." As a young man Smohalla experienced a religious revelation which had a profound influence on his life and the Wanapums. Concern over increasing white influence on Wanapum culture prompted Smohalla to journey to La Lac, a sacred mountain of his people, in search of his *wot,* or guardian spirit. While awaiting the appearance of his spirit he fasted and meditated, and according to legend, died on the mountain. However, his spirit was refused entry into the "land of the dead" and Smohalla was ordered to return to his people and save them from cultural extinction, which could only be prevented by rejecting white influences and returning to the traditional sacred beliefs and doctrines of the Washani religion.

Washani is a Shahaptian word for "dancers" but it can also be translated as "worship." Inherent in the faith is the concept of the "dreamer-prophet." A dreamer holds a sacred place in Wanapum culture because it is believed that he has experienced a temporary death, followed by a visit to the spirit world, and a subsequent return to earth with a message from the Creator. This temporary death has sometimes been described as a "vision." Over the centuries the Washani religion has gone through three phases: the aboriginal or pre-European phase, a Christianized variation related to the coming of the Europeans, and finally a revitalized version, with Smohalla and other dreamer-prophets of the mid to late nineteenth century. A dreamer-prophet is said to appear amongst the Wanapums during a time of crisis, which is often a precursor to the end of the Wanapum world. This prophetic crisis may be natural phenomena, such as an earthquake or flood, or it may be precipitated by intruders such as white settlers. The dreamer-prophet, through his teachings and example, prepares the Wanapums for a subsequent renewal of life following the crisis.

Became a Holy Man

Smohalla, like other Wanapums, believed that the *Nami Piap* or Creator, was responsible for creating the world, that certain peoples were selected to inhabit specific regions, and that an earth spirit or Mother Earth would provide sustenance in the form of fish and game for its inhabitants. He also mirrored the Wanapum belief that the land must not be disturbed by being divided into parcels. Smohalla believed that the white man's practices of land ownership and farming were an affront to the Creator.

When Smohalla returned from his journey to La Lac his tale of death and resurrection made him revered by his people and he soon gained a reputation as a visionary able to foresee the future and approaching doom. It was around this time that he took the name Smohalla. As Smohalla's reputation as a holy man grew so did the jealousy of his enemies. Sometime in the early 1850s he aroused the enmity of Moses, the chief of a band of Sinkiuse Indians living nearby. The two leaders met in battle and Smohalla was stricken and left to die. But Smohalla did not die, and upon regaining consciousness slipped away unseen to the Columbia River where he came upon an unattended boat in which he drifted downriver. Smohalla was eventually rescued by some white men and he purportedly wandered down the Pacific coast eventually reaching Mexico and then returned to his homeland by way of Arizona, Utah, and Nevada. Upon reaching his people his stature as a dreamer was further enhanced as he was again seemingly resurrected from the dead. Smohalla then found himself the most important spiritual leader of the Wanapums.

Following the Yakima Wars of 1855 and 1856, many of the tribes of the Columbian Plateau (but not the Wanapums) unsuccessfully tried to stand up to the U.S. Army and repulse further white intrusions. Smohalla then moved his band of followers to the region of the Priest Rapids on the Columbia River because of the abundance of fish and game in the region. There he established a lodge with his ten wives and named his eldest daughter his spiritual successor. However, she became ill, died shortly thereafter, and was buried in a canoe on a sandy rise overlooking the Colombia River. When the tribal rites at the grave ended, Smohalla remained alone at the site in mourning. He had not returned to his lodge by the next day and worried villagers hurried to the gravesite only to find that Smohalla had died there during the night. His body was removed to the village where it was cleansed, dressed in buckskin, and adorned with yellow paint and strips of otter fur in anticipation of a funeral befitting a great leader. However, the next morning's funeral ceremony was abruptly interrupted when Smohalla's body began twitching. His eyes soon opened and he rose to his knees, but remained silent. Frightened villagers ran from the lodge which Smohalla, now very much alive, walked out of two days later. The dreamer-prophet had once again been resurrected from the dead, carrying a message from *Nami Piap,* the Creator. The message was delivered later that day at a spot on the Columbia River known as Water-Swirl-Place.

Taught Songs and Dances

Smohalla told his people that *Nami Piap* would not allow Smohalla's spirit to remain in the land of the dead. Instead, he was commanded to return to his people and instruct them in a special dance and teach them 120 new songs which were to be added to their religious rituals. According to *American Indian Quarterly,* Smohalla was also ordered by the Creator to "teach the Wanapums and others to be good, do good, and live like Indians. Give them this song and show them this dance."

The *washat,* or dance, was an intricate ritual involving seven *kookoolots,* or drums, which symbolized life. The dancers, both men and women, held eagle and swan feathers which represented flight from the earth to the spirit world. Smohalla conducted the ceremonial dance holding a triangular flag on which was drawn a five-pointed star and a red circle on a white, yellow, and blue background. During the dance a *qualal qualal,* or brass bell, symbolized the heart and was rung to keep time and announce to *Nami Piap* that the dance was underway.

Smohalla's emerging religious doctrines formalized traditional Washani beliefs in the goodness of the Creator and the bountiful earth which sustained them. The Wanapums long believed that the salmon was created first and the huckleberry last. Thus did Smohalla have these foods served as Communion first and last at thanksgiving ceremonies. He also had a dogmatic opposition to the white concept of land ownership, farming and cultivation.

Smohalla's influence over the Wanapums was truly profound, as his religious teachings were deeply rooted in and complemented the spiritual traditions of his people his. Smohalla was militant in his beliefs and demanded strict allegiance from his followers, especially in regard to the rejection of the white man's culture and its attendant trappings. Smohalla rejected the white work ethic and federal reservation policies, and although he opposed Christianity many Christian ceremonial practices became incorporated into dreamer ceremonies over the decades. He did not advocate violence against whites. He did, however, garner the enmity of federal bureaucrats who implemented Indian policy from the belief that their Native American wards should be Christianized.

Teachings Spread

Smohalla's teachings and variations on his teachings spread to other Native American tribes of the Columbian Plateau. Many other, however, chose to be Christianized and live on reservations. A schism soon developed between the two groups with federal agents favoring the latter. Even though Smohalla remained non-violent, many of the hostile actions on non-treaty Native Americans, especially during the Nez Percé War of 1877, were blamed on the dreamer teachings. Soon all followers of the dreamer faith came to be regarded as fanatics and their religion an impediment to the further civilizing of the region.

During the early 1890s the federal government intensified efforts to place all Native Americans on reservations, and with access to their traditional hunting and fishing grounds becoming increasingly difficult the Wanapums had little choice but to comply. By then even Smohalla was living on the Yakima Reservation where he died in 1895. Before his death Smohalla had named his son Yo-Yonan as his successor. Yo-Yonan died in 1917 and Smohalla's nephew Puck Hyah Toot conducted religious ceremonies in a longhouse at Priest Rapids until his death in 1956. As late as 1975 religious ceremonies were still being held by various succeeding dreamer-prophets and Smohalla's beliefs were still providing spiritual guidance to the Wanapums and other Native Americans of the Pacific Northwest.

Further Reading

Trafzer, Clifford E., and Margery Ann Beach, "Smohalla, The Washani, and Religion as a Factor in Northwestern History," in *American Indian Quarterly,* 1985, pp. 309-324.

Malone, Dumas, *Dictionary of American Biography,* Charles Scribner's Sons, 1935, pp. 371-72.

Ruby, Robert H., and John A. Brown, *Dreamer-Prophets of the Columbian Plateau,* University of Oklahoma Press, 1989.

Relander, Click, *Drummers and Dreamers,* Caxton Printers Ltd., 1956.

Hirschfelder, Arlene, and Paulette Molin, *The Encyclopedia of Native American Religions,* Facts On File, 1992.

Hodge, Frederick Webb, *Handbook of American Indians North of Mexico,* Pageant Books, Inc., 1960.

Swanton, John R., *The Indian Tribes of North America,* United States Government Printing Office, 1952. □

Tobias George Smollett

Of the major 18th-century novelists and satirists, the British author and physician Tobias George Smollett (1721-1771) is most clearly identified with the picaresque tradition of novel writing.

The variety and extent of Tobias Smollett's interests, his phlegmatic Scottish nature, the grossness and bite of his satires, and the keenness of his caricatures distinguish the man and his works. The acts of shocking violence and brutality and the coarseness of language that Smollett incorporated into his novels set him off from the three other principal English novelists of the mid-18th century: Samuel Richardson, best known for his massive and powerful epistolary novel, *Clarissa;* Henry Fielding, the satirist and novelist of English manners most frequently remembered for *Tom Jones;* and Laurence Sterne, whose experiments with structure in *Tristram Shandy* produced a work unique in the fiction of the period. Like his contemporary, friend, and fellow physician Oliver Goldsmith, Smollett earned his living primarily as a professional writer rather than from his medical practice.

Early Life

Smollett was born of a good family in Dunbartonshire, Scotland, on March 19, 1721, the third child of Archibald and Barbara Smollett. He studied medicine at the University of Glasgow during the 1730s, but he did not receive his formal medical degree from Marischal College, Aberdeen, until 1750. After a brief term as an apprentice surgeon in Glasgow in 1739, Smollett moved to London in order to pursue his literary ambitions. Financial necessity led him to take a post as surgeon's mate aboard H.M.S. *Chichester* in 1740. His grim exposure to life in the Royal Navy provided him with many of the vivid scenes of life at sea that he later incorporated into *Roderick Random* and other novels.

Smollett returned to London from the West Indies briefly in 1742, but he soon sailed back to Jamaica, where he married Anne Lassalls, an heiress, probably in 1743. In

1744, at the same time that he was trying to establish a medical practice in London, Smollett began to publish a series of minor poems and attempted unsuccessfully to have his first play, an ill-starred tragedy entitled *The Regicide,* produced. Of the occasional odes that Smollett published between 1744 and 1747, the best was his movingly patriotic *The Tears of Scotland* (1746). The most noteworthy of his Juvenalian verse satires, *Advice* (1746) and *Reproof* (1747), merely furthered his growing reputation as a quarrelsome Scotsman outraged by the refined vices of London.

Roderick Random

The Adventures of Roderick Random, published in "two neat Pocket-Volumes" in 1748, made Smollett a controversial literary celebrity. The success of his raw, bold story of a young man's progress through the world was immediate, impressive, and prolonged. While some critics attacked Smollett for the viciousness of his characters, the indecency of his language, and the carelessness of his prose, the English public enjoyed Smollett's vivid depiction of the horrors of naval warfare, the rapid pace of his narrative, the brutality that marked individual scenes, and the colorful—if roughly drawn—caricatures that abounded in the novel. As young Roderick moves from adventure to adventure, he observes the grasping, vicious nature of most of the human beings whom he encounters and quickly learns that he can survive in the world only by using his cunning and native wit.

In 1748 Smollett also published his laborious translation of Alain René Lesage's *Gil Blas* in four volumes, began work on a translation of Cervantes's *The History and Adventures of the Renowned Don Quixote* (not published until 1755), and completed a second abortive dramatic piece entitled *Alceste.* After *The Regicide* had been published in 1749, the cantankerous Smollett, in ill health, made his first extensive visit to the Continent.

Peregrine Pickle

In 1751 Smollett released his second picaresque novel, *Peregrine Pickle,* widely read because of its magnificently drawn naval characters and because of Smollett's bitter, personal attacks on such prominent English figures as Henry Fielding and David Garrick. Peregrine, like Roderick Random, must learn to live by his wits in a world that Smollett depicts as corrupt and unfeeling. In the same year Smollett began reviewing books for the *Monthly Review,* an activity that he expanded later for the *Critical Review.*

Ferdinand Count Fathom

Smollett's third novel, *The Adventures of Ferdinand Count Fathom,* appeared early in 1753. Again the story of a rogue moving through vicious elements in society, it was financially less successful than his first two works of fiction. Smollett continued to supplement his meager medical income by undertaking hackwork for various booksellers in London during this period. By 1756, in fact, he had largely abandoned his medical practice. Although he was deeply involved in establishing and contributing to the *Critical Review* in 1756, he did not find the venture commercially profitable until 1762.

Real financial success from his writing came to Smollett only with the publication of the four volumes of his *Complete History of England* in 1757-1758, a project begun in 1755 and already being revised before the end of 1758. Smollett's farce, *The Reprisal; or, The Tars of Old England,* was successfully produced at the Theatre Royal in Drury Lane in 1757. By 1759, although he was only 38 years old, he was already suffering so severely from the asthma and associated complicating disorders that eventually led to his death that he sought feverishly but unsuccessfully to obtain a diplomatic post that would take him to a warmer climate to live and work.

Sir Launcelot Greaves and Editorial Work

During 1760-1761 Smollett published his fourth novel, *The Adventures of Sir Launcelot Greaves,* in the *British Magazine,* which he had helped to found. The novel, although an unsuccessful attempt to translate the Don Quixote story into 18th-century English characters and situations, was the first considerable English novel ever to be published serially. Smollett also undertook a *Continuation of the Complete History of England* (five volumes of which were published between 1760 and 1765), engaged in virulent political controversy, and in 1761 agreed to contribute to and help prepare a 36-volume edition of *The Works of M. de Voltaire* (1761-1769). By 1763, in broken health and mourning the death of his daughter, Elizabeth, who had been born in 1747 or 1748, Smollett sailed for France, where he remained for 2 years.

In 1766 Smollett published two important volumes of his *Travels through France and Italy,* a popular compendium of observations on character, customs, commerce, the arts, and antiquities. Although he traveled constantly through England and Scotland between 1765 and 1768, he was finally forced by his deteriorating health to leave England forever and to move to Italy in 1768. Smollett is usually considered to be the author of *The Adventures of an Atom* (1769), a satire that pretended to be about Japan but was, in fact, a coarse and violent attack on important political issues and personages in the early years of the reign of George III.

Humphrey Clinker

While living in Il Gardino, Italy, Smollett completed work on his last and finest novel, *The Expedition of Humphrey Clinker,* which was published in three volumes in June 1771. His only epistolary novel, *Humphrey Clinker* reflects a more careful structure, a more balanced view of human nature, and a greater control of style and character than any of his earlier fiction. The novel describes the travels of Matthew Bramble, various members of his family, and their companions through England, Wales, and Scotland in a series of letters written from startlingly different points of view. While Matt's letters, for example, criticize the noise and pollution of London and Bath, those of his niece, Lydia, describe the excitement, the bustle, and the charm of these cities with relish and delight. In depicting Matthew Bramble's progress from sickness to health during the novel, Smollett drew much from his own adventures traveling through England. Smollett died in Italy in 1771.

Further Reading

Major biographical studies of Smollett are Louis L. Martz, *The Later Career of Tobias Smollett* (1942); George M. Kahrl, *Tobias Smollett: Traveller-Novelist* (1945); Lewis M. Knapp, *Tobias Smollett: Doctor of Men and Manners* (1949); and Robert D. Spector, *Tobias Smollett* (1968). Important critical studies of Smollett are Fred W. Boege, *Smollett's Reputation as a Novelist* (1947), and G. S. Rousseau and P. G. Boucé, eds., *Tobias Smollett: Bicentennial Essays Presented to Louis M. Knapp* (1971). Useful chapters on Smollett are in the following works: Alan D. McKillop, *The Early Masters of English Fiction* (1956); Ian Watt, *The Rise of the Novel* (1957); Robert Alter, *Rogue's Progress* (1964); and Ronald Paulson, *Satire and the Novel in Eighteenth Century England* (1967). Recommended for general historical and social background are J.H. Plumb, *England in the Eighteenth Century* (1950); A. H. Humphreys, *The Augustan World* (1954); and R.J. White, *The Age of George III* (1968).

Additional Sources

Smeaton, William Henry Oliphant, *Tobias Smollett,* Norwood, Pa.: Norwood Editions, 1977. ☐

Michael Smuin

Award winning dancer-choreographer-director, Michael Smuin (born 1938) had a wide-ranging career filled with numerous honors in the theater, television and film.

Michael Smuin was born on October 13, 1938, in Missoula, Minnesota, of parents involved in community theater. His mother was an actress and his father was a skier who also ran a meat market. Michael's earliest memories include family Christmas parties with Missoula relatives, plus his passion for the dancing of Gene Kelly and Fred Astaire, his movie idols. He wanted to dance like them and was serious in attending tap dance classes at a young age.

At the age of eight he was a member of The Wise Guys, a group of youngsters who sang, tapped, and told jokes for such groups as the Chamber of Commerce, Kiwanis Club, and Red Cross. When Ballet Russe de Monte Carlo came to town in a one-night stand, Michael became an instant convert to ballet. Encouraged by his parents, he spent several summers in Salt Lake City, where he studied ballet with William Christenson, director of Ballet West. Then for his last year in high school and two years in college, he studied ballet at the School of The San Francisco Ballet, a company directed by William's brothers Lew and Harold. "They," says Smuin, "refined the skills I had already been working on, and helped me understand not only tradition but how a company operates, from backstage to box-office."

In 1958, the day after school closed for summer vacation he was off with the company for a nine-week tour of South America, mostly split week engagements. It meant that in addition to daily class, rehearsals in strange theaters, and performances, twice a week the male dancers assisted with "breaking up" the show—loading and unloading floor, sets, curtain, and props onto and off vans.

A year later he was with the company in a three-month tour of the Middle East. It was there that he really understood that dance is an international language, despite its different accents. He learned, too, that touring can be educational. He remembered well the audiences that included Haile Selassie and Gamal Abdel Nasser. As usual, he asked a lot of questions until he was satisfied that he understood. It was then, too, that he became aware of his interest in doing choreography, a different skill from dancing, and he started what became a life-long habit, carrying a small notebook with him wherever he might be. Every night before going to bed he made notes of his observations and reflections of the day. He later added details of the current production, including sketches of stage business.

In 1961 he was drafted for Army training, where he found more to learn. Before that he had become leading dancer of the San Francisco Ballet, its ballet master, and its resident choreographer. Released from the Army in 1962, he returned to San Francisco to choreograph a tap ballet for the company. Its success proved to be the spring-board for new adventure.

He made a dancing debut on Broadway in Bob Fosse's *Little Me.* He began work on film and television offers and, in addition, from 1963 to 1966, made intermittent night club and summer hotel engagements with his wife, Paula

Tracy, in a cabaret act aptly titled "Paula and Michael." In 1966 he joined American Ballet Theater (ABT). There he gained much recognition as a performer, especially for his in-depth characterizations in ballets by Frederick Ashton, Leonide Massine, Michael Fokine, and Jerome Robbins. He cherished all of them, but it was his role in Robbins' *Fancy Free* of which he was especially proud. Not only was he doing those and other new roles but he also choreographed six works ("some good, some not so good," he said).

He continued on in New York and on tour with the ABT until 1973, turning down television and film offers. However, he accepted the invitation to be co-artistic director of the San Francisco Ballet, his starting point. He became artistic director, and before he left there in 1985 he had choreographed 30 works for the company and produced 120 ballets. He commissioned composers and designers with fresh and lively points of view and gained large subscription audiences. There were a series of nationwide television presentations, including three of his full-length ballets: *Cinderella* (1973), *Romeo and Juliet* (1976), and *The Tempest* (1980), the latter two winning Emmys. There were some interesting on-leave ventures as well. From 1976 to 1979 he served as member and co-chairman of the National Endowment for the Arts Dance advisory panel. In 1980 he traveled to China as a member of the first official U.S. dance study team. Asked to be show doctor for Broadway's *Sophisticated Ladies,* he viewed it carefully; he found music, casting, and other elements excellent, but the script lacking in definition. Invited to redo the script, he did. The smash hit result brought him the 1981 Outer Critics Circle Award and two Tony Award nominations, one for choreography, one for direction.

In January 1982 Gregory Hines and Michael Smuin tap danced together at a premiére at the San Francisco Opera House. In March 1982 sections of three of Smuin's ballets were part of the television presentation *In Performance at the White House.* In October 1982 he choreographed the fight scenes for Francis Coppola's movie *Rumble Fish,* and soon after collaborated with him in a film-plus-live performance of *Romanze.* He conceived, produced, and directed San Francisco's Golden Gala program in January 1983. In April of the same year he received the prestigious Dance Magazine Award as "man of the theater in the truest character of the American dance artist . . . electic and virtuoso . . . electrifying vitality and elan."

Other awards include two Emmys, one for choreography, one for direction, for *A Song for Dead Warriors,* nationally broadcast in January 1984. He received the Award of Honor for Achievement in the Arts from the San Francisco Arts Commission. He was head choreographer for Coppola's film *Cotton Club* and choreographed Mozart's *Piano Concerto No. 21* for television and the hugely successful *To the Beatles.* In 1985 he choreographed *Brahms-Haydn Variations* and in 1986 a ballet based on *Children of Paradise,* the French film classic, with music by Piaf.

He won a 1986-1987 Emmy award for direction for voice/dance, another area he planned to explore further. He staged the fight scenes for Michael Ritchie's film *Golden Girl,* and, with his incredible versatility, soon after staged a ballet for Leslie Caron, Mikhail Baryshnikov, and Rudolph Nureyev plus male chorus for a combined American Ballet Theatre-Paris Opera Ballet gala at the Metropolitan Opera House.

In 1987 he directed a theater production of Nagle Jackson's *Faustus in Hell* for the American Conservatory Theatre, as well as George Bernard Shaw's *Saint Joan* for the Stratford Shakespeare Festival. He did a music video for Linda Ronstadt to the song "When You Wish Upon a Star" featuring Cynthia Gregory and Disney's Jiminy Cricket. Additionally, he directed/co-produced the AIDS benefit "Aid and Comfort" for television broadcast.

In 1988 Smuin created the choreography for Luis Valdez' television special and was director/choreographer of the Linda Ronstadt touring show *Canciones de mi Padre.* He also choreographed a scene for Chevy Chase and 625 extras in the Michael Ritchie movie *Fletch Saved.*

For his choreography for the Lincoln Center's *Anything Goes,* the 1988 revival of the Cole Porter musical (which he later re-created in London), Smuin received a Tony award, a Fred Astaire award, and the Drama Desk award.

During the 1989 summer vacation in the Tracy-Smuin beach house in Hawaii, he viewed six hundred hours of film and tape in preparation for the February 1990, 50th Anniversary Gala of the ABT, in which excerpts from 30 ballets, in film and live performance, were seamlessly presented in an enticing entertainment. In 1990 Smuin was developing a film, which he was to direct, based on Gore Vidal's mystery thriller *Death in the Fifth Position.*

But before that, there was still another Broadway choreography/directing assignment, a new musical drama based on James Clavell's best-selling novel *Shogun,* which opened in fall 1990. Prior to rehearsals, Smuin made four trips to Japan to consider a Japanese English-speaking cast, a concept he finally rejected in favor of American-Japanese actors/dancers/singers. However, he imported consultants to prepare the cast for proper tea service, drum dance, different levels of bowing for differing castes, and other such niceties about which he is precise.

Filmmaker Coppola spoke of Michael Smuin as "a most cordial person" who "moves a show with an electric pace and stunning effect." Tap dancer Gregory Hines said, "Michael's special. He recognizes at once the accent and rhythm required for theatricalization, and surprising for someone of his intensity, he's patient, very patient. No hysterics. Multi-talented, he knows what he wants and he works for it."

When asked if he would be interested in heading a ballet company again, Smuin replied, "After twelve years with the San Francisco Ballet I'm well acquainted with the ecstacy and the agony of that position, and although I'm flattered to be asked, I'd say 'no.' There are still many untried avenues in theater arts that challenge me. I seem to care deeply about the possibilities that exist in the Americanization of dance and its sister arts." What he didn't count on was a request to contribute his directing and choreography talents for a San Francisco Foundation for the Arts fund raiser in 1994. In response to this request he brought together a troupe of young, energetic and talented dancers performing a potpourri of dance that was distinctly American. The sell-out first performance lead to more than a five-week run, followed by sold out performances in Los Angeles and New York.

This troupe of dancers became the famed Smuin Ballets/SF performing to sell out audiences nationwide. The troupe with appearances at Carnegie Hall and the Joyce Theater in New York maintained an exhausting schedule with more than 70 performances in some years. Smuin described the troupe as "a very American company with a huge vocabulary of dance styles." The Smuin Ballets/SF gained a popular following with selections set to music ranging from Chopin and Bartok to the Righteous Brothers and Willie Nelson. Smuin ballets that the company introduced include: *The Christmas Ballet* (1995), choreographed to music from the Renaissance and Baroque periods mixed with rhythm and blues, *Frankie and Johnny* (1996), billed as the first mambo ballet, and *Cyrano* (1997), based on the life and loves of Cyrano de Bergerac.

Further Reading

Most of the information on Smuin can be found in such trade publications as *Variety*. There is a brief biography of Smuin together with a lengthy exposition of how he developed *Shogun* by Joseph McLellan, in *The Washington Post* (September 2, 1990). □

Jan Christian Smuts

The South African soldier, statesman, and philosopher Jan Christian Smuts (1870-1950) was one of the founders of the Union of South Africa and an architect of the League of Nations and of the United Nations.

Jan Smuts the second son of Jacobus Abraham Smuts, a prosperous farmer and a member of the Cape Legislative Assembly, was born on May 24, 1870, on a farm in the Malmesbury district of the Cape Colony (Cape Province). He began his formal education at the age of 12, when he entered a boarding school at Riebeek West. Although he was shy and physically weak, Smuts possessed a great zeal for learning. Four years later he entered Victoria College at Stellenbosch and there compiled a brilliant academic record. While a student at Stellenbosch, Smuts met Sybella Margaretha Krige, whom he later married. In 1891 Smuts won the Ebden scholarship and went to Christ's College, Cambridge, to study law.

Early Career

In 1895 Smuts returned to South Africa, settled at Cape Town, and was admitted to the bar. Because of his reserved ways, however, he was not immediately successful; consequently, he developed an interest in journalism and politics. In politics he was initially attracted to Cecil Rhodes, who was prime minister at that time. After the Jameson Raid was made and Rhodes's part in it became known, Smuts repudiated Rhodes. He moved to Johannesburg and resumed the practice of law.

In Johannesburg, Smuts quickly won the recognition of Paul Kruger, the president of Transvaal, and in 1898 Smuts was appointed state attorney of the republic. He became attached to the Boer cause and, when the Boer War began, published a propaganda pamphlet in 1899 entitled *A Century of Wrong*. During the war Smuts discovered that he was a natural fighter, and he became a leader of one of the most successful of the Boers' guerrilla bands. At the end of the war, in 1902, Smuts participated in the peace negotiations at Vereeniging.

Smuts-Botha Government

After the war Smuts returned to Pretoria, Transvaal, and once again practiced law. A few years later he reentered politics. In 1904 Smuts joined Louis Botha to launch a political party, Het Volk (The People). The party's aim was to work for responsible government. The following year Smuts was sent to England to carry his party's demands directly to Henry Campbell-Bannerman's new Liberal government. When the British prime minister approved of the Het Volk request, not only did the Boer Republic regain its self-government but also Smuts regained his British sympathies.

For the 15-year period from 1904 to 1919, the Smuts-Botha combination was the great fact of South African poli-

tics. These two former Boer generals collaborated to produce qualities needed for political leadership. Smuts was a scholar and a reformer in politics who combined vision and ambition; he remained the source of ideas and the power behind the scenes. In 1906, when Transvaal was granted responsible government, he supported Botha for the premiership of the republic, and he himself became colonial secretary and minister of education. Later, when his great dream of the Union of South Africa became a reality in 1910, Smuts worked hard to have Botha accepted as the first premier of South Africa. He himself accepted the portfolios of mines, defense, and interior. Botha and Smuts merged their Het Volk party with other provincial parties and formed the South African party.

World War I

At the outbreak of World War I, the South African Parliament voted to enter the hostilities on Britain's side. Some of the Boers, however, disapproved of this policy and revolted. Smuts participated in the suppression of this rebellion. Afterward Botha and Smuts resumed their campaign against the Germans in Southwest Africa. The campaign was a striking success, and once again Smuts was hailed as a brilliant soldier. In 1916 he accepted the command of the imperial forces in East Africa and was commissioned a lieutenant general in the British army. The following year, at Botha's request, he proceeded to England as the South African representative to the forthcoming Imperial Conference. The British prime minister, David Lloyd George, offered Smuts a position in the British War Cabinet.

By the end of the war Smuts had acquired his great reputation as a soldier and statesman. He published an influential pamphlet in December 1918 entitled. *The League of Nations: A Practical Suggestion,* and he played an important role at the Paris Peace Conference in 1919. A champion of a lenient peace, he was greatly disillusioned by the Versailles settlement.

Premiership and World War II

When Botha died in August 1919, Smuts became prime minister of South Africa. In 1924, however, he was defeated, and he then began a long period of opposition. During these years his fame as a scholar continued to grow. In 1925 Smuts wrote *Holism and Evolution,* a philosophical work in which he offered an explanation of the unitary character of all things. Smuts was reconciled with his old opponent Gen. James Hertzog in 1933. A year later they formed a fusion party, the United South African National party. Smuts served until 1939 as minister of justice. Upon the outbreak of World War II, Hertzog wanted to declare South Africa neutral. Smuts opposed this idea, and in September 1939 he was called to the premiership. As during World War I, he displayed qualities that marked him as a war leader of the first order. At the end of the war, Smuts went to San Francisco and helped to create the United Nations.

In May 1950 Smuts suffered a heart attack. He died on September 11.

Further Reading

The best biography of Smuts is W. Keith Hancock, *Smuts* (2 vols., 1962-1968), superbly written and rich in primary material. F.S. Crafford, *Jan Smuts: A Biography* (1943), is a useful study. Other biographies include René Kraus, *Old Master: The Life of Jan Christian Smuts* (1944), and, by Smuts's son, Jan C. Smuts, *Jan Christian Smuts: A Biography* (1952). The Smuts-Botha collaboration is well depicted in Basil Williams, *Botha, Smuts and South Africa* (1946). Alan Paton's recent biography of Jan Hofmeyr, *Hofmeyr* (1964; abridged 1965 edition entitled *South African Tragedy*), is particularly important for the last period of Smuts's career. For general background see Eric A. Walker, *A History of South Africa* (1928; 3d ed. 1957).

Additional Sources

Beukes, Piet, *The romantic Smuts: women and love in his life,* Cape Town: Human & Rousseau, 1992.

Cameron, Trewhella, *Jan Smuts: an illustrated biography,* Cape Town: Human & Rousseau, 1994.

Friedman, Bernard, *Smuts: a reappraisal,* New York: St. Martin's Press, 1976.

Ingham, Kenneth, *Jan Christian Smuts: the conscience of a South African,* New York: St. Martin's Press, 1986.

Meiring, Piet, *Smuts the patriot,* Cape Town: Tafelberg, 1975. ☐

Snorri Sturluson

The Icelandic statesman Snorri Sturluson (1179-1241) was his country's most renowned historian. Although some might with justice question his accuracy, few would deny that he was a literary genius creatively writing from the viewpoint of his own times.

The life of Snorri Sturluson was as eventful as the lives of the Norse heroes about whom he wrote. The son of a chieftain in the western fjords, he was brought up by the powerful chief Jon Lofstsson, who awakened in him an interest in poetry and history. Two successful marriages gave prestige and wealth. Ambitious and a shrewd politician, he twice became president of the Legislative Assembly and as such was the supreme magistrate in Iceland. At times he could be passionate, mean, and untrustworthy if judged by modern standards rather than Viking standards. He was not so bloodthirsty and cruel as his opponents, and his political victories were not marked by maimings and killings.

Snorri traveled twice to Norway: once to avert a Norwegian military expedition to Iceland, and a second time to escape capture and perhaps death at the hands of his brother Sighvatr and his nephew Sturla. With the defeat of his enemies, he returned to Iceland hoping to regain political power but was killed at his estate at Reykholt by his son-in-law Gissur Thorvaldson, who was acting as the agent of the Norwegian king Haakon IV (the Old). He died on Sept. 22, 1241, an Icelandic patriot. By 1262 Iceland had become a tributary to the Norwegian crown.

His writings rather than Viking deeds and intrigue make Snorri one of the most important figures in Scandinavian history. More than any other person, he preserved the knowledge of the skalds and their poetry. He used them extensively in his histories, and the second part of his *Prose Edda* is a catalog of kennings, whose use in poetry is illustrated by examples. The *Heimskringla* (Sagas of the Norwegian Kings) shows him as both poet and historian. A highly creative literary genius, he brings the work to a climax in the *Saga of St. Olaf.* In addition he was probably the author of *Egil's Saga,* which is the story of a renowned 10th-century Icelandic Viking poet who fought as a mercenary in Norway.

Snorri was a key figure culminating the Icelandic renaissance. The *Heimskringla,* a work of unique literary achievement, is the single most important source for events that transpired in Norway from the 6th to the late 12th century.

Further Reading

Most of the editions of the writings of Snorri contain extensive introductions dealing with his life. *The Prose Edda,* translated by Jean I. Young (1966), and the *Heimskringla,* translated by Samuel Laing (rev. ed., 3 vols., 1906), are excellent. Peter Hallberg, *The Icelandic Sagas* (trans. 1962), adds much information on Snorri's life and times. □

Charles Percy Snow

The English novelist and physicist Charles Percy Snow (1905-1972) wrote "Strangers and Brothers," a series of novels depicting the professional and intellectual classes and detailing the struggles involved in the pursuit of ambition and the exercise of power.

On Oct. 15, 1905, C. P. Snow was born into a working-class family in Leicester. He graduated from Leicester University with a first in chemistry and a master of science degree in physics. In 1930 Snow received a doctorate in physics from Cambridge, where he remained until 1950 as a fellow and as an administrator.

Deeply involved in molecular research during the 1930s, Snow turned to writing fiction for relaxation. His first novel, *Death under Sail* (1932), was a detective story. His second, *The Search* (1934), concerning scientific research, began the novelistic exploration of the personal lives and public ambitions of the British professional and intellectual classes that later achieved its fullest expression in the novels of the "Strangers and Brothers" series. In 1940 the first novel of this series, from which it takes its title, was published. *Strangers and Brothers* introduced many of the characters who appeared in the later novels, particularly Lewis Eliot, the narrator of all of them and the subject of two.

During World War II Snow gave up writing to become the director of technical personnel for the Ministry of Labour. In 1943 he was made a commander of the British Empire, and in 1945 he was named a civil service commissioner with the responsibility of selecting scientists for government projects, a post he held until 1960.

After the war, Snow returned to writing and published the second volume in his series, *The Light and the Dark* (1947). Lewis Eliot's struggles for happiness in love and success in his career were recorded in *Time of Hope* (1949) and *Homecoming* (1956).

In 1950 Snow married the English novelist Pamela Hansford Johnson. In 1951 the fourth novel of the series *The Masters,* was published. *The New Men* (1954), which dealt with scientists involved in developing the atomic bomb, was the fifth novel in the series. In 1957 Snow was knighted. A year later the seventh novel in the series, *The Conscience of the Rich,* appeared. It concerned the struggle for independence of a talented young man who resists his wealthy father's attempts to dominate him.

During the 1950s Snow lectured frequently. His most controversial lecture, "The Two Cultures and the Scientific Revolution," concerned the dangerous communication gap between humanist and scientific intellectuals. In 1960 he published *The Affair,* the eighth novel in his series. *Corridors of Power,* a study of the exercise of power at the highest levels of government, appeared in 1964. *The Sleep of Reason,* issued in 1968 as the tenth novel in the series, concerned the details of a lurid torture-murder. Snow also published lectures, criticism, and a volume of biographical studies, *Variety of Men.*

Further Reading

Two worthwhile studies of Snow's work are Frederick R. Karl, *C. P. Snow: The Politics of Conscience* (1963), and Jerome Thale, *C. P. Snow* (1964).

Additional Sources

De la Mothe, John, *C.P. Snow and the struggle of modernity,* Austin: University of Texas Press, 1992.

Halperin, John, *C.P. Snow—an oral biography: together with a conversation with Lady Snow (Pamela Hansford Johnson),* New York: St. Martin's Press, 1983.

Snow, C. P. (Charles Percy), *The physicists,* Boston: Little, Brown, 1981.

Snow, Philip, *Stranger and brother: a portrait of C.P. Snow,* New York: Scribner, 1983, 1982. □

Edgar Snow

An American journalist and author, Edgar Snow (1905-1972) acquainted the Western world with the Communist movement in China and was for many years the only American writer with regular access to Chinese Communist leaders.

The son of a printer and editor, James Edgar, and Anna Catherine (Edelman) Snow, Edgar Parks Snow was born on July 19, 1905, in Kansas City, Missouri. In 1923 he attended Kansas City Junior College; then transferred to the University of Missouri, from which he graduated in 1926; and in 1927 went to Columbia University's School of Journalism for a year. Eager to travel, he began work as a foreign correspondent for the New York *Sun* in 1928, visiting Hawaii and Central America. Snow then went to China, where he remained for the next 12 years. Travelling extensively, Snow became acquainted with many of China's future leaders and wrote many firsthand reports of major news events, including the Sino-Soviet hostilities in Manchuria during 1929 and 1930, the agrarian revolt in Indo-China in 1930, and the Tharawaddy uprisings against British rule in Burma.

In 1936, when the regime of Generalissimo Chiang Kaishek was reporting the rumor that Mao Tse-tung had died, Snow trekked across China, slipped through the Nationalist lines, and crossed the hills of Shensi to enter a village just south of the Great Wall where he met with the Red Army that had just concluded its historic Long March from southern China. For the next five months he travelled with the Chinese Red Army and lived with Mao in the caves of Yenan. His articles and photographs for various publications broke a news blockade on the Communist leaders and on their war tactics and objectives.

The publication in 1937 of his book *Red Star Over China* quickly earned Snow the reputation of the Western world's expert on Communists in China. An international

bestseller, Snow's prophetic account of the guerrilla movement and its leaders predicted that they would ultimately win the civil war. He reported with exuberance on the discipline and idealism of the insurgents; he recounted Mao's version of his pre-1936 career and of the Communist program for China; he suggested that Mao's policies enjoyed widespread support in the countryside; and he depicted the Communists as a formidable nationalist and anti-Japanese force, not the bandits claimed by Chiang Kai-shek.

Another prophetic work, *The Battle for Asia,* published in 1941, predicted many of Japan's military victories and foresaw the challenge to the whole colonial system that would result from World War II. Although not a Communist himself, Snow actively sympathized with the Communist movement in China. During the Cold War, he was blacklisted in the United States and had to earn his livelihood on free-lance sales to foreign journals. He continued to travel extensively in China after the successful Communist revolution in 1949, and Snow was the only American journalist to be granted frequent interviews with Chairman Mao and Premier Chou En-lai. His favorable impressions of the new society in China and of the progress made toward improving the quality of Chinese life were published in 1962 in *The Other Side of the River.*

In 1970, during his last trip to China, the Chinese showed their admiration for Snow by inviting him to stand atop the Tienamen Gate in Peking with Chairman Mao during the celebration of National Day. On this final visit, moreover, Chow told Snow that "the door is open" for improved relations with the United States, hinting that the Chinese leaders would welcome a summit meeting with President Nixon. When the president began to prepare for his visit to the People's Republic of China, Snow was in Switzerland dying of cancer. Premier Chou En-lai sent a special medical team to attend his friend, but Snow died on February 15, 1972, almost at the very time of President Nixon's triumphant arrival in Shanghai.

Snow's final book, *The Long Revolution,* an account of his last trip to China and his many talks with Mao, was published posthumously in 1972. He was survived by his second wife, Lois Wheeler, a stage and film actress whom he married in 1949, and two children of his second marriage, Sian and Christopher. Wanting to belong partly in China and partly in the United States, Snow directed that his remains rest in a garden at Peking University and also near "the Hudson River, before it enters the Atlantic to touch Europe and all the shores of mankind of which I felt a part."

Further Reading

Snow's major writings on China include *Red Star Over China* (1937), *Random Notes on Red China* (1957), *Journey to the Beginning* (1958), *The Other Side of the River* (1962), *Red China Today* (1971), and *The Long Revolution* (1972). He also authored *The Battle for Asia* (1941), *People on Our Side* (1944), *The Pattern of Soviet Power* (1945), and *Stalin Must Have Peace* (1947). Biographical data appear in his obituaries in the *New York Times* (February 16, 1972) and *Nation* (February 28, 1972).

Additional Sources

China remembers Edgar Snow, Beijing, China: Beijing Review: Distributed by China Publications Centre (Guoji Shudian), 1982.

Farnsworth, Robert M., *From vagabond to journalist: Edgar Snow in Asia, 1928-1941,* Columbia, MO: University of Missouri Press, 1996.

Hamilton, John Maxwell, *Edgar Snow, a biography,* Bloomington: Indiana University Press, 1988.

Thomas, S. Bernard, *Season of high adventure: Edgar Snow in China,* Berkeley: University of California Press, 1996. □

Olympia Snowe

Olympia Snowe (born 1947) overcame the early deaths of both of her parents and her first husband to build a strong political career grounded in fiscal conservatism and to forge a fulfilling personal life based on a strong second marriage and community involvement.

Olympia Snowe's career is characterized by a number of firsts. Most notably, when she was elected to Congress from the Maine second congressional district in 1978 at the age of 31, she was the youngest Republican and the first Greek American woman to serve in Congress. As a U.S. Senator representing the state of Maine, Snowe is well-known for her work on budget-deficit reduction, fiscal issues, health care, women's issues, and foreign affairs.

Snowe was born Olympia Jean Bouchles in 1947 in Augusta, Maine. Her father, George, emigrated to the United States from Mytilene, Greece, and her mother, Georgia Goranites Bouchles, was a second-generation Greek whose parents had come to America from Sparta. Snowe's parents died when she was young, and she was raised by her Aunt Mary and Uncle James Goranites of Auburn, Maine. After attending St. Basil's Academy in Garrison, New York, Snowe completed her secondary education at Edward Little High School in Auburn. She went on to receive a degree in political science from the University of Maine at Orono in 1969.

Elected to Senate

Snowe sparked her political career from the ashes of tragedy. She was first elected to the Maine House of Representatives in 1973 to fill the seat that was left vacant by her first husband, Peter Snowe. She was re-elected to the seat for a full two-year term in 1974. When Snowe's term was up in the House, she ran for, and was elected to, the Maine Senate in 1976, where she chaired the Joint Standing Committee on Health and Institutional Services. In this position, she gained recognition for her work on health care issues and for sponsoring legislation in the health field. She is also a strong advocate for children's and family issues. "We are here today to send one unmistakable message to deadbeat par-

ents," she declared in a statement released by her office on March 29, 1995. "To deadbeat parents we are saying your days of parental irresponsibility are over. We must act now to bring hope and financial stability to the millions of children and their single-parents who depend on support from absent parents—and that means both mothers and fathers."

In 1978 Snowe was elected to the U.S. House of Representatives from Maine's second congressional district, where she earned respect for her leadership as cochair of the Congressional Caucus for Women's Issues. She was also a member of the House Budget Committee and the House Foreign Affairs Committee, and was a leading member of the former House Select Committee on Aging, where she served as ranking Republican on its Subcommittee on Human Services.

Grass-roots Supporter

Snowe served eight terms in the U.S. House before her election to the U.S. Senate in 1994. She carried over her strong Maine ties into her political career, becoming known as a grass-roots supporter. In her campaign, she emphasized local issues, such as the closing of the Loring Air Force Base in northern Maine and the possibility of the closing of another, the Portsmouth Naval Shipyard in Kittery, Maine.

In the 104th Congress, Snowe is a member of the Senate Committee on Commerce, Science, and Transportation, where she serves on the Subcommittees on Fisheries and Oceans; Merchant Marine and Surface Transportation; and Consumer, Foreign Commerce, and Tourism. Snowe also serves on the Senate Budget Committee; the Senate Committee on Small Business; and the Senate Committee on Foreign Relations, where she chairs the subcommittee on International Operations and serves on the subcommittees on European Affairs, Near Eastern and South Asian Affairs, and African Affairs.

Snowe is married to former Maine governor John R. McKernan, Jr. and lives in Auburn, Maine, where she is a member of the Holy Trinity Greek Orthodox Church of Lewiston-Auburn. She is an active member of many civic and community groups. ☐

Sir John Soane

Sir John Soane (1753-1837) was one of England's most original and distinguished architect in the neoclassic idiom.

The son of a bricklayer, John Soane was born on Sept. 10, 1753, at Goring-on-Thames, Reading. He entered the office of George Dance, Jr., surveyor to the city of London, in 1768, and in 1771 was admitted to the Royal Academy Schools, where he was awarded the Silver and Gold Medals. He was an assistant to Henry Holland from 1772 to 1778 and was probably responsible for designing the Entrance Hall at Claremont House, Surrey, rebuilt by Holland for Lord Clive.

In 1778 Soane traveled to Italy on a king's studentship. There he met the eccentric bishop of Derry (later Marquess of Bristol) and in 1780 returned to England with him, encouraged by dazzling promises of elaborate building commissions. These did not materialize, but eventually Soane established a successful practice, chiefly building small houses in Norfolk and Suffolk. In 1788 he was selected as surveyor to the Bank of England.

In 1806 Soane became professor of architecture at the Royal Academy, and from 1807 until his death he delivered a famous series of elaborately illustrated lectures. In 1814 he became one of three "attached architects" to the Board of Works.

Soane's outstanding achievement was the rebuilding of the Bank of England (1788-1830), in which he gave the fullest expression to the highly personal style that he evolved. This was a primitive kind of neoclassicism, in which he abandoned the conventional orders of columns, entablature, and pediment in the interiors and replaced them by a system of flat wall surfaces with shallow recessions and with a severe linear ornament of incised lines and fluting. Structurally he made great use of shallow domes, clerestory lighting, segmental arches, pendentives, lantern lights, and mirror friezes, by these means often creating a sense of infinity within a confined space. His facades, in which he employed the classical orders, possess great dignity and elegance.

Other important works are Shotesham, Norfolk (1785-1788), Chillington, Staffordshire (1786-1789), the Chapel at

Wardour Castle, Wiltshire (1788), Tyringham, Buckinghamshire (1793-1800), Aynhoe Park, Northamptonshire (1800-1804), Pitzhanger Place at Ealing (now the Public Library, 1800-1803), Moggerhanger, Bedfordshire (1806-1811), and Dulwich College Picture Gallery in London (1811-1814).

Soane designed his own house in Lincoln's Inn Fields, London (1812-1813), and adapted it as a museum "for the study of architecture and the allied arts"; his collection of drawings, models, casts, paintings, sculpture, antiquities, and architectural fragments survives intact, and the house is now a public museum. He died there on Jan. 20, 1837.

Further Reading

Soane's own work, *The Union of Architecture, Sculpture and Painting* (1827), contains a full description of Sir John Soane's Museum. The most detailed monograph on Soane is Arthur T. Bolton, *The Works of Sir John Soane* (1924). Harry J. Birnstingl, *Sir John Soane* (1935), is a brief monograph containing good photographs of the Bank and other principal works. The excellent work by Dorothy Stroud, *The Architecture of Sir John Soane* (1961), incorporating the most recent research, is particularly well illustrated with modern photographs, including many of the country houses not shown in other works. A general account of Soane's style and influence is in John Summerson, *Architecture in Britain, 1530-1830* (1963).

Additional Sources

Du Prey, Pierre de la Ruffiniere, *John Soane, the making of an architect,* Chicago: University of Chicago Press, 1982.

Du Prey, Pierre de la Ruffiniere, *John Soane's architectural education, 1753-80,* New York: Garland Pub., 1977.

Watkin, David, *John Soane,* London: Academy Editions; New York: St. Martin's Press, 1983. □

Mário Soares

Mário Soares (born 1924) was the first socialist president of Portugal and a long-time opponent of the right-wing Salazar regime.

Mário Alberto Nobre Lopes Soares was born in Lisbon on December 7, 1924. As a young boy he was greatly influenced by his father, a militant republican who spent considerable time in prison, in exile, or in hiding for his political activism. In the mid-1930s Soares' father started a private school, the *Colégio Moderno,* that reflected his deep-seated republican and liberal views. The young Soares subsequently lived and attended classes at this well-known private high school in Portugal. Later, Mário Soares attended the Classical University of Lisbon, where he became a student leader opposed to the right-wing authoritarian government of the day. In time he earned degrees in history, philosophy, and law, which, along with the influence of his father, prepared him well for his future role as one of Portugal's leading political activists.

For most of his adult life Mário Soares was an opponent of the fascist government of Antonio de Oliveira Salazar (1932-1968), which had come to power after a military government overthrow of the Portuguese Republic in 1926. Both Salazar's so-called "New State" and the six-year successor regime of Marcello Caetano (1968-1974) drew the opposition of Mário Soares. By the time the dictatorship fell in 1974 Soares had been jailed 12 times on political grounds, banished for almost one year to the former Portuguese territory of São Tomé, and exiled for four years to France (1970-1974). Soares, however, was implacable. As one of his close friends stated: "Nothing gets him down. He is an optimist. He is a fighter. . . ." One noteworthy act of defiance performed by Soares was his prison wedding to Maria Barroso, an actress he had met at the university. She later headed the *Colégio Moderno* founded by Soares' father.

Soares' political fortunes rose with the emergence of the Portuguese Socialist Party (PSP). First founded in 1875, it was strongly suppressed with the rise of Salazar's dictatorship. However, in 1964 Soares and his allies played a leading role in founding the Portuguese Socialist Action, which led to the clandestine reconstruction of the PSP in the early 1970s. In 1969 Soares represented Portugal at the 11th congress of the Socialist International in Eastbourne. Following this congress he came to know many of the leading European socialists in the late 1960s and early 1970s; among them were Olaf Palme of Sweden, Willy Brandt of West Germany, and Bruno Kreisky of Austria. During his long exile in France he also became a close acquaintance of François Mitterrand.

Due in part to the protracted rebellion in Portugal's African colonies (Angola, Mozambique, and Portuguese Guinea) and the general state of the economy, young military officers overthrew the Caetano regime on April 25, 1974. Known as the Armed Forces Movement, the new leadership chose General Antonio de Spinola as the head of a new government that pledged to restore democracy to Portugal. When Soares returned to his country from Paris, he was quickly mobbed by thousands of his admirers. In the first military-controlled government following the overthrow Soares served as foreign minister and oversaw the granting of independence to the African colonies. In elections to a constituent assembly in April of 1975 Soares' PSP emerged as Portugal's strongest party, winning 116 seats out of 250.

The year 1975 proved to be a crucial year for the "Portuguese Revolution" and the political career of Mário Soares. Following the radicalization of the Armed Forces Movement, influenced by the Moscow line of the Communist Party of Portugal, Soares was compelled to resign as foreign minister, and in July he quit the government altogether and called for rallies and demonstrations against the Communists. Increased Communist influence in the government as well as an unsuccessful coup attempt by Spinola eventually motivated a moderate military faction in the Armed Forces Movement backed by Soares to call for elections in 1976. Soares' PSP won these elections with approximately 35 percent of the vote, winning 107 of the 263 seats in a new assembly. Soares then became Portugal's first constitutionally elected prime minister since the revolution of 1974 and served in this office from 1976 to 1978. In 1976, too, Soares was elected vice-president of the Socialist International.

Soares' popularity and that of his party, however, declined in the following years due to austerity measures that the government imposed in order to obtain a loan from the International Monetary Fund. The representation of Soares' PSP in parliament dropped to 74 seats in the 1979 elections and to 66 seats in the 1980 elections. Defections from the PSP and the party's declining political fortunes at the polls influenced Soares to resign as secretary general of the Socialist Party in 1979. One year later, however, he resumed his duties as leader of the PSP.

By 1983 the popularity of the PSP was on the rise once again. Soares' effective opposition politics may be partially credited for this renewal. In the April 1983 elections the PSP won 36 percent of the vote and 101 seats in parliament; it subsequently formed a coalition government with the Social Democratic Party. Following the 1983 elections Soares was appointed to his former position as prime minister. However, in the October 1985 elections he and his party suffered a humiliating defeat, winning only 20 percent of the vote.

Nevertheless, Soares decided to run in the 1986 presidential elections, and four months later defeated the conservative candidate Diogo Freitas do Amaral by 151,000 votes. Soares thus became Portugal's first civilian president in 60 years. His tenacity and superior debating skills contributed to this victory. At the end of Soares' five-year term in 1991, his popularity was such that he was faced with only token opposition, and was easily re-elected, taking 70% of the popular vote. In 1996, socialist candidate Jorge Sampaio was elected to succeed Soares, who had to give up the presidency after two consecutive terms.

Soares played a primary role in engineering the entry of Portugal into the European Economic Community (1986). His goal was to modernize Portugal's economy, the most backward in Western Europe, and to tie his nation closer to Western states. Portugal's integration into the economy of Western Europe strengthened the economy of Soares' country and stabilized the Portuguese political system. At home, Soares instituted popular informal town meetings with the citizens, and he rarely interefered with the work of the cabinet or legislature.

Perhaps the most distinguished characteristic of Mário Soares as a politician was his ability to rebound after a loss. "There are victories and defeats in politics," he was quoted as saying after his 1986 presidential victory, "and what is necessary is to maintain your convictions, to keep battling."

Further Reading

For a sympathetic account of Soares' life see Hans Janitschek's *Mário Soares: Portrait of a Hero* (1985). Two excellent studies of contemporary Portugal are found in Walter C. Opello, Jr.'s *Portugal: From Monarchy to Pluralist Democracy* (1991), and in Eric Solsten, ed., *Portugal: A Country Study* (Federal Research Division, Library of Congress,1993). □

Anatoly Alexandrovich Sobchak

Anatoly Alexandrovich Sobchak (born 1937), a popular democratic leader of Russia, was elected mayor of St. Petersburg (formerly Leningrad) in 1990.

Anatoly A. Sobchak, the urbane mayor of St. Petersburg (named Leningrad in the Soviet era) often mentioned as a future president of Russia, began his life far from the city in which he became famous. Sobchak was born in Chita, east of Lake Baikal in the Soviet far east, an area with a long revolutionary history. Both his grandfather and his father worked for the railroad and participated in the revolution and consolidation of Soviet power in Siberia. Although his family was a humble one, Sobchak revealed that his Czech grandmother tutored the family in the manners of the intelligentsia, which perhaps contributed to his demeanor and image. Like other families, the Sobchaks experienced the cruel hand of Stalinism when his grandfather was arrested in the late 1930s. His father fought in World War II, while his mother earned a meager salary to support the family.

Young Sobchak was selected to go to Leningrad University, a rare honor for someone from the remote provinces. After the university, he worked at first in the Stavropol region and later attended graduate school in Leningrad. He became a resident of Leningrad, building his career as an attorney and as a professor in the Law Department of Leningrad University. Unlike most prominent figures of the Soviet era, Sobchak was not a long-time member of the Communist party of the Soviet Union (CPSU). He joined the party in 1988 during the opening of the ranks (called *perestroika*) because he believed reforms would have to begin within the CPSU, the most entrenched structure in that society. His public life began as a response to Gorbachev's initiatives in *perestroika* in the late 1980s and was fueled by a desire to advance the reform movement.

In 1989 Sobchak was nominated and elected to the new parliament, the Congress of People's Deputies. His "I, Too, Have a Dream" speech to secure the nomination was inspired by Martin Luther King Jr.'s famous speech. Sobchak was subsequently elected by the People's Deputies to the smaller, more powerful standing parliament, the Supreme Soviet. In his early political career in the Congress, Sobchak moved slowly and carefully, observing his colleagues, aware of the entrenched power and the fragility of the new democratic movement. He approached the national political arena not as a long-time bureaucrat (*apparatchik*) but as a critic of the Soviet state structure, theoretically based on the local Soviets or councils that for many years had been rubber stamps for the party. Boris Yeltsin, elected to the new Congress and the Supreme Soviet, also criticized the status quo but had been part of the system for many years before he was removed from the Politburo in 1987.

Sobchak worked with Andrei Sakharov to abolish Article VI, which gave special status to the CPSU, from the Soviet Constitution, continuing the struggle after Sakharov's death. In March 1990 the article was removed despite Gorbachev's continuing opposition. A confrontation between the leaders of reform and the party old guard at the 28th Party Congress in July 1990 resulted in the resignation of numerous reform leaders, including Sobchak.

In 1990 when Sobchak was elected chairman of the Leningrad city council, and shortly afterward mayor of Leningrad, he was already a politician with a national following. After 1992 Sobchak was viewed as an important leader of independent Russia, a significant voice in Russia's democratic movement, and an articulate spokesperson for the new Russia. He was criticized, however, as were other Russian leaders, for sometimes wanting to govern without accountability to anyone. In addition, his reputation as a democrat was clouded by a minor furor over an elaborate tsarist-style ball he and his wife sponsored during a time of general economic hardship. Sobchak, however, remained widely respected by Russia's intelligentsia and was one of numerous academics who made a successful transition into politics during the Gorbachev era.

Sobchak was successful in changing the name of the former Leningrad to St. Petersburg. He achieved significant progress in St. Petersburg despite its serious economic problems. The city's economy was built on the defense industry, which faced cutbacks and conversion. It is in a region with few natural resources and is dependent on other areas for raw materials and food. His goal was to develop the city as a center for free enterprise, emphasizing finance, tourism, and trade. He was able to designate it a free economic zone and to create a municipal bank to handle foreign exchange and regulate other banking activity. He encountered considerable frustration in his efforts to transform the city into a financial center, primarily because of its financial and economic backwardness in respect to Moscow, which widely outdistanced Leningrad in employment, income, banking activity, access to currency, and infrastructural soundness.

By 1991 many people began to perceive the mayor of Leningrad as the most articulate and progressive alternative to Gorbachev. In August 1991 Sobchak was involved in the anti-coup movement against the conservative party and government officials, who had tried to remove Gorbachev and reverse the reforms. He led demonstrations in Leningrad and was in frequent contact with Yeltsin, who led the resistance at the parliament building in Moscow. After the coup had failed, Sobchak tried to prevent the dissolution of the parliament and the union, realizing that rapid disruption of existing structures and the end of the Soviet Union could be more problematic than working within a less than perfect system. In post-Soviet Russia, supporters of reform advocated differing paths, and at times Sobchak disagreed with Yeltsin on the pace and course of reform.

A tall, handsome man, Sobchak had a commanding presence and good speaking skills that were assets in Russia's expanded use of television in politics and elections. In the parliamentary elections of December 1993, he was a leader of one of several competing reform parties and was perceived as a possible future presidential candidate. He was also well respected abroad, where he made numerous appearances as mayor of Leningrad

Sobchak had difficulty in dealing with a cumbersome city council apparatus. He was criticized for an intransigent administrative style. In *The Struggle for Russia* (1995), Yeltsin wrote that "Sobchak had to change in his job as St Petersburg's town governor' from his old image as a liberal, from a well-respected politician and law professor to a harsh, authoritarian administrator." Sobchak's image as a haughty national leader in-waiting did not enhance his local popularity as mayor. In a period of economic decline and hardship, he also suffered, with others, from a general public disillusionment with the fathers of liberal economic reforms. He was perceived by many Russians as cold and detatched. He alienated many with his strong anti-communist positions and was accused of spending more time away from the city than in it.

Sobchak was unexpectedly defeated in the second round of the 1996 mayoral elections by Vladimir Yakovlev, an economist specializing in municipal affairs and Sobchak's Deputy Mayor responsible for housing. The campaign was recriminatory, with accusations by Sobchak and his wife, Lyudmila Narusova, a deputy to the state Duma from St. Petersburg, that Yakovlev, who spent far more than the 125-million-ruble limit on his campaign, had exerted pressure on the local media to provide favorable coverage for Yakovlev. Yakovlev and media employees retorted that Sobchak, who as mayor had a weekly call-in television show with a huge regular audience, and Narusova had regularly attempted to dictate coverage during his term of office.

Narusova, an influential woman like Raisa Gorbacheva, was both admired and resented by others in political life. She and Sobchak had two daughters. Although successful in his own political career, Sobchak had reservations about politicians and political life. He functioned both as a political actor and as an observer of the very process in which he participated. His ambivalence can be summarized in a passage from his book, *For a New Russia:* "If we overcome the system's resistance and build a market economy, powerful democratic forces capable of preventing any relapse into the past will appear. Then we . . . will feel free to go back to our private lives. We are mere recruits, and most of us dream of completing the work that was suspended in spring 1989 until better times. I dream of my books, my research, and the joys of life within a Russian intellectual's compass."

Further Reading

Anatoly Sobchak, *For a New Russia* (1992) is an interesting chronicle of the years 1985 to 1991 and includes an autobiographical sketch of his life. It is a useful resource to understand the man and his thinking. David Remnick, *Lenin's Tomb: The Last Days of the Soviet Empire* (1993) offers insights on Sobchak's role in the anticoup movement. Stephen Sestanovich's article, "Amateur Hour," in the *New Republic* (January 27, 1992) gives a good analysis of Sobchak and his views on politics. Articles on Sobchak's public activities can be found in *The Economist, Central European,* and *World Press Review.* See especially Peter Kurth, "Great Prospekts," *Condé Nast Traveler* (February 1994). The *Soviet Biographical Service* provides well-updated information on public figures. Events of the Post-Soviet period are discussed in Boris Yeltsin, *The Struggle for Russia* (1995) and G.D.G. Murrell, *Russia's Transition to Democracy* (1997). □

Robert Mangaliso Sobukwe

Robert Mangaliso Sobukwe (1924-1978), who helped found and led the Pan-African Congress, was a militant opponent of white supremacy in South Africa.

Robert Sobukwe was born in the South African town of Graaff-Reinet on December 5, 1924. His mother was a South African of Xhosa background; his father was from Lesotho and had been both a worker in the Graaff-Reinet water system and a woodcutter. Like most Black families in South Africa, Sobukwe's was poor. With financial help from the local Methodist mission, Sobukwe went to Healdtown, a Methodist boarding school, and was an outstanding student.

In the late 1940s he went on to Fort Hare University College, the only such institution open to Blacks, and was elected president of the Students' Representative Council. At Fort Hare he also joined the African National Congress (ANC), the principal organ of Black resistance to race discrimination, and became associated with its Youth League. Begun by Anton Lembede, Nelson Mandela, and others in the 1940s, the Youth League challenged the moderate policies of older ANC leaders.

After graduation from Fort Hare, Sobukwe took a teaching position, from which he was fired in 1952 for participating in the ANC's Defiance Campaign, a mass refusal to obey apartheid laws. He then taught in the languages program of the University of Witwatersrand in Johannesburg.

In the mid-1950s Sobukwe opposed the ANC's policy of allying itself with anti-apartheid organizations of other races. This led him and others to leave the ANC in 1959 and found the Pan-African Congress (PAC), which rejected cooperation with other races. Sobukwe was elected its first president.

Convinced that a direct challenge to the apartheid government would spark a mass uprising, the PAC planned a nationwide attack on South Africa's hated pass laws—laws that forced Blacks to carry identity cards to certify their right to be in areas reserved for whites. The demonstration on March 21, 1960, did not attract mass participation. But in one of the few places where the turnout was heavy, the township of Sharpeville, the police fired on the crowd, killing 67 and wounding hundreds more. Many victims were shot in the back as they fled. This event profoundly altered South African history.

In the aftermath of the Sharpeville killings, the government declared a state of emergency. Sobukwe and other anti-apartheid leaders were jailed and the PAC and the ANC

were outlawed. As a result, both groups decided that because decades of peaceful protest against race discrimination had led only to intensified violence by the state, violent countermeasures were necessary. For the next 30 years both groups launched occasional raids and sabotage campaigns against the state. The ANC became more popular than the PAC among Blacks during this period. The armed struggle and other factors culminated in the government legalizing the PAC and the ANC in 1990, releasing Mandela and other leaders, and beginning negotiations that were eventually to lead to the end of apartheid, though the process was a bloody one.

After his arrest in 1961, Sobukwe denied the legitimacy of the judicial system that tried him and refused to defend himself. He served a prison term from 1961 to 1964. In prison he studied law by correspondence and earned a degree. Upon release he was re-arrested immediately under what came to be known as the "Sobukwe clause"—Article 4 of the General Law Amendment Act of 1963—which allowed the government to detain indefinitely without trial anyone who, having completed a prison sentence, was deemed by the minister of justice to be a danger to the state.

In 1969 Sobukwe was allowed to settle in the town of Kimberly but was banned—prohibited from speaking in public or being quoted and from participating in any group activity. He could not leave the Kimberly area; nonetheless, he practiced law until his death from cancer in 1978.

From all reports, Sobukwe was a reluctant, self-effacing leader who radiated warmth, generosity, and intellectual vigor. An instructor at Fort Hare reported that he was "by far the most brilliant fellow we have at college .... It is doubtful if Fort Hare will ever get the like of him in the foreseeable future." One of his colleagues referred to "his clear, incisive mind ..., his glowing honesty ..., his concern for the welfare of each of us, his willingness to assist in whatever capacity." One student of Black politics concluded that his activity was "wholly the product of a sense of duty, never an outlet for frustrated ambition."

Sobukwe's reason for rejecting cooperation with white and Asian anti-apartheid groups was that he believed that years of white supremacy had conditioned whites to be dominant and Blacks to be submissive. Blacks thus needed psychological independence. He admitted that "there are Europeans who are intellectually converts to the African's cause, but, because they materially benefit from the present set-up, they cannot completely identify with that cause." Real democracy, he argued, can come only when Blacks "by themselves formulate policies and programmes and decide on the method of struggle without interference from ... the minorities who arrogantly appropriate to themselves the right to plan and think for the African." These ideas draw much from the "Africanist" philosophy articulated earlier by Anton Lembede. It was refined and extended by Stephen Biko in the 1960s and 1970s.

Sobukwe was aware of the danger that this would become an anti-white, rather than a more precise anti-white supremacy, position. He frequently stated that, even though Blacks must be independent of the influence of sympathetic whites, ultimately loyalty to Africa was the crucial requirement for citizenship in a liberated South Africa. Whites and Asians would have full rights, so long as they viewed themselves as Africans and acted accordingly.

Before his death Sobukwe worried that younger PAC militants, unwilling to see the subtleties in the PAC philosophy, would develop hatred of whites, rather than of apartheid. The fact that in the 1990s the PAC boycotted negotiations, announced a policy of "one settler, one bullet," and was linked to random killings of whites during the difficult transition to a post-apartheid society suggest that his fears were realized.

Further Reading

Benjamin Pogrund's *Sobukwe and Apartheid* (1991) is a highly personal biography. For a superb study that places Sobukwe's life and ideas in a larger context, see Gail Gerhart's *Black Power in South Africa* (1978). Peter Walshe's *The Rise of African Nationalism in South Africa* (1971) and Tom Lodge's *Black Politics in South Africa since 1945* (1983) are also valuable.

Additional Sources

Pheko, S. E. M., *The land is ours: the political legacy of Mangaliso Sobukwe,* New York: Pheko & Associates, 1994.

Pogrund, Benjamin, *How can man die better: Sobukwe and apartheid,* London: P. Halban, 1990. □

Socrates

The Greek philosopher and logician Socrates (469-399 B.C.) was an important formative influence on Plato and had a profound effect on ancient philosophy.

Socrates was the son of Sophroniscus, an Athenian stone mason and sculptor. He learned his father's craft and apparently practiced it for many years before devoting his time almost completely to intellectual interests. Details of his early life are scanty, although he appears to have had no more than an ordinary Greek education. He did, however, take a keen interest in the works of the natural philosophers, and Plato (*Parmenides,* 127C) records the fact that Socrates met Zeno of Elea and Parmenides on their trip to Athens, which probably took place about 450 B.C. Socrates wrote nothing; therefore evidence for his life and activities must come from the writings of Plato and Xenophon. It is likely that neither of these presents a completely accurate picture of him, but Plato's *Apology, Crito, Phaedo,* and *Symposium* contain details which must be close to fact.

From the *Apology* we learn that Socrates was well known around Athens, that uncritical thinkers linked him with the rest of the Sophists, that he fought in at least three military campaigns for the city, and that he attracted to his circle large numbers of young men who delighted in seeing their pretentious elders refuted by Socrates. His notoriety in Athens was sufficient for the Athenian comic poet Aristophanes to lampoon him in *The Clouds,* although the Socrates who appears there bears little resemblance to the dialectician in Plato's writings. His endurance and prowess in military campaigns are attested by Alcibiades in the *Symposium.* He tells of Socrates's valor in battle, which allowed Alcibiades to escape when he was in a perilous situation. He also recounts an incident which reveals Socrates's habit of falling into a kind of trance while thinking. One morning Socrates wandered a short distance off from the other men to concentrate on a problem. By noon a small crowd had gathered, and by evening a group had come with their bedding to spend the night watching him. At the break of day, he offered up a prayer to the sun and went about his usual activities.

In addition to these anecdotes about Socrates's peculiar character, the *Symposium* provides details regarding his physical appearance. He was short and Silenus-like, quite the opposite of what was considered graceful and beautiful in the Athens of his time. He was also poor and had only the barest necessities of life. He was not ascetic, however, for he accepted the lavish hospitality of the wealthy on occasion (Agathon, the successful tragic poet, was host to the illustrious group in the *Symposium*) and proved himself capable of besting the others not only at their esoteric and sophistic sport of making impromptu speeches on the god Eros but also in holding his wine. Socrates's physical ugliness was no bar to his appeal. Alcibiades asserts in the same dialogue that Socrates made him feel deep shame and humiliation over his failure to live up to the high standards of justice and truth. He had this same effect on countless others.

His Thought

There was a strong religious side to Socrates's character and thought which constantly revealed itself in spite of his penchant for exposing the ridiculous conclusions to which uncritical acceptance of the ancient myths might lead. His words and actions in the *Apology, Crito, Phaedo,* and *Symposium* reveal a deep reverence for Athenian religious customs and a sincere regard for divinity. Indeed, it was a divine voice which Socrates claimed to hear within himself on important occasions in his life. It was not a voice which gave him positive instructions, but instead warned him when he was about to go astray. He recounts, in his defense before the Athenian court, the story of his friend Chaerephon, who was told by the Delphic Oracle that Socrates was the wisest of men. That statement puzzled Socrates, he says, for no one was more aware of the extent of his own ignorance than he himself, but he determined to see the truth of the god's words. After questioning those who had a reputation for wisdom and who considered themselves, wise, he concluded that he was wiser than they because he could recognize his ignorance while they, who were equally ignorant, thought themselves wise. He thus confirmed the truth of the god's statement.

Socrates was famous for his method of argumentation. His "irony" was an important part of that method and surely helped account for the appeal which he had for the young and the disfavor in which he was held by many Athenians.

An example comes from the *Apology*. Meletus had accused Socrates of corrupting the youth. Socrates begins by asking if Meletus considers the improvement of youth important. He replies that he does, whereupon Socrates asks who is capable of improving the young. The laws, says Meletus, and Socrates asks him to name a person who knows the laws. Meletus responds that the judges there present know the laws, whereupon Socrates asks if all who are present are able to instruct and improve youth or whether only a few can. Meletus replies that all of them are capable of such a task, which forces Meletus to confess that other groups of Athenians, such as the Senate and the Assembly, and indeed all Athenians are capable of instructing and improving the youth. All except Socrates, that is. Socrates then starts a parallel set of questions regarding the instruction and improvement of horses and other animals. Is it true that all men are capable of training horses, or only those men with special qualifications and experience? Meletus, realizing the absurdity of his position, does not answer, but Socrates answers for him and asserts that if he does not care enough about the youth of Athens to have given adequate thought to who might instruct and improve them, he has no right to accuse Socrates of corrupting them.

Thus the Socratic method of argumentation begins with commonplace questions which lead the opponent to believe that the questioner is a simpleton, but ends in a complete reversal. It is a method not calculated to win friends, especially when used in public.

Socrates's true contributions to the development of ancient thought are difficult to assess. Plato's dialogues, although they are our single most important source, are not entirely reliable because Socrates is used, especially in the later dialogues, merely as a mouthpiece. It is probable, however, that the Socrates we find in the *Apology Crito,* and a few of the other early dialogues represents a fair approximation of the man and his thinking. Thus his chief contributions lie not in the construction of an elaborate system but in clearing away the false common beliefs and in leading men to an awareness of their own ignorance, from which position they may begin to discover the truth. Socrates's contribution, then, was primarily the negative one of exposing fallacies, but equally important was the magnetism of his personality and the effect which he had on the people he met. It was his unique combination of dialectical skill and magnetic attractiveness to the youth of Athens which gave his opponents their opportunity to bring him to trial in 399 B.C.

His Death

Meletus, Lycon, and Anytus charged Socrates with impiety and with corrupting the youth of the city. Since prosecution and defense speeches were made by the principals in Athenian legal practice, Socrates spoke in his own behalf. It is uncertain if the charges were the result of his associations with the Thirty or resulted from personal pique. Callias, Plato's uncle, had been the leader of the unpopular Thirty, but it is difficult to imagine that Socrates could have been considered a collaborator when in fact he risked death by refusing to be implicated in their crimes. He had, however, made a great number of enemies for himself over the years through his self-appointed role as the "gadfly" of Athens, and it is probable that popular misunderstanding and animosity toward his activities helped lead to his conviction. His defense speech was not in the least conciliatory. After taking up the charges and showing how they were false, he proposed that the city should honor him as it did Olympic victors. He was convicted and sentenced to death. Plato's *Crito* tells of Crito's attempts to persuade Socrates to flee the prison (Crito had bribed the jailer, as was customary), but Socrates, in an allegorical dialogue between himself and the Laws of Athens, reveals his devotion to the city and his obligation to obey its decrees even if they lead to his death. In the *Phaedo,* Plato recounts Socrates's discussion of the immortality of the soul; and at the end of that dialogue, one of the most moving and dramatic scenes in ancient literature, Socrates takes the hemlock prepared for him while his friends sit helplessly by. He died reminding Crito that he owes a cock to Aesculapius.

Socrates was the most colorful figure in the history of ancient philosophy. His fame was widespread in his own time, and his name soon became a household word although he professed no extraordinary wisdom, constructed no philosophical system, established no school, and founded no sect. His influence on the course of ancient philosophy, through Plato, the Cynics, and less directly, Aristotle, is incalculable.

Further Reading

Sources for Socrates's life are the dialogues of Plato, especially the *Apology, Crito, Phaedo,* and Alcibiades's speech in the *Symposium,* and Xenophon's *Memorabilia,* all of which are available in a variety of editions and translations. A comprehensive and major study of Socrates's thought is Norman Gulley, *The Philosophy of Socrates* (1968). See also Eduard Zeller, *Socrates and the Socratic Schools* (1885; 3d rev. ed. 1962); A. E. Taylor, *Socrates* (1933); and Anton-Hermann Chroust, *Socrates: Man and Myth* (1957).

A dramatic version of Socrates's accusation, self-defense, imprisonment, and death is rendered in simplified, colloquial English by I. A. Richards in *Why So Socrates? A Dramatic Version of Plato's Dialogues Euthyphro, Apology, Crito, Phaedo* (1964). Critical treatment of Socrates and his place in the development of ancient thought is in Eduard Zeller, *Outlines of the History of Greek Philosophy* (trans. 1890; 13th ed. revised by Wilhelm Nestle, 1931); John Burnet, *Greek Philosophy* (1914); and Wilhelm Windelband, *History of Ancient Philosophy,* translated by Herbert E. Cushman (1956). □

Frederick Soddy

The English chemist Frederick Soddy (1877-1956) shared in the discoveries of atomic disintegration and of helium production during radioactive decay and introduced the term "isotope" to nuclear science.

Frederick Soddy was born at Eastbourne, Sussex, on Sept. 2, 1877. He studied at Eastbourne College; University College, Aberystwyth; and Merton College, Oxford, where in 1898 he received his degree in chemistry.

Radioactivity Studies at Montreal

Having accepted a demonstratorship in chemistry at McGill University, Montreal, Soddy found himself increasingly attracted by the work being done by Ernest Rutherford, then research professor of physics at the university. He joined Rutherford's team and brought to it his valuable experience as a chemist.

In a study of the radioactivity of thorium, Rutherford and Soddy added ammonia to a solution of a thorium salt, so precipitating out thorium hydroxide. When the insoluble material had been filtered off, the remaining solution still showed radioactivity. They established that this was due to a highly radioactive substance which they called thorium-X. Detailed measurements were made of the radioactivity of solution and precipitate over a number of weeks, and it became clear that different chemical species were involved in the process of radioactive decay over the period studied.

Further evidence for a strangely new kind of disintegration came from Rutherford's and Soddy's examination of the behavior of uranium, which when pure, emitted alpha particles only. The beta emission often encountered must therefore come from some other substance. Rutherford had already noted a gaseous emanation from thorium; now, with Soddy, he suggested that it belonged to the inert gas family. Also, they removed all doubts about the existence of a similar emanation from radium by condensing it with liquid air.

Soddy, who had long been interested in the historical problem of alchemy, now used the alchemical term "transmutation" to describe the changes that are accompanied by radioactive emission. Rutherford adopted the concept, and in 1903 they announced the general theory of radioactive disintegration. They proposed that radioactivity was an atomic phenomenon and that radiation was an accompaniment of chemical transmutations of the atoms themselves. This theory, though often bearing Rutherford's name alone, was in fact a product of the joint activity of Rutherford and Soddy.

Helium Studies at London

In 1903 Soddy left Montreal for London, drawn by the reputation of Sir William Ramsay at University College. Soddy was anxious to study further the gases associated with radioactive materials. Ramsay's laboratory, internationally acclaimed for the addition of the inert gases to the periodic table, was almost the only place where minute quantities of rare gases could be successfully examined.

Ramsay had recently acquired a small amount of radium bromide, and he and Soddy examined the gaseous emanations which were pumped off. After removal of oxygen and other common gases, the residue was examined spectroscopically. It was found to give the same spectrum as helium. When the gas was cooled by liquid air to remove the helium, the residue, as expected, gave no helium spectrum; but after a few days the helium line reappeared. Clearly helium had formed as a product of radioactive decay. Soddy concluded that the helium originated with the alpha particles, which were thus helium nuclei—a view later confirmed by Rutherford. Ramsay and Soddy showed that the other gaseous emanations were true inert gases.

Defining the Isotope at Glasgow

In 1904 Soddy moved to the University of Glasgow to take up a special appointment as lecturer in physical chemistry (including radiochemistry). During his first few years he made steady progress in purifying radioactive materials. In 1908 he married Winifred Beilby, only daughter of George Beilby of the Cassell Gold Extracting Company, which provided financial support for a research program in which Soddy was engaged involving methods of extraction for possible substitutes for radium. This project yielded few results of importance.

In 1910 Soddy turned his attention to the short-lived radioelements, collaborating with Alexander Fleck. They decided to establish the chemical characteristics of every known member of the disintegration series. They showed that in several cases a number of intermediates were chemically identical and inseparable from one another, yet underwent radioactive decay in quite different ways. Thus identical chemical properties were shown by radium-B, thorium-B, actinium-B, and lead.

Soddy's first generalization on these mysteries came in his rule that loss of an alpha particle from an atom with an even number in the periodic table produces an atom with the next lower even number. In subsequent changes, however, when alpha emission does not take place, a reversion to the original "family" may occur, and the products will be chemically inseparable from the starting material, even though the atomic weights vary. Complementary to this alpha-particle rule is the one that in beta emissions an atom moves up one place in the periodic table. In 1913 Soddy combined the alpha and beta rules into the group displacement law: one alpha emission causes a shift two places back in the periodic table, and one beta emission causes a shift one place further on. Hence a sequence of alpha-beta-beta emissions would mean a return to the original place in the table.

The underlying concept, that more than one kind of atom might be assignable to the same chemical "space," was daring and revolutionary. In December 1913 Soddy brought matters to a head by writing a letter to *Nature* in which he proposed that such chemically inseparable species should be termed "isotopes." In modern parlance, they differ from each other in mass but not in overall nuclear charge. The group displacement law and the related concept of isotopy were soon confirmed.

In 1914 Soddy became professor of chemistry at Aberdeen. His fortunes here were immediately and drastically affected by the war. He was able to complete some of the work begun in Glasgow, but his radiochemical researches were brought to a premature end by the special wartime demands made upon his laboratories.

Oxford and Retirement

With the ending of the war the future held great promise for radiochemical studies in Britain. In 1919 Soddy was appointed Lee's professor of inorganic and physical chemistry at the University of Oxford. Two years later he received the Nobel Prize in chemistry for his contributions to radiochemistry and, particularly, to the concept of isotopes.

It was widely hoped that, under Soddy's leadership, a British school of radiochemistry would emerge at Oxford that would complement the work of the atomic physicists at the Cavendish Laboratory in Cambridge. Unfortunately this was not to be, for his output of original work in science was negligible. In 1936 he resigned his chair. The death of his wife no doubt contributed to his discontent, but this cannot explain the full measure of his apparent disenchantment with experimental work.

Soddy was an extremely talented writer, and to some extent his literary gifts may have interfered with his laboratory research. His first book, *Radioactivity,* appeared in 1904. For many years, beginning in 1904, he contributed articles on radioactivity to the *Annual Reports* of the Chemical Society. *The Interpretation of Radium* (1909) was a popular treatise deriving much from his Glasgow lectures. *The Chemistry of the Radioelements* (1910) was a concise and reliable summary of the contemporary position. Later works included *The Interpretation of the Atom* (1932) and *The Story of Atomic Energy* (1947). He also wrote several books on economic theory. He died on Sept. 21, 1956, in Brighton.

Further Reading

Muriel Howarth, *Pioneer Research on the Atom* (1958), contains a biography of Soddy. The Royal Society of London, *Biographical Memoirs of Fellows of the Royal Society,* vol. 3 (1957), has a biography of Soddy by Sir Alexander Fleck. Additional material is in Henry A. Boorse and Lloyd Motz, eds., *The World of the Atom* (2 vols., 1966).

Additional Sources

Frederick Soddy (1877-1956): early pioneer in radiochemistry, Dordrecht; Boston: D. Reidel Pub. Co.; Hingham, MA, U.S.A.: Sold and distributed in the U.S.A. and Canada by Kluwer Academic Publishers, 1986.

Merricks, Linda, *The world made new: Frederick Soddy, science, politics, and environment,* New York: Oxford University Press, 1996. □

Nathan Söderblom

The Swedish churchman Nathan Söderblom (1866-1931) was an important leader in the ecumenical movement for the unification of Christian Churches. He won the Nobel Peace Prize in 1930 for his efforts in the area of international understanding.

Theologically and intellectually the life of Nathan Söderblom was characterized by tensions. His father was a fervent Pietist minister of Swedish yeoman stock, and his mother came from a liberal Danish background. Nathan Söderblom was born Lars Jonathan Söderblom on Jan. 15, 1866, in Trönö (Hälsingland). As a young man, he pursued theological studies at the University of Uppsala. During the period he was minister of the busy Swedish church at Paris (1894-1901), Söderblom earned his theological doctorate at the Sorbonne (1901). Returning to Sweden, he became professor of the history of religion at Uppsala, and from 1914 to 1931 he served as vice chancellor of the university. After becoming archbishop, Söderblom never lost sight of the many Swedes who had emigrated to the United States. When he visited the United States in 1923, this concern and his ecumenical mission caused some friction. Such crises of modernity notwithstanding, Söderblom's scholarly and intellectual achievements were considerable. His quest for the uniqueness of Christianity was grounded on theological competence within the Christian tradition as well as on an application of the canons of historical criticism to the study of both Christian and non-Christian religions.

Söderblom had first established himself as a promising scholar in the history of religion through the publication of his dissertation, *La vie future d'après le Mazdaisme.* Many other books followed. In 1914 he published *Origins of Belief in God,* in which he summarized the involved and heated debate on this subject. As an alternate route to evolution, he outlined an inquiry into the psychological prerequisites of religion. His clear distinction between high gods and monotheism and his rejection of

protomonotheism have become part of scholarly tradition. In his emphasis on the holy as the basic constituent of religion, he anticipated Rudolf Otto. On the theological side, Söderblom viewed the uniqueness of Christianity in its character as a religion of historic revelation, against the mysticisms of infinity, pantheisms, and deisms. According to Söderblom, the tension between the transcendence and the nearness of God, between His perfections and His presence, and between ethics and religious experience inherent in this dynamic concept found its original unity in the person of Jesus Christ. This ensured the redemptive rather than the arbitrary character of history. Moreover, Söderblom overcame the then prevalent notion that a personal god belonged to an obsolete, earlier, and less ethical stage in religion. He emphasized that the center of Christianity was neither doctrines nor institutions but the person of Jesus Christ.

Söderblom died in Uppsala on July 12, 1931.

Further Reading

The best biography of Söderblom, which also gives an idea of the scope of his mind, is Bengt Sundkler, *Nathan Söderblom: His Life and Work* (1968). ☐

Dorothee Soelle

Dorothee Soelle (born 1929), German theologian, political activist, and feminist, was a leader among the generation of liberation theologians who reinterpreted the Christian message within the context of socialism and pacifism.

Dorothee Soelle was born September 30, 1929, in Cologne, West Germany, to a middle-class Protestant family. Her father was a lawyer who attempted to maintain a distance from both the Hitler regime and the church. He impressed upon the young Dorothee the importance of education and a disregard for material wealth. Despite parental indifference to religion Dorothee became interested in the church (Evangelical Church of the Rhineland) and theology as a high school student. She studied philology, philosophy, theology, and German literature at the Universities of Cologne, Freiburg, and Göttingen and was awarded the doctoral degree by the University of Göttingen in 1959, where her teachers were Friedrich Gogarten and Ernst Käsemann.

She taught German and theology in high school from 1954 to 1960, when she became a research assistant at the Philosophical Institute of Aachen until 1962. At that time she returned to Cologne to teach in the Institute of Germanic Philology at the university. She was a lecturer on the theological faculty of the University of Mainz from 1972 to 1975. Unable to secure a permanent position in a German university because of her political activities, she was the Harry Emerson Fosdick Visiting Professor at Union Theological Seminary in New York beginning in 1975. She spent half of each year in the United States and half in Germany, where she continued to be one of the leading spokespersons against nuclear proliferation and the oppressive South American and South African regimes and a critic of capitalism.

She married Fulbert Steffensky, a professor of religion and education at the University of Hamburg who in the 1970s was co-founder with Soelle of the religiously oriented, socially active Politisches Nachtgebet. Founded initially as a protest against First World countries' intervention in Vietnam, the group also addressed itself to problems of economic and social discrimination in West Germany. Soelle had two daughters and a son by a first marriage, and she and Steffensky had a daughter, Mirjam.

The content of Soelle's works is theological and political, but their styles are diverse and include books of poetry. Among her more important works are *Christ the Representative* (1967), *The Truth Is Concrete* (1967), *Beyond Mere Obedience* (1968), *Suffering* (1973), *Political Theology* (1974), *Death by Bread Alone* (1975), *Choosing Life* (1980), *The Arms Race Kills* (1982), *Of War and Love* (1983), *The Strength of the Weak: Toward a Christian Feminist Identity* (1984), and numerous articles. In 1995 Soelle co-authored, *Great Women of the Bible in Art and Literature* with J.H. Kirchberger and Hebert Haag.

Soelle's first book, *Christ the Representative,* was her response to the then-current "death of God" theology. It reflects her effort to understand and to reconcile the reality of what had happened in World War II (symbolized by Auschwitz) with the idea of an all-seeing, all-loving God "who leads all things to Good." In *Christ the Representative* Soelle declared an end to the traditional "vertical" idea of God as the all-powerful lord of history controlling the world from above. In God's place, as God's representative, is the Christ who suffers and dies with us; but as Christ represents God, humans must also represent Christ to each other. This became the foundation upon which Soelle developed her theology in social and political terms.

In her book *Political Theology* Soelle worked from a base of the existential theology of Rudolf Bultmann to build a foundation for her political theology. Bultmann's theology, she argued, is truncated; he properly grounds theological reflection in an understanding of the structures of concrete human existence, but fails to see that that existence is inherently social and not simply individual. Forgiveness is inseparable from responsibility and is socially mediated. God does not offer private forgiveness, but rather, as we learn from the Sermon on the Mount, "admonishes us to go and first be reconciled to our brother" (Matthew 5:14). Resurrection occurs within the context of history as we bring about an end to oppression and transform those social structures that are its cause.

In later years, as a direct outgrowth of her political and social activism grounded in theological reflection, there emerged a new emphasis in Soelle's thought: on the one hand contemporary feminism and on the other Christian mystical tradition. Soelle understood feminist theology as a liberation theology and always dealt with the oppression and liberation of women together with the issues of racism and exploitation of the proletariat. In that context she referred to sexism as the "colonialization" of women. The task of both an authentic Christianity and an authentic politics can only be human liberation, which integrally involves militant action against the madness of nuclearism. The creation of genuinely non-exploitative human society inherently entails the building of the peaceable kingdom, of shalom with all its fullness of meaning.

Soelle defined mysticism as the Cognitio Dei Experimentalis, the "perception of God through experience." It is in mystical experience—which Soelle did not regard as esoteric but as widely experienced by ordinary people—that the contemporary Christian feminist can find warrant for a direct, personal-social, anti-authoritarian, and creative relationship to the Christian tradition and to contemporary structures of oppression. Soelle emphasized in this connection the subversive, "anarchical" character of the mystical tradition.

For Soelle the only mode of theological reflection appropriate to both the nature of Christian faith and the task of liberation in the real human world was "inductive" and "narrative." Theology may be grounded firmly in the concrete experiences of people undergoing suffering and incompleteness in their lives, rather than beginning "deductively" with doctrines. Soelle's own theological writing, especially during the 1970s and early 1980s, was a remarkably successful synthesis of the personal and the intellectual, the concrete and the analytical, the imaginative and the thoroughly knowledgeable. It was a theological style which provided an entirely congruent medium for her unification of feminism, mysticism, and socialist pacifism.

Further Reading

There does not appear to be any full studies of the life or work of Dorothee Soelle. Some of her work tends to be autobiographical in nature (*Death by Bread Alone* offers some personal insights). There is a short biographical sketch in the introduction to the English translation of *Political Theology* by John Shelley. Peter Hodgson comments on *Christ the Representative* in his book *Jesus—Word and Presence* (1971). Reactions from the Jewish perspective are found in the book *Contemporary Christologies: A Jewish Response* (1980) by Eugene B. Borowitz. Soelle was a frequent contributor to *Christianity and Crisis* and other liberal Christian periodicals. □

Sol Ch'ong

Sol Ch'ong (ca. 680-750) was an eminent Korean Confucian scholar of the Silla dynasty. He made significant contributions to the field of education through the development of a system for writing Korean. He was known as one of the Ten Confucian Sages of Silla.

Sol Ch'ong, whose literary appellation was Pingwoldang (Ice Moon Hall), came from the Sol clan of Kyongju, the capital of ancient Silla. By the time Kim Pusik included Sol Ch'ong's biography in his *History of the Three Kingdoms* in the 13th century, much information concerning Sol Ch'ong's career had been lost.

Silla had a strong caste system called Bone Ranks, and Sol came from one of the eminent families. His grandfather had held high office in the government before Silla unified the Korean peninsula, and his father, Wonhyo, was an eminent monk in this predominantly Buddhist kingdom. Wonhyo married a royal princess who gave birth to Sol Ch'ong. Wonhyo is known to have written at least 12 volumes on Buddhism and was considered one of the Ten Buddhist Saints of Silla. Together with the monk Ŭisang, he founded the Pomosa Temple, which stands near Pusan today.

Sol Ch'ong rose to high position in the National Academy, where his principal duties involved translating dispatches into Chinese for the King. As one of the three most famous Confucian scholars in Silla—Kang Su and Ch'oe Chiwon were the others—Sol lectured on the Confucian classics in the Korean vernacular.

Inasmuch as Korea had come under Chinese influence long before the Christian era and before the Koreans developed a means of writing their language, Chinese was utilized to record ideas and transact business. Sol Ch'ong was reputed to have invented *idu,* a system which enabled Koreans to write noun and verb inflections used in their language between Chinese characters to render Chinese into Korean grammar. In a similar manner, pure Korean words could be written by using Chinese characters for their phonetic values. However, the existence of the Royal Tour Monuments, erected on North Han Mountain in the reign of King Chinhŭng (reigned 540-575) and inscribed in *idu,* indicates that the system originated much before Sol's birth. It is probable that Sol Ch'ong's fame stems from his collection and organization of *idu* symbols rather than from their invention.

One original work by Sol Ch'ong is mentioned in the *History of the Three Kingdoms* and is titled *The Flower King's Warning* (*Hwa Wang Kye*). It was said to have been an allegorical work which presented court personages as residents of the Flower Kingdom.

In 1022 a memorial ceremony was held for Sol in the National Shrine, and he was enshrined in the Soak Academy in Kyongju.

Further Reading

Because of the scarcity of factual data relating to his career, there are no comprehensive works on Sol Ch'ong in Western or Asian languages. For general background see Edwin O. Reischauer and John K. Fairbank, *A History of East Asian Civilization,* vol. 1: *East Asia: The Great Tradition* (1958), and Peter H. Lee, *Korean Literature: Topics and Themes* (1965). □

Juan Díaz de Solís

Juan Díaz de Solís (ca. 1470-1516), the pilot major of Castile, sailed under the Spanish flag to explore the Americas, where he discovered the Río de la Plata.

Juan Díaz de Solis was evidently born in Portugal, although his ancestry was Spanish. As a young man, he visited India perhaps several times as a seaman in Portuguese service. Dissatisfied with his meager and often unpaid wages, he served for a time with French corsairs. When he and his French associates captured a Portuguese caravel returning from the Gold Coast, this made his return to Portugal impossible, so he transferred his services to Spain. He had by this time become a skilled pilot.

Solís was in Spain by 1508, and in that year he embarked on a discovery voyage with Christopher Columbus's former companion Vicente Yáñez Pinzón. Their exact route is a matter of dispute, but they attempted to find the much-sought strait to the Spice Islands and spent part of their time exploring the coast of Veragua (Nicaragua).

Upon returning to Spain in 1509, Solís was imprisoned because he and Pinzón had quarreled; the authorities at this point favored the older navigator. A more careful review of the matter soon followed, and Solís was released. He now enjoyed the esteem of King Ferdinand V, and when Amerigo Vespucci, the first pilot major of Castile, died in February 1512, Solís became his successor.

As pilot major, Solís embarked in 1515 on his last voyage, the purpose of which was to find a passage into the Pacific Ocean. Once in the Pacific, he was to proceed to the Far East if possible. The three caravels allotted him were small so that they could explore shallow coastal waters that vessels of greater draft could not penetrate. The Portuguese knew the purpose of Solís's voyage and, fearing to lose their monopoly on the Oriental trade, attempted unsuccessfully to sabotage the undertaking before Solís left Sanlúcar de Barrameda on Oct. 8, 1515.

After carefully working its way down the Brazilian coast, Solís's expedition entered the Río de la Plata. He explored the Uruguayan coast as far as Martin Garcia Island, and near here he went ashore with a party, including his two principal officers, Pedro de Alarcón and Francisco Marquina. Suddenly a band of Indians, presumably Charrúa, burst upon them and killed the landing group in plain view of those on shipboard. The leaderless expedition returned as quickly as possible to Spain and arrived there on Sept. 4, 1516.

Further Reading

Major accounts of Solís are in Spanish. In English, some information on him is in Pietro Martire d'Anghiera, *De orbe novo* (trans., 2 vols., 1912). The Solís discoveries receive attention in Germán Arciniegas, *Amerigo and the New World* (trans. 1955); and the voyages are placed in historical perspective in Charles E. Nowell, ed., *Magellan's Voyage around the World* (1962). □

Solomon

Solomon (reigned ca. 965-ca. 925 B.C.) was a king of the ancient Hebrews. He rebuilt the city of Jerusalem and erected the first Hebrew temple there. His wisdom is proverbial.

Solomon was the youngest son of David and Bathsheba. He inherited an empire that extended in the northeast to the Euphrates, in the southeast to the Gulf of Aqaba, and in the southwest to the borders of Egypt and Philistia.

Solomon ruled as a grand monarch, supreme in power and regal in splendor. History and legend have endowed him with great gifts, of which his wisdom is the most famous. Impartial and eager for wisdom and understanding, he was famous as a wise and evenhanded judge. Three sections of the Bible are ascribed to his authorship: Proverbs, Ecclesiastes, and the Song of Solomon (Song of Songs).

The King's reign was a peaceful one. With consummate diplomatic skill he entered into numerous friendly alliances with the great powers of his time, often securing them through marriage. His most important marriage was with the Pharaoh's daughter. It secured peace on his southern border and kept the road open to Ezion-geber, site of his iron and copper refinery.

Solomon believed that his kingdom and especially his capital city of Jerusalem should reflect the power and glory of Israel's king. He undertook a series of elaborate building

operations, fortifying the strategic and economic towns within his realm. In Jerusalem he built luxurious palaces, completed the defense wall around the city, and erected a magnificent temple on Mt. Moriah.

Solomon also sponsored industrial and commercial enterprises that brought him wealth. He built a great fleet, sending naval expeditions along the coast of the Red Sea and through the Mediterranean as far as Spain. He carried on an extensive caravan trade to Arabia and Egypt, developed copper and iron mines, and built refineries for smelting.

Heavy expenses caused Solomon to severely regulate the fiscal administration of Israel. The cost of maintaining his court necessitated the collection of extremely high taxes. To raise these taxes, he consolidated his administration, creating 12 new districts with royal officers in charge of each.

Despite the magnificence of Solomon's rule, the people were dissatisfied and harbored many grievances against him. His death was immediately followed by a rebellion of the northern tribes and the division of his kingdom.

Further Reading

Although there is no single authoritative biography of Solomon, there are numerous volumes of fiction, making it difficult to distinguish between the historical and the legendary. The best shorter essays are in Rudolph Kittel, *Great Men and Movements in Israel* (1929), and James Fleming, *Personalities of the Old Testament* (1939). The best treatment of Solomon is in the Holy Scriptures, supplemented with the commentaries published by each of the major religious groups. For historical background the following works are recommended: W. F. Albright, *From the Stone Age to Christianity* (1940); Max I. Margolis and Alexander Marx, *A History of the Jewish People* (1944); S. W. Baron, *A Social and Religious History of the Jews,* vol. 1 (1952); and Martin Noth, *The History of Israel* (1958). □

Solon

The Greek statesman and poet Solon (active 594 B.C.) formulated an influential code of laws and has been regarded as the founder of Athenian democracy.

As a statesman, Solon put principles before expediency. Elected chief magistrate in 594 B.C., he was given special powers to deal with the emergency brought on by civil war. The war had arisen mainly because of the oppression of the poor by the rich, who were entitled under the existing laws to tie some bankrupt debtors to the land and exact a sixth part of the produce (hence the victims were called *hectemoroi,* "sixth-parters") and to sell others into slavery. Solon canceled all debts. He freed the land and those tied to it, and he purchased the freedom of those who had been enslaved. He enacted new laws of debt which were the same for both groups. "The laws I passed were alike for low-born and for high-born; my aim was straightforward justice for each." He proclaimed a general amnesty except in cases of bloodshed or an attempted coup d'etat. The principles of habeas corpus and of equality before the law were thus implemented by Solon. The price was a grave economic crisis, during which he banned the export of foodstuffs except olive oil, always plentiful in the land of the olive. For the future he took steps to align Athens commercially with Corinth, the leading exporter to overseas markets.

Reorganization of Athenian Institutions

The principles enunciated by Solon were in advance of the existing constitution. In 592 he was entrusted with full legislative powers. As he had done in regard to debt, he abolished distinctions of birth in politics. Henceforth all Athenians were classified by income into four groups. Liability for tax and military service and eligibility for office were defined in terms of the new classification. For example, the lowest group—that of the *thetes*—paid no tax, provided no equipment, and was not eligible for any office, whereas the next lowest—that of the *zeugitae*—paid tax at the lowest rate, provided body armor, and was eligible for minor offices. The effective organ in the existing constitution was the Areopagus Council, recruited from former magistrates, who held office for life. Solon introduced alongside it a second house, the Council of Four Hundred, nominated by Solon no doubt for their liberal and progressive views. The new house was designed not only to break the monopoly of the Areopagus Council but also to guide the Assembly

of Citizens (*Ekklesia*), in which men of all classes sat. This Assembly was sovereign in theory; but at a time of social and economic disruption Solon did not intend it to be sovereign in practice. He regarded the two councils as stabilizers. "The ship of state, riding upon two anchors, will pitch less in the surf and make the people less turbulent." In particular, the Assembly was debarred from considering any motion on which the Council of Four Hundred had not already reported its own recommendation. Thus snap decisions were ruled out.

Politics and justice were closely related in ancient society. Solon championed the poor more in justice than in politics. Every citizen was to have the right of appeal against the edict of a magistrate. Every citizen was to be entitled to prosecute at law. And every citizen was to be eligible to sit on a new court of state, the *Heliaea,* or People's Court, before which appeals were heard (the actual panel for each case being selected by lot). He drew up a new code of laws, designed to protect the underprivileged and the deprived. Only fragments survive.

Having established the basic equalities on which a democratic society is founded, Solon went into voluntary exile for 10 years. Returning to find party strife, he censured the leaders and the people for their stupidity. He died at an advanced age.

His Poetry

Solon's poetry, esteemed for its ideas rather than its literary form, was a basic element in Athenian education. His few extant poems reveal an original and profound thinker. Earlier poets had attributed to the gods not only natural calamities such as epidemics or drought but also national and individual disasters, and they had deduced that the gods always punished wickedness. Solon first distinguished between events beyond human control and events within human control; and he thought more deeply about the ways of the gods. Thus in a poem written during a civil war at Athens, Solon attributed the destruction of society not to the gods but to the citizens. It was their greed, cruelty, and injustice which had caused chaos. Order could be restored only if the citizens agreed to obey the laws. "Where law reigns, all human affairs are sensible and sound." In essence, men are responsible for human relations within a group; and if they are to achieve order within the group, they must seek social justice and they must accept the reign of law.

In his longest surviving poem Solon reflected on a man's personal aspirations. Success is not his to command. It is the gods who give success and who take success away. Their purposes are not clear. Success is not awarded in accordance with human merits. "Many bad men are rich, many good men are poor." "One who tries to work well falls without any premonition into utter disaster, while complete success is granted by the gods to a bad worker." In the long run wickedness is punished but not necessarily the actual sinner. Sometimes "the innocent pay—the children of the sinner or his descendants thereafter." These ideas are the stuff from which Attic tragedy and indirectly later tragedy were made. Intellectual awareness and religious faith were fused to produce the tragic view of man.

Further Reading

Solon's poems are translated in Kathleen Freeman, *The Work and Life of Solon* (1926). Ancient sources on Solon include the biography by Plutarch and Aristotle's *Athenaion politeia.* Modern works include Ivan M. Linforth, *Solon the Athenian* (1919); W. J. Woodhouse, *Solon the Liberator* (1938); and N. G. L. Hammond, *A History of Greece* (2d ed. 1967). ☐

Joseph Baer Soloveitchik

The Jewish theologian/philosopher Joseph Baer Soloveitchik (1903-1993) was able to use his extensive knowledge of rabbinical tradition and of secular and non-Jewish thought to illuminate both the contemporary Jewish situation and the circumstances of modern man in general. During his lifetime, he ordained over 2000 rabbis.

Joseph Baer Soloveitchik was born in 1903 in Pruzhan, Poland, into one of the most distinguished rabbinical families in Eastern Europe. His grandfather Rav Chaim Soloveitchik had pioneered a new method of talmudic study and had thereby created one of the main religious and intellectual streams within modern Orthodox Jewry. After receiving an excellent traditional Jewish education at home under the tutelage of his father, Rav Moses Soloveitchik, the young Soloveitchik at the age of 20 took the dramatic action, given his family background, of going to Germany to study at the University of Berlin. And it was here, after nearly a decade of secular studies, that he received his Ph.D. in philosophy in 1931 for a dissertation dealing with Herman Cohen's neo-Kantian philosophical outlook. It was also here that he met and married Dr. Tonya Lewit (who died in 1967). In 1932, with doctorate in hand, he went to the United States and settled in Boston. In 1933 he began to teach rabbinics at the Rabbi Isaac Elchanan Seminary of Yeshiva University (New York City), and in 1941, following his father's death, he acceded to its head (as *Rosh Yeshiva*).

Soloveitchik's fame as a theologian-philosopher rested upon his unique control of the whole range of rabbinical tradition as well as the main sources of modern secular and non-Jewish thought. As few others, he was able to bring together these two disparate traditions in such a way as to illuminate both the contemporary Jewish situation and the circumstances of modern man in general. He exerted his influence in two very different ways. The first, and most important, was through his teaching at Yeshiva University, where several generations of young American Orthodox rabbis became his students and "disciples." The second was through his diverse essays, many of which have been collected into published volumes. The most important of these were *Halakhic Man* (English translation, 1984); *Shiurei Ha-Rav* (1978); *On Repentance* (1984); and the essays "The Lonely Man of Faith" (*Tradition,* 7 [Summer 1965]) and "Confrontation" (*Tradition,* 6 [Spring-Summer-1964]).

Soloveitchik's work is not easy to summarize because it was not presented in a systematic fashion, but its essential features can be summarized. His primary concern was to analyze—and draw subtle distinctions between—different understandings of the human condition—for example, between what he perceived to be the character of "technological" man who asked the pragmatic and scientific question "How does the cosmos function?" and "religious" man who asked rather the metaphysical question "Why is there a cosmos at all?"; or again to distinguish among "rational man," "religious man" in general, and "halakhic man" (the man who lives according to Jewish law—that is, *halakah*). The purpose of making such discriminations for Soloveitchik was that they reveal human-kind's complex character, a complex character which cannot ultimately be satisfied through the cultivation of only one aspect—for example, the pragmatic scientific-rational side of the human personality. The whole person, the religious-moral, as well as the intellectual-acquisitive, aspects of life require proper attention and development.

His world-view revealed deep affinities with the modern school of thought known as Existentialism. Like the existentialist philosophers he emphasized, as was indicated in the title of his most famous essay, the characteristics of "The Lonely Man of Faith," his studies were preoccupied with the themes of human anxiety, loneliness, alienation, guilt, repentance, and suffering and how these conditions were to be overcome through a personal and authentic relation to God.

He was above all else a deeply committed, profoundly learned Jew who wished to examine, explain, and justify the workings of the rabbinic tradition to modern individuals. His truly unique contribution was his halakhic orientation, his continued effort to elaborate and defend the need for the *halakah* (religious law) as the most appropriate means by which Jews can enter into a proper dialogical relationship with God. According to this perspective the appropriate divine-human dialogue was created when mankind willingly brings its will into conformity with the Divine Will as revealed in the *Torah* (the Hebrew Bible), as interpreted by the rabbinic tradition (the *Halakah,* religious law).

In addition to contributing to the theoretical debate over these complex theological issues, Soloveitchik also influenced American and world Jewry by his championing of Zionism and by his deep commitment to the state of Israel.

During his lifetime, Soloveitchik ordained more than 2000 rabbis. He died in his home in Brookline, Massachusetts, at the age of 90, on April 8, 1993.

Further Reading

Readers now have access to many of Soloveitchik's own writings, some written originally in English, many translated from Yiddish and Hebrew. The most important were the essays "The Lonely Man of Faith," *Tradition,* (Summer 1965; republished as a book by Doubleday in 1992), which gave his view of human nature, and "Ish-Ha-Halachah," now available in an English translation under the title *Halakhic Man,* edited and translated by Lawrence Kaplan (1984). A number of his oral discourses, translated by Pinchas Peli, appeared in *On Repentance* (1984). These materials were a good source for coming to an appreciation of his style as well as his control of all traditional Jewish sources. The same was true of the second collection of his discourses, published under the title *Shiurei Ha-Rav* (*Discourses of the Rav,* 1978). For a general study of Soloveitchik's views see Aharon Lichtenstein's essay on Soloveitchik in *Great Jewish Thinkers* edited by Simon Novack (1985), which included biographical details. For discussion of his theological and philosophical work see the respective "Introduction(s)" by Lawrence Kaplan and Pinchas Peli to the volumes edited by them and cited above. See also the exegesis of his position provided by Eugene Borowitz in his *Choices in Modern Jewish Thought* (1983) and Steven T. Katz, *Jewish Philosophers* (1975). ☐

Vladimir Sergeevich Soloviev

The Russian philosopher and religious thinker Vladimir Sergeevich Soloviev (1853-1900) was an early exponent of the ecumenical movement. He was also a leader of the modern reaction against extreme rationalism.

Vladimir Soloviev was born on Jan. 28, 1853, the second son of a distinguished historian. He graduated from Moscow Gymnasium No. 1 in 1869 and entered the science faculty at Moscow University. Three years later he transferred to the philosophy faculty, graduating in 1873, and then attended classes in the seminary of the St. Sergius Monastery. He also studied European philosophy in preparation for his master of arts thesis, an attack on materialism which was accepted in 1874 (*The Crisis of Western Philosophy*). He lectured for a year at Moscow University and then took a leave in England. In the British Museum he had a vision of a beautiful woman whom he identified as Sophia, or the Divine Wisdom (he had first seen her when he was only 9 years old). This time she told him to go to Egypt, where in November 1875 she appeared to him in the desert.

This desert vision changed Soloviev's life. He became increasingly interested in religion. In 1877 he took a post in the Education Ministry in St. Petersburg, where he was close to Slavophile circles. In 1878 he completed his *Treatise on God-Manhood.* Two years later his doctoral dissertation (*Critique of Abstract Principles*) was accepted. His public lecturing was suppressed after April 1881 because of his appeal to spare the lives of those who had assassinated Alexander II, an appeal which incensed the authorities.

The decade from 1881 to 1890 was the fullest in Soloviev's life, a period of intense work for the reconciliation of the churches. He worked closely with J. G. Strossmayer, Archbishop of Djakovo (in what is now Yugoslavia), who wished to unite the Slavs with the West under the Pope. In 1888 Soloviev traveled to Paris with his latest book (written in French), *Russia and the Universal Church,* but had little success with French Catholics.

The last decade of Soloviev's life was one of frustration and growing darkness. He continued to write profusely, notably, *Three Meetings* (1897) and *The Justification of the Good* (1898). His 1898 trip to Egypt greatly depressed him. In the last year of his life he published *Three Conversations,* which he considered his most important book, even though it repudiated much of his earlier work. He died at Uzkoe, the estate of the Trubetskoys, on Aug. 13, 1900.

Further Reading

S.L. Frank, ed., *A Solovyev Anthology* (1950), is poorly translated but remains much better than any of the books in English about Soloviev. Probably the best concise treatment of Soloviev's life and ideas is the chapter on him in Nicolas Zernov, *Three Russian Prophets* (1944). Written from the Roman Catholic point of view, Maurice d'Herbigny, *Soloviev: A Russian Newman* (trans. 1918), is rather turgid and one-sided; the chapter on Soloviev in Karl Pfleger, *Wrestlers with Christ* (trans. 1936), is cursory; and Egbert Munzer, *Solovyev: Prophet of Russian Western Unity* (1956), is intellectually shoddy.

Additional Sources

Stremooukhoff, D., *Vladimir Soloviev and his messianic work,* Belmont, Mass.: Nordland Pub. Co., 1980, 1979.

Sutton, Jonathan, *The religious philosophy of Vladimir Solovyov: towards a reassessment,* New York: St. Martin's Press, 1988.

□

Alexander Isayevich Solzhenitsyn

Although his works were banned in the Soviet Union, the Soviet novelist Alexander Isayevich Solzhenitsyn (born 1918) won the Nobel Prize for literature in 1970.

Alexander Solzhenitsyn, descended from a family of Cossack intellectuals, was born in Koslovodsk, a resort town in the northern Caucasus, on December 11, 1918, a year after the Bolsheviks had stormed to power throughout Russia. His petit bourgeois family moved to the southern Russian port city of Rostov-on-Don when Solzhenitsyn was a child, and there he grew up. His father, an office worker, died when Solzhenitsyn was still young, and his mother, a schoolteacher, brought the boy up. He studied at the University of Rostov, majoring in physics and mathematics, and received a degree in 1941.

Military Service and Imprisonment

In 1941 Solzhenitsyn's life changed drastically. After the Germans attacked the Soviet Union in June 1941, Solzhenitsyn was drafted into the Red Army as a private and was sent to artillery school. He was "a spare man with dark, intense eyes and a brooding, lined face." After his graduation from the artillery course in 1942, Solzhenitsyn became commander of an artillery battery, serving with distinction and almost continuously at the front for three years. Wounded several times, he was twice decorated for bravery. Toward the war's end Solzhenitsyn, now a captain, commented derogatorily about Stalin's conduct of the war—referring to him as "the whiskered one"—in a letter to a friend. He was arrested and sentenced to eight years in prison.

Most of Solzhenitsyn's imprisonment was spent in a labor camp—probably Karaganda in Kazakh S.S.R. While a prisoner, he probably underwent an operation for cancer. On March 5, 1953—the day Stalin died—he was released from the labor camp and deported for life from the European part of the Soviet Union.

Solzhenitsyn spent his period of enforced exile in the Dzhambul Oblast of Soviet Central Asia as a teacher. He also began to write down the experiences he had undergone as a prisoner. During this period, too, he apparently had another operation for cancer, this one in a hospital in Tashkent. He was freed from exile in 1956 and was officially rehabilitated in 1957.

First Publication

Following his release, Solzhenitsyn settled in Ryazan, an industrial town about 110 miles southeast of Moscow, where he taught mathematics and physics. His wife, Natalya, had divorced him during his imprisonment, but she reportedly divorced her second husband and rejoined Solzhenitsyn in Ryazan. Drawing on his prison camp experiences and his observation of life in a small Russian town, Solzhenitsyn continued to write. In autumn 1962 he submitted the fourth draft of a novella to *Novy Mir,* the Soviet literary journal. The manuscript of *One Day in the Life of Ivan Denisovich* was submitted by that journal's liberal editor, Aleksandr Tvardovsky, to the Communist Party Central Committee, who gave it to Premier Nikita Khrushchev. The Premier, in an attempt to fortify his anti-Stalinist line, authorized its publication in *Novy Mir* in November 1962. The novella was a sensational success, gaining for its author admission to membership in the Union of Soviet Writers.

One Day in the Life of Ivan Denisovich was the first published work to describe life in one of Stalin's labor camps in detail. It followed its protagonist, Shukhov, a humble farm laborer serving a ten year term on false espionage charges, through a single day in a bleak Arctic camp. The simple, futile, and monotonous horror of the labor camp system emerged strongly.

Minor Works

Solzhenitsyn published two anti-Stalinist short stories in the January 1963 issue of *Novy Mir:* "Incident at Krechetovka Station" and "Matryona's House." The first told of a military commandant of a railroad station in World War II who denounced a seemingly innocent man to the secret police and later regretted it. The second told of the struggle for survival of a poor and unassuming peasant woman. In summer 1963 Solzhenitsyn published another story in *Novy Mir,* "For the Good of the Cause," which tells in ironic terms a tale of Khrushchevan bureaucrats acting in the manner of junior Stalins.

Solzhenitsyn was nominated in 1964 for the Lenin Prize for literature, but he did not receive the award. After Khrushchev's removal from the Soviet premiership in October 1964, Solzhenitsyn encountered steadily increasing difficulties in publishing his work in the Soviet Union. In 1966 he published a short story, "Zakhar-Kalita"; it was his last to be published in the Soviet Union.

In May 1967 Solzhenitsyn issued a plea to the Fourth National Congress of Soviet Writers. He called for an end to "the oppression, no longer tolerable, that our literature has been enduring for decades, [which] gives people who are unversed in literature arbitrary control over writers." He revealed that his literary archives, dating back about 20 years, had been confiscated, including the manuscripts of several novels and plays that had been denied publication. "My work has thus been finally smothered, gagged, and slandered," he concluded.

Many of the Soviet Union's leading writers and intellectuals sided with Solzhenitsyn, but the government continued to denounce him and to prohibit publication of his works. In April 1968 Solzhenitsyn protested that Soviet secret agents had sent a manuscript of his novel *Cancer Ward* to publishers in the West in order to discredit him in Russia. At about the same time another manuscript of his, *The First Circle,* also found its way to the West.

Two Masterpieces

The First Circle was published in English translation in the United States in 1968. Its title derived from Dante's *Inferno,* in which the first circle was that portion of hell occupied by the pre-Christian philosophers. The setting of the novel was Mavrino *sharashka,* a scientific institute near Moscow. Its inmates were technicians and scientists who were working to perfect an eavesdropping machine. Panoramic in scope and in effect a history of the Stalinist era, the novel was harshly satiric in tone.

Solzhenitsyn's next work to be published in the West, *Cancer Ward,* appeared in 1969. A more emotional and reflective book than its predecessors, *Cancer Ward* recounted the day-to-day events in the lives of critically ill patients in an overcrowded hospital in Soviet Central Asia. It was partly based on the author's own struggle against cancer. The inmates of the hospital, perhaps because of the hopelessness of their situations, seemed to have achieved a freedom and serenity denied to the healthy.

After the publication of his books in the West and their sensational impact there, Solzhenitsyn continued to be denounced in the Soviet Union. He lived in Ryazan and maintained an apartment in Moscow. He was described as "a vigorous, burly . . . man with a booming voice—

possessed equally by his love for Russia and his passion for freedom" and as an "irreverent individualist" who "wears good clothes . . . but in haphazard combinations."

In 1970 Solzhenitsyn was awarded the Nobel Prize for Literature, but was unable to leave the Soviet Union to accept it. In 1974 he was finally banished from the U.S.S.R. because of his controversial writings, most notably *The Gulag Archipelago* (1973). Ultimately, Solzhenitsyn settled in the United States where he lived until 1994, when he returned to Russia after the fall of the Soviet Union.

Over the years, Solzhenitsyn has hammered away at an ambitious project, *The Red Wheel* series, which chronicles WWI in the books *August 1914* (1971), *October 1916* (1984), and *March 1917* (1986). In 1997, despite ailing health, he continued to work on the next installment in the series.

In 1994 Solzhenitsyn returned to his native country, and received a mixed reception. While immensely popular with some, many regarded his nationalist views as outmoded. He felt that too much emphasis was being placed on the economy, and that what most needed attention was the moral aspect of his homeland, saying, "We must build a moral Russia, or not at all . . . we must preserve and nourish all the good seed which miraculously have not been trampled down." Such views were unpopular at a time when many Russians were forced to wait as long as three months to receive their wages. He had a national talk show for a brief period, but it was canceled in 1995, and after that time he disappeared from the public eye.

In May 1997 Solzhenitsyn was hospitalized for a heart ailment at 78 years of age. Reflecting on his waning popularity, Joseph Epstein wrote in *Commentary,* "Even his American publisher has said that he does not anticipate a large sale for the next installment of *The Red Wheel.* The interest is just not there anymore."

Further Reading

There were a number of excellent biographies and discussions of Solzhenitsyn, including Steven Allaback's *Alexander Solzhenitsyn* (1978); Francis Barker's *Solzhenitsyn: Politics and Form* (1977); and Stephen Carter's *The Politics of Solzhenitsyn* (1977). An excellent, extensive discussion of the man and his work can be found in Helen Muchnic, *Russian Writers: Notes and Essays* (1971). Solzhenitsyn's earlier works were discussed in Vera Alexandrova, *A History of Soviet Literature* (trans. 1963), and Marc Slonim, *Soviet Russian Literature: Writers and Problems* (1964; rev. ed. 1967). *Solzhenitsyn: A Documentary Record,* edited with an introduction by Leopold Labedz (1971), recounted Solzhenitsyn's struggle for creative freedom. His censorship problems were also recounted in Abraham Brumberg, ed., *In Quest of Justice: Protest and Dissent in the Soviet Union Today* (1970). □

Werner Sombart

The German economic historian Werner Sombart (1863-1941) is known for his work in two fields: socialism and capitalism. He began as an admirer of Marxian socialism and ended as its bitter critic. Several of his works on the history of capitalism are regarded as classics in spite of many errors of fact.

Werner Sombart was born on Jan. 19, 1863, at Ermsleben. His father was a prosperous landowner and a member of the Prussian Diet and of the Reichstag. Young Sombart was educated at Pisa and the University of Berlin, where he studied under Adolf Wagner and Gustav von Schmoller. He received a doctorate in 1888 and became secretary of the Bremen Chamber of Commerce. In 1890 he became extraordinary professor of economics at the University of Breslau, where he remained until 1905. His radical views on social and economic reform did not please the Prussian government, and in spite of his outstanding performance as a scholar and a teacher he was given no promotion while he remained at Breslau.

In 1905 Sombart was named to a chair at the Handelshochschule (Commercial College) in Berlin. In 1917 he succeeded Wagner as professor of economics at the University of Berlin, where he remained until his retirement in 1931. Sombart died in Berlin on May 13, 1941.

In his early years Sombart was an admirer and friendly critic of Karl Marx and Marxism, and even after he had swung to the extreme right and had become a bitter if not vitriolic critic of Marx, he spoke at times of his own work as a continuation and completion of Marx's. Sombart's early publications were on trade unionism and socialism, both of

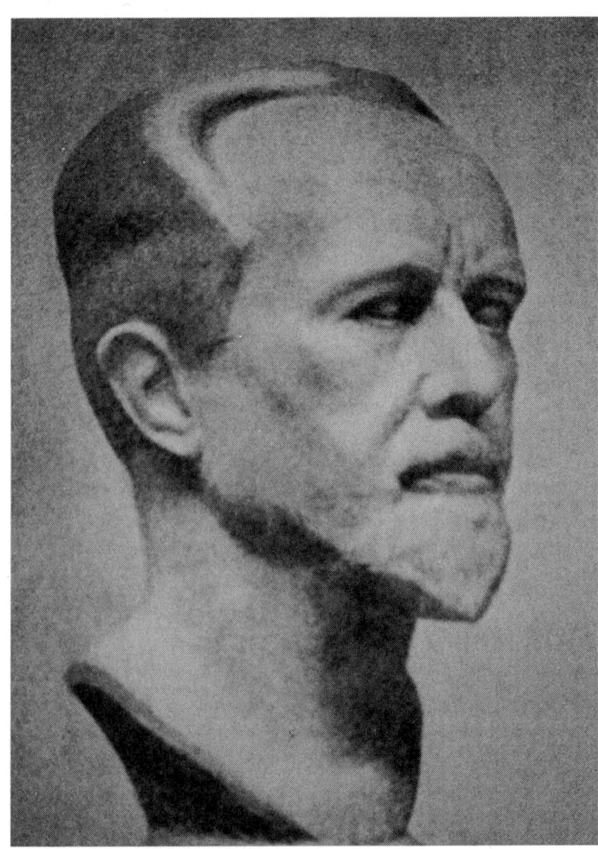

which he looked upon favorably. But his *Socialism and the Social Movement* is a good example of the shift in his viewpoint. The first nine editions were sympathetic to socialism, but the tenth was a bitter attack on Marxism and Soviet socialism. The last (1934) edition was a thinly disguised apology for the Nazi system.

Sombart's work on the history of capitalism is spread over a large number of volumes, beginning with his classic *Der Moderne Kapitalismus* (1902-1927; Modern Capitalism) and includes a number of ancillary studies of which *The Jews and Modern Capitalism* (1911; trans. 1913) is probably the best known. His approach is the very antithesis of that of Marx. Instead of presenting history as the resolution of a universal law, Sombart presents it as the outcome of unique social forms and forces. Whereas Marx would stress the role of the material in establishing the ethos of an age, Sombart explains material developments as the result of the ethos, for instance, the role of Judaism in the development of capitalism. Although the detailed accuracy of much of Sombart's work may be, and in fact has been, questioned, his overall conception of the history of modern capitalism is widely accepted among economic historians.

Further Reading

A full-length study of Sombart's economic views is Mortin J. Plotnik, *Werner Sombart and His Type of Economics* (1937). A survey of Sombart's social and economic philosophy by F. X. Sutton is in Harry E. Barnes, ed., *An Introduction to the History of Sociology* (1948). Sombart's career is also examined in Ben B. Seligman, *Main Currents in Modern Economics: Economic Thought since 1870* (1962).

Additional Sources

Mitzman, Arthur, *Sociology and estrangement: three sociologists of Imperial Germany,* New Brunswick, N.J., U.S.A.: Transaction Books, 1987. □

Duke of Somerset

The English statesman Edward Seymour, 1st Earl of Hertford Duke of Somerset (ca. 1506-1552), who served as lord protector, favored Protestantism, union with Scotland, and economic change.

Edward Seymour was the son of Sir John Seymour of Wolf Hall, Wiltshire. The flowering of Henry VIII's passion for Jane Seymour, Edward's younger sister, opened the gates to royal preferment. One week after Jane's marriage to Henry (March 30, 1536), Edward was created Viscount Beauchamp of Hache, and 3 days after the christening of his nephew Edward, he was made Earl of Hertford (Oct. 18, 1537). Henry VIII's death (Jan. 28, 1547) provided him with his opportunity. With the cooperation of Henry's secretary, he kept Henry's death a secret until he secured possession of his 9-year-old nephew, now Edward VI. He made known Henry's death at a council meeting on Jan. 31, 1547, and secured assent to his becoming lord protector; later he became Duke of Somerset (Feb. 16, 1547).

On Easter, 1548, Somerset instituted a new religious service. The first Act of Uniformity, prescribing the new service and commanding the use of an English Prayer Book, passed in 1549. The tone was Protestant, the emphasis on transforming the Mass into a commemorative act. Somerset's dream of Scottish union foundered on his inability to complete arrangements for marrying Edward VI to Mary, Queen of Scots, who instead married Francis, the Dauphin of France. In 1548 Somerset issued a proclamation forbidding enclosure and set up an investigatory commission which led to discontent among landowners. Moreover, his plan to place a head tax on sheep aroused opposition.

The revolts of 1549—the rebellion in the western counties of Devonshire and Cornwall, a reaction to the Prayer Book; and Ket's Rebellion in Norfolk, originating from economic discontent—caused further dissatisfaction. John Dudley, the Earl of Warwick, who had successfully crushed Ket's Rebellion, gained control of the council, and Somerset was sent to the Tower on Oct. 14, 1549. Released later, he was ordered to appear before the council on Oct. 4, 1551, the same day that Warwick became Duke of Northumberland. Somerset was sent to the Tower on October 16 and executed after trial at Tower Hill on Jan. 22, 1552.

Handsome and personally gracious, Somerset was an ambitious man who lacked the patience to bring his visionary ideas to fruition. A successful general who beat the Scots

at Musselburgh (Sept. 10, 1548), the last pitched battle fought between the two countries, he did not pay enough attention to the practical politics which might have prevented his fall. His enduring monument is the part he played in the advance of Protestant views and the promulgation of Thomas Cranmer's magnificent Prayer Book.

Further Reading

The best book for the details of Somerset's policies is A. F. Pollard, *England under Protector Somerset: An Essay* (1900). For a view of religious change see Jasper Ridley, *Thomas Cranmer* (1962), and A. G. Dickens, *The English Reformation* (1964; rev. ed. 1967). Consult the admirable work by S. T. Bindoff, *Ket's Rebellion, 1549* (1949), for an analysis of agrarian discontent. □

Edith Anna OEnone Somerville

Edith Anna OEnone Somerville (1858-1949), who in collaboration with her cousin Violet Martin published under the pseudonym "Somerville and Ross," wrote the popular *Experiences of an Irish R. M.* stories, as well as one of the finest Irish novels of the 19th century, *The Real Charlotte.*

Although she was born (May 2, 1858) on the island of Corfu, where her father, Lieutenant-Colonel Thomas Henry Somerville, was stationed, Edith Anna OEnone Somerville returned by the age of one to Ireland, where she lived most of the rest of her life and where her stories and novels are set. Her mother was Adelaide Eliza Coghill. Edith was the eldest of eight children, all of them boys except Edith and one sister. Upon his retirement in 1859 her father returned the family to his home at Drishane House in the parish of Castlehaven in the western part of County Cork. The Somervilles (and also the Martins, to which family Edith's cousin Violet belonged) were a part of the so-called "Ascendency"—middle-class families of Anglo-Irish descent.

Edith's early years were devoted to riding and painting. The latter interest she pursued seriously, studying at the South Kensington School of Art and the Royal Westminster School in London and in Düsseldorf and Paris (in the latter place she apprenticed under Colarossi and Délécluse). She continued to paint all her life, a practice which undoubtedly influenced her literary style (critics have noted a painterly quality in her pictorial descriptions). Eventually she had successful shows of her art in London and New York, and she contributed illustrations to the literary works she did with Martin and alone. The rest of her education was conducted by governesses and briefly at Alexandra College in Dublin.

Edith's real contribution lay in the field of literature, however. The event that precipitated this commitment was her fateful meeting, on January 17, 1886, with her second cousin Violet Martin. Edith later called that January encounter "the hinge of my life, the place where my fate, and hers, turned over" (*Irish Memories*). Not only did the women shortly begin collaborating in literature (their first book, *An Irish Cousin,* was begun in 1887), they soon contracted what was known in this country as a "Boston marriage," a life long commitment between two women. Their partnership lasted until Violet's untimely death in 1915 and produced 14 books, including *The Real Charlotte* (1894), considered by some to be the finest Irish novel of the 19th century; *Some Experiences of an Irish R. M.* (1899); and *Further Experiences of an Irish R. M.* (1908).

While *The Real Charlotte* is a darkly tragic, realistic work, the *R. M.* stories are light-hearted and comic, though also realistically set in the Irish countryside and faithfully capturing the local Munster dialect. The comic premise of the stories is the clash that occurs between Anglo-Irishman Major Yeates, the "Resident Magistrate" (a position established throughout the British empire to oversee dependencies' legal and administrative systems) and the customs of various eccentric Irish villagers. The *R. M.* stories were enormously popular and gave authors "E. OE. Somerville and Martin Ross" an international reputation. The stories' popularity continued into the 1980s; in 1982 a "Masterpiece Theatre" adaptation, "The Irish R. M.," was produced for British television. It aired on American public television in 1984.

Somerville and Ross also published several travel sketches, including *Naboth's Vineyard* (1891), about the French wine country; *In the Vine Country* (1893), which recorded tours in Wales and Denmark; and *Beggars on Horseback* (1895), which recounted a riding tour the women took through Wales, a kind of pilgrimage to the home of the celebrated "Ladies of Llanghollen," a similar female couple of the early 19th century. The third and final volume of the *R. M.* stories, *In Mr. Knox's Country,* appeared in 1915, the year of Martin's death.

That event devastated Edith, who thought she would never write again. However, she soon developed an interest in spiritualism, then very popular, by which people attempt to communicate with the dead. Through the use of "automatic writing," a spiritualistic technique, Edith came to believe that Violet was dictating messages to her. In this way she was able to resume writing, firmly convinced that their literary partnership could continue as it was. She, therefore, retained the "Somerville and Ross" designation on most subsequent works of her authorship. Of these 15 further books some are reminiscences, such as *Irish Memories* (1917); some are miscellaneous collections (of both her and Martin's work), such as *Strayaways* (1920); and many are novels, including *Mount Music* (1919), *An Enthusiast* (1921), *The Big House of Inver* (1925, considered her best work of this period), *French Leave* (1928), and *Sarah's Youth* (1938).

In her later years Edith travelled widely, including trips to Denmark, France, Italy, and the United States, the last of which she recorded in *The States Through Irish Eyes* (1930). She developed an intense friendship with English composer

Ethel Smythe, who helped promote public recognition of Somerville's accomplishment. In 1941 the Irish Academy of Letters awarded her the Gregory gold medal, its most important honor. She remained an ardent feminist, was chair of the Munster Women's Franchise League, and continued to ride, paint, and write into her final years. On October 8, 1949, Edith Somerville died in Castletownshend, where she is buried beside her beloved cousin and collaborator, Violet Martin.

Further Reading

The *Irish R. M.* stories are currently available in paperback. Biographies include Geraldine Cummins, *Dr. E. OE Somerville: A Biography* (1952); Maurice S. Collis, *Somerville and Ross: A Biography* (1968); and Violet G. Powell, *The Irish Cousins: The Books and Background of Somerville and Ross* (1970). A short introduction is John Cronin, *Somerville and Ross* (1972), and a more scholarly study is Hilary Robinson, *Somerville & Ross: A Critical Appreciation* (1980).

Additional Sources

Lewis, Gifford, *Somerville and Ross: the world of the Irish R.M.*, Harmondsworth, Middlesex, England; New York, N.Y., U.S.A.: Viking, 1985. □

Anastasio Somoza

The Nicaraguan dictator and military leader Anastasio Somoza (1896-1956) used his position as commander of the national guard to overthrow the government in 1936, and he assumed the presidency in 1937. He ruled Nicaragua as a personal fief and was a hated symbol to many democrats.

Anastasio Somoza, born in San Marcos on Feb. 1, 1896, to Julia García and Anastasio Somoza, a coffee planter, received primary education in his village. After attending the Instituto Nacional de Oriente in Granada, Nicaragua, he went to Philadelphia to study at the Peirce School of Business Administration. While in Philadelphia he met his future wife, Salvadora Debayle, of a prominent Nicaraguan family. Returning to Nicaragua, he entered business; not very successful, he took various jobs before entering political life.

During the Liberal revolution against Emiliano Chamorro and Adolfo Diaz (1926-1927), Somoza joined the Liberal cause. When the Liberals returned to power after the United States-supervised election of 1928, Somoza rose in Nicaraguan politics. Reports attributed this rise to his talent as an interpreter during negotiations ending the revolution and to his charm and dancing ability.

Offices held by Somoza included administrator of taxes and, later, governor of the department of León, minister to Costa Rica, and undersecretary and secretary for foreign relations. When the United States prepared to withdraw marines and turn officerships in the United States-trained national guard over to Nicaraguans, President José Moncada selected Somoza as commander.

After marine withdrawal on Jan. 2, 1933, and after the guerrilla chief Augusto Sandino made peace with the government in February, strong hostility developed between Somoza and Sandino. This animosity climaxed on the night of Feb. 21, 1934, when members of the national guard abducted and shot Sandino, who was in Managua.

When Somoza, maneuvering for the presidency, became convinced that President Juan Bautista Sacasa was attempting to stall his bid for the high office, he forced the President and the Vice President to resign in June 1936. Following an interim government Somoza was inaugurated on Jan. 1, 1937, after his election in December.

Somoza occupied the presidency until 1956, with the exception of one term, when Leonardo Argüello was allowed the office in 1947. Argüello, too independent, was ejected and replaced by one of Somoza's aged uncles, Victor M. Román y Reyes. Somoza resumed the presidency in 1950, after his uncle's death.

While attending a banquet in León on Sept. 21, 1956, celebrating his renomination by the National Liberal convention, Somoza was shot by Rigoberto López Pérez. Somoza died on September 29 in Panama and was buried in Managua.

Further Reading

Manuel Cordero Reyes, *Nicaragua under Somoza* (1944), is a short anti-Somoza essay by a former Nicaraguan public official. Some discussion of Somoza is in a number of general works: John D. Martz, *Central America: The Crisis and the Challenge* (1959); Neill Macauley, *The Sandino Affair* (1967); and William Kamman, *A Search for Stability: United States Diplomacy toward Nicaragua, 1925-1933* (1968). □

Anastasio Somoza Debayle

Anastasio Somoza Debayle (1925-1980) became president of Nicaragua in an election in 1967 which was marred by fraud. His rule was marked by corruption and repression. Opposition to him grew until he was forced to flee to the United States in 1979.

Anastasio Somoza Debayle was born in Leon, Nicaragua, on December 5, 1925, the last of three children of Salvadora Debayle and Anastasio Somoza Garcia. The family moved to Managua, where his father rose rapidly in politics, becoming commander of Nicaragua's only armed force, the National Guard, in 1933. In 1937 General Somoza Garcia used his position to install himself as president of Nicaragua.

After a few years of primary education, Anastasio Somoza Debayle was sent to the United States to study, first in Tampa, then at La Salle Academy in New York. While there he was commissioned a lieutenant in the Guard and promoted to captain when he graduated. In 1943 he entered West Point, graduating from the war-shortened course in 1946. Returning to Nicaragua he was promoted to major and, shortly thereafter, to lieutenant colonel and made the Guard's chief of staff. In 1950 he married Hope Portocarrero. This union produced five children.

In 1956 Anastasio Somoza Debayle was made a colonel and became acting commander of the Guard while his father, who had dominated Nicaragua for 20 years, prepared to run again for president. But in September 1956 General Somoza Garcia was shot, dying a few days later. While Anastasio Somoza Debayle held command of the military, his older brother, Luis, was installed as president and nominated by the Somoza-controlled Liberal Party for the 1957 presidential elections. In the aftermath of his father's death, Anastasio supervised the brutal interrogation of opposition political leaders, but failed to locate evidence of their participation in the assassination.

In 1963, over Anastasio's objections, Luis Somoza allowed a hand-picked political supporter, Rene Shick, to become president. Luis, responding to U.S. pressures, favored a slow loosening of family controls and a liberalization of the regime, while Anastasio wanted full family control and his own turn in the presidency. In 1967, having promoted himself to major general, Anastasio fulfilled his ambition, becoming president in an election marred by fraud and violence. That same year Luis died, removing the major check on Anastasio's power and ambition.

General Somoza Debayle's first term as president was marked by increased corruption, conflicts within the National Guard and the Liberal Party, and growing opposition to Somoza rule. The president appointed relatives to numerous key posts. His illegitimate half-brother, Jose Somoza, became the Guard's inspector general. The Somozas used their positions to expand the family's dominance over the economy and increase their already huge personal fortunes. A Marxist guerrilla group, the Sandinista National Liberation Front (FSLN), launched several assaults against the government, but all were crushed by the National Guard. General Somoza Debayle's ability to retain control was facilitated by a period of rapid economic growth which saw the per capita GDP (gross domestic product) increase by 8 percent between 1968 and 1971.

Responding to internal and external pressures, General Somoza Debayle reached an agreement with part of the political opposition, providing for the installation of a three member junta, including one opposition member, to govern the nation from May 1972 until December 1974. This agreement reflected a classic Somoza tactic of dividing and co-opting the political opposition. The junta was installed, but General Somoza Debayle, who remained Guard commander, held the real power in the nation.

This arrangement was disrupted in December 1972 when an earthquake devastated Managua. The general, supported by the U.S. ambassador, brushed aside the junta and took direct control of the nation. The Somozas and the Guard took advantage of the earthquake to further enrich themselves, extending their interests into areas such as banking which they had previously ignored. These actions produced widespread resentment and drove much of the middle and upper classes into open opposition. The Roman Catholic Church also became critical of the regime.

In 1974, in a rigged election, Somoza won a six-year presidential term. A few months later, FSLN guerrillas took numerous prominent Nicaraguans hostage, forcing the regime to release political prisoners and pay a large ransom. Somoza responded to this humiliation by instituting a state of seige and press censorship. Relations with the United States deteriorated, especially when Jimmy Carter became president in 1977.

In July 1977 Somoza suffered a major heart attack. Although he recovered, this emboldened his opponents to increase their attacks on the regime. In January 1978 the opposition's most prominent leader, newspaper editor Pedro Joaquin Chamorro, was assassinated. While no direct evidence of the general's involvement was ever found, this produced massive public demonstrations and a business-sponsored national strike. Somoza refused to step down, but ultimately made some concessions to domestic and international pressures, including lifting the state of seige. In August 1977 FSLN commandos seized the National Palace, taking the entire Congress hostage. They negotiated the release of several more prisoners and were flown to Panama. Almost immediately, armed uprisings broke out in several cities. General Somoza used the Guard to crush the rebels, but the brutality of these actions increased domestic and international opposition. Trying to retain power, he agreed to a U.S.-sponsored mediation process with the opposition, but this collapsed when he refused the mediators' proposals for a national plebescite on his future. Responding to this, the United States suspended aid and reduced its presence in Nicaragua.

General Somoza's efforts in early 1979 to shore up his regime proved unavailing. In late May FSLN guerrillas launched a major offensive and foreign governments began to withdraw recognition. In June the Organization of American States (OAS) adopted a resolution calling for Somoza's resignation. While proclaiming his intention to finish his term, Somoza began negotiations with the U.S. ambassador to obtain asylum in the United States. On July 17, 1979, he turned over the presidency to Francisco Urcuyo and fled to Miami. When Urcuyo balked at transferring power to a FSLN-designated junta, the Carter administration blamed Somoza and threatened to deport him. After the FSLN took power, Somoza, with his half-brother and his mistress, moved to Paraguay. There, on September 17, 1980, he was assassinated by Argentinian radicals. He was buried in Miami.

Further Reading

The only full treatment of Anastasio Somoza Debayle's career is Bernard Diedrich, *Somoza and the Legacy of U.S. Involvement in Central America* (1981). Anastasio Somoza Debayle and Jack Cox produced a distorted defense of the regime in *Nicaragua Betrayed* (1980). For a history of the Somoza dynasty through 1976 see Richard Millett, *Guardians of the Dynasty* (1977). A description of the 1978-1979 revolution which toppled Somoza is found in John A. Booth, *The End and the Beginning: The Nicaraguan Revolution* (1982). □

Stephen Sondheim

Active in major Broadway productions of American musical theater beginning in 1957, composer and lyricist Stephen Sondheim (born 1930) redefined the Broadway musical form with his innovative and award winning productions. He continued to be a major force in the shaping of this genre into the 1980s.

American composer and lyricist Stephen Sondheim is mainly known for his stage works, which included *A Funny Thing Happened on the Way to the Forum* (1962); *Anyone Can Whistle* (1964); *Company* (1970); *Follies* (1971); and *A Little Night Music* (1973). He is known for his collaborations with Leonard Bernstein as lyricist for *West Side Story* (1957) and *Candide* (1974), and with Richard Rogers on *Do I Hear a Waltz* (1965). Sondheim's partnership with the director/producer Hal Prince resulted in Tony Awards for Best Musical Scores for three consecutive years (1971-1973), and *Pacific Overtures* (1976) was hailed as a landmark in American musical theater because of its masterful use of traditional Japanese theater elements. In 1984, Sondheim paired himself with James Lapine to put together *Sunday in the Park with George,* a musical inspired by a Georges Seurat painting.

Sondheim was born into a prosperous business family on March 22, 1930. He studied piano for two years while very young and continued his interest in the musical stage throughout his education. Sondheim's parents divorced in 1942 and his mother took up residence in Doylestown, Pennsylvania, close to the summertime residence of Oscar Hammerstein II. As a friend of Hammerstein's son, Sondheim was able to ask the famous librettist for an evaluation of his first stage work, a high school production produced at the age of 15. Hammerstein's critical evaluation of *By George* initiated a four-year relationship that was decisive in formulating the young artist's style. As Hammerstein's personal assistant, Sondheim gained entry into the world of professional theater.

While attending Williams College he performed duties in the preparation and rehearsals of the Rogers and Hammerstein productions of *South Pacific* and *The King and I.* Upon graduation he won the Hutchinson Prize, which enabled him to study composition at Princeton University with Milton Babbitt.

Sondheim began his professional career in television by writing scripts for the *Topper* and *The Last Word* series and incidental music for the Broadway musical *Girls of Summer.* Shortly thereafter he made the acquaintance of Arthur Laurents, who introduced him to Jerome Robbins and Leonard Bernstein as the possible lyricist for *West Side Story,* which was produced in 1957. The young songwriter found himself involved in one of the most successful shows ever produced on Broadway. Sondheim followed this success by collaborating on the Broadway production of *Gypsy*

in 1959, distinguishing himself as one of the great young talents in American musical theater.

Intent on broadening his talents, Sondheim sought productions where he could use his musical as well as lyrical expertise. He produced *A Funny Thing Happened on the Way to the Forum* in 1962 . . . a bawdy farce based on the plays of Plautus. The show had an impressive run of almost 1,000 performances, won the Tony Award for Best Musical, and was made into a successful film in 1966.

Sondheim followed with two less successful ventures: *Anyone Can Whistle* (1964) and *Do I Hear a Waltz* (1965). Although both failed commercially, Sondheim contributed songs of high quality.

In 1970 Sondheim produced *Company,* which once again won him unanimous praise from the critics. The production was awarded the Drama Critics and Tony Awards for Best Musical of the season, and Sondheim received awards for the best composer and best lyricist. One critic commented that *Company* "is absolutely first rate . . . the freshest . . . in years . . . This is a wonderful musical score, the one that Broadway has long needed. . . ." The following year Sondheim produced *Follies,* a retrospective of the Ziegfield Follies, in which the composer blended the nostalgia of popular songs of the past with his own style of sentimental ballad. He was awarded both the Drama Critics and Outer Critics Circle Awards for Best Musical of 1971.

In *A Little Night Music* (1973) Sondheim exposed his strong background in classical music. It was described by critics as reminiscent of Mahler, Strauss, Ravel, Liszt, and Rachmaninoff. Another Tony Award winner, *A Little Night Music* also included his first commercial hit song, "Send in the Clowns."

Noteworthy as a relentless innovator, Sondheim collaborated with Hal Prince on *Pacific Overtures* (1976). In an attempt to relate the westernization of Japan with the commercialized present, Sondheim fused the unlikely elements of Haiku poetry, Japanese pentatonic scales, and Kabuki theater with contemporary stage techniques in a production that was hailed as a successful Broadway hit. He followed this with *Sweeney Todd* (1979), the melodramatic story of the demon barber of Fleet Street who conspired with the neighborhood baker to supply her with sufficient barbershop victims for her meat pies. Less funny than tragic, *Sweeney Todd* explored the dark side of the 19th-century English social system.

Sondheim's talent derived from his ability to cross genres of music and theater to offer Broadway audiences works of remarkable craft on unexpected subjects that challenged and tested the form of the American musical. Sondheim explored issues of contemporary life; marriage and relationships in *Company;* madness and the human condition in *Anyone Can Whistle;* nostalgia and sentiment in *Follies;* Western imperialism in *Pacific Overtures;* and injustice and revenge in *Sweeney Todd.*

Sondheim avoided filler in his lyrics and concentrated on direct impact through verbal interplay. His lyrics were witty without his ever sacrificing integrity for superficially clever rhyme. Similarly, he maintained his musical individuality even while operating in the adopted Eastern musical style of *Pacific Overtures.* Sondheim's consistent ability to merge words and music that hint at the deeper personality beneath the prototype character distinguished him as a composer of rare ingenuity and talent.

Side by Side by Sondheim, a musical tribute to the artist, was successfully produced in 1976. Sondheim's later works included the film score for *Reds* (1981) and *Sunday in the Park with George* (1984), which won a 1985 Pulitzer Prize. *Into the Woods* was another musical hit on Broadway in 1987.

Sondheim participated on the council of the Dramatists Guild and served as its president from 1973 to 1981. He was elected to the American Academy of Arts and Letters in 1983. He won the 1990 Academy Award for Best Original Song for "Sooner or Later (I Always Get My Man)" from the movie *Dick Tracy.*

Sondheim composed the music for the ABC television presentation *Time Warner Presents the Earth Day Special* (1990). In 1992, he declined a National Medal of Arts Award, from the National Endowment for the Arts.

Further Reading

The reader should consult the excellent biography *Sondheim and Company* (1974) by Craig Zadan; David Ewen's *Popular American Composers* (1st Supplement, 1972); *The World of Musical Comedy* (1980) by Stanley Green; and "The Words and Music of Stephen Sondheim" by Samuel G. Freedman, which appeared in the *New York Times Magazine* on April 1, 1984. □

The Song Sisters

By marrying men of political distinction and adhering to their own political pursuits, the Song sisters—who included Ailing (1890-1973), Meiling (born 1897), and Qingling (1892?-1981) Song—participated in Chinese political activities and were destined to play key roles in Chinese modern history.

Charlie Song and Guizhen Ni had three daughters and three sons, all of whom received American educations at their father's encouragement. Though dissimilar political beliefs led the Song sisters down different paths, each exerted influence both on Chinese and international politics; indeed, Meiling's influence in America was particularly great.

In childhood, Ailing was known as a tomboy, smart and ebullient; Qingling was thought a pretty girl, quiet and pensive; and Meiling was considered a plump child, charming and headstrong. For their early education, they all went to McTyeire, the most important foreign-style school for Chinese girls in Shanghai. In 1904, Charlie Song asked his friend William Burke, an American Methodist missionary in China, to take 14-year-old Ailing to Wesleyan College, Georgia, for her college education. Thus, Ailing embarked on an American liner with the Burke family in Shanghai, but when they reached Japan, Mrs. Burke was so ill that the family was forced to remain in Japan. Alone, Ailing sailed on for America. She reached San Francisco, to find that Chinese were restricted from coming to America and was prevented from entering the United States despite a genuine Portuguese passport. She was transferred from ship to ship for three weeks until an American missionary helped solve the problem. Finally, Ailing arrived at Georgia's Wesleyan College and was well treated. But she never forgot her experience in San Francisco. Later, in 1906, she visited the White House with her uncle, who was a Chinese imperial education commissioner, and complained to President Theodore Roosevelt of her bitter reception in San Francisco: "America is a beautiful country," she said, "but why do you call it a free country?" Roosevelt was reportedly so surprised by her straightforwardness that he could do little more than mutter an apology and turn away.

In 1907, Qingling and Meiling followed Ailing to America. Arriving with their commissioner uncle, they had no problem entering the United States. They first stayed at Miss Clara Potwin's private school for language improvement and then joined Ailing at Wesleyan. Meiling was only ten years old and stayed as a special student.

The First and Second Revolution

Ailing received her degree in 1909 and returned to Shanghai, where she took part in charity activities with her mother. With her father's influence, she soon became secretary to Dr. Sun Yat-sen, the Chinese revolutionary leader whose principles of nationalism, democracy and popular livelihood greatly appealed to many Chinese. In October of 1911, soldiers mutinied in Wuhan, setting off the Chinese Revolution. Puyi, the last emperor of China, was overthrown and the Republic of China was established with Sun Yat-sen as the provisional president. Charlie Soong informed his daughters in America of the great news and sent them a republican flag. As recalled by her roommates, Qingling climbed up on a chair, ripped down the old imperial dragon flag, and put up the five-colored republican flag, shouting "Down with the dragon! Up with the flag of the Republic!" She wrote in an article for the Wesleyan student magazine:

> One of the greatest events of the twentieth century, the greatest even since Waterloo, in the opinion of many well-known educators and politicians, is the Chinese Revolution. It is a most glorious achievement. It means the emancipation of four hundred million souls from the thralldom of an absolute monarchy, which has been in existence for over four thousand years, and under whose rule "life, liberty, and the pursuit of happiness" have been denied.

However, the "glorious achievement" was not easily won. When Qingling finished her education in America and went back in 1913, she found China in a "Second Revolution." Yuan Shikai, who acted as president of the new Republic, proclaimed himself emperor and began slaughtering republicans. The whole Song family fled to Japan with Sun Yat-sen as political fugitives. During their sojourn in Japan, Ailing met a young man named Xiangxi Kong (H.H. Kung) from one of the richest families in China. Kong had just finished his education in America at Oberlin and Yale and was working with the Chinese YMCA in Tokyo. Ailing soon married Kong, leaving her job as secretary to Qingling, who firmly believed in Sun Yat-sen's revolution. Qingling fell in love with Sun Yat-sen and informed her parents of her desire to marry him. Her parents, however, objected, for Sun Yat-sen was a married man and much older than Qingling. Charlie Soong took his family back to Shanghai and confined Qingling to her room upstairs. But Qingling escaped to Japan and married Sun Yat-sen after he divorced his first wife.

Meanwhile, Meiling had transferred from Wesleyan to Massachusetts's Wellesley College to be near her brother T.V. Song, who was studying at Harvard and could take care of her. When she heard of her parent's reaction to Qingling's choice of marriage, Meiling feared that she might have to accept an arranged marriage when she returned to China; thus, she hurriedly announced her engagement to a young Chinese student at Harvard. When her anxiety turned out to be unnecessary, she renounced the engagement. Meiling finished her education at Wellesley and returned to China in 1917 to become a Shanghai socialite and work for both the National Film Censorship Board and the YMCA in Shanghai.

Ailing proved more interested in business than politics. She and her husband lived in Shanghai and rapidly expanded their business in various large Chinese cities including Hongkong. A shrewd businesswoman, who usually stayed away from publicity, Ailing was often said to be the mastermind of the Song family.

Qingling continued working as Sun Yat-sen's secretary and accompanied him on all public appearances. Though shy by nature, she was known for her strong character. After the death of Yuan Shikai, China was enveloped in the struggle of rival warlords. Qingling joined her husband in the campaigns against the warlords and encouraged women to participate in the Chinese revolution by organizing women's training schools and associations. Unfortunately, Sun Yat-sen died in 1925 and his party, Guomindang (the Nationalist party), soon split. In the following years of struggles between different factions, Chiang Kai-shek, who attained the control of Guomindang with his military power, persecuted Guomindang leftists and Chinese Communists. Qingling was sympathetic with Guomindang leftists, whom she regarded as faithful to her husband's principles and continued her revolutionary activities. In denouncing Chiang's dictatorship and betrayal of Sun Yat-sen's principles, Qingling went to Moscow in 1927, and then to Berlin, for a four year self-exile. Upon her return to China, she continued criticizing Chiang publicly.

In 1927, Chiang Kai-shek married Meiling, thereby greatly enhancing his political life because of the Song family's wealth and connections in China and America. Whereas Qingling never approved of the marriage (believing that Chiang had not married her little sister out of love), Ailing was supportive of Chiang's marriage to Meiling.

Seeing in Chiang the future strongman of China, Ailing saw in their marriage the mutual benefits both to the Song family and to Chiang. Meiling, an energetic and charming young lady, wanted to make a contribution to China. By marrying Chiang she became the powerful woman behind the country's strongman. Just as Qingling followed Sun Yat-sen, Meiling followed Chiang Kai-shek by plunging herself into all her husband's public activities, and working as his interpreter and public-relation officer at home and abroad. She helped Chiang launch the New Life Movement to improve the manners and ethics of the Chinese people, and she took up public positions as the general secretary of the Chinese Red Cross and the secretary-general of the commission of aeronautical affairs, which was in charge of the building of the Chinese air force. Under her influence, Chiang was even baptized.

Meiling's marriage to Chiang meant that the Song family was deeply involved in China's business and financial affairs. Both Ailing's husband Kong and her brother T.V. Song alternately served as Chiang's finance minister and, at times, premier. In 1932, Meiling accompanied her husband on an official trip to America and Europe. When she arrived in Italy, she was given a royal reception even though she held no public titles.

The Xi-an Incident

In 1936, two Guomindang generals held Chiang Kai-shek hostage in Xi-an (the Xi-an Incident) in an attempt to coerce him into fighting against the Japanese invaders, rather than continuing the civil war with Chinese Communists. When the pro-Japan clique in Chiang's government planned to bomb Xi'an and kill Chiang in order to set up their own government, the incident immediately threw China into political crisis. In a demonstration of courage and political sophistication, Meiling persuaded the generals in Nanjing to delay their attack on Xi-an, to which she personally flew for peace negotiations. Her efforts not only helped gain the release of her husband Chiang, but also proved instrumental in a settlement involving the formation of a United Front of all Chinese factions to fight against the Japanese invaders. The peaceful solution of the Xi-an Incident was hailed as a great victory. Henry Luce, then the most powerful publisher in America and a friend to Meiling and Chiang, decided to put the couple on the cover of *Time* in 1938 as "Man and Wife of the Year." In a confidential memo, Luce wrote "The most difficult problem in Sino-American publicity concerns the Soong family. They are . . . the head and front of a pro-American policy.

"The United Front was thereafter formed and for a time it united the three Song sisters. Discarding their political differences, they worked together for Chinese liberation from Japan. The sisters made radio broadcasts to America to appeal for justice and support for China's anti-Japanese War. Qingling also headed the China Defense League, which raised funds and solicited support all over the world. Ailing was nominated chairperson of the Association of Friends for Wounded Soldiers.

Meiling's Appeal to United States for Support

The year 1942 saw Meiling's return to America for medical treatment. During her stay, she was invited to the White House as a guest of President Franklin Roosevelt and his wife Eleanor. While there, she was asked by the President how she and her husband would deal with a wartime strike of coal miners, and she was said to have replied by drawing her hand silently across her throat. In February of 1943, she was invited to address the American Congress; she spoke of brave Chinese resistance against Japan and appealed to America for further support:

> When Japan thrust total war on China in 1937, military experts of every nation did not give China a ghost of a chance. But, when Japan failed to bring China cringing to her knees as she vaunted, the world took solace . . . . Let us not forget that during the first four and a half years of total aggression China had borne Japan's sadistic fury unaided and alone.

Her speech was repeatedly interrupted by applause. In March, her picture again appeared on the cover of *Time* as an international celebrity. She began a six-week itinerary from New York to Chicago and Los Angeles, giving speeches and attending banquets. The successful trip was arranged by Henry Luce as part of his fund-raising for United China Relief. Meiling's charm extended past Washington to the American people, and the news media popularized her in the United States and made her known throughout the world. Indeed, her success in America had a far-reaching effect on American attitudes and policies toward China.

Soon afterward, Meiling accompanied Chiang to Cairo and attended the Cairo Conference, where territorial issues in Asia after the defeat of Japan were discussed. The Cairo Summit marked both the apex of Meiling's political career and the beginning of the fall of Chiang's regime. Corruption in his government ran so rampant that—despite a total sum of $3.5 billion American Lend-Lease supplies—Chiang's own soldiers starved to death on the streets of his wartime capital Chongqing (Chungking). While China languished in poverty, the Songs kept millions of dollars in their own American accounts. In addition to the corruption, Chiang's government lost the trust and support of the people. After the victory over Japan, Chiang began a civil war with Chinese Communists, but was defeated in battle after battle. Meiling made a last attempt to save her husband's regime by flying to Washington in 1948 for more material support for Chiang in the civil war. Truman's polite indifference, however, deeply disappointed her. Following this rebuff, she stayed with Ailing in New York City until after Chiang retreated to Taiwan with his Nationalist armies.

Ailing moved most of her wealth to America and left China with her husband in 1947. She stayed in New York and never returned to China. She and her family worked for Chiang's regime by supporting the China Lobby and other public-relations activities in the United States. Whenever Meiling returned to America, she stayed with Ailing and her family. Ailing died in 1973 in New York City.

Differing Beliefs and Efforts for a Better China

Meanwhile, Qingling had remained in China, leading the China Welfare League to establish new hospitals and provide relief for wartime orphans and famine refugees. When Chinese Communists established a united government in Beijing (Peking) in 1949, Qingling was invited as a non-Communist to join the new government and was elected vice-chairperson of the People's Republic of China. In 1951, she was awarded the Stalin International Peace Prize. While she was active in the international peace movement and Chinese state affairs in the 1950s, she never neglected her work with China Welfare and her lifelong devotion to assisting women and children. Qingling was one of the most respected women in China, who inspired many of her contemporaries as well as younger generations. She was made honorary president of the People's Republic of China in 1981 before she died. According to her wishes, she was buried beside her parents in Shanghai.

Because of their differing political beliefs, the three Song sisters took different roads in their efforts to work for China. Qingling joined the Communist government because she believed it worked for the well-being of the ordinary Chinese. Meiling believed in restoring her husband's government in the mainland and used her personal connections in the United States to pressure the American government in favor of her husband's regime in Taiwan. Typical of such penetration in American politics was the China Lobby, which had a powerful sway on American policies toward Chiang's regime in Taiwan and the Chinese Communist government in Beijing. Members of the China Lobby included senators, generals, business tycoons, and former missionaries. In 1954, Meiling traveled again to Washington in an attempt to prevent the United Nations from accepting the People's Republic of China. After Chiang's death and his son's succession, Meiling lived in America for over ten years. The last remaining of three powerfully influential sisters, she now resides in Long Island, New York.

Further Reading

Eunson, Roby. *The Soong Sisters.* Franklin Watts, 1975.
Fairbank, John. *China: A New History.* Belknap Press of Harvard University Press, 1992.
Hahn, Emily. *The Soong Sisters.* Greenwood Press, 1970.
Li Da. *Song Meiling and Taiwan.* Hongkong: Wide Angle Press, 1988.
Liu Jia-quan. *Biography of Song Meiling.* China Cultural Association Press, 1988.
Seagrave, Sterling. *The Soong Dynasty.* Harper and Row, 1985.
Sheridan, James E. *China in Disintegration.* The Free Press, 1975.
□

Sŏnjo

The Korean king Sŏnjo (1552-1608) ruled from 1567 to 1608. His reign was marked by factional strife, serious economic and social discord, and two destructive Japanese invasions.

Sŏnjo, formally named Yi Kong and known before his accession as Prince Hasŏng, was born on Nov. 26, 1552, the third son of Prince Tŏkhŭng, a younger brother of the kings Injong (reigned 1544-1545) and Myŏngjong (1545-1567). When Myŏngjong died without an heir, he gave his deathbed approval to the designation of Sŏnjo as his successor. The 14-year-old boy took the throne on Aug. 7, 1567. For the first year of his reign the queen dowager served as regent, but when the chief officials urged that Sŏnjo, though so young, was ready for rule, the dowager yielded, and from 1568 on the royal decisions were Sŏnjo's.

At first it seemed that Sŏnjo's actions might help to dissolve the political strife of the preceding 50 years, during which a succession of bloody power struggles among the gentry had resulted in death for many political leaders and long exile in the countryside for many more. Sŏnjo decreed posthumous rehabilitation for some of the key victims and called many survivors back to service. But the long years of exile and retirement had produced new divisions in the gentry that only intensified the factional discord. While Sŏnjo was widely regarded by contemporaries as an ideal monarch for his model Confucian behavior, he left the political initiative to the gentry and was never able in his lifetime to control their bitter infighting.

Sŏnjo's unwillingness to assert leadership was tragically demonstrated in 1592, when the Japanese dictator Hideyoshi launched the first of his two devastating invasions of Korea. Koreans had had signs of the coming storm since 1590, but the political rivalry fatally frustrated defense planning, and when the hordes arrived in 1592, Korea was woefully unprepared. As the Japanese sped toward Seoul, the court frantically evacuated the city. In the emergency Sŏnjo designated his second son, Prince Kwanghae, as crown prince and dispatched the other princes into hiding in the mountains. Accompanied by a small escort, he then hurried to safety in Tiju (Ŭiju), a small town on the Yalu River, where he set up temporary court and awaited the Chinese reply to his desperate pleas for military aid. Chinese troops came the next year, and this, in conjunction with Korean naval successes on the southern coast and the Japanese inability to hold positions far from their coastal bases, resulted in a general Japanese retreat in the spring of 1593. But when Sŏnjo shortly afterward returned to Seoul, two of his sons were Japanese prisoners, his capital was devastated, and his politicians as quarrelsome as ever. The princes were released in 1593 as part of a truce; the peace talks which followed this agreement, however, collapsed in 1596, and early in 1597 the Japanese invaded again. The new offensive was quickly blunted, and in late 1598, following a deathbed order by Hideyoshi, the Japanese troops withdrew and Sŏnjo's worst ordeal was over.

In Sŏnjo's last years a heated controversy arose concerning his successor. Crown Prince Kwanghae was clearly competent and had performed many assignments during the war years with distinction. Yet he was the son of a consort, not of the Queen, who had died childless in 1600. However, when Sŏnjo's second wife, Queen Inmok, gave birth to a son in 1606, the members of one political faction seized the opportunity to attempt to depose Prince Kwanghae. Sŏnjo and another faction stoutly defended the crown prince, however, and he indeed succeeded when Sŏnjo died 2 years later.

Sŏnjo was dedicated to Confucianism. He encouraged the establishment of Confucian academies in the countryside, sponsored vernacular translations of the Confucian classics, and issued many proclamations commending agriculture, economy, filial piety, and other Confucian verities. He was especially known for his personal frugality, dressing simply and eating sparsely. This frugality extended even to his favorite avocations, painting and calligraphy: critics 200 years later marveled at the fact that one of his finest calligraphic specimens was written on the back of a government memorandum.

Sŏnjo died on March 16, 1608. His tomb, known as Mongnŭng, is in Yangju.

Further Reading

There is no biography of Sŏnjo in English. Some details of his reign can be found in standard survey histories, of which two are Takashi Hatada, *A History of Korea,* translated and edited by Warren W. Smith, Jr., and Benjamin H. Hazard (1969); and Woo-keun Han, *The History of Korea,* translated by Kyung-sik Lee and edited by Grafton Mintz (1970). □

Susan Sontag

Among the literary stars of the radical 1960s, Susan Sontag (born 1933) produced numerous works evaluating and commenting on contemporary life and literature. Her essays appeared in nearly every major publication beginning in 1962, and her assessment of topics such as "camp," pornography, and the Vietnam war earned her a wide readership, well into the 1990s.

Susan Sontag was born on January 28, 1933, in New York City, the daughter of a travelling salesman and a teacher. She recalled that as a child her ambition was to be a chemist, although she had always spent a great deal of time writing. When the family moved to California, she entered North Hollywood High School, graduating at 15. She then entered the University of California at Berkeley, but soon transferred to the University of Chicago. She received a B.A. in philosophy in 1951, a year after her marriage to Philip Rieff, a sociologist. Their son, David, was born in 1952.

Sontag studied at Harvard, receiving her M.A. from the graduate school there and completing all but her dissertation for a Ph.D. She taught at various schools, including Columbia University, Sarah Lawrence College, and Harvard. In 1957 she was awarded a grant from the American Association of University Women which allowed her to study at the Sorbonne, in Paris. The following year she and Rieff divorced, although they collaborated on *Freud: The Mind of the Moralist,* published in 1959.

Sontag worked as editor of *Commentary* and settled in New York City with her son. In 1961 she wrote *The Benefactor,* a novel in the style of the French *récit* (a type of narrative). She also began contributing regularly to such publications as the *Partisan Review,* the *Nation,* and the *New York Review of Books.* Observers soon hailed Sontag as a leading voice in contemporary criticism, and in 1964 she won *Mademoiselle* magazine's merit award.

Her statements on "camp" in the fall 1964 issue of *Partisan Review* were received with delight as she exploded then-current myths concerning the meaning and content of art. In a collection of essays published in 1966 (*Against Interpretation*) Sontag said, "The function of criticism should be to show how the work of art is what it is . . . rather than to show what it means."

Although sometimes accused of "intellectual snobbery," she was generally accepted as the *enfant terrible* on the New York intellectual scene in the 1960s. She received the George Polk Memorial Award in 1966, along with a Guggenheim fellowship. That same year she was also nominated for a National Book Award for Arts and Letters. In 1967 Sontag was a juror at the Venice Film Festival, and she selected movies for the New York Film Festival. Her own film-making efforts led to *Duet for Cannibals* (1969); *Brother Carl* (1971); *Promised Lands* (1974); and *Unguided Tour* (1983). In 1976 Sontag received further awards, including the Arts and Letters Award of the American Academy of Arts and Letters. She was a MacArthur Foundation Fellow from 1990-1995.

Sontag wrote *Trip to Hanoi* in 1968 in which she explored her reactions to a two-week trip to North Vietnam, and in 1969 she published *Styles of Radical Will.* The latter discussed, among other things, the value of pornography as a distinct literary form. Another of her fiction works, *Death Kit* (1967), permitted Sontag to contrast her views on reality and dream, but the book was reviewed in the *New York Times* as one that "skips, shuffles, and snoozes."

Making her home in New York City, in an apartment that overlooked the Hudson River, Sontag travelled extensively. She spent a number of months each year in Europe, and although she was a sought-after lecturer, she appeared only rarely. Sontag limited her speaking engagements since they were, in her word, often "exploitative."

Sontag published *On Photography* in 1977 and *I, etcetera,* a collection of short stories, in 1978. Also in 1978 she brought out *Illness as Metaphor,* which was prompted in part by her own battles with cancer.

In 1992, Sontag published her first novel in 25 years, *The Volcano Lover.* During the 1990s, she also published a collection of stories, *The Way We Live Now* (1991); some essays, *Paintings* (1995); and a play, *Alice in Bed* (1993). In 1996, she edited, *Homo Poeticus* by Danilo Kis, a compilation of essays on social conditions and trends. Also in 1996, Sontag wrote a long commentary for the *New York Times Magazine,* entitled *The Decay of Cinema,* which discusses the death of cinephilia—the love of movies as an art form.

Further Reading

For a biography of Susan Sontag, see Liam Kennedy's *Premature Postmodern—Susan Sontag: Mind as Passion* (Manchester, 1995). Sontag's own earlier works were perhaps the best insight into her character. They included: *The Benefactor* (1963); *Death Kit* (1967); *Against Interpretation* (1966); *Trip to Hanoi* (1968); *Styles of Radical Will* (1969); and *Illness as Metaphor* (1978). □

Sophocles

The Greek tragedian Sophocles (496-406 B.C.) ranks foremost among Greek classical dramatists and has been called the poet of Greek humanism par excellence.

The son of Sophilus, a well-to-do industrialist, Sophocles was born in Colonus near Athens and grew up in the most brilliant intellectual period of Athens. Nothing concrete is known about his education, though it is known that he had a reputation for learning and esthetic taste. He was well versed in Homer and the Greek lyric poets, and because of his industriousness he was known as the "Attic Bee." His music teacher was a great man of the old school, Lamprus. Tradition says that because of his beauty and talent Sophocles was chosen to lead the male chorus at the celebration of the Greek victory at Salamis.

In 468 B.C., at age 28, Sophocles defeated Aeschylus in one of the drama contests that were then fashionable. During the remainder of his career he never won less than second prize and gained first prize more than any other Greek tragedian. He was also known for his amiability and sociability which epitomized the ideal Athenian gentleman (*kaloskagathos*). In public life he distinguished himself as a man of affairs. In 443-442 he held the post of *Hellenotamias,* or imperial treasurer, and was elected general at least twice. His religious activities included service as priest of the healing divinity, and he turned over his house for the worship of Asclepius until a proper temple could be built. For this he was honored with the title *Dexion* as a hero after his death. He is reported to have written a paean in honor of Asclepius. Sophocles had two sons, Iophon and Sophocles, by his first wife, Nicostrata, and he had a third son, Ariston, by his second wife, Theoris.

Style and Contributions to Theater

Of approximately 125 tragedies that Sophocles is said to have written, only 7 have survived. Since we have but a fraction of the plays he wrote, general comments on Sophoclean drama are based on the extant plays. However, Plutarch tells us that there were three periods in Sophocles's literary development: imitation of the grand style of Aeschylus, use of artificial and incisive style, and use of the best style and that which is most expressive of character. It is only from the third period that we have examples.

It is often asserted that Sophocles found tragedy up in the clouds and brought it down to earth. For Aeschylus, myth was an important vehicle for ideas, for highlighting man's relation to the gods. Sophocles dealt with men and showed how a character reacts under stress. The tragedy of Sophocles has been described as a tragedy of character as contrasted to Aeschylus's tragedy of situation. Sophocles's principal subject is man, and his hero is suffering man. The protagonist is subjected to a series of tests which he usually surmounts.

It was Sophocles who raised the number of the chorus from 12 to 15 members and initiated other technical improvements, such as scene painting and better tragic masks. He abandoned the tetralogy and presented three plays on different subjects and a satyr play. A supreme master in the delineation of character, he is credited with the invention of the heroic maiden (Antigone, Electra) and the ingenuous young man (Haemon). Sophocles's choral songs are excellent and structurally, as well as situationally, beautiful.

The Plays

The dates of the seven extant plays of Sophocles are not all certain. Three are known: *Antigone,* 442/441; *Philoctetes,* 409; and *Oedipus at Colonus,* 401 (posthumously). C. H. Whitman has argued for 447 for the *Ajax,* about 437-432 for the *Trachiniae,* about 429 for the *Oedipus Rex,* and 418-414 for the *Electra.*

In the *Ajax,* the hero, whom the *Iliad* describes as second only to Achilles, is humiliated by Agamemnon and Menelaus when they award the arms of Achilles to Odysseus through intrigue. He vows vengeance on the Greek commanders as well as on Odysseus, but the goddess Athena makes him believe that he is attacking the Greeks when he is in fact attacking sheep. When he realizes his folly, he is so appalled that he commits suicide. Menelaus and Agamemnon try to prevent a proper burial, but Odysseus intercedes to make it possible. In the *Ajax,* Sophocles is pointing up the tragedy that may result from an insult to a man's *arete* (Homeric recognition of a man's excellence).

The *Antigone* is one of three plays on the Oedipus theme written over a period of some 40 years. Antigone is the young princess who pits herself against her uncle, King Creon. She defies his cruel edict forbidding burial of her brother Polyneices who, in attempting to invade Thebes and seize the throne from his brother Eteocles, slew him in mortal combat and, in turn, was slain. Against the pleas of her sister Ismene and fiancé Haemon, Antigone goes to her death holding to her defiance.

The *Antigone* has been interpreted as depicting the conflict between divine and secular law, between devotion to family and to the state, and between the *arete* of the heroine and the inadequacy of society represented by an illegal tyrant.

In the *Trachiniae,* Heracles's wife, Deianira, worries about the 15-month absence of her husband, who has acquired a new love, Princess Iole, and is bringing her home. In her sincere attempt to regain her husband's love, Deianira sends him a poisoned robe which she falsely believes has magical powers to restore lost love. Her son Hyllus and her husband, before dying, denounce Deianira, who commits suicide.

In this play Sophocles poignantly raises the question, "Why can knowledge hurt?" He stresses the dilemma of the person who unintentionally hurts those whom he loves. The question of the role of knowledge in human affairs prepares us for the *Oedipus,* his greatest play and the work that Aristotle considered the perfect Greek play and many have considered the greatest play of all time.

Oedipus Rex is a superb example of dramatic irony. It is not a play about sex or murder; it is a play about the inadequacy of human knowledge and man's capacity to survive almost intolerable suffering. The worst of all things happens to Oedipus: unknowingly he kills his own father, Laius, and is given his own mother, Jocasta, in marriage for slaying the Sphinx. When a plague at Thebes compels him to consult the oracle, he finds that he himself is the cause of the affliction.

No summary can do this amazing play justice. Sophocles brings up the question of justice. Why is there irrational evil in the world? Why does the very man who is basically good suffer intolerably? The answer is found in the concept of *dikē*—balance, order, justice. The world is orderly and follows natural laws. No matter how good or how well intentioned man may be, if he violates a natural law, he will be punished and he will suffer. Human knowledge is limited, but there is nobility in human suffering.

The *Electra* is Sophocles's only play that can be compared thematically with works of Aeschylus (*Libation Bearers*) and Euripides (*Electra*). Again Sophocles concentrates on a character under stress. Described as the most grim of all Greek tragedies, *Electra* suggests a flaw in the universe. It is less concerned with moral issues than the other two Electra plays. An oppressed and harassed Electra anxiously awaits the return of her avenging brother, Orestes. He returns secretly, first spreading the news that Orestes was killed in a chariot accident. Electra is constantly at the tomb of her father but is warned by her sister, Chrysothemis, about her constant wailing. Clytemnestra, disturbed by an ominous dream, sends Chrysothemis to offer libations at the tomb. A quarrel between Clytemnestra and Electra demonstrates the impossibility of reconciliation between mother and daughter. A messenger announcing the death of Orestes and carrying an urn with his ashes stirs up maternal feelings in Clytemnestra, despair in Chrysothemis, and determination to wreak vengeance on her mother and Aegisthus, her mother's consort, in Electra. The appearance of Orestes rejuvenates Electra, and together they do away with Clytemnestra and Aegisthus. The chorus rejoices that justice has triumphed.

The *Electra* of Sophocles may have been written as an answer to Euripides's *Electra.* Matricide and murder are fully justified, Clytemnestra and Aegisthus are completely and utterly evil, and Electra avenges her father's death relentlessly and almost psychopathically.

In the *Philoctetes,* Odysseus is sent with young Neoptolemus, the son of Achilles, from Troy to the allegedly uninhabited island of Lemnos to bring back Philoctetes with his bow and his arrows to effect the capture of Troy. Urged by Odysseus to do his assignment, Neoptolemus, after gaining Philoctetes's confidence suffers pangs of conscience over the old man and refuses to deceive him. He returns Philoctetes's weapons and promises to take him home. A *deus ex machina* finally convinces Philoctetes to return to Troy voluntarily. The *Philoctetes* clearly shows how man and society can come into conflict, how society can discard an individual when it does not need him, and how the individual with technological knowhow can bring society to its knees.

The *Oedipus at Colonus,* produced posthumously, is the most loosely structured, most lyrical, and longest of Sophoclean dramas. It brings to a conclusion Sophocles's concern with the Oedipus theme. Exiled by Creon, in concurrence with Eteocles and Polyneices, Oedipus becomes a wandering beggar accompanied by his daughter Antigone. He stumbles into a sacred grove of the Eumenides at Colonus, and the chorus of Elders is shocked to discover his identity. Oedipus justifies his past and asks that Theseus be summoned. Theseus arrives and promises him asylum, but Creon, first deceitfully, then by force, tries to remove Oedipus. Theseus comes to the rescue and thwarts Creon. The arrival of his son Polyneices produces thunderous rage in Oedipus, who curses both him and Eteocles. Oedipus soon senses his impending death and allows only Theseus to witness the event by which he is transfigured into a hero and a saint.

"Many are the wonders of the world," says Sophocles in the first *stasimon* of the *Antigone,* "but none is more wonderful than man." Sophocles's humanism is nowhere more concisely manifest than in this famous quotation. Man is able to overcome all kinds of obstacles and is able to be remarkably inventive and creative, but he is mortal and hence limited, despite an optimistic, progressive outlook. Suffering is an inherent part of the nature of things, but learning can be gained, and through suffering man can achieve nobility and dignity.

Further Reading

The bibliography on Sophocles is extensive, and in recent years some very stimulating and imaginative interpretations have appeared. Among the most significant works are C.M. Bowra, *Sophoclean Tragedy* (1944); Robert F. Goheen, *The Imagery of Sophocles' Antigone* (1951); Cedric H. Whitman, *Sophocles: A Study of Heroic Humanism* (1951); Sinclair M. Adams, *Sophocles the Playwright* (1957); Bernard M.W. Knox, *Oedipus at Thebes* (1957); George M. Kirkwood, *A Study of Sophoclean Drama* (1958); H.D.F. Kitto, *Sophocles, Dramatist and Philosopher* (1958); and Michael J. O'Brien, ed., *Twentieth Century Interpretations of Oedipus Rex* (1968). □

Thomas Octave Murdoch Sopwith

During a long life, British aviation industrialist, Sir Thomas Octave Murdoch Sopwith (1888-1989) was a race car driver, yachtsman, speed record holder, balloonist, pioneer pilot, and engineer.

Thomas Sopwith was born January 18, 1888, into a family distinguished for several generations in engineering and business. As the eighth child, and first boy, he was named Thomas Octave Murdoch Sopwith. What he began in 1913 would grow to become half of the British aerospace industry in the post-World War II era. However, he avoided public prominence throughout his life.

Sopwith did not distinguish himself academically in the private schools he attended as the son of a reasonably well-off family. While still young he lost his father in a hunting accident. He went on to study engineering and his elder sisters began to make good marriages for themselves. Though not rich, he inherited an income and the unshakable support of his sisters. With a friend, seventeen-year-old Thomas began a business in the motor trade that soon grew into a successful Rolls-Royce dealership. It was the first instance of what proved to be a remarkable soundness of judgment in business.

He enjoyed motor racing, speedboats, and sailing yachts, as well as ballooning, which then was stylish and put him in contact with prominent people. Returning home aboard his yacht in the summer of 1910, he discovered that there was an airplane nearby. He took a ride aloft and immediately caught, as he said, the "flying bug."

The "Flying Bug" Leads to the Camel

After too few lessons he bought a primitive airplane and tried to fly. His subsequent crash landing was not unusual. Soon he possessed Britain's 31st aviator's certificate and an expensive hobby. Wishing to recoup expenses, a solution lay in winning some of the easy money then offered as prizes. Quickly he captured several distance prizes. The following year, 1911, he made a successful American tour.

With his winnings he started his first aviation business, a flying school. Among his important, well-placed students was Major Hugh Trenchard, later "father of the Royal Air Force" (RAF). However, the lack of a good aircraft led Sopwith to build his own. He was relatively successful selling them in the small prewar market and won the 1914 Schneider Trophy. However, no one was prepared for World War I's demand. Thomas Sopwith had nearly completed his career as a pilot but had just begun his life as an airplane engineer and industrialist. His company went from ten employees to several thousand. Despite the enormous and disruptive growth, he created a flow of new airplanes of which the remarkable Camel was the most famous. By the end of 1918, 18,000 Sopwith airplanes had been built.

The Armistice brought a depression, and peacetime offered no compensating uses of aircraft. He paid off creditors and liquidated the Sopwith company. He started a new small company building motorcycles under the Hawker name, after pilot Harry G. Hawker. As aviation recovered, Sopwith would become a behind-the-scenes chairman in a successful industrial empire.

The Hurricane in World War II

The Hawker Aircraft company was successful with several metal biplanes in the mid-1920s; however, modern monoplane designs were rebuffed. The company became an ever more successful exporter while supplying the RAF with a majority of its inventory. Sopwith added enormously to his aviation holdings in the 1930s by purchasing Avro, Armstrong Whitworth, and other major firms. Acquisitions of such size were, he said, the most frightening moments of his career. Almost equally bold was his next decision. He recognized the inevitability of war and began building a new monoplane fighter without a government order. In World War II the extra months of Hurricane fighter production helped save England. His wartime factories also produced airplanes of enduring fame, including Britain's best bombers, the Lancaster, and the Allies' first jet fighter, the Meteor.

As always, Sopwith remained in the background and deflected any attention to the managers of his industrial groups. Even as chairman he spoke little unless it was necessary, but behind the scenes his influence and probing questions tended to settle matters. He was known for his charming manner and could be very convincing. All admired his ability to select the most able managers, delegating to them control of individual companies. He always described his successes in business and so many fields as "pure luck."

Sopwith was best known publicly as a yachtsman. In 1913 he held the world powerboat speed record at 55 miles per hour. In 1934 he sought to win the America's Cup for Britain but lost in a questionable decision. Trying again in 1937, he was fairly beaten. He had long been moving in the highest social circles, having married Beatrix Hore-Ruthven, of Irish nobility, in 1914. Following her death, he married Phyllis Brodie in 1932 and had one son, Thomas Edward.

Another War, Another Fighter Plane

Following "England's finest hour," the postwar years were a disappointment. British aviation suffered particularly. Government decisions injured the home industry, which also suffered from too many small firms. In the 1960s the government ordered the firms to merge. His companies, called the Hawker Siddeley group, had created some of the finest postwar fighters and bombers, even created the "jump-jet," a whole new type of airplane. In the 1982 Falkland Islands War the Harrier jump-jet, a single seat V/STOL (vertical/short takeoff and landing), played an important part in Great Britain's defeat of Argentina. Still, individually, British firms lacked the depth needed to compete with America and had more than their share of problems, including the Hawker Siddeley group. Sopwith's competing factories merged along with outsiders to form one of two major British combines. His group was one of the largest in the world, with a combined employment that reached 130,000. Finally the government dictated a single state-owned aviation company and Hawker Siddeley became a non-aviation firm. However, by 1963, at 75 years old, Sopwith had retired as chairman and assumed an ever smaller role.

Usually engaged in several interests, he never gave work undivided attention, interspersing hunting, travel, and other diversions. Honors, politics, or office of any sort played little role for him, although he was knighted in 1953. He died January 27, 1989.

Further Reading

Until almost the end, Sopwith resisted biographers, with two significant exceptions. His years through approximately 1920 are covered in *Sopwith—The Man and His Aircraft* by Bruce Robertson (1970) and his complete life appeared in *Pure Luck: The Authorized Biography of Sir Thomas Sopwith, 1888-1989* by Alan Bramson (1990). The influence of Sopwith can be indirectly seen in the many books on British aircraft, but the common biographical sources are weak. □

Albert Sorel

The French diplomatic historian Albert Sorel (1842-1906) was distinguished for his major work, *Europe and the French Revolution,* which influenced profoundly the interpretation of the French Revolution.

Albert Sorel was born to a wealthy industrial family of Honfleur. Although his father wanted him to join the family business, he showed from a very early age an interest in literature and history, and by the age of 18 he was publishing numerous poems in local journals. By 1863 Sorel published a series of articles in which he argued that a general history of France could not be written without previous histories of the villages and cities of the country, allowing the picture of the whole to be built up by a mosaic of parts. These interests were to appear later in his most famous work.

After finishing his studies, Sorel received his father's permission to seek work in Paris. With the assistance of François Guizot, he was attached to the Ministry of Foreign Affairs in 1866. While at the Ministry, between 1866 and 1871, Sorel proved himself an astute diplomat. At the same time, he composed poetry and music and published two novels. During and after the Franco-Prussian War of 1870 he served as chief assistant to France's primary negotiator and assured himself of a brilliant future as a diplomat.

Sorel's career was not to be as a diplomat, however. Because he felt that his German wife, whom he married shortly after the war, would be put in a difficult position because of strong anti-German feelings in France, he retired from political life, took a position as a professor at the newly established École des Sciences Politiques, and devoted the rest of his life to one work, *Europe and the French Revolution.*

After a series of detailed preparatory studies, Sorel published his masterwork in eight volumes between 1885 and 1904. His object was to study the struggle between the Old Regime (*ancien régime*) of Europe and the Revolution. The Revolution was neither a perversion of the past nor a totally new creation. Alexis de Tocqueville had discovered that much of the internal policy of the Revolution had been a continuation of that of the Old Regime, and Sorel argued that the foreign policy of the Revolution was a natural outgrowth of that of the European Old Regime.

As the "Enlightened Despots" had ruthlessly partitioned Poland under the guise of establishing natural frontiers, so the Revolution's foreign policy was based on might rather than right, and the noble ideas of rational reform were lost in the struggle for alleged natural frontiers. In the later volumes, Sorel even argued that Napoleon's expansionist policies were a continuation of practices common in a morally bankrupt Europe.

Sorel's work, particularly the early volumes, placed the Revolution in a general European context and contributed to an understanding of the most general and most fundamental forces affecting the entire course of 19th-century European history.

Sorel died one of the most respected and most influential of modern historians, his work forcing men to study the quality of the most basic structures of a society rather than simply placing blame or credit on individuals or groups.

Further Reading

There are brief accounts of Sorel in G.P. Gooch, *History and Historians in the Nineteenth Century* (1913; 2d ed. rev. 1952), and James Westfall Thompson, *A History of Historical Writing* (2 vols., 1942). For Sorel's place in French historiography see Paul Farmer, *France Reviews Its Revolutionary Origins* (1944). Stanley Mellon, *The Political Uses of History* (1958), is a provocative study of the role of French historiography itself. □

Georges Sorel

The French philosopher and political and social thinker Georges Sorel (1847-1922) has been said to have inspired both Communist and Fascist ideologists.

Georges Sorel, born into a bourgeois family in Normandy, became a civil engineer working for the government. At the age of 45 he retired on a small pension and spent the remainder of his life living in the suburbs of Paris studying, reflecting, and writing.

Sorel belonged to the generations of Frenchmen who were greatly affected by the French defeat of 1870 and the civil war of the Paris Commune in the following year. He meditated on the ways whereby society could be held together. His first published work was on the Bible and on the educational value of the biblical story. Then he wrote about Socrates, the arrogant intellectual who by his questioning undermined the certainties of others, and about the decline of the ancient world. During the 1890s Sorel fell under the influence of Marxism and admired a philosophy which he considered to be objective. But he was quickly caught up in the Dreyfus Affair and with the movement which sought to put right the injustice which had been committed in imprisoning a Jewish army officer, Capt. Alfred Dreyfus, as a spy. This led him to proceed to a revision of Marxism and reappraise socialism in terms of action.

In Sorel's two most famous works, *Reflections on Violence* and *The Illusions of Progress* (both 1908), he expressed his scorn for the bourgeoisie and for bourgeois values. He believed that the proletariat was now ready to seize power, not through Socialist politicians or parliamentary and trade union politics, since these were a part of bourgeois deceit and decadence, but through the general strike. However, they would have to isolate themselves, indulge in class war, and engage in physical clashes with employers and with the state authorities. In this way the workers would become pure and heroic, would be held together by their struggle, and would found a new civilization.

Thus Sorel emphasized violence, emotion, and myth as the means of overthrowing the prevailing decadence and demoralization. On the type of society which would emerge after the general strike had made its break-through, Sorel was vague. But he believed that once the organized workers

had succeeded, their cohesion and enthusiasm would engender further cooperation and progress.

Before 1914 Sorel became interested in the movement of monarchist nationalism; he admired Lenin; and he made some equivocal references to Benito Mussolini, who came to power within a few weeks of Sorel's death.

Further Reading

Studies of Sorel include Richard D. Humphrey, *Georges Sorel: Prophet without Honor* (1951); James H. Meisel, *The Genesis of Georges Sorel* (1951); and Irving L. Horowitz, *Radicalism and the Revolt against Reason: The Social Theories of Georges Sorel* (1961). Also useful is H. Stuart Hughes, *Consciousness and Society* (1958).

Additional Sources

Meisel, James Hans, *The genesis of Georges Sorel: an account of his formative period, followed by a study of his influence,* Westport, Conn.: Greenwood Press, 1982, 1951.

Portis, Larry, *Georges Sorel,* London: Pluto Press, 1980. □

Pitirim A. Sorokin

The Russian-American sociologist, social critic, and educator Pitirim A. Sorokin (1889-1968) was a leading exponent of the importance of values and broad knowledge in an era dominated by science and power.

Pitirim Sorokin was born in the village of Turya, Russia, on Jan. 21, 1889. His training was concentrated at the University of St. Petersburg, though he also studied at the Psycho-Neurological Institute in the same city. From 1914 to 1916 he taught at the institute and then at the university, where he was a professor of sociology from 1919 to 1922.

After serving as secretary to Kerensky, Sorokin was forced to leave the country by the Soviet government. A brief period in Czechoslovakia was followed by several lectureships in the United States, where he was appointed professor of sociology at the University of Minnesota (1924-1930). Sorokin founded the department of sociology at Harvard University, where he remained until his retirement in 1959. He was elected president of the American Sociological Association (1965) and continued to attend professional meetings all over the world until 1968.

Sorokin's massive publication list and personal influence encompassed many areas. During the Minnesota period, he was interested in social class, social change, and rural community life. The key works of that period were *Social Mobility* (1927) and *Contemporary Sociological Theories* (1928). In the former he distinguished vertical and horizontal forms of mobility and showed the importance of institutional channels as mechanisms of mobility. The latter work provided a unique and critical summary of numerous sociological theories, with particular emphasis on the shortcomings of nonhuman and excessively abstract explanations.

Though Sorokin and his associates cumulated and ordered a considerable body of material on rural-urban contrasts (*Principles of Rural-Urban Sociology,* 1929; *A Systematic Source Book in Rural Sociology,* 1930-1932), social change and its consequences came to be his major focus for many years. After analyzing the causes of revolution in *The Sociology of Revolution* (1925), he began the imposing four-volume study called *Social and Cultural Dynamics* (1937-1941). This work revolved around the controversial thesis that genuine change is traceable to basic cultural presuppositions which undergird each major social institution, and that these presuppositions change because each type apprehends only a portion of complex societal experience. Sorokin therefore posited a series of varyingly recurrent cycles in social change, from ideational (religious-intuitional) to sensate (objective-materialistic) to idealistic (a mixture of the preceding types).

From this standpoint, Sorokin criticized the application of natural science viewpoints to social science, first in *Sociocultural Causality, Space, and Time* (1943) and with gusto in *Fads and Foibles in Modern Sociology* (1956). In a related vein, he wrote as a sociological Jeremiah against the excesses of modern sensate culture—especially in such books as *The Crisis of Our Age* (1941), *Man and Society in Calamity* (1942), *The Reconstruction of Humanity* (1948), and *SOS: The Meaning of Our Crisis* (1951).

As an antidote, Sorokin's last 2 decades of life were devoted to the cause of altruism and love, for which he established a research institute at Harvard. Some results of this interest were published in *Altruistic Love* (1950), *Forms and Techniques of Altruistic and Spiritual Growth* (1954), and *The Ways and Power of Love* (1954). However, Sorokin's fame rests on his scholarship and encouragement of sociological theory. His final work, *Sociological Theories of Today* (1966), was a detailed critique of trends in sociology since 1925. He died at Winchester, Mass., on Feb. 10, 1968.

Further Reading

Sorokin wrote two autobiographical works: *Leaves from a Russian Diary* (1924; rev. ed. 1950) and *A Long Journey* (1963). The latter is more comprehensive and illuminates his thinking during his long career in the United States. In addition, Frank R. Cowell, *History, Civilization, and Culture* (1952), provides a summary of Sorokin's approach to social change. Two volumes of appreciation and some critical analysis of his work appeared in 1963: Edward A. Tiryakian, ed., *Sociological Theory, Values, and Sociocultural Change: Essays in Honor of Pitirim A. Sorokin,* and Philip J. Allen, ed., *Pitirim A. Sorokin in Review.* See also Jacques J. P. Maquet, *The Sociology of Knowledge* (trans. 1951), and, for Sorokin's period at Harvard, Paul Buck, ed., *Social Sciences at Harvard, 1860-1920: From Inculcation to the Open Mind* (1965).

Additional Sources

Johnston, Barry V., *Pitirim A. Sorokin: an intellectual biography,* Lawrence, Kan.: University Press of Kansas, 1995.

Sorokin and civilization: a centennial assessment, New Brunswick, N.J.: Transaction Publishers, 1995. □

Tawaraya Sotatsu

Tawaraya Sotatsu (ca. 1570-ca. 1643) is considered among the giants of Japanese painting. His work is typically Japanese both in its choice of subject matter and in its rather abstract, decorative design.

Little is known about the life and artistic career of Sotatsu. It is believed that he came from a family of well-to-do cloth merchants and that he grew up in the Kyoto area. The first fact about his life is that in 1602 he was employed to repair the famous 12th-century sutra scrolls which the Taira family had dedicated to the Itsukushima shrine. Even more significant is the fact that in 1630 the rank of *hokkyo* was bestowed upon him, indicating that by this time the artist must have achieved considerable fame and success. The few other references to Sotatsu suggest that he was part of a circle of influential Kyoto tea masters and esthetes and that he collaborated at various times with the famous calligrapher and lacquer artist Koetsu, who was related to him by marriage.

In contrast to many other artists of the early Edo period, who painted Chinese subjects in a Chinese style, Sotatsu worked in a very Japanese manner which was based on the Yamato-e and Tosa traditions of native painting. It is significant that one of his most famous works is a copy of the 13th-century Yamato-e scroll dealing with the life of the priest Saigyo and that before this he had been engaged in repairing another celebrated example of narrative scroll painting. From these works he derived his interest in subjects taken from Japanese history and literature such as the *Tale of Genji* and the *Ise Monogatari.* When choosing landscapes for his paintings, he also selected typically Japanese ones, such as the pine-covered islands of Matsushima, rather than the Chinese scenery represented by the artists of the Kano school. Not only is Sotatsu's subject matter typically Japanese, but his style is too, for he used bright colors and gold leaf applied in flat areas, thus achieving abstract, decorative patterns of great beauty and sensitivity.

Among the numerous works attributed to Sotatsu, the most remarkable is a pair of six-panel screens depicting episodes from the *Tale of Genji* (in the Seikado, a museum near Tokyo). Other fine paintings by Sotatsu are in the Daigoji, a temple near Kyoto, with which the artist seems to have had some sort of connection. One of the outstanding works there is a pair of two-panel screens depicting the classical Bugaku dance; another work consists of fan paintings mounted on a screen. All these works are typical for Sotatsu in their use of colorful, almost abstract decorative designs and in their dependence on the Yamato-e pictorial tradition. The finest example of this type of Sotatsu painting in America is a pair of folding screens depicting Matsushima (Freer Gallery, Washington). Another fine example is the deer scroll (Museum of Art, Seattle), which combines delicate pictorial designs executed by Sotatsu in gold and silver with calligraphy by his friend Koetsu.

Although Sotatsu's fame rests primarily on these screens and horizontal hand scrolls, he also painted numerous smaller pictures in the form of fans, album leaves, and hanging scrolls, some of the scrolls being in monochrome rather than color. Here again the question of authenticity is much debated, for Sotatsu had many followers and imitators who continued his type of painting after his death. The most famous of these artists were his son Sosetu and, somewhat later, Korin.

Further Reading

The best and most complete book is Yuzo Yamane, ed., *Sotatsu* (Tokyo, 1962), which although written in Japanese, contains a summary and descriptions of plates in English. Briefer studies in English are Judith and Arthur Hart Burling, *Sotatsu* (1962), and Ichimatsu Tanaka, ed., *Tawaraya Sotatsu,* adapted into English by Elise Grilli (1956). For general background see Hugo Munsterberg, *Arts of Japan* (1957), and Peter C. Swann, *Art of the World: Japan* (1966). □

Jacques Germain Soufflot

The French architect Jacques Germain Soufflot (1713-1780) was in the forefront of those responsible for launching the neoclassic movement that was to sweep over Europe in the early 19th century.

Jacques Germain Soufflot was born in Irancy, Yonne, on July 22, 1713. After briefly studying law in Paris, he traveled to Italy, where his interest turned irrevocably to architecture, and in 1733 he was admitted to the French Academy in Rome. He was in Lyons by 1739, where he published a book on St. Peter's.

Soufflot's design for the enormous Hôtel Dieu (1742) in Lyons made his name known in Paris and brought him to the attention of the influential Marquis de Marigny, brother of Madame de Pompadour and later *directeur des bâtiments.* In 1750 Soufflot accompanied Marigny to Italy, where they examined the recent excavations at Herculaneum and measured the Greek temples at Paestum; the architect's *Suite de plans de trois temples à Péstum* was published in 1764.

Soufflot also appreciated the Gothic style, whose structural qualities he particularly admired. His paper *De l'architecture Gothique,* read in 1742, reveals an awareness of the Gothic structural lightness and soaring elegance, which he wished to apply to buildings cast in the classic mode.

Although Soufflot built two town houses in Paris and several garden pavilions at Ménars for Marigny, these architectural accomplishments pale beside his imaginative design for the church of Ste-Geneviève (now the Panthéon) in Paris; begun in 1756, it was finished in 1792, 12 years after his death in Paris on Aug. 29, 1780. The structure was the first of its kind in France to convey a true feeling of Roman classicism. The hugely scaled hexastyle Corinthian portico was inspired by the Temple at Baalbek or the Roman Pantheon. The peripheral walls are starkly simple, the only embellishment being a continuous entablature with a carved frieze of decorative festoons. The building is a Greek cross in plan; its multidomes recall the disposition of St. Mark's in Venice and St-Front at Périgueux. The interior provides a sense of monumental ordered elegance and a certain "sublime simplicity" much sought after in the subsequent neoclassic movement. A multitude of colossal but slender Corinthian columns conveys, however, something of the lightness of the Gothic idiom.

Most unusual is the treatment of the vast dome, which, though inspired by St. Peter's in Rome and more particularly by St. Paul's in London by Sir Christopher Wren, rests not on the usual heavy piers but on daringly light supports. Although they were later reinforced by his pupil Jean Baptiste Rondelet, the original delicate piers must have produced a feeling of airy fantasy akin to that of the works of Giovanni Battista Piranesi.

Further Reading

There is no biography of Soufflot in English. Material on his life and work is in William Henry Ward, *The Architecture of the Renaissance in France* (1911; 2d ed. 1926), and Reginald Blomfield, *A History of French Architecture from the Death of Mazarin till the Death of Louis XV, 1661-1774* (2 vols., 1921). A brief appraisal of Soufflot's work is in Emil Kaufmann, *Architecture in the Age of Reason* (1955). ☐

Pierre Soulages

Pierre Soulages (born 1919), a French painter, was one of the major abstractionists of the School of Paris. His work was characterized by broad strokes of paint that created a tonality of light and dark and by a subdued palette.

Pierre Soulages was born on December 24, 1919, in Rodez, a region where prehistoric and Romanesque artifacts abound. This art had a profound influence on his work. When he was quite young, he began to draw and paint.

After graduating from high school in 1938, Soulages went to Paris. He enrolled in the École des Beaux-Arts to study painting but quickly became dissatisfied with the type of work that was encouraged at the school. After seeing exhibitions of works by Paul Cézanne and Pablo Picasso, he decided to leave school and return to Rodez.

Soulages served in the French army (1939-1940) and then worked as a farmer in Montpellier until 1945. He did not paint during this time, but he read French poetry voraciously. He met the painter Sonia Delaunay and first heard abstract painting discussed.

Soulages's career as a painter began in 1946, when he and his wife, Colette, moved to Paris. Within a year he became known for his bold black-and-white abstractions. Self-taught and independent of any artistic movement, he explored the painter's means of expression and developed his own nondescriptive and poetic style. Abstract painting, which until the war had been a peripheral mode of expression in France, was at this time emerging as the new French style. Soulages was one of the painters responsible for this development.

By 1949, when he had his first one-man show in Paris, Soulages had found the direction his work took in subsequent years. He renounced his earlier calligraphic style with its emphasis on movement and line for a planar and monumental style in which luminous blacks predominate. In paintings like *July 4, 1956,* typically titled by date alone, Soulages's lifetime interest in Romanesque architecture manifested itself in the massive brushstrokes and planes and in the play of dark against light.

In 1953 Soulages won a prize at the São Paulo Biennial. In 1959 he made a trip to Japan. Although he continued to restrict himself to a classical purity of expression, he gradually allowed color to emerge in his paintings.

After 1970 Soulages began to produce larger compositions and larger-scale works. His later work also included aquatints and lithographs. From 1975 onward he produced several bronzes related to the irregular shapes of the plates used to make his prints. In 1979 he began creating very large paintings that relied for effect on contrasting texture, rhythm, and brushwork.

He continued to exhibit worldwide and resided in Paris.

Further Reading

Pierre Daix, *Pierre Soulages,* Neuchatel, 1991; Bernard Ceysson, *Soulages,* Crown, 1980; J.J. Sweeney, *Soulages,* New York Graphic Society Ltd., 1972; and J.J. Sweeney, *Soulages: Paintings since 1963* (1968), a catalog with a short but enlightening commentary on his development as a painter. Soulages was also quoted and represented in Andrew C. Ritchie, ed., *The New Decade: 22 European Painters and Sculptors* (1955). □

Pierre Soulé

Pierre Soulé (1801-1870), French-born American politician, lawyer, and diplomat, was active in Louisiana politics and pre-Civil War diplomacy.

Pierre Soulé was born at Castillon-en-Couserans on Aug. 31, 1801. Before completing religious training at the Jesuit Collège de l'Esquille at Toulouse, Soulé left and became an anti-Bourbon conspirator. He was exiled to Navarre until pardoned in 1818. Soulé returned to Bordeaux, completed college, and moved to Paris to study law, completing this in 1823. For his activities in the republican movement against Charles X and as publisher of *Le Nain jaune,* Soulé was arrested in April 1825, convicted, and imprisoned. He escaped to England and emigrated to Haiti in 1825. He finally settled in New Orleans.

Soulé became an active criminal lawyer, orator, financier, and Democratic politician. In 1846 he was elected to the Louisiana Legislature; at the end of the year he went to the U.S. Senate to fill an unexpired term. Elected to a full term in 1848, Soulé became the leader of the Southern faction of the Democratic party. For his activities on behalf of Franklin Pierce in the election of 1852, Soulé was appointed minister to Spain.

Since Soulé was known in Europe as an advocate of American annexation of Cuba and a dangerous republican, his appointment was a diplomatic blunder. His appointment was further compromised when he visited republican exiles in London and interfered with Franco-Spanish relations in Paris. Arriving at his post in Madrid, Soulé sent an impertinent note to the Queen, for which he was rebuked by the Spanish Foreign Office. Later he fought two duels and was ostracized by Spanish society.

Determined to secure Cuba for the United States, on his own initiative Soulé used the *Black Warrior* incident (involving the illegal seizure of an American ship in Cuba) to threaten Spain with war if it did not sell Cuba. Later, instructed to purchase or otherwise promote the "detachment" of Cuba from Spain, Soulé conspired with Spanish republicans and became involved in a plot to assassinate Napoleon III. On Oct. 14, 1854, Soulé met with the American ministers to England and to France at Ostend, Belgium, and at Aix-la-Chapelle, Rhenish Prussia, and drew up the so-called Ostend Manifesto. The document, justifying vigorous action for the annexation of Cuba, was repudiated by Secretary of State William Marcy, and in

December Soulé resigned his post, returning to New Orleans.

Between 1854 and 1861 Soulé practiced law. He advocated a canal project across the Isthmus of Tehuantepec in Mexico and was a leader of the Democratic party in Louisiana. A unionist during the secession crisis of 1861, Soulé supported Louisiana during the Civil War. For opposing the administration of occupied Louisiana by Union general Benjamin Butler during the war, he was arrested in 1862 and imprisoned in New York. After his release Soulé broke parole, escaped to Nassau, and made his way to Richmond, Va. Although he served the Confederacy between September 1863 and June 1864, he was kept from a position of importance by Judah Benjamin and President Jefferson Davis. Soulé died on March 26, 1870.

Further Reading

There is no biography of Soulé, but information on his background is in A. A. Ettinger, *The Mission to Spain of Pierre Soulé, 1853-1855* (1932). □

Henrique Teixeira de Sousa

Henrique Teixeira de Sousa (born 1919) of Cape Verde was regarded as one of the most prolific and best-known novelists of Portuguese-speaking Africa.

Henrique Teixeira de Sousa was born on September 6, 1919, in Bernardo Gomes on the small volcanic island of Fogo. Fogo, which means "fire" in Portuguese, was one of Cape Verde's leeward islands situated in the South Atlantic some 350 miles from the west African country of Senegal.

Although of Portuguese stock and thus superficially white, Sousa believed that on his mother's side he had African ancestry. His father, originally from Cape Verde's Brava Island, was the captain of a sailing ship that traveled regularly to neighboring Fogo, where he settled after meeting and marrying Sousa's mother.

At the age of 17, while attending high school in the city of Mindelo, on the windward island of São Vicente, Sousa published his first piece of fiction. This story, written in Portuguese, carried the title of "Chuba qu'é nós governador," which was Cape Verdean creole for, literally, "the rain is our governor." The young Sousa intended the governor metaphor as a somewhat cryptic protest against Cape Verde's status as a colony of Portugal. In other words, the regime appointed governors to rule the colony but neglected to deal with the island's endemic social and economic problems, many of which were caused by frequent and extended drought.

After high school in Cape Verde, Sousa studied medicine in Portugal. In 1945 he graduated as a medical doctor from the University of Lisbon. He then embarked for Timor, in the far-off Indonesian island chain, to assume an internship in the then Portuguese colony's general hospital. By the late 1950s Sousa realized his dream of a post in Cape Verde, first on his native Fogo and then on the Island of S.Vicente.

Despite his unbroken dedication to the practice of medicine, Sousa also devoted himself to writing. After his first literary effort in 1936, Sousa published a number of short stories, four novels (an unprecedented number by Cape Verdean standards), and several essays. "A estrutura social da Ilha do Fogo em 1940" (The Social Structure of Fogo Island), published originally in 1947, and "Sobrados, lojas e funcos" (Mansions, Shops, and Shanties), which appeared in 1958, were two essays that explore the same issues on which Sousa based his short stories and novels. One of these stories was the acclaimed "Na corte de El-Rei D. Pedro" ("In the Court of King Dom Pedro"), in which the hero played out the tragic and comic drama inspired by social transitions on the island of Fogo. In 1972 Sousa brought together this and nine other of his short stories, most previously published in journals and anthologies, in a volume titled *Contra mar e vento* (Against Sea and Wind). The story from which the collection derived its title has as its protagonist a sailor modeled on Captain John, the author's father.

The first of Sousa's novels, *Ilhéu de contenda* (*Isle of Contention*), which he finished writing in 1974, on the eve of the overthrow of Portugal's colonialist regime, was published in 1978. In this monumental work the author depicted the major social transitions that occurred on Fogo with the social and economic decline of the landed gentry, of mainly European origin, and the ascendancy of a chiefly *mestiço* (mixed-race) middle class. In 1985 he published *Capitão-de-mar-e-terra* (a variation of *Capitão-de-mar-e-guerra,* a Portuguese navy term for a senior sea captain), a novel that treated the time-honored themes of the sea and Cape Verdeans' legendary wanderlust.

Xaguate (*The Xaguate Hotel*), published in 1988, initiated a new phase in Sousa's writing and gave a unique twist to Cape Verdean fiction. To paraphrase the promotional blurb on the novel's back cover, this story was about returning rather than departing. Historically, much of Cape Verdean literature deals with the climatic and economic harshness of life on the islands that has resulted in the often massive emigration to such countries as Portugal, Brazil, and especially the United States. Sousa, whose own father eventually emigrated to Massachusetts, fashioned the story of *Xaguate* around Cape Verdean immigrants who, after decades in America, returned home to live on their native islands.

Sousa proved himself to be even more innovative in *Djunga,* a novel published in 1989. *Djunga,* which was the creole nickname of one of the main characters, was a metanovel. In other words, it was a novel about writing a novel, perhaps the great Cape Verdean novel. And like *Xaguate,* it took place after Cape Verde's independence from Portugal.

Cape Verde gained its independence in 1975, the year Sousa resettled in Portugal. In an extensive interview with Michel Laban, in the latter's volume *Cabo Verde: Encontro com escritores* (*Cape Verde: An Encounter with Writers*), Sousa explained why he left his native islands. He cited his disagreement with certain of the ruling party's policies.

Sousa offered, however, familial, not political, concerns as his principal reason for remaining in Lisbon.

Despite his disagreement with certain aspects of his homeland's post-colonial policies, Sousa remained one of Cape Verde's favorite sons. Moreover, Henrique Teixeira de Sousa continued to be one of the most celebrated of Cape Verdean authors, both at home and elsewhere in the Portuguese-speaking world.

Further Reading

Only one of Sousa's works of fiction has appeared in English. "Na corte de El-Rei D. Pedro," translated by Donald Burness, appeared under the title "In the Court of King Dom Pedro" in *Across the Atlantic: An Anthology of Cape Verdean Literature.* Edited by Maria Ellen, this anthology, published in 1988 by Southeastern Massachusetts University, was in fact a rare collection of Cape Verdean prose and poetry in English translation. There was likewise very little in English about Sousa and his works. In Russell Hamilton's *Voices from an Empire: A History of Afro-Portuguese Literature* (1975) several pages were devoted to Sousa's essays and stories. For the English-speaking reader interested in learning about Sousa's Cape Verde there were a few worthwhile historical accounts, such as D. Abshire's and M. Samuels' somewhat dated, but still informative, *Portuguese Africa: A Handbook* (London, 1969). Also worthy of mention were two books that, even though they focus on Cape Verdeans in America, specifically in southern New England, shed light on many of the issues and themes dealt with in Sousa's novels. The studies in question are D. Machado's *Cape Verdean Americans: Their Culture and Historical Background* (1978) and M. Halter's *Between Race and Ethnicity: Cape Verdean American Immigrants, 1860-1965* (1993). □

John Philip Sousa

At the end of the 19th century the name of the American bandmaster and composer John Philip Sousa (1854-1932) was virtually synonymous with the music of marches.

John Philip Sousa was born on Nov. 6, 1854, in Washington, D.C. His father was Portuguese, his mother German. At the age of 10 Sousa began violin lessons and later studied music theory and composition. By the time he was 13 he could play a number of band instruments and enlisted in the Marine Band. He was playing in civilian orchestras as well and subsequently got a discharge from the Marine Band. At 18 he became director of the orchestra at a variety house in Washington and later led orchestras for a comedy troupe and for Morgan's Living Pictures.

In 1876 Sousa joined the orchestra conducted by Jacques Offenbach at the Centennial Exposition in Philadelphia. The musical sensation of the exposition, however, was Patrick Gilmore, and it was here that Sousa first heard and admired Gilmore's band. After playing for a number of Philadelphia theaters, Sousa returned to Washington in 1880 to become director of the U.S. Marine Band, a post he held for 12 years. He reorganized the band, altered its instrumentation, raised its prestige, and built up its library.

In 1892 Sousa formed his own band, capitalizing on his fame by calling it the New Marine Band. A concert band rather than a marching band, it made its first public appearance in September 1892 in Plainfield, N.J. Its initial season was only a moderate financial success, primarily because of an unwise selection of cities for the tour. The following year at the World's Columbian Exposition in Chicago the band attracted thousands of people to each concert. So popular were Sousa's programs that after a few weeks Theodore Thomas, the musical director of the exposition, canceled the more elaborate symphonic and choral events he had planned for the fair, feeling they could not compete. Charles Harris's sentimental ballad "After the Ball" became a national hit during the fair as played by Sousa; its success set a new trend in American popular music.

Soon Sousa's band, operating without any subsidy, proved an economic as well as a musical success. It played for most of the important expositions after 1893, made annual tours through the United States and Canada, and was acclaimed on four trips to Europe and on one venture around the world. Sousa was decorated by the crowned heads of Europe and by various academies and societies. When the United States entered World War I, he was made a lieutenant in the Naval Reserve.

Sousa's fame as a composer was related to his success as a bandleader. Although his marches earned him the title of "March King," he nevertheless was influenced strongly

by the style of Offenbach. Sousa's renowned marches include *The Stars and Stripes Forever, The Washington Post, The High School Cadets,* and *The Gladiator.* These are characterized by a strong rhythmic propulsion, jaunty, memorable tunes, and more wideranging harmony than normally found in marches. Many of his best marches came from operettas, and some were originally sung.

Sousa's exposure to Offenbach, coupled with the astonishing American success of Gilbert and Sullivan, convinced him to try composing for the stage. He wrote 10 comic operas, achieving greatest acclaim for *The Bride Elect, El Capitan,* and *The Free Lance.* For some of his operettas he wrote the lyrics and libretto as well. He composed many other works of miscellaneous variety and wrote three novels. His autobiography is considered among the most readable memoirs in American letters.

Like Patrick Gilmore, Sousa wanted to create commercial music for pure entertainment. His understanding of the great music of the past or of his own day was slight. He succeeded in bringing high-quality military music to the public, achieving an instrumentation for the concert band that permitted effects as soft as those of a symphony orchestra. Artistic results were of secondary importance to Sousa; his first concern was to entertain his audiences. During his 40 years as bandmaster, Sousa lifted the concert band to popular heights it had never attained before, grossed an estimated $40 million, and was one of the most respected musicians of his generation. He died on March 6, 1932, in Reading, Pa.

Further Reading

The best account of Sousa's career is his *Marching Along: An Autobiography* (1928). Interesting and informative studies are Mina Lewiton, *John Philip Sousa: The March King* (1944), and Kenneth Walter Berger, *The March King and His Band* (1957). There is valuable material on Sousa in Harry Wayne Schwartz, *Bands of America* (1957). Wilfrid Mellers, *Music in a New Found Land* (1964), contains a penetrating evaluation of his work.

Additional Sources

Bierley, Paul E., *John Philip Sousa, American phenomenon,* Columbus, Ohio: Integrity Press, 1986?, 1973.

Delaplaine, Edward S. (Edward Schley), *John Philip Sousa and the national anthem,* Frederick, Md.: Great Southern Press, 1983.

Heslip, Malcolm, *Nostalgic happenings in the three bands of John Philip Sousa,* Laguna Hills, Calif.: M. Heslip, 1982.

Sousa, John Philip, *Marching along: recollections of men, women, and music,* Westerville, OH: Integrity Press, 1994. □

Martim Afonso de Sousa

Martim Afonso de Sousa (ca. 1500-1564) was a Portuguese colonizer and viceroy who founded the first permanent Portuguese settlement in South America, and served as viceroy of India.

The exact date of the birth of Martim Afonso de Sousa remains unknown, but some authorities arbitrarily give 1500. He was born in Vila Viçosa and grew up closely attached to the royal court. Disturbed by increasing foreign commerce along the Brazilian coast, Portugal's King João III decided to send an expedition to his South American colony to drive away the interlopers, further explore the coast, and establish at least one permanent settlement. In 1530 he selected Martim Afonso de Sousa and delegated extensive powers to him as "chief captain of the fleet and lands" of Brazil. Under the command of Sousa, a fleet of five ships embarked for Brazil in December 1530. After reconnoitering the coast from Pernambuco to the Rio de la Plata, Sousa founded the settlement of São Vicente in 1532. As the official chronicler of the expedition, Pero Lopes de Sousa, put it, "To all of us this land seemed so good that Captain Martim de Sousa decided to settle it."

The Portuguese built a chapel, a small governmental headquarters, two tiny fortresses, and quarters for the men. Capt. Sousa appointed municipal officers and distributed the land with lavish generosity. Wheat, grape vines, and sugarcane were planted; cattle were introduced; and the first sugar mill was put into operation in 1533. On the plateau high above São Vicente, Sousa established a second small settlement, Piratininga, near present-day São Paulo. Returning to Portugal in 1533, Sousa left behind a viable colony. The King rewarded him with extensive lands in southern Brazil, including the captaincy of São Vicente. Sousa never returned to Brazil, but his captaincy continued to prosper.

In 1534 the King dispatched Sousa to the East as the chief captain of a new expedition. He spent 5 years fighting Portugal's rivals and enemies along the Indian coast before sailing back to Lisbon. In 1542 the Crown appointed him viceroy of India, a post he held for 3 years, the customary tour of duty. Once again he made the long sea voyage back to Lisbon, this time to occupy a post on the Council of State. Few facts are known about the last decades of his life. He died on July 21, 1564, in Lisbon.

Further Reading

The most extensive source in English for material on Sousa is Elaine Sanceau, *Captains of Brazil* (Porto, Portugal, 1965). See also Alexander Marchant, *From Barter to Slavery: The Economic Relations of Portuguese and Indians in the Settlement of Brazil, 1500-1580* (1942), No. 1, Series 60, in the Johns Hopkins University Studies in Historical and Political Science. For general background consult João P. Calogeras, *A History of Brazil* (trans. 1939), and Pollie E. Poppino, *Brazil: The Land and People* (1968). □

David H. Souter

David H. Souter (born 1939), a New Hampshire state attorney and state supreme court judge, was appointed to the U.S. Supreme Court in the fall of 1990 as the 105th justice in the nation's history.

David H. Souter was born on September 17, 1939, in Melrose, Massachusetts. At age 11, Souter and his parents moved to Weare, New Hampshire, near Concord, where his father, a banker, could lead a slower-paced life necessitated by a heart condition. Souter was a lifelong bachelor and lived with his widowed mother until she entered a nursing home several years before his nomination to the U.S. Supreme Court. He was still living in the family's farmhouse in Weare when President George Bush plucked him from obscurity to place him on the nation's highest court in 1990.

By educational background, Souter seemed a worthy candidate for the U.S. Supreme Court. He attended public elementary schools and Concord High School, where he was elected president of the National Honor Society and was voted "most literary," "most sophisticated," and, prophetically, "most likely to succeed." He entered Harvard College in 1957 and majored in philosophy, writing his senior honors thesis on the jurisprudence of Justice Oliver Wendell Holmes. After graduating *magna cum laude* and Phi Beta Kappa, he won a Rhodes scholarship to attend Magdelan College at Oxford University, where he studied law and philosophy for two years. In 1963 he enrolled in Harvard Law School, from which he received his LL.B. degree where he reportedly did well, but failed to make the law review.

Graduating from Harvard Law in 1966, Souter returned home to Weare and began his legal career in the Concord law firm of Orr & Rena. He found private practice unsuited to his tastes, however, and turned to the public sector. In 1968 he joined the staff of the New Hampshire attorney general. Warren Rudman, who was destined to become a senator from the Granite State and who would play a key role in supporting Souter's eventual U.S. Supreme Court nomination, became attorney general of New Hampshire in 1970 and promoted Souter to be his top aide. Rudman resigned as attorney general in 1976 and persuaded Governor Meldrim Thomson to name Souter as his successor.

In his two-year service as state attorney general, from 1976 to 1978, Souter personally argued several controversial religion cases. In one, he defended Governor Thompson's desire to fly the American and state flags at half-staff on Good Friday. He also defended the state's attempts to prosecute residents who for religious reasons covered up the state motto—"Live Free or Die"—on their license plates. The state was unsuccessful in both cases.

Nevertheless, Souter's service was rewarded by a judicial appointment to the state superior court in 1978. He served there for five years before Governor John Sununu, who would become President Bush's chief of staff, named him to the New Hampshire Supreme Court in 1983. In the spring of 1990 President Bush nominated Souter to the U.S. Court of Appeals for the First Circuit in Boston. He had yet to write an opinion for that court, or indeed even be assigned an office, when the president made his surprise announcement nominating him to the U.S. Supreme Court on July 23, 1990.

Justice William Brennan's retirement from the seat that Souter was named to fill had been equally surprising. Although Brennan was 84, he had remained a vigorous member of the Court through its 1989-1990 term. Indeed, he had fashioned slim, but victorious, majorities for the dwindling liberal bloc in his last contentious cases involving flag-burning and affirmative action. Yet Justice Brennan had suffered a slight stroke early in the summer of 1990 and his physician urged him to retire. He did so reluctantly, citing the incompatibility of the burdens of the Court with his fragile health.

President Bush vowed to make quick work of the selection process for Brennan's replacement. The administration had compiled a list of potential nominees during Bush's first year in office, and his advisers turned to it as deliberations began immediately after Brennan sent his letter of resignation to the White House. Within three days Bush had his man. He passed over the runner-up, Judge Edith Jones of the Fifth Circuit Court of Appeals in Texas, for the less-well-known Souter. In the aftermath of the denial of Judge Bork's nomination to the high court because of his staunchly conservative paper trail, Souter's very obscurity was the overwhelming deciding factor in his favor.

Yet Souter's past did contain several clues to his jurisprudence. In a 1986 dissenting opinion on the New Hampshire Supreme Court, Souter wrote that "the court's interpretive task is to determine the meaning of [constitutional language] as it was understood when the framers proposed it." On one of the most controversial issues of the day—abortion—Souter also expressed a restraintist position toward procedural aspects of judging, even if his personal and professional views on the topic were unknown. As a superior-court judge in 1981, Souter wrote a letter to the state legislature to argue for the rejection of a provision of a bill that would have required teenagers seeking abortions to obtain permission from a judge if they could not get their parents' consent. Souter maintained that the provision "would express a decision by society, speaking through the legislature, to leave it to individual judges . . . to make fundamental moral decisions about the interests of other people without any standards to guide the individual judge. . . ."

Souter's nomination cleared the Senate Judiciary Committee by a vote of 13 to 1. The full Senate was equally favorable, approving Souter by a vote of 90 to 9. The new justice was sworn in October 9, 1990, and began work on the fall term of the Court almost immediately. (A second new justice took a seat on the Supreme Court for the 1991 fall term when Justice Thurgood Marshall resigned because of failing health and was replaced by Clarence Thomas).

As a Justice, Souter focused on legal process in many of his decisions. In his dissent of *Missouri v. Jenkins* he began with: "The Court's process of orderly adjudication has broken down in this case," Some critics claimed that his focus on process was an attempt to flee substance. Important opinions written by Souter included issues related to free speech and separation of church and state in *Rosenberger v. University of Virginia* (free speech and a student run newspaper) and *Lee v. Weissman* (separation of church and state).

Further Reading

Because of David Souter's relatively obscure background, there was no major studies of his life and career. *Time* magazine (August 5, 1990) and the *New York Times* (July 25, 1990) offered detailed journalistic analyses of Souter. For the voting in the Judiciary Committee and later the full Senate see the *Washington Post* (September 27 and October 2, 1990). Other articles on Souter have appeared in *Rocky Mountain News* July 25, 1993) and *The Courier-Journal, Louisville, KY* (March 21, 1993). Reviews of Souter's performance as a Justice can be found in legal and political journals such as *Almanac of the Federal Judiciary* and *Policy Review.* □

Chaim Soutine

Chaim Soutine (1894-1943), a Russian painter of the School of Paris, was the main representative in France of a dynamic expressionism.

Chaim Soutine was born in Smilovitch near Minsk, the tenth of 11 children of a poor village tailor. Life in Smilovitch was typical of the Jewish ghetto in prewar Russia, and young Soutine escaped from it, first to Minsk (1907) and then to Vilna, where he studied at the School of Fine Arts (1910-1913).

Soutine then went to Paris. After studying briefly at the Atelier Cormon, he began to work on his own. He never exhibited the pictures of his early period; he often destroyed and sometimes repainted them. Only the exhibition of the Indépendants in 1937 disclosed the range and power of this ecstatic visionary who depicted the tragic melancholy of being.

Without the help of the art dealer Leopold Zborowski, to whom Soutine was introduced by his painter friend Amedeo Modigliani, Soutine might have despaired of his vocation. In 1919 Zborowski sent him to Céret in the Pyrenees, where Soutine stayed for 3 years and executed 200 paintings. Here he freed himself from the impact which Tintoretto, El Greco, Gustave Courbet, and, in particular, Rembrandt had made upon his sensitive mind, and here he created the series of frenetically painted landscape visions which established his name, such as *View of Céret* (ca. 1919) and *Gnarled Trees* (ca. 1921). The expressionist style is also typical of his portraits and still lifes, mainly dead fowl and carcasses, which, by their very subject matter, are symbols of mortality, for example, *Woman in Red* (ca. 1922) and *Carcass of Beef* (ca. 1925).

In 1925 Soutine was in Cagnes, where he suffered an emotional crisis. In 1927 he painted his famous series of choir boys. In 1929 Monsieur Marcellin Castaing and his wife offered Soutine a home in their castle near Chartres; here for a time he found peace of mind. His gift for portraiture is again seen in the fine portrait of Madame Castaing (ca. 1928).

Although Soutine traveled a great deal in France, he always returned to Paris. The German occupation worsened his already Kafkaesque state of anxiety, and he fled to the village of Champigny-sur-Vende in the Touraine to escape deportation. He died on Aug. 9, 1943, in Paris after an operation for stomach ulcers.

Further Reading

Jean Leymarie, *Soutine* (trans. 1964), includes an important introduction by the artist's friend Marcellin Castaing, an analysis of the art by Leymarie, and fine color plates. A monograph on the artist is Raymond Cogniat, *Soutine* (1952). See also the exhibition catalogs of the Museum of Modern Art, *Soutine* (1950); the Arts Council of Great Britain, *Chaim Soutine, 1894-1943* (1963); and the Los Angeles County Art Museum, *Chaim Soutine* (1968).

Additional Sources

Werner, Alfred, *Chaim Soutine,* New York: H. N. Abrams, 1977.

□

Souvanna Phouma

The Lao prince and political leader Souvanna Phouma (1901-1984) played a political balancing role during the first decade and a half of Lao independence that may have permitted the survival of the badly splintered Southeast Asian nation.

Born on October 7, 1901, in Luang Prabang in then French-ruled Laos, Prince Souvanna Phouma was educated as an engineer in France. Highly Frenchified in manner, he subsequently served as an engineer in the public transport department upon his return from France. He supported the 1945 declaration of independence, made by King Sisavangvong with strong Japanese encouragement; and, when French troops returned to reoccupy the country, he joined the national resistance movement (Lao Issara) in neighboring Thailand.

Following French acquiesence in partial independence, Souvanna Phouma served as minister of public transport, minister of planning, and minister of posts and telegraphs in 1950-1951. Premier during the years when Lao independence was finally completely obtained (1951-1954), he fell from office shortly thereafter. He returned as premier in 1956 and successfully negotiated a coalition government with the Pathet Lao, allies of Ho Chi Minh's Viet Minh in neighboring Vietnam.

An early advocate of neutralism, Souvanna Phouma fell again as premier in 1958—partly in response to American pressure for a stronger anti-Communist position. The shortsightedness of this pressure was evidenced when the Pathet Lao resumed their armed revolt and air force captain Kong Le staged an initially successful coup (1960). Souvanna Phouma reluctantly supported the Kong Le forces, which further splintered Lao political life.

The Souvanna Phouma-Kong Le neutralists cooperated with the Communist Pathet Lao in the Lao civil war of the early 1960s, partly because the anti-Communists left them with no alternative. Souvanna Phouma played a major role in 1962, at the time of the Geneva Agreement on Laos, in reconciling the three major political factions, which formed a new coalition government.

Souvanna Phouma was premier in the government formed in 1962 and remained in this position throughout the decade. The Communists resumed their revolt in 1963, however, and Souvanna Phouma's neutralists and the rightists subsequently drew closer together. Souvanna Phouma solicited American economic and military aid to preserve Lao independence in the light of increasing intervention by the Communist Vietnamese, whose numbers in Laos by 1970 approximated 60,000.

The tragedy of Souvanna Phouma was that he devotedly pursued a policy of neutrality for his country but ultimately had to call on the United States to assure the survival of his nation. His triumph was that he did this with such skill that the Soviet Union, Communist China, and North Vietnam were not able to mount a convincing propaganda case that Souvanna Phouma had abandoned his neutralists approach. Although most of eastern Laos was in Communist hands throughout the 1960s, the Communist powers continued to recognize his regime as the legitimate government of Laos. Souvanna Phouma did not hold Laos together in the 1960s, but he kept more of it in one piece than probably anybody anticipated.

In 1971 the South Vietnamese government sent troops into Laos in an effort to stop the flow of military supplies from North Vietnam along the Ho Chi Minh Trail. Objecting to the influence of the North Vietnamese over the Pathet Lao, Souvanna Phouma began working with the United States government and gave approval to U.S. air raids on Pathet Lao forces. After the United States began to withdraw from Vietnam, the government and the Pathet Lao agreed on a cease fire in 1973, and a coalition government was formed in which he allied himself once again with his brother and the Pathet Lao. With North Vietnam's victory, however, the Pathet Lao moved to dominate the coalition. He was ousted in 1975 when they abolished the monarchy and established the People's Democratic Republic of Laos.

After 1975 Souvanna Phouma was seen at official gatherings and was allowed to attend high-level government meetings. He served as an adviser to the government until his death in 1984.

Further Reading

There was no biographical study of Souvanna Phouma, probably the most important Lao political figure of his times. His importance, however, came through in several excellent studies dealing with various crises in which he was a participant. The best of them was *Anatomy of a Crisis: The Laotian Crisis of 1960-1969,* the last book by the late Bernard B. Fall, edited and completed by Roger M. Smith (1969). Another excellent book on the same subject was Arthur J. Dommen, *Conflict in Laos* (1964). An account by a Laotian who himself figured prominently in events in his country was Sisouk Na Champassak, *Storm over Laos* (1961). An update of the narrative begun in the more specific studies of the major crises in the start of the 1960s was Hugh Toye, *Laos: Buffer State or Battleground* (1968).

See also Perry Stieglitz, *In a Little Kingdom: The Tragedy of Laos, 1960-1980* (M.E. Sharpe, 1990); William Bouarouy, *The Roots of the Conflicts in Indochina: With Chronology of Laos History, & Major Successive Political Events in Laos from 1316 Through 1975* (Asian-Americans Research Center & Publishing Agency, 1992); and Timothy Castle, *At War in the Shadow of Vietnam: United States Military Aid to the Royal Lao Government, 1955-1975* (Columbia University Press, 1995). □

Wole Soyinka

The Nigerian playwright Wole Soyinka (born 1935) was one of the few African writers to denounce the slogan of Negritude as a tool of autocracy. He also was the first black African to be awarded the Nobel Prize in Literature.

Wole Soyinka was born July 13, 1934 in Abeokuta a village on the banks of the River Ogun in the western area of Nigeria. His mother was a Christian convert so devout that he nicknamed her "Wild Christian" and he father was the scholarly headmaster of a Christian primary school whom he nicknamed "Essay"—a play on his occupation and his initials S.A. Soyinka was educated through the secondary level in Ibadan and later attended University College, Ibadan, and the University of Leeds, from which he graduated with honors. He worked for a brief period at the Royal Court Theatre in London before returning to Nigeria in 1960. His play, "The Invention" was staged in 1957 at the Royal Court Theatre. At that time his only published works were poems such as "The Immigrant" and "My Next Door Neighbour," which appeared in the magazine *Black Orpheus.*

Two of Soyinka's plays, *The Lion and the Jewel* and *The Swamp Dwellers,* were performed by students at Ibadan in 1960. Later that year his play *A Dance in the Forest* was produced for the Nigerian independence celebrations. In 1963 Oxford University Press issued a collection of his plays. These were *The Trials of Brother Jero, The Strong Breed, The Swamp Dwellers,* and *The Lion and the Jewel.* He also continued to publish poetry in *Black Orpheus* and other journals, and he was very active in theater group activities in Nigeria.

In the plays written and produced in the early 1960s, Soyinka showed his ability to project traditional Nigerian themes and stories through English instead of Yoruba. He was recognized as a dramatic poet and skilled dramatic craftsman. The plays dealt with a great diversity of theme—from the farce of *The Trials of Brother Jero,* to the romanticism of *The Lion and the Jewel,* to the tragedy of *The Strong Breed.* Soyinka was concerned with universal problems, and his plays examined town life, a retrograde countryside, and the ambitions of the "new" Nigerians.

Perhaps the best example of the juxtaposition of the past and present was in *A Dance in the Forest.* Three guilty persons were lured into a deep woodland where they were confronted with their spirit counterparts from the past. Selfishness, dishonesty, and lust were personified as elements in all societies—past and present.

The worsening political situation in Nigeria was reflected in Soyinka's theme for *Kongi's Harvest,* first performed at the Dakar Festival of Negro Arts in 1965. The theme was the establishment of a dictatorship in an African state; and the venal politician, the uncommitted, corrupt traditional ruler, and the ruthlessness of a man driven toward power were all displayed. In *Idanre and Other Poems,* published in 1967, Soyinka ceased being a satirist and became a gloomy visionary. The title poem, reciting a creation myth, stressed the symbols of fire, iron, and blood, which were central to the poet's view of the modern African world.

Soyinka became a vocal critic of Negritude, accusing politicians of using it as a mask for autocracy. His increasing use of polemic against social injustice and his demands for freedom coincided with the military takeover in Nigeria and the later drift toward civil war. Soyinka was arrested by the Nigerian government in October 1967, was accused of spying for Biafra, and was kept in detention in the north for two years, after which he returned to his position as head of the drama department at Ibadan. Much of his creative attention following his release went into filming *Kongi's Harvest,* in which he also played the leading role.

Soyinka's Nigeria was a country in transition, attempting to mold itself out of a variety of tribal cultures and a turbulent European colonization. Soyinka did not romanticize his native land, nor was he willing to see African culture as a flat symbol of primitiveness. He was as willing to charge Nigerian politicians and bureaucrats with barbarity and corruption as he was to condemn the greed and materialism of the west. These attitudes were even more prevalent after his second incarceration on the trumped up spying charges. His work took on a darker and angrier tone. When he was released from prison in 1969, Soyinka left Nigeria and did not return until the government changed in 1975. Soyinka's prison diary, published in 1972 *The Man Died: Prison Notes of Wole Soyinka* was a fragmented and grim account of the days he spent incarcerated, often in chains. Along with his verses that captured the essence of his prison experience, *The Man Died* provided invaluable context for Soyinka' subsequent imagery in his works.

Soyinka's post-prison works striked readers as more angry and despairing than his earlier ones. The play *Madmen and Specialists* was about a young doctor who returned from war trained in the ways of torture and practices his new skills on his seemingly mad old father. Charles Larson in *New York Times Review of Books* called the play "a product of those months Soyinka spent in prison, in solitary confinement, as a political prisoner. It is, not surprisingly, the most brutal social criticism he has ever published."

Yet not all his post prison works were filled with despair. *Ake: The Years of Childhood* and its prequel *Isara: A Voyage around Essay* were beautiful memoirs of both his own childhood with its strong Yoruba background and his father's youth in a changing Nigeria. *Isara,* published in 1988 after his father's death, reconstructed his father's divided life and tried to reconcile two conflicting cultures—African and Western–that trapped him between.

In 1986 Soyinka was awarded the Nobel Prize for literature in recognition of his accomplishments. The prize committee recognized him for his commitment to render the full complexity of his African culture In addition to his literary output, Soyinka had produced two essay collections that define his literary philosophy *Myth Literature and the African World* (1976) and *Art Dialog and Outrage* (1991, 1994) in which Soyinka asserted that critics must approach African literature on its own terms rather than by standards established in western cultures. African literature was not monolithic and needs to be seen as a variety of voices, not merely one speaker.

In 1994, Soyinka escaped to Paris, just ahead of being arrested by the militarist government for his advocacy of democracy. In 1997, the same government charged him with treason, claiming he was involved in a series of bombing of army sites.

Further Reading

For a selection of his work see Soyinka's *Five Plays* (1964). A fine biographical, critical study was Gerald Moore, *Wole Soyinka* (1972). There was a good discussion of Soyinka in the essay by Martin Esslin, "Two Nigerian Playwrights," in Ulli Beier, ed., *Introduction to African Literature* (1967), and also in Wilfred F. Cartey, *Whispers from a Continent: The Literature of Contemporary Black Africa* 1969). See also *The Emergence of African Fiction* (1972) and *The Novels of Wole Soyinka* (1990); and *The Man Died: Prison Notes of Wole Soyinka* (1972). □

Paul Henri Spaak

The Belgian statesman Paul Henri Spaak (1899-1972) was an architect of the Benelux association of his country with the Netherlands and Luxembourg and a supporter of Western European military, economic, and political unity during the Cold War.

Paul Henri Spaak was born near Brussels on Jan. 25, 1899. His father was the writer Paul Spaak. Interned by the Germans during World War I, the younger Spaak thereafter studied law in Brussels. He was sent to the Chamber of Deputies in 1932 and rose through a number of Cabinet positions to become Belgium's first Socialist prime minister, in 1938. Despite his early experiences, Spaak was during this period a believer in Belgian neutrality and worked to disassociate his government from the Locarno Pact.

The experiences of World War II decisively affected Spaak's orientation. During the war he served as foreign minister in the Belgian government-in-exile in London. Returning to Brussels in 1944, he continued to serve in postwar coalition governments as foreign minister (1945-1947). He was again prime minister from March 1947 to August 1949, and foreign minister from April 1954 to May 1957. Spaak resigned his government position in 1957, but as head of the Socialist party, he became deputy prime minister in yet another coalition government in 1961.

During the postwar years Spaak's interest in and commitment to international organization enhanced his reputation. Already during the war he had worked toward the Benelux customs union (finally launched in 1948). He also promoted the idea of a Western European defense pact, then rejected on the grounds that it would lead to rivalry with the Soviets over the fate of Germany—a not altogether inaccurate prognostication.

Spaak's Western European defense plan was realized in the North Atlantic Treaty, which he signed in 1949. Meanwhile, he had been elected (January 1946) president of the General Assembly of the United Nations. As one of the staunchest of European integrationists, he was made president of the Consultative Assembly of the Council of Europe (May 1951) and of the General Assembly of the European Steel and Coal Community (1952). From late 1957 to 1961, Spaak capped his career as a supporter of European unity by serving as the chairman of the Atlantic Council and secretary general of the North Atlantic Treaty Organization.

During Spaak's period of greatest activity, the unity he sought and partially achieved was economic. The Belgian statesman desired political unification but not on the basis of the Common Market countries alone. He therefore argued against further moves in this direction until the economic integration of Britain into Europe had been accomplished. He retired from political life in 1966 and died in Brussels on June 30, 1972.

Further Reading

Spaak wrote a very interesting account of his 30 years in public service: *The Continuing Battle: Memoirs of a European, 1936-1966* (1972). J. H. Huizinga, *Mr Europe: A Political Biography of Paul Henri Spaak* (1961), deals with Spaak's life and work. For background on postwar Europe and its new arrangements see Max Beloff, *The United States and the Unity of Europe* (1963). □

Lazzaro Spallanzani

The Italian naturalist Lazzaro Spallanzani (1729-1799) was one of the founders of modern experimental biology.

Lazzaro Spallanzani was born in Scandiano on Jan. 12, 1729. He entered a Jesuit college at the age of 15 and later studied law at Bologna, but very early he became interested in physics and developed an overall knowledge of nature. He took orders in 1755 and is therefore often referred to as the Abbé Spallanzani. That year he began to teach logic, metaphysics, and classics at Reggio. In 1757 he was appointed to the chair of mathematics and physics at the university there; later he taught at the University of Modena.

In 1765 Spallanzani began publishing his numerous scientific works. Most of them are motivated by a philosophy of science which nowadays could be called reductionist, namely, a belief that most phenomena are reducible to physical and chemical explanation. In 1769 he accepted the chair of natural history at the University of Pavia, remaining at this post until his death on Feb. 11, 1799.

Spallanzani is well known for one of his major works on microscopical observation that concerned the systems of spontaneous generation, and was an attempt to disprove J. T. Needham's and the Comte de Buffon's theory in support of spontaneous generation. Although his experimentation was exact, and he did prove that some organisms can live in a vacuum for many days (anaerobiosis), his theory was not comprehensive enough. Thus Spallanzani did not succeed in establishing in a final way that the theory of spontaneous generation was wrong. He also did important work in embryology. He was an ovarian preformationist, and through his experiments with artificial fertilization using filtered semen he pointed out the need for the physical contact between the spermatozoa and the ovule. He thus disproved the fertilizing power of the seminal fluid. Yet he did not fully understand the process, and in plants he described fertilization as being effected by the spermatic vapor of the pollen and not by any of the visible parts of it. In his

studies on regeneration of animals he practically established the modern lines of animal morphology.

Spallanzani also worked on problems of circulation, gastric digestion, respiration, the hearing of bats, the electricity of torpedo fish, and the reproduction of eels. As a result of these studies he gave experimental proof of the action of gastric juice on foodstuffs. He theorized that this action was not putrefaction or vinous fermentation, as others had thought, but acid fermentation; however, he was unable to isolate acid from the gastric mixture. His experiments on respiration provided evidence that tissues use oxygen and release carbon dioxide.

Especially noteworthy is the long trip Spallanzani undertook in Sicily and the neighboring volcanic areas. With systematic measurements and exact physical methods he established that there was nothing mysterious about the fire in the volcanoes; on the contrary, the same physical laws which apply on the surface of the earth are the ones which create volcanoes and which are acting in the heart of the earth. He succeeded in measuring the heat in one of the volcanoes and expressing it in degrees Fahrenheit, which were used in regular terrestrial measuring. His description of these areas is rich—not only in describing nature but also the social habits, customs, and crafts of the inhabitants and the ways of primitive science.

Further Reading

Spallanzani's life and career are well covered in Paul De Kruif, *Microbe Hunters* (1926), and Wade W. Oliver, *Stalkers of Pestilence: The Story of Man's Ideas of Infection* (1930). Spallanzani is also discussed in Joseph Needham, *A History of Embryology* (1934; 2d ed. 1959), and Arthur William Meyer, *The Rise of Embryology* (1939). □

Muriel Sarah Spark

Muriel Sarah Spark (born 1918) wrote biography, literary criticism, poetry, and fiction, including the novel that was considered her masterpiece, *The Prime of Miss Jean Brodie.*

Born in Edinburgh on February 1, 1918, Muriel Spark worked in the Political Intelligence Department of the British Foreign Office in 1944-1945, was the general secretary of the Poetry Society from 1947 to 1949, and served as the editor of *Poetry Review* in 1949. She was the founder of the literary magazine *Forum* and worked as a part-time editor for Peter Owen Ltd.

In the early 1950s Spark published her first poetry collection, *The Fanfarlo and Other Verse* (1952), and built a solid reputation as a biographer with *Child of Light: A Reassessment of Mary Wollstonecraft Shelley* (1951); *Emily Bronte: Her Life and Work* (1953); and *John Masefield* (1953). She also edited *A Collection of Poems* by Emily Bronte (1952), *My Best Mary: The Letters of Mary Shelley* (1954), and, most important, *Letters of John Henry Newman* (1957).

While working in these areas of nonfiction, Spark was undergoing a crisis of faith and was strongly influenced by the writings of Newman, the 19th-century Anglican clergyman who became a convert to Roman Catholicism and eventually a cardinal in that faith. While she was dealing with her crisis, she received financial and psychological assistance from Graham Greene, also a Roman Catholic convert, and was eventually converted herself, a move that had significant influence on her novels.

Spark published the first of those novels, *The Comforters,* in 1957 and followed that with *Robinson* in 1958, the same year she authored her first short-story collection, *The Go-Away Bird and Other Stories.* In this same period she began writing radio plays, with *The Party Through the Wall* in 1957, *The Interview* in 1958, and *The Dry River Bed* in 1959.

It was in 1959 that Spark had her first major success, *Memento Mori,* with some critics comparing her to Ivy Compton-Burnett and Evelyn Waugh. She followed this with *The Ballad of Peckham Rye* in 1960, writing a radio play based on the novel that same year; *The Bachelors,* also in 1960; and *Voices at Play* in 1961, likewise turned into a radio play.

In 1961 she also published the novel generally regarded as her masterwork, *The Prime of Miss Jean Brodie,* subsequently made into a play, a hit on both sides of the Atlantic in the years 1966-1968; a film in 1969; and a six-part adaptation for television, another transatlantic success,

in 1978 and 1979. This was the portrait of a middle-aged teacher at the Marcia Blaine School for Girls in Edinburgh in the 1930s who has gathered around her a coterie of five girls, "The Brodie Set." Jean Brodie was one of those delightful eccentrics, common in English fiction, who walked a tightrope over the abyss of caricature but never tumbled in. She saw her task as "putting old heads on young shoulders" and told her disciples that they were the *créme de la créme.* In 1939 she was forced to retire on the grounds that she has been teaching fascism, the accusation made by the girl who eventually became a nun and defended herself against charges of betrayal by observing that "It's only possible to betray where loyalty is due." Critic George Stade probably best defined Spark's attitude toward Jean Brodie by pointing out that the novel embodied "the traditional moral wisdom that, if you are not part of something larger than yourself, you are nothing."

In 1962 Spark's sole venture into theater, *Doctors of Philosophy,* was presented in London and was not a resounding success. She returned to fiction and wrote The *Girls of Slender Means* (1963); *The Mandelbaum Gate* (1965); *Collected Stories I* (1967); *The Public Image* (1968); *The Very Fine Clock* (1968), her only work for juveniles; *The Driver's Seat* (1970); *Not To Disturb* (1971); and *The Hothouse by the East River* (1973).

Also in 1973 Sharp published another outstanding novel, *The Abbess of Crewe,* a work alive with paradox. To win election as abbess, the protagonist, Sister Gertrude, studied Machiavelli; once in charge, she combined an extreme conservatism in religious matters with the installation of electronic devices in the abbey and enlisted the aid of two Jesuit priests in exposing the affair between Sister Felicity and a young Jesuit. Released from the abbey, Sister Gertrude roamed the Third World like a loose cannon, indulging in such projects as mediating a war between a tribe of cannibals and a tribe of vegetarians. The novel was filmed in 1976 under the title *Nasty Habits.*

Subsequently there came the novels *The Takeover* (1976); *Territorial Rights* (1979); *Loitering with Intent* (1981); *A Far Cry from Kensington* (1987); *The Only Problem* (1988); *Symposium* (1990); *Reality and Dreams* (1997); and two collections of short stories, *Bang-Bang You're Dead and Other Stories* (1982) and *The Stories of Muriel Spark* (1985). In 1992, she published *Curriculum Vitae: Autobiography.*

Her twentieth novel, *Reality and Dreams* explored the boundaries and connections between realities and dreams in a story about a dream-driven film director who feels and seeks to be Godlike in his work, a theme which illustrated the aptness of critic Frank Kermode's insight that in Spark's novels portrayed a connection between fiction and the world, and between the creation of the novelist and the creation of God.

Much of the criticism about Spark's work focused on the extent to which her Catholicism influenced her writing; that is, was she a Catholic novelist or a novelist who was incidentally a Catholic? The former view was upheld by American critic Granville Hicks, who termed her "a gloomy Catholic, like Graham Greene and Flannery O'Connor, more concerned with the evil of man than the goodness of God." J.D. Enright, on the other hand, felt that, unlike Paul Claudel or François Mauriac or Graham Greene, she had no interest in force-feeding Catholicism to her readers. Religion aside, Duncan Fallowell summed up her fiction in this way: "She is the master, and sometimes mistress, of an attractive, cynical worldliness which is not shallow." And that observation probably best encapsulated British critical opinion, which has been generally kind, if not generous, to her work for four decades.

In 1993, Spark was made Dame Muriel Spark, Order of the British Empire.

Further Reading

Obviously Spark's 1992 autobiography was essential reading. Otherwise, studies of her and her work abound. The best overview can be found in Joseph Hynes' *Critical Essays on Muriel Spark* (1992). There were about a dozen volumes by individual authors (some of the critics included in Hynes' collection). The most recent were the six works, all titled *Muriel Spark,* by Peter Kemp (1974); Allan Massie (1979); Velma B. Richmond (1984); Alan N. Bold (1986); Dorothea Walker (1988); and Page Norman (1990). ☐

Jared Sparks

Jared Sparks (1789-1866), American editor, Unitarian minister, and historian, pioneered in publishing the source documents of American history.

Jared Sparks was born on May 10, 1789, on an impoverished farm in Willington, Conn. He graduated from Harvard in 1815, studied theology at the Harvard Divinity School, and was briefly a magazine editor. He was a Unitarian minister from 1819 to 1829, when he bought the *North American Review* and became its editor.

In the summer of 1823 he wrote in his diary, "Meditating on the importance of having a new history of America." The next year he began preparing an edition of George Washington's writings. His great ambition was to write the full history of the American Revolution. He gathered materials for this theme in archives of the original 13 states and in Europe.

Sparks published a series of volumes, beginning with the *Life and Travels of John Ledyard* (1828), concerning the famous traveler from Connecticut. In the next 2 years *The Diplomatic Correspondence of the American Revolution,* in 12 volumes, appeared. A subsidy from the Federal government aided in its publication. *The Life of Gouverneur Morris,* in three volumes, followed in 1832. Between 1834 and 1837 *The Life and Writings of George Washington* appeared in 12 volumes. One volume contained the biography, the rest included Washington's letters and public papers. Sparks was also preparing an edition of Benjamin Franklin's writings. Ten volumes of *The Works of Benjamin Franklin* were published between 1836 and 1840; one volume was devoted to biography. The *Washington* and the *Franklin* were Sparks's most creditable achievements.

The energetic historian also projected a "Library of American Biography." Through the lives of distinguished men, readers could trace a connected history of the nation. Eventually 25 volumes were published containing 60 biographies, of which Sparks wrote 8. In 1853 the *Correspondence of the American Revolution, Being Letters of Eminent Men to George Washington,* in four volumes, appeared.

Sparks filled vast gaps in American historiography, but his weaknesses were many. He was uncritical in depicting his subjects, whom he was inclined to portray without blemish. He lacked the literary gifts of other contemporary historians. As editor, he altered documents or omitted them if unfavorable to the image he wished to project. Yet the sheer volume of his productivity transformed the character of American historical writing.

Sparks was well rewarded. Americans avidly read books on the American Revolution. Sparks taught the subject at Harvard after 1839 and lectured on the Revolution to large public audiences. In 1849 he was elected president of Harvard, but he was an unhappy administrator, resigning after 4 years. The hectic early years gave way to a quiet period of correspondence with younger historians and public figures. He died in Cambridge, Mass., on March 14, 1866.

Further Reading

The best source is Herbert B. Adams, *The Life and Writings of Jared Sparks* (2 vols. 1893), the official biography based on Sparks's papers. John S. Bassett edited the *Correspondence of George Bancroft and Jared Sparks, 1823-1832* (1917). Bassett's *The Middle Group of American Historians* (1917) has an important chapter on Sparks. A briefer summary of Sparks's achievement may be found in Michael Kraus, *The Writing of American History* (1953). □

Spartacus

Spartacus (died 71 B.C.) was a Thracian gladiator who led a slave war in Italy against the Romans. He plundered most of Italy before being defeated and killed in a pitched battle.

It is not known how Spartacus became a gladiator. He is said to have fought either with or against the Romans. Eventually he found himself in the gladiator school of Gnaeus Lentulus Batiatus at Capua. From there in 73 B.C. some 70 gladiators escaped and fled to Mt. Vesuvius, where they were joined by slaves and farm workers from the countryside. Spartacus with the help of two Celts, Crixus and Oenomaos, led them, forging the motley group into a first-class fighting force.

Roman response to the uprising was at first slow and inadequate. Spartacus defeated local levies led by a propraetor and a praetor in three sharp engagements. The slaves then broke out of Campania and raided all of southern Italy, eventually establishing winter quarters at Thurii and Metapontum in Lucania. There their forces grew to 70,000 men.

In 72 the Senate assigned both consuls and four legions to the war against the slaves. After a minor engagement at Mt. Garganos in which Crixus was killed, Spartacus defeated the two consuls in separate battles in central Italy. At this point he attempted to lead the slaves north to freedom beyond the Alps. But after they defeated the governor of Cisalpine Gaul at Mutina (Modena), they elected to turn back to Italy to plunder and enrich themselves. Spartacus not only threatened Rome itself but again defeated both consuls in a major battle in Picenum. The Romans no longer dared face him in the field. He then returned to southern Italy and again made Thurii his headquarters.

In the autumn of 72 the Senate transferred the command against the slaves to Marcus Licinius Crassus, who held no public office at the time. He recruited six additional legions and took up a protective position in south-central Italy. After an initial defeat Crassus won a victory over a contingent of the slaves. That winter he built a wall and ditch across the toe of Italy to contain Spartacus, whose attempts to escape to Sicily with his army failed.

Spartacus (center, leaning toward ground)

Early in the spring of 71 Spartacus broke through Crassus' lines but suffered two defeats at his hands in Lucania. He then retired again to Bruttium (Calabria), where he defeated two of Crassus' lieutenants who were following him. Encouraged, Spartacus's men persuaded him to risk a major battle with Crassus. In it Spartacus and 60,000 of his men fell. Spartacus's body was never found. Stragglers from the massacre were caught in Etruria by Pompey, summoned by the people from Spain to help end the war. In a final act of cruelty Crassus crucified 6,000 prisoners along the Via Appia from Capua to Rome.

Although Spartacus has been justly lauded as a bold leader, the slave war was not a revolt of the lower classes against the bourgeois leadership of Rome. Spartacus got almost no support from the Italian population, which remained loyal to Rome. Nonetheless, Spartacus has been idolized by revolutionaries since the 18th century. From 1916 to 1919 the German Socialists styled themselves "Spartacists" when they tried to foment a proletarian revolution after World War I. Spartacus's stout resistance against the Romans has been a popular theme among poets and novelists, for example, Arthur Koestler in *The Gladiators* (1939) and Howard Fast in *Spartacus* (1951).

Further Reading

The principal sources for Spartacus are Plutarch and Appian. For additional details see *The Cambridge Ancient History,* vol. 9: *The Roman Republic, 133-44 B.C.,* edited by S. A. Cook, F. E. Adcock, and M. P. Charlesworth; and H. H. Scullard, *From the Gracchi to Nero: A History of Rome from 133 B.C. to A.D. 68* (1959; 2d ed. 1963). □

Charles Clinton Spaulding

Business executive Charles Clinton Spaulding (1874-1952) was one of the most prominent and influential African American entrepreneurs of the 20th century, achieving success in both the banking and insurance professions. He was president of the North Carolina Mutual Insurance Company, the largest African American business in the country; a leading proponent of the Negro Business Movement of the period; and a civic and social leader in the tradition of Booker T. Washington.

Charles Clinton Spaulding, the third of fourteen children, was born on a farm near Whiteville in Columbus County, North Carolina, in 1874. His parents, Benjamin Mclver and Margaret Moore Spaulding, were prosperous landowners of free ancestry who were respected leaders of the community. Young Spaulding spent his early years working on the family farm and exhausting the limited possibilities for education in his rural community.

In the mid 1890s he made his way to Durham to join his uncle, Aaron McDuffie Moore, a practicing physician, and to avail himself of the city's greater educational opportunities. Here he enrolled in the Whitted School, from which he graduated in 1898 at the age of 23 with what was then considered a high school diploma. Although he continued self-education throughout his life and enjoyed the mentorship of his uncle, it was from this base of formal education and family background that Spaulding rose from farm worker to a position of regional and national prominence.

Activities as a Businessman

Spaulding's first job following graduation was as manager of a grocery concern in which 25 African American men had invested $10 each. The venture was unsuccessful, however, and Spaulding was left with bare shelves and $300 indebtedness from the insolvent business. Following this failure he entered the field of insurance, a newly-emerging profession among African Americans. In 1899 he became general manager of the North Carolina Mutual and Provident Association, a small industrial assessment organization founded by Durham barber John Merrick and Spaulding's uncle Aaron Moore. As the sole employee, Spaulding served also as promoter, agent, clerk, bookkeeper, office boy, and janitor. In 1909 the firm achieved the status of old line legal reserve life insurance company and changed its name to North Carolina Mutual Life Insurance Company. Spaulding succeeded to the presidency of the company in 1923 and was for many years the pivotal figure in an organization that, rising from a situation where the company in 1899 did not have enough money on hand to pay its first death claim, came to hold distinction as the largest African American business in the country.

By 1921 Spaulding had also assumed leadership of the Mechanics and Farmers Bank and the Mutual Building and Loan Association, two organizations founded in Durham by the organizers of North Carolina Mutual. In addition, he was vice president of the Bankers Fire Insurance Company and the Southern Fidelity Mutual Insurance Company. These enterprises made Durham one of the leading centers of African American business achievement in the first half of the 20th century and, in large measure, provided the financial sustenance for the early economic growth of African Americans in North Carolina and the region. In his capacity as executive of these enterprises, Spaulding sought to map a program of social service that stretched beyond the routine functions of a business corporation to include the expansion of home ownership, business growth, and general race uplift.

Spaulding was widely involved in the larger arena of African American business beyond Durham. He belonged to the inner circle of the National Negro Business League, founded by Booker T. Washington in 1900, serving as secretary-treasurer as well as chairman of the executive committee during the 1920s. Similarly, he provided leadership in the National Negro Insurance Association and the National Negro Bankers Association. In recognition of his outstanding contributions to the management and direction of business activities, Spaulding was awarded the Harmon Foundation Award for Distinguished Achievement in Business in 1926. In his lifetime numerous other awards, honors, and honorary degrees also accrued to Spaulding in recognition of his success in the fields of life insurance and finance and for his contribution to the progress of African Americans in their struggle for economic and civic emancipation.

Follows Booker Washington's Economic Philosophy

It was said that Spaulding was the greatest living exponent of the economic philosophy popularized by Booker T. Washington. Like Washington, Spaulding believed in harmonious racial understanding and tolerance, and he praised the opportunities available to African Americans in the South. He also extolled the idea that integrity, character, and achievement would equate eventually with acceptance and citizenship for African Americans. Spaulding viewed business and economic success, along with intelligence, vision, and cooperation, as powerful weapons in the battle to destroy race prejudice in America. He believed, particularly, that African Americans could surmount racial prejudice and strengthen their positions in society by evidencing success in the financial and business areas. He asked only that equal opportunities be afforded.

Through his work in civic, educational, and social organizations, he sought to foster opportunities for African Americans. He served on a number of boards of trustees of African Americancolleges and universities, including Howard, Shaw, and North Carolina College. He was the first African American elected to the board of the Slater Fund and was the regional broker for the Rosenwald Fund. His views on education, race, and social issues impacting opportunity were disseminated also through his membership on the boards of the Southern Educational Foundation and the North Carolina Commission on Interracial Cooperation.

At the national level, Spaulding's activities with the National Urban League and the New Deal were directed at broadening opportunities as well. He was appointed national chairman of the Emergency Advisory Council of the Urban League, a body organized to enlist support for the New Deal among African Americans. He used this position and his national contacts to advance opportunities for African Americans in the region. His work in the New Deal earned him recognition as the leading Democrat in North Carolina. Spaulding married twice and raised four children. He died in Durham on August 1, 1952, his 78th birthday.

Further Reading

An excellent scholarly essay on Spaulding has been written by Walter Weare in *Black Leaders of the Twentieth Century* (1982), edited by John Hope Franklin and August Meier. A good deal of information on Spaulding is also available in Weare's study of North Carolina Mutual Insurance Company, titled *Black Business in the New South* (1973). Short biographical sketches may be found in several other sources: Edgar A. Toppins, *Biographies of Notable Black Americans* (1961); *Negro History Bulletin* (Vol. XVI); and *Black Enterprise* (Vol. VI). Spaulding's own views on several issues can be found in "50 Years of Progress," a series published by the *Pittsburgh Courier* (1950). □

John Hanning Speke

An English explorer of Africa, John Hanning Speke (1827-1864) solved the riddle of the Nile River by discovering its source during the course of an epic journey to and through the Great Lakes region of eastern Africa.

Ever since the time of Herodotus, men had sought and speculated about the fountains—the ultimate origins—of the river that provided Egypt's life-blood and sustained classical as well as modern civilizations throughout much of its length. Ptolemy had hinted at the Nile's beginning in equatorial Africa, but only the 19th-century search for the sources of the main, or White, Nile (in the late 18th century James Bruce had seen the Blue Nile flow from Lake Tana in Ethiopia) produced John Speke's confirmation.

John Speke was born at Jordans, Somersetshire, on May 4, 1827. He joined the Indian army in 1844 and saw considerable action in the Punjab campaign. He liked to fight but was bored by the longueurs between periods of combat. Appropriately, he spent his local leaves shooting game in Tibet.

In 1854 Speke obtained overseas leave in order to join Richard Burton in Somalia. While Burton was journeying to the "forbidden city" of Harar, Speke twice went eastward to Bunder Gori, a nearby Somali town. In an attack in 1855 by Somali on the British camp near Berbera, Speke almost died from wounds before he and Burton fled to Aden.

Early Explorations

Speke served as a captain in a Turkish regiment at Kertch during the Crimean War (1855-1856) and then returned to Africa as second-in-command of Burton's expedition to the lakes of the eastern interior. The Royal Geographical Society was sponsoring this attempt to locate the rumored Sea of Ujiji and to ascertain the sources of the Nile.

Guided by Arabs and Africans, the expedition attained the Sea of Ujiji (modern Lake Tanganyika) in 1858. Speke's eyes were then too clouded with ophthalmia for him to see the waters of the lake, but he had already learned that Tanganyika was but one of the component lakes—Victoria and Nyasa being the others—of the Sea of Ujiji. He had also surmised or gathered that it was from Victoria that the Nile River flowed north to Egypt. Despite the opposition of Burton, he tested this hypothesis later in 1858.

From Tabora, Speke took a "flying trip" to the southern end of the lake along a route known but relatively little frequented by traders. Reaching the lake after several detours, he at last caught a murky glimpse of the southern waters of what he called Victoria Nyanza (Lake Victoria). With only the evidence of hearsay, Speke decided that this lake was in fact the source of the Nile.

Sources of the Nile

Two years later the Royal Geographical Society commissioned Speke to demonstrate his belief. Accompanied by James Augustus Grant, a colleague from the Indian army, Speke reached Tabora in 1861, and they set out around the western side of Victoria Nyanza to Buganda, the capital of which they reached early in 1862. After several months the kabaka, or king, Mutesa, gave Speke permission to travel to the Nile and then northward.

In July 1862 Speke stood above a point where the waters of the Victoria Nyanza cascaded down the White Nile on their way to Alexandria. "I saw," the exultant explorer wrote, "that old father Nile without any doubt [rose] in the Victoria Nyanza, and, as I had foretold, that [that] lake [was] the great source of the holy river which cradled the first expounder of our religious belief." Grant and Speke proceeded down the Nile, but they were inhibited from following its course, and from visiting other lakes of which they had heard rumor, by African warfare.

Even after Speke had seen the waters of Victoria coursing over Ripon Falls and down the Nile, however, there were some who remained unconvinced that Herodotus's fabled fountains had in fact been found. Burton was a leading critic: Speke had not, he said, followed the Nile the entire way from Victoria to Gondokoro. At a meeting of the august British Association for the Advancement of Science in September 1864, it was arranged that Burton and Speke present their theories. But on the day before the debate Speke went partridge shooting at Neston Park near

Bath, mishandled a gun while crossing a stone wall, and fatally shot himself.

The effect of Speke's discoveries, which he embodied in two narratives—*Journal of the Discovery of the Source of the Nile* (1863) and *What Led to the Discovery of the Source of the Nile* (1864)—was to direct European interest to the peoples and regions near the headwaters of the Nile. Subsequent European enterprise, and the way in which Buganda was regarded as a prize at the time of the scramble for Africa, indicated the result of Speke's journey to the Nile for both Africans and Europeans.

Further Reading

Speke's own journals contain the most detailed discussions of his activities in Africa. Alexander Maitland's *Speke* (1971) is the only biography. The best short study is Roy Charles Bridges, "John Hanning Speke: Negotiating a Way to the Nile," in Robert I. Rotberg, ed., *Africa and Its Explorers* (1970). Speke also figures prominently in two recent biographies of Sir Richard Burton: Byron Farwell, *Burton* (1963), and Fawn Brodie, *The Devil Drives* (1967). See also James A. Grant, *A Walk across Africa* (1864). □

Cardinal Francis Joseph Spellman

Cardinal Francis Joseph Spellman (1889-1967), archbishop of New York, was for 25 years the best-known and most influential leader of American Catholicism.

Francis Joseph Spellman was born in Whitman, Mass., on May 4, 1889. Educated at Fordham College in New York and the North American College in Rome, he was ordained in 1916 and served for 2 years as a curate at All Saints Church in Roxbury. In 1922 he was appointed vice-chancellor of the Boston archdiocese, and he served on the editorial staff of the diocesan paper, the *Pilot.* From 1925 to 1932 he was attached to the Secretariat of State in Rome and then was appointed auxiliary bishop to Cardinal William O'Connell of Boston.

During his years in Rome, Spellman was a close friend of Eugenio Pacelli, papal secretary of state, who became Pope Pius XII in 1939. That year the new pope appointed Spellman archbishop of New York. In 1946 Spellman became a member of the College of Cardinals, and in following years he was regarded as the most powerful and influential leader of the Catholic hierarchy in the United States. His public friendship with President Franklin Roosevelt added to his fame and prestige.

An active, vigorous leader and a talented administrator, Spellman was also a highly successful fund raiser. During his tenure as New York's archbishop, he vastly expanded the diocese's system of hospitals, orphanages, schools, and charitable agencies, undertaking new construction totaling over $500 million. As bishop for the U.S. Armed Forces, he traveled widely to visit American troops around the world and to oversee the work of Catholic chaplains. He supported a strong American foreign policy and frequently warned against the danger of communism. His activities in support of public aid for parochial schools and his militant opposition to birth control, pornography, and communism embroiled him in numerous controversies, as did his actions forbidding Catholics to see certain motion pictures. Toward the end of his life his strong support for American participation in the Vietnam War aroused militant opposition within and without the Church.

In addition to his enormous pastoral and administrative work, Cardinal Spellman wrote several volumes of poetry and a novel, *The Foundling* (1951), which was a national best seller. He died in New York City on Dec. 2, 1967.

Further Reading

The authorized biography of Spellman is Robert J. Gannon, *The Cardinal Spellman Story* (1962).

Additional Sources

Cooney, John, *The American pope: the life and times of Francis Cardinal Spellman,* New York, N.Y.: Times Books, 1984. □

Hans Spemann

The German experimental embryologist Hans Spemann (1869-1941) was awarded the Nobel Prize in Physiology or Medicine for his discovery of the organizer effect in embryonic development.

Hans Spemann, son of Wilhelm Spemann, a publisher, was born in Stuttgart on June 27, 1869. After a period in his father's business and military service, he became a medical student at the University of Heidelberg, spent a period at the University of Munich, and in 1894 transferred to Würzburg. There he abandoned medicine for science, studied under Theodor Boveri, who greatly influenced his future research, and graduated in 1895.

Spemann then began research in the Zoological Institute at Würzburg, where he became a lecturer in 1898. In 1908 he was appointed professor of zoology and comparative anatomy in the University of Rostock, and in 1914 associate director of the Kaiser Wilhelm Institute for Biology at Berlin-Dahlem. He was called to the chair of zoology in the University of Freiburg in Breisgau in 1919, from which post he retired in 1935. Spemann devoted his scientific career to the study of the causes that act on the cells of the earliest embryos, leading to their differentiation and specialization for different functions.

Foundation of Experimental Embryology

The science of experimental embryology (or developmental mechanics) was founded about 1890 by Wilhelm Roux and Hans Driesch. Roux destroyed one of the two blastomeres formed by the first division of a fertilized frog's egg. He found that the other blastomere continued to develop, but it formed half an embryo. Then Driesch separated the two blastomeres of a sea urchin's egg and removed one entirely. The remaining blastomere formed, not half an embryo, but a normal embryo of small size.

It was well known that the eyeball developed from the optic cup, a protuberance from the primitive brain, and that the lens arose in the epidermis overlying the optic cup. Why the epidermis thickened and became transparent at the appropriate point was unknown, and the question was whether there was some unknown connection between optic cup and potential lens. In 1901 Carl Herbst found that, in abnormal embryos showing a single (median) optic cup, only one lens developed and that at a point opposite the cup. This strongly favored an influence exerted by the cup on the overlying ectoderm.

Spemann's Classical Experiments

This paper by Herbst fired Spemann's enthusiasm, and in the same year he demonstrated that the epidermis showed no change if the eye rudiment was destroyed. He suggested that proof of the correlation could be obtained if the optic cup was brought into contact with a foreign part of the epidermis, either by transplanting the optic cup or the epidermis overlying it. W. H. Lewis performed these experiments satisfactorily in 1904. During the next 6 years Spemann published his experiments on the eye and also his technique and instruments for "microsurgery." It was shown that practically any part of the epidermis could form a lens if it was activated by some influence in the optic cup.

Spemann then experimented on the amphibian gastrula, the early embryo consisting of undifferentiated cells forming a hollow sphere, with a mouth (the blastopore) opening to the exterior. He frequently transplanted minute pieces of the gastrula from one area of its surface to another, and he always found—with one exception—that the transplants developed according to their new positions. The exception was a transplant from the upper lip of the blastopore, which in its new position developed into a small secondary embryo. In 1918 Spemann thought that the whole of the secondary embryo was formed by the implanted material, so that the ectoderm (upper layer) of the implant formed the medullary plate (subsequently forming the central nervous system), and the lower layer developed into the notochord and muscular system. He concluded therefore that the blastopore region was already differentiated at that stage, while all other cells in the gastrula were still undifferentiated.

Further work then led Spemann to think that possibly the primitive nervous system of the secondary embryo was formed by induction from the ectoderm of the host tissue. To decide the point it was necessary to distinguish implanted tissue from host tissue. Until then his transplants had been from one part to another of the same embryo, but in 1921 he decided that the answer lay in using two embryos, of the same age but of different species. In 1924 Spemann and Hilde Mangold published their results. For the implant and the host they used respectively gastrulas of the newts *Triton cristatus* (almost colorless) and *Triton taeniatus* (highly pigmented). Implant and host cells were thus easily distinguished. In innumerable experiments they found that the graft disappeared below the gastrula surface to form the mesodermal elements (notochord and muscles) of the secondary embryo. Above it the ectoderm of the host was induced to form, from host material, the neural tube of the secondary embryo.

Organizer Effect

From these "heteroplastic transplants" Spemann concluded that the upper lip of the blastopore, when brought into contact with other cells of the gastrula, could exert an influence to induce them to become differentiated to form a medullary plate. This influence he called an "organizer." In all vertebrate embryos it is the first step in the series of differentiations that result in the fully formed fetus. He therefore termed the influence of the blastopore lip the "primary organizer." The formation of the optic cup being a sequel to this action, he called the organizer in the optic cup a "secondary organizer." Further development is due to chains of induction by successive orders of organizers. Spemann believed that the action of the organizer was transferred by a chemical substance; but he, and other scientists such as Joseph Needham and C. H. Waddington, succeeded only partially in identifying it.

Spemann was awarded the Nobel Prize in 1935, and he received many other honors, including the title of *Geheimrat* (Privy Councilor). He died at Freiburg on Sept. 9, 1941.

Further Reading

There is a biography of Spemann in *Nobel Lectures, Physiology or Medicine, 1922-1941* (1965), which also includes his Nobel Lecture. For his work see his *Embryonic Development and Induction* (1938); see also C. H. Waddington, *The Nature of Life* (1961), and J. Needham, *Biochemistry and Morphogenesis* (1942). □

Herbert Spencer

Herbert Spencer (1820-1903) was an English philosopher, scientist, engineer, and political economist. In his day his works were important in popularizing the concept of evolution and played an important part in the development of economics, political science, biology, and philosophy.

Herbert Spencer was born in Derby on April 27, 1820. His childhood, described in *An Autobiography* (1904), reflected the attitudes of a family which was known on both sides to include religious nonconformists, social critics, and rebels. His father, a teacher, had been a Wesleyan, but he separated himself from organized religion as he did from political and social authority. Spencer's father and an uncle saw that he received a highly individualized education that emphasized the family traditions of dissent and independence of thought. He was particularly instructed in the study of nature and the fundamentals of science, neglecting such traditional subjects as history.

Spencer initially followed up the scientific interests encouraged by his father and studied engineering. For a few years, until 1841, he practiced the profession of civil engineer as an employee of the London and Birmingham Railway. His interest in evolution is said to have arisen from the examination of fossils that came from the rail-road cuts.

Spencer left the railroad to take up a literary career and to follow up some of his scientific interests. He began by contributing to *The Non-Conformist,* writing a series of letters called *The Proper Sphere of Government.* This was his first major work and contained his basic concepts of individualism and laissez-faire, which were to be later developed more fully in his *Social Statics* (1850) and other works. Especially stressed were the right of the individual and the ideal of noninterference on the part of the state. He also foreshadowed some of his later ideas on evolution and spoke of society as an individual organism.

A System of Evolution

The concept of organic evolution was elaborated fully for the first time in his famous essay "The Developmental Hypothesis," published in the *Leader* in 1852. In a series of articles and writings Spencer gradually refined his concept of organic and inorganic evolution and popularized the term itself. Particularly in "Progress: Its Law and Cause," an essay published in 1857, he extended the idea of evolutionary progress to human society as well as to the animal and physical worlds. All nature moves from the simple to the complex. This fundamental law is seen in the evolution of human society as it is seen in the geological transformation of the earth and in the origin and development of plant and animal species.

Natural selection, as described by Charles Darwin in the *Origin of Species,* published in 1859, completed Spencer's evolutionary system by providing the mechanism by which organic evolution occurred. Spencer enthusiastically elaborated on Darwin's process of natural selection, applying it to human society, and made his own contribution in the notion of "survival of the fittest." From the beginning Spencer applied his harsh dictum to human society, races, and the state—judging them in the process: "If they are sufficiently complete to live, they do live, and it is well they should live. If they are not sufficiently complete to live, they die, and it is best they should die."

Spencer systematically tried to establish the basis of a scientific study of education, psychology, sociology, and ethics from an evolutionary point of view. Although many of his specific ideas are no longer fashionable, Spencer went a long way in helping to establish the separate existence of sociology as a social science. His idea of evolutionary progress, from the simple to the complex, provided a conceptual framework that was productive and that justifies granting to him the title father of comparative sociology. His views concerning a science of sociology are elaborated in two major works, *Descriptive Sociology* (published in 17 volumes, 1873-1934) and *The Study of Sociology* (1873).

Spencer was particularly influential in the United States until the turn of the century. According to William Graham Sumner, who used *The Study of Sociology* as a text in the first sociology course offered in an American university, it was Spencer's work which established sociology as a separate, legitimate field in its own right. Spencer's demand that historians present the "natural history of society," in order to furnish data for a comparative sociology, is also credited with inspiring James Harvey Robinson and the others involved in the writing of the New History in the United States.

Economic Theories

Social philosophy in the latter part of the 19th century in the United States was dominated by Spencer. His ideas of laissez-faire and the survival of the fittest by natural selection fitted very well into an age of rapid expansion and ruthless business competition. Spencer provided businessmen with the reassuring notion that what they were doing was not just ruthless self-interest but was a natural law operating in nature and human society. Not only was competition in harmony with nature, but it was also in the interest of the general welfare and progress. Social Darwinism, or Spencerism, became a total view of life which justified opposition to social reform on the basis that reform interfered with the operation of the natural law of survival of the fittest.

Spencer visited the United States in 1882 and was much impressed by what he observed on a triumphal tour. He prophetically saw in the industrial might of the United States the seeds of world power. He admired the American industrialists and became a close friend of the great industrialist and steel baron Andrew Carnegie.

By the 1880s and 1890s Spencer had become a universally recognized philosopher and scientist. His books were published widely, and his ideas commanded a great deal of respect and attention. His *Principles of Biology* was a standard text at Oxford. At Harvard, William James used his *Principles of Psychology* as a textbook.

Although some of Spencer's more extreme formulations of laissez-faire were abandoned fairly rapidly, even in the United States, he will continue to exert an influence as long as competition, the profit motive, and individualism are held up as positive social values. His indirect influence on psychology, sociology, and history is too strong to be denied, even when his philosophical system as a whole has been discarded. He is a giant in the intellectual history of the 19th century.

Spencer spent his last years continuing his work and avoiding the honors and positions that were offered to him by a long list of colleges and universities. He died at Brighton on Dec. 8, 1903.

Further Reading

By far the best source on Spencer's life, education, and the development of his major ideas is his own *An Autobiography* (2 vols., 1904). Two of the more reliable and critical biographical works are Josiah Royce, *Herbert Spencer: An Estimate and Review* (1904), and Hugh Elliot, *Herbert Spencer* (1917). For a careful study of Spencer's impact upon American intellectual history see Richard Hofstadter, *Social Darwinism in American Thought* (1944; rev. ed. 1955). Recommended for general historical background are Ernest Barker, *Political Thought in England, 1848-1914* (1915; 2d ed. 1963), and William James Durant, *The Story of Philosophy* (1926; 2d ed. 1967).

Additional Sources

Hudson, William Henry, *An introduction to the philosophy of Herbert Spencer: with a biographical sketch,* New York: Haskell House Publishers, 1974.

Kennedy, James Gettier, *Herbert Spencer,* Boston: Twayne Publishers, 1978.

Thomson, J. Arthur (John Arthur), *Herbert Spencer,* New York: AMS Press, 1976.

Turner, Jonathan H., *Herbert Spencer: a renewed appreciation,* Beverly Hills, Calif.: Sage Publications, 1985. □

Stephen Harold Spender

Sir Stephen Harold Spender (1909-1995), poet, critic, translator, travel writer, and English man of letters, first came to prominence as a poet of social protest in the 1930s.

Stephen Spender was born February 28, 1909, the son of well-to-do, accomplished parents. His father, Edward Harold Spender, was himself a novelist and journalist. Stephen attended the University College School and then matriculated at University College, Oxford, where he became active in both literary and political circles, editing university poetry anthologies and debating current issues while forging his own poetic style.

Spender was of the first generation for whom World War I had ceased to be an important symbolic experience (as it had been for such writers as Aldous Huxley and Evelyn Waugh). For him, rather, it was the economic and political dislocations which followed—labor unrest; rising unemployment, especially after 1929; the upsurge of Fascist-Nazi totalitarianism—which fired a lively imagination from the first, both poetic and critical. Although he had a long and creative career, continuing in productivity well after World War II, Spender will probably best be remembered as part of a twin spearhead of English social protest (with his friend W. H. Auden) of the 1930s. Other poets in this group included C. Day Lewis and Louis MacNeice.

The poetry of these young poets tended at first to be too precious, marred and obscured by an excessively private imagery, but Spender's deep sympathies with ordinary people enabled him to simplify his expression for a more direct communication in *Poems* (1933), the first significant collection of his work. Here, in "Without That Once Clear Aim," he lamented that "on men's buried lives there falls no light." The ideal affirmed was a democratic socialist one:

No spirit seek here rest. But this: No man
Shall hunger: Man shall spend equally.
("Not Palaces, An Era's Crown")

Spender praised the concept of a collective industrialism: the owner-worker, joyously contributing his labor as part of a meaningful community:

They think how one life hums, revolves and toils,
One cog in a golden singing hive.
("The Funeral," 1934)

With the development of a growing, menacing fascism on the European continent during the 1930s Spender's industrial images, in protest, became enriched by the addition of those from modern warfare. (Spender spent considerable time in Germany during these years.) The dictator's ticking bomb explodes, silencing the heartbeat of a civilian child:

The timed, exploding heart that breaks
The loved and little hearts.
("The Bombed Happiness," 1939).

For Spender, the most important political event during these years was the Spanish Civil War (1936-1939). Along with many of his generation, he saw this conflict as a dress rehearsal of the titanic conflict between democracy and totalitarianism which was to culminate almost immediately afterward in World War II. Partisanship for the Republican side in Spain, against the eventually triumphant General Franco, inspired Spender's poetry. Some of his best work from this time was collected as *Poems for Spain* (1939). Earlier, in the same vein of politically radical expression, are *Vienna* (1934), a long didactic poem, and *Trial of a Judge* (1937), a verse play. As a critic defending the imaginative writer's social role Spender made a significant prose statement in *The Destructive Element* (1934).

At the end of the 1930s, when the nature of Stalinist rule had become more evident—especially after the Stalin-Hitler pact of 1939—Spender became disillusioned with Russian Communism (this process having begun with a falling out at a writers' conference in Spain two years earlier). Especially eloquent testimony of this disenchantment with Communism can be found in Spender's essay in *The God That Failed* (1949).

During World War II Spender served as a fireman in the National Fire Service. An earlier marriage, to Frances Marie Inez in 1936, had been dissolved, and in 1941 he married again, to Natasha Litvin, with whom he had a son and daughter. After the war Spender worked for the United Nations, serving as counsellor for the Section on Letters of the U.N. Economic and Scientific Committee (UNESCO) in 1947.

Another aspect of this writer's contribution was his editorial work. He co-edited *Horizon* magazine from 1939 to 1941; later he held the same post with *Encounter* (1953-1967). As a latter day romantic and social critic, it was not surprising that Spender was drawn to sympathetic figures from the past: he edited a book of Shelley's verse (1971) and a volume of D. H. Lawrence's writings (1973). Two years later he paid homage to an old friend by editing *W. H. Auden: A Tribute.*

A particularly happy aspect of Spender's postwar life and work was the numerous positions held on the New World side of the Atlantic. He held the Elliston Chair of Poetry, University of Cincinnati (1953) and the Beckman Professorship, University of California (1959); he was poetry consultant to the Library of Congress (1965); he gave the Clark Lectures on Poetry in Cambridge, Massachusetts, in 1966 and the Mellon Lectures in Washington, D.C. in 1968. Other teaching positions in the United States were at Cornell College, Vanderbilt, Connecticut, Loyola, and Northwestern. He was an honorary member of the American Academy of Arts and Letters. In England, Spender was professor of English, University College, London University (1970-1977). He took this position after becoming interested in the student radicalism of the 1960s, which he analyzed in *The Year of the Young Rebels* (1969). Spender was awarded the Queen's Gold Medal for Poetry in 1971 and was knighted in 1982.

He was also a translator of note. Spender's rendition of Shiller's *Mary Stuart* appeared in 1958 and was produced at the Old Vic Theater three years later. He translated the entire Oedipus Trilogy in 1983, staged by the Oxford Playhouse that year. *World Within World,* his autobiography, appeared in 1951; *Learning Laughter,* a record of his travels in Israel, the next year. Throughout this entire postwar period Spender continued to write poetry, collections of this verse appearing from time to time: *Poems of Dedication* (1946); *Collected Poems* (1954); *Selected Poems* (1965); *The Generous Days* (1971); *Collected Poems 1978-1985* (1985); and *Dolphins* (1994).

In 1993, Spender filed a plagiarism lawsuit regarding a novel which he asserted was taken from his own autobiography. The suit was settled in 1994. He died in London on July 17, 1995.

Further Reading

Other books by Spender included a reminiscence, *The Thirties and After* (1978); *China Diary* (1982), another travel piece (with David Hockney); an anthology of short fiction, *Engaged in Writing* (1958); and a collection of his journals 1939-1983 (published in 1986). D.E.S. Maxwell analyzed Spender's poetry in the context of his early contemporaries in *Poets of the Thirties* (1969). W.D. Jacobs wrote a shorter critical assessment, "The Moderate Poetical Success of Stephen Spender," in *College English* 17 (1956). The poet, Joseph Brodsky, wrote a lengthy commentary, *English Lessons from Stephen Spender* for the *New Yorker* (1996), in which he reminisced about his 23-year friendship with Spender. □

Philipp Jakob Spener

The German theologian Philipp Jakob Spener (1635-1705) tried to infuse a new spirit into the formal Lutheranism of the 17th century. He is consequently regarded as the father of the movement called Pietism, which resulted from his efforts.

Philipp Spener was born at Rappoltsweiler in Upper Alsace on Jan. 23, 1635. His first university experience began at Strassburg, where he studied history, philosophy, philology, and theology from 1651 to 1659. He then continued his studies at Basel, Tübingen, and Geneva. At Geneva he became familiar with Reformed teachings and, although a Lutheran, seems to have been much impressed with them. In 1663 he returned to Strassburg, where he was made an assistant preacher. Three years later he was called to Frankfurt am Main to become the senior pastor of the Lutheran church. In this position Spener attempted to raise the level of the religious life of the congregation by meaningful reforms. He strengthened Church discipline, emphasized training of the young and use of the catechism, and established the practice of confirmation.

In order to aid in the program of spiritual reformation, Spener arranged small gatherings of interested churchgoers in private houses for cultivation of Christian life by study of the Bible, prayer, and discussion of Sunday sermons. From the name of these groups, the *collegia pietatis,* is derived the name of this movement for the restoration of a spiritualized Christian faith—namely, Pietism. While in Frankfurt, Spener also provided the theoretical foundation for the Pietist movement in his book *Pia desideria.* In this work, published in 1675, he spelled out some measures which he considered important for the improvement of the life of the Church. These included use of prayer instead of arguments to settle religious differences, Bible study, improved education of theologians, more stress on a personal and practical Christianity, meaningful and practical sermons instead of learned declamations, and more control of the Church by the congregation instead of ministers and princes.

Spener's criticism of the established Lutheran Church led to much opposition from Church and state officials, who accused him of being untrue to Lutheran doctrines. As a result, in 1686, Spener accepted the invitation of the elector of Saxony to become the chief court chaplain at Dresden, then a very important position in German Lutheranism. Spener soon found himself in conflict with the clergy in Saxony, the theological faculties at Leipzig and Wittenberg, and the elector himself. Consequently, Spener gladly accepted an invitation to become provost of the Church of St. Nicholas in Berlin in 1691. Here he was soundly supported by Elector Frederick III of Brandenburg-Prussia and, as a result, exercised much influence over Church conditions. Because of his ascendancy, the new University of Halle, founded by the elector in 1694, became the cultural center of Pietism. Although his later years were marred by bitter controversies with his opponents, he continued to preach conscientiously until his death on Feb. 5, 1705.

Further Reading

A short but informative biographical sketch of Spener can be found in F. Ernest Stoeffler, *The Rise of Evangelical Pietism* (1965). The Pietistic movement in western Germany and Spener's relationship to it are discussed in Paulus Scharpff, *History of Evangelism* (trans. 1966). See also Gerald R. Cragg, *The Church and the Age of Reason, 1648-1789* (1960), and John P. Dolan, *History of the Reformation* (1964). □

Oswald Spengler

The German philosopher Oswald Spengler (1880-1936) is famous for his *Decline of the West.* He held that civilizations, like biological organisms, pass through a determinable life cycle and that the modern West was approaching the end of such a cycle.

Oswald Spengler was born at Blankenburg am Harz on May 29, 1880, the son of a postal official. Although mathematics and natural science were his major subjects at the University of Halle, he received his doctorate for a dissertation on Heraclitus in 1904. After recovering from a nervous breakdown in 1905-1906, Spengler taught in secondary schools until a small inheritance from his mother allowed him in 1911 to move to Munich as a private scholar. Spengler never married.

Exempted from military service because of poor health, Spengler wrote the major part of *The Decline of the West* during the war years under conditions of great economic hardship. The first volume appeared in 1918, the second in 1922.

The Decline of the West is an impassioned attack against the values of modern post-Enlightenment civilization—of intellect, social equality, peace, and urban culture. Borrowing from the anti-intellectualist tradition of German conservative thought, he rejects the possibility of scientific history. History is never "correct" or "erroneous" but only "deep" or "shallow." Human history as such has no meaning. In place of the traditional Europeocentric conception of a linear history of human civilization, Spengler offers a "Copernican" view of history in which Western (or Faustian) civilization since A.D. 1000 constitutes merely one of eight historic cultures. Each culture has a wholly individual way of looking at the world which permeates all its cultural expressions, even its mathematics and science. No understanding is possible between men of different cultures. Nevertheless, the similarity of the life processes of birth, growth, and decay makes possible a "comparative morphology of history." A culture is born out of the historyless mass of humanity the moment "a great soul awakens."

All cultures in their beginning are aristocratic, dominated by the heroic estates of the warrior noble and priest. The maturation of a culture is a process of intellectualization, urbanization, social leveling, and the growing domination of money. In this process the creative essence of the culture is progressively lost until the culture, now become shallow, gives way to a soulless megalopolitan "civilization." In the West this transformation occurred in the 19th century. Democracy, behind which hides the dictatorship of money, then opens the path to Caesarism and the dissolution of the culture into total formlessness. Democracy, parliamentarism, egalitarianism, proletarian socialism, pacifism, humanitarianism, and attempts at "world improvement" and social reform, Spengler concluded, were all symptoms of a decadent civilization. The moral to be learned from world history is that "ever in History it is life and life only—race quality, the triumph of the will to power" which counts.

The Decline of the West catapulted Spengler to fame. He became a political prophet for disillusioned German national conservatives stunned by defeat in World War I. Beginning with his essay "Prussianism and Socialism" (1920), in which he sought to lay the basis for a new revolutionary conservatism which identified socialism with service to the state, Spengler devoted himself to free-lance political writings against the Weimar Republic, which he detested. Despite his strident opposition to democracy, his idealization of authoritarian and military values, and his almost paranoid racism, he regarded the Nazis with mistrust. As an elitist, he was repelled by their demagogic appeal.

The Nazis regarded Spengler as one of their intellectual forerunners. Adolf Hitler received him in 1933. Nevertheless the critical tone of his *Hour of Decision* (1933) resulted in the condemnation of the book and the man by the Nazis. Spengler died on May 8, 1936.

Further Reading

The best English-language introduction to Spengler's thought is H. Stuart Hughes, *Oswald Spengler: A Critical Estimate* (1952). Other books include E. H. Goddard and P. A. Gibbons, *Civilisation or Civilisations: An Essay on the Spenglerian Philosophy of History* (1926), and William Harlan Hale, *Challenge to Defeat: Modern Man in Goethe's World and Spengler's Century* (1932). An extensive discussion of Spengler is in Pitirim A. Sorokin, *Modern Historical and Social Philosophies* (1963; first published in 1950 as *Social Philosophies of an Age of Crisis*), and a brief chapter on him is in Erich Heller, *The Disinherited Mind* (1952).

Additional Sources

Fischer, Klaus P., *History and prophecy: Oswald Spengler and The decline of the West,* Durham, N.C.: Moore Pub. Co., 1977.

Hughes, H. Stuart (Henry Stuart), *Oswald Spengler,* New Brunswick, U.S.A.: Transaction Publishers, 1992. □

Edmund Spenser

Edmund Spenser (ca. 1552-1599) ranks as the foremost English poet of the 16th century. Famous as the author of the unfinished epic poem *The Faerie*

***Queene,* he is the poet of an ordered yet passionate Elizabethan world.**

Edmund Spenser was a man of his times, and his work reflects the religious and humanistic ideals as well as the intense but critical patriotism of Elizabethan England. His contributions to English literature—in the form of a heightened and enlarged poetic vocabulary, a charming and flexible verse style, and a rich fusing of the philosophic and literary currents of the English Renaissance—entitle him to a rank not far removed from that of William Shakespeare and John Milton.

Spenser was the son of a London tailor, but his family seems to have had its origins in Lancashire. The poet was admitted to the newly founded Merchant Taylors' School about 1561 as a "poor scholar." There his headmaster was the patriotic and scholarly Richard Mulcaster, author of several books on the improvement of the English language. The curriculum at Mulcaster's school included Latin, Greek, and Hebrew; music and drama were stressed; and the English language was also a subject of study—then a novelty.

In 1569 Spenser went to Cambridge, where he entered Pembroke College as a sizar (a student who earns his tuition by acting as a servant to wealthy students). He spent 7 years at the university, gaining his bachelor of arts degree in 1572 and his master of arts degree in 1576. Records of the period reveal that Spenser's health was poor but that he had an excellent reputation as a student. He studied Italian, French, Latin, and Greek; read widely in classical literature and in the poetry of the modern languages; and authored some Latin verse. At Cambridge, Spenser came to know Gabriel Harvey, lecturer in rhetoric and man of letters, who proved to be a faithful and long-term friend and adviser. Among his fellow students were Lancelot Andrewes, later a learned theologian and bishop, and Edward Kirke, a future member of Spenser's poetic circle.

Diplomatic Activities

After completing his studies, Spenser seems to have spent some time in Lancashire, possibly with his relatives. This sojourn in the north increased his familiarity with the northern dialect, which later exerted a considerable influence on the language of *The Shepherd's Calendar.* Shortly after leaving the university, Spenser also spent time in the service of the powerful Earl of Leicester, regarded as the head of the Puritan faction in the government. Some hints in Spenser's correspondence and in his published works suggest that he may have traveled as an envoy for Leicester to Ireland, Spain, France, and Italy. In any case, in 1578 Spenser was named secretary to the former master of his college, John Young, now bishop of Rochester. Spenser probably composed the major part of *The Shepherd's Calendar* at Rochester.

By Easter 1579, Spenser was back in London, in daily contact with Gabriel Harvey and Edward Kirke, and much involved in literary discussions, especially those about Harvey's project of introducing classical Latin and Greek nonrhyming meters into English verse. Probably at this time Spenser made the acquaintance of Sir Philip Sidney, the poet and courtier.

The Shepherd's Calendar

By now Spenser had written a considerable quantity of poetry, but he had published nothing. Upon the advice of his friends he decided to make his literary debut with *The Shepherd's Calendar* (1579), which he dedicated to Sidney. This work, consisting of 12 pastoral eclogues, uses the pastoral conventions as vehicles of allegorical and satirical allusions to contemporary political and religious problems, as well as to the poet's own life and loves. Spenser in this work shows the influence of such classical and foreign models as Virgil, Jacopo Sannazaro, and Clément Marot, but he also acknowledges a considerable debt to Geoffrey Chaucer and to other English sources. The work is especially important for its naturalization in English of a variety of poetic forms—dirges, complaints, paeans—and for its attempt to enrich the English poetic vocabulary through foreign borrowings and through the use of archaic and dialect words.

Allusions and letters from this period of Spenser's life show that he was busy with a variety of literary projects. Spenser was already at work on *The Faerie Queene* and on a number of the poems eventually collected in his *Complaints.* Meanwhile, he was also studying law and hoping for a place in diplomacy or civil service. His efforts were rewarded in 1580, when, through the influence of the Earl of Leicester, he was named secretary to Lord Grey, the new lord deputy of Ireland. That same year Spenser accompanied Grey to Dublin.

Ireland was to remain Spenser's home for the rest of his life. Grey was recalled in 1582, but Spenser remained, holding a variety of government posts and participating at first in the cultivated life of Dublin Anglo-Irish society. Increasingly, however, the poet's financial interests and administrative duties took him to Munster (southern Ireland). In 1586 he leased Kilcolman Castle in County Cork, and he lived there after 1588.

The Faerie Queene

For some years Spenser had been working on *The Faerie Queene.* By 1589 three books were complete. When Sir Walter Raleigh visited the poet in the early autumn of that year, Raleigh was so impressed with this work that he took Spenser with him back to England. In November 1589 they arrived in London; and early in the following year the first three books of Spenser's most famous work were published, with an elaborate dedication to Queen Elizabeth I. Spenser's ambition was to write the great English epic. His plan was to compose 12 books, each concerned with one of the 12 moral virtues as classified by Aristotle. Each of these virtues was to be embodied in a knight. Thus the poem would combine elements of the romance of chivalry, the handbook of manners and morals, and the national epic.

The Faerie Queene can be read on various levels: as an allegory of the eternal struggle between good and evil in every form; as a poetic statement of an ethical system; and as a historical allegory portraying the struggle between the pure Protestant traditions of England and the manifold threats of England's Roman Catholic neighbors. Allusions to contemporary political and religious controversies are numerous. The philosophy underlying Spenser's epic combines three strands. Platonism, which (as seen through the eyes of Renaissance commentators) stressed the harmony between love and beauty on the human and divine levels, is blended with the less imaginative and more concrete Aristotelianism of the scholastic tradition, with its disciplined analysis and careful reflection on the moral life, which Spenser had probably learned in school. These two elements are penetrated by a strong Calvinistic Christianity, stressing man's weakness, his need for a strict moral life, and the total dependence of humanity on the atonement of Christ. Thus the work itself is a fine example of an attempted synthesis between the traditions of Christianity and those of classical antiquity that characterizes all the best productions of the Renaissance.

Spenser's style is distinctively his own: he attempted to create a remote, old-fashioned atmosphere through the use of archaic diction, strange neologisms, and forgotten terms of chivalry. Yet, because of his clear and straightforward syntax, few of his passages are obscure, even to a modern reader. For his verse form, Spenser created a new stanza which has since been often imitated in English literature. It consists of nine lines, eight lines of iambic pentameter concluding with an Alexandrine (iambic hexameter), arranged in the rhyme scheme ababbcbcc. The harmonious and orderly movement of this Spenserian stanza fits the slow, ample, and cumulative pace of the whole work.

The publication of the first three books of *The Faerie Queene* met with much acclaim. Spenser remained in London for more than a year, enjoying fame and making many friends; but he did not succeed in attaining a sufficiently lucrative post in the home government. Spenser was now by no means a poor man, and his wealth was increased by the substantial annual pension that was the reward for his poem. But in courtly circles he was a decidedly minor figure. In 1591, probably in the spring, Spenser returned to Ireland, famous but disappointed.

The *Complaints*

Before leaving London, Spenser prepared for publication a collection of minor poems under the title of *Complaints.* A hint of Spenser's mood at this time might have been expressed in this volume's subtitle: *Sundry Small Poems of the World's Vanity.* However, most of its contents had been composed years before. The most important of the poems in this volume is "Mother Hubberd's Tale," a satire that had gained notoriety a decade earlier. This poem satirizes Queen Elizabeth's projected marriage to the French Catholic Duke of Alençon—a prospect that had greatly alarmed the Puritan faction at court. The work is important not only because of its political implications but also because of its express and able use of medieval English sources and conventions. Its plot is drawn from William Caxton's translation of the French beast allegory *Renard the Fox,* and its verse and narrative style betray clear Chaucerian influences.

Also included in the *Complaints* were revised and enlarged versions of Spenser's youthful translations from Joachim du Bellay and Petrarch; a poem entitled "The Ruins of Time" celebrating the family of the Earl of Leicester and Sir Philip Sidney; and another called "Tears of the Muses," which lamented the poverty and neglect suffered by poets. Somewhat lighter in tone is "Virgil's Gnat," a free translation of the *Culex,* a humorous ancient poem attributed to Virgil. In this work Spenser tells allegorically of his discomfiture resulting from the adverse political reactions to "Mother Hubberd's Tale." "Muiopotmus; or, The Fate of the Butterfly" was probably an entirely new work written during Spenser's stay in London.

Other Works

Late in 1591, after returning to Ireland, Spenser wrote the greater part of "Colin Clout's Come Home Again," an idealized poetic autobiography dedicated to Raleigh. It ranks as one of Spenser's most charming poems, narrating in the allegorical terms of the then popular pastoral convention the story of his reception in London and his impressions (mostly negative) of court life. Shortly afterward Spenser compiled a collection of poems dedicated to the memory of Sir Philip Sidney. To this collection he contributed the first elegy, "Astrophel." This collection was published together with "Colin Clout's Come Home Again" in 1595.

Meanwhile, Spenser was courting Elizabeth Boyle, an Anglo-Irish woman of a well-connected family. They were married on June 11, 1594. His sonnet sequence "Amoretti" and his "Epithalamion" together form an imaginatively enhanced poetic chronicle of his courtship and marriage. Some of the "Amoretti" sonnets were probably written earlier, but Spenser intended this collection to represent the fluctuations and the emotions of his love for his wife. Written in frequent imitation of such French and Italian sonneteers as Philippe Desportes and Torquato Tasso, Spenser's sonnets, representing one of the most popular poetic forms of his period, are graceful if not great. However, his "Epithalamion" is generally acknowledged to rank among the greatest love poems in English. In this poem a lover's passion blends with a deeply religious sensibility, calling upon both classical myth and medieval legend to create an intricate pattern of allusions and evocations.

Late in 1595 Spenser returned to London, again staying for more than a year. He published during this visit to the capital three more books of *The Faerie Queene;* the "Prothalamion," written to celebrate the double wedding of two daughters of the Earl of Worcester; and the "Four Hymns," poems that concern his Platonic conceptions of love and beauty. During this stay he seems also to have composed or at least to have revised his *View of the Present State of Ireland,* a prose tract in which he defended the policies of his earlier patron, Lord Grey, in dealing with rebellious Irish subjects and in which he proposed a program for first subjugating the Irish people and then reforming their government on the model of the English administrative system. Surprisingly, this pamphlet, so in tune with much of governmental opinion, did not receive permission for publication during Spenser's lifetime and was first published in 1633.

Final Period

Spenser seems to have returned to Ireland sometime in 1597 and to have resumed his work on *The Faerie Queene.* Two more cantos of a succeeding book were published posthumously in 1609, but most of what he wrote in these years has been lost. Spenser was temporarily without political office, but in September 1598 he was named sheriff of Cork. He had hardly taken control of that office before, in October of the same year, the Earl of Tyrone's rebellion, a generalized revolt of the Irish people, broke out in Munster. Spenser's castle was burned, and the poet was forced to flee with his family, which now included four young children.

In December the provincial governor sent Spenser as a messenger to Queen Elizabeth. He arrived in the capital at the end of 1598, much weakened by the hardships of the preceding months. Spenser presented his messages to the Queen, together with a personal statement reiterating his position on the Irish question. Soon after his arrival he became seriously ill, and he died in London on Jan. 16, 1599. Spenser was buried near other poets in Westminster Abbey.

Further Reading

The Works of Edmund Spenser: A Variorum Edition was edited by Edwin Greenlaw and others (9 vols., 1932-1949). A smaller edition of the *Poetical Works of Edmund Spenser* was edited by J. C. Smith and Ernest de Sélincourt (3 vols., 1909-1910). H. S. V. Jones, *A Spenser Handbook* (1930), is still useful as a general introduction to the works. A thorough biographical study by Alexander C. Judson, *The Life of Edmund Spenser* (1945), was published as volume 3 of the Variorum Edition.

Important critical studies include Leicester Bradner, *Edmund Spenser and the Faerie Queene* (1948); William Nelson, *The Poetry of Edmund Spenser* (1963); and C. S. Lewis, *Spenser's Images of Life,* edited by Alastair Fowler (1967). Helpful studies of particular aspects of Spenser's work are Edwin Greenlaw, *Studies in Spenser's Historical Allegory* (1932); C. S. Lewis, *The Allegory of Love* (1936); Ruth Mohl, *Studies in Spenser, Milton, and the Theory of Monarchy* (1949); and E. M. W. Tillyard, *The English Epic and Its Background* (1954). A work on Spenser's reputation through the centuries is William R. Mueller, ed., *Spenser's Critics* (1959). Waldo F. McNeir and Foster Provost compiled an *Annotated Bibliography of Edmund Spenser, 1937-1960* (1962).

For general background see S. T. Bindoff, *Tudor England* (1951); Hallet Smith, *Elizabethan Poetry* (1952); and C. S. Lewis, *English Literature in the Sixteenth Century: Excluding Drama* (1954).

Additional Sources

Rambuss, Richard, *Spenser's secret career,* Cambridge England; New York: Cambridge University Press, 1993.

Shire, Helena Mennie, *A preface to Spenser,* London; New York: Longman, 1978.

Spenser and Ireland: an interdisciplinary perspective, Cork: Cork University Press, 1989.

Spenser's life and the subject of biography, Amherst: University of Massachusetts Press, 1996.

Tuckwell, William, *Spenser,* Norwood, Pa.: Norwood Editions, 1975.

Waller, Gary F. (Gary Fredric), *Edmund Spenser: a literary life,* New York: St. Martin's Press, 1994. □

Count Mikhail Mikhailovich Speranski

The Russian statesman and reformer Count Mikhail Mikhailovich Speranski (1772-1839) is known for his governmental reforms, based on the doctrine of separation of legislative, executive, and judicial powers.

Mikhail Speranski was born on Jan. 12, 1772, to a village priest and received his education in a theological seminary. He taught in an ecclesiastical institution but soon transferred to the civil service. Because of his personality, intelligence, and capacity for work, as well as the patronage of the princes Alexander and Alexis Kurakin and Count Victor Kochubey, Speranski had a rapid rise and a brilliant career. At the request of the minister of interior, Kochubey, in 1803 Speranski prepared one of his first drafts of constitutional reforms. In 1808 Czar Alexander I appointed him assistant minister of justice and in 1810 secretary of state. Speranski's influence with Alexander was very great from 1809 to the beginning of 1812. A contemporary wrote: "M. Speranski is the emperor's factotum, a kind of minister of innovations. He is not allied with anyone. His influence extends to everything."

Government Reforms

In 1808 Alexander commissioned Speranski to draft a plan of constitutional reform. Speranski recommended reforms of the government based on the doctrine of separation of powers—legislative, executive, and judicial—all of them emanating from the czar. The right to vote was to be given to property owners. However, his reforms overlooked the emancipation of the serfs and excluded the servile population from participation in government. Although he leaned toward the eventual abolition of serfdom, he nevertheless realized the obstacles facing this action.

Alexander rejected his recommendations of separation of powers, but he accepted his idea of a state council, one suffering from obvious limitations. It was an appointed body; its decisions were not binding on the emperor; and it was denied the prerogative of legislative initiative. But from the point of view of constitutional theory the creation of a state council was significant. For the first time in Russian history a clear-cut distinction was made between a law, that is, a measure examined by the state council and approved by the czar, and an executive order.

Czar Alexander approved Speranski's legislation of 1810-1811 for the reconstruction of the executive departments. Speranski was also responsible for raising the civil service standards: an appointment to positions above a specified rank was conditional on the passing of a stiff examination or the holding of a college degree.

Speranski's financial program was very unpopular because it called for the suspension of issues of paper currency, the curtailment of expenditures, increases in direct and indirect taxation, and an emergency tax on incomes derived from landed estates. It is safe to conclude that these infringements of the privileges of the bureaucratic and landowning classes, rather than any organized opposition to Speranski's constitutional views, hastened his fall from power during the second half of Alexander's reign.

In 1826, however, Speranski was appointed by Nicholas I to a committee formed to codify Russian law. Under his able leadership the committee's work was fruitful in 1833 with the publication of the complete collection of the laws of the Russian Empire, which contained 35,993 enactments. Count Speranski died in St. Petersburg on Feb. 23, 1839.

Further Reading

Marc Raeff, *Michael Speransky: Statesman of Imperial Russia, 1772-1839* (1957), is an excellent biography and the only one in English. Additional material on Speranski is in Allen McConnell, *Tsar Alexander I: Paternalist Reformer* (1970).

Additional Sources

Raeff, Marc, *Michael Speransky, statesman of imperial Russia, 1772-1839*, Westport, Conn.: Hyperion Press, 1979. □

Elmer A. Sperry

The technical achievements of Elmer A. Sperry (1860-1930) made him one of the most prolific and capable inventors in American history. Like other successful inventors, he knew how to mix finance, engineering, and management to develop unique inventions into commercial products.

Born on October 21, 1860, Elmer Sperry grew up near the small town of Cortland, New York. His mother died a few hours after his birth, and he was raised in a devout Baptist home by an aunt and his grandparents. Sperry showed a natural aptitude and interest in mechanical things during his youth.

While in high school Sperry did well in science and drawing. The drawing skills would prove important in his later years as he visualized and communicated to others his many inventions. Sperry constantly read in the technical library of the local Young Men's Christian Association (YMCA), and during a YMCA-sponsored trip to the 1876 Centennial Exposition in Philadelphia he was exposed to the inventions and technical achievements of booming America.

Arc Light System

At the age of 19 Sperry invented an electrical regulator, part of an electric light circuit. Helped by the Cortland Wagon Company, which had a strong engineering department, Sperry acquired the tools, supplies, assistants, legal assistance, and other institutional support he needed to develop his invention into a complete arc light system. He moved to Chicago and, backed by money from hometown Cortland and from investors in Chicago whom he met through the Baptist community, he started selling his system there.

Although Sperry's system was technically capable, it could not compete with its better-financed and better-run competitors. His company failed after about five years. But the particular needs of arc light systems had forced him to learn about automatic controls and feedback systems, on which he spent much of his future career.

Commitment to Research and Development

Through his wife, the former Zula Goodman of Chicago, Sperry had access to many people with money to invest and positions of power and influence. A good speaker, a charming person, and an enthusiastic booster of his projects—in addition to being technically gifted—Sperry had acquired the skills he needed for a consistently successful career.

To avoid the routine, day-to-day engineering required by his first company, Sperry created a new company devoted to research and development. The new company let Sperry do what he did best: finding new ideas, directing the building of working models, and looking for problems that his inventions could solve. Sperry deliberately avoided manufacturing, selling to other companies the production rights to his inventions.

For the next 20 years, Sperry entered a series of new fields just as they began rapid development. He chose fields that were attracting lots of financial investors, which provided the money needed for his inventive activity. He worked in the fields of electric light and power, mining machinery, electric traction (streetcars), automobiles, batteries, and industrial chemistry.

Before inventing, Sperry always carefully analyzed earlier work to identify critical problems and to find existing inventions to which he could add his own expertise. Sperry concentrated on electrically-based inventions, such as electrical machinery and electrochemistry. In each field, he tried to solve critical problems that were holding it back.

The Gyro

In 1907 Sperry became interested in using gyroscopes to provide stability to moving vehicles. Other inventors had designed "gyrostabilizers" that could help ships avoid the rolling caused by waves and wind. If you try to tip a spinning gyroscope, it will turn to one side in a predictable way—called "precession." In the same way, the force of a spinning gyrostabilizer pushed a rolling ship in the opposite direction from the push of the waves. Sperry invented a motion sensor, a motor to amplify the effect of the sensor on the gyroscope, and an automatic feedback and control system. All worked together to make a much more effective gyrostabilizer.

Because he had analyzed the market for gyrostabilizers, Sperry was able to put himself in the right place at the right time. The U.S. Navy was building new, mammoth battleships that would be unusable without some form of sophisticated stabilizer. The Navy provided critical development support for Sperry, including the men, materials, and money needed to build models and experiment with ever-larger gyros. Navy support replaced the private financial investment on which Sperry had relied in the past.

In 1910 Sperry created a company to specialize in gyroscopes. Over the next 20 years Sperry and his company invented, among other things, a gyrocompass, a stabilizer for airplanes, gunfire control systems, and an automatic pilot for planes. Like so many of his earlier inventions, these often relied on automatic control and feedback systems.

Although Sperry had become well-known in technical circles, World War I placed him high in the public's awareness and provided him with much material success. His inventions were used heavily by the British, Russian, German, and American navies. As the second most famous inventor in America (after Thomas Edison), he served on the Naval Consulting Board and directed some of its major projects. He won many international awards, helped create the American Institute of Electrical Engineers and the American Electro-Chemical Society, and was a leading member of many other professional organizations.

During the final decade of Sperry's life he further developed many of the systems he had started during the World War I years, adapting them to peacetime uses (such as taking a searchlight invented for antiaircraft warfare and using it as a beacon for the new airmail service). Sperry did not invent in isolation, but tried to take existing devices and methods and apply them to new areas. This was one of the critical elements of his style as an inventor and researcher.

By the time of his death in 1930, Sperry met regularly with Rockefellers, presidents, ambassadors, and others. His biographer has called him "the father of automatic feedback and control systems."

Further Reading

The most complete treatment of Sperry—including many technical details about his work—is in Thomas Parke Hughes, *Elmer Sperry: Inventor and Engineer* (1971). For a more contemporary perspective, see the obituary which appeared in J. C. Hunsaker, "Biographical Memoir of Elmer Ambrose Sperry, 1860-1930," *Biographical Memoirs, National Academy of Sciences* 28 (1954).

Additional Sources

Hughes, Thomas Parke, *Science and the instrument-maker: Michelson, Sperry, and the speed of light,* Washington: Smithsonian Institution Press: for sale by the Supt. of Docs., U.S. Govt. Print. Off., 1976. □

Steven Spielberg

Steven Spielberg (born 1947) was one of the wealthiest and most powerful movie-makers in Hollywood. The director of such elaborate fantasies as *Close Encounters of the Third Kind* and *E.T., The Extra-Terrestrial,* he was regarded as a man who understood the pulse of America as it would like to see itself.

Steven Spielberg was born in Cincinnati, Ohio, on December 18, 1947. He was the oldest of four children. His father, Arnold, was an electrical engineer who worked in what was then a newly emerging field: computers. His mother, Leah, had been a concert pianist. The only boy among his siblings, he was doted on by his mother and three sisters; therefore, it is not surprising that he grew up having his own way and feeling that he was the center of the universe. Indulged throughout his childhood at home, he was not so treated at school where he displayed little enthusiasm for his studies and was rewarded with average grades at best.

Like many American families of the postwar years, the Spielbergs moved frequently. Spielberg's father was an executive and corporate promotions caused the family to move to Haddonfield, New Jersey; then to suburban Phoenix; and thereafter to the emerging bedroom communities of what would be known as "Silicon Valley" near San Jose, California. The original name of this region, "The Land of the Heart's Desire," provided an interesting counterpoint when one considers the sorts of movies that Spielberg would make, for it seems as though almost all of his films, even ones that he does not actually direct, were a combination of technical wizardry (highlighted by gadgets and toys) and wee-ripened sentimentality.

Learning to Use a Camera

The first film that Spielberg recalled seeing in a movie theater was *The Greatest Show on Earth,* a spectacular 1952 circus epic directed by Cecil B. De Mille. Little Steven began shooting 8mm films with his family's home movie camera. He recorded camping trips and other such cinematic ephemera but soon grew dissatisfied with them. He began to film narrative movies, attempting to actually set up shots with different angles and primitive special effects. By the time he was 12 years old he actually filmed a movie from a script using a cast of actors. At age 13 he made "Escape to Nowhere," which lasted 40 minutes and was about a war. He grew increasingly ambitious and three years later filmed a feature-length science fiction movie which he entitled "Firelight." This movie was 140 minutes long and had a complex plot involving astronomers, eerie lights in the evening sky, and a rather violent encounter with some aliens.

At this point in his life Spielberg may have had cause to regret his, at best, lackadaisical efforts toward schoolwork. His poor grades in high school prevented him from entering the University of Southern California or U.C.L.A. He was

accepted at the California State College at Long Beach, from which he was graduated in 1970 with a B.A. in English. In lieu of a film program, he went to the movies and saw every film that he could. He also cajoled his way past the guards at Universal Studios and watched major projects being filmed.

He continued to make films, though, and prepared a short subject, "Amblin'," which he later used at the 1969 Atlanta film festival. It also won an award at the Venice film festival, and got him a seven-year contract at the studio whose gates he used to crash—Universal. Studio executives had been so impressed with "Amblin'," a simple story about a boy and girl who hitchhike from the Mojave Desert to the ocean, that they released it with *Love Story,* a major hit of 1970.

Spielberg began his career as a professional by directing several episodes for television programs that were being shot at Universal. First among these was the pilot episode of Rod Serling's *Night Gallery,* which starred the legendary Hollywood star Joan Crawford. He went on to direct episodes of *Marcus Welby, M.D., Owen Marshall, Columbo, The Psychiatrists,* and *The Name of the Game.* The first "movie" that he directed professionally was a film made for television, *Duel;* it was released theatrically in Europe and Japan to rave reviews. Here in the United States it was generally regarded as one of the greatest movies ever made for television. It starred Dennis Weaver as a hapless suburbanite involved in a deadly battle of wits with an 18-wheeler. It was a variation on the "heart of darkness" theme, which showed how easily the smooth skin of civilization peeled off, revealing the human savage underneath.

Spielberg made two other movies for television, *Something Evil* and *Savage.* By that time he was being courted by every studio in Hollywood due to the phenomenal success of *Duel.* The made-for-television movie, which had cost only $350,000 to produce, grossed between $5,000,000 and $6,000,000 in its foreign releases. Spielberg was not overwhelmed, however, by the quality of the properties that he was offered and withdrew from the studio mainstream for a year in order to develop a project of his own.

Directing What He Wanted

What he came up with was *The Sugarland Express,* a drama about a gritty and determined, if somewhat dim, woman, played by Goldie Hawn, who browbeats her husband into breaking out of jail in order that they may kidnap their baby from its foster home. A spectacular car chase ensues after the couple steals a police cruiser. The film was a critical success but a commercial failure. Nonetheless, it led to the breakthrough film of Spielberg's career, the spectacularly successful *Jaws* (1974).

Even by this stage of his career, certain salient features had emerged. *Jaws* would spiral hopelessly over budget. There would be enormous technical difficulties, which Spielberg would overcome brilliantly, but at a staggering cost. The studio executives would later lament that they had a property which no one knew how to film. The haphazard approach and free and easy financing would be a hallmark of film making through the rest of the decade. Directors reigned supreme as several studios went into bankruptcy. Spielberg felt quite comfortable in this atmosphere wherein his every whim was dutifully responded to as though it were holy writ.

Despite bringing in *Jaws* at 100 percent *over* its $3,500,000 budget, Spielberg became Hollywood's anointed director of the moment when the film grossed over $60,000,000 in its first month. The film was as popular with critics as with the public. It was an unabashed triumph. Spielberg was now in a position to do whatever he wanted. He embarked on a film whose subject had obsessed him since his childhood.

Close Encounters of the Third Kind was perhaps his most personal film. It dealt with the heroic efforts of average middle-Americans to make contact with visitors from another planet. For all of its staggering special effects, its power derived from its strongly human base, its exploration of what people will do when they find that they have the opportunity to make their dreams come true. Perhaps no other film of Spielberg's had come so close to capturing the wonder that he seems to be seeking in the medium that Orson Welles called "the ribbon of a dream."

The next film that he directed, *1941,* was an overblown disaster. It was a case study in overdoing the "erector-set" approach to filmmaking. Despite the accusation of the most important film critic in America, the *New Yorker*'s Pauline Kael, that he was responsible for infantilizing American culture, Steven Spielberg was responsible both for many successful films of his own direction and for the creation of dozens of film projects. He helped to define the film of the post-studio era, in that he was one of the young directors responsible for the power of the director in our time.

The "Indiana Jones" trilogy (1981-1989), *E.T.: The Extra-Terrestrial* (1982), and *The Color Purple* (1985) exemplified Spielberg at his best and worst. The "Indiana Jones" pictures mixed a loving affection for old-time movie serials with a contemporary sensibility—one with an unfortunately high tolerance for excessive violence, however. *Indiana Jones and the Temple of Doom* (1984), the second installment of the series, necessitated the creation of a new rating code, "PG-13," due to its gratuitous gore. *E.T.* (1982) swept the nation, and its catchphrase, "Phone home!" was heard around the world. Less successful was the reception of *The Color Purple.* Spielberg was accused of patronizing African-Americans and prettifying rural Southern poverty. He attempted to defend himself by citing his fidelity to Alice Walker's novel, but this tack satisfied neither his film detractors nor the fans of the book.

Spielberg was a great favorite among his fellow directors, such as George Lucas and John Landis. He stood by the latter when he was implicated in the deaths of three cast members of *Twilight Zone: The Movie,* a film which Spielberg also worked on. In 1991 Spielberg directed a big-budget movie about Peter Pan, called *Hook.* As Spielberg continued to direct and produce he seemed to grow more and more powerful. The fact that he was never satisfactorily recognized by the Motion Picture Academy of Arts and Sciences seemed less and less relevant. He was able to make any film that he wanted and seemed totally uninterested in courting the public or the critics. The tremendous wealth that he gained from making his films as he saw fit would seem to be his justification.

The subject of one of the longest and most intensive pre-release hypefests in film history, was the media blitz surrounding Spielberg's 1993 mega-hit *Jurassic Park*. The story centered around a present day theme park that featured genetically engineered dinosaurs as the main attraction. The movie was a box office and home theater success. Spielberg released the sequel entitled *The Lost World: Jurassic Park* in 1997.

Perhaps the most poignant of Spielberg's movies was the black and white, critically-acclaimed *Schindler's List*. Released in late 1993, the movie was filmed in Poland, and was a lengthy, Holocaust drama. It was a fictionalized account of real life instances in which an amoral German businessman had a change of heart and saved the lives of thousands of Jews who worked in his factory. The movie brought respect to Spielberg as both a film maker and an individual. The picture won the 1993 Best Picture Academy Award and Spielberg won for Best Director.

Spielberg married actress Amy Irving in 1985. They had one son, Max, before a 1989 divorce. He later married actress Kate Capshaw, and they had five children.

Further Reading

There was a critical account of Spielberg's cinematic product by Donald R. Mott and Cheryl M. Saunders, *Steven Spielberg* (1986). It was an overwritten and unsatisfactory text. One would do better to consult *The Steven Spielberg Story* by Tony Crawley (1984). Chapters on Spielberg appeared in *The Movie Brats* by Michael Pye and Linda Myles (1979) and in *A Cinema of Loneliness* by Robert P. Kolker (1988). Spielberg was also discussed in Stephen Farber's *Outrageous Conduct: Art, Ego, and the "Twilight Zone" Case* (1988). For an in-depth portrayal of Spielberg, see "Peter Pan Grows Up" by Richard Corliss and Jeffery Ressner in *Time* (May 19, 1997) magazine. □

Baruch Spinoza

The Dutch philosopher Baruch Spinoza (1632-1677) ranks as a major thinker in the rationalist tradition, and his *Ethics* is a classic of Western philosophy. In his writings the crucial issues of metaphysics are exemplified more clearly than in any thinker since Plato.

Baruch, or Benedict, Spinoza was born on Nov. 24, 1632, in Amsterdam, where his family had settled after fleeing religious persecution in Portugal. His grandfather, Abraham, was the acknowledged leader of the Jewish community, and his father was a successful merchant and active in civic affairs. Michael Spinoza had three children, of whom the future philosopher was the only son. Spinoza's mother died when he was 6, and his father and one sister died by the time he was in his early 20s. Little is precisely known about his early education except that biblical and Talmudic texts were studied at the synagogue school and that the young Spinoza showed a facility for languages and eventually mastered Spanish, Portuguese, Dutch, Hebrew, Latin, Greek, and German. In 1656 Spinoza was expelled by his congregation on charges of atheism. The edict asked for God to curse him and warned "that none may speak with him by word of mouth, nor by writing, nor show any favor to him, nor be under one roof with him." The philosopher responded with calm detachment and Christianized his name to Benedict.

Teacher and Lens Grinder

For the next 4 years Spinoza worked as a teacher in a private academy in Amsterdam run by Francis van den Ende, a former Jesuit, a doctor, and a political activist. His future interests in mathematics, physics, and politics supposedly stem from this period. From 1660 to 1663 he lived near Leiden among a free religious sect who called themselves Collegiants, and there he wrote *Principles of Cartesianism, Short Treatise on God, Man and His Well-being,* and the first book of *Ethics*.

Spinoza then moved to a suburb of The Hague, where he worked as a lens grinder. The *Ethics* was completed between 1670 and 1675. In 1670 he anonymously published his *Theological-Political Treatise*. In addition to these not very extensive writings, Spinoza conducted a large correspondence with various scientists and philosophers. Two of the most important were Henry Oldenburg, the first secretary of the British Royal Society, and Gottfried Wilhelm von Leibniz, who visited him in 1676. Three years previ-

ously Spinoza had declined a professorship at the University of Heidelberg in order to preserve his "freedom of philosophizing." The same intellectual integrity is seen also in a letter to a former student who accused Spinoza of intellectual presumption. While acknowledging that he had not written the best philosophy, he stated "I do know that I think the true one." Spinoza died in The Hague on Feb. 20, 1677, of consumption aggravated by inhaling dust while polishing lenses.

Origins of Rationalism

Rationalism is the name ascribed to a movement of thought that originated in the 17th century, and it is usually associated with the names of René Descartes, Leibniz, and Spinoza. The point of departure for all rationalists is subjectivity: a discovery of the philosophic implications of the person with a heightened sense of his uniqueness, his inviolability, and, above all, the power of knowledge. Descartes began his career as a highly original mathematical physicist. He generalized from his conception of the method of mathematical reasoning and believed that its proper application might guarantee local certitude in all areas of knowledge. The justification of his theory of reasoning led Descartes to several metaphysical commitments concerning the nature of reality.

In simplest terms, Descartes maintained that God was a supreme rationalist who had created an orderly universe that could be known by following the clear and distinct ideas of reason. In order to avoid the determinist and irreligious implications of such a conception of the universe, Descartes separated the mind as a free spiritual power from the physical world of determined mechanical relations. With this step a set of contradictory dualisms between subject and object, thought and extension, spirit and nature, God and world, and freedom and necessity were bequeathed to philosophy. The only work that Spinoza published under his own name was *René Descartes' Principles of Philosophy* (1663), and although the book was mainly expository, he could not forbear pointing out that Descartes's errors resulted from his inability to follow out the metaphysical implications of the logic of rationalism, especially with respect to the notion of substance.

Spinoza's *Ethics*

Spinoza's *Ethics* consists of five books. Oddly enough, the first is about God and the meaning of substance. The second book deals with the mind and knowledge. The third, fourth, and fifth books seem concerned with topics usually associated with ethical discussions: the passions, human enslavement to the emotions, and finally human freedom by virtue of intellect. Hence the central concern of the treatise is to move from a consideration of God to the realization of human freedom by an analysis of knowledge and passion and their conflict. Thus, for Spinoza, an ethic that studies the purpose of life is simultaneously a metaphysic, a theory of knowledge, and a psychology of human nature.

This is made clearer if one is familiar with an earlier and unpublished work, which he called *On the Improvement of the Understanding.* In a highly personal manner Spinoza began by saying that he resolved to seek true happiness and joy "after experience had taught me that all the usual surroundings of social life are vain and futile." Men everywhere esteem "riches, fame, and the pleasures of sense," but their pursuit seems to diminish rather than to enhance men's lives through frustration or overindulgence. The only remedy for the wretchedness of life is to improve or literally "cure" the mind. Man's attitude toward reality is equal to his sense of what is true and important. In a striking passage Spinoza wrote: "All these evils seem to have arisen from the fact that happiness or unhappiness is made wholly to depend on the quality of the object which we love. When a thing is not loved, no quarrels will arise concerning it—no sadness will be felt if it perishes—no envy if it is possessed by another—no fear, no hatred, in short no disturbances of the mind."

Nature of Reality

Because of man's "mixed perceptions" and confused knowledge, he desires perishable objects. To see reality clearly, man would need an exact knowledge of himself and of general nature in order to understand the extent to which they can be modified in the search for lasting happiness. This can be accomplished only by a more and more inclusive understanding of reality. Imagine, Spinoza wrote to a correspondent, a parasite living in the bloodstream being asked to describe its environment. From its perspective each drop of blood would seem to be separate. But, in truth, the action of each independent drop can be understood only as a determined part of a larger system. And this system, in turn, is a small part of a larger whole. The ultimate aim of philosophic knowledge is what Spinoza called a "synoptic intuition" of all reality as a deductive system. And this is why the *Ethics* begins with a consideration of God as substance. In Spinoza's view the task is not so much to explain God as to understand what it means to be a man.

The *Ethics* is subtitled *More Geometrics,* and its geometrical method, using axioms, postulates, and definitions to prove its propositions, relates to the content as well as to the technique of exposition. As a rationalist, Spinoza aimed at nothing less than total certitude, and the clearest way was to utilize deductive reasoning. But the content of the system is such that the truth of each proposition depends, in part, on its necessary connection with the others.

The first book of the *Ethics* draws out the implications of one of the central assumptions of the Western metaphysical tradition: that the intrinsic order of nature is an effect of an ordering mind, God. The startling conclusion that Spinoza draws is that the words nature, substance, and God are interchangeable. There can be only one such being, who is self-caused and of which everything else is an effect. An effect manifests only what it has received from its cause, and the causal principle can only communicate what it is. With these axioms Spinoza argued monism, or the oneness of reality, in proposition after proposition; and the effect that, if God is *causa sui* and first cause (and if there is no such cause, then there is no reality), such an entity must be understood as an "absolutely infinite being." In logic, at least, there cannot be an infinite being and something else.

Thus all finite existence must be rooted in a necessary existent, and there is one system of nature in which all limited things begin or cease inevitably according to causal sequences and interdependencies. Spinoza adopted a scholastic distinction to express the only conceivable differences that can be predicated of infinite being: *Natura Naturans* is nature as active or is God as the free cause that brings all things to pass according to necessary principles, and *Natura Naturata* is nature as passive or existent at any one moment.

Nature and Origin of the Mind

Spinoza's argument is conducted a priori, or without appeal to experience, and its truth or falsity rests on what the concept of substance entails logically. Accordingly, God exists by definition, or negatively one must posit a reason for the nonexistence of such a being and again only God would suffice. For him, reason is identical with cause, and the only legitimate distinctions that one can impute to the reason of the universe is to logically separate that which causes and that which is caused.

The second book of *Ethics* examines the nature and origin of the mind. An infinite substance possesses infinite attributes, but the mind perceives only two: thought and extension. Yet the relation between mind and matter is not dualistic but one of identity, for "thinking substance and extended substance is one and the same substance comprehended now under this and now under that attribute." To understand this doctrine, sometimes referred to as "psychophysical parallelism," the mind must overcome its reliance on sense knowledge ("opinion") and even advance beyond scientific understanding ("adequate ideas") of cause-and-effect relations to a synoptic vision ("intuition") of the complete system of reality. In this perspective the mind of man is an individually existing modification of infinite intelligence, the body is the object of that idea, and the two are like different sides of a coin.

With this understanding of man's place in nature, Spinoza took up the questions of moral life. Action occurs when an individual is the cause of his own conduct, and a passion when he is the partial cause. Virtue is the power of knowing how to act in accord with nature, whereas men suffer in proportion to the number of inadequate ideas that they have.

The essence of man is the struggle "to preserve in being." Adequate ideas replace passions, rational self-control supplants the impotence of desires. The issue is life itself: whether one is ensnared in "human bondage" as a prey to the whims of desire or external persons or objects, or one achieves the freedom that Spinoza calls "blessedness" and that is virtue's own reward. He was enough of a psychologist to see that ultimately passions can be overcome only by stronger passions. Thus in cultivating a knowledge and intellectual love of God man comes to know himself and to experience a freedom from external restraint.

Further Reading

For studies of Spinoza consult the following works: F. Pollock, *Spinoza: His Life and Philosophy* (1880); E. Caird, *Spinoza* (1902); H. A. Wolfson, *The Philosophy of Spinoza* (1934); and S. Hampshire, *Spinoza* (1956). ☐

Benjamin Spock

Benjamin Spock (born 1903), pediatrician and political activist, was most noted for his authorship of *Baby and Child Care,* which significantly changed predominant attitudes toward the raising of infants and children.

Benjamin McLane Spock was born on May 2, 1903, in New Haven, Connecticut, the oldest child in a large, strict New England family. His family was so strict that in his 82nd year he would still be saying "I love to dance in order to liberate myself from my puritanical upbringing." Educated at private preparatory schools, he attended Yale from 1921 to 1925, majoring in English literature. He was a member of the racing crew that represented the United States in the 1924 Olympic Games at Paris, finishing 300 feet ahead of its nearest rival. He began medical school at Yale in 1925, and transferring to Columbia University's College of Physicians and Surgeons in 1927. He had, by this time, married Jane Davenport Cheney, whom he had met after a Yale-Harvard boat race.

Spock had decided well before starting his medical studies that he would "work with children, who have their whole lives ahead of them" and so, upon taking his M.D. degree in 1929 and serving his general internship at the prestigious Presbyterian Hospital, he specialized in pediatrics at a small hospital crowded with children in New York's Hell's Kitchen area. Believing that pediatricians at that time were focusing too much on the physical side of child development, he took up a residency in psychiatry as well.

Between 1933 and 1944 Spock practiced pediatric medicine while at the same time teaching pediatrics at Cornell Medical College and consulting in pediatric psychiatry for the New York City Health Department. On a summer vacation in 1943 he began to write his most famous book, *Baby and Child Care,* and he continued to work on it from 1944 to 1946 while serving as a medical officer in the Navy.

The book sharply broke with the authoritarian tone and rigorous instructions found in earlier generations of babycare books, most of which said to feed infants on a strict schedule and not to pick them up when they cried. Spock, who spent ten years trying to reconcile his psychoanalytic training with what mothers were telling him about their children, told his readers "You know more than you think you do. . . . Don't be afraid to trust your own common sense. . . . Take it easy, trust your own instincts, and follow the directions that your doctor gives you." The response was overwhelming. *Baby and Child Care* rapidly became America's all-time best-seller except for Shakespeare and the Bible; by 1976 it had also eclipsed Shakespeare.

After his discharge from the Navy, Spock became associated with the famous Mayo Clinic (1947-1951) and then became a professor of child development at the University of Pittsburgh (1951-1955) and at Case Western Reserve (1955-1967). His political activism began during this period, growing logically out of his concern for children. A healthy environment for growing children, he believed, included a radiation-free atmosphere to breathe and so, in 1962, he became co-chairman of SANE, an organization dedicated to stopping nuclear bomb tests in the Earth's atmosphere. The following year, in which the United States did ratify a nuclear test ban treaty, he campaigned for Medicare, incurring the wrath of the American Medical Association, many of whose members were already suspicious of a colleague who wrote advice columns for the *Ladies Home Journal* and *Redbook* instead of writing technical monographs for the medical journals.

Spock was an early opponent of the Indo-China war; his view on that subject, *Dr. Spock on Vietnam,* appeared in 1968. As the war escalated, so did antiwar protest, in which Spock participated vigorously, marching and demonstrating with militant youths who had not yet been born when he began his medical career. Conservatives accused him of having *created,* in large measure, the youth protest movement of the 1960s. Ignoring his many admonitions to parents in *Baby and Child Care* that they should "set limits," his political opponents accused Spock of teaching "permissiveness," by which they claimed an entire generation of American youth had been raised and ruined. In vain Spock pointed out that similar student protests were happening in Third World countries where his book enjoyed no circulation and were not happening in Western Europe countries where it sold well.

Because of his own strict personal upbringing and his acute moral sense, Spock may have intended a lot less when he told parents to "relax" than some of them realized. In 1968 he revised *Baby and Child Care* to make his intentions more clear, now cautioning his readers "Don't be afraid that your children will dislike you" if you set those limits and enforce them. Nevertheless, that 1968 edition showed a 50 percent drop in sales, mainly, Spock thought, because of his stand on Vietnam.

On May 20, 1968, along with several other leading war protesters, Spock was put on trial for conspiracy. The charge was that he had counseled young people to resist the draft. In the superheated political atmosphere of the times he was convicted, but on appeal the verdict was set aside on a technicality. Some indignant readers returned their well-thumbed copies of *Baby and Child Care* in order to prevent further undermining of their children's patriotism. To many other readers, however, the government's indictment of the baby doctor seemed rather like prosecuting Santa Claus.

Two books published in 1970, *Decent and Indecent: Our Personal and Political Behavior* and *A Teenager's Guide to Life and Love,* made it clear that Spock was a good deal more of a traditional moralist than either his friends or his enemies were aware. He had been driven into the antiwar and other reform movements by the same imperious, old-fashioned conscience that propelled some of his opponents in exactly the opposite direction.

At the same time the doctor showed himself capable of growing and changing. His social activism mutated into socialism, and in 1972 he ran for president on the People's Party ticket. He was also capable of admitting a mistake. Badgered for some five years on the lecture platform by feminist objectors to the gender-role stereotypes of fathers and mothers as they appeared in *Baby and Child Care,* he eventually conceded that much of what they had said had been right. In 1976, 30 years after its initial publication, Spock brought out a third version of the famous book, deleting material he himself termed "sexist" and calling for greater sharing by fathers in the parental role. He also yielded 45 percent of subsequent book royalties in the divorce settlement that year with his wife, who contended she had done much more of the work on *Baby and Child Care* than he had ever acknowledged. Spock was remarried in the fall of 1976 to Mary Morgan Councille.

Formally retired in 1967, Spock was the kind of person who in spirit never really retires. Contemplating his own death as his health began to fail in the 1980s, he wrote in 1985 (at the age of 82) that he did not want any lugubrious funeral tunes played over him: "My ideal would be the New Orleans black funeral, in which friends snake-dance through the streets to the music of a jazz band." He had chronic bronchitis and suffered a stroke in 1989. His wife, Mary, collaborated with Spock on his autobiography, *Spock on Spock,* which was published in 1989. His book *A Better World for Our Children* was published in 1994 and explored the relationship between child-rearing and politics.

According to an article in the *Detroit Free Press,* Spock said "When I look at our society and think of the millions of children exposed every day to its harmful effects, I am near despair."

Further Reading

Lynn Z. Bloom wrote a perceptive study entitled *Doctor Spock: Biography of A Conservative Radical* (1972). Doctor Spock's own writings, in addition to the famous baby book, included *Decent and Indecent* and *A Teenager's Guide to Life and Love,* both published in 1970. An account of the conspiracy trial was Jessica Mitford's *The Trial of Dr. Spock, the Rev. William Sloane Coffin, Jr., Michael Ferber, Mitchell Goodman, and Marcus Raskin* (1969). Changes in Spock's thinking after the Bloom book appeared were briefly noted in M.A. Kellogg's "Updating Dr. Spock," *Newsweek* (March 3, 1976). A mellow valedictory statement by Spock, "A Way To Say Farewell," appeared in *Parade Magazine* on March 10, 1985.

See also *Spock on Parenting* (1988); *Spock on Spock: A Memoir of Growing Up With the Century* (1989); and *A Better World for Our Children* (National Press Books, 1994). □

Alexander Spotswood

Alexander Spotswood (1676-1740), a British soldier, became lieutenant governor of the Virginia colony in America.

Alexander Spotswood was born in Tangier, Morocco, where his father was an army physician at an English military base. The family had been prominent in Scottish public life and strongly committed to the Stuarts during the Puritan Revolution. Young Spotswood entered the army in 1693, serving an initial term as ensign in Flanders. During the War of the Spanish Succession he was appointed lieutenant quartermaster general, later rising to the rank of lieutenant colonel. Wounded in the Battle of Blenheim, he was a prisoner of war until the Duke of Marlborough negotiated his release. On June 23, 1710, he assumed the office of lieutenant governor of Virginia.

The appointment of a British officer to serve in the Colonies was in keeping with the pattern of royal appointments in the mid-18th century. Furthermore, at a time when the colonial assemblies were taking a dominant role, a governor with military experience seemed well inclined to reassert the power of the mother country.

Spotswood impressed Virginians with his ability during 12 years as lieutenant governor. From the first he tried to develop effective means of limiting land grants to actual settlers (not speculators); successfully explored the West; wanted to control tobacco production; offered protection against pirates; reformed the systems of finance, local courts, and the militia; and sought unsuccessfully to impose his will on the Anglican Church in Virginia. Spotswood's emphasis on the power of his office, however, combined with his lack of tact in dealing with members of the council, provoked bitter quarrels and demands for his removal. He was relieved of office in 1722. Ironically, at the end, he understood that the need for harmony with the assembly would mean substantial concessions to colonial autonomy.

As a civilian, Spotswood cast his lot with Virginia. He became a Virginia gentleman, retiring to his estates at Germanna, where he produced iron and looked after the 85,027 acres he had acquired in Spotsylvania County. Returning to England in 1724, he married Anne Butler Brayne, with whom he had four children. He was appointed deputy postmaster general for the American colonies in 1730. He received the position of major general at the onset of the war with Spain in 1739. He died in Annapolis, Md., on June 7, 1740, while preparing to take part in the conflict.

Further Reading

The best study of Spotswood is by Leonidas Dodson, *Alexander Spotswood: Governor of Colonial Virginia, 1710-1722* (1932). A recent brief but shallow biography is Walter Havighurst, *Alexander Spotswood: Portrait of a Governor* (1967). Both are supplemented by an appraisal of Spotswood's controversies with the legislature in Richard L. Morton, *Colonial Virginia* (2 vols., 1960). □

Frank Julian Sprague

Frank Julian Sprague (1857-1934), American electrical engineer and inventor, successfully used electricity to power vehicles and is known today as the

father of electric traction. His electric motor-driven streetcar revolutionized urban transportation.

Frank Sprague was born in Milford, Conn., on July 25, 1857, but lived with relatives in North Adams, Mass., after 1866. Demonstrating an aptitude for science and mathematics, Sprague secured an appointment to the U.S. Naval Academy in 1874. After graduation in 1878 and 2 years at sea, he pursued his electrical studies relentlessly.

In 1883 Sprague joined Thomas Edison's staff, but he soon withdrew to form the Sprague Electric Railway and Motor Company. He soon marketed a "constant speed" motor for industrial use but subcontracted its manufacture so he could devote himself to electric traction development. In 1887 he contracted to electrify a new street railway in Richmond, Va. Despite having to devise the entire system from scratch, he completed the installation of a 12-mile, 40-car system in 1888.

By 1890 over 200 electric street railways were in operation or under construction; half of these used Sprague equipment, and 90 percent of them were based on his patents. In 1890 the Edison General Electric Company acquired Sprague's business, but Sprague left to establish the Sprague Electric Elevator Company. He developed and installed electric elevators in several New York buildings before selling out to the Otis Elevator Company.

Having worked out a system of multiple-unit control for elevators, Sprague sought to apply it to railways. He realized that trains made up of individually motorized cars controlled by a single operator had enormous advantages. His multiple-unit system, installed in Chicago in 1897-1898, was adopted generally for subway, elevated, and suburban service. Thus the basis for the modern rapid transit system was complete. Sprague continued to advance the application of electrical engineering. He worked on automatic railroad signaling and elevator control systems, and during World War I he served on the Naval Consulting Board.

Sprague was energetic and resourceful. He was an enthusiastic gardener and enjoyed art and music. Twice married, he was the father of four children. He received many professional honors before his death on Oct. 25, 1934.

Further Reading

Sources on Sprague's life are limited; Harold C. Passer's biographical sketch in William Miller, ed., *Men in Business* (1952), is the best available. Accounts of the development of electric traction can be found in the popularly written book by John Anderson Miller, *Fares, Please!* (1941), and the scholarly book by George W. Hilton and John F. Due, *The Electric Interurban Railways in America* (1960; rev. ed. 1969). □

Squanto

Squanto (1585?-1623) was the guide for many of the Pilgrim settlers of the Plymouth Colony.

Squanto is remembered as the interpreter, guide, and agricultural advisor who shepherded the Pilgrim settlers of Plymouth Colony through their precarious early existence in the New World and did more than anyone else to secure the survival of the settlement.

Squanto was a member of the Patuxet band of the Wampanoag tribe, which dominated the area in which the colonists eventually settled. He first enters written history in 1614, as one of 20 Patuxet Indians kidnapped by English explorer Thomas Hunt. Hunt carried his captives to Spain, where he sold them into slavery. Squanto, however, was one of a number who were rescued by Spanish friars, and he eventually made his way to England, where he next surfaced in the employ of John Slaney, whose interests extended to exploration in the New World. He sent Squanto along on an expedition to Newfoundland in 1617; there the Indian met explorer Thomas Dermer, with whom he returned to England the following year. Squanto's relation to Slaney and Dermer may have been in the nature of indentured servant; he may have hoped to earn his passage home. In any event, he traveled once again to the New World with Dermer in 1619, coming to rest in the Patuxet region of his birth.

In 1617, during Squanto's absence, a great epidemic—perhaps the plague—swept the Indian populations in the Massachusetts Bay region, and the Patuxet band was particularly hard hit. Indeed, they were virtually wiped out. Squanto returned to find the village of his youth abandoned.

Squanto (left)

He left Captain Dermer to go in search of survivors, but returned to his aid when Dermer ran afoul of hostile Indians. Squanto remained with Dermer until Dermer was mortally wounded in a skirmish with the Pokanoket Wampanoag. Squanto was then taken prisoner.

Some historians have theorized that when Squanto was dispatched in 1621 as emissary to the English settlers, he may have still been living with the Wampanoag as a captive. This would explain the later reports of antagonism between him and Massasoit, who had become Sagamore, or civil chief, of the Wampanoag confederation in the wake of the epidemic. It was Massasoit who sent Squanto to the English at Plymouth, Massachusetts, where they had settled on the former lands of the Patuxet in November of 1620.

The English—weakened from their journey, hungry, and ill—kept their distance from the Indians during the first winter of their residence; half of the Pilgrims died before spring. The Wampanoag, who had had mixed experiences with Europeans, watched the newcomers with a wary eye. In March, Massasoit felt the time was right to approach the English and sent Squanto and a companion to reassure them of the friendly intentions of the Indians. The two arranged for a conference between the English leaders and Massasoit. That meeting resulted in the historic treaty in which the Wampanoag and the English pledged mutual peace and friendship.

"Sent of God"

Squanto was sent to live with the English settlers. His guidance proved so indispensable to them that Plymouth Governor William Bradford was moved to declare him a "spetiall instrument sent of God for [their] good."

Squanto's role in introducing the English to neighboring tribes was particularly crucial. His extensive travels had provided him with unique qualifications as intermediary between the cultures. Thus it was possible for the colonists to establish vital trade relationships, thereby enabling them to secure seeds and other supplies necessary to life in New England, as well as animal pelts which they sent to England to repay investments and secure English goods.

Tradition has it that Squanto taught the English, most of whom had not been farmers in their native country, to plant Indian corn and other local vegetables, and to insure the success of the crop by the use of fish fertilizer. The English believed the practice of fertilizing with fish to be traditional among the Indians. In recent years, however, this has come into question among historians, some believing that Squanto learned the practice in Europe or in Newfoundland.

Steeped in Conflict

Squanto's career was not without controversy. There are reports that he sought to increase his status among the Indians by exaggerating his influence with the English and alarming neighboring Native American groups with reports that colonists kept a plague (he may have meant gunpowder) buried underground that could be released at any time. There is also evidence that he tried to undermine Massasoit's relationship with the English. A crisis developed in 1622 when Squanto perpetrated an elaborate ruse to try to convince the English that Massasoit was plotting with the hostile Narragansett tribe to destroy the Plymouth Colony and that an attack was imminent. The deception was quickly discovered; however, Massasoit was sufficiently incensed to demand Squanto's life. The Plymouth settlers were very angry with Squanto in the wake of the fiasco, even to the extent that Governor Bradford admitted to Massasoit that Squanto deserved death for his act of betrayal. It was a measure of the colonists' dependence on him that they nevertheless protected him from Massasoit's vengeance.

In November of 1623, with the arrival of additional English settlers who came ill-prepared for the approaching New England winter, Squanto guided an expedition from Plymouth to trade with Cape Cod Indians for corn. He fell ill with what William Bradford, who led the foray, described as an "Indianfever" and died within a few days. According to Bradford, as quoted by John H. Humins in *New England Quarterly,* the dying Squanto expressed his wish to "go to the Englishmen's God in Heaven" and "bequeathed his little property to his English friends, as remembrances of his love." Some observers, including Humins, contend that Squanto's legendary role as the Pilgrims' savior has been largely exaggerated. "His struggle for power with Massasoit . . . has not been adequately noted in histories about the period," noted Humins, "[and] in fact jeopardized the plantation's relationship with the Indians." However, Squanto remains a key figure in American folklore—and the classic symbol of Thanksgiving.

Further Reading

Salisbury, Neal, *Manitou and Providence: Indians, Europeans, and the Making of New England, 1500-1643,* New York, Oxford University Press, 1982.

Thacher, James, *History of the Town of Plymouth from its First Settlement in 1620, to the Present Time,* third edition, Yarmouthport, Massachusetts, Parnassus Imprints, 1972.

Vaughan, Alden T., *New England Frontier: Puritans and Indians, 1620-1675,* Boston, Little, Brown, 1965.

Ceci, Lynn, "Squanto and the Pilgrims," *Society,* 27, May/June 1990; 40-44.

Humins, John H., "Squanto and Massasoit: A Struggle for Power," *New England Quarterly,* 60, March 1987; 54-70. □

Ssu-ma Ch'ien

Ssu-ma Ch'ien (145-ca. 90 B.C.), who has been described as the "Grand Historian of China," held the office of T'ai-shih, or director of astrology, in the imperial government. He completed a draft history of mankind started by his father.

In his capacity as court official, Ssu-ma Ch'ien became involved in political rivalries. He defended Li Ling, an officer who had led a force of infantry against China's enemies in central Asia. Li Ling had been fighting at a great distance from his base and had been forced to surrender after a prolonged and gallant struggle. For espousing Li Ling's cause, Ssu-ma Ch'ien suffered disgrace and punishment by castration.

Earlier Histories

The work produced by Ssu-ma Ch'ien and his father, Ssu-ma T'an, constitutes China's first systematic history. It was written as a matter of private initiative. Before this time a number of works had been written which can be regarded as historical documents or chronicles, such as the *Shu-ching* (Book of Documents), the *Ch'un-ch'iu* (Spring and Autumn Annals), the *Tso chuan* (Tso's Commentary), and the *Kuo-yü* (Discourses of the States). By the time of Ssu-ma Ch'ien, some of these works were held in great repute, for instance, the *Shu-ching* and the *Ch'un-ch'iu.* These were said to have been selected or compiled by Confucius for didactic purposes and included accounts of solemn speeches or oaths taken by some of China's very early kings as well as chronological records of incidents that had occurred at some of the lesser courts established in China between 722 and 481 B.C. Some of the works included a highly varied content—the trivialities of court procedure, the observance of religious cults, and political, dynastic, and matrimonial intrigues.

In all these works there is no attempt at an ordered review of human development. The sense of chronology varies widely, and the treatment of and emphasis on different aspects are highly diverse. With the *Shih-chi,* or *Historical Records,* of Ssu-ma Ch'ien, a new type of purposeful record was evolved. Divided into 130 chapters, the work was designed as no less than a history of mankind from earliest times until the contemporary age. From the outset a contrast was drawn, implicitly and at times explicitly, between the Chinese, who were fortunate enough to enjoy life under the dispensation of the emperor, and those other mortals who lived beyond the pale of civilization as barbarians.

Owing partly to the nature of the source material available to Ssu-ma Ch'ien and partly to political, social, and dynastic differences, there is a very considerable variation in the *Shih-chi*'s treatment of China before the imperial period (before 221 B.C.) and during the Ch'in (221-207 B.C.) and Han (from 202 B.C.) dynasties. For the preimperial period Ssu-ma Ch'ien could draw on material of the type mentioned and on a number of works that have long since been lost; for the imperial period he was able to consult the records of the imperial administration, edicts issued from the throne, and reports submitted by officials. In addition, he had acquired considerable information during his own wanderings in China and from his personal observations.

Historical Records

The 130 chapters of the *Shih-chi* are divided into Annals of the Kings and Emperors (12 chapters), Tables (10), Treatises (8), Accounts of Certain Families (30), and Biographies (70). The Annals extend back to the reigns of sovereigns of the Shang-yin kingdom and before, and end with that of the contemporary Han emperor (Wu-ti). These chapters are written in a terse style, recording acts or utterances with which the emperor was personally concerned—edicts, acts of worship, the establishment of imperial consorts or heirs, military campaigns, the submission of foreigners, and reports of phenomena and rarities observed on earth and in the heavens. These events are arranged in strict chronological order, with precisely defined dating.

The Tables are set out in rows and columns indicating the succession of rulers (in the preimperial age) and of noblemen and officials (in the Han period), together with short notes on the circumstances in which a nobility or senior office was created, filled, vacated, or subjected to change. The eight Treatises are studies of subjects chosen for their overriding importance in the conduct of human and imperial affairs, for instance, ceremonials, music, state cults, calendars, economic balance, and waterways. These chapters include notes on the observation of events and accounts of the reaction of officials and their submissions and cover the practices of both the preimperial and the imperial ages.

The Accounts of Certain Families are concerned with the houses of the nobility and the rulers who played a prominent part in China's political history before its unification under one empire in 221 B.C. and trace the fortunes of those families during their political vicissitudes. The Biographies, which constitute over one-half of the entire work, are concerned with individuals of importance who influenced the development of the Han dynasty or took part in political events in the previous century or so. The subjects of the Biographies include members of the imperial family, statesmen, officials and men of letters, and military officers. In some cases two or more individuals are treated together in the same chapter, if their careers were similar or if their contributions to history were of the same type. In addition, some of these chapters are monographs that concern the growth and origins of foreign communities and their relations with China.

It is by no means clear on what sources Ssu-ma Ch'ien could draw for these chapters, but there are some obvious points at which his personal contribution is discernible. Appended at the end of many chapters are short appreciations in which an attempt is made to evaluate the subject of a biography or even an emperor; although the choice of subjects for treatment as biographies may have been partly affected by political considerations, the method of treatment—the combination of several persons together for comparison and the selection of material for inclusion—may be due to Ssu-ma Ch'ien's personal judgment. In addition, it is likely that in including the texts of certain earlier works such as the *Shuching* (Book of Documents), Ssu-ma Ch'ien deliberately simplified the linguistic style of the original in order to ease the task of his reader.

Strictly speaking the *Shih-chi* is not a "Dynastic History," insofar as it covers long periods of time before the creation of a single imperial dynasty and does not cover the complete period of the Han dynasty, which lasted for a century or so after Ssu-ma Ch'ien's death; and it remained for Pan Ku to compile a history which did treat the whole of this dynastic period. However, the form, treatment, and arrangement of the *Shih-chi* and its effect on subsequent histories are such that it is regarded as the first of China's 26 Dynastic, or Standard, Histories, which cover the history of imperial China from 221 B.C. until A.D. 1910.

The *Shih-chi* is in fact dynastically centered, with its main emphasis being the rise of the Han dynasty to its exalted position. In addition, it provides documentary evidence to support the claim of the Han emperors that they enjoyed that position justifiably and with the blessing of heaven. Such purposes or characteristics persist in the later Dynastic Histories, which are concerned with the events of single dynastic periods. Ssu-ma Ch'ien's pioneer work has been held up as a model for subsequent historians and writers of prose.

Further Reading

An English translation of those chapters of the *Shih-chi* that concern the Han period was published by Burton Watson as *Records of the Grand Historian of China* (2 vols., 1961). For a translation of 47 chapters of the *Shih-chi* into French see E. Chavannes, *Mémoires historiques* (1895-1905; repr. 1967); this work includes a detailed introduction. In *Ssu-ma Ch'ien, Grand Historian of China* (1958) Burton Watson assesses Ssu-ma Ch'ien's work and his contribution to historical writing. Dealing with the development of historical writing in China are Charles S. Gardner, *Chinese Traditional Historiography* (1938; repr. 1961), and W. G. Beasley and E. G. Pulleyblank, *Historians of China and Japan* (1961). Also useful are William T. de Bary and others, eds., *Sources of Chinese Tradition* (1960), and Burton Watson, *Early Chinese Literature* (1962).

Additional Sources

Durrant, Stephen W., *The cloudy mirror: tension and conflict in the writings of Sima Qian,* Albany: State University of New York Press, 1995. □

Ssu-ma Hsiang-ju

Ssu-ma Hsiang-ju (ca. 179-117 B.C.) was a leading Chinese poet of the Western Han period. He also explored and colonized lands that lay to the southwest of imperial territory.

Born in western China, Ssu-ma Hsiang-ju served as an official at the court of the king of Liang, who enjoyed certain local rights of government subject to the overall authority of the central government. Later Ssu-ma served as the leader of two missions which were sent to make contacts with the unassimilated tribes of the southwest; and following his reasonably successful achievements there, he was brought to the attention of the Emperor's court at Ch'ang-an.

Of six long poems attributed to Ssu-ma Hsiang-ju, two are probably not authentic. In addition he composed a number of essays in prose, including one which concerned some of the religious observances of state. It is possible that by this contribution, together with other references in his poems, he helped to persuade the emperor, Han Wu-ti, to conduct the supreme ceremonies of *Feng* and *Shan* on Mt. Tai in 110 B.C.

His Poetry

In his poetry Ssu-ma developed the tradition of the South, which was associated with the old kingdom and culture of Ch'u. This type of poetry was distinct from the poetry of the North and was clearly traceable to beginnings made in the *Ch'u tz'u,* or Songs of Ch'u. In developing a form of poetry known as the *fu,* Ssu-ma made an important contribution to the growth of Chinese literature.

The *fu* was a type of rhymed or rhythmical prose, often introduced by a short narrative written in free prose. Unlike other forms of poetry, it was not intended for musical accompaniment but was devised for recitation at the court. *Fu* are usually long and are characterized by a richness of expression that sometimes appears to be excessively decorative.

In the case of Ssu-ma Hsiang-ju's work, this effect was achieved at a time when the Chinese written language was still developing and many units of vocabulary were being evolved. As a literary form, the *fu* was didactic and descriptive rather than lyrical, romantic, or epic. Thus in the *Shang-lin fu,* or *fu* on the Shang-lin, which was an imperial pleasure and hunting ground, Ssu-ma Hsiang-ju describes the scenery and the palace buildings or pavilions before proceeding to the hunting scenes themselves; he then describes some of the spectacles that were presented for the amusement of the Emperor, such as dancing and musical performances.

In Ssu-ma Hsiang-ju's hands the *fu* was used to synthesize a number of literary elements that had previously been discrete. He wrote *fu* for the pleasure of the Emperor and called on fantasy and riddles in order to excite the attention of his audience. At the same time Ssu-ma Hsiang-ju was ready to allude to topical matters and events, partly as a means of reminding the Emperor and his officials where the path of duty led; he was more attracted to the Confucian than the Taoist attitude to life.

Further Reading

The definitive study of Ssu-ma Hsiang-ju is in French: Yves Hervouet, *Un poète de cour sous les Han: Sseuma Siang-jou* (1964). A study of his life and work is in Burton Watson, *Early Chinese Literature* (1962). See also his biography in Ssu-ma Ch'ien, *Shih chi,* translated by Burton Watson as *Records of the Grand Historian of China* (2 vols., 1961). □

Ssu-ma kuang

Ssu-ma kuang (1019-1086) was one of the greatest Chinese historians and a leading conservative statesman.

The family home of Ssu-ma Kuang was in Shan-chou, Shansi, but he was born, on Nov. 17, 1019, in Kuang-shan, Hunan, where his father was serving as subprefect. Ssu-ma's mother was the daughter of an editor of the imperial archives. Ssu-ma is said to have been a precocious child, filled with enthusiasm at the age of 6 for the *Tso-chuan,* the great historical work in the form of a commentary on the *Spring and Autumn Annals.* He passed the highest civil service examination in 1038 at the age of 19 and obtained the *chin-shih* degree, thereby qualifying for appointment as an official.

After serving in a number of official posts in the provinces and in the capital, including a tour in the Institute of History, Ssu-ma became administrator of the Bureau of Policy Criticism in 1061 and went on to become a Hanlin academician in 1067 and for a short time an executive censor during the same year. In 1070 he left the capital because of his opposition to the policies of Wang An-shih, then in power. In the years preceding the conflict with Wang, Ssu-ma demonstrated his Northern conservative political orientation when he proposed a system of regional quotas in the examination system to put an end to the preponderance of successful candidates from the capital region and the southeast. In this he disagreed with Ou-yang Hsiu, as he did again when Ou-yang supported Emperor Ying-tsung's wish to honor his deceased father as "emperor" even though he owed the throne to his uncle and adopted father, Emperor, Jen-tsung.

Opponent of Wang An-shih

Ssu-ma and his fellow Northerners objected to what they considered Wang's opinionated and arrogant adherence to his policies without regard for the opposition they aroused, the way in which the individual reform programs were maladministered by selfish officials, and the actual content of the various measures.

Suspicious of the growing money economy, opposed to state spending on the grounds that it was the people who had to pay for it, and placing their faith in the reform of men rather than of institutions, they viewed with dismay the increased use of money and the extension of state activities engendered by Wang's program. Yet, unlike the more moderate southwestern opponents of Wang, Ssu-ma and his associates offered few constructive alternatives. The conflict with Wang also reflected disagreements on the classics and differences in philosophical orientation.

A History of China

Even before his departure from the capital in 1070 Ssu-ma had occupied himself with history and had completed some of the groundwork for his monumental history. In 1064 he presented to the throne a chronological table of events covering the period from the beginning of the Warring States (403 B.C.) to the end of the Five Dynasties (A.D. 959), and in 1066 he presented to the Emperor a chronicle of the history of the Warring States period (403-221 B.C.). He was commissioned to continue his work, and two scholars were assigned to assist him. The following year he read the work completed to date to the Emperor, who graced it with a preface from his own hand and gave it the title *Tzu-chih t'ung-chien* (Comprehensive Mirror for Aid in Government).

In 1070 Ssu-ma was transferred to the Ch'ang-an region but was granted a sinecure in Loyang the following year, and in 1072 he obtained the transfer to Loyang of his library and the office for writing the history. He was now able to devote himself completely to his history, carefully working through the long draft compiled by his associates and selecting the material to be incorporated in the finished work. In the process he consulted over 300 sources, including not only various kinds of historical writing but a wide range of literary works. These he handled with great care, and, in an important departure from previous practice, Ssu-ma included in the completed work a section of "examinations of differences" in which he discussed discrepancies between the sources and explained the reasons for his selections.

As indicated by the title, the work was intended to offer guidance for government, and Ssu-ma fully shared the Confucian belief in the didactic function of history; but he was convinced that an accurate account of the facts would clearly convey the moral lessons of the past, and in dealing with such problems as the question of the legitimacy of governments in periods of division, he chose to apply objective rather than moral criteria.

Ssu-ma completed the *Tzu-chih t'ung-chien* in 1084 and presented it to the throne in that year. In 1085, after the death of Emperor Shen-tsung, Ssu-ma returned to the capital and was appointed executive of the Chancellery. Promoted to chief councilor in the second month of 1086, he had the satisfaction of obtaining the reversal of many of Wang Anshih's reforms before his death on October 11 of that year.

Further Reading

Achilles Fang translated a section of the *Tzu-chih t'ung-chien* as well as the sources used by Ssu-ma Kuang in his *The Chronicle of the Three Kingdoms, 220-265,* vol. 1, edited by Glen W. Baxter (1952), and vol. 2, edited by Bernard S. Solomon (1965). For a valuable discussion of Ssu-ma's historiography see E. G. Pulleybank's essay, "Chinese Historical Criticism: Liu Chih-chi and Ssu-ma Kuang," in William G. Beasley and E. G. Pulleybank, eds., *Historians of China and Japan* (1961), which is also useful for background on Chinese historiography as a whole. Also useful for general historical background are William T. de Bary and others, eds., *Sources of Chinese Tradition* (1960), and James T.C. Liu and Peter J. Golas, *Change in Sung China: Innovation or Renovation?* (1969). □

Germaine de Staël

The French-Swiss woman of letters and novelist Germaine de Staël [full name Anne Louise Germaine Necker, Baronne de Staël-Holstein, historically referred to as Madame de Staël] (1766-1817) greatly influenced European thought and literature with her enthusiasm for German romanticism.

Germaine de Staël was born Anne Louise Germaine Necker in Paris on April 22, 1766. Her father was Jacques Necker, a man of modest origins, who had risen to become Louis XVI's finance minister. Her mother Suzanne, though stiff and cold, entertained the leading intellectuals and politicians of the day in her famous salon. Staël's natural genius was thus nurtured from her infancy. The child adored her father—to the point of deploring that she was born too late to marry him—and he adored and pampered her. Madame Necker was intensely jealous of their mutual adoration; she and Staël bitterly resented one another. The three were bound together by a complex web of passions and hostilities, and their family life was characterized by emotional frenzy.

When she was 20 years old, Staël made a loveless marriage to the Swedish ambassador to France, Baron Erik Magnus de Staël-Holstein. Though he grew to love her, she lived with him only at strategic intervals when the origin of a child she was carrying might arouse suspicion. Only one of her five children was fathered by him.

Staël did, however, profit from her husband's diplomatic immunity by remaining in Paris during most of the French Revolution. Her salon became a center of political intrigue for those who favored a modern constitutional monarchy and a bicameral legislature. During the Terror she courageously arranged and financed the escape of numerous constitutionalist friends.

Although Staël was not considered a woman of traditional beauty, her brilliance and wit attracted some of the leading intellectuals and political figures of her day. Her love affairs were continuous, intense, and simultaneous. She never ended a love affair, and often as many as five lovers lived with her. She spent much of her life in exile, always surrounded by a small court of French émigrés and admirers. Her first lover was Charles Maurice de Talleyrand, and another was August Wilhelm von Schlegel, the German scholar and poet. But it was Benjamin Constant, a French-Swiss writer, who became the passion and torment of her life. They lived together for 12 turbulent years. Constant's novel *Adolphe* examines their relationship.

In 1797 Staël welcomed Napoleon Bonaparte to Paris as France's deliverer; within a few years she grew to detest him. Napoleon resented both her interference in politics and her unorthodox views. He repeatedly confiscated her manuscripts and banished her from Paris.

Her Works

Staël's first publication was *Lettre sur Jean-Jacques Rousseau.* It appeared in 1788, and in it she identified herself with enlightenment and reason. Her book *De l'Influence des passions sur le bonheur des individus et des nations* was issued in 1796. In it she expressed her belief in a system that considered the absolute liberty of the moral being the most essential element in his welfare and his most precious and inalienable right.

In 1800 Staël advanced her "theory of lights" in *De la littérature considérée dans ses rapports avec les institutions sociales.* In this book she held the belief that there was a constant progression of literature toward the light of perfection. In 1802 she published a novel, *Delphine.* An immediate success, it related the life of a beautiful and intelligent woman who sought happiness through love. Napoleon was enraged by *Delphine* because it praised liberalism, divorce, the British, and Protestantism. He declared it immoral, antisocial, and anti-Catholic. Staël was banished from Paris. Making a trip to Germany, she immersed herself in the society and culture of that country.

Continuing her travels into Italy, Staël found inspiration for her second novel there, *Corinne ou l'Italie,* published in 1807. At once a love story and a guidebook to Italy, this novel's heroine, as in *Delphine,* was a beautiful and brilliant woman who became a victim of society.

The fruits of Staël's sojourn in Germany appeared in 1810. *De l'Allemagne* ranked as one of the seminal works of early romantic thought. In it she made a famous distinction between two types of literature: that of the north (Germany, England, and Scandinavia) she found romantic, original, and free; that of the south (France and Italy) she found classical, formal, and conventional. In *De l'Allemagne* Staël examined the history, culture, and national character of Germany. She encouraged the rise of German consciousness and held it up as a model for France. Her book ended with a plea for enthusiasm and sentiment, which she understood to be the original "fact" of the human soul.

Napoleon was incensed by this call for German nationalism. He labeled the book "anti-French," destroyed the first edition, and exiled Staël to her home, the Château Coppet on Lake Geneva. At Coppet her activities were closely watched, and her mail was intercepted.

Staël's only comfort in despair was a new romance. Her husband had died, and in 1811 she married a 24-year-old Italian lieutenant named Rocca. In 1812 she escaped from Coppet and traveled to Russia, Sweden, and England. In 1814, after the fall of Napoleon, she returned to Paris. The Restoration disappointed her. Opium and insomnia, too many years on the edge of hysteria, and unending "enthusiasm" had all taken their toll. On July 14, 1817, paralyzed from a stroke, Staël died in her sleep.

Literary historians and critics have traditionally characterized Staël's work as providing a transition between the Enlightenment and Romanticism, but recent scholarship has provided new insights into its originality and historical importance. Staël's novels have been reinterpreted as expressions of a uniquely female literary vision. Her work has also been viewed as the struggle of an exceptional intellect to transcend the social and creative constraints imposed on the women of her time.

Further Reading

See Vivian Folkenflik, *An Extraordinary Woman: Selected Writings of Germaine de Staël* Columbia University, 1995; Madelyn Gutwirth, *Madame de Staël, Novelist: The Emergence of the Artist as Woman* Books on Demand, 1994; John Isbell, *The Birth of a European Romanticism: Truth and Propaganda in Staël's De L-Allemagne* Cambridge University, 1994; Gretchen Besser, *Germaine de Staël: Revisited* Maxwell Macmillan, 1994; Charlotte Hogsett, *The Literary Existence of Germaine de Staël* Southern Illinois University, 1987; ed. Madelyn Gutwirth et. al., *Germaine de Staël: Crossing the Borders* Rutgers, 1991; and ed. Eva Sartori, *French Women Writers: A Bio-Bibliographical Source Book,* Greenwood, 1991. Maurice Levaillant's informed and readable *The Passionate Exiles: Madame de Staël and Madame Récamier* (1956; trans. 1958) gave a broad picture, while J. Christopher Herold, *Mistress to an Age: A Life of Madame de Staël* (1958) described the author of *Corinne* with a just mixture of irony and compassion. Also useful were David G. Larg, *Madame de Staël: Her Life as Revealed in Her Work 1766-1800* (1924; trans. 1926), a good if pedantic treatment, and Wayne Andrews, *Germaine: A Portrait of Madame de Staël* (1963). □

Nicolas de Staël

The French painter Nicolas de Staël (1914-1955) was a major painter of the School of Paris. His work is characterized by a simplification of forms and the application of paint in thick slabs.

Nicolas de Staël was born on Jan. 5, 1914, in St. Petersburg, the son of a wealthy baron. Nicolas's mother encouraged him to draw and paint at a very early age. In 1919 the Russian Revolution forced the family into exile in Poland. Within 2 years his parents were dead, and Nicolas was sent to Brussels to study humanities. In 1932 he entered the Royal Academy of Art there.

During the 1930s Staël embarked on a series of travels to see as many kinds of art as possible. In the Netherlands he was particularly impressed by the works of Rembrandt and Jan Vermeer, and in Paris he was very moved by the paintings of Paul Cézanne, Henri Matisse, and Georges Braque. He traveled in Spain, Italy, Morocco, and Algeria and then settled in Paris in 1938. When World War II broke out, Staël joined the French Foreign Legion and fought in Tunisia for a year.

In 1942 Staël's individual style began to emerge. He gave up direct representation for a highly sensuous, nonfigurative approach, as in his *Composition 45* (1945). He became friends with Braque and André Lanskoy, whose work he greatly admired and who encouraged and advised him. Staël's life had been one of extreme poverty, but by 1948, when he became a French citizen, he was beginning to be successful. Although he was painting nonfigurative pictures, he did not consider himself an abstract painter. "One does not start from nothing, and a painting is always bad if it has not been preceded by contact with nature."

In 1951 Staël made a trip to London, where he became familiar with the work of J. M. W. Turner and John Constable, an interest that presaged his return to nature in 1952. That year he executed a series of paintings of football players. He began to paint directly from nature and, greatly influenced by Gustave Courbet, developed a highly personal style of landscape painting. Staël applied brilliant flat colors with a minimum of detail to suggest the essence of a vista; this suggestive simplification of a recognizable scene was one of his contributions to the development of modern painting. It is exemplified in *Landscape, Sky, Blue and Gray* (1953).

A dedicated artist who lived for painting, Staël had achieved wealth and fame when, on March 16, 1955, he committed suicide in Antibes.

Further Reading

The best book on Staël, a thoughtful analysis of his life and work, is Douglas Cooper, *Nicholas de Staël* (1961). Roger van Gindertael, *Nicolas de Staël* (1960; trans. 1961), is a brief but perceptive appreciation and critique by one of Staël's friends. □

Georg Ernst Stahl

The German chemist and medical theorist Georg Ernst Stahl (1660-1734) was the founder of the phlogiston theory of combustion and the author of a theory of medicine based upon vitalistic ideas.

Georg Stahl was born on Oct. 21, 1660, at Anspach in Bavaria, the son of a Lutheran pastor. Although brought up in an extremely pious and religious household, he early showed an enthusiasm for chemistry. By the age of 15 he had mastered a set of university lecture notes on the subject as well as a difficult treatise by Johann Kunckel.

Stahl studied medicine at the University of Jena, where he graduated in 1683. Here he came under the influence of iatrochemical theories, which gave an interpretation of physiological processes in terms of chemistry. He was later to become a strong opponent of this school of medical theory. Following graduation he taught at the University of Jena for 10 years.

In 1694 Stahl was invited to fill the second chair of medicine at the newly founded University of Halle. He owed his appointment to the recommendation of the holder of the first chair of medicine, Friedrich Hoffmann. They made Halle one of the most important medical schools of the early 18th century, although their careers there were punctuated by frequent quarrels. For 22 years Stahl lectured at Halle and wrote an impressive list of works on chemistry and medicine. His lectures were said to have been dry and intentionally difficult; he is alleged to have had a low opinion of the intellectual capacity of his students at Halle.

Stahl's most notable contribution to chemistry was his famous phlogiston theory of combustion, which became one of the main unifying theories of 18th-century chemistry. He maintained that all substances which burned contained a combustible principle called phlogiston (from the Greek *phlogos,* a flame) which was liberated during the combustion process. This principle of phlogiston was present not only in such obviously combustible substances as wood, wax, oils, and other organic materials but also in inorganic substances such as sulfur and phosphorus and even in metals. Thus when a metal was calcined by heating (a process now known as oxidation), the metal was said to lose its phlogiston. Conversely, when the metallic calx was reduced again to the metal, phlogiston was taken up.

This theory also offered the first explanation of why charcoal was used in the smelting of metallic ores. Charcoal was a substance rich in phlogiston (since on burning it left no residue), and in the smelting process the phlogiston passed from the charcoal to the ore to give the pure metal. One of the major achievements of this theory was that it offered a comprehensive explanation of so many seemingly disparate chemical phenomena. In developing his theory, Stahl drew from the earlier ideas on combustion of the late-17th-century German chemist J.J. Becher.

As a medical theorist, Stahl opposed the purely chemical and mechanistic explanations of living phenomena current in his time. He emphasized the gulf between living and nonliving materials, stating that the distinctive feature of the former was that they possessed a soul which prevented their decomposition. His reintroduction of animistic or vitalistic ideas into physiology had great influence on 18th-century medical theory.

Stahl retired from academic life in 1716 to take up appointment as physician to King Frederick I of Prussia. He held this post until his death on May 14, 1734.

Further Reading

There is no major study of Stahl's life in English, but for his contributions to chemistry see John M. Stillman, *The Story of Alchemy and Early Chemistry* (1960); and James R. Partington, *A History of Chemistry,* vol. 2 (1961). ☐

Joseph Stalin

The Soviet statesman Joseph Stalin (1879-1953) was the supreme ruler of the Soviet Union and the leader of world communism for almost 30 years.

Under Joseph Stalin the Soviet Union greatly enlarged its territory, won a war of unprecedented destructiveness, and transformed itself from a relatively backward country into the second most important industrial nation in the world. For these achievements the Soviet people and the international Communist movement paid a price that many of Stalin's critics consider excessive. The price included the loss of millions of lives; massive material and spiritual deprivation; political repression; an untold waste of resources; and the erection of an inflexible authoritarian system of rule thought by some historians to be one of the most offensive in recent history and one that many Communists consider a hindrance to further progress in the Soviet Union itself.

Formative Years

Stalin was born Iosif Vissarionovich Dzhugashvili on Dec. 21, 1879, in Gori, Georgia. He was the only surviving son of Vissarion Dzhugashvili, a cobbler who first practiced his craft in a village shop but later in a shoe factory in the city. Stalin's father died in 1891. His mother, Ekaterina, a pious and illiterate peasant woman, sent her teen-age son to the theological seminary in Tpilisi (Tiflis), where Stalin prepared for the ministry. Shortly before his graduation, however, he was expelled in 1899 for spreading subversive views.

Stalin then joined the underground revolutionary Marxist movement in Tpilisi. In 1901 he was elected a member of the Tpilisi committee of the Russian Social Democratic Workers party. The following year he was arrested, imprisoned, and subsequently banished to Siberia. Stalin escaped from Siberia in 1904 and rejoined the Marxist underground in Tpilisi. When the Russian Marxist movement split into two factions, Stalin identified himself with the Bolsheviks.

During the time of the 1904-1905 revolution, Stalin made a name as the organizer of daring bank robberies and raids on money transports, an activity that V. I. Lenin considered important in view of the party's need for funds, although many other Marxists considered this type of highway robbery unworthy of a revolutionary socialist.

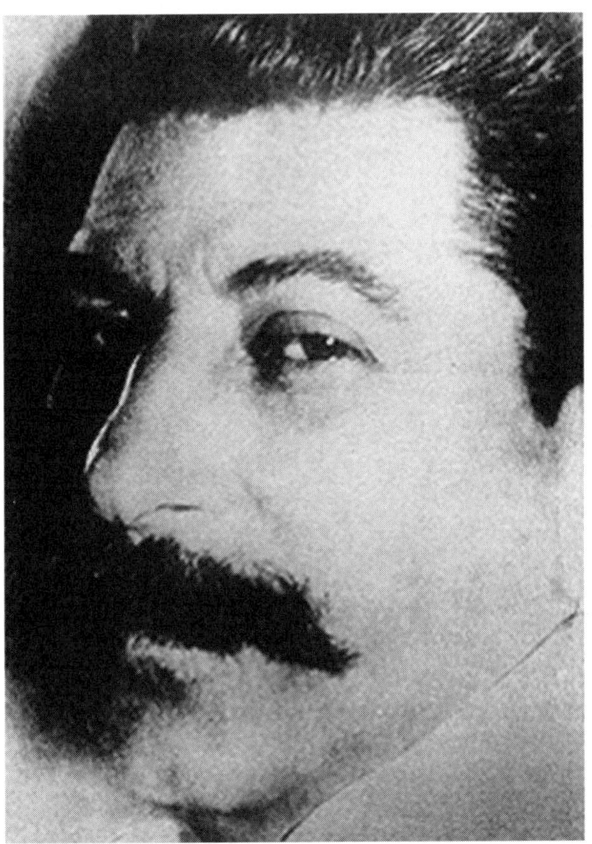

Stalin participated in congresses of the Russian Social Democratic Workers party at Tampere, London, and Stockholm in 1905 and 1906, meeting Lenin for the first time at these congresses. In 1912 Stalin spent some time with Lenin and his wife in Crakow and then went to Vienna to study the Marxist literature concerning the nationality problem. This study trip resulted in a book, *Marxism and the National Question*. In the same year Lenin co-opted Stalin into the Central Committee of the Bolshevik party.

Stalin's trips abroad during these years were short episodes in his life. He spent the major portion of the years from 1905 to 1912 in organizational work for the movement, mainly in the city of Baku. The secret police arrested him several times, and several times he escaped. Eventually, after his return from Vienna, the police caught him again, and he was exiled to the faraway village of Turukhansk beyond the Arctic Circle. He remained here until the fall of czarism. He adopted the name Stalin ("man of steel") about 1913.

First Years of Soviet Rule

After the fall of czarism, Stalin made his way at once to Petrograd, where until the arrival of Lenin from Switzerland he was the senior Bolshevik and the editor of *Pravda,* the party organ. After Lenin's return, Stalin remained in the high councils of the party, but he played a relatively inconspicuous role in the preparations for the October Revolution, which placed the Bolsheviks in power. In the first Cabinet of the Soviet government, he held the post of people's commissar for nationalities.

During the years of the civil war (1918-1921), Stalin distinguished himself primarily as military commissar during the battle of Tsaritsyn (Stalingrad), in the Polish campaign, and on several other fronts. In 1919 he received another important government assignment by being appointed commissar of the Workers and Peasants Inspectorate. Within the party, he rose to the highest ranks, becoming a member of both the Political Bureau and the Organizational Bureau. When the party Secretariat was organized, he became one of its leading members and was appointed its secretary general in 1922. Lenin obviously valued Stalin for his organizational talents, for his ability to knock heads together and to cut through bureaucratic red tape. He appreciated Stalin's capabilities as a machine politician, as a troubleshooter, and as a hatchet man.

The strength of Stalin's position in the government and in the party was anchored probably by his secretary generalship, which gave him control over party personnel administration—over admissions, training, assignments, promotions, and disciplinary matters. Thus, although he was relatively unknown to outsiders and even within the party, Stalin doubtless ranked as the most powerful man in Soviet Russia after Lenin.

During Lenin's last illness and after his death in 1924, Stalin served as a member of the three-man committee that conducted the affairs of the party and the country. The other members of this "troika" arrangement were Grigori

Zinoviev and Lev Kamenev. The best-known activity of this committee during the years 1923-1925 was its successful attempt to discredit Leon Trotsky and to make it impossible for him to assume party leadership after Lenin's death. After the committee succeeded in this task, Stalin turned against his two associates, who after some hesitation made common cause with Trotsky. The conflict between these two groups can be viewed either as a power struggle or as a clash of personalities, but it also concerned political issues—a dispute between the left wing and the right wing of bolshevism. The former feared a conservative perversion of the revolution, and the latter were confident that socialism could be reached even in an isolated and relatively backward country. In this dispute Stalin represented, for the time being, the right wing of the party. He and his theoretical spokesman, Nikolai Bukharin, warned against revolutionary adventurism and argued in favor of continuing the more cautious and patient policies that Lenin had inaugurated with the NEP (New Economic Policy).

In 1927 Stalin succeeded in defeating the entire left opposition and in eliminating its leaders from the party. He then adopted much of its domestic program by initiating a 5-year plan of industrial development and by executing it with a degree of recklessness and haste that antagonized many of his former supporters, who then formed a right opposition. This opposition, too, was defeated quickly, and by the early 1930s Stalin had gained dictatorial control over the party, the state, and the entire Communist International.

Stalin's Personality

Although always depicted as a towering figure, Stalin, in fact, was of short stature. He possessed the typical features of Transcaucasians: black hair, black eyes, a short skull, and a large nose. His personality was highly controversial, and it remains shrouded in mystery. Stalin was crude and cruel and, in some important ways, a primitive man. His cunning, distrust, and vindictiveness seem to have reached paranoid proportions. In political life he tended to be cautious and slow-moving. His style of speaking and writing was also ponderous and graceless. Some of his speeches and occasional writings read like a catechism. He was at times, however, a clever orator and a formidable antagonist in debate. Stalin seems to have possessed boundless energy and a phenomenal capacity for absorbing detailed knowledge.

About Stalin's private life, little is known beyond the fact that he seems always to have been a lonely man. His first wife, a Georgian girl named Ekaterina Svanidze, died of tuberculosis. His second wife, Nadezhda Alleluyeva, committed suicide in 1932, presumably in despair over Stalin's dictatorial rule of the party. The only child from his first marriage, Jacob, fell into German hands during World War II and was killed. The two children from his second marriage outlived their father, but they were not always on good terms with him. The son, Vasili, an officer in the Soviet air force, drank himself to death in 1962. The daughter, Svetlana, fled to the United States in the 1960s.

Stalin's Achievements

In successive 5-year plans, the Soviet Union under Stalin industrialized and urbanized with great speed. Although the military needs of the country drained away precious resources and World War II brought total destruction to some of the richest areas of the Soviet Union and death to many millions of citizens, the nation by the end of Stalin's life had become the second most important industrial country in the world.

The price the Soviet Union paid for this great achievement remains staggering. It included the destruction of all remnants of free enterprise in both town and country and the physical destruction of hundreds of thousands of Russian peasants. The transformation of Soviet agriculture in the early 1930s into collectives tremendously damaged the country's food production. Living standards were drastically lowered at first, and more than a million people died of starvation. Meanwhile, Stalin jailed and executed vast numbers of party members, especially the old revolutionaries and the leading figures in all areas of endeavor.

In the process of securing his rule and of mobilizing the country for the industrialization effort, Stalin erected a new kind of political system characterized by unprecedented severity in police control, bureaucratic centralization, and personal dictatorship. Historians consider his regime one of history's most notorious examples of totalitarianism.

Stalin also changed the ideology of communism and of the Soviet Union in a subtle but drastic fashion. While retaining the rhetoric of Marxism-Leninism, and indeed transforming it into an inflexible dogma, Stalin also changed it from a revolutionary system of ideas into a conservative and authoritarian theory of state, preaching obedience and discipline as well as veneration of the Russian past. In world affairs the Stalinist system became isolationist. While paying lip service to the revolutionary goals of Karl Marx and Lenin, Stalin sought to promote good relations with the capitalist countries and urged Communist parties to ally themselves with moderate and middle-of-the-road parties in a popular front against the radical right.

From the middle of the 1930s onward, Stalin personally managed the vast political and economic system he had established. Formally, he took charge of it only in May 1941, when he assumed the office of chairman of the Council of Ministers. After Nazi Germany invaded the Soviet Union, Stalin also assumed formal command over the entire military establishment.

Stalin's conduct of Russian military strategy in the war remains as controversial as most of his activities. Some evidence indicates that he committed serious blunders, but other evidence allows him credit for brilliant achievements. The fact remains that under Stalin the Soviet Union won the war, emerged as one of the major powers in the world, and managed to bargain for a distribution of the spoils of war that enlarged its area of domination significantly, partly by annexation and partly by the transformation of all the lands east of the Oder and Neisse rivers into client states.

Judgments of Stalin

Stalin died of a cerebrovascular accident on March 5, 1953. His body was entombed next to Lenin's in the mausoleum in Red Square, Moscow. After his death Stalin became a controversial figure in the Communist world, where appreciation for his great achievements was offset to a varying degree by harsh criticism of his methods. At the Twentieth All-Union Party Congress in 1956, Premier Nikita Khrushchev and other Soviet leaders attacked the cult of Stalin, accusing him of tyranny, terror, falsification of history, and self-glorification.

Further Reading

Two excellent biographies of Stalin are Boris Souvarine, *Stalin: A Critical Study of Bolshevism* (trans. 1939), and Isaac Deutscher, *Stalin: A Political Biography* (1949; 2d ed. 1967). A good brief survey of his life is Robert D. Warth, *Joseph Stalin* (1969). Lenin, Trotsky, and Stalin are the subjects of Bertram D. Wolfe, *Three Who Made a Revolution* (1948). Stalin figures prominently in Nikita Khrushchev's memoirs, *Khrushchev Remembers* (trans. 1971); however, the authenticity of the memoirs is not completely established.

Many of the countless books dealing with Soviet affairs between 1923 and 1953 necessarily must deal with Stalin extensively, particularly such standard works as Edward H. Carr's massive multivolume study, *A History of Soviet Russia* (9 vols., 1951-1969); Merle Fainsod, *How Russia Is Ruled* (1953; rev. ed. 1963); Frederick L. Schuman, *Russia since* 1917 (1957); and Leonard Schapiro, *The Communist Party of the Soviet Union* (1959). Of the numerous works by former Communist leaders who dealt with Stalin and later denounced him, several are noteworthy: Leon Trotsky, *Stalin: An Appraisal of the Man and His Influence,* edited and translated by Charles Malamuth (1941; new ed. 1967); Ruth Fischer, *Stalin and the German Communist Party* (1948); Alexander Orlov, *The Secret History of Stalin's Crimes* (1953); and Abdurakhman Avtorkhanov, *Stalin and the Soviet Communist Party: A Study in the Technology of Power* (1959). Various assessments of Stalin and his conduct of Soviet affairs are given in T.H. Rigby, ed., *Stalin* (1966). Stalin figures prominently in the best account of the purges of the 1930s, Robert Conquest, *The Great Terror: Stalin's Purge of the Thirties* (1968).

Studies of the Soviet army and its officer corps under Stalin include John Erickson, *The Soviet High Command* (1962); Alexander Werth, *Russia at War* (1964); and Seweryn Bialer, ed., *Stalin and His Generals: Soviet Military Memoirs of World War II* (1969). □

Myles Standish

Myles Standish (ca. 1584-1656), a professional English soldier hired by the Pilgrims to direct their military affairs, gave great service to New Plymouth in America and won personal glory.

Little is known of Myles Standish's early life, other than that he probably came from Lancashire, England, and had fought the Spaniards in the Netherlands. Hired by the Leiden Pilgrims to manage the military defenses of the prospective colony, Standish was not a member of the Leiden congregation, although he quickly became a loyal supporter of the Pilgrim venture.

When he arrived in New England, Standish's first responsibility was to give practical assistance in the explorations for a permanent place for settlement. Standish participated in the venture that discovered corn (later used as seed to save the colony from starvation) and in the expedition that made initial contact with the Indians and later landed at the future site of the colony. Once the colony was begun, he turned his attention to building its defenses. He supervised construction of the town fort and directed the organization and training of the local militia.

Standish also commanded military expeditions sent out from Plymouth to aid allies or to suppress enemies. Once he led a party of Pilgrims to aid Squanto and a group of friendly Indians. Another time he helped an English village at Wessagussett (Weymouth) threatened by Indian attack. There Standish demonstrated his personal courage when, in a conference with the Indians, he had the doors to the building barred and then called for an assault on the potential enemy, personally killing the Indian leader.

Perhaps the most entertaining example of Standish's military leadership was his seriocomic capture of Thomas Morton of Merrimount in 1628. Morton's emphasis on riotous living, selling firearms to the Indians, and paying high prices for furs threatened the piety and profit of New Plymouth. Standish led the assault on Merrimount. In a maneuver similar to the one used against the Indians at Wessagussett, he barred the doors and made ready to battle Morton. Mor-

ton and his two associates were "soe steeled with drink," however, that they could not resist capture.

Standish was the colony's first agent to return to England, and he also served as envoy to other New England colonies. He was known for his aggressiveness and quick temper. But it was as the Pilgrims' military adviser and commander that he made his greatest contribution. He developed a strong defensive posture for New Plymouth and directed the colony's militia with an exceptional degree of personal heroism and dedicated leadership. He died in Duxbury, Mass., on Oct. 3, 1656.

Further Reading

There is no recent biography of Standish. One of the best sources of information is William Bradford, *Of Plimouth Plantation,* edited by Samuel Eliot Morison (1952). Specific information, as well as general background, is in George F. Willison, *Saints and Strangers* (1945); Bradford Smith, *Bradford of Plymouth* (1951); and George D. Langdon, Jr., *Pilgrim Colony: A History of New Plymouth, 1620-1691* (1966). □

Leland Stanford

Leland Stanford (1824-1893), American railroad builder and politician, was one of the founders of the Central Pacific and Southern Pacific railroads and served as California's governor and then U.S. senator.

Leland Stanford, born on March 9, 1824, in Watervliet, N.Y., was one of eight children of a prosperous farmer who also dabbled in various local bridge and road contracts. Leland received a formal education until the age of 12, had 3 years of tutoring at home, and then returned to school. He became an apprentice in an Albany law office and 3 years later gained admission to the bar.

In 1848 Stanford opened a law office at Port Washington, Wis.; meanwhile, his brothers sensed the lure of fortune in California and opened a mercantile business in Sacramento. In 1850 Stanford married Jane Elizabeth Lathrop. Two years later his law office burned down, and he decided to relocate in California. His brothers helped him establish a mining store in Cold Springs, but it did not do well so he opened a business at Michigan Bluff, which was successful. He also engaged in mining on a small scale.

In 1856 Stanford moved to Sacramento, where he started business with a brother and quickly entered politics. He met defeat in a race for Republican state treasurer in 1857, and 2 years later he lost the gubernatorial contest. His golden opportunity came in 1861, when the Civil War split the Democratic party, and he won the governor's office with less than the combined vote of his two Democratic opponents. Though he served only one term, he was able to keep California in the Union. His administration also encouraged the passage of several acts designed to aid the proposed

transcontinental railroad, in which he had a large financial interest.

In 1861 Stanford, Collis P. Huntington, Charles Crocker, and Mark Hopkins organized the Central Pacific Railroad, which built east to join the westward-progressing Union Pacific Railroad. The two joined at Promontory Point, Utah, in May 1869. Stanford became president of the Central Pacific, Huntington handled eastern financial and political arrangements, Crocker supervised construction, and Hopkins looked after company finances. Stanford's excellent reputation in California allowed the Central Pacific access to considerable sums of construction money. Also, as a stockholder in the construction companies, he enjoyed great personal profit.

Stanford remained president of the Central Pacific until his death. In 1870 the Southern Pacific was incorporated to build in southern California and eventually to reach New Orleans, La. Fourteen years later a holding company, the Southern Pacific Company, merged the Southern Pacific Railroad, Central Pacific, and others into one combine. Stanford was president of the combine from 1885 to 1890.

In 1890 Stanford and Huntington split over Stanford's renewed political ambitions. After he left the governor's office in 1863, he had remained active in influencing legislation in California. In 1885 he had declared his candidacy for the U.S. Senate and had defeated A. A. Sargent on a strictly party vote. Sargent was a personal friend of Huntington, and in 1890 Huntington managed to have Stanford replaced as Southern Pacific president. Stanford's senatorial career was undistinguished.

Stanford endowed a new institution, the Leland Stanford Junior University, in 1885 in memory of his son, who had died at the age of 15. Stanford died in Palo Alto on June 21, 1893.

Further Reading

No recent work on Stanford has appeared. Two biographies are George T. Clark, *Leland Stanford, War Governor of California, Railroad Builder and Founder of Stanford University* (1931), and Hubert H. Bancroft, *History of the Life of Leland Stanford* (1952). Stanford's role in the Central Pacific is examined in Oscar Lewis, *The Big Four* (1938).

Additional Sources

Lewis, Oscar, *The big four: the story of Huntington, Stanford, Hopkins, and Crocker, and of the building of the Central Pacific,* New York: Arno Press, 1981, 1938.

Regnery, Dorothy F., *The Stanford House in Sacramento: an American treasure,* Stanford, Calif. (P.O. Box 2328, Stanford University, Stanford 94305): Stanford Historical Society, 1987. □

Constantin Stanislavsky

The Russian actor and director Constantin Stanislavsky (1863-1938) originated a system of acting. He was a cofounder of the Moscow Art Theater, where his productions achieved the zenith in 20th-century naturalism.

Constantin Stanislavsky was born Constantin Sergeyevich Alexeyev on Jan. 18, 1863, in Moscow. He was the son of a rich industrialist. His stage name, Stanislavsky, was taken from an actor whom he met in amateur theatricals. Stanislavsky's excellent classical education included singing, ballet, and acting lessons as well as regular visits to the opera and theater. By the age of 14 he was acting in performances at the family estate, where his father had built a theater. After completing his formal education, Stanislavsky entered the family business, enthusiastically devoting himself at the same time to a career in semiprofessional theater. Beginning in 1888 he directed and acted in performances for the Society of Art and Literature, which he had founded, and he continued these productions until 1897 under the sponsorship of the Hunting Club.

On June 22, 1897, Stanislavsky met Vladimir Nemirovich-Danchenko, a successful playwright and teacher in the Moscow Philharmonic Society School, at a Moscow restaurant in order to discuss the reform of the Russian stage. Out of their 18-hour meeting came the establishment of the Moscow Art Theater as a protest against the artificial theatrical conventions of the late 19th century. Although the opening production in October 1898 of Alexey Tolstoy's *Tsar Fyodor Ivanovich* was a tremendous popular success because of its realism, it was with Anton Chekhov's *The Seagull* in December that Stanislavsky discovered a play ideally suited to his artistic aspirations and naturalistic methods. In the next 2 decades the Moscow Art Theater attained international recognition with productions widely ranging in style: Maxim Gorky's sociopolitical drama *The Lower Depths* (1902), Leonid Andreyev's symbolic *The Life of Man* (1907), Maurice Maeterlinck's enchanting fairy tale *The Blue Bird* (1908), and *Hamlet* with settings by Gordon Craig (1911).

During this period Stanislavsky worked out his theories by exploring the most difficult problems of acting with his company. An indication of the success of his system was the emergence from his training methods of all the best Russian actors of the early 20th century. Rehearsals, which often resembled acting classes, began with discussions of the "super-objective" and the "through action" of the play, and at the same time the actor examined the previous history of his character, the "pre-text." Stanislavsky believed that, through study of the play, analysis of the role, and recall of previous emotions, the actor could arrive at the "inner truth" of a part by actually experiencing the emotions he conveyed to the audience. Furthermore, the actor must never lose control of his creation and must have the technical discipline to repeat his previously experienced emotions at every performance. The actor's interpretations must be unified in the same way that the central idea of the play was realized through the unity of direction, acting, and production design. This training, which aimed at stimulating the artistic intelligence of the actor, developing his inner discipline, and providing perfect control of such external means as voice, diction, and physical movement, came to be known in the United States as the "Method."

Opposed to the acrobatics and constructivism of avant-garde directors, Stanislavsky continued to present his prewar repertory for 5 years after the 1917 Revolution, and then he traveled with his company in western Europe and the United States from August 1922 to September 1924.

My Life in Art, the only book by Stanislavsky to be published in the Soviet Union during his lifetime, appeared in 1924. In response to criticisms that he had never staged contemporary Communist plays, Stanislavsky directed several dramas of revolutionary significance. Even so, he was attacked by proletarian critics for catering to "progressive bourgeois" audiences. Determined to maintain his integrity and the high standards of production upon which the Moscow Art Theater was founded, he resisted pressures to force his company to perform plays unworthy of its distinguished tradition. Fortunately for Stanislavsky, by the 1930s Communist theoreticians had elected to explain his system in terms of dialectical materialism. The Moscow Art Theater was venerated as the fountainhead of "social realism," and Stanislavsky occupied once again a central position in the Russian theater. During his last years he concentrated on giving the final touches to his writings. Stanislavsky died in Moscow on Aug. 7, 1938.

Further Reading

Stanislavsky's writings include *My Life in Art,* translated by J. J. Robbins (1924); and *An Actor Prepares* (1936; rev. ed. 1956), *Building a Character* (1949), *Stanislavsky's Legacy* (1958; rev. ed. 1968), and *Creating a Role* (1961), all translated by Elizabeth Reynolds Hapgood. The standard biography is David Magarshack, *Stanislavsky: A Life* (1950). Discussions of the system are in Robert Lewis, *Method—or Madness* (1958); Christine Edwards, *The Stanislavsky Heritage* (1965); and Sonia Moore, *The Stanislavski System* (1965).

Additional Sources

Benedetti, Jean, *Stanislavski: a biography,* New York, NY: Routledge, 1990.

Jones, David Richard, *Great directors at work: Stanislavsky, Brecht, Kazan, Brook,* Berkeley: University of California Press, 1986.

Magarshack, David, *Stanislavsky: a life,* Boston: Faber and Faber, 1986. □

Sir Henry Morton Stanley

Sir Henry Morton Stanley (1841-1904), British explorer and journalist, opened Central Africa to exploitation by Western nations.

Henry Stanley was originally named John Rowland. He was born near Denbigh Castle, Wales, to John Rowland, a farmer, and an unmarried woman. The boy lived with his maternal grandfather until he was about 6, when his grandfather died. The youngster was sent to a workhouse, where he remained until the age of 15, when he ran away.

Young Rowland lived on a hand-to-mouth basis with various relatives until he was 18, when he signed on as a cabin boy and shipped to New Orleans. There a cotton broker, Henry Morton Stanley, adopted him and gave him his name. Stanley's adopted father died without providing for him. The young man volunteered as a Confederate soldier and was captured at Shiloh. He was released from prison by changing sides and finished the war in the Union Navy.

After the war Stanley became a newspaper correspondent. He covered Indian campaigns in the American West. In 1868 he went to Abyssinia to cover a British expedition. In 1869 the publisher of the *New York Herald* commissioned Stanley to find Dr. David Livingstone, a Scottish missionary explorer, lost somewhere in Central Africa. Stanley found Livingstone at Ujiji in 1871 after an 8-month search. They did some exploring together, and when Livingstone died in 1873, Stanley stepped into his shoes.

In 1874 Stanley began a 3-year journey to measure the lakes of Central Africa. From 1879 to 1884 he opened the Congo River Basin and laid the groundwork for the Congo Free State after setting up 21 trading posts along the river. Between 1887 and 1890 he led a mission to rescue Emin Pasha, the governor of Equatoria. Stanley settled the question of the source of the Nile and opened a vast territory

which accelerated the desire of European countries to control African soil.

On July 12, 1890, Stanley married Dorothy Tennant. In 1895 he became a member of Parliament, and 4 years later he was knighted, receiving the Grand Cross of the Bath. He died on May 10, 1904, in London.

Further Reading

The Autobiography of Henry M. Stanley, edited by his wife (1909), is invaluable; Stanley wrote the first nine chapters before his death, and Lady Stanley drew the remainder from her husband's journals, letters, and notebooks. Among Stanley's many works are *How I Found Livingstone* (1872), *Through the Dark Continent* (2 vols., 1878), and *In Darkest Africa* (2 vols., 1890), adventure stories of the first magnitude. *Stanley's Despatches to the New York Herald, 1871-1872, 1874-1877,* edited by Norman R. Bennett (1970), provides the complete series of Stanley's despatches as a reporter, along with scholarly annotations. Sir Reginald Coupland, *Livingstone's Last Journey* (1947), is an interesting study. □

Wendell Meredith Stanley

The American virologist Wendell Meredith Stanley (1904-1971) convinced the world that viruses are physicochemically definable particles showing some properties of living material.

On Aug. 16, 1904, W. M. Stanley was born in Ridgeville, Ind. At the age of 16 he entered Earlham College in Richmond, Ind., where he majored in chemistry and mathematics and excelled in football. Upon graduating, he considered a career as an athletic coach. A visit to the University of Illinois at Urbana in connection with his contemplated football career culminated in a fortuitous interview with Roger Adams, professor of chemistry. Three years of graduate work under Professor Adams followed.

After graduating, Stanley married a collaborator, Marian Jay, and they spent a year at the University of Munich. In 1931 he joined the Rockefeller Institute in New York City. The following year he transferred to its newly established laboratory of plant pathology at Princeton, N.J., where he did his important research, the crystallization of the tobacco mosaic virus, which within 3 years led to a short epochmaking paper in *Science* and to many more publications, lectures, and world renown within 6 years.

Origin of Molecular Virology

Viruses differ from bacteria and other microorganisms in replicating not on nutrient media but only in living cells. Stanley, as a chemist, knew that purification should lead to pure and usually crystallizable materials. He was working at a time when mysterious enzymes were proved to be crystallizable proteins. He employed these protein methods and succeeded in 1935 in obtaining pure tobacco mosaic virus, free from plant material and infective when introduced into susceptible plants. The crystals seen by Stanley are now called paracrystals because the rod-shaped virus particles are arranged in only two-dimensional order (lengthwise).

All-important was Stanley's recognition that viruses could be obtained in pure form and studied by physical and chemical methods, like proteins and other simpler biologically active compounds. And, more important than this recognition, in which he was not alone, was his willingness and ability to "sell" this concept to the scientific community, and his success in overcoming the skepticism of those virologists and biologists who retained vestiges of vitalist philosophy and wanted the seemingly living viruses to retain a shroud of mystery and to resist the efforts of chemists. Concerning the question whether viruses are living or not, we now know that they carry the same principal genetic capabilities as living cells but lack all metabolic capabilities. Thus viruses need the energy and materials produced in living cells for their replication. They are half alive.

Move to the West

The next turning point for Stanley came about through another fortuitous circumstance. Gordon Sproul, president of the University of California, was looking for a man to head a new biochemistry department at Berkeley. He and Stanley met when their planes were grounded by fog, and they agreed in principle on a joint future. The creation of a separate research laboratory, the Virus Laboratory, by the California Legislature was part of the deal. In 1948 Stanley moved to Berkeley, successfully staffing both the biochemistry department and the Virus Laboratory in the course of the next 5 years.

Stanley's interest had turned from plant viruses to human pathogens, particularly influenza virus. During World War II his prime aim was the development of a vaccine against this virus. At Berkeley, research proceeded on plant, bacterial, and animal viruses; Stanley's greatest interest was in animal viruses, with poliomyelitis as the focal point. In subsequent years his interest turned more toward tumor-causing viruses. Several of these had been described as having elicited tumors in chickens or rabbits that resembled human malignant tumors. The belief that many or all malignant tumors might be due to viruses found a new proponent and prophet in Stanley. This aspect of his career received crowning recognition when he served as president of the Tenth International Cancer Congress in 1970.

Stanley received many honors and awards. Besides the Nobel Prize in chemistry in 1946, shared with John Northrop and James Sumner, there was a Presidential Certificate of Merit and the Franklin Medal in 1948, an American Cancer Society award in 1959, and over a dozen honorary doctorates. Stanley retired as director of the Virus Laboratory in 1969. He died in Salamanca, Spain, on June 15, 1971.

Further Reading

Stanley's perspective on virology is illustrated in a book by himself and Evans G. Valens, developed from a series of filmed lectures by staff members, *Viruses and the Nature of Life* (1961). A biographical sketch of Stanley is in Nobel Foundation, *Chemistry: Including Presentation Speeches and Laureates' Biographies* (3 vols., 1964-1966). Stanley's career and researches at the Rockefeller Institute are discussed in detail in George W. Corner, *A History of the Rockefeller Institute, 1901-1953: Origins and Growth* (1964). A more personal viewpoint is expressed by R. E. Shope in volume 5 of *Perspectives in Virology* (1967), an issue dedicated to Stanley. A recent textbook on molecular virology by Heinz Fraenkel-Conrat, *The Chemistry and Biology of Viruses* (1969), describes the development of this research field since it was opened up by Stanley in 1935. □

Edwin McMasters Stanton

Edwin McMasters Stanton (1814-1869), American lawyer, was a member of both James Buchanan's and Abraham Lincoln's Cabinets.

Edwin M. Stanton was born in Steubenville, Ohio, on Dec. 19, 1814. He attended a private school and a Latin academy, but on his father's death in 1827 he was forced to accept a job in a local bookstore. After working there for 3 years he borrowed enough money from his mother's lawyer to enter Kenyon College in Gambier, Ohio. At the beginning of his second year, family finances became so strained that he had to return to his old employer.

However, Stanton wanted to study and did so in a law office in Steubenville. In 1835 he passed his bar examination. Later that year he became a partner in a law office in Cadiz, Ohio. His reputation as a capable lawyer was soon established, and he was now able to take care of his own family and to marry Mary Lamson. He moved back to Steubenville, where he formed a partnership.

Stanton had meanwhile been dabbling in local politics, and in 1837 he was elected county prosecuting attorney on the Democratic ticket. In 1842 he was appointed reporter of the Ohio Supreme Court and was gaining a reputation as a hardfisted, ingenious lawyer. A move to Pittsburgh in 1847 opened the way for Stanton to become connected with cases in which large sums of money were involved and to which national attention was attracted. He was important in the famous McCormick patent infringement case and, especially, the revelation of frauds in California land grants. He was soon well known and was in 1860 named U.S. attorney general in President James Buchanan's Cabinet. Stanton became secretary of war in President Lincoln's Cabinet in 1862. He reorganized the War Department and did a creditable job of meeting army needs. Yet his blunt and high-handed manner made enemies, and he played no little part in the divided character of Lincoln's Cabinet.

After Lincoln's assassination, Stanton went on to serve President Andrew Johnson, but he supported the Radical element in Congress against both the President and the Supreme Court. When Johnson asked for Stanton's resignation, Stanton refused; Johnson suspended him and ordered Ulysses S. Grant to take over the department.

Five months later, with the Radicals in control of Congress, the Senate voided Johnson's suspension and ordered Stanton to return to his department. In response Stanton remained day and night in his office while President Johnson's appointee was refused control. Not until Johnson's impeachment trail did Stanton resign. Broken in health and in dire financial straits, he died in Washington on Dec. 24, 1869, just a few days after Grant, now president, named him to the Supreme Court.

Further Reading

The most complete work on Stanton is Benjamin P. Thomas and Harold M. Hyman, *Stanton: The Life and Times of Lincoln's Secretary of War* (1962). Another biography is Fletcher Pratt, *Stanton: Lincoln's Secretary of War* (1953). Stanton figures prominently in studies of Lincoln's administration: Burton J. Hendrick, *Lincoln's War Cabinet* (1946), and James G. Randall, *Lincoln, the President* (4 vols., 1946-1955). Intimate views of Stanton and other members of Lincoln's government are in Howard K. Beale, ed., *The Diary of Gideon Welles* (3 vols., 1960).

Additional Sources

Thomas, Benjamin Platt, *Stanton, the life and times of Lincoln's Secretary of War,* Westport, Conn.: Greenwood Press, 1980.

□

Elizabeth Cady Stanton

The writer and reformer Elizabeth Cady Stanton (1815-1902) was perhaps the most gifted and versatile feminist leader in American history.

Elizabeth Cady was born in Johnstown, N.Y., on Nov. 12, 1815. The daughter of a judge, she became a feminist while still a child after hearing her father inform abused women that they had no legal alternative but to endure mistreatment by their husbands and fathers. She had the best education then available to women. While completing her studies at the Troy Female Seminary, she experienced a nervous collapse on hearing the great revivalist James Finney preach; henceforth she had an intense hostility toward organized religion.

In 1840 Elizabeth Cady married the abolitionist leader Henry B. Stanton. Although he sympathized with her ambitions, he was not wealthy, and she remained home with her five children for many years. All the same, she was able to do some writing and speaking for the feminist cause. In 1848 she organized America's first woman's-rights convention, held in Seneca Falls, N.Y., where the Stantons resided. She also composed a declaration of principles, which described the history of mankind as one of "repeated injuries and usurpations on the part of man toward woman, having in direct object the establishment of an absolute tyranny over her." Despite opposition, she persuaded the convention to approve a resolution calling for women's suffrage.

During the Civil War, Stanton and her friend and ally Susan B. Anthony created the National Woman's Loyal League to build support for what became the 13th Amendment to the Constitution. Once the slaves were free, the two worked to ensure that women would be enfranchised along with the freedmen. However, their work was seen as a threat to the black franchise. If the struggle to enfranchise black males was associated with votes for women, it was thought, neither black men nor women of any color would get the vote. But this opposition only made the Stantonites more stubborn. Their campaign finally divided the women's suffrage movement into two camps: their own New York-based band of uncompromising radicals, the National Woman Suffrage Association, and a more conservative group, the American Woman Suffrage Association, which was centered in Boston and accepted the primacy of black suffrage. There were several ideological differences between the two organizations, and a good deal of personal animosity developed. By 1890, however, these were overcome, and the two organizations merged into the National American Woman Suffrage Association, with Stanton as president.

Although Stanton remained active into old age, she was less concerned with suffrage and more interested in divorce reform and other matters during her last years. A fluent and witty writer, she collaborated with Anthony and Matilda Gage on the first three volumes of the massive *History of Woman Suffrage* and edited *The Woman's Bible.* Mrs. Stanton also wrote articles on a variety of subjects for the best contemporary magazines. She died on Oct. 26, 1902, in New York City.

Further Reading

Mrs. Stanton's autobiography, *Eighty Years and More* (1898), is engaging; it should be supplemented by Harriet Stanton Blatch and Theodore Stanton, eds., *Elizabeth Cady Stanton as Revealed in Her Letters, Diary and Reminiscences* (2 vols., 1922). Volumes 1-3 of the *History of Woman Suffrage* (1881-1888), which she edited with Susan B. Anthony and Matilda Joslyn Gage, contain important material, as does volume 4 (1903), edited by Susan B. Anthony and Ida Husted Harper. A good biography is Alma Lutz, *Created Equal: Elizabeth Cady Stanton, 1815-1902* (1940). □

Starhawk

Starhawk (Miriam Simos; born 1951) was a leading theoretician and practitioner of feminist Wicca (witchcraft) in the United States.

On June 17, 1951, Miriam Simos (who later took the name Starhawk) was born in St. Paul, Minnesota. Educated in public schools, she regularly attended Hebrew study sessions after school and later frequently credited her Jewish upbringing as a major influence on evolving religious and political sensibilities. In 1982 she received a Master's degree in the feminist therapy program at Antioch University West. She worked as a psychotherapist in San Francisco from 1983 to 1986, then taught at Antioch West and other colleges in the San Francisco Bay Area. She traveled widely, lecturing and teaching the art of ritual-making to various members of the clergy, therapists, and personal-growth seekers.

Starhawk was a major voice in the feminist spirituality movement. Her view of witchcraft as "Goddess Religion" and the model of nurturing strength she saw in the figure of the historical witch caused a resurgence of interest in "neo-pagan" traditions. Her first book, *The Spiral Dance: A Rebirth of the Ancient Religion of the Great Goddess* (1979, and Tenth Anniversary Edition, 1989), was a panoramic introduction to the movement adherents called "Wicca." It was also heralded as a manifesto for a truly feminist religion that welcomed men. Starhawk explored the roots of the Wiccan revival in earliest prehistory, comparing witchcraft more to tribal, shamanic practices than the world religions of the patriarchal era. She traced the persecution of native European, nature-based religions into the mass witch-hunts of medieval times. She contended that the Roman Catholic Inquisition drove paganism underground, passed on secretly until its re-discovery in the 20th century.

The Spiral Dance presented an eclectic mix of theology, feminist theory, mind-expanding exercises, poetry, and rituals for celebrating the ancient seasonal festivals of the year. In it Starhawk espoused three principles central to her theology. Goddess was seen as immanent in the world. All things were interconnected; therefore, "magic" ("the art of changing consciousness at will") must be ethical and include a focus on social justice. Goddess Religion fostered community to re-define maleness/femaleness and to transform a deteriorating planet into a place for life-affirming culture.

In her next work, *Dreaming the Dark: Magic, Sex, and Politics* (1982), Starhawk elaborated the role of ritual as an agent of societal change. Advocating the fusion of spirituality and politics, she developed her theories of the "culture of estrangement," the patriarchal mainstream based on "power-over," and the emerging Goddess-centered communities which emphasize "power-from-within." Her experience in the 1981 blockade of the Diablo Canyon Nuclear Power Plant in coastal California formed the backdrop of the work. Confronting "the dark"—her own fear of nuclear annihilation—she wove historical material from 16th-and 17th-century Europe with personal reflections from the women's jail near the power plant.

Positing magic as directed energy, an art, and as will, she argued that it necessitates an "ethics of integrity," which demands consistency between images and actions. Yet these "are not based on absolutes imposed upon chaotic nature, but upon the ordering principles inherent in nature." She pondered that if such political events as the blockade are acts of magic (aimed at changing consciousness), then applying the principles of magic to political actions can make the latter more effective. The results of this cross-pollination were several exercises for consensus group process and an analysis of political groups from a magical world view.

In *Dreaming the Dark* Starhawk contended that when we recoil from words like "Witch" and "Goddess," our discomfort is a sign of potential liberation into new thought forms. She added that the God, consort or son of the Goddess, can become an image to guide men back into the "mother-ground," healing their separation from woman and from nature. The Goddess and God, she asserted, "can become doorways leading out of patriarchal cultures, channels for the powers we need to transform ourselves, our visions, and our stories."

In a later edition, Starhawk remarked that she no longer accepted the psychological theories she learned in graduate school. Instead, she came to hold more accountable the cultural systems of control and domination that bear down on the individual and on groups. Her third work, *Truth Or Dare: Encounters with Power, Authority and Mystery* (1987), synthesized her views on personal development, political action, and witchcraft into a "psychology of liberation." Again, autobiographical accounts of the antinuclear movement were abound. This time she identified a third form of power in political communities, "power-with," described as "the art of gaining influence and using it creatively to empower." Power-from-within and power-with, she argued, can overthrow the internal Judge, Conqueror, and Censor, thus changing their manifestations in patriarchal culture.

True to form, scholarship had its place in this multifaceted work as well. An important chapter focused on the transition from matrifocal to patriarchal times in the Middle

East. Through Starhawk's poetry throughout the work, the Sumerian Goddess Inanna points the way for feminist women and changing men who would confront authority and encounter mystery.

In 1988 Starhawk was teaching at the Institute in Culture and Creation Spirituality in Oakland, California, headed by the renegade Roman Catholic priest Matthew Fox. When Fox was investigated and silenced by the Vatican late that year, he showed the press a letter from Cardinal Ratzinger of the Vatican's Congregation for the Doctrine of the Faith. It urged him to "disassociate himself" from "wicca, the ideology of Starhawk." In response, Starhawk remarked that she was puzzled by the cardinal's apprehension, for it was the Church who had burned witches, not the other way around.

During the 1990s, Starhawk continued her Wicca evangelicalism through teaching week-long "Witch Camps" and working in the Covenant of the Goddess, a legally recognized Church since 1975. She was also active in demonstrations against the clear cutting of old growth redwoods. Keeping up with the electronic age Starhawk established a home page on the Internet providing information on her appearances and witch camps. She published *Walking to Mercury* (1997), a prequel to *The Fifth Sacred Thing. Mercury,* the story of Maya Greenwood's wild experiences with magic, sex, and politics in the sixties, has been portrayed as an autobiographical work. Starhawk denied that the work was autobiographical, but that Maya "often does things I thought about doing."

Further Reading

There was no biography of Starhawk. She was profiled in Michele Jamal's *Shape Shifters: Shaman Women in Contemporary Society* (1987). Starhawk's works were woven with autobiographical content: see especially the introduction to *The Spiral Dance* (1989) and preface to *Dreaming the Dark* (1988). She published other accounts of her experiences in small pagan-feminist journals; see especially *Woman of Power* (Summer 1988) and *Reclaiming,* the newsletter of Starhawk's own collective. An entertaining account of Starhawk's involvement in the first International Pagan Spirit Gathering can be found in "Pagan Spirit Journal No. 1." □

Danielle Steel

Danielle Steel (born 1947) is an internationally bestselling author of over thirty romance novels. Since publishing her first book in 1973, Steel has acquired an enormous following of loyal, avid readers.

Steel was born on August 14, 1947, in New York City, the only child of John Schuelein-Steel, a member of Munich's wealthy Lowenbrau beer family, and Norma Schuelein-Steel, an international beauty from Portugal. Steel's parents divorced when she was seven or eight years old. Afterwards, she was raised by relatives and servants in Paris and New York. She graduated from the Lycee Francais when she was not quite fifteen and in 1963 entered New York's Parsons School of Design. However, she soon abandoned her dream of becoming "the new Chanel" when the pressure to succeed caused her to develop a stomach ulcer. She then enrolled at New York University, where she studied until 1967. When she was eighteen, Steel married her first husband, a French banker with homes in New York, San Francisco, and Paris. Within a few years, she became bored with her jet-setting lifestyle and, against her husband's wishes, decided to find a job. In 1968, she was hired as vice president of public relations and new business for Supergirls, a Manhattan public relations and advertising agency. A few years later the five-woman firm began to falter and Steel was looking to the future.

One of her clients, then the editor of *Ladies' Home Journal,* suggested she try writing, so Steel isolated herself at her home in San Francisco and wrote her first book, *Going Home.* Published by Dell paperbacks in 1973, the novel had moderate sales. Around the same time, Steel's marriage broke up, and she turned to writing in earnest. However, she composed five more novels that were rejected before *Passion's Promise* was published by Dell in 1977. During these years she also wrote advertising copy as well as poems about love and motherhood that appeared in women's magazines. Some of these poems were included in the abridged edition of her only volume of poetry, *Love Poems: Danielle Steel* (1981), which came out in 1984. After *Passion's Promise,* Dell published three more of Steel's romances: *The Promise* (1978), a novelization of a screenplay by Garry Michael White, *Now and Forever* (1978), which was

adapted for a film released by Inter Planetary Pictures in 1983, and *Season of Passion* (1979). Sales of *The Promise,* Steel's first big success, reached two million copies in 1979, and in the same year she signed a six-figure contract with Dell.

Steel set a grueling pace for herself, composing two to three novels a year, and in the early 1980s several more best-selling paperbacks appeared. In addition, Dell's affiliate, Delacorte, began publishing Steel's books in hardcover. *Thurston House* (1983) was the last of her novels to originate as a paperback. Steel tailors her work habits to meet family considerations. In 1981 she married John Traina, a shipping executive who, like herself, had two children. The couple has since produced five children together. Steel works in concentrated marathon sessions, which affords her blocks of time she can devote to her large family. Unlike many of her heroines, Steel shies away from the limelight, refusing to do promotional tours, and lives a relatively quiet life that is frequently far from glamorous. When writing, she has been known to work eighteen-hour days, typing away on a 1948 metal-body Olympia in a flannel nightgown.

Though she is an extremely wealthy woman—she recently signed a sixty-million-dollar contract with Delacorte—Steel shows no signs of relaxing her frantic pace. In 1994 she published three more novels, *Accident, The Gift,* and *Wings,* and since 1989, she has produced two series of books for children, the "Max and Martha" series and the "Freddie" series. Steel's romances feature both contemporary and historical settings, and their exotic and exciting locales offer readers fast-paced escape from the routine of daily life. They typically focus on a glamorous, well-to-do heroine who proves that women can "have it all": love, family, and career. However, Steel's characters are beset by obstacles on their road to fulfillment; often they are confronted with the task of rebuilding their life after an emotionally crippling tragedy. Sometimes Steel's heroines have one or more unlucky romances before they find lasting love, but all their relationships with men lead them to increased self-awareness, which, in many cases, helps them to establish successful careers.

A sampling of Steel's plots illustrates these themes. The heroine of *Passion's Promise* is a beautiful young journalist, Kezia St. Martin, who temporarily puts her career on hold to be with her lover, who is a social activist. The romance ends in tragedy but it provides St. Martin with the grounding she needs to come to terms with her family's affluence and to realize her goal of becoming a renowned writer. *Family Album* (1985) is about a famous actress who forsakes stardom to marry a wealthy playboy, watches anxiously as her husband squanders their fortune, and then achieves success as an Oscar-winning director. *Zoya* (1988) traces the eventful and dramatic life of the beautiful and resourceful Russian countess Zoya Ossupov. When the violent October Revolution explodes, she loses her position, wealth, and much of her family, and she flees to Paris, where she falls in love with a wealthy American army officer, whom she marries. Zoya and her husband live an exciting life in New York City during the Roaring Twenties but her happiness is destroyed once again when the stock market crashes, bankrupts her husband, and causes him to suffer a fatal heart attack. Another marriage brings more heartache. Zoya's second husband, a Seventh Avenue mogul who helps her launch a chain of department stores, enlists in the armed forces after the Japanese attack on Pearl Harbor and is killed in action. Brokenhearted, but not broken, Zoya summons her courage and makes a new life for herself. *Message from Nam* (1990) takes the lovely, intelligent Paxton Andrews from her native Savannah, Georgia, to her college years at the University of California, Berkeley, where she studies journalism, and then to her life as a war correspondent in Vietnam. Paxton loses her first two loves to the war. When a third boyfriend is reported missing in action, Paxton abandons hope that he is still alive, but they finally find each other, and they take one of the last helicopters home from Saigon.

In *Kaleidoscope* (1987) and *No Greater Love* (1991) Steel turns her attention to the love shared by siblings. *Kaleidoscope* is the story of three young sisters who are separated after their father kills their mother in a jealous rage and then commits suicide; the girls grow up living completely different lives yet after many trials and tribulations they are eventully reunited. One of the sisters survives the horrors of rape and incest to become a powerful television network executive. *No Greater Love* concerns a twenty-one-year-old woman, Edwina Winfield, who takes it upon herself to care for her younger brothers and sisters after their parents die on the Titanic, a tragedy that also claims the life of Edwina's fiance. Edwina's burdens are eased by her family's wealth, but she nonetheless makes great sacrifices and endures much loneliness in an effort to keep her brothers and sisters together.

In a few of her novels, Steel shifts her focus to male characters. *Fine Things* (1987), for example, is about a department store executive, Bernard Fine, whose beloved wife dies from cancer a few years after their marriage, and *Daddy* (1989) describes the emotional recovery of Oliver Watson after his wife of eighteen years abandons him and their three children. *Secrets* (1985), another uncharacteristic novel, has six major characters, all of whom work on the set of a television soap opera.

While Steel can lay claim to one of the largest readerships in popular fiction, she is anything but a favorite among critics. Even when reviewers acknowledge that Steel is a commercial writer who does not pretend to write serious literature, they seem compelled to point out what they see as major weaknesses in her novels: bad writing, shallow characterization, preposterous plot twists, unconvincing dialogue, and rigid adherence to the "poor little rich girl" formula. Her novels are also faulted as being unrealistic because they focus on the lives of the wealthy and privileged. Critics reserve their harshest comments for Steel's prose style, which is generally considered to be sloppy and careless. A number of critics have expressed amazement that Steel's books do not undergo more extensive editing, and some have appeared to take delight in pointing out her run-on sentences, non sequiturs, and frequent repetition of certain words and phrases. In a review of *Daddy,* for example, Edna Stumpf remarked, "Ms. Steel plays with the themes of love and work like a child with a Barbie doll. She strips a life down, only to dress it up in billows of her famous free-associative prose, as scattered with commas as a Bob Mackie gown is with bugle beads." While some critics might prefer to dismiss Steel without comment, her enormous popularity makes her impossible to ignore. Beginning with her third hardcover, *Crossings* (1982), all of Steel's novels have received coverage in the *New York Times Book Review.* Steel responded to her critics in the Spring, 1987, issue of *Booktalk:* "Each book is different. I do historical plots, books about men, about women, about totally different things. I don't think the press likes big commercial authors. I have seen devastating reviews on my books, Jackie Collins', Judith Krantz', and Sidney Sheldon's books. We all get beaten up by the press. They usually pick a remote, esoteric writer to do the review, which is so unfair. There is obviously something to our books or millions of people wouldn't be buying them." Despite their low appraisals of Steel's talents as a writer, critics concede that her tear-jerking tragedies and happy endings meet some need in her millions of readers, be it a desire for satisfying diversion or for emotional catharsis.

Steel's fans have also been able to enjoy her stories in the form of television movies. In 1986 *Crossings* was presented as an ABC miniseries starring Cheryl Ladd, Jane Seymour, and Christopher Plummer; NBC made television movies from *Kaleidoscope* and *Fine Things* in 1990, and aired *Palomino* (1981), *Changes* (1983), and *Daddy* in 1991; a miniseries called *Danielle Steel's "Zoya,"* with Melissa Gilbert and Bruce Boxleitner. Several of Steel's other novels, including *Thurston House* and *Wanderlust* (1986), have also been optioned for television films and miniseries.

Further Reading

Bestsellers 89, Issue 1, Gale, 1989.
Bestsellers 90, Issue 4, Gale, 1991.
Chicago Tribune, June 3, 1996; December 29, 1996.
Chicago Tribune Book World, August 28, 1983.
Detroit Free Press, December 1, 1989.
Detroit News, September 11, 1983.
Globe & Mail (Toronto), July 9, 1988.
Library Journal, September 1, 1993; October 15, 1993. □

David Martin Scott Steel

The British politician Sir David Martin Scott Steel (born 1938) was a Scottish member of Parliament and leader of the Liberal Party beginning in 1976.

David Steel was born on March 31, 1938, in Kirkcaldy, Scotland. His father was the Very Rev. Dr. David Steel, a Calvinist minister. From the age of 11 to 15 Steel was with his family in Kenya, Africa where he developed a sympathetic understanding of the plight of Black Africans. (He was president of the Anti-Apartheid Movement of Great Britain from 1966 to 1969.) He was educated at the Prince of Wales School in Nairobi, and afterwards, back in Scotland, at George Watson's College and at Edinburgh University, where he earned an M.A. in 1960 and an LL.B. in 1962.

At Edinburgh University he joined the Liberal Party, and it provided him with a career for life. He was not able to join the Labour Party because he did not feel "socialist" enough; and he could not accept the Tory Party for its going to war with Egypt over the Suez Canal in 1957. He joined the Liberals, knowing that it was a small party and was unlikely to win electoral votes. The Liberals were strong in Wales and Scotland (the so-called "Celtic fringe") and weak in heavily-populated areas.

As a student he became good friends with Jo Grimond, the leader of the Liberal Party, and managed his election as rector of Edinburgh University. Upon graduation in 1960 Steel was chosen as assistant secretary of the Liberal Party.

He married Judy MacGregor, a college contemporary, in 1962, and when he was elected to a seat in the House of Commons in 1965 they lived in Ettrick Bridge in the Scottish Borders country. At 26, he was the youngest member of Parliament. Steel was organized, hard-working, even-tempered, and rational, which showed up in his work in the House of Commons. The first legislation for which he gained a distinct recognition was his Private Member's Bill to reform the out-of-date abortion law. The law was enacted in 18 months, and it took political skill and very hard work on Steel's part (1967).

Jo Grimond was weary of his job as leader of the party and resigned in 1967; Jeremy Thorpe took his place. The

Liberal Party of Gladstone, Asquith, and Lloyd George now experienced a leader—Thorpe—who came to grief on a sordid scandal involving his liaison with a male model and his misuse of party funds (1976). Steel, who had been chief whip and the effective second man in the party, was a candidate for leader to replace Thorpe; he fought a bitter election for that post against John Pardoe and won.

During Steel's early days in the job of leader of the Liberals, the prime minister was James Callaghan (Labour, 1976-1979). Steel struck an understanding with Callaghan ("the Lib-Lab Pact," as some unhappy Liberals called it), about how the Liberals would react to the Conservative (Margaret Thatcher's) motion of no-confidence in Callaghan's government. The Liberals would support the Labour government, provided that they had some say over policy. For instance, there was to be no more nationalization of industry. The experiment lasted 18 months; Steel ended it in the autumn of 1978.

In May 1979 the Conservatives, under Thatcher, swept the board in the election. During the next few months, private conversations between Steel and his friend Roy Jenkins (home secretary in Labour governments of the 1960s and 1970s and president of the European Community in 1979) explored how to form a new party—the Social Democrats—which Jenkins would lead. The Social Democratic Party (SDP) emerged 15 months later, in March 1981, when the "Gang of Four" (ex-Labour ministers) combined: Jenkins, David Owen, Shirley Williams, and William Rodgers. Reputedly, the "Fifth Wheel" was Steel who encouraged the rest to escape from the Labour Party.

In a previous meeting with Jenkins, Steel promised to form an "alliance" between his Liberals and the new party, the Social Democrats. At one time Steel looked for an outright merger of the Social Democrats and the Liberals to form a third party opposing the Conservative and Labour parties. A large segment of the British electorate wanted that too, he thought.

The election of June 1983 was disappointing for the SDP and for Steel's Liberals. Thatcher and her Conservative Party were triumphant in the Falklands War (1982), and that victory over Argentina carried the Tories to victory at election time. SDP strength dwindled to six members of Parliament (at the outset there were 26 members). The Liberals, in contrast, stood at a steady 17 members, but were chagrined at the loss by the SDP. Maybe the British electorate did not want a third party at all.

Two of the Gang of Four lost their seats in Parliament, leaving David Owen (foreign secretary under Callaghan, 1976-1980) and Jenkins. Owen replaced Jenkins as Social Democratic leader, much to Steel's surprise.

The "two Davids"—Steel and Owen—were facing each other. Which would be leader of the merged parties, if they did in fact merge? David Owen had more ministerial ("front-bench," as the English say) experience, and he had more ideas than Steel. David Steel had more members of Parliament behind him and was a television professional (he had been a broadcaster). Perhaps Steel was the first British politician of the television era.

Meanwhile, the Labour Party was not finished. Neil Kinnock, a Welshman, emerged at the leader of the Labour Party (1983). Like Steel, he had an accent that exempted him from any note of class in the class-ridden English society. The leaders of both the Labour and the Liberal parties were from the "Celtic fringe" now—Wales and Scotland. Kinnock's rise in the public-opinion polls was at the expense of David Owen and the Social Democratic Party, not at the expense of David Steel and the Liberals. In the 1987 parliamentary election Thatcher's Conservatives won 376 seats, Kinnock's Labourites 229, and the "Alliance" only 22 seats—17 Liberals and 5 Social Democrats. Both minor parties then voted to work out a merger. David Owen resigned in protest, leaving David Steel the clear leader in the merged party.

In 1990 Steel became a "Knight Commander of the Order of the British Empire" (KBE). The next year, Sir David Steel was awarded the title "Her Majesty's Deputy Lieutenant (DL) for Roxburghshire, Ettick and Lauderdale." He held the post as joint Chairman of the Scottish Constitutional Convention from 1991-1993. An Honorary Doctorate of Merit was bestowed on Steel by the President of the Federal Republic of Germany in 1992.

Further Reading

Additional information on David Steel and the political climate in which he functioned can be found in Hugh Stephenson, *Claret and Chips: the Rise of the SDP* (London, 1982); Cyril Smith, *Big Cyril* (London, 1977); and John Newhouse, "Profiles: David Steel," *New Yorker* (May 21, 1984). David Steel, *High Ground of Politics* (London, 1979) and *A House Divided* (London, 1980) provided insights on Steel's philosophy and politics. Steel's autobiography *Against Goliath* was published in 1990 and as a paperback in 1991. □

Sir Richard Steele

The British essayist, dramatist, and politician Sir Richard Steele (1672-1729) is best known for his collaboration with Addison on a series of essays for the *Tatler* and the *Spectator*.

Richard Steele was born in Dublin, Ireland, in March 1672. The exact date of his birth is not known, but he was baptized on March 12. Steele's father, an attorney, died in 1676, and his mother died the next year. He was placed under the guardianship of his maternal uncle, Henry Gascoigne, who was secretary and confidential agent to the Duke of Ormonde. In 1684 he began attending Charterhouse School, London, where he met Joseph Addison. Both Steele and Addison went to Oxford, Steele entering Christ Church in 1689 and transferring to Merton College in 1691. His Oxford career was undistinguished, and he left in 1692 without taking a degree in order to volunteer for cadet service under the command of the Duke of Ormonde. Steele then served in the Life Guards and later transferred to the Coldstream Guards. In 1695 Lord Cutts, to whom Steele had dedicated a poem on the funeral of Queen Mary, became Steele's patron. Steele first served him as private secretary and then became an officer in Cutts's regiment in 1697. Two years later Steele received a captaincy in a foot regiment.

During these years of military service in London, Steele became acquainted with a circle of literary and artistic figures, and he began to write. His first comedy, *The Funeral, or Grief A-la-mode,* was performed successfully at Drury Lane Theatre in 1701. This play was a satire on the new profession of undertaking. It was followed by *The Lying Lover, or The Ladies' Friendship* in 1703. His third comedy, *The Tender Husband, or The Accomplished Fools,* produced in 1705, achieved some success, perhaps because Addison helped him write it.

A constant need for money dominated much of Steele's life because his spending habits were impulsive and extravagant. In 1705 he married an elderly and propertied widow, Margaret Stretch. She died in 1706, leaving him an annual income of £850, and in 1707 Steele married Mary Scurlock (died 1718), the "Dear Prue" of a series of delightful letters he addressed to her. They had four children, but only Elizabeth, the eldest daughter, survived to maturity. Steele lived in considerable style after his second marriage, and his habits continued to be free-spending and improvident. He left the army in 1707, or perhaps earlier, and in the years following secured several minor appointments.

On April 12, 1709, Steele launched his own paper, the *Tatler,* to be published three times weekly. Partly a newspaper and partly a journal of politics and of society events, the *Tatler* soon featured essays on general questions of manners, morality, and entertainment. The great majority of the *Tatler* issues were authored by Steele, Addison writing about 46 by himself and about 36 in conjunction with Steele. The *Tatler,* though prosperous, discontinued publication for obscure reasons on Jan. 2, 1711.

The first issue of the *Tatler's* brilliant successor, the *Spectator,* appeared on March 1, 1711. It was a joint venture of Steele and Addison, who was the chief contributor to the new paper. However, in this paper, as in the *Tatler,* Addison followed Steele's choice of subjects. The Steele-Addison literary partnership ranks as one of the most successful in the history of English literature. Both men were Whigs and sympathized with the moral attitudes of England's rapidly growing middle class. They differed greatly in temperament, Steele being impulsive and warmhearted and Addison restrained and sedate. The *Spectator* had a run of 555 daily numbers, discontinuing publication on Dec. 6, 1712. Of this number, Steele authored about 240 issues.

Steele made many additional forays into periodical journalism. The most notable of these, some of which were purely political, were the *Guardian* (March 12-Oct. 1, 1713); the *Englishman* (Oct. 6, 1713-Feb. 11, 1714; July 11-Nov. 21, 1715); and the *Lover* (Feb. 25-May 27, 1714), which saw the publication of 40 essays by Steele. The *Plebeian* (1718), Steele's most famous political journal, involved him in a dispute with Addison, whose death in 1719 frustrated Steele's attempt at reconciliation.

During these years Steele served as the chief Whig propagandist; as the principal journalist of the Whigs in opposition, he was the antagonist of Jonathan Swift, who held the corresponding job for the Tories. Steele's writings frequently made his political career perilous. Appointed commissioner of stamps in 1710, he was forced to resign from this office in 1713. That same year he was elected to Parliament from Stockbridge, but he was expelled in 1714 on a charge of sedition.

After the accession of George I to the English throne in 1714, Steele obtained a number of political favors. In 1715 he was knighted and was reelected to Parliament. Steele's intemperance gradually undermined his health, and he suffered from gout for many years. In 1722 he wrote his last and most successful comedy, *The Conscious Lovers.* In 1724—still notoriously improvident, impulsive, ostentatious, and generous—Steele was forced to retire from London because of his mounting debts and his worsening health. He went to live on his wife's estate of Llangunnor in Wales, and in 1726 he suffered a paralytic stroke. His health broken, Steele died at Carmarthen, Wales, on Sept. 1, 1729.

Further Reading

Most of Steele's works are available in modern editions. *The Tatler* was edited by George A. Aitken (4 vols., 1899) and *The Spectator* by Donald F. Bond (5 vols., 1965). The standard biographies of Steele are George A. Aitken, *The Life of Richard Steele* (2 vols., 1889), and Willard Connely, *Sir Richard*

Steele (1934). Other studies of value include George S. Marr, *The Periodical Essayists of the Eighteenth Century* (1923); F. W. Bateson, *English Comic Drama, 1700-50* (1929); John Loftis, *Steele at Drury Lane* (1952); Rae Blanchard, ed., *The Englishman: A Political Journal* (1955); Arthur R. Humphreys, *Steele, Addison and Their Periodical Essays* (1959); and Bertrand A. Goldgar, *The Curse of Party: Swift's Relations with Addison and Steele* (1961). □

Vilhjalmur Stefansson

The Canadian-American Arctic explorer, scientist, and author Vilhjalmur Stefansson (1879-1962) discovered new lands and became an authority on Eskimo life and language.

Vilhjalmur Stefansson was born near Arnes, Manitoba, on Nov. 3, 1879, of Icelandic parents recently settled in Canada. The family soon moved to North Dakota, where Stefansson grew up. A brilliant student despite little formal schooling, he entered the University of North Dakota but was expelled in 1902 for excessive absences. Transferring to the University of Iowa, within a year Stefansson received credit by examination for 4 years of college, after which he studied religious folklore and anthropology at Harvard University.

Stefansson's fieldwork began with trips in 1904 and 1905 to study the language and dietary habits of the Icelanders. In 1906 he signed on the Leffingwell-Mikkelsen Arctic expedition as its ethnologist. He arranged to meet the expedition in the North, but it failed to reach Stefansson at the Mackenzie River delta, so he spent the winter among the Eskimo, learning much of their way of life. From 1908 until 1912 Stefansson led an expedition back to the Arctic, exploring northern Alaska and the Canadian archipelago. This trip led to his discovery of the Copper (blond) Eskimo. From 1913 to 1918 he headed a Canadian government-sponsored expedition in the Arctic, during which he tested his controversial theories on diet and survival: he believed that explorers could live off the wildlife in the Arctic, even on the polar ice floes, by adapting Eskimo ways. Despite dissension among some of his subordinates and the loss of one ship, Stefansson and two companions traveled 500 miles across the moving ice of Beaufort Sea to Banks Island in dramatic proof of these ideas.

Upon returning to the United States in 1918, Stefansson made several lecture tours and began to establish himself as an expert on polar subjects through his numerous writings. His first major work was *My Life with the Eskimo* (1913), and he amplified his unconventional views of the North as he discussed his 5-year sojourn in *The Friendly Arctic* (1921). He stressed the economic potential of the Arctic and predicted transpolar trips by both airplanes and submarines. He also developed at this time what had started as a hobby—a collection of polar literature now considered the finest in the world.

From 1932 to 1945 Stefansson served as an adviser on northern operations to Pan-American Airways, and he performed similar services for the military during World War II. He prepared Arctic manuals and language guides and demonstrated survival techniques.

Stefansson, who married Evelyn Schwartz Baird in 1941, spent the last 15 years of his life in Hanover, N.H., where he served as Arctic consultant to the Northern Studies program at Dartmouth College and continued lecturing, teaching, and writing. A witty, gifted, and inspiring conversationalist and teacher, the iconoclastic Stefansson was as effective in assisting others and furthering Arctic knowledge as he had been as an explorer and scientist. The author of more than a score of books and several hundred articles, Stefansson died in Hanover on Aug. 26, 1962.

Further Reading

The best source on Stefansson's life is his brilliant *Discovery: The Autobiography of Vilhjalmur Stefansson* (1964), completed just weeks before his death. An excellent study of Stefansson and his expeditions is Leslie H. Neatby, *Conquest of the Last Frontier* (1966). His exploits are recounted in Laurence Patrick Kirwan, *A History of Polar Exploration* (1960).

Additional Sources

Diubaldo, Richard J., *Stefansson and the Canadian Arctic,* Montreal: McGill-Queen's University Press, 1978.

Hunt, William R., *Stef: a biography of Vilhjalmur Stefansson, Canadian Arctic explorer,* Vancouver: University of British Columbia Press, 1986.

Vilhjalmur Stefansson and the development of Arctic terrestrial science, Iowa City, Iowa: University of Iowa, 1984. □

Lincoln Steffens

Lincoln Steffens (1866-1936) was the most famous of the American muckraker journalists of the period 1903-1910. His exposés of corruption in government and business helped build support for reform.

Lincoln Steffens was born on April 6, 1866, in Sacramento, Calif. The son of a wealthy businessman, he went to an expensive military academy where he began showing signs of the rebelliousness that would eventually lead him to political radicalism. After barely graduating from the academy, he went to the University of California at Berkeley, where he became convinced that the answers to the great questions of life and politics lay in the study of philosophy. Upon graduating in 1889, he continued his pursuit of "culture" in Europe, studying at universities in Germany and France.

When Steffens returned to New York in 1892, secretly married to an American girl he had met in Germany, he found a $100 check from his father and a note saying that this was the last subsidy. Steffens got a job as police reporter for the *New York Evening Post.* He soon became fascinated with the tangled web of corruption that ensnared the police department and municipal government in general. He wrote of this for the *Evening Post* in the 1890s, as did other journalists. But he became famous for this only in 1903, when, as an editor of *McClure's Magazine,* he began a series of articles on corruption in various American cities entitled "The Shame of St. Louis," "The Shame of Minneapolis," and so on, which portrayed a pattern of shocking corruption in municipal government throughout the country.

The publication of Steffen's articles, in conjunction with the first chapters of Ida Tarbell's exposé of the Standard Oil Company, led to a sharp climb in *McClure's* circulation, and soon many other magazines were competing to boost their circulations by exposing the ills of American government. This type of writing was derided by President Theodore Roosevelt as "muckrake" journalism, and the term stuck.

Steffen's series, published as *The Shame of the Cities* (1940), became a best seller. Its popularity was well deserved, for Steffens's work stood far above most of the other muckraking exposés of municipal corruption in terms of both literary style and intellectual perception. He was not interested in merely exposing corrupt bosses. Indeed, his affection for many of those colorful characters shows through in his work. He wanted to expose the pattern of corruption and the real villains, the supposedly respectable, honest businessmen whose bribes and greed fueled the whole system.

The decline of muckraking journalism about 1910 coincided with Steffens's growing doubts as to its effectiveness. He increasingly doubted the effectiveness of reform politics, which seemed to seek to eradicate the symptoms of corruption rather than its causes. With the outbreak of the Mexican Revolution in 1910, he became fascinated by the idea of revolution and wrote many articles in the succeeding decade supporting the more radical revolutionaries. He saw the revolution as an attempt to uplift Mexico by eliminating the two most corrupting factors: American domination and capitalism.

Steffens was coming to associate the economic system of capitalism with the cause of social corruption; the apparent success of the Bolshevik Revolution seemed to bear him out. In 1921, returning from a trip to the Soviet Union, he uttered his famous words, "I have seen the future, and it works."

Like many liberals and radicals, Steffens found the United States of the 1920s a very uncongenial place. He moved to Europe and settled in a villa in Italy, where he became mildly enamored with Mussolini's revolution and began working on his autobiography. *The Autobiography of Lincoln Steffens* hit the United States at just the right time. Published in 1931, after 2 years of the Great Depression, it chronicled Steffens's mental journey from oversophisticated intellectual to reformer to revolutionary in a way that struck a deep chord among many people who felt that they should travel the same route. Although he never joined the Communist party, Steffens clearly indicated his thought that only something like a Communist revolution could save the

United States. However, it was not just what he said but how he said it that made the book an instant success, for he wrote with wit, charm, and compassion. His autobiography is certainly one of the most interesting, literate, and thought-provoking autobiographies of the 20th century. He died in Carmel, Calif., on Aug. 9, 1936.

Further Reading

The best book on Steffens is his *Autobiography* (1931). His *The Shame of the Cities* (1904; repr. 1957) reveals that he was not as naive a muckraker as his *Autobiography* would indicate. Interesting insights can be gleaned from *The Letters of Lincoln Steffens,* edited by Ella Winter and Granville Hicks (2 vols., 1938). A useful collection of many of his articles is *The World of Lincoln Steffens,* edited by Ella Winter and Herbert Shapiro (1962). Louis Filler, *Crusaders for American Liberalism* (1950), is a standard work on the muckrakers. Also useful is David M. Chalmers, *The Social and Political Ideas of the Muckrakers* (1964). A provocative chapter on Steffens is in Christopher Lasch, *The New Radicalism in America, 1889-1963* (1965), and a lively sketch of him is in Arthur and Lila Weinberg, *Some Dissenting Voices* (1969), a discussion of the American spokesmen for human dignity from 1833 to 1938.

Additional Sources

Horton, Russell M., *Lincoln Steffen,* New York, Twayne Publishers 1974.

Kaplan, Justin, *Lincoln Steffens; a biography,* New York, Simon and Schuster 1974.

Palermo, Patrick F., *Lincoln Steffens,* Boston: Twayne Publishers, 1978.

Stinson, Robert, *Lincoln Steffens,* New York: F. Ungar Pub. Co., 1979. □

Edward Steichen

Edward Steichen (1879-1973) was an American photographer, painter, and museum curator who helped transform photography into an art form. At the turn of the century his photographs were hailed for their artistic quality. In the 1920s he produced a new style of fashion illustration and portraiture for magazines.

Edward Steichen was born in Luxembourg on March 27, 1879. The family settled in Hancock, Michigan, in 1881, where the father worked in a copper mine. Eduard—as he then spelled his name—went to Pio Nono College near Milwaukee in 1888 and showed such talent for drawing that on leaving school he became an apprentice at a Milwaukee lithographing company. In 1895 he bought a camera. Three years later his photographs, which a critic called "ultra expressionistic," were accepted at the Second Philadelphia Salon of Pictorial Photography.

Meanwhile, Steichen had organized the Milwaukee Art Student's League and served as its first president. He decided to study painting in Paris, and on his way there in 1900 he stopped in New York to meet Alfred Stieglitz, who was America's foremost photographer and leader of a movement to gain for photography recognition as a fine art. They became close friends. Steichen was confounder with Stieglitz of the Photo-Secession, an organization dedicated to photography as a fine art, and its exhibition gallery, called "291." The gallery exhibited photographs and introduced to America paintings, drawings, and sculpture by such modern artists as Paul Cézanne, Henri Matisse, Pablo Picasso, and Constantin Brancusi. Steichen's photographs were widely exhibited; among the most famous were his portraits of J. P. Morgan and Auguste Rodin.

During World War I Steichen was in command of all aerial photography of the American Expeditionary Force; he retired as lieutenant colonel in 1919 and settled in Voulangis, France. He gave up painting and abandoned the soft-focus and heavily retouched style that had won him fame as a photographer. He used the camera directly, emphasizing sharpness and texture. In 1922 he returned to America and a year later opened a commercial studio in New York, specializing in advertising photography. For *Vanity Fair* and *Vogue* magazines he produced fashion illustrations and portraits of outstanding personalities. He closed his studio in 1938 to devote his time to plant breeding. When America entered World War II, he was commissioned lieutenant commander and put in command of all Navy combat photography.

At the age of 68 Steichen was named director of photography at the Museum of Modern Art in New York. Of the many exhibitions he created, the largest and most famous was "The Family of Man." This exhibition of 503 photographs toured throughout America and overseas. The book

of the same title became a best seller. His involvement as a curator helped promote photography to the status of an acknowledged art form. In 1961 Steichen held an exhibition of his own photography at the Museum of Modern Art; a year later he retired to Connecticut. His autobiography, *A Life in Photography,* appeared in 1963, the same year he was awarded the Medal of Freedom by President John F. Kennedy.

In later life Steichen continued to experiment with new photographic techniques. At his 90th birthday celebration, he said, "When I first became interested in photography, I thought it was the whole cheese. My idea was to have it recognized as one of the fine arts. Today I don't give a hoot . . . about that. The mission of photography is to explain man to man and each man to himself. And that is no mean function. Man is the most complicated thing on earth and also as naive as a tender plant."

He died in Connecticut in 1973.

Further Reading

Steichen's own account was *A Life in Photography* (1963). Biographies included: Penelope Niven's *Steichen: A Biography* (Crown, 1997); Patricia Johnston's *Real Fantasies: Edward Steichen's Advertising Photography* (University of California Press, 1997); and Eric Sandeen's *Picturing an Exhibition: The "Family of Man" & 1950s America* (University of New Mexico Press, 1995). An old biography is Carl Sandburg, *Steichen, the Photographer* (1929). A large, representative selection of Steichen's work was New York Museum of Modern Art, *Steichen the Photographer* (1961), exhibition catalog with text by Sandburg, Alexander Liberman, and Steichen and chronology by Grace M. Mayer. □

Edith Stein

German philosopher Edith Stein (1891-1942) was a leading proponent of the phenomenological school of thought led by Edmund Husserl in the first half of the twentieth century. In her writings, Stein attempted to reconcile phenomenology with her Catholic beliefs in works on Thomas Aquinas, St. John of the Cross, and the topic of women in the Church. A Jew by birth who converted to Catholicism, she was killed in a Nazi concentration camp and beatified as a Catholic martyr in 1987.

The twentieth-century German philosopher Edith Stein was a student of Edmund Husserl and a prominent supporter of his theories on phenomenology. Born into a Jewish family, Stein's search for spiritual truth led her first to atheism and later to the Roman Catholic Church, where she eventually became a Carmelite nun. She attempted to connect her philosophical and religious beliefs in her writings that discussed topics such as the role of women in the Catholic Church, Thomism, and the mysticism of St. John of the Cross. She is considered a martyr by both Jews and Catholics for her death in the concentration camps of the Nazi regime during World War II.

Edith Stein was born on October 12, 1891, in Breslau, Germany. She was the youngest of eleven children born to Jewish lumber merchants hailing originally from Silesia (now part of Poland); four of her siblings had died before Stein's birth. Stein's father died when she was only a year old, leaving her mother, Auguste Stein, in charge of the debt-ridden business and the surviving children. Because her mother was required to devote most of her time to work outside the home, her oldest daughter, Else, took on much of the responsibility of raising the other children. As a child, Stein became known for her intelligence and sense of humor—she would often recite poetry and make clever remarks. But she disliked her reputation as "the smart one" of the family and began to develop a more isolated, introspective nature in her early school days. She attended the Victoria School in Breslau, where she not only began classes early, but quickly became the best student in her grade. Her love of learning extended to her hours at home as well, where she spent much of her free time reading.

Religious Crisis Led to Atheism

At the age of 13, Stein underwent a crisis of faith and decided to leave school. Although she no longer believed in God, she did not discuss her beliefs with her family and continued to attend religious services. Thinking that she was suffering from poor health, her mother sent her to rest at the home of her sister Else, who had married and moved to Hamburg. After eight months in Hamburg, Stein came to terms with her new ideas and decided to devote her life to teaching and the pursuit of the truth. She returned to Victoria School and completed her coursework in anticipation of attending college.

She began her advanced education at the University of Breslau in 1911. In the hopes of gaining some insight into the mysteries of human experience and the soul, she took a psychology course, but was disappointed at its emphasis on quantitative experimentation. About this time she read the philosophical work *Logische Untersuchungen* ("Logical Investigations") by Edmund Husserl. Husserl, who was a professor of philosophy at Göttingen University, was the founder of the school of thought known as phenomenology, an examination of the development of human consciousness. The book was a revelation to Stein, who decided that she wanted to study with Husserl himself. She transferred to Göttingen, where she was one of the first female students to attend the university. There she found a group of philosophers who shared her interests, and she was encouraged by Husserl, who told her that the practice of phenomenology could lead her to the truth she sought.

Became Leading Phenomenologist

It was at Göttingen that Stein was first exposed to the Roman Catholic faith. A fellow student, Max Scheler, who was also a Jew by birth but would later convert to Catholicism, gave lectures on religious philosophy that introduced Stein to the tenets of the faith. Scheler's work involved the ranking of human values, and he placed religious values as the factor that defines humanity. While his teachings showed Stein the richness of the Christian faith, it also made her reflect on her own lack of religious beliefs and started her on her own search for religious meaning. She was also influenced in this thinking by another phenomenologist who converted to Christianity, Adolf Reinach.

With the beginning of World War I in 1914, Stein volunteered her services at a hospital that treated soldiers suffering from cholera, typhus, and dysentery. The hospital closed a year later, and Stein returned to the university and completed her doctoral studies. She had selected the idea of empathy as the subject of her investigations in phenomenology, and Husserl was very impressed with her work. Although he had several distinguished students, including the philosopher Martin Heidegger, Husserl considered Stein to be the best student he had ever had. When in 1916 he took a professorship at the University of Freiburg, Husserl requested that Stein join him as his graduate assistant. That year she completed her doctoral dissertation, "The Problem of Empathy," and received her doctoral degree with honors. She was then hired as a faculty member at Freiburg, where she taught phenomenology and helped Husserl to edit his manuscripts. She was very successful at Freiburg and soon became known as a top philosopher at the university.

Converted to Catholicism

Stein's interest in Catholicism increased in 1917 with the death of her friend Reinach, who had been killed in battle at Flanders. She was approached by Reinach's widow, who asked her to organize her husband's academic papers. In Reinach's writings, she found many references to Jesus Christ, and this led her to read the New Testament. These experiences convinced Stein that she believed in God and the divinity of Jesus Christ, but she did not yet take steps to convert to an organized religion. She returned to her work in philosophy, applying to Göttingen to work as a professor. But the school's longstanding ban on female professors was upheld, despite a glowing recommendation from Husserl. Stein returned to Breslau in 1919 to teach and continue her research. It was during this period, in 1921, that she finally was inspired to commit to the Catholic Church. While visiting friends in Bergzabern, Germany, that summer, she discovered the autobiography of St. Teresa of Avila. She found herself unable to put down the book, and after spending a whole night reading it, she was certain that she was ready for conversion. She attended her first Mass and requested that the priest baptize her, but she found that she had to complete a period of instruction first. She returned to her work in Breslau but came back to Bergzabern to be baptized on January 1, 1922.

Stein felt that her new religious life included a calling to serve in a religious order, but she did not do this immediately out of respect for her mother, who was quite disturbed by her daughter's conversion. Instead, she began working at a girl's school in Speyer, Germany, run by Dominican nuns. She followed the Dominican's practices closely, even though she was not one of them, accepting only enough money to cover basic living expenses. During her stay at Speyer, she was encouraged by the Jesuit priest and philosopher Erich Przywara not to abandon her academic work. At his urging, she began a German translation of a Latin work on truth by St. Thomas Aquinas. Through her study of Aquinas and her discussions with Przywara, she was convinced that she could serve God through a scholarly search for truth. Her writing and translations became popular and Stein was invited to lecture for a number of groups on religious and women's issues in Germany, Switzerland, and Austria. By 1931, these experiences had convinced her that she should leave Speyer and return to her philosophical work full-time.

Completes Book on Jewish Life

The academic world in the 1930s, however, was growing increasingly anti-Semitic, and Stein found that she was not welcome at the schools at Freiburg and Breslau. She finally managed to obtain a lecture position at the Educational Institute in Münster in 1932. There she continued her work on Scholasticism and phenomenology, but she also felt the need to address the increasing hatred and violence that she witnessed around her. Attacks on Jews were becoming frequent and in 1933, the Nazi leader Adolf Hitler came to power in Germany. One result of the rise of Hitler was that Stein, along with other Jews in university positions, was fired from her job. She felt that she had a unique opportunity and responsibility, as a Jewish-born Catholic, to bridge the gap of understanding between Christians and Jews. To accomplish this, she penned the book *Aus dem Leben einer Jüdischen Familie,* or "Life in a Jewish Family," which tried to show the similar human experiences of Jews and Christians in their daily lives.

In 1933, Stein felt that she was ready to devote her life more completely to religious pursuits. She applied to the Carmelite convent in Cologne, and at the age of 42, was accepted as an initiate to the order. There she took the religious name Teresa Benedicta a Cruce, in honor of St. Benedict and St. Teresa of Avila as well as the Passion of Christ. She was encouraged by her superiors to continue her philosophical writings, which included an attempt to combine the thoughts of Husserl and Aquinas in her book *Endliches und ewiges Sein* ("Finite and Eternal Being"), completed in 1936. Under the anti-Jewish laws in effect then, however, the book was refused for publication and was not printed until 1950.

After the Kristallnacht, a night in which numerous Jewish businesses and synagogues were vandalized and burned in Germany, Stein realized that she was no longer safe in her native country. Also wishing to avoid bringing harm to her Carmelites sisters by her presence in their convent, she moved to a Carmelite convent in Echt in the Netherlands on December 31, 1938. In Echt, she was joined by her sister Rosa, who had also converted to Catholicism. Although still not completely out of danger, Stein attempted to return to a normal pattern of life, instructing younger women in Latin and training her sister Rosa as a Carmelite. She also continued her writing, completing a phenomenological work on the life of the mystic St. John of the Cross entitled *Kreuzewissenschaft: Studie über Joannes a Cruce* ("The Science of the Cross: A Study of Saint John of the

Cross''), a book that also would not see publication until after the war.

Killed in Concentration Camp

In 1942, the Nazis began removing Jews from the Netherlands, and Stein urgently applied for a Swiss visa in order to transfer to a convent in Switzerland. Her sister was unable to arrange similar travel arrangements, however, and Stein refused to leave without her. On August 2, 1942, the sisters were removed from the convent at Echt by Nazi troops and transported to a concentration camp at Amersfoort for a few days before being sent on to the Auchwitz camp in Poland. While nothing is know about their last days or the exact circumstances of their deaths, it is assumed that the women were among the many people killed in the Nazi gas chambers, placed in mass graves on the site, and later cremated.

In 1987, decades after the travesties of the Jewish Holocaust, Stein was beatified by Pope John Paul II, who lauded her as a Catholic martyr and also praised her phenomenological works. This created controversy among Jewish groups, who were upset that she was remembered in this way since the reason she was killed was because she was a Jew, not because she was Catholic. In an apologetic statement, John Paul II acknowledged that her fate was a symbol of the great loss of Jewish life during World War II. This discussion highlighted the difficult, but important place that Stein holds among both Jews and Catholics. She is remembered by many people for her untiring search for truth in both the philosophical and spiritual realms and her attempts to use this knowledge to promote peace and understanding in the face of hatred and war.

Further Reading

Graef, Hilda C., *The Scholar and the Cross: The Life and Work of Edith Stein,* Newman Press, 1955.

Herbstrith, Waltraud, *Edith Stein: A Biography,* translated by Bernard Bonowitz, Harper & Row, 1985.

Nota, John H., ''Misunderstanding and Insight about Edith Stein's Philosophy,'' *Human Studies,* Vol. 10, 1987, pp. 205-12.

Oben, Freda Mary, *Edith Stein: Scholar, Feminist, Saint,* Alba House, 1988.

Posselt, Sister Teresia Renata de Spriritu Sancto, *Edith Stein,* translated by Cecily Hastings and Donald Nicholl, Sheed & Ward, 1952. ☐

Gertrude Stein

American writer Gertrude Stein (1874-1946) was a powerful literary force in the period around World War I. Although the ultimate value of her writing was a matter of debate, in its time it profoundly affected the work of a generation of American writers.

Gertrude Stein was born in Allegheny, Pennsylvania, on February 3, 1874, the youngest of five children of affluent German-Jewish-American parents. As a child, she lived in Vienna and Paris but grew up mainly in Oakland and San Francisco, California. Her early formal education was spotty, but she was an avid reader and had a strong interest in art. With only a year of high school, she managed to be admitted in 1893 to Radcliffe College, where she specialized in psychology and became a favorite of William James. He discovered her great capacity for automatic writing, in which the conscious mind is suspended and the unconscious directly evoked. The exaltation of the primitive mind at the expense of the sophisticated mind was to become an important principle in Stein's esthetic theory and is manifest in most of her writing.

The Expatriate

Stein did not take a degree at Radcliffe or at Johns Hopkins, where she studied medicine for 4 years. In 1903 she went to Paris and took up residence on the Left Bank with her brother Leo. In 1907 she met Alice B. Toklas, a wealthy young San Franciscan who became her lifelong companion and secretary, running the household, typing manuscripts, and screening visitors. France became their permanent home.

In her early Paris years Stein established herself as a champion of the painting avant-garde. With her inherited wealth she patronized young artists and knew virtually all of the important painters, including Pablo Picasso, who did a famous portrait of her, Henri Matisse, Juan Gris, André

Derain, and Georges Braque. Her brother Leo became a famous art critic, but their relationship, which had been extremely close, became permanently estranged in 1912 because of a disagreement over his marriage.

Stein's first two books, *Three Lives* (1909) and *Tender Buttons* (1915), stirred considerable interest among a limited but sophisticated audience, and her home became an informal salon visited by many creative people, including American composer Virgil Thomson, British writers Ford Madox Ford, Lytton Strachey, and Edith Sitwell, and American writers Ezra Pound, Elliot Paul, Sherwood Anderson, F. Scott Fitzgerald, and Ernest Hemingway. It was to Hemingway that Stein characterized the disenchanted expatriate veterans as a "lost generation."

A woman with deep black eyes and a supremely self-assured manner, Stein was frequently intimidating, impatient with disagreement, and prone to alienate associates. The stylistic innovations and peculiarities of her writing appealed primarily to a small coterie, but her prestige as a taste maker was lifelong.

Stein's 1934 visit to the United States for the opening of her opera *Four Saints in Three Acts,* with music by Virgil Thomson, culminated in an enormously successful university lecture tour. During the German occupation of France, both Stein and Toklas lived briefly in Culoz, returning to Paris in 1944. Stein's reactions to World War II were recorded in *Paris, France* (1940) and *Wars I Have Seen* (1945), and her interest in the soldiers was reflected in the idiomatic conversations of *Brewsie and Willie* (1946), which was published a week before her death, on July 27, 1946, in Neuilly.

Her Writings

Stein's first book, *Three Lives,* her most realistic work, foreshadowed her more abstract writings and evinced a number of influences: neoprimitivist painting, Flaubert's *Trois contes,* and automatic writing. "Melanctha," the best of the three novelettes that constituted the book, was an especially tender treatment of an impulsive, flirtatious African-American woman whose relations with men were recorded in a colloquial, deliberately repetitious style intended to capture the immediacy of consciousness; indeed, incremental repetition is the crucial element of Stein's style, which was perhaps most accurately called "subjective realism."

Stein wanted to give literature the plastic freedom that painting has, and *Tender Buttons* was a striking attempt at verbal "portraits" in the manner of the cubist painters. The denotative value of words was almost entirely abandoned; instead, words were used in a connotative, associative, and surrealistic way.

The Making of Americans: Being a History of a Family's Progress (1925) gave character analysis within a family chronicle, although it was chiefly concerned with the servants and only marginally with the family members. In the 1930s and 1940s she concentrated on memoirs, esthetic theory, plays, and art criticism. *How to Write* (1931) and *The Geographical History of America: The Relation of Human Nature to the Human Mind* (1936) explained the theoretical basis of her literary practice.

The Autobiography of Alice B. Toklas (1933), written as if by Toklas, was an autobiography of Stein. Unexpectedly intelligible and charming, it became a best seller. Critic F. W. Dupee called it "one of the best memoirs in American literature." A sequel, *Everybody's Autobiography* (1937), described Stein's visit to America, and *Portraits and Prayers* (1934) was a collection of verbal pictures of her Paris circle.

Stein's libretto for *Four Saints in Three Acts* (1934) was a study of the attraction of opposites—the ascetic and the compassionate. Similar to her nondramatic work in its surrealism and plotlessness, shored up by music and spectacle, it was better received than most of her writings. *Picasso* (1939) was an erratic, witty, sometimes illuminating study of the development of the great painter's art. Her three wartime books and *In Savoy; or Yes Is for a Very Young Man: A Play of the Resistance in France* (1946) showed unexpected social concern.

After Stein's death, there were numerous publications of the works she left behind. Some of the more notable are *The Previously Uncollected Writings of Gertrude Stein* and *Dear Sammy: Letters from Gertrude Stein and Alice B. Toklas.* These works were released in 1974 and 1977 respectively. In 1996 Stein's *Four Saints in Three Acts* was remade into an avant-garde opera.

Further Reading

Stein remains a controversial figure. The closest to a definitive study was Richard Bridgman, *Gertrude Stein in Pieces* (1970). The most adulatory study was William G. Rogers, *When This You See, Remember Me: Gertrude Stein in Person* (1948); and the most damaging books were by her brother, Leo Stein, *Appreciations: Painting, Poetry and Prose* (1947), and by Benjamin L. Reid, *Art by Subtraction: A Dissenting Opinion on Gertrude Stein* (1958). The best studies were in Edmund Wilson, *Axel's Castle* (1931); Donald Sutherland's sympathetic and judicious critical work, *Gertrude Stein: A Biography of Her Work* (1951); John Malcolm Brinnin's biography, *The Third Rose: Gertrude Stein and Her World* (1959); Allegra Stewart, *Gertrude Stein and the Present* (1967); and Norman Weinstein's scholarly *Gertrude Stein and the Literature of the Modern Consciousness* (1970). Stein was discussed in George Wickes, *Americans in Paris* (1969). Information regarding the new opera based on Stein's work can be read about in *Time* (March 11, 1996). □

Baron Heinrich Friedrich Karl vom und zum Stein

The Prussian statesman Baron Heinrich Friedrich Karl vom und zum Stein (1757-1831) was the initiator and planner of the Prussian recovery after the collapse of 1806.

Baron Stein was born in Nassau on Oct. 26, 1757, the scion of an ancient knightly family. He studied at the University of Göttingen and entered the Prussian administrative service as an expert on mining in 1780. He served reliably but without extraordinary distinction in that capacity for a quarter century. Most of his service was in the detached Prussian provinces of Cleves and Jülich, a circumstance that led him to conclude that centralized absolutism of the sort that characterized most 18th-century states could not be made to work very well. In 1804 he was appointed minister of commerce but was dismissed after 2 years by Frederick William III for insisting too stridently on administrative reform.

Stein retired to his residence at Nassau and composed a memorandum in which he declared that the only way that Prussia could recover from its collapse at the hands of Napoleon was to turn away once and for all from sterile absolutism and to associate all of its people with the Crown in the great work of regeneration. This argument so impressed the King that he not only recalled Stein but appointed him prime minister with extensive and unprecedented powers (1807). Stein at once proclaimed an end to serfdom and opened all professions to every citizen. He decentralized the administration, transforming the larger towns into practically self-governing units, while standardizing administrative procedures throughout the realm. He also laid plans for calling to life elective assemblies which would share in the power of the Crown and which would be elected by all landowners.

Stein was unable to effect this last reform, as his conduct of foreign policy brought about his fall. Unable to obtain from a victorious Napoleon a reduction of the enormous indemnities he was demanding from Prussia, Stein tried to convince the Austrians to join Prussia in a renewal of the war. These negotiations came to the attention of the French, and at their insistence, Stein was once again dismissed (1808). Four years later he was called to Russia as special adviser to Czar Alexander I and there worked on behalf of the Russian government to bring Prussia back into the war against Napoleon, which he succeeded in doing in 1813. In his exile he had concluded that only a united Germany could prevail among its more powerful neighbors. But, as this notion pleased neither his King nor the all-powerful Austrian chancellor Prince Metternich, who preferred to see Germany continue divided into a multitude of independent and powerless states, many of which would be dependent on Austria's goodwill, Stein found himself isolated at the Congress of Vienna. He retired into private life in 1816 and died at his castle, Kappenberg, on June 29, 1831.

Further Reading

Information on Stein and his times can be found in Guy S. Ford, *Stein and the Era of Reform in Prussia* (1922); Walter M. Simon, *The Failure of the Prussian Reform Movement, 1807-1819* (1955); Hajo Holborn, *A History of Modern Germany,* vol. 2 (1964); R. C. Raack, *The Fall of Stein* (1965); and K. S. Pinson, *Modern Germany* (2d ed. 1966). □

John Ernst Steinbeck

John Ernst Steinbeck (1902-1968), American author and winner of the Nobel Prize in 1962, was a leading exponent of the proletarian novel and a prominent spokesman for the victims of the Great Depression.

John Steinbeck was born on Feb. 27, 1902, in Salinas, Calif., the son of a small-town politician and schoolteacher. He worked as a laboratory assistant and farm laborer to support himself through 6 years of study at Stanford University, where he took only those courses that interested him, without seeking a degree. In 1925 he traveled to New York (by way of the Panama Canal) on a freighter, collecting impressions for his first novel. *Cup of Gold* (1929) was an unsuccessful attempt at psychological romance involving the pirate Henry Morgan.

Undiscouraged, Steinbeck returned to California to begin work as a writer of serious fiction. A collection of short stories, *The Pastures of Heaven* (1932), vividly detailed rural life among the "unfinished children of nature" in his native California valley. His second novel, *To a God Unknown* (1933), his strongest statement about man's relationship to the land, reveals a strain of neo-primitive mysticism later to permeate even his most objectively deterministic writings. With *Tortilla Flat* (1935) Steinbeck received critical and popular acclaim, and there are many critics who consider this humorous and idyllic tale of the Monterey paisanos Steinbeck's most artistically satisfying work.

Steinbeck next dealt with the problems of labor unionism in *In Dubious Battle* (1936), an effective story of a strike by local grape pickers. *Of Mice and Men* (1937), first conceived as a play, is a tightly constructed novella about an unusual friendship between two migratory workers. Although the book is powerfully written and often moving, its theme lacks the psychological penetration and moral vision necessary to sustain its tragic intention.

Steinbeck's series of articles for the *San Francisco Chronicle* on the plight of migratory farm laborers provided material for *The Grapes of Wrath* (1939), his major novel and the finest proletarian fiction of the decade. The struggle of a family of Oklahoma tenant farmers, forced to turn over their land to the banks and journey across the vast plains to the promised land of California—only to be met with derision when they arrive—is a successful example of social protest in fiction, as well as a convincing tribute to man's will to survive. *The Grapes of Wrath* combines techniques of naturalistic documentation and symbolic stylization, its episodic structure being admirably held together by the unifying device of U.S. Highway 66 and by lyrical interchapters which possess a Whitmanesque expansiveness. The novel's weaknesses lie in occasional lapses into sentimentality and melodramatic oversimplification, Steinbeck's tendency to depict human relationships in biological rather than psychological terms, and the general absence of philosophical vision and intellectual content. It received the Pulitzer Prize in 1940.

During World War II Steinbeck served as a foreign correspondent; from this experience came such nonfiction as *Bombs Away: The Story of a Bomber Team* (1942); his dispatches of 1943, collected as *Once There Was a War* (1958); and *A Russian Journal* (1948) with photographs by Robert Capa. More interesting nonfiction of this period is *The Sea of Cortez,* coauthored with marine biologist Edward F. Ricketts. This account of the two explorers' research into sea life provides an important key to many of the themes and attitudes prevalent in Steinbeck's novels.

Steinbeck's fiction during the 1940s includes *The Moon Is Down* (1942), a tale of the Norwegian resistance to Nazi occupation; *Cannery Row* (1944), a return to the milieu of *Tortilla Flat; The Wayward Bus* (1947); and *The Pearl,* a popular allegorical novella written in a mannered pseudobiblical style about a poor Mexican fisherman who discovers a valuable pearl which brings ill fortune to his family.

In the 1950s Steinbeck's artistic decline was evident with a series of novels characterized by their sentimentality, pretentiousness, and lack of substance. The author received modest critical praise in 1961 for his more ambitious novel *The Winter of Our Discontent,* a study of the moral disintegration of a man of high ideals. In 1962 *Travels with Charley,* a pleasantly humorous account of his travels through America with his pet poodle, was well received. Following the popular success of the latter work, Steinbeck was awarded the Nobel Prize.

Steinbeck's finest novels are a curious blend of scientific determinism, romantic mysticism, and a rudimentary, often allegorical, type of symbolism. His work remains popular in both the United States and Europe, chiefly for its social consciousness and compassion and the narrative qualities exhibited in the early novels. Although he refused to settle into political conservatism in his later years, his all-embracing affirmation of American values and acceptance of all national policies, including the Vietnam War, lost him the respect of many liberal intellectuals who had once admired his social commitments. He died on Dec. 28, 1968, in New York City.

Further Reading

There is no biography of Steinbeck. Critical studies of his work are Harry T. Moore, *The Novels of John Steinbeck: A First Critical Study* (1939; 2d ed. 1968), and Peter Lisca, *The Wide World of John Steinbeck* (1958). Peter Covici, ed., *The Portable Steinbeck* (1943; 3d ed. 1963), contains an extensive introduction to the writer and his works by Louis Gannett. For brief but important criticism see Edmund Wilson, *The Boys in the Back Room* (1941), and those chapters devoted to Steinbeck in such studies of American literature as Maxwell Geismar, *Writers in Crisis* (1942); Wilbur M. Frohock, *The Novel of Violence in America, 1920-1950* (1950; 2d ed. 1957); and Frederick J. Hoffman, *The Modern Novel in America* (1951). The most comprehensive collection of Steinbeck criticism is E. W. Tedlock, Jr., and C. V. Wicker, eds., *Steinbeck and His Critics: A Record of Twenty-five Years* (1957). □

Gloria Steinem

The feminist and journalist Gloria Steinem (born 1934) was active in many liberal causes beginning in the mid-1950s and was the first editor of *Ms.* magazine. She became a leading spokeswoman of the feminist movement and helped shape the debate over women's enfranchisement.

Gloria Steinem was born on March 25, 1934, in Toledo, Ohio. Her father was an antique dealer and her mother was a newspaperwoman. She was the granddaughter of the noted suffragette, Pauline Steinem. Given her family's background, it was not surprising that she became a feminist and a journalist. But her life followed a winding path which began in her youth, when she travelled around the country with her parents in a trailer.

When she was only 8 years old her parents divorced, leaving Steinem to live the next several years with her mother in bitter poverty. Her mother suffered from depression so severe that she eventually became incapacitated, required young Steinem to care for her. At the age of 15 she went to live with her sister, ten years her senior, in Washington, D.C., and from there she entered Smith College. When she graduated from Smith in 1956 (Phi Beta Kappa and *magna cum laude*), she won a fellowship to study in India for two years.

Steinem's experience in India broadened her horizons and made her aware of the extent of human suffering in the world. She realized for the first time the high standard of living most Americans take for granted was not available to all. She commented at the time that "America is an enormous frosted cupcake in the middle of millions of starving people." She returned with a strong sense of social injustice and embarked on her career as a journalist.

In 1960 she moved to New York and began writing freelance articles for popular magazines. She also did some script writing for the popular television show *That Was the Week That Was.*

One of her first major assignments in investigative journalism was a two-part series for *Show* magazine on the working conditions of Playboy bunnies. In order to do research for the article, Steinem applied for a job as a Playboy bunny and was hired. She held the position for three weeks in order to do research. The articles that she wrote as a result of her experience exposed the poor working conditions and meager wages of the women who worked long hours in the lavish clubs where rich men spent their leisure time. Years later, in 1970, she published a lengthy interview with Hugh Hefner, founder and editor of *Playboy* magazine. In that dialogue Steinem debated Hefner on issues such as women's rights, the "sexual revolution," consumerism, and the "Playboy philosophy."

In 1968 Steinem joined the founding staff of *New York* magazine and became a contributing editor. She established a column, "The City Politic," and wrote in support of causes on the American left. During these years Steinem moved into politics more directly, working for Democratic candidates such as Norman Mailer, John Lindsay, Eugene McCarthy, Robert Kennedy, and later George McGovern. She also worked with Cesar Chavez in his efforts on behalf of the United Farm Workers.

Steinem's feminist concerns were first sparked when she went to a meeting of the Redstockings, a New York women's liberation group. Although she went as a journalist with the intention of writing a story about the group, she found herself deeply moved by the stories the women told, particularly of the dangers of illegal abortions.

Gloria Steinem's commitment to the political causes of the New Left provided a natural path into her later career as a feminist leader. During the years she spent establishing herself as a journalist she was deeply involved in the political movements that were stirring thousands of her generation to action. The civil rights movement and the movement against the Vietnam War involved young women as well as men who dedicated themselves to building a future based on racial justice and peace. Out of these movements sprang the rebirth of feminism, which had remained dormant for several decades. Women discovered their organizing skills in the process of participating in the political left during the late 1950s and early 1960s, and by the late 1960s they began mobilizing on their own behalf. The new movement for women's liberation began at the grass roots level and swelled to mass proportions within a few short years.

By the late 1960s Steinem had gained national attention as an outspoken leader of the women's liberation movement, which continued to grow and gain strength. In 1971 she joined Bella Abzug, Shirley Chisholm, and Betty Friedan to form the National Women's Political Caucus, encouraging women's participation in the 1972 election. Steinem herself was active in the National Democratic Party Convention in Miami that year, fighting for an abortion plank in the party platform and challenging the seating of delegations that included mostly white males. Those efforts drew attention to the issue of underrepresentation of women in politics and the centrality of political issues for women's lives.

In that same year of 1972 Steinem, as part of the Women's Action Alliance, gained funding for the first mass circulation feminist magazine, *Ms.* The preview issue sold out, and within five years *Ms.* had a circulation of 500,000. As editor of the magazine Steinem gained national attention as a feminist leader and became an influential spokeswoman for women's rights issues.

Steinem's editorship of *Ms.* did not prevent her from continuing her active political life. In 1975 she helped plan the women's agenda for the Democratic National Convention, and she continued to exert pressure on liberal politicians on behalf of women's concerns. In 1977 Steinem participated in the National Conference of Women in Houston, Texas. The conference was the first of its kind and served to publicize the number of feminist issues and draw attention to women's rights leaders.

Steinem continued to speak and write extensively. In 1983 she published her first book, *Outrageous Acts and Everyday Rebellions.* The book included her recollections of the past, such as her experience as a Playboy bunny, and also highlighted the lives of other notable 20th-century women. In 1986 she published *Marilyn: Norma Jean,* a sympathetic biography of the unhappy life of the film star whom she knew personally. In her books Steinem argued for the causes that occupied her energies for two decades. She continued to call for an end to women's disadvantaged condition in the paid labor force, for the elimination of sexual exploitation, and for the achievement of true equality of the sexes.

Revolution From Within: A Book of Self-Esteem was published in 1992, in which Steinem attempted to provide "... a portable friend. It's self-help and inspiration, with examples of what some people have done and a glimpse of the extraordinary potential of the unexplored powers of the brain and how much our ideas of reality become reality." In 1994, Steinem published another book, *Moving Beyond Words,* wherein her views on publishing, society and advertising were expressed.

In 1997, Steinem spoke out against the movie *The People vs. Larry Flynt* in a *New York Times* editorial (January 7, 1997). She has also been the subject of an A&E Biography (television show) profile.

Further Reading

Numerous articles have been written and interviews published with Gloria Steinem from the mid-1960s into the 1980s. Her own book *Outrageous Acts and Everyday Rebellions* (1983) was a good starting point for information concerning her life and her beliefs. She has also been featured extensively in magazines such as *Cosmopolitan* (July 1990); *Time* (March 9, 1992); *Progressive* (June 1995; and *Mother Jones* (November 1995). She was listed in *Political Profiles,* Vol. 5: *The Nixon/Ford Years* (1979).

See also these selections written by Gloria Steinem: *A Thousand Indias* (1957); *Marilyn: Norma Jean* (1986); *Revolution from Within: A Book of Self-Esteem* (Little, Brown, 1992); and *Moving Beyond Words* (Simon & Schuster, 1994) □

Charles Proteus Steinmetz

The German-born American mathematician and electrical engineer Charles Proteus Steinmetz (1865-1923), by devoting himself to industrial research, made fundamental contributions to the development of both electricity and the industrial laboratory.

Charles Steinmetz was born Karl August Rudolf Steinmetz on April 9, 1865, in Breslau. His father worked for the government railway service, and Karl was encouraged to attend the university and pursue his intellectual curiosities. He had been deformed since birth and had lost his mother at the age of one year but found solace and excitement in the affairs of the mind. He entered the university at Breslau in 1883 and specialized in mathematics and the physical sciences. He also read widely in economics and politics, and in 1884 he associated himself with the Socialist party in Breslau. As he pursued his scientific education, he also continued his political activities, a pattern he was to continue throughout his life.

As ghost editor of the Breslau Socialist newspaper, *People's Voice,* Steinmetz attracted the attention of the police. In 1888, just as he had finished the work for his doctor's degree, he learned of plans for his arrest and fled to Switzerland. He never received his degree. He emigrated to the United States in 1889.

Steinmetz went to work in Yonkers, N.Y., for the electrical inventor Rudolph Eickemeyer, who put him to the task of improving alternating-current devices. In the course of this work he tackled the problem of hysteresis, or the loss of efficiency in electric motors due to alternating magnetism. There was some disagreement among electrical engineers whether such a loss even existed, and none had ever been able to measure it. Working from known data, Steinmetz applied mathematics of a very high level not only to demonstrate that hysteresis existed but to measure its exact effect in any given case. In 1892 he read two papers on the subject to the American Institute of Electrical Engineers.

One result of Steinmetz's growing reputation was his employment by General Electric Company in its consulting department. GE was then pioneering in the establishment of industrial research in the United States. The hiring of a mathematician of Steinmetz's caliber was thus a sign of the firm's growing recognition of the fact that it could not depend indefinitely upon buying patents that were independently and randomly arrived at but would have to begin a

systematic search for innovation within the firm itself. He worked first at Lynn, Mass., but soon he was moved to the head plant at Schenectady, N.Y., and given the designation of consulting engineer. This position left him comparatively free to pursue his own researches into electrical phenomena.

In his work for GE, Steinmetz applied his unique grasp of mathematics to electrical problems. He preferred not to be tied too closely to the ongoing work of the research laboratory but continued to work on practical as well as theoretical problems: batteries, incandescent and arc lights, and the artificial propagation of lightning in the laboratory all received his attention. This last success, with its giant spark crackling across the laboratory, had a dramatic impact upon a public already convinced that science was a fertile source of "miracles."

Throughout these years Steinmetz maintained his interest in public service and refused to allow his experiments, scientific writing, and teaching responsibilities at Union University to prevent him from discharging his duties as a citizen. He followed the Russian Revolution of 1917 with interest and in 1922 wrote to Lenin offering his services to the Soviet Union. Steinmetz was president of Schenectady's school board (1912-1923) and common council (1916-1923). In 1922 he ran unsuccessfully for the office of state engineer on the Socialist and Farmer-Labor tickets. He died in Schenectady on Oct. 26, 1923.

Further Reading

There are several biographies of Steinmetz, including John T. Broderick, *Steinmetz and His Discoveries* (1924); John E. Hammond, *Charles Proteus Steinmetz: A Biography* (1924); and Jonathan N. Leonard, *Loki: The Life of Charles Proteus Steinmetz* (1929), the last a more popular work. The technical context can be found in Kendall Birr, *Pioneering in Industrial Research: The Story of the General Electric Research Laboratory* (1957).

Additional Sources

Garlin, Sender, *Three American radicals: John Swinton, crusading editor: Charles P. Steinmetz, scientist and socialist: William Dean Howells and the Haymarket Era,* Boulder: Westview Press, 1991.

Kline, Ronald R., *Steinmetz: engineer and socialist,* Baltimore: Johns Hopkins University Press, 1992. □

Frank Stella

Frank Stella (born 1936), American painter, was one of the most dominant and influential figures in abstract painting during the 1960s through the 1990s.

Frank Stella was born in Malden, Massachusetts, on May 12, 1936. He attended the Phillips Academy in Andover (1950-1954), where he studied painting with Patrick Morgan. Stella graduated from Princeton University with a bachelor of arts degree in history in 1958. Because Princeton did not offer a degree in studio art, his development during these years was largely the result of self-teaching. However, he received important advice and encouragement from the painter Stephen Greene and the art historian William Seitz, both then teaching at Princeton.

Stella's first important group show was the Museum of Modern Art's "Sixteen Americans," held in 1959; this exhibition established him as one of the most radical young artists working in the United States. He instantly gained notoriety for his *Black Paintings,* a series of linear shapes and squares in various shades of black. A year later he had his first one-man show in New York City. Throughout the 1960s he exhibited regularly, and his work was included in numerous national and international group shows, the most important of which were the São Paulo Biennial and the Fogg Museum of Art's "Three American Painters," both held in 1965. His reputation and influence grew steadily, and in 1970 he was honored with a retrospective exhibition by the Museum of Modern Art.

From the time of his first one-man show, Stella's art revealed constant growth and change. Between 1958 and 1966 his primary concern was with shape—or, more precisely, with the relationship between the literal shape of a particular painting and the depicted shapes on the surface of the painting. Throughout most of this period his imagery consisted of slender bands of color that followed the outline of the literal shape of the picture support. But the supports themselves were shaped in a variety of ways, ranging from

squares and rectangles to trapezoids, hexagons, and even zigzags. In pursuing this concern, Stella single-handedly liberated painting from its traditional formats.

A major accomplishment of Stella's concern with shape was realized in 1966 in a series of paintings called the "Irregular Polygons." In these he abandoned the imagery of stripes, choosing instead to create literal and depicted shapes of a wholly abstract variety. One of the great achievements of the "Irregular Polygons" was that they rendered shape purely pictorial—that is, their shapes were felt to belong exclusively to the medium of painting.

Beginning in 1967 Stella worked on a group of paintings known as the "Protractor Series." Their imagery consisted of sweeping arcs of brilliant color. They marked a new direction in his work; he seemed to be aligning himself more with the coloristic exuberance of Henri Matisse than with the structural austerity of Pablo Picasso.

Stella's style has always been in an evolutionary format. Art critic Carol Diehl wrote in *ARTnews* that "Stella, unlike others of his stature, uses his fame as a platform from which he takes the risk of failing. Even at his worst, he's interesting, and each new turn provokes speculation as to what he'll do next."

In 1970, at the age of 33, the Museum of Modern Art in New York gave Stella a retrospective. That same year, Stella introduced the "Polish Village" series, artwork made up of paper, felt, and painted canvas pasted on a stretched canvas. The series lasted until about 1974, and included shapes of wood and homosote, turning the collage into low-relief works. In 1975, he started the "Brazilian" constructions, first made of honeycomb aluminum. These were angular and linear, with hot colors. He followed this with the "Exotic Birds," sculptures of both low and high relief from aluminum shapes that often had colors smeared on them. In 1977, he expanded to the "Indian Birds" series, in which the aluminum shapes jutted outward from curved sections of heavy steel mesh.

This series eventually gave way to the "Circuit" series of 1981. These shapes were even more intricately interlaced than previous works, and full of glitter. The next year, the "Shards" series was introduced, composed of left over pieces of metal from previous works on a squared-off aluminum sheet. This series featured sparkling zigzags and miscellaneous shapes. Wooden dowels, wire mesh and perforated strips of metal appeared in his next series, called "Playskool," which Stella produced from 1982-83. The next year, he unveiled "Cones and Pillars"—rows of stripes in varying widths, almost resembling schematics in massive volume.

In 1986, Stella wrote a book, *Working Space,* which was based on a series of lectures he did at Harvard University. The following year, he held retrospective at the Museum of Modern Art, displaying his works from 1970 through 1987.

Stella was very active in producing new works during the 1990s. His art literally continued expanding, including murals 100 feet to a full block long. He also produced abstract sculptures made of cast-plaster, Styrofoam, stainless steel, brass, and fiberglass. In 1990, he exhibited a block-long mural in Los Angeles for the Gas Company Tower in downtown. In 1993, his works became part of the architectural structure of the new Prince of Wales Theatre in Toronto. The lobbies on three floors and two grand stairwells contained nine computer-generated murals from Stella, three of which were more than 60 feet long. The fluid, dreamy patterns on the dome of the theater were designed by photo-plotting cigar smoke rings blown by the artist. 3-D reliefs were cast on the side panels of the aisle seats, and painted a velvet red.

In 1995, Stella exhibited at the Knoedler Gallery in New York, and unveiled *Loohooloo,* a fiberglass mural 97 feet long that bulged out four feet in a smooth, pillow-like fashion. Every inch was covered with twisted grids, graphic designs, and graffiti-style markings. Stella called these combinations of wild colors and patterns "color density." That year, Stella also exhibited a series of 30-year-old sketchings he made in Spain in the early 1960s that disclosed how he worked out ideas about shaped canvases. The show was particularly intriguing because it revealed ideas that later would culminate in his eccentric architecture of the "Polish Series" from the early 1970s, and the metal relief "Brazilian" series of the mid to late 1970s.

In 1995, he exhibited six large stainless steel sculptures at the newly opened Gagosian Gallery, each named after a small town in the Hudson River Valley of New York. They invoked metaphors of both the landscape and industry of the area, suggesting smokestack-filled factories and rolling countryside. The largest was 8 feet tall and 18 feet in depth, named Bear Mountain.

At the Reina Sofia gallery in Madrid in 1996, Stella held another retrospective, displaying 45 works dating from 1958 up through 1994. Art critic George Stolz wrote in *ARTnews* that "ever since the 'Black Paintings,' nothing seems to have been discarded. Each successive variation, motif, or technique has been added to the sum of all that preceded it." He said the show testified that Stella "now might be considered America's greatest living baroque painter."

Further Reading

The most brilliant essay on Stella was in the Fogg Art Museum's exhibition catalog by Michael Fried, *Three American Painters* (1965). Also see William Rubin's catalog for the Stella retrospective at the Museum of Modern Art, *Frank Stella* (1970), especially rich in illustrations. □

Joseph Stella

Joseph Stella (1877-1946), Italian-born American futurist painter, is best known for his dynamic interpretations of Brooklyn Bridge at night, with its dazzling automobile headlights and soaring crystalline forms.

Joseph Stella was born in Muro Lucano, a mountain village close to Naples. When he was 19, he went to America to study medicine and pharmacology. In 1897 he began to paint and enrolled as a full-time student at the Art Students League and then at the New York School of Art, studying under William Merritt Chase. Stella's earliest painting emulates the manner of Chase, who admired Diego Velázquez, Édouard Manet, and Frans Hals and interpreted American subjects with breadth of handling and richness of palette. Stella made several drawings of immigrants and miners for the magazines *Outlook* and *Survey*.

By 1910 Stella was back in Europe. He spent about a year in Italy and then went to Paris, where he met Henri Matisse, Pablo Picasso, and a number of the Italian futurists, including Umberto Boccioni, Carlo Carrà, and Gino Severini. Stella's enthusiasm for their art was not immediately translated into his own work, but after he returned to the United States late in 1912 he began his first large futurist painting, *Battle of Lights, Coney Island.* In this picture, forms are fractured and faceted to form a phantasmagoria of fragmented amusement-park architecture, disembodied by light and bright colors. It owes much to Severini in its conception. When the painting was exhibited in New York City, knowing art patrons admired it, but the general reception was negative.

Stella refined and applied his futurist approach to the American industrial scene, glorifying it by lending to it a precisionist character not unlike that of Charles Sheeler and Niles Spencer.

In 1920 Stella executed his first "Brooklyn Bridge" painting. He was to return to the theme as late as 1939 in his *Brooklyn Bridge: Variations on an Old Theme.* In these two paintings the scintillating and iridescent light patterns and hyperbolic sweep of steel are fixed by a taut, overriding symmetrical composition.

Stella became an American citizen in 1923. He made numerous trips abroad during the 1920s and 1930s. Visits to North Africa and Barbados inspired him to depict the spirit of a tropical environment in lush color and strong, centrally located forms. He also composed small, delicate, and intimate collages somewhat in the spirit of Paul Klee and Arthur Dove. Stella's development as an artist was marked by impulsiveness and surprising shifts and turns. He died in New York City on Nov. 5, 1946.

Further Reading

Irma B. Jaffe, *Joseph Stella* (1970), is the most complete study of the artist. Recommended for general background are Milton W. Brown, *American Painting: From the Armory Show to the Depression* (1955); and Daniel M. Mendelowitz, *A History of American Art* (rev. ed. 1970).

Additional Sources

Jaffe, Irma B., *Joseph Stella,* New York: Fordham University Press, 1988. □

Stendhal

The works of the French author Stendhal (1783-1842) mark the transition in France from romanticism to realism. His masterpieces—*The Red and the Black* and *The Charterhouse of Parma*—provide incisive and ironic depictions of love and the will to power.

Stendhal was born Marie Henri Beyle on Jan. 23, 1783, in Grenoble. He was thus a child of the 18th century who lived well into the 19th. He early developed a dislike for his father and an undue attachment to his mother. She died when he was 7 years old. Stendhal soon displayed the customary pattern that develops from such emotional situations: a hatred for authority and a search for a surrogate mother.

Early Training and Career

Stendhal's schooling was under the Ideologues, a group of 18th-century investigators of psychology, a training that set him apart from the later romantic authors. From this schooling, as well as from an intensive study of Ideologue writings (especially those of Destutt de Tracy) that he began in 1804, Stendhal formed his world view. He sought to understand man by learning the workings of his mind and above all his emotions, the latter of which Stendhal believed were rooted in man's physiological nature. Stendhal hoped through this study to be able to dominate those about him.

The principal keys were consciousness of self, awareness of the primal role of will, and excellence of memory in order to ensure recall of all relevant facts. In the happiness principle (*la chasse au bonheur,* the pursuit of happiness) Stendhal saw the central dynamic drive of man.

In 1800 Stendhal accompanied Napoleon Bonaparte on his heroic crossing of the Alps into Italy, first coming at this time to know and love Italy. He rapidly became a functionary of some importance under the Napoleonic Empire and spent the years 1806-1810 in Germany, where, among other places, he stayed for a time in the town of Stendhal, from which he derived his pseudonym. In 1814, with the collapse of the Empire, Stendhal settled happily in Italy, renouncing forever his dreams of a major public career. He preferred Italy to his native land, for, probably erroneously, he believed it a more fertile soil for the cultivation of the passions.

Doctrine of "Beylism"

An elusive personality, the end product of a process of disillusionment, Stendhal showed a mocking exterior, ironic and skeptical, that masked his sensitive and wounded heart. He gradually elaborated a doctrine he called "egotism" or "Beylism." Stendhal later wrote of this doctrine in detail in a series of works not published until long after his death: his *Journal* (1888), his *Life of Henri Brûlard* (1890), and his *Memoirs of Egotism* (1892). The doctrine, the name of which is deceptive to speakers of English, urges a deliberate following of self-interest and views the external world solely as a theater for personal energies. The "will to glory" is no more than the doctrine's external manifestation. Its essence is inward, an intense study of the self in order to give to the fleeting moments of life all the density of which they are capable. Although this is an admittedly elitist doctrine, Stendhal excused and justified it by his total sincerity. It ultimately proposes self-knowledge, not self-interest, to enhance the cult of the will, and it proposes the energy to develop an ever present sense of what one owes to oneself. To Stendhal, Italy and Napoleon were the supreme models of his doctrine. He proposed them to the "Happy Few" as guides, for he believed that the elite alone possess sufficient independence of judgment and strength of will to dare to be themselves. They alone may seek the supreme goal—happiness and the complete conscious realization of self—through self-analysis leading to self-knowledge and an awareness of how all others also seek their own ends; through a conscious hypocrisy to conceal their own goals; and through an unabating honesty with self.

Early Writings

Stendhal's early works little suggest the sincerity of his approach. His *History of Painting in Italy* and *Rome, Naples, and Florence,* both written in 1817, contain interesting original elements among many plagiarized passages. In 1821 Stendhal was suspected as a spy and forced to leave Italy but not before completing much of the work on his first major publication, *On Love* (1822). This study of love, today highly prized, sold only 17 copies during his lifetime. It is a rationalist's account of the ultimate emotional experience. Through a witty analogy Stendhal suggested that the initial manifestation of love is no more than a "crystallization" about the loved one of qualities the lover wishes to find in him or her—a matter (to use a later terminology) of projection and ego-satisfaction little dependent upon the real qualities of the person who is loved. It is a form of self-love, then, and not real love. For Stendhal, if love is to be complete, it must become a discovery of the loved person and a loss of self in love of the other. This total absorption is the supreme manifestation of the ego, a transcendent state to which all art and nature then contribute.

Stendhal's *Racine and Shakespeare,* a minor foray into the developing battle of romanticism in France, appeared in 1823. In 1827 he published his first major novel, *Armance,* a psychological study marred by a lack of clarity (a fatal fault in such analyses).

The Red and the Black

In 1831, taking advantage of a momentary easing of the censorship, Stendhal published *The Red and the Black.* Although it is today acclaimed as a masterpiece, it had to wait 50 years and long after the death of its author to begin to achieve that status. It is the best single work in which to study Stendhal.

The plot of *The Red and the Black* (like those of many other French novels of the 19th century) is based on a widely reported criminal case of the day. Stendhal adopted its outline, changing the names of the characters and providing his own account of their motivations. His hero, Julien Sorel, of a peasant family, is placed as tutor in the minor noble family of the Rênals in a small village in Savoy, the region in which Stendhal had passed his childhood. Julien seduces Madame de Rênal, leaving her when scandal is about to break out in order to enter a seminary and pursue studies for the priesthood. He next becomes the secretary of the aristocratic Marquis de la Môle in Paris, where he seduces the marquis's daughter, Mathilde. As he is about to marry her, Madame de Rênal writes a damaging letter to the marquis. Julien, infuriated, makes an unsuccessful attempt to kill Madame de Rênal. For this crime he receives the sentence of execution.

The "Black" of the title represents the Roman Catholic Church; the "Red" is a broader symbol, suggesting the Revolution, the Republic, the Empire of Napoleon, and more generalized concepts of courage and daring. Julien, a fervent admirer of Napoleon, is born too late for the Red; but he "knows how to choose the uniform of his century" and opts for the priesthood, the Black. The novel is, in this regard, a satiric portrayal of France under the Restoration, the conservative reaction that followed the Empire and that depended for its continuance upon repressing young men like Julien. In his flaming speech at his trial Julien accuses his accusers of being no better than himself and of punishing him for being "a plebian in revolt."

Julien Sorel's Character

Julien's character is complex but clearly delineated, so that *The Red and the Black* is also, and more importantly, a study of love. Physically weak, Julien is scorned by his father and brothers; he early loses his mother. He uses his keen intelligence to serve his ambition and little understands how much he seeks a mother in all women. His need is to dominate, not only society but especially a woman. Madame de Rênal is a maternal type of woman; he plans her seduction coldly. But Stendhal wisely has Julien win her only when he lacks the strength to continue his foolish stratagems and bursts into tears in her bedroom. For almost the first time, Julien is honest with himself and with her. Julien thus also provides that moment of the unexpected (*l'imprévu*), which Stendhal deemed essential to love. For a brief time Julien passes from self-love to real love, but soon his wounded vanity drives him back to ambition. The two themes, love and the revolutionary spirit, blend in a terrifying spectacle as his sufferings make him an enemy dangerous to society and fatal to any woman who loves him. His chosen method, hypocrisy, gains him rapid success, but it denies him the possibility of full love.

In Julien's affair with Mathilde, on the one hand, Stendhal satirizes the decadent Parisian nobility of the Restoration and, on the other, with the rigor of a mathematical demonstration, he pushes Julien into the seduction. The relationship offers the occasion to contrast an ambitious and calculating love to Madame de Rênal's selfless devotion. Julien can control Mathilde only by keeping his emotions constantly in check; it is always a battle between them for domination, and the revolutionary theme returns.

After his attempted murder of Madame de Rênal, Julien, contrasting her devotion with the self-seeking vanity of Mathilde, discovers the real nature of love. Renouncing both ambition and hypocrisy, he gives himself wholly to Madame de Rênal, who forgives him and returns his love. She spends long hours in prison with him, thus allowing Stendhal to depict his concept of one person's fully developed love for another person. Julien is serenely happy despite his death sentence. His will to power has been set aside for higher goals; his pursuit of happiness has been successful.

In its acceptance of love as the supreme experience of life, *The Red and the Black* is romantic. In its sensitive and sympathetic analysis of motives and of feeling and response, it derives from the 18th century. It foreshadows the return of psychological analysis in the novel, a return that characterized France at the end of the 19th century, when *The Red and the Black* began first to be appreciated. In the delicate irony of its presentation (not always translatable into English) it is, however, Stendhal's work alone.

The Charterhouse of Parma

In 1831 Stendhal returned to Italy. In 1834 he began his novel *Lucien Leuwen* (not published until 1890), an attack on the July Monarchy. In 1839 he published his second great work, *The Charterhouse of Parma.* A complex novel set in Italy, it analyzes, even more delicately than does *The Red and the Black,* the variations and nuances of love. Again a prison serves as the paradoxical setting. The book is also important for its satiric portrayal of the Battle of Waterloo, at which the hero, Fabrice, is in fact present without ever being sure whether the action is really a battle or not.

More important is the detailed portrait of Fabrice's aunt, La Sansévérina, who is in love with him but whose love is not returned. Her quiet self-command, the fullness with which she lives a major role in the court at Parma, and her ease in handling her lover, the Prime Minister, and the ruler, who also loves her, make her one of Stendhal's most complex characters, perhaps his best delineation, and certainly one of the greatest female characters in French fiction. The ending of this novel is seriously truncated. Its last words are a dedication (in English): "To the Happy Few." The novel, little admired on its publication, did at least receive praise from Honoré de Balzac.

On March 22, 1842, Stendhal died in Paris. Almost a hundred years passed before he was understood as a major figure of world literature.

Further Reading

Autobiographical works by Stendhal are *The Life of Henri Brûlard* (trans. 1939), *Memoirs of Egotism* (trans. 1949), and *The Private Diaries of Stendhal* (trans. 1954). Jean Dutourd, *The Man of Sensibility* (trans. 1961), is a series of essays on various aspects of Stendhal's personality. Robert M. Adams, *Stendhal: Notes on a Novelist* (1959), contains a short biography and general criticism of the fiction. Introductions to Stendhal's work are Howard Clewes, *Stendhal: An Introduction to the Novelist* (1950), and Wallace Fowlie, *Stendhal* (1969), which emphasizes Stendhal's contributions to the evolution of the novel.

Useful studies include Frederick C. Green, *Stendhal* (1939); Matthew Josephson's excellent *Stendhal: or, The Pursuit of Happiness* (1946), which lays great weight on psychological factors; John Atherton, *Stendhal* (1965), an analysis of the concepts which motivate and form the personalities of Stendhal's characters; Armand Caraccio, *Stendhal* (trans. 1965), divided into a biography and a perceptive study of the novels; and Victor Brombert, *Stendhal: Fiction and the Themes of Freedom* (1968).

Varied critical opinion on Stendhal appears in Victor Brombert, ed., *Stendhal: A Collection of Critical Essays* (1962). Harry Levin, *The Gates of Horn: A Study of Five French Realists* (1963), contains a penetrating chapter on Stendhal; and Stendhal figures prominently in Joseph Wood Krutch, *Five Masters: A Study in the Mutations of the Novel* (1930), and Raymond Giraud, *The Unheroic Hero in the Novels of Stendhal, Balzac and Flaubert* (1957). For background see Martin Turnell's two works, *The Novel in France* (1951) and *The Art of French Fiction* (1959).

Additional Sources

Alter, Robert, *A lion for love: a critical biography of Stendhal,* Cambridge, Mass.: Harvard University Press, 1986, 1979.

Fineshriber, William H., *Stendhal, the romantic rationalist,* Philadelphia: R. West, 1977 c1932.

Jameson, Storm, *Speaking of Stendhal,* London: Gollancz, 1979.

May, Gita, *Stendhal and the Age of Napoleon,* New York: Columbia University Press, 1977.

Stendhal, *Memoirs of an egotist,* London: Chatto and Windus, 1975. □

Nicolaus Steno

The Danish naturalist Nicolaus Steno (1638-1686) established the law of superposition and the law of constancy of interfacial angles.

Nicolaus Steno, originally Niels Stensen, the son of a goldsmith, was born in Copenhagen on Jan. 10, 1638. He entered the University of Copenhagen in 1656 to begin studies in medicine which he continued in Amsterdam and Leiden. After studying anatomy in Paris in 1664, he went to Florence in 1665. He became court physician to the Grand Duke of Tuscany, Ferdinand II, who subsidized Steno's scientific interests.

During this period Steno investigated the geology of Tuscany with its related mineralogical and paleontological problems. His *De solido intra solidum naturaliter contento dissertationis prodromus* (1669; Introduction to a Dissertation concerning a Solid Body Enclosed by Process of Nature within a Solid) was one of the most fundamental contributions to geology because of Steno's qualities of observation, analysis, and inductive reasoning at a time when scientific research was nothing but metaphysical speculation. Contrary to many other works of the 17th century, it had an impact on contemporary scientists through three Latin editions and its translation into English by Henry Oldenburg in 1671.

The *Prodromus* is divided into four parts. The first contains an investigation on the origin of fossils. The second part analyzes the following fundamental problem: "given a substance having a certain shape, and formed according to the laws of nature, how to find in the substance itself evidences disclosing the place and manner of its production." The third part discusses different solids contained within a solid in relation to the laws discovered and presented in the previous part. This is the section dealing mostly with crystallography. The fourth part is largely a consideration of the geological changes which Steno was able to interpret from his observations throughout Tuscany.

A fundamental part of *Prodromus* concerns the aspects and the mechanism of the growth of crystals, which are also solids within solids. In that respect Steno discovered the fundamental law of crystallography known as the "law of constancy of interfacial angles," which states that regardless of the variations in shape or size of the faces of a crystal, the interfacial angles remain constant. At the end of *Prodromus,* Steno in a series of diagrams illustrates the geological history of Tuscany. These sections, the earliest of their type ever prepared, fully substantiate the claim that Steno is one of the founders of stratigraphy and historical geology and perhaps the first geologist in the modern sense.

Steno, in his general concept of the universe, adopted the doctrine of the four Aristotelian elements: fire, earth, air, and water. However, his concept of matter was Cartesian, since he considered a natural body as an aggregate of imperceptible particles subject to the action of forces as generated by a magnet, fire, and sometimes light.

In paleontology, Steno clearly understood the organic origin of fossils and their importance as indicators of different environments of deposition. Assuming that strata had been deposited in the form of sediments from turbid waters under the action of gravity, Steno established some of the fundamental principles of stratigraphy: deposition of each bed upon a solid substratum, superposition of younger strata over older ones, and occurrence of all beds except the basal one between two essentially horizontal planes. In structural geology, Steno visualized three types of mountains: mountains formed by faults, mountains due to the effects of erosion by running waters, and volcanic mountains formed by eruptions of subterranean fires.

In 1672 Steno became professor of anatomy in Copenhagen. As a Catholic, he encountered so much religious intolerance from the Protestant community that he returned to Florence, where he was put in charge of the education of Cosimo III, the son of the Grand Duke. In 1675 Steno took Holy Orders, and a year later Pope Innocent XI appointed him bishop of Titopolis and apostolic vicar of northern Germany and Scandinavia. He died in Schwerin on Nov. 26, 1686.

Further Reading

The most comprehensive biography of Steno, including the translation of all his geological works, is in *Steno: Geological Papers,* edited by Gustav Scherz and translated by Alex J. Pollock (1969). Some biographical information on Steno is in Gustav Scherz, ed., *Historical Symposium on Nicolaus Steno* (1965). Other accounts of his life and contributions to geology are in Sir Archibald Geikie, *The Founders of Geology* (1897); Karl von Zittel, *History of Geology and Palaeontology* (1901); and Frank D. Adams, *The Birth and Development of the Geological Sciences* (1938).

Additional Sources

Moe, Harald, *Nicolaus Steno: an illustrated biography: his tireless pursuit of knowledge, his genius, his quest for the absolute,* Copenhagen: Rhodos, 1994.

Scherz, Gustav, *Niels Steensen (Nicolaus Steno), 1638-1686: the goldsmith's son from Copenhagen who won world fame as a pioneering natural scientist but who sacrificed science to become a celebrated servant of God,* Copenhagen: Royal Danish Ministry of Foreign Affairs, 1988. ☐

Stephen

Stephen (c. 1096-1154) was king of England from 1135 to 1154. His claim to the throne was contested by his cousin Matilda, and his reign was disturbed by civil war. He eventually accepted Matilda's son Henry as his heir.

Stephen was the third son of Stephen, Count of Blois and Chartres, and Adela, daughter of William I of England. His uncle, King Henry I of England, gave him lands in England and Normandy and in 1125 arranged his marriage to Matilda, heiress of the Count of Boulogne. She brought him not only her rich and strategically important county but also large estates in England; Stephen became one of the most powerful men in England.

In December 1126 King Henry, having no legitimate male heir, made the nobility do homage to his daughter, Matilda, widow of Emperor Henry V, as Lady (Domina) of England and Normandy. Stephen was the first to swear, but on King Henry's death (Dec. 1, 1135) he hurried to England, gained the support of the citizens of London, and at Winchester, where his brother was bishop, won over the heads of the administration, the justiciar and the treasurer. On December 22 Stephen was crowned by the archbishop of Canterbury. Stephen bought, or rewarded, support by issuing a charter of liberties, promising reforms, and confirming to the bishops "justice and power" over the clergy.

At first Stephen appeared secure. His rival, Matilda, seems to have been unpopular, and she was now married to Geoffrey, Count of Anjou, a hereditary enemy of the Normans. Stephen marched against Geoffrey in 1137, but his army was demoralized by the defection of the powerful Earl of Gloucester, illegitimate son of King Henry, who soon declared openly for Matilda, his half sister. Stephen left Normandy, and it was conquered piecemeal by Geoffrey.

In 1138 King David I of Scotland, Matilda's uncle, launched an attack on England; though defeated at the Battle of the Standard in August, he remained a rallying point for the opposition. In 1139 Stephen arrested (by trickery) the heads of the royal administration: Roger, Bishop of Salisbury, his son, and his two nephews. The Church was upset by the incident because three of the four were bishops; the nobility, because it made the King seem untrustworthy.

On Sept. 30, 1139, Matilda landed at Arundel, and Stephen quixotically gave her safe conduct to the Earl of Gloucester's castle at Bristol. She had little success until, in February 1141, Stephen was captured by the earl in battle at Lincoln. Matilda was recognized by the Church as Lady of England, but she was driven from Westminster before her intended coronation, and in September the earl was captured. The earl and the King were then exchanged, and from that time a stalemate was established. The southwest was controlled by the earl for Matilda; most of the rest of England was ruled by Stephen. But everywhere new castles were built from which landowners could defend their property and defy authority, and there were pockets of resistance throughout the country which Stephen could not eliminate; Wallingford was held for Matilda during the whole of his reign, and Framlingham from 1141 onward. Though the royal chancery functioned and the Exchequer may have met, orders could not always be enforced or money collected. Traitors could not be punished or violence controlled.

In these circumstances, the decisive factor was the conquest of Normandy by the Count of Anjou, who made over the duchy to his son Henry in 1150. The nobles of England were mostly Normans; they were anxious for a negotiated peace so that they could preserve their Norman properties. At the same time the bishops refused to consecrate Stephen's elder son Eustace as coruler and heir to the throne unless they had permission from the Pope, and the Pope was hostile. After the death of Eustace (Aug. 17, 1153) Stephen met Henry at Winchester and on November 6 recognized his hereditary right to the throne of England, retaining the kingdom for himself for life. He adopted Henry as his "son and heir," thus excluding his younger son from the succession. Stephen died on Oct. 25, 1154, and Henry took peaceful possession of England (as Henry II).

Further Reading

R. H. C. Davis, *King Stephen, 1135-1154* (1967), is a short and lucid biography. H. A. Cronne, *The Reign of Stephen* (1970), is more detailed; for the general reader there is a good account by John Tate Appleby, *The Troubled Reign of King Stephen* (1970). For general historical background see Austin Lane Poole, *From Domesday Book to Magna Carta, 1087-1216* (1951; 2d ed. 1955).

Additional Sources

Davis, R. H. C. (Ralph Henry Carless), *King Stephen, 1135-1154,* London; New York: Longman, 1990.

Stringer, K. J. (Keith John), *The reign of Stephen: kingship, warfare, and government in twelfth-century England,* London; New York: Routledge, 1993. □

Stephen I

Stephen I (ca. 973–1038) was king of Hungary, who went from pagan tribal leader to Christian leader of a powerful nation in the space of one generation and left a remarkable imprint on the history of Europe and the world.

The Hungarian kingdom was established by descendants of Arpad, a Magyar nomad from the steppes of Asia whose horsemen had terrorized central Europe in the first half of the 10th century. After a decisive defeat by the Germans at Lechfeld, just south of Augsburg, Bavaria, in 955, the Magyars, under Arpad's great grandson Taksony, settled down in what is now Hungary.

Taksony's son, the duke Géza, established a semblance of order and initiated moves to Christianize the Magyar/Hungarians by appealing to the Holy Roman Emperor Otto I for Christian missionaries. His move has been termed the "Quedlinburg Mission." Fortunately, for the Hungarians, Otto did not take the request seriously. Although a number of German Benedictine missionaries came to the Hungarian lands and began the process of Christianization, their methods were so crude that they caused many problems and delayed progress.

When Géza died in 997, his son Stephen took a more direct action some three years later by appealing to Pope Sylvester II, asking that he be baptized and crowned Christian king of Hungary. This move reduced the possibility that the Holy Roman Emperor might assume the role of feudal lord over Hungary, making the Hungarian ruler his vassal.

Acting quickly, Sylvester II sent a bishop and a group of clergy; he also sent a crown which was slightly damaged en route. When the coronation took place on Christmas Day in the year 1000, that same crown with its bent cross was set on Stephen's head; the defect remains to this day, symbolizing the origin and function of the crown and its wearer.

Stephen was faced with great problems from all sides as he began the task of organizing, defending, Christianizing, and bringing his nation into the European fold. One of these problems was the revolt of a cousin who ruled in Transylvania. Koppàny claimed not only the throne, but the hand of Stephen's widowed mother. Immediately moving against him, Stephen finally defeated Koppàny, executing him in 1003. Then another Magyar—known only by the title Gyula—claimed the rule in Transylvania and usurped it. He too was disposed of by the new king, who was actively supported by German knights in the service of his wife/queen, Gisela, a Bavarian princess.

Stephen established the seat of his kingdom at Esztergom, site of an old Roman settlement called Strigonium, allegedly where the Roman Emperor Marcus Aurelius wrote his *Meditations.* He lost no time in setting up a number of bishoprics and instituting a vigorous program of Christianization of his people. Some have reported that this was accomplished through forceful means—in much the same manner as the Frankish king Clovis Christianized his pagan tribesmen in the sixth century, and the Emperor Constantine his Roman subjects in the fourth century.

Stephen I ruled for four decades. Considering that his father Géza, who began the first attempts to Christianize the Magyars, had been anything but successful, Stephen achieved nearly miraculous results, leaving a clear majority of his subjects following the new religion at his death in 1038. In addition to establishing dioceses for the propagation of the faith, Stephen established schools and churches and encouraged his nobility to endow monasteries. He also invited Jewish and Muslim traders into the kingdom to build up the economy, ordering a strict toleration of their religious practices in order to profit from their trading activities.

He sponsored the drafting and enactment of law codes for his new nation, in what appears—retroactively—to be a close adaptation of what other European monarchs of the period were accomplishing. One element that makes Stephen's legal pronouncements different from the others is that he sought, with some degree of success, to prevent Hungary from becoming a theocratic protectorate. The laws were Christianized versions of Magyar customs and traditions; they reflected the need of his people as much as the requirement for order.

He allied himself with the Byzantine emperor, Basil II, in his battle with the Bulgarian ruler John Vladislav in 1018, the results of which action saw the establishment of pilgrimage routes to Jerusalem through Constantinople. In later years, Stephen's treatment of Bulgarian prisoners was humane and considerate and led to a satisfying relaxation of tensions between the two kingdoms. This was especially fruitful when the German emperor Conrad II launched attacks against the western parts of Hungary in 1030. Since he didn't have to worry about his eastern and southern flanks, Stephen was able to concentrate his forces and defeat the Germans in the west, forcing their withdrawal.

Stephen's personal life included a series of tragedies. His only son Imre (Emeric), who enjoyed a reputation for virtue and valor, died in what has been reported as a hunting accident (killed by a "wild boar"). But Stephen Sisa, in his book *The Spirit of Hungary,* alleges that the death was a successful assassination attempt by the Thonuzoba family, who were resisting conversion to Christianity. Sisa points out that the term, *thonuzoba,* means "wild boar" in the language of the Petcheneg (a pre-Christian steppe-dwelling people, some of whom settled in Transylvania). Because he had led an exemplary life and was well-loved by the Hungarian peoples who had accepted Christianity, Imre was canonized in the late 11th century, at about the same time as his father.

The successful implantation of a substantial group of non-Slavs in Eastern Europe in the midst of what was becoming a Slavic empire is one of the minor mysteries of European history. To the north, the Poles held sway, but the Hungarians successfully intermarried with Polish aristocracy, and it is a verified fact that Stephen sent to Poland two young men who might become eligible for his throne when their lives appeared to be in danger. They subsequently returned after Stephen's death and each of them later ruled for brief periods. To the east, Bulgars could have posed threats to the peace of the kingdom, yet Stephen, through careful diplomacy, managed to keep the Bulgarian rulers either pacified or immobilized. To the northeast the Bohemians (Czechs) represented a highly developed culture that acted as a buffer for their Slavic brothers to the east, while they did not pose any kind of a threat to the Magyar kingdom. Other minor groupings of Slavs—including Slovenes, Slovaks, Croats, Ruthenians, White Russians, Ukrainians, Serbians, Vlachs (Rumanians)—formed a demographic ring around the Carpathian Basin. Yet the Magyars/Hungarians survived and prospered. Their history and their historians assert that the chief architect of this was Stephen—Saint Stephen—whose vision and energy made the beginnings possible.

Further Reading

Kosztolnyik, Z. J. *Five Eleventh Century Hungarian Kings: Their Policies and Their Relations with Rome.* East European Monographs, distributed by Columbia University Press, 1981.

Sisa, Stephen. *The Spirit of Hungary: A Panorama of Hungarian History and Culture.* Ontario, Canada, 1983 (2nd edition published in U.S., 1990).

Sugar, Peter A., ed. *A History of Hungary.* Indiana University Press, 1990.

Dragomir, Sylvius. *The Ethnical Minorities in Transylvania.* Sonor Printing, 1927.

Ignotus, Paul. *Hungary: Nations of the Modern World.* Praeger, 1972.

Konnyu, Leslie. *A Condensed Geography of Hungary.* American-Hungarian Review, 1971. □

St. Stephen Harding

The English monastic reformer and medieval abbot St. Stephen Harding (died 1134) helped to found the reformed Benedictine monastery of Cîteaux, France. The spirit and organization of the Cistercians, which date from his abbacy, reflect St. Stephen's ideas.

Before the Norman invasion of England, Stephen was a monk in the Benedictine abbey of Sherborne, Dorset. He left England during the troubled times that followed the Norman conquest. After a pilgrimage to Rome, Stephen lived in the Benedictine monastery in Langres, France. There he hoped to resume a quiet life of work and prayer. Stephen found monastic life at Langres appalling. The fat and prosperous monks were more concerned with local politics than their spiritual duties. To escape this undesirable environment, Stephen and 19 other monks decided to found a new monastery where they could live according to the ideals of St. Benedict. In 1098 they settled at Cîteaux in a deserted part of Burgundy near Dijon.

About 1109 Stephen became this group's third abbot. Although he succeeded in maintaining his fellow monks' sense of purpose and dedication, very few recruits joined their ranks. Stephen became discouraged about the future of their venture, and he was on the verge of resigning as abbot in 1112, when a young man named Bernard with 30 of his relatives and friends knocked on the door of the abbey and asked that they be admitted as novices: Soon more and more young men joined. Bernard was sent out in 1115 to start a new abbey at Clairvaux. From this time on, Cîteaux's growth was spectacular.

Stephen put his monastic ideals into writing in the "Charter of Charity." This code, dating from about 1119, became the main constitutional paper of the Cistercians. It provided that the monks would not wear any unnecessary clothes or eat any food not prescribed by the Rule of St. Benedict. The monastery would not own property except the land on which its buildings stood. The monks would grow all the food they needed, and everything produced would belong to all alike. The monks would not engage in any business with neighboring people. The life of each monk would be one of concentrated prayer and serious work.

By the time Stephen Harding died in 1134, his organizational ability and powers of leadership had fashioned a large and important movement in the Roman Catholic Church in France. By 1153 the monasteries founded from Cîteaux numbered 338.

Further Reading

Louis J. Lekai gives details of St. Stephen Harding's important contributions in *The White Monks: A History of the Cistercian Order* (1953). Archdale A. King, *Citeaux and Her Elder Daughters* (1954), also has a helpful chapter on the saint. G. G. Coulton wrote a sobering study of some of the unwholesome aspects of Stephen Harding's monastery in *Five Centuries of Religion,* vol. 1 (1923).

Additional Sources

M. Raymond, Father, O.C.S.O., *Three religious rebels: the forefathers of the Trappist,* Boston, MA: St. Paul Books & Media, 1991, 1986. □

Sir Leslie Stephen

The English historian, critic, and editor Sir Leslie Stephen (1832-1904) was one of the great popularizers of Victorian thought and literature.

Leslie Stephen was born in London on Nov. 28, 1832, the son of Sir James Stephen, a leading Evangelical and distinguished undersecretary in the Colonial Office. By birth and education Leslie was a member of the Victorian intellectual aristocracy, and his upbringing was typical of his class and time. Educated at Eton and at Trinity Hall, Cambridge, he first determined on an academic career, which required his entry into Anglican orders. He was ordained deacon in 1855 and priest in 1859. A few years later, in a typically Victorian intellectual crisis which led him to religious doubt as a result of his reading of the works of J. S. Mill, he resigned his Cambridge fellowship and in 1867 began a literary career.

The whole of Stephen's outlook for the rest of his life was shaped by this early crisis. Increasingly he came under Darwinian influences and moved steadily toward agnosticism. In 1875 he resigned his priesthood. His first and most important work, *English Thought in the Eighteenth Century* (2 vols., 1876), revealed the full scale of his agnostic values and assumptions. For Stephen, with his strong Evangelical background, the great goal of 19th-century philosophy was to preserve the ethics of theism in an increasingly nontheistic world. Between 1878 and 1882 he wrote a work of philosophical synthesis which he hoped would win him a reputation as a major thinker by putting the traditional ethics on a scientific base of utilitarianism and Darwinism. The work, entitled *The Science of Ethics* (1882), was such a failure that it permanently altered Stephen's career and caused him to devote the rest of his life to high-level journalism and editing.

From 1882 to 1889 Stephen was editor of the *Dictionary of National Biography,* and during this time 26 volumes appeared; he also contributed 378 biographical articles. He produced, in addition to a number of lesser works, two substantial studies, *The English Utilitarians* (1900) and *English Literature and Society in the Eighteenth Century,* which was published on the day of his death, Feb. 22, 1904.

Stephen was neither a great thinker nor an original scholar. His writings, though often lucid and intelligent, were Victorian period pieces which reveal as much about the author and the age in which he lived as they do about their subjects.

Further Reading

The fullest biography is still Frederic W. Maitland's happy memoir, *Life and Letters of Leslie Stephen* (1906). Noel G. Annan, *Leslie Stephen: His Thought and Character in Relation to His Time* (1952), is an intellectual biography. A brief consideration of Stephen as historian is Sidney A. Burrell's essay, "Sir Leslie Stephen (1832-1904)" in Herman Ausubel and others, eds., *Some Modern Historians of Britain* (1951).

Additional Sources

Annan, Noel Gilroy Annan, Baron, *Leslie Stephen,* New York: Arno Press, 1977.

Annan, Noel Gilroy Annan, Baron, *Leslie Stephen: the Godless Victorian,* Chicago: University of Chicago Press, 1986, 1984.

Annan, Noel Gilroy Annan, Baron, *Leslie Stephen, his thought and character in relation to his time,* New York: AMS Press, 1977.

MacCarthy, Desmond, *Leslie Stephen,* Philadelphia, Pa.: R. West, 1978. □

Alexander Hamilton Stephens

Alexander Hamilton Stephens (1812-1883) was a U.S. congressman, vice president of the Confederacy, and briefly governor of Georgia.

Alexander H. Stephens was born on Feb. 11, 1812, in Wilkes County, Ga. Sickly almost from infancy and orphaned at the age of 14, Stephens received little education until he went to a small academy in Washington,

Ga. He graduated from the University of Georgia in 1832 at the head of his class. Two years later he was admitted to the Georgia bar.

Acutely aware of his era's political issues, Stephens criticized the idea of nullification but upheld the right of a state to secede from the Union. In 1836 Stephens was elected to the state legislature. In 1843, elected to the U.S. Congress, Stephens consistently, but moderately, championed Southern interests. He endorsed the Compromise of 1850 but warned the North that any conciliation must be reasonable toward the South. He collaborated in forming Georgia's short-lived Constitutional Union party and helped draft the "Georgia Platform," which combined acceptance of the Compromise of 1850 with strict Northern observance of the Fugitive Slave Law.

In 1852 Stephens and other Georgia Whigs voted for Daniel Webster for president, despite the fact that Webster had died before the election. Thereafter Stephens became identified with the Democratic party, still carefully guarding his habitual political independence. Stephens's view of the slavery question evolved from his initial denial that he defended slavery to a support of the system as best for the inherently inferior black and, finally, to plans for reopening the foreign slave trade.

Stephens retired from Congress in 1859, asserting his concept of society to be hierarchical. "Order is nature's first law," he said, "with it comes gradation and subordination." During the secession crisis after Abraham Lincoln's election in 1860, he counseled moderation. Voting for Georgia's secession in January 1861, Stephens was quickly elected vice president of the Confederacy.

However, Stephens's scruples and his constitutional restraint made him dissatisfied with the Confederate government. He found fault with numerous government practices, conscription and suspension of habeas corpus, in particular. After the war, Stephens counseled acceptance of its result and of the Reconstruction plans. He wrote several popular books on the war and American history. Elected to Congress in 1872, he again proved a master parliamentarian and guardian of the public interest. After resigning from Congress in 1882, he was elected governor of Georgia but died on March 4, 1883, a few months after his inauguration.

Further Reading

The recent account of Stephens is Rudolph R. Von Abele, *Alexander H. Stephens* (1946), a critical study not always scholarly in documentation. Eudora Ramsay Richardson, *Little Aleck: A Life of Alexander H. Stephens, the Fighting Vice-president of the Confederacy* (1932), emphasizes Stephens's personal life but lacks satisfactory analysis. The political background and Stephens's role are well covered in Burton. J. Hendrick, *Statesmen of the Lost Cause: Jefferson Davis and His Cabinet* (1939), and Rembert W. Patrick, *Jefferson Davis and His Cabinet* (1944).

Additional Sources

Knight, Lucian Lamar, *Alexander H. Stephens, the sage of Liberty Hall: Georgia's great commoner,* Liberty Hall, Ga.?: United Daughters of the Confederacy, Georgia Division, 1994.

Norwood, Martha F., *Liberty Hall, Taliaferro County, Georgia: a history of the structures known as Liberty Hall and their owners from 1827 to the present,* Atlanta: Georgia Dept. of Natural Resources, Office of Planning and Research, Historic Preservation Section, 1977.

Schott, Thomas Edwin, *Alexander H. Stephens of Georgia: a biography,* Baton Rouge: Louisiana State University Press, 1988. □

James Stephens

The fame of the Irish novelist and poet James Stephens (1882-1950) rests almost entirely upon a single masterpiece, the novel *The Crock of Gold.* His minor works consist of humorous fiction based on Irish folklore and lyric poems.

James Stephens was born on Feb. 2, 1882 (the same day James Joyce was born), to a poor family living in a slum area of Dublin. He was largely self-educated and was working in a solicitor's office when the poet George Russell (known as AE) discovered him. In physical appearance he resembled a leprechaun, less than 5 feet in height, with a droll face and dark complexion, a prototype of the comic Irishman. Married and with two children, he divided his time between Dublin and Paris until the outbreak of World War II. He made his debut as a successful broadcaster for the BBC in 1928 with a personal reminiscence of John

Millington Synge. Although he disassociated himself from Irish neutrality during the 1940s, declaring himself "an Irishman who wished to elect himself an Englishman for the duration," he was honored for his service to the cause of Irish independence and was active in the Sinn Fein movement from its beginnings. Until his death on Dec. 26, 1950, he was assistant curator of the Dublin National Gallery.

Stephens's proficiency in the Gaelic language and his extensive collection of Irish folklore and legends made him a master of the Irish oral tradition. His fables and tales are a blend of philosophy and nonsense, aimed at creating for Ireland "a new mythology to take the place of the threadbare mythology of Greece and Rome." His masterpiece, *The Crock of Gold* (1912), a modern fable, employs leprechauns and spirits in a half-concealed burlesque of Irish philosophy that derides the imprisonment of the human intellect by doctors, lawyers, priests, professors, and merchants; at the same time, it presents a humorous commentary on the Irish battle of the sexes. This work won the Polignac Prize for fiction in 1912. *The Charwoman's Daughter* (1912) enjoyed great success in America under the title *Mary, Mary*.

Stephens's graphic eyewitness account of the events of Easter Week, *The Insurrection in Dublin* (1916), was reprinted in 1965. His third novel, *Deirdre* (1923), won the Tailteann Gold Medal for fiction in 1923. Thirteen volumes of lyric poems have established his reputation as a poet; among the best of these are his first, *Insurrections* (1909), *Songs from the Clay* (1915), *Strict Joy* (1931), and his last, *Kings and the Moon* (1938). *Etched in Moonlight* (1928), a collection of short stories, exhibits the same genius for language and love of Irish lore as was found in his popular collection *Irish Fairy Tales* (1920). Stephens's linguistic wizardry and lyric gifts led James Joyce to remark that if he died before completing *Finnegans Wake,* James Stephens was the only man who could finish it.

Further Reading

There is no definitive biography of Stephens. The most valuable studies of his works (including much helpful information on his life) are Birgit Bramsbäck, *James Stephens: A Literary and Bibliographical Study* (1959), and Hilary Pyle, *James Stephens: His Work and an Account of His Life* (1965). The critical and biographical commentaries in Lloyd Frankenberg's edition of Stephens's unpublished writings, *James, Seumas and Jacques* (1964), and Frankenberg's *A James Stephens Reader* (1962) also provide much useful information.

Additional Sources

Bramsbeack, Birgit, *James Stephens: a literary and bibliographical study,* Philadelphia: R. West, 1977.

Finneran, Richard J., *The olympian & the leprechaun: W. B. Yeats and James Stephens,* Dublin: Dolmen Press; Atlantic Highlands, N.J.: distributed by Humanities Press, 1978. □

Uriah Stephens

Uriah Stephens (1821-1882), American labor leader prominent in founding the Knights of Labor, remained its leader for a decade.

Uriah Stephens was born in Cape May, N.J., on Aug. 3, 1821. He studied to be a Baptist preacher, but financial problems forced him to become apprenticed to a tailor. He apparently continued to study in his spare time but in 1845 moved to Philadelphia and practiced his trade full time.

In 1855 Stephens journeyed through the West Indies, Mexico, and Central America, settling in California. In 1858 he returned to Philadelphia. An antislavery Republican, Stephens supported the Union after hostilities began.

Stephens early joined the trade union movement. He helped organize the Garment Cutters' Association of Philadelphia (1862) and was active in its affairs. Late in 1869, however, having fallen on bad times, the union disbanded. Stephens and eight others, seeking to maintain a workers' organization, soon founded the Noble and Holy Order of the Knights of Labor.

Stephens influenced the Knights' peculiar character. A religious mysticism led him to emphasize the fraternal solidarity of labor. Thus he eschewed craft divisions and advocated admission to and equality in the Knights of all workers, regardless of religion, political affiliation, or race.

The Knights' characteristic ritual and secrecy were due to Stephens. An active Freemason, Odd Fellow, and Knight of Pythias, Stephens concluded that the stability of these long-lived organizations lay in their ritual and secrecy. He

devised a ceremony for the Knights based largely on the Masonic tradition and insisted that the union keep even its name secret from nonmembers. There were practical reasons for these policies, too. Secrecy was a necessity in an age when unions were weak and employers inclined to use violent retaliation to break them up.

Stephens maintained his policies as the union grew from 9 members in 1869 to 9,000 in 1878. In 1878 he was elected the first grand master workman of the union. But by now Stephens was distracted by politics and spent much of his time running for Congress on the Greenback party ticket. He resigned as head of the union, but the Knights reelected him. After another year he resigned anew and was succeeded by Terence V. Powderly.

Powderly and Stephens quarreled immediately because Powderly had pushed modification of the Knights' ritual and abandonment of its secrecy in order to placate the Catholic Church. Stephens remained an inactive member until his death on Feb. 13, 1882. He had pioneered in many workable and successful labor union policies.

Further Reading

Information on Stephens is in the standard histories of the labor movement during this period. The most comprehensive is Norman J. Ware, *The Labor Movement in the United States, 1860-1895* (1929), still the definitive work on Stephens's Knights of Labor. Foster Rhea Dulles, *Labor in America* (1949; 3d ed. 1966), is informative, as, to a lesser extent, are Henry Pelling, *American Labor* (1960), and Thomas R. Brooks, *Toil and Trouble: A History of American Labor* (1964). □

George and Robert Stephenson

The English railway engineers George Stephenson (1781-1848) and his son, Robert Stephenson (1803-1859), pioneered in steam railway engineering, which led directly to the onset of the railway age in Britain.

George Stephenson was born on July 9, 1781, at Wylam, near Newcastle-upon-Tyne. He followed his father's trade of colliery engineman with its concomitant migratory life. A natural mechanical bent led him to positions of increasing responsibility. In 1804 at Killingworth Colliery he took charge of a winding engine belonging to the Grand Allies, an important group of coal masters who controlled the pits. By 1812 Stephenson had become engine wright at Killingworth and was charged with maintaining the Grand Allies' machinery at all their collieries. He also acted as an adviser to other colliery owners. In 1815 he invented a safety lamp for miners at about the same time as did Sir Humphry Davy.

During the Napoleonic Wars coal masters became increasingly interested in developing the steam railway locomotive invented by Richard Trevithick in 1804. In 1813 Stephenson was commissioned to build a locomotive for Killingworth, and his first engine, the *Blucher,* ran in 1814. In design he closely followed the successful Blenkinsop and Murray rack locomotives, except that he depended solely on adhesive weight to draw a worthwhile load. Over the next years Stephenson laid down a number of new colliery railways and made improvements on the locomotives as well as on the rails. In 1821 he was named engineer on the Stockton and Darlington Railway.

Stephenson had only a most elementary education and seemingly lacked the capacity to grasp concepts, but he had great powers of observation, keen mechanical intuition, and remarkable foresight for the potential of the steam railway. His only son, Robert, was born on Oct. 16, 1803, at Willington Quay near Newcastle and was intensively schooled from earliest youth. He made the detailed survey for the Stockton and Darlington line for his father. This railway was constructed under George Stephenson's direction in 1822-1825 and employed locomotives which were built at the engine works he established in Newcastle in 1823 as Robert Stephenson and Company.

In 1824 George became engineer of the Liverpool and Manchester Railway project. That year Robert left for South America to direct mining operations in Colombia, where he remained until 1827. During his absence George thoroughly bungled the survey and estimate for the Liverpool and Manchester line, which led to the denial of parliamentary authority for the line in 1825, but the following year it was granted. In 1827 Robert became manager of the Newcastle works. In 1829 the directors of the Liverpool and Manchester line offered a prize for the best locomotive. At

George Stephenson

the famous Rainhill trials held in October, the *Rocket,* designed by Robert with a multitube boiler, easily won the day. The following year the Liverpool and Manchester Railway was opened.

The next major undertaking in which George Stephenson was concerned was the Grand Junction Railway, connecting Liverpool and Manchester with Birmingham, which was authorized in 1833. The survey and the northern half of the line were made by Joseph Locke, the Stephensons' ablest assistant. On the southern half George Stephenson again proved to be incompetent, and he was replaced by Locke in 1835. On the London and Birmingham Railway, authorized in 1832, Robert Stephenson had sole control of the survey; he became engineer in chief in 1833 and completed the line in 1838. George learned his lesson, and on important lines laid out between 1835 and 1840 he applied his rule-of-thumb genius to the choice of route, leaving details and organization to assistants.

In 1843 George Stephenson retired to Chesterfield, Derbyshire. He was the first president (1847-1848) of the Institution of Mechanical Engineers. He died on Aug. 12, 1848, at Chesterfield.

Robert Stephenson's engineering ability was most clearly shown in the great tubular bridges of unprecedented size on the Chester and Holyhead Railway, designed and built from 1845 to 1850 under his supervision. He died in London on Oct. 12, 1859.

Further Reading

George Stephenson, about whom literary battles raged over his alleged and disputed inventions for decades after his death, has occasioned several biographies. Samuel Smiles, *The Life of George Stephenson* (1857; new ed. 1864), is a classic. A definitive biography of his son is J. C. Jeaffreson, *The Life of Robert Stephenson* (1864; 2d ed. 1866). L. T. C. Rolt, *The Railway Revoultion: George and Robert Stephenson* (1962), shows great insight, and Michael Robbins, *George and Robert Stephenson* (1966), is a short, well-written account.

Additional Sources

Beckett, Derrick, *Stephensons' Britain,* Newton Abbot, Devon; North Pomfret, Vt: David & Charles, 1984.

Robbins, Michael, *George & Robert Stephenson,* London: H.M.S.O., 1981.

Rolt, L. T. C., *George and Robert Stephenson: the railway revolution,* Westport, Conn.: Greenwood Press, 1977, 1960. □

Alojzije Stepinac

A fervent Croatian nationalist, Catholic, and anti-Communist, Alojzije Stepinac (1898-1960) became a world-wide symbol of Roman Catholic resistance to Communism when he was imprisoned by the Communist regime of Yugoslavia in 1946.

Robert Stephenson

Alojzije Aloysius Stepinac was born to a large prosperous peasant family in the village of Krašić, Croatia, about 40 miles from Zagreb, then a part of Austria-Hungary, on May 8, 1898. After completing high school, he was drafted into the Hungarian army in World War I. Wounded and captured by the Italians, he subsequently joined and fought with the Allied-sponsored Yugoslav Volunteer Corps at Salonika. By 1919 he had earned several decorations for valor and had attained the rank of second lieutenant.

After the war, Stepinac attended the University of Zagreb in the new state of Yugoslavia, and in 1924 he enrolled in the Gregorian University in Rome to prepare for the Roman Catholic priesthood. A brilliant student, he earned doctorates in philosophy and theology and was ordained a priest in 1930. He returned to Yugoslavia to serve as a parish priest in the slums of Zagreb. Thereafter, his rise in the church hierarchy was extremely rapid, propelled by his growing reputation for deep piety and capable administration as well as his friendship with Papal Secretary of State Eugenio Cardinal Pacelli, who was to become Pope Pius XII in 1939. Stepinac was appointed secretary to Archbishop Ante Bauer of Zagreb, then (in 1934) titular Archbishop of Nicope and co-adjutor to Bauer, and finally (in 1937) Archbishop of Zagreb. The new primate of Yugoslavia was one of the youngest archbishops in Roman Catholic history.

In 1941, when Yugoslavia fell before the attack of Nazi Germany, Croatia declared itself an independent state. In reality, it became a puppet ally of Germany under the fascist (Ustaša) regime of Ante Pavelić. Stepinac, a dedicated Croatian patriot, accepted the Pavelić government as the legitimate representative of Croatian aspirations to political self-determination. To the very last days of World War II he publicly exhorted his clergy as well as the Croatian masses to support and defend the Ustaša state. He himself accepted the post of Supreme Apostolic VicarGeneral of the Croatian army and became a member of the ruling Council of State. His other actions and attitudes are in dispute. His defenders insist that, unlike other prominent Croatian Catholic churchmen, and at great personal risk to himself, Stepinac denounced the barbarous Nazi racial theories and practices adopted by the Ustaši and that he conducted extensive relief work among Christian and Jewish war refugees, even hiding them in episcopal buildings. They also deny that he condoned the forced conversions of Orthodox Christians to Catholicism or the notorious massacres of many thousands of Serbs, Jews, Slovenes, and anti-fascist Croats.

At war's end Marshal Tito's partisans took control of a reunited Yugoslavia and set up a Communist state. In November 1945 Stepinac was arrested, then released, ostensibly at the order of Tito himself. In a pastoral letter, Stepinac openly denounced Communism. He adamantly refused to accept the new regime's secularization of education and the destruction of the Catholic Church's privileges and the nationalization of its property. In September 1946 he was arrested and charged with wartime collaboration with the fascist regimes of Germany, Italy, and the Ustaša, as well as other war crimes and crimes against the new Yugoslav state. In October 1946 he was found guilty by the Supreme Court at Zagreb and sentenced to the confiscation of all of his property, the loss of his civil rights for five years, and imprisonment at hard labor for 16 years in Lepoglava Prison. The Vatican promptly excommunicated all persons connected with his arrest and trial. The tall, ascetic prelate quickly became a world-wide symbol of the growing church-state conflict in the new Soviet satellites of Eastern Europe.

In prison, the sentence of hard labor was not enforced. Stepinac was permitted to live in modest but clean quarters, to receive books, and to perform religious services and take communion. When Tito broke with the Soviet bloc in 1948, Stepinac's imprisonment threatened to embarrass his attempts to improve Yugoslav relations with the West. Stepinac was, therefore, released in December 1951, but was forbidden to act as a bishop and restricted to his native village of Krašić. There he served as a simple parish priest to the local inhabitants, numbering about 400 persons. In November 1952 the Papacy announced Stepinac's long-awaited elevation to the rank of cardinal. The following month Yugoslavia, in return, severed diplomatic relations with the Vatican. Stepinac did not go to Rome to be invested as a Prince of the Church, knowing that he would not be permitted to return home by the Yugoslav government. He also refused to go abroad for treatment of a blood-clotting problem (polycythemia) from which he suffered after 1953. Two American physicians were, however, permitted to come to Yugoslavia to treat him and to operate to remove blood clots from his bloodstream. He died of a heart ailment complicated by pneumonia in Krašić on February 10, 1960.

His tomb in Zagreb has since become a place of pilgrimage for Croatian nationalists.

Further Reading

Two widely-available books in English about Stepinac are both Catholic defenses of the prelate: Anthony H. O'Brien, *Archbishop Stepinac, the Man and His Case* (1947), and Richard Pattee, *The Case of Cardinal Aloysius Stepinac* (1953). The latter work consists mostly of a large number of documents bearing on the specific charges in the indictment against Stepinac. For a more balanced treatment of Stepinac as well as the Vatican's generally ambiguous attitude toward the Croatian fascist regime, see Fred Singleton, *Twentieth-Century Yugoslavia* (1976).

Additional Sources

Alexander, Stella, *The triple myth: a life of Archbishop Alojzije Stepinac,* Boulder: East European Monographs; New York: Distributed by Columbia University Press, 1987. □

Otto Stern

The German-born American physicist Otto Stern (1888-1969) discovered the atomic-and molecular-beam technique and used it to provide the first direct proof of spatial quantization.

Otto Stern was born on Feb. 17, 1888, in Sorau, Upper Silesia. In 1906 he entered the University of Breslau, completing his doctoral degree in physical chemistry in 1912. He then went to the University of Prague to study under Albert Einstein and, when Einstein moved to the Swiss Federal Institute of Technology (FIT) in Zurich, Stern followed him, becoming lecturer at the FIT in 1913.

The following year Stern accepted a similar position in theoretical physics at the University of Frankfurt am Main but almost immediately found himself in military service. After the war and a brief period at the University of Berlin during 1918, Stern returned to Frankfurt. There, turning from theory to experiment, he conceived and carried out the first of the atomic-and molecular-beam experiments which brought him an international reputation and, ultimately, the Nobel Prize in 1943.

Stern realized that electrons rotating about the nucleus of an atom possess "orbital angular momentum" and produce a magnetic moment along the axis of rotation. This magnetic moment gives rise to a magnetic field identical to one which would be set up by a tiny bar magnet positioned on the axis of rotation of the electron. Therefore, if a beam of atoms, each possessing a magnetic moment, is sent through a nonuniform external magnetic field, each atom will experience a net force, the magnitude of which depends on the orientation of the magnetic moment of the atom with respect to the direction of the external magnetic field.

In the classical theory, all orientations of the atom's magnetic moment are possible, so that the external field should deflect as many atoms above as below the original beam direction, causing the beam to simply spread out. Instead, using a beam of silver atoms, Stern and Walter Gerlach found that the beam was actually split up into two separate beams, one above, the other below, the original beam direction. This observation completely contradicted classical theory; it showed that not all orientations of the atom's magnetic moment are possible; that is, it showed that there exists "spatial quantization."

In later years, whether as a lecturer at Frankfurt, as a full professor at Rostock and Hamburg, or (after fleeing Nazi persecution) as a research professor of physics at the Carnegie Institute of Technology in Pittsburgh, where he remained from 1933 until 1945, Stern devised a number of other experiments exploiting the atomic-and molecular-beam technique he developed. For example, he checked the accuracy of the Maxwell-Boltzmann velocity distribution for gas molecules; he measured nuclear magnetic moments and the magnetic moment of the proton; finally, he observed the wave nature of helium and hydrogen atoms by diffracting beams of these atoms.

In 1945, the same year in which he retired and took up residence in Berkeley, Calif., Stern was elected to the National Academy of Sciences, one of a number of honors he received during his lifetime. He died in Berkeley on Aug. 17, 1969.

Further Reading

Stern gave an account of his experiments in his Nobel lecture, reprinted in *Nobel Lectures in Physics,* vol. 3 (1964). For the importance of his work in the context of the times see Max Jammer, *The Conceptual Development of Quantum Mechanics* (1966). □

Laurence Sterne

The British novelist Laurence Sterne (1713-1768) produced only two works of fiction, but he ranks as one of the major novelists of the 18th century because of his experiments with the structure and organization of the novel.

The English novel came of age in the 18th century. Daniel Defoe had contributed realistic detail in the 1720s; Samuel Richardson had showed the dramatic intensity inherent in the epistolary novel; Henry Fielding had combined the satirical portrayal of contemporary manners with elaborate and carefully worked-out plots. Laurence Sterne, however, published the single most idiosyncratic novel of the century, *The Life and Opinions of Tristram Shandy* (1760-1767). The apparent plotlessness of *Tristram Shandy,* the endless digressions and wordplay, and the use of the narrator's psychological consciousness as the governing structure in the novel make Sterne unique among the early masters of the English novel and suggest a tie to the stream-of-consciousness novelists who appeared later.

Biography and Early Work

Sterne was born in Clonmel, Ireland, on Nov. 24, 1713, the son of an English army officer, Roger Sterne, and an Irish mother, Agnes. After spending his early years moving about with his father's regiment, he attended school in Yorkshire from 1723 to 1731. Sterne received a bachelor of arts degree from Jesus College, Cambridge, took orders in 1737, and in 1738 became the vicar at Sutton-in-the-Forest, near York, the first of several benefices in and near York that he held. His marriage to Elizabeth Lumley in 1741 proved unhappy.

In 1743 Sterne published his first verses, "The Unknown World, Verses Occasioned by Hearing a Pass-Bell," in the *Gentleman's Magazine*. But neither his verses nor his second work, *A Political Romance* (1759), later called *The History of a Good Warm Watch,* a work that had grown out of a quarrel with fellow clerics, had prepared the English reading audience for the first two volumes of *Tristram Shandy,* which were published early in 1760.

The enormous popularity of Sterne's unusual novel quickly made him a celebrity and gave him social access to the great houses of London and Bath. In 1762 the consumption that plagued his entire life forced him to abandon London society and to seek better health in France. During the last winter before his death, Sterne readied his *A Sentimental Journey* for the press and carried on a curious platonic affair with Mrs. Eliza Draper, the wife of a Bombay official in the East India Company. Sterne's letters to Mrs. Draper were collected in the *Journal to Eliza.*

Sterne's irascibility and bawdy humor were well known to his congregations and to the English public. His local reputation around York was based, at least in part, on his eccentric dress and habits, his mordant wit, and his fund of indecorous anecdotes. It is said that he preached sermons on brotherly love with unusual rancor and ill temper. He died in London on March 18, 1768.

Tristram Shandy

With the London publication of volumes 1 and 2 of *Tristram Shandy* on Jan. 1, 1760, Sterne was launched as a successful author. There were baffled readers, bored readers, and indignant readers, but as Sterne observed, even those who condemned the book bought it. Samuel Richardson found the work "too gross to be inflaming," and Horace Mann noted: "I don't understand it. It was probably the intention that nobody should." Within a few months, Sterne had become a literary lion in London. He admitted that he intended to publish additional volumes as part of the novel "as long as I live, 'tis, in fact, my hobbyhorse." Sterne published volumes 3-6 in 1761; volumes 7 and 8 appeared in 1765; and in 1767, not long before Sterne's death, volume 9 appeared. Although Dr. Samuel Johnson observed of Sterne's novel that "nothing odd will do long," it has survived both neglect and the attacks of critics, and it continues to please, puzzle, and attract more readers than any other 18th-century English novel.

The apparently chaotic structure and puzzling chronology of *Tristram Shandy* are easily clarified. For example, Tristram is born on Nov. 5, 1718; attends Jesus College, Cambridge; and begins his latest volume on or about Aug. 12, 1766. Parson Yorick dies in 1748. Sterne's intention, of course, was to experiment with the straight-forward chronological development of plot that had previously characterized English fiction. By dramatically scrambling chronological and psychological durations, he emphasized the dual nature of time, something to which an individual responds both by reason and by emotion. Despite the immediate confusions of the book, with its blank pages, marbled pages, squiggles, erudite references, footnotes, and puzzling time sequence (Tristram is not born until a third of the way through the work), the novel has an artistic structure of its own, a coherence that resides primarily in the character of Tristram, who holds together all of the elements of the novel, shifting his attention from character to character and from idea to idea. Influenced by the work of John Locke, Sterne concentrated less on the passage of time as the clock measures it than on mental time, in which events can move more or less quickly than clock time. Because the consciousness of the narrator is the unifying factor in the novel, *Tristram Shandy* can be considered a completed work.

The characters in *Tristram Shandy* deserve special note because of their idiosyncracies. Tristram himself seems so scatterbrained that he cannot organize his thoughts. He is quickly and easily diverted from whatever topic he is discussing to frequent digressions. While Mrs. Shandy, Obadiah, Susanna, and Dr. Slop never escape from actuality, "My Father" and Uncle Toby ride special "hobbyhorses." "My Father" believes that life should be presided over by theory, but he never troubles to see that life is so ordered. Indeed, life seems less important to him than the idea and contemplation of it. He propounds his theory of noses (the longer the better), of names (Tristram is the worst of all possible names), and of education (the Tristapedia) in the course of the novel. Although Uncle Toby is literally too sentimental to harm a fly, he is so obsessed with warfare, military campaigns, and battle strategy that he can regret that the Peace of Utrecht has ended war in Europe.

Tristram Shandy is bawdy, satiric, humorous, sentimental, filled with Sterne's extensive learning and crammed with footnotes and foreign languages. Much of the novel is made up of talk about Sterne's writing chores and his rhetorical relation to the reader. The book stands as a rich catalog of the possibilities of misunderstanding and confusion inherent in language.

A Sentimental Journey

Parson Yorick, who dies in *Tristram Shandy,* was habitually identified with Sterne, an identification that he himself promoted in 1760 and again in 1766 by publishing his sermons under the title *The Sermons of Mr. Yorick.* This identification is also apparent in the brief *A Sentimental Journey through France and Italy* (1768), a reworking of volume 7 of *Tristram Shandy.* In both works Parson Yorick is a whimsical, good-hearted, slightly daffy character. The *Journey,* employing typical Sternean techniques, follows Yorick on a tour through France and Italy punctuated with misadventures, sexual ploys, and the usual fill of digressions and abrupt shifts in topic and tone. Sterne's *Sermons,* from which he earned a considerable income, shows the development of a moral theory that is more imaginative than his orthodox religion and more complex as a philosophy.

Sterne's fiction exhibits his ability to give immediacy to a dialogue; to handle dramatic techniques with great skill; to capture idiom with delightful mimicry; to quote frequently—if not always accurately—from the Bible and William Shakespeare and other English authors; and to present his ideas with a witty indecision that charms the reader even as it goads his patience.

The small number of letters that form Sterne's correspondence exhibit his playfulness with language and provide an intensely personal view of him. Unfortunately, many of Sterne's letters were burned by John Botham or mutilated by Sterne's daughter, Lydia, before their first publication in 1775.

Further Reading

Two important biographical studies of Sterne are Wilbur L. Cross, *The Life and Times of Laurence Sterne* (1908; 3d rev. ed. 1929), and Lodwick Hartley, *This Is Laurence* (1943). Major critical studies of *Tristram Shandy* include John L. Traugott, *Tristram Shandy's World: Sterne's Philosophical Rhetoric* (1954); William B. Piper, *Laurence Sterne* (1966); Melvyn Nero, *Laurence Sterne as Satirist* (1969); and William Holtz, *Image and Immortality: A Study of Tristram Shandy* (1970). Lodwick Hartley, *Laurence Sterne in the Twentieth Century: An Essay and a Bibliography of Sternean Studies, 1900-1965* (1966), is an indispensable review of Sterne scholarship. Valuable essays on Sterne's works are included in Dorothy Van Ghent, *The English Novel: Form and Function* (1953); Ian P. Watt, *The Rise of the Novel: Studies in Defoe, Richardson and Fielding* (1957); and Wayne C. Booth, *The Rhetoric of Fiction* (1961).

Additional Sources

Cash, Arthur H. (Arthur Hill), *Laurence Sterne, the early & middle years,* London; New York: Routledge, 1992.

Cash, Arthur H. (Arthur Hill), *Laurence Sterne, the later years,* London; New York: Routledge, 1992.

Connely, Willard, *Laurence Sterne as Yorick,* Westport, Conn.: Greenwood Press, 1979. □

Edward R. Stettinius Jr.

Edward R. Stettinius, Jr. (1900-1949), was an American industrialist and public servant and a secretary of state in President Franklin Roosevelt's Cabinet.

Edward Stettinius, Jr., was born in Chicago, Ill., on Oct. 2, 1900. His father was a partner of financier J. P. Morgan. He received his education at the Pomfret School and the University of Virginia. In 1924 he joined the General Motors Company as a stock clerk at 44 cents an hour. His rise in business was rapid; in 1931 he became General Motors vice president in charge of public and industrial relations. In 1934 he became chairman of the finance committee of the U.S. Steel Corporation, and in 1938 he became chairman of the board.

Stettinius's political views were liberal, and he served in Franklin Roosevelt's administration, first on the Industrial Advisory Board of the National Recovery Administration (1933), then as chairman of the War Resources Board (1939), and finally as administrator of the Lend-Lease Program (1941). He was beyond question a brilliant administrator and in addition a warm human being.

In October 1943 Stettinius succeeded Cordell Hull as secretary of state. In this capacity he undertook a reorganization of the department, sought to bring it into closer relations with other parts of the government, improved the relations of the department with the public at large, and labored vigorously in the creation of the United Nations.

Stettinius cannot be regarded, however, as one of America's great secretaries of state. This was partly a result of President Roosevelt's methods, for Roosevelt's conduct of foreign policy was highly personal. But Stettinius played a useful and competent role in organizing the Dumbarton Oaks Conferences, with representatives of the other Great Powers, which paved the way for the UN conference at San Francisco.

In the winter of 1945 Stettinius accompanied President Roosevelt to the Yalta Conference in the Crimea, at which the Big Three, Roosevelt, Winston Churchill of England, and Joseph Stalin of the U.S.S.R., attempted to plot the future course of international affairs. Stettinius appears to have acquiesced in the most vulnerable agreement made at the conference, by which the Soviet Union was promised nu-

merous concessions in the Far East. This agreement was kept secret and has been sharply criticized; but it must be remembered that at this time the entry of Russia into the war in the East was regarded as indispensable for victory over Japan.

Stettinius led the American delegation to the UN conference at San Francisco. His organization of American opinion for the support of the conference was impressive, and his dignity and good humor were generally praised. Soon after the death of Roosevelt, Stettinius's career as secretary came to an end. For a time he served as rector of the University of Virginia. He died of a heart attack in February 1949.

Further Reading

Stettinius wrote two books, *Lend-Lease: Weapon for Victory* (1944) and *Roosevelt and the Russians: The Yalta Conference* (1949). Several chapters on him by Richard L. Walker are in Samuel Flagg Bemis, ed., *The American Secretaries of State and Their Diplomacy,* vol. 14 (1965). □

Baron Frederick William Augustus von Steuben

Baron Frederick William Augustus von Steuben (1730-1794), a German officer who fought with the colonists in the American Revolutionary War, was best known as the drillmaster of the Army.

On Sept. 17, 1730, Frederick William von Steuben was born in Prussia, the son of an army officer. At the age of 16 he entered the service of the king of Prussia as a lieutenant and served with distinction for 17 years. Part of that time he was an aide-de-camp to the king, Frederick the Great, which provided him with valuable experience in the organization, training, supplying, and disciplining of an army.

In 1763, at the close of the Seven Years War, Steuben left the army and during the next 14 years found employment at the courts of several of the rulers of German principalities. Wishing to return to military life, he sought unsuccessfully to gain a commission in various armies. In Paris in 1777, he met Benjamin Franklin and Silas Deane, the representatives of the American colonies in France. Impressed by his training and experience, they sent him to America with a letter recommending him to the Continental Congress. The Congress accepted Steuben's offer of his services, and in February 1778 he joined the Army under Gen. Washington in winter quarters at Valley Forge.

The Army was in a desperate state—cold, hungry, ill-clad, discontented; it was this ragged body of men that Washington ordered Steuben to train. Knowing no English and acting through interpreters, Steuben drilled the men, taught them tactics, and instilled discipline. His success was

astonishing, and soon he had transformed the "rag, tag, and bobtail" into a body of soldiers who could march, maneuver in column and line, do the manual of arms, carry, load, and fire the musket, and use the bayonet. In the process, he had raised the morale of the Army. He also drew up tables of organization for infantry, artillery, cavalry, and engineers.

In May 1778 a grateful Congress conferred upon Steuben the title of inspector general with the rank of major general. The following year Steuben wrote a manual on infantry drill, *Regulations for the Order and Discipline of the Troops of the United States;* called the "Blue Book," this became the military bible of the Army until 1812. Alexander Hamilton summed up the consequence of Steuben's work at the Battle of Monmouth (June 28, 1778) with the observation that he "had never known til that day the value of discipline."

After 2 years' training troops, Steuben longed for a command. He received this in 1780, when he was sent to Virginia to take over a division. In 1784 he left the Army, became a citizen by acts of the Pennsylvania and New York legislatures, and settled down on a 1,600-acre farm in Oneida County, N.Y., a grant by the state in recognition of his wartime service. He died in Steubenville, N.Y., on Nov. 28, 1794.

Further Reading

The standard biography is John McAuley Palmer, *General Von Steuben* (1937). Still useful is Joseph B. Doyle, *Frederick William Von Steuben and the American Revolution* (1913).

Additional Sources

Steuben: the baron and the town, Remsen, NY: Remsen-Steuben Historical Society, 1994.

Ueberhorst, Horst, *Friedrich Wilhelm von Steuben, 1730-1794: soldier and democrat,* Mèunchen; Baltimore: Moos, 1981. □

John Stevens

The American engineer and inventor John Stevens (1749-1838) was one of the country's earliest experimenters with steamboats. He spent his entire career promoting better transportation in the form of steam railroads, canals, and steamboat lines.

John Stevens was born in New York City, where his father was a shipowner and shipmaster and a wealthy landowner prominent in politics. Young Stevens was raised in Perth Amboy, N.J., and educated primarily by tutors until he attended King's College (now Columbia University), from which he graduated in 1768. Three years later he was admitted to the bar but never practiced law as a profession. During the American Revolution he rose to the rank of colonel, largely for his efforts in raising funds for the patriot cause. He married in 1782 and 2 years later acquired at auction a large tract of land around the present site of Hoboken, N.J., which he developed.

In 1788 Stevens saw John Fitch's steamboat on the Delaware River and became convinced of the bright future for that mode of transportation. Within a few months he petitioned the New York Legislature to grant him the exclusive privilege of steam navigation within the state, but that privilege went to another. Frustrated by his attempts to gain patents from the several states, he aided in drawing up the first Federal patent law in 1790. In August 1791 he was awarded a patent for improvements in steam machinery.

Stevens's father died in 1792, and for the next few years he was busy administering the family estates. About 1797 he entered into partnership with Nicholas I. Roosevelt and Chancellor Robert R. Livingston to build and operate steamboats. The partners differed over such matters as the proper way of applying steam (Stevens preferred the use of screw propellers), and no successful boat was ever built by the group. Stevens then became consultant for the Manhattan Company, which was building a water system for the city of New York, and in 1802 he became head of the Bergen Turnpike Company.

In 1804 Stevens achieved a measure of success with his small steamboat *Little Juliana* and began to build a larger boat, the *Phoenix,* in 1806. Before he could get it into operation, however, Robert Fulton successfully ran the *Claremont* on the Hudson River (1807). The *Phoenix* was sent by sea to the Delaware River and put into ferry service between Philadelphia and Trenton.

About 1810 Stevens turned his steamboat interests over to his sons, who became prominent engineers in their own

right, while he concentrated on the development of steam railroads, which he preferred to the more popular canals. In 1825 he constructed and operated on his estate the first steam locomotive built in the United States. He was a leader in establishing the utility of steam railroads in the United States.

Further Reading

The standard biography of Stevens is Archibald Douglas Turnbull, *John Stevens: An American Record* (1928). An older book, which gives information on his sons as well, is R. H. Thurston, *The Messrs. Stevens, of Hoboken, as Engineers, Naval Architects and Philanthropists* (1874). The best book on early steamboat developments, including those of Stevens, is James Thomas Flexner, *Steamboats Come True: American Inventors in Action* (1944). □

John Paul Stevens

John Paul Stevens (born 1920), appointed to the Supreme Court by President Richard Nixon in 1975, became a member of the "liberal" voting group on the Court which included Justices William J. Brennan and Thurgood Marshall.

Illinois native John Paul Stevens was a Phi Beta Kappa first-in-his-class University of Chicago *magna cum laude* graduate and law review graduate of Northwestern University. He clerked for Supreme Court Associate Justice Wiley B. Rutledge 1947-1948. He was serving on the U.S. Court of Appeals for the Seventh Circuit when President Ford selected him in 1975 as his sole appointment to the U.S. Supreme Court. He was speedily confirmed 98 to 0.

On the Court, Justice Stevens—its junior justice for almost six years until Justice Sandra Day O'Connor replaced Justice Stewart in late 1981—confounded prognosticators who thought they knew him as well as those who did not. Widely considered a "sure swing vote" in the Court's center, then generally composed of Justices White and Stewart, often joined by Justice Powell and occasionally by Justice Blackmun, he soon proved to be found far more frequently with the "liberal bloc" of Justices Brennan and Marshall, and increasingly so with the passing of time.

Stevens was not as doctrinaire as the other two liberals in all facets of civil rights and liberties, and he resolutely parted company with them on such high visibility issues as "reverse discrimination." Nevertheless his "pro rights" or "pro individual" score was consistently high, exceeded only by his two libertarian brethren and by Justice Blackmun in racial discrimination litigation. The women's rights group which opposed his nomination because of his alleged "blatant insensitivity" to sex discrimination quickly began to hail him as both sensitive and free of preconceived notions. Voting rights, free speech, free exercise of religion, separation of church and state, civil rights for African-Americans, children, and prisoners, and not excluding the criminal justice sector—the Stevens' record in all of these areas drew praise from liberal constituencies.

A "gadfly to the brethren," a personal loner, a legal maverick, he consistently challenged his colleagues. Always well-prepared and soft-spoken in his frequent colloquies with counsel in oral argument, he probed like a veritable explorer and was replete with novel legal theories. The latter was particularly notable in cases involving constitutional interpretation, where his jurisprudence permitted him a great deal more latitude than in statutory construction problems. A student of history, and beholden to the tenets of *stare decisis* he nonetheless recognized the importance of the moving finger of time—or, as Justice Oliver W. Holmes expressed it, he "felt necessities of the time." Yet, as he demonstrated so fervently in such stream-of-consciousness cases as *Bakke,* he did not ignore legislative language or clear legislative intent in favor of judicial fiat.

Although respectful and courteous, Stevens found it difficult to subsume his own ideas and interpretations to others in order to forge a numerically united front. This was in part because he wrote more dissenting and concurring opinions than any of his colleagues while lamenting the plethora of opinions handed down by the Court and the cascading number of cases accepted for review! He disagreed with the majority in fully 50 of 91 divided opinions in the 1983-1984 term. To dissent, of course, is one thing; but to engage in a flood of concurring opinions is quite another—for they all-too-often muddied the constitutional law waters and laid themselves open to the charge that they were ego trips.

Stevens found it extremely difficult to join a majority or dissenting opinion without some comment. Thus, in the delicate and difficult July 1983 holding in *Barefoot* v. *Estelle,* in which a badly divided Court upheld the expedited handling of a death row case, Stevens dissented from Justice White's controlling opinion on the procedural issue; but he then concurred in the majority's sanction of the prosecution's use of psychiatric testimony—thereby casting the Court's vote into a 5:3 equation. And early in 1984 he deemed it necessary not only to be the sole dissenter in an "original jurisdiction" jurisdictional case dispute, but he also filed a partial concurrence. That he was not the only justice to engage in that type of perfectionism does not gainsay the unfortunate effect it had upon the judicial process, let alone the public's comprehension.

In 1992, Stevens wrote the opinion for *Cipollone* v. *Liggett Group, Inc.,* in which the Court, by a 7-2 vote, ruled that cigarette manufacturers could be sued under state products liability laws, particularly those grounded in charges of fraud or misrepresentation about the dangers of cigarette smoking. A rash of lawsuits broke out country-wide. In March, 1997, the Liggett Group announced a sweeping settlement in 22 states that were suing the tobacco industry to recover Medicaid costs. This followed a public admission by Liggett officials that tobacco is addictive and causes cancer and heart disease.

If Stevens was not a jurisprudential or tactical on-bench leader, he was nonetheless an unceasing stimulator of reflection, of innovation, of disciplined literateness (witness his majority opinion for the 5:4 Court in the 1984 "Home Video Taping" case), and of cerebral combat in constitutional law logic and theory. His gift for elegant, pungent expression will grace the Court's annals.

Further Reading

The literature on Justice Stevens was sparse. A commendable early appraisal was Leonard Orland's "John Paul Stevens" in Leon Friedman (editor), *The Justices of the United States Supreme Court, 1789-1978* (1980). Justice Stevens' opinions—several of which were mentioned in this article—represented a good measure of his jurisprudence. In general, see Henry J. Abraham, *Justices and Presidents: A Political History of Appointments to the Supreme Court* (1985). ☐

Nettie Maria Stevens

Biologist Nettie Maria Stevens (1861-1912) discovered that chromosomes determine sex.

Nettie Maria Stevens was a biologist and cytogeneticist and one of the first American women to be recognized for her contributions to scientific research. "She . . . produced new data and new theories," wrote Marilyn Bailey Ogilvie in *Women in Science,* "yet beyond these accomplishments passed along her expertise to a new generation. . . . illustrat[ing] the importance of the women's colleges in the education of women scientists." Although Stevens started her research career when she was in her thirties, she successfully expanded the fields of embryology and cytogenetics (the branch of biology which focuses on the study of heredity), particularly in the study of histology (a branch of anatomy dealing with plant and animal tissues) and of regenerative processes in invertebrates such as hydras and flatworms. She is best known for her role in genetics—her research contributed greatly to the understanding of chromosomes and heredity. She theorized that the sex of an organism was determined by the inheritance of a specific chromosome—X or Y—and performed experiments to confirm this hypothesis.

Stevens, the third of four children and the first daughter, was born in Cavendish, Vermont, on July 7, 1861, to Ephraim Stevens, a carpenter of English descent, and Julia Adams Stevens. Historians know little about her family or her early life, except that she was educated in the public schools in Westford, Massachusetts, and displayed exceptional scholastic abilities. Upon graduation, Stevens taught Latin, English, mathematics, physiology and zoology at the high school in Lebanon, New Hampshire. As a teacher she had a great zeal for learning that she tried to impart both to her students and her colleagues. Between 1881 and 1883, Stevens attended the Normal School at Westfield, Massachusetts, consistently achieving the highest scores in her class from the time she started until she graduated. She worked as a school teacher, and then as a librarian for a number of years after she graduated; however, there are gaps in her history that are unaccounted for between this time and when she enrolled at Stanford University in 1896.

In 1896, Stevens was attracted by the reputation of Stanford University for providing innovative opportunities for individuals aspiring to pursue their own scholastic interests. At the age of thirty-five she enrolled, studying physiology under professor Oliver Peebles Jenkins. She spent summers studying at the Hopkins Seaside Laboratory, Pacific Grove, California, and pursuing her love of learning and of biology. During this time, Stevens decided to switch careers to focus on research, instead of teaching. While at Hopkins she performed research on the life cycle of *Boveria,* a protozoan parasite of sea cucumbers. Her findings were published in 1901 in the *Proceedings of the California Academy of Sciences.* After obtaining her master's degree—a highly unusual accomplishment for a woman in that era—Stevens returned to the East to study at Bryn Mawr College, Pennsylvania, as a graduate biology student in 1900. She was such an exceptional student that she was awarded a fellowship enabling her to study at the Zoological Station in Naples, Italy, and then at the Zoological Institute of the University of Würzburg, Germany. Back at Bryn Mawr, she obtained her doctorate in 1903. At this time, she was made a research fellow in biology at Bryn Mawr and then was promoted to a reader in experimental morphology in 1904. From 1903 until 1905, her research was funded by a grant from the Carnegie Institution. In 1905, she was promoted again to associate in experimental morphology, a position she held until her death in 1912.

While Stevens' early research focused on morphology and taxonomy and then later expanded to cytology, her most important research was with chromosomes and their relation to heredity. Because of the pioneering studies performed by the renowned monk Gregor Mendel (showing how pea plant genetic traits are inherited), scientists of the time knew a lot about how chromosomes acted during cell division and maturation of germ cells. However, no inherited trait had been traced from the parents' chromosomes to those of the offspring. In addition, no scientific studies had yet linked one chromosome with a specific characteristic. Stevens, and the well-known biologist Edmund Beecher Wilson, who worked independently on this type of research, were the first to demonstrate that the sex of an organism was determined by a particular chromosome; moreover, they proved that gender is inherited in accordance with Mendel's laws of genetics. Together, their research confirmed, and therefore established, a chromosomal basis for heredity. Working with the meal worm, *Tenebrio molitor,* Stevens determined that the male produced two kinds of sperm—one with a large X chromosome, and the other with a small Y chromosome. Unfertilized eggs, however, were all alike and had only X chromosomes. Stevens theorized that sex, in some organisms, may result from chromosomal inheritance. She suggested that eggs fertilized by sperm carrying X chromosomes produced females, and those by sperm carrying the Y chromosome resulted in males. She performed further research to prove this phenomenon, expanding her studies to other species. Although this theory was not accepted by all scientists at the time, it was profoundly important in the evolution of the field of genetics and to an understanding of determination of gender.

Stevens was a prolific author, publishing some thirty-eight papers in eleven years. For her paper, "A Study of the Germ Cells of *Aphis rosae* and *Aphis oenotherae,*" Stevens was awarded the Ellen Richards Research Prize in 1905, given to promote scientific research by women. Stevens died of breast cancer on May 4, 1912, before she could occupy the research professorship created for her by the Bryn Mawr trustees. Much later, Thomas Hunt Morgan, a 1933 Nobel Prize recipient for his work in genetics, recognized the importance of Stevens' ground-breaking experiments, as quoted by Ogilvie in the *Proceedings of the American Philosophical Society,* "Stevens had a share in a discovery of importance and her name will be remembered for this, when the minutiae of detailed investigations that she carried out have become incorporated in the general body of the subject."

Further Reading

Ogilvie, Marilyn Bailey, *Women in Science: Antiquity through the Nineteenth Century,* Massachusetts Institute of Technology, 1986.

Isis, June, 1978, pp. 163–72.

Proceedings of the American Philosophical Society, Held at Philadelphia for Promoting Useful Knowledge, Volume 125, American Philosophical Society, 1981, pp. 292–311. □

Thaddeus Stevens

Thaddeus Stevens (1792-1868), American congressman, was the leading Radical Republican in the Civil War era.

Thaddeus Stevens, the son of an unsuccessful farmer who subsequently deserted his family, was born on April 4, 1792, in Danville, Vt. Despite his impoverished background and a deformity of the feet, he graduated from Dartmouth in 1814 and became a successful lawyer in Gettysburg, Pa. An Anti-Mason, he became a Whig when that party absorbed his in the mid-1830s. Elected to the state legislature in 1833, he remained for 8 years, becoming noted for his campaign to extend the state's free school system. An early and intense opponent of slavery, he defended fugitive slaves in the courts and, at the Pennsylvania constitutional convention of 1837, unsuccessfully fought black disenfranchisement.

Stevens's intelligence and absolute mastery of political invective made him a frequent spokesman for his party, but his occasional erratic and impulsive actions and his singular ability to end up on the losing side in intraparty struggles kept him from achieving high office. In 1841, failing to get a post in President William Henry Harrison's Cabinet, he retired from the legislature and moved to Lancaster.

Stevens was elected to Congress in 1848 and 1850, becoming noted for his attacks on the South during debates on the Compromise of 1850. Once the slavery question seemed settled, Stevens's antislavery stance seemed inopportune, and he was not renominated in 1852. Revitalization of the slavery issue after 1854 brought him back into politics as a Know-Nothing and then as a Republican when that party emerged in the 1850s. In 1858, again elected to Congress, he renewed his bitter enmity toward Southern slaveholders.

In 1861 Stevens became chairman of the powerful House Ways and Means Committee and helped to secure passage of the legislation needed to finance the Civil War. He and other Radical Republicans urged Abraham Lincoln to pursue an uncompromising war policy to restore the Union, secure freedom for the slaves, and destroy the political power of the slaveholders. Stevens advocated military emancipation, use of African American troops, and confiscation of Confederate property. He insisted that the Southern states not be restored to the Union until they had been thoroughly reconstructed, arguing that by seceding they had lost all rights under the Constitution and were conquered provinces subject to congressional control. Stevens particularly wanted the economic and political power of the planters decreased and schools, land, and ballots provided for the freedmen.

Stevens served on the crucial Joint Committee on Reconstruction in the postwar period, guiding much of its legislation, including the 14th Amendment, guaranteeing civil rights for the freedmen, through the House. An adroit parliamentarian, Stevens intimidated opponents. Yet many of his more radical proposals were never passed. Many Northerners were simply not ready to accept the social implications of radical measures designed to uplift the blacks.

Stevens's views on Reconstruction clashed with President Andrew Johnson's more conservative course. The President's veto of the civil rights and Freedmen's Bureau bills in 1866 and his violent personal attack on Stevens prompted Stevens and other Republicans to break openly with Johnson and to push through a much more stringent congressional Reconstruction program over the President's opposition.

In 1868 Stevens served on the committee that drafted the articles of impeachment against Johnson and was a manager of the case before the Senate. Johnson was acquitted in May, and Stevens died on August 11 in Washington. He requested that he be buried in a black cemetery to "illustrate in my death the principles which I advocated through a long life—Equality of Man before his Creator." Stevens's tragedy lay in the nation's unreadiness to begin the social and economic reforms necessary to make legal guarantees for blacks meaningful.

Further Reading

Richard N. Current, *Old Thad Stevens: A Story of Ambition* (1942), is a scholarly, somewhat hostile analysis that finds Stevens primarily motivated by political ambition. Ralph Korngold, *Thaddeus Stevens: A Being Darkly Wise and Rudely Great* (1955), and Fawn M. Brodie, *Thaddeus Stevens: Scourge of the South* (1959), are sympathetic to Stevens, as is Hans Trefousse, *The Radical Republicans* (1969), a useful analysis of the ideas and political situation of that group. □

Wallace Stevens

American poet Wallace Stevens (1879-1955) was a virtuoso of language, a master of rhyme and verbal music, of gay and thoughtful rhythms, and of precise and exotic diction.

Wallace Stevens was a successful lawyer and businessman, as well as an important poet. But too much has been made of the combination of esthete and businessman in him. Poetry for him was an irresistible urge ("one writes poetry because one must"), whereas business success was largely a means to attain the independence and privacy he needed for his poetry. He was from the start a poet's poet, a brilliant craftsman, but general critical acclaim came slowly. His early verse shows the influence of the French symbolists—the romantic skepticism, irony, dandified wit, and self-deprecation of Charles Baudelaire, Stéphane Mallarmé, and Jules Laforgue. Stevens stood apart from groups, but he shared the imagists' devotion to concrete images and the general commitment of modernists to learning, discriminating diction, wit, and the merging of thought and feeling. Beneath the surface of his cosmopolitan verse, an American heart beats, acknowledging attachments to Pennsylvania, Connecticut, his adopted state, and Florida, a vacation state. In "The Comedian as the Letter C" he wrote that "his soil is man's intelligence." Stevens was an heir of Walt Whitman, who employed free forms, foreign phrases, and references to music. Stevens's approximately 400 published poems and his few essays and published talks are largely devoted to converting the diversity of reality, its "fragrances" and "stinks," to poetry's order and harmony.

Stevens was born on Oct. 2, 1879, in Reading, Pa. He was educated locally and from 1897 to 1900 at Harvard, where he absorbed something of Professor George Santayana's estheticism. After college he worked briefly as a *New York Herald Tribune* reporter and attended New York University Law School (1900-1903). He was admitted to the bar in 1904 and began practicing law in New York City. He married Elsie V. Kachel in 1909 and they had one daughter. All the while he was writing poetry, and as the poetic renascence in America and England gathered momentum, he began to associate with other poets, such as Alfred Kreymborg, William Carlos Williams, E. E. Cummings, and later Marianne Moore. In 1914, at the age of 35, this large, competent man, who spoke softly and seldom, submitted a group of poems to *Poetry* magazine, which printed four under the dandyish pseudonym of "Peter Parasol."

First Poems

In 1915 "Peter Quince at the Clavier" appeared, an important poem employing a variety of economical forms—three-line unrhymed stanzas, stanzas with irregular rhymes and different numbers of lines, and couplet stanzas. In it a man improvising at a clavier speaks or thinks of a beloved, and his imagination associates the sound of the music, his desire, and the ancient myth of Susanna and the elders.

Particular beauties, he finds, are "momentary in the mind," but our hunger for beauty itself is passed on immortally in the blood.

The same year "Sunday Morning," one of Stevens's most celebrated poems, appeared. The poem is skeptical, but regretfully so. A complacent lady in a peignoir, having coffee and oranges in a sunny room, finds it possible to put off "the dark/ Encroachment of that old catastrophe," Christ's martyrdom. She suspects that the "comforts of the sun" are "all of paradise that we shall know," though she still feels "The need of some imperishable bliss." In a naturalistic cosmos, on the "wide water" of history, "unsponsored, free," she can unite herself to the passing delights of her tasteful room and the world outside.

In 1916 Stevens joined the legal department of the Hartford Accident and Indemnity Insurance Company in Hartford, Conn., but he returned to New York occasionally to see literary friends. He published two short plays, "Three Travelers Watch the Sunrise" (1916) and "Carlos among the Candles" (1917), both embodying the influence of symbolist theory and Japanese No plays. In 1919 Stevens enjoyed the first of the Florida vacations that occasioned a number of poems. Publishing regularly in little magazines, he had put approximately 100 poems into print when, at the age of 44, he published his first volume of verse, *Harmonium* (1923).

Harmonium

Most notices of *Harmonium* were unfavorable. The book demonstrated, nevertheless, that Stevens had perfected his use of Gallicisms, rare words, and "gaudy" language; of unusual titles and color symbols; and of short imagistic lyrics and long meditative poems, usually about poetry. The title and exuberant musical effects of "Bantams in Pine-woods," beginning "Chieftain Iffucan of Azcan in caftan/ Of tan with henna hackles, halt!" illustrate two of these characteristics. The poem contrasts bantams absorbed in concrete particularities with the inflated crowing of a "universal cock." "Thirteen Ways of Looking at a Blackbird," "Le Monocle de Mon Oncle," "To the One of Fictive Music," and "The Emperor of Ice Cream" all became familiar pieces.

The character of Crispin in the long and difficult "The Comedian as the Letter C" is, up to 1923, Stevens's most effective representation of the artist. A performer-transformer in quest of deep realities, he is both the earth's highest creature and a limited clown subject to chance and change. Crispin's far, dreamlike voyages ultimately return him to his home continent and to the world within himself. Some critics look upon this thoughtful poem with its unusual vocabulary as a bridge between Stevens's early inclination toward virtuoso performances and a final concentration on the penetration of reality.

Stevens's poetic activity fell off after *Harmonium.* This has been attributed to efforts to advance his business career (he became a vice president of his insurance company in 1934) and to the fact that his Crispin-like quest took longer than he had expected. In 1930 his poems began to appear again, and he published a second edition of *Harmonium* (1931), its status as a classic of modern poetry now secure.

It was 1935 before Stevens issued a new volume, *Ideas of Order.* Here Stevens was still meditating on the poetic process but with a new elegiac note, a new uneasiness about a reality that included the Great Depression and forebodings of international violence. "Academic Discourse at Havana" notes that "a grand decadence settles down like cold." What is "the function of the poet" in such a cultural setting? Is it to speak an "epitaph" or "An infinite incantation of our selves/ In the grand decadence of the perished swans"? In "Ideas of Order at Key West" two men walk on the shore and discuss the sea (reality) and the "Blessed rage to order." The person in "Anglais Mort à Florence" finds that the pleasures of spring, Brahms's music, and the imaginative moon are waning with age and that he has become increasingly dependent on social order and memory.

The long title poem of *The Man with the Blue Guitar* (1937) represents an advance in Stevens's meditations on poetry. The guitarist is the poet, and the blue guitar his imagination. The guitarist says, "'Things as they are/ Are changed upon the blue guitar.'" The author adds that in our secular world "Poetry/ Exceeding music must take the place/ Of empty heaven and its hymns." And later he declares that "Poetry is the subject of the poem,/ From this the poem issues and/ To this returns. . . ." Men are most alive in their imaginations, and the artist who imagines the materials of the world most truly and austerely into art is the most alive of men. In "Mystic Garden and Middling Beast" Stevens again affirms the responsible hedonism of such men who are "Happy rather than holy" and "whose heaven is in themselves."

Late Writings

At 60 Stevens began his unusually productive last period. *Parts of a World* (1942) is a collection of raw fragments of reality that were preliminaries to the final synthesizing meditations of later volumes. "Loneliness in Jersey City" presents an urban barrenness amusingly humanized by "Polacks" playing concertinas. Other poems are addressed to poetry and the fiction-making mind of the poet-hero, "the central man," "the glass man," who is as "responsive as a mirror with a voice."

Notes toward a Supreme Fiction (1942) is an extended poem of 30 lesser poems with prologue and epilogue embodying Stevens's mature ideas about poetry. Like much of his late verse, it is sparse, dense, and as a result at times obscure. To the ears of some critics it is also prosaic. Assessing the relationship of poetry and philosophy, imagination and reality, Stevens concludes that the true poet seeks the Supreme Fiction, the absolute but unattainable poem. He strives to enter into the changing fragments of this world and to discover by will or by chance order and unity. Though the results are only partial and unstable, he is compelled to go on seeking.

Esthétique du Mal (1944), another long poem, accepts the inevitable deprivation and suffering of man and the necessity for evil in order to define good. Poetry or language at its best, like faith in God, can help us convert these inevitabilities into joy: "Natives of poverty, children of malheur,/ The gaiety of language is our seigneur."

Stevens's new collection, *Transport to Summer* (1947), included *Notes toward a Supreme Fiction* and *Esthétique du Mal.* "Credences of Summer" is a lyrical celebration of the high point of reality (greenness) and of the year, "green's green apogee." "Dutch Graves" grew out of a visit to his old family home and cemetery in Tulpehocken, Pa. This poem and an essay published in 1948 both dwell on the decay of the religious vision, the fiction or myth that gave direction to his ancestors' lives.

Auroras of Autumn (1950) won the Bollingen Prize. The volume contains one of Steven's most penetrating statements on his poetic theory. In "An Ordinary Evening in New Haven" the meditator states, "'We seek/ Nothing beyond reality. Within it/ Everything . . . The search for reality is as momentous as/ The search for God,'" adding that a philosopher seeks "'an interior made exterior'" and a poet "'the same exterior made/ Interior. . . . '" *The Necessary Angel: Essays in Reality and Imagination* (1951) contains pithy and closely reasoned essays and lectures.

Stevens's *Collected Poems* (1954) received the Pulitzer Prize and the National Book Award. At this time he refused a Harvard professorship, though he relished the idea of concentrating on poetry, but he feared that the appointment would force his retirement from business, since he had already worked several years beyond the statutory retirement age of 70. The decision was of little consequence, for he died on Aug. 2, 1955. The dedicated imaginer of the things of this world, like the subject of "A Child Asleep in Its Own Life" from his *Opus Posthumous* (1957), was asleep in his poems, the "sole emperor" of what he had regarded outwardly and known inwardly.

Further Reading

Stevens's daughter, Holly Stevens, selected and edited his *Letters* (1966). Stevens's *Opus Posthumous* was edited by Samuel F. Morse (1957). Morse's *Wallace Stevens: Poetry as Life* (1970) is comprehensive and combines biography with scholarly criticism of the work.

A general study is William Van O'Connor, *The Shaping Spirit: A Study of Wallace Stevens* (1950). Two introductions to Stevens's work are Frank Kermode, *Wallace Stevens* (1960), and Henry W. Wells, *Introduction to Wallace Stevens* (1964). More specialized studies include Robert Pack, *Wallace Stevens: An Approach to His Poetry and Thought* (1958); Daniel Fuchs, *The Comic Spirit of Wallace Stevens* (1963); John J. Enck, *Wallace Stevens: Images and Judgments* (1964); Joseph N. Riddel, *The Clairvoyant Eye: The Poetry and Poetics of Wallace Stevens* (1965); Herbert J. Stern, *Wallace Stevens: Art of Uncertainty* (1966); and Ronald Sukenick, *Wallace Stevens, Musing the Obscure: Readings, an Interpretation, and a Guide to the Collected Poetry* (1967). Essays on Stevens by various critics are in Ashley Brown and Robert S. Haller, eds., *The Achievement of Wallace Stevens* (1962), and Marie Boroff, ed., *Wallace Stevens: A Collection of Critical Essays* (1963).

Additional Sources

Bates, Milton J., *Wallace Stevens: a mythology of self,* Berkeley: University of California Press, 1985.

Brazeau, Peter, *Parts of a world: Wallace Stevens remembered: an oral biography,* San Francisco: North Point Press, 1985, 1983.

Richardson, Joan, *Wallace Stevens,* New York: Beech Tree Books, 1986-c1988.

Stevens, Holly, *Souvenirs and prophecies: the young Wallace Stevens,* New York: Knopf, 1977, 1976.

Wallace Stevens: a celebration, Princeton, N.J.: Princeton University Press, 1980. □

Adlai Ewing Stevenson

Adlai Ewing Stevenson (1900-1965), American statesman and diplomat, was twice Democratic candidate for president.

Adlai Stevenson was born in Los Angeles, Calif., on Feb. 5, 1900, of a family prominent in Bloomington, Ill. He was the grandson of Adlai E. Stevenson, the vice president under Grover Cleveland. Graduating from the public schools, he attended Choate Academy, an eastern private school. He finished Princeton University in 1922 and graduated from Northwestern University Law School in 1926. Admitted that year to the Illinois bar, he began law practice in Chicago. He early showed studious tastes, especially for history and international affairs.

Stevenson became familiar with farm needs and policies around Bloomington. He combined intense faith in democracy with a strong desire to encourage thinking upon the issues of the time. His principles were also influenced by work in Franklin Roosevelt's New Deal administration. He worked for the Chicago Foreign Policy Association and the Chicago Bar Association and helped to promote the civil rights movement. In 1946-1947 he served as United States delegate to the General Assembly of the United Nations.

In 1948 Stevenson was elected governor of Illinois. His administration of the state, though ambitious and vigorous, was hampered by Republican legislative opposition and a division of sentiment between rural and industrial Illinois. Nevertheless, having attracted wide attention through speeches and articles, he was nominated for president on the Democratic ticket in 1952. Though defeated by Dwight Eisenhower, he maintained his place as leader of the Democratic party, representing its more studious, liberal element.

Stevenson ran against Eisenhower again in the presidential race of 1956. A lonely, thoughtful man, with a tinge of melancholia which made him seem unhappy despite his warm humor and flashing wit, he appeared colorless compared with Eisenhower. He later declared that one of his principal disappointments in 1956 was the failure to provoke a real debate on the issues. Stevenson's contribution to public discussion was, nevertheless, large and unique, for he appraised the importance of issues in the revolutionary new era.

After John F. Kennedy was elected president, Stevenson made no secret of his wish to be appointed secretary of state. Made ambassador to the United Nations instead, he was deeply disappointed. He felt humiliated when, as America's UN representative, he had to explain and defend policies and actions of other men, some of which, like the Bay of Pigs invasion in Cuba in April 1961, he did not approve. But he was an immovable supporter of the United States against Soviet policies and threats and especially distinguished himself in refuting and denouncing the U.S.S.R.'s position in UN debate. On Oct. 25, 1962 he demanded that the Soviet ambassador to the UN state honestly whether the U.S.S.R. was placing missiles and sites in Cuba. When Soviet Ambassador Zorin replied evasively, "I am not in an American courtroom, sir," Stevenson thundered, "You are in the court of world opinion right now." While still ambassador to the United Nations, Stevenson died suddenly in London on July 14, 1965.

Further Reading

Bert Cochran, *Adlai Stevenson: Patrician among the Politicians* (1969), views Stevenson as a member of an American ruling upper class. Other biographical works include Kenneth Sydney Davis, *The Politics of Honor: A Biography of Adlai E. Stevenson* (1957; rev. ed. 1967); Stuart Gerry Brown, *Conscience in Politics: Adlai Stevenson in the 1950's* (1961) and *Adlai E. Stevenson, a Short Biography: The Conscience of the Country* (1965); Herbert J. Muller, *Adlai Stevenson: A Study in Values* (1967); and Richard J. Walton, *The Remnants of Power: The Tragic Last Years of Adlai Stevenson* (1968). Composite views of Stevenson are offered by Alden Whitman and the *New York Times as Portrait: Adlai E. Stevenson: Politician, Diplomat, Friend* (1965), and Edward P. Doyle, *As We Knew Adlai: The Stevenson Story by Twenty-two Friends* (1966). Also useful is Rockefeller Brothers Fund, *Prospect for America: The Rockefeller Panel Reports* (1961). □

Robert Louis Stevenson

The Scottish novelist, essayist, and poet Robert Louis Stevenson (1850-1894) was one of the most popular and highly regarded British writers of the end of the 19th century. He played a significant part in the revival of the novel of romance.

During Robert Louis Stevenson's youth the romantic novels of Sir Walter Scott and his followers had been eclipsed by the realism of William Makepeace Thackeray and Anthony Trollope. Writing in conscious opposition to this trend, Stevenson formulated his theoretical position in his essays "A Gossip on Romance" (1882), "A Humble Remonstrance" (1884), and "The Lantern-bearers" (1888). Romance, he wrote, is not concerned with objective truth but rather with things as they appear to the subjective imagination, with the "poetry of circumstance." Romance, according to Stevenson, avoids complications of character and morality and dwells on action and adventure.

Stevenson was born on Nov. 13, 1850, in Edinburgh, the son of a noted lighthouse builder and harbor engineer. Though robust and healthy at birth, Stevenson soon became a victim of constant respiratory ailments that later developed into tuberculosis and made him skeletally thin and frail most of his life. By the time he entered Edinburgh University at the age of 16, ostensibly to study engineering, Stevenson had fallen under the spell of language and had begun to write. For several years he attended classes irregularly, cultivating a bohemian existence complete with long hair and velvet jackets and acquainting himself with Edinburgh's lower depths.

Early Works

When he was 21 years old, Stevenson openly declared his intention of becoming a writer against the strong opposition of his father. Agreeing to study law as a compromise, Stevenson was admitted to the Scottish bar in 1875. Having traveled to the Continent several times for health and pleasure, he now swung back and forth between Scotland and a growing circle of artistic and literary friends in London and Paris. Stevenson's first book, *An Inland Voyage* (1878), related his adventures during a canoe trip on the canals of Belgium and France.

In 1876 in France, Stevenson had met an American woman named Fanny Osbourne. Separated from her husband, she was 11 years older than Stevenson and had two children. Two years later Stevenson and Osbourne became lovers. In 1878 Osbourne returned to California to arrange a divorce, and a year later Stevenson followed her. After traveling across America in an emigrant train, Stevenson arrived in Monterey in poor health. After his marriage, a stay in an abandoned mining camp, later recounted in *The Silverado Squatters* (1883), restored his health. A year after setting out for the United States, Stevenson was back in Scotland. But the climate there proved impossible, and for the next 4 years he and his wife lived in Switzerland and in the south of France.

Despite ill health these years were productive. In his collections *Virginibus puerisque* (1881) and *Familiar Studies of Men and Books* (1882) Stevenson arrived at maturity as an essayist. Addressing his readers with confidential ease, he reflected on the common beliefs and incidents of life with a mild iconoclasm, a middling disillusionment.

The stories Stevenson collected in *The New Arabian Nights* (1883) and *The Merry Men* (1887) range from detective stories to Scottish dialect tales. The evocation of mood and setting that he practiced in his travel essays was used to great effect here. Despite his theory of romance, he was unable entirely to keep away from moral issues in these stories, but he was rarely successful in integrating moral viewpoint with action and scene.

Early Novels

Treasure Island (1881, 1883), first published as a serial in a children's magazine, ranks as Stevenson's first popular book, and it established his fame. A perfect romance according to Stevenson's formula, the novel—riding over all the problems of morality and character that might have arisen—recounts a boy's involvement with murderous pirates. *Kidnapped* (1886), set in Scotland shortly after the abortive Jacobite rebellion of 1745, has the same charm. In its sequel, *David Balfour* (1893), Stevenson could not avoid psychological and moral problems without marked strain. In *The Strange Case of Dr. Jekyll and Mr. Hyde* (1886) he dealt directly with the nature of evil in man and the hideous effects of a hypocrisy that seeks to deny it. This work pointed the way toward Stevenson's more serious later novels. During this same period he published a very popular collection of poetry, *A Child's Garden of Verses* (1885).

After the death of his father in 1887, Stevenson again traveled to the United States, this time for his health. He lived for a year at Saranac Lake, N.Y., in the Adirondacks. In 1889 Stevenson and his family set out on a cruise of the South Sea Islands. When it became clear that only there could he live in relative good health, he settled on the island of Upolu in Samoa. He bought a plantation (Vailima), built a house, and gained influence with the natives, who called him Tusifala ("teller of tales"). By the time of his death on Dec. 3, 1894, Stevenson had become a significant figure in island affairs. His observations on Samoan life were published in the collection *In the South Seas* (1896) and in *A Footnote to History* (1892). Of the stories written in these years, "The Beach of Falesá" in *Island Nights' Entertainments* (1893) remains particularly interesting as an exploration of the confrontation between European and native ways of life.

Later Novels

The Master of Ballantrae (1889), set in the same period as *Kidnapped,* showed a new sophistication in Stevenson's use of the elements of romance. Its basic theme involved complexities of character that his earlier romances had deliberately avoided. In the more advanced *Weir of Hermiston,* the legends of the romantic Scottish past saturate the setting and serve as a symbolic background for a tragic conflict between the primitive energies of a father and his sensitive, effete son. Left unfinished at his death, this novel would have ranked as Stevenson's greatest work. While living in the South Pacific, Stevenson also collaborated on three novels with his stepson Lloyd Osbourne.

Further Reading

The best biographies of Stevenson are David Daiches, *Robert Louis Stevenson* (1947), and Joseph C. Furnas, *Voyage to Windward: The Life of Robert Louis Stevenson* (1951). Recommended critical studies include David Daiches, *Stevenson and the Art of Fiction* (1951); Robert Kiely, *Robert Louis Stevenson and the Fiction of Adventure* (1964), and Edwin M. Eigner, *Robert Louis Stevenson and Romantic Tradition* (1966).

Additional Sources

Bell, Ian, *Dreams of exile: Robert Louis Stevenson, a biography,* New York: H. Holt, 1993.

Hammond, J. R. (John R.), *A Robert Louis Stevenson chronology,* New York: St. Martin's Press, 1996.

McLynn, F. J., *Robert Louis Stevenson: a biography,* New York: Random House, 1994. □

Alexander Turney Stewart

In the mid-19th century Alexander Turney Stewart (1803-1876) was America's leading retail dry-goods merchant and an outstanding dry-goods wholesaler. His innovations in merchandising profoundly affected American retail trade.

Alexander Stewart was born on Oct. 12, 1803, in Lisburn, County Antrim, Ireland. With his inheritance, he opened a retail store in New York City in 1823, having emigrated to the United States somewhat earlier. A merchandising genius, he introduced a new type of dry-goods store in 1846 that was the precursor of the department store. In this mercantile showplace, Stewart sold a wide range of merchandise. Successful, this store was expanded so that by 1850 Stewart had the largest establishment of this kind in New York City, the largest mercantile center in the nation. In 1862 he again pioneered when he erected a grander store constructed on iron structural beams.

Mid-19th-century America witnessed the development of three variants of mass marketing: the department store, the mail-order house, and the chain store. These all possessed certain common attributes, many of which Stewart innovated. For example, he early used the one-price system, without bargaining, as well as cash buying in large quantities and selling at low prices. These innovations are related to large-scale enterprise. "He was the first retailer to departmentalize his merchandise, thus preparing the way for the future department store." After all, a department store presupposes a degree of decentralization and autonomy for each of the departments. In an age in which domestic commerce was dominated by the wholesaler, Stewart employed vertical integration: he was his own wholesaler and manufacturer and also maintained his own European buying organization. These techniques reduced costs and selling prices. The result of such policies was an unequaled sales volume in millions of dollars. This merchant prince became one of the richest Americans of his day.

Another of Stewart's accomplishments was the creation of a sizable, effective sales and supporting staff. To motivate his managers, he allowed them to share in profits, though not in ownership. However, Stewart's enterprise began to decline as key personnel were not replaced and Stewart became involved in outside affairs. His enterprise did not survive mismanagement by those who succeeded him. The hulk of the concern was sold to John Wanamaker, the prime Philadelphia merchant, in 1896.

Outside of his business, Stewart's career was undistinguished, although he did sponsor one of the early "model towns," Garden City, N.Y. He became a War Democrat during the Civil War. Appointed secretary of the Treasury in 1869 by President Ulysses S. Grant, he never held the position, since business people were disqualified by law.

He died on April 10, 1876, in New York City, having profoundly affected American retail trade.

Further Reading

Ralph Merle Hower, *History of Macy's of New York, 1858-1919: Chapters in the Evolution of the Department Store* (1943), presents material on the history of retailing, as does John W. Ferry, *A History of the Department Store* (1960). Also useful is Philip S. Foner, *Business and Slavery* (1941).

Additional Sources

Elias, Stephen N., *Alexander T. Stewart: the forgotten merchant prince,* Westport, Conn.: Praeger, 1992. □

Dugald Stewart

The Scottish philosopher Dugald Stewart (1753-1828) was a proponent of Reid's commonsense philosophy in Scotland.

Dugald Stewart was born on Nov. 22, 1753, in Edinburgh. His father was a professor of mathematics at the University of Edinburgh. At 13 young Dugald himself entered the university, studying moral philosophy under Adam Ferguson, who had been strongly influenced by Thomas Reid. Later, at the insistence of Ferguson, he went to hear Reid lecture at Glasgow University. Returning to Edinburgh, he became conjoint professor of mathematics with his father. In 1783 he married Helen Bannatyne, who died in 1787, leaving one son. After the death of his father he assumed the chair of mathematics, and a few years later (1785) he was made professor of moral philosophy. In 1790 he married Helen D'Arcy Cranston, by whom he had a son and a daughter. She was a brilliant and cultured woman who was an able critic of his writings.

Stewart's chief concern was to formulate a philosophy of mind through the use of the inductive method of Sir Francis Bacon. He intended to show that the phenomena of consciousness are connected by laws, discovered through the inductive method, and that such laws explain the constitution and operation of mind. Most of his writings do not depart from this major concern. His *Elements of the Philosophy of the Human Mind* was published in three volumes (1792, 1814, 1827). In 1793 he published his *Outlines of Moral Philosophy,* a summary of his views. In 1803 he was made editor of the *Edinburgh Gazette,* a position given to him because of his political loyalty. In 1810 he brought out *Philosophical Essays* and, a year later, *Biographical Memoirs of W. Robertson, Adam Smith and Thomas Reid.* He published *Dissertation on the Progress of Metaphysical and Ethical Philosophy* in two parts (1815, 1821). In 1822 he suffered a stroke from which he partially recovered. The stroke apparently affected his speech but left his mind clear. Shortly before his death, his *View of the Active and Moral Powers of Man* was published (1828).

Stewart died on June 11, 1828, while on a visit to a friend. As more than one interpreter has indicated, his most

appropriate memorial is found not in his writings but in his pupils, who included Lord Brougham, Lord Palmerston, Sir Walter Scott, and James Mill.

Further Reading

The Collected Works of Dugald Stewart was edited by William Hamilton, with a brief sketch of Stewart's life by John Veitch (11 vols., 1854-1860). A chapter on Stewart's life and work is in Henry Laurie, *Scottish Philosophy in Its National Development* (1902). Also helpful is Daniel S. Robinson, *The Story of Scottish Philosophy* (1961). □

Potter Stewart

U.S. Supreme Court Justice Potter Stewart (1915-1985) was a strong supporter of civil rights and of First and Fourteenth amendment rights to freedom of expression. During the Burger Court period of his service he functioned as "swing man" with Justice Byron R. White.

Born in Michigan in 1915, Potter Stewart was later a resident and Republican political activist in Ohio. After graduating from Yale and Cambridge, Stewart became President Eisenhower's fourth appointee to the Supreme Court in October 1958. "Ike" promoted him from the U.S. Court of Appeals for the Fifth Circuit, whence he

had sent him four years earlier. Initially serving under a recess appointment, the 39-year-old jurist ran into a bitter and protracted confirmation battle in the Senate, chiefly in view of his liberal record on racial matters. Spearheading the opposition was the powerful leader of the strong Southern bloc, Richard B. Russell, a Democratic Senator from Georgia whose loyalists delayed confirmation for almost seven months. When the appointment came to a vote, it was 70 to 17.

Justice Stewart lived up fully to the expectations of President Eisenhower and the Southern senators. He charted a generally progressive-conservative or moderately liberal course, depending upon one's perception. During the hey-day of the Warren Court he was more often than not found on the cautiously conservative or "centrist" side, especially in matters concerning law and order and reapportionment and redistricting. But his stance on racial and sexual discrimination and in particular on the First and Fourteenth amendments' guarantee of freedom of expression found him only slightly less pro-individual or progroup than his most advanced libertarian contemporaries, such as Justices Douglas, Brennan, and Marshall. Thus, although yielding to no one in his devotion to the tenets of federalism, Stewart brooked no equivocation with egalitarian constitutional guarantees and commands. And some of his well-known opinions in the constitutional "disaster area" of obscenity testify to his generous approach to freedom of speech and press as well as privacy. Hence his exasperated concurring observation in *Jacobellis* v. *Ohio* (1964) (involving the movie *Les Amants*) that, under the First and Fourteenth amendments, criminal laws in this area are *faute de mieux* ("for want of better") limited to hard-core pornography—which, he went on to say, he could characterize only with "I know it when I see it."

Stewart had hardly assumed his seat on the bench in 1958 when he gave notice of his opposition to censorship of any kind by writing the Court's unanimous opinion that struck down the New York Board of Regent's proscription of the film version of D. H. Lawrence's *Lady Chatterley's Lover,* warning that the advocacy of ideas was not subject to censorship; that by doing so the state had "struck at the very heart of constitutionally protected liberty." At the same time, however, Stewart was not about to be a party to a policy that, in his view, transformed the Bill of Rights "into a suicide pact"—as Justice Jackson had warned so eloquently in 1949 in *Terminiello*—a commitment to law enforcement that might well mean giving the benefit of the doubt to government rather than the individual. Consequently, it was natural for Stewart to line up with likeminded Justices Clark, Harlan, and White in the realm of criminal procedure in dissenting from such celebrated and contentious 5:4 rulings as those in *Escobedo* v. *Illinois* and *Miranda* v. *Arizona.*

Stewart, high in President Nixon's esteem, was being seriously considered for promotion to Chief Justice upon Earl Warren's retirement in 1969—and he might very well have been nominated. But in a long talk with the president in the Oval Office, he asked Nixon to remove him from the list of possibilities, believing strongly that the interests of the tribunal warranted an appointment from outside its membership, and that promotion from within was delicate and difficult and had not worked well for the Court in the on-the-record instances of Associate Justices Edward D. White and Harlan F. Stone.

After Chief Justice Earl Warren's and Justice Abe Fortas' departures from the bench, followed two years later by the departures of Justices Black and Harlan, Stewart and Byron R. White became the "swing men" on what had by then become the Burger Court. It was a role admirably suited for the cautious, judicious, fair-minded student of judicial power, whom Court historians have adjudged to merit a high "average" ranking. It was a role he comfortably continued until he issued the surprise announcement of his retirement at the end of the 1980-1981 term of Court, having served 23 years. At 66, he was one of the younger Justices on the bench and in excellent health; but, as he told the press conference in which he informed the country that he had decided to step down: "I'm a firm believer that it's better to go too soon than stay too long." He died of a stroke four years later, on December 7, 1985.

Although Stewart would not have won a prize for being the hardest worker on the Court, he always relished his tasks thereon and he never missed a single day of oral argument. The jurist, whom the senior correspondents of the press corps pronounced "our best friend on the Court since Hugo Black," penned some 300 opinions for the Court and another 350 in concurrence or dissent. He may not be identified with many of the Court's landmark decisions—with the possible exceptions of his majority opinions in *Katz* v. *United States* (an important 1967 case broadening the protection against wiretapping) and *Gregg* v. *Georgia* (upholding capital punishment under carefully-controlled circumstances in 1976), his concurring opinions in the 1972 *Furman* v. *Georgia* capital punishment case and in the 1971 *Pentagon Papers* case, and his stirring dissenting opinion in the 1980 *Fullilove* v. *Klutznick* case that sanctioned a ten percent "set aside" racial quota for construction work on federally funded projects. Yet he will be remembered as a principled constitutionalist who had that all-too-rare ability to write both simply and clearly.

Further Reading

The literature on Justice Stewart is thin. A good analysis is Jerold H. Israel's "Potter Stewart" in Leon Friedman and Fred L. Israel (editors), *The Justices of the United States Supreme Court, 1789-1978* (1980). For a thorough sketch of Stewart's early career see John P. Frank, *The Warren Court* (1964) and H. M. Barnett and K. Levine, "Mr. Justice Stewart," *New York University Law Review* 40 (1965). Generally, see Henry J. Abraham, *Justices & Presidents: A Political History of Appointments to the Supreme Court,* 2d ed. (1985). □

Henry William Stiegel

Henry William Stiegel (1729-1785), a German-born American iron founder and glassmaker, is best known for the colorful blown glass associated with his name.

Henry Stiegel was born near Cologne and emigrated to Philadelphia in 1750 with his widowed mother and younger brother. After a year or so in Philadelphia, he went to work in Lancaster County for an iron founder, whose daughter, Elizabeth Huber, he married in 1752. By 1756 Stiegel had become a partner in the ironworks, which was run on a cooperative basis, and he renamed it Elizabeth Furnace. In 1760 he became a subject of Great Britain. By then he was an important community leader and a lay delegate to the Lutheran Ministerium of Pennsylvania.

Elizabeth Furnace was modernized, and a small company town was built around it. Under Stiegel's energetic influence the foundry produced stoves, heating devices, and almost every kind of object that could be made of iron. By the 1760s Stiegel had acquired a second ironworks, Charming Forge, near Womelsdorf, Pa., and a large amount of land at what later became the town of Manheim. His first wife had died, and he married again.

In 1763 Stiegel produced, on an experimental basis, his first glassware at Elizabeth Furnace. There were 10 craftsmen, supervised by his brother Anthony. The initial output of the factory—window glass and green bottles—sold quickly. Shortly thereafter Stiegel made a trip to England to study advanced methods and technology of glass production.

Upon his return to America, Stiegel and his partners lost no time in setting up a glassworks at Manheim. On Nov. 11, 1765, the enterprise went into operation. The first two seasons were fairly prosperous, but business subsequently declined until 1769, when Stiegel built a larger glassworks which was staffed with over 130 workers, including Venetians, Germans, Irish, and English. Distributing agencies were set up in a number of Pennsylvania cities and later in Baltimore, New York, and Boston as well.

With the glassworks prospering, Stiegel lived in great luxury. He might have survived his extravagance had times not been bad. Money became increasingly tight in the Colonies and taxes more oppressive. He mortgaged his two ironworks and real estate to build a second glass factory but continued to live beyond his means. By 1772 he was surrounded on all sides by debtors. In 1774 he was put in debtors' prison. When he was freed on Christmas Eve, all his belongings were confiscated. In 1776 the new owner of Elizabeth Furnace, which was making cannonballs for the Continental Army, gave him employment. When the battlefront changed, this manufacture was discontinued, and Stiegel was again jobless. He died in poverty on Jan. 10, 1785.

Further Reading

A full-length biography of Stiegel, and an analysis of the product he created, is Frederick William Hunter, *Stiegel Glass* (1914). He figures prominently in two general works on glassware: George S. and Helen McKearin, *American Glass* (1941) and *Two Hundred Years of American Blown Glass* (1950). □

Alfred Stieglitz

Alfred Stieglitz (1864-1946), American photographer, editor, and art gallery director, was a leader in the battle to win recognition for photography as an art.

Alfred Stieglitz was born in Hoboken, N.J., on Jan. 1, 1864. In 1871 the family moved to New York City, where Stieglitz attended elementary schools and the College of the City of New York until 1881. He then studied at the Realgymnasium in Karlsruhe, Germany, and the Berlin Polytechnic Institute. He enrolled in the photographic courses of Hermann Wilhelm Vogel, an outstanding photographic scientist. As a student, he traveled extensively throughout Europe and, beginning in 1886, sent photographs to competitions. By 1890, when he returned to America, he was already famous.

In the United States, Stieglitz continued to photograph, using the newly invented hand camera and surprising his contemporaries with such a technical tour de force as "Winter on Fifth Avenue," taken in 1893 during a blizzard. He organized competitions and exhibitions in camera clubs and from 1890 to 1895 was in the photoengraving business. He was editor of the *American Amateur Photographer* (1893-1896), *Camera Notes* (1897-1902), which was the official organ of the Camera Club of New York, and *Camera Works* (1902-1917).

When the National Arts Club of New York invited Stieglitz to hold an exhibition in 1902, he showed the work of those American photographers in whom he believed. He described the exhibition as the work of the Photo-Secession. Thus an informal society was formed that dominated art photography in America for 15 years. His chief colleague was a young photographer and painter, Edward Steichen, who assisted him in the society's Little Galleries, which came to be known as "291" from the Fifth Avenue address.

In 1907 Stieglitz began to show works of art other than photography at "291." In 1908 he exhibited drawings by the sculptor Auguste Rodin and drawings, lithographs, etchings, and watercolors by Henri Matisse—the first American exhibition of this modern artist. "291" became the most progressive art gallery in the country, showing the work of Pablo Picasso, Constantin Brancusi, Henri de Toulouse-Lautrec, and young Americans such as John Marin.

In 1910 Stieglitz organized a vast exhibition of pictorial photography in Buffalo, N.Y. He helped the Association of American Painters and Sculptors to organize the "International Exhibition of Modern Art" in 1913. During the exhibition he showed his own photographs at "291" as a demonstration of the esthetic differences between photography and other visual media.

The "Photo Secession" disbanded in 1917, "291" closed, and *Camera Work* ceased publication, but Stieglitz continued to photograph and exhibit. He made penetrating portraits of his friends and associates. In answer to a challenge that his photographs' power was due to his hypnotic influence over his sitters, Stieglitz began to photograph clouds, to show, as he wrote in 1923, "that my photographs were not due to subject matter." He called these photographs "Equivalents," and they almost rivaled abstract art in their beauty of form and chiaroscuro.

In 1929 Stieglitz opened An American Place, a gallery where he showed paintings by contemporary Americans and, later, photographs. From the windows of this 17th-floor gallery and from his apartment he photographed New York City. He died on July 13, 1946.

Further Reading

Dorothy Norman, *Alfred Stieglitz: Introduction to an American Seer* (1960), whose text consists mainly of Stieglitz's recollections as told to the author, is handsomely illustrated; the detailed chronology is invaluable. Doris Bry, *Alfred Stieglitz, Photographer* (1965), reproduces, in original size, 62 photographs in the collection of the Museum of Fine Arts, Boston; the text is concerned with Stieglitz's photographic activity. *America and Alfred Stieglitz: A Collective Portrait,* edited by Waldo Frank and others (1934), contains many brilliant essays which illuminate Stieglitz's philosophy and the breadth of his concern for the arts in America. Herbert J. Seligmann, *Alfred Stieglitz Talking* (1966), is a vivid journal of the author's visits with Stieglitz from 1925 to 1931.

Additional Sources

Eisler, Benita, *O'Keeffe and Stieglitz: an American romance,* New York: Doubleday, 1991.

Kim, Yong-gwon, *Alfred Stieglitz and his time: an intellectual portrait,* Seoul, Korea: American Studies Institute, Seoul National University, 1978.

Lowe, Sue Davidson, *Stieglitz: a memoir/biography,* New York: Farrar Straus Giroux, 1983.

Norman, Dorothy, *Alfred Stieglitz: an American seer,* New York: Aperture, 1990.

Whelan, Richard, *Alfred Stieglitz: a biography,* Boston: Little, Brown, 1995. □

Flavius Stilicho

Flavius Stilicho (died 408) was a Roman general of Vandal origin who maintained the territorial integrity of the Western Roman Empire during the reign of the emperor Honorius.

The father of Stilicho was from the German tribe of the Vandals but served with distinction as a cavalry officer in the Roman army. Stilicho's mother was Roman. His early career included both diplomatic and military experience. He was sent on a mission to Sapor III, king of the Sassanian Persians, to arrange for the partition of Armenia (383 or 387). His early military exploits included victories over the Visigoths, Bastarnae (ca. 391), and Franks (395). He held various military offices, and after Emperor

Theodosius defeated the rebel Eugenius (394), he promoted Stilicho to the rank of master of infantry and cavalry for Italy. The Emperor further showed appreciation for the ability of Stilicho by marrying him to his niece Serena. On his deathbed Theodosius appointed Stilicho guardian of his two sons, Honorius, who would rule in the West, and Arcadius, who would rule in the East. Thus Theodosius left them in the hands of a talented man whose barbarian ancestry would prevent him from aspiring to become emperor. But the very division of power further weakened the empire, already staggering under severe barbarian pressures on the frontier.

Honorius was too young and incompetent to manage the empire, and the responsibility fell heavily upon Stilicho. His problems were enormous. Virtually no region of the frontier was secure, and one area could be defended only by withdrawing troops from another, exposing that area in turn to barbarian assaults. Thus in 406, when Stilicho defeated an invasion of Italy by the German Radagaisus, he was forced to draw troops from the Rhine and British frontiers, leaving those open to invasion.

Foreign problems were compounded by domestic revolt. In 398, Gildas, the governor of North Africa, revolted and cut off the vital grain supply for the city of Rome. Stilicho raised grain from Gaul and Spain and marshaled forces which defeated Gildas and restored Africa to the empire.

However, the major rival to Stilicho was Alaric the Goth. Four times in his career, Stilicho faced Alaric. He was about to crush Alaric when he was called back by order of the emperor Arcadius. In 397 he confronted Alaric in Greece but was forced to make peace when Gildas revolted. In 402 Alaric invaded Italy. Stilicho checked him in battle (April 6) but negotiated peace rather than crushing him. In 403 Alaric again invaded Italy and was defeated by Stilicho near Verona. This time also, Stilicho did not eliminate his rival.

The failure of Stilicho to annihilate Alaric was the result of other challenges. The first derived from his being semibarbarian and therefore suspect by the still-powerful Italian nobility. Stilicho tried to appeal to that group. He slowed down such antipagan acts of the emperors as temple closings and even restored the altar of victory, a symbol of the old Roman paganism, to the Senate house. He also reduced the burdens of taxation and military recruiting which were levied on the Italian upper classes. These gestures were not successful in winning support, and toward the end of his career he took a more antipagan stance. In 407 he proposed a law which confiscated all pagan property and destroyed all pagan altars. With animosity toward him strong among the Romans, Stilicho needed the potentially powerful assistance that Alaric's forces could provide.

A second area of concern was the Eastern Empire. This was largely independent of Stilicho's control, and in fact, with Arcadius coming under the control of Stilicho's archenemy Rufinus, it became actually hostile. The major area of contention was Illyria, which was a buffer zone between the two parts of the empire and also an important recruiting ground for soldiers. Stilicho arranged the murder of Rufinus but even then did not succeed in dominating the East. After the death of Arcadius, Stilicho had plans for seizing the Eastern throne for Honorius, but his own fall prevented that. Again, Alaric and his Goths, who generally were settled close to the border of the two empires, could be extremely useful as friends of Stilicho against the Eastern emperors.

During the first decade of the 5th century, the power of Stilicho seemed secure. The Emperor had married two of Stilicho's daughters in succession. He had been consul four times. However, trouble continued. A rival, Constantine, led a revolt in Britain and rapidly seized control of Gaul. The Italians were hostile toward the Vandal. Factions in the court led by a palace official, Olympus, were turning Honorius away from him. Finally Stilicho was arrested and on Aug. 22, 408, was executed. For 40 years no barbarians held a comparable high place in the Western Roman Empire.

Further Reading

Much material on Stilicho is contained in the poems of Claudian. These are highly rhetorical and eulogistic but have a core of historical fact. Fragments from ancient historians on Stilicho are given in Colin D. Gordon, *The Age of Attila: Fifth Century Byzantium and the Barbarians* (1960). The best modern account in English is still John B. Bury, *History of the Later Roman Empire* (2 vols., 1931). □

Clyfford Still

Clyfford Still (1904-1980) was one of the pioneers of Abstract Expressionism, although throughout his life he chose isolation from other styles and most other artists.

Clyfford Still was born in 1904 in Grandin, North Dakota. During his childhood he was interested in music, literature, and poetry, as well as art. A graduate of Spokane University, Still received an M.A. from Washington State College, where he later taught from 1933 to 1941. He lived for a time in Alberta, Canada, and also taught briefly at the College of William and Mary (1943-1945) and at the California School of Fine Arts.

Being something of a renegade from the art establishment, Still rarely exhibited his work. In 1943 he showed 22 canvasses at the San Francisco Museum of Art; in 1946 he had a one-man show at Peggy Guggenheim's New York gallery; and in 1959 he had a major retrospective exhibition at the Albright-Knox Art Gallery in Buffalo. He also had major one-man shows at the San Francisco Museum in 1976 and at the Metropolitan Museum of Art in 1979.

Still always saw himself as a visionary artist, rather than as one who belonged to a movement. He criticized European modernism for its "sterility" and denied all artistic influences upon his work. Although his style of the 1930s bears some resemblance to Picasso's and his canvasses of the 1940s relate to the satanic, grotesque imagery of some forms of Surrealism, Still consistently rejected all such associations. He also rejected the Classical heritage which forms the basis of Western art and disaffiliated himself from the traditional values of the art world, all of which he saw as decadent and profane. In fact, between 1952 and 1967 Still refused to exhibit in New York because he felt the city was too corrupt for his work. In spite of his having gained an early reputation as a "difficult artist," Still enjoyed a long and successful career.

Philosophically, Still is most often associated with artistic loners such as William Blake and Albert Pinkham Ryder. On a deeper level, his obsession with the theme of the dualism of good and evil is symbolized through his use of light and dark. Critics have drawn parallels between Still's art and Manichaeanism, a heretic faith which originated in Persia in the third century A.D. and which taught the release of the spirit from matter through asceticism. The philosophy is based on separate, but opposing, realms of darkness and light which symbolize the elements of evil and good. Still vehemently rejected any such associations, always negating any attempts to "explain" his works. The fact that his canvasses are untitled, being identified only by dates and letters, helped to create an aura of ambiguity around his art.

In spite of an overall sense of unity in his work, Still's style changed and evolved over the years. His figurative work of the 1930s, rich with interpenetrating forms, gave way in the 1940s to primitive and satanic images. Later in the 1940s, working in a monochromatic palette and using heavy impasto, Still began creating non-representational paintings filled with ragged, flame-like forms. His work of the late 1940s and early 1950s seems to echo the earth tones and open spaces of the Western plains where he grew up, although the artist refused to acknowledge any connections between his paintings and the natural landscape. Often aggressive in mood, the canvasses are rough in texture like the earth itself and are very expressionistic.

During the 1950s Still's paintings became larger in scale and lighter and brighter in color. Sometimes areas of the canvas were left unpainted. By this point in his career the artist seemed free of the dark imagery of the underworld. A mood of spiritual aspiration, reflected in the vertical application of the paint, pervades the work. His friendship with the color-field painter Mark Rothko may have been influential in this move towards an emphasis on size and color. Yet Still retained his textured, tactile surface in contrast to Rothko's color staining. The justapositions of light and dark and the dematerialization of forms remained constant.

Still's work from the 1960s is soft, sensuous, and lyrical in comparison with that of two decades earlier. This shift in his style came at a time when he personally withdrew even further from society, leaving New York to live and work in rural Maryland near Westminster, where he stayed until his death in 1980. However, in 1964 Still gave a group of 31 paintings to the Albright-Knox Art Gallery in Buffalo, and in 1976 he made a similar presentation of 28 works to the San Francisco Museum of Modern Art.

Clyfford Still's career focused on human aspiration, the personal search for identity, and the liberation of the spirit. Although his jealously guarded privacy kept him from becoming known to the general public, he was, nevertheless, one of the early pioneers of Abstract Expressionism, and he greatly influenced such better known painters as Barnett Newman and Mark Rothko.

Still had a wife, Patricia, and two daughters, Diane and Sandra.

Further Reading

Several journal articles provide useful information about Clyfford Still: Hubert Crehan, "Clyfford Still: Black Angel in Buffalo," *Art News* 58 (December 1959); Robert Rosenblum, "Abstract Sublime," *Art News* 59 (February 1961); and J. B. Townsend, "interview with Clyfford Still," *Albright-Knox Gallery Notes* 24 (Summer 1961). The following exhibition catalogues are also helpful: Albright-Knox Art Gallery, *Paintings of Clyfford Still* (1959); Buffalo Fine Arts Academy, *Clyfford Still, Thirty-three Paintings in the Albright-Knox Art Gallery* (1966); San Francisco Museum of Modern Art, *Clyfford Still* (1976); and Metropolitan Museum of Art, *Clyfford Still* (1979). Still's work is also discussed in Peter Selz, *Art in Our Times* (1981). ☐

William Still

William Still (1821-1902), African American abolitionist, philanthropist, and business person, became an important strategist for the Underground Railroad and wrote an account of the hundreds of slaves he aided in their flight to freedom.

William Still was born free on Oct. 7, 1821, in Shamong, Burlington County, N.J. He was the youngest of 18 children born to parents who had been slaves. His father had purchased freedom. His mother had escaped slavery with two of her four children. His parents settled on a 40-acre plot near Medford, N.J.

At the age of 23 and self-taught, Still went to Philadelphia, where he held a number of jobs before joining the staff of the Pennsylvania Society for Promoting the Abolition of Slavery, as janitor and mail clerk. During the 14 years he spent with the society, his responsibilities grew, and he took a special interest in assisting runaway slaves, often boarding them in his home.

In 1852 Still was named chairman of a committee of four acting for the Vigilance Committee of Philadelphia. The committee offered financial assistance to escaping slaves, and Still was especially effective in finding board and lodging for them among the black population of Philadelphia.

Still recorded the information he got from interviewing slaves so that he could reunite friends and relatives. During one interview, he discovered that the slave he was trying to help was his own brother, left behind when their mother escaped 40 years before. His careful records later became the documentation for his famous book, *The Underground Railroad* (1872).

When abolitionist John Brown raided Harpers Ferry, Va., in 1859, Still sheltered some of Brown's men who were

able to escape the law, as well as some members of Brown's family. Still was constantly in danger of prosecution, and had his detailed records been discovered, they probably would have sent him and other members of the Vigilance Committee to prison. Charges were brought against him several times, but only once was he unable to clear himself, and this was in a civil suit brought by a former slave whose motives and character Still had challenged.

In 1855 Still visited Canada to see how the refugees from slavery who had settled there were faring. He was impressed by their determination and published an account of their achievement. He was also active in civil rights efforts for blacks in the North, especially in Philadelphia. He helped organize and finance a society to collect information on black life, was responsible for the establishment of an orphanage for children of black soldiers and sailors, and organized a Young Men's Christian Association for blacks. Still's book, *The Underground Railroad,* differs from most accounts of the time in emphasizing the bravery and ingenuity of the escaping slaves rather than the heroism of the railroad's white conductors.

Further Reading

Sources for biographical information on Still are Wilhelmina S. Robinson, *Historical Negro Biographies* (1967); William J. Simmons, *Men of Mark* (1969); and August Meier and Elliot Rudwick, eds., *The Making of Black America* (2 vols., 1969). □

William Grant Still

William Grant Still (1895-1978) has been called the dean of African American composers. Throughout his distinguished career he composed in many styles, frequently utilizing black motifs.

William Grant Still was born in Woodville, Mississippi. In his early years he took violin lessons and was exposed to a wide variety of music, ranging from spirituals and hymns to opera. He majored in science at Wilberforce University but soon found himself composing, arranging, and conducting the school band. He decided to become a composer and studied at Oberlin and the New England Conservatory.

After serving in the Navy during World War I, Still went to New York City to work in W. C. Handy's music publishing company. He participated actively in the musical world, playing jazz and directing the Black Swan Phonograph Company. In addition, he studied with the avant-garde composer Edgard Varèse, who proved to be an important mentor.

During the 1920s Still began to compose serious concert works. Among these were *Darker America* (1924) and *From the Land of Dreams* (1925), the latter work showing the influence of Varèse. When Howard Hanson led the Rochester Philharmonic in a performance of Still's *Afro-American* Symphony in 1931, it marked the first time a symphonic work by a black composer was performed by a leading symphony orchestra. The work later received hundreds of performances in the United States and abroad. As the composer noted, "I knew I wanted to write a symphony; I knew that it had to be an American work; and I wanted to demonstrate how the blues, so often considered a lowly expression, could be elevated to the highest musical level." The *Afro-American* Symphony was the second part of a symphonic trilogy, consisting also of *Africa* (1930) and the *Symphony in G Minor,* subtitled *Song of a New Race* (1937).

During the 1930s Still worked as a free-lance arranger and a staff composer for network radio. He orchestrated musical comedies and wrote for outstanding personalities such as Artie Shaw and Paul Whiteman. In 1934 a Guggenheim fellowship enabled Still to devote himself entirely to composition. His first opera, *Blue Steel,* was based on the story of a black worker and incorporated African-American folk music. Another "first" in Still's career occurred in 1949, when the New York City Opera Company presented his second opera, *Troubled Island;* this was the first time that a leading opera company produced a work by an African-American composer.

Still composed background music for motion pictures and television, including the film *Pennies from Heaven* and the television show *Gunsmoke.* This versatile composer also wrote ballets, chamber music, many solo songs and spirituals, and choral works. His later works, such as *The*

Prince and the Mermaid (1966), continued to indicate his originality within conventional modes of expression.

Still's career was replete with musical scholarships and honorary degrees in music. In 1971, he received an honorary doctorate in music from the University of Arkansas. In 1976, the American Society of Composers, Authors and Publishers (ASCAP) honored Still with a scroll for his "extraordinary contributions to the literature of symphonic music, opera, ballet, chamber music, songs and solo works."

Still was producing or revising earlier works even while in his late seventies. He was saluted on his 75th birthday with an all-Still concert by the Oberlin (Ohio) Orchestra, which presented the world premiere of his *Symphony No. 5, Western Hemisphere.* This four-movement piece was originally composed in 1937, and revised in 1970. In 1974, Opera/South in Jackson, Mississippi, presented the world premiere of Still's *A Bayou Legend,* originally composed in 1941. The libretto was written by Still's wife, Verna Arvey. This opera was later performed in Los Angeles in 1976 as part of the U.S. Bicentennial celebration and Black History Week, and was telecast on Public Broadcast Service (PBS) in 1981.

Columbia Records released a new recording of Still's *Afro-American* Symphony in 1974. The next year, Still was honored on his 80th birthday at the University of Southern California with a program of his works. In 1977, Opera Ebony revived Still's two-act opera *Highway 1 USA* in New York.

Still died on December 3, 1978 in Los Angeles. The William Grant Still Community Arts Center was dedicated in Los Angeles shortly before his death, and a memorial concert featuring his key compositions was presented at the University of Southern California in May 1979. Still's accomplishments clearly placed him among the foremost composers of his day.

Further Reading

The only book written on Still was by his wife, Verna Arvey, in *William Grant Still* (1939). It was a valuable, short source work but stopped at 1939. A good survey of Still's career through 1971 was found in Eileen Southern's, *Music of Black Americans* (1971). □

Joseph Warren Stilwell

Joseph Warren Stilwell (1883-1946) was the Army officer in charge of U.S. affairs in China during World War II.

Joseph Stilwell was born on March 19, 1883, at Palatka, Fla. He graduated from the U.S. Military Academy in 1914. During World War I he served with the IV Corps in combat intelligence, winning the Distinguished Service Medal.

In 1919 Stilwell was appointed to study Chinese at the University of California, Berkeley. The following year he sailed for the first of three tours of duty in China. After 1935 he served as military attaché to the Chinese government. Stilwell's work as a tactician and trainer impressed his superiors in Washington.

Following the Japanese assault on Pearl Harbor in December 1941, the U.S. War Department, to sustain and strengthen Chinese resistance to the Japanese invaders, ordered Stilwell to improve the Chinese army as chief of staff to Generalissimo Chiang Kai-shek, take command of all United States forces in the China-Burma-India theater, and direct all Chinese forces in Burma (now Myanmar). In April 1942, however, the Japanese defeated Stilwell's forces in Burma and cut off the Burma Road, a Chinese supply line. When the road was finally reopened in 1945, it was named after Stilwell.

Known as "Vinegar Joe" because of his integrity, his refusal to ingratiate himself with others, and the demands he placed on those around him, Stilwell despised Chiang Kai-shek and made no effort to conceal it. He recoiled at the administrative paralysis in the wartime Chinese capital. Three times, directly and indirectly, Chiang sought Stilwell's recall. In 1944 Stilwell was to command all Chinese forces, but Chiang managed through President Franklin Roosevelt to force Stilwell's removal from China. Stilwell warned the American government against the Chinese central government, placing more faith in the more efficient Chinese Communists at Yenan. At the time of his death at San Francisco, Calif., on Oct. 12, 1946, Stilwell commanded the 6th Army.

Further Reading

Of interest for its comments on men and events is Theodore White, ed., *The Stilwell Papers* (1948). The best book on Stilwell is Barbara W. Tuchman, *Stilwell and the American Experience in China, 1911-45* (1970). Other important studies of Stilwell's wartime experiences in China are Charles F. Romanus and Riley Sunderland, *Stilwell's Mission to China* (1953) and *Stilwell's Command Problems* (1956). Books dealing with Stilwell's experiences in Burma are Jack Belden, *Retreat with Stilwell* (1943), and Fred Eldridge, *Wrath in Burma: The Uncensored Story of General Stilwell and International Maneuvers in the Far East* (1946). Claire Lee Chennault, *Way of a Fighter: The Memoirs,* edited by Robert Hotz (1949), contains observations on Stilwell's activities in China.

Additional Sources

The Stilwell papers, New York, N.Y.: Da Capo Press, 1991. □

Henry Lewis Stimson

The American lawyer and statesman Henry Lewis Stimson (1867-1950) was twice secretary of war and once secretary of state.

Henry Stimson was born on Sept. 21, 1867, in New York City of a family of substantial means. He was educated at Phillips Exeter Academy, Yale University (class of 1888), and Harvard Law School (class of 1891). He then joined one of the most prestigious law firms in New York.

Stimson became a highly successful lawyer and a rich man, but he was deeply interested in public affairs. From 1906 to 1909, as U.S. district attorney in New York, he distinguished himself by his energy in carrying out the trust-busting policies of President Theodore Roosevelt. In 1910 Roosevelt persuaded him to run for the governorship of New York. Never very impressive as a public speaker, and handicapped by the nationwide reaction against the Republican party, to which he belonged, Stimson lost. From 1911 to 1913 he was secretary of war in the administration of President William Howard Taft. Never one to avoid responsibility, he worked to improve the armed services under his control. In private life from 1913 to 1917, he enlisted in the Army with the coming of World War I, serving briefly in France.

In 1927 President Calvin Coolidge appointed Stimson to a mission to Nicaragua. He helped bring the civil war there to a conclusion and laid the foundations for what came to be known as the good-neighbor policy toward Latin America. From December 1927 to March 1929 he served a brilliantly successful term as governor general of the Philippines.

Stimson was secretary of state in the administration of President Hoover from 1929 to 1933. Stimson faced a multitude of vexing problems, made more difficult by strained relations with the President, who in many ways wanted to be his own secretary. Most important was the situation in the Far East. In 1931 the Japanese army began conquering the Chinese province of Manchuria (hitherto under a limited Japanese occupation) and set up a puppet regime. The League of Nations attempted to arrest the aggression without result. Stimson, unable to cooperate with the League, addressed identical notes to Japan and China declaring that the United States did not intend to "admit the legality of any situation or recognize any treaty or agreement which violated the rights of the United States or of the Republic of China." This later became known as the Stimson Doctrine, but it was ineffectual in ending the dispute.

In 1933 Stimson resumed his law practice. When the Democrats came to power, President Franklin Roosevelt appointed him secretary of war in 1940. Though Stimson was a Republican, he accepted and brilliantly administered the War Department. He chose remarkable lieutenants and must be credited with a great accomplishment. He had a part in developing and launching the atomic bomb. His critics have alleged that he took insufficient measures to warn the American Army leaders at Pearl Harbor before the Japanese attack. He resigned as secretary in 1945 and died in Huntington, Long Island, on Oct. 20, 1950. Few men have ever served the U.S. government more usefully or with greater devotion.

Further Reading

Stimson's account of his activities, written with McGeorge Bundy, is *On Active Service in Peace and War* (1948). Studies of Stimson are Richard N. Current, *Secretary Stimson: A Study in Statecraft* (1954), and Elting E. Morison, *Turmoil and Tradition: A Study of the Life and Times of Henry L. Stimson* (1960).

Additional Sources

Hodgson, Godfrey, *The colonel: the life and wars of Henry Stimson, 1867-1950,* Boston: Northeastern University Press, 1992. □

James Stirling

James Stirling (1926-1992) was a frequently honored British architect and city planner, whose work influenced architecture in Britain and Western Europe (particularly Germany) beginning in the 1960s. Two good examples of his work may be found in the United States, although the bulk of his buildings are in England.

James Stirling (he never used his middle name or initial) was born in Glasgow, Scotland, on April 22, 1926. His father was a marine engineer. He was raised and educated in Liverpool—Quarry Bank High School, Liverpool School of Art, and the University of Liverpool School of Architecture—finishing at the School of Town Planning and Regional Research, London (1950-1952). He served as a lieutenant in the paratroops, 1942-1945, and participated in the D-Day landing in France with the 6th Airborne Division.

After three years as an assistant with the firm of Lyons, Israel and Ellis (1953-1956), Stirling entered private practice with James Gowan as a partner (1956-1963) and then with Michael Wilford as a partner beginning in 1971.

Although the curriculum where Stirling trained as an architect was based on the classicism of the Ecole des Beaux-Arts, Stirling's early work, beginning with his thesis project in 1950 (a community center and town center plan for Newton Aycliffe), appeared to owe most to the then prevailing International Style as practiced by Le Corbusier. Much of the work Stirling did in this decade was small scale houses or housing complexes, nearly all to be built from the traditional red brick and designed with reference to the traditional English forms of warehouses, factories, barns, etc. The architecture was unquestionably modern: functional, austere (no surface ornament), and with volumes defined by clean lines and open spaces. What was markedly different about his work was its humanistic side: an unmistakable concern for communal vitality and integration in terms of space and circulation of people. Architecture was, as Stirling said, "not a question of style or appearance; it is how you organize spaces and movement for a place and activity."

In the 1960s Stirling exploded on the international art scene with two famous—and shocking—buildings: the Leicester University engineering building (1959) and the Cambridge University History Faculty Building (1964). These were both thoroughly modern constructivist designs that depended upon technical innovation, demonstrated the truth in the cliche that "form follows function," and exhibited no concessions to their surroundings. Both were built of brick and red tiles in the tradition of Victorian architecture, but with massive amounts of greenhouse glazing used on chamfered surfaces as a kind of glass skin. They were, in fact, proof that new methods and materials were a vital aspect of progressive architecture. Although the extrovert quality of these buildings was a surprise, they and their successors (which used precast concrete and even prefabricated plastic to demonstrate their self-reliance) helped change the course of British architecture from a flat blandness to one showing careful use of numerous materials within a rigorously functional design.

The Two United States Buildings

By the 1970s Stirling's work took another turn: his buildings began to show a greater interest in their context, in symmetry, and in historical allusion. The two examples of Stirling's completed commissions in America appeared during this period. The first, an extension of the School of Architecture at Rice University, was commissioned in 1979 and completed in 1981; the second, the Sackler Museum at Harvard University, was also commissioned in 1979 but was not completed until 1985. The Rice building, "a lesson in restraint," was the ultimate in contextual architecture. Both the materials and the design forms were the same as the original buildings, but Stirling used and interpreted them in witty and off-beat ways (for example, a two story arch on the main facade included a round window near the top set decidedly off-center) to give life and light to this addition.

The Sackler Museum, on the other hand, was a free standing building, located on a small lot across from the Fogg Museum, with which it was intended to be connected by an enclosed catwalk over an entrance that some said recalls the ancient Lion Gate at Mycenae and others insisted was Superman's Fortress of Solitude. The exterior of the building was striped orange and grey brick, and the interior continued this color pattern. The use of color was a characteristic of Stirling, who saw architecture as an expression of art, not merely of social planning and engineering. The Sackler Museum, called by one critic a "mixture of historical motifs with raw industrialism," was dominated by a monumental staircase that provided the necessary sense of seriousness for a museum while skillfully dividing the building into gallery space and office space. Another skillful touch by Stirling showed in the changing size of the exhibit rooms, which encouraged the public to move along through the exhibit areas. One eminent critic called the building "remarkable for the creative virtuosity with which its functions are accommodated. . . . It is knowledgeable, worldly, elitist and difficult. . . ."

Commission for Science and Art

Notable among Stirling's later constructed buildings are the Wissenschaftszentrum (Science Museum) in Berlin and two additional structures: the Clore Gallery for the Turner bequest at the Tate Gallery in London and the Neue Staatsgalerie in Stuttgart. The Clore Gallery, an L-shaped addition to a neoclassic structure, relied for effect on the familiar Stirling signature of mullioned glass, colored building materials (including green window frames, purple and turquoise moldings, and pink railings against yellow stucco and Portland stone), and simple geometric forms and apparently random fenestration punched and cut into the building. The exhibition areas for displaying the Turner paintings were cleverly designed to be awash with natural light. The Staatsgalerie, characterized by Paul Goldberger of the *New York Times* as "arguably the one building that sums up the current concerns of Western architecture better than any other built in this decade," contained all the Stirling signatures, plus a superb solution to two site problems: the need to serve as a connector between the old museum and a theater and the requirement to incorporate the legally mandated footpath through the building space.

Stirling received numerous awards and other expressions of public acclaim for his work. He was made an honorary member of the Akademie der Kunste in Berlin in 1969, an honorary fellow of the American Institute of Architects in 1976, and a fellow of the Royal Society of Arts in 1979. He received the Royal Institute of British Architects Gold Medal in 1980 and the Pritzker Prize (the "Nobel Prize" for architecture) in 1981. He died at the age of 66 in 1992.

Further Reading

The bibliography of articles and monographs about Stirling and his work is constantly growing. A great deal of this was published in specialized architectural magazines and journals—particularly British publications, but increasingly those in the United States, Germany, and elsewhere in Europe. Many of these, along with essays by American critics, have been reprinted in volumes about Stirling. The two best of these were *James Stirling: Architecture Design Profile* (1982) and *James Stirling: Buildings and Projects,* introduction by Colin Rowe, complied and edited by Peter Arnell and Ted Bickford (1984). The strength of these two publications was in their lists, descriptions, and photographs of plans from all of Stirling's important work. The second volume contained about 300 bibliographic citations to periodical literature dealing with specific Stirling buildings, as well as a list of 21 articles by Stirling, numerous general articles, and a list of the 16 major exhibitions of Stirling's work. Also see Michael Wilford and Thomas Muirhead, *Purple Passages—James Stirling, Michael Wilford and Associates: Buildings and Projects, 1975-1992* (1994). □

Max Stirner

The German philosopher Max Stirner (1806-1856) had considerable international influence as the outstanding German "theoretician of anarchism."

Max Stirner, whose real name was Johann Caspar Schmidt, was born on Oct. 25, 1806, in Bayreuth. After studying theology and philology in Berlin, Erlangen, and Königsberg, he returned to Berlin, where he spent practically the rest of his life. He taught at a private girls' school until he married a wealthy woman whose money he used partly to write his *magnum opus, Der Einzige und sein Eigentum* (1844; *The Ego and His Own*), and partly to speculate in the milk business. The latter activity resulted in his imprisonment for unpaid debts, and his wife became disillusioned with him and left him. He died from the bite of a poisonous fly on June 26, 1856.

Stirner's philosophy maintained that only the individual counted: He was the center of the world, and his thoughts and feelings determined the scale of social and, specifically, moral values. Outside the individual nothing existed but the creation of the individual. Stirner's philosophy represents probably the acme of subjectivism in the history of philosophy of the Western world.

Stirner was against all social conventions and demanded the abolition of the state. He opposed all the philosophies of his time that were known to him, including German idealism, French materialism, British empiricism, and international socialism (communism).

A great number of brilliant thinkers admired him, from Ivan Turgenev and Fyodor Dostoevsky to George Bernard Shaw and André Gide. A great number of brilliant thinkers fought him, the most famous among them Friedrich Engels and Karl Marx.

After Stirner's death his name was lost among those of a lot of minor figures, but in the 1890s he became well known again through the efforts of John Henry Mackay. A Stirner renaissance set in. It was not that his philosophy became popular but that Mackay resurrected him in the form of a father of modern anarchy. In fact, however, Stirner never was politically active as an anarchist. Yet his writings became not only part but a standard element of anarchist teaching. If Marx said that philosophers ought not only to interpret the world but to change it, one can say of Stirner that while he was alive he tried to "interpret away" the world and after his death he came to inspire those who wanted to change it partly by blowing it up and partly by dissolving it into millions of small social units.

Further Reading

No book has been published in English dealing extensively with Stirner. Some information can be found in Paul Eltzbacher, *Anarchism: Seven Exponents of the Anarchist Philosophy* (1908; rev. ed. 1970); George Woodcock, *Anarchism: A History of Libertarian Ideas and Movements* (1962); and Irving L. Horowitz, *The Anarchists* (1964). □

Karlheinz Stockhausen

The German composer Karlheinz Stockhausen (born 1928) was one of the most influential composers of the post-World War II period. His works embodied most of the advanced musical tendencies of his time.

Karlheinz Stockhausen was born August 22, 1928, in a suburb of Cologne, the son of a schoolteacher. He did not show any particular interest in music until after his demobilization from the army at the close of World War II in 1945. Then he studied musicology at the University of Cologne and music at the Musikhochschule, supporting himself by playing the piano in dance bands. His first compositions date from 1950, strongly influenced by Arnold Schoenberg and Anton Webern, and have complex serial plans and pointillistic texture.

In 1951 Stockhausen attended the Summer Course for New Music in Darmstadt, the center for many of the postwar developments in music. Here he became acquainted with Olivier Messiaen and Pierre Boulez. He found their ideas—mainly concerning the serialization of durations, dynamics, and other parameters—so stimulating that he spent the next year in Paris, where he attended Messiaen's classes at the conservatory and worked in Pierre Schaeffer's newly established *musique-concrète* laboratory.

Upon his return to Germany, Stockhausen studied physics and acoustics at the University of Bonn, and in 1953 he joined the electronic music studio of the Cologne Radio. His *Electronic Studies* (1953) and *The Song of the Youths* (1955) were early landmarks in the medium, and the latter work was one of the first "space" compositions in that it was conceived to be heard from five separated loudspeakers.

In the mid-1950s Stockhausen became interested in writing compositions in which the form was fluid, to be determined by the performer at the time of performance. His best-known piece of this type was *Piano Piece XI.* It consisted of 19 fragments printed on a large roll of paper. The performer was instructed to look at random at the sheet of music and begin with any fragment that catches his eye. At the end of each group of notes he read the tempo, dynamic, and attack indications that follow and next looked at random at another group, which he then played in accordance with its indications. When a group was arrived at for the third time, one possible realization of the piece was completed. In any performance some sections of the piece may be omitted, and no two performances were ever apt to be the same.

In this kind of music, sometimes called aleatory, or chance music, there was a drastic abrogation of the composer's traditional rights and privileges. It was a style that interested many composers in the following years.

Stockhausen next turned to compositions calling for large groups of instruments, sometimes combined with electronic sounds, in which spatial effects play a role. *Gruppen* (1955-1957) calls for 109 instruments arranged in three groups, the performers seated in front of and at the left and right of the audience. The groups played separately and in various combinations in a texture that was so thick that it was impossible to distinguish individual sounds. *Carré* (1960) was for four orchestras and four choruses. The orchestras were located against the four walls of the room;

the audience sat in the middle so as to hear the sounds coming from all sides.

Momente (1961, revised 1965) was another huge sound conglomerate, calling for soprano, four choral groups, and 13 instruments. "In this piece," Stockhausen said, "the distinction between sound and music disappears." It started with the sounds of handclapping, and then words, grunts, whispers, and shouts were added, giving the impression that one was listening to a political meeting. The piece lasted almost an hour and has been described as containing "everything—parody, persiflage, wit, childlikeness, psalmody, and electronic, yet man-made sounds." Another vast montage was *Hymnen* (1966-1971), based on the national anthems of many countries. The anthems were so distorted that they were rarely identifiable.

Stockhausen said that there was no musical causality in these pieces. "Although one moment may suggest the one which follows it, the connection is in no way causal, and it would be equally possible for a different moment to follow." Concentrated listening, then, was not called for; one could listen, or not, to any or all sections.

In some later compositions Stockhausen returned to smaller groups, combining live performance with on-the-spot electronic manipulation of the sounds. His *Solo* (1969) was written for any melody instrument with feedback. It called for one instrumentalist and four assistants, who electronically altered the sounds. *Microphonie 1* (1964) consisted of sounds emanating from a large tam-tam altered through electronic means. One heard the natural sounds along with the manipulated ones. For the Tokyo Expo 70, Stockhausen wrote "continuous" music that was heard as people, coming and going, were in the room in which it was played.

In spite of the completely revolutionary character of his various kinds of music, Stockhausen enjoyed great success. He had the advantage of the Cologne Radio to publicize and present his compositions, as well as the influential Summer Course for New Music in Darmstadt. His compositions were recorded and reviewed by critics as soon as they were written. He made worldwide lecture and concert tours and had several teaching appointments at American universities.

As part of the U.S. Bicentennial celebration, West Germany commissioned Stockhausen to write a cantata as a gift to the U.S., called *Sirius.* This piece was written for trumpet, clarinet, soprano, and bass, and included electronic sounds. The following year, Stockhausen unveiled a new work called *Zodiac,* a series of twelve melodies of the star signs for melody and keyboard instruments. This was originally composed two years earlier for music boxes, but Stockhausen rewrote them for formal instrumentation.

The year 1977 also marked the beginning of an operatic work that would progress for the next two decades. Stockhausen began composing *Licht* (meaning Light), which when completed would be representative of the seven days of the week. The first three acts were *Michaels Jugend* (1979), *Michaels Reise* (1978); and *Michaels Heimkehr* (1980). This massive work featured solo voices, solo instruments, dancers, choirs, orchestras, ballet, and electronic music. *Donnerstag aus Licht* was released in 1981, followed by *Montag aus Licht* in 1988. *Dienstag aus Licht* was written in 1990-91 (two parts), and *Freitag aus Licht* was presented in three parts from 1991 through 1994.

Throughout his career, Stockhausen has written more than 250 performance works, and has made more than 100 records. He wrote a book, *Stockhausen on Music,* in 1989, and since 1991, has been working on a project to put his entire works on CD. He has been cited for many awards, including the Picasso Medal, UNESCO (1992) and the Edison Prize from Holland (1996). He served as Professor of Composition, Cologne State Conservatory, and has been a visiting professor of music at the University of Pennsylvania and University of California.

Further Reading

Stockhausen was discussed in Effie B. Carlson, *Twelve Tone and Serial Composers* (1970); David Ewen, *Composers of Tomorrow's Music* (1970); and Peter S. Hansen, *An Introduction to Twentieth Century Music* (3d ed. 1971). *Stockhausen on Music* was published by Marion Boyars Publishers (1989). □

Robert Field Stockton

Robert Field Stockton (1795-1866), American naval officer, politician, and promoter of internal improvements in the nation, was very important in the conquest of California and served briefly in the U.S. Senate.

Born on Aug. 20, 1795, at Princeton, N. J., Robert F. Stockton was the son of a prominent lawyer and U.S. senator. Robert entered the College of New Jersey at the age of 13, studying mathematics and languages, but withdrew to accept an appointment as a midshipman in 1811 aboard the *President,* flagship of Commodore John Rodgers. During the War of 1812 Stockton was aide-de-camp to Rodgers and was cited for his conduct.

Following the War of 1812, Stockton fought against the Algerian pirates and from 1816 to 1820 cruised the Mediterranean aboard the *Washington* and the *Erie,* rising to command the latter. He fought two duels during this time. Active in the American Colonization Society, in 1821 he commanded the *Alligator,* which took Dr. Eli Ayres to Africa to secure the land that would become Liberia. In 1822 Stockton helped suppress piracy in the West Indies and then did duty with the surveying team along the southern coast of the United States (1823-1824 and 1827-1828).

In 1828 Stockton inherited the family estate of Morven at Princeton. For the next 12 years he was on furlough and leave of absence, investing the family fortune in the Delaware and Raritan Canal (and serving as its first president) and in the Camden and Amboy Railroad. In 1838 he was promoted to captain and returned to active duty, but in 1840 he took a leave of absence to campaign for William

Henry Harrison's election. He was offered the post of secretary of the Navy, but he declined in order to promote the building of steam vessels for the Navy.

The Mexican War began, and in October 1845 Stockton sailed to the Pacific in command of the *Congress.* At Monterey, Calif., on July 23, 1846, he assumed command of the Pacific fleet. Quickly he enrolled the army of the Bear Flag Revolt into his force and won a victory over the Mexican troops, proclaiming the war to be at an end on August 17. He next intended an invasion of Mexico at Acapulco but had to abandon that plan during the Mexican counterrevolution in California. The province was secured in January 1847.

Replaced as commander of the Pacific naval squadron, Stockton made his way to Washington, where he resigned from the Navy. That fall the legislature of New Jersey elected him to the U.S. Senate; he served until Jan. 10, 1853, working for Navy reforms and expanded harbor defenses. In 1856 he almost became the presidential candidate of the American party, and in 1861 he was a delegate to the Washington Peace Conference. He served as president of the Delaware and Raritan Canal until his death on Oct. 7, 1866.

Further Reading

Very little has been written about this hero, for whom the city of Stockton, Calif., was named. Samuel J. Bayard, *A Sketch of the Life of Com. Robert F. Stockton* (1856), was intended as a campaign biography. Considerable information can be obtained from Alfred Hoyt Bill, *A House Called Morven* (1954). □

Solomon Stoddard

Solomon Stoddard (1643-1728/1729), American colonial Congregational clergyman, was for nearly 60 years the dominant civil and religious figure in western Massachusetts.

One of 15 sons, and grandnephew of John Winthrop, Solomon Stoddard was born in Boston in September 1643. He graduated from Harvard in 1662. He became the college's first librarian (1667-1674), though during part of this period he served as Congregationalist chaplain to Bermuda. He preached at Northampton after 1669; asked to be regular pastor, he formally accepted in 1672 and continued in that post until his death. In 1670 he married Esther Warham Mather; the couple had 12 children.

As pastor, Stoddard accepted the Puritan "Half-way Covenant," approved by the Synod of 1662, but soon came to feel it inconsistent to deny Communion to those who had been baptized but lacked a conversion "experience." Seeking to convert the unregenerate, he began teaching that Communion was itself a converting ordinance, and he extended membership privileges to penitents professing faith, irrespective of their certainty of their salvation. This "Stoddardeanism" was accepted by the Reforming Synod of 1679, but Increase Mather and others objected, believing that it made the Church (by opening membership to all) indistinguishable from the world at large. Stoddard defended his position in a series of trenchant pamphlets.

Stoddard was a highly effective minister; his open invitation combined with warnings of damnation to produce great increases in Church membership. During five "harvests" (periods of revivals) between 1679 and 1719, many—young people especially—were converted. He taught his grandson (and associate pastor) Jonathan Edwards the revival methods which produced religious "experiences," though Edwards later rejected Stoddardean leniency in acceptance into Church membership.

Liberal with respect to membership, Stoddard was conservative in other areas. He wanted the Church to be governed by a synod, leaving the laity only the right of electing their ministers. He berated wicked behavior and extravagant dress, helped engender the province's sumptuary laws (1676), and condemned worldly trends at Harvard. His letters to Boston shaped governmental policy, particularly concerning frontier defenses, and he so controlled his congregation that critics called him "Pope."

Impressive in appearance and conversation, Stoddard was an original and forceful writer, publishing over 20 pamphlets and sermons. Significant among these were *The Doctrine of Instituted Churches* (1700), *The Inexcusableness of Neglecting the Worship of God, under a*

Pretence of Being in an Unconverted Condition (1708), *The Efficacy of the Fear of Hell to Restrain Men from Sin* (1713), and *An Answer to Some Cases of Conscience Respecting the Country* (1722). He died on Feb. 11, 1728/1729.

Further Reading

John Langdon Sibley, *Biographical Sketches of Graduates of Harvard University,* vol. 2 (1881), gives most of the facts of Stoddard's life. Ola Elizabeth Winslow, *Jonathan Edwards* (1940), contains illuminating information concerning Edward's grandfather. See also James R. Trumbull, *History of Northampton, Massachusetts* (2 vols., 1898-1902). □

Bram Stoker

Bram Stoker (1847-1912) is best known as the author of *Dracula* (1897), one of the most famous horror novels of all time.

Abraham Stoker was born in Clontarf, Ireland in 1847. He was a sickly child, bedridden for much of his boyhood. As a student at Trinity College, however, he excelled in athletics as well as academics, and graduated with honors in mathematics in 1870. He worked for ten years in the Irish Civil Service, and during this time contributed drama criticism to the Dublin *Mail.* His glowing reviews of Henry Irving's performances encouraged the actor to seek him out. The two became friends, and in 1879 Stoker became Irving's manager. He also performed managerial, secretarial, and even directorial duties at London's Lyceum Theatre. Despite an active personal and professional life, he began writing and publishing novels, beginning with *The Snake's Pass* in 1890. *Dracula* appeared in 1897. Following Irving's death in 1905, Stoker was associated with the literary staff of the London *Telegraph* and wrote several more works of fiction, including the horror novels *The Lady of the Shroud* (1909) and *The Lair of the White Worm* (1911). He died in 1912.

Although most of Stoker's novels were favorably reviewed when they appeared, they are dated by their stereotyped characters and romanticized Gothic plots, and are rarely read today. Even the earliest reviews frequently decry the stiff characterization and tendency to melodrama that flaw Stoker's writing. Critics have universally praised, however, his beautifully precise place descriptions. Stoker's short stories, while sharing the faults of his novels, have fared better with modern readers. Anthologists frequently include Stoker's stories in collections of horror fiction. "Dracula's Guest," originally intended as a prefatory chapter to *Dracula,* is one of the best known.

Dracula is generally regarded as the culmination of the Gothic vampire story, preceded earlier in the nineteenth century by Dr. William Polidori's "The Vampyre," Thomas Prest's *Varney the Vampyre,* J. S. Le Fanu's *Carmilla,* and Guy de Maupassant's "Le Horla." A large part of the novel's initial success was due, however, not to its Gothicism but to the fact, noted by Daniel Farson, that "to the Victorian reader it must have seemed daringly modern." An early reviewer of *Dracula* in the *Spectator* commented that "the up-to-dateness of the book—the phonograph diaries, typewriters, and so on—hardly fits in with the mediaeval methods which ultimately secure the victory for Count Dracula's foes." Stoker utilized the epistolary style of narrative that was characteristic of Samuel Richardson and Tobias Smollett in the eighteenth century, and that Wilkie Collins further refined in the nineteenth. The narrative, comprising journal entries, letters, newspaper clippings, a ship's log, and phonograph recordings, allowed Stoker to contrast his characters' actions with their own explications of their acts.

Some early critics noted the "unnecessary number of hideous incidents" which could "shock and disgust" readers of *Dracula.* One critic even advised keeping the novel away from children and nervous adults. Initially, *Dracula* was interpreted as a straightforward horror novel. Dorothy Scarborough indicated the direction of future criticism in 1916 when she wrote that "Bram Stoker furnished us with several interesting specimens of supernatural life always tangled with other uncanny motives." In 1931 Ernest Jones, in his *On the Nightmare,* drew attention to the theory that these "other uncanny motives" involve repressed sexuality. Critics have since tended to view *Dracula* from a Freudian psychosexual standpoint; however, the novel has also been interpreted from folkloric, political, feminist, medical, and religious points of view.

Today the name of Dracula is familiar to many people who may be wholly unaware of Stoker's identity, though the popularly held image of the vampire bears little resemblance to the demonic being that Stoker depicted. Adaptations of *Dracula* in plays and films have taken enormous liberties with Stoker's characterization. A resurgence of interest in traditional folklore has revealed that Stoker himself did not conform to established vampire legend. Yet *Dracula* has had tremendous impact on readers since its publication. Whether Stoker evoked a universal fear, or as some modern critics would have it, gave form to a universal fantasy, he created a powerful and lasting image that has become a part of popular culture.

Further Reading

Concise Dictionary of British Literary Biography, Volume 5: *Late Victorian and Edwardian Writers, 1890-1914,* Gale, 1991, pp. 310-16.

Farson, Daniel, *The Man Who Wrote Dracula: A Biography of Bram Stoker,* Joseph, 1975, St. Martin's, 1976.

Glut, Donald F., *The Dracula Book,* Scarecrow Press, 1975.

Leatherdale, Clive, *Dracula: The Novel and the Legend,* Aquarian Press, 1985.

Ludlam, Harry, *A Biography of Dracula: The Life Story of Bram Stoker,* St. Martin's, 1976.

McNally, Raymond T., editor, *A Clutch of Vampires,* New York Graphic Society, 1974.

McNally, Raymond T., and Radu Florescu, *In Search of Dracula: A True History of Dracula and Vampire Legends,* Warner, 1976. □

Carl B. Stokes

Carl B. Stokes (1927-1996), mayor of Cleveland, Ohio, was the first elected black mayor of a major American city.

Born of a poor black family in Cleveland on June 21, 1927, Carl Stokes was raised by a hardworking mother (his father died when Carl was 3) who constantly stressed the value of education. After receiving his discharge from the Army, he attended West Virginia College and the Cleveland College of Western Reserve. He received a BS degree from the University of Minnesota Law School (1954) and the JD degree from the Cleveland-Marshall Law School (1956). He passed the bar examination in 1957.

In 1962 Stokes resigned as Cleveland's assistant prosecutor and with his brother founded the law firm of Stokes and Stokes. Stokes was elected to the Ohio House of Representatives in 1962 and was twice reelected. In the House he served on committees of judiciary, industry and labor, and public welfare. While urging civil rights and welfare bills, he sponsored a measure empowering the governor to send in national guard troops to defuse a potential riot.

In 1965 Stokes lost the Cleveland mayoral election by a small margin. Deciding to run again in 1967, Stokes worked hard to win the white vote by showing that he was a moderate who was concerned with the welfare of all Cleveland citizens regardless of race. By winning the primary, Stokes became a symbol not for Cleveland alone but for the United States; several national news magazines and Ohio newspapers made this point. The *Cleveland Plain Dealer* said, "By electing Carl Stokes in the primary we have shown the nation, indeed the world that Cleveland is today the most mature and politically sophisticated city on the face of the earth."

Stokes next faced Republican Seth C. Taft, scion of the famous family, in the mayoral election. Stokes refused to make race an issue in the campaign and based his candidacy on his abilities as a politician. In television debates between the candidates, Stokes showed his expertise concerning urban problems. Cleveland's leading industrialist and its leading banker supported Stokes, while economically disadvantaged blacks raised $25,000 for his campaign. The election was close, with Stokes winning with 20 percent of the white vote and 96 percent of the black vote.

As mayor, Stokes addressed a number of immediate problems typical in urban America. He made a special effort to reduce crime by using more policemen but insisting that the police treat all citizens with courtesy and respect. He won praise for his handling of a disturbance which followed the ambush of a white policeman by black nationalists in 1968. He fired an administrative assistant because of her interest in an illegal liquor establishment, saying that maximum integrity was "imperative" for all members of his administration.

Stokes's reelection in 1969 revealed that he again received practically all of the black vote and the majority of votes in 8 of the 11 all-white wards. His administration continued to battle problems such as pollution, housing, urban renewal, and federal assistance to state education. In 1970, the National League of Cities, comprised of mayors and county officials from across the country, voted Stokes as its first black president-elect. However, Stokes did not run for mayor in 1971, and in 1972 made a major switch in careers. He became the first black anchorman to appear daily on a New York City television outlet, WNBC, NBC's flagship station. He was with WNBC for eight years, serving as urban affairs editor and foreign correspondent to Africa.

Stokes returned to Cleveland and became the first black lawyer to serve as general counsel to a major American labor union, the United Auto Workers. He jumped back into the political arena, being elected as a judge in Cleveland's Municipal Court. With that election, he completed service in all three branches of government—legislative, executive and judicial.

In 1994, Stokes served in the Clinton Administration as U.S. Ambassador to the Republic of Seychelles, a cluster of islands in the Indian Ocean off the coast of Africa. He served in that post until he was forced to take a medical leave of absence, suffering from cancer of the esophagus. He died in Cleveland on April 3, 1996.

During his life, Stokes was awarded 12 honorary degrees from various institutions, including Cleveland-Marshall Law School, Tufts University, and Oberlin College.

Further Reading

Kenneth G. Weinberg, *Black Victory: Carl Stokes and the Winning of Cleveland* (1968), is good. Information on Stokes's election is also in Leonard I. Ruchelman, ed., *Big City Mayors* (1969). A good background study is Chuck Stone, *Black Political Power in America* (1968). Stokes's administration is analyzed in "Carl Stokes," a chapter by James F. Barnes in *Seven on Black: Reflections on the Negro Experience in America,* edited by William G. Shade and Roy C. Henenkohl (1969). □

Piotr Arkadevich Stolypin

The Russian statesman and reformer Piotr Arkadevich Stolypin (1862-1911) is known for his victory over anarchist forces, for his attempt to transform the Russian autocratic monarchy into a constitutional one, and for his land reform.

Piotr Stolypin was born in Baden. A country squire and landlord in Kovno, he was named marshal of the nobility of that province from 1887 to 1902. In 1903 he was appointed governor of the adjoining province of Grodno and a year later was transferred in the same capacity to Saratov on the Volga. There he ruthlessly put down the peasants, and his determination and personal courage led to his appointment as minister of the interior in 1906. Later that year he became prime minister.

Stolypin was the most competent and clear-sighted official to serve Czar Nicholas II. His policy was twofold—to bring law and order to society and to institute reform. An enemy of revolution and a conservative, Stolypin tried to break up the revolutionary groups and also to undermine their popular support through social and political reforms. As a monarchist and a constitutionalist, he wished to work harmoniously with the elected Duma in the passage of reform legislation.

An intelligent and well-educated man, Stolypin pondered for some time the poor condition of the Russian villages and concluded that the low level of rural economy was due to the fact that the land did not belong to the peasants. He realized also that Russia could not become a strong power until the majority of the Russian population—the peasants—became interested in the preservation of individual property. The Revolution of 1905 with its agrarian excesses only strengthened Stolypin's conviction on this point. He came to believe finally that the primary need of Russia was the creation of a class of well-to-do landowners.

Under Stolypin's agrarian reform law peasants made remarkable progress in obtaining private land ownership. Stolypin spared no money in order to consolidate and to increase the peasantry. He encouraged the practice of granting the peasants small credits; he maintained an army of land experts, land surveyors, and agronomists; and he spent large sums of money on public education.

Stolypin's creative efforts in the work of the state were not always within the limits of the constitutional order at which he aimed. The introduction of local assemblies in the western province aroused the entire Russian people against him. The left wing and the center were indignant at such a

flagrant violation of the constitution, and the right wing was indignant at his treatment of its leaders in the State Council. Stolypin was killed in Kiev on Sept. 18, 1911. His assassin was a double agent whose motives remain cloudy to this day.

Further Reading

The only full-length study of Stolypin in English is by his daughter Maria Bock, *Reminiscences of My Father, Peter A. Stolypin* (trans. 1970). Vladimir I. Kokovtsov, *Out of My Past* (trans. 1935), and Vladimir I. Gurko, *Features and Figures of the Past: Government and Opinion in the Reign of Nicholas II* (trans. 1939), are memoirs by czarist officials and contain useful material on Stolypin. A biographical sketch of Stolypin is in Arthur E. Adams, ed., *Imperial Russia after 1861* (1965). □

Edward Durrell Stone

The American architect, educator, and designer Edward Durrell Stone (1902-1978) was an early practitioner of the International Style, but took his architecture in a new direction after 1940. He was particularly known for his design for the U.S. embassy in New Delhi, India, and for the Kennedy Center in Washington, D.C.

Edward Durrell Stone was born in Fayetteville, Arkansas, on March 9, 1902. He attended the University of Arkansas (1920-1923) located in his home town, but received no degree. His first job—for the firm of Coolidge, Shepley, Bulfinch and Abbott in Boston—was to work on the restoration of Massachusetts Hall at Harvard as an apprentice to Henry R. Shepley (1923-1925). In 1926 Stone won the competition for a special scholarship to Harvard and attended for one year. Eclecticism was on the way out in architecture, and Stone switched to MIT (Massachusetts Institute of Technology) where Jacques Carlu was beginning to experiment with modern design. The following year Stone won the Rotch travelling scholarship for two years of study and travel in Europe.

His return to America in November 1929 coincided with the stock market crash. He managed to join the firm of Schultze and Weaver in New York and worked on the design for the interior of the Waldorf-Astoria Hotel. In 1930 he married Orlean Vandiver, whom he had met in Europe. Stone also worked with the consortium of architects designing Rockefeller Center, New York (1929-1935). He was appointed chief designer of the two theaters: Radio City Music Hall and The Center Theater. During this period Stone met Howard Myers, the editor of *The Architectural Forum* and a leading exponent of modern architecture. Their friendship was life-long.

Striking Out on His Own

In 1933 Stone became an architect in his own right with the commission for the Mandel House in Mount Kisco, New York (1933-1935). He made use of an open plan, concrete, steel, glass block, and strip windows in this modern house and saw it as the first house in the East in the International Style. He built several other private residences, but the Depression made commissions scarce and he went to work for Wallace K. Harrison.

During this time the informal headquarters for architects and journalists in New York City was Rose's Restaurant on West 51st Street. Rose was considered a patroness of the arts as she provided meals to sustain artists and others between odd jobs.

From 1935 to the beginning of World War II Stone supplemented his income by teaching advanced design at New York University's night school of architecture. His students were men working in architectural offices who could not afford full-time studies. He again turned to teaching in the late 1940s for three years at Yale, in 1953 for one year at Princeton, and in 1955 and 1957-1959 at the University of Arkansas, Fayetteville.

In 1937 the trustees of the Museum of Modern Art (MOMA) formed a building committee to select architects to design a new building on West 53rd Street in New York City. Stone and Philip L. Goodwin, one of the trustees, were named associate architects for the design (1937-1939). Open flexible gallery space capable of change for exhibitions was required, and as a result Stone and Goodwin placed the auditorium in the basement, the stairs and service facilities at one end of the building, and office spaces and the library on the upper floors. A walled garden for sculpture was set to the rear of the building as an oasis from the hectic pace of the city. The design for this important building was done in the International Style.

Disenchantment with International Style

Toward the end of the 1930s Stone began to question the use of the International Style in residential design. Generally, it had not won acceptance because it was sparse and cold. The style had begun shortly after World War I in a period of deprivation. Economics was the prime consideration, and the use of reinforced concrete—a less expensive material—and the exclusion of ornament from the design reduced the expense of a building. Even more influential on Stone's change of mind was the cross-country trip to California he took in 1940. During this trip he saw the "good" and "bad" architecture of the United States and visited Frank Lloyd Wright at Taliesin in Wisconsin. On the return trip he visited Taliesin West near Phoenix, Arizona, where he became more aware of how Wright attuned each complex to the natural beauty of its site: the pastoral green of Wisconsin and the harsh desert environment of Arizona. Stone viewed his repudiation of the International Style as trading a European style architecture for an indigenous style which would be strongly influenced by Wright's work.

Collier's magazine provided an opportunity for Stone to design in this new direction. Stone and John Fistere, a journalist who wrote on architecture, were asked to design *Collier's* "House of Ideas" (1940), which would make new ideas in home furnishings and building materials available to the public. Located on the terrace adjacent to Rockefeller Center's International Building, Stone introduced the use of natural redwood for the exterior walls and plywood as an interior surface material.

During World War II Stone served as a major in the U.S. Air Force (1942-1945) and worked as an architect designing buildings and ground facilities (hangars and runways). After World War II he established an office in Great Neck, Long Island, and designed houses. One of these residences was for Bernard Tomson, a lawyer who took an interest in the legal aspects of the architectural profession and eventually wrote a column and a book for architects to help them with their business affairs. Stone moved his offices to New York City and was joined by his nephew, Karl J. Holzinger, Jr., who worked with him for seven years. Commissions were primarily for residential designs which were done in an indigenous style based on modular wooden construction.

Building at Home and Abroad

After World War II Stone was asked to design a modern resort hotel in Panama which called for special consideration of the extremes of the equatorial climate. The design problems worked out for El Panama Hotel, Panama City (1946), were further refined when Stone designed resort hotels in San Salvador (1952) and Montego Bay, Jamaica (1952).

In 1948 Stone was asked to design a fine arts group for the University of Arkansas, Fayetteville, to include facilities for architecture, painting, sculpture, music, and theater. Stone physically integrated the arts in three separate elements (a three-story classroom building, a concert hall, and a theater and library) linked by an exhibition gallery.

The Peruvian government selected Stone and Alfred Aydelott to design a general and maternity hospital for 900 patients in Lima (1950). Stone believed there was no more difficult or complicated architectural project than a hospital. This one took several years to complete, and it was necessary for the designers to live there for about six months in the early stages. While there, Stone travelled to Cuzco and Machu Picchu and started a collection of Pre-Incan pottery.

Stone credited his second marriage with bringing order to his life. On a night flight from New York City to Paris in 1953 he met Maria Elena Torchio, the American-born daughter of a Florentine architect and a Barcelona mother, and they were married in June 1954 in Beirut, Lebanon, by the archbishop of the Greek Orthodox Church.

In order to take architecture out of politics, the U.S. State Department appointed a board comprised of Henry R. Shepley, Ralph Walker, and Pietro Beluschi to advise them in selecting an architect to design the U.S. embassy at New Delhi, India. Stone was awarded the commission in 1954 and found he had to deal with a subtropical climate. Some of the devices he used to compensate for the extreme heat were a water garden for its cooling effect, terrazzo grilles for the external walls for their light filtering qualities, and a large rectangular canopy extending beyond the walls of the building for its shading ability. Stone placed his classical building on a platform so that automobiles could be parked in the space below, thus preventing their visual intrusion on the building. An Indian religious leader, Mohan Singh, and his son, Daljit, were chosen as builders. They brought the workers and their families to live at the site where they fabricated the building materials. The U.S. embassy was literally built by hand with a combination of Eastern and Western skills.

Toward a More Romantic Style

In 1955 Stone was asked to design a hospital and medical center for the city of Palo Alto, California, and Stanford University. He found it necessary to open an office in Palo Alto. The design he arrived at was to be compatible with the original quadrangle of three-story buildings designed by Shepley, Rutan, and Coolidge. Because this was earthquake country, reinforced concrete was the preferred building material. To imitate the rough stone of the earlier buildings, Stone created a geometric pattern in the concrete by nailing wooden blocks onto the casting forms. In the same year Stone designed a pharmaceutical plant for the Stuart Company in Pasadena. The company's founder, Arthur Hanisch, gave Stone a large site and a free hand to design the plant and amenities (recreation areas, courtyards, and a swimming pool) for the employees. The morale of the workers and the prestige of the company were influenced by the architecture, a trend recognized by corporations in the 1950s.

An American Institute of Architects (AIA) committee of five architects selected Stone to design the U.S. Pavilion

(1957-1959) for the Brussels Exposition. The irregular site seemed best served by a circular building, and Stone adapted the principle of the bicycle wheel (inner and outer rings connected by radiating spokes) combined with translucent plastic panels to cover the 350 foot diameter interior open space of his design. This space allowed the United States to honor the Belgians' request to preserve the 11 willow trees planted 50 years earlier by King Albert. The white, crystal, and gold pavilion with its plaza and reflecting pool drew a cover story by *TIME* and an invitation from the Russians for Stone to visit their country.

Stone had long held the conviction that row housing made better use of land than the free-standing house on an individual lot. The open countryside around towns and cities should be preserved. *LIFE* was doing a series of essays on more livable homes and in 1958 asked Stone for a design. He suggested a row house development, noting that there was much historical precedent for it and that the "urban sprawl" of the American subdivision might be abandoned for it.

This same year Huntington Hartford chose Stone to design his gallery of modern art to be located at Columbus Circle in New York City. Due to the small site, Stone arranged the galleries vertically and selected poured concrete for its plastic possibilities. The entire building was surrounded by an arcade which provided protective covering for prospective museum goers. The romantic design Stone used here was in sharp contrast to the severe International Style he had used 20 years earlier for the MOMA.

The Kennedy Center and Work in New York

In the fall of 1958 Stone began work on a plan for the National Cultural Center (Kennedy Center) in Washington, D.C. (1958-1971). He developed two schemes for the 11-acre site on the Potomac River which included an opera house, a concert hall, and a theater under one roof with parking facilities at a lower level. The first scheme placed the three auditoria around a grand central circular hall, while the second scheme arranged them in a row and separated them by entrance lobbies. Cost was the deciding factor in the selection of the second scheme. Hopes for a truly national cultural center of stature would have been better served by the first scheme. The critics used terms such as bland and uninspiring to describe the Kennedy Center.

As Stone designed more complex and larger scale projects, such as the State University of New York at Albany campus (1962), he turned to an academic style of architecture that sought formal simplicity. Though work such as this received less than complimentary acclaim, Stone retained his popular appeal.

One of his last works, the PepsiCo World Headquarters, Purchase, New York (1971-1973), was representative of the low suburban office building. In a move from Park Avenue to an old polo field, PepsiCo acquired a 112-acre site where building height was restricted to 40 feet by a local zoning code. Stone designed a series of seven three-storied buildings to be set on a mounded site of ten acres. He created an interplay between the buildings and open spaces, with each building connected to its neighbor only at the corner. Patterned precast concrete panels were used to enrich the exterior surfaces of these low horizontal structures, while sculpture was placed in the surrounding landscape.

Further Reading

Numerous articles on Stone may be found in *The Architectural Forum* and *The Architectural Record.* Additional material may be found in *Progressive Architecture* and other American architectural journals. Stone is listed in *Contemporary Architects* edited by Muriel Emanuel (1980). Stone wrote two books: *The Evolution of an Architect* (1962) and *Recent and Future Architecture* (1967). Information on the International Style is provided in Henry-Russell Hitchcock and Philip Johnson, *The International Style: Architecture Since 1922* (1932). □

Harlan Fiske Stone

Harlan Fiske Stone (1872-1946), as chief justice of the U.S. Supreme Court, at first could not be classified either as conservative or liberal but finally stood with the liberal justices.

Harlan Fiske Stone was born in Chesterfield, N.H., on Oct. 11, 1872. The family soon moved to Amherst, Mass. Harlan's father was a farmer, and the sons did the typical farm chores.

Stone attended public school in Amherst and then, after 2 years of high school, enrolled in the Massachusetts Agricultural College. He led his fellow students in a number of pranks; for one of these he was expelled. He was accepted by Amherst College, graduating in 1894. He was bent on a career in medicine. At Amherst he tutored other students and sold typewriters and insurance. He was elected to Phi Beta Kappa, was business manager of the school paper, and played on the football team. Somewhere along the way, he gave up the idea of medicine for a career in law. To earn the money for law school, he taught high school science. In 1896 he entered the Columbia University School of Law, supporting himself by teaching history. In June 1898 he received his law degree and soon passed his bar examinations.

Stone joined the well-known New York City legal firm of Sullivan and Cromwell, later moving to another firm. He married Agnes Harvey in 1899, and the couple had two sons.

Law School Dean and Attorney General

In his early days in practice Stone supplemented his income by lecturing at Columbia School of Law. He became a professor in 1902, resigning in 1905 to give full time to the firm of Satterlee, Canfield and Stone. Stone appeared to be perfectly content making money until, in 1910, he became dean of the Columbia School of Law. The work as dean was most rewarding. Stone managed to continue his

law practice, teach, and also advise and counsel students. He was one of the most loved and revered Columbia professors of that day.

This so-called conservative lawyer proved to be most liberal in defending his faculty. When the university decided to dismiss two professors because of their pacifist speeches, he worked out a settlement between the teachers and Columbia president Nicholas Murray Butler. Stone was much upset by the U.S. attorney general's "Red raids."

Yet there were too many examples of Stone's conservatism to convince his fellow faculty members that he was in any way liberal. His courses in personal property, mortgages, and equity law were geared conservatively. In 1923 his conservatism seemed confirmed when he resigned as dean to become a partner in the Sullivan and Cromwell firm. During the next year he handled corporation and estate work. In 1924 President Calvin Coolidge, who had known Stone in Amherst, named him U.S. attorney general. The appointment was well received by the banking and business community.

As U.S. attorney general, Stone moved quickly to rid the department of those involved in the "Red scare" regime. He also made an appointment that years later would remain controversial when he made J. Edgar Hoover head of the Bureau of Criminal Investigations (later the Federal Bureau of Investigation). Stone also moved against the Aluminum Corporation of America as a violator of the antitrust laws. This corporation was under control of the family of Andrew Mellon, who was then secretary of the treasury. Before this case could be readied for court, President Coolidge named Stone an associate justice of the Supreme Court.

Supreme Court Justice

Stone's new appointment ran into some difficulties. Some people suggested that he was pushed onto the Court to get him out of the attorney general's office. However, the appointment was confirmed. On the bench Stone moved slowly. Justice Louis Brandeis, a liberal, along with Oliver Wendell Holmes, tried to give Stone a much broader view of the Constitution. In time the liberals on the Court were considered to be Brandeis, Holmes, Stone, and later Benjamin Cardozo.

The question of the constitutionality of many of President Franklin Roosevelt's New Deal laws eventually confronted the Supreme Court. Stone met these challenges and remained liberal in his thinking. He concurred in the Court's decision on the unconstitutionality of the National Recovery Administration. He supported the majority in the famous *NLRB v. Jones and Laughlin Steel Corporation* (1937), which preserved the National Labor Relations law.

With Chief Justice Charles Evans Hughes's resignation in 1941, President Roosevelt named Stone to the position. However, Stone is remembered for his work as an associate justice rather than for his achievements as chief justice because, as presiding officer, he was unable to head the Court as efficiently as had his predecessor. Stone looked upon the Constitution as a broad charter of government. He summed up his philosophy by stating: "I have nothing personally against the world in which I grew up. That world has always made me very comfortable. But I don't see why I should let my social predilections interfere with experimental legislation that is not prohibited in the Constitution."

One of the most important pieces of New Deal legislation was the Agricultural Adjustment Act of 1933. It was inevitable that the Supreme Court would be asked to rule on its constitutionality. In *U.S. v. Butler* (1936) a majority of the Court declared the AAA constitutional. Justice Stone wrote a strong dissenting opinion. He revealed his conception of judicial functions when he declared: "The power of courts to declare a statute unconstitutional is subject to two guiding principles of decision which ought never to be absent from judicial consciousness. One is that courts are concerned only with the power to enact statutes, not with their wisdom. The other is that while unconstitutional exercise of power by the executive and legislative branches of the government is subject to judicial restraint, the only check upon our own exercise of power is our own sense of self-restraint."

Stone was not a colorful figure, but he was a human one. He died in Washington on April 22, 1946. If one was to seek among Stone's utterances for a phrase that would summarize his contributions, it might be: ". . . the Constitution has not adopted any particular set of social and economic ideas, to the exclusion of others, which however wrong they seemed to me, fair-minded men might yet hold."

Further Reading

The best general study of Stone is Alpheus Mason, *Harlan Fiske Stone: Pillar of the Law* (1956). An excellent survey of Stone as chief justice is in Alpheus Mason, *The Supreme Court from Taft to Warren* (1958). A complete discussion of Stone's dissent in *U.S. v. Butler* is in Walter F. Murphy, *Congress and the Courts: A Case Study in the American Political Process* (1962). Kenneth Urmbreit brings the man into focus in *Our Eleven Chief Justices: A History of the Supreme Court in Terms of Their Personalities* (1942). □

I. F. Stone

The American journalist I. F. Stone (1907-1989) published the iconoclastic political newsletter *I. F. Stone's Weekly* from 1953 to 1971. A critic of the Cold War and McCarthyism, his opposition to the Vietnam War helped to change public opinion in the United States.

Born Isador Feinstein on December 24, 1907, in Philadelphia, I. F. Stone was the son of Bernard and Katherine Feinstein. His parents were Russian Jewish immigrants who owned a dry goods store in Haddonfield, New Jersey. At age 14 Stone made his journalism debut by publishing a five-cent monthly paper called *The Progress*. As a journalist he became known for his outspoken but hopeful views.

During high school he covered Haddonfield as a correspondent for the *Camden Evening-Courier*. After graduating in 1924 he studied philosophy at the University of Pennsylvania, but was more interested in the newsroom than in the classroom. While a student he worked full time as a copy editor and rewrite man for the *Philadelphia Inquirer*. He left school to take a job as a reporter and editor with the *Camden Courier-Post*. In 1929, Stone married Esther Roisman and together they had three children.

Stone was legendary among American journalists for his intense political commitments and his unwillingness to compromise his beliefs. Beginning with Jack London's novel *Martin Eden*, Stone's radical, utopian outlook emerged from his independent reading. In the 1930s he supported the Popular Front in its opposition to Adolf Hitler. Although his thinking was never dependent on any party or ideology, he later became isolated during the McCarthy period when his strong views collided with the prevailing consensus.

Following a move to New York City, he served as an editorial writer for the *New York Post* from 1933 to 1939. His first book, *The Court Disposes* (1937), defended President Roosevelt's attempts to expand the Supreme Court. In 1938 Stone became an associate editor of the liberal weekly *The Nation* and in 1940 he became its Washington editor. In *Business as Usual* (1941) he criticized the country's defense mobilization program.

Although he was not a religious man, Stone was concerned with the political and human rights situation in the Middle East. In 1945 he reported on the Jewish struggle to establish a homeland in Palestine. In 1946 he accompanied Jewish survivors of Nazi concentration camps as they secretly migrated from Eastern Europe to Palestine. His experience was first printed in the experimental newspaper *PM*, for which he had begun writing in 1942, and later as *Underground to Palestine* (1946). In 1948 he covered the Jewish-Arab War which led to the creation of Israel.

After World War II Stone became a relentless critic of the emerging Cold War. When *PM* folded in 1948, Stone wrote first for the *New York Star* and then for the *Daily Compass*. In the fall of 1950 he went to Paris as European correspondent for the *Compass*. He conducted an investigation into the origins of the Korean War which was published as *The Hidden History of the Korean War* (1952). Calling it "a case study in the Cold War," it questioned the official explanations for why America entered the Korean War.

While the book was largely ignored, its style became the model for a new publication that Stone started out of professional necessity. In the late fall of 1952 the *Daily Compass* collapsed and Stone was out of a job. Since many publications would not hire him due to his political convictions, he launched his own political newsletter, *I. F. Stone's Weekly*. The first issue debuted on January 17, 1953.

To the original 5,300 subscribers of *I. F. Stone's Weekly* he wrote, "This weekly represents an attempt to keep alive through a difficult period the kind of independent radical journalism represented in various ways by *PM*, the *New York Star*, and the *Daily Compass*."

In its early days, Stone viewed *I.F. Stone's Weekly* as "the journalistic equivalent of the old-fashioned Jewish momma-and-poppa grocery store." While radical in viewpoint, the newsletter was conservative in format. Since he had no access to inside information, he was forced to rely on official documents for his sources. He quickly acquired a reputation for indicting the government with its own evidence.

Stone's style as a journalist was recognizable not only by his incisive criticism and ability to extract precious information out of material other journalists ignored, but also by his sense of historical perspective. In the 1950s the *Weekly* covered topics ranging from McCarthyism, defense spending, and the Soviet Union to the Supreme Court and civil rights.

Stone will be long remembered for his sustained criticism of America's involvement in Vietnam, which he began discussing as early as 1954. By 1963 he explained the failed efforts to impose stability on South Vietnam. "You can't go on pouring napalm on villages and poison on crops, uprooting the people and putting them in prison-like compounds and expect to be liked," he wrote.

In 1964, Stone was the only American journalist to challenge President Johnson's account of the fateful Gulf of Tonkin incident, which was used to obtain the congressional authority to escalate the war in Vietnam. Throughout the 1960s and early 1970s he persisted in exposing the horrors and fallacies of America's Vietnam policies. While he relied on public records to support his case, he also took his own trip to South Vietnam in 1966. As public disapproval of the war mounted, the increasingly popular Stone found a growing audience for the *Weekly.*

Stone once told his wife, "I'm going to graduate from a pariah into a character, and then if I last long enough I'll be regarded as a national institution." By the last years of the *Weekly* he had over 70,000 subscribers. When a collection of his essays appeared in 1970 he was called one of "the finest fog-cutters in Washington," and he was even saluted by *TIME* magazine. In 1971 he received a George Polk Memorial award.

Stone closed the *Weekly* at the end of 1971 because of poor health and became a contributing editor for the *New York Review of Books.* He soon retired to become a classical scholar, studying the origins of freedom of thought in Athens at the time of Socrates. In 1981 he came out of retirement to write articles for *The Nation* and the *New York Times* Op-ed page in response to actions of the Reagan administration.

Stone died on June 18, 1989, at age 81, after he underwent surgery in a Boston Hospital and suffered a heart attack. In September 1994, the FBI released information stating he had been under close scrutiny for the past 30 years. This was not an easy task since the FBI's records listed Stone under many different names. The FBI's file on Stone, a 4 1/4-inch, 1,794-page stack of paper, was released to the public under the Freedom of Information Act. Much information is blacked out and 332 pages were withheld. The file reveals as much about bureau operations in those days as about Stone. It also illustrates how difficult it was for the FBI to obtain incriminating evidence against this maverick who for six decades offered opinions on everything political.

Was Stone a Communist? From 1941 to 1971 the FBI tried to find an answer to this question. Stone traveled throughout the United States making speeches to leftist audiences. He began some of his speeches, "Fellow Communists and FBI agents ... " He denounced the House Committee on Un-American Activities and the Smith Act, which required the registration of foreigners, and the McCarran Act, which required Communists to register as foreign agents. On a passport application he refused, "as a matter of principle," to indicate whether or not he was a Communist. Ultimately, the FBI was never able to confirm that Stone was a committed Communist.

Since 1990, The Nation Institute/I.F. Stone Award has been presented to students who exhibit excellence in journalism. Candidates for the award must embody the same uniquely independent journalistic tendencies, investigative zeal, commitment to human rights, and desire to expose injustice that were I. F. Stone's trademark and legacy.

Further Reading

The best way to understand Stone's contribution as a journalist is to examine the many collections of his writings. They include *The Truman Era* (1953); *The Haunted Fifties* (1963); *In a Time of Torment* (1967); *Polemics and Prophecies 1967-70* (1970); and the one-volume anthology *The I. F. Stone's Weekly Reader* (1973). The best account of his life and style as a journalist is contained in the documentary film "I. F. Stone's Weekly," produced by Gerry Bruck. Updated information can be gathered from the *Los Angeles Times* "FBI Surveillance of I. F Stone Proved One Thing: Agents Couldn't Spell," September 25, 1994. □

Lucy Stone

Lucy Stone (1818-1893), American abolitionist, temperance worker, and woman's-suffrage leader, was the first important suffragist to retain her maiden name after marrying.

Lucy Stone was born in West Brookfield, Mass., on Aug. 13, 1818. At the age of 16 she began teaching school. For 9 years she saved her money and pursued her own studies. With some help from her father she finished her education at Oberlin College in 1847. That year she gave her first lecture on woman's rights from the pulpit of her brother's church. The following year she became an agent for the Antislavery Society. It was still rare for a woman to speak in public, rarer still for one to speak on woman's rights. The Antislavery Society disliked having the two causes confused, and so a compromise was arrived at by which Stone spoke for abolition on weekends, leaving the rest of the week free for woman's rights.

In 1855 Stone married noted abolitionist Henry B. Blackwell. The marriage service was distinguished by a joint protest against woman's disadvantaged state and a pledge that both partners would have absolutely equal rights in marriage. Blackwell was as good as his word. He became an ardent feminist and devoted much of his own time to the cause. Their daughter, Alice Stone Blackwell, became a feminist and helped bring to completion her parents' great work.

After the Civil War, Stone broke with the radical feminists over the question of giving precedence to black males in the suffrage struggle. More committed to the antislavery movement than women like Susan B. Anthony and Elizabeth Cady Stanton, Stone accepted the argument that by confusing women's suffrage with black suffrage both would be lost and that the black's need was at this moment greater. In 1869 she was one of the organizers of the American Woman Suffrage Association, which differed from the Stantonites' organization, the National Woman Suffrage Association, in being more conservative and in having male members.

On Jan. 8, 1870, the American Association brought forth its paper, the *Woman's Journal,* as a rival to the National's weekly. Edited by Stone, Blackwell, and Mary Livermore, *Woman's Journal* appealed to the growing number of clubwomen, professional women, and the like who were reaching for greater freedom but were not yet ready to commit themselves to equal suffrage. Alice Stone Blackwell succeeded her parents as its editor, and, after the vote had

been won, the magazine continued as the *Woman Citizen,* the organ of the League of Women Voters.

When the two wings of the suffrage movement were reunited in 1890 as the National American Woman Suffrage Association, Stone became one of its officers. She died on Oct. 18, 1893, in Boston.

Further Reading

Volumes 1 (1881) and 2 (1882) of the *History of Woman Suffrage,* edited by Elizabeth Cady Stanton, Susan B. Anthony, and Matilda Joslyn Gage, are helpful. Mrs. Stone's daughter, Alice Stone Blackwell, published an affectionate account, *Lucy Stone: Pioneer of Women's Rights* (1930). A thorough study is Elinor Rice Hays, *Morning Star: A Biography of Lucy Stone, 1818-1893* (1961). □

Oliver Stone

Oliver Stone's harrowing movies about life in an era bereft of morals have earned both lofty praise and stern condemnation. Stone (born 1946) is a pioneer writer-director of films that show the direct human consequences of national policy, whether it is set in the halls of government or in the board rooms of corporate financiers.

"Taking their cues from front-page headlines," wrote Patrick Goldstein in the *Los Angeles Times,* "Stone's moody, tumultuous films walk the thin line between outrage and outrageousness."

New York Times critic Janet Maslin observed that Stone "isn't one to regard moviegoing as a passive experience. Part of his method is to make audiences squirm." In works such as *Platoon, Wall Street,* and *Born on the Fourth of July*—all of which he wrote as well as directed—Stone has dared to confront the consequences of faulty values as the patriotism, greed, or naivete of his characters lead them into peril. During the 90s Stone's work became bolder, beginning with the controversial *JFK* and proceeding to the surrealistic horror of *Natural Born Killers* and the tragic history of *Nixon.* The filmmaker's increasingly wild visual style and loose interpretations of historical events—not to mention his occasionally blood-spattered scenarios—have made him a target. Republican Presidential hopeful Bob Dole lambasted him for his violence, while others have never forgiven his speculations about President Kennedy's assassination in *JFK.* "It's sad," Stone said of such acrimony in *Premiere,* "because you try to reach out and show people that you are rational and open to discourse."

Right-Wing Upbringing

Stone was born and raised in New York City, the son of a successful stockbroker. His childhood years were marked by all the privileges of wealth—private schooling, summer vacations in France, and most importantly, a sense of patriotism born of comfortable circumstances. "My father was

right-wing; he hated [President Franklin] Roosevelt all his life," Stone told *Film Comment.* "I grew up in that Cold War context that we all did, from the Fifties on, learning to fear Russians and hate Communism like cancer." Stone was in his junior year at the Hill School, a Pennsylvania college prep academy, when his parents announced their decision to divorce. In the subsequent family skirmish, Stone discovered that his father was in fact deeply in debt and that the values on which he had founded his life were quite thin. Stone entered Yale University in 1965, but after only one year he decided to quit college in order to find more meaningful experiences.

Late in 1965 Stone took a job teaching English at the Free Pacific Institute in Saigon, South Vietnam. His arrival in that war-torn country coincided with the first major commitment of American troops to the conflict. Stone told *Time* magazine that Saigon at the time had a "Dodge City" atmosphere. "There were guys walking around with pistols, no curfews, shoot-outs in the streets," he said. Stone left his post after six months and shipped out on a merchant tanker bound for the United States. While crossing the Pacific he began to work on a novel, and he continued to write it during a brief stay in Mexico and another futile attempt at college. The finished manuscript, entitled *A Child's Night Dream,* was more than four hundred pages in length. Stone was unable to find a publisher for it, and this rejection—combined with his father's condescending paternal attitude—pushed him to enlist in the Army. However, Stone continued to work on the novel, eventually expanding it to 1,100 pages. It was finally published by St. Martin's Press and released in 1997.

Shaped By Vietnam Experience

A number of interviewers have questioned Stone about his decision to fight in Vietnam. He could have missed the war entirely by staying in college, but instead he not only joined the service but insisted on infantry duty in the war zone. "I thought war was it; it was the most difficult thing a young man could go through," Stone told *Interview* magazine. "It was a rite of passage. And I knew it would be the only war of my generation, so I said, 'I've gotta get over there fast, because it's going to be over.' There was also a heavy streak of rebelliousness in the face of my father, and I think I was trying to prove to him that I was a man, not a boy." Stone was not long in discovering that the realities of combat were a far cry from his romantic notions about action, manhood, and adventure. "Vietnam completely deadened me and sickened me," he told the *Washington Post.* Assigned to a unit patrolling the Cambodian border, Stone was involved in several deadly skirmishes. He was wounded twice, once by gunshot and once by shrapnel, and he often witnessed the brutalization of Vietnamese civilians by American soldiers. "There was such a dog-tired, don't-give-a-damn attitude over there, such anger and frustration and casual brutality," he said in *Interview.* "I remember being so tired that I wished the North Vietnamese Army would come up and shoot me, just to get this thing over with."

Filmmaking Became New Goal

Stone was discharged after one tour and returned to America "very mixed up, very paranoid and very alienated," he told the *Washington Post.* He has since said that he might have succumbed to despair had he not felt a spark of optimism—perhaps he had survived Vietnam in order to "do something" with his life. Using his G.I. Bill benefits, he enrolled at New York University, where he began to study filmmaking with Martin Scorsese. Suddenly Stone had definable career goals: he wanted to write screenplays and make movies. Stone graduated from New York University in 1971 and within two years had sold his first project to a small Canadian film company. His writing and directorial debut was *Seizure,* a horror story about a writer whose fantastic creations come to life.

Seizure received lukewarm reviews and very little play at the box office, and its author-director entered a stagnant period marked by heavy drug and alcohol use. Stone finally pulled himself together during the Bicentennial celebrations in 1976 and decided to write a screenplay about his experiences in Vietnam. Between 1976 and 1978 Stone scripted two monumental stories on the war, *Platoon* and *Born on the Fourth of July,* based on the autobiography of crippled war veteran Ron Kovic. No studio would touch either property; the screenplays were deemed too violent and too negative. Stone's writing talents were recognized, however, and he was invited to work on other, less controversial themes.

Oscar for *Express* Script

In 1977 Stone was hired to write the screenplay for *Midnight Express,* a drama based on the true-life imprisonment of Bill Hayes. The film offers a sensational depiction of Hayes's capture and incarceration in a Turkish jail, where only the most brutal and powerful could survive the tortures inflicted by the guards and other inmates. *Midnight Express* created a critical firestorm when it was released in 1978. Many reviewers decried its gratuitous violence and its racist implications against the Turks. The controversy helped to create an audience for the movie; it turned a neat profit and garnered five Academy Award nominations. Stone himself won his first Oscar for best screenplay adaptation, and Hollywood's doors began to open to him.

Still Stone could not find backing for *Platoon.* Instead he wrote and directed a low-budget horror movie called *The Hand,* starring Michael Caine as a writer whose severed limb takes on a life of its own and begins to kill people. Although critics praised the stylishness of the work, it did little box office business, and Stone was reduced to the role of mere screenwriter again. In 1982 he wrote a script for John Milius's *Conan the Barbarian,* but the finished film bore little resemblance to his original idea. He then worked on the sensational *Scarface,* the story of a ruthless cocaine dealer. The violent and profane film also provoked controversy, but for Stone it was a very important project. Having suffered from the effects of drug abuse himself, he used his work on *Scarface* as his own farewell to drugs. In between these projects he continued to try to sell *Platoon* and *Born on the Fourth of July,* often meeting with last-minute frustration as financing would once again fall through.

Heightened Reality

Two more Stone projects, *Year of the Dragon* and *Eight Million Ways To Die,* were filmed in 1986. Both suffered at the hands of Hollywood "committees," and Stone became determined to exercise more control over his work. He became an independent filmmaker, and with the backing of a small British production company, finally saw his pet projects come to fruition. First he filmed the low-budget drama *Salvador,* based on the violent tactics of the American-supported Salvadoran army. The film did not receive wide distribution, but it was praised by critics, especially those with left-wing sensibilities. Hemdale, the British firm that produced Salvador, then gave Stone the money to do *Platoon.*

The script Stone used was essentially the one he had written in 1976, based on himself and composites of other soldiers he had known. The movie, Stone told *People,* is "heightened reality." He added: "I pushed beyond the factual truth to the spiritual . . . no, to a greater truth. This is the spirit of what I saw happening." An ensemble cast performance, Platoon follows a young grunt (Charlie Sheen) into the brutal arena that was Vietnam. Its violence and pessimism notwithstanding, the film won a number of important Oscars, including best picture and best director. "*Platoon,*" wrote Pat McGilligan in *Film Comment,* "takes the futility of the war and the rape of Vietnam for granted, and instead focuses on the searing intimacy of fear and hate; on the psychology of the battlefield; on the civil war-within-the-war, the left-wing versus the right-wing (as it were) of the soldiery and the command. . . . *Platoon* is an ugly, painful, doom-laden film, with much that is honest and beautiful and, yes, good. Apart from its intrinsic historical value as the first feature film directed by a former vet, I believe Stone when he says his goals in making it were in part modest and private. Rather than affecting a grand, universal statement about men in war, he is content to exorcise his own ghost from Vietnam."

Hit Mainstream, Caused Outrage

Stone followed Platoon with his first big-budget project, *Wall Street.* Another critical and commercial success, *Wall Street* explores the seduction of a young stockbroker by an older and completely ruthless business tycoon. Following *Wall Street* Stone was finally able to find the money to film *Born on the Fourth of July.* When he tried to have the movie made in the 1970s he planned to use Al Pacino in the lead; in the late 1980s he turned to another Hollywood superstar, Tom Cruise. Cruise gives an affecting performance as the raging Ron Kovic, who endures not only the horror of battle but the humiliation of helpless paraplegia. "Although Mr. Kovic's personal ordeal and Tom Cruise's fiery performance occupy center stage in the movie, and although the film addresses every intimate aspect of Mr. Kovic's struggle," wrote Maslin, it isn't this private story that makes the film such an emotional powerhouse. It is Mr. Stone's ability to surround his central figure with huge, vivid tableaux that wrenchingly depict the progress of a nation; his chilling vision of the forces that shape American notions of manhood, and the consequences they may bring; and his way of grafting sights, sounds and sensations together so breathlessly, making the whole film hurtle forward at such a breakneck pace."

Born on the Fourth of July brought Stone yet another Academy Award for best director. The early 1990s find him hitting his stride as one of the most important writer-directors in Hollywood. He next explored 1960s counterculture with his psychedelic rock opus *The Doors.* This film was something of a preamble to his most controversial feature, *JFK,* in which Kevin Costner portrayed Jim Garrison, the Texas Attorney General who battled what the film views as a conspiracy to cover up the real circumstances behind the death of President John F. Kennedy in 1963. The film's mixture of hallucinatory sequences and historical details infuriated many, but even his detractors had trouble denying the power of Stone's cinematic vision; as a result, many reviews ended up calling *JFK* brilliant claptrap.

After *JFK,* Stone's alleged paranoia and fondness for conspiracy theories was the source of a million show-business jokes; the cable comedy network Comedy Central even offered "Oliver Stone's Paranoia Web Site." The filmmaker demonstrated he had a sense of humor about the matter when he played a conspiracy nut in the political comedy *Dave.*

Stone returned to the Vietnam nightmare for 1993's *Heaven and Earth,* this time dealing with the war's impact and aftermath from the point of view of a Vietnamese woman. Though a good-faith effort on Stone's part to trascend the male-centered, American perspective he'd previously emphasized with regard to Vietnam, the film was pounded by reviewers.

Outrageous *Killers,* Balanced *Nixon*

Stone came raging back, however, with 1994's wildly experimental and brutally violent *Natural Born Killers.* Loosely based on a script by Quentin Tarantino, the film chronicles the murderous odyssey of two disturbed young lovers, played by Woody Harrelson and Juliette Lewis, and the twisted opera of celebrity that grows around them. Cinematographer Robert Richardson told *Time,* "the making of the film resembled throwing paint at the canvas—you don't know if you're making art. The only rule was that you could change your mind." The film was a sensation, and inspired condemnation from Dole and others about its brash treatment of violence, which was portrayed as a sickness spreading through popular culture—thus serving as a handy tool in an election season.

Stone's next film assayed the story of another American President. Though many expected his biopic of Richard Nixon—who resigned in disgrace after being implicated in the controversy known as Watergate—to be a hatchet job on an easy Republican target. After all, many reasoned, Nixon prolonged the war in Vietnam; it would be easy enough to lay the pain of the filmmaker's whole generation at the late leader's feet. But Stone preferred to tell a more complex tale. As he told *Entertainment Weekly,* "the character [of Nixon] is so fascinating. He's this contradiction of idealism and corruption. He saw greatness and understood the meaning of it. But the weapons that allowed him to rise to the top were also the weapons that destroyed him." Casting British actor Anthony Hopkins in the title role, Stone earned near-unanimous praise for his emotionally deep and even-handed portrait of Nixon. The film earned numerous Academy Award nominations, and—perhaps more satisfyingly for Stone—the recognition that he could transcend his political agendas to make universally appealing cinema. "You have to make films as an idealist," he told *Film Comment* some years earlier. "You've got to make them to the greater glory of mankind. Then, even if you fail, even if the film doesn't work, you do not have to be ashamed, because you tried." Stone added: "I've grown with each of my films. . . . None of them has been a waste of time for me. That's important. I've educated myself. I've gotten better. I've learned more about my craft. I'm just at the beginning of a road. I'm learning how to make movies."

Stone's next film, 1997's *U-Turn,* depicts the story of a drifter (Sean Penn) who encounters a town's strange inhabitants in a plot that involves sex, murder, and betrayal. Filmed in Superior, Arizona, the cast also includes Nick Nolte, Billy Bob Thornton, Jon Voight, Claire Danes, and Jennifer Lopez. The director opted for a small budget for this project, making the film in six weeks. Although it is based strictly on fiction, *U-Turn,* like many of Stone's films, contains very controversial material.

Further Reading

American Film, December, 1987.
Entertainment Weekly, January 12, 1996.
Film Comment, February, 1987.
Interview, February, 1987.
Los Angeles Times, December 24, 1989; July 30, 1996.
Newsday, December 14, 1986. Newsweek, January 9, 1989.
New York Times, May 15, 1981; April 13, 1987; December 31, 1989.
People, June 1, 1981; March 2, 1987; January 11, 1988.
Premiere, January 1996.
Rolling Stone, January 29, 1987.
Time, December 5, 1983; January 26, 1987; August 29, 1994.
USA Today, August 7, 1996.
Village Voice, December 26, 1989.
Wall Street Journal, February 13, 1996.
Washington Post, January 11, 1987; July 19, 1996. □

Robert Anthony Stone

Robert Anthony Stone (born 1937) was an American novelist whose preoccupations were politics, the media, and the random, senseless violence and cruelty that pervade contemporary life both in the United States and in parts of the world where United States' influence has extended, such as Latin America and Vietnam. His vision of the world is dark but powerful.

Robert Anthony Stone was born in Brooklyn, New York, on August 21, 1937, to C. Homer and Gladys Catherine (Grant) Stone. His mother had been a teacher, but her career was cut short by schizophrenia. Her husband having deserted his family, she supported herself and her son by working as a chambermaid. The two lived in a succession of rooming houses and welfare hotels. Stone attended a parochial school, Archbishop Malloy High School, until he was asked to leave because of truancy and atheistic beliefs.

For a year he lived in New Orleans, which was later to provide the setting for his first novel. It was here that he joined the Navy in 1955. He was discharged in 1958, and the following year he married Janice C. Burr, a social worker. The couple had two children, Ian and Deirdre. He studied for one year at New York University and then attended Stanford.

His first novel, *A Hall of Mirrors* (1967), won him the William Faulkner Foundation Award. In 1982 he was awarded the John Dos Passos Prize for literature, and he also won an award for literature from the American Academy and Institute of Arts and Letters. He taught at various colleges and universities, including Harvard. He lived in the early 1990s in Amherst.

The mirrors to which *A Hall of Mirrors* alluded are a recurring theme in the novel. The various characters bear either physical or psychological scars, and Stone seems to be saying that mirrors reflect the scars that life has bestowed on us but that they do not show how or why we have

obtained those scars. Rheinhardt, the protagonist of the novel, is a musician who finds employment in New Orleans with a high-powered, right-wing evangelist and radio station owner who uses the air waves to mercilessly exploit his listeners and employees in the furtherance of his ideas.

In the 1960s Stone came to know many of the figures of the Beat Generation—Allen Ginsberg, Neal Cassady, and others. He joined in the famous cross-country bus ride of the Merry Pranksters, a ride described hilariously by Tom Wolfe in his book *The Electric Kool-Aid Acid Test.* A fellow passenger on the bus was Ken Kesey, author of *One Flew Over the Cuckoo's Nest,* with whom he formed a long-lasting friendship. Not surprisingly, Stone experimented with drugs and later attributed the discovery of a spiritual aspect of his life to this experimentation.

Not even his earlier experiments with drugs, however, were able to prepare him for what he found in Saigon (now Ho Chi Minh City), Vietnam, where he traveled in 1971 and from where he sent a series of reports to the *Manchester Guardian.* Out of his first-hand observations of the drug trade came his classic novel *Dog Soldiers* (1974), which helped to establish his reputation as a writer. This novel was later made into the movie *Who'll Stop the Rain* (1978) staring Nick Nolte, Tuesday Weld, and Michael Moriarty.

Stone wrote out of his own experience. For him, fiction was another way to get at the truth without being fettered by facts. He said that fiction purifies reality, renders it into the insubstantiality of the dream, and there is certainly a dreamlike quality in all of his writing. As early as *A Hall of Mirrors* this aspect is evident. His handling of the episode involving Rheinhardt's adventures in Lake Ponchartrain takes on a quality so primordial as to suggest that the shock of recognition which the reader experiences may well be owing to the collective unconscious, which by definition is common to all humanity.

A Flag for Sunrise (1982) grew out of three visits which Stone made to Nicaragua, the first of which was undertaken merely as a scuba diving vacation. He was repelled by the casual and pervasive use of violence that characterized the Somoza regime. In the novel, however, Stone created his own country. In one especially graphic episode Father Egan, an American missionary who is one of the chief characters of the novel, is asked by an army officer to dispose of the body of a young American girl. The officer, who has murdered her, has stuffed her body into his refrigerator. The novel abounds in atrocities.

Children of Light (1986) deals with the film industry and is set in Hollywood, or at least part of it is. It is as bleak as his other works. Other American authors have also written novels about Hollywood—F. Scott Fitzgerald, Nathanael West, Norman Mailer—and though there may have been a comic moment here or there, theirs have been as grim as his.

Stone believed that humor can mitigate the cruelty of human existence. He was serious about the craft of writing and considered that there is an indissoluble connection between fiction and morality, and that for that reason, the writer must do his best and never pander to political or commercial considerations. In other words, fiction must not corrupt itself, for in its pure state, it links humanity together and helps overcome isolation. In times of various kinds of disorder and upheaval, as for instance revolution and war, he saw the individual as being subsumed in the group; nevertheless, the individual comes to see himself at such a time for what he is. Stone seems to have applied this credo to his own work. Though his work often deals with violence, he never sensationalizes it. It is there to show the darker side of human existence, but one is sure that Stone hopes to see humankind rise above individual violence and war.

Other works by Stone included *Outerbridge Reach* (1992) and *Bear and His Daughter* (1997), both published by Houghton-Mifflin. *Bear and His Daughter* represented a departure from Stone's novel writing and was a collection of six previously published short stories plus a new novella for which the volume is named.

Further Reading

Additional information on Robert Stone can be found in Eric James Schroeder, "Two Interviews: Talks with Tim O'Brien and Robert Stone," in *Modern Fiction Studies* (Spring 1984), and in Robert Stone, "The Reason for Stories: Toward a Moral Fiction," *Harper's* (June 1988), which is about his ideas on fiction. Paul Gray provides a lengthy review of *Bear and His Daughter* in *Time* magazine (April 7, 1997). ☐

Marie Stopes

Best known for her work as a pioneer in popularizing the use of birth control in the United Kingdom, Marie Stopes (1880-1958) was also a prolific writer. While attracting the condemnation of the Catholic Church for her staunch advocacy of contraception and her establishment of Great Britain's first birth control clinic, Stopes' work as a social reformer would also pave the way for an increasing public acceptance of books on the subject of human sexuality.

Marie Stopes was a British scientist and writer who became an active proponent of sexual education and birth control in the early twentieth century. In books such as *Married Love* (1918), Stopes became one of the first people to publicly discuss romantic and sexual happiness in marriage. She also provided information on contraception through her clinics, lectures, and books, including *Wise Parenthood* (1918). While much of Stopes's information and advice was criticized by medical professionals and officials of the Roman Catholic church, her books enjoyed wide sales, demonstrating the public's need for the kind of well-explained practical advice that she offered.

Marie Charlotte Stopes was born in Edinburgh, Scotland, on October 15, 1880. Her parents were both well-educated with successful careers: her father, Henry Stopes, was an architect, and her mother, Charlotte Carmichael

Stopes, was a Shakespeare expert who had been the first female graduate of a Scottish university. The family moved to London after Stopes's birth, and there she was educated at home by her mother until the age of 12. She was then sent to Edinburgh to begin classes at St. George's School. After a short period there, she moved to North London Collegiate, where she distinguished herself as a top student. Stopes attended University College, where she focused first on chemistry and later switched to an honors botany program. In 1902, she received her bachelor of science degree with honors in botany and geology.

Continuing to prepare herself for a scientific career, Stopes went to the Botanical Institute of Munich University in Germany. There, she conducted her doctoral research on the reproduction processes of cycads, a type of tropical plant. She was awarded a doctoral degree with highest honors in 1904. Returning to England, she earned a doctor of science degree from London University, becoming the youngest person in Britain to do so. The same year, she overcame another boundary by becoming the first woman to join the science faculty of Manchester University. Stopes had a very successful scientific career; she conducted well-respected research on the history of angiosperms and she also studied the composition of coal. Her work earned her a grant from the British Royal Society, an organization of leading scientists, which allowed her to travel to Japan to conduct research in 1907 and 1908. This award was another first for a woman.

Returning to her post at Manchester for a time, Stopes published the first of her scientific works, *Ancient Plants,* published in 1910. In 1913, she accepted a position at University College and for the next seven years she lectured in paleobotany and wrote other books in her fields of specialty. These included *The Constitution of Coal,* published in 1918, and *The Four Visible Ingredients in Banded Bituminous Coal: Studies in the Composition of Coal,* published in 1919.

In 1911, Stopes married Reginald Ruggles Gates, a Canadian botanist; she did not take his surname, however, and would retain her maiden name throughout her life. The marriage was not successful, primarily due to Stopes's discovery that her new husband was impotent. She filed for an annulment, which was granted in 1916. The experience apparently left a strong impression on Stopes, who increasingly turned her energies from her scientific research and teaching to writing on the topics of love, marriage, and sex. After completing her first book in this area, *Married Love,* she found that publishers were unwilling to handle a book that engaged in such unabashed discussions of sexual relationships. In order to get her work published, Stopes sought financial backing elsewhere. During this time, she met the wealthy pilot Humphrey Verdon Roe, who shared her interests in promoting birth control. Roe agreed to lend her the money to publish the book, which was finally printed in 1918. Stopes and Roe were married that year in a civil ceremony at a registry office in May and a religious ceremony on June 19. In July of 1919, Stopes delivered a stillborn son, a tragedy for which she held her doctors responsible. This event may have played a role in her strong distrust of doctors for the rest of her life. Roe and Stopes were successful in having a child in 1924, when their son Harry Stopes-Roe was born.

Married Love was a great success. Her marriage manual did not present many new ideas, but was unique in presenting instruction and advice with uncomplicated language that was accessible to a wide audience. Her main contribution was promoting the idea that people should expect and strive for happiness in their personal and sexual relationships, a fairly radical idea for the time. The book drew a substantial amount of letters from readers, most of whom desired information on birth control. Stopes willingly obliged her readers by compiling her ideas on the topic in the book *Wise Parenthood* in 1918. In the book, she suggested that a cervical cap be used for contraception; she felt that this was the best method to use and never supported any other methods despite the criticism she received from medical doctors on the subject. *Wise Parenthood* continued Stopes's practice of providing often unavailable information on reproduction by using detailed drawings of human anatomy to educate readers about the physical facts of sexuality.

Other books on sex, marriage, and birth control by Stopes followed throughout the 1920s and early 1930s, including *A Letter to Working Mothers* (1919), *Radiant Motherhood* (1920), and *Enduring Passion* (1928). In addition, in 1921 she and her husband founded the first birth control clinic in London, the Mother's Clinic. The early 1920s brought a number of attacks on Stopes's work. Doctors criticized her promotion of the cervical cap, arguing that it was one of the most harmful methods of birth control for women. A Roman Catholic doctor, Halliday Sutherland, wrote a treatise accusing Stopes of using poor women for birth control experiments; she vehemently denied the charges and countered by suing Sutherland for libel. The highly publicized trials that followed ultimately resulted in Sutherland being cleared of the charges, but brought Stopes an incredible amount of attention, resulting in her popularity as a public speaker. She also published a formal rebuttal to the Church's attacks on her work in the 1933 book, *Roman Catholic Methods of Birth Control.*

Stopes's later years were marked by a growing sense of frustration and isolation. She and Roe were separated in 1938, at which time she moved into a home in Norbury Park in England. After she expressed disapproval over her son's marriage, she also lost touch with him for a long time. She reportedly became disillusioned with her humanitarian causes and retreated into literary pursuits, producing a number of poorly-received collections of love poetry such as *Love Songs for Young Lovers* (1939), *We Burn* (1950), and *Joy and Verity* (1952). The battles that she did take on were obscure and unsuccessful, notably her fight to obtain a state pension for the poet Lord Alfred Douglas. She held the belief that physical health could be maintained with a regimen of cold baths and drinking a daily glass of sea water; because of this and her distrust of doctors, she did not immediately seek medical attention when signs of illness appeared. She was finally diagnosed with advanced breast cancer, but refused standard treatment. Instead she underwent some holistic therapy in Switzerland before returning to Norbury Park and dying on October 2, 1958.

A flamboyant and often arrogant figure who considered herself the best authority on the topics of love, marriage, sex, and birth control, Stopes was criticized during her lifetime for advancing ideas that were in some cases outdated and not proper for all people. But much of the opposition she encountered also stemmed from the fact that she dared to address topics that were still considered improper for public discussion at that time. Fighting this mentality, which she felt led to ignorance and unhappiness in sexual matters, Stopes provided information that was eagerly sought by the public. Her success in changing attitudes about romantic relationships and parenthood was apparent in the popularity of her books and the enormous public response that they generated.

Further Reading

Adam, Corinna, "The Disappointed Prophetess," *New Statesman,* August 8, 1969, pp. 177-78.

Aylmer, Maude, *The Authorized Life of Marie C. Stopes,* Williams and Norgate, 1924.

Briant, Keith, *Passionate Paradox: The Life of Marie Stopes,* W. W. Norton, 1962.

Hall, Ruth, *Passionate Crusader: The Life of Marie Stopes,* Harcourt Brace Jovanovich, 1977. □

Thomas Stoppard

One of England's most important playwrights, Tom Stoppard (born 1937) was popular in the United States as well. His two great stage successes were *Rosenkrantz and Guildenstern Are Dead* and *The Real Thing.*

The son of a doctor for the Bata shoe manufacturing company, Thomas Straussler (Stoppard) was born on July 3, 1937, in Zlin, Czechoslovakia. According to Nazi racial laws there was "Jewish blood" in the family, so his father was transferred to Singapore in 1939, taking the family with him. When the Japanese invaded that city in 1942, the women and children were taken to India. Dr. Straussler stayed behind and was killed.

Stoppard attended an American boarding school in Darjeeling. In 1945 his mother married Kenneth Stoppard, a British Army major, and both of her sons took his name. The Stoppards went to England, where Stoppard's stepfather worked in the machine-tool industry. Thomas continued his education at a preparatory school in Yorkshire.

At age 17 he felt that he had had enough schooling and became first a reporter and then a critic for the *Western Daily Press* of Bristol from 1954 to 1958. He left the *Press* and worked as a reporter for the *Evening World,* also in Bristol, from 1958 to 1960. Stoppard then worked as a freelance reporter from 1960 to 1963. During these years he experimented with writing short stories and short plays. In 1962 he moved to London in order to be closer to the center of the publishing and theatrical worlds in the United Kingdom.

His first radio plays for the BBC (British Broadcasting Company)—*The Dissolution of Dominic Boot* and *M Is for Moon Among Other Things*—were aired in 1964, with two more, *Albert's Bridge* and *If You're Glad I'll Be Frank,* following in 1965. His first television play, *A Separate Peace,* appeared the next year, as did his only novel, *Lord Malquist and Mr. Moon,* and the stage play that established his reputation as a playwright, *Rosenkrantz and Guildenstern Are Dead.*

Rosenkrantz and Guildenstern Are Dead takes two minor characters in Shakespeare's *Hamlet* and shows us the world of the Danish prince from a different perspective. Critic Charles Marowitz dubbed the show a "play-beneath-the-play." But it was more than an oblique look at a dramatic classic. It was an examination of existentialist philosophy when the protagonists learn that they are to die and accept their fate. As Marowitz put it, the play "demonstrates a remarkable skill in juggling the donnees of existentialist philosophy. . . . We are summoned, we come. We are given roles, we play them. We are dismissed, we go." America's influential critic Harold Clurman wrote, "Based on a nice conceit, it is epigrammatically literate, intelligent, theatrically clever." The play earned Stoppard his first Tony award.

That same year, 1966, Stoppard produced *Tango,* based on a work by Slawomir Mrozek, and in 1967 he produced two television plays, *Teeth* and *Another Moon Called Earth.*

The year 1968 saw another television play, *Neutral Ground,* and two short works for the theater; *Enter a Free Man* and *The Real Inspector Hound.* Of the former, critic Brendan Gill wrote that it has "a plot of no very great originality . . . an ending too neat for its own good," while of the latter another critic, Clive Barnes, opined that it was a "spinoff" from *Rosenkrantz and Guildenstern.* He went on, "Here it is two critics watching a conventional murder mystery who eventually find themselves dragged into the action of the play. In a sense the same existentialist attitude. . . ."

In 1970 Stoppard returned to the BBC with the two radio plays, *Artist Descending a Staircase* and *Where Are They Now,* and authored the television plays *The Engagement* and *Experiment in Television* as well as the stage work *After Magritte.* It was about this time that Stoppard became acquainted with Ed Berman from New York City's Off-Off-Broadway, who was attempting to establish an alternative theater in London. For him Stoppard composed *Dogg's Our Pet,* produced in 1971 at the Almost Free Theater; the feeble double bill of *Dirty Linen* and *New-found-land* in 1975; and *Night and Day* in 1978.

In 1972 Stoppard had presented *Jumpers,* his second major work, which begins with circus acts and evolves into religious and moral philosophy. As critic Victor Cahn put it, "The specific philosophical problem at the basis of George's [the protagonist's] inquiry is whether moral judgments are absolute or relative, whether their truth lies in correspondence with the facts of the world or whether they are . . . personal expressions of emotion." *Jumpers* did not enjoy the same critical acclaim that had greeted *Rosenkrantz and Guildenstern.* Stanley Kauffmann labeled it "fake, structurally and thematically," while John Simon wrote that "there is even something arrogant about trying to convert the history of Western culture into a series of blackout sketches, which is very nearly what *Jumpers* is up to." Stoppard wrote the television play *One Pair of Eyes* with Clive Exton the same year.

Two years later he produced his third major work, *Travesties.* It was based on the coincidence that Russian exile politician V. I. Lenin, Irish novelist James Joyce, and the father of the French Dadaist movement in literature and art, Tristan Tzara, were all in Zurich, Switzerland, at times during World War I. It is assumed that they never met in actuality, but their interaction in Stoppard's play illuminates the question of what constitutes art. The author's conclusion seems to be that its sole function is to make the meaninglessness of life more bearable.

In 1977 Stoppard offered *Every Good Boy Deserves Favour,* a tour de force premiered by the Royal Shakespeare Company and the 100-piece London Symphony Orchestra conducted by Andre Previn at the Royal Festival Hall. Brought to the United States, it was presented at the Metropolitan Opera House in New York with an 81-piece orchestra. The play concerns a dissident in an Iron Curtain country who has been placed in a mental institution. Its attack on the totalitarian state was the author's strongest political statement up to that time. That same year he was named a Commander of the British Empire (CBE).

In 1979 came three plays; *Undiscovered Country,* based on Austrian playwright Artur Schnitzler's *Das weite land; Dogg's Hamlet;* and *Cahoot's Macbeth.* In 1982 his fourth major work was produced. *The Real Thing* won Stoppard his second Tony award in 1984. More psychological than his previous plays, *The Real Thing* concerns a literary man whose love is unfaithful to him and how he copes with his disillusionment. Again critical opinion was divided: Benedict Nightingale in the *New Statesman* summarized it this way: "He has maintained his humour, increased his complexity, and deepened his art." Robert Brustein, on the other hand, saw it as "another clever exercise in the Mayfair mode, where all of the characters . . . share the same wit, artifice and ornamental diction."

Stoppard summed up his life's work as an attempt to "make serious points by flinging a custard pie around the stage for a couple of hours."

Further Reading

There are three good biographies and studies: *Tom Stoppard* by Felicia Hardison Londre (1981), *Tom Stoppard* by Joan Fitzpatrick Dean (1981), and *Beyond Absurdity: The Plays of Tom Stoppard* by Victor L. Cahn (1979). Another worthwhile appreciation is the chapter on Stoppard in *The Second Wave: British Drama for the Seventies* by John Russell Taylor (1971). Also see Dean, Joan Fitzpatrick, *Tom Stoppard: Comedy as a Moral Matrix,* (University of Missouri Press, 1981). □

Theodor Storm

The German poet and novelist Theodor Storm (1817-1888) ranks as one of the finest lyric poets in German literature, but modern readers know him best for his novellas, a form in which he was a recognized master.

Theodor Storm was born on Sept. 14, 1817, at Husum, an old coastal town in Schleswig. His father, of humble origin, was an attorney, but his mother, whose interest in family life, art, and nature Storm inherited, had a patrician heritage. From 1837 to 1842 he studied law, principally at Kiel, where he became a friend of Theodor Mommsen, later a celebrated historian, and his brother, together with whom he published a volume of poetry in 1843. A volume of his own poetry, issued in 1852, was expanded through a seventh edition in 1885. In 1843 Storm began to practice law at Husum, and he married Konstanze Esmarch 3 years later. They had seven children.

Mood Novels

All of Storm's works have a lyrical quality, but shifting emphases allow them to be divided into groupings. His first novella, *Immensee* (1850), is the most popular of his stories. A charming, romantic idyll, it is told through the technique of reminiscence, has little action, and projects a lyrical mood of melancholy and resignation. Storm treated the same theme in *Ein grünes Blatt* (1855) and in *Späte Rosen* (1861). The device of reminiscence also occurs in *Auf dem Staatshof* (1851), *Im Schloss* (1861), and *Sankt Jürgen* (1867).

When Storm's native province came under Danish dominion (1853), his staunch patriotism prompted his voluntary exile, first to Potsdam, then to Heiligenstadt (1856), where he became a district judge. Schleswig's liberation in 1864 enabled Storm to return to Husum. But the years of exile had been a harshly bitter experience. An additional blow was the death of his wife a year later. Though Storm soon married again happily, his tragic sense of life had been quickened. Most of his later stories reveal a certain pessimism, an increasingly deterministic conception of life, and a note of dismay in the face of life's transitoriness and enigmatic quality.

Realistic and Historical Novels

Until 1870 Storm's narratives dealt with sentimental situations that emphasized mood. A change in his style occurred during the following decade, beginning with *Draussen im Heidehof* (1871). The novellas of this period exhibit a greater realism of execution and logic of motivation. An element of drama in the action, which remains psychological in character, was also introduced. Representative stories include *Viola Tricolor* (1873), *Pole Poppenspäler* (1874), *Psyche* (1875), and *Ein stiller Musikant* (1875). Storm next turned to the production of a number of historical novels. This group includes *Aquis Submersus* (1875), thought by some critics to be his finest novella, as well as *Carsten Curator* (1877), *Renate* (1878), and *Eekenhof* (1879), all of which rank among his best tales. These stories show man in his lonely struggle against a dark and often tragic destiny.

Storm spent the years after 1880 in retirement. He died on July 4, 1888, at Hademarschen. Some of the finest of his more than 50 novellas derive from this period. These works are marked by the fullest realization of his powers as a narrator of man's conflicts with his fellowman. Outstanding among his late works are *Die Söhne des Senators* (1881), *Hans und Heinz Kirch* (1883), *Ein Fest auf Haderslevhuus* (1885), and *Der Schimmelreiter* (1888).

Further Reading

Two works in English on Storm are by Otto Wooley, *Studies in Theodor Storm* (1943) and *Theodor Storm's World in Pictures* (1954). Thomas Mann, *Essays of Three Decades* (1948), contains a chapter on Storm. For background see John G. Robertson, *A History of German Literature* (1902; rev. ed. 1970).

Additional Sources

Jackson, David A., *Theodor Storm: the life and works of a democratic humanitarian,* New York: Berg: St. Martin's Press distributor, 1992. □

Joseph Story

Joseph Story (1779-1845), American jurist and statesman, was an associate justice of the Supreme Court and a prolific and influential legal publicist.

Joseph Story was born in Marblehead, Mass., on Sept. 18, 1779. He graduated with honors from Harvard in 1798. After studying in the offices of Samuel Putnam and Samuel Sewall, he was admitted to the bar in 1801. He practiced in the local, state, and lower Federal courts, specializing in commercial and maritime law, and rose rapidly to the top of the profession. At the same time he began his career in legal scholarship, editing works on pleading (1805), shipping (1810), and assumpsit (1811).

Story entered politics as a Jeffersonian Republican. From 1805 to 1811 he was a leading member of the Massachusetts House of Representatives and during 1811 was Speaker. He championed judicial reform, including a successful attempt to raise judicial salaries and an unsuccessful effort to establish a chancery court. In the winter of 1808/1809 he served in the U.S. House of Representatives. President James Madison appointed him to the Supreme Court in November 1811.

Story quickly won respect among his fellow justices. During the War of 1812 he steadfastly backed national authority. His exposition of admiralty law during this period and thereafter helped lay the foundations for that branch of American jurisprudence. His opinion in *Martin v. Hunter's*

Lessee (1816) was a major decisional link in the chain of nationalism forged by the Court under Chief Justice John Marshall. Like Marshall, Story was dedicated to the sanctity of property rights, and his opinions consistently favored national expansion of business and commerce. His opinion in *Terrett v. Taylor* (1815) and concurrence in *Dartmouth College v. Woodward* (1819) were instrumental in shielding corporations from state interference. In commercial law he was during his tenure the most influential justice on the Court.

After 1837 Story was progressively alienated by the states'-rights tendency of the Court under Chief Justice Roger B. Taney, and he continued to defend the "old law" in biting dissents. While performing his judicial duties, he also taught at the Harvard Law School, which, through his efforts, pioneered in formal legal education. From his teaching came a series of commentaries on the main branches of American law.

Story was a leader in the Massachusetts constitutional convention of 1820 and drafted legislation on bankruptcy, crimes, and admiralty jurisdiction. He died on Sept. 10, 1845.

Further Reading

Story's son's work, William W. Story, ed., *Life and Letters of Joseph Story* (2 vols., 1851), remains a valuable account of Story's life and career. Henry Steele Commager's "Joseph Story" in *The Gaspar G. Bacon Lectures on the Constitution of the United States, 1940-1950* (1953) is a very readable summary. Gerald T. Dunne, *Justice Joseph Story and the Rise of the Supreme Court* (1971), and James McClellan, *Joseph Story and the American Constitution* (1971), are the fullest and most analytical studies of Story to date. General histories of the Supreme Court and biographies of other justices can be consulted for information on Story. Among the most useful are Albert J. Beveridge, *The Life of John Marshall* (4 vols., 1916-1919); Charles Warren, *The Supreme Court in United States History* (3 vols., 1922; rev. ed., 2 vols., 1926); Carl B. Swisher, *Roger B. Taney* (1935); and *The Role of the Supreme Court in American Government and Politics,* vol. 1: *1789-1835* (1944), by Charles G. Haines, and vol. 2: *1835-1864* (1957), on the Taney period, by Haines and Foster H. Sherwood.

Additional Sources

Newmyer, R. Kent, *Supreme Court Justice Joseph Story: statesman of the Old Republic,* Chapel Hill: University of North Carolina Press, 1985. □

Veit Stoss

The German sculptor Veit Stoss (ca. 1445-1533) perfected the expressive late Gothic style in his early masterpiece, the high altar of the Virgin Mary in Cracow, Poland. His late sculpture shows his mastery of a new, abstract, Renaissance-inspired art.

Born either in Swabia or Nuremberg, Veit Stoss worked in Cracow, Poland, between 1477 and 1496, when he became a citizen of Nuremberg. In 1503 he falsified papers and was condemned to death. He was reprieved but branded on the cheeks with hot irons. He nevertheless continued to work in Nuremberg until his death.

Stoss's most impressive and important work is the high altar (1477-1486) of the parish church of the Virgin Mary in Cracow. It is an elaborate polychromed wood structure, with two sets of wings which depict in relief sculpture the life of the Virgin and of Christ. In the center is the Death of Mary in the presence of the Apostles. In the openwork Gothic superstructure Christ ascends into heaven with her soul, and at the top of the altarpiece Mary is crowned Queen of Heaven by the Trinity. The entire altarpiece is a blaze of gold and strong colors, especially blue, and the excitement continues in the style of the carving. Drapery folds, deeply undercut, break crisply and swirl about, forming animated patterns in light and shade. The altarpiece is a technical tour de force that overwhelms the beholder.

The first accredited works by Stoss after his return to Nuremberg are the three stone reliefs (1499) of the Passion in the choir of St. Sebald. They are of remarkable formal concentration and enormous power, as is the wooden crucifix from the same period and church (now on the high altar of the church of St. Lorenz).

High above this altar in St. Lorenz, suspended in midair, is Stoss's famous *Great Rosary,* or *Salve Regina* (1517-1518). A wooden chaplet of carved roses and medallions representing the Seven Joys of Mary surround the life-size figures of Gabriel and the Annunciate Virgin. The style is crisp and somewhat nervous in this very dramatic conception, which honors the Cult of the Rosary, promulgated in the late 15th century by the Dominicans.

There is just a hint of calm and relaxation, as well as a breath of the new spirit of the Renaissance, in the masterpiece of Stoss's late style, the *Adoration of the Shepherds* altarpiece (1520-1523), carved for a church in Bamberg (now in the Cathedral). The wood was purposely left uncolored, in the new Renaissance feeling for the medium that Stoss's contemporary Tilman Riemenschneider shared.

Stoss's genius was so strong that it was apparently impossible for forceful individuals to develop in his school in Nuremberg.

Further Reading

There is no biography of Stoss in English. Theodore Müller, *Sculpture in the Netherlands, Germany, France, and Spain, 1400-1500* (trans. 1966), has excellent biographical and critical material on Stoss. Recommended for background are Charles Louis Kuhn, *German and Netherlandish Sculpture, 1280-1800* (1965), and Hanspeter Landolt, *German Painting: The Late Middle Ages, 1350-1500* (trans. 1968). □

Samuel A. Stouffer

Samuel A. Stouffer (1900-1960) was an American sociologist and statistician. He was among the leaders in applying rigorous methodology to sociological investigations.

Samuel Stouffer was born in Sac City, Iowa, on June 6, 1900. After receiving a bachelor's degree at Morningside College in Iowa (1921), he took graduate work at Harvard University and then at the University of Chicago, where he obtained a doctorate in sociology (1930). He taught at the universities of Chicago and Wisconsin and worked with several governmental agencies during the 1930s. During World War II he was director of the professional staff of the Information and Education Department of the War Department. In that position, he directed an important series of studies on attitudes of servicemen. In 1946 he went to Harvard, where he was director of the Laboratory of Social Relations and professor of sociology until his death on Aug. 24, 1960.

Stouffer's work was marked by a dominant interest in the use of varied research techniques, rather than a sustained focus on one or two topical areas in sociology. His doctoral dissertation dealt with the relative merits of the case-study method and the statistical approach. In the 1930s he critically reviewed data on marriage in his *Research Memorandum on the Family in the Depression* (1937), and he began to investigate the area of opinion research and mass communications, incorporating his findings in a chapter of Paul F. Lazarsfeld's *Radio and the Printed Page* (1940).

A sophisticated use of statistical methods by Stouffer was first widely recognized in his analysis of factors in migration (1940). He theorized that the number of migrants between two communities not only was influenced by the opportunities at the receiving community, but was modified or reduced by the presence of opportunities between home community and potential destination. By ingenious use of local rental data, he was able to obtain enough confirmation to stimulate several comparable studies of this basic problem that accurately described and partially explained migrant patterns in the United States.

Stouffer's stature as a research sociologist rests on his experience with survey research techniques, which came to fruition in studies on attitudes and difficulties of American military men during World War II. These were published in four volumes known as *The American Soldier* (1949-1950), with Stouffer as leading researcher, editor, or contributor. Stouffer and his associates not only developed useful research techniques (such as scalogram analysis), but demonstrated the importance of relativity in people's judgments of both their rewarding and frustrating social experiences.

In the last decade of his career, Stouffer turned to the study of attitudes in situations of conflicting values and roles. He became interested in the actual barriers to educational advancement and mobility among youngsters and, more generally, in the study of the compromises made by people faced by inconsistent moral directives. His major work in this area was the national survey on differences in tolerance of nonconformity, published as *Communism, Conformity, and Civil Liberties* (1955). Stouffer was able to show that tolerance was connected with education, urban residence, and personal optimism.

Further Reading

Several of Stouffer's articles and addresses are collected in his *Social Research to Test Ideas: Selected Writings* (1962), which includes a summary of his career by Paul F. Lazarsfeld. □

Luther (Lou) McKinley Stovall

Lou Stovall (born 1937) was credited by artists and critics alike with helping to transform the concept of silkscreen printmaking from a commercial craft to a true art form. He was also an accomplished draftsman, as well as a designer and builder of fine furniture.

Luther McKinley (Lou) Stovall was born in Athens, Georgia, on New Year's Day, 1937. When he was still a young boy his family moved to Springfield, Massachusetts, where Stovall's interest in printmaking was born. It was while working at a summer job in a grocery store that young Stovall discovered a printmaker making "Sale" signs for the store. Before returning to school at summer's end, he had begun assisting the printer.

Stovall's formal art education began in 1956 at the Rhode Island School of Design, where he studied for a semester before having to return home to help his family. In 1962 he enrolled at Howard University in Washington, D.C., under James A. Porter, the department head who became Stovall's adviser and mentor and who had written the definitive book on African American art. Stovall continued his printmaking studies at Howard under James Lesesne Wells, himself a renowned printmaker. When he graduated in 1966 with a BFA degree in art history Stovall had already established himself as a talented printmaker.

Following his graduation, Stovall began working as head designer at a sign shop in a Washington, D.C., suburb. He fulfilled his job responsibilities during the day and would then work on his own designs after hours. It was during this period at Botkin's Sign Shop in Silver Spring, Maryland, that Stovall produced countless posters for community, government, and labor groups and collaborated with Lloyd McNeill, a musician and fellow artist, on posters for jazz workshops.

By 1968 Stovall had opened his own studio (Workshop, Inc.), teaching silkscreen techniques to other artists while further refining his own style. He was joined thereafter by his assistant, Diane (Di) Bagley, who was later to become his wife and occasional collaborator.

Traditionally, the silkscreening process entails the cutting of a stencil, which is attached to the silkscreen in areas where the artist wishes to prevent the color from coming through. The color is then spread over the stencil with a rubber blade, where it passes onto the exposed silkscreen underneath. For each additional color used in a particular print, the artist must cut a new stencil. It is not unusual for a printmaker to cut dozens of stencils in order to complete a single silkscreen design.

By utilizing tools and techniques not customarily associated with silkscreening, Stovall's prints exhibit an intricacy not usually attained with the medium. In addition to the use of the traditional stencil and rubber blade, or "squeegee," Stovall painted directly on the silkscreen, using a color blocking lacquer. On other occasions he used sponges and large brushes to achieve subtle shading. When customary tools proved insufficient for his needs, Stovall created his own instruments in order to produce the thin, engraving-like lines found in many of his works.

Although he readily admitted to a fascination with the human form, Stovall's art never depicted people. Instead, he imbued his birds and landscapes with a human gracefulness.

It is from nature that Stovall received much of his inspiration. He was perhaps best known for his circular prints of flowers and landscapes, depicting flowing streams and graceful trees. In his trees, a favorite subject, Stovall's intricate style can be easily detected. One can almost feel the textures he has depicted on the trunks. In 1986, upon request, he made the print, *American Beauty Rose* for the Washington, D.C., Area Host Committee 1988 Democratic National Convention.

Besides producing his own designs, Stovall was frequently commissioned to make silkscreen prints of other artists' work, including that of Joseph Albers, Leon Berkowitz, Peter Blume, Alexander Calder, Chun Chen, Gene Davis, Tom Downing, Sam Gilliam, Sidney T. Guberman, Selma Hurwitz, Jacob Kainen, Jacob Lawrence, Robert Mangold, Mathieu Mategot, Pat Buckley Moss, Robert Newman, Paul Reed, Reuben Rubin, Roy Slade, Brockie Stevenson, Di Stovall, Franklin White, and James L. Wells.

Stovall's sensitivity to line and form was repeated in the furniture which he designed and built in his studio. He was sometimes commissioned to create both the furniture and artwork for a client and frequently built the frames for displaying his silkscreens.

Stovall's work has enjoyed exhibition throughout the United States, as well as in Japan and Moscow, USSR. (now part of the Federation of Russian Republics). He has also been featured in various fundraising events and benefits, making special contributions to diverse groups from Amnesty International to The Environmental Law Institute.

Further Reading

Stovall is listed in *Who's Who in American Art* (various editions). Keith Morrison, *Art in Washington and Its Afro-American Presence: 1940-1970* (1985) offers a look at the work of Stovall, his contemporaries, and some of the artists who influenced them. Jacquelyn Bontemps' catalogue, *Choosing,* offers another view of Stovall's silkscreens. *Through Their Eyes: The Art of Lou and Di Stovall* was published in conjunction with the Stovalls' exhibit at the Anacostia Neighborhood

Museum, Washington, D.C., in 1983. Also available through the Smithsonian Museum/Anacostia Neighborhood Museum is a video in which Stovall explains his craft. It was shown in conjunction with *Through Their Eyes.* In 1993, Stovall was interviewed for Ken Oda's *Newsletter,* a monthly newsletter for art collectors and professionals in the Washington, D. C., area. □

Harriet Elizabeth Beecher Stowe

The impact created in 1852 by the novel *Uncle Tom's Cabin* of Harriet Elizabeth Beecher Stowe (1811-1896) made her the most widely known American woman writer of the 19th century.

Harriet Beecher Stowe's personality and her work are mint products of her culture. They represent a special combination of rigid Calvinist discipline (fight against it though she tried), sentimental weakness for the romanticism of Sir Walter Scott and Lord Byron, and a crusading sense of social and political responsibility.

"Hattie" Beecher was born in Litchfield, Conn., on June 14, 1811, into a family of powerful and very demanding individuals. Her father, Lyman Beecher, was a fiery, evangelical Calvinist who drove his six sons and two daughters along the straight and narrow path of devotion to God, to duty, and to himself. Her mother, Roxana Foote Beecher, died when she was 4, leaving a legacy of quiet gentleness and a brother—the Beecher children's uncle Samuel Foote. Uncle Sam, retired sea captain, brought a sense of romance and adventure into the household, as well as a measure of warm tolerance which might otherwise have been absent.

In October 1832 the family moved to Cincinnati, where the elder Beecher became director of the Lane Theological Seminary and where his older daughter, Catherine, opened her Western Female Institute, a school in which Harriet taught.

In 1834 she began writing for the *Western Monthly Magazine* and was awarded a $50 prize for her tale "A New England Sketch." Her writing during the next 16 years was to be sketchy indeed, for on Jan. 6, 1836, she married Calvin Ellis Stowe, a professor in the Lane Seminary, and they had seven children during a period of financial hardship. At the same time she did, however, have the opportunity to visit the South, and she observed with particular attention the operation of the slave system there. The atmosphere at the Lane Seminary was abolitionist in the extreme, but Harriet herself did not at that time espouse this position. In 1849 she published her first volume, *The Mayflower,* a slender book but one which convinced her husband that she should aspire seriously to a literary career.

Uncle Tom's Cabin

In 1850 Calvin Stowe was called to a chair at Bowdoin College in Brunswick, Maine, where they had their last child. She then set about writing *Uncle Tom's Cabin,* which first appeared in serial form in 1851-1852 in the *National Era,* a Washington, D.C., antislavery newspaper. The book was published in 1852 in a two-volume edition by the house of John P. Jewett and sold 300,000 copies in its first year—10,000 in the first week. During the first 5 years of its publication, the book sold half a million copies in America alone.

Though *Uncle Tom's Cabin* was received with wild attention, its reception was (except for the abolitionist press) almost uniformly hostile. Not only in the South, where each newspaper was a sea of fury, but also in the North there were universal charges that the world of the slave had been melodramatically misrepresented. The action of the book traces the passage of the slave Uncle Tom through the hands of three owners, each meant to represent a type of Southern figure. The first is a benevolent planter, the second a highbred gentleman, and the last the infamous Simon Legree, who causes the death of Uncle Tom. The fortunes of the slaves in the book curve downward, and the finally successful dash for freedom taken by George and Eliza constitutes the high drama of the book. But the overall treatment of slave and master reveals something far more complex than an abolitionist tract: the high, eloquent style contains much that is warmly, even fiercely sympathetic to the world of the old South.

Stowe answered her critics in 1853 with *A Key to Uncle Tom's Cabin,* a book designed to document the facts of the novel, but she also responded to her success by traveling widely, receiving in England and on the Continent a perfect wave of acclamation. In 1856 she published her novel *Dred: A Tale of the Great Dismal Swamp.* This, too, was a slave novel, and its reception was hardly less enthusiastic than that of *Uncle Tom's Cabin.* In England alone, during the first month, over 100,000 copies were sold. Although Stowe then turned to a less didactic dimension, producing a series of novels based on New England and drawing heavily on local color, her reputation for years to come was connected with the didactic power of her first two novels. Indeed, when she was introduced to Abraham Lincoln in 1862, he is said to have exclaimed, "So this is the little lady who started our big war!"

Later Years

In 1869 Stowe again toured Europe, renewing an earlier friendship with Lord Byron's widow. As a result, the novelist published *Lady Byron Vindicated* (1870), charging the dead poet with having so violated his marriage vows as to have had an incestuous relationship with his sister. Byron was a legend by this time, and the charges resulted in alienating much of Stowe's hitherto loyal British audience. Undisturbed, however, she continued her series of novels, poems, and sketches, as well as her autobiography, never wanting for a devoted and enthusiastic American audience.

The later years of her life were spent, in large part, in Florida, where she and her husband tried, with only moderate success, to manage the income from her literary activities. Stowe died in Hartford, Conn., on July 1, 1896.

Further Reading

Forrest Wilson, *Crusader in Crinoline: The Life of Harriet Beecher Stowe* (1941), consolidates earlier work. Lyman Beecher Stowe, *Saints, Sinners and Beechers* (1934), supplies the crucial family context. See also John R. Adams, *Harriet Beecher Stowe* (1963). For critical works consult Harry Birdoff, *The World's Greatest Hit: Uncle Tom's Cabin* (1947); Charles H. Foster, *The Rungless Ladder: Harriet Beecher Stowe and New England Puritanism* (1954); Joseph Chamberlin Furnas, *Goodbye to Uncle Tom* (1956); and Edmund Wilson; *Patriotic Gore: Studies in the Literature of the American Civil War* (1962). A complete list of Mrs. Stowe's work can be found in Robert E. Spiller and others, eds., *Literary History of the United States,* vol. 3 (1948; 3d ed. 1963). □

Strabo

Strabo (ca. 64 B.C.-ca. A.D. 23) was a Greek geographer and historian who saw the final collapse of the Roman Republic and the creation by Augustus of the Roman Empire. He wrote large-scale works in his fields.

Strabo was born in the Greek city of Amisea in the district of Pontus, probably in the winter of 64/63 B.C. He came from a wealthy and distinguished family and had an excellent education, first in Asia Minor and later in Rome, which he first visited sometime before the death of Julius Caesar in 44. He returned to Asia Minor but in 29 went back to Rome. There he met several prominent men, including Aelius Gallus, who obtained for him a grant of Roman citizenship. When Gallus went to Egypt as governor in 28 or 27, Strabo accompanied him, toured the province with him, and probably took part in Gallus's unsuccessful expedition into Arabia. Strabo stayed in Egypt for a time after Gallus's recall, but eventually he returned to Rome, where he lived for many years, devoting himself to studying and writing. He may have spent his last years in his native city and died probably in A.D. 23 or 24.

Historical and Geographical Works

Strabo's history, now lost, had the modest title of *Historical Notes* but was in fact a large-scale history in 43 books. It was essentially a continuation of the great work of the Greek historian Polybios and covered the history of the Greco-Roman world from 144 to 30 B.C.

Strabo's *Geography,* also a substantial work, was in 17 books. It has survived complete, except for the end of book 7, and was finished sometime between A.D. 17 and 23, though some sections were clearly written much earlier. In the first two books, Strabo examines the theoretical basis of his subject and discusses the views of his predecessors, especially Eratosthenes. The rest of the work contains a detailed descriptive geography of the world as known in his time, starting with Spain and continuing through the other European lands to Greece, Asia Minor, and further Asia (that is, India, Persia, and Syria) and concluding with Egypt and North Africa. In each country he discusses not only the main

physical features but also its products and the character and history of its inhabitants. To some extent he depended on his own observations, but for the most part he drew his material from the works of earlier writers. He usually showed good sense in choosing his sources, though sometimes the information he derived was outdated. In general the *Geography* is a very valuable compilation of facts and gives an interesting picture of the world as it was known to educated men in the Augustan Age. But it was not merely a collection of data; Strabo wrote fine Greek prose and used considerable artistry in the organization of his material, making his opus the best of its kind to be handed down from antiquity.

Further Reading

The only complete modern translation of Strabo, with an introduction on his life and works, is *The Geography of Strabo* by Horace L. Jones (8 vols., 1917-1933). Numerous extracts in translation are in Eric H. Warmington, *Greek Geography* (1934). Henry F. Tozer, *History of Ancient Geography* (1897; 2d ed. 1964), still the standard work on the science of geography in Greco-Roman times, contains a good brief account of Strabo and his geographical work.

For a good account of the growth of geographical knowledge see Max Cary and Eric H. Warmington, *The Ancient Explorers* (1929). Max Cary, *Geographic Background of Greek and Roman History* (1949), a survey of Mediterranean geography with special reference to classical times, contains excellent sections on Greece, Asia Minor, and Italy. An interesting discussion of Strabo and other Greek writers in the context of Roman society in the Augustan Age is in Glen W. Bowersock, *Augustus and the Greek World* (1964). The best account of the Roman world during Strabo's lifetime is in Howard H. Scullard, *From the Gracchi to Nero* (1959; 2d ed. 1963). □

John Strachan

John Strachan (1778-1867) was the first Anglican bishop of Toronto and one of the most important members of the ruling oligarchy in Upper Canada. He was also an educator and the founder of the University of Toronto.

John Strachan was born on April 12, 1778, at Aberdeen, Scotland. He was educated at the University of Aberdeen and at St. Andrews. In 1799, unable to find an attractive living in Scotland, he emigrated to British North America and during the next 12 years taught school in Upper Canada.

In May 1803 Strachan accepted orders in the Church of England. In 1812 he was made rector of York (Toronto) and chaplain to the troops. By the end of the War of 1812 he had emerged as one of the prominent men of York. He was rewarded in 1815 with an appointment as an honorary member of the governor's executive council, and in 1817 he became a full member.

In 1820 Strachan became a member as well of the legislative council, and from 1818 to 1828 he acted as the chief adviser to the lieutenant governor, Sir Peregrine Maitland. In May 1823, in addition to his other duties, Strachan was appointed president of the Board of the General Superintendence of Education.

In 1825 Strachan was appointed archdeacon of York. By the mid-1830s, as his religious duties became more burdensome, he withdrew more and more from participation in political affairs. On Aug. 4, 1839, he was consecrated the first bishop of Toronto in Lambeth Palace Chapel. The balance of his long life was to be devoted to his diocese and to education.

In 1827 Strachan had obtained a royal charter for the founding of the University of King's College, York, but the first classes were not held until 1843. Through the 1840s Strachan had to oppose a number of governmental plans to secularize the university, and he finally lost this struggle in 1850. He immediately began to plan for a new university which would be under the control of the Church of England, and Trinity College admitted its first students in January 1852.

In 1854 Strachan lost another lengthy battle when the clergy reserves were secularized; with their secularization went the last hope of establishment for the Church of England in Canada. He died in Toronto on Nov. 1, 1867.

Further Reading

John L. H. Henderson, ed., *John Strachan: Documents and Opinions* (1969), is an excellent collection of Strachan's writings which reveals much of the man and his times. George Spragge edited many of Strachan's letters in the *John Strachan Letter*

Book, 1812-1834 (1946). Alexander Bethune wrote a life of his episcopal predecessor, *Memoir of the Right Reverend John Strachan* (1870). Two recent studies are Sylvia Boorman, *John Toronto: A Biography of Bishop Strachan* (1969), and John L. H. Henderson, *John Strachan, 1778-1867* (1969), a brief but useful and sympathetic portrait.

Additional Sources

Phelps, Dorothy J., *John Strachan comes to Cornwall, 1803-1812,* Cornwall, Ont.: Vesta Publications, 1976. □

Giles Lytton Strachey

Giles Lytton Strachey (1880-1932) was an English biographer and critic known for his satire of the Victorian Era.

Lytton Strachey was born in London on March 1, 1880. He was the eleventh of thirteen children of an upper-middle-class family. His father, Sir Richard Strachey, was a colonial Indian civil servant and civil engineer and a British army general; he was a typical Victorian explorer/scientist. Sir Richard's second wife, Lytton's mother, was the daughter of Sir J. P. Grant of Rothiemurchus and was keen on French literature; she influenced Lytton's precocious literary talent. Even though Lytton's family members on both sides were well-connected and prosperous, the large parental home in unfashionable Bayswater was "suffocating" to him. He was a spoiled child, of frail health, and always withdrawn. Even so, he had an iron will and sat in cultural judgment of the world his parents inhabited: the Victorian era.

For primary education Strachey went to uncongenial upper-class boarding schools in Derbyshire and to Leamington College. He left the "petticoat world of Victorian schoolrooms" for Liverpool University in 1897, where Professor Walter Raleigh, his tutor in history and literature, was the main object of Lytton's hero worship. He began a new six-year phase of his life at Cambridge: the world suddenly opened up in 1899.

It was at Trinity College, and later at King's College, that he met most of his intellectual friends, among them the philosopher G. E. Moore (1873-1958), the economist John Maynard Keynes (1883-1946), the novelist E. M. Forster (1879-1970), the critic and publisher Leonard Woolf (1880-1969), and the art critic Clive Bell (1881-1964). As Cambridge undergraduates they were privileged to join a society called "The Apostles", an elite, exotic group devoted to the arts and an ambivalent way of life in which traditional wisdom and customary middle-class morals were discarded, especially where sex was concerned. The Apostles were personally affected by the philosophy of G. E. Moore. Lytton Strachey saw in Moore's doctrines the importance of aesthetic experience and the gospel of personal friendship. These were the attributes of the "good life." But "friendship" meant, for Strachey, homosexual love. He turned a blind eye to Moore's inherent puritanism. Strachey and Maynard Keynes were often furiously in love with the same male students, and often Keynes won the upper hand.

After partly failing in Cambridge (with a second-class degree and no fellowship at Trinity), Strachey went to London to endure 13 years of penny-pinching frustration as a weekly reviewer for the *Spectator,* edited by his pedigreed cousin. He fell in with the Bloomsbury Group, the same sort of society in London as the Cambridge Apostles (their leading members were the same). One of the leading "Bloomsberries" was the "stream of consciousness" novelist Virginia Woolf (1882-1941), the sister of Vanessa Bell. Lytton had previously proposed marriage to Virginia (which he did not mean), but she had turned him down. Of all the Bloomsberries, Strachey took precedence (for instance, the Bloomsbury Group began to decline after his own death in 1932).

In 1912 Strachey published his first book, on French literary history, *Landmarks in French Literature,* designed to awaken English readers to the charms of Racine and French classics. Two years later, World War I broke out. The war was a direct challenge, as Lytton saw it, to Bloomsbury pacifist ı ·inciples. He managed to be a "conscientious objector" to the war. To the standard question; "If a German soldier tried to rape your sister, what would you do?" Strachey slyly replied; "I would try to interpose my own body." The war was of no consequence to Lytton's endless "partying" in country houses, nor to his writing schedule. He published his major book, *Eminent Victorians,* in 1918.

"Eminent" in the book's title was satirical. The themes, common to the four biographical sketches of the volume, were the sacred icons of Victorian sentiment: patriotic fervor and Christian messianic zeal, the ideal of the "public" school, and humanitarianism, as opposed to what Strachey thought were the perils of upper-class education, self-interested do-goodism, and, above all, the sins of Victorian imperialism. The four objects of Strachey's satire were Cardinal H. E. Manning, formerly a prominent Anglican member of the Oxford Movement, converted to Catholicism in 1851; Florence Nightingale, the "Lady with the Lamp," a founder of nursing and active with the wounded in the Crimean War; Thomas Arnold of Rugby School; and General C. G. "Chinese" Gordon, the pious hero killed by Mahdi raiders in the siege of Khartoum in 1885.

Strachey's book of polemical essays caused a popular sensation. Almost instantly the postwar era plunged into "anti-Victorianism." The war-weary generation wanted to hear this wholesale assault on past idols. But in his next book, *Queen Victoria* (1921), Strachey was seduced by his subject. "Mordant irony" was replaced by grudging respect for the queen, even though Strachey felt himself amused by her antics. Seven years later he produced *Elizabeth and Essex* (1928), a book full of vulgarized Freudianism that tampered with actual Tudor history. Strachey was not a historical revisionist; for that he would have to have been a scholar. He was rather an artist with words.

His biographical creed was to paint a picture of the person from the author's viewpoint—never mind the scholarly inhibitions, never mind the search to find "the truth" of any human situation so far as is possible. He had a "laughing admiration" for the satirists of the 18th century, like Voltaire (1694-1778). He saw religion as Voltaire saw it, as a "ludicrous anachronism." Careers in public service were mainly full of political intrigue. But human relationships were the nexus of life itself. Strachey eschewed the standard "two fat volumes" of Victorian biographies (he saw these tomes as "hagiographies": treatment of the illustrious dead). He favored for himself brief biographies, the art of which rested on the subject's motive and personality as he saw it.

Strachey was fairly tall and excessively thin, with a disguising rust beard and a shrill voice. He wore bookworm spectacles. He had an air of sick, melancholic sadness; he sagged. With true friends he was quick of mind, caustic, and conspicuously, bitingly witty. In addition, he was overtly, ardently homosexual. The conspiracy of public silence by which the Apostles, Bloomsbury Group, and other circles in England kept hidden from the world their sexual proclivities is yet to be studied. Strachey's painstaking biographer, Michael Holroyd, revealed the Strachey letters, laying it all out in two volumes in 1967 and 1968 ("two fat volumes," as Strachey would have said). The Bloomsberries would "jump from sex to sex in making love."

The decline of Strachey's reputation came soon after his death. The humbug of the "eminent" Victorians was an easy target for Strachey to satirize, but it led critics to accuse him of caricature. It is hard for the satirist not to treat the world and its problems as pure comedy. There was an element of theater, of almost pantomime, in Strachey's treatment of the Victorians. One critic in 1931 isolated one word, "preposterous," which Strachey used over and over again, about his stick-figure characters. Leonard Woolf (1960) was on target, when he described the critic as "a strange character."

Irony is one thing; but it conceals too much from the author himself. Strachey was one of the literary influences that partly destroyed the ghost of the Victorian era in the 1920s.

Strachey died of cancer on January 21, 1932, surrounded by his friends, at Ham Spray House, Hungerford. Carrington committed suicide immediately after his death.

Further Reading

As mentioned in the text, the definitive biography of Strachey is Michael Holroyd, *Lytton Strachey: A Critical Biography* (2 vols., 1967, 1968). Authors who discuss Strachey in magazines include Edwin Muir, *Nation and Athenaeum* (April 25, 1925); John Raymond, *New Statesman and Nation* (April 16, 1955); Scott James, *BC/Longmans* (1955); Gertrude Himmelfarb, *New Republic* (May 28, 1968); and Noel Annan, *New York Review of Books* (June 6, 1968). See also David Cecil, *DNB,* (*Dictionary of National Biography;* London, 1931-1940). An interesting account of Strachey and other members of the Bloomsbury group is provided by John Keith Johnstone, in *The Bloomsbury Group; a study of E.M. Forster, Lytton Strachey, Virginia Woolf, and Their Circle* (Noonday Press, 1954). □

Antonio Stradivari

Italian violin maker Antonio Stradivari (c. 1644-1737) created instruments that are still considered the finest ever made. The new styles of violins and cellos that he developed were remarkable for their excellent tonal quality and became the basic design for all modern versions of the instruments.

Antonio Stradivari, also known by the Latin form of his name, Antonius Stradivarius, was a master craftsman who revolutionized the design of the violin. The instruments that he crafted in the late 1600s and early 1700s are considered to be the finest ever made because of the unsurpassed quality of their tone. Of the approximately 650 of his violins known still to exist, many continue to be played by musicians today. Stradivari also accomplished a similar redesign of the cello, setting the standard for the styles of violins and cellos used in later centuries. But the exact qualities of Stradivari's creations have never been able to be reproduced, making the stringed instruments that bear his name the most valuable and sought after in the world.

There were no records of Stradivari's birth, but based on the documentation of his age that accompanied his signature on some of the instruments he created late in his life, it was assumed that he was born in 1644. There was also little that is known about his youth. He was probably born in Cremona, Italy, the city where his family had been established for five centuries, and he was the son of Alessandro Stradivari. Cremona was a town that had been renowned for its master violin makers for nearly 100 years. Its leading craftsman during Stradivari's early life was Niccolo Amati, who represented the third generation of his family to contribute to the development of the traditional violin style popular at that time. Stradivari was probably apprenticed to Amati by the early 1660s and under his direction learned the craft of violin making.

Experimented with Violin Design

By 1666, Stradivari was producing instruments independently as well as continuing to work at his mentor's shop, which he probably did until Amati's death in 1684. In 1667, he was married to Francesca Feraboschi and set up his own household and shop; the couple eventually had six children and two of their sons would follow in their father's footsteps as violin makers. In the decade or so before 1680, Stradivari created a wide variety of stringed instruments, including guitars, harps, lutes, and mandolins. He continued to follow Amati's basic design for violins, but during this time he began experimenting with improvements in tone and design. The small number of instruments he created were primarily sold in Cremona, and he was not well-known outside the city in these years.

The Stradivari family moved to a new house at No. 2, Piazza San Domenico in 1680, and the building would serve as the violin maker's home and workshop for the rest of his life. Here he matured in his art and created his greatest works, most notably the violins that set the standard for perfection in the music world. In the 1680s, he continued to develop his own style, deviating from Amati's design to create a more solid-looking violin that used new materials and finishes. The resulting instruments during this time created a more powerful sound than earlier violins, and musicians from outside Cremona began to seek out instruments from his workshop as his fame grew. Upon Amati's death in 1684, Stradivari was considered the city's greatest violin maker.

Despite his considerable success with his designs, Stradivari continued to look for ways to improve his violins. In the 1690s, he experimented with the length of the instrument, creating what was known as the "long pattern" or "long Strad"—a violin that was 5/16 of an inch longer than the traditional pattern. The result was a deeper, fuller tone that was quite distinct from the lighter sounds of other Cremona instrument makers. Stradivari's wife died in 1698, and she was honored with a large funeral. In the summer of the following year, the craftsman married his second wife, Antonia-Maria Zambelli. He had five more children from this marriage, but none of them ever entered the instrument-making business.

Created Finest Works in "Golden Period"

The years from 1700 to 1720 were the greatest of Stradivari's career and the era was often referred to as the "golden period" of the artisan. It was during this time that he perfected his violin design and created his finest instruments. He discontinued his work with the long pattern during this time, instead creating violins that blended the qualities of the dark, rich tones of his earlier instruments with the brighter, sweet sounds of the traditional Cremona violin. Not only was his design revolutionary, but the materials he used also helped to create his unique effects. He selected excellent wood, such as maple, for his violins and developed the orange-brown varnish that became a trademark of his work. His works from this period were so magnificent that some violins created at this time have developed individual identities and reputations. Some of the most famous include the 1704 "Betts" violin, now in the United States Library of Congress, the 1715 "Alard," which is considered the finest Strativarius in existence, and the 1716 "Messiah," an instrument that Stradivari never sold and is now in the best condition of any of his surviving pieces.

The cello also underwent a similar transformation at the hands of Stradivari during the golden period. Cellos before his time were larger than modern instruments and served primarily as an accompaniment instrument in the bass range. But performers seeking to use the cello for solo performances wanted a smaller instrument that was more expressive in tone. Stradivari became interested in this growing need among musicians and between 1707 and 1710 created a number of smaller cellos that became the models for modern instruments.

After 1720, Stradivari continued to produce violins and other stringed instruments, but the number of items decreased through the years. And while his work maintained a high level of quality, it began to show the effects of failing eyesight and a less steady hand. His sons, Francesco and Omobono, had become assistants of their father in his business, and they began to collaborate with him and another employee, Carlo Bergonzi, to produce instruments that bear the inscription of being created "under the discipline of Antonio Stradivari." But Stradivari also produced instruments on his own until his death at the age of 93 on December 18, 1737. His second wife had died just nine months earlier. They were both buried in a tomb located just across the street from their house at the Chapel of the Rosary of the Church of San Domenico. By the 1800s, the chapel had fallen into disrepair and was eventually demolished. All that remained of Stradivari's final resting place was the stone bearing his name that had appeared on his tomb; it was now located in the Cremona Civic Museum, which also housed personal items belonging to Stradivari, including original drawings and designs for his instruments.

Quality Instruments Remain Unequaled

Although Stradivari is best remembered for his exceptional violins, the patterns that he created have become the basis for instruments used today. Some of the secrets of his craft have never been completely unraveled, however, despite investigations into the materials that were used in Strativarius violins. While his accomplishments may never be duplicated, it was generally assumed that the beautiful sound of his instruments was due to the unique combination of design, materials, and workmanship that Stradivari had developed during his long and successful career. Many people felt that his instruments were the best ever produced, and their use by leading musicians hundreds of years after his death were a testament to the genius of Stradivari.

Further Reading

Balfoort, Dirk J., *Antonius Stradivarius,* translated by W. A. G. Doyle-Davidson, Continental Book Company (Stockholm), 1947.

Hill, W. Henry, Arthur E. Hill, and Alfred E. Hill, *Antonio Stradivari: His Life and Work (1644-1737),* William E. Hill and Sons, 1902. □

1st Earl of Strafford

The English statesman Thomas Wentworth, 1st Earl of Strafford (1593-1641), was lord deputy of Ireland from 1632 to 1640. In Ireland he autocratically enforced, with his hated policy of "Thorough," the King's rule and the King's peace. Later he became Charles I's chief adviser.

Thomas Wentworth was born on April 13, 1593. He derived from a knightly family long established at Wentworth-Woodhouse, Yorkshire. He was educated at Cambridge and at the Inns of Court, London. He spent a year traveling on the Continent after his marriage to the eldest daughter of the Earl of Cumberland. Upon his return to England he was elected to Parliament from Yorkshire in 1614.

In 1621 Wentworth was again elected knight of the shire, and the courtier Lord (George) Calvert was his fellow member. Wentworth evidently supported Calvert's policy of peace with Spain. He joined the critics of the Duke of Buckingham, who favored war with Spain. For this reason he was excluded from Parliament by being made a sheriff of Yorkshire.

In 1625 the widowed Wentworth married Arabella Holles, second daughter of the Earl of Clare. She was the sister of Denzil Holles, a leader of the parliamentary opposition. Wentworth's continued opposition to war with Spain led him to move to the ranks of the opposition in the first year of Charles I's reign. In 1627 Wentworth's opposition went so far that he refused to pay a forced loan and was imprisoned for 6 months.

King Charles I sought Wentworth's adherence by creating him baron and viscount in 1628 and by naming him lord president of the Council of the North. As lord president, Wentworth carried out, in cooperation with the King, the tasks of orderly civil government, which were congenial to him. Any derogation of royal power in the North was quickly punished.

Lord Deputy of Ireland

On Jan. 12, 1632, Wentworth was named lord deputy of Ireland. He determined to bring a maximum portion of land in Ireland under the direct administration of the Crown and to improve the royal income and power. He brought his harsh rule of "Thorough" to Ireland. The philosophy of "Thorough" was summed up in Wentworth's words: "Princes are to be the indulgent nursing fathers to their people. . . . [The people] repose safe and still under the protection of their sceptres." Wentworth summoned the Irish Parliament in 1634, and it granted a large tax revenue to the government. He initiated a program of clearing the Irish Channel of pirates in order to stimulate trade, and he patronized the linen industry in order to increase customs revenues. To the Anglican Church, that faithful adjunct of royal power, he often restored Church lands that had been alienated to Protestant laymen. Finally, he left the titles of Catholic landlords uncertain as the prelude to a massive expropriation and resettlement by English colonists. Wentworth's wealth increased enormously. He farmed the Irish customs at a profit and acquired five manors representing nearly 60,000 acres. He remained lord president of the North and derived large revenues from there, especially from fines on Roman Catholics (recusants).

In 1639 Wentworth returned to England in order to defend his treatment of subordinate English officials. He was exonerated, created 1st Earl of Strafford, and became a chief adviser to Charles I. Created lord lieutenant of Ireland in 1640, Strafford raised a largely Catholic Irish army to use against the Scots. He was forced, however, to leave this army in Ireland.

Strafford also recommended a Parliament that he expected to dominate, but when it did not cooperate, he concurred in its dismissal. His military efforts proved unavailing against Scotland, and when Parliament was again summoned in November 1640, its chief order of business was the destruction of Strafford. He ably defended himself against an impeachment of treason. But he was powerless against the legislative device of a bill of attainder, which defined his autocratic acts in Ireland and in managing the war against the Scots as a constructive subversion (treason) against the whole frame of legal government in England. After long hesitation, Charles I signed the bill, and Strafford was beheaded on May 12, 1641.

Strafford's career represented the tension between parliamentary allegiance and royal service that so acutely divided his generation. His increasingly extreme advocacy of royal authority led to his fate on Tower Hill.

Further Reading

The standard biography, *Strafford* by C. V. Wedgwood (1935), was revised as *Thomas Wentworth, First Earl of Strafford, 1593-1641: A Revaluation* (1961), as a result of the publication of Hugh F. Kearney's influential *Strafford in Ireland, 1633-41: A Study in Absolutism* (1959).

Additional Sources

Kearney, Hugh F., *Strafford in Ireland, 1633-41: a study in absolutism,* Cambridge; New York: Cambridge University Press, 1989.

Timmis, John H., *Thine is the kingdom: the trial for treason of Thomas Wentworth, Earl of Strafford, First Minister to King Charles I and last hope of the English Crown,* University: University of Alabama Press, 1975 1974. □

Mark Strand

The fourth Poet Laureate of the United States (1996-1997), Mark Strand (born 1934) wrote poems on subjects ranging from dark and terrible wrestlings with one's fears and alter egos to joyous celebrations of life and light.

Mark Strand, the fourth American poet to be given the title of Poet Laureate, once remarked that he was intrigued by the epigraph from Jorge Luis Borges' story, "Tlon, Uqbar, Orbis Tertius": "while we sleep here, we are awake elsewhere and that in this way every man is two men."

Borges' idea, interestingly enough, describes the diversities and paradoxes inherent in the creative spirit of Mark Strand himself and the major themes and motifs that his poems and fictions dealt with over the years.

At times Strand's poetic voice is plain and conversational, sparse of detail almost to a fault, and filled with dark images of menace and foreboding; at other times, however, it is lively and sensuous, rich in specifics of time and place and abundantly joyous in its celebration of life and light.

In the title poem of his first volume, *Sleeping with One Eye Open* (1964), Strand introduces us to a nameless persona who speaks fearfully of the intense terror he feels while he lies in bed one night unable to sleep.

> The shivers
> Wash over
> Me, shaking my bones, my loose ends
> Loosen,
> And I lie sleeping with one eye open,
> Hoping
> That nothing, nothing will happen.

In *Reasons for Moving* (1968), his second volume, Strand continued to explore this theme of menace and foreboding. In "Violent Storm" his terrified persona finds himself threatened by a loud and terrible storm. He fears the coming of the night and the horrible uncertainty of what the darkness may bring.

> A cold we never knew invades our bones.
> We shake as though the storm were going to hurl
> us down
> Against the flat stones
> Of our lives. All other nights
> Seem pale compared to this, and the brilliant rise
> Of morning after morning seems unthinkable.

Judging from the merely external circumstances and events of Mark Strand's own life, such gut-wrenching fears and existential angst seem unwarranted, if not exaggerated.

He was born on April 14, 1934, in the quiet village of Summerside on Prince Edward Island in Canada to Robert Strand and the former Sonia Apter. He was educated at Antioch College in Ohio where he received his BA. Later, he went on to Yale where he studied painting under Josef Albers. When he decided that he was not quite good enough to become a major painter, Strand began to write. By the time he graduated he had already won two highly acclaimed awards, the Cook and Bergin prizes, for his collection of poetry. In 1960 he went to Italy with a Fulbright scholarship to the University of Florence. The following year he married Antonia Ratensky and had a daughter, Jessica. In 1974 he divorced and married Julia Garretson. He taught in over a dozen prestigious colleges and universities, earning numerous honors and awards for his poetry and fiction. Nevertheless, like the "man who is two men," Mark Strand is much more than the highly successful poet and popular professor who is very much at home in the world.

In *Darker* (1970), his third volume of poetry, his personae wrestle endlessly with their terrors and obsessions. This time, however, the enemy is no longer an outside force like the night or a violent storm. Now the enemy has become the *Self* itself, that haunting, elusive, bewildering alter ego with which so many of Strand's poetic counterparts are so obsessed.

"In Celebration" in his fourth volume, *The Story of Our Lives* (1973), Strand's speaker vividly expresses this idea when he remarks that "by giving yourself over to nothing, you shall be healed."

In "To Begin" Strand's persona becomes the artist-creator who knows full well the emptiness of the false Self and the "black map" of nothingness that is the world. He survives and endures, however, by attempting to shape words and images that will give life to new worlds and a new, more powerful Self. "He stared at the ceiling / and imagined his breath shaping itself into words."

Like every artist, and certainly every poet, however, the speaker also knows the terror of beginning anew, of facing again and again the blank canvas or the blank page.

In the dark he would still be uncertain about how
to begin.
He would mumble to himself; he would follow
his words to learn where he was.
He would begin.
And the room, the house, the field,
the woods beyond the field, would also begin,
and in the sound of his own voice beginning
he would hear them.

And yet, despite all his fortitude, Strand's persona comes once again to realize the frustration inherent in his paradoxical situation. Like the speaker in "The Untelling," he learns that the more he attempts to do and say, the less he will accomplish and succeed.

His pursuit was a form of evasion:
the more he tried to uncover
the more there was to conceal
the less he understood.
If he kept it up,
he would lose everything.

In Strand's fifth volume of poetry, *The Late Hour* (1978), several of his speakers try to avoid the whole question of self-confrontation and authentic self-realization by simply immersing themselves in the purely sensual pleasures of life and forgetting everything else. In "Pot Roast," another celebration of sorts, the protagonist recalls his childhood after inhaling the steam that rises from a plate of meat. He remembers the gravy, its odor of garlic and celery, and how he enjoyed sopping it up with pieces of bread.

And now
I taste it again
The meat of memory.
The meat of no change.
I raise my fork
and I eat.

In "For Jessica, My Daughter," Strand attempts to stay the terror of loss and confusion by celebrating the love that binds people together in a life filled with loss and separation.

Afraid of the dark
in which we drift or vanish altogether,
I imagine a light
that would not let us stray too far apart,
a secret moon or mirror,
a sheet of paper,
something you could carry
in the dark
when I am away.

For Strand, writing itself is the central paradox, the imagined light that will vanish the darkness but one day vanish itself like so many of his own "poems of air . . . too light for the page." But he continued to write, remembering and reinventing his life and Canadian childhood in such descriptive and nostalgic poems as "Shooting Whales," "Nights in Hackett's Cove," "A Morning," and "My Mother on an Evening in Late Summer" from his sixth and most personal and concretely detailed collection, *Selected Poems,* in 1980 (reissued in 1990).

Other poetry volumes by Strand include: *The Continuous Life* (1990) and *Dark Harbor* (1993) both Published by Alfred A. Knopf. He also translated Portuguese and Spanish poetry. In addition to his poetry, Strand wrote a long prose-poem, *The Monument* (1978); a collection of fiction, *Mr. and Mrs. Baby and Other Stories* (1985); three children's books, *The Planet of Lost Things* (1982), *The Night Book* (1985), and *Rembrandt Takes A Walk* (1986).

In addition to poetry, Strand has written works of art criticism, *Art of the Real: Nine American Figurative Painters* (1983) and *William Bailey* (1987). Strand was awarded the Rebekan Johnson Bobbitt National Prize for Poetry in 1992 and the Bollingen Prize in Poetry in 1993. In 1995 *The New Republic* magazine announced Strand's selection to replace Mary Jo Salter as their poetry editor. Strand was elected to the Board of Chancellors of the Academy of American Poets in 1996.

He also translated and edited numerous anthologies of modern poetry and Latin American fiction.

Further Reading

In addition to the works by Strand cited in the text see David Kirby, *Mark Strand and the Poet's Place in Contemporary Culture* (1990) and Richard Howard, *Alone with America: Essays on the Art of Poetry in the United States Since 1950* (1971). See also the following biographical/critical sources: *Yale Review* (Autumn 1968); *Contemporary Literature* (1969); *Virginia Quarterly Review* (Summer 1969); *Antioch Review* (Fall/Winter 1970-1971); and Carolyn Riley, editor, *Contemporary Literary Criticism,* Volume VI (1976). □

Ruth May Strang

The many-sided interests of Ruth May Strang (1895-1971) over her 40 years at Columbia University and the University of Arizona earned international respect for her achievements in the fields of student guidance, reading and communication, child study, mental health, and development and adjustment.

Ruth May Strang was born on April 3, 1895, in Chatham, New Jersey. She grew up in the greater New York City area, spending the first ten years of her life on the family farm in South Jamaica, New York. Her father, Charles Garret Strang, gave up his interest in becoming a lawyer to provide much needed help on the family farm. His career disappointment appeared to leave a strong impression on young Ruth. Her father was the disciplinarian in the family, while her mother, Anna Bergen Strang, a "gentle woman," "always a lady," would be "likely to cry" when the children were bad.

Strang was the youngest of three children. Her two older brothers (one 15 years older) were concerned about her choice of a career over attention to family. This was to create a lasting tension in her relations with them. She attended Adelphi Academy in Brooklyn, was active on the school's basketball team, and participated as a member of the German and Walking Clubs. After graduation she studied household science at Pratt Institute in Brooklyn (1914-1916) and for a while was employed as an assistant to an interior decorator.

Strang's memory of her childhood was one of tension and conflict. As the only girl, her role, as viewed by her parents, was a domestic one. "I was not expected to go to college and my school marks were accepted without special comment." She remembers having no "clearly defined self-image during childhood or adolescence. I did what my hands found to do but always wanted to do something new and different." Ruth's strong sense of individuality made it difficult to find a role model. She wanted to be original—different. Even the characters she read about in fiction were not complete models, "although they had certain qualities" she wanted to appropriate. This memory of her early years at home and in school was to leave a lasting influence on her approach to career choice and opportunity throughout her life. She recalled later in life that the "atmosphere of anxiety" in which she was reared "may have reinforced a strong persistent tendency to worry and to anticipate the worst, to see a calamity in every opportunity."

Career and Honors

Strang's career was one of success over "calamity." Unplanned, it developed as opportunities appeared. "I developed my interests and abilities and doors seemed to open." She launched her career in education by teaching home economics in New York City public schools from 1917 to 1920. Recognizing that as a teacher she needed to broaden her education, Strang enrolled at Columbia University's Teachers College and earned her B.S. degree in home economics in 1922. While working on the M.A. degree (1923-1924) she worked as a research assistant in nutrition. As a Ph.D. student Strang worked as an instructor in health education and supervised health education at Teachers College's Horace Mann School. During her last year of doctoral study Strang worked as a research assistant in psychology.

Upon completion of the doctorate in 1926, opportunity opened its door and Strang accepted a year-long research fellowship at Teachers College in student personnel work, a field in its infancy. At the time only one book and a few scattered articles represented the total field. Dean James Russell had handed her the challenge to build a body of subject matter in the field. Student personnel work and its related fields were to dominate Strang's professional interests for the remainder of her career. A close associate, Amelia Melnik, said that "it became evident to Dr. Strang that the field was as many sided as the human personality with which it is connected."

Strang spent the summers of 1926, 1927, and 1928 at North Carolina College for Women in Greensboro as head resident and instructor in psychology. In 1929 Strang was appointed assistant professor of education at Teachers College. She was promoted to associate professor in 1936 and to full professor in 1940. This relatively rapid rise in rank was quite significant for a woman in higher education in the 1920s and 1930s.

Charles Burgess has noted that Ruth Strang played a part in forming a "new minority of American Women—the female professor." It was "one thing to get through the door of academe," said Burgess, "and quite another thing for a woman to pass beyond the level of instructor or assistant professor." Strang was one of the few who succeeded. She did so in a male world by building a "usefully protective reputation as a 'loner' as one who did her work with quiet dispatch . . . and left departmental affairs to men—and to more socially aggressive women—on the faculty.

Strang remained at Teachers College until she reached the mandatory retirement age of 65. She continued her work at the University of California at Berkeley during the summer session of 1960. In the fall of that year she accepted a position as professor of education at the University of Arizona at Tucson. In 1968 she went to the Ontario Institute for Studies in Education at Toronto as Peter Sandiford Visiting Professor. In 1955 Strang became president of the National Association of Remedial Teachers, and from 1935 to 1960 she edited the *journal of the National Association of Women Deans and Counselors.* In 1960 Strang was chairman of the National Society for the Study of Education. She was a director of the American Association for Gifted Children and a fellow of the American Public Health Association, the American Association of Applied Psychology, and the Royal Society of Health in Great Britain.

Ideas and Contributions

According to one biographer, Strang's ideals rested on some of the most familiar values of the American experience: the Protestant ethic and those values associated with small-town rural America. It was especially the Protestant ethic that was central to her philosophy of life. Hard Work, duty, and stewardship were guideposts. Strang believed that humans were duty bound to give returns for their gifts "in the forms of self-development and social usefulness." Burgess noted that "the former had the latter as its crowning achievement."

Strang's educational philosophy was represented in her own version of the child-centered approach enhanced by child study. To Strang, "learning children as well as teaching them" was essential. Although her professional attention through the years was given to a wide range of educational matters from nutrition, child study, and mental health to reading improvement, Strang's abiding commitment was to student guidance in all of its dimensions. A former student remembered a comment Strang made toward the end of a course. "If you remember nothing else from our work together, remember that it is the guidance point of view that must permeate your entire school and build its esprit." Strang found her "greatest classroom interests" in her course on the role of the teacher in personnel work.

Strang's devotion to her work completely ruled out marriage. Not too long before her death she wrote: "My work has always been so exacting and demanding that social activities other than those directly related to my work have been crowded out. My chief satisfactions have been the responsiveness of classes and other audiences, the success and friendship of my students, the excitement of new ideas, and the 'things of beauty' that John Keats describes."

Death came in January 1971 after a long illness. Strang was 75 years old. She left no immediate survivors.

Further Reading

Ruth May Strang is listed in *Biographical Dictionary of American Educators, Who's Who in America* (1960-1961), and *Who's Who of American Women* (1961). There is no major biographical treatment of her life available. Two works, however, are important: Ruth M. Strang, "An Autobiographical Sketch," and Charles Burgess, "Ruth Strang: A Biographical Sketch." Each appeared in *Leaders in American Education,* The Seventieth Yearbook of the National Society of Education, Part II (1971). Appearing in that same edition is a selected bibliography of Strang's massive publications. Helpful concerning the last years of Strang's life are the obituaries appearing in the *New York Times* (January 5, 1971); *Journal of Reading* (April 1971), *National Association of Women Deans and Counselors Journal* (Spring 1971), and the *Reading Teacher* (April 1971). Essential in appreciating Strang's massive research and writing contributions is Amelia Melnik, "The Writings of Ruth Strang," *Teachers College Record.* The bibliography was grouped under eight areas in education: guidance and student personnel, reading and communication, health education, psychology and mental health, general education, gifted children, and groups work. Three types of contributions were given: research studies, summaries of research for professional workers, and practical books and articles and books for administrators, teachers, parents, children, and young people. □

Lee Strasberg

Lee Strasberg (1901-1982) was best known as a founding member of the Group Theatre and as the main teacher of "Method" acting in the United States.

Lee Strasberg was born Israel Strasberg in Galicia, then part of Austria-Hungary, on November 17, 1901. He was brought to Manhattan's Lower East Side at age seven. Strasberg's father was a garment worker and was active in a trade union which supported community theater. It was in this Yiddish Theatre that Strasberg was first exposed to the naturalistic style of acting. While he was still a young boy he joined the amateur Progressive Dramatic Club, whose leaders were quite familiar with the theories of Constantine Stanislavsky, the great acting coach and director of the Moscow Art Theatre.

After leaving Townsend Harris High School in 1918 to work as a clerk in a wig factory, he studied acting at the American Laboratory Theatre under Richard Boleslavsky and Maria Ouspenskaya, both former students of Stanislavsky. He also gained his first experience as a director as a member of an amateur theatrical group that produced plays in the Christie Street Settlement House, a social center on the Lower East Side.

Strasberg's professional career in the theater began when he joined the Theatre Guild as an actor and assistant stage manager in 1924. It was at the Theatre Guild that Strasberg met Harold Clurman and Cheryl Crawford, two young Theatre Guild staffers who were dissatisfied with the commercial bent of the New York theater scene. Strasberg, Clurman, and Crawford began to meet informally with other similarly discontented young theater people, and eventually these informal meetings grew into rehearsals and workshops. In 1931 the Theatre Guild released the rights to Paul

Green's *The House of Connelly* to the young idealists, and the Group Theatre was born on Broadway.

The Group Theatre was a unique establishment in the history of the American theater. Under the leadership of Strasberg, Clurman, and Crawford, the Group attempted to establish a company of actors, designers, directors, and playwrights who would create artistically notable works for the Broadway stage while maintaining social accountability. The Group Theatre's policies and practices fostered the talents of such notable names as Lee J. Cobb, Clifford Odets, and Elia Kazan (who started with the Group as an intern actor), among others. Strasberg blossomed as a director and acting coach with the Group, achieving his greatest success with Sidney Kingsley's *Men in White* (1933), for which the author won the 1934 Pulitzer Prize. In his account of the Group Theatre, *The Fervent Years* (1957), Harold Clurman described Strasberg as "one of the few artists among American theatre directors. He is the director of introverted feeling, of strong emotion curbed by ascetic control. . . . The effect he produces is a classic hush, tense and tragic. . . . The roots are clearly in the intimate experience of a complex psychology, an acute awareness of human contradiction and suffering."

Strasberg left the Group in 1937 and pursued interests in Hollywood through most of the 1940s. He returned to Broadway to direct occasionally, achieving success with such works as Clifford Odets' *Clash by Night* (1941). He returned to New York to stay in 1948 to become the director and dominant force of the Actors Studio, an organization started by Kazan, Crawford, and Robert Lewis. The Studio was to be a workshop and training ground for actors, not a vehicle for public performance. Strasberg was the artistic director and guiding spirit of the Actors Studio for 34 years, from 1948 until his death in 1982, and his reputation as America's finest acting teacher spread worldwide by the 1970s, resulting in frequent invitations to lecture and teach in Europe. Strasberg's influence on American acting is undeniable and measurable. At his 75th birthday it was estimated that actors trained by him had received 24 Academy Awards and 108 nominations.

Strasberg's effectiveness as a teacher derived from his interest in the psychology of dramatic interpretation and from his emphasis on the actor's private personality as the raw material from which performance should be created. Combining the theories of Stanislavsky and some modern psychology, he urged his students to create "backlife" for their characters, previous and subsequent histories based on assumptions from facts in the script. The areas examined were from the most tragic (such as loss of a parent) to the most mundane (such as brushing one's teeth). The object of this training was to break down the artificiality of acting by instilling in the actor such a familiarity with the character that the role ceased to be distinct from the actor's self. In this way, the personality of the performer became a functional part of stage technique.

Strasberg was married three times: to Nora Z. Krecaun in 1926 (she died in 1929), to Paula Miller in 1934 (who died in 1966), and to Anna Mizrahi in 1968. He had four children: two by Miller (Susan—an actress—and John) and two by Mizrahi (Adam and David). Strasberg's career as a stage actor ended in 1929 with his retirement, and his career as a film actor began in 1974 with his role as Hyman Roth in *The Godfather, Part II,* for which he received an Academy Award nomination for best supporting actor in 1975. His other film appearances included *The Cassandra Crossing* (1976), *Boardwalk* (1979), *Going in Style* (1979), and *And Justice for All* (1980). His television appearances included roles in *The Last Tenant* (1981) and *Skokie* (1981).

Strasberg died of a heart attack on February 17, 1982, in New York City, several days after appearing in a benefit chorus line at Radio City Music Hall.

Further Reading

Strasberg and the Group Theatre are discussed in Harold Clurman, *The Fervent Years* (1957). Strasberg's personal papers are at the Wisconsin Center for Theatre Research, University of Wisconsin. His book on directing, *A Dream of Passion* (1982), is unpublished.

Additional Sources

Adams, Cindy Heller, *Lee Strasberg, the imperfect genius of the Actors Studio,* Garden City, N.Y.: Doubleday, 1980.

Strasberg, Lee, *A dream of passion: the development of the method,* New York, N.Y.: New American Library, 1988, 1987. □

Isidor Straus

The American merchant Isidor Straus (1845-1912) was the owner of the department store R. H. Macy and Company and a U.S. congressman.

Isidor Straus was born on Feb. 6, 1845, in Otterberg, Germany, of a cultivated family. His father, a successful landowner and merchant, suffered political repression and emigrated to America in 1852. After traveling as a merchant in the South, he established a general store in Talbotton, Ga., bringing his wife and four children over in 1854. Isidor was the eldest of this family which was destined for distinction. He took responsibility for family affairs and was the real business head.

Straus was educated in local public schools but was prevented from going to West Point by the Civil War. He first worked in the family store; then a local business group sent him to Europe to buy ships and run the Union blockade, exporting cotton directly. This plan was abandoned, and Straus was left stranded in London with his life savings ($1,200 in gold) stitched into his underwear. He worked for 6 months in a Liverpool office and began trading Confederate bonds on the Amsterdam and London markets. He returned home with $12,000 and set up in business with his father, importing crockery.

L. Straus and Son (1866) did very well. His brother Nathan decided to reach more customers by opening departments inside existing great stores. They took over R. H. Macy's basement in 1874 and soon were doing over 10 percent of all Macy's business. Outlets were opened in big department stores in Chicago, Boston, and Philadelphia (Wanamaker's). They bought factories in Europe and began domestic crockery manufacture also. In 1888 the two brothers became partners in Macy's and in 1896 sole owners. Isidor reorganized the store; he was the business brains, Nathan the idea man. Straus' careful management built Macy's into the "biggest department store in the world."

Straus emphasized underselling, advertising, and the use of odd prices. From 1893 to 1919 the brothers also controlled a Brooklyn department store, and the two stores cooperated in joint purchasing, foreign buying, joint ownership of drug and food processing, and, in general, exchange of information. But the Straus family fortune was built essentially on Macy's.

Straus was a warm friend of President Grover Cleveland and a Gold Democrat of the Carl Schurz variety. He fell out with the party when it adopted free silver under William Jennings Bryan. He worked for Cleveland's reelection in 1892 and declined the office of postmaster general. Straus also firmly opposed the protective tariff. He served in Congress (1893-1895) but refused renomination. He worked for various charities and was a founder-member of the American-Jewish Committee. He drowned when the *Titanic* went down on April 15, 1912.

Further Reading

The best source on Straus is Ralph M. Hower, *History of Macy's of New York* (1943), which makes use of Straus's unpublished autobiographical essay. Isidor's brother Oscar S. Straus produced his own recollections, *Under Four Administrations, from Cleveland to Taft* (1922), but devoted little space to Isidor. □

David Friedrich Strauss

David Friedrich Strauss (1808-1874), the German historian and the most controversial Protestant theologian of his time, was one of the first to make a clear distinction between Jesus the historical figure and Jesus the subject of Christian belief.

David Strauss was a highly intelligent student at the famous Tübinger Stift, the school at which G. W. F. Hegel, Friedrich Hölderlin, and F. W. J. von Schelling had studied. As a theologian, he employed the dialectical method of Hegel. In 1835-1836 he wrote the book on the subject which was to concern him for the greater part of his life, the *Life of Jesus.* His main thesis was that the Jesus of biblical writings is not the real Jesus of history but a person transformed by the religious consciousness of Christians. Therefore, he stated that the basis of Christian belief and theology cannot be explained by scientific methods since Christianity is not based upon historical knowledge but upon a myth. Furthermore, it is impossible to analyze the life of Jesus under the aspects of a historical person and save his divine nature.

This book was a challenge to the entire Protestant theology of the time, and Strauss became intensely involved in polemics and discussions. Due to his reputation he was unable to obtain a teaching position at any university. He defended his theological position in many pamphlets, yet began to compromise to satisfy his critics. However, in a new book, *Christian Doctrine in Its Historical Development and Its Struggle against Modern Science* (1840-1841), he again stressed the scientific point of view in evaluating the Bible, the Church, and dogmas. He was convinced that the positions of Church and science could not be unified.

After 1841 he separated from his wife, withdrew from theology, and began a career as a writer. He concentrated on biographies of poets from southern Germany and history. Among his elegantly written biographies we find essays on A. J. Kerner, Eduard Mörike, J. L. Uhland, C. F. Schubart, and Voltaire. During the French-German war in 1870-1871, he corresponded with the French historian Ernest Renan. These letters were published and publicly discussed.

In 1864 Strauss again tried to cope with the problem of the life of Jesus but in a more moderate way. He accepted many of the arguments of his earlier enemies. But this new *Life of Jesus* was not challenging and did not attract the same attention as his work of 1836. In 1872 he again attacked the basis of Christian theology. His last book, *The Old and New Faith,* ordered his thoughts under four questions: Are we still Christians? Have we still religion? How do we conceive the world? How do we arrange our life? He denied that Christianity had any relevance for a modern, educated man. For religious feelings he substituted worship of the universe. The world should be understood in a scientific and materialistic way. Human life should be ordered by a concern for the good of man. This book was rejected almost unanimously by friends and opponents. The most famous attack was led by Friedrich Nietzsche. This reaction was the disappointment of Strauss's last years. He died in Ludwigsburg, the place of his birth, on Feb. 8, 1874.

Further Reading

Recommended for the study of the life and thought of Strauss are the relevant chapters in the following works: Sidney Hook, *From Hegel to Marx* (1936); Albert Schweitzer, *The Quest of the Historical Jesus: A Critical Study of Its Progress from Reimarus to Wrede,* translated by W. Montgomery (1948); Karl Barth, *Protestant Thought: From Rousseau to Ritschl,* translated by B. Cozens (1959); and Karl Löwith, *From Hegel to Nietzsche: The Revolution in Nineteenth-century Thought,* translated by David E. Green (1964).

Additional Sources

Cromwell, Richard S., *David Friedrich Strauss and his place in modern though,* Fair Lawn, N.J., R. E. Burdick 1974. □

Franz Josef Strauss

The West German politician Franz Josef Strauss (1915-1988) was a founder of the Christian Social Union and its standard bearer for four decades. He was minister president of Bavaria beginning in 1978.

Franz Josef Strauss was born on September 6, 1915, in the Bavarian capital of Munich. A butcher's son, raised a strict Catholic, he proved to be a brilliant student until he was drafted September 1, 1939. He served two years on the eastern front, became an artillery officer, and ended World War II in American captivity.

In 1945 Strauss was active in founding the Christian Social Union (CSU), the quasi-independent Bavarian sister party to the larger Christian Democratic Union (CDU) led by Konrad Adenauer, West German chancellor from 1949 to 1963. Strauss quickly gained attention for his slashing speeches as a CSU parliamentary deputy. Short, stout, and earthy, the energetic Strauss seemingly personified the conservative majority of Bavaria. He was chairman and undisputed leader of the CSU beginning in 1961 and served as minister president of Bavaria beginning in 1978. This controversial and colorful right-wing politician's great frustration, however, was his inability to duplicate on the national level the power and authority he achieved in his regional base of Bavaria.

In 1953 Strauss entered the Adenauer cabinet and was soon dubbed "the elbow minister" for his ability to push himself to the top. After a brief stint as minister of nuclear power he became minister of defense in 1956. The Federal Republic had just instituted conscription, and when the North Atlantic Treaty Organization (NATO) decided in 1957 to authorize the use of tactical nuclear arms, Strauss squashed the call for a "nuclear free" Central Europe. He forced parliament to vote in favor of nuclear arms. He also argued that West Germany must obtain nuclear weapons to remain on equal footing with her NATO allies. When the Kennedy administration resisted this goal, insisting on U.S. control, Strauss sought cooperation with General de Gaulle's France to build a Europe of states willing to share nuclear weapons. As a "German Gaullist," Strauss was viewed with suspicion by the supporters of Adenauer's heir apparent, Ludwig Erhard, who favored a pro-American, "Atlantic" posture. The liberal press also started writing in ominous tones that Strauss might become a hawkish foreign minister, or even Adenauer's ultimate successor.

Strauss helped bring upon himself the great crisis of his career in the "Spiegel Affair" of 1962. *Der Spiegel,* a weekly news magazine, published an article criticizing the West German army's lack of preparedness and Strauss' stewardship of it. Two weeks later, police seized the magazine's office and arrested the publisher and other journalists, claiming they had leaked defense secrets. Strauss tried to minimize his own role before parliament, only to have it become known that he had personally authorized the arrest of the article's author, an arrest which was legally questionable since it took place outside the country. Demonstrations against the defense minister rocked a hitherto docile public, and Adenauer's small coalition partner, the Free Democratic party, forced Strauss' resignation from the cabinet. Bavarians stood by their beleaguered leader, however, and voted an increased mandate to the CSU.

Driven from national office and hounded by an often vindictive press, Strauss studied economics at the University of Innsbruck. He then staged an impressive political comeback. He was instrumental in toppling the Erhard government of 1963-1966 and helped fashion the "Great Coalition" of 1966-1969. The coalition was headed by a new CDU chancellor, Kurt Georg Kiesinger, and the Social Democratic vice-chancellor and foreign minister, Willy Brandt. Strauss became minister of finance and surprised his critics by working harmoniously with the Social Democratic minister of economics to tackle the economic recession.

When the coalition broke apart and the CDU/CSU was forced into opposition for the first time after the Social Democrat (SPD) victory in the election of 1969, Strauss became the leading critic of Willy Brandt's conciliatory foreign policy towards Eastern Europe. Strauss maintained the traditional West German rejection of the 1945 settlement, arguing that Brandt was bargaining claims away for uncertain promises. But public opinion was tiring of Cold War intransigence, with even Strauss' CDU ally moving towards acceptance of the treaties with the East. Although Strauss was able to keep the CDU from accepting the treaties, he could prevent neither their passage nor the reelection of the Brandt government in 1972.

The tensions within the CDU/CSU opposition became ever more strained in the 1970s. The maverick Strauss tried to become a dominating voice, but also threatened to make the CSU a national splinter party of the right. Divided, the CDU/CSU opposition was defeated in the 1976 national election by a Social Democratic/Free Democratic alliance led by Chancellor Helmut Schmidt. Strauss finally became the CDU/CSU chancellor candidate in 1980. This electoral confrontation between Strauss and Schmidt was billed as the "clash of giants," but no clear issues emerged. The campaign turned out to be a national referendum on Strauss. The liberal-social democratic coalition united against him with the emotional slogan "Stop Strauss!" In victory, however, the Social Democratic/Free Democratic alliance would quickly disintegrate, and Schmidt was out of office by 1983.

Although the 1980 election was supposed to be Strauss' "last hurrah," he remained a formidable figure in West German politics for several years thereafter.

In 1983-84, Strauss served in the largely honorary post of president of the Bundesrat, in the upper house of the federal parliament. He lost his wife in a fatal car accident shortly thereafter. He died in Regensburg, Bavaria on October 3, 1988.

Further Reading

There is no biography in English of Strauss. Michael Balfour's *West Germany* (2nd ed., 1982) provides an informative sketch. See also Ronald F. Blum, *German Politics and the Spiegel Affair* (1968). In 1985, a commemorative *Festschrift* honoring Strauss's 70th birthday was published, with a preface by Ronald Reagan and contributions by Margaret Thatcher and Helmut Schmidt, among others. ☐

Johann Strauss Jr.

Johann Strauss, Jr. (1825-1899), Vienna's greatest composer of light music, was known for his waltzes and operettas. His music seems to capture the height of elegance and refinement of the Hapsburg regime.

Johann Strauss, Jr., was the eldest son of Johann Strauss, Sr., a famous composer and conductor, known as "the father of the waltz." Although the elder Strauss wanted his sons to pursue business careers, the musical talents of Johann, Jr., quickly became evident, and he composed his first waltz at the age of 6. Behind his father's back, his mother secretly procured a musical education for her son. At the age of 19 he organized his own small orchestra, which performed some of his compositions in a restaurant in Hietzing. When his father died in 1849, Strauss, combined both bands and became their leader and ultimately earned his own nickname, "the king of the waltz."

Strauss toured throughout Europe and England with great success and also went to America, conducting mammoth concerts in Boston and New York. He was the official conductor of the court balls in Vienna (1863-1870) and during this time composed his most famous waltzes. They include *On the Beautiful Blue Danube* (1867), probably the best-known waltz ever written, *Artist's Life* (1867), *Tales from the Vienna Woods* (1868), and *Wine, Women, and Song* (1869). He elevated the waltz from the atmosphere of the beer hall and the restaurant to that of the aristocratic ballroom.

In 1863 Jacques Offenbach, Paris's most popular composer of light operas, visited Vienna, and the two composers met. The success of Offenbach's stage works encouraged Strauss to try writing operettas. He resigned as court conductor in 1870 to devote himself to the composition of operettas. Of these, three remain consistently in the repertoire today. The finest of them, *Die Fledermaus* (1874; *The Bat*), is probably the greatest operetta ever written and a masterpiece of its genre. The lovely *Du und Du* waltz is made up of excerpts from this work. His two other most successful operettas were *A Night in Venice* (1883), from which he derived the music for the *Lagoon Waltz,* and *The Gypsy Baron* (1885), from which stems the *Treasure Waltz.*

Strauss continued to compose dance music, including the famous waltzes *Roses from the South* (1880) and *Voices of Spring* (1883). This last work, most often heard today as a purely instrumental composition, was originally conceived with a soprano solo as the composer's only independent vocal waltz. He wrote more than 150 waltzes, 100 polkas, 70 quadrilles, mazurkas, marches, and galops. His music combines considerable melodic invention, tremendous verve, and brilliance with suavity and polish, even at times an incredibly refined sensuality.

Further Reading

The best-known biographies of Strauss in English are Heinrich Eduard Jacob, *Johann Strauss, Father and Son: A Century of Light Music* (1940), and David Ewen, *Tales from the Vienna Woods: The Story of Johann Strauss* (1944). □

Leo Strauss

One of the most controversial thinkers of modern times, Leo Strauss (1899-1973), a German Jew, was a Socratic political philosopher. As he considered the civic duty of a Socratic to be to question and criticize reigning dogmas, he aroused bitter opposition from established academic and intellectual authorities.

Leo Strauss was born to a rural, orthodox family living in the village of Kirchhain in the province of Hesse, Germany, on September 20, 1899. He graduated from the Gymnasium Philippinum in Marburg in 1917 and served until the end of World War I in the German army of occupation in Belgium. With war's end, Strauss entered upon the study of mathematics, natural science, and, above all, philosophy at the Universities of Marburg, Frankfurt am Main, Berlin, and Hamburg. In 1921 he received his doctorate from Hamburg, with a dissertation on the theory of knowledge of Friedrich Jacobi, written under the supervision of the neo-Kantian Ernst Cassirer.

By this time Strauss had moved far from his orthodox roots. But the shattering power of Nietzsche's critique of rationalism in all its forms led Strauss away from his initial philosophic position as a neo-Kantian and compelled him to acknowledge the as yet unmet challenge of religious faith. Strauss' subsequent encounter with Martin Heidegger and Franz Rosenzweig confirmed the deep inadequacy of Kantian thought. On the other hand, post-doctoral study under Edmund Husserl at Freiburg fueled Strauss' consuming need to seek the possibility of a "philosophy as rigorous science" that could withstand Nietzsche's great critique and meet the challenge posed by faith. Meanwhile, in his early twenties, if not before, Strauss became convinced of the political unviability of the existence of Jews in Germany and became an active leader of Zionist youth. He thus found himself in the grip of a total dilemma: he could not simply accept traditional Jewish faith but he could not find in modern rationalism (science) and in modern liberal society a foundation for moral and civic life. The mature Strauss came to see the problem of being a Jew as a clue to the insolubly problematic character of all political life.

The abiding theme of Strauss' mature philosophic reflection was what he called, following Spinoza, the "theologico-political problem." This problem has several facets. First and foremost is the question whether or not God exists, and, in the second place, what difference God's existence or nonexistence makes, above all for our understanding of justice or the common good. Does justice, and hence the good society, ultimately require divine support, and faith in that support, or is there a natural, purely rational basis for justice? Does justice rest ultimately on *divine* right and law; and, if so, how does one decide between the various competing religions; or, alternatively, does justice rest ultimately on *natural* right and law, and, if so, how does "philosophy as rigorous science" discover the principles of natural right? By insisting on these questions, Strauss set himself in radical opposition to almost all the reigning dogmas of the 20th century, which try to avoid or ignore or suppress these questions by such dodges as relativism, pragmatism, existential commitment, religious faith, or ideology of one sort or another, including uncritical acceptance of the basic norms of modern liberal-democratic culture.

To begin to deal with the theologico-political problem, the young Strauss undertook a study of the original foundations of modern science in the critique of religion carried out by Spinoza and Hobbes. As a research assistant in the Academy of Jewish Research in Berlin (1922-1935), Strauss published his first book, *Spinoza's Critique of Religion* (1930), and helped edit the collected works of Moses Mendelssohn. Dissatisfaction with Spinoza led Strauss back to Spinoza's great antagonist, Moses Maimonides, the preeminent exponent of Aristotelian and Platonic or classical rationalism in the Middle Ages. Through Maimonides and his

Islamic philosophic teachers, especially Farabi, Strauss rediscovered what he came to believe to be the decisive superiority of classical rationalism as epitomized in Socrates and the Socratic way of life. Strauss' second book, *Philosophy and Law* (1935), announced this discovery to the world and set the agenda for all Strauss' subsequent work, elaborated in some 13 other books, the most important of which are *Persecution and the Art of Writing* (1952), *Natural Right and History* (1953), *The City and Man* (1963), and *Xenophon's Socratic Discourse* (1970).

When the Third Reich began persecuting Jews Strauss found refuge from the Nazis first in France and England and finally in the United States, where he settled permanently in 1937. He was professor of political philosophy at the New School for Social Research from 1938 to 1949, and then at the University of Chicago from 1949 until 1967. In America he mounted a searing critique of relativistic social science and of democratic dogmatism. He insisted, in his words, that "precisely because we are friends of liberal democracy we cannot be its flatterers." The highest civic duty of the Socratic, he insisted, was to criticize the reigning dogmas, and in a liberal democracy this means the duty to criticize democracy, liberalism, individualism, and egalitarianism. Like Socrates, he aroused, and continues to arouse even after his death, bitter opposition from all established academic and intellectual authorities. He was an extraordinarily influential teacher and left behind scores of students, numbering in the hundreds and perhaps thousands, some of whom are prominent and influential not only in the university but in journalism and the national government.

Further Reading

For an introduction to Strauss, see Thomas Pangle, editor, *The Rebirth of Classical Political Rationalism* (1989) and the "epilogue" to Leo Strauss and Joseph Cropsey, editors, *History of Political Philosophy,* 3rd edition (1987). Strauss' autobiographical essay was published as the preface to the English translation of *Spinoza's Critique of Religion* (1965). □

Richard Strauss

Richard Strauss (1864-1949), the German composer and conductor, is known especially for his operas and symphonic poems linked to his phenomenal mastery of the orchestra. He was the chief exemplar of post-Wagnerian tastes and techniques.

Richard Strauss was born in Munich to a mother who was a talented amateur musician and a father who was the principal horn player in the Court Opera. Piano lessons with his mother began at the age of 4; at 8 he started violin study. In his own words, however, he was a bad pupil because he did not enjoy practicing. His pleasure even then was in composing, which he tried first when he was only 6. Thereafter he composed steadily while receiving regular instruction in music theory from various local musicians. Meanwhile his general education was furthered at the Royal Gymnasium and for a year at the University of Munich.

Strauss was obviously headed toward a career in composition, for by the age of 20 he had turned out a large and quite respectable collection of piano pieces, songs, chamber music, choruses, and orchestral works, including two symphonies and two concertos. He also got into print very early with the *Festival March,* written in 1876. This music, as far as one can judge from the available examples, was extremely conservative in tone, modeled after Felix Mendelssohn, Robert Schumann, and Johannes Brahms. It clearly carried the mark of his father's tutelage, which Strauss said kept him from hearing anything but classical music until he was 16.

The progressive movements of the 19th century touched Strauss only after he took up conducting and settled in 1885 into his first post as director of the Meiningen orchestra. There he became acquainted with a violinist named Alexander Ritter, who opened Strauss's mind to the "advanced" music and ideas of Hector Berlioz, Franz Liszt, and Richard Wagner—men whose names were anathema in his father's house.

The effect of this awakening was first apparent in a symphonic fantasy, *Aus Italien,* written in 1886 while Strauss was on a visit to Italy. Full alignment with the newer currents was signaled by his entry into the field of program music cultivated years before by Liszt. The result was a series of nine single-movement, orchestral tone poems beginning with *Macbeth* (1890), ending with *Eine*

Alpensinfonie (1915), and covering a range of subject matter from medieval legend in *Till Eulenspiegels lustige Streiche* (1895) to Strauss's own domestic life in *Symphonia Domestica* (1903). *Don Juan* (1888), *Till,* and *Don Quixote,* (1897) are generally the most favored of these works. In principle, however, Strauss's method remained constant. The shaping of each piece was guided by a poetic idea to which his music was linked in a more intimate and detailed way than in earlier programmatic scores. Yet he avoided becoming a mere illustrator by insisting that the composition must also develop "logically from within" to produce a satisfying musical form. And at every point he demonstrated his unsurpassed virtuosity in orchestration.

With the tone poems Strauss came into his own as a composer. He also became increasingly successful as a conductor, performing throughout Europe, especially Germany, where he held positions in Munich, Weimar, and Berlin, and in New York City. By the time he was 30, he was a celebrity on two counts. But there was much more to come after he turned to opera composition.

Strauss, as he said, may have put off composing for the theater from awe of Wagner. Once started, however, he gave it his main attention for almost 40 years, producing 15 operas in that period. The first two, *Guntram* (1893) and *Feuersnot* (1901), were failures. Then came *Salome* (1905), *Elektra* (1908), *Der Rosenkavalier* (1910), and *Ariadne auf Naxos* (1912), which are possibly his best and certainly the most frequently played of all. *Salome,* with its shocking, perverse sensuality, and *Elektra,* which goes beyond that in violence and unremitting tension, are prime examples of German expressionism in its most lurid phase. They also show Strauss at the peak of his modernity in respect to musical vocabulary and technique. In *Der Rosenkavalier* he reverted to a sweetly diatonic strain cast much of the time in waltz rhythm; in *Ariadne* he looked still farther back as he applied classical methods to the ingenious idea of presenting an antique myth simultaneously with a sketch out of the commedia dell'arte. Of his remaining operas, *Die Frau ohne Schatten* (1917), *Arabella* (1932), and *Capriccio* (1941) are the most interesting, although none has won repertory status.

After *Capriccio* Strauss returned to earlier interests in concerto composition, chamber music, and songs, the peak of this final effort being the *Metamorphosen* for 23 solo strings (1945). Grave and Wagnerian in tone, it recalls Strauss's ties to the Germany of his youth and sounds an affecting though belated finale to an era that had long since been closed out by composers such as Igor Stravinsky, Arnold Schoenberg, and Béla Bartók.

Further Reading

Strauss's *Recollections and Reflections* were edited by Will Schuh (1953). Two biographical studies are George R. Marek, *Richard Strauss: Life of a Non-hero* (1967), and Ernst Krause, *Richard Strauss: The Man and His Work* (trans. 1969). Joseph Kerman, *Opera as Drama* (1956), offers a biting censure of the Straussian dramaturgy, while William Mann, *Richard Strauss: A Critical Study of the Operas* (1964), is generally sympathetic. Strauss's historical position is outlined in Gerald Abraham, *A Hundred Years of Music* (1938; 3d ed. 1964), and Adolfo Salazar, *Music in Our Time* (trans. 1946).

Additional Sources

Kennedy, Michael, *Richard Strauss,* Oxford, England: Clarendon Press, 1995. ☐

Robert Schwarz Strauss

Robert Schwarz Strauss (born 1918) was a master fundraiser and strategist for the Democratic Party between 1968 and 1980, active in both Texan and national campaigns. He later served as U.S. Ambassador to Russia under President George Bush.

Robert Schwarz Strauss was born in Lockhart, Texas, on October 19, 1918. He grew up in Stamford, Texas, the son of a small-town merchant who ran a dry-goods business. Robert helped out behind the counter as he grew up. Despite his family's modest circumstances and the fact that the country was in the midst of the Depression, Strauss entered the University of Texas at Austin. There he got his first taste of politics when he worked as a clerk at the state capitol in order to support himself at school. While at the University of Texas, he met and began a long-lasting friendship with John B. Connally, future governor of Texas. In 1937 he worked on the campaign of Lyndon B. Johnson, who was making his first run for elected office. Johnson ran for Congress on a New Deal platform of support for Franklin D. Roosevelt. The excitement of politics captured Strauss' imagination.

In 1941 Strauss graduated from the University of Texas Law School and joined the Federal Bureau of Investigation. He worked as a special agent for the FBI until 1945, when he resigned and helped found a law firm—Akin, Gump, Strauss, Hauer & Feld—which became a prestigious law firm in Dallas. Prudent investments in real estate and radio stations made him a wealthy man by the early 1960s. In 1964 he was named president of the Strauss Broadcasting Company.

Strauss re-entered politics in 1962 when his friend John Connally ran for the governorship of Texas. Strauss served as a chief fund raiser for the successful campaign and was appointed by Connally to the state banking board, where he served for six years.

In 1968 Strauss began his long association with the national Democratic Party when Connally appointed him to the Democratic National Committee. He was to become an important political force in the party for the next 12 years.

Strauss managed the 1968 Humphrey-Muskie campaign in Texas, demonstrating both a mastery of finances (a campaign chest that ended in the black) and an ability to negotiate an acceptable middle ground among disparate elements of the Democratic Party. This would be his trademark as he continued his political career.

In 1970 Strauss was elected treasurer of the Democratic National Committee and was charged with reducing the 1968 party debt of $9,300,000 to manageable proportions. It was a gigantic undertaking. Yet by the end of his tenure in July 1972 Strauss had reduced the debt by one-half, funded the 1972 Democratic National Convention, and placed the credit of the national party on a solid basis. During the 1972 campaign he served as chairman of the National Committee to Re-elect a Democratic Congress.

After the disastrous defeat of Senator George McGovern in 1972, disaffected elements of the Democratic Party representing the old established conservative wing made their bid to regain control of the party structure. Their opening gambit was to challenge Jean Westwood for the party chairmanship. Robert Strauss was their candidate. After an acrimonious, month-long struggle, Strauss was elected Democratic Party chairman, promising to use his talents to bring the party together again. "I am a centrist, a worker, a doer, a putter-together, and those talents belong to you."

Strauss began immediately the task of conciliation between the "new" political forces that had emerged in 1972—women, African Americans, and the young—and the "old guard" Democratic establishment of labor, urban machines, and the South. The task was to define a party in which George McGovern, Shirley Chisholm, George Wallace, Mayor Daley, and George Meany could all find a place and contribute towards winning a national election. That he succeeded was evident in 1976 when Jimmy Carter was elected president. Carter called Strauss "the greatest party chairman I have ever known."

President Carter quickly tapped Strauss to participate in a panel with ten other high level officials to select personnel for the Carter administration. In March 1977, Strauss' own nomination as special representative for trade negotiations was confirmed by the Senate. The post carried with it the rank of ambassador, and Strauss was widely regarded as an excellent choice.

In April 1979, following the Camp David accords, Strauss was named U.S. ambassador-at-large for negotiations on Palestinian autonomy on the West Bank and the Gaza Strip. While his open negotiating manner had been an asset to him on the domestic political scene, Strauss appeared to be less effective in the Middle East. He soon left this post to become chairman of President Carter's reelection committee in November 1979. In consideration of his services to the nation, Strauss was awarded the Medal of Freedom—the highest civilian award given by the United States—by President Carter in January 1981.

After the defeat of Jimmy Carter, Strauss resumed the practice of law as a partner in his old law firm. In 1983 he was appointed by President Reagan to the Bipartisan Commission on Central America Policy headed by Henry Kissinger. In the 1984 presidential campaign he was called on to canvass party leaders for advice on behalf of Walter Mondale, but played no larger role. He formed a bipartisan committee with Melvin Laird to study the primary system's place in electoral politics in March 1985. Strauss served as United States Ambassador to Russia from 1991-1993 under President George Bush.

Further Reading

There is no biography yet of Robert Strauss. Material can be found by checking the entries in *Who's Who in America,* the yearly index of *Facts on File,* the *New York Times,* and the *Washington Post.* ☐

Igor Fedorovich Stravinsky

The Russian-born composer Igor Fedorovich Stravinsky (1882-1971) identified himself as an "inventor of music." The novelty, power, and elegance of his works won worldwide admiration before he was 30. Throughout his life he continued to surprise admirers with transformations of his style that stimulated controversy.

Every aspect of music was renewed again and again in the work of Igor Stravinsky. Rhythm was the most striking ingredient, and his novel rhythms were most widely imitated. His instrumentation and his ways of writing for voices were also distinctive and influential. His harmonies and forms were more elusive. He recognized melody as the "most essential" element. Even if his rhythm and his sheer sound sometimes seemed independent of melody, stimulating composers like Edgard Varèse, Olivier Messiaen, Elliott Carter, Pierre Boulez, and Karlheinz

Stockhausen to explore further possibilities of such independence, Stravinsky's own works constituted integral melodies, as much as Claude Debussy's or Ludwig van Beethoven's or Carlo Gesualdo's, if not quite Wolfgang Amadeus Mozart's. Stravinsky constantly subordinated all "technical apparatus" to what he recognized in 1939 as "a general revision of both the basic values and the primordial elements of the art of music," a revision continuing throughout his life. "The so-called crisis of means," he insisted in 1966, "is interior."

Beginnings in Russia

Stravinsky was born at Oranienbaum near St. Petersburg on June 17, 1882. Although his father was a star singer of the Imperial Opera, he rather expected the boy to become a bureaucrat. Igor finished a university law course before he made the decision to become a musician. By this time he was a good amateur pianist, an occasional professional accompanist, an avid reader of avant-garde scores from France and Germany, and, of course, a connoisseur of Italian, French, and Russian opera.

The closest friend of Stravinsky's youth was Stephan Mitusov, stepson of a prince. Stravinsky acknowledged that Mitusov was "a kind of literary and theatrical tutor to me at one of the greatest moments in the Russian theater." Mitusov translated the poems of Paul Verlaine that Stravinsky set to music in 1910, and he arranged the libretto of Stravinsky's opera *The Nightingale* (1908-1914).

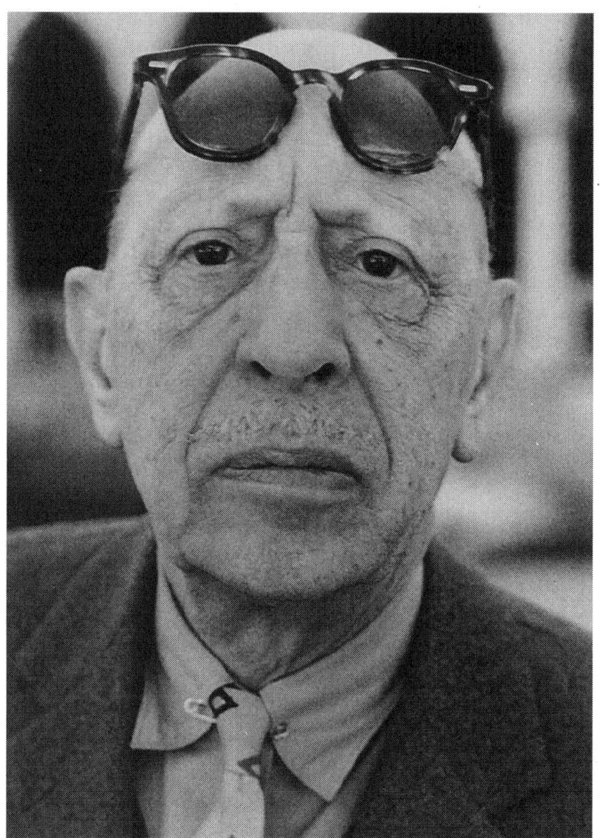

One of Stravinsky's classmates at the university was Vladimir Rimsky-Korsakov, son of the composer, whose reputation as master orchestrator and teacher at the St. Petersburg Conservatory surpassed the fame of his operas. Stravinsky became Rimsky's apprentice; he did not enter classes at the conservatory but worked privately and intensely at his home. For the sake of the most advanced craftsmanship, Stravinsky gladly submerged his independent taste, confident that he could exercise it later. As demonstration of his learning, with few original features, he composed his Symphony in E-flat (1905-1907), dedicated to his teacher. For Madame Rimsky, there was a charming *Pastorale* (1907) for wordless voice and piano, later to become a favorite in various instrumental arrangements. For a wedding present to Rimsky's daughter Nadia and his favorite pupil, Maximilian Steinberg, Stravinsky composed a brilliant short fantasy for orchestra, *Fireworks* (1908). When Rimsky died in the same year, Stravinsky wrote a funeral dirge which he later recalled as the best of his early works; it was not published, and the manuscript was lost.

Scandal, Glory, and Misunderstanding in France

The great impresario Sergei Diaghilev, hearing *Fireworks,* recognized both the mastery and the budding originality. He at once enlisted Stravinsky to make some orchestral arrangements of Chopin for the season of Russian ballets that he was producing in Paris. Then Diaghilev assigned him bigger tasks, for which Stravinsky postponed his opera *Nightingale.* Diaghilev soon brought him into the center of an illustrious group of artists in Paris and during the next few years evoked his utmost daring in collaborations with Michel Fokine and Vaslav Nijinsky, among others.

Each of Stravinsky's three ballets for Diaghilev's company scandalized the first audiences. Each quickly became a classic. Each is unique. *Firebird* (1910) surpasses all Rimsky's variegated splendor and sweetness. *Petrushka* (1911) brings a new fusion of irony and pathos to the piano, the trumpet, and the dance. The *Rite of Spring* (1912-1913) is a frenzied breakthrough of 20th-century affinities to prehistoric mankind. Genteel audiences were provoked to riotous protest. The three ballets together made Stravinsky's influence on all the arts enormous and established him alongside older composers like Maurice Ravel and Arnold Schoenberg as a leader of a heroic musical generation.

Among countless testimonials to the power of the *Rite,* one by John Dos Passos is typical: to him it seemed "just about the height of what could be accomplished on the stage. . . . Stravinsky's music got into our blood. For months his rhythms underlay everything we heard, his prancing figures moved behind everything we saw. . . . The ballet would do for our time what tragedy had done for the Greeks."

The young hero was a small man with a big face. Stravinsky's elegant clothes, his thin hair brushed straight back, and a very thin mustache contrasted with his bulging nose, readily grinning or smacking lips, busy bright eyes, and huge ears. In speech and action he exuded aggressive energy, like that of the *Rite of Spring,* matched and controlled by correspondingly fastidious craftsmanship. Nijinsky described him as "like an emperor ... but cleverer."

World War I interrupted the expansion of Diaghilev's enterprise, and the Russian Revolution uprooted Stravinsky from the home to which he had been returning from Paris. During the war he lived in Switzerland, where he collaborated with the poet C. F. Ramuz on a series of astonishing works based on folklore and, to some extent, on popular music, including ragtime. The most surprising and appealing of these was *The Soldier's Tale* (1918) for narrator, three dancers, and seven instrumentalists. This work deeply influenced Bertold Brecht, Jean Cocteau, and other dramatists of the 1920s, as well as composers and performers of each later generation. Stravinsky's new turn to concision and counterpoint in *The Soldier's Tale* was often compared with the contemporary trend of his new friend, the Spanish painter Pablo Picasso, who was to work with him on his next Diaghilev assignment, *Pulcinella* (1920).

But another ballet, begun in 1914, composed in 1917, and finally orchestrated only in 1923, was the grandest fulfillment of these years: *Svadebka* (*Les Noces,* or *The Little Wedding*) for chorus and four solo singers in the pit, with four pianos and percussion. Here the barbaric power of the *Rite* and the modern concision of *The Soldier's Tale* met in an austere affirmation of love—too austere to be recognized as affirmation by many people. Alongside these very diverse major works were several smaller ones, for voices and for instruments in various combinations, all of which won frequent performance only much later. Outstanding among these was a memorial to Debussy, *Symphonies for Wind Instruments.*

A short comic opera, *Mavra* (1922), revealed a new lyricism in Stravinsky's complicated development. *Mavra* was a declaration of continuity with the Russian traditions of Aleksandr Pushkin, Mikhail Glinka, and Peter Ilyich Tchaikovsky. Though it was not a popular success (to Stravinsky's great disappointment), it influenced young men like Darius Milhaud, Francis Poulenc, Kurt Weill, Sergei Prokofiev, and Dmitri Shostakovich as much as had the *Rite.* For them, as for their contemporary Paul Hindemith, Stravinsky seemed now to have left not only Ravel but Schoenberg and his school in a backwater of history; Stravinsky belonged with the young. Stravinsky's instrumental works of the 1920s, including the Piano Concerto, the Octet for winds, the Sonata, and the Serenade in a for piano solo, justified the slogan "Back to Bach," though just what Stravinsky meant by the slogan was seldom fully grasped despite his meticulous qualifications.

An opera-oratorio, *Oedipus Rex* (1927), and a "white" ballet, *Apollo* (1928), both defined and transcended the "neoclassicism" that was much talked about between the wars. That Stravinsky's taste was by no means so narrow as this fashionable label suggests is indicated by the next ballet, *The Fairy's Kiss* (1928), a new tribute to Tchaikovsky, making use of themes from Tchaikovsky's songs and piano pieces. The Divertimento for orchestra and the Capriccio for piano and orchestra likewise testify to Stravinsky's continuing versatility. But these works dissatisfied some admirers of *Mavra* as much as those of the *Rite,* without winning the bigger audience of Tchaikovsky's symphonies, not to mention the ever-growing mass of consumers of other music.

The death of Diaghilev in the year the Great Depression began (1929) marked the end of an epoch, the extinction of a social focus for much of Stravinsky's work. Though he was to become a French citizen in 1934, he was not able to win in France the recognition and security he needed. He found some solace with friends like the French poet Paul Valéry, the philosopher Jacques Maritain, and the philosopher-critic Pierre Souvchinsky. These thinkers, more than any musician, helped him seek order and discipline "at a time," as he wrote, "when the status of man is undergoing profound upheavals. Modern man is progressively losing his understanding of values and his sense of proportions." Stravinsky reaffirmed membership in the Orthodox Church, which he had neglected since adolescence.

The *Symphony of Psalms* (1930) for chorus of men and boys and orchestra without violins became the most widely known of all Stravinsky's works after the *Rite.* At first its gravity seemed incongruous with the worldliness of the ballets; after it got to be familiar, it was often recommended as a good starting point for acquaintance with Stravinsky's work as a whole.

The theatrical works *Persephone* (1934) and *A Game of Cards* (1936) were as obviously unique as the *Symphony of Psalms.* They were somewhat subordinate to a series of purely instrumental works on a grand scale: the Violin Concerto (1931), Duo concertante for violin and piano (1932), Concerto for two pianos (1935), Concerto for chamber orchestra ("Dumbarton Oaks," 1938), and Symphony in C (1940). If composers like Arthur Honegger, Bohuslav Martinu, Walter Piston, Roger Sessions, and Benjamin Britten abstracted from Stravinsky's procedures models for their own various recurring problems, this was irrelevant to the lasting values of the Stravinsky works, for he continued to set himself fresh problems and to find fresh solutions.

The true sequel to the *Symphony of Psalms* was to be liturgical. From 1942 to 1948 Stravinsky worked intermittently on an uncommissioned setting of the Ordinary of the Roman Catholic Mass for chorus and winds. He had been spurred to this work by Mozart's Masses but not in any obvious way; rather, he said, "As I played through these rococo-operatic sweets-of-sin, I knew I had to write a Mass of my own, but a real one." And on another occasion he said, "One composes a march to facilitate marching men, so with my Credo I hope to provide an aid to the text. The Credo is the longest movement. There is so much to believe."

Stravinsky's tone in language matches the aggressive originality of his music. His originality, nevertheless, is at the service of orthodox belief, and his polemics are written "not in my own defense, but in order to defend in words all music and its principles, just as I defend them in a different way with my compositions."

Renewals in America

When he settled in the United States in 1939, Stravinsky renewed his interest in popular music long enough to compose several short pieces culminating in the *Ebony Concerto* (1946) for Woody Herman's band. His arrangement of the *Star-spangled Banner* (1944) was too severe to become a favorite. Several projects for film music were begun, and though none was completed, the music for them found various proper forms; most expansive, and at moments reminiscent of the *Rite,* was the *Symphony in Three Movements* (1945).

A collaboration happier even than that with Diaghilev developed with the New York City Ballet under George Balanchine. The first fruit of this collaboration was *Orpheus* (1948). From then on, though *Agon* (1957) was the only later piece composed especially for dance, the ballet made use of many old and new works, illuminating and popularizing them, gratifying and inspiring the composer as did comparatively few other performances of his work. *Apollo* and *Orpheus* rivaled the *Firebird* in the New York City Ballet repertory, and the symphonies, concertos, and miscellaneous pieces came to life.

At last Stravinsky was able to undertake a full-length opera, *The Rake's Progress* (1948-1951). This was a fulfillment not merely of his celebrated anti-Wagnerian stylistic principles but also of capacities and aspirations that had seemed only natural at the outset of his career and of his mature ethical and religious concerns. On the advice of his friend Aldous Huxley, he applied to the poet W. H. Auden for a libretto, to be based on his own vision derived from William Hogarth's prints of *The Rake's Progress.* Auden's work, in collaboration with Chester Kallman, provided an ideal "fable," embodying elements of farce, melodrama, pastoral, and allegory. The music includes some of Stravinsky's most melodious ideas, contrasting with bold dry recitative, colorful choruses, and concise episodes for the Mozartean orchestra. Performed all over the world, *The Rake's Progress* was especially successful in versions designed by Ingmar Bergman and Gian Carlo Menotti.

The young conductor Robert Craft became a devoted aide of Stravinsky while he worked on the opera. Soon Craft's pioneering work with the music of Anton Webern aroused Stravinsky's interest. During the 1950s, alongside several younger composers in Europe and America, Stravinsky deeply studied Webern and gradually absorbed new elements into his own still evolving, still very individual, style. Some old friends, like Poulenc, unable to keep up the pace, felt betrayed. But now, as in the 1920s, Stravinsky belonged with the young.

The Cantata on medieval English poems (1952) and the Septet (1953) show a new density of contrapuntal ingenuity in the service of wonderfully lively expression. The moving Song with dirge canons in memory of Dylan Thomas (1954) is still more densely made, with every note accountable as part of a five-note series continually varied. In the oratorio *Canticum sacrum* in honor of St. Mark (1956), there are passages with Webernish sounds and silences, melodies made mostly of wide skips, and series of twelve notes treated according to Schoenberg's technique. Similar passages in *Agon* (1953-1957), a plotless ballet for twelve dancers, are combined with references to 16th-century dances and strong C-major cadences in a fantastic synthesis.

Threni, i.e., Lamentations of Jeremiah (1958) for solo voices, chorus, and orchestra appeared as a major historical landmark, for in this work Stravinsky made the twelve-tone technique a "point of departure" throughout, as he continued to do in later compositions. Of these the largest ones are settings of religious texts: *A Sermon, a Narrative, and a Prayer* (1961), *The Flood* (1962), *Abraham and Isaac* (1963), and *Requiem Canticles* (1966). Some smaller vocal works deserve a place beside the larger ones: the unaccompanied Anthem on stanzas from T. S. Eliot's *Quartets, The dove descending breaks the air* (1962), the setting for voice and three clarinets of Auden's *Elegy for J. F. K.* (1964), and even the song for voice and piano on Edward Lear's poem *The Owl and the Pussycat* (1968). In each of these works the complexities of rhythm and sound, as well as the fascinating harmony and counterpoint, serve to clarify and intensify the meanings of the texts.

Stravinsky's major instrumental works after the Septet were the Movements for piano and orchestra (1959) and the Variations for orchestra (1964), both of which were interpreted in ballets by Balanchine that could disarm any candid critic of the music. Both were "major" despite a brevity worthy of Webern—the Movements about 10 minutes, the Variations less than 5. Balanchine simply had the Variations played three times, with the threefold dance accumulating power.

Stravinsky died on April 6, 1971, in New York City. He was buried with pomp in Venice.

Assessments of the Composer

The poet Herbert Read declared in 1962 that Stravinsky was "the most representative artist of our own 20th century." The critic François Michel a year earlier gave a reason for calling him "the greatest musician of our epoch"—he was "the only one who could transform its characteristic defects, which he took upon himself, into ways of seeing the truths of all time." The publisher Ernst Roth in 1967 went further, hailing Stravinsky as "the most prophetic of all men of our time. His life is like a symbol of future mankind."

That same year Stravinsky characteristically made fun of "the natural desire to cling to an old man in hopes that he can point the road to the future. What is needed, of course, is simply *any* road that offers enough mileage and a good enough safety record. And my road . . . will soon become a detour, I realize . . . but I hardly mind that. Detours are often pleasant to travel, far more so than those super-turnpikes on which the traffic has yet to discover that the race is not always to the swift."

Further Reading

With his *Autobiography* (1936), Stravinsky became an important writer on music. His *Poetics of Music* (1942; translated by Arthur Knodel and Ingolf Dahl, 1947) is his most systematic literary work, unique among discussions of music for its authority and scope. But these books, he said later, were "much less like me, in all my faults, than my conversations," which he compiled in collaboration with Robert Craft in a series of volumes: *Conversations* (1959), *Memories and Commentaries* (1960), *Expositions and Developments* (1962), *Dia-*

logues and a Diary (1963), *Themes and Episodes* (1966), and *Retrospectives and Conclusions* (1969).

The most comprehensive collection of facts about his life and all his works is Eric W. White, *Stravinsky* (1966). Other studies include Heinrich Strobel, *Stravinsky: Classic Humanist* (1955); Roman Vlad, *Stravinsky* (trans. 1960; repr. 1968); and Robert Siohan, *Stravinsky* (1969). □

Sir Peter Fredrick Strawson

Peter Fredrick Strawson (born 1919) was regarded as one of the most prominent philosophers of the 20th century. He was especially active in the movement known as ordinary language philosophy.

Sir Peter Fredrick Strawson was born November 23, 1919. He received his master's degree in philosophy from St. John's College, Oxford University, in 1940. After serving in the British Armed Forces during World War II, where he achieved the rank of captain, Strawson began his professional career in philosophy as a lecturer at the University College of North Wales. In 1948 he was appointed lecturer in philosophy at Oxford University, serving first as praelector and later as reader in philosophy. In 1968 Strawson succeeded Gilbert Ryle as Waynflete Professor of Metaphysical Philosophy at Magdalen College, Oxford University, where he remained into the 1990s. Strawson was a member of the British Academy and an honorary member of the American Academy of the Arts and Sciences. In 1977 he was appointed Knight Bachelor.

Strawson's work influenced 20th-century philosophy considerably, especially the movement known as ordinary language philosophy. In an early article, entitled "On Referring," he launched an attack against Bertrand Russell's famed "theory of definite descriptions." Russell had argued that propositions must be either true, false, or meaningless. Strawson did not disagree totally with Russell, but he felt that the theory was inadequate for showing that meaning is a function of a sentence. He believed that a sentence could have a sense or convey meaning without one knowing whether the constituents of the sentence actually exist. For example, the sentence "the present King of France is bald," might be uttered during a play. In this case, all those involved in the situation—that is, the actors and the audience—would understand the meaning of the sentence without entertaining the question of its truth or falsity.

The situation or context in which a sentence is made was important for Strawson. This notion carried over into his first book, *Introduction to Logical Theory*. While Strawson did not deny the validity of logical axioms, he did assert that logic as a discipline is limited in its ability to analyze language. Logic's primary business is to establish rules of entailment—that is, rules for showing how one statement follows from another. So limited, logic is unable to show the sense of an expression. For example, if one were asked, "Are you looking forward to going?" he might answer, "I am and I'm not." Logic would construe this statement as a contradiction. However, ordinary language analysis might reveal that the speaker meant that in certain respects he was looking forward to going while in other respects he was not. Strawson's primary objective in this work was to establish that ordinary language analysis is a primary discipline, whereas logic is a second order discipline, or one that takes place after situational analysis. As such, logic is descriptive, showing the form of the language but not the content.

Strawson's most significant impact on philosophy derived from his second book, *Individuals*. In many ways *Individuals* is a working out of themes implicit in earlier work. The work might be termed an essay in "descriptive metaphysics." Strawson believed that a more exact analysis of what there "really" is will be gained by description rather than by speculation. First, Strawson utilized the Kantian notion that all perception takes place in a spatio-temporal framework. Given this, what is basic to all perception is that it is of particular objects. In that many statements can be made about an object, and since Strawson was seeking to find the basis of all perception, he had to qualify exactly what he was trying to establish. The criteria used toward this end was that objects must be identifiable in a spatio-temporal conceptual scheme. In other words, quantitative statements are to be understood as the basic object statements. This means that the objects of a statement must be locatable in a spatial and temporal scheme without relying upon anything else for their construal. Further, objects of this scheme must be re-identifiable in the same sense over a lapse of time. This is possible with quantitative statements only, not with qualitative statements. Quantitative statements are made of an object, if that object is locatable in space and time, without depending upon anything else for that identity except the scheme itself. This is not the case with qualitative statements. Qualitative statements are attributive; hence, they presuppose an object already identified before they are applied. For example, to say of someone that he is wise means that one is applying the attribute of wisdom to a subject already identified. In other words, quantitative statements do not depend upon anything else, but qualitative statements depend on quantitative identities already established. Thus Strawson concluded that matter is to be understood as the basic particular upon which al statements about reality are grounded.

Strawson took the implications of his metaphysics seriously, especially when dealing with the traditional problem of how the mind and body are related. He asserted that the whole problem is a confused one. Further, he said that The concepts "mind" and "body" are abstract or second order concepts. Both concepts presuppose something even more basic, which Strawson argued is the concept of the "person." The person is what is given in perception. The distinction between the mind and body is made after the person has already been identified. Likewise, the person is re-identifiable by virtue of publicly observable behavior.

Part two of *Individuals* is more or less a working out of the first part from a strictly linguistic perspective. It deals in part with the relation of the subject to predicate and how particulars and universals are to be construed in discourse. Strawson drew a distinction between the logical and grammatical subjects of a sentence. For example, wisdom, or a derivative of the term, could be the grammatical subject of a sentence. In this case, however, the term would have no referent unless the logical subject stood in the position of predicate in the sentence. The logical subject must always be a particular, whereas the grammatical subject need not be. As a particular, the logical subject is always complete; that is, it is not dependent upon anything else. The logical subject is based upon an empirical fact—that is, a particular material object. The universal is introduced into discourse by its relation to the logical subject. As such, it is incomplete. In other words, the universal is dependent upon the logical subject and not on an empirical fact. Thus, the logical subject cannot be applied to anything other than the fact with which it has been identified. On the other hand, the universal may be applied to another subject, if the situation demands, since it is not rooted directly in fact nor identifiable directly in a spatio-temporal framework.

Strawson did much work after the publication of *Individuals*. Most of this work was a more specific, albeit brilliant, explication of his earlier work. Nonetheless, Strawson's earliest work was the most significant and the most likely to assure him a prominent role in the history of philosophy.

Further Reading

A good general essay on Strawson's philosophy can be found in the *Encyclopedia of Philosophy*. Numerous critiques of Strawson have been offered by noted philosophers. Of particular interest are: Bertrand Russell, "Mr. Strawson on Referring," *Mind* (1957); W. V. O. Quine, "Mr. Strawson on Logical Theory," in Quine's book *The Ways of Paradox* (1966); and A. J. Ayer's critique of Strawson's analysis of the person found in *The Concept of the Person* (1963). Other critiques can be found listed in the *Philosophers Index*.

Strawson's own works, also listed in the *Philosophers Index*, include the following books: *Introduction to Logical Theory* (1952), *Individuals* (1959), *The Bounds of Sense* (1966), *Logico-Linguistic Papers* (1971), *Freedom and Resentment* (1974), *Subject and Predicate in Logic and Grammar* (1974), and *Scepticism and Naturalism: Some Varieties* (1985). The reader should also note two of Strawson's early articles as extremely important works by Strawson. They are "On Referring" and "Truth." These two articles, and others, can be found in most any reputable anthology on the philosophy of language. □

Sir Arthur Ernest Streeton

The Australian landscape painter Sir Arthur Ernest Streeton (1867-1943) was a leading member of the Heidelberg school, the Australian version of impressionism.

Arthur Streeton was born at Mount Duneed, Victoria, on April 8, 1867. He showed an early aptitude for sketching and, moving to Melbourne, became a lithographer's apprentice. While still in his teens he began studying at the National Gallery School.

When the painter Tom Roberts returned to Melbourne in 1885, the impressionist principles he brought back inspired a group of young artists. This became the Heidelberg school (named from the locale of the group's principal painting camp, overlooking the river Yarra, near Melbourne). Streeton joined the group in 1886 and was deeply influenced by impressionism. But he saw the need to stress high-key tonal values in order to translate into paint "the blue of the Australian skies and the clear transparency of Australian distances," and he struck out on a new course.

After the sale of a landscape in 1888 Streeton decided to abandon lithography. His artistic skill matured quickly, and *Golden Summer* and *Still Glides the Stream* (both 1888) were among his most notable paintings. In 1889 he and the Heidelberg group exhibited "9 × 5 Impressions"—mainly paintings on cigar-box lids—and the proceeds enabled Streeton to pursue his career. Much of his finest work was done in the next few years, such as the *Purple Noon's Transparent Might* (1896).

In 1898 Streeton went to London. On his return to Melbourne in 1907 he had a successful exhibition with good sales. His *Australia Felix* dates from this year. A one-man show in Sydney and a second in Melbourne followed. Back in London, he had little difficulty in securing commissions. The Paris Salon awarded him its Gold Medal in 1909.

Streeton joined the British army as a private in 1914. After being invalided out, early in 1918 he was commissioned by the Australian government as a war artist. After spending 2 years in Melbourne and then revisiting London, Streeton decided in 1923 to return permanently to Victoria. From his home in the picturesque hill country east of Melbourne, he continued to paint in his established manner. He was knighted in 1937 and died at Olinda, Victoria, on Sept. 1, 1943.

Streeton was a pioneer of the heroic impressionism which dominated the nation's art for half a century, beginning in the 1880s. In settings of well-clothed rolling countryside, his paintings invested the continent's inner pastoral lands with a truly Arcadian grandeur. His contemporaries saw him as a true product of "the sun and soil of his land," and he was acknowledged to be "a natural technician, with virtuosity and technical perfection including correct drawing and balanced design."

Further Reading

James Gleeson's commentary in his extensively illustrated review, *Masterpieces of Australian Painting* (1969), contains a significant survey of Streeton's life and work. His role in the development of Australian impressionism and its offshoots is detailed in Alan McCulloch, *The Golden Age of Australian Painting* (1969). The rise of the Heidelberg school and Streeton's role in it are also related by Elizabeth Young in *Australian Painting: Colonial, Impressionist, Contemporary*

(1962), the catalog for the Australian Art Exhibition in London and Ottawa.

Additional Sources

Dutton, Geoffrey, *Arthur Streeton, 1867-1943: a biographical sketch,* Brisbane: Oz Pub. Co., 1987, 1988 printing.

Wray, Christopher, *Arthur Streeton: painter of light,* Milton, Qld.: Jacaranda, 1993. □

Gustav Stresemann

Gustav Stresemann (1878-1929) was one of Germany's outstanding diplomats and a leading political figure of the post-World War I Weimar Republic. He championed a policy of postwar reconciliation and cooperation in Europe.

Gustav Stresemann was born in Berlin on May 10, 1878, the son of a small businessman. His involvement in his family's business and the difficulties of small businesses in general influenced Stresemann to study economics and political science at the University of Berlin, from which he received a doctorate.

Stresemann's first job, in a small business, carried him into the arena of liberal politics. In 1902 he founded the Association of Saxon Industrialists, serving as its director from then until 1918. Stresemann entered the Reichstag in 1907 as a deputy of the strongly nationalist, economically liberal National Liberal party. He was reelected in 1914, and his fervent nationalism and extraordinary parliamentary skill quickly earned him the chairmanship of his party in July 1917.

After the end of World War I, during which he had supported the monarchy and an annexationist policy, Stresemann founded the conservative German People's party. As leader of this group, he hoped to reconcile Germany with its former enemies and to regain for his country a position of international respect.

Stresemann became chancellor in 1923 at the height of the postwar inflation. His government lasted only 100 days—from Aug. 13 to Nov. 23, 1923—but it mastered the inflation and firmly established a new foreign policy of economic understanding with France over the reparations question.

In 1923 Stresemann also became foreign minister, a post he held until his death. Stresemann ended the occupation by French and Belgian troops of the Ruhr in 1924. Against bitter attacks from nationalists he defended Germany's acceptance of the Treaty of Versailles as a reality and as the only realistic starting point for a successful foreign policy. In cooperation with the British ambassador Lord D'Abernon and the French foreign minister Aristide Briand, Stresemann rapidly recaptured a position of international prestige and prosperity for Germany. He then began a gradual revision of the treaty. German reparations were drastically reduced in the Dawes Plan of 1924. The Locarno Pact of 1925, which guaranteed Germany's western borders and reassured France, gained admission for Germany to the League of Nations in 1926, and it left the door open for Stresemann to pursue future border modifications in the East. The removal of Allied controls in the years following permitted Germany to regain much of its freedom as a great power, including the opportunity for clandestine rearmament.

The special cooperation between Stresemann and Briand, the cornerstone of Germany's international diplomacy, earned the two statesmen the Nobel Peace Prize in 1926. However, an agreement to resolve all remaining problems between France and Germany, negotiated by the two diplomats at Thoiry in 1926, failed to survive the growing national opposition in both countries. A further reduction of the Versailles reparations, gained in the Young Plan of 1929, ranks as Stresemann's last success. He died of a stroke on Oct. 3, 1929, in Berlin.

Further Reading

Stresemann's papers, collected and screened by his former secretary, were translated and edited in slightly condensed form by Eric Sutton, *Gustav Stresemann: His Diaries, Letters and Papers* (3 vols., 1935-1940). Although there is no definitive biography of Stresemann, there are several fine, balanced studies. Henry L. Bretton, *Stresemann and the Revision of Versailles* (1953), emphasizes Stresemann as the skillful manipulator of peaceful diplomacy. Hans Gatzke, *Stresemann and the Rearmament of Germany* (1954), portrays him as an upright, great statesman and nationalist unabashedly two-faced about German armament. Stresemann's role in German politics is discussed in Henry A. Turner, *Stresemann and the Politics of the Weimar Republic* (1963). Marvin L. Edwards, *Stresemann and the Greater Germany, 1914-1918* (1963), treats the war years. Of the many earlier, favorable accounts of the foreign minister as the "good European," two stand out: Rochus von Rheinbaben, *Stresemann: The Man and the Statesman* (1929), written with Stresemann's help, and Antonina Vallentin, *Stresemann* (trans. 1931). □

August Strindberg

August Strindberg (1849-1912) is considered Sweden's greatest author. Although his reputation outside Sweden rests on his plays, in Sweden he is equally important for his stories, novels, poetry, and autobiographical works.

August Strindberg was born on Jan. 22, 1849, in Stockholm. His father, although poor, came from a good family; his mother had been a servant. Family life was disharmonic; Strindberg felt he had been an unwanted child, and he suffered as well from the class distinction between his parents. He began writing plays while a student at Uppsala University. His first mature play, *Master Olof* (1872), written when he was 23 years old, is considered Sweden's first great drama. It was rejected by the Royal Dramatic Theater because of its "irreverent"—that is, realistic—treatment of Swedish national heroes and because it was written in prose, unthinkable for tragedy at the time. The play gives an excellent picture of Strindberg's radical intellectual interests then: Jean Jacques Rousseau, Søren Kierkegaard, Henrik Ibsen, the Danish literary reformer George Brandes, and the English historian Henry Buckle.

During these years Strindberg led an unruly life with a circle of young bohemians and earned his living as a private tutor, insurance agent, journalist, translator (of, among others, Mark Twain and Bret Harte), and assistant in the Royal Library. He married Siri von Essen in 1877; this marriage was the longest and most decisive of his three marriages, which all ended in divorce.

In spite of *Master Olof* and other, lesser works, Strindberg was unknown when, in 1879, he published the novel *The Red Room.* This work was Sweden's first realistic novel, a robust satire on just about everything Strindberg had observed in the Stockholm of the 1870s. The novel was a scandal and made him famous overnight.

In the early 1880s Strindberg's work reflected the happy years of his marriage to Siri and his growing confidence as a writer. His most successful play of the time, *Lucky Per's Journey* (1882), was written for his actress-wife. However, he began to make enemies, especially when he ventured into history-writing from a then radical point of view. He responded, typically, with another social satire, *The New Kingdom* (1882), much more bitter and personal than *The Red Room,* which stirred up more hostility. He fled Sweden with his family in 1883, but before leaving he

published a collection of angry poems which, in form and style, were completely new in Swedish literature.

In 1884 appeared a collection of stories, *Married* (the second, harsher collection appeared in 1886), which reflected in their bold treatment of sexual matters the influence of French naturalism. However, what outraged the public was the first clear evidence in the stories of Strindberg's lifelong hatred of the feminist movement and the emancipated woman. In his views on these questions, Strindberg stood alone among major Scandinavian authors. A man who three times married ambitious, career-minded women, he insisted that a woman's place is in the home. Thus he lost the support of many liberal friends.

Mental Crisis

Strindberg's enemies—their ranks now greatly increased—found a trivial occasion to bring a charge of blasphemy against him. To save his publishers, he returned to Sweden, stood trial, and was acquitted. The strain, however, was too much, and the trial marked the acceleration of the persecution complex that led, a decade later, to a period of nearly total madness.

In spite of the damage caused by the trial, the strain of trying to support a growing family by his pen, and even, for a time, a total boycott of his work in Sweden, Strindberg produced many of his greatest works in the last half of the 1880s. These include the plays upon which his European reputation was first based—the naturalistic dramas *The Father* (1887), *Miss Julie* (1888), and *Creditors* (1889)—and the autobiographical novels *The Son of a Servant* and *The Confession of a Fool* (the latter a ruthlessly one-sided account of his marriage to Siri von Essen). Characteristically, in the midst of his growing personal troubles, he wrote one of his happiest, freshest novels, *The People of Hemsö* (1887).

Strindberg's European reputation grew, and his plays created sensations when they were performed in private theaters (to escape police censorship) in Denmark, Germany, and France. However, overwork and the nightmarish breakup of his first marriage led to further deterioration of his mental health, and he rejected the offers of producers and turned to science (believing he could synthesize elements) and then to alchemy (to make the gold he sorely needed), and finally he began to study the occult and write for occult journals.

In studying mysticism, theosophy, and especially the works of the Swedish mystic Emanuel Swedenborg, Strindberg felt he had found an answer to why he (and mankind generally) suffered so much. In finding an answer, he recovered his sanity, and a new, perhaps the greatest, period of his authorship began.

Later Career

From the "Inferno" crisis—named for the remarkable account he wrote of the years of near madness, *Inferno* (1897)—until his death in 1912, Strindberg wrote 29 plays, a volume of poetry, and about 15 volumes of prose. The most important plays of his last period, the expressionistic period, are *To Damascus I-III* (1898-1904), *There Are Crimes and Crimes* (1899), *Easter* (1901), *The Dance of Death* (1901), *Crown Bride* (1902), *A Dream Play* (1902), and the "chamber plays" he wrote for his own theater in 1907. He also wrote a number of historical dramas, the best of which is *Gustaf Vasa,* and a final, autobiographical play, *The Great Highway* (1909). Of his prose work, mention should be made of the gripping, personal novels *Alone* (1903) and *The Scapegoat* (1907) and the remarkable diary *Blå böcker* (1907-1912; Blue Books).

Strindberg's last years were comparatively calm, broken only by the "feud" occasioned by the novel *Svarta fanor* (1907; Black Banners), a final, savage attack on his enemies, real and imagined, all readily identifiable in the book. He died alone, as he had lived, on May 14, 1912, in Stockholm.

Critical Assessment

Strindberg's contribution to world drama was in two areas—naturalism and expressionism. The naturalistic works, including such plays as *The Father* and *Miss Julie,* follow the example of Émile Zola and other French writers in striving to present as scientific and objective a picture of life as possible. However, as a playwright, Strindberg was superior to Zola and most other naturalists. His superiority lies just in his refusal to burden his plays with the mass of natural scientific documentation naturalism demanded. He was forced by his own restless, impatient nature—and his great dramatic sense—to seek daring shortcuts to what he wanted to express. Furthermore, Strindberg became increasingly interested in "inner states," especially the "battle of wills," and in the power of mental suggestion, from his readings of pre-Freudian psychologists, criminologists, and authors such as Edgar Allan Poe and Friedrich Nietzsche. Finally, the problems his plays dealt with—often the battle between the sexes—were too personal for him to always achieve naturalistic objectivity. His woman figures are often "vampires" (Tekla in *Creditors,* for example), and their victims are often recognizable as Strindberg himself. For these reasons, many of Strindberg's naturalistic plays threaten constantly to break out of their naturalistic mold, and in their savagery, their heightened realism, they point ahead to the expressionistic plays which follow the "Inferno" crisis.

The expressionistic plays—such as *To Damascus, The Dance of Death,* and *The Ghost Sonata*—depart, at their most extreme, from the naturalistic plays in that Strindberg attempts to dramatize directly his emotions and view of life, neglecting almost totally a logically developed plot, psychological motivation, and realism in stage setting. Strindberg came to believe that life is a hideous dream and, in a number of these later plays, dramatizes this view. There is a kind of "realism" in even the most extreme of these plays, however—they are none of them like the moody, vague, symbolist plays of Maurice Maeterlinck, for example—but it is the aching, sharp-edged, hallucinatory realism of nightmare, not of our waking life.

The themes of the later plays are the same as in Strindberg's earlier work: life's pervasive, incomprehensible cruelty and the battle of wills in which the weaker is mercilessly destroyed. But now there is a much more overt metaphysical perspective: life is a kind of hell, or purgatory, from which we will someday be released; there are "powers" that punish us for our sins; and "mankind is to be pitied."

Strindberg's influence on world drama continues to be considerable. European expressionism around World War I owed much to his later plays, Pär Lagerkvist in Sweden and Eugene O'Neill in America believed him to be the portal figure in 20th-century drama, and the seeds of much recent experimental drama can be traced back to Strindberg too.

Further Reading

Useful accounts in English of Strindberg's life are Elizabeth Sprigge, *The Strange Life of August Strindberg* (1949), and Brita M. E. Mortensen and Brian W. Downs, *Strindberg: An Introduction to His Life and Work* (1949). The older and still sound biography by V. J. McGill, *August Strindberg: The Bedeviled Viking* (1930), slights the latter half of Strindberg's life and has not been revised to accommodate the findings of more recent scholarship.

Critical works dealing with Strindberg's drama include Martin Lamm, *Modern Drama* (trans. 1952); Walter Gilbert Johnson, *Strindberg and the Historical Drama* (1963); Maurice Jacques Valency, *The Flower and the Castle: An Introduction to Modern Drama* (1963); and Carl Enoch William Leonard Dahlstrom, *Strindberg's Dramatic Expressionism* (2d ed. 1965). For Strindberg's contribution to the novel see the excellent work by Eric O. Johannesson, *The Novels of August Strindberg: A Study in Themes and Structure* (1968). Alrik Gustafson, *A History of Swedish Literature* (1961), contains a critical bibliography of sources on Strindberg's life and work in Swedish and English.

Additional Sources

Dittmann, Reidar, *Eros and psyche: Strindberg and Munch in the 1890s,* Ann Arbor, Mich.: UMI Research Press, 1982.

Lagercrantz, Olof Gustaf Hugo, *August Strindberg,* New York: Farrar, Straus, Giroux, 1984.

Meyer, Michael Leverson, *Strindberg,* New York: Random House, 1985.

Strindberg, August, *Inferno and From an occult diary,* Harmondsworth, Eng.; New York: Penguin Books, 1979. □

Alfredo Stroessner

Alfredo Stroessner (born 1912) became president of Paraguay in 1954, and ruled as a dictator until he was overthrown and forced into exile in 1989.

Alfredo Stroessner was born on Nov. 3, 1912, at the southeastern Paraguayan border city of Encarnación. His father, Hugo Stroessner, was a German immigrant who became a mechanic and ironworker. His mother, Heriberta Matiauda, was the daughter of a prominent Encarnación family whose roots stemmed from Paraguay's independence era. His wife, Eligia Mora Delgado, was likewise a descendant of an old Paraguayan family. The Stroessners had two sons and a daughter.

A dedicated professional soldier with an unswerving sense of patriotism, Stroessner began his military career at the outbreak of the Chaco War with Bolivia. First serving at the siege of Paraguay's Boquerón outpost in September 1932 as a military college cadet commanding an infantry platoon, he was subsequently commissioned in the field as a second lieutenant and transferred to the artillery, his favored service branch. As a mortar platoon commander, he served with distinction throughout the remainder of the war and received numerous citations.

Promoted to captain in 1936, Stroessner rose swiftly in rank and became general of division in 1951. Post-Chaco service was highlighted by his participation as a loyal army officer in the major 1947 revolution, in which he was commended for his success in blocking Paraguay's southern borders against rebelling army and navy units.

In 1954, he led the coup d'etat which toppled the government of President Federico Cháves. Formally inaugurated as president in August 1954, he was successively reelected, although he sometimes had little or no opposition. Stroessner's administration was founded on an alliance between the military and the dominant Colorado Party. Certain political parties were allowed to exist, while others were banned.

Part of Stroessner's success not only came from his strong rule over his country, but also because of a relatively solid and stable economy he brought to Paraguay. The country's economy grew at a rate uncommon for Latin American nations at the time.

A confirmed anti-Communist, Stroessner nullified all subversive attempts in Paraguay, supported U.S. inter-American objectives, including participation by a Paraguayan contingent in the Dominican Republic episode, and received both U.S. economic assistance and Peace Corps projects in the 1960s. In 1968, following his third reelection, he formally visited Washington—the second Paraguayan president to have been officially invited to the United States.

Under Stroessner's rule, there was no free press. Newspaper presses and radio transmitters were routinely destroyed by police aligned with the Colorado Party. *The Progressive* magazine noted three examples: Aldo Zuccolillo, publisher of *ABC Color,* Paraguay's largest newspaper, was jailed, and his paper shut down for five years. Radio Nanduti was off the air for two years after its transmitter was demolished. Reporter Alejandro Mella Latorre was jailed and tortured for 8 1/2 years.

According to *Newsweek,* "Party membership [in the Colorado Party] was a prerequisite for getting most jobs in government service, the military, or even in nursing or teaching. Stroessner's tools were violence and fear. Critics of the government disappeared, only to show up again floating face down in the muddy Paraguay River."

After 35 years of rule, Stroessner's empire began to crumble. The U.S. started to pressure his government to reform in the late 1970s and 1980s, after human rights violations came to light. Then the economy, which had been quite strong, began to slow, and inflation soared to 30 percent. Street protests, unthinkable a few years earlier, began appearing in 1986. In 1988, Pope John Paul II toured South America, and called for major reforms in Paraguay. Stroessner became ill, and while recovering from prostate surgery, his former right-hand man, Andres Rodriguez, led a military coup and overthrew Stroessner in February, 1989.

Stroessner was originally placed under house arrest, and later allowed to go into exile in Brazil. In 1996, he was reportedly living in a closely guarded mansion in Brazil, occasionally fishing, and keeping a low profile.

Further Reading

References to Stroessner are in George Pendle, *Paraguay* (1954; 3d ed. 1967); Hubert Herring, *A History of Latin America* (1955; 3d rev. ed. 1968); and Philip Raine, *Paraguay* (1956). □

Josiah Strong

Josiah Strong (1847-1916) was one of America's leading religious and social voices during the late nineteenth and early twentieth centuries.

A clergyman who proposed revolutionary religion-oriented solutions to perceived inequities in America's social and economic network, Josiah Strong adhered to a brand of Christianity that came to be known as Christian Socialism. The impact of his words and actions was felt beyond the borders of religion, however. In the 1890s he also emerged as one of the country's strongest voices in support of American imperialism, a philosophy that held that the nation needed to expand its sphere of influence around the world to ensure its continued primacy and to save heathen cultures. The support of Strong and other American religious leaders lent America's expansionist impulse a veneer of righteousness and altruism.

Wrote Influential Book *Our Country*

Strong was born into an Illinois family with deep colonial roots. When he was five years old, Strong's family moved to Hudson, Ohio, and it was there that he spent the rest of his childhood. He attended Western Reserve College, graduating in 1869, and entered seminary school at Lane Theological Seminary. He was ordained two years later, shortly after marrying Alice Bisbee.

The newlyweds settled in Cheyenne, Wyoming, where he served as pastor of the community's Congregational church. In 1873, though, Strong returned to Western Reserve, where he taught and served as the campus chaplain. The next several years were marked by continued migration from one post to another, eventually landing at Central Congregational Church in 1884. During his stint at Central, Strong was asked to update a manual used by the Congregational Missionary Society. The result was *Our Country* (1885), one of the most influential books of the late nineteenth century.

In *Our Country,* Strong articulated some of his most strongly held beliefs. Rich in idealistic exhortation and social commentary, the booklet offered previously unexplored religion-based prescriptions for addressing America's social and industrial ills. Strong paid particular attention to the nation's overcrowded and poverty-riddled cities, which he saw as endangered by immigrant-based political parties and fiscal irresponsibility. "The city is the nerve center of our civilization. It is also the storm center," he wrote. "It has become a serious threat to our civilization." *Our Country* also made the minister's imperialist leanings clear. Like many proponents of American expansionism at the turn of the century, Strong contended that the moral superiority of the nation's white population made America duty-bound to help "lift up" the inferior members of other nations. The Anglo-Saxon race, he wrote, was "of unequaled energy, with all the majesty of numbers and the might of wealth behind it." As possessor "of the largest liberty, the purest Christianity, the highest civilization," Strong argued that it was the Anglo-Saxons' duty to stretch its influence over all the earth. Many expansionists, including Strong, pointed to America's burgeoning economic power as a sure sign of its superiority. They felt that foreign trade could be a tremendously effective mechanism in realizing America's ambitions of empire. "The world is to be Christianized and civilized," remarked Strong. "And what is the process of civilizing but the creating of more and higher wants. Commerce follows the missionary."

Developed Philosophies of Christian Socialism

Our Country vaulted Strong into the national limelight and led to his appointment as secretary of a Protestant ecumenical agency known as the American Evangelical Alliance. In 1893 he published a second book, entitled *The New Era,* which enjoyed a similarly enthusiastic reception. In *The New Era,* which was translated into a number of different languages, Strong articulated the philosophies that became cornerstones of a movement that came to be known as Christian Socialism or the Social Gospel. Strong insisted that people could create an ideal society akin to the Kingdom of God through programs of fundamental social change. Although Strong's first two works were perhaps his most influential, he continued to author books throughout his career. These included *The Twentieth Century City* (1898), *Religious Movements for Social Betterment* (1900), *The Next Great Awakening* (1902), *The Challenge of the City* (1907), *My Religion in Everyday Life* (1910), *Our World: The New World Life* (1913), and *Our World: The New World Religion* (1915). He also founded a monthly periodical entitled *The Gospel of the Kingdom* in 1908.

As secretary of the American Evangelical Alliance, Strong had hoped to unite various denominations under a single banner of social outreach, but disagreements with other religious leaders during his tenure in the Alliance gradually convinced him to pursue other avenues. In 1898 he resigned from his secretary position to found the League for Social Service (known as the American Institute for Social Service after 1902). He was also an important contributor to the establishment of the Federal Council of the Churches of Christ. An untiring champion of the tenets of the Social Gospel, Strong maintained a vigorous schedule of lecturing and writing.

In the early 1900s Strong extended his involvement beyond America's shores. He extended a "Safety First" movement intended to curb accidents to several South American nations, and in 1904 he founded the British Institute of Social Service in England. He died in New York City on April 28, 1916.

Further Reading

Pratt, Julius W., *Expansionists of 1898,* Peter Smith Co., 1952.
Strong, Josiah, *Our Country,* American Home Missionary Society, 1885. □

Friedrich Georg Wilhelm von Struve

The German-born Russian astronomer and geodesist Friedrich Georg Wilhelm von Struve (1793-1864) is noted for his observations of double stars and for the measurement of the meridional arc from the north coast of Norway to Ismail on the Danube.

On April 15, 1793, F. G. W. von Struve was born in Altona, then part of the Holy Roman Empire. After escaping in 1808 from a French press gang seeking recruits for Napoleon's army, he entered the University of Dorpat (now Tartu in Estonia). His brother, Karl, taught philology there, and the younger Struve decided to follow his footsteps; he completed his studies and received a degree in philology by December 1810.

Under the influence of the physicist Georg Friedrich Parrot, Struve developed an interest in the exact sciences, especially astronomy. In 1812 he began his first astronomical observations at Dorpat Observatory, and later he was appointed extraordinary professor of mathematics and astronomy as well as observer there. From 1818 to 1838, under Struve's leadership, the work at Dorpat Observatory achieved international acclaim, particularly after 1824, when Struve received the Fraunhofer equatorial telescope with the 9.6-inch achromatic objective lens—the largest aperture for its day.

Struve elected to study double (binary) stars with his newly acquired telescope. From November 1824 to February 1827, he spent 320 hours in the course of 138 nights, observing roughly 400 stars per hour, for a total of 120,000 stars, of which 2,200 were doubles. He published his studies on multiple-star systems in *Catalogus novus* (1827), *Mensurae micrometricae* (1837), and *Positiones mediae* (1852). His examination of binary stars demonstrated that Isaac Newton's law of gravitation operates outside the solar system and is therefore a universal law and that multiple-star systems are not rare. For his scientific accomplishments Struve was elected to full membership in the St. Petersburg Imperial Academy of Sciences.

In 1830 Czar Nicholas I set aside land in the Pulkovo Hills outside St. Petersburg as the site for a new astronomical observatory and selected Struve for the commission responsible for its construction. When the Pulkovo Observatory opened in 1839, it could boast not only of Struve's being its first director but also of housing a telescope with a 15-inch objective lens. It was the best-equipped observatory in Europe.

At Pulkovo Observatory, Struve continued observing binary stars and moved into the areas of practical astronomy and geodesy. The observatory's staff also made numerous measurements of geographic points in Russia to supply information necessary for road building, railways, and military needs, and in 1845 Struve helped to found the Russian Geographical Society. After his death on Nov. 23, 1864, his son, Otto Wilhelm Struve, continued the Struve dynasty in Russian astronomy; his directorship of Pulkovo Observatory began in 1858 and lasted until 1899.

Further Reading

There is no definitive biography of Struve in English or Russian. Scattered references to his accomplishments appear in the technical work by Robert G. Aitken, *The Binary Stars* (1918); in Hector MacPherson, *Makers of Astronomy* (1933); in the highly readable book by Pierre Rousseau, *Man's Conquest of the Stars* (trans. 1959); and in Alexander Vucinich, *Science in Russian Culture* (1963). □

Gilbert Stuart

Gilbert Stuart (1755-1828), American painter, was the classical portraitist of the early republic, painting likenesses that hovered between meticulous representations and idealized generalizations. He created the iconic image of George Washington as the Father of His Country.

Gilbert Stuart was born in North Kingston, R.I., on Dec. 3, 1755. At the age of 13 or 14 he studied art with the Scottish painter Cosmo Alexander in Newport. With Alexander he made a tour of the South and a journey to Edinburgh, where Alexander died in 1772. For about a year Stuart remained, poverty-stricken, in Scotland, but finally, working as a sailor, he managed to get back to America. There he executed a few portraits in a hard limner fashion. With the Revolutionary War threatening, his family, who had Tory sympathies, fled to Nova Scotia, and Stuart sailed for London, where he remained from 1775 to 1787.

For the first 4 or 5 years, Stuart served as the first assistant of American expatriate painter Benjamin West, who had rescued him from poverty. From the first, Stuart showed an interest only in portraiture and had no desire to go into the branch of history painting West practiced. After his apprenticeship, Stuart became London's leading portrait painter, next to Joshua Reynolds and Thomas Gainsborough, whose style he emulated, as in a rare full-length portrait of William Grant of Congalton as *The Skater* (ca. 1782). For a while Stuart lived in splendor, but being a bad businessman and a profligate spender, he was in constant debt. He lived in Ireland from 1787 to 1792 and then returned to America to make a fortune, he said, by painting Washington's portrait. He worked in New York, Philadelphia, and Washington until 1805, when he permanently established his studio in Boston.

Stuart's Portraits of Washington

From the first, Stuart seems to have been awed by Washington. "There were features in his face," he observed, "totally different from what I had observed in any other human being. The sockets of the eyes, for instance, were larger than what I ever met with before. . . . All his features were indicative of the strongest passions." Because of the painter's carefree, libertine ways, Washington behaved coldly toward him. It may have been partly because of this that Stuart interpreted Washington in an aloof and imperious manner, rather than in the more intimate way that Charles Wilson Peale did. Yet it was Stuart who created the iconic image of Washington recognized by generations of Americans.

Stuart painted Washington at a time when the general's physique was beginning to break down and he was wearing false teeth. But there is no hint of this in any of Stuart's portraits. Without obvious flattery, still catching the essential character, he presented careful regularizations and glosses. He made three basic versions of Washington as an elder statesman—all remote, dignified, with a wonderful sense of composure, without exterior paraphernalia or insignia to identify his rank—and based all his future portraits of Washington on them.

The three versions were the Vaughan portrait, showing the right side of Washington's face (1795, original destroyed), the full-length Landsdowne portrait (1796), and the unfinished Athenaeum portrait (1796). After a while, Stuart could produce Washington's features rapidly, with little effort. At the end of his life, according to his daughter, he could dash off portraits of Washington at the rate of one every 2 hours. So popular were the portraits that inferior artists made large sums of money by copying the copies.

Stuart's Other Portraits

By 1792 Stuart's portraits had evolved into remote, detached images like the three main versions of Washington. This had not been the case in England, where, following Gainsborough, he included something of the sitter's environment. For example, *The Skater* has a bit of landscape and other figures skating in the background; the portrait of Sir Joshua Reynolds (1784) contains part of a curtain and a table with a scroll, and the costume is detailed. But in America, Stuart usually painted the head and shoulders against a bare background. At the end of his career, he would suggest but a hint of the lace of the upper part of the coat or dress by a few quick strokes, or he hired a drapery painter to do this work. Stuart came to specialize in painting faces—nothing more.

No one challenged Stuart's position as the foremost American portraitist of his day. Five presidents and numerous leaders of society sat for him. Among Stuart's American portraits are those of Isabella Henderson Lenox (ca. 1810), Gen. Horatio Gates (ca. 1794), and John Adams (1823). The Lenox portrait is a good example of Stuart's drawing-room portraits of wealthy women. The lady's hair is gathered up in a neat bunch in the back, but the curls fall loosely on her forehead; her neck seems to be gracefully elongated and her eyes slightly enlarged. The outlines are soft. There is a hint of a shadow on her neck. Nothing in the background detracts attention from the sitter's face, which is placed equidistant from the two vertical edges of the canvas. The figure is in three quarter pose. The elegant gown is sketchily indicated; the face is rendered with more detail.

In the portrait of Gen. Gates, Stuart caught something of the pomposity of the man, who had desired to replace Washington as commander in chief—but the painting is still flattering. Stuart does not get to the core of his subject's personality as John Singleton Copley does. Gates's bearing is noble, his eyes look boldly at the observer, but no trace of his inner thoughts can be discerned. Stuart paints only the appearance, but the most generous appearance possible.

Stuart's portrait of John Adams shows the former president at the age of 90. Again Stuart paints external appearances, but here he catches sympathetically the look of old age. Adam's hand is held like a claw, his eyes are watery and look ahead vacantly, the muscular structure of his mouth has weakened, and the skin is soft and saggy. Yet there is nothing repulsive or demeaning; there is still about the figure a sense of aristocracy and high office.

Stuart's Technique

Unlike Copley, who laboriously worked first on one part and then on another part of his portraits, Stuart worked on all parts of the canvas at once. Copley was still tied to the linear tradition of the limners, but Stuart utilized the loose, painterly treatment of contemporary English artists. First he blocked in the principal shapes with the brush (there were no preparatory drawings), and then he put in the opaque colors of the face, which he covered with transparent and semitransparent hues. The final effect was one of freshness and spontaneity. The strokes were applied quickly but surely.

Stuart used few colors—vermilion, lake, and a few others—but he had special mixtures for reflections and shadows. The colors were not blended into one another, for he took care to avoid muddiness, yet there were small gradations between one tone and another. As the opaque underpainting shone forth through the transparent hues, the texture of flesh was suggested remarkably well. Stuart once said that flesh "is like no other substance under heaven. It has all the gaiety of a silk-mercer's shop without its gaudiness of gloss, and all the soberness of old mahogany without its sadness." His technique may be observed in the unfinished portrait of Mrs. Perez Morton (ca. 1802). Here the entire canvas has been worked on. But while the face is complete down to its transparent hues, the arms and veil are still in the sketched-in state.

Stuart set the standard for portrait painting in America in the first half of the 19th century. Because he worked so rapidly, he was able to execute over a thousand commissions in America (besides the numerous Washingtons), and his work could be seen widely. All important American portrait painters in the decades following him either studied briefly with him or, more usually, learned from his works. Among these many artists were Thomas Sully, John Wesley Jarvis, Samuel F. B. Morse, Chester Harding, John Neagle, Ezra Ames, Matthew Jouett, and Mather Brown.

Further Reading

A comprehensive biography, including recently discovered material, is Charles Merrill Mount, *Gilbert Stuart* (1964). Lawrence Park, *Gilbert Stuart: An Illustrated Descriptive List of His Works* (4 vols., 1926), is the most complete catalog of the paintings, with biographical sketches in the first volume. □

James Ewell Brown Stuart

James Ewell Brown Stuart (1833-1864), known as Jeb Stuart, ranks among the most effective cavalry officers in American military history for his exploits in the Civil War.

Jeb Stuart was born in Patrick County, Va., on Feb. 6, 1833. Educated at home and at Emory and Henry College, he entered the U.S. Military Academy in 1850 and graduated thirteenth in the class of 1854. On Nov. 14, 1855, he married Flora Cooke; they had three children.

Commissioned brevet second lieutenant in the Mounted Rifles, Stuart was transferred to the 1st U.S. Cavalry in 1855. In October 1859 he served as aide to Col. Robert E. Lee in capturing John Brown at Harpers Ferry, Va. He resigned his commission when Virginia seceded from the Union, and as the Civil War began he accepted appointment as colonel of the 1st Virginia Cavalry.

Assigned to Gen. Joseph E. Johnston in the Shenandoah Valley, Stuart quickly distinguished himself for daring. Gallantry at First Manassas (Bull Run) in July 1861 earned him a brigadier general's wreath. In June 1862 Gen. Lee ordered him to reconnoiter Gen. George B. McClellan's rear positions on the Virginia Peninsula. Leading 1,200 men, Stuart won lasting renown with his "Ride around McClellan." Promoted to major general in July 1862, he took command of the cavalry division of Lee's Army of Northern Virginia.

Stuart became one of the most skilled scouts and intelligence officers in the war. He distinguished himself in the campaign of Second Manassas, and in the invasion of Maryland he and his dismounted troopers proved stubborn fighters. In December 1862 Stuart's horse artillery helped stall the attack on Stonewall Jackson's corps at Fredericksburg. Perhaps his most decisive action came during Jackson's march to intercept Gen. Joseph Hooker in the Virginia

Wilderness in April 1863. Assigned the task of discovering enemy plans and screening the Confederate advance, Stuart, plumed hat everywhere in evidence, his banjo-playing companion, "Sweeny," in tow, did superbly. When Jackson was mortally wounded in the Battle of Chancellorsville on May 2, Stuart took temporary command of the II Corps and handled it well in the action of May 3.

At Brandy Station, Va., Stuart's cavalry was surprised and sorely tested for the first time. In the Gettysburg campaign, Stuart's love of adventure led him to his one glaring blunder; when Lee most needed him, Stuart was away on a raid toward Washington, D.C. Rejoining the army on July 2, Stuart's command had no decisive part in the Battle of Gettysburg.

Stuart did not disappoint Lee again. With dwindling manpower and scant forage, he managed Lee's cavalry adroitly through the winter and spring of 1863-1864. On May 11, 1864, Stuart halted Gen. Philip Sheridan's big corps heading for Richmond, but he was wounded at Yellow Tavern and died the next day. His death removed a quality of zeal from Lee's cavalry and left a permanent gap in Southern leadership.

Further Reading

The best biography of Stuart is John W. Thompson, Jr., *Jeb Stuart* (1930). More recent is Burke Davis, *Jeb Stuart: The Last Cavalier* (1957). See also W. W. Blackford, *War Years with Jeb Stuart* (1945). Stuart's relations with Lee are admirably treated in Douglas Southall Freeman, *R. E. Lee* (4 vols., 1934-1937) and *Lee's Lieutenants* (3 vols., 1942-1944). □